CORPORATE TAX DIGEST

by

JAMES A. DOUGLAS
Member, New York Bar

JAMES STANISLAW
Member, New York and California Bars

WARREN, GORHAM & LAMONT
Boston • New York

Copyright © 1987 by
WARREN, GORHAM & LAMONT, INC.
210 SOUTH STREET
BOSTON, MASSACHUSETTS 02111

ALL RIGHTS RESERVED

No part of this book may be reproduced in any form, by photostat, microfilm, xerography, or any other means, or incorporated into any information retrieval system, electronic or mechanical, without the written permission of the copyright owner.

ISBN 0-88712-622-7

Library of Congress Catalog Card No. 86-51378

PRINTED IN THE UNITED STATES OF AMERICA

How to Use This Book

The *Corporate Tax Digest* provides a comprehensive reference to federal corporation tax cases and rulings rendered since 1954. All relevant reported decisions of federal courts and agencies have been carefully reviewed, selected, and edited to present concise and easily understandable abstracts of complex cases. Because the law of federal taxation changes constantly, however, the reader should check the continued validity of the point of law in any given case.

Digest Contents and Citations. Each digest summarizes the facts, gives the holding, and states the name of the case or ruling and the volume and page number of the law reporters where the decision or ruling is printed. Citations to reporters published by Commerce Clearing House and Prentice-Hall are provided for convenience.

Digest Organization and IRC References. The digests are organized under alphabetical topic headings. The Index of Contents, in the front of the book, lists each topic heading and its page number in the text. In addition, the headings are printed at the top of each page in the text where digests of cases on that topic appear. If material on a particular Code section or case is needed, reference can be obtained by consulting the Table of IRC Sections or the Table of Cases at the end of the book.

Index of Contents

Accelerated Depreciation (*See* Depreciation and Amortization)
Accounting Methods (*See also* Bad Debts; Inventories) 1
   In General 1
   Accrual Method 1
   Change of Method 1
   Installment Sales 2
Accumulated Earnings Tax 3
   In General 3
   Accumulated Earnings Credit 5
   Accumulated Taxable Income 6
   Burden of Proof 7
   Consolidated Groups 11
   Contingent Liabilities 13
   Dividends Paid Deduction 13
   Expansion Plans 14
   Liquidating Distributions 21
   Passive Investment Income 22
   Reasonable Business Needs 23
   Tax-Avoidance Purpose 37
Acquiring Corporations, Carry-Over of Tax Attributes By (*See* Reorganizations—Carryover of Net Operating Losses and Other Tax Attributes)
Acquisitions (*See* Reorganizations)
Acquisitions to Avoid Tax (*See also* Net Operating Losses; Reorganizations—Carry-Over of Losses and Tax Attributes) 41
Affiliated Corporations (*See also* Allocation Among Related Taxpayers; Consolidated Returns; Related Taxpayers) 53
   In General 53
   Affiliated Group Defined 54
   Control Defined 56
   Excess Loss Accounts 58
   Net Operating Loss Carry-Overs 59
   Tax-Avoidance Purpose 60
Agency (*See* Business Expenses—Deductible by Whom)
Allocation Among Related Taxpayers (*See also* Affiliated Corporations; Consolidated Returns; Related Taxpayers) 63
   In General 63
   Arm's-Length Transaction Defense 65
   Business Purpose Defense 70
   Conduit Theory 73

   Methods of Reallocation 75
   Related Taxpayers Defined 79
   Sham Transactions 80
Amortization (*See* Depreciation and Amortization)
Anticipatory Assignment of Income (*See* Assignment of Income)
Assessment and Collection (*See also* Procedure) 82
   In General 82
   Liens & Priorities 82
   Transferee Liability 82
   Withholding Requirements 84
Assignment of Income (*See also* Capital Gains and Losses) 87
Associations Taxable as Corporations 88
   In General 88
   Post-Dissolution Activities 88
   Professional Associations 90
   Trusts and Trustees 90
Assumption of Liabilities (*See* Liabilities, Assumption Of)
Attribution Rules (*See also* Redemptions—Attribution Rules) 93
Avoidance of Tax (*See* Accumulated Earnings Tax; Acquisitions to Avoid Tax; Tax Avoidance)
Bad Debts (*See also* Capital Contributions; Debt vs. Equity) 94
   In General 94
   Bona Fide Indebtedness Requirement 95
   Business vs. Nonbusiness Debts 98
   Deduction For 102
   Reserves For 104
Bargain Purchases (*See* Compensation for Personal Services; Dividends and Distributions—Bargain Purchases and Sales)
Bargain Sales (*See* Compensation for Personal Services; Dividends and Distributions—Bargain Purchases and Sales)
Basis of Property (*See also* Liquidations—Basis of Property Received; Reorganizations; Tax-Free Exchanges; Tax-Free Incorporations) 105
Bonds and Debentures 107
   In General 107

v

Index of Contents

Bond Discount and Premiums 108
Deduction of Interest Paid 111
Equity Investments Distinguished 115

Bonuses (*See* Business Expenses—Bonuses; Compensation for Personal Services—Bonuses; Dividends and Distributions—Bonus Payments)

Boot (*See* Reorganizations—Boot)

Bribes (*See* Business Expenses—Bribes and Other Illegal Expenses)

Burden of Proof (*See* Accumulated Earnings Tax—Burden of Proof; Procedure)

Business Expenses (*See also* Dividends and Distributions) 122
In General 123
Bonuses 127
Bribes and Other Illegal Expenses 127
Capital Expenditures Distinguished 128
Deductible by Whom 130
Interest Expenses 133
Liquidating Expenses 134
Medical Expenses 135
Ordinary and Necessary Requirement .. 136
Organizational Expenses 140
Payment of Claims 140
Payments to Related Taxpayers 141
Payments to Stockholders' Beneficiaries 141
Profit Motive Requirement 142
Salaries 143
Stockholders' Expenses 144
Substantiation 144
Travel and Entertainment Expenses 144

Business Needs (*See* Accumulated Earnings Tax—Reasonable Business Needs)

Business, Sale or Purchase Of (*See* Acquisitions to Avoid Tax; Reorganizations)

Business Purpose (*See* Redemptions; Reorganizations)

Cancellation of Indebtedness 146

Capital Assets (*See* Capital Gains and Losses—Capital Asset Defined)

Capital Contributions (*See* Contributions to Capital)

Capital Expenditures (*See* Business Expenses—Capital Expenditures Distinguished)

Capital Gains and Losses 148
In General 148
Assignment of Income 149
Capital Asset Defined 149
Holding Period 151
Ordinary Gains/Losses Distinguished .. 151

Carry-Back and Carry-Over (*See* Consolidated Returns—Net Operating Loss Carry-Overs; Net Operating Loss—Carry-Back; Net Operating Loss—Carry-Forward; Reorganizations—Carry-Over of Net Operating Losses and Other Tax Attributes)

Change of Accounting Methods (*See* Accounting Methods—Change of Method)

Character of Gain or Loss (*See* Capital Gains and Losses)

Charitable Contributions 155

Classification of Entities for Tax Purposes (*See* Associations Taxable as Corporations; Corporations as Taxable Entities)

Clearly Reflecting Income (*See* Allocation Among Related Taxpayers)

Closely Held Corporations (*See* Affiliated Corporations; Allocation Among Related Taxpayers; Consolidated Returns; Compensation for Personal Services; Dividends and Distributions; Related Taxpayers)

Collapsible Corporations 157
Definition 157
Liquidation Of 163
Realization of Substantial Part of Income Exception 166
Three-Year Holding Period Exception .. 169

Collection of Taxes (*See* Assessment and Collection)

Compensation for Personal Services 171
In General 171
Bonuses 173
Dividend Equivalence 179
Held Reasonable 181
Held Unreasonable 194
Loans Distinguished 204
Past Services 204

Complete Liquidations (*See* Liquidations)

Compliance (*See* Assessment and Collection; Procedure; Tax Avoidance)

Consent Dividends (*See* Accumulated Earnings Tax; Personal Holding Companies)

Consolidated Returns (*See also* Affiliated Corporations) 207
In General 208
Control Defined 211
Elections 213
Excess Loss Account 216
Intercorporate Transactions 216
Net Operating Loss Carry-Overs 218

Continuity of Interest (*See* Reorganizations—Continuity of Interest)

INDEX OF CONTENTS

Contributions (*See* Charitable Contributions; Contributions to Capital)

Contributions to Capital (*See also* Bad Debts; Debt vs. Equity) 222
   In General 222
   Distinguished From Debt 226
   Preferred Stock 248

Controlled Corporations (*See* Affiliated Corporations; Consolidated Returns; Transfers to Controlled Corporations)

Corporate Divisions (*See* Reorganizations—Spin-Offs and Other Divisive Reorganizations)

Corporate Entities (*See* Associations Taxable as Corporations; Corporations as Taxable Entities)

Corporate Income (*See* Taxable Income of Corporations)

Corporate Liquidations (*See* Liquidations)

Corporate Redemptions (*See* Redemptions)

Corporate Reorganizations (*See* Reorganizations)

Corporate Separations (*See* Reorganizations—Spin-Offs and Other Divisive Reorganizations)

Corporations as Taxable Entities 250

Death Taxes, Redemption of Stock to Pay (*See* Redemptions—Redemptions to Pay Death Taxes)

Debentures (*See* Bonds and Debentures)

Debts (*See* Bad Debts) 255

Debt vs. Equity (*See also* Bad Debts; Bonds and Debentures—Equity Investments Distinguished; Contributions to Capital) .. 255
   In General 255
   Bona Fide Indebtedness 257
   Intent of Parties 266
   Thin Capitalization 268

Deductions (*See particular items, such as* Business Expenses; Charitable Contributions)

Depreciation and Amortization 271
   In General 271
   Recapture Of 272

Discharge of Debt (*See* Cancellation of Indebtedness)

Discount Bonds (*See* Bonds and Debentures—Bond Discount and Premiums)

DISC (*See* Domestic International Sales Corporations)

Disguised Dividends (*See* Dividends and Distributions)

Distributions (*See* Dividends and Distributions)

Distributions in Kind (*See* Dividends and Distributions)

Distributions of Stock and Rights Thereto (*See* Dividends and Distributions—Stock Dividends and Rights; Reorganizations)

Dividend Equivalence (*See* Compensation for Personal Services—Dividend Equivalence; Dividends and Distributions; Redemptions—Dividend Equivalence; Reorganizations)

Dividends and Distributions (*See also* Compensation for Personal Services—Dividend Equivalence; Earnings and Profits; Redemptions—Dividend Equivalence; Reorganizations) 273
   In General 273
   Bargain Purchases and Sales 277
   Bonus Payments 282
   Cancellation of Indebtedness 282
   Capital Gains Distinguished 284
   Disallowed Corporate Expenses 285
   Disguised and Constructive—Generally .. 287
   Distribution of Stock of Controlled Corporation 291
   Diverted Funds 292
   Dividends in Kind 293
   Earnings and Profits 293
   Excessive Salaries 295
   Guarantor Fees 296
   Intercorporate Transfers 296
   Life Insurance Premiums 298
   Loans Distinguished 299
   Payments Benefiting Stockholders 304
   Payments to Stockholders' Beneficiaries 309
   Satisfaction of Stockholder Obligations .. 312
   Stock Dividends and Rights 316
   Stockholder Use of Corporate Property 320
   Taxable Party 322
   Withdrawals by Stockholders Treated as Dividends 323

Dividends Paid Deduction (*See* Accumulated Earnings Tax; Personal Holding Companies)

Dividends Received Deduction 335

Divisive Reorganizations (*See* Reorganizations—Spin-Offs and Other Divisive Reorganizations)

Domestic International Sales Corporations 337

Dummy Corporations (*See* Associations Taxable as Corporations; Corporations as Taxable Entities)

Earned Surplus (*See* Earnings and Profits)

Index of Contents

Earnings and Profits (*See also* Dividends and Distributions) 337
Entertainment Expenses (*See* Business Expenses—Travel and Entertainment Expenses)
Essentially Equivalent to a Dividend (*See* Compensation for Personal Services—Dividend Equivalence; Dividends and Distributions; Redemptions—Dividend Equivalence; Reorganizations)
Exchanges—Tax-Free (*See* Reorganizations; Tax-Free Exchanges; Tax-Free Incorporations)
Expenses (*See* Business Expenses)
Fair Market Value (*See* Valuation of Property)
Family Transactions (*See* Related Taxpayers)
Foreign Corporations 342
Foreign Tax Credit (*See* Foreign Corporations)
Forgiveness of Debts (*See* Cancellation of Indebtedness)
Goodwill 343
Holding Companies (*See* Affiliated Corporations; Consolidated Returns; Personal Holding Companies)
Holding Period (*See* Capital Gains and Losses—Holding Period)
Illegal Income and Transactions (*See* Business Expenses—Bribes and Other Illegal Expenses)
Income (*See* Taxable Income of Corporations; Taxable Income of Stockholders)
Income Splitting (*See* Affiliated Corporations; Allocation Among Related Taxpayers)
Incorporations (*See* Reorganizations; Transfers to Controlled Corporations)
Indebtedness (*See* Bad Debts; Cancellation of Indebtedness)
Installment Obligations (*See* Accounting Methods—Installment Sales)
Installment Reporting (*See* Accounting Methods—Installment Sales)
Installment Sales (*See* Accounting Methods—Installment Sales)
Intercompany Transactions (*See* Affiliated Corporations; Allocation Among Related Taxpayers; Dividends and Distributions—Intercorporate Transfers)

Interest Expense (*See* Business Expenses—Interest Expenses)
Interest Income 345
Inventories (*See also* Accounting Methods) 345
Investment Tax Credit 347
Involuntary Conversions (*See also* Liquidations—Involuntary Conversions) ... 347
Judicial Doctrines (*See* Redemptions—Business Purpose)
Kickbacks (*See* Business Expenses—Bribes and Other Illegal Expenses)
Liabilities, Assumption Of (*See also* Cancellation of Indebtedness) 348
Like-Kind Exchanges 352
Liquidating Trusts 353
Liquidations 353
  In General 353
  Assignment of Income Doctrine 357
  Basis of Property Received 360
  Expenses Incurred in Liquidation 363
  Involuntary Conversions 365
  Liquidating Corporation's Gain or Loss 368
  Liquidating Distributions 371
  Liquidation of Subsidiaries 373
  One-Month Liquidations 375
  Partial Liquidations 379
  Reincorporations 385
  Stockholders' Gain or Loss 389
  Twelve-Month Liquidations—In General 392
  Twelve-Month Liquidations—Sale of Assets 399
  Twelve-Month Liquidations—Sale of Contracts 403
  Twelve-Month Liquidations—Sale of Inventory 403
  Twelve-Month Liquidations—Sale of Receivables 405
  Unused Bad Debt Reserve 406
Loans (*See* Bad Debts; Bonds and Debentures; Cancellation of Indebtedness; Dividends and Distributions—Loans Distinguished)
Loss Corporations (*See* Acquisitions to Avoid Tax; Consolidated Returns; Net Operating Losses)
Losses (*See also* Bad Debts; Business Expenses; Capital Gains and Losses; Net Operating Losses) 407
Market Value (*See* Valuation of Property)
Mergers (*See* Reorganizations)
Mitigation (*See* Procedure)

Index of Contents

Multiple Corporations (*See* Affiliated Corporations)

Net Operating Losses (*See also* Affiliated Corporations—Net Operating Loss Carry-Overs; Consolidated Returns—Net Operating Loss Carry-Overs; Reorganizations—Carry-Over of Net Operating Losses and Other Tax Attributes) 409
    Carry-Back of Net Operating Loss 409
    Carry-Forward of Net Operating Loss .. 411
    Loss Limitations 416

Nontaxable Exchanges (*See* Like-Kind Exchanges; Reorganizations; Transfers to Controlled Corporations)

Operating Losses (*See* Net Operating Losses)

Ordinary and Necessary (*See* Business Expenses—Ordinary and Necessary Requirement)

Parent Corporation (*See* Affiliated Corporations)

Partial Liquidations (*See* Liquidations—Partial Liquidations; Redemptions—Partial Liquidations)

Party to a Reorganization (*See* Reorganizations)

Payment of Tax (*See* Assessment and Collection)

Personal Compensation (*See* Compensation for Personal Services)

Personal Holding Companies 417
    In General 417
    Deficiency Dividends 420
    Dividends Paid Deduction 422
    Exemptions From Personal Holding Company Status 423
    Personal Holding Company Defined ... 426
    Personal Holding Company Income 431

Premium, Bond (*See* Bonds and Debentures—Bond Discount and Premiums)

Procedure (*See also* Assessment and Collection) 437
    In General 437
    Mitigation 439
    Penalties and Interest 439
    Refunds 440
    Returns 441

Professional Service Corporations (*See* Associations Taxable as Corporations—Professional Associations)

Proof of Expenditures (*See* Business Expenses—Substantiation)

Reasonable Salaries (*See* Compensation for Personal Services)

Recapitalizations (*See* Reorganizations—Recapitalizations)

Recapture of Depreciation (*See* Depreciation and Amortization—Recapture Of)

Recognition of Gain or Loss (*See* Capital Gains and Losses; Liquidations; Redemptions; Reorganizations; Transfers to Controlled Corporations)

Redemptions (*See also* Dividends and Distributions; Liquidations; Reorganizations) 442
    In General 442
    Attribution Rules 445
    Business Purpose 452
    Dividend Equivalence 454
    Effect on Redeeming Corporation 462
    Effect on Remaining Stockholders 463
    Gift Consequences 463
    Meaningful Reduction of Stockholder's Interest 464
    Partial Liquidations 469
    Redemptions by Affiliated Corporations 470
    Redemptions of Preferred Stock 474
    Redemptions to Pay Death Taxes 477
    Satisfaction of Stockholder Obligations .. 479
    Substantially Disproportionate Redemptions 483
    Termination of Stockholder's Interest ... 487

Reincorporations (*See* Liquidations—Reincorporations; Reorganizations)

Related Taxpayers (*See also* Affiliated Corporations; Allocation Among Related Taxpayers; Compensation for Personal Services; Dividends and Distributions—Payments to Stockholders' Beneficiaries; Transfers to Controlled Corporations) 493
    In General 493
    Expenses 495
    Losses 497
    Sales—In General 497
    Sales—Depreciable Property 500

Rents (*See also* Business Expenses; Dividends and Distributions) 502
    In General 502
    Deductibility Of 504

Reorganizations (*See also* Liquidations—Reincorporations; Transfers to Controlled Corporations) 509
    In General 509
    Acquisition of Assets (C Reorganizations) 514
    Acquisition of Stock (B Reorganizations) 518
    Boot 526
    Business Purpose 529

ix

Index of Contents

Carry-Over of Net Operating Losses and
Other Tax Attributes 532
Changes in Identity or Form (F
Reorganizations) 543
Continuity of Business 544
Continuity of Interest 546
Dividend Equivalence 549
Expenses 550
Mergers (A Reorganizations) 551
Recapitalizations (E Reorganizations) . . . 557
Reverse Acquisitions 559
Spin-Offs and Other Divisive
Reorganizations (D Reorganizations)–
Generally 559
Spin-Offs and Other Divisive
Reorganizations–Active Business
Requirement 568
Step-Transaction Doctrine 573

Research Expenditures (*See* Business
Expenses–In General)

Reserves (*See* Bad Debts–Reserves For;
Liquidations–Unused Bad Debt Reserve)

Retained Earnings (*See* Earnings and
Profits)

Rights, Stock (*See* Dividends and
Distributions–Stock Dividends and Rights)

Royalties 577

Salaries (*See* Compensation for Personal
Services; Dividends and Distributions–
Excessive Salaries)

Section 306 Stock 579

Section 1244 Stock 583

Securities (*See* Bonds and Debentures;
Capital Gains and Losses; Reorganizations;
Tax-Free Incorporations)

Sham Transactions (*See also* Allocation
Among Related Taxpayers–Sham
Transactions; Tax Avoidance) 585

Spin-Offs, Split-Offs, and Split-Ups (*See*
Reorganizations–Spin-Offs and Other
Divisive Reorganizations)

Splitting of Income (*See* Affiliated
Corporations; Allocation Among Related
Taxpayers)

Statutory Mergers (*See* Reorganizations–
Mergers)

Step-Transaction Doctrine (*See*
Reorganizations–Step-Transaction Doctrine;
Transfers to Controlled Corporations–Step-
Transaction Doctrine)

Stock Redemptions (*See* Redemptions)

Stock Retirement (*See* Liquidations;
Redemptions; Reorganizations)

Stock Rights (*See* Dividends and
Distributions–Stock Dividends and Rights)

Stock, Sales Of 587

Stock vs. Debt (*See* Bonds and Debentures;
Contributions to Capital; Debt vs. Equity)

Straw Corporations (*See* Associations
Taxable as Corporations; Corporations as
Taxable Entities)

Subsidiaries (*See* Affiliated Corporations;
Consolidated Returns)

Substantiation (*See* Business Expenses–
Substantiation)

Substituted Basis (*See* Basis of Property)

Successor Corporations (*See* Affiliated
Corporations; Net Operating Losses;
Reorganizations–Carry-Over of Net
Operating Losses and Other Tax Attributes)

Surplus (*See* Earnings and Profits)

Taxable Income of Corporations (*See also*
Capital Gains and Losses) 589

Taxable Income of Stockholders (*See also*
Capital Gains and Losses; Dividends and
Distributions) 591

Tax Avoidance (*See also* Acquisitions to
Avoid Tax; Allocation Among Related
Taxpayers; Reorganizations; Sham
Transactions) 592

Tax-Benefit Rule 595

Tax-Exempt Organizations 597

Tax-Free Exchanges (*See* Involuntary
Conversions; Like-Kind Exchanges;
Reorganizations; Transfers to Controlled
Corporations)

Tax-Free Incorporations (*See*
Reorganizations; Transfers to Controlled
Corporations)

Tax-Free Reorganizations (*See*
Reorganizations)

Tax Shelters (*See* Tax Avoidance)

Thin Capitalization (*See* Debt vs. Equity–
Thin Capitalization)

Trade or Business, Definition Of (*See*
Business Expenses–Profit Motive
Requirement; Reorganizations–Spin-Offs
and Other Divisive Reorganizations–Active
Business Requirement)

Transferee Liability (*See* Assessment and
Collection–Transferee Liability)

Transfers to Controlled Corporations (*See
also* Reorganizations) 599
In General 600

Index of Contents

Basis of Property Transferred 603
Control Defined 605
Step-Transaction Doctrine 607
Taxable Transfers 608
Tax-Free Transfers 614

Travel and Entertainment Expenses (*See* Business Expenses–Travel and Entertainment Expenses)

Twelve-Month Liquidations (*See* Liquidations–Twelve-Month Liquidations)

Undistributed Income (*See* Accumulated Earnings Tax; Personal Holding Companies)

Unreasonable Accumulations of Surplus (*See* Accumulated Earnings Tax)

Unrelated Business Income (*See* Tax-Exempt Organizations)

Useful Lives (*See* Depreciation and Amortization)

Valuation of Property 622

Withholding of Tax (*See* Assessment and Collection–Withholding Requirements)

Worthless Securities (*See* Bad Debts; Capital Gains and Losses; Contributions to Capital; Debt vs. Equity; Losses)

Year Deductible (*See* Accounting Methods; Bad Debts; Inventories)

Year Includible in Income (*See* Accounting Methods)

TABLE OF IRC SECTIONS T-1

TABLE OF TREASURY REGULATIONS T-7

TABLE OF REVENUE RULINGS T-9

TABLE OF CASES T-17

ACCELERATED DEPRECIATION

(*See* Depreciation and Amortization)

ACCOUNTING METHODS

(*See also* Bad Debts; Inventories)

In General	1
Accrual Method	1
Change of Method	1
Installment Sales	2

In General

Deferral of oil burner service income permitted for preconsolidation period since method of accounting commercially acceptable. Taxpayer was on a fiscal year ending June 30. Although taxpayer was engaged in servicing oil burners during the entire year, most of the taxpayer's expenses were incurred during the winter months. For its own accounting purposes, taxpayer deferred all service income and accrued an equal amount of such income monthly. Since taxpayer was acquired by a consolidated group on January 10, 1963, it filed a short period return for the six-month period July 1, 1962 to December 31, 1962. The IRS contended that Schlude, 372 US 128, required that all income received by taxpayer be included in the short period return. *Held:* For taxpayer. The court held that Schlude was inapplicable. Regulation § 1.1502-32A read in conjunction with Section 446 permits taxpayer to use regular method of accounting for short period returns preceding affiliation so long as method is commercially acceptable and is ordinarily used in the trade. Petroleum Heat & Power Co., 405 F2d 1300, 69-1 USTC ¶ 9190 (Ct. Cl. 1969).

Accrual Method

Corporation denied salary deduction for compensation paid over two and a half months after close of year. Taxpayer reported its income on the basis of a fiscal year ending June 30 and the accrual method of accounting. As of June 30, for each of the years in question, it accrued bonuses for its employees. These bonuses were not paid until December, in accordance with determinations of the respective amounts of the bonuses made in September by a 52 percent stockholder officer. Taxpayer claimed a deduction for the bonus accruals in question. *Held:* For the IRS. In authorizing the bonuses, the board of directors did not designate the amounts payable to the individual recipients. Taxpayer was unable to establish that the apportionment was made prior to September 15, the date on which the statutory period of Section 267(a)(2) expired. The right, as distinguished from the power, to receive funds controls the doctrine of constructive receipt. A shareholder's controlling position does not mandate a finding of constructive receipt when this power does not coexist with a right. Accordingly, the deductions for the bonus accruals were denied. Lacy Contracting Co., 56 TC 464 (1971).

Change of Method

Incorporation following business change from cash to accrual method of accounting causes acceleration of the Section 481 income adjustment that is otherwise allowed to be spread over a 10-year period. Taxpayer owned and operated a sole proprietorship using the cash receipts and disbursements method of accounting. In 1968, taxpayer was required to report a net increase of income which he was permitted to spread over 10 years. In 1970, taxpayer incorporated his sole proprietorship. Taxpayer continued to report the Section 481 adjustment on his personal tax return. The IRS claimed that the incorporation accelerated the realization of the remaining eight years of income from the Section 481 adjustment. In particular, the IRS asserted that the incorporation constituted a "cessation of business," which is an acceleration

Accounting Methods: *Installment Sales*

event under Section 481. The Tax Court held for the IRS. *Held:* Affirmed. Section 481 and the Revenue Procedures that apply Section 481 focus on the taxpayer and not on his business. Thus, although taxpayer had been actively engaged in business as a proprietor, he thereafter converted his proprietary interest into stock; the holding of such stock does not constitute a business. The fact that the taxpayer was an officer and employee of the newly formed corporation was immaterial. Further, the court found that the acceleration of income under Section 481 was not inconsistent with the otherwise nontaxable treatment of the incorporation under Section 351. Dean R. Shore, 631 F2d 624, 80-2 USTC ¶ 9759, 46 AFTR2d 80-6104 (9th Cir. 1980).

Carry-over permitted transitional adjustment resulting from a change of accounting method. In a transaction in which Section 381(a) was applicable, the unreported portion of a transitional adjustment resulting from a change in accounting method that was allocated over a period of years was carried over to the acquiring corporation. Rev. Rul. 68-527, 1968-2 CB 162.

Installment Sales

Taxpayer denied use of installment method as he received 30 percent of sales price in year of sale. Taxpayer was the majority stockholder and ultimate decision maker of *R* Corporation. Taxpayer sold two mineral leases to *R* for $2 million. *R* paid taxpayer $50,000 in cash, and in lieu of the formal assumption of taxpayer's mortgage, *R* gave taxpayer a $1,950,000 promissory note payable in monthly installments of not less than $25,000, plus interest. *R*'s promissory note was secured by taxpayer's own promissory note to a bank, which was, in turn, secured by the mortgage on the leases. Taxpayer elected to report his gain from the lease sale on the installment basis pursuant to Section 453. The district court agreed with the IRS that the taxpayer was not entitled to use the installment method to report his gain. *Held:* Affirmed. Where payments received by the taxpayer in the year of sale of the real property exceeded 30 percent of the sales price, the taxpayer was not permitted to report his gain from the sale on the installment method. *R* reimbursed taxpayer for interest payments made on the mortgage, which represented an indirect assumption of the mortgage. Thus, the amount of the mortgages was included in the computation of the 30 percent. Republic Petroleum Corp., 613 F2d 518, 80-1 USTC ¶ 9279, 45 AFTR2d 80-1045 (5th Cir. 1980).

Use of installment method required receipt of at least two payments. Taxpayer and *A* Corporation were wholly owned by *M*. Taxpayer, who was engaged in the rental and management of real estate, sold rental property to *A*, who then assumed a $400,000 mortgage and executed a $100,000 purchase-money mortgage due in 11 years. No payment was made in the year of sale and the only payment called for was the $100,000 payment due 11 years hence. The IRS determined that taxpayer could not use the installment method to report the gain on the sale. Instead, the gain was reportable as ordinary income under Section 1239(a) because taxpayer and *A* were both owned by *M*. Thus, the sale was an indirect one between an individual and the vendee corporation. *Held:* For the IRS, in part. In order for a sale to qualify under Section 453 for use of the installment method of reporting gain, there must be more than a single, future payment. Where corporations were bona fide, capital gains treatment was available to intercorporate transactions. Taxpayer argued that under Section 1239(a), "individual" was equivalent to "corporation" through the use of the word "indirect"; this argument was not valid. 10-42 Corp., 55 TC 593 (1971), acq. 1979-1 CB 11.

Distributions of installment obligations. A corporation recognized gain at the time it distributed installment obligations acquired in prior years upon the sale of land used in its business with outstanding balances greater than fair market value, which was greater than basis. The recognition of gain does not result in an increase in the amount of distribution, an increase in the basis of the obligations in the hands of the shareholders, or adjustments of the decrease in earnings and profit. Rev. Rul. 74-337, 1974-2 CB 94.

ACCUMULATED EARNINGS TAX

In General	3
Accumulated Earnings Credit	5
Accumulated Taxable Income	6
Burden of Proof	7
Consolidated Groups	11
Contingent Liabilities	13
Dividends Paid Deduction	13
Expansion Plans	14
Liquidating Distributions	21
Passive Investment Income	22
Reasonable Business Needs	23
Tax-Avoidance Purpose	37

In General

Instructions to jury in accumulated earnings case were adequate. Taxpayer, a family corporation, operated an oyster packing plant on leased land. Because taxpayer feared loss of its lease, the authorized capital stock of the corporation was increased to finance the contemplated move. No other plans were drawn up, although taxpayer's deceased president had consulted an attorney about the cost of replacing the land and equipment. The IRS determined taxpayer to be subject to the accumulated earnings tax. At the district court level, the jury was given instructions to determine if taxpayer was subject to the tax. The judge noted that a closely held corporation was not held to the same strict formalities as a large publicly held corporation. The IRS contended that the instructions were improper. *Held:* For taxpayer. Where the jury instructions, as a whole, fairly and adequately stated the legal principles involved concerning the accumulated earnings tax, affirmance of the court below was required. Disapproval of certain portions of the instructions concerning closely held corporations, and also the time when intent was to be examined, were insufficient to overrule the lower court. Hogg's Oyster Co., 676 F2d 1015, 82-1 USTC ¶ 9353, 49 AFTR2d 82-1383 (4th Cir. 1982).

No Section 531 tax on accumulations, distribution of which exceeded 1971 anti-inflation guidelines. Taxpayer paid no dividends during its 1971-1972 fiscal year, during which federal dividend "guidelines", part of the current wage-price antiinflation guidelines, restricted payment of dividends. It was not clear how the guidelines applied to closely held corporations. The IRS imposed the Section 531 tax on taxpayer's full accumulations, contending that a corporation must have paid the highest dividend permitted under the guidelines for excess accumulations to be free of penalty tax. *Held:* For taxpayer, in part. The IRS' demand to pay up to the dividend limit violated the spirit of the guidelines and forced taxpayers to walk on a razor's edge between Section 531 and the antiinflation rules. But the tax may be imposed on accumulations that could have been paid out within the guidelines. Estate of Lucas, 657 F2d 841, 81-2 USTC ¶ 9782, 48 AFTR2d 81-5836 (6th Cir. 1981).

Interest on accumulated earnings tax deficiency begins only after the IRS has given notice and demand for its payment. Taxpayer filed its income tax return for the years 1954 through 1960 by the appropriate due dates, and paid the taxes shown to be due on the face of the returns. After an audit, the IRS assessed taxpayer, on July 9, 1965, for accumulated earnings tax for the years 1954 through 1960. Included in the assessment was a charge for interest on this tax computed from the due dates of the various returns involved. The taxpayer asserted that interest on the accumulated earnings tax assessed did not begin until notice and demand was made for its payment. The District Court held for the IRS. *Held:* Reversed. Because the accumulated earnings tax is not self-assessing, the normal rules for interest accrual did not apply. The liability for such interest arises when liability for the accumulated earnings tax arises, i.e., only after the IRS has given notice and demand for its payment. Loper, 444 F2d 301, 71-2 USTC ¶ 9514, 28 AFTR2d 71-5074 (6th Cir. 1971).

Interest on deficiencies in accumulated earnings tax is collectible from date of notice and demand and not from due date of return. IRS mailed corporate taxpayer a deficiency notice

Accumulated Earnings Tax: *In General*

with respect to an accumulated earnings tax liability. Thereafter, the Tax Court held taxpayer liable for certain deficiencies. Taxpayer sent in the amounts within 10 days of notice and demand for payment in an effort to stop the running of interest on the deficiencies determined against it. Taxpayer filed a claim for refund on a portion of the interest paid on the accumulated earnings tax, which was denied. Thereafter, the district court held against the taxpayer because it failed to demonstrate that the interest on the redetermined deficiencies in accumulated earnings tax was collectible from it only from and after the date of sending the formal notice and demand, rather than the due date of its federal income tax return. *Held:* Reversed. Accumulated earnings tax was an addition to regular income tax. Where taxpayer paid the tax within 10 days of notice and demand for payment, taxpayer was not chargeable with interest. Interest did not accrue from the due date of taxpayer's federal income tax return. Bardahl Mfg. Corp., 452 F2d 604, 72-1 USTC ¶ 9158, 29 AFTR2d 72-321 (9th Cir. 1971).

Section 531 assertion was no surprise. Contending that taxpayer was a mere holding or investment company, the IRS asserted the tax on accumulated earnings. The Tax Court sustained the determination. It held that taxpayer was clearly an investment company after it sold its business assets. As such, taxpayer was prima facie subject to the tax. *Held:* Affirmed. The record did not support taxpayer's contention that it was taken by surprise by the IRS' argument that taxpayer was a mere holding company. The claim of surprise was a "resourceful afterthought." Rhombar Co., 386 F2d 510, 67-2 USTC ¶ 9743, 20 AFTR2d 5764 (2d Cir. 1967).

Court properly excluded evidence of subsequent distributions in sustaining accumulated earnings tax. The district court held taxpayer liable for the accumulated earnings tax. On appeal, taxpayer contended that the lower court erred in excluding evidence that taxpayer's shareholder did not enjoy a tax saving until 1959 as the result of taxpayer's delaying distributions for one year. Taxpayer also claimed the court's charge to the jury was prejudicial. Taxpayer's last argument was that the court improperly excluded certain "expert" testimony. *Held:* Affirmed. Occurrences in 1959 were not relevant to the key issue of taxpayer's intent to retain unreasonable accumulations in 1958. Taxpayer's failure to object to the district court's charge to the jury precluded him from doing so at the appellate level. The district court did not abuse its discretion in determining that taxpayer's witnesses did not qualify as experts. Stevenson, 378 F2d 354, 67-2 USTC ¶ 9498, 19 AFTR2d 1641 (2d Cir. 1967).

Imposition of accumulated earnings tax on non-publicly held corporation was not a violation of due process or equal protection. On motion for summary judgment, taxpayer, a nonpublicly owned corporation, claimed that it was denied due process of law and equal protection of law because of the uneven application of the accumulated earnings tax to corporations; it claimed that publicly owned corporations are exempt and application of the tax is limited to nonpublicly owned corporations. On this basis, taxpayer sought a refund of accumulated earnings tax. *Held:* For the IRS. The accumulated earnings tax can apply to publicly held corporations. Accordingly, taxpayer's claim was not valid. Alphatype Corp., 76-2 USTC ¶ 9730, 38 AFTR2d 76-6019 (Ct. Cl. 1976).

Interest on accumulated earnings tax accrues only from date of notice and demand. Taxpayer paid 1958–1962 assessments of accumulated earnings tax, including interest from the due dates of the returns, within 10 days of notice and demand. Taxpayer argued that it was entitled to a refund of the interest because (1) under Section 6601(f)(3), interest was due only if the tax was not paid within 10 days of notice and demand, or (2) under Section 6601(a), "the last date prescribed for payment" was the date of notice and demand. *Held:* For taxpayer. (1) Section 6601(f)(3), which includes interest on penalties, additional amounts, or additions to the tax, covers the accumulated earnings tax, which is not self-assessable and is an addition to the regular income tax. (2) Even if Section 6601(a) applied, no interest was due under

ACCUMULATED EARNINGS TAX: *Accumulated Earnings Credit*

Section 6601(f)(4) because the last date prescribed for payment of the Section 531 tax is the date of notice and demand pursuant to Sections 6601(c) and 6155. Motor Fuel Carriers, Inc., 420 F2d 702, 70-1 USTC ¶ 9191, 25 AFTR2d 70-492 (Ct. Cl. 1970).

No pre-trial ruling on whether Section 534 statement shifted burden of proof. Taxpayer filed a statement under Section 534 setting forth the grounds on which it relied in establishing that its earnings and profits were not accumulated beyond its reasonable needs. Taxpayer then made a motion requesting the Tax Court to determine whether the statement was sufficient to shift to the IRS the burden of proving an unreasonable accumulation. *Held:* Motion denied. The Tax Court found no occasion for changing its consistent practice of refusing to rule on this question prior to trial. The Shaw-Walker Co., 39 TC 293 (1962).

Negligence penalty can be asserted where accumulated earnings tax applies. The amount of an accumulated earnings tax under Section 531 is an "additional amount" where the computation of interest is concerned but not for purposes of the negligence penalty of Section 6653(a). Accordingly, where the facts and circumstances are sufficient, a negligence penalty may apply. The IRS indicated that it would not automatically assert the penalty in every case. Rev. Rul. 75-330, 1975-2 CB 496.

No interest due on accumulated earnings tax if paid within 10 days of notice and demand. As a result of recent court decisions, the IRS conceded that no interest is due on accumulated earnings tax if paid within 10 days of notice and demand. If not paid within such time, interest accrues on the unpaid amount from the date of notice and demand to the date of payment. Rev. Rul. 66-237 revoked. Rev. Rul. 72-324, 1972-1 CB 399.

Section 531 resulted in a deficiency for interest computation. In reviewing the history of present Section 531, the IRS concluded that a tax imposed under that section was an additional Chapter 1 tax. Such an amount was a deficiency and was therefore subject to all provisions applicable to the assessment and collection of deficiencies and the computation of interest thereon. Therefore, the date the liability for the accumulated earnings tax under Section 531 arose was to be determined in the same manner as in the case of any other deficiency for interest computations under Section 6601. Rev. Rul. 66-237, 1966-2 CB 508.

Accumulated Earnings Credit

Imposition of accumulated earnings tax upheld; no evidence of reasonable business needs or minimum credit applicable. Taxpayer corporation accumulated net income after taxes of $313,000 during the first three years of its existence and did not declare any cash dividends, although it declared stock dividends of $150,000. If cash dividends had been declared, they would have been subject to tax at rates of 55 percent to 68 percent. In addition, taxpayer made loans and purchased securities unrelated to its business. The IRS determined that the taxpayer had been availed of to avoid taxes by allowing earnings and profits to accumulate and that no part of such earnings were retained for the reasonable needs of the business. Taxpayer contended that the needs of the business included a possible relocation of the business, diversification of products, and cash requirements for the next year. *Held:* For the IRS. There were no positive steps taken to relocate other than the purchase of a vacant tract. The need asserted by the taxpayer was based solely on a local news story stating that the property was to be condemned, but the threat was a long-range projection at best. Investments in unrelated businesses indicated that taxpayers attempted to put its surplus to work, and this constituted a strategy to avoid the income tax on the stockholders. No part of the cash was needed for future operation because anticipated future revenues exceeded projected expenditures. The needs of the business must be credible and supported by testimony, and taxpayer did not sustain this burden. Taxpayer was not permitted any general credit, since no part of the accumulation was required for the needs of the business. Further, taxpayer was not permitted a minimum credit for 1955

ACCUMULATED EARNINGS TAX: *Accumulated Taxable Income*

under Section 535(c)(2) because, when stock dividends were taken into earnings and profits, the accumulation exceeded $60,000. E-Z Sew Enters., Inc., 260 F. Supp. 100, 66-2 USTC ¶ 9599, 18 AFTR2d 5607 (ED Mich. 1966).

Separate surtax exemptions and Section 531 minimum credit allowed where several corporations are formed for valid business reasons. Taxpayer corporations were organized by the same individual to sell soft goods in several department stores. One corporation paid interest on a loan from the individual. The IRS, under Section 269(a), claimed that each corporation was not entitled to separate $25,000 surtax exemptions or full minimum accumulated earnings credit of Section 535(c)(2), since they were formed for the principal purpose of avoiding income tax. The interest deduction was also disallowed. *Held:* For the taxpayer, in part. The corporations were formed for the valid business reasons of being able to sell, manage, secure capital, and insulate obligations of the separate units. No tax consequences were considered when the corporations were formed. Since Section 269 did not apply, each corporation was also entitled to a full minimum credit, and there was no accumulated earnings tax. The interest deductions were denied, since taxpayer failed to prove that the corporation was obligated to pay the interest. Lake Textile Co., 28 TCM 246, ¶ 69,044 P-H Memo. TC (1969).

Corporation selling insurance policies is not service corporation. With respect to tax years ending after 1981, a corporation engaged in the business of selling insurance policies for insurance companies is not a service corporation as described in Section 535(c)(2) It is therefore entitled to a minimum accumulated earnings credit of $250,000. Rev. Rul. 84-101, 1984-2 CB 115.

Business needs not considered in computing accumulated earnings credit of investment company. Reasonable business needs such as working capital and liquidity were not considered in computation of the accumulated earnings credit of a company determined to be a mere holding or investment company under Section 533(b). Rev. Rul. 77-368, 1977-2 CB 201.

Prior year's accumulated earnings tax may be used as a credit to meet reasonable needs of current year. In determining if there is an unreasonable accumulation of earnings and profits in the current year, the prior year's accumulated earnings tax may be taken into consideration. However, pursuant to Regulation § 1.535-3(b)(1)(ii), the accumulated earnings and profits of the prior year must be analyzed to determine whether any portion of its accumulation may be used in computing the credit for the current taxable year. Rev. Rul. 70-301, 1970-1 CB 138.

Accumulated Taxable Income

Proceeds from sale of corporate assets not subject to accumulated earnings tax. The IRS attempted to impose the accumulated earnings tax in a year in which taxpayer corporation sold substantially all of its operating assets. A district court held for taxpayer. *Held:* Affirmed. The appellate court found that no permanent or semipermanent investment of the sales proceeds was made in the disputed year. The cash proceeds were retained in a savings account for the reasonably anticipated needs of the business. There was no tax avoidance in the accumulation at either shareholder or corporate levels. Starman Inv., Inc., 534 F2d 834, 76-1 USTC ¶ 9376, 37 AFTR2d 76-1294 (9th Cir. 1976).

Sale of all corporate assets shortly before close of tax year (without intent to reinvest) triggers accumulated earnings tax, where distribution of sales proceeds occurred after the close of such year. In February 1968, taxpayer sold its assets and its stockholders decided it should dissolve. Thus, by February 29, 1968, the end of its tax year, taxpayer no longer had any business needs or future business plans that would require reinvestment of its profits. Taxpayer distributed a portion of its sale proceeds on April 30, 1968 and retained the balance. The IRS assessed accumulated earnings tax for the year ending February 29, 1968. *Held:* For the IRS. Since taxpayer, by its board and stockholders, intended to dissolve after sale of its assets, it no longer had any "reasonable business needs" for its undistributed earnings. Lynch, 74-1 USTC ¶ 9273, 33 AFTR2d 75-847 (CD Cal. 1974).

Unpaid deficiency not deductible in computing accumulated earnings. Taxpayer was held liable for the accumulated earnings tax. In computing its 1974 income subject to the tax, the taxpayer reduced its accumulated taxable income by the amount of a deficiency asserted for 1974. *Held:* For the IRS. The Tax Court held that the corporation could not reduce its accumulated taxable income by the amount of the deficiency because, although it did not contest the deficiency, an unpaid deficiency is by definition a contested liability and therefore may not be used to reduce accumulated taxable income. Doug-Long, Inc., 73 TC 71 (1980).

Interest-bearing warrants received for services performed were current assets in determining accumulations penalty. Taxpayer, engaged in paying contract work for municipalities, was paid with interest-bearing special assessment warrants. The IRS imposed an accumulations penalty, contending that the interest-bearing warrants were current assets; as such, the current assets were in excess of current liabilities in an amount more than that required for the corporation's working capital needs and other reasonable business needs. *Held:* For the IRS. The warrants were current assets, as they were readily marketable, and taxpayer had sold some of them in prior years. They were included as current assets on taxpayer's financial statements. Taxpayer would not have been able to obtain a surety bond if these warrants had not been considered current assets by the surety company and taxpayer had treated the warrants as current assets. Ready Paving & Constr. Co., 61 TC 826 (1974).

Tax-exempt income and Section 531. Since the Section 531 tax is imposed on a corporation's "accumulated taxable income," tax exempt interest is omitted from the calculation. However, such income is included in earnings and profits to determine whether they have been accumulated beyond a reasonable need. Rev. Rul. 70-497, 1970-2 CB 128.

Burden of Proof

Accumulated earnings tax imposed; taxpayer fails to meet burden of showing reasonable accumulation. On the issue of whether taxpayer was used by its stockholders in 1956 for the purpose of avoiding income tax by permitting its earnings and profits to accumulate, it listed five major grounds in its Section 534 statement, namely: (1) to provide for expansion of business and replacement of plant; (2) to acquire business enterprises through purchase of stock and assets; (3) to provide for working capital; (4) to provide for investments or loans to suppliers or customers; and (5) to provide for continuation of business when the principal stockholder officer died. The corporation had accumulated a surplus of $3 million as of December 31, 1955, when its current assets were over $2.3 million and its total current liabilities only $350,000. *Held:* For the IRS. The court thought it evident that all the "commitments" given by taxpayer as reasons for its accumulation in 1956 could have been met by the accumulated surplus at the beginning of the year. Youngs Rubber Co., 331 F2d 12, 64-1 USTC ¶ 9416 (2d Cir. 1964).

Taxpayer allowed to show need for part of surplus accumulation. Taxpayer was engaged in a trucking business. Almost all its equipment was leased or financed through banks. It contended that its earnings must be accumulated for the construction of a terminal building and for the purchase of new equipment. The district court found that taxpayer had no definite plans for the construction of a terminal building. It also concluded that from its history of financing equipment purchases it was not necessary to accumulate funds for such purpose or for additional working capital. *Held:* Vacated and remanded. In the trial of the case, neither side considered the possibility of establishing a credit for that part of the accumulation which could be shown to be reasonable. While the burden of proof was on the taxpayer to establish the credit, if any, to which it was entitled, the court vacated the

ACCUMULATED EARNINGS TAX: *Burden of Proof*

judgment, in the interest of fairness, to permit additional testimony on this issue. Motor Fuel Carriers, Inc., 322 F2d 576, 63-2 USTC ¶ 9697, 12 AFTR2d 5554 (5th Cir. 1963).

Burden of proof shifted to the IRS in accumulated earnings tax case; first appeal case reverses Tax Court. Taxpayer corporation submitted a 24-page statement of its reasons for accumulating surplus and argued that this shifted the burden of proof on the issue of accumulation beyond reasonable business needs, according to the provisions of Section 534. Nevertheless, the Tax Court found that the tax applied because the proscribed purpose of avoiding surtax was present. Taxpayer was in the business of importing Swiss watch movements. Taxpayer's statement showed that it had large outstanding commitments at various times and had to advance substantial customs duties. The IRS' only evidence of unreasonable business needs was the substantial investment in marketable securities, which taxpayer alleged might be required to meet these commitments. *Held:* Reversed. The court found that the IRS had failed to meet its burden of proof as to reasonable business needs. It was an error for the Tax Court to bypass this issue and move directly to the question of the surtax avoidance purpose. Gsell & Co., 294 F2d 321, 61-2 USTC ¶ 9671, 8 AFTR2d 5507 (2d Cir. 1961).

Section 531 statement did not shift burden of proof; not enough facts. Taxpayer, the Dixie Hotel in New York's Time Square area, never paid dividends; it had an accumulated surplus of about $700,000 at the end of the year 1952. The Tax Court found that the burden of proof was on the taxpayer because the statement it filed attempting to shift the burden of proof gave merely the grounds that it urged would justify the accumulation but did not give sufficient facts to prove the reasonableness of the accumulation. The Tax Court upheld the penalty tax. *Held:* Affirmed. Taxpayer did nothing but recognize future problems and discuss possible and alternative solutions. Definiteness of plan, coupled with action taken toward its consummation, are essential. Taxpayer also contended its retention of earning and profits was per se reasonable, since these were substantially less than its operating costs over 1 million per year. This rule of thumb may be proper for administrative convenience, but the needs of the particular business as they existed in the particular year were decisive. Dixie, Inc., 277 F2d 526, 60-1 USTC ¶ 9419, 5 AFTR2d 1239 (2d Cir.), cert. denied, 364 US 827 (1960).

Taxpayer failed to show need for part of surplus accumulation. Taxpayer was engaged in a trucking business. Almost all of its equipment was leased or financed through banks. It contended that its earnings must be accumulated for the construction of a terminal building and for the purchase of new equipment. The district court found that taxpayer had no definite plans for the construction of a terminal building. It also concluded that from taxpayer's purchase history, it was not necessary to accumulate funds for the purchase of financing equipment or for additional working capital. At trial, neither side considered the possibility of establishing a credit for that part of the accumulation that could be shown to be reasonable. The Fifth Circuit therefore remanded the case for a determination of whether a partial credit was applicable. *Held:* On remand, the district court found that no part of the earnings was accumulated for reasonable business needs. Taxpayer's financial history showed no need to accumulate earnings to meet competition. Motor Fuel Carriers, Inc., 244 F. Supp. 380, 65-2 USTC ¶ 9454 (ND Fla. 1965).

IRS not required to show theory for imposing accumulated earnings tax. Taxpayer moved for the production of documents showing the computations and analyses upon which the IRS based its assessment of the penalty tax on an unreasonable accumulation of earnings. *Held:* Motion denied. Taxpayer had the burden of proving that the accumulation was necessary under Section 531. Taxpayer's success did not depend upon the theory used by the IRS in asserting Section 531. Unistruck Corp., 65-1 USTC ¶ 9349 (ED Mich. 1965).

A Section 534(c) statement must provide facts sufficient to show the basis of the asserted

Accumulated Earnings Tax: Burden of Proof

grounds, and the grounds generally require a mere denial of unreasonable accumulation. Taxpayer's corporation moved for a pretrial ruling that its Section 534(c) statement relating to the grounds for the accumulation of its earnings was sufficient to shift the burden of proof of unreasonable accumulations to the IRS. *Held:* For the IRS. While a Section 534(c) statement need not contain sufficient evidence to prove the grounds set forth, it must provide facts sufficient to show the basis of the asserted grounds (namely, the ultimate and supporting facts on which the taxpayer will rely). However, as to those grounds requiring merely a denial, the denial alone will generally suffice. Further, the opportunity for discovery does not affect the scope of the facts that must be included, since the purpose of Section 534(c) is to precipitate administrative level settlement. Rutter, 81 TC 937 (1983).

Burden of proof in accumulated earnings tax case determined. The IRS notified taxpayer that it proposed to issue a notice of deficiency for the accumulated earnings tax on May 15, 1979 and advised taxpayer that it had 60 days to submit a statement explaining why it believed it was not subject to the tax. On June 25, 1979, the IRS mailed the taxpayer a notice of deficiency under Section 534(b). Taxpayer did not respond to that notice, but filed a timely petition with the Tax Court. Taxpayer contended that it should be excused from submitting the Section 534(c) statement because the IRS mailed the notice of deficiency before the Section 534(c) response was due. *Held:* For taxpayer. The deadline for submitting the Section 534(c) statement was extended, since taxpayer's belief that the notice of defiency excused compliance with Section 534(c), although erroneous, was reasonable and no prejudice would result. Manson W. Corp., 76 TC 1161 (1981).

Corporation fails to justify surplus accumulation. Since 1863, taxpayer and its predecessors had operated a cigar manufacturing business that became the largest in the New England area. In 1956, the corporation, a pioneer in new processes and machinery to the industry, began experimenting with a new kind of binder for cigars. This new binder substituted a sheet composed of finely ground tobacco for the less economical tobacco leaf. Although the principal officer and stockholder investigated the feasibility of manufacturing the binder, the corporation continued to purchase the binder from outside firms. By utilizing the new binder, the corporation was able to reduce its inventory of leaf tobacco and to invest the freed funds in securities. In 1958, the controlling group of stockholders sold their stock to new owners. The parties set a price based upon a balance sheet for September 30, 1957, and the seller warranted that between that date and the date of sale, January 1, 1958, no dividends were paid. For the period from 1956 to the date of sale, the IRS asserted the tax on excessive accumulation of surplus. *Held:* The accumulation was excessive. The funds released by the inventory reduction were sufficient to provide a capital for the establishment of a plant to produce the new binder. No further retention of earnings was necessary because current assets adequately covered operating expenses. In arriving at its decision, the court did not consider a $160,000 loan to a stockholder evidence of an excessive accumulation. The repayment of the loan negated the presumption of the regulations. The conversion of the accumulation to capital gain by the sale tended to establish intent. The consequence of a dividend to any individual stockholder had no bearing on intent. The warranties contained in the sales contract did not prevent a dividend, but assured the buyer of an adjusted price if the corporation did not pay a dividend. Apollo Indus., Inc., 44 TC 1 (1965).

Corporation failed to prove reasonableness of accumulations. The IRS assessed accumulated earnings tax against taxpayer, which operated a real estate business. The corporation did not pay a dividend for over 30 years, and during the years in question had more than $500,000 in working capital. Taxpayer cited several reasons for the accumulations, such as plans to renovate deteriorated buildings, to redeem a shareholders' stock when he died, to establish a self-insurance fund, and to cover anticipated future losses. *Held:* For the IRS.

Accumulated Earnings Tax: *Burden of Proof*

Taxpayer failed to establish sufficient evidence of the purported needs, or that specific and definite plans for use of the funds existed. Boshwit Bros., 43 TCM 906, ¶ 82,156 P-H Memo. TC (1982).

Accumulated earnings tax on unreasonable accumulation appropriate. Taxpayer corporation, an insurance agency, accumulated earnings of about $200,000 for 1965 and 1966. The IRS asserted the accumulated earnings tax. Taxpayer argued that it had plans to build new facilities and to hire outside salesmen. *Held:* For the IRS. The justifications for the accumulation were insufficient. There was no indication that taxpayer intended or needed to construct a new building. The amount of funds on deposit with and the business received from a savings and loan association was not shown. There was no showing of a reasonable business need to hire outside salesmen [or the cost of such a hiring.] Furthermore, no dividends had been paid since incorporation in 1955. Thus, a tax-avoidance purpose motivated the retention of earnings. The application of the accumulated earnings tax was appropriate. Bohac Agency, Inc, 30 TCM 979, ¶ 71,228 P-H Memo. TC (1971).

Mere holding company failed to meet burden of proof to overcome unreasonable accumulations. Taxpayer corporation operated an auto dealership under a Ford franchise in Illinois. In 1955, when its president obtained a Cadillac franchise in Milwaukee, taxpayer was required to surrender its Ford franchise. Taxpayer sold its business, and its activities thereafter consisted of loans, investments, and rental of real estate. The IRS contended that taxpayer engaged in no business activities during the taxable years and was therefore a holding or investment company under Section 533(b), and thus was liable for the accumulated earnings tax. Taxpayer maintained that the purpose of the accumulation was to have sufficient funds to operate a Cadillac franchise in Illinois that it reasonably anticipated obtaining. *Held:* For the IRS. Evidence established that taxpayer had no reasonable anticipation of obtaining a Cadillac franchise in Illinois during the years in issue or in the reasonably foreseeable future, and also that as of the beginning of each of the years in issue, taxpayer's already accumulated earnings and profits were ample to finance operations under such a franchise if one were obtained. Nodell Motors Inc., 26 TCM 1027, ¶ 67,209 P-H Memo. TC (1967).

Office equipment manufacturer liable for accumulated earnings tax. After the IRS asserted an accumulated earnings tax penalty against taxpayer, it filed a statement pursuant to Section 534(c) giving five reasons why the earnings were not accumulated beyond the reasonable needs of the business. The grounds were that taxpayer needed the earnings (1) to provide sufficient working capital for normal operations, (2) to replace fixed assets, since taxpayer believed in internal financing, (3) to provide funds for development of a new product, (4) to repurchase executive stock pursuant to a plan on which the holders were relying, and (5) to increase its sales to banks. *Held:* For the IRS. The penalty was sustained. Taxpayer's statement was too general to shift the burden of proof to the IRS. The grounds listed in the statement were insufficient to justify taxpayer's extremely liquid position whereby approximately 50 percent of its total assets were in cash or cash equivalents. Shaw-Walker Co., 24 TCM 1709, ¶ 65,309 P-H Memo. TC (1965).

Family investment company liable for the Section 531 tax. Taxpayer, a family corporation in the investment business, was notified pursuant to Section 534(a) that the IRS intended to issue a deficiency notice based on an asserted accumulated earnings tax. Taxpayer submitted a timely statement to justify its accumulation. *Held:* For the IRS. Even if all the "grounds" submitted by taxpayer were true, there was no justification for accumulating any current earnings and profits, since taxpayer did not even justify its retention of $625,500 that it had accumulated *prior* to the taxable year. Taxpayer failed to show by a preponderance of evidence that it was not availed of for the purpose of avoiding the income tax with respect to its shareholders. Otmar Real Estate Corp., ¶ 65,189 P-H Memo. TC (1965).

ACCUMULATED EARNINGS TAX: Consolidated Groups

Accumulation of earnings to meet performance bond requirements is reasonable. The IRS determined that taxpayer, a building contractor, was liable for the accumulated earnings tax. Taxpayer made interest-free loans to its stockholders, invested a large part of its retained earnings in marketable securities, and had a working capital ratio in excess of eight to one. In order to shift the burden of proof to the IRS, taxpayer submitted a Section 534 statement that supported its retention of earnings on the grounds that the accumulation was (1) to provide for bona fide expansion of business, (2) to provide necessary working capital for performance bond requirements, and (3) to provide a safeguard against business hazards. *Held:* For taxpayer. The IRS did not carry its burden of proof. The accumulation of earnings was not beyond the corporation's reasonable business needs because, in order to qualify for performance bonds, the corporation was required to retain working capital equal to at least 10 percent of its work program in addition to its need for operating capital. Since all of the corporation's working capital was not always immediately required, the fact that it invested part of its earnings in securities did not establish that it might not have needed the proceeds. Also, taxpayer's jobs in progress increased so that it needed its working capital for bona fide expansion of business. Vuono-Lione, Inc., 24 TCM 506, ¶ 65,096 P-H Memo. TC (1965).

Accumulated earnings tax assessed in absence of proof of reasonable business need. The IRS assessed the accumulated earnings tax against taxpayer corporation, a vendor of canned foods. During the years involved, 100 percent of taxpayer's stock was owned by its president and his wife, and its earnings had increased approximately $21,000 per year. The corporation never paid a dividend or a salary to its president. Taxpayer did not submit to the IRS a Section 534 statement. Taxpayer contended that the accumulation was essential to meet seasonal fluctuations of inventory and accounts receivable. *Held:* For the IRS. Taxpayer failed to establish the reasonableness of the accumulation to meet the special requirements of its operations. Evidence supporting its seasonal sales activities was in vague and generally unconvincing terms. Perfection Foods, Inc., 24 TCM 61, ¶ 65,015 P-H Memo. TC (1965).

Consolidated Groups

Determination of applicability of accumulated earnings tax to four related corporations. Taxpayer corporations, *A, B, C,* and *D,* were members of a controlled group engaged in the automobile dealership business. The district court jury found that taxpayers were liable for the accumulated earnings tax because of unreasonable accumulations. *Held:* Reversed as to *A, B,* and *C.* As to *A,* jury instructions regarding operating and credit cycles were erroneous. As to *B* and *C,* the IRS' working capital calculations were improper. However, the fact that *B* and *C* were finance companies did not make the operating cycle theory inapplicable. *A, B,* and *C* were entitled to new trials. *D,* however, was liable for the accumulated earnings tax, since it had no inventory or receivable cycles and could demand payment of receivables and delay payment of obligations to related companies. Central Motor Co., 583 F2d 470, 78-2 USTC ¶ 9608, 42 AFTR2d 78-5581 (10th Cir. 1978).

Accumulations to make loans to affiliated corporation were unreasonable. Taxpayer corporation leased property to Princeton, Inc. Both corporations were controlled by the same individuals. In response to the IRS' assertion of the accumulated earnings tax, taxpayer claimed that the accumulations were justified because loans had to be made to Princeton since (1) both corporations were units in a single business enterprise, and (2) Princeton was taxpayer's only tenant and needed the loans to stay in business. The Tax Court upheld the accumulated earnings tax assessment. *Held:* Affirmed. The court dismissed taxpayer's first contention as a matter of law, since the "reasonable needs" must be of the *taxpayer's* business. The stockholders chose to operate through two corporations rather than one, and were bound by the consequences of their choice. It held the second contention not supported by the facts. Princeton did not need the loans to stay in business. It earned sizable profits in the years involved, and paid dividends on both its common and preferred stock. Taxpayer, on the other hand, never paid a dividend despite substantial earnings. Further, Princeton was not the only possible tenant: after Princeton's business was sold, taxpayer rented the property to an outsider for more than twice the old rental. Factories Inv. Corp., 328 F2d 781, 64-1 USTC ¶ 9306, 13 AFTR2d 880 (2d Cir. 1964).

Wholly owned subsidiary may accumulate earnings for parent's needs if parent's earnings are insufficient. Parent corporation allowed its wholly owned subsidiary to accumulate earnings. The facts showed that this accumulation was in excess of the subsidiary's reasonably anticipated needs within the meaning of the accumulated earnings tax section. The facts, however, also showed that parent's "reasonably anticipated needs" exceeded its accumulated earnings. *Held:* For taxpayer. A wholly owned subsidiary may accumulate excess earnings if parent's accumulated earnings are insufficient to cover its "reasonably anticipated needs" for accumulated earnings tax purposes. Inland Terminals, Inc., 477 F2d 836, 73-1 USTC ¶ 9387, 31 AFTR2d 73-1170 (4th Cir. 1973).

Reasonable needs of the business do not include needs of sister corporation. *A* Corporation was one of a group of corporations involved in the construction business. All of the corporations were owned by the same individuals in approximately the same percentages, and a majority of each corporation was held by an individual, *H*. *H* operated the corporations together and the accumulated earnings of *A* were reflected almost entirely in quick assets used to obtain bonding on the construction work sister corporations undertook as general contractors. However, *A* did not undertake any construction work on its own. *A* submitted bids on most of the jobs and received a management fee. The bonding company required the general contractor to maintain a minimum of liquid assets. The corporations entered into an indemnity agreement cross-guaranteeing the bonding company against loss from default of any corporation, and the bonding company treated all of the corporations as a single entity for bonding purposes. The IRS determined that the earnings and profits of *A* were excessive and imposed an accumulated earnings tax. The taxpayer contended that the needs of the sister corporations required the accumulation. *Held:* For the IRS. The accumulation of earnings and profits on behalf of another, related taxpayer is not an accumulation related to the reasonable business needs of the taxpayer. *A* never actually performed any construction work and could not justify the accumulation by claiming that it needed a large amount of liquid assets to cover construction costs. Nor does the indemnification agreement justify the accumulation, since *A* did not engage in general contracting. Accordingly, the benefits it received from the agreement were negligible. Chaney & Hope, Inc., 80 TC 263 (1982).

Consolidated group was not liable for accumulated earnings tax. Taxpayer, the parent corporation of a group of affiliated corporations that filed consolidated returns, computed its liability for the accumulated earnings tax and made appropriate distributions to its shareholders to reduce its accumulated taxable income to zero. The computation of the amount of the distribution was based on the parent's separate taxable income, rather than on the affiliated group's consolidated income. The IRS assessed a deficiency based on imposition of the accumulated earnings tax on the amount of accumulation from the consolidated income. The taxpayer moved for summary judgment on the grounds that the consolidated return regulations were ambiguous and should be strictly construed against the IRS. *Held:* For taxpayer. Before 1966, the consolidated return regulations supported the IRS' position; however, the 1966 amendments to those regulations did not provide for the computation of accumulated taxable income for purposes of the accumulated earnings tax. Because of the ambiguity, and since the taxpayer made a good faith estimate of what was required, taxpayer's motion was granted. Gottesman & Co., 77 TC 1149 (1981).

Accumulated Earnings Tax: *Dividends Paid Deduction*

Contingent Liabilities

Unrealistic contingent liability on lawsuit not a defense to accumulated earnings tax. Taxpayer's principal defense to an assessment for unreasonable accumulation of surplus was that, as an architectural engineering company, it had a contingent liability for injuries arising out of an accident on a construction project. The Tax Court found that both taxpayer's attorney and the attorney for those injured in the accident knew that not even a prima facie case for tort liability could be established against taxpayer, a nominal defendant in the action. The Tax Court, therefore, held taxpayer liable for the tax. Noting that taxpayer's balance sheet did not even show a reserve for this contingent liability, the court also relied on the facts that reasonable business needs do not cover such unrealistic contingencies, and that taxpayer's dividends were not significant compared to the amount of prior and current accumulations. Taxpayer's short-term borrowing, from 4 to 14 days, was repaid in such short time as to indicate its financial strength, not weakness. *Held:* For the IRS. The Tax Court's findings were amply supported by the record. The court also affirmed the denial of a deduction for accrued income tax in computing the amount of the accumulation, since taxpayer was on the cash basis. Gordon Turnbull, Inc., 373 F2d 91, 67-1 USTC ¶ 9221, 19 AFTR2d 609 (5th Cir.), cert. denied, 389 US 842 (1967).

Court rejects medical corporation's claim that it accumulated earnings to cover legal damage awards in excess of earnings, as corporation's accumulations exceeded its reasonable needs. Taxpayer, a professional corporation, was wholly owned by Dr. Booth. Taxpayer was under a contract with a hospital to manage the hospital's pathology department, and agreed to maintain malpractice insurance coverage to at least a certain level. The contract was for a period of 10 years, unless terminated by the earlier death or disability of Dr. Booth. Taxpayer carried malpractice insurance sufficient to cover the contract requirements. The IRS assessed taxpayer for accumulated earnings tax. Taxpayer argued that the accumulations were necessary to insure against awards in lawsuits which exceeded its insurance coverage, and to purchase new equipment if its contract was canceled by the hospital. *Held:* For the IRS. Evidence showed that the level of insurance maintained by taxpayer and its doctors was sufficient to satisfy the hospital contract requirements, and that legal awards of damages in the area of taxpayer's practice did not exceed the level of insurance maintained by taxpayer. Further, it was unlikely that the need for more medical equipment would soon arise, since the hospital contract had more than seven years left to run and could only be terminated by the earlier death or disability of Dr. Booth. Taxpayer's accumulations exceeded its reasonable needs and thus, taxpayer was liable for the accumulated income tax. Earnest Booth, M.D., P.C., 44 TCM 595, ¶ 82, 423 P-H Memo. TC (1982).

Taxpayer's accumulation of earnings was reasonable liability. The IRS sought to impose the penalty tax on earnings accumulated by a corporation engaged in the importation of optical goods. Taxpayers asserted that the accumulation was made to insulate the company against a possible adverse outcome in a trademark infringement suit. *Held:* For taxpayer. The possibility of the liability arising was a realistically foreseeable contingency. The accumulations were not excessive in light of the potential liability. Steelmasters, Inc., 35 TCM 1460, ¶ 76,234 P-H Memo. TC (1976).

Dividends Paid Deduction

Distribution to 50 percent shareholder disallowed in calculating dividends paid deduction. Taxpayer corporation was deemed liable for the accumulated earnings tax by the IRS. Taxpayer corporation claimed the redemption of all the stock of a 50 percent shareholder as a dividends paid deduction in computing accumulated taxable income. The IRS disallowed the deduction; this was the issue contested by taxpayer corporation. *Held:* For the IRS. The distribution to the 50 percent shareholder was preferential, not pro rata; therefore, no part of such distribution could be used for the dividends paid deduction.

ACCUMULATED EARNINGS TAX: *Expansion Plans*

King Flour Mills Co., 325 F. Supp. 1085, 71-1 USTC ¶ 9292 (D. Minn. 1971).

Distribution under Section 303 does not qualify as dividend distribution for Section 535. A corporation made a distribution in order to pay death taxes under Section 303. The distribution did not meet the requirements of Section 302 or 346 and could not be used as a dividends paid deduction in computing accumulated taxable income under Section 535. Rev. Rul. 70-642, 1970-2 CB 131.

Dividends paid deduction for accumulated earnings tax allowed even though recipient not a stockholder at end of prior year. In December 1966, taxpayer, a calendar year corporation, declared a dividend payable to record owners as of January 31, 1967. On January 8, 1967, another corporation had acquired all the stock of taxpayer. On March 12, 1967, the dividend was paid. The IRS ruled that for purposes of the accumulated earnings tax under Section 531, the dividends paid were includable in the dividend deduction of taxpayer. The Code does not require a recipient of a dividend to be a stockholder at the end of the prior taxable year. Rev. Rul. 68-409, 1968-2 CB 252.

Expansion Plans

Earnings subject to Section 531 tax when expansion plan was abandoned. The sole stockholder of taxpayer corporation at first planned to buy a new factory to expand its manufacturing activities, but abandoned the plan when other corporations became interested in buying his company. The corporation's stock ultimately was sold by the stockholder. The Tax Court held that taxpayer's accumulated earnings became subject to the Section 531 tax in the year the plan was abandoned. *Held:* Affirmed. When the stockholder became more interested in a cash buyout of his shares than in expanding the business, there was no longer justification for retaining the earnings. Brookfield Wire Co., 667 F2d 551, 82-1 USTC ¶ 9120, 49 AFTR2d 82-505 (1st Cir. 1981).

Vagueness of expansion plans justifies accumulated earnings tax. Taxpayer was engaged in the printing business and the Tax Court found that its plans to enter the real estate business insufficiently specific and definite. The Tax Court upheld the IRS' imposition of the accumulated earnings tax. *Held:* Affirmed. The lower court's findings of fact and conclusions of law were not erroneous. Union Offset, 603 F2d 90, 79-2 USTC ¶ 9550, 44 AFTR2d 79-5652 (9th Cir. 1979).

Plans for expansion deemed definite. The lower court held that taxpayer, a motor fuel carrier, was liable for the accumulated earnings tax, since its plans for expansion were found indefinite. *Held:* Reversed. Accumulations to finance the expansion of service by establishing a new truck terminal were found to be reasonable and necessary. Motor Fuel Carriers, Inc., 559 F2d 1348, 77-2 USTC ¶ 9661, 40 AFTR2d 77-5807 (5th Cir. 1977).

Abandonment of specific plan for expansion of business set stage for imposition of accumulated earnings tax. Taxpayer accumulated earnings during the period that it maintained specific plans to expand its business. In a later year, it abandoned these plans and did not replace them with a specific plan for use of the accumulated earnings. The IRS imposed the accumulated earnings tax at this point. *Held:* For the IRS. Once expansion plans were abandoned earnings should have been distributed. Roth Properties Co., 511 F2d 526, 75-1 USTC ¶ 9337, 35 AFTR2d 75-1093 (6th Cir. 1975).

Accumulated earnings tax upheld due to unrelated investments and lack of definite plans for diversification. The Tax Court upheld the IRS' imposition of the accumulated earnings tax against taxpayer corporation. *Held:* Affirmed. It was not shown that the lower court's findings were clearly erroneous. The evidence indicated that taxpayer was interested in acquiring unrelated real estate investments, and that plans for diversification were indefinite and vague. Finally, it was not shown by a clear preponderance of evidence that this accumulation was not for the purpose of avoiding income tax with respect to

ACCUMULATED EARNINGS TAX: *Expansion Plans*

stockholders. Atlantic Commerce & Shipping Co., 500 F2d 937, 74-2 USTC ¶ 9624, 34 AFTR2d 74-5667 (2d Cir. 1974).

Accumulation of earnings is reasonable for accumulated earnings tax only if accumulated for uses that are definite and not remote. Taxpayer, a newspaper publisher, was assessed accumulated earnings tax. Taxpayer claimed that the accumulation was intended to cover a six-month working capital reserve, as well as the modernization of its facilities and the commencement of a Sunday edition. The IRS claimed that the extent to which the taxpayer accumulated its earnings was unjustified. *Held:* For the IRS. First, the court held that a working capital reserve covering more than three months was unreasonable. Evidence also showed that at the time of the accumulation, the taxpayer's plans concerning modernization and an extra edition on Sunday were not sufficiently definite to justify the extent of the accumulation. Cheyenne Newspapers, Inc., 494 F2d 429, 74-1 USTC ¶ 9294, 33 AFTR2d 74-893 (10th Cir. 1974).

Manufacturer liable for accumulated earnings tax. The district court held taxpayer, a manufacturer of replacement parts for weaving looms, liable for the accumulated earnings tax under Section 531 for 1959, 1960, and 1961. During this period, taxpayer claimed deductions for payments of $400,000 to relatives of its president; its accumulated earnings increased from $1.7 million to $2.2 million. *Held:* Affirmed. The lack of specificity of its future plans for use of the accumulated earnings was not excused by the fact that taxpayer was small and conducted its operations in an informal manner. Bahan Textile Mach. Co., 453 F2d 1100, 72-1 USTC ¶ 9184, 29 AFTR2d 72-418 (4th Cir. 1972).

Corporation must have specific plans to justify its accumulation of earnings. Taxpayer was a newspaper publisher that accumulated substantial earnings over a period of years to be applied toward a new office building, remodeling of offices, replacement of its printing press, and retirement benefits for its principal officer. The district court held that the accumulations were reasonable in view of taxpayer's particular business and its needs. *Held:* Reversed, in major part. Taxpayer failed to establish specific and definite plans for constructing a new office building or remodeling its offices. The case was remanded for the taking of further evidence on the retirement reserve. Oklahoma Press Publishing Co., 437 F2d 1275, 71-1 USTC ¶ 9218, 27 AFTR2d 71-656 (10th Cir. 1971).

Unreasonableness of accumulated earnings determined by conditions in year involved, not subsequent events. Taxpayer, a beer distributor corporation with accumulated earnings and profits of approximately $246,000 at the end of the taxable year 1957, contended that it was not subject to the accumulated earnings tax for that year because (1) it planned to use the accumulated funds to finance expansion into a neighboring county in the event that a forthcoming local option election should legalize beer sales in that county; (2) it planned in 1957 to acquire additional warehouse facilities and did acquire land for this purpose in 1958; (3) it had made certain deposits with the city and county taxing authorities to secure payment for beer taxes, and such deposits were not available for dividends; and (4) the competition in the area was severe. The district court found that these reasons were sufficient to forgo imposing the tax for the year 1957, but that a subsequent event required that the accumulated earnings tax be imposed for 1958 when accumulations amounted to approximately $269,000. The subsequent event was that the warehouse site had been rendered unsuitable for a warehouse because the property could not be served by a railroad spur. The fact that this land could not be used in the expansion plans indicated that in 1958 taxpayer used the land for the purpose of avoiding income tax by its stockholders. *Held:* Reversed, as to the year 1958. The unreasonableness of the accumulation should have been determined by the conditions as they existed in the year involved, not by subsequent events. As of the end of 1958, taxpayer could not have known that its recently acquired warehouse site could not be used. Sterling Distribs., Inc., 313 F2d 803, 63-1 USTC ¶ 9288, 11 AFTR2d 767 (5th Cir. 1963).

Accumulated Earnings Tax: *Expansion Plans*

Unreasonable accumulations by garment manufacturer. Taxpayer, a closely held family corporation engaged in the garment manufacture business, paid dividends in most years of less than 10 percent of its profits after taxes and made investments in assets not connected with its business. Taxpayer contended that it adopted a plan to erect a new plant and needed the accumulated earnings to reduce whatever borrowings might be necessary when the plan was put into effect. *Held:* For the IRS. The court, in affirming the Tax Court, found the plan was quite general, not only as to the type of plant, but also as to the time of implementation, and was not within the reasonably calculated future. Thus, the taxpayer was held to have accumulated surplus unreasonably for the purpose of preventing imposition of surtaxes on its stockholders. Accordingly, taxpayer was subject to the penalty tax. Barrow Mfg. Co., 294 F2d 79, 61-2 USTC ¶ 9637, 8 AFTR2d 5330 (5th Cir. 1961), cert. denied, 369 US 817 (1962).

Accumulated earnings tax levied where expansion purpose not proved. Two corporations whose stock was held almost entirely by one individual were engaged in the metal cabinet business. In 1947 both corporations adopted resolutions creating various reserves amounting to a total of about $2 million primarily for self-insurance and contemplated expansion. The IRS determined that both corporations were used during the years 1952 through 1954 to avoid tax on its stockholders by accumulating earnings unreasonably, and assessed the penalty tax. The Tax Court sustained the IRS, holding that taxpayers did not shift the burden of proof under Section 534 (which shifts the burden of proof to the IRS when taxpayer files the requisite statement) on the question of reasonableness of the accumulation since the facts submitted in taxpayer's Section 534 statement were not sufficiently detailed to support the grounds relied on in such statements. The Tax Court found that the contemplated expansion was not supported by plans, or by a course of conduct directed to expansion and, in fact, that no expansion took place. *Held:* Affirmed. The appellate court found the Tax Court's conclusion supported by the record, and so found it unnecessary to decide the burden of proof issue. American Metal Prods. Corp., 287 F2d 860, 61-1 USTC ¶ 9332, 7 AFTR2d 1005 (8th Cir. 1961).

Business needs must be considered in Section 531 cases even if motive for accumulation was tax avoidance. Taxpayer, an automobile dealer, having been notified of a proposed penalty for unreasonable accumulation of surplus, submitted a statement alleging that earnings had not been accumulated beyond its reasonable business needs, since it planned to modernize and expand. The IRS imposed the penalty and was upheld by the Tax Court. Under a 1955 amendment, the burden of proving absence of business need was shifted to the IRS when taxpayer filed the statement. However, the Tax Court pointed out that the ultimate burden rested on the taxpayer to rebut the presumption that one of the purposes of the accumulation was the avoidance of a dividend tax on the stockholders. The Tax Court found affirmative evidence of the condemned purpose in taxpayer's failure to pay dividends for 20 years, in its making unsecured and interest-free loans to taxpayer's principal stockholder, in its failure to pay salaries to its officer stockholders, and in the unduly low rent paid to its stockholder for the use of his property. *Held:* Reversed and remanded. The Tax Court erred in failing to consider reasonable business needs. That question could not be bypassed by focusing on the motive for accumulation. To the extent that Pelton Steel Casting, 251 F2d 278 (7th Cir. 1958), was inconsistent with this reasoning, the court disagreed. Young Motor Co., 281 F2d 488, 60-2 USTC ¶ 9658 (1st Cir. 1960).

Corporation unreasonably accumulated profits where expansion plans were nebulous. The district court decided that the taxpayer corporation, practically all of whose sales were made to a commonly controlled corporation that occupied the same premises, accumulated 99 percent of its earnings during 1950 through 1953 for the purpose of preventing imposition of surtax on its controlling stockholder. The taxpayer appealed. *Held:* Affirmed. Despite some testimony that the corporation was accumulating funds in contemplation of future expansion, that it would be in need of additional machinery and equipment, and that it was somewhat fearful of refunds pursuant to renegotiation contract, there was no evidence, according to the court, of "anything more than nebulous plans" for future expansion of the corporation. The finding of the district court that the business was not a new one, that it grew out of a prior organization, militated against the taxpayer's argument that it needed to accumulate profits because it was running a new business. Engineering Corp. of Am., 284 F2d 302, 60-2 USTC ¶ 9804 (7th Cir. 1960).

One-year operating expense test does not justify avoidance of accumulated earnings tax. Taxpayer corporation argued that the IRS should not have imposed the accumulated earnings tax because taxpayer had to accumulate one year's operating expenses to meet its working capital needs, and taxpayer claimed to be self-insured to the extent of approximately $100,000 for fire damage to buildings and contents. *Held:* For the IRS. The court held that the one-year operating expense method was inapplicable because taxpayer was a service company that collected 90 percent of its receivables within 60 days and had a six to one current ratio and no inventory requirements. Self-insurance was not necessary, since taxpayer already carried $30,000 worth of insurance on its buildings; that was deemed adequate. In further support of the IRS' position, the court found that there were no real plans for expansion, taxpayer had been able to make loans to officer shareholders, unrelated assets had been purchased, and failure to distribute earnings in the years in question had caused the shareholders to pay less tax than if the earnings had been distributed. Coastal Casting Serv., Inc., 70-2 USTC ¶ 9716 (SD Tex. 1970).

Expansion of plants in order to maintain a competitive position overcomes accumulated earnings tax. Taxpayer brought suit to recover deficiencies assessed and paid under Section 531. The corporation was founded in the early 1900s, and present ownership was acquired in 1931 on foreclosure. The company began to show substantial earnings in the years during which the tax was assessed. In the three years in issue, the alleged excess accumulations totaled $1.3 million. Taxpayer contended that the accumulations were required to meet business needs that required at least $3.2 million for fixed asset acquisitions. The corporation, which was engaged in the manufacture of paper, did in fact expend such sums in expanding two of its plants. In addition, it contended that additional new machinery and plant costs were required at a cost of $3.75 million, that it had to prepare to expend additional sums to meet the problem of stream pollution, and therefore, its working capital did not exceed the reasonable needs of the business. *Held:* For taxpayer. A taxpayer must rebut the determination that the earnings were permitted to accumulate for the proscribed purpose of avoidance of the tax on the stockholders. This could be done by showing that the accumulations were not beyond the reasonable needs of the business. In this case, taxpayer did so by showing definite plans and projects for expansion that it could finance through operations without reborrowing. In addition, working capital was no more than sufficient for currrent operations. There were no loans or unrelated investments of any consequence, and management's desire to have funds available was undoubtedly influenced by the early unsuccessful history of the corporation. Mohawk Paper Mills, Inc., 262 F. Supp. 365, 67-1 USTC ¶ 9108 (NDNY 1966).

No accumulated earnings penalty where initial steps taken to expand facilities. Taxpayer corporation's existing plant facilities had reached their maximum production capacity and it became obvious that a larger plant would produce substantial savings. Taxpayer took some initial steps in this direction and purchased a 10 acre tract of land for the construction of a new plant. However, there were no specific working plans or drawings for the plant and no contract had been let. The IRS imposed the accumulated earnings tax. *Held:* For taxpayer. Taxpayer was not liable for the accumulated earnings tax. Taxpayer's ratio of current assets to current liabilities was less than that of comparable food companies and

ACCUMULATED EARNINGS TAX: *Expansion Plans*

its number of months' cash requirement was in line with that of other companies. The court concluded that taxpayer was not formed or availed of for the purpose of avoiding the income tax with respect to stockholders. Lewis Food Co., 64-1 USTC ¶ 9386 (SD Cal. 1964).

Surplus accumulation of insurance brokerage was reasonable. In a case involving the penalty tax on unreasonable surplus accumulations levied against an insurance brokerage corporation, taxpayer showed that its current ratio was less than that of a publicly held company in the field. Taxpayer also contended that it required a large surplus for future expansion and because of the slowness of its receivables. *Held:* For taxpayer. The surplus accumulated was reasonable. The court also held that for this purpose investment securities should be valued at cost because the taxpayer could not be expected to use the unrealized appreciation in its business. Harry A. Koch Co., 228 F. Supp. 782, 64-1 USTC ¶ 9401, 13 AFTR2d 1241 (D. Neb. 1964).

No Section 531 tax where corporation was entering new business and diversifying. Taxpayer's cash position was $86,312, with its liabilities amounting to $50,000 on a bank note, $57,000 for income taxes, and $40,000 due to stockholders. It expected to buy a greater amount of inventory and to invest heavily for plant and equipment. Furthermore, it contemplated production of a new item at a cost of $200,000 and the acquisition of a new business for more than $500,000. *Held:* For taxpayer. There was no unreasonable accumulation as taxpayer's financial picture, anticipated expenditures, and plans to enter a new business were sufficient justification to accumulate. Buffalo Batt & Felt Corp., 64-2 USTC ¶ 9724 (WDNY 1964).

Accumulation for working capital and expansion was not unreasonable. Taxpayer corporation accumulated earnings which ranged from $78,000 in 1955 to $109,000 in 1957. It paid a Section 531 assessment for 1956 and 1957 and sued for refund. Taxpayer presented evidence that (1) working capital to meet current operating expenses required a retention of $35,000 to $50,000; (2) it planned to replace existing facilities and to build a new plant at an estimated cost of $156,000 to $181,000. Land was acquired for this purpose in 1961 at a cost of $26,000 and bids were being taken for the erection of a plant and the purchase of machinery; (3) cash dividends had been paid every year from 1955 through 1962; and (4) none of the directors were related and only 6 of 15 stockholders were related by marriage. *Held:* For taxpayer. The court found that taxpayer had proved its case by a preponderance of the evidence and was entitled to a refund. Independent Laundry & Linen Serv., Inc., 62-2 USTC ¶ 9803 (SD Ind. 1962).

Accumulated earnings tax imposed on holding company. Taxpayer's only activity was owning waterhouses that it leased to an operating company wholly owned by its sole stockholder. The taxpayer obtained estimates for renovating the warehouses and constructing a new one, but these plans were abandoned. The IRS imposed the accumulated earnings tax, contending that taxpayer was a mere holding company under Section 533(b), which was prima facie evidence that it was used to avoid tax on shareholders. *Held:* For the IRS. The taxpayer was a mere holding company. It had no activities except holding property and collecting the income from it. The plans to renovate were insufficient due to their abandonment. H.G. Cockrell Warehouse Corp., 71 TC 1036 (1979).

Expansion plans defeat accumulated earnings tax. Taxpayer was a retailer corporation. IRS determined that it was subject to the accumulated earnings tax. *Held:* For taxpayer. Taxpayer did not permit its earnings and profits to accumulate beyond the reasonable needs of its business, which included reasonably anticipated needs. The operating cycle method is most appropriate here to compute ordinary working capital requirements. In addition, taxpayer definitely established its requirement for accumulated earnings and profits for future needs. Plans for the acquisition of warehousing facilities were definite, feasible, and never postponed, and were in fact accomplished within a reasonable period. In

ACCUMULATED EARNINGS TAX: *Expansion Plans*

view of the accumulated earnings credit, it was unnecessary to consider if taxpayer was availed of for the proscribed purpose. Magic Mart, Inc., 51 TC 775 (1969).

Corporation's assets fully committed to reasonable needs of the business, and definite plans for expansion existed. Taxpayer, a family corporation, was engaged in the manufacture and sale of cement and cinder blocks. Although incorporated in 1928, it operated with hand machinery and inadequate facilities until it recapitalized and expanded in 1957. It then opened expanded facilities at its present location, and began construction of another plant in a neighboring county. The construction was completed in 1960 at a cost of $450,000 and was financed in part by an $85,000 mortgage that was paid off in two years. Minutes of board meetings held in 1961 also evidenced plans to study future expansion of present facilities and to purchase additional machinery as an alternative to the acquisition of additional land at a prohibitive cost. Taxpayer developed the area adjacent to its plant for commercial tenants by advancing up to $180,000 to a sister corporation for this purpose. In 1965, it began construction of a new plant. Between 1957 and 1966, taxpayer invested over $1.8 million in plant, machinery, and equipment. Throughout its existence, taxpayer maintained a "no borrowing" policy. Taxpayer also paid materials bills promptly in order to take advantage of cash discounts despite financing of its own customers for extended periods. It also maintained a program of financial aid to employees to help them through periods of difficulty and to enable them to purchase homes. From 1961 through 1963, taxpayer advanced over $100,000 to a manufacturer of steel trusses used in the cement block industry, and from 1959 through 1964, was engaged in negotiations for the purchase of a controlling interest in another cinder block company. Taxpayer paid dividends on Class B nonvoting common stock as required but paid no dividends on Class A voting common stock during the years in issue. The IRS assessed the tax on the entire undistributed earnings and profits for the years 1961 through 1963. *Held:* For taxpayer. Although the IRS contended that taxpayer could have distributed the receivables from its sister corporation and the truss manufacturer, the retention of such assets was not determinative of an unreasonable accumulation. The crucial question of whether accumulated earnings and profits were sufficiently committed to business operations and anticipated needs involves essentially a factual determination, and the court found that the accumulations did not exceed such needs. Although there was evidence that the loans were substantially to benefit the shareholders, approximately 50 percent of the working capital was required to meet current working capital requirements calculated under the *Bardahl* formula. In addition, the court rejected the IRS' contention that taxpayer did not have adequate plans for expansion under Section 537. Faber Cement Block Co., 50 TC 317 (1968).

Accumulation equaling one year's operating expenses found reasonable. The IRS determined that for the years 1954 through 1957 taxpayer's earnings and profits, ranging from $1.8 million to $2.4 million, constituted an unreasonable accumulation. Taxpayer advanced 25 reasons for the accumulation, including the need for a parking lot, air conditioning, new equipment, an elevator, and the need to buy out minority stockholders in an affiliate. *Held:* For taxpayer. The Tax Court abstained from substituting its judgment for the business judgment of taxpayer's officers, and after noting that the accumulations approximated one year's operating expenses, that taxpayer's manner of doing business justified an accumulation to meet one year's operating expenses, that substantial dividends had consistently been paid (even in one loss year), and that competitive conditions in taxpayer's industry had to be met, found the accumulations reasonable. James M. Pierce Corp., 326 F2d 67, 64-1 USTC ¶ 9173, 13 AFTR2d 358 (8th Cir. 1964).

Pending business contingency precludes application of the accumulated earnings tax. Taxpayer, an incorporated dairy business, contended it had accumulated earnings to acquire plastic bottling equipment. The IRS argued that the taxpayer lacked any plan, and

ACCUMULATED EARNINGS TAX: *Expansion Plans*

applied the accumulated earnings tax. *Held:* For taxpayer. While the court agreed that the taxpayer did not have a specific, definite, and feasible plan to acquire the equipment, the taxpayer was faced with a pending business contingency. In order to remain competitive, it had to accumulate earnings in anticipation of developing the plastic packaging capability. Summit Farms, Inc., ¶ 81,556 P-H Memo. TC, 42 TCM 1240 (1981).

Corporation not liable for accumulated earnings tax. Taxpayer, a trucking corporation, accumulated liquid assets in order to purchase new equipment and acquire interstate operating rights. The IRS argued, inter alia, that taxpayer could meet its needs through borrowing and therefore imposed the accumulated earnings tax. *Held:* For taxpayer. Taxpayer's reasonably anticipated business needs justified the accumulations. Taxpayer was not required to finance expansion through borrowing. C.E. Estes, Inc., 41 TCM 354, ¶ 180,504 P-H Memo. TC (1980).

Accumulated earnings tax imposed where taxpayer did not pursue plan for expansion of its business. Taxpayer accumulated earnings while planning to develop or acquire a business to supply it with raw materials. Subsequently, the IRS imposed the accumulated earnings tax on taxpayer. *Held:* For the IRS. Based on evidence showing that taxpayer ceased serious efforts to expand its business, the court determined that taxpayer's accumulation of earnings in later years was unreasonable. Standard Corrugated Case Corp., 32 TCM 1302, ¶ 73,276 P-H Memo. TC (1973).

Definite expansion plans were reasonably anticipated needs of a business sufficient to overcome accumulated earnings tax. Taxpayer, a holding company of a machine tool business that was expanding to produce a new, large product, was determined to be liable for the accumulated earnings tax by the IRS. *Held:* For taxpayer. The earnings and profits of the company were not permitted to accumulate beyond the reasonable needs of its business, which included at least $3 million a year for additional machinery and increased inventory requirements and plant expansion in addition to other sums related to its new product. The plans for the use of these funds were specific, definite, and feasible, making them appear reasonable at the time of accumulation. Kingsbury Invs., Inc., 28 TCM 1082, ¶ 69,205 P-H Memo. TC (1969).

Accumulated earnings were for new plant; despite 10-year delay, plans were not indefinitely postponed. Taxpayers, bottling corporations, advertised by use of signs, clocks, and scoreboards placed near customers' premises and deducted the expenses in the year in which they were incurred. The IRS disallowed the deduction, claiming the expenses to be amortizable. The IRS also determined that one of the taxpayers was subject to the accumulated earnings tax. *Held:* For the IRS, in part. The advertising expenses, including installation costs, were amortizable because the signs had a useful life of at least five years. Any change in taxpayers' accounting methods was necessary to clearly reflect their incomes. The single taxpayer was not subject to the accumulated earnings tax. Although taxpayer had no need to accumulate earnings and profits for its present plant, it did need all its net liquid assets to pay material and operating costs for a cycle in its peak season along with carrying receivables and inventories. Taxpayer also needed its total accumulated earnings, some $1.6 million, for the reasonably anticipated needs of its business, and in building and equipping a new plant, over $2 million. There was a need for a new and larger plant, and there was a specific and definite plan to build it. Despite the problems that had arisen beginning in 1958 and had caused the deferment of plans for 10 years, the plans had not been postponed indefinitely, which would have disqualified them from being within the reasonable needs of the business for Section 531 tax purposes. Alabama Coca-Cola Bottling Co., 28 TCM 635, ¶ 69,123 P-H Memo. TC (1969).

No accumulated earnings tax where reasonably anticipated needs included a continuous expansion program. Taxpayer had a large reserve of accumulated earnings to finance new production facilities for its beer plant. The IRS asserted that the accumulation was unreasonable. *Held:* For taxpayer. The accumulation was reasonable considering the vast building program. Also, funds were needed for increases in inventories, greater production and administration costs, and a pending $14 million damage suit for which there was no insurance. Coors, 27 TCM 1351, ¶ 68,256 P-H Memo. TC (1968).

Expansion plans exempt newspaper publisher from Section 531 tax. Taxpayer, the tenth largest newspaper publisher in the country, continually looked for newspapers to purchase. It followed a policy of paying cash for the papers instead of financing the purchases by debt. The principal economic reasons for expansion were the fact that a publisher can only significantly increase its circulation by purchasing newspapers and to provide greater opportunities for its young executives. In addition, the publishers were quite anxious to have their political opinions read by the largest possible group of people. The IRS assessed the accumulated earnings tax for 1959 and 1960 because taxpayer neither acquired any papers in those years nor had any written offers to purchase. Taxpayer paid no dividends during these two years when its surplus rose from $7.7 million to $9.6 million. *Held:* For taxpayer. The accumulation was justified. Because of the "unique and unusual" problems of acquiring a newspaper, taxpayer's plans for expansion were as definite as they could be. Negotiations for purchase take a long time. At the time of trial, taxpayer had just about concluded negotiations for a purchase that had begun with oral proposals during the years at issue. Further, taxpayer was faced with a potential antitrust liability during 1959 and 1960 and was justified in setting aside funds to provide a cushion against that liability. Freedom Newspapers, Inc., 24 TCM 1327, ¶ 65,248 P-H Memo. TC (1965).

Needs of business justified retention of earnings until expansion program abandoned. Taxpayer corporation's petroleum trucking business was threatened and ultimately affected by a railroad's construction of a petroleum pipeline. In an effort to avert or minimize this competitive threat to its business, taxpayer considered two courses of action in 1955: the construction of a new terminal and the expansion of its dry-freight hauling business. The first course of action was abandoned in 1958, and the second in 1956. In 1956 taxpayer's directors established a pension plan for its salaried employees and declared an intention to fund prior service benefits as soon as the plan was approved. The IRS assessed the accumulated earnings tax against taxpayer corporation for the years 1955 through 1957. *Held:* For taxpayer, in part. Taxpayer's directors had concluded in good faith in 1955 and 1956 that the company should retain earnings for the purpose of expansion and liquidating its obligation to the pension trust. Furthermore, the record disclosed that taxpayer's working capital was not excessive in view of its operating costs, and its current ratios compared favorably with those of other trucking companies. However, the same conclusion was not possible for 1957 since, by the end of 1956, taxpayer had abandoned its intention to expand its dry-freight business and there was no need to accumulate its 1957 earnings to meet the current anticipated needs. Also, amounts expended for replacement of engines, petroleum tanks, and truck cabs in the truck fleet constituted capital expenditures rather than deductible repairs. LaSalle Trucking Co., 22 TCM 1375, ¶ 63,274 P-H Memo. TC (1963).

Liquidating Distributions

Liquidating distributions have no effect on court's finding of proscribed purpose for accumulated earnings. In June 1969, taxpayer, who had been inactive for two years, collected a judgment of over $300,000. At the end of 1959, taxpayer had retained earnings of about $1 million. On March 1, 1960, taxpayer adopted Section 337; liquidating distributions were made in April and June 1960. Taxpayer contended that (1) pursuant to Section 563, dividends paid within two and a half months of year end were deductible from accumulated earnings; (2) Section 562 treats liquidating distributions as dividends; (3) taxpayer could have paid its liquidating distribution between March 1 and March 15 and avoided the accumulated earnings tax; (4) taxpayer's stockholders would have a capital

Accumulated Earnings Tax: *Passive Investment Income*

gain regardless of whether liquidating distributions were made prior to March 15 or thereafter; and (5) therefore, the proscribed purpose of tax avoidance did not exist. The district court held for the IRS. *Held:* Affirmed. Since there was no valid reason for the accumulation of earnings, the accumulated earnings tax was properly assessed. The fact that there was a statutory means of avoiding the tax had no bearing on the fact that the accumulation was improper. Ray, 409 F2d 1322, 69-1 USTC ¶ 9334 (6th Cir. 1969).

Passive Investment Income

Advances to investment company do not establish unreasonable accumulation. Taxpayer, a family corporation in the baking business, acquired four predecessor corporations in 1955 in a tax-free reorganization. Its accumulated earnings and profits at that time exceeded $2 million. Taxpayer also acquired a 98 percent interest in an investment company. Taxpayer filed consolidated returns with the investment company and advanced substantial sums to it during the period 1956 through 1958. During the same period, taxpayer paid no dividends. The IRS asserted the accumulated earnings tax for 1956 through 1958; it was sustained in part by the Tax Court, which held that the amounts advanced to the affiliated company represented unreasonable accumulations, but that earnings retained in excess of the advances were for the reasonable needs of the business. The Tax Court noted that although a parent may accumulate earnings to meet its subsidiary's need for funds, it cannot do so if the subsidiary is a passive investment company. *Held:* Reversed regarding the holding that the advances to the affiliate represented unreasonable accumulations. Investments in properties unrelated to the activities of the business *may* indicate that earnings have been accumulated beyond the reasonable needs of the business. In this case, however, taxpayer had specific plans for expansion and improvement that demonstrated its reasonable need for funds in excess of retained earnings. Mead's Bakery, Inc., 364 F2d 101, 66-2 USTC ¶ 9555, 18 AFTR2d 5205 (5th Cir. 1966).

Tanning corporation with substantial unrelated investments was not liable for the accumulated earnings tax. Taxpayer corporation, in the tanning business, was deemed liable for the accumulated earnings tax by the IRS, which supported its case by stressing taxpayer's substantial passive investments and the high bracket of its leading shareholder. *Held:* For taxpayer. Taxpayer's retention of approximately 50 percent of its earnings was for maintenance and repair of its aging facility and other definite business needs, including a reserve for building or purchasing a new plant. In view of taxpayer's erratic sales performance over the years, it was reasonable to maintain a substantial portfolio of unrelated investments to cushion the bad years. Finally, the tax bracket of the leading shareholder was not controlling on the question of corporate intent. A.F. Gallun & Sons Corp., 510 F. Supp. 630, 81-1 USTC ¶ 9471, 47 AFTR2d 81-1157 (ED Wis. 1981).

Accumulated earnings tax inapplicable where taxpayer was not a mere holding or investment company. The IRS held that taxpayer corporation was liable for accumulated earnings tax because it was a mere holding or investment company and had unreasonably accumulated earnings. *Held:* For taxpayer. Taxpayer owned material amounts of stock of two corporations that were involved in noninvestment activity and therefore could not be considered a mere holding or investment company. Furthermore, business needs justified its earnings accumulation. Empire Land Corp., 473 F. Supp. 1289, 79-2 USTC ¶ 9549, 44 AFTR2d 79-5613 (D. La. 1979), aff'd (5th Cir. 1980).

Where making of mortgage loans is a regular business activity, it cannot be the basis for a Section 531 attack. A corporation that owned and managed apartment buildings since 1933 was personally supervised by its sole shareholder. Over the years, the corporation used its profits to make mortgage loans. Corporate officers investigated loan prospects and participated in negotiations for loans. Other than these loans and $500,000 in government bonds, taxpayer purchased no securities. Taxpayer also did not make any loans to its

Accumulated Earnings Tax: *Reasonable Business Needs*

stockholder. In asserting the tax on accumulated earnings, the IRS regarded the mortgage loans as investments representing funds retained in excess of the reasonable needs of the business. Taxpayer stated that the purpose of the accumulation was to provide funds for rehabilitation of buildings, a self-insurance reserve, apartment house operations, and mortgage loans. *Held:* For taxpayer. The Tax Court held that the accumulation was reasonable. The corporation did initiate a costly program for the repair of its old buildings. However, the main flaw in the IRS' argument was that the making of mortgage loans was a business, not an investment as contended by the IRS. The extent of taxpayer's involvement in the making of the loans qualified this activity as a separate business. Sandy Estate Co., 43 TC 361 (1965), acq. 1965-2 CB 6.

Reasonable Business Needs

Accumulated earnings tax imposed on holding company upheld; accumulation of earnings and profits not justified by possible future need of cash. Taxpayer corporation was in the business of buying and selling stocks, making loans, and operating an insurance company. The purchase of its stock was limited to full-time officers, employees, and directors of a bank, and the stock contained a first option to the corporation to repurchase. From the date of incorporation, taxpayer paid no dividends; management did not consider it prudent to pay dividends in the absence of sufficient funds on hand to redeem all the shares. Taxpayer initially borrowed sums for the redemption of stock, if it became necessary, and for the purchase of investments. The district court agreed with the IRS and found that the corporation was formed or availed of for the purpose of avoiding the income tax with respect to stockholders by permitting earnings and profits to accumulate instead of being distributed, in violation of Section 532(a). It based its decision on taxpayer's failure to offer convincing proof that its accumulated earnings were necessary for reasonable business needs, or reasonably anticipated business needs. *Held:* Affirmed. The fact that taxpayer might need money in the future to redeem stock or to repay loans did not justify its accumulation of earnings and profits. It had to take into account the availability of future earnings and profits, which could be used for these purposes. Firstco Co., 607 F2d 704, 80-1 USTC ¶ 9127, 45 AFTR2d 80-898 (5th Cir. 1979).

Taxpayer's earnings and profit accumulated beyond reasonable business needs. Taxpayer, a manufacturer and reconditioner of automotive parts, permitted its earnings and profits to accumulate instead of being divided or distributed. The IRS found that the amount accumulated was beyond the reasonable needs of the business and imposed the accumulated earnings tax. The Tax Court found for the IRS. *Held:* Affirmed. There was no proof that the lower court's findings were clearly erroneous. Alma Piston Co., 579 F2d 1000, 78-2 USTC ¶ 9591, 42 AFTR2d 78-5320 (6th Cir. 1978).

Ninth Circuit reverses district court's factual analysis of reasonable needs for business attempting to purchase leased premises. Taxpayer was a corporation formed to operate a ballroom and an adjoining cocktail lounge. The business was operated in premises that were owned by an elderly woman, who was unrelated to any of the stockholders. In 1957, taxpayer first sought to purchase the property but was repeatedly rebuffed by its owner. For a period of not less than 13 years, taxpayer persisted in its efforts to purchase, eventually offering three times the amount of its initial proposal. In the meantime, the IRS determined that the taxpayer's retained earnings of $415,766 in 1968 were unreasonable, and it asserted the accumulated earnings tax under Section 537. The district court held for the IRS. *Held:* Reversed. the evidence produced at trial showed that in 1968 taxpayer made a bona fide offer to purchase the property for $300,000, and that the owner refused to sell only because of her unwillingness to part with the business. When combined with an estimated $75,000 for repairs and $100,000 in needed working capital, the resulting figure of $475,000 representing the reasonable needs of the business fully justified retained earnings of $415,766. The fact that taxpayer's sole stockholder was in a position to loan up to $200,000 to facilitate the purchase was not determinative. Myron's Enters., 548 F2d 311, 39 AFTR2d 77-693, 77-1 USTC ¶ 9253 (9th Cir. 1977).

Court determines amount of unreasonable accumulation. Taxpayer, a family owned corporation, was engaged in the publication of a daily newspaper and the operation of a radio station. Beginning in 1943, taxpayer established and maintained various reserves for anticipated business needs. The district court found the practice to be in comformity with the general policy of taxpayer, and other newspapers similarly situated, which believed it essential to maintain complete independence, financial and professional, in their operation. Taxpayer's officers testified that the accumulated earnings were needed to construct a new office building because urban renewal might condemn the present building and the town was expected to grow. No evidence was introduced concerning the condemnation issue. Other reserves were accumulated to replace the press and update equipment. The Tenth Circuit found that in view of the pre-existing accumulation of earnings and the life insurance on the president's life, taxpayer had the burden of explaining why further additions to the retirement reserve were necessary during the years in question. The Tenth Circuit concluded that it could not sustain the lower court's finding that the 1962 addition of $20,000 to the retirement reserve was within the reasonable needs of the business, and that taxpayer failed to negate the presumptive tax-avoidance purpose. The case was then remanded to the district court for a recomputation of the allowable judgment. *Held:* For taxpayer, in part. Where a review of the evidence established the accumulation to be reasonable, and to represent an actual need of taxpayer in the specific year, taxpayer was entitled to accumulate earnings. Specifically, the court held the accumulations to be reasonable and not for the purpose of avoiding income tax on its stockholders in 1962, a portion thereof to be unreasonably accumulated in 1963, and all of the accumulations in 1964 to be unreasonably accumulated for the purpose of avoiding tax on its stockholders. Oklahoma Press Publishing Co., 75-2 USTC ¶ 9514, 35 AFTR2d 75-1383 (10th Cir. 1975).

Use of 19-day operating cycle deemed proper. The district court held that taxpayer's two wholly owned baking corporations were subject to the accumulated earnings tax because no reasonable business necessity supported their accumulation of earnings. *Held:* Affirmed. Use of a 19-day operating cycle as a measure of reasonable business needs deemed proper. Hardin, 461 F2d 865, 72-1 USTC ¶ 9464, 29 AFTR2d 72-1446 (5th Cir. 1972).

Real estate developer not liable for accumulated earnings tax because profits were accumulated for the reasonable needs of the business. Taxpayer was a closely held corporation that had two classes of stock and an initial capitalization that consisted principally of developed real estate. The corporation developed real estate and leased stores and apartments. It also sought to purchase additional tracts of unimproved land for the same purposes. The corporation continued a modest real estate operation that became successful, expanded, and continued to be managed conservatively. It secured operating funds from its operations, since banks would not loan money on undeveloped land. During the years in issue, taxpayer was faced with cancellation by several of its best lessees and felt it necessary to accumulate funds to remodel in order to obtain renewals. The IRS determined that earnings and profits had been accumulated to avoid tax on stockholders and that taxpayer's plans with respect to future acquisitions and development were not sufficiently definite. The district court held for the IRS. *Held:* Reversed. Although taxpayer had no binding option to purchase a particular parcel, this did not detract from the conclusion that it was retaining funds for such a purchase, and that the retention of funds was for the reasonably anticipated business needs of the business. The outlines for expansion and the contingencies to which the business was subject were sufficiently certain to justify the accumulation. Indeed, to have held otherwise and to have required taxpayer to declare and pay dividends would have left the corporation with inadequate reserves to meet the contingencies of repairs and remodeling, let alone the purchase of additional land. Dahlem Found., Inc., 405 F2d 993, 69-1 USTC ¶ 9129 (6th Cir. 1968).

Reasonable business needs adequately considered by Tax Court. Taxpayer, a closely held corporation, maintained 12 gasoline service stations and dealt in industrial petroleum products. It never paid cash dividends althought it had repeatedly issued stock dividends by capitalizing its earnings to the extent of $900,000. Taxpayer alleged that the primary purpose of accumulating its earnings was to accumulate cash to finance the expansion of its business facilities, but it was unable to show a plan for such expansion. Although taxpayer carried on its business with substantial borrowed working capital, it owned investments in unrealted enterprises. Taxpayer did not file a Section 534 statement. The Tax Court held that taxpayer was subject to the accumulated earnings tax. *Held:* Remanded. The Tax Court gave weight to the payment of stock dividends which is not a factor in showing an unreasonable accumulation. The Tax Court should give futher consideration to the needs for inventory and possible expansion. Sears Oil Co., 359 F2d 191, 66-1 USTC ¶ 9384, 17 AFTR2d 833 (2d Cir. 1966).

Accumulated earnings tax imposed where accumulation was not for the reasonable needs of the business. Taxpayer was a close corporation. It had earnings of $334,000 in 1959, of which it retained $129,000. Its accumulated earnings and profits were almost $2.8 million. In 1959, it paid dividends of $12,000. Total dividends paid from 1948 through 1959 were $184,000. At the end of 1959, the corporation had cash and government securities in excess of $1 million dollars, and its working capital ratio was greater than six to one. The district court sustained the imposition of the accumulated earnings tax. *Held:* Affirmed The accumulated earnings tax under Section 531 was properly imposed. Taxpayer failed to carry its burden of proof that the 1959 accumulation was for the reasonable needs of the business. Taxpayer's contention that earnings were accumulated to redeem stock from the estates of its elderly shareholders after their deaths was rejected since this was not a corporate purpose. Dickmam Lumber Co., 355 F2d 670, 66-1 USTC ¶ 9203, 17 AFTR2d 249 (9th Cir. 1966).

Accumulated earnings tax imposed despite good dividend record. Taxpayer, a family owned corporation, was primarily engaged as an insurance agent and broker. It had an accumulation of earnings and profits exceeding $1.5 million at the end of 1956, $1.7 million at the end of 1957, $1.8 million at the end of 1958, and $1.9 million at the end of 1959. The IRS asserted accumulated earnings tax penalties for those years. In rebuttal, taxpayer produced evidence showing it had paid substantial dividends and salaries to it shareholders during this period. It also showed the absence of repeated loans to stockholders or corporate expenditures for their benefit. The Tax Court found for the IRS, reasoning that although the record of substantial dividend and salary payments was impressive, it was not conclusive. In reaching its determination, the Tax Court considered the following factors controlling: (1) taxpayer's investments and retention of securities unrelated to its business; (2) the making of large loans to an unaffiliated but related inactive corporation; and (3) the fact that if taxpayer had paid out its additional earnings, the principal and controlling stockholders would have been subject to a very large additional personal income tax. *Held:* Affirmed. The initial determination as to whether a business unreasonably accumulates earnings was one of fact. Thus, the decision of the Tax Court must stand if it is supported by the record. In this case, the record showed that the reasonable needs of the business fell considerably below the amount accumulated. Van Hummell, Inc., 364 F2d 746, 66-2 USTC ¶ 9610, 18 AFTR2d 5500 (10th Cir. 1966), cert. denied, 386 US 956 (1967).

Real estate corporation has unreasonable accumulated surplus. Originating as a spin-off from an automobile dealership, taxpayer's sole business activity was renting a building to the dealer. It also owned a parcel of vacant land that was being held for expansion of the dealership operation, but only vague building plans were made. Taxpayer had current assets of over $600,000 and no liabilities. *Held:* For the IRS. The court held that taxpayer's accumulated earnings were in excess of its reasonable needs and therefore assessed the Section 531 penalty tax. Fenco, Inc., 348 F2d 456, 65-2 USTC ¶ 9535 (4th Cir. 1965).

No one-year expense test for determining reasonableness of accumulation. Taxpayer corporations operated motion picture theatres and were part of extensive business interests carried on by one family. The corporations had accumulated large surpluses and sought to prevent the imposition of the penalty surtax by contending that they needed the accumulations to meet the competition of drive-in theatres and television and to refurnish and refurbish their theatres. On the facts, the Tax Court found the earnings accumulated prior to the taxable years in issue were more than sufficient to meet any reasonable needs of their business immediately or prospectively, as evidenced by extensive loans to several of the family enterprises. *Held:* Affirmed. The court rejected taxpayer's argument that the accumulations were not reasonable as a matter of law because they represented less than a year's expense requirements. Latchis Theatres of Keene, Inc., 286 F2d 237, 61-1 USTC ¶ 9171 (1st Cir. 1961).

Bar in Reno needed part of its accumulated earnings. Taxpayer operated a bar in a leading Reno gambling establishment. Taxpayer's sole stockholder was also a principal stockholder of the gambling firm. In the years 1950 through 1954, taxpayer paid no dividends but had a surplus ranging from $292,000 to $639,000. The IRS imposed the accumulated earnings tax on taxpayer for each of those years. *Held:* For taxpayer, in part. The Tax Court found that several expenditures made by taxpayer represented its reasonable business needs and justified taxpayer's failure to pay dividends, thus preventing the surplus accumulation tax in three of the five years involved. The reasonable needs were (1) $500,000 for a stock option on a one-half interest in the gambling firm in order to prevent the sale of the stock to a competitor and possible injuries to taxpayer's business; (2) the purchase for $150,000 of Old West relics to decorate the bar and attract tourists; (3) $15,000 a year for 10 years to be paid to the owners of these memorabilia to promote and exploit their presence on taxpayer's premises; (4) purchase of a motel and coffee shop for $225,000 to accommodate taxpayer's patrons; and (5) $100,000 for the purchase of liquor in anticipation of Korean War shortages. Raymond I. Smith, Inc., 292 F2d 470, 61-2 USTC ¶ 9562 (9th Cir.), cert. denied, 368 US 948 (1961).

Accumulation of earnings and profits held reasonable as there was a shortfall in taxpayer's needed working capital. Taxpayer was a closely held corporation engaged in tool and die work. Because the machine tool industry was highly sensitive to fluctuations in the economy and was subject to obsolescence resulting from technological changes, taxpayer accumulated earnings. The IRS determined that the taxpayer was subject to an accumulated earnings tax. *Held:* For taxpayer. The accumulation of earnings and profits was not unreasonable where application of the *Bardahl* formula indicated that there was a shortfall in taxpayer's needed working capital. Thus taxpayer's controlling stockholder and president did not use the corporation for the purpose of avoiding income tax. GROB, Inc., 565 F. Supp. 391, 83-1 USTC ¶ 9401, 52 AFTR2d 83-5094 (ED Wis. 1983).

Taxpayer not liable for accumulated earnings tax where accumulations did not exceed capital needs. Taxpayer was actively engaged in business as a general and farm merchandiser and sold fertilizer, insecticides, pesticides, seed, and farm equipment. Taxpayer was formed by heirs to continue the deceased proprietor's farming and mercantile business. Taxpayer accumulated earnings in order to carry customers on credit through the farming season, and for new farming equipment. The IRS imposed an accumulated earnings tax on taxpayer. *Held:* For taxpayer. Taxpayer was not liable for an accumulated earnings tax where its available working capital and reasonably anticipated receipts for the subject year did not exceed its working capital needs for normal operation, for foreseeable future needs, and for stated contingencies. Taxpayer was not availed of for the purpose of avoiding income tax with respect to its stockholders by permitting earnings and profits to accumulate beyond the reasonable anticipated needs of the business. Consideration was given to the company's current and foreseeable capital needs for technology, modernization, possible crop failure, and so forth. W.G. Clark, 81-1 USTC ¶ 9377, 47 AFTR2d 81-1093 (EDNC 1980).

IRS's imposition of accumulated earnings tax upheld in major part. The IRS held that five corporate taxpayers had accumulated earnings and profits beyond their reasonable needs with a view to avoiding tax on their shareholders, and consequently they were subject to the accumulated earnings tax. *Held:* For the IRS, in major part. As to one year of one taxpayer, the jury found that the requisite intent did not exist. Central Credit, 76-1 USTC ¶ 9321, 37 AFTR2d 76-1051 (DNM 1976).

IRS's imposition of accumulated earnings tax rejected. The IRS asserted the accumulated earnings tax against taxpayer, a title company. *Held:* For taxpayer. It was reasonable for taxpayer to accumulate liquid reserves of $200,000 for the construction of a building and to accumulate liquid reserves as protection against uninsured losses equal to at least three months' operating expenses. Inter County Title Co., 75-2 USTC ¶ 9845, 36 AFTR2d 75-6395 (ED Cal. 1975).

Railroad not liable for accumulated earnings tax. The IRS sought to impose the accumulated earnings tax against taxpayer, a closely held railroad. *Held:* For taxpayer. Taxpayer's surplus accumulation was reasonable when such business needs as maintenance of roadways and equipment, purchase of new cars and new office building and maintenance shop, extension of existing lines, and the development of a trucking operation were considered. Taxpayer's business needs were far beyond the assets available to meet such needs. Also, there was no tax avoidance at the individual level. Sandersville RR Co., 385 F. Supp. 59, 74-2 USTC ¶ 9584 (MD Ga. 1974).

Jury determines no unreasonable accumulation of earnings. Upon auditing taxpayer corporation's tax return, the IRS determined that taxpayer had accumulated its earnings and profits beyond the reasonable needs of its business, and, in accordance with Section 531, assessed additional taxes. Taxpayer paid the additional taxes and sued for a refund on the basis that it had not unreasonably accumulated earnings and profits in the year in question. *Held:* For taxpayer. The court observed that under Section 531, an accumulated earnings tax applies to every corporation formed or availed of for the purpose of avoiding the income tax with respect to its stockholders, or the stockholders of any other corporation, by permitting earnings and profits to accumulate instead of being distributed. Since the need to retain earnings and profits was directly connected to the needs of the corporation itself and there was a bona fide business purpose for retention, taxpayer had established by a preponderance of the evidence that it did not permit its earnings and profits to accumulate beyond its reasonable needs for the business year. Hence, taxpayer was not subject to the accumulated earnings and profits tax. Hurst-Rosche, Inc., 73-2 USTC ¶ 9562, 32 AFTR2d 73-5456 (SD Ill. 1973).

Reasonable business needs preclude accumulated earnings tax. The IRS asserted the accumulated earnings tax against taxpayer, a corporation whose activities included oil and gas production and real estate. *Held:* For taxpayer. The court found that dividends were paid regularly prior to the years in question and that during the disputed years, taxpayer made actual expenditures in excess of cash earnings plus noncash deductions acquiring additional tangible assets and for other business purposes. It therefore had to partly finance such expenditures by borrowing. Finally, it is held that taxpayer had not been formed or availed of for the purpose of avoiding tax to shareholders. American Trading &

Accumulated Earnings Tax: *Reasonable Business Needs*

Prod. Corp., 362 F. Supp. 801, 72-1 USTC ¶ 9432, 29 AFTR2d 72-1301 (D. Md. 1972).

Jury finds taxpayer not liable for accumulated earnings tax on the basis of reasonable needs of the business and whether purpose of accumulation was tax avoidance. Taxpayer corporation, which had only one stockholder, filed its tax return for the fiscal year and paid the taxes shown to be due. Upon an audit, the IRS determined that taxpayer had accumulated earnings and profits beyond the reasonable needs of the business and accordingly assessed additional taxes. Taxpayer paid the tax and sued for a refund on the basis that it did not unreasonably accumulate earnings and profits, or if it did, that the purpose of such accumulation was not the avoidance of taxes for its stockholder. *Held:* For taxpayer. To decide whether the accumulated earnings tax should be imposed, the court instructed the jury that it had to decide two issues, namely, whether taxpayer did accumulate earnings and profits beyond the reasonable needs of the business in the year in question and, if so, whether or not one purpose for that accumulation was the avoidance of income tax at the stockholder level. In concluding that taxpayer was not subject to the accumulated earnings tax, the jury carefully considered all facts and circumstances, including the financial condition of both taxpayer and its sole stockholder, the intent of the parties, and whether taxpayer had a specific, definite, or feasible plan or need for the use of the accumulation. Art Sawyer, Inc., 72-2 USTC ¶ 9732, 30 AFTR2d 72-5711 (ED Mich. 1972).

Jury determines that taxpayer did not accumulate earnings beyond its reasonable needs. The IRS determined that taxpayer had allowed its earnings and profits to accumulate beyond the reasonable needs of its business. After the IRS assessed the accumulated earnings tax against taxpayer, taxpayer paid the tax under protest and instituted suit to recover the amounts. *Held:* For taxpayer. In determining whether taxpayer was liable for the accumulated earnings tax, the jury first considered whether the earnings and profits had been accumulated beyond the reasonable present and future needs of the business. Reviewing factors such as the amount needed for working capital and existing plans for expansion at the time of the accumulation, the jury found that taxpayer did not accumulate earnings and profits beyond its reasonable needs. Eberle Tanning Co., 342 F. Supp 1039, 72-1 USTC ¶ 9398, 30 AFTR2d 72-5469 (MD Pa. 1972).

Jury finds earnings are not unreasonably accumulated. The IRS determined that taxpayer, a refining corporation, permitted its earnings and profits to accumulate beyond its needs in order to avoid taxes at the stockholder level. The IRS assessed an accumulated earnings tax. *Held:* For taxpayer. Where the jury determined that taxpayer had not accumulated its earnings and profits beyond its reasonable business needs, it was not liable for an accumulated earnings tax. The jury was told to review reasonable needs including reasonably anticipated needs of the future, and to examine the definiteness of future plans. Sunnyland Ref. Co., 72-1 USTC ¶ 9125, 28 AFTR2d 71-6142 (ND Ala. 1971).

Capital outlays to prepare coal reserves for mining preclude Section 531 tax. Taxpayer, a coal mining company, was assessed a Section 531 tax on its accumulated earnings. It contended that it needed the funds in its business. *Held:* For taxpayer. Taxpayer was not formed or availed of to avoid tax on its shareholders. Its deep coal reserves would be in demand in the near future. Substantial capital outlays would be needed to mine them. This would require all of taxpayer's resources plus additional borrowed amounts. Templeton Coal Co., 301 F. Supp. 592, 69-1 USTC ¶ 9300 (SD Ind. 1969).

Manufacturing corporation found not to have permitted an accumulation of income beyond reasonable business needs. Taxpayer corporation was engaged in the manufacture of tractor trailers and the operation of a foundry and a farm. It had current assets in excess of current liabilities, but in earlier years was compelled to use current earnings and bank borrowing to finance operations. After discussions for the years in issue, taxpayer's di-

Accumulated Earnings Tax: *Reasonable Business Needs*

rectors declared that no dividend should be paid. The decision was based on the projection of cost of operations, the working capital available, and the need to borrow to take the benefit of extended credit. The IRS determined that taxpayer had permitted its earnings to accumulate beyond reasonably anticipated business needs to avoid the tax on shareholders and assessed the accumulated earnings tax. *Held:* For taxpayer. Taxpayer offered convincing and uncontradicted testimony that, under the operating cycle theory, its working capital must be available to meet the needs of the business and to provide for capital acquisitions. The earnings were therefore not permitted to accumulate beyond such reasonable business needs despite the nonpayment of a dividend in either taxable year. R.C. Tway Co., 68-2 USTC ¶ 9597 (WD Ky. 1968).

Court finds corporation accumulated earnings and profits for reasonably anticipated future business needs. Taxpayer corporation was formed through the merger of three corporations that had been engaged in the manufacture of wooden pails and tubs. All of taxpayer's stock was owned by the two families that had controlled the prior corporations. It decided to enter into the manufacture of corrugated boxes. Directors representing both controlling families consulted frequently, both orally and in writing, concerning the declaration of dividends. Both parties were mindful of taxpayer's position at the bottom of the corrugated box manufacturing ladder and their low standing in comparison to other larger and more nationally known firms. In order to diversify, taxpayer hired a consulting firm to advise them how they might enter the plastics industry. This study, as well as others, began just one year after taxpayer began to realize substantial profits after many years of losses or small earnings. During the three taxable years in issue and the three subsequent taxable years, taxpayer steadily improved its earnings, paid dividends of approximately 25 percent therefrom, and accumulated the remainder. In addition, taxpayer had sufficient net current assets to cover the operating costs for the business cycle. The IRS assessed the accumulated earnings tax.

Held: For taxpayer. There is no single approach to all cases, no governing mathematical formula, and no generally applicable observations that govern. All relevant facts must be considered and the facts here showed that the earnings and profits were accumulated to meet reasonably anticipated future business needs. Taxpayer had specific and feasible plans to use such accumulations to meet a reasonable expansionist and diversification program that was to have resulted in the implementation of new projects within a reasonable time. Consummation of this intent was reasonably foreseeable, and taxpayer's directors were motivated by an intent to maintain and advance the corporate business, not to avoid taxation. New England Wooden Ware, 289 F. Supp. 111, 68-2 USTC ¶ 9568 (D. Mass. 1968).

Corporation did not accumulate earnings and profits beyond reasonable business needs. Taxpayer corporation argued that retained earnings were to replace capital assets and acquire inventory. It also claimed it had a policy of not borrowing. The IRS claimed that taxpayer had unreasonable accumulated earnings. *Held:* For taxpayer. Accumulated earnings tax did not apply. Anticipated needs must be based on specific, definite, and reasonable plans. The jury found that the accumulations were for reasonable business needs. Mobile Press Register, Inc., 67-2 USTC ¶ 9595, 20 AFTR2d 5086 (SD Ala. 1967).

Accumulation of earnings held valid without formal plan for use as taxpayers had various finacial commitments. Taxpayer corporations were engaged in the bakery business and controlled by the same individuals. Taxpayers enjoyed substantial profits from their operations and paid no dividends in the years in question. There was no formal plan for the specific use of their retained earnings. The IRS determined that taxpayers had unreasonably accumulated earnings and were subject to an accumulated earnings tax. *Held:* For taxpayers. Although there were no specific plans to use retained earnings, the existence of large outstanding purchase commitments, the carrying of their own collision insurance, and the constant need to update equipment justified the accumulation of earnings for corporate expansion. Hardin's Bakeries, Inc., 293 F. Supp. 1129, 67-1 USTC ¶ 9253 (SD Miss. 1967).

Section 531 penalty tax not imposed where earnings and profits accumulation was to meet reasonable needs of speculative business. Taxpayer, a corporation engaged in constructing shopping centers, started in business with a paid-in-capital of $63,000. At the beginning of the three years in issue, the book value of the capital stock had risen to $306,000, and the surplus to $273,000. During this time, there was no additional investment by shareholders, so that the entire growth in net worth had come from the earnings and profits. Eighty-five percent of the stock was owned by one person, with the remaining shares owned by other members of his family. Cash dividends had been paid regularly on preferred stock, but infrequently on common stock. Whatever dividends were paid on the common stock were paid reluctantly by management, against the advice of its accountants and attorneys. Nervertheless, the IRS assessed deficiencies under Section 531, contending that earnings and profits at the beginning of the period were sufficient to meet the anticipated business needs of the corporation. Taxpayer introduced evidence bearing on the speculative nature and hazards of the business, difficulties and protracted periods of collection, fluctuations in volume, and working capital ratios. The court found that large cash reserves were required to meet current operations during peak construction periods and to meet the requirements of bonding companies. *Held:* For taxpayer. For the reasons and facts stated, taxpayer met his burden of proving that the earnings were not retained for any purpose other than to meet the reasonable needs of the business. Dahlem Constr. Co., 268 F. Supp. 103, 66-2 USTC ¶ 9772 (WD Ky. 1966).

Music publisher unreasonably accumulated surplus. Taxpayer was a leading publisher of sheet music in the United States. It brought action to recover the penalty tax on unreasonable surplus accumulation. At the end of the fiscal year in question, it had net current assets of over $1.3 million. Apparently the IRS allowed $330,000 as a reasonable reserve. *Held:* For the IRS. Taxpayer did have need for funds to buy the publishing rights to songs from new shows, to acquire other catalogs, and to pay advance royalties, but the reserve allowed by the IRS was sufficient for the reasonably anticipated needs. Chappell & Co., 66-1 USTC ¶ 9124 (SDNY 1965).

Penalty tax imposed on broadcasting company's surplus accumulation. The penalty tax for unreasonable accumulation of surplus was asserted against taxpayer, a corporation engaged in radio and TV broadcasting. Taxpayer contended that a large accumulation was necessary because of the possibilty of losing its network affiliation. The accumulation would also allow taxpayer to purchase certain operating equipment which might be required by the FCC to curb interference between broadcasting channels. Taxpayer had only one stockholder. *Held:* For IRS. The penalty tax was properly imposed. While the loss of a network affiliation would be extremely costly to taxpayer, the court noted that such situations were rare in the broadcasting industry. The court also considered the need for funds to purchase new equipment and determined that the resources of taxpayer were ample for this purpose. Havens & Martin, Inc., 65-1 USTC ¶ 9417 (ED Va. 1965).

Jury found accumulation unreasonable. All of taxpayer corporation's stock was owned by one individual. Taxpayer's accumulated earnings at the beginning of 1954 totaled $623,000; from 1954 through 1956 they were in excess of $150,000. *Held:* For the IRS. The jury's determination was based on the following considerations: the finacial status of taxpayer and its affiliate; changes in taxpayer's products; the tax bracket of both taxpayer and its stockholder; the postponement of plans for the use of the accumulation; and the unissued stock which could be used to raise additional capital. American Lawn Mower Co., 63-2 USTC ¶ 9779 (SD Ind. 1963).

Accumulated Earnings Tax: *Reasonable Business Needs*

Jury found no unreasonable accumulation by newspaper fearing competition. Taxpayer published the only daily newspaper in the community. It feared that a competitive weekly paper would become a daily. Part of the surplus funds would be needed for additional promotion and other expenses to meet the expected competition. Funds were also needed for a new press and possibly a new building. *Held:* For taxpayer. The jury found that taxpayer's surplus was not accumulated beyond business needs. Times Publishing Co., 63-1 USTC ¶ 9325 (WD Pa. 1963).

Jury found surplus accumulation reasonable where amount is within what a prudent businessman would accumulate for corporate business purposes. The IRS determined that taxpayer, a limestone and cement corporation, had accumulated earnings beyond its present and anticipated reasonable needs for the purpose of avoiding income tax on its stockholders. Accordingly, an accumulated earnings tax was assessed against the corporation. *Held:* For taxpayer. Where a jury found the accumulation not beyond what a prudent businessman would accumulate for corporate business purposes for present and anticipated needs, the accumulation was reasonable. The jury considered whether taxpayer had a specific, feasible, and definite plan, and whether taxpayer might undertake other related lines of business. It also examined past retained earnings to decide if they were adequate for the business needs, for taxpayer motivation, and so forth. The jury found no tax-avoidance motives. Fischer Lime & Cement Co., 63-2 USTC ¶ 9664, 12 AFTR2d 5540 (WD Tenn. 1963).

Accumulation of surplus to rehabilitate property was reasonable. The principal asset of taxpayer corporation was a single parcel of commercial real estate. Over the years it had been rented to a number of different tenants. The corporate directors concluded that the maximum income could be realized by rehabilitation of the property to make it suitable for rental to a single tenant. It was determined that an expenditure of $150,000 would be required for this purpose. *Held:* For taxpayer. The court found that this was a reasonable purpose for the accumulation of surplus sufficient to avoid the penalty tax. Leedy-Glover Realty & Ins. Co., 62-1 USTC ¶ 9102 (ND Ala. 1961).

Earnings needed for business; no penalty tax despite redemption of principal stockholder's stock. Spurred by the redemption of the stock of a principal stockholder, the IRS asserted the accumulated earnings tax against taxpayer corporation, a wholesale liquor dealer. *Held:* For taxpayer. Examining its needs for inventory, and considering that it had always paid substantial dividends, the court found that the surplus was being accumulated for reasonable business needs. Barrett Hamilton, Inc., 59-2 USTC ¶ 9710, 4 AFTR2d 5612 (ED Ark. 1959).

Court held that earnings set aside to redeem minority stockholders' interests were not a reasonable business need; thus, taxpayer was subject to the accumulated earnings tax. In May 1970, taxpayer sold its assets to another company. Taxpayer then placed these funds in short-term, income-bearing securities pending the decision of its board as to its future activities. The majority stockholder (and chief operating officer) of taxpayer wanted taxpayer to redeem the minority stockholders' stock, and then remain in existence as an investment or holding company. However, the majority stockholder died before firm plans could be made for the redemption of the minority stockholders' interests, and only three months after the sale. From that point on, taxpayer was relatively inactive and engaged solely in winding up its affairs. It was not until October 15, 1970, that the reconstituted board of directors met, and decided to redeem the minority stockholders' stock and continue on as an investment company entirely owned by the majority stockholder's family. The IRS assessed the accumulated earnings tax for taxpayer's taxable year ending August 31, 1970. *Held:* For the IRS. When the "reasonably anticipated needs" test is applied under the accumulated earnings tax, the planned "needs" must be specific and definite (not vague or uncertain), and supported by real considerations during the year in issue (and not by use of changed circumstances or intentions subsequent to the year end). Beyond the costs of its Section 303 redemption, which are expressly defined as a "reasonable need" by Section 537(b)(2), taxpayer had no "reasonable need," for its earnings. In particular, accumulations to redeem the minority stockholders' interests were not a "reasonable need," since such a redemption would be for the benefit of the majority stockholder's family and heirs. Finally, taxpayer could not rebut presumption of tax-avoidance purpose, since no board activities evidencing a contrary intent occurred before the end of the tax year 1970. Thus, taxpayer was subject to the accumulated earnings tax. JJJ Corp., 576 F2d 327, 78-1 USTC ¶ 9453, 42 AFTR2d 78-5024 (Ct. Cl. 1978).

Imposition of penalty upheld. The IRS imposed the accumulated earnings tax, contending that the earnings accumulation was not related to any reasonable business purpose but was used to redeem a stockholder's 50 percent interest in taxpayer corporation. *Held:* For the IRS. In a related issue, the court held that interest on the penalty assessment was not recoverable, even though improperly computed, since the refund claim failed to raise the issue of interest. John B. Lambert & Assocs., 76-2 USTC ¶ 9776, 38 AFTR2d 76-6207 (Ct. Cl. 1976).

Liability for accumulated earnings tax determined. Taxpayer, a radio audience rating business, contended that it was not liable for the penalty tax, since its accumulated earnings were necessary to meet expenses incurred during the operating cycle, the cost of inventory, and operating costs during the period required to collect accounts receivable. *Held:* For taxpayer. The Court of Claims found that the accumulation of earnings was for a valid business purpose. Hooper, Inc., 539 F2d 1276, 76-2 USTC ¶ 9538, 38 AFTR2d 76-5417 (Ct. Cl. 1976).

Accumulations not unreasonable where management determines that higher reserves were required because of impending strike. Due to an impending strike and increased orders from customers who were enlarging their own inventories in anticipation of the strike, taxpayer had an exceptionally profitable year. The IRS contended that taxpayer was subject to accumulated earnings tax. *Held:* For taxpayer. Due to the strike and the resulting economic turmoil, the normal cash flow utilization formula contained in *Bardahl* for determining working capital needs may not have provided sufficient flexibility to meet cash requirements. The IRS' analysis did not adequately take into account the vagaries of the market situation in which taxpayer expected to, and did, find itself at the end of the year. The court refused to substitute its business judgment for that of corporate management. Accordingly, imposition of the accumulated earnings tax was held improper. Dielectric Materials Co., 57 TC 587 (1972).

Liability on subsidiary's obligation avoids Section 531 tax. Taxpayer formed a wholly owned subsidiary to enter into the motel business. The subsidiary borrowed $540,000 on two notes. The taxpayer was primarily liable on the note for $190,000, and its real property was mortgaged to secure the loan. The second note was secured by a mortgage on the balance of taxpayer's other property. A joint venture, consisting of an unrelated corporation and taxpayer's subsidiary, agreed to be responsible for the payment of the second note. During the years at issue, the taxpayer had from $80,000 to $100,000 available for dividends. *Held:* For taxpayer. Because the taxpayer needed at least $200,000 in working capital to meet the reasonably anticipated needs of its motel venture, it was not liable for the Section 531 tax. Montgomery Co., 54 TC 986 (1970), acq. 1970-2 CB xx.

Accumulated earnings tax imposed where stockholder capital was $90. Taxpayer corporation had accumulated profits of $530,000 from prior years and $260,000 for the current year. Its year-end balance sheet showed current assets of $1.2 million (of which $820,000 was in cash) and current liabilities of $750,000. The IRS asserted that the accumulated earnings penalty tax applied. *Held:* For the IRS. Taking into account prior accumulations, the current accumulation was beyond the reasonable needs of the business. Moreover, there was sufficient cash available to pay dividends, even after taking current liabilities into account, since the cash to be generated by new business could be used to pay some of the liabilities. Since the taxpayer earned a substantial profit every year and never paid a dividend, since it had ample surplus and cash, and since the stockholders, whose original investment in the corporation was $90, were aware of the high tax on dividends paid to them, taxpayer was availed of for the purpose of avoiding the tax on the stockholders. Electric Regulation Corp., 40 TC 757 (1963).

Personal holding company tax avoided but accumulated earnings tax imposed. Taxpayer had been a personal holding company for over 20 years. In 1956, on advice of tax counsel, it invested in oil and gas working interests so that it no longer was a personal holding company. Taxpayer added over $500,000 to its earnings and profits for the year and paid a $2 dividend compared with almost $20 the year before. Taxpayer's president justified the low dividend on the basis of a short cash position. It had made more than $2.5 million noninterest loans to its stockholders. Taxpayer was assessed as a personal holding company, but at trial the IRS abandoned this attack and asserted liability for the accumulated earnings tax. *Held:* For the IRS, on the issue of accumulated earnings tax. The retained earnings were not shown by a preponderance of the evidence to be within the reasonable needs of the business. A noncash dividend in the form of discharge of the loans due the corporation could have been made. That this would not be desirable to the stockholders was immaterial. Nemours Corp., 38 TC 585 (1962).

Surplus penalty imposed; accumulation was beyond reasonable business needs. Taxpayer's sole stockholder was a partner in a well-known textile commission house, Iselin-Jefferson. Taxpayer was used to hold securities and real estate, to carry out some sporadic investments in textiles, and to provide managerial services, under contract with various textile mills. Its accumulated earnings rose from $249,000 at the start of the three-year period involved, to $472,000 at the close of the period. During the same period, taxpayer's ratio of current assets to current liabilities increased from 11 to 1 to 31 to 1. Taxpayer did not pay any dividends during its nine-year existence. The IRS imposed an accumulated earnings tax. *Held:* For the IRS. The court found that there were no reasonable business needs sufficient to justify the accumulation, that various ventures contemplated were unrelated to taxpayer's business, and that the accumulation enabled taxpayer's principal stockholder to avoid payment of a dividend tax. The court briefly noted that taxpayer's statement of business needs, filed pursuant to Section 534, was too general and vague to shift the burden of proving unreasonable accumulation to the IRS. Wellman Operating Corp., 33 TC 162 (1959).

Taxpayer held liable for accumulated earnings tax. Taxpayer corporation, a wholesale distributor of meat products, accumulated substantial earnings and profits in two consecutive years. The IRS determined that the taxpayer had been availed of by its controlling stockholder for the purpose of avoiding taxes by allowing its earnings and profits to accumulate beyond its reasonable business needs. The taxpayer argued that its sister corporation's business needs should also be considered when determining the reasonable business needs. *Held:* For the IRS. Because the taxpayer's controlling stockholder attempted to avoid tax by having the taxpayer accumulate earnings and profits in excess of its reasonable business needs, the taxpayer was liable under Section 531 for the accumulated earnings tax. The business needs of the taxpayer's sister corporation could not be considered in determining the reasonable business needs of the taxpayer. Feilen Meat Co., 48 TCM 440, ¶ 84,341 P-H Memo. TC (1984), aff'd (8th Cir. 1985).

Earnings were accumulated beyond the reasonable needs of the business. The IRS assessed the accumulated earnings tax on taxpayer corporation, who argued that it needed to accumulate its earnings in order to bid on certain contracts and to enter a new business. *Held:* For the IRS. Taxpayer had no written records of its bids on the contracts, it made

Accumulated Earnings Tax: *Reasonable Business Needs*

large loans to related businesses and stockholders without interest and unevidenced by written documents, it maintained a large portfolio of unrelated investments, and its liquidity was high during the years in question. Therefore, the accumulation was beyond the reasonable needs of the business. Petrozello Co., 46 TCM 63, ¶ 83,250 P-H Memo. TC (1983), aff'd (3d Cir. 1984).

Bardahl formula may be computed using peak-cycle method. Taxpayer was in the office design business and also furnished office equipment and supplies. Taxpayer's president was also its majority stockholder. The IRS notified taxpayer of a proposed deficiency stemming from an accumulated earnings tax under Section 531. Pursuant to Section 534(c), taxpayer submitted a statement of the reasons for the accumulations. These included the expansion of the corporation's business and its building, the maintenance of a minimum net worth imposed by a real estate mortgage, and sufficient working capital necessary for it to meet its operating cycle requirements. Both parties agreed that use of the *Bardahl* formula was an appropriate way to measure the working capital requirements of taxpayer's business. Under this formula, the length of an operating cycle was converted into a percentage of one year and multiplied by the total operating expenses, not including depreciation and federal income taxes. An operating cycle consisted of an inventory cycle, which was determined by dividing a monthly inventory by the cost of goods sold, and an accounts receivable cycle, which was determined by dividing a monthly accounts receivable by the net sales. These two amounts were added together and represented the total length of one operating cycle in terms of a decimal part of one year. The IRS sought to use $182,097 as an average value for working capital, whereas taxpayer contended that $250,000 represented its working capital for the year in question. *Held:* For taxpayer. Where evidence indicated taxpayer's business was cyclical in nature with ending balances of inventory and accounts receivable very low, taxpayer was allowed to use an average of the highest three consecutive months to adjust accounts receivable upward in order to more accurately measure working capital requirements under the *Bardahl* formula. State Office Supply, Inc., 43 TCM 1481, ¶ 82,292 P-H Memo. TC (1982).

Earnings held to exceed reasonable needs of the business after considering taxpayer's trade payables, working capital requirements, business needs, and the shortage of supplies. Taxpayer was engaged in the retail sale of gasoline and the wholesale trade of kerosene and fuel oil. From 1971 to 1974, taxpayer's year-end retained earnings nearly tripled to more than $3.8 million. Although taxpayer's CPA suggested taxpayer distribute a dividend in 1972, it made no distributions until 1974. Through the rules of attribution, taxpayer's entire stock was owned by *W*. The IRS determined that taxpayer was liable for the accumulated earnings tax, pursuant to Section 531 for its taxable year 1974. *Held:* For the IRS. Accumulated earnings tax was imposed where the court determined that taxpayer had unreasonably accumulated earnings for the purpose of avoiding taxes with respect to its stockholders. The accumulation was unreasonable, since taxpayer's liquid assets exceeded its reasonable business needs. Considered by the court were taxpayer's trade payables, working capital requirements, business needs, and the shortage of supplies. Owner *W* had knowledge of a possible accumulated earnings tax problem; thus, taxpayer had the proscribed purpose for accumulating earnings. Williams Oil Co., 42 TCM 851, ¶ 81,461 P-H Memo. TC (1981).

Redemption of 95 percent owner does not justify earnings accumulation. Taxpayer, a corporation charged with accumulating earnings in excess of reasonable business needs, argued that it needed the funds to redeem the shares of its 95 percent owner. If the business were not passed in this fashion to the minority shareholder, the company would have to liquidate. *Held:* For the IRS. The stock redemption was primarily motivated by the personal situation of the majority shareholder. Lamark Shipping Agency, 42 TCM 38, ¶ 81,284 P-H Memo. TC (1981).

Accumulated Earnings Tax: *Reasonable Business Needs*

Lumber manufacturer held liable for unreasonable accumulated earnings tax using a modified *Bardahl* formula. Taxpayer corporation was engaged in the manufacture and sale of lumber products. Logs remained at the mill up to four weeks, and the lumber required anywhere from 30 to 90 days to be air dried. Taxpayer's inventory consisted of different types of wood, each requiring different times to dry, and some wood was kiln-dried. In 1970 and 1973, taxpayer paid stock dividends, but it paid no cash dividends until 1973. Taxpayer did not pay dividends because it felt it needed the cash for current operations and expansion. The IRS determined that taxpayer allowed its earnings and profits to accumulate beyond the reasonable needs of its business and that it was liable for an accumulated earnings tax. *Held:* For the IRS. Accumulated earnings tax was imposed on taxpayer where its available working capital exceeded its operating expenses and reasonable business needs. The appropriate method to be used in determining what was a reasonable amount of working capital to be maintained by taxpayer for its business was the *Bardahl* formula, with certain modifications reflecting the taxpayer's individual circumstances. Suwannee Lumber Mfg. Co., 39 TCM 572, ¶ 79,477 P-H Memo. TC (1979).

Manufacturing corporation's accumulations justified. The IRS determined that a manufacturing corporation and a related corporation that leased property to it unreasonably accumulated their earnings. *Held:* For taxpayers, in part. The manufacturer's accumulations were needed to redeem a dissenting shareholder's stock and to provide self-insurance for the company, but the lessor corporation had no business reason for accumulating its earnings in two of the three years at issue. Wilcox Mfg. Co., 38 TCM 378, ¶ 79-092 P-H Memo. TC (1979).

Accumulated earnings and profits were for reasonable business needs. Taxpayer, a retail clothing store, had accumulated earnings and profits for 1971–1973 of $530,000. The IRS determined deficiencies in the accumulated earnings tax of approximately $5,000 for each year in question. *Held:* For taxpayer. Although no specific plan for remodeling, moving, and expansion was formulated by taxpayer, the underlying circumstances and taxpayer's manifestation of intent supported taxpayer's assertion that the funds were accumulated in part for such projects. In addition, it was found that the funds were needed for contingent liabilities and working capital needs. Marie's Shoppe, Inc., 36 TCM 1548, ¶ 77,381 P-H Memo. TC (1977).

Accumulated earnings determined reasonable. Taxpayer corporation, a clinical pathology laboratory, saved money to purchase a new machine. The IRS imposed an accumulated earnings tax. *Held:* For taxpayer. Although gross receipts in 1968 and 1969 exceeded $200,000, and no dividends were paid to the sole stockholder, taxpayer intended to purchase the new machinery and actually did purchase equipment in 1971 and 1972. Thus, the accumulated earnings were not unreasonable and no tax was applicable. North Valley Metabolic Laboratories, 34 TCM 400, ¶ 75,079 P-H Memo. TC (1975).

Accumulated earnings tax determined. Taxpayer, a building construction corporation, received rental income from a building it specifically designed and put up for one tenant. The IRS assessed an accumulated earnings tax. *Held:* For the IRS. The earnings were accumulated beyond the reasonable needs of the business. No dividends were paid for 25 years. When the IRS first questioned the accumulation, the corporation then distributed all of its earnings. The possibility that the tenant might not renew its lease, and actually threatened to cancel its lease, was not sufficient need for the accumulation. Therefore, the accumulated earnings tax was properly imposed. Hamabe Realty Corp., 33 TCM 1029, ¶ 744,233 P-H Memo. TC (1974).

Accumulation for reasonable needs not taxable. Taxpayer corporation, pursuant to its board of directors' resolutions, established a capital items reserve fund, which was equal to depreciation and amortization deductions, and a mortgage retirement fund. The IRS assessed an accumulated earnings tax. *Held:* For taxpayer. The accumulation of earnings

Accumulated Earnings Tax: *Reasonable Business Needs*

was for the reasonable needs of the business. Taxpayer's board had made plans to erect a new office building and over several years actively sought funds, tenants, and made drawings. During the period in question, distributions were made to stockholders. Thus, the accumulations were not unreasonable, but had a business related purpose; the accumulated earnings tax was not applicable. Starks Bldg. Co., 32 TCM 1201, ¶ 73,256 P-H Memo. TC (1973).

Accumulated earnings tax determined. Taxpayer, a realty trust, was organized by a corporation to hold real estate and construct improvements on it. The stockholders were the beneficiaries. The IRS asserted an accumulated earnings tax. *Held:* For the IRS. The accumulations were beyond taxpayer's reasonable needs. Although new improvements may have been necessary, it was likely that funds would be sought and available from sources other than retained earnings. If funds had been distributed to the beneficiaries, their tax liabilities would have increased significantly. Taxpayer had net increases in income each year in which it accumulated funds and could not show a reasonable business need for the funds. Powder Mill Realty Trust, 32 TCM 707, ¶ 73,149 P-H Memo. TC (1973).

Accumulated earnings tax applicable where accumulation unnecessary for reasonable business needs. Taxpayer, a corporation engaged in road paving, accumulated earnings during operating years and later sold its operating assets. The IRS assessed an accumulated earnings tax for the years in question. *Held:* For the IRS. Taxpayer retained cash reserves in excess of what was needed for one operating cycle. The contention that funds were necessary for certified checks to be submitted with government bids was rejected. Since future plans to resume business operations were vague and indefinite, such plans did not constitute a reasonable need for an accumulation. Finally, taxpayer, a closely held corporation, never paid dividends and maintained large amounts of cash and liquid investments. This retention of earnings resulted in a substantial tax savings to stockholders. Based on these factors, the Section 531 tax was properly imposed. Mimmac Corp., 31 TCM 375, ¶ 72,096 P-H Memo. TC (1972).

Accumulated earnings tax inapplicable where accumulation necessary for business. The IRS claimed that taxpayer corporation unreasonably accumulated its earnings and imposed an accumulated earning's tax under Section 531. *Held:* For taxpayer, in part. The evidence presented clearly demonstrated that taxpayer needed its entire accumulated earnings in all of the years in question for the reasonable needs of its business for (1) working capital, (2) financing a program of modernization of plant and equipment, and (3) expansion, all of which are acceptable reasons for accumulation under Regulation §§ 1.537-2(b)(4), 1.537(b)(1), and 1.537(b)(2). Walton Mill, Inc., 31 TCM 75, ¶ 72,025 P-H Memo. TC (1972).

Reasonable business needs for Section 531 tax determined under operating cycle test. Taxpayer corporation was a sales organization that distributed oil additives manufactured by a sister corporation to various unrelated blenders and distributors that were under franchise contracts. It was stipulated that in a business such as taxpayer's, an operating cycle consists of the period of time that begins when (1) cash is converted into inventory, (2) inventory is converted into sales and accounts receivable, and ends when cash is realized upon collection of the receivables. This period was converted into a decimal equivalent of the year. This figure was then multiplied by the known cost of goods sold and other operating costs of a full year to determine the anticipated cost of operating taxpayer's business during one full operating cycle in the following year. Under this approach, the IRS determined that taxpayer, during its taxable years 1956 through 1959, was liable for the accumulated earnings tax imposed by Section 531. *Held:* For the IRS for the years 1957 and 1958, but taxpayer was entitled to an accumulated earnings credit equal to its undistributed taxable income for 1956 and 1959. Thus, the accumulated earnings tax was not applicable for 1956 and 1959. The approach of *Bardahl Manufacturing Corp.,* TC Memo. 1965-200, was applica-

ACCUMULATED EARNINGS TAX: *Tax-Avoidance Purpose*

ble here, namely, that taxpayer should have sufficient liquid assets on hand to pay all of its current liabilities and any extraordinary reasonably anticipated expenses, plus enough to operate the business during one operating cycle. It is also found that for 1959, taxpayer needed additional funds to defend itself against a breach of contract suit brought against it by a foreign distributor. Bardahl Int'l Corp., 25 TCM 935, ¶ 66,182 P-H Memo. TC (1966).

Advertising agency liable for accumulated earnings tax. Taxpayer was the fifth largest advertising agency in the United States. As a result of its policy of retaining a major portion of its earnings, taxpayer was extremely liquid from 1957 through 1961. As a result of this high degree of liquidity and the relatively large amount of accumulated earnings, the IRS asserted the accumulated earnings tax. *Held:* For the IRS, in part. The accumulated earnings tax was imposed for 1958, 1959, and 1961. Large cash balances may be maintained where there is a sufficient business need for them. However, taxpayer's claim of reasonable business needs to finance slow-paying clients, to provide for loss of major clients, to plan for foreign expansion, and to finance a stock redemption plan in order to keep three key employees justified only part of the accumulations. Ted Bates & Co., 24 TCM 1346, ¶ 65,251 P-H Memo. TC (1965).

Manufacturer of auto clutches not subject to accumulated earnings tax. Taxpayer, a manufacturer of automobile clutches for Ford, had accumulated earnings of more than $2.6 million on December 31, 1953. The IRS imposed the accumulated earnings tax. *Held:* For taxpayer. The court found that taxpayer, for the years in issue, 1954 through 1958, did not accumulate earnings and profits beyond the reasonable needs of its business, including reasonably anticipated needs, and was not availed of for the purpose of avoiding the income tax with respect to its stockholders. The earnings and profits were accumulated (1) to provide the corporation with additional working capital to carry peak amounts of accounts receivable arising from delays by Ford in approving initial prices for newly designed clutches and in approving price increases for other clutches, and (2) to provide capital for the diversification of taxpayer's product line necessitated by the decline of the clutch business after the introduction by Ford in 1951 of automobiles equipped with automatic transmissions. Alma Piston Co., 22 TCM 948, ¶ 63,195 P-H Memo. TC (1963).

Accumulated earnings tax not applicable where taxpayer anticipated large construction contracts. The IRS determined that taxpayer, a construction contractor, was subject to the accumulated earnings tax for the years 1954 through 1957. Prior to 1954 taxpayer was engaged in a large contract road construction business. It was shown that the last of the large road construction contracts was concluded sometime in 1954 or 1955, and that the company had reasonable expectation of obtaining additional large contracts through 1955. Although it sold most of its heavy equipment in 1955, it kept the proceeds in liquid assets, since it seemed wiser to sell the old equipment and buy new equipment if a contract were obtained. *Held:* For taxpayer, in part. The court concluded that the taxpayer's accumulation of earnings and profits at the end of 1954 and 1955 did not exceed the amount that a prudent businessman would consider appropriate for the then present and reasonably anticipated future business needs of taxpayer. It concluded differently, however, with respect to 1956 and 1957, in which years taxpayer had no large road construction contracts and could not have anticipated any. McMinn, Jr., 21 TCM 913, ¶ 62,165 P-H Memo. TC (1962).

Tax-Avoidance Purpose

Mere presence of tax-avoidance motive sufficient for imposition of accumulated earnings tax. Taxpayer corporation was engaged in the manufacture and sale of bubble gum, and in the operation of a farm. Taxpayer was wholly owned by *W*, and made no loans to *W* and provided no benefits other than a salary. Taxpayer made no investments in unrelated businesses and declared no dividends during a period in which it had significant accumulated earnings. At the district court level, the

ACCUMULATED EARNINGS TAX: *Tax-Avoidance Purpose*

jury found for the IRS after rejecting instructions that the avoidance had to be the purpose for the accumulation in order to impose the accumulated earnings tax. The Sixth Circuit reversed and remanded for a new trial. Certification was granted to resolve the dispute among the circuits. *Held:* Affirmed. The proper instruction to a jury was that the mere presence of any intention to avoid individual taxation was sufficient reason to impose the accumulated earnings tax, assuming the accumulations were not for a reasonable business purpose. Donruss Co., 393 US 297, 89 S. Ct. 501, 69-1 USTC ¶ 9167 (1969).

Accumulated earnings tax imposed regardless of no increase in earnings and profits of taxable year in question; gifts of stock to exempt charities were followed by redemptions of said stock for the purpose of tax avoidance. Taxpayer was engaged in the sale and distribution of auto parts. Its president and sole stockholder, *T*, never received compensation for his services as an officer, and taxpayer paid no dividends from 1959 to 1967. Over the years, *T* donated stock to charities and afterwards redeemed the donated stock. At the end of 1968, the year in question, *T* had redeemed all the donated stock and was taxpayer's sole stockholder. The IRS determined that taxpayer was subject to an accumulated earnings tax. With respect to 1968, the Tax Court found no increase in taxpayer's earnings and profits for the year because of its stock redemption: The Tax Court further found that the IRS had erred in assessing an accumulated earnings tax. *Held:* Reversed and remanded. The fact that earnings and profits had not increased in 1968 did not prevent the imposition of tax under Section 531, where the corporation fell under Section 532. The repetitive cycles of gifts of stock to exempt charities followed by redemptions of the donated stock demonstrated *T's* intention to avoid income tax. The charitable deductions were enhanced by the retention of corporate earnings and provided shelters against other taxable income. Thus, the redemptions kept *T* in control. GPD, Inc., 508 F2d 1076, 75-1 USTC ¶ 9142, 35 AFTR2d 75-348 (6th Cir. 1974).

Taxpayer liable for accumulated earnings tax where earnings were accumulated beyond reasonable needs of business and where one purpose of accumulation was the avoidance of tax. Taxpayer was originally chartered in 1939 to issue contracts of insurance against various hazards. During the years 1963 through 1965, taxpayer did not maintain a sales force, and its primary income was from the sale and rental of real properties and management of its investment portfolio. Taxpayer contended that the reason it had to accumulate earnings was that under state law, new insurance companies were required to have a minimum initial capital and surplus of $600,000. The IRS determined that taxpayer had unreasonably accumulated its earnings and profits. *Held:* For the IRS. Taxpayer was liable for the accumulated earnings tax where one purpose for the accumulation was the avoidance of taxation. There was no justification for accumulating earnings because taxpayer was in a lower income tax bracket than the corporation. Industrial Life Ins. Co., 481 F2d 609, 73-2 USTC ¶ 9533, 32 AFTR2d 73-5273 (4th Cir. 1973), cert. denied, 414 US 1143 (1973).

Imposition of accumulated earnings tax upheld. The Tax Court held that taxpayer corporation was availed for the purpose of avoiding income taxes on its sole stockholder when it unreasonably accumulated its earnings and profits. *Held:* Affirmed. Taxpayer did not prove under Donruss that avoidance of income tax on its stockholder was not one of the purposes for the accumulation. Also, in computing the accumulated earnings tax, there was no statutory authority for a deduction for keyman insurance premiums. Novelart Mfg. Co., 434 F2d 1011, 70-2 USTC ¶ 9717, 26 AFTR2d 70-5837 (6th Cir. 1970).

Realty company had unreasonable surplus accumulation. An individual transferred investment securities and real estate to taxpayer corporation. Over the years, taxpayer accumulated $265,000 of surplus and paid no dividends. *Held:* For the IRS. The IRS assessed the accumulated earnings tax against taxpayer. The surplus was unreasonably accumulated to avoid surtax on the stockholder. The penalty tax was properly imposed. The findings of the district court were not clearly erroneous and were affirmed. Carlen Realty Co., 345 F2d 998, 65-1 USTC ¶ 9425 (5th Cir. 1965).

Unreasonable surplus accumulation demonstrated by loans to related companies for unrelated activities. Interest-free loans of over $350,000 were made by taxpayer to four corporations owned or controlled by taxpayer's sole stockholder. Most of these loans were for activities unrelated to taxpayer's business. The IRS imposed the accumulated earnings tax on the corporation. *Held:* For the IRS. These loans and the use of corporate funds for the personal expenses of the stockholder were evidence that the surplus was being unreasonably accumulated for the purpose of avoiding surtaxes. The penalty tax was upheld. An example of the use of funds for personal expenses, the deduction of which the district court disallowed, was the payment of a nurse for the care of the principal stockholder. Although the nurse performed some secretarial duties, her work was primarily for his personal comfort. Cummins Diesel Sales of Ore., Inc., 321 F2d 503, 63-2 USTC ¶ 9641, 12 AFTR2d 5296 (9th Cir. 1963).

Accumulated earnings tax imposed on unreasonable accumulation as there were no "specific, definite and feasible" plans for the use of the funds, and there was a tax-avoidance motive. Taxpayer corporation filed its returns for 1961 and 1962 and paid the regular corporate income taxes due. After audit, the IRS assessed a deficiency by applying the accumulated earnings tax to what it felt were unreasonable accumulations motivated by tax-avoidance purposes. *Held:* For the IRS. In its instructions to the jury, the district court defined an unreasonable accumulation of earnings to be "an accumulation that exceeds the amount a prudent businessman would consider appropriate for the present business purposes and for the reasonable anticipated future needs of the business." To justify the accumulation for future needs, the business must have had "specific, definite and feasible" plans at the end of each year for the use of the accumulated funds. To impose this tax, the court noted, there must also be a tax-avoidance motive for the excessive accumulations. That generally comes from the desire to avoid individual tax that would be due if the earnings were distributed to the stockholders as dividends. Once an unreasonable accumulation is found, the tax-avoidance purpose is presumed. Under these instructions, the jury found both an unreasonable accumulation and a tax-avoidance purpose to justify the imposition of the accumulated earnings tax. R.W. Mitscher Co., 71-1 USTC ¶ 9177, 27 AFTR2d 515 (WDNY 1970).

Accumulated earnings tax not applicable despite accumulations beyond reasonable business needs. Taxpayer, an engineering and sales corporation, accumulated earnings of well over $100,000 in each of the three years in issue. Testimony indicated that the controlling stockholder was motivated by his experiences during the depression of 1929 and was convinced that the business should retain vast liquid reserves to provide a cushion against depression and to service long-term contracts. The financial history of the business indicated that it was highly suseptible to contract cancellations and to manufactures' delays and policy changes. The IRS determined that the accumulated earnings tax was applicable and assessed deficiencies. *Held:* For taxpayer. Although income was permitted to accumulate far beyond the reasonable needs of the business, the evidence did not indicate that the corporation was formed or availed of for the purpose of avoiding the income tax on its shareholders. T.C. Heyward & Co., 66-2 USTC ¶ 9667 (WDNC 1966).

Earnings not unreasonably accumulated for various reasons. The IRS determined that taxpayer, a bolt and nut manufacturing corporation, had unreasonably accumulated earnings for the purpose of avoiding tax on its stockholders. The jury was instructed to consider several factors in determining whether earnings were unreasonably accumulated: the amount that a prudent businessman would retain, the intentions of the directors and eventual use of the earnings: the amount accumulated; conditions in the idustry as a whole; and the definiteness of plans for using the earnings. *Held:* For taxpayer.

ACCUMULATED EARNINGS TAX: *Tax-Avoidance Purpose*

Reviewing the evidence, the jury found that the accumulations were reasonable. Therefore, no further determination regarding tax avoidance was necessary. Harrison Bolt & Nut Co., 64-2 USTC ¶ 9631, 14 AFTR2d 5360 (D. Md. 1964).

Accumulation of earnings was beyond reasonable business needs. Taxpayer, engaged in leasing old, run-down business properties, accumulated earnings for the purpose of refurbishing the structures. The plans and estimates for this work were vague and indefinite. The 25 percent stockholder did not want the company to declare dividends, whereas the remaining stockholders did desire dividends, but because the bylaws required an 80 percent vote for payment of dividends, none was paid. *Held:* For the IRS. Taxpayer failed to prove that the reasonable needs of the business required the accumulation of earnings. There were no specific, definite, and feasible plans for reinvesting the funds into the business. Further, the refusal of the 25 percent stockholder to permit payment of dividends was for the purpose of avoiding the income tax he would have been required to pay if taxpayer had paid dividends or a salary to him. Atlantic Properties, Inc., 62 TC 644 (1974).

Unreasonable accumulation without tax-avoidance purpose does not invoke Section 531 tax. Taxpayer, whose stock was owned by a single individual, operated a newspaper that showed steady growth from 1940 through 1959. During this period, a heavy investment was made in plant and equipment, and employees entered profit-sharing arrangements. From 1954, dividends average about 29 percent of net profit after taxes. No shareholder loans were made, but investments were made in U.S. bonds and in the stock of other newspapers. In 1958 and 1959, the accumulated earnings totaled $746,000 and $905,000, respectively. The IRS asserted the Section 531 penalty tax. The taxpayer submitted a statement justifying its accumulations on seven grounds. *Held:* For taxpayer. The statement was sufficient to shift the burden of proof to the IRS, although the need for a reserve for competition and for business reserves was not considered applicable. The size of the accumulations was not the crucial factor. After examining the evidence the court concluded that while the accumulated earnings were somewhat beyond the reasonable foreseeable business needs, the conservative policies of management, not any tax-avoidance motive, were the only reason for retaining the earnings. The Section 531 tax was therefore not applicable. Bremerton Sun Publishing Co., 44 TC 566 (1965).

Taxpayer accumulated earnings beyond reasonably anticipated business needs and was availed of to avoid income taxes. By 1960, taxpayer had an earned surplus of almost $500,000 that increased regularly, including about $60,000 in 1960 and 1961. No dividends were ever distributed, and no salary was ever paid to the 90 percent stockholder and principal officer. The IRS computed an accumulated earnings tax for 1960 and 1961. *Held:* For the IRS. The accumulation exceeded the reasonable needs of the business as it was placed in unrelated investments. Taxpayer was in an extremely liquid position, the small working capital needs were easily covered because gross receipts exceeded total costs, and receivables were quickly collected. The accumulation was also beyond the reasonably anticipated needs of the business. Taxpayer's four reasons for accumulation were all insufficient. A reserve for self fire insurance was not based on any facts and was too high, and earlier funds were already sufficient. There were no definite expansion plans, although taxpayer had been thinking about them since 1927. A large order was more than five years away and was uncertain. Finally, maintenance of large deposits in its customer banks was unnecessary, as contracts were granted under competive bidding. Also, there was no evidence that one of the accumulation purposes was not the avoidance of income tax with respect to the already wealthy majority stockholder. Federal Ornamental Iron & Bronze Co., 28 TCM 391, ¶ 69,072 P-H Memo. TC (1969).

Construction corporation not liable for accumulated earnings tax. Taxpayer corporation was in the heavy construction business. Contracts were obtained principally by competitive bidding on a lump sum or fixed unit-price basis. The corporation did not subcontract and assumed the risks of bad weather, strikes, subsoil conditions, increases in costs of material and equipment, and other hazards. The IRS determined that taxpayer was liable for the accumulated earnings tax for 1958 through 1960 on the grounds that the retained earnings increased in the three years from $486,000 to $3,379 million, that its cash account increased from $294,000 to $689,000, and that at the end of each year the ratio of current assets to current liabilities was in excess of four to one. *Held:* For taxpayer. The penalty tax was not sustained. Taxpayer's accumulation of earnings was not for the purpose of avoiding income tax on its stockholders but to protect itself and its stockholders from losses arising from the unusually large risks inherent in the heavy construction business and for increasing its net worth to be qualified for bidding on increasingly larger contracts. Oman Constr. Co., 24 TCM 1799, ¶ 65-325 P-H Memo. TC (1965).

Retained earnings were for future expansion, not to avoid tax. Taxpayer corporation was organized in 1930 to take over an unsuccessful rubber tire company. The tire business was soon dissolved and the corporation concentrated on the manufacture of rubber hoses, a material used in the construction of railroads. Although initial profits were small, taxpayer nevertheless earned money every year and paid a dividend every year since 1932. During 1960 and 1961, taxpayer accumulated over $300,000, which increased its surplus to over $1.5 million. Taxpayer's policy was to finance operations and expansions out of earnings and not to rely on debt. The IRS alleged that taxpayer was liable for the accumulated earnings tax for 1960 and 1961. *Held:* For taxpayer. The undistributed earnings and profits for 1960 and 1961 were not beyond the reasonably anticipated needs of the business. The accumulation was needed to help finance a new plant, expand the existing plant, finance a pension plan, and for other business reasons. Taxpayer had a history of conservative financial management and a large minority interest was owned by a trust. In addition, the excellent dividend record was adequate proof that the corporation was not availed of to avoid tax on its stockholders. Carolina Rubber Hose Co., 24 TCM 1159, ¶ 65,229 P-H Memo. TC (1965).

ACQUIRING CORPORATIONS, CARRY-OVER OF TAX ATTRIBUTES BY

(*See* Reorganizations—Carry-Over of Net Operating Losses and Other Tax Attributes)

ACQUISITIONS

(*See* Reorganizations)

ACQUISITIONS TO AVOID TAX

(*See also* Net Operating Losses; Reorganizations—Carry-Over of Losses and Tax Attributes)

Purchase of corporate stock by related trust was a sham. District court held that a transaction wherein a trust organized by taxpayer shareholders purchased all the outstanding corporate stock was void because the transaction served no other purpose than tax avoidance. Therefore, amounts receive by taxpayers as deposits on an option, which had been assigned to the corporation, were held to be ordinary income to taxpayers in 1963, the year of the trust purchase. *Held:* Affirmed the basis of the lower court's opinion. Peters, 527 F2d 1174, 76-1 USTC ¶ 9260 (5th Cir. 1976).

Deduction of post-acquisition net operation losses denied. The IRS determined that taxpayer corporation acquired five subsidiaries for the principal purpose of filing a consolidated return in order to utilize the subsidiaries' anticipated post-acquisition operating losses to offset taxable income. The operating loss deductions were then denied under Section 269. The district court held for the taxpayer on the theory that Section 269 was inapplicable to post-acquisition losses. *Held:*

Reversed and remanded. The lower court's decision violated both the literal language of Section 269 and the purpose of the statute as revealed by the legislative history. Hall Paving Co., 471 F2d 261, 73-1 USTC ¶ 9161, 31 AFTR2d 73-514 (5th Cir. 1973).

Where evidence indicated that the purpose of a merger was to gain use of the losses of a liquidated corporation, court held under Section 269 that the company could not use said losses to offset its post-merger profits. In July 1957, as a result of earlier negotiations, taxpayer's parent caused one of its subsidiaries to merge into Hollander, Inc., which after the merger became the taxpayer. At the time of the merger, Hollander's sole assets consisted of the stock of the newly acquired subsidiary and its large tax losses. Prior to acquiring this subsidiary, Hollander had liquidated all of its assets and as a result had only cash and its losses. To acquire the subsidiary, Hollander used all of its cash and obtained loans secured by collateral. The funds were lent by a person closely associated with taxpayer's parent. Under the collateral loan agreements, the lender had the right to require Hollander to merge with another business that was able to meet certain specific requirements. Taxpayer's predecessor met these precise requirements. After the merger, the taxpayer was owned 64 percent by its parent and 36 percent by the public (including Hollander's stockholders). In the years following the merger, taxpayer claimed Hollander's losses as offsets to its taxable income. The IRS disallowed, under Section 269, the deduction of these losses. *Held:* For the IRS. Evidence indicated that the principal purpose of the merger was to obtain Hollander's losses. Specifically, Hollander's sole business was that of its newly acquired subsidiary. The taxpayer's parent could easily have acquired Hollander's subsidiary before it was acquired by Hollander: In fact, the parent was instrumental in providing the collateral for loans Hollander needed to acquire the subsidiary. Since the taxpayer's parent could have acquired the subsidiary directly, the only possible purpose the parent could have had for allowing Hollander to acquire the subsidiary first was to permit the taxpayer's parent to obtain both the subsidiary and Hollander's losses. PEPI, Inc., 448 F2d 141, 71-2 USTC ¶ 9631, 28 AFTR2d 71-5586 (2d Cir. 1971).

Utilization of net operating loss carry-overs after sale to another corporation was for the principal purpose of tax avoidance. S, a wholly owned subsidiary of W, engaged in manufacturing furniture, incurred net operating losses of approximately $600,000 prior to its acquisition by K. K purchased the stock of S for $235,000, an amount equal to the net book value of S's assets. At the time of its purchase, S had started to show some profit; however, such profits were not sufficient to absorb any material amount of its net operating loss carry-overs. A short time after the acquisition, K merged its wholly owned subsidiary, C, into S; on the first post-acquisition return, S deducted its net operating loss carry-overs of approximately $600,000 from the combined income of C's business ($976,000) and S's business ($35,000), resulting in a reduction of tax of about $300,000. The IRS disallowed the net operating loss carry-over of S on the ground that the principal purpose for the acquisition of S was to avoid payment of income taxes. The Tax Court found for the IRS. *Held:* Affirmed. Although the acquisition might have been consummated even if there weren't opportunity for tax avoidance, tax avoidance was above all other motives, thus satisfying the principal purpose test of Section 269(a). Scroll, 447 F2d 612, 71-2 USTC ¶ 9588, 28 AFTR2d 71-5434 (5th Cir. 1971).

Net operating loss carry-overs disallowed where tax evasion was the principal purpose for acquisition of taxpayer. Taxpayer and its acquirer's corporation were merged, the acquirer getting the benefit of $225,000 of taxpayer's net operating loss to offset his corporation's gain. He paid, at most, $65,000 for the loss benefit and $255,000 for property. The IRS disallowed the loss carry-over deductions under Section 269, and also certain capital loss carry-overs. The Tax Court held for the IRS. *Held:* Affirmed. Although taxpayer claimed it had been acquired principally for a business purpose, Section 269(a) was applicable and the deduction was disallowed because the consideration paid was substantially disproportionate to the sum of the corporate property and the tax benefit acquired. Because it was impossible to determine the fair market value of a note and preferred stock exchanged for common stock or the fair market value of the common stock, which was sold for $1, the capital loss and the carryovers were correctly disallowed. Hart Metal Prods. Corp., 437 F2d 946, 71-1 USTC ¶ 9186, 27 AFTR2d 71-546 (7th Cir. 1971).

Net operating loss carry-over was disallowed where acquisition was chiefly to evade or avoid taxes. Taxpayer acquired a corporation whose only product was in decreasing demand and that incurred increasing losses totaling almost $60,000. Shortly after acquisition, the corporation was liquidated; taxpayer used its net operating losses, which the IRS disallowed. The Tax Court held for the IRS. *Held:* Affirmed. Taxpayer's business reasons for the acquisition were questionable and secondary in purpose to evading or avoiding taxes by use of the disallowed loss carryovers. Brumley-Donaldson Co., 443 F2d 170, 71-1 USTC ¶ 9422 (9th Cir. 1971).

Separate corporations were formed for tax avoidance. The IRS held that the formation of separate corporations to operate barges and vessels was motivated principally for purposes of tax avoidance in order to secure the benefit of multiple surtax exemptions. Such a setup was deemed to be in violation of Section 269. The district court held for the IRS. *Held:* Affirmed. Although limitation of liability was asserted as a reason for separate incorporation, such limitation existed already to a substantial extent under the law of the United States. There may have also been nontax motives for separate corporations, but tax avoidance was the principal purpose for the separation. Bay Sound Transp. Co., 410 F2d 505, 69-1 USTC ¶ 9371, 23 AFTR2d 69-1289 (5th Cir. 1969).

Carry-over of preacquisition losses denied where the principal purposes of the acquisition was tax evasion. *H* purchased taxpayer, a corporation with a record of net operating losses. A year later taxpayer was merged into another of *H*'s corporations. Taxpayer's income tax return claimed a carry-over deduction for losses it sustained during the four years previous to *H*'s purchase, as well as losses incurred after the purchase. The Tax Court agreed with the IRS in stating that the claimed deduction should be disallowed in its entirety. Both the Tax Court and the IRS claimed that the deduction was contrary to Section 269, and was inconsistent with the special limitations on operating loss carryovers in Section 382. *Held:* Affirmed, in part. The statutory presumption of Section 269(c) holds that the principal purpose of an acquisition is the evasion of taxes. Where this presumption was not overcome, the preacquisition losses were disallowed. However, the advance of money to taxpayer to help it financially after the acquisition indicated that the post-acquisition losses were not designed as a means of tax avoidance and therefore were allowed. Herculite Protective Fabrics Corp., 387 F2d 475, 68-1 USTC ¶ 9157 (3d Cir. 1968).

Section 269 not applicable to merger with corporation controlled by stockholders of acquiring corporation. A corporation that incurred losses in the shipping business was merged in 1956 with a corporation in the dairy and grocery store business. The shipping corporation was dormant for several months prior to the merger. Shortly before the merger, controlling shareholders of the shipping corporation increased their holdings in the dairy corporation to achieve control. The district court found that the principal purpose of the merger was tax avoidance. It therefore held that under Section 269 the net operating losses of the shipping corporation could not be applied against taxpayer's profits from the store business. *Held:* Reversed and remanded. Section 269 by its terms did not apply to the merger, since immediately before the merger, taxpayer's stockholders controlled both corporations. The only acquisition to which the statute may have applied was the purchase by the controlling stockholders of their additional interest in the dairy corporation. The purchase could be viewed as an integral component of a plan leading to the merger and the ultimate securing of the tax benefit. Realistically, however, it would seem that sound business practice, and not tax avoidance, led to this acquisition of control, with its attendant benefits. In any event, the district court did not consider this issue, and the case was remanded. Southland Corp., 358 F2d 333, 66-1 USTC ¶ 9347, 17 AFTR2d 673 (5th Cir. 1966).

Acquisition of loss corporation stock was for tax avoidance. "National" acquired the assets of taxpayer at a foreclosure sale. Taxpayer, a manufacturer of micrometers, had incurred large operating losses. Later, National acquired the stock of taxpayer and assumed the liabilities due former stockholders. These liabilities were later converted to debenture bonds. Shortly thereafter, National sold taxpayer's stock to Green and Turbo, two related corporations engaged in the manufacture of aircraft parts, for $30,000. Green and Turbo were then merged into taxpayer, the surviving corporation, and operations continued, with micrometers accounting for less than 6 percent of post-merger sales. Taxpayer carried forward its premerger net operating losses and deducted interest on the debentures. The Tax Court disallowed both deductions. *Held:* Affirmed. Although business purpose existed, taxpayer failed to establish by a preponderance of the evidence that the principal purpose of the acquisition was not to evade or avoid federal income tax. Prior to the acquisition taxpayer was a moribund corporation with liabilities far in excess of its assets, with a 10 year loss history and a potential net operating loss carry-over of $332,000, a definite factor in the acquisition, and with problematic chances for future profits. J.T. Slocomb Co., 334 F2d 269, 64-2 USTC ¶ 9592, 14 AFTR2d 5086 (2d Cir. 1964).

Loss carry-over disallowed on acquisition to avoid tax. Taxpayer corporation was organized in 1949 to develop and market cornpickers. It sustained losses from 1950 through 1953 and then abandoned that business. Benjamin A. Snyder and his brother each acquired 31 percent of the taxpayer's outstanding shares at its organization and purchased the remaining shares for a nominal price in 1953. Snyder was also the sole stockholder of a corporation engaged in the business of buying and selling molasses and he owned, as an individual, tank cars for transporting the molasses, from which he received rental income. On September 1, 1953, Snyder, after becoming taxpayer's sole stockholder and owner of its notes payable, sold his tank cars to taxpayer. From that date until the end of the taxpayer's fiscal year ending February 28, 1954, its sole income was rent from the use of the tank cars. This income was offset on its tax return by a claimed net operation loss deduction derived from its cornpicker business. On March 1, 1954, the molasses corporation merged into the taxpayer. The Tax Court found that Snyder acquired control in 1953 to get the benefit of the loss carry-over. *Held:* Affirmed. The court rejected taxpayer's contention that he already had control by attribution of his brother's stock. The court agreed with the Tax Court and other circuits that Section 269 was applicable to disallow the loss in this situation. Snyder Sons Co., 288 F2d 36, 61-1 USTC ¶ 9312, 7 AFTR2d 875 (7th Cir.), cert. denied, 368 US 823 (1961).

Loss deduction on sale of building owned by acquired corporation was proper; tax avoidance absent as a principal purpose of acquisition. Taxpayer was engaged in construction of industrial buildings, and, in order to acquire certain property, acquired a controlling interest in the stock of another corporation. The acquired corporation was under financial stress and sold a building it owned at a substantial loss to finance a new factory-office complex under construction by taxpayer. The IRS conceded that the principal purpose of the acquisition was not tax avoidance, but disallowed the loss deduction claimed on a consolidated return on the grounds that it was attributable to events preceding affiliation. *Held:* For taxpayer. In acquiring control and filing a consolidated return, taxpayer did not have an improper tax-avoidance purpose. The loss incurred on the sale of the building was not a deduction attributable to events preceding the date of affiliation. Anderson & Son, Inc., 68-2 USTC ¶ 9573 (ND Ill. 1968).

Jury found evidence failed to establish that the principal purpose of acquisition of stock was not tax avoidance. Taxpayer acquired the stock of an investment company, which had a substantial net operating loss carry-over. The IRS disallowed the net operating loss carry-over under Section 382(a) after it determined that the purchase of the stock, and losses, was for the principal purpose of tax evasion, or avoidance, and that taxpayer did not continue the business after the purchase. *Held:* For the IRS. A jury found that the evidence indicated that the purchase of the corporate stock and the acquisition of its loss carry-overs was for the principal purpose of evading, or avoiding, taxes. It also found that after the change in ownership the business was not carried on in substantially the same way. Trade Winds Inv., Inc., 68-1 USTC ¶ 9247, 21 AFTR2d 810 (WD Tex. 1968).

Losses of discontinued business deductible against profits of business transferred from stockholders. Shortly after its incorporation in New York in March 1951, taxpayer's predecessor acquired the assets of a woodworking business for $50,000. The corporation financed the purchase with its initial paid-in-capital and a $35,000 5-year bank loan. The corporate stockholders, four equal partners in a management consultant business, guaranteed payment of $15,000 of the loan. In its first two years of operation, taxpayer's predecessor lost $11,000 annually. In 1953, when it discontinued its woodworking business and attempted to sell or rent its assets, the corporation continued to operate at a loss, the result of interest, insurance costs, and taxes. From 1953 through 1956, taxpayer's predecessor incurred annual net losses averaging $5,000. The stockholders financed the losses through loans. In early 1957, one of the partners retired, and the remaining partners acquired his interests. They then transferred the assets of their management consultant business to the corporation, which repaid their advances. On June 30, 1957, the corporation sold the assets of the woodworking business. The corporation claimed the losses incurred in prior years as deductions against its income from the management consultant business. Taxpayer, which was organized in Delaware at the end of 1957 to succeed to the business of its predecessor, made similar claims in filing its income tax returns for subsequent years. The IRS denied the deductions for the loss carry-overs on the ground that the losses were not incurred by the same business that had earned the profits. The IRS also relied on Section 269 in denying deductions for the loss carry-overs. *Held:* For taxpayer. The necessity for the stockholders to keep taxpayer's predecessor going in order not to lose their investment, as well as to protect against loss under their personal guarantees, indicated that, contrary to the IRS' argument, there was no de facto dissolution of the corporation when the woodworking business was discontinued. Thus, there was no acquisition of corporate control within the meaning of Section 269 when the partners transferred their partnership assets to a corporation that they had previously controlled. The subsequent change in state of incorporation was of no consequence on this point. The economic losses that taxpayer's predecessor sustained in the years following its incorporation made it unrealistic to assume that its incorporation was intended to evade or avoid taxes in 1957. Section 382 did not apply to deny the loss carry-over, because there was not the requisite change in stock ownership to bring its provisions into effect. The *Libson Shops* doctrine did not apply because (1) the transaction was governed by the 1954 Code and (2) common owners absorbed their own partnership business into their own corporation. Wofac Corp., 269 F. Supp. 654, 67-2 USTC ¶ 9532 (DNJ 1967).

Purchase of corporate control was motivated by tax avoidance. Taxpayer was one of a number of associates who bought the outstanding stock and $700,000 of debenture notes of Olivier from the corporation's stockholder. At the time of purchase, Olivier had a net operation loss carry-over. The corporation also had an agreement with the stockholders of Whitten, a profitable corporation, to purchase all the latter's stock. When Olivier redeemed the notes, taxpayer reported the excess over purchase price of the notes as capital gain. The IRS contended that the excess was ordinary income, arguing that the associates acquired control of Olivier for the principal purpose of tax evasion or tax avoidance. *Held:* For the IRS. The IRS argued that the associates acquired Olivier to use its loss carry-over to offset the profits of Whitten (even though it was not so used) and to draw down the earnings of Whitten as capital gain in the form of payments on the Olivier notes. Ullman, 66-1 USTC ¶ 9442 (ND Ala. 1966).

Net operating loss carry-over disallowed where tax avoidance was principal purpose of corporate control. The IRS disallowed net operating loss carry-overs of taxpayer's controlled corporation on the theory that pursuant to Section 269, control of such corporation was acquired for the principal purpose of avoiding federal income tax. *Held:* For the IRS. Taxpayer failed to overcome the presumption of correctness of the IRS' determination. Furthermore, taxpayer failed to substantiate the losses claimed. Jupiter Corp., 83-1 USTC ¶ 9168, 51 AFTR2d 83-823 (Cl. Ct. 1983).

Subsidiaries were not acquired to evade or avoid tax. Taxpayer, a corporation engaged in the turkey farming business, formed two subsidiaries to operate various phases of the business. The parent company reported with the accrual method of accounting, and the subsidiaries adopted the cash method. The subsidiaries suffered operating losses for the initial year, primarily as a result of not considering closing inventories when computing income, and the parent filed a consolidated return with the subsidiaries and carried back the net operation losses against the parent's income. The IRS increased the group's consolidated income under Section 269, contending that the acquisition's primary purpose was to obtain the benefit of adopting the cash method of accounting for the subsidiaries. *Held:* For taxpayer. The principal purpose of the acquisition was not to avoid or evade tax but to achieve business benefits. The parent was forced to compete in the processing and marketing of turkeys, and the subsidiary corporations were formed to limit the parent's liability. Rocco, Inc., 72 TC 140 (1978).

Company with carry-over loss was not acquired to avoid tax. Taxpayer acquired all the stock of Magnolia in a reorganization under the Bankruptcy Act. Subsequently, Magnolia was merged into the taxpayer, which claimed operating loss deductions based on a carry-over of Magnolia's loss sustained priority and during its bankruptcy. The IRS disallowed the losses on the basis of Sections 269, 381, and 382. *Held:* For taxpayer. The IRS did not meet its burden of proving that the acquisition was principally motivated by tax avoidance. The length of time between the acquisition and the merger (three years) was an important factor, and it did not matter that tax avoidance might have been a reason for the merger. Additionally, other factors indicated a non-tax-avoidance motive for the merger. Daytona Beach Kennel Club, Inc., 69 TC 1015 (1978).

A parent's purchase of assets and transfer of assets to a subsidiary was viewed as the subsidiary's purchase of the assets, thereby avoiding application of Section 269. Taxpayer was the wholly owned subsidiary of its parent corporation. Taxpayer was unprofitable and, as a consequence, had unused net operating losses. As part of a plan to increase taxpayer's profitability and thus use its net operating losses, taxpayer's parent acquired income-producing assets from an unrelated company. The parent immediately transferred these assets to taxpayer, which assumed its purchase liability for these assets. Taxpayer's parent acquired stock in two other companies and transferred the stock to taxpayer, which assumed the parent's liability for such stock. Taxpayer soon thereafter redeemed this stock for part of the companies' assets. The IRS sought, under Section 269 to prevent taxpayer's using its net operating losses against the income produced by these assets in later years. The issue before the court was whether taxpayer acquired these assets from its parent on a cost basis or on a carry-over basis. In the latter case, Section 269 would prevent taxpayer's using its net operating losses because, under Section 269(a)(2), taxpayer's basis in the assets would have been determined according to the basis that its parent had in such assets. *Held:* For taxpayer. Taxpayer and the IRS conceded that the asset purchase and asset transfer to taxpayer were part of a single plan. Accordingly, taxpayer was viewed as the purchaser of the assets, and so its basis in the assets was a cost basis. Therefore, Section 269 did not apply. Omealia Research & Dev., Inc., 64 TC 491 (1975).

Section 269 requires adjustment of depreciation and loss where plan to purchase corporation's asset was changed to purchase of such corporation's stock. Taxpayer revised its plans to purchase outright X Corporation's sole asset, a yacht, when it was learned that the yacht in X's hands had a depreciable basis significantly higher than its value. Taxpayer instead acquired X's stock in exchange for its own stock equal in value to the yacht. The following year after attempting to charter the yacht, taxpayer sold it. For both years (the year of acquisition and the year of sale), taxpayer filed a consolidated return with X, claiming depreciation on the yacht. Taxpayer also claimed a loss in the year of sale. *Held:* For the IRS. The IRS, under Section 269, asserted that the depreciable basis of the yacht was its fair market value. Accordingly, it reduced the post-transaction depreciation deductions and determined that taxpayer had a gain on sale of the yacht. Under the circumstances, it was clear that the manner in which the taxpayer acquired the yacht was dictated by tax-avoidance purposes. Canaveral Int'l Corp., 61 TC 520 (1974).

Principal purpose of acquisition of taxpayer's stock held to have been tax avoidance; preacquisition losses not deductible. Taxpayer was engaged in the business of wholesale and retail sales of hardware and industrial supplies. It incurred net operating losses from 1950 through 1954. In 1955, a new group, with interests in companies engaged in the manufacture and retail sale of steel and building materials, became interested in acquiring taxpayer's stock. They determined that taxpayer's inventory was worth only half of its book value because some items were obsolete and unsalable. They were also aware that the net operating losses might be available as tax deductions. They thereupon purchased the capital stock and acquired for a nominal consideration taxpayer's indebtedness to two affiliated companies. Indebtedness was subsequently cancelled. During the three years following the acquisition, taxpayer and several other companies participated in a contract for the sale of steel used in a government project. Although taxpayer sustained losses in 1955 and 1957, it realized net profits in all years subsequent to the acquisition. Taxpayer continued to operate at the same location until the termination of its lease, whereupon it purchased its own building at a location on the same road some three miles away from the original location. The manager was employed under a five-year contract, but the number of other employees had risen from one to seven. The value of the inventory had also increased by 50 percent over the acquisition cost. Taxpayer deducted the net operating losses for the period prior to acquisition against income thereafter, but the IRS disallowed the deduction on the grounds that the principal purpose of the acquisition was the avoidance or evasion of the income tax. *Held:* For the IRS, in part. Regarding the losses incurred prior to acquisition, Section 269(a) provides that if any person or persons acquire control, and the principal purpose of such acquisition is tax avoidance, then the net operating loss deduction is disallowed. Although the price paid for the capital stock was less than the adjusted basis of the corporate property, and taxpayer contended that the acquiring group would have purchased its stock if only to acquire the inventory, the court was not convinced that the principal purpose for the acquisition of the stock was not the acquisition of the carry-overs. There was no evidence that the previous stockholders would have been willing to sell the inventory without disposing of the stock. In addition, the tax-avoidance motive was further evidenced by the knowledge of the contract under which taxpayer and others were to profit on the sale of steel for the government project during the three years after acquisition. Regarding the losses subsequent to acquisition, neither Section 269 nor 382 was applicable, but the IRS nevertheless contended that the losses were not deductible for failure to establish that the acquisition of corporate stock and accounts receivable, on which the claimed loss was based, became worthless after acquisition rather than before. The evidence, however, pointed to worthlessness occurring after acquisition; consequently, the loss was deductible. Industrial Suppliers, Inc., 50 TC 635 (1968).

Section 269 bars net operating loss deduction where acquired company had been inactive. The managing stockholder of a corporation engaged in road excavation suffered from arthritis and was unable to tend adequately to corporate affairs. As a result, the corporation incurred operating losses for a number of years. Finally, the corporation went into de facto liquidation by completing its existing contracts, selling its equipment, and paying its outstanding debts. At this time, one of the stockholder's relatives, who also operated a road construction business, purchased the stock of the corporation. This relative had operated his own business profitably for some time. By conducting some of his operations through the deactivated corporation, he was able to use its net operating loss carry-forward as a deduction against current income. The IRS disallowed the loss. *Held:* For the IRS. The carry-forward losses were not deductible. The testimony at the trial did not substantiate that the excess over book value paid for the stock was for anything other than acquiring the tax loss. The purpose of the acquisition was to avoid tax. If this intention exists, Section 269 provides that the IRS may deprive a taxpayer of the benefits of the transaction. H.F. Ramsey Co., 43 TC 500 (1964).

Post-acquisition losses of acquired corporation allowed when business reasons prompted acquisition. Taxpayer and Missourian were controlled by two brothers. Missourian's operations became unprofitable from 1953 through 1957 and taxpayer advanced large sums of money to it. In 1955, the brothers contributed their stock in Missourian to taxpayer on advice by bankers that this would produce a better credit picture for financing of the group. Additional reasons were to consolidate the management of the corporation and to replace obsolete equipment in the loss corporation. Consolidated returns were filed from 1955 through 1957. When Missourian showed a profit from 1958 through 1960, separate returns were filed. The Commissioner disallowed post-acquisition losses of the subsidiary on the consolidated return filed by the taxpayer. *Held:* For taxpayer. The losses were allowed. There were valid business reasons for the acquisition and the acquired corporation was not a "shell." Taxpayer anticipated that the losses would continue only for a short period before turning profitable, and that was what actually happened. Naeter Bros. Publishing Co., 42 TC 1 (1964).

Section 269 applied where principal purpose of acquiring corporation was to obtain net operating loss carry-over. Taxpayer, a sales corporation with large losses, discontinued operations. The corporate shell was sold for $500 to another corporation, which transferred its sales operations to taxpayer. Taxpayer claimed net operating loss carry-overs, which the IRS denied under Section 269. *Held:* For the IRS. The acquisition of taxpayer was for the principal purpose of securing the benefit of the loss. The contention that taxpayer was acquired to protect a trade name was not supported by the facts. The stockholders of the acquiring corporation knew of taxpayer's financial difficulties and receivership, even if they did not know the exact amount of the loss carry-over benefit. Moreover, the loss carry-over would also be denied under Section 382, since there was no continuance of the business of the acquired corporation. Taxpayer was inactive for two years before the sales operations of the acquiring corporation were transferred to it. Regulation § 1.382(a)-1(h)(6), which provides this rule, is valid. Fawn Fashions, Inc., 41 TC 205 (1963).

Stockholders of loss company bought profitable business and then sold their stock to its old owners; carry-over denied. Taxpayer was an automobile agency owned by two CPAs who also had a professional practice. The taxpayer suffered substantial losses in each of two years. Thereafter, the following transactions, which the court found were all preplanned, occurred. The accountants bought the stock of a profitable fire screen business operated

ACQUISITIONS TO AVOID TAX

by a businessman who was a client of theirs. They dissolved that corporation and transferred its assets to the auto agency corporation; the former operator of the business continued as its manager. Shortly thereafter the accountants sold their stock to trusts for the children of the former operator of the business; one of the accountants was a trustee. The IRS asserted that the whole purpose of the scheme was the avoidance of tax by the acquisition of the loss corporation. *Held:* For the IRS. Noting that taxpayer had abandoned the position that Section 269 is inapplicable to the acquiring corporation, the Tax Court denied it the right to offset the auto losses against the screen profits. Temple Square Mfg. Co., 36 TC 88 (1961).

Carryover of net operating losses not allowed where business purchase was designed to obtain losses. Taxpayer, in the business of developing and marketing cornpickers, suffered net operating losses. *S* became the majority stockholder of taxpayer and transferred tank cars he owned to taxpayer for the transportation of molasses. *S* then merged his wholly owned corporation, which bought and sold molasses, into taxpayer. Taxpayer no longer operated the cornpicker business. Taxpayer carried over the net operating losses from the cornpicker business against the subsequent earnings of the molasses business. The IRS disallowed the deductions. *Held:* For the IRS. Where the principal purpose for acquiring control of a corporation was to evade or avoid taxes by securing the benefit of the corporation's net operating losses, the losses could not be offset against the acquiring corporation's profits. Snyder Sons Co., 34 TC 400 (1960).

Taxpayer's principal purposes in acquiring a company that had large net operating losses was not tax avoidance. Taxpayer corporation acquired the assets and liabilities of an unrelated company through its wholly owned subsidiary in a nontaxable transaction under Section 368(a)(1)(C). On the consolidated returns it filed for itself and its subsidiaries, the taxpayer deducted the acquired company's large net operating losses. The IRS claimed that the taxpayer's principal purpose in acquiring the company was to evade or avoid income tax by utilizing the net operating losses of the acquired company, and disallowed the deduction under Section 269. *Held:* For taxpayer. Taxpayer's principal purpose in acquiring the company was not to avoid or evade tax but to obtain the company's cash, which it needed to expand its business, and to make the stockholders of that company stockholders of taxpayer so that it could offer its stock over the counter and raise badly needed capital. In addition, the testimony of taxpayer's management revealed that the acquired company's net operating losses were considered to be of little value to taxpayer, since taxpayer had large net operating loss carry-overs of its own. Fairfield Communities Land Co., 47 TCM 1194, ¶ 84,100 P-H Memo. TC (1984).

Net operating loss benefits not denied to purchase of stock where valid business reasons exist for acquiring the stock and where the business is not substantially changed. Taxpayer corporation conducted a fixed airport operation *T*. From 1966 through 1970, taxpayer reported net operating losses, which it applied against its taxable income. Taxpayer then acquired *P* airport. Taxpayer lost enormous sums of money from the air carrier service at *P* airport. Taxpayer sold the right to operate scheduled airlines to *S*, and its subsidiary airline. *T* sold the land at *P* airport, and all of its outstanding stock to *M*. Had *M* not purchased the stock, it would have been required to obtain new licenses which would have caused a closure of the airport for two or three weeks. After the purchase, *M* discontinued the air taxi service, but continued all other aspects of the business. The IRS determined that the principal purpose for the purchase of the stock by *M* was tax evasion, and accordingly the net operating loss carry-overs should be denied under Section 269. Additionally, the IRS contended that *M* should not be permitted the benefit of those same carry-over losses pursuant to Section 382(a), because *M* did not continue substantially the same business. *Held:* For taxpayer. Where bona fide business reasons existed for acquiring the corporate stock, such a finding was sufficient to place the transaction outside the

49

scope of Section 269. Further, the elimination of one portion of taxpayer's business following the change of ownership of its stock did not result in a substantial change in its business. Therefore, the corporation was not denied the carry-over of losses. Princeton Aviation Corp., 47 TCM 575, ¶ 83,735 P-H Memo. TC (1983).

Loss corporation permitted to use its tax benefits to reduce tax liability on income generated by acquired profitable enterprise, as there were valid business reasons for doing so. Taxpayer had incurred net operating losses and investment tax credit carry-overs, and was in danger of failing without the infusion of additional capital. X Corporation had a profitable income-producing business that was, however, dependent on a single unrelated customer. The principal stockholders of X Corporation (who also held stock in taxpayer) acquired control of taxpayer and caused X Corporation to transfer its assets and liabilities to taxpayer in exchange for taxpayer's stock. X Corporation also acquired the balance of taxpayer's stock by exchanging its stock for taxpayer's stock. Both X Corporation and taxpayer were operated separately by taxpayer. The IRS, under Section 269, disallowed taxpayer's use of its net operating losses and credits against the income generated by the consolidated businesses. *Held:* For taxpayer. The evidence did not indicate that the principal purpose of the above transaction was tax avoidance. The court found that the main purposes of the transaction were (1) to provide taxpayer with capital, (2) to achieve economy in administering both businesses, (3) to provide diversity of investment, and (4) to create a vehicle for future business acquisitions and diversification. It was clear that the use of taxpayer's tax benefits was considered, and that this consideration dictated the form of the transaction. However, this did not per se trigger application of Section 269. Stange Co., 36 TCM 31, ¶ 77,007 P-H Memo. TC (1977).

Acquisition of loss corporation with business purpose, followed by merger with profitable corporation, did not bar net operating loss carry-over. R Corporation, the survivor of a statutory merger with O Corporation, sought to offset its net operating loss carry-overs against the post-merger profits of the acquired business. The IRS contended that the common parent, K, had acquired R as part of a unified transaction, intending to carry out the merger in order to utilize R's losses. The IRS sought to disallow the losses under Section 269. *Held:* For taxpayer. Taxpayer showed that K had a business purpose in acquiring R and that the later merger was a separate transaction. Key Buick Co., 35 TCM 1359, ¶ 76,303 P-H Memo. TC (1976).

Net operating loss carry-over deduction of inactive business denied as acquisition was to avoid tax. Taxpayer went into bankruptcy and its stock was acquired by a party that operated the same business. Taxpayer took a deduction for its net operating losses. The IRS disallowed the deductions. *Held:* For the IRS. In order for the loss deduction to be available, taxpayer must continue substantially the same business; that was not done here, where the corporation was inactive at the time stock ownership changed. Regulation § 1.382(a)-1(h)(6). Taxpayer's discontinuance was permanent, not temporary, as evidenced by the voluntary petition of bankruptcy, the selling of all assets by the trustee in bankruptcy, and the commencement of operation 18 months after cessation. Thus, the net operating loss carry-over deductions were disallowed. Utah Bit & Steel, Inc., 29 TCM 224, ¶ 70,050 P-H Memo. TC (1970).

Acquisition of loss corporation not for tax evasion or avoidance. A garment subcontractor acquired the stock of taxpayer, a contract garment manufacturer. Taxpayer had adequate plant and facilities, good customers, a competent labor force, and an available net operating loss carry-over. The IRS disallowed the deduction of the net operating loss carry-over to taxpayer, contending that the acquisition was for the principal purpose of tax evasion or avoidance by the purchasing corporation's "funneling" of income to taxpayer in order to utilize the latter's loss. *Held:* For taxpayer. The principal purpose of the acquisition was to turn taxpayer into a profitable enterprise. Furthermore, there was no indication of any improper intercompany "funnelling" of income. Accrued interest expense on a note given to the sellers in partial payment of the stock was disallowed because the amount of the liability at the time of the accrual was not certain. The obligation of taxpayer to pay the note, plus interest thereon, was by the terms of the note contingent upon a judicial determination that the net operating loss carry-overs would be available. Superior Garment Co., 24 TCM 1571, ¶ 65,283 P-H Memo. TC (1965).

Net operating loss carry-over permitted where acquisition of control is for valid business reasons. Taxpayer corporation manufactured machines that were used in railroad construction. To obtain needed plant space with a minimum of cash outlay, taxpayer entered into an agreement in 1956 with Turner Corporation, a manufacturer of farm machinery. Taxpayer was to manage and control the latter's business in return for an option to buy Turner's stock out of future earnings prior to 1961. Taxpayer pumped some of its own manufacturing operations into Turner, and although it made an effort to continue with the manufacture of farm machinery, it was eventually forced to terminate the farm division. Turner suffered losses from 1956 through 1960. In February 1960, taxpayer exercised its option to acquire all the Turner stock at a cost of $250,000. At that time, Turner's assets had risen to a net value of $350,000. A few months later, taxpayer and Turner were merged. After the merger, taxpayer sought to deduct Turner's premerger losses. The IRS denied the deduction under Section 269. *Held:* For taxpayer. Taxpayer was entitled to the net operating loss carry-over deduction. Section 269 was inapplicable, since the purpose of the acquisition was to exploit the benefit of the value of Turner's assets over the option price of the stock, not to obtain the advantage of the loss carry-overs. The fact that after acquiring control, taxpayer elected to merge because it was to its tax advantage to do so was not determinative of any issue. Kershaw Mfg. Co., 24 TCM 228, ¶ 65,044 P-H Memo. TC (1965).

Loss carry-over of acquired corporation permitted upon evidence of lack of intent to evade or avoid taxes. Taxpayer, engaged in the manufacture of costume jewelry, sustained net operating losses for the years 1954 through 1957. In March 1958, all of taxpayer's stock was acquired by a competitor. The new owners also paid $9,900 to the old stockholders for two corporate notes having a fair market value of $99,000. The new owners acquired taxpayer for its inventory of tools, molds, models, and other items so that they could have taxpayer's line available for the coming selling season. They were not advised of the net operating losses during the negotiations for the sale of the business. Taxpayer, under its new ownership, operated at a profit and sought to carry forward its pre-1958 net operating losses against post-1957 income. The IRS disallowed the carry-over under Section 269, contending that the principal purpose for the acquisition was tax avoidance. *Held:* For taxpayer. The net operating loss carry-over was allowed. The principal purpose of the acquisition was not for avoidance of tax by securing the benefit of the loss deduction, but for a bona fide business reason. The court also found that there was no change of business under the provisions of Section 382(a) as a ground for disallowing the net operating loss carry-over. Taxpayer continued substantially the same business after the acquisition. However, the retirement of the corporate notes for full face value was deemed to be a redemption of part of the stockholders' equity, not the payment of true debt, and therefore constituted a dividend to the extent of current earnings and profits. When originally issued, the notes represented advances by the then-sole shareholder that were intended as an additional equity investment. Barclay Co., 23 TCM 1695, ¶ 64,279 P-H Memo. TC (1964).

Net operating loss carry-over allowed where purpose of stock acquisition was not tax avoidance. In March 1954, taxpayer, a manufacturer of hats, acquired the stock of Young's, a corporation operating a chain of retail stores. Taxpayer acquired Young's stock to preserve Young's as a market and retail distributor of taxpayer's hats. Prior to 1954, Young's was the largest single retailer of taxpayer's hats in the New York City area, accounting for almost 50 percent of the total sales therein, and was also the largest single retailer of taxpayer's hats in the United States. Young's sustained substantial net operating losses prior to its acquisition by taxpayer. In 1956 Young's was liquidated into taxpayer and dissolved. In its return for that year taxpayer claimed as a deduction Young's available net operating losses. The IRS disallowed the deduction, contending that taxpayer's principal purpose for the acquisition was the avoidance of tax. *Held:* For taxpayer. The net operating loss deduction was permitted. There was substantial evidence showing that tax avoidance was not the principal purpose of the acquisition. Stetson Co., 23 TCM 876, ¶ 64,146 P-H Memo. TC (1964).

Section 269 applies to acquisition by one corporation of another even though both are controlled by same stockholder. Two brothers acquired control of an ice manufacturing company in January 1956. In 1957, after the corporation had reacquired the shares held by its minority stockholders, the brothers transferred their stock to taxpayer, a milling company in which they were the sole stockholders. The milling company, as parent, then liquidated the ice company pursuant to the nonrecognition provisions of Section 332, and continued to operate the ice business together with its own milling business. It sought to deduct the net operating loss carry-overs of the ice company prior to the merger, as well as the losses from the ice business after the merger. The IRS denied the deductions for the claimed losses. *Held:* For the IRS. The principal purpose of taxpayer's acquisition was the evasion or avoidance of tax by securing the benefits of the net operating loss carry-overs as well as the subsequent losses from the ice business. Section 269 applies to the acquisition of control of one corporation by another even if they are both owned by the same stockholder. As long as the principal purpose of tax evasion or avoidance is present, the section can also apply to deny the acquiring corporation post-acquisition as well as preacquisition losses. Brick Milling Co., 22 TCM 1603, ¶ 63,305 P-H Memo. TC (1963).

Transfer of a business without change to acquired loss corporation; loss carry-over denied. A partner in a successful tool and die business acquired in 1953 the stock of a loss corporation which had engaged in a general woodworking business. The physical assets of the corporation consisted of an old plant building and obsolescent machinery. The partnership transferred its assets to the corporation, which thereafter changed its name and continued the partnership business without change. None of the assets of the predecessor business were continued in use by the corporation. The IRS disallowed the loss carry-over claimed by the corporation. *Held:* For the IRS. The court found that the loss corporation was acquired for the principal purpose of obtaining the loss carry-overs, and concluded that the corporation could not properly carry over to its taxable years 1953 and 1955 the business operating losses of the predecessor business for 1951 and 1952. Continental Mach. & Tool Corp., 21 TCM 517, ¶ 62,096 P-H Memo. TC (1962).

Acquisition of loss corporation to operate successful business was to avoid tax; carry-over denied. Taxpayer corporation conducted a snack bar and beer business in Athens, Georgia. It consistently lost money, and for a period of six months prior to the sale of its stock to Davis, the business was completely closed down. Davis, after acquiring the stock, utilized the corporation to operate a new cafeteria and a previously successful restaurant business, both in Atlanta, Georgia. He sought to apply the corporate net operating loss carry-over against its current operations. The IRS found that Davis' principal purpose in acquiring the stock of taxpayer was to avoid income tax by securing the benefit of a deduction, credit, or allowance which he would not otherwise enjoy. *Held:* For the IRS. Taking all factors into consideration, the court agreed and sustained the disallowances of the carry-over of the prior year's operating losses. The Huddle, Inc., 20 TCM 745, ¶ 61,150 P-H Memo. TC (1961).

"Control," for Section 269 purposes, acquired in merger. *M* Corporation, owned 45 percent of *N* Corporation. *M*'s sole stockholder owned 10 percent of *N*. A statutory merger was effected to secure a tax benefit that was otherwise unavailable. Since no attribution rules apply for purposes of Section 269, *M* did not have control before the merger. However, *M* acquired control of *N*'s two subsidiaries within the meaning of Section 269(a)(1) on the merger. Rev. Rul. 80-46, 1980-1 CB 62.

Section 269(a)(2) inapplicable when trust and trust beneficiaries each own corporations that are parties to a statutory reorganization. The stock of one corporation, a party to statutory reorganization, was owned by family members, and the stock of the other party to the reorganization was owned by a trust whose beneficiaries were the same family members. It was held that the stockholders controlled both corporations directly or indirectly prior to the reorganization, causing Section 269(a)(2) to be inapplicable. Rev. Rul. 70-638, 1970-2 CB 71.

IRS finds substance, not form, controlling in Section 269 situation; corporation's acquisition lacked substance as it was merely the initial step of a prearranged plan of liquidation. In January 1961, taxpayer, an individual, purchased all the stock of unrelated *X* and *Y* corporations, each of which was engaged in an active business. In the five-year period preceding the acquisition, both corporations operated at a profit. During 1961 and 1962 the corporations were operated separately and both corporations showed a small profit. During 1963, 1964, and 1965 both corporations incurred substantial losses. In 1964, the federal government initiated procedures to condemn a portion of *Y*'s land. In February 1966, in anticipation of the large gain to be realized from the condemnation, taxpayer contributed his *X* stock to *Y*. Five days later, *X* was liquidated into *Y* so that the losses of both businesses could be used to partially offset *Y*'s gain. Ruling on the applicability of Section 269, the IRS held that although, in form, *Y* acquired control of *X*, the transitory control lacked substance since it was merely the initial step of a prearranged plan to liquidate *X* into *Y*. Thus, the "essential nature of the transaction" involved in the present case was the indirect acquisition by *Y* of the *X* property. Accordingly, since Section 269(a)(1) pertains only to the acquisition of control of a corporation and not to the acquisition of its assets, the section was not applicable to the described transaction. Moreover, Section 269(a)(2) was not applicable since taxpayer owned all the stock of each corporation prior to the acquisition of *X*'s property by *Y*. Rev. Rul. 67-202, 1967-1 CB 73.

AFFILIATED CORPORATIONS

(*See also* Allocation Among Related Taxpayers; Consolidated Returns; Related Taxpayers)

In General	53
Affiliated Group Defined	54
Control Defined	56
Excess Loss Accounts	58
Net Operating Loss Carry-Overs	59
Tax-Avoidance Purpose	60

In General

Losses of a Western Hemisphere Trade Corporation offset profits of remainder of consolidated group, not profits of affiliated public utility corporations, in determining consolidated income subject to additional 2 percent tax. Taxpayer filed consolidated tax returns with its affiliated corporations for the years 1955 through 1957. One of the affiliated corporations was a Western Hemisphere Trade Corporation, which operated at a loss. Two of the affiliated corporations were regulated public utilities, which were profitable. The IRS contended that in determining the additional 2 percent tax, which was then applicable, on the group's consolidated income, the loss of the Western Hemisphere Trade Corporation offset the profits of the regulated public utility corporations, and not the profits of the other affiliated corporations. Since the income of the regulated public utilities, like the income of the Western Hemisphere Trade

AFFILIATED CORPORATIONS: *Affiliated Group Defined*

Corporation, was exempt from the additional tax, the IRS' determination had the effect of increasing taxpayer's overall tax liability. Taxpayer claimed that the loss of the Western Hemisphere Trade Corporation offset the income of the affiliated corporations subject to the additional 2 percent tax. *Held:* For taxpayer. Although the legislative history is not clear on this point, the policy motivations for enacting the separate exemptions clearly indicate that they are unrelated. Furthermore, when the Senate Finance Committee recommended enactment of the exemption from the 2 percent tax for regulated public utilities, it said that the exemption was to be applied "in a manner similar to the provision applicable to Western Hemisphere Trade Corporations." In the case of the latter provision, there was an intraclass calculation. To net these intraclass calculations now would not apply the provision for regulated public utilities in a manner similar to that previously applied in the case of Western Hemisphere Trade Corporations. Sinclair Oil Corp., 392 F2d 249, 68-1 USTC ¶ 9268, 21 AFTR2d 926 (Ct. Cl. 1968).

Application of Section 334(b)(2)(B) to an affiliated group. The IRS ruled that the stock ownership requirements of Section 334(b)(2)(B) are met even when no member of an affiliated group owns 80 percent of the shares where the members of the group purchased for cash all outstanding shares of a corporation whose assets were distributed to the members in a year to which Section 332 applies. Rev. Rul. 74-441, 1974-2 CB 105.

100 percent dividend received deduction not affected by a reorganization that created a holding company parent. A corporation engaged in manufacturing operated three subsidiaries. The parent corporation formed a holding company. *H*, which in turn formed *S*, a new subsidiary. *P* was merged into *S*. The stockholders of *P* exchanged their stock for stock in *H*. As a result, *H* owned all the stock in *PS*, which in turn owned the stock of the three subsidiaries. The IRS ruled that the affiliated group would be considered as one and the same for purposes of the 100 percent dividend received deduction of Section 243(a). Rev. Rul. 72-274, 1972-1 CB 97.

Affiliated Group Defined

Tax Court refuses to find controlled group. A corporate taxpayer was owned 70 percent by a shareholder who, for Section 1563 purposes, was deemed to own 100 percent of another corporation in the same line of business. Taxpayer was owned 30 percent by another shareholder who had no interest in the second corporation. The IRS disputed the taxpayer's right to a full surtax exemption under Section 11(d). *Held:* For taxpayer. Following its decision in Fairfax Auto Parts of N. Va., Inc., 65 TC 798 (1976), rev'd, 548 F2d 501 (5th Cir. 1977), the Tax Court refused to include the stock of a shareholder who did not own stock in both corporations in the calculations of the 80 percent test of Section 1563(a)(2)(A). Allen Oil Co., 38 TCM 355, rev'd, 614 F2d 336, 80-1 USTC ¶ 9156, 45 AFTR2d 80-560 (2d Cir. 1980).

Reciprocity as to disposition of shares negates disallowance of multiple surtax exemptions. The IRS held that for the years 1966, 1967, and 1968, three taxpayer corporations were a controlled group within the meaning of Section 1563(a)(2) as it then existed, so that they had to apportion a single surtax exemption. The IRS' determination was based on the fact that common shareholder *H* owned more than 80 percent of the stock of each corporation when the shares held by employees were excluded from the total stock figure for Section 1563(a)(2) purposes. Such exclusion was deemed justified under Section 1563(c)(2)(B)(ii), since the shares owned by the employees were substantially restricted as to disposition. The Tax Court found for the IRS. *Held:* Reversed. The restriction was found to be reciprocal in that it restricted common owner H as well as the employees. Such reciprocity was an exception to Section 1563(c)(2)(B)(ii); therefore, the employees' stock was included in the Section 1563(a)(2) determination, so that *H* owned less than 80 percent of each of the three companies. Superior Beverage Co. of Marysville, Inc., 525 F2d

AFFILIATED CORPORATIONS: *Affiliated Group Defined*

186, 75-2 USTC ¶ 9808, 36 AFTR2d 75-6233 (9th Cir. 1975).

IRS cannot relitigate controlled-group issue it previously lost. A Tax Court decision holding that taxpayer corporations are not members of a brother-sister controlled group under Section 1563 applied to 1976. Taxpayers sued for refunds for 1973 through 1975. The IRS argued that it was not collaterally estopped from raising the controlled-group issue based on the fact that the value of the corporation's stock varied in the years previous to 1976. *Held:* For taxpayers. The "value" issue in the control test was implicitly decided in the Tax Court case. The IRS could not relitigate it. Joe Esco S.W. Tire Co., 582 F. Supp. 993, 84-1 USTC ¶ 9160, 53 AFTR2d 84-756 (WD Okla. 1983).

Corporation was a component member of a controlled corporate group. Taxpayer was a wholly owned subsidiary of Allied. On May 5, 1965, taxpayer acquired all the stock of Crossett, a corporation formed on that day by a corporation other than taxpayer or its parent. Subsequently, the stockholders and directors of Crossett passed a resolution to liquidate and dissolve the company, and a certificate of dissolution was filed on May 6, 1965. Crossett filed a corporate income tax return for its taxable year beginning May 5, 1965 and ending May 6, 1965, claiming a full $25,000 exemption from surtax. The IRS determined that Crossett was a member of the controlled group; therefore, two thirds of its claimed surtax exemption should be disallowed. *Held:* For the IRS. Crossett was one of three members of a controlled group of corporations for one half or more of the days preceding the last day of its taxable year, even though the year only comprised two days. Therefore, Crossett did not qualify as an excluded member of the group. Allied Util. Corp., 64 TC 1024 (1975).

Newly organized subsidiaries qualified as old members of affiliated group. Taxpayer, a parent corporation of an affiliated group, filed a consolidated return. In the year following a consolidated return change of ownership (CRCO), taxpayer, pursuant to a bankruptcy plan of reorganization, organized two wholly owned subsidiaries by transferring to them the assets and liabilities of two of its divisions that had existed prior to the CRCO. On the consolidated return it filed for the year following the CRCO, taxpayer used a net operating loss carry-over attributable to years preceding the CRCO to offset the profits of the new subsidiaries. Since all of the assets and businesses of the new subsidiaries had been derived from the taxpayer parent corporation, the subsidiaries are treated as "old members" of the affiliated group for purposes of the limitations contained in Regulation § 1.1502-21(d) on the use of net operating loss carry-overs. Thus, the taxpayer may carry over its net operating losses from years preceding the CRCO and apply it against the new subsidiaries' profits. Rev. Rul. 84-33, 1984-2 CB 186.

Regulation § 1.1502-75(d)(2)(ii) applied to certain mergers. *P, S,* and *T* were the common parent, first-tier subsidiary, and second-tier subsidiary, respectively, of a Section 1504(a) affiliated group that filed a consolidated return. Pursuant to a plan of reorganization, *T* merged into *P*, and *S* became the parent corporation. The IRS determined that the merger of a second-tier subsidiary into the common parent of an affiliated group does not cause the termination of the affiliated group. Rev. Rul. 82-152, 1982-2 CB 205.

Aggregate stock ownership rules. Under Section 332, the aggregate stock ownership rules do not serve to prevent recognition of gain or loss of a wholly owned foreign subsidiary's transfer of all its assets, subject to liabilities, to the parent's wholly owned U.S. subsidiary that owns no shares in the foreign subsidiary and files a consolidated return with the parent. Rev. Rul. 74-598, 1974-2 CB 287.

Two corporations deemed brother-sister where majority shareholder owned only two-thirds interest in one of the corporations under Section 1563(a)(2). A majority stockholder owned 69 percent of the outstanding stock of one corporation and 90 percent of another. The remaining stock of both corporations was owned by unrelated parties. The IRS stated that if, under state law, the majority stockholder could effectively control each corporation and substantially restrict or limit minority stock dispositions, then the stock of such minority stockholders must be considered as "excluded stock" within the meaning of Section 1563(c)(2)(B). Rev. Rul. 70-252, 1970-1 CB 186.

Failure to issue stock certificates does not destroy affiliation. Taxpayer organized a subsidiary as a sales agent. The subsidiary sold taxpayer's products. Although the parent had not been issued any stock, it managed and controlled the subsidiary. The taxpayer and the subsidiary could file a consolidated return, since they were an affiliated group. Taxpayer had all the rights of ownership of at least 80 percent of the stock. Formal certificates did not need to be issued. (GCM 2019 superseded). Rev. Rul. 69-591, 1969-2 CB 171.

Control Defined

In applying the 80 percent test under Section 1563(a)(2), consideration was given only to stock held by stockholders with actual interests in all corporations making up the purported controlled group. Vogel owned 77.49 percent of taxpayer's outstanding stock, and another unrelated stockholder owned the balance. Vogel also owned 87.5 percent of Vogel Popcorn Co. Vogel's co-stockholder in taxpayer owned no part of Vogel Popcorn Co. Taxpayer claimed that it was entitled to refund, since it and Vogel Popcorn were not a "controlled group," and thus were not required to split one surtax exemption as originally filed. *Held:* For taxpayer. Regulation § 1.1563-1(a)(3) (1981) was invalid to the extent that it took into account, for purposes of Code Section 1563(a)(2)'s 80 percent requirement, stock held by a stockholder who owned stock in only one corporation of the controlled group. Vogel Fertilizer Co., 455 US 16 (1982).

Corporations are part of brother-sister controlled group. The Tax Court held that three corporations were brother-sister corporations and thus were entitled to only one surtax exemption. Additionally, it held that taxpayers failed to justify a 3 percent write-off of ending inventory. *Held:* Affirmed. Taxpayers need not own stock directly before they can be considered one of the five or fewer persons owning stock. Both corporate and family attribution rules may be applied in the same application. Finally, taxpayers failed to justify their write-down of inventory. Complete Fin. Corp., 766 F2d 436, 85-2 USTC ¶ 9505, 56 AFTR2d 85-5438 (10th Cir. 1985).

Controlled group existed where employees' stock was restricted. In 1967, taxpayer acquired 100 of the 250 shares of N, and all of N's stockholders entered into an agreement that the taxpayer would have a right of first refusal if any other shareholder wanted to sell his stock. In 1972, taxpayer acquired 75 additional shares of N's stock, and the balance continued to be held by two of N's employees. The IRS determined that taxpayer and N constituted a controlled group of corporations. Taxpayer contended it and N were not a controlled group. *Held:* For the IRS. The right of first refusal held by the taxpayer was a substantial restriction on the sale of N stock. Accordingly, the stock held by the two N employee shareholders was excluded stock. Since that stock was treated as not outstanding, N was a wholly owned subsidiary of the taxpayer, and the two corporations constituted a parent-subsidiary controlled group. Tribune Publishing Co., 731 F2d 1401, 84-1 USTC ¶ 9424, 53 AFTR2d 84-1210 (9th Cir. 1984).

Right to file consolidated returns denied to brother-sister corporations. Two corporations owned by the same individual filed a consolidated return. The IRS contended that the two corporations were not members of an affiliated group within the meaning of Section 1501. *Held:* For the IRS. The Tax Court held that the corporations could not file consolidated returns. Section 1504 defines an affiliated group as a number of corporations connected by a common parent corporation. Since there was no parent corporation, there was no affiliation. Ray Eng'g Co., 347 F2d 716, 65-2 USTC ¶ 9510, 16 AFTR2d 5021 (3d Cir. 1965).

AFFILIATED CORPORATIONS: *Control Defined*

Eighty percent test under Section 1563 for determining controlled group clarified. Principal business activity of taxpayer (B&M) throughout its corporate life was real estate rentals. Some of taxpayer's investors formed a separate corporation, *K*, in the same line of business. Taxpayer *H* was in commercial trucking, and its subsidiary, *G*, manufactured wire harnesses for the appliance industry. During 1974 and 1975, B&M and *K* filed elections allocating the $25,000 surtax exemption between themselves, whereas *H* and *G* filed a consolidated return and did not allocate the surtax exemption between themselves. The IRS determined B&M, *H*, and *K* to be members of a controlled group of brother-sister corporations within Section 1563(a)(2) during this period, and disallowed the amounts claimed on the returns as a surtax exemption under Section 11(d). Each corporation was allowed one third of the exemption. *Held:* For taxpayers. Under Vogel Fertilizer Co., 455 US 16 (1982), each member of the stockholder group must own stock in each brother-sister corporation for purposes of the 80 percent test. Accordingly, Regulation § 1.1563-1(a)(3) was an unreasonable implementation of the statute, and therefore invalid to the extent that it prescribed otherwise. B&M Investors Corp., 78 TC 165 (1982).

Eighty percent test of Section 1563(a)(2) applied only with respect to stockholders of both corporations. Three stockholders owned all of taxpayer's stock and 78 percent of another corporation's stock. A fourth person owned the remaining 22 percent of this other corporation. The IRS claimed that taxpayer and this other corporation were a "brother-sister controlled group." *Held:* For taxpayer. Under Section 1563(a)(2), the 80 percent test is determined with respect to stockholders owning stock in both of the corporations that are being tested for an affiliated relationship. Charles Baloian Co., 68 TC 620 (1977), aff'd (9th Cir. 1982).

Regulation § 1.1563-1(a)(3) held invalid by Tax Court; taxpayer must own stock in each member of the brother-sister controlled group. *H* owned all the stock of taxpayer corporation and 55 percent of the outstanding stock of a second corporation. An unrelated party held the other 45 percent of the stock in the second corporation. Each corporation utilized a full surtax exemption of $25,000 in computing their tax liabilities. The IRS determined the corporations to be within the definition of a brother-sister controlled group contained in Section 1563(a)(2), and disallowed the double exemption. *Held:* For taxpayer. Stock ownership was not to be taken into account for purposes of the 80 percent test unless the person owned stock in each member of the brother-sister controlled group. Therefore, the 45 percent stock ownership by the unrelated party could not be counted for purposes of the 80 percent test. Fairfax Auto Parts of N. Va., Inc., 65 TC 798 (1976).

Constructive stock ownership did not reduce actual ownership for purposes of Section 1563. Hansen Building, Inc. owned more than 80 percent of taxpayer's capital stock. An employee of taxpayer owned a small percentage of the stock and had an option to acquire unissued stock of the taxpayer to increase his ownership to 25 percent. Taxpayer contended that this constructive ownership resulted in Hansen owning 75 percent for purposes of Section 1563. Therefore, multiple surtax exemptions without an increase in the basic tax rate could be claimed by both companies. *Held:* For the IRS. The constructive ownership provisions of the Code are of consequence only regarding the person whose percentage of equity ownership is in question. The provisions cannot be used to reduce another shareholder's percentage of interest. This is true whether dealing with issued or unissued stock. Thus, the employee's option did not reduce Hansen's ownership, and the companies were a parent-subsidiary controlled group of corporations. For this reason they were limited to one surtax exemption. Northwestern Steel & Supply Co., 60 TC 356 (1973).

Stock subject to right of first refusal was excluded in determining "control" for purposes of limitation on multiple use of surtax exemption. The stockholders of *X* Corporation (taxpayer) formed *Y* Corporation. *Y* shares were

AFFILIATED CORPORATIONS: *Excess Loss Accounts*

subject to a right of first refusal, except those shares held by its principal stockholder. The IRS asserted that X and Y were commonly controlled organizations, and thus, each did not independently qualify for its own surtax exemption. Taxpayer argued that there was no common control if the restricted stock held by Y's employees was considered. *Held:* For the IRS. The restricted rights on Y stock were substantial, and thus such stock was excluded in determining the principal stockholder's control, for this purpose, over Y Corporation. Barton Naptha Co., 56 TC 107 (1971).

Stock attribution under state law yields controlled group. Taxpayer owned all of X Corporation stock and two thirds of Y corporation stock. The other one third of Y was owned by taxpayer's son-in-law. The issue was whether X and Y were members of a controlled group because of the effect of community property on the attribution rules. *Held:* For the IRS. Under California law, the taxpayer's daughter deemed to own one-half of her husband's Y stock; such amount was attributed to taxpayer under Section 1563(e)(6). Thus, X and Y were members of a controlled group and entitled to only one surtax exemption under Section 1561(a). Aero Indus. Co., 40 TCM 147, ¶ 80,116 P-H Memo. TC (1980).

Stockholder must own stock in all corporations to be counted in Section 1563 80 percent test. Taxpayer argued that it was not a member of an affiliated group under Section 1563, since one of its stockholders, who did not own stock in all of the corporations, could not be counted under the 80 percent test. Three prior Tax Court cases supported the taxpayer's position. The IRS, noting that two of those cases were reversed on appeal, urged the court to change its mind. *Held:* For taxpayer. The Tax Court maintained that its earlier position was correct. A shareholder must own stock in all of the corporations to be counted in the 80 percent test. Delta Metalforming Co., 37 TCM 1485, ¶ 78,354 P-H Memo. TC (1978), aff'd, 632 F2d 442, 81-1 USTC ¶ 9108, 47 AFTR2d 81-459 (5th Cir. 1980), cert. denied, 445 US 906 (1982).

Stock ownership by wives does not invoke Section 269. Taxpayer corporations were owned 20 percent by two men. The balance of the stock was owned by their wives. In an earlier action, the IRS successfully denied the surtax exemptions on the grounds that the taxpayers were acquired to evade taxes under Section 269. The case was reversed and remanded for a determination of whether the husbands had beneficial ownership of their wives' stock. *Held:* For taxpayers. There was no evidence that the wives held the stock in a fiduciary capacity or otherwise for the benefit of their husbands. The wives had control of their respective corporations, but had no controlling interest in any other corporation; the acquisition of control of only one corporation does not permit disallowance of the surtax exemption to that corporation under Section 269. The court of appeals' narrow remand mandate prevents any reconsideration of attribution rules or "actualities of the situation" in determining control. Dewmar Constr. Co., 28 TCM 826, ¶ 69,165 P-H Memo. TC (1969).

Subsidiary stock owned by employees of the subsidiary that is subject to a purchase option are excluded in determining whether a controlled group exists. A domestic corporation owned 100 percent of $S1$ and 78 percent of $S2$ and $S3$. The remaining stock of the subsidiaries was owned by employees of these companies. However, the stock was subject to a purchase option by an unrelated corporation. The stock held by the employees would be excluded in determining whether a controlled group existed for purposes of Section 1563(a)(1) as there were substantial restrictions on the employee stock. Rev. Rul. 70-470, 1970-2 CB 182.

Excess Loss Accounts

Application of investment adjustment regulations resulting in excess loss account upheld. From 1966 to 1972, taxpayer was an affiliated group of corporations filing consolidated returns. Because one member of the group distributed stock from earnings and profits accumulated prior to affiliation, the investment adjustment regulations required taxpayer to reduce the distributing corporation's stock basis by the same amount: $4.9 million in distributions was subtracted from a basis of 0.25 million, which had been carried over as a result of the corporation entering the group through a B reorganization. The result was a sizable negative adjusted basis. In 1972, when taxpayer disaffiliated, the IRS claimed an "excess loss account," which produced a deficiency of $1.4 million in corporate taxes. The Claims Court found that taxpayer's attacks on the validity of Regulation § 1.1502-32(b)(2)(iii)(b) dealing with investment adjustments were inaccurate. It found that the IRS was not estopped from a literal application of the regulation because in 1968 and 1971 the Treasury published proposals to amend the regulation, proposals that would create an exception for taxpayer's situation. The court found a variance in taxpayer's Section 243 dividend taxation argument. *Held:* Affirmed. An affiliated group that files a consolidated return is required to include excess loss account in income on the termination of the affiliated group, in a manner proper to the application of the existing regulations. However, there was no variance in taxpayer's attacks on the regulation generally, as opposed to application to taxpayer's particular carry-over basis situation. Garvey, 726 F2d 1569, 84-1 USTC ¶ 9214, 53 AFTR2d 84-776 (Fed. Cir. 1984), cert. denied, 105 S. Ct. 99 (1984).

Gain deferred on intercompany sale of stock with excess loss account. Taxpayer and X corporation were members of an affiliated group of corporations that filed a consolidated income tax return. P owned all the stock of taxpayer and taxpayer owned all the stock of X. Taxpayer utilized the losses of X in excess of its basis in taxpayer's stock, and thus created an excess loss account with respect to the X stock. Taxpayer sold the X stock to P for cash at its fair market value during a consolidated return year end. Subsequently, taxpayer and X became brother-sister corporations, with P as the common parent. The IRS ruled that taxpayer had an excess loss account in X's stock, which was not included in taxpayer's income on the sale of X stock to P. The excess loss account was treated as deferred gain, and was to be includible in taxpayer's income on the occurrence of the events specified in Regulation §§ 1.1501-13(d), 1.1501-13(e), and 1.1501-13(f). All of this followed because the sale of the X stock occured during a consolidated return year between members of the consolidated group, and the sale of the X stock constituted a deferred intercompany transaction. Rev. Rul. 81-81, 1981-1 CB 451.

Net Operating Loss Carry-Overs

Net operating loss of one company not allowed as offset against other company's income in later year. On July 1, 1957, the properties and operating authorities of H, a regulated transportation company, were transferred to X, and the stock of X was transferred to taxpayer. The IRS contended that X's existence began when its charter was issued on May 13, 1955. *Held:* For the IRS. As X had adopted a calendar year, its 1957 tax year began on January 1, 1957 and ended on December 31, 1957, instead of including only the short period from July 1 to December 31, 1957, even though it had no assets or income until July 1, 1957. Thus, X and taxpayer were not members of the same affiliated group for each day of X's 1957 taxable year, and X's net operating loss could not be used to offset taxpayer's income for 1964. Braswell Motor Freight Lines, 72-2 USTC ¶ 9675 (ND Tex. 1972).

Loss disallowed when sale of parent's stock to sister corporation was not bona fide. In the course of a tax-free liquidation, taxpayer, at the direction of its parent corporation, sold stock in the parent to another controlled subsidiary corporation. The parent financed the sale by a loan. Taxpayer attempted to deduct its loss on the sale under Section 165. Citing Regulation 1.165-1(b), the IRS denied the deduction on the ground that the sale was not a bona fide transaction. In rebuttal, taxpayer argued that the purchaser needed the shares to build up its working capital, and that the parent did not want the shares because (1) the Interstate Commerce Commission would prevent the parent from disposing of them; (2) the shares would be non-voting, treasury stock; and (3) the shares would be subject to various after acquired mortgage property clauses. *Held:* For the IRS. Taxpayer's arguments that the transaction did not take the shape it did for tax reasons were not persuasive. The purchaser would have been at least as well off if the shares had been contributed to it. Nothing indicated that the Interstate Commerce Commission would have prevented the parent from disposing of the shares. There was also no evidence that the shares would have become subject to the after acquired clauses. In any event, the restrictions imposed by the clauses would have been minimal. The parent's desire for its management to retain voting control over the shares was not a business purpose justifying recognition of the loss. Northern Pac. Ry. Co., 378 F2d 686, 67-2 USTC ¶ 9501 (Ct. Cl. 1967).

Transfer of houses was to use up affiliates' net operating losses. Taxpayer corporation, owner of 421 houses, transferred the houses to its affiliated corporation, each of which had available separate net operating loss carryovers. The separate affiliates sold the houses. The IRS reallocated the entire installment gain to taxpayer under Section 482. *Held:* For the IRS. The primary purpose of the transfer was to enable the affiliates to make use of their separate net operating loss carryovers and thus to avoid tax. The court also ruled that, in determining the extent that pre-affiliation operating losses of the affiliates could be applied to the consolidated income, the amount of the consolidated net income, prior to application of any net operating loss carry-over, was to be prorated among all affiliates reporting separate incomes, whether or not such affiliate had a separate net operating loss carry-over, on the basis the income reported by such affiliates bore to the total of the income reported by all affiliates reporting income. The amount of income so allocated to each affiliate having a separate net operating loss carry-over was the maximum extent to which such separate net operating loss carry-over could be used in computing the taxable consolidated income. Foster, ¶ 66,273 P-H Memo. TC (1966).

Tax-Avoidance Purpose

Tax avoidance not a factor in applying Section 1563. The IRS and a lower court held that X Corporation and Y Corporation were a controlled group, and therefore were entitled to only one corporate surtax exemption between them. The taxpayers argued that Section 1563 was inapplicable since tax avoidance was not present. *Held:* Affirmed. The attribution rules of Section 1563 represent a mechanical test to be applied without regard to any taxpayer motives. Yaffee Iron & Metal Corp., 593 F2d 832, 79-1 USTC ¶ 9268, 43 AFTR2d 79-845 (8th Cir.), cert. denied, 444 US 843 (1979).

Related realty corporations were entitled to separate surtax exemptions. In March 1957, an individual organized five corporations (taxpayers) and transferred improved real property to each. Subsequently, he gave 40 percent of the stock of each taxpayer to his son. From 1958 through 1959, the IRS argued that four of the taxpayers were not entitled to surtax exemptions under Section 269. *Held:* For taxpayers. The individual's principal purpose in acquiring taxpayers was not tax avoidance but estate planning, flexibility in managing and developing the real estate, and obtaining mortgage financing without personal liability. 800 S. Fourth St., Inc., 70-1 USTC ¶ 9222, 25 AFTR2d 70-580 (WD Ky. 1970).

Multiple surtax exemption was allowed where principal purpose of spin-off was not tax avoidance. A corporation transferred its road paving equipment to newly formed taxpayer in exchange for all of taxpayer's stock. Taxpayer carried on the road paving business formerly conducted by its parent. The IRS disallowed the surtax exemption under Section 1551, contending that the major purpose of the spin-off was tax avoidance. Taxpayer contended that the major purpose for its creation was to avoid the Ohio sales tax, which would have been imposed on the parent, and also to alleviate or reduce labor problems. *Held:* For taxpayer. The material fact in this case was the determination that incorporation of the taxpayer was necessary in order to avoid the Ohio sales tax. Since this was the

AFFILIATED CORPORATIONS: *Tax-Avoidance Purpose*

principal purpose of the formation of taxpayer corporation, not the securing of another surtax exemption, the determination of the IRS was erroneous. Melvin Asphalt Prods. Corp., 66-2 USTC ¶ 9671 (SD Ohio 1966).

Jury found no tax-avoidance purpose in multiple corporations. Taxpayer parent corporation created two wholly owned subsidiaries, one to construct churches, and the other to construct private homes. Both subsidiaries claimed the full surtax exemptions for the disputed taxable years. The IRS determined each corporation to be entitled to only one-fifth of a surtax exemption. *Held:* For taxpayer. After being instructed in the applications of Section 269, a jury found no tax-avoidance purpose in the formation of taxpayer's subsidiaries. The apparent, although not factually stated, reason for two distinct businesses was the relative risk factor. Security Homes, Inc., 63-1 USTC ¶ 9297, 11 AFTR2d 890 (DND 1963).

Tax evasion finding was fatal to corporation's surtax exemption. Taxpayer was one of a group of eleven corporations all controlled by the same stockholder. The IRS disallowed the surtax exemption under Section 269. *Held:* For the IRS. In holding for the IRS, the court found no need for the use of multiple corporations and regarded the reasons given for their use as having little substance. The incorporations resulted merely in an old business being conducted in a new manner. The court found credible the testimony of a former employee (an admitted embezzler) to the effect that it was a common practice for the corporations to "balance out" the income each year. The court, therefore, held that the evidence indicated that the primary purpose of taxpayer's information was tax evasion. Fine Realty, Inc., 209 F. Supp. 286, 62-2 USTC ¶ 9758, 10 AFTR2d 5751 (D. Minn. 1962).

Court finds valid business purpose for multiple incorporations of family partnership's stores and allows use of multiple surtax exemptions. Thirteen retail stores were owned and operated by the same family partnership. A central warehouse operated by the partnership serviced all of these stores. To achieve continuity of the business on the demise of any partner, and for any other estate planning purposes, it was decided that each profitable store would be separately incorporated. There were several reasons for this: (1) the partners believed that separate incorporation of each store would help to avoid unionization of their employees; (2) it would enable a store, through greater independence from the partnership, to develop a more local image and to have greater control of its business operations in the hands of its local manager; (3) it would avoid certain minimum wage laws; and (4) it would provide stock incentive plans for managers in their particular store. After incorporation, the partnership rendered buying, warehousing, and administrative services to the corporations for a fee determined by prorating the gross sales of both the incorporated and unincorporated stores. The IRS challenged, under Section 269, the multiple claims to the surtax exemption made by each incorporated store on its return. *Held:* For taxpayer. The evidence indicated clearly that the principal purpose was not to avoid income tax. Evidence indicated strong business purpose for multiple incorporations. The Louisville Store of Liberty, Ky., Inc., 376 F2d 314, 67-1 USTC ¶ 9375, 19 AFTR2d 1186 (Ct. Cl. 1967).

Increased bank credit valid reason for multiple corporations. Taxpayer was a manufacturer of a patented agricultural cutting machine. The machines were distributed in various regions by eight affiliated corporations. Although each had its own bank account and kept separate books, these companies had no inventory and were dependent upon the manufacturing company for management services. Salesmen were compensated on a commission basis and provided their own office and transportation facilities. The individual firms were able to obtain bank loans that in total exceeded the possible credit obtainable by a combined company, as their financing bank was subject to a maximum on loans to individual firms. In 1963, the manufacturing company went public and all the affiliates were merged. For the years 1957 and 1958, the IRS attributed to taxpayer the incomes of the affiliates. *Held:* For taxpayer. The Tax

AFFILIATED CORPORATIONS: *Tax-Avoidance Purpose*

Court held that the affiliates were viable entities and were not established to obtain surtax exemptions. Increased borrowing power was a substantial business reason for separate corporations. In addition, there was no evidence of any artificial shifting of income. Bush Hog Mfg. Co., 42 TC 713 (1964), acq. 1962-2 CB 4.

Tax avoidance not the principal purpose for 67 multiple corporations. Taxpayers, 67 corporations, were all involved in the production or sale of plastic hobby kits and other plastic products. The stock of these corporations was owned largely by three individuals. The IRS determined that the principal purpose of the formation of the numerous corporations was tax evasion or avoidance, and it therefore sought to allocate the $25,000 corporate surtax exemption among the various corporations. *Held:* For taxpayers. The court, having found that taxpayers had established by a preponderance of evidence that a tax-avoidance purpose did not exceed in importance any other purpose, ruled in favor of taxpayers. In reaching its decision, the court considered the fact that the procedure of forming one corporation for each product had been used in the past for the purpose of establishing the relative interests of several independent investors, that the stockholders were aware of the tax disadvantages of a multiple corporate structure in not being able to set off losses of one corporation against gains of another, and that two of the three stockholders who invested in the corporations considered it of extreme importance that they be protected as to monetary risks. The Royle Co., 22 TCM 747, ¶ 63,157 P-H Memo. TC (1963).

Multiple corporations justified where major purpose is to reduce risks inherent in taxpayer's business. Taxpayer conducted a poultry-rendering business as a sole proprietor. In 1952, as a result of his concern about his personal liability in the event of a serious accident involving one of his trucks and the heavy risks of product contamination, he separated the proprietorship into three corporations—a land-owning corporation to hold title to his real estate, a manufacturing corporation to perform the rendering operation, and a trucking corporation to haul the raw materials and finished products. Taxpayer and his wife owned all the stock of the three corporations. To avoid having the trucking corporation come under the jurisdiction of the Interstate Commerce Commission, its charter was amended to permit it to buy and sell raw materials on its own account. Thereafter, the trucking corporation purchased raw materials, which it sold to the rendering corporation for processing. On completion of the rendering process, the rendering corporation sold the finished products to the trucking corporation, which in turn sold them to its customers. The IRS contended that the multiple corporations were formed for the principal purpose of tax evasion and denied the surtax exemptions, relying on Sections 269 and 1551. *Held:* For taxpayer, in part. The rendering and truck corporations were "acquired" or formed for bona fide business reasons (i.e., to insulate taxpayer from risks inherent in the manufacturing and trucking operations of the rendering business) and would have been created absent any tax advantage. The court did, however, sustain the IRS' denial of the surtax exemption for the real estate corporation on the grounds that it was a mere corporate shell to hold title to the real estate and served no bona fide business purpose. The court also rejected the IRS' alternative argument that the income of the trucking corporation should be allocated to the rendering corporation under Section 482. It found that the transactions between the two entities were fair and at arm's length. Esrenco Truck Co., 22 TCM 287, ¶ 63,072 P-H Memo. TC (1963).

Surtax exemptions allowed when the establishment of separate corporations to avert threat of unionization is deemed proper purpose. Taxpayer was in the business of manufacturing and selling concrete and related products. An active union movement existed in the area, and the home builders, who were not unionized and were the taxpayer's major customers, believed it was essential to have a nonunion source of concrete. To avoid the threat of unionization, the taxpayer decided to separate the manufacturing functions from the sales and delivery functions by setting up separate entities for each. The plan proved successful. The IRS disallowed the $25,000 surtax exemptions of the new corporations on the ground that the transfer of property to them from taxpayer was made with the major purpose of securing surtax exemptions. *Held:* For taxpayer. The court found that tax savings were neither a major nor the principal purpose for which the new corporations were formed, and that the corporations would have been formed regardless of whether tax savings would have resulted. Pre-Mixed Concrete, Inc., 21 TCM 1601, ¶ 62,301 P-H Memo. TC (1962).

AGENCY

(*See* Business Expenses—Deductible by Whom)

ALLOCATION AMONG RELATED TAXPAYERS

(*See also* Affiliated Corporations; Consolidated Returns; Related Taxpayers)

In General	63
Arm's-Length Transaction Defense	65
Business Purpose Defense	70
Conduit Theory	73
Methods of Reallocation	75
Related Taxpayers Defined	79
Sham Transactions	80

In General

Taxpayer had adequate notice that IRS would argue Section 482 reallocation. The Tax Court refused to permit the IRS to argue that income should be reallocated among various entities under Section 482 because the IRS had formally notified taxpayers of that theory five days before the trial, which the court held was too late. *Held:* Reversed. The Revenue Agent's Report, which taxpayers had long before the trial, relied heavily on Section 482; thus, the court held that taxpayers had sufficient notice. Abatti, 644 F2d 1385, 81-1 USTC ¶ 9442, 48 AFTR2d 81-5020 (9th Cir. 1981).

Taxpayer failed to prove that transfer leaseback was rescinded. Taxpayer transferred his restaurant to a partnership composed of four corporations he controlled. The partnership leased the restaurant back to him. He claimed that in a later year he had rescinded the transfer leaseback so that he could deduct the restaurant's loss on his own return. The Tax Court held that the transfer was not rescinded, and reallocated loss and depreciation deductions to the partnership. *Held:* Affirmed. The various entities had no documentation of the purported rescission. Erickson, 598 F2d 525, 79-2 USTC ¶ 9444, 44 AFTR2d 79-5241 (9th Cir. 1979).

Under Section 482 charitable deduction from gift of stock was reallocated from parent to wholly owned subsidiary which had made a dividend distribution of the stock to its parent. Taxpayer owned all the stock of Building Co., which, in turn, owned 10 percent of the stock of Center, Inc. The stock of Center, Inc. had a sudden increase in value, and Building Co. declared a dividend of its Center, Inc. stock. Taxpayer donated these shares to charity. The IRS disallowed the charitable deduction under Section 482, and allocated it to Building Co. Taxpayer argued that intercorporate dividend distributions are not the kind of transactions that would occur between uncontrolled taxpayers; therefore, Section 482 is inapplicable to this type of transaction. *Held:* For the IRS. The purpose of Section 482 is to prevent distortions arising from the use of tax advantages not available in arm's-length transactions. Accordingly, Section 482 can be applied to distortions in the net incomes of parent and subsidiary corporations. The stock was intended to be donated to charity, but instead the subsidiary made a distribution of stock to the parent, who would gain a greater tax advantage from the charitable deduction. Northwestern Nat'l Bank of Minn., 556 F2d 890, 77-2 USTC ¶ 9479, 40 AFTR2d 5156 (8th Cir. 1977).

ALLOCATION AMONG RELATED TAXPAYERS: *In General*

IRS cannot allocate income to taxpayer that cannot legally receive it. Taxpayer bank made credit life insurance available to borrowers. A separate corporation from the bank, but having the same stockholders, received commissions from sales. State law prohibited the bank from selling insurance. The IRS sought to allocate the commission income to the bank under Section 482. *Held:* For taxpayer. The IRS cannot allocate income to a taxpayer that is prohibited by law from receiving the income. Bank of Winnfield & Trust Co., 540 F. Supp. 219, 81-1 USTC ¶ 9292, 49 AFTR2d 82-1265 (WD La. 1982).

Refunds resulting from Section 482 allocation not income. The IRS, pursuant to Section 482, reduced taxpayer's rental deductions with regard to rents paid to a related corporation. Taxpayers contended that the repayment to them of the excess rent was not income. *Held:* For taxpayers. Although taxpayers had not observed all of the procedural requirements of Rev. Proc. 65-17, it had made an agreement with the IRS pertaining to refund of the excess rentals without tax consequences. Gentry, Jr., 76-2 USTC ¶ 9713 (ND Tex. 1976).

Interest on tax from Section 482 reallocation runs from filing date. Taxpayer paid additional tax based on a Section 482 adjustment concerning dealings with its foreign subsidiaries. It argued that interest on the tax ran only from the time the IRS demanded payment, not from the date of the return based on Motor Fuel Carriers, Inc., 420 F2d 702 (Ct. Cl. 1970), which reached a similar conclusion on the Section 531 tax. *Held:* For the IRS. Unlike the Section 531 penalty tax, the added tax from a Section 482 reallocation is part of taxpayer's regular income tax liability, so the normal rules on interest apply. Morton-Norwich Prods., Inc., 602 F2d 270, 79-2 USTC ¶ 9483, 44 AFTR2d 79-5346 (Ct. Cl. 1979), cert. denied, 445 US 927 (1980).

Allocation under Section 482 upheld. A banking corporation distributed appreciated U.S. Treasury bonds and notes to its parent holding company as a dividend in kind, anticipating the sale or redemption of such obligations to avoid the impact of Section 482. The IRS allocated the gain realized on the sale of the notes to the banking corporation under Section 482. *Held:* For the IRS. The income from the sale of the notes that the taxpayer distributed as a dividend in kind was allocable to the taxpayer under Section 482, since the taxpayer's invested money was invested and produced the income. Southern Bank Corp., 67 TC 1022 (1977).

Untimely arguments for reallocation of income not permitted. Taxpayer, *R*'s sister corporation, purchased equipment on credit and leased it to *R*. Taxpayer purchased some trailer-trucks, which turned out to be unsatisfactory, and therefore taxpayer convinced the seller to repurchase the trucks. Because the repurchase deprived *R* of low rentals, *R* and taxpayer entered an agreement granting *R* the right to receive any profit on the sale of the trucks. The IRS determined that taxpayer realized a gain equal to the difference between the selling price and the basis of the trailer. During trial, taxpayer offered uncontradicted evidence showing that the gain was attributable to *R*. On brief, the IRS offered theories for the first time based on an arm's-length approach and adequacy of consideration for reallocating the gain between the parties. *Held:* For taxpayer. The IRS failed to inform taxpayer in the statutory notice, in its answer, or at trial of its theories for sustaining a deficiency. Thus, the court could not consider these untimely arguments in its decision. Accordingly, taxpayer received none of the gain from the sale of the trailer-trucks. Riss, Sr., 57 TC 469 (1971).

Income reallocated from controlled corporations to stockholders. Stockholders rented property to two corporations that they controlled and operated, at less than the fair market rental value of the land. The IRS reallocated income to the stockholders. *Held:* For the IRS. Income equal to the fair market rental value of the property was imputed to the stockholders under Section 482. The insolvency of the corporation was not a defense to the reallocation, provided that the corporations had sufficient gross income to pay the reallocated amounts. Thomas, 46 TCM 974, ¶ 83,462 P-H Memo. TC (1983).

Rental income reallocated due to invalid profit-sharing ratio. Taxpayer corporations, producers of sand and gravel and owned by one family, entered a partnership to operate various mining sites and to apportion profits and losses. The partnership entered into an agreement with an unrelated corporation to purchase and lease equipment and remove sand and gravel. The IRS reallocated the rental income among the corporations. *Held:* For the IRS. The partnership's profit-sharing ratio used to allocate rent had no valid foundation. Taxpayers could not prove that the IRS' allocation, based on relative gross dollar volume of sales from each corporation's respective plant site, was arbitrary or unreasonable. Such reallocation of income was upheld. Also, Section 482 could be used to reallocate taxable income among the partners. Upon the unrelated corporation's exercise of an option to purchase machinery and lease interests, taxpayers claimed that the portion of the sales proceeds allocable to the leasehold was not ordinary income. However, no part of the sales proceeds was allocable to the leaseholds because the total required payments had already been made by prior rental payments, and the lessee corporation had already acquired the leases. Also, taxpayers did not establish the amount of income from mining and therefore could not establish any allowable depletion deduction. Finally, the corporation's payment of expenses for test borings on land sold to its stockholder and certain payments for the stockholder's car, travel, and entertainment expenses were for his personal use. They were not deductible items, and thus constituted additional income to the stockholder. Rodebaugh, 33 TCM 169, ¶ 74,036 P-H Memo. TC (1974).

Liquidated subsidiary could deduct expenses which were given a basis in the hands of the parent, which later deducted same expenses. A wholly owned subsidiary was liquidated pursuant to Section 332. Various agricultural expenses had been incurred, which were not inventoried at the end of the subsidiary's final tax year. The parent allocated basis to these costs pursuant to Section 334(b)(2). In South Lakes Farms, Inc., 36 TC 1027 (1961) aff'd, 324 F2d 837 (9th Cir. 1963), the Tax Court indicated that this did not violate the "clearly reflects income requirement" of Section 446(b) or the allocation of deduction provision of Section 482. On appeal, the court decided that the subsidiary did not have to report income on the additional ground of a "tax benefit." The IRS originally acquiesced in the decision on the grounds held for in the Tax Court. Due to confusion with the additional ground in the Ninth Circuit's decision, the IRS withdrew this acquiescence. Rev. Rul. 77-67, 1977-1 CB 33.

Section 164(d) not applicable to dissolutions but Section 482 might be applied. Taxpayer, an accrual basis corporation, had not elected to accrue real property taxes ratably under Section 461(c). In the past, it had accrued its real estate taxes on April 1. The corporation was dissolved on June 30, 1960 and accrued the real estate taxes for the real property year ending December 31, 1960 on its return for the short period January 1 through June 30, 1960. The principal asset distributed was real estate. The IRS ruled that Section 164(d), which provides for the allocation of real property taxes between a seller and buyer of real estate, has no application to a dissolution of a corporation. However, this does not prevent such an allocation under Section 482, which grants discretionary power in order to reflect income clearly. In the instant case, the inclusion of more than a pro rata amount of real estate taxes in taxpayer's final return would not clearly reflect income; the IRS requires an allocation under Section 482 between the corporation and the distributee of the real estate. Rev. Rul. 62-45, 1962-1 CB 27.

Arm's-Length Transaction Defense

Determination of fair market rent. The IRS determined that rent payments made for land and improvements subleased by the taxpayer to a related corporation were not at arm's length, and applied Section 482 to reconstruct income. *Held:* For the IRS. The fact

ALLOCATION AMONG RELATED TAXPAYERS: *Arm's-Length Transaction*

that the sublessee was unable to pay did not establish that the rent was at arm's length, because a new sublessee would have been found had an uncontrolled sublessee continually defaulted as did the sublessee here. The court found that the comparative, or market data, approach was suitable for determination of the fair rental value of the land under Section 482. Due to lack of comparable rental property in the area, the fair rental value of the improvements was properly computed by using the investor's approach: fair rental value equals 10 percent of the fair market value, or cost less depreciation of the leased improvements. Powers, 724 F2d 64, 53 AFTR2d 84-413 (7th Cir. 1984).

Section 482 reallocation between three family corporations was upheld where lessor charged lessee excessive rental. Taxpayer and his sons held all the stock of taxpayer corporation, as well as Rental and Charter Corporations, during 1973 and 1974. Collectively, the three comprised the board of directors and officers of all three corporations. Taxpayer transferred equipment to Rental, and a vehicle and airplane to Charter. During 1973 and 1974, Rental's sole business was leasing equipment to taxpayer; Charter's sole business was leasing trucks, automobiles, and an airplane to taxpayer. The IRS determined that the rental payments to Charter and Rental were not at arm's length. Relying on Section 482, the IRS reallocated an amount of the rental income to taxpayer, and disallowed rental expenses in the same amount, as these expenses did not constitute ordinary and necessary business expenses under Section 162. The Tax Court upheld the reallocation because taxpayer could not show the rental was at arm's length. *Held:* Affirmed. The findings of the Tax Court were not clearly erroneous. Reallocation of income and deductions between three family corporations was upheld where lessor charged lessee excessive rental. Taxpayers elected to operate through separate corporations and reallocation was reasonable. White Tool & Mach. Co., 677 F2d 528, 49 AFTR2d 82-1343 (6th Cir.), cert. denied, 459 US 903 (1982).

Allocation of rent income between related parties was proper. Taxpayer and his son controlled F Corporation. Taxpayer constructed, equipped, and furnished a motel that he rented to F. Under the lease, rent was fixed at a minimum amount less than the allowable depreciation on the motel plus an additional amount based upon revenues. The IRS allocated additional rent income to the taxpayer under Section 482, arguing that the lease agreement was not an arm's length transaction. *Held:* For the IRS. The rental to F constituted a trade or business. The taxpayer did not prove that the rent charged to F was the amount that would have been charged to an unrelated party in an arm's-length transaction. The allocation did not create income where none had existed. Fegan, 81-1 USTC ¶ 9436 (10th Cir. 1981).

Shipping fees between related corporations were set at arm's length and not subject to reallocation under Section 482. Taxpayer was a major vertically integrated producer of steel, and additionally owned iron ore mines around the world. Taxpayer incorporated a subsidiary in Liberia with its principal place of business in the Bahamas as a carrier for its ore. During 1957 through 1960, there was no information publicly available from which a "market price" for the carriage of iron ore by sea could be determined. The IRS determined that the subsidiary had overcharged taxpayer by 25 percent and reallocated income from the subsidiary to taxpayer. The Tax Court agreed that the reallocation was justified because it found that taxpayer's motives were designed to protect its subsidiary, to give it more profits, and to shelter income from taxation. *Held:* Reversed. Where taxpayer has shown that the price it paid a controlled corporation for a service was the amount that would have been charged for the same or similar services in an independent transaction with or between unrelated parties, it earned the right to be free from a Section 482 reallocation despite other evidence tending to show that its activities resulted in a shifting of tax liability among controlled corporations. United States Steel Corp., 617 F2d 942, 80-1 USTC ¶ 9307, 45 AFTR2d 80-1081 (2d Cir. 1980).

Allocation Among Related Taxpayers: *Arm's-Length Transaction*

Section 482 allocations of interest in loans did not depend on whether loans produced income. The IRS held that interest income reported by taxpayer was understated to the extent that taxpayer failed to charge arm's-length interest on monies advanced to related entities. The Tax Court upheld the IRS' allocation, stating that taxpayer had not shown that the borrowers did not realize gross income from the use of the loans. *Held:* Affirmed, but for different reasons. Section 482, dealing with allocation of income, applies where the loans are not made at arm's length, as was the situation here. The Tax Court's test of whether the debtor uses the loan to produce income was rejected. Fitzgerald Motor Co., 508 F2d 1096, 75-1 USTC ¶ 9275, 35 AFTR2d 75-832 (5th Cir. 1975).

Section 482 reallocation involving Western Hemisphere subsidiary remanded. The IRS determined that all of the income of taxpayer's Western Hemisphere Trade Corporation subsidiary, which acted as a distributor for taxpayer under Section 482, should be reallocated. The district court held that no reallocation was necessary. *Held:* Remanded. The profit margin realized by taxpayer was not the same as the profit that would have been made in an arm's-length sale to other distributors. Therefore, a partial reallocation was proper. Baldwin-Lima Hamilton Corp., 435 F2d 182, 70-2 USTC ¶ 9725, 26 AFTR2d 70-5881 (7th Cir. 1970).

Stockholder's lease of corporate assets fails to shift corporate losses. Taxpayer formed six subsidiaries to construct garden apartments under FHA-approved loans. The buildings, which contained 56 apartments, consistently showed losses and a high percentage of vacancies. Soon, the subsidiaries were unable to make repairs and pay their mortgage commitments. To remedy this, taxpayer leased 55 of the 56 apartments and agreed to pay all operating expenses. Despite taxpayer's efforts to improve the operation by making repairs and hiring a new manager, the losses continued because of the general economic decline of the area. The IRS disallowed, under Section 482, the losses claimed by taxpayer and determined that they should be allocated back to the subsidiaries. The Tax Court held for the IRS. *Held:* Affirmed. The evidence did not sustain taxpayer's contention that the rent and expenses were reasonable in amount or that there existed fair prospect of profit from anticipated subleasing. Financial aid to the corporations and tax deductions for taxpayer were apparently strong incentives for entering into the leases. Baldwin Bros., 361 F2d 668, 66-1 USTC ¶ 9464, 17 AFTR2d 1171 (3d Cir. 1966).

Transactions between related partnership and corporation were at arm's length. A partnership, formed by the principal stockholders of a construction corporation, originally confined its activities to renting equipment to the corporation. In later years, it took construction contracts of the same general nature as those of the corporation. The IRS reallocated certain items of income between the corporation and the partnership. *Held:* For taxpayer. The court found that the transactions were conducted at prices which reflected arm's-length dealings and that the rental paid for construction equipment by the corporation to the partnership was reasonable. The court also determined the depreciation rate on certain equipment. Tillotson, 202 F. Supp. 925, 62-1 USTC ¶ 9337, 9 AFTR2d 1011 (D. Neb. 1962).

Royalties paid to related corporation were deductible. Taxpayer, a wholly owned American subsidiary of a foreign corporation, conducted field tests of various chemical products. Following that, the parent corporation filed patent applications in 32 countries. The taxpayer undertook the work required to obtain the required governmental approval for marketing the products in the United States and was subsequently granted nonexclusive licenses to manufacture and market certain of these products in exchange for a 10 percent royalty. Following this, the taxpayer received the exclusive licensing rights in the United States in exchange for the 10 percent royalty payments. The IRS disallowed the claimed royalty deductions on the grounds that the parties were involved in a joint research project, the results of which were equally available to each for exploitation without the need for royalty payments. *Held:* For taxpayer. The taxpayer's involvement in developing the chemical products was peripheral and did not constitute a joint venture. The parent had previously negotiated with an unrelated U.S. party for a nonexclusive license to manufacture and sell the product. That party would have paid royalties of 10 percent to 12.5 percent. Since this established that an unrelated party would have paid at least 10 percent, the royalties were realistic. Therefore, the IRS abused its discretion under Section 482 when it determined that the royalty agreement was not entered into in an arm's-length transaction. Ciba-Geigy Corp., 85 TC 172 (1986).

Allocation of income and expenses of professional corporation to its sole stockholder not permitted. Taxpayer operated two sole proprietorships, a private psychiatric hospital and a clinical psychiatric practice. In 1971, the taxpayer incorporated the clinical practice and entered into an exclusive employment agreement with the corporation for his services. The corporation billed private patients for the taxpayer's services. It also billed the taxpayer's private psychiatric hospital for services rendered by the taxpayer to hospital inpatients. The IRS reallocated to the taxpayer's hospital all the income the corporation received for billing the hospital and reallocated the remainder of the corporation's income to the taxpayer. *Held:* For taxpayer. Taxpayer established that the corporation carried on a business during the years at issue, since it hired employees, subscribed to periodicals, paid operating expenses, rendered bills and other correspondence on its own stationery, and provided psychiatric services to the hospital and individual patients. In addition, the terms of the employment contract between the taxpayer and his corporation, and the contract between the corporation and the hospital represented arm's-length transactions, since taxpayer asked a reasonable amount for his services and the compensation he received from his corporation was also reasonable. The Tax Court rejected the IRS' attempt to use ink analysis to prove "backdating" of taxpayer's employment contract. Ink analysis is not a recognized science and the IRS' ink library is not sufficiently complete to be respected. Pacella, 78 TC 604 (1982).

Court determined that income and deductions of closely held personal service corporation should not be reallocated or adjusted under Sections 482, 269, or 61. Taxpayer held significant stock interests in X and Y Corporations. Taxpayer, along with others, formed Z Corporation to render management services to X and Y. Taxpayer entered into an exclusive employment contract with Z Corporation, and thereunder rendered management services on Z's behalf to X and Y. Owner employees often form sham personal service corporations in order to gain tax benefits available to them only through a corporation, such as pension and profit-sharing plans. As part of its campaign against such practice, the IRS disallowed X's and Y's deductions for amounts paid to Z, and further adjusted X's, Y's, and Z's income and deductions for the years involved under the "clear reflection of income" principles. *Held:* For taxpayer. The court held that (1) since payments to Z reflected arm's-length charges for the services rendered, no adjustment to income or deductions was required under Section 482; (2) Section 269 does not apply because although taxpayer attempted to gain a better retirement plan than X or Y could offer to him, he was foiled by the aggregation of X's, Y's, and Z's retirement plans; (3) Z could not be defined as a sham corporation since it carried on actual business activities; and (4) the evidence did not support application of assignment of income principles that would enable Z's income or deductions to be attributed to X or Y. Achiro, 77 TC 881 (1981).

Corporation recognized, but Section 482 applied. Taxpayers were physicians and were equal owners of a professional medical corporation. They created a Subchapter S corporation and assigned all its stock to members of their families. The Subchapter S corporation provided X-ray services to the medical corporation and operated from the medical corporation's premises without paying rent. Its clients were not aware that it was a separate entity. The IRS argued that the Subchapter S corporation was a sham. *Held:* For taxpayer, in part. The Subchapter S corporation had an employee who performed services on a continuing basis, and the corporation borrowed money and paid its taxes and suppliers. Thus, it was not a sham. However, the rates charged by the Subchapter S corporation for its services were not at arm's length and the excess charge was reallocable to the professional corporation. Furthermore, income was reallocated to reflect the Subchapter S corporation's payment of its own rent, utilities, and insurance. Also, because taxpayers continued to control the Subchapter S corporation and did not deal with it at arm's length, the purported transfer of the stock to the family members was disregarded, the taxpayers were deemed the owners of that corporation and were taxable on its distributions. Bell III, 45 TCM 97, ¶ 82,660 P-H Memo. TC (1982).

Applicability of Section 482 to personal service corporation determined. The IRS argued that taxpayer, the sole nonresident alien stockholder and employee of a domestic corporation, should report the income earned by his personal service corporation as his. *Held:* For taxpayer, in part. The taxpayer acted as employee-agent of the corporation, which controlled the performance of the services that gave rise to the income. The corporation was a separate legal entity and could not be disregarded under the substance over form doctrine. Under Section 482, the salary received by taxpayer during certain years was an arm's-length salary. However, when the corporation's earnings increased, taxpayer's salary should have also been increased to reflect the arm's-length compensation. To that extent, part of the corporation's income was reallocable to taxpayer as compensation. Morrison, 44 TCM 1459, ¶ 82,613 P-H Memo. TC (1982).

Reallocation of income between related corporations unnecessary for arm's-length transactions. Taxpayer parent, a manufacturer, sold its products to a wholly owned subsidiary created for the purpose of marketing outside the United States. The IRS allocated a portion of the subsidiary's income and all of its income from Canadian sales to the parent. *Held:* For taxpayer. No allocations of income were necessary as the product sales were made at arm's-length prices, as indicated by the comparable uncontrolled price method, that is, actual prices paid by unrelated companies for similar products. Furthermore, the parent did not receive a constructive dividend or a bargain purchase because of the sale and resale of stock between its subsidiaries or the acquisition of stock of unrelated companies. The court determined that the allocation of a subsidiary's income to the parent, because of an interest-free loan between them, was an imputation of interest income, which is not allowed under Section 482. Since the transfer of unpatented technology under four or five agreements did not convey all substantial rights in the property, the proceeds were ordinary income; the proceeds of the fifth contract, which conveyed all rights, were entitled to capital gain treatment. PGG Indus., Inc., 29 TCM 1710, ¶ 70,354 P-H Memo. TC (1970).

Section 482 adjustments upheld where related taxpayers rental charges, not arm's-length arrangement. Taxpayer, as sublessee, made rental payments totaling $79,000 to another corporation that was controlled by the same stockholders. The second corporation, already losing money elsewhere, was a lessee paying rent of $24,700 to a third unrelated corporation. The IRS, while not denying the existence of the intermediary corporation, reallocated taxpayer's excess rental payments back to taxpayer, claiming the parties were not dealing at arm's length. *Held:* For the IRS. The only reason the lease was arranged through the intermediary was to take advantage of its losses to offset the excess rental payments and to gain a greater rental deduction for the successful taxpayer. Taxpayer was also denied rental deductions to the intermediary for furniture and air conditioning because, although they were placed on the intermediary's books as assets, there was no proof that taxpayer bought them on behalf of the intermediary. Bluefeld Caterer, Inc., 28 TCM 315, ¶ 69,056 P-H Memo. TC (1969).

Allocation Among Related Taxpayers: *Business Purpose Defense*

Business Purpose Defense

Excessive rent deductions disallowed in transfer and leaseback. Taxpayers transferred improved real estate to a controlled corporation and leased it back under a "net" lease. The corporation used the rent payments to finance a profitable auto leasing business. The IRS disallowed taxpayers' deduction for rent payments. *Held:* For taxpayers, in part. The transfer was not a sham because it served a legitimate business purpose, but the IRS properly disallowed a portion of the deduction under Section 482 because the rent was excessive. Peck, 752 F2d 469, 55 AFTR2d 85-804 (9th Cir. 1985).

Court approves doctor's formation of corporation for purpose of obtaining pension and medical plans. Taxpayer, a doctor, formed a corporation through which he conducted his profession. Taxpayer, the sole stockholder and employee of the corporation, formed the corporation to establish and maintain for himself a pension and medical plan. The corporation replaced taxpayer as a member of a medical partnership. Compensation paid by the corporation to taxpayer was approximately equal to his earnings prior to formation of the corporation. The IRS taxed taxpayer on amounts received by the corporation in respect of services performed by taxpayer. *Held:* For taxpayer. While Section 482 can be applied in this kind of situation, under the facts, taxpayer's return clearly reflected income. However, he was taxable on checks made payable to him by the partnership which he endorsed over to the corporation. Further, even though taxpayer formed the corporation to avail himself of tax benefits available only to businesses conducted in the corporate form, his formation of the corporation did not lack business purpose. Daniel Keller, 723 F2d 58, 83-2 USTC ¶ 9740, 53 AFTR2d 84-404 (10th Cir. 1983).

Proceeds from the sale of property should be imputed to the corporation only if sale was in fact made by corporation. Taxpayer was director, secretary, and attorney-in-fact of a family owned corporation which faced imminent bankruptcy. The sale of the corporation's extensive timberland holdings was planned as the solution to the financial difficulties, and was specifically structured to avoid double taxation. The timberlands were first distributed to taxpayer and stockholders as tenants in common. Several paper companies were then invited to submit sealed bids for the land, a purchaser was selected, and the proceeds of the sale were paid to taxpayer and stockholders in pro rata portions. Taxpayer reported his portion of the proceeds and claimed long-term capital gains status. The corporation did not report the gains from the sale received by its stockholders on its corporate income tax, nor did it treat them as additions to its earned surplus on the corporation's books. The IRS assessed a deficiency against taxpayer, and determined that the gain on the sale of the lands should have been imputed to the corporation because the distribution lacked a normal and justifiable commercial motivation and was made for the principal purpose of avoiding tax. The district court held for the IRS. *Held:* Reversed. The court stated that the proceeds of the sale of property distributed by a corporation to its stockholders should be imputed to the corporation only if the sale was in fact made by the corporation, and not by the stockholders. The court must find that the corporation actively participated in the transaction that produced the income for it to be imputed. The court relied on the finding of the district court, which stated that the corporation had neither negotiated the sale prior to the distribution of the lands to stockholders nor participated in the sale after the distribution in determining that imputation had been improper. The corporation could not be charged with tax liability for a transaction in which it had no involvement or control. Hines, Jr., 477 F2d 1063, 73-1 USTC ¶ 9403, 31 AFTR2d 73-1215 (5th Cir. 1973).

Loss on sale to a related corporation disallowed. Taxpayer corporation sold trailers to a related corporation and claimed a loss on the sale. The Tax Court disallowed this claim. *Held:* Affirmed. The sale was deemed to lack a business purpose and therefore the loss was not recognized. Transport Mfg. & Equip. Co. of Del., 431 F2d 729, 70-2 USTC ¶ 9604, 26 AFTR2d 70-5501 (8th Cir. 1970).

Allocation Among Related Taxpayers: Business Purpose Defense

Transfers from parent to subsidiary were for sound business reasons; allocations of income by the IRS to the former were arbitrary. Taxpayer corporation was organized to conduct the same business in the Northeast as was conducted by another corporation in the Midwest. Ten years after its incorporation, taxpayer's subsidiary was incorporated to sell related products at wholesale, but it subsequently became inactive. Taxpayer employed two persons to run its business. These two owned a one-third interest and were not related to the owners of the two-thirds interest, who were also the sole stockholders of the third corporation. When a substantial customer moved its plant from the area serviced by the third corporation to that serviced by taxpayer, the owners of the one-third interest recommended that the third corporation cease making shipments to them and that the account be serviced by the then-inactive subsidiary. Subsequent to the transfer of the account, the parties agreed on a fee to be paid by the subsidiary to the third corporation for services rendered in connection with the account. The IRS allocated all the income of the subsidiary to taxpayer under Section 482 and was upheld in the Tax Court. *Held:* Reversed. The Tax Court, in sustaining the IRS' determination that the use of the subsidiary was motivated by tax avoidance, found that the purpose was to take advantage of the subsidiary's net operating loss carry-over. It held that taxpayer had not sustained its contention that the allocation was not necessary to clearly reflect income. The court felt, however, that taxpayer had shown sufficiently sound business reasons for the transactions involving the subsidiary, and to hold otherwise would be to substitute the IRS' judgment for that of taxpayer's officers and directors without the factual showing of an unlawful purpose. The financial welfare of the minority interests was dependent upon the arrangement; the fee arrangement with the third corporation was considered adequate compensation for their not taking the account. The IRS' arbitrary allocation of all the income of the subsidiary to taxpayer was not justified. Braun Co., 396 F2d 264, 68-1 USTC ¶ 9430, 21 AFTR2d 1438 (2d Cir. 1968).

Expenses incurred prior to incorporation were not allocable to the corporate entity. Taxpayers transferred a farm they operated to their controlled corporation pursuant to Section 351. Before this incorporation, taxpayers deducted expenses incurred in planting crops. However, the profits from such crops were reported by the newly formed corporation, as that entity had harvested and sold the crops. The IRS, pursuant to Section 482, reallocated the expenses to the corporation. *Held:* For taxpayer. The incorporation was motivated by banking considerations, not tax avoidance. Unlike similar cases in which the IRS' reallocation was upheld, taxpayer's expense deductions did not give rise to a net operating loss for the year. Fanning, 568 F. Supp. 823, 83-2 USTC ¶ 9430, 52 AFTR2d 83-5481 (ED Wash. 1983).

Section 482 allocation deemed unnecessary. A related group of corporations were engaged in operating department stores at separate locations. Their parent purchased merchandise and supplied administrative and managerial assistance to the operating corporations. A second related group of corporations operated and leased real estate to third parties and to the first related group. The IRS disregarded the existence of the subsidiaries and allocated the income of each related group to their respective parents. *Held:* For taxpayer. The allocation of income under Section 482 to the parent corporations was improper. The operating and property subsidiaries were operated as independent concerns, carried on substantial business with third parties, and conducted business affairs within the corporate group on an arm's-length basis. Delhar, Inc., 71-1 USTC ¶ 9107 (SD Fla. 1970).

Gain on stock sale allocated to subsidiary that originally owned the stock. Subsidiary A paid a property dividend consisting of 52,638 shares of Z Corporation to its parent, P Corporation. Subsequently, P sold the Z stock at a gain and offset the gain against a net operating loss carry-over. The IRS, pursuant to Section 482, allocated the gain to A. *Held:* For the IRS. There existed a prior plan for the sale of the dividend shares, and the transfer to P was not undertaken for an acceptable business purpose. Ruddick Corp., 83-2 USTC ¶ 9480, 52 AFTR2d 83-5677 (Cl. Ct. 1983), aff'd, 732 F2d 168 (Fed. Cir. 1984).

Intercompany pricing policies were not correct. Taxpayer organized a wholly owned subsidiary in Puerto Rico as a possessions corporation. The taxpayer transferred manufacturing intangibles for two products to the subsidiary, and the subsidiary became the sole manufacturer of the products and sold them to the taxpayer. The price the subsidiary charged the taxpayer was equal to the wholesale price less discounts of 40 percent to 58 percent to allow the taxpayer to recover its costs and earn a predetermined profit. The IRS reallocated to the taxpayer the income attributable to the patents and the related manufacturing know-how. The taxpayer contended the reallocation was improper, since it did not take into account the subsidiary's ownership of the manufacturing intangibles. *Held:* For the IRS, in part. The transfer of ownership of manufacturing intangibles cannot be disregarded, and all of the income generated by those assets cannot be reallocated to the taxpayer. The transfer was motivated by a bona fide business consideration and the subsidiary did not dispose of the assets following the transfer. The income earned by the use of those assets belongs to the subsidiary because the subsidiary earned it through the use of its own property in its business. However, a reallocation of income to the taxpayer is required because the prices the subsidiary charged shifted profits to itself, distorting the income. Eli Lilly & Co. Subsidiaries, 84 TC 996 (1985).

No reallocation of income from controlled foreign corporation. Taxpayer, a produce distributor in Florida, acted as a selling agent for Cuban farmers. One of these farmers invited taxpayer to participate in a joint farming venture. Expecting that he would be able to purchase produce from the venture, taxpayer agreed to furnish capital for the venture. Being fearful of subjecting his produce business to the risks of farming, taxpayer decided to incorporate his interest in the joint venture. An attorney advised him to form a Panamanian corporation. Taxpayer purchased produce from the venture at current U.S. prices. Because of favorable market conditions, the joint venture was very successful. The profits of the Panamanian corporation accumulated in Panama until the joint venture disbanded because of the Cuban revolution. Taxpayer liquidated the Panamanian corporation and reported a capital gain. The IRS contended that the income of the Panamanian corporation should be reallocated to taxpayer and reported as ordinary income. *Held:* For taxpayer. The Panamanian corporation was a valid entity created for sound business reasons. Since the principal purpose of the acquisition was not to avoid tax, Section 269 did not apply. Furthermore, the wording of Section 269 is too narrow to permit the allocation of income other than between "corporations or properties." Siegel, 45 TC 566 (1965), acq. 1966-2 CB 7.

Reallocation of income of suburban retail store to main store is proper. Taxpayer for many years had been in the retail men's clothing business at a downtown city location. A separately incorporated store was opened in the suburbs, with essentially the same officers, directors, and stockholders. The advertising, buying, display, and sales forces of both stores were supervised by the downtown store. The lease for the suburban store and much of the capitalization of that corporation were obtained on the basis of guarantees by the principals of the established downtown store. Under Section 482, the IRS allocated all of the suburban corporation's taxable income to the taxpayer. *Held:* For the IRS. The court found that the business of the second corporation was essentially conducted as a branch operation and that no business need for the second corporation existed except for the additional surtax exemption. Hambergers York Road, Inc., 41 TC 821 (1964), acq. 1965-2 CB 5.

Related corporate income not allocated to partnership. Taxpayers formed a law partnership and a management corporation. The IRS reallocated corporate income to the partners through the partnership. *Held:* For taxpayers. The corporation was a valid, separate, and distinct business that earned the fees, and the reallocation to the partnership was therefore unreasonable. Since the fees were earned by the corporation, its dividend and interest income did not constitute 60 percent of its adjusted gross income, and the personal holding company tax was not applicable. Medical expenses made on behalf of employees under a medical reimbursement plan were deductible, and finally, expenses incurred in maintaining nonrental personal vacation property were not deductible. Gettler, 34 TCM 442, ¶ 75,087 P-H Memo. TC (1975).

Conduit Theory

Gain from stock sale by controlled corporation allocated to shareholder under Section 482. Taxpayer contributed stock to his controlled corporation, which then immediately sold the stock. The bulk of the sales' proceeds were distributed to taxpayer or to entities controlled by taxpayer. The IRS used Section 482 to reallocate the gain from the stock sale to taxpayer. The Tax Court found for the IRS. *Held:* Affirmed. The corporation had large net operating loss carry-overs to absorb the gain. Considering the substance-over-form doctrine, the corporation was found to be a conduit for the sale of appreciated securities by taxpayer. Stewart, 714 F2d 977, 83-2 USTC ¶ 9573, 52 AFTR2d 83-5885 (9th Cir. 1983).

All of subsidiaries' restaurant business attributed to taxpayer. Taxpayer corporation owned 100 percent of the stock of 10 subsidiaries; each subsidiary operated a separate restaurant. All 10 subsidiaries had the same officers and were charged fees for subfranchises and management by taxpayer corporation. In addition, taxpayer corporation owned two other corporations that sold food supplies to the restaurant-subsidiaries. The IRS contended that taxpayer's related corporate entities were to be disregarded for income tax purposes and that all income and deductions were attributable to taxpayer corporation. The Tax Court held for the IRS and stated that taxpayer's fee structure, which was not at arm's length, was used for shifting income in order to obtain tax advantages for taxpayer. *Held:* Affirmed. The facts indicated that in substance, taxpayer had conducted an integrated business enterprise through its division's setup as wholly owned subsidiaries. This was so, even though taxpayer claimed that there were business reasons other than tax advantages for this multicorporate arrangement. Wisconsin Big Boy Corp., 452 F2d 137, 71-2 USTC ¶ 9755, 28 AFTR2d 71-6044 (7th Cir. 1971).

Allocation not justified as taxpayer did not earn income. The IRS allocated to taxpayer banks reinsurance premiums on policies written by related companies. The policies involved taxpayers' customers. The Tax Court upheld the IRS. *Held:* Reversed. Taxpayers did not earn the premiums, and although they physically received the premium payments, they acted only as a conduit to pass such payments on to the related entities that were legally entitled to them. Thus, there had been no assignment of income. First Sec. Bank of Utah, 436 F2d 1192, 71-1 USTC ¶ 9169, 27 AFTR2d 71-472 (10th Cir. 1971).

Court permits allocation, under Section 482, of 100 percent of the net income of corporations not held to be sham entities. Taxpayer was the principal corporation in a group of 11 corporations that were under the direct or indirect control of the same interests. Of the remaining 10 corporations, half were foreign and half were domestic. All of the corporations were involved in the purchase and resale of chemicals. Taxpayer did the shipping and bookkeeping for all of the corporations and received consideration for its services. The domestic corporations, unlike the foreign corporations, incurred significant operating expenses owed to unrelated persons. The IRS, under Section 482, allocated the net incomes of all the corporations to taxpayer. The Tax Court held in favor of the IRS. *Held:* Reversed, in part. The IRS should not have allocated the net incomes of the domestic corporations to taxpayer. The domestic corporations, through their expenses, were able to show that they carried on substantial income-producing activities. No evidence was offered to show that the foreign corporations earned the income they reported through services or risking of capital. Philipp Bros.

Allocation Among Related Taxpayers: *Conduit Theory*

Chems., 435 F2d 53, 70-2 USTC ¶ 9723, 26 AFTR2d 70-5877 (2d Cir. 1970).

Payment of 90 percent of income is reallocated to payor corporation due to taxpayer's interest in the operation of the corporation. Taxpayer corporation entered into an agreement with Fairmount, a loss corporation, under which the latter was to furnish the necessary capital for taxpayer to conduct two horse racing meets. The controlling stockholders of Fairmount owned 2 percent of taxpayer. Their cousin owned the rest. Taxpayer agreed to operate the meets "for the benefit of Fairmount" and to receive 10 percent of the net profits for this service. Pursuant to this agreement, taxpayer paid 90 percent of the income received from the meets to Fairmount. The IRS reallocated all the profits to taxpayer. *Held:* For IRS. No true agency relationship existed between taxpayer and Fairmount. Taxpayer operated the property as if it were its own and did all the things necessary to earn the income. The court also rejected an alternative contention that the two corporations acted as joint venturers. Charles Town, Inc., 372 F2d 415, 67-1 USTC ¶ 9243 (4th Cir.), cert. denied, 389 US 841 (1967).

Co-tenant's income and expenses must be allocated among them where parties are separate corporate entities. Taxpayer and SAVI, adjacent irrigation companies, formed SARD to facilitate the successful operations of their irrigation businesses. Eventually SARD held a one-third interest in certain lands jointly with taxpayer and SAVI. SARD reported all the rental income and expenses attributable to the jointly held properties on its federal income tax return. The IRS reallocated the rental income and expenses according to the proportional shares held by the co-tenant. *Held:* For the IRS. Where the evidence indicated that the parties were separate corporate entitles, the fact that one corporation performed functions as an agent for the others in no way permitted it to report on its own return the entire rental income and expense from those lands on which it was a co-tenant. Anaheim Union Water Co., 35 TC 1072 (1961), modified, 321 F2d 253, 63-2 USTC ¶ 9589, 12 AFTR2d 5181 (9th Cir. 1963).

Profits of insurance agency taxable to banking corporation where transferred without consideration to stockholders. Taxpayer, a banking corporation, purchased an insurance agency in 1947 and operated the agency on the bank premises with bank employees. No rent was paid by the insurance activity to taxpayer. In 1951, taxpayer's directors, who were also the stockholders, voted to transfer the insurance business to themselves. Although this was done, the operation continued to use taxpayer's facilities. In 1956, the directors filed a partnership agreement pursuant to local law, and in 1957 they prepared and filed a partnership tax return. At no time did any of the directors make a contribution to the capital of the agency. The IRS contended that the entire income from 1951 through 1957 was includible in taxpayer's gross income. *Held:* For the IRS. The conduct of the parties was insufficient to uphold the contention that the insurance agency was a partnership, not a department of the taxpayer corporation. Bank of Kimball, 200 F. Supp. 638, 62-1 USTC ¶ 9228 (DSD 1962).

Section 482 applied to allocate fees between related corporations to controlling stockholder. Taxpayer controlled two corporations. One of the corporations entered into a contract to provide management services to the other. The services were in fact rendered by taxpayer. In its original opinion, Rubin, 51 TC 251 (1968), the Tax Court held that the net fees were taxable to taxpayer under Section 61 and principles enunciated in Lucas v. Earl, 281 US 111 (1930). The Second Circuit, in Rubin, 429 F2d 650 (1970), reversed and remanded to determine the case under Section 482. *Held:* For the IRS. Under controlling case law, income received by a corporation for services performed by an individual in control of corporate affairs is properly held subject to the IRS' power of allocation under Section 482. A stockholder's business activity may constitute a trade or business within the meaning of the statute where the stockholder operated an independent business and assigned a portion of the income to the corporation. Accordingly, based on the facts, taxpayer was taxable under Section 482 on the net fees. It was further held that taxpayer had fair warning of the IRS' intention to use Section 482. Rubin, 56 TC 1155 (1971).

Panamanian corporation's income only partially allocated to domestic owners. Taxpayers organized a partnership in 1955 for the purpose of conducting a construction business. In 1957, they organized a domestic corporation and transferred the business to it. Another corporation had been organized in 1953 under Panamanian laws. This corporation did no business until 1956. In 1956, the taxpayers were awarded contracts by the navy for the construction of missile tracking stations in the Caribbean. As the Panamanian corporation had no credit rating, the contracts were undertaken in the name of the partnership. The work was actually done by the Panamanian company, but considerable services, such as obtaining of performance bonds and purchasing materials, were rendered by the domestic companies. Income from these contracts was recorded by the foreign corporation. The IRS reallocated the entire income to the partnership and the domestic corporation. *Held:* For taxpayer. The Tax Court concluded that the allocation of the entire net income was unreasonable. The Panamanian corporation was a valid entity, which performed substantial services as a subcontractor. However, since the partnership and the domestic corporation were the prime contractor and the purchaser of materials, the Tax Court held that part of the net profit should be allocated to them. The court exercised its discretion by determining the percentages of net income allocable to each company. Nat Harrison Assocs., 42 TC 601 (1964), acq. 1965-2 CB 5.

Reallocation of income proper. Taxpayer divided his cleaning business into two corporations in order to satisfy the needs of a particular customer. The IRS reallocated the income of the new corporation back to the original corporation. *Held:* For the IRS. The IRS did not abuse its discretion in making the reallocation. The second corporation merely owned the cleaning contract with the customer and performed no services to earn income. Although separate records were kept, there was no evidence to show that the two companies operated under an arm's-length arrangement. Thus, the reallocation of income was proper. Marcus, 34 TCM 722, ¶ 75,158 P-H Memo. TC (1975).

Methods of Reallocation

Section 482 used to reduce cost of goods sold. Taxpayer was owned by two brothers. The brothers and another individual later formed a second corporation (International). International encountered financial difficulties and transferred its assets to taxpayer in exchange for taxpayer's assumption of International's liabilities. Because taxpayer and International were under common control, the IRS sought to allocate income to taxpayer under Section 482 by reducing taxpayer's cost of goods sold. *Held:* For the IRS. Taxpayer paid an excessive price for International's assets. The reallocation was proper, and an addition to tax was sustained. Mornes, Inc., 696 F2d 1000 (8th Cir. 1982).

Taxpayer failed to prove that a Section 482 allocation was arbitrary. The lower court held that a reallocation of a portion of corporate income by the IRS to a related entity was improper under Section 482 as was a finding by the IRS that certain dividend income was constructively received by taxpayer parents even though distributed to their children. *Held:* Reversed. Taxpayers failed to show that the IRS' determination was arbitrary, nor did they specify what the terms and prices would have been in an arm's-length transaction. Engineering Sales Inc., 510 F2d 565, 75-1 USTC ¶ 9347, 35 AFTR2d 75-1122 (5th Cir. 1975).

Arm's-length standard upheld for Section 482 allocation. Taxpayer, pursuant to an agreement with its wholly owned foreign subsidiary, paid the latter commissions and discounts that were roughly twice as large as those allowed to uncontrolled foreign sales representatives. The Tax Court sustained the IRS' arm's-length bargaining standard in disallowing half of the allocation. Taxpayer, relying on International Can. Corp., 308 F2d 520 (1962), contended that under Section 482, the question was whether the income reported by taxpayer was a fair and reasonable return on its retained manufacturing activity. *Held:* Affirmed. Where the extent of the income is largely determined by the terms of business transactions entered into between two controlled corporations, it is not unreasonable to construe "true" taxable income as that which would have resulted if the transactions had been at arm's length between unrelated parties. International Canadian did not hold that the arm's-length standard was improper. It merely held that it was not "the sole criterion" for determining the true net income of each controlled taxpayer. Oil Base, Inc., 362 F2d 212, 66-2 USTC ¶ 9497, 17 AFTR2d 1280 (9th Cir. 1966), cert. denied, 385 US 928 (1966).

Deductions of related, dissimilar businesses can not be reallocated on ratio of gross income. Several stockholders of the taxpayer (a bank) were interested in entering the insurance business. Since state law prevented a bank from engaging in the insurance business, taxpayer's stockholders (except one) formed an insurance partnership, which conducted its business on taxpayer's premises and paid no rent. Taxpayer paid for the partnership's telephone, advertising, office supplies, and postage. The IRS contended that taxpayer was taxable on the income derived by the partnership from the insurance business, since taxpayer and the partnership were operated as one for all but tax purposes. In the alternative, the IRS contended that certain of taxpayer's expense deductions were the partnership's expenses and were not deductible by taxpayer, invoking Section 482, which authorizes the IRS to reallocate expenses between related taxpayers. The Tax Court found two separate entities despite the close relationship of the parties. However, it disallowed a portion of taxpayer's deductions based on a ratio of insurance gross income to total gross income. *Held:* Reversed. The appellate court found the Tax Court's method of allocation unreasonable. There was no finding that these deductions were substantially the same for both businesses: on the contrary, the evidence indicated a wide divergence in the operating expenses of both businesses and that some of the expenses were not common to both entities. The court reversed and remanded. Campbell County State Bank, Inc., 311 F2d 374, 63-1 USTC ¶ 9162, 11 AFTR2d 374 (8th Cir. 1963).

IRS allocation of income improper. The IRS allocated operating revenues and deductions among four commonly controlled bus companies under Section 482. The allocations were made on the basis of the corporations' respective operating revenues and the number of their buses in operation. One of the corporations, operating out of state, was financially involved with the other three only because it had paid standard charges for bus repairs. *Held:* For taxpayer. It was not necessary to include the out-of-state corporation in the allocation in order to clearly reflect the income of the four corporations. Futhermore, it was improper to allocate a bonus paid by the only profitable corporation, since the bonus was based on earnings. In any event, the fair and reasonable method for making the allocation was bus mileage, not the hybrid method employed by the IRS, since, in the motor transportation industry, the matter of bus mileage is of paramount importance and governs most matters of this kind. IRS allocation was further criticized for being based on operating revenues, not gross income, and for not being based on the identical taxable period for all the parties. As a result of denying the allocation, an unreasonable accumulations tax had to be recomputed. Oklahoma Transp. Co., 272 F. Supp. 729, 67-1 USTC ¶ 9467 (WD Okla. 1966).

***Cohan* rule applies to allocation of expenses between related taxpayers.** Taxpayer was a banking corporation. Its stockholders operated an insurance agency on taxpayer's premises as a partnership. Insurance was sold by taxpayer's employees and the insurance agency advertising was included in taxpayer's normal business advertising. The IRS compared taxpayer's income with that of the partnership and thereby arrived at a ratio that reallocated 12 to 14 percent of taxpayer's deductions to the agency. *Held:* For taxpayer. In holding the ratio unreasonable, the district court noted that space occupied, employee's time devoted to insurance, and the office sup-

Allocation Among Related Taxpayers: *Methods of Reallocation*

plies consumed must be allocated under the *Cohan* rule. Although no records were kept of the actual division of work and expenses, it was likely that the insurance activity required less capital than the bank. Bank of Kimball, 200 F. Supp. 638, 62-1 USTC ¶ 9228 (DSD 1962).

Crop-growing expenses allocated to corporate seller. Before transferring its farm to a controlled corporation in a tax-free exchange, taxpayer incurred all the expenses incident to growing the crops. The crops were then sold by the corporation. The IRS allocated the expenses to the corporation. *Held:* For the IRS. Under Section 482, this allocation was necessary to put the transaction on the same basis as it would have been if the parties had dealt at arm's length. Rooney, 189 F. Supp. 733, 61-1 USTC ¶ 9141 (ND Cal. 1960).

Section 482 interest allocation made on an individual subsidiary basis. Taxpayer was a holding company that lent money to its various subsidiaries. On audit, the IRS adjusted taxpayer's interest income pursuant to Section 482 with regard to those subsidiaries to which taxpayer charged less than 4 percent interest. The interest rate was adjusted to 5 percent in accordance with existing regulations, and a correlative adjustment was made to the returns of the involved subsidiaries. *Held:* For the IRS. The court rejected taxpayer's argument that total interest income from loan transactions with all subsidiaries as a whole should have been considered in determining an arm's-length rate. The IRS' individual loan approach was supported by Liberty Loan Corp., 498 F2d 225 (8th Cir. 1974). Aristar Inc., 553 F2d 644, 77-1 USTC ¶ 9361, 39 AFTR2d 77-1567 (Ct. Cl. 1977).

Allocation and computation of interest income between controlled corporations was proper. Taxpayer corporation and *D* Corporation were owned by the same individuals. During 1971 and 1972, the taxpayer loaned money interest-free to *D*. *D* paid the balance at the end of each fiscal year by borrowing from banks, then borrowing from taxpayer to pay the bank loans. The IRS computed interest on these advances at a 5 percent rate and allocated the income to the taxpayer. *Held:* For the IRS. The taxpayer and *D* were owned and controlled by the same interests within the meaning of Section 482. The interest period properly commenced upon inception of the indebtedness, and interest was properly computed with reference to the outstanding daily balance rather than the outstanding monthly balance. Collins Elec. Co., 67 TC 911 (1977).

Income allocated between related parties. Taxpayers were partners in a partnership and controlled a corporation. The partnership sold new equipment to the corporation at a discount. The IRS allocated income to the partnership in an amount equal to the difference between the profit the partnership would have made had it sold the equipment to the corporation for the list price and the profit actually realized and reported by the partnership in respect to the sales. *Held:* For taxpayers, as to IRS' method. Although the IRS was authorized under Section 482 to allocate income between related entities regardless of whether income was actually realized within the controlled group, the allocation was only authorized if it reflected an arm's-length price for the sales. The IRS acted arbitrarily and unreasonably in determining the arm's-length price. Here, the arm's-length was more accurately determined by the cost-plus method, since the equipment was not resold. Edwards, 67 TC 224 (1976).

Arm's-length price between unrelated companies upheld. Taxpayers, two brothers, owned the controlling interest in *D,* a Texas corporation. *D* purchased tile from *C*, a Mexican corporation (controlled by one of the brothers) for resale in the United States. The price paid for the tile was substantially higher than the customs value as determined by the U.S. Bureau of Customs. The IRS allocated income from the foreign company, *C*, to the domestic company, *D*, based upon an alleged non-arm's-length price between related entities, then imputed dividend income and a fraud penalty to the shareholders. *Held*: For taxpayers. *D* and *C* were not owned or controlled by the same interest within the meaning of Section 482. *D* paid an arm's-length price for the tile purchased from *C*; the deter-

Allocation Among Related Taxpayers: *Methods of Reallocation*

mination by the Customs Bureau was not binding in determining the validity of the price charged, since it was based on an incorrect assumption as to the quality of the tile purchased. Furthermore, no part of the payments made by *D* were dividend income to the taxpayers, and no fraud penalty was applicable. Brittingham, 66 TC 373 (1976).

Comparable prices used to determine income of related corporations. During the years in question, taxpayer paid a Virgin Islands and a Puerto Rican corporation excessive prices for terrazzo strip and rod. The corporations were controlled by the same interest as taxpayer. The IRS contended that taxpayer at all times owned the materials used in fabrication of the strip and rod; accordingly, the IRS reallocated income to taxpayer. *Held*: For taxpayer. The IRS' basic premise was erroneous and consequently the reallocations of income, unsupported by industry standards and practice, were arbitrary and unreasonable. Taxpayer showed that the procedures it followed were similar to unrelated situations. By use of the comparable uncontrolled price method as described in Regulation § 1.482-2(e)(2)(i), an arm's-length price for the sales in question could be determined. Accordingly, gross income was reallocated and determined. American Terrazzo Strip Co., 56 TC 961 (1971).

Evidence showing arm's-length price between parent and subsidiary overcomes allocation of income. The IRS made substantial allocations of the sales income of taxpayer's foreign subsidiary to taxpayer. In making these allocations, the IRS relied on the Treasury Department's Source Book of Statistics of Income for 1960 and 1961. At trial, the IRS announced a new position to the effect that the subsidiary was a combination export manager with a nominal net profit margin of 2 percent of sales. *Held*: For taxpayer. The original allocation of income based on the Source Book of Statistics of Income was arbitrary and unreasonable. There was no indication in the record to show that the operations of the unnamed corporations in the applicable asset category were in any way comparable to the operations of the subsidiary. Rather, the evidence emphasized a lack of comparability. Likewise, the position taken by the IRS at trial that the subsidiary was a combination export manager was erroneous. The functional disparity between the two was amply demonstrated by the record. It was further held that the existence of a long-standing, interest-free indebtedness from another subsidiary to taxpayer did not justify the allocation of a portion of the subsidiary's investment income. PPG Indus., 55 TC 928 (1971).

Income from franchises allocated to parent corporation as taxpayer generated income by conducting an integrated business enterprise through divisions set up as wholly owned subsidiaries. Taxpayer corporation owned a series of restaurants, which were set up and operated as subfranchises, and a series of commissaries, which were set up and operated as adjuncts to the restaurants. By virtue of taxpayer's ownership of the subsidiaries, and its subfranchise agreement, taxpayer had the power and authority to determine all policy matters with respect to the financial affairs and operations of the restaurants. Taxpayer also determined leasehold obligations, personnel practices and procedures, advertising, purchases, and sales of goods. Taxpayer's personnel would occasionally step in to perform particular restaurant functions. Taxpayer charged a fee based on a sliding scale percentage of gross sales for its services. The IRS allocated all of the gross income and deductions of taxpayer's subsidiaries to taxpayer under Section 482. *Held*: For the IRS. The allocation was not arbitrary, capricious, or unreasonable. The record sustained the IRS' determination that taxpayer generated income for the years in issue by conducting an integrated business enterprise through its divisions set up as wholly owned subsidiaries. Marc's Big Boy–Prospect, Inc., 52 TC 1073 (1969).

Reasonableness of income reallocation determined. Taxpayer corporation and a partnership supplying taxpayer with materials were both controlled by the same interests. Based on the supplier's large profit and taxpayer's smaller profit on a greater sales volume, the IRS reallocated income to taxpayer. *Held*: For the IRS, in part. Although some realloca-

ALLOCATION AMONG RELATED TAXPAYERS: *Related Taxpayers Defined*

tion of income was required, the IRS' real location based solely on profit margins was unreasonable. Different cost elements in sales items and the lack of comparability to other unrelated supplier-seller transactions led to a lesser reallocation of only $100,000 to taxpayer. Furthermore, an accumulated earnings tax was appropriate. There was a $5.5 million earned surplus account, a seven to one current ratio, and no specific, definite, or feasible plan to purchase new equipment. A proposed stock redemption was motivated by personal, not business, needs. Annual compensation of $14,000 to each of two shareholder employees who also ran their own private business was unreasonable to the extent of $9,000 for one and the entire $14,000 for the other shareholder. Finally, cars used for business and depreciation deductions were allowed, while club dues and certain entertainment expenses, not substantiated, were not deductible. Cadillac Textiles Inc., 34 TCM 295, ¶ 75,046 P-H Memo. TC (1975).

Advance charter hire payment from domestic corporation to its foreign subsidiary produces interest allocation under Section 482. *P*, a domestic corporation, and *S*, its wholly owned foreign subsidiary, entered into an agreement to have ships constructed by a foreign shipyard. The ships would be owned by *S* and chartered from *S* by *P*. An agreement was negotiated with authorities in *S*'s country of incorporation whereby *P* would make advance charter payments to *S* to defray construction costs. The advances would not be treated as a loan, and no interest would be charged. The IRS ruled that under Section 482, interest could be allocated to reflect the arm's-length rate for use of the advance. Further, *P* could not defer the interest income, since it was under no U.S. or foreign legal disability preventing it from receiving the interest. Rev. Rul. 76-243, 1976-1 CB 134.

Bargain sales price to sister corporation is increased under Section 482. Property was sold for less than its arm's-length price to a sister corporation. It was determined that one of the principal purposes of the transaction was the avoidance of federal income tax. The income of the brother corporation was to be increased under Section 482 to reflect the arm's-length price of the property sold. However, the provisions of Rev. Proc. 65-17 would not be applicable because one of the principal purposes of the transaction was the avoidance of federal income tax. Rev. Rul. 69-630, 1969-2 CB 112.

Related Taxpayers Defined

Customs duty value of merchandise did not control value for Section 482 purposes. IRS adjusted the income of taxpayer and another corporation under Section 482. The two corporations involved were taxpayer (owned principally by two brothers and their relatives) and a Mexican corporation (owned by one of the brothers and his mother, who held no interest in taxpayer). The Section 482 claim concerned the pricing of tile sold by the Mexican corporation to taxpayer. In determining the value of the tile, the district court relied on the value for customs duty purposes. *Held*: For taxpayer. First, the district court relied on the value for customs purposes in the face of clear evidence of a higher value; this was erroneous. Intangible benefits under the sales contract (e.g., first call on production) that were not considered in the customs value of the tile could be considered for income tax purposes. Further, application of Section 482 was questionable, since there was insufficient evidence of common control and advantage. In particular, the brother with the greater, and thus controlling, interest in taxpayer had no interest in the Mexican corporation. Accordingly, overpaying for tile would have been detrimental to his personal interests. Dallas Ceramic Co., 598 F2d 1382, 79-2 USTC ¶ 9500, 44 AFTR2d 79-5367 (5th Cir. 1979).

Income allocated from controlled garage corporations to related apartment corporations. The IRS allocated to apartment corporations all of the income and expenses of controlled garage corporations organized to serve the tenants and to operate garages located in the basements of apartment houses. The evidence presented indicated that although some corporate formalities were maintained, employees of the garages performed services for the apartments, executive control was centralized, no lease or other agreement regarding occupancy or control of the garage premises existed, and garage rentals were received by the apartment corporations and classified by the garages as receivables. *Held:* For the IRS. There was no arm's-length relationship between the corporations, nor was there a business reason for having separate garage entities. The IRS acted within its powers under Section 482 in allocating income and expenses to the apartment corporations, since the purpose of the arrangement was primarily to obtain tax savings through the splitting of income. Shaker Apartments Inc., 66-2 USTC ¶ 9538 (ND Ohio 1966).

Two corporations found related for purposes of Section 482 despite lack of common control. A management company was formed to operate taxpayer's electrical contracting business. Taxpayer's sole stockholder owned 40 percent of the stock, her two daughters owned 10 percent, and her former manager owned 50 percent. The management company adopted a qualified pension plan for its two principal stockholders, its only employees. The IRS had previously found that a pension plan adopted by taxpayer was unqualified because it discriminated against lower paid employees. The IRS determined that the management fee paid by taxpayer was excessive, and reallocated income and expenses under Section 482. *Held:* For the IRS. Although the two corporations were not commonly controlled, there was a common design to shift income under Brittingham, 66 TC 373 (1976), aff'd, 598 F2d 1375 (5th Cir. 1979). Taxpayer's sole stockholder benefited from the additional corporate surtax exemption and from her participation in a deferred compensation plan. Garbini Elec., Inc., 43 TCM 919, ¶ 82,159 P-H Memo. TC (1982).

Sham Transactions

IRS cannot allocate income to taxpayer where personal service corporation was a viable and taxable entity, and not a sham. Taxpayer, who had worked for several years as a manufacturers' sales representative, formed a personal service corporation. Taxpayer owned 98 percent of the stock, and worked exclusively for his corporation. The corporation received some commissions at formation from work the taxpayer had performed prior to incorporation. The corporation paid the taxpayer a salary for his work. The Tax Court determined that the corporation was a viable, taxable entity and not a mere sham, but disregarded its findings. It concluded that control over 98 percent of the commission income remained with the taxpayer, and thus such income was taxable to him and not the corporation. The Seventh Circuit found that receipt of the commissions through the taxpayer's personal service corporation did not violate Section 61 assignment of income rules. It also found that tax avoidance was not the sole purpose of incorporation, and that the corporation was not a sham. On remand, the Tax Court found that income received by the taxpayer's personal service corporation could be allocated to the taxpayer under Section 482. *Held:* Reversed and remanded on other points. Because taxpayer worked exclusively for the corporation, and because there was no shifting of income, Section 482 could not be applied to allocate income received by the corporation to taxpayer. Foglesong, 691 F2d 848, 82-2 USTC ¶ 9650, 50 AFTR2d 82-6026 (7th Cir. 1982).

IRS' reallocation of income upheld. The IRS reallocated income from two corporations, engaged in the production of rental income and the furnishing of entertainment services, to the three individuals who formed the corporations. The district court upheld the IRS. *Held:* Affirmed. The appellate court found that the corporations were not engaged in a valid business or commercial activity, but were a mere tax saving device. McGuire, 71-1 USTC ¶ 9304 (2d Cir. 1971).

IRS successfully applies Sections 482 and 269 to disallow losses and reallocate income between entertainer and his poultry business. Taxpayer owned all of the stock of a corporation which both owned and operated a poultry business. The corporation also offered the taxpayer's services as an entertainer. The corporation earned income from taxpayer's performances far in excess of the $50,000 it paid

Allocation Among Related Taxpayers: *Sham Transactions*

him annually for such services. The corporation offset this excess income with the substantial losses it realized in the poultry business. The corporation did nothing to promote or aid taxpayer in the entertainment business. Further, contracts with the corporation for taxpayer's services required the taxpayer's guarantees. The IRS reallocated to the taxpayer, under Section 482, amounts earned by the corporation as entertainment income and, under Section 269, disallowed the corporation's losses in excess of the Section 270 $50,000 loss limitation on individuals. *Held:* For the IRS. Taxpayer controlled two businesses: a poultry business and an entertainment business. Contrary to taxpayer's claims, an individual can be a business separate from his corporation. Under Section 482, the IRS is empowered to allocate income and deductions from one of these businesses to the other to clearly reflect income. Accordingly, allocation of a major portion of the corporation's entertainment income to the taxpayer was, under the facts, appropriate. Evidence shows that the taxpayer organized the corporation as a means of claiming losses in excess of the Section 270 limit. Accordingly, the IRS correctly applied Section 269. Borge, 405 F2d 673, 69-1 USTC ¶ 9131, 23 AFTR2d 69-320 (2d Cir.), cert. denied, 395 US 933 (1968).

IRS reallocates income shifted between related corporations. Two corporations were commonly owned and controlled. One of the corporations incurred net operating losses. To enable it to take advantage of such losses, it leased profitable theatres from the other corporation and offset its losses against the income earned under the theatre leases. The IRS reallocated the income back to the profitable corporation, and the Tax Court upheld the reallocation. *Held:* Affirmed. The purpose of Section 482 is to prevent the avoidance of tax or the distortion of income by shifting profits from one business to another. Section 482 enables the IRS to arrive at the true net income of each controlled taxpayer. Spicer Theatre, Inc., 346 F2d 704, 65-2 USTC ¶ 9468, 15 AFTR2d 1172 (6th Cir. 1965).

Partnership that leased rental property from controlled corporations was no sham; Section 482 allocation denied. From 1919 through 1955, a group of real estate corporations with extensive holdings had leased their properties to a management partnership composed of two brothers. When one of the brothers died, a new partnership was formed by the families of both brothers to continue the operation. New leases were then executed. Twelve of the partners were also stockholders of the corporations, and no capital was contributed to the new partnership. The partnership's profits were substantial, while the profits of the corporations were nominal. *Held:* For taxpayer. The court, in rejecting the IRS' dual contentions that the partnership was a sham and that the income should be reallocated, found that a legitimate business purpose existed (centralized management) and that valuable services were performed for the corporations. It accordingly held that the partnership was no sham. Common control or the fact that the corporation could have done their own management are not reasons for the application of Section 482. Interior Sec. Corp., 38 TC 330 (1962), acq. 1962-2 CB 4.

Earnings "shifted" to affiliated loss corporation are reallocated. Taxpayer entered into a contract with a dormant loss corporation, *X*, whereby the latter agreed to act as the taxpayer's packer in connection with taxpayer's carrot packing and marketing business. All the working capital, labor, and equipment required for the packing operation were supplied to *X* Corporation by taxpayer. The IRS allocated to taxpayer all of *X*'s gross income and deductions except the deduction for its net operating loss carry-over. *Held:* For the IRS. The substance of the entire transaction was to shift income, which in fact had been earned by taxpayer, to *X* so that it could be offset by *X*'s net operating loss carry-over. The IRS was therefore correct in allocating to the taxpayer, under Section 482, the earnings shifted to the corporation. Pacific Northwest Food Club, Inc., 23 TCM 29, ¶ 64,008 P-H Memo. TC (1964).

Partnership income not attributable to related corporation. Taxpayer corporation was formed in 1950, and since its inception it operated as a plumbing and heating contractor. In 1953, taxpayer's two stockholders formed a separate partnership to engage wholly in the selling of heating and plumbing supplies. The partnership had its own capital furnished by the partners, carried on a bona fide business operation, and kept its own separate books and accounts. The IRS, under Section 482, took the income of the partnership and added it to the income of taxpayer. *Held:* For taxpayer. There was no justification for the IRS' holding that the partnership was a fiction or a sham. A taxpayer is held free to choose the type of organization or form in which he will cast his business activities. Union Plumbing & Heating, Inc., 21 TCM 281, ¶ 62,050 P-H Memo. TC (1962).

AMORTIZATION

(*See* Depreciation and Amortization)

ANTICIPATORY ASSIGNMENT OF INCOME

(*See* Assignment of Income)

ASSESSMENT AND COLLECTION

(*See also* Procedure)

In General	82
Liens and Priorities	82
Transferee Liability	82
Withholding Requirements	84

In General

IRS rules on interest due where corporation, facing net operating loss, extends period for paying taxes. Based on a detailed factual situation, the IRS has held that when a corporation elects to pay its taxes in installments under Section 6152 and also extends the period for payment because of an expected net operating loss under Section 6164, interest runs on the amount deferred under Section 6164 from the original due date only on that amount not deferred under Section 6152. Interest runs from the due date of the second installment on the remaining portion of the amount subject to the Section 6164 election. Rev. Rul. 82-48, 1982-1 CB 211.

Liens and Priorities

IRS does not have to assert tax liens against a corporation before imposing Section 6672 penalty. The IRS imposed the Section 6672 penalty against an executive whose corporation paid "net wages" but no payroll taxes. *Held:* For the IRS. The penalty can be imposed even if, as the corporate executive proposed, the IRS did not assert tax liens to protect its interests, and did not seek first to collect the taxes in bankruptcy court. Kraus, 85-1 USTC ¶ 9310, 55 AFTR2d 85-116 (EDNY 1985).

Transferee Liability

No third-party liability for employment taxes without proper notice. The IRS imposed third-party liability for employment taxes on a bank for paying the employees of a borrower's employees when the borrower failed to pay payroll taxes. The bank claimed that the IRS failed to give notice of its assessments for unpaid payroll taxes against the borrower. *Held:* For taxpayer. Section 6203 required the IRS to notify the bank of the assessments; failure to give the notice prevents the IRS from using Section 3505 to impose liability on the bank. Merchants' Nat'l Bank of Mobile, 84-2 USTC ¶ 9674, 54 AFTR2d 84-5752 (SD Ala. 1984).

Liquidation of a subsidiary does not result in a double tax to stockholders of parent. Parent corporation was formed in 1953 as a holding company for a wholly owned subsidiary that was actively engaged as a water supplier. On July 15, 1957, the subsidiary adopted a plan of complete liquidation and made a bulk sale of all its operating assets within the following 12-month period; the parent company was also liquidated within the same 12-month period. The IRS contended that taxpayer shareholders of parent were taxable on the subsidiary's sale proceeds that they received from parent. Furthermore, the IRS held that since the subsidiary was not liquidated within two years after acquisition, such subsidiary by virtue of Sections 332 and 337(c)(2) was taxable for gains it realized on liquidation. Taxpayers, as transferees, were therefore liable for the same tax a second time. *Held:* For taxpayer. Substance governs over form. Since the parent was only a holding company, it was disregarded as a separate taxable entity so that taxpayers were only taxable on the proceeds distributed to them from the sale and were not liable a second time as transferees. Manilow, 315 F. Supp. 28, 70-2 USTC ¶ 9564 (ND Ill. 1970).

Transferee-stockholders liable for unpaid corporate income taxes when reserves used to discharge local liens. Taxpayers were transferees of the assets of a corporation that was liquidated under Section 333. At the time of liquidation, corporation had set aside a reserve to meet tax liabilities, but was later required to use the reserve to pay local liens for special assessments. The IRS assessed deficiencies against taxpayers, contending that under the trust fund theory, they were liable to the full value of the assets received. Taxpayers contended that at time of dissolution, the corporation was not insolvent. *Held:* For the IRS. Sufficient evidence established that the corporation was rendered insolvent by the liquidation; hence, taxpayers were liable as transferees. The fact that there was no notation on books indicating liability for local assessments was illusory. The crucial fact was that when the taxes became due, the corporation had insufficient funds to pay them, the result of failure to set aside sufficient reserve. Drew, 367 F2d 828, 66-2 USTC ¶ 9739 (Ct. Cl. 1966).

Cancellation of stockholder's debt yields transferee liability. Taxpayer's wholly owned corporation paid him a dividend in 1972 by cancelling his debt. The corporation was insolvent at the time of the cancellation and the dividend violated state law. The corporation's assets were insufficient to pay its tax deficiencies and the IRS imposed transferee liability for these deficiencies on the taxpayer. The taxpayer claimed that the dividend was not a transfer of property but a book entry, and accordingly, he was not liable as a transferee. *Held:* For the IRS. The book entry canceling the debt constituted a real reduction in the corporation's assets as well as an increase in the taxpayer's assets. Notwithstanding the fact that the taxpayer had reported the dividend as income on his 1972 income tax return, he remained liable for the corporation's unpaid tax liability. Segura, 77 TC 734 (1981).

Recoupment of taxes paid on corporate distributions denied to transferees. Opinion filed September 25, 1969. The Tax Court held that taxpayers were liable for corporate taxes as transferees of assets. Taxpayers claimed in the instant case that they were entitled to a recoupment of taxes paid on corporate distributions due to the fact that they were liable as transferees. *Held:* For the IRS. When a taxpayer has received an amount from a corporation under a claim of right and paid a tax on the receipt, he is not entitled to recover the tax paid under a doctrine of equitable recoupment when it is later determined that he is liable as transferee for the tax of the corporation making the distribution to him. It was further held that since no taxpayer had received transferred assets equal to the corporate tax liability, the rate and starting date of interest on the transfers was to be determined under state law. Accordingly, interest commenced on the date of the deficiency notice because interest was allowable only on liquidated claims under state law. Maynard Hosp., Inc., 54 TC 1675 (1970).

Post-dissolution recovery held not taxable to corporation. Taxpayers (husband and wife) were the sole stockholders of *X* Corporation, which for many years had operated a motion picture theatre. The corporation was dissolved in 1949, and all its assets were distributed to taxpayers. In 1953, a suit was instituted by *X* against Loew's, Inc. and other film distributors for alleged violation of antitrust laws, loss of profits, and damages incurred by the corporation, for the years 1932 through 1948. The case was settled in 1956, and taxpayers received a net settlement of $32,000.

Assessment and Collection: Withholding Requirements

Taxpayers treated this as long-term capital gain taxable to them; the IRS asserted that the award was taxable to X Corporation and that taxpayers were liable as transferees. The IRS case was based on a state statute under which a corporation's existence is deemed to continue for the purpose of winding up its affairs. *Held:* For taxpayer. The Tax Court found that this provision would only be of help to the IRS if the claim against Loew's were retained by X Corporation. However, the parties stipulated that *all* assets had been distributed. There were no unpaid liabilities and no affairs to wind up, and the evidence indicated that X was "dead" after 1949. The fact that the suit was brought in X's name and the taxpayers' names as "trustees in dissolution" was merely a matter of form. Poro, 39 TC 641 (1963), acq. 1963-2 CB 5.

Transferee liable for transferor corporation's tax. Taxpayer and his wife each owned 50 percent of a corporation engaged in the sale of boats. Pursuant to a divorce, the corporation was sold and all the proceeds distributed to the wife in exchange for claims for alimony or support. The corporation had understated its income, and the IRS asserted liability against the husband as a transferee of the corporate assets. *Held:* For the IRS. Although the wife received all the proceeds from the sale, taxpayer was relieved of his indebtedness to her in exchange for assigning her his 50 percent interest in the sale proceeds. Accordingly, taxpayer was liable as a transferee under Section 6901 for the entire tax of the transferor corporation. Cockey, 46 TCM 1564, ¶ 85,609 P-H Memo. TC (1983).

Transferee of assets liable for corporation's underpayment. A close corporation transferred its assets without consideration to its majority shareholder; it was thus unable to pay its federal tax liabilities. The IRS assessed deficiencies and fraud penalties against the shareholder as transferee. *Held:* For the IRS. Under local law, the transfers constituted a fraud on the government which was a creditor of the corporation. Estate of Taylor, 41 TCM 44, ¶ 80,426 P-H Memo. TC (1980).

Corporation could not offset excess of operating expenses over ordinary income against capital gain. Taxpayer was the surviving corporation in a merger. After Y Corporation transferred all of its assets to taxpayer without consideration, it ceased to exist. In its fiscal year immediately preceding the merger, Y's operating expenses exceeded its ordinary income. On its return, Y sought to offset the excess of expenses against its capital gain in computing the Section 1201(a) alternative tax. The IRS assessed a deficiency against taxpayer as transferee of Y's assets. *Held:* For the IRS. Taxpayer was liable for Y's tax deficiency as a transferee under Section 6901. Section 1201(a) does not permit the offset of excess operating expenses against capital gain. These expenses were deductible, if at all, as a net operating loss carry-over to prior or subsequent years. KDI Navcor, Inc., 35 TCM 341, ¶ 76,077 P-H Memo. TC (1976).

Withholding Requirements

Chairman of the board not a responsible person for purposes of payroll withholding taxes. Taxpayer, a practicing attorney, served as chairman of the board of a publicly held corporation. He had no authority to sign checks, and did not participate in day to day operations. Additionally, he did not own a significant fraction of the corporation's stock. The IRS assessed the 100 percent penalty for failure to pay withholding tax against him as a responsible person. The Claims Court concurred. *Held:* Reversed. Taxpayer was not a responsible person, since there was no evidence he had control over such functions, nor did he willfully fail to pay over taxes. Godfrey, Jr., 748 F2d 1568, 84-2 USTC ¶ 9974, 55 AFTR2d 85-409 (Fed. Cir. 1984).

Taxpayer fails to disprove liability under Section 6672. Taxpayer, who admitted that he was a "responsible person," denied that he was liable for the Section 6672 penalty. *Held:* For the IRS. Taxpayer failed to refute with specific evidence, the evidence that he had willfully failed to pay over the corporation's taxes. Braswell, 85-2 USTC ¶ 9685, 56 AFTR2d 85-6218 (SD Ala. 1985).

Treasurer obligated to pay over payroll taxes even if he faced being fired. Taxpayer, treasurer of a corporation, argued that he should not be liable for the Section 6672 penalty because he would have been fired if he had paid overdue payroll taxes. *Held:* For the IRS. Taxpayer's desire to keep his job did not excuse his informed decision to not use available corporate funds to pay the taxes. Freeman, 603 F. Supp. 272, 85-1 USTC ¶ 9255, 55 AFTR2d 85-982 (D. Ariz. 1985).

Board of directors' order did not excuse president from Section 6672 liability. Taxpayer, a corporate president, was assessed the Section 6672 penalty for not paying over employment taxes of his corporation. *Held:* For the IRS, in part. An order from the board of directors to pay other debts before the taxes does not excuse taxpayer from responsibility. Taxpayer, however, is not responsible for taxes not withheld during a period after he resigned his corporate office. Carr, 85-2 USTC ¶ 9542, 56 AFTR2d 85-5723 (ND Ill. 1985).

No right to contribution among Section 6672 penalty recipients. Taxpayers, officers of a corporation that did not pay over employment taxes, were assessed Section 6672 penalties. They sought contributions from other taxpayers who were also assessed the penalty. The other taxpayers argued that there was no right to contribution. *Held:* There is no right to contribution among taxpayers who are subject to Section 6672 penalties. This right would damage the penal nature of the penalty. Rebelle III, 85-2 USTC ¶ 9493 (MD La. 1985).

Agent for major stockholder of corporation liable under Section 6672. Taxpayer ran a corporation under a power of attorney granted by its major shareholder, who was hospitalized. After the corporation failed to pay withholding taxes and became bankrupt, the IRS imposed the Section 6672 penalty against taxpayer. *Held:* For the IRS. Taxpayer's status as agent of the owner does not preclude "responsible person" status. Taxpayer had enough control over the corporation's financial affairs to make him responsible for the unpaid taxes. Blais, 85-2 USTC ¶ 9684 (D. Mass. 1985).

IRS need not give notice to lender in collecting payroll taxes of borrower. The IRS claimed taxpayer was liable for unpaid payroll taxes because it loaned funds to an employer for the specific purpose of paying wages, with actual notice or knowledge that the employer did not intend or would not be able to make timely payment of its employees' withholding taxes. Taxpayer claimed it was not liable because it did not receive timely notice of assessment of the withholding taxes against the employer. *Held:* For the IRS. A lender's liability is not dependent on receipt of notice. National Acceptance Co., 603 F. Supp. 1351, 85-1 USTC ¶ 9362, 55 AFTR2d 85-1408 (ED Mich. 1985).

Taxpayer defeats "responsible person" charge. The IRS assessed the Section 6672 penalty against the secretary/treasurer of a corporation. *Held:* For taxpayer. The president, not the secretary/treasurer, handled all corporate finances. Because the secretary/treasurer had very limited power over finances, he was not responsible for making payments. Abramson, 85-1 USTC ¶ 9380, 55 AFTR2d 85-1479 (EDNY 1985).

Taxpayer may be liable under Section 6672 even if IRS drops other methods of collecting payroll taxes. Taxpayers were employees of a corporation that failed to pay payroll taxes. Taxpayer stated that one of its customers owed it money that could be used to pay the taxes. The IRS asserted a claim against that customer, but later dropped the claim. Taxpayers argued that the IRS could not then assert Section 6672 penalties against them personally. *Held:* For the IRS. The method chosen by the IRS to collect payroll taxes is irrelevant to the issue of Section 6672 liability, unless there is an abuse of discretion by the IRS. There was none in this case. Young, 609 F. Supp. 512, 85-1 USTC ¶ 9247, 55 AFTR2d 85-1056 (ND Tex. 1985).

Taxpayer is responsible person for withholding taxes. Taxpayer was president, director, and stockholder of a corporation that failed to pay over withholding taxes. He admitted his duty to withhold and file quarterly tax returns, but claimed he should be absolved because he had also relied on the treasurer of the corporation. *Held:* For the IRS. Taxpayer admitted he was a responsible person. The failure was willful since he preferred other creditors to the IRS. Grant, 85-1 USTC ¶ 9385, 56 AFTR2d 85-5414 (D. Vt. 1985).

Taxpayer liable for failure to pay over withholding taxes for only one quarter. Taxpayer was a stock-holder, director, and arguably secretary/treasurer of the corporation at issue. The IRS assessed the 100 percent penalty for failure to pay over withholding taxes. *Held:* For taxpayer, in part. He was not a signatory to any bank account or tax documents. His "control" of the financial affairs differed from time to time. In the first two of the three quarters in issue, he was not a responsible person, but in the fourth quarter he was. Chartrand, 84-2 USTC ¶ 10,013, 55 AFTR2d 85-777 (ND Cal. 1984).

Willfulness not negated by reliance on attorney. Taxpayer, president of a corporation, was charged with the 100 percent penalty for failure to pay over withholding taxes. Taxpayer argued that the failure to pay was not willful because a bankruptcy attorney had advised him that the withholding taxes would not have to be paid if a petition of bankruptcy were filed. *Held:* For the IRS. The clear weight of authority is that willfulness is not negated because the action was taken in good faith and with reasonable cause. Alioto, 593 F. Supp. 1402, 84-2 USTC ¶ 9736, 54 AFTR2d 84-5753 (ND Cal. 1984).

Officers of youth-hiring organization liable for unpaid payroll taxes. Taxpayers, officers of an organization that hired minority youth, received funding from several agencies. The budget it submitted to the agencies sought only enough funds to pay the net payroll of the hired youth, not the payroll taxes. The IRS imposed the Section 6672 penalty against them. *Held:* For the IRS. The taxpayers' failure to request enough funds for payroll taxes, while reporting to the IRS that the taxes were withheld, was a willful act. Taxpayers could have paid the taxes with other funds. Latimer, 593 F. Supp. 881, 84-2 USTC ¶ 9769, 54 AFTR2d 84-5933 (ND Ill. 1984).

Taxpayer was "responsible person" despite only 20 percent ownership of business. Taxpayer, who was vice-president and 20 percent owner of a failed corporation, was ruled liable by the IRS for the Section 6672 penalty. *Held:* For the IRS. Taxpayer had equal control with the president over decisions on which creditors to pay, knew of the unpaid payroll taxes, but took no action to pay them while paying other expenses. Millson, 84-2 USTC ¶ 9741 (NDNY 1984).

Finance director and treasurer a responsible person for paying over withholding taxes. Taxpayer was a corporation's treasurer and finance director. The IRS claimed he was a responsible person who willfully failed to cause payment to the IRS of withheld payroll taxes. *Held:* For the IRS. Taxpayer was apprised of the corporation's financial condition. He had the power to cause payment, and at certain times actually prevented payment to the IRS. He acted willfully by preferring other creditors to the IRS. Edmiston, 84-2 USTC ¶ 9578, 54 AFTR2d 84-5574 (MD Tenn. 1984), aff'd (6th Cir. 1985).

Three executives liable for company's payroll taxes. After a faltering restaurant corporation failed to pay its payroll taxes, the IRS imposed liabity under Section 6672 against its president and two taxpayers, each of whom functioned as treasurer at different times. *Held:* For the IRS. All were involved in decisions to pay food suppliers and other creditors instead of the IRS when cash flow became tight. Ronholt, 84-2 USTC ¶ 9678, 54 AFTR2d 84-5884 (WD Wash. 1984).

President not excused from Section 6672 penalty by reliance on company's sole stockholder. Taxpayer, president of a failed corporation, argued that he was not responsible for the company's unpaid withholding taxes under Section 6672 because he was relying for tax payment on the company's controlling shareholder, who sent bad checks to the IRS for the taxes. *Held:* For the IRS. Taxpayer signed other corporate checks and had control over the company's finances, so he was a "responsible person." He could have demanded proper payment of the taxes or else resigned. Lucas, 84-2 USTC ¶ 9818, 54 AFTR2d 84-6289 (Bankr. D. Conn. 1984).

Secretary of corporation not liable for withholding taxes. The IRS maintained that the taxpayer, the corporation's secretary, was liable for its unpaid withholding taxes. Taxpayer had ended day-to-day involvement in the business by the time of the failure to withhold the taxes. *Held:* For taxpayer. A corporation's officer is not always a responsible person. His lack of involvement in the business at the time of the withholding precluded the element of willfullness. Potozky, 85-1 USTC ¶ 9438 (Cl. Ct. 1985).

Volunteer trustee may be held liable under Section 6672. The IRS ruled that a volunteer member of a board of trustees of a Section 501(a) charitable organization may be found to be responsible for collecting and paying over employment and withholding taxes, and be held liable for the 100% penalty under Section 6672. The fact that the trustee is a voluntary member of the board of trustees is not determinative of his liability. Rather, the voluntary trustee's liability depends upon whether he is found to be a responsible person who willfully failed to pay over withholding taxes. Rev. Rul. 84-83, 1984-1 CB 264.

ASSIGNMENT OF INCOME

(*See also* Capital Gains and Losses)

Stockholder received ordinary income to the extent that interest on loan was supposedly forgiven. D Corporation, owned by taxpayer and his son, entered into an agreement with a purchaser calling for the sale of D's major assets, which would be followed immediately by liquidation. Thereafter, D sold its assets for $700,000 and paid taxpayer $400,000 due on outstanding debentures. D further paid taxpayer $170,000 in payment of an open account. Taxpayer forgave $38,875 in accrued interest that D owed him, and D liquidated by paying $65,000 to both taxpayer and his son. The Tax Court held for taxpayer, stating that the $38,875 in forgiven accrued interest was not ordinary income to taxpayer. *Held*: Reversed. Taxpayer exercised significant control over the disposition of the proceeds and in fact received the proceeds under an assignment of income theory. Dwyer, 622 F2d 460, 80-2 USTC ¶ 9545, 46 AFTR2d 80-5471 (9th Cir. 1980).

Transfer of liquidating corporation's stock resulted in anticipatory assignment of income. Taxpayer corporation transferred to its majority stockholder, in redemption of its stock, shares in another corporation that had adopted a plan of liquidation. Although the transfer was made before the first liquidating distribution, the IRS held that taxpayer's transfer of the corporate stock constituted an anticipatory assignment of the liquidating proceeds and consequently taxed the resultant capital gain to taxpayer. The lower court upheld the IRS. *Held:* Affirmed. There existed only a remote and hypothetical possibility that the liquidation would be abandoned, so that at the time of transfer the liquidation plan was practically certain to be completed. This result was not changed by the fact that the transfer had been made to facilitate the payment of inheritance taxes. Dayton Hydraulic Co., 592 F2d 937, 79-1 USTC ¶ 9213, 43 AFTR2d 79-649 (6th Cir.), cert. denied, 444 US 831 (1979).

Dissolving corporate collection agency deemed not taxable on unearned fees. Taxpayer was a collection agency entitled to a fee for its services only on collection of the delinquent account assigned to it. It dissolved and transferred in liquidation some $5 million in accounts receivable it held as agent of the various creditors. The transferee valued the possibility of its earning fees by collecting these accounts at $300,000 and paid capital gain tax on the liquidation based on that value. The IRS asserted that taxpayer had income in the amount of this $300,000 in the year of dissolution. *Held:* For taxpayer. The Tax Court held that taxpayer could have no income from these accounts because no right to a commission arose until collection. Furthermore, the anticipatory assignment of income theory was not applicable here; although taxpayer had made some attempts to collect these accounts, income did not arise until collection was made. United Mercantile Agencies, 34 TC 808 (1960).

Court upheld IRS assertion of assignment of income doctrine to tax assignors on income paid to assignees. X owned all of taxpayer's and Management Corporation's stock. X assigned $75,000 from a third party for investment advice rendered and to be rendered. The assignment was made in exchange for real estate shared by taxpayer. Under the assignment, taxpayer was committed to lend this amount to X if, as, and when received. Notwithstanding the assignment, X received almost all of the $75,000 directly from the third party. Additionally, taxpayer assigned its right to receive payment under an agreement (which assigned a real estate purchase contract to the third party) to Management Corporation. The IRS, under the assignment of income doctrine, asserted that the assignments involved were ineffective in transferring the incidence of taxation. *Held:* For the IRS. Amounts paid were taxable to the assignors. Realty Settlement Corp., 40 TCM 569, ¶ 80,282 P-H Memo. TC (1980).

ASSOCIATIONS TAXABLE AS CORPORATIONS

In General	88
Post-Dissolution Activities	88
Professional Associations	90
Trusts and Trustees	90

In General

Oil development group taxable as a corporation. A number of investors in oil leases on nearby land agreed with three organizers to develop the properties as a unit. Each investor gave the organizers a power of attorney to arrange for the development of the property, to enter into operating agreements, and so forth. These powers of attorney were revocable on 10-days' notice. The district court held, considering the revocability of the power, that the group did not have the degree of centralized management necessary to classify it as a corporation for tax purposes. *Held:* Reversed. The court looked to the practical effect of the organization and found that it achieved substantially the operating advantages of a corporation. Stierwalt, 287 F2d 855, 61-1 USTC ¶ 9330 (10th Cir. 1961).

Title holding corporation not taxable. X Corporation was organized to hold title to property being purchased by the stockholders as beneficial owners. This apparently was a common practice in Florida. The land was subdivided and sold in several transactions over a period of years. The IRS imposed the corporate income tax, for which the stockholders sought a refund. *Held:* For taxpayer. The court found that the corporation served no purpose other than holding naked title. It was not considered a corporation for tax purposes and the real ownership was considered to be that of the stockholders. Refund of the corporate income tax paid was allowed. Miles, 61-2 USTC ¶ 9521 (SD Fla. 1961).

No liquidation of association solely by operation of amended regulations. Where an organization that was formerly considered an association taxable as a corporation loses this status under Regulation § 301.7701 (effective for years beginning after 1960), it is deemed to have been liquidated if there was no *voluntary* action taken by its members to restore its status as a partnership. The new regulations have added new criteria for determining whether an association may be taxed as a corporation. Any association which, as a result of these amendments, *involuntarily* loses its classification as a corporation will not be subject to the liquidation provisions of Section 331. Rev. Rul. 63-107, 1963-1 CB 71.

Post-Dissolution Activities

Corporation that retained assets remained in existence for federal tax purposes even though its existence terminated under state law. Taxpayer and two others were stockholders of T, a New Jersey corporation, which filed its fiscal income tax return for the fiscal year ending September 30, 1960. The minutes of a special meeting of its board of directors, dated September 19, 1960, contained a resolution that the corporation be dissolved, and a state certificate of dissolution was issued in December 1960. The corporation's assets were to be distributed to the stockholders, subject to the payment of one claim by RCA. The corporation issued promissory notes to RCA, payable starting in April 1962, to pay off this claim. Due to federal antitrust action, a claim against RCA ripened. This claim by the corporation was in the hands of attorneys after September 30, 1960, and the matter was settled in June 1961, at which time the notes previously issued to RCA were cancelled in exchange for a release of the corporation's claim against RCA. The corporation paid for legal services in connection with this settlement in November 1961. As of September 30, 1960, $100,000 of corporate funds were invested in a note of another corporation, M. Payments representing interest on the note were received by the corporation in each month from October 1960 through July 1961. This interest was deposited in a corporate bank account that was maintained until November 1961. The corporation retained title to M notes until July 1961, at which time they were cancelled and new notes were issued to the stockholders. Because they complied with state law, gave the IRS notice of the dissolution, closed the corporation's accounts and distributed its assets, taxpayers claimed that the corporation was not required to file returns for periods subsequent to September 30, 1960. The IRS claimed that the corporation did indeed retain assets, namely the notes and RCA claim, and that it was therefore taxable on interest on the notes as well as on the proceeds of the settlement of the claim. Relying on Regulation § 1.6012-2(a)(2), the Tax Court held the corporation liable. *Held:* Affirmed. Where a corporation retains assets, it continues to be taxable for federal tax purposes even though it is in the process of liquidation and has terminated its legal existence under state law. The corporation had and claimed assets, it made efforts to realize on its claim; it had certain debts; and it regularly distributed money to attorney-creditors as well as to stockholders. T retained $12,000 of assets, exclusive of the notes and claim and kept a bank account until November 1961 and made deposits through that period. The corporation also retained its RCA claim and never assigned it. It, not the stockholders, retained the attorneys to prosecute the claim. Messer, 438 F2d 774, 71-1 USTC ¶ 9214, 27 AFTR2d 71-621 (3d Cir. 1971).

Post-dissolution activities give rise to corporate tax liabilities. Taxpayers were trustees of two affiliated corporations. One of the corporations had been dissolved in 1928, and the other corporation's charter had expired in 1937. Both corporations had, since 1928, received payments from the Mixed Claims Commission as compensation for World War I losses. They defended a lawsuit in the 1930s, pursued claims against various governments until 1958, and owed liabilities and paid fees to attorneys and the taxpayer trustees during the post-dissolution period. *Held:* For the IRS. The court found these activities more than sufficient to conclude that the corporations were in existence and not "dead and buried." Thus, there was a liability for corporate income taxes for the years 1949, 1953, and 1954. Hersloff, 310 F2d 947, 63-1 USTC ¶ 9123, 10 AFTR2d 6072 (Ct. Cl. 1962).

Dissolved corporation no longer alive for tax purposes. In 1928 and 1937, two corporations dissolved, leaving to their directors, as trustees for stockholders, the task of collecting certain war claims. The IRS found that the trustees were subject to corporate tax. In Hersloff, 310 F2d 947 (Ct. Cl. 1962), the Court of Claims found that the dissolved corporations still existed for tax purposes. For later years, the trustees again contested the corporate tax. *Held:* For taxpayer. In the years treated by the Claims Court, the trustees were active in prosecuting the war claims. Since that time, the trustees merely collected income from awards. The corporations were fully liquidated for tax purposes. Hersloff, 46 TC 545 (1966).

Associations Taxable as Corporations: *Professional Associations*

Professional Associations

Professional corporation's income not taxed to doctor. Taxpayer physician contracted to perform services for a hospital as an independent contractor, and then assigned his rights under the contract to his professional corporation. The IRS sought to attribute the corporation's income from the contract to the taxpayer. *Held:* For taxpayer. The corporation was not a sham, the taxpayer was not an employee of the hospital, and there was no distortion of income that justified the use of Section 482. McGee, 81-1 USTC ¶ 9184, 47 AFTR2d 81-913 (D. Neb. 1980).

Certain new Colorado and New Hampshire professional organizations taxable as corporations. The IRS announced that professional service organizations that are formed and operated under either the Colorado Rules of Civil Procedure, Chapter 22, Rule 265, as amended on May 1, 1982, or the New Hampshire Professional Associations Act, as amended on February 1, 1982, will be classified as corporations for tax purposes. Rev. Rul. 82-212, 1982-2 CB 401.

Organization was corporation. An individual formed a professional service organization under the Professional Service Corporation Act of one of the states listed in Rev. Rul. 70-101. The IRS ruled that the organization was a corporation for purposes of the Code, and the criteria in the regulations under Section 7701 did not need to be applied. Rev. Rul. 77-31, 1977-1 CB 409.

California professional service organization trust is taxed as a corporation. The IRS stated that a California professional service organization operating in the form of a business trust was taxable as a corporation. The trust instrument in the particular case possessed a preponderance of corporate characteristics. Rev. Rul. 72-75, 1972-1 CB 401.

Trusts and Trustees

Trust held taxable as a corporation where property was transferred to trustees who had broad management powers and the responsibility of dividing profits annually. A closely held family corporation operated a meat packing business and owned the physical properties, including the plant, premises, and improvements. In 1950, it decided to discontinue the processing business, but leased the plant to an unrelated corporation for the same purposes on a 20-year lease with options to renew or purchase. Shortly thereafter, the lessor corporation voted to liquidate within two years and gave notice of the plan to the IRS. The plan was carried out, and the properties were conveyed to some of the former stockholders and officers as trustees. In 1963, the property was sold and the proceeds distributed to the beneficiaries of the trust as final distributions. The trust filed fiduciary income tax returns for the interim years, and the IRS assessed deficiencies for the years 1960 through 1963 on the grounds that the trust was an association taxable as a corporation. The trust agreement provided the issuance of certificates of shares to the beneficiaries and gave the trustees the power to manage and control the property with broader powers to convey the property and borrow, mortgage, and call meetings of the certificate holders. The trust was to continue in effect for 75 years unless sooner terminated by sale of the real estate. The actual trust activity, however, consisted mainly of the collection of rent and sales of some small parcels. *Held:* For the IRS. The purpose of the trust had to be gathered from the entire agreement. The fact that only one major piece of property was involved was not material in determining whether the trust's objective was to carry on a business. Also, the lack of formal meetings, resolutions, bylaws, minute books, seals, and other corporate analogies was not controlling. There were associates because the corporate stockholders of the former entity surrendered their shares of stock in return for certificates of shares in the trust. There was also an objective to carry on a business and to divide the gains, and the powers granted to the trustees were broad enough to enable it to carry on the same business of the former corporation for a period up to 75 years. Abraham, 406 F2d 1259, 69-1 USTC ¶ 9226 (6th Cir. 1969).

Associations Taxable as Corporations: *Trusts and Trustees*

Corporate characteristics render a trustee taxable as a corporation. Taxpayer, trustee for five separate real estate management trusts, filed corporate income tax returns for both trusts for the years 1938 through 1956. In 1957, it filed fiduciary income tax returns for the years 1953 through 1956, and it filed a claim for refund of the corporate taxes paid in those years. The IRS argued that the trustee was taxable as a corporation. *Held:* For the IRS. Since the trusts had all the corporate attributes and were a medium for actively conducting a business, they were associations taxable as a corporation. These attributes were found by the district court to be perpetual existence, centralized management, ease of transferability of certificates of beneficial interest, and limited liability. Mid-Ridge Inv. Co., 324 F2d 945, 63-2 USTC ¶ 9827 (7th Cir. 1963).

Real estate trust not taxable as corporation. In 1907, 13 persons bought a piece of unimproved real estate, taking title in the name of a trustee. For 50 years, until the property was sold, they rented to various parking lot operators. The trustee collected the rent, paid the real estate taxes, and distributed the balance to the beneficiaries. The IRS asserted that the trust was an association taxable as a corporation. *Held:* For taxpayer. The trust was not engaged in a business operation. Further, the duties of the trustee were ministerial and did not constitute centralized management. Rohman, 275 F2d 120, 60-1 USTC ¶ 9292, 5 AFTR2d 871 (9th Cir. 1960).

Trust taxable as corporation during period of liquidation. Taxpayer was a trust with transferable certificates of beneficial interest. It had extensive holdings of ranch properties, livestock, and corporate securities and concededly was taxable as a corporation in the years of its ordinary business operations. However, taxpayer contended that it was not so taxable after the term of the trust had expired and it had determined to liquidate. Because of the nature of its properties, several years were required for an orderly liquidation. *Held:* For the IRS. The district court concluded, and the appellate court affirmed, that the trust's purpose during those years was still to carry on a business, although with the ultimate purpose of liquidation, and that its status as an association taxable as a corporation continued during the liquidation period. Mullendore Trust Co., 271 F2d 748, 59-2 USTC ¶ 9747 (10th Cir. 1959).

Real estate trust held taxable as a corporation; notes held to be common stock. Taxpayer was organized as a real estate trust in 1911. Its indenture provided for a 30-year life, the issuance of $2 million of 4 percent bonds, interest payable semiannually, and power in the trustees to manage the property transferred to the trust or subsequently acquired, to collect rents and profits, and to rent, sell, lease, and mortgage. The indenture also provided for regular and special meetings of the bondholders, who were to govern by majority vote according to one vote for each bond outstanding, and for the adoption by the bondholders of bylaws providing for the internal management and government of the trust. In 1940, the bondholders unanimously voted to extend taxpayer's life for another 30-year period. In the last two years of the period, taxpayer held title to 13 or 14 apartment buildings and 5 contiguous parking lots. As a matter of practice, taxpayer did not pay its bondholders interest at the rate of 4 percent per annum, but paid such amounts as the bondholders determined would be appropriate in advance of a year on the basis of the prior year's earnings. In 1925, the IRS determined that taxpayer was taxable as a corporation, and for all subsequent years taxpayer filed a corporate return. In 1960 and 1961, taxpayer claimed it was not taxable as a corporation; alternatively, it claimed that it could deduct payments to its bondholders as interest. *Held:* For the IRS. There are five factors of particular importance in determining whether an association is taxable as a corporation. These factors are: (1) continuity of interest, (2) transferability of interest, (3) title in a single entity, (4) limited liability, and (5) centralized management. An analysis of the facts here indicated that all five factors were present. Hence, taxpayer was taxable as a corporation. The facts also established that, whatever the original intent and practice, taxpayer had so evolved that its securities, which as pieces of paper had all the indicia of interest-bearing secured obligations, had in fact as a matter of practice and law become pure equity obligations. Payments on the securities therefore were not deductible as interest. National Sav. & Trust Co., 205 F. Supp. 325, 68-1 USTC 9371, 22 AFTR2d 5548 (DDC 1968).

Liquidating trust not taxable as association. Real estate was transferred to a trust under which the real estate would be manged by three trustees, one representing each branch of a family who had long been hostile to each other. The net income of the trust was to be paid to eight beneficiaries in equal shares. Each of the beneficiaries could at any time by an instrument in writing bring about the termination of the trust. The trust was, in any event, to be terminated on the sale of the real estate. The IRS contended that the trust was an association taxable as a corporation under Section 7701(a)(3) and assessed corporate income taxes against the trust. An association taxable as a corporation exists when (1) two or more persons associate themselves in a joint enterprise, (2) there is a substantial resemblance to a corporation, and (3) the business is carried on for a profit. *Held:* For taxpayer. This trust, the court held, met the first of those three requisites, but failed to meet the other two. The power to terminate the trust by any of the beneficiaries precluded continuity of life, which is one of the prime features of a corporation. In addition, the trust was not engaging in business for profit since its purpose was to sell or dispose of the real estate. Every trust involves some business activity, but in this case, it did not appear to have involved more than what was required to conserve the value of the property and to obtain a satisfactory price for it. Walker, 194 F. Supp. 522, 61-1 USTC ¶ 9473, 7 AFTR2d 1641 (D. Mass. 1961).

Entity taxable as a corporation. Taxpayer created a trust of which he was one of three trustees and the sole beneficiary. The trust's terms stipulated that it was to continue for 20 years after the death of the original trustees, unless it was terminated earlier by a majority vote of the trustees. The trustees had broad powers to conduct the trust affairs, and each could bind the trust in all matters relating to trust property. The trustees' and beneficiary's liability was limited to the trust property, and the beneficiary was required to obtain consent of all trustees in order to transfer any shares of the trust. The beneficiary taxpayer claimed deductions for losses incurred by the trust. The IRS disallowed the deductions, contending that the trust was an association taxable as a corporation. *Held:* For the IRS. The trust was an association taxable as a corporation, since it had associates, an objective to carry on a business for joint profit, continuity of life, centralization of management, and limited liability for its members. Therefore, taxpayer could not deduct the losses of the trust on his return. Hynes, Jr., 74 TC 1266 (1980).

IRS okays fixed investment trust's automatic reinvestment plan. A fixed investment trust is not reclassified as an association taxable as a corporation where (1) it adopts an automatic reinvestment plan under which certificate holders use distributions to purchase certificates in new fixed investment trusts, and (2) there is no change in, or addition to, the assets of the original trust. This plan does not result in the power to vary the investment of the certificate holders within the meaning of Regulation § 301.7701-4(c). Rev. Rul. 81-238, 1981-2 CB 248.

A fixed investment trust is a trust. The IRS ruled that a fixed investment trust established by a stockbroker that deposited municipal securities with a trustee bank in exchange for 20,000 ownership units that were sold to investor clients qualifies as a trust and not as an association. Rev. Rul. 73-460, 1973-2 CB 424.

Trust to dispose of bankrupt's assets is not association taxable as a corporation. A partnership and its partners, which had been engaged in the contracting business, were adjudicated bankrupts in 1959. A group of the creditors acquired the partnership assets from the trustee in bankruptcy, and under a trust agreement completed the construction of unfinished residences. The trust sold the residences, distributed the proceeds, and terminated in 1961. Since the purpose of the trust was to liquidate and distribute assets, and since the activities carried on were reasonably necessary and consistent with this purpose and were made to dispose of the assets as soon as possible, the trust arrangements did not constitute an association taxable as a corporation. The creditors were regarded as the owners of the trust and had to include in their income all items of income, deductions, and credits as if received directly, in accordance with Sections 671 and 677. The portion of the FMV of the property allocable to each creditor's claim against the partnership was the unadjusted basis of the property in the hands of the creditor. Proper additions to basis included bankruptcy costs, construction costs, accrued real estate taxes, and other capital expenditures. Rev. Rul. 63-228, 1963-2 CB 229.

ASSUMPTION OF LIABILITIES

(*See* Liabilities, Assumption Of)

ATTRIBUTION RULES

(*See also* Redemptions—Attribution Rules)

IRS rejected First Circuit's family hostility exception to attribution rules. All of the stock of a corporation was owned by three individuals and five trusts. The corporation redeemed the stock held by four trusts that were for the benefit of an individual stockholder's children. Before the redemption, each trust owned, actually and constructively, 31 percent of the corporation's stock, and afterwards, each owned 33 percent solely by attribution under Section 318 of the Code. Although family hostility prevented the trusts from exercising actual control over such stock, The IRS held that Section 318 applies nevertheless, and that the redemption was not a distribution in exchange for stock under Section 302(a). In so holding, the IRS rejected a First Circuit case to the contrary. Half Trust, 510 F2d 43 (1st Cir. 1975), rev'g 61 TC 398 (1973). Rev. Rul. 80-26, 1980-1 CB 66.

Corporation's unexercised option to purchase stock from stockholder does not trigger attribution. A corporation had 100x shares of common stock outstanding. All of the stock was owned by *A*, *B*, and *C*, who were unrelated individuals. *A* owned 50x shares and *B* and *C* each owned 25x shares of the common stock. The corporation had an option to purchase the 25x shares of its common stock that were owned by *B*. On these spare facts, the IRS held that since the corporation did not acquire voting or other rights as a stockholder by acquiring its own stock through exercise of the option, it was not considered, under Section 318(a)(4), to be the owner of the stock that it had an option to acquire from *B* for the purpose of making *A* the indirect owner of such stock. Rev. Rul. 69-562, 1969-2 CB 47.

Remaindermen no longer excluded from attribution rules. For purposes of determining stock ownership in restricted stock options and for personal holding companies, the IRS has ruled that stock held by a trust is considered to be owned by its present or future beneficiaries in proportion to their actuarial interests. Under the former rule, as reflected in Steuben Sec. Corp., 1 TC 395 (1943), and Rev. Rul. 58-325, 1958-1 CB 212, the stock ownership rules were applied only to present interests in a trust and excluded remainder or other remote interests, whether vested or contingent. The current rule was derived from Tuboscope Co., 268 F2d 233 (5th Cir. 1959), in which the court pointed out that under the old rule the statute could be thwarted by the simple expedient of an inter vivos trust. Accordingly, Rev. Rul. 58-325 is revoked, and the IRS will not follow that part of the *Steuben* decision which conflicts with the new rule. Rev. Rul. 62-155, 1962-2 CB 132.

AVOIDANCE OF TAX

(*See* Accumulated Earnings Tax; Acquisitions to Avoid Tax; Fraud; Tax Avoidance)

Bad Debts: *In General*

BAD DEBTS

(*See also* Capital Contributions; Debt vs. Equity)

In General	94
Bona Fide Indebtedness Requirement	95
Business vs. Nonbusiness Debts	98
Deduction For	102
Reserves For	104

In General

Section 482 allocation of interest income does not produce a bad debt. The IRS, under Section 482, allocated interest income from two corporations to a partnership, the partners of which controlled the corporations. The Tax Court upheld these allocations. The partners then claimed a bad debt deduction equal to the interest allocated to the partnership. The Tax Court denied the deduction. *Held:* Affirmed. A Section 482 allocation does not create an obligation from the corporations to the partnership, so there is no bad debt. Allowing the deduction would produce a double deduction, since the IRS had allowed the corporations to deduct the allocated interest. Cappuccilli, 668 F2d 138, 82-1 USTC ¶ 9118, 49 AFTR2d 82-509 (2d Cir. 1981), cert. denied, 459 US 822 (1982).

Overall loss on brewery venture allowed; it was not a bad debt. Taxpayer decided to go into the brewery business and contracted to buy the stock of an existing company and certain assets used in its business. About two years later, upon the discovery of unrecorded liabilities, taxpayer exercised his right to rescind the contract. A receiver was appointed, and after long negotiations the whole business was sold to outsiders. The Tax Court said that taxpayer had only a nonbusiness bad debt (treated as a short-term capital loss under the Code). *Held:* Reversed. Taxpayer suffered a loss on a transaction entered into for profit. Taxpayer's claim arising out of advances to the company was rejected by the receiver; therefore the Tax Court's finding that taxpayer had a bad debt was wrong. Protzmann, 276 F2d 684, 60-1 USTC ¶ 9387 (1st Cir. 1960).

IRS' bad debt calculation not responsive to business conditions. Taxpayer, an automobile dealer, computed his deduction for bad debts in accordance with industry standards. The IRS computed the deduction by applying the five-year-experience formula of *Black Motor Co. Held:* For taxpayer. The IRS' calculation was found to be insufficient and not responsive to changes in taxpayer's business conditions. Richardson, 330 F. Supp. 102, 71-2 USTC ¶ 9562, 28 AFTR2d 71-5375 (SD Tex. 1971).

Consolidated return regulations did not require deferral of pre-affiliation bad debt. Taxpayer corporation's board of directors voted to charge off as worthless a debt from *Y* corporation. Later that year, taxpayer purchased 89 percent of *Y*'s stock and filed a consolidated return. The IRS held that taxpayer's bad debt deduction must be deferred under Regulation § 1.1502-14(d). *Held:* For taxpayer. The bad debt may have been recognized at the time of the directors' vote, although it was not recorded on the taxpayer's books until after the purchase of *Y*. The regulation does not require deferral of a preacquisition bad debt. Velvet O'Donnell Corp., 51 AFTR2d 83-778 (Cl. Ct. 1983).

Advances to subsidiary not bad debts. Taxpayer's subsidiary sustained operating losses for more than 10 years and remained in business only because taxpayer did not press for payment of its account receivable. Taxpayer wrote off the excess of the account receivable over the net realizable value of the subsidiary's assets in liquidation and then sold its holdings in the subsidiary to taxpayer's parent company for net book value less the sum owned to taxpayer. Taxpayer continued to make credit sales to its former subsidiary. The IRS disallowed the deduction. *Held*: For the IRS. Reliance on liquidating book value to establish the collectible portion of the debt requires an actual intention to liquidate at that time. The subsequent actions of taxpayer and its parent company evidenced the fact that the intent was to maintain the subsidia-

BAD DEBTS: Bona Fide Indebtedness Requirement

ry's existence. Sika Chem. Corp., 64 TC 856 (1975).

Advances to corporation for business purpose constituted deductible loss. The two stockholders of taxpayer, a building block manufacturer, had their partnership advance money on the partnership's behalf to a mineral manufacturer. The partnership received taxpayer's notes, and taxpayer received notes from the new company. When the mineral company went out of business, taxpayer had to make payments to the partnership. It deducted these amounts as ordinary losses. The IRS disallowed the loss deductions. *Held*: For taxpayer. Taxpayers had the money put into the mineral company for the business purpose of acquiring a source of the mineral. There was no investment motive, and the payments were deductible as ordinary losses. Furthermore, the payments to the partnership were not dividends to taxpayer's stockholders, as taxpayer and the partnership were separate entities. Taxpayer intended to assume the risks of the venture, and the payments represented repayments to its indebtedness to them as guarantors of the notes. Pumi-Blok Co., 31 TCM 197, ¶ 72,048 P-H Memo. TC (1972).

Pre-insolvency advances were bad debts; post-insolvency advances were capital investments. Taxpayer corporations, engaged in the manufacture of textiles, organized a new corporation, Tuftwick, to manufacture bedspreads. One of taxpayers acquired 40 percent of Tuftwick's stock by crediting Tuftwick's account for $60,000. Advances were also made by both taxpayers to Tuftwick to help it get needed working capital. By 1952, Tuftwick became insolvent and was finally dissolved in 1958. In 1957, taxpayers claimed business bad debt deductions for their uncollectible advances. *Held*: For taxpayers, in part. Advances made prior to 1952 resulted in bad debts. The new corporation was not undercapitalized merely because it started business with a small amount of cash on hand. It was able to buy raw materials from taxpayers on credit, had adequate plant facilities, and had a regular cash supply from a factoring arrangement. Moreover, its capitalization of $150,000 was judged by expert testimony to be adequate. However, advances made after Tuftwick became insolvent in 1952 were not bad debts, since there was by then no reasonable hope of recovering them. Scotland Mills, Inc., 24 TCM 265, ¶ 65,048 P-H Memo. TC (1965).

Subsidiary may be liquidated and operated as a branch without jeopardizing bad debt deduction. A creditor-parent entered into a statutory merger with its wholly owned subsidiary. It later liquidated the subsidiary and operated it as a branch. The parent was still entitled to bad debt and worthless security deductions that may have resulted. (Rev. Rul. 59-296 amplified.) Rev. Rul. 70-489, 1970-2 CB 53.

Bad debt possible on liquidation of subsidiary. A transfer by a wholly owned subsidiary of all of its assets to its parent corporation in partial satisfaction of a bona fide debt does qualify either as a nontaxable liquidation of a subsidiary or a a tax-free reorganization, since all of the subsidiary's property is worth less than the debt, and thus no part of the transfer is attributable to the parent's stock interest. Accordingly the parent is entitled to a bad debt deduction for the unsatisfied portion of the debt. Rev. Rul. 59-296, 1959-2 CB 87.

Bona Fide Indebtedness Requirement

Advances of corporation to unprofitable subsidiary held to be debt. Taxpayer was organized in 1961 to provide engineering services for the electronics industry. Over the years, it prospered, and in 1968, it acquired IT in a stock-for-stock exchange. After the acquisition, IT continued its corporate existence as taxpayer's subsidiary. Taxpayer advanced cash to IT to finance the company's day-to-day operations. The advances were not evidenced by promissory notes, and no interest was charged. The advances were carried on taxpayer's books as accounts receivable and on IT's books as accounts payable. Taxpayer's president testified that the advances were considered loans and that taxpayer expected repayment. It was understood that taxpayer

BAD DEBTS: *Bona Fide Indebtedness Requirement*

would advance to IT whatever funds were necessary for it to continue ongoing operations, and that these payments would be repaid as soon as IT became profitable. Due to IT's financial failure, taxpayer liquidated the subsidiary. In its 1971 federal income tax return, taxpayer claimed a bad debt deduction for losses regarding the advances that it suffered upon the liquidation. The Court of Claims held that taxpayer was entitled to a bad debt deduction for the amounts advanced to its failed subsidiary. The court found that the advances were made with an expectation of repayment and that the subsidiary's assets were properly given nominal valuations at liquidation. Although IT was thinly capitalized, optimistic projections of profitability, and treatment on the books evidenced intent to repay the advances. *Held*: Affirmed. Where advances were made for valid business reasons, and the evidence indicated that they were loans and not equity investment, the corporation was allowed a bad debt deduction for advances made to its subsequently liquidated subsidiary. Electronic Modules Corp., 695 F2d 1367, 83-1 USTC ¶ 9113 (Fed. Cir. 1982).

Insolvent corporation denied bad debt deduction for advances to insolvent stockholder. Over a two-year period, a stockholder withdrew from his wholly owned corporation amounts in excess of $1.3 million. The stockholder executed notes in consideration for three withdrawals, and the corporation entered them as loans on its books. When its stockholder failed to repay these amounts, the corporation claimed a bad debt deduction. *Held*: For the IRS. The evidence clearly showed that the withdrawals were never intended to be loans. First, at the time that the loans were made, both the corporation and its stockholder were insolvent or on the brink of insolvency. Further, the notes stated no maturity date or interest, and no collateral was provided by the stockholder. The mere fact that the stockholder had borrowed and repaid much smaller amounts in the past was found to be immaterial. Transamerica Ins. Co., 492 F2d 1240, 74-1 USTC ¶ 9326, 33 AFTR2d 74-999 (4th Cir. 1974).

No bad debt deduction for advances to affiliate. Elbeco and Eastern were wholly owned subsidiaries of a common parent. From 1950 through 1953, Elbeco advanced to Eastern over $1 million on unsecured demand notes. No interest was provided, and none was paid. It was also shown that Eastern had insufficient assets to meet its outstanding indebtedness. The IRS denied Elbeco a bad debt deduction. *Held*: For the IRS. The court noted that there was no reasonable expectation that the advances made would be repaid and that there was no bona fide intent to create a debtor-creditor relationship. Accordingly, no bona fide indebtedness was created that could be the subject of a bad debt deduction. Ludwig Baumann & Co., 312 F2d 557, 63-1 USTC ¶ 9261 (1963).

Bad debt deduction allowed on advances to foreign subsidiary. Taxpayer organized a subsidiary to carry out a short-term project in the Dutch East Indies. A subsidiary was organized because taxpayer did not want to risk its own resources. Taxpayer advanced $564,000 to the wholly owned subsidiary. The subsidiary issued only six shares of $5 stock. The district court disallowed the bad debt deduction of $467,000 after $97,000 of assets was received upon winding up the subsidiary. *Held*: Reversed. Despite the extremely thin capitalization, the parties intended the advances to have the character of debt. The operation of the subsidiary was to be completed in a short time. Byerlite Corp., 286 F2d 285, 61-1 USTC ¶ 9138, 6 AFTR2d 6069 (6th Cir. 1960).

Lack of intent to repay loan between related corporation dooms bad debt deduction. Taxpayer filed its 1969 income tax return claiming a bad debt deduction resulting from the worthlessness of a note it had received in 1965 from a related corporation. The two corporations were set up by the same individual in an attempt to conceal certain transactions from the Securities and Exchange Commission. The IRS disallowed the deduction in full. *Held*: For the IRS. The district court found that there was no security for the note, and no interest or principal was payable until five years of the making thereof. From this, the court concluded that there was never an intent to repay the note; therefore, the alleged "debt" was not bona fide. Caletta Blueberry Co., 76-2 USTC ¶ 9508, 38 AFTR2d 76-5306 (SD Fla. 1976).

Worthless claim from extension of credit to commonly controlled corporation was deductible. Taxpayer extended credit on open account to one of its former operating divisions that had been spun off and incorporated as a subsidiary of a corporation under the same control as taxpayer. After the spin-off, the operating division continued to operate in the same manner as before. The division was unsuccessful, and its indebtedness to taxpayer was $235,000 as the result of the 1952 spin-off, as contrasted to a capitalization of $5,000. Its indebtedness grew to $445,000 in 1956 when a fire that destroyed taxpayer's inadequately insured properties left it with approximately $65,000 in assets. Taxpayer wrote off $405,000 of the indebtedness in the year of the fire and claimed a bad debt deduction for this amount. The IRS denied the deduction on the grounds that (1) the spin-off was motivated by tax-avoidance purposes, (2) the indebtedness in fact was an equity investment, and (3) the claim for indebtedness was not worthless in the year claimed. *Held*: For taxpayer. By exercising its statutory authority to allocate income and deductions among related taxpayers, the IRS could prevent the controlled group of corporations from claiming both the bad debt deduction for the unpaid advances, as taxpayer did, and a second deduction for the losses incurred by the feed division, as the controlled parent unsuccessfully attempted to do in filing a consolidated return. This fact, coupled with the fact that the spinoff was motivated by the desire to defeat efforts at unionization, indicated that the purpose for the spin-off was a business purpose and not a tax-avoidance purpose. The IRS' argument that the advances to the feed division were capital contributions shrank to almost nothing the circumstances under which corporations under common control can safely occupy a debtor-creditor relationship. The pertinent fact in this case was that taxpayer had a bona fide expectation of repayment based upon its misplaced confidence in the ultimate success of the feed division. The court also found that the amount due on open account constituted a debit and was worthless when claimed. American Processing & Sales Co., 371 F2d 842, 67-1 USTC ¶ 9189, 19 AFTR2d 533 (Ct. Cl. 1967).

Bad debt deduction allowed only when true loan relationship was intended and existed between parties. Taxpayer corporation, other corporations, and individuals made several loans to a mine leasing development corporation. When the mine failed, taxpayer and others deducted the loans as bad debt losses and business expenses. The IRS disallowed the deductions. *Held*: For the IRS, in part. The original unpaid loans were deductible as bad debts, since they were advanced at a time when profits and repayment looked good, and the developer was not undercapitalized. As to the individuals, the amounts were nonbusiness bad debts. Advances made at the time of an SBA loan and thereafter were not deductible as bad debts, since there was a failure to show that a bona fide debtor-creditor relationship was intended, and that there was a reasonable expectation of repayment. The amounts were also not deductible as expenses of the parties except for the lessor corporation, which had a substantial and direct business interest in the mine's development. Certain bad debt deductions related to uncollectible accounts receivable were allowed, since there was a reasonable expectation of repayment when they were created. Taxpayer received funds from a stockholder that were considered equity contributions; therefore, no interest deductions were allowable. Fifteen percent of the deficiency, not 25 percent, was proper as an addition to tax, since taxpayer filed his return three months late, and having no taxable income was not an adequate excuse to prevent the penalty. Christie Coal & Coke Co., 28 TCM 498, ¶ 69,092 P-H Memo. TC (1969).

Taxpayer's bona fide loan, primarily related to his own business, allowed as a business bad debt. Taxpayer, a fabric sytlist, formed his own corporation, loaned it $50,000, and was not repaid upon a creditor action. The IRS ruled that it was a nonbusiness bad debt loss,

BAD DEBTS: Business vs. Nonbusiness Debts

the deduction being limited to $1,000. *Held*: For taxpayer. There was a bona fide intention and a realistic prospect of repayment. Note and interest payments, the necessary formalities, were also present. The loan, made for the purpose of creating and protecting taxpayer's job, was primarily related to his business, investment motives being secondary. Estate of Avery, 28 TCM 364, ¶ 69,064 P-H Memo. TC (1969).

Advance to related corporation was a bona fide loan, but not worthless. Taxpayer, a family-held corporation in the real estate business, advanced $100,000 to a sister corporation in the insurance agency business. The borrower, a major tenant in taxpayer's building, expected to receive the covering payments from its local agents in a relatively short time. Both parties entered the advance on the books as a loan, and substantial payments were begun within two months and continued with some regularity until almost half the advance was repaid. In March 1960, because of financial difficulties, the borrower transferred its entire insurance business to an unrelated company in consideration of the latter's assuming the borrower's liabilities other than the debt to taxpayer. The borrower remained in existence after the transfer, retaining its other assets and liabilities. Taxpayer advanced an additional $350 to the borrower in June 1960 and sought to deduct in that year as a worthless debt the unpaid balance of the $100,000 as well as the $350. *Held*: For the IRS, in part. The deduction was denied. The $100,000 advance was intended to be, and in fact was a loan. The fact of common ownership, and control of the lender and borrower at the time the loan was made did not preclude the existence of a real debtor-creditor relationship. In addition to evidence indicating that the parties intended a loan at the time of the advance, there was also evidence of a business purpose in making the advance. The evidence concerning the $350 advance at the time that the borrower had lost its business and was engaged only in paying creditors establishes that this advance was not a bona fide loan. A bad debt deduction was, however, denied for 1960, since the debtor was shown to have possessed sufficient assets to meet its debts in that year. Irbco Corp., 25 TCM 359, ¶ 66,067 P-H Memo. TC (1966).

Business vs. Nonbusiness Debts

Corporation's payment of shockholder's guarantee produces dividend income, nonbusiness bad debt to stockholders. Taxpayers guaranteed, as individuals, a loan to a client of the corporation that they controlled. When the client defaulted, the corporation paid on the guarantee. The Tax Court held that taxpayers realized dividend income from that payment, and that taxpayers were limited to a nonbusiness bad debt (short-term capital loss). *Held*: Affirmed. The guarantee was undertaken by taxpayers primarily to increase their investment in the business, not to increase their own salaries. Tennessee Sec., Inc., 674 F2d 570, 82-1 USTC ¶ 9297, 49 AFTR2d 82-1102 (6th Cir. 1982).

Payments on behalf of stockholder's corporation held part equity. Taxpayer sought a bad debt deduction for payments he made on his wholly owned corporation. The IRS denied the deduction. *Held*: For the IRS. Since some of the payments were made pursuant to a guarantor agreement, they were bona fide debt, but not business debt. The other payments were contributions to capital that raised taxpayer's stock basis, but were not currently deductible. Morey, Jr., 37 TCM 1712, ¶ 78,412 P-H Memo. TC (1978), aff'd, 615 F2d 1357 (4th Cir. 1980).

Business bad debt deduction denied for advances to controlled corporation. Taxpayers, a partnership and an individual who were in the business of oil leasing, organized a corporation to sell air conditioners. They each invested $5,000 in stock, and each advanced $25,000 for working capital. As the corporation actually engaged in business, taxpayers made additional cash advances substantially in proportion to the stockholdings. No notes or other evidence of indebtedness were ever issued for any of the advances, nor was there any fixed date for repayment. After several years of unsuccessful operation, the corporation wound up its affairs in 1954. Taxpayers claimed business bad debt deductions for the advances. Although they proved that they had invested previously in various ventures, they were unable to convince the Tax Court that they were sufficiently active as promoters to be entitled to the deduction. At the most, the advances were nonbusiness bad debts. However, the Tax Court held that in reality the advances were contributions to capital. *Held*: Affirmed in part and reversed in part. The appellate court agreed that the debts were not business bad debts. However, it reversed the Tax Court's holding that the advances were capital contributions, finding them to be nonbusiness bad debts because the corporate manager had created an unexpected obligation that taxpayers had to pay. Bodzy, 321 F2d 331, 63-2 USTC ¶ 9599, 12 AFTR2d 5166 (5th Cir. 1963).

Payments of interest and expenses by taxpayer as guarantor of corporate indebtedness deemed deductible only as a nonbusiness bad debt loss. Taxpayer, the owner of all the stock of two separate corporations, had guaranteed some of the corporations' indebtedness. Upon being required to pay principal, interest, and some other expense items as guarantor of the corporate obligations, taxpayer contended that he should be allowed to deduct as interest or expense such items paid by him. The IRS contended that no interest or expense deduction should be allowed taxpayer for the interest or expense payments made by him as guarantor. *Held:* For the IRS. The court stated that a deduction for interest cannot be taken unless the indebtedness is that of taxpayer. The taxpayer here was liable only as a guarantor or surety of the obligation. The guarantor's loss was a loss from a nonbusiness bad debt. Taxpayer argued that alternatively, the corporate identities should be ignored because the corporations were insolvent at the time of the loans. The court stated, however, that the situation did not call for a disregard of the corporate entity in order to give taxpayer stockholder the tax deductions. Where a corporation is formed and operated for business purposes, it has an identity for tax purposes separate from that of its sole stockholder. Here, the separate entities were taxpayer's creation, and taxpayer could not escape the tax consequences of their separate existence. Nelson, 281 F2d 1, 60-2 USTC ¶ 9591, 6 AFTR2d 5150 (5th Cir. 1960).

Lawyer-investor denied business bad debt deduction. Taxpayer, a lawyer, agreed to back a former client who was engaged in the development of a revolutionary machine. The lawyer advanced substantial sums of money, but the project was a failure. He claimed a business bad debt deduction for the amounts advanced. On the ground that the lawyer was not in the separate business of promoting, financing, managing, or making loans to businesses, the Tax Court held that this was not a business bad debt. Further, the court noted that taxpayer did not show that he had ever reported ordinary income from a profitable venture, suggesting that there was a separate business only where there was material and continuous business activity. Protecting, enhancing or managing one's investments, no matter how extensive or time-consuming, is not a separate trade or business. *Held:* Affirmed. The court commented that while the Tax Court might not unreasonably have reached an opposite view, its find of fact was not clearly erroneous. Taxpayer relied on Biblin, 227 F2d 692 (1959), but he did not show that he contributed substantially 50 percent of his time to business promotion as did the taxpayer there. Rollins, 276 F2d 368, 60-1 USTC ¶ 9357, 5 AFTR2d 1124 (4th Cir. 1960).

Taxpayer's corporate interest not business related. The IRS held that taxpayer was not entitled to a business bad debt deduction for a loss on stock and notes of a corporation. *Held:* For the IRS. The facts did not support taxpayer's contention that his interest in the corporation was business related. McCurdy, 328 F. Supp. 1068, 71-1 USTC ¶ 9444 (SD Ohio 1971).

Losses on loans by majority stockholder employee to corporation were nonbusiness bad debts. Taxpayer claimed that he loaned approximately $900,000 to a construction corporation of which he was a corporate employee and majority stockholder. The alleged loans became worthless when the business

BAD DEBTS: *Business vs. Nonbusiness Debts*

failed, and taxpayer claimed that the loans were bad business debts. The IRS determined the advances to the corporation to be capital investments; alternatively, if they were loans, they created nonbusiness bad debts. *Held:* For the IRS. Where the evidence indicated that an advance was a loan by a corporate employee but that the employee failed to show by a preponderance of the evidence that protection of his job and salary as an employee was significant motivation for making the advancement, the loans were nonbusiness bad debts. Davis, 69-1 USTC ¶ 9408, 23 AFTR2d 69-1461 (NM 1969).

"Advances" by principal stockholder not deductible as business bad debts. Taxpayer was actively engaged in the lumber business. He had formerly conducted business as a sole proprietor and later as a partnership. He then organized a corporation to which some of the partnership assets were transferred in exchange for 60 percent of the capital stock. The corporation was unable to obtain loans from banks, but obtained one from the SBA upon the guarantee of the taxpayer and his advance to the corporation of additional funds. These conditions and others were met, but the corporation was unable to meet the loan installments. Subsequently, a fire at the sawmill destroyed the corporation's assets, and the insurance proceeds were sufficient only to pay the SBA loan. The Tax Court expressed its doubt that the advances were a genuine indebtedness, but decided in favor of the IRS on the grounds that the advances were not so proximately related to the taxpayer's trade or business as to give rise to a business bad debt. *Held:* Reversed. Whether the advances constituted a genuine indebtedness was a question to be decided in light of the particular case. Here the advances were evidenced by promissory notes that bore 4 percent interest, were conventional in form, and were not dependent upon earnings for repayment. While they were required to be subordinated to the SBA loan, they were not subordinated to any other creditors and were payable on demand after retirement of the six-year SBA loan. Whether the loss was incurred in the taxpayer's trade or business is a question of fact, unless the determination involves the interpretation of a statute. Taxpayer contended that his trade or business consisted of supplying managerial services to the corporation, but it was held in Whipple 373 US 1963, that the furnishing of such services to one of several corporations cannot constitute an independent trade or business when the taxpayer's motivation is one of an investor. However, the IRS' reliance on Whipple conflicted with the stipulation in the Tax Court that the corporation was not formed merely for investment purposes and the evidence that the taxpayer was in the independent business of selling timber to various entities, including the corporation. The facts of the case supported the taxpayer's contention that the investment in the corporation was motivated primarily by the expectation of gain from such sales of timber at a profit. This was supported further by the SBA agreement that provided that the corporation could not pay taxpayer a salary without its permission. Lundgren, 376 F2d 623, 67-1 USTC ¶ 9389, 19 AFTR2d 1407 (9th Cir. 1967).

Loan to wholly owned corporation held deductible as business bad debt. In 1954, taxpayer purchased all the stock of an automobile dealership for $60,000. His plan was to eventually sell the stock to an experienced manager he employed to run the business on a day-to-day basis while taxpayer and his wife made the major policy decisions as chief corporate officers. From 1954 to 1960, taxpayer made 20 advances to the corporation totaling $135,000. When the corporation went bankrupt in 1961, $105,000 of the advances still were unpaid. Taxpayer claimed this amount as a business bad debt. The IRS contended the advances were capital contributions and were not made in taxpayer's trade or business. From 1948 to 1960, taxpayer had participated in numerous other business ventures, five times as a lender and four times as an investor, and investigated still other opportunities. He had not devoted his full time to any one venture. *Held:* For taxpayer. Nothing prevents a shareholder from also being a creditor of his corporation for tax purposes. The intent in the latter regard is determinative. The testimony established that

BAD DEBTS: *Business vs. Nonbusiness Debts*

taxpayer's intent was to loan funds to the corporation. The corporation was not thinly capitalized, since it had $60,000 of physical assets and no debts when taxpayer acquired it. The facts also established taxpayer was in the business of seeking out business opportunities that he could profitably finance or promote. Thus, his loss was deductible as a business bad debt. Elliott, 268 F. Supp. 521, 67-1 USTC ¶ 9368 (D. Ore. 1967).

Stockholder loan is business debt. Taxpayer had for many years been engaged in the business of conducting activities connected with the aviation industry. Most of these activities were carried on through wholly owned corporations. During the years 1951 through 1956, taxpayer caused five corporations to be formed, including *X* Corporation, to which taxpayer advanced $205,000. Only $3,600 was repaid, leaving a balance of $201,400. Taxpayer deducted this as a business bad debt, which the IRS disallowed. *Held:* For taxpayer. Taxpayer's business "was a myriad of activities all directly connected with aviation." He was involved, not merely as an investor, but he worked in, made important decisions in, and put up money to enable the business to operate. The opinion says: "What the IRS urges, as we see it, is that if one embodies his business in the corporate forms, he may, in fact, spend his days in overalls working at a bench in his factory, but in law he will be regarded as engaged only in cashing dividend checks and clipping coupons." Maytag, 289 F2d 647, 61-1 USTC ¶ 9424 (Ct. Cl. 1961).

Stockholder's guarantee of his corporation's line of credit gives rise to nonbusiness bad debts. Taxpayer stockholder of Windor Inc., a manufacturer of finished windows, guaranteed Windor's accounts payable to its suppliers. Subsequently, Windor's stock became worthless and taxpayer was called upon to make payments on his guarantees. The IRS disallowed taxpayer's bad debt deduction, claiming that the payments were indirect capital contributions to Windor. *Held:* For taxpayer. Taxpayer made no direct payments to Windor, and the payments to suppliers under taxpayer's guarantees were made when Windor had ceased doing business and had made an assignment for the creditors' benefit. Since taxpayer's day-to-day involvement with Windor was minimal and his making of guarantees was not motivated by a desire to protect his job, he was entitled to a nonbusiness bad debt deduction. Teakle, 36 TCM 1542, ¶ 77,380 P-H Memo. TC (1977).

Guarantee of loan to corporation yields nonbusiness bad debt deduction. Taxpayer attorney received, for no consideration, stock in a corporation created by one of his clients. Taxpayer guaranteed a loan to the corporation and sought a business bad debt deduction when he had to make good on the guarantee. *Held:* For the IRS. The loan was not incurred in his trade or business. On the facts, taxpayer's primary motive was to enhance his chances for profits on his stockholdings, not to insure a continued flow of business from the client. Higgins, 35 TCM 962, ¶ 76,220 P-H Memo. TC (1976).

Taxpayer stockholder who guaranteed loans to his three close corporations was limited to nonbusiness bad debt deduction. Taxpayer owned and was the chief employee of *A, B,* and *C* Corporations, which were engaged in the raising of chickens. He entered into an agreement with *X* Corporation to supply *X* with chickens, and bought a 25 percent interest in *X*. In order to adequately supply *X*, taxpayer took out loans to expand *A, B,* and *C*, and guaranteed these loans personally, also pledging his *X* stock as security. Upon the bankruptcy of *A, B,* and *C*, taxpayer suffered losses on the payment of their debts as guarantor. He sought a business bad debt deduction. *Held:* For the IRS. Taxpayer was limited to a nonbusiness bad debt (short-term capital loss) deduction. Applying Generes, 405 US 93 (1972), the court found that taxpayer's dominant motive in guaranteeing the loans was to protect his investment in *X*, not to protect his employment with *A, B,* and *C*. Miller, 35 TCM 721, ¶ 76,162 P-H Memo. TC (1976).

Loan by stockholder a nonbusiness bad debt as taxpayer was not in the business of promoting, managing, financing, and making loans to

BAD DEBTS: *Deduction For*

enterprises. Taxpayer made loans on unsecured notes to a corporation of which he was a stockholder. Subsequent to the loans, an involuntary petition of bankruptcy was filed against the corporation, and it was later adjudged bankrupt. Taxpayer filed a proof of claim with the referee in bankruptcy, but no part of the unsecured claim was paid. Taxpayer, a farmer, claimed the amounts as business losses for tax purposes. The IRS determined the bad debt resulting from the loan to be a nonbusiness bad debt. *Held:* For the IRS. The court held that the corporate loan made by taxpayer that became a bad debt was a nonbusiness bad debt because taxpayer was not engaged in the business of promoting, managing, financing, and making loans to enterprises. Zeigenhorn, 19 TCM 344, ¶ 60,066 P-H Memo. TC (1960).

Deduction For

Advances to failing corporation not loans; bad debt deduction denied. Taxpayers, stockholders of a corporation, advanced approximately $98,000 to protect their original capital investment of $5,000. The advances were not evidenced by written instruments, and no interest was paid or accrued on the books of the corporation. No date or schedule of repayment was established, and only a minor repayment was ever made. Each year of continued operations resulted in increasing deficits, precluding reasonable hope that any substantial portion of the advances could ever be returned. Taxpayers sold the stock at the stated price of their original capital investment and assigned the receivables for $20,000, claiming a fully deductible business bad debt loss of approximately $78,000 on the sale of the receivables. The district court directed a verdict that the loss was from the sale of a capital asset in favor of the IRS. *Held:* Affirmed. The evidence showed that the funds were advanced by taxpayers to protect and expand the original capital investment. Taxpayers placed those funds at the risk of the success of the venture. Further, even if it assumed that the advances were loans or debts, the advances could not be charged off as bad business debts because the receivables were not charged off on the books and records of tax-payers prior to the sale. Taxpayers were not entitled to a bad debt deduction when the debt was no longer owned. Wachovia Bank & Trust Co., 288 F2d 750, 61-1 USTC ¶ 9362 (4th Cir. 1961).

Shareholder denied ordinary loss on business bad debt deduction for advances to corporation. The IRS contended that taxpayer was not entitled to an ordinary loss or business bad debt deduction where, pursuant to an indemnification agreement, she made unrecovered advances to her corporation. She was not entitled to a loss deduction because her advances merely subrogated her to the creditor's rights against the corporation. *Held:* For the IRS. The court found that as to the business bad debt deduction, the evidence showed her dominant motive for the advances was not protection of her corporate salary, but profit and protection of her son-in-law's salary. Lemoge, 378 F. Supp. 228, 74-1 USTC ¶ 9232, 33 AFTR2d 74-653 (ND Cal. 1974).

Bad debt deduction released in bankruptcy settlement; no deduction on behalf of another. The creditor stockholder of a bankrupt municipal securities company claimed a bad debt deduction for unpaid claims. The IRS disallowed the deduction, contending that taxpayer had released the claims in the bankruptcy settlement, and so the debt no longer existed. Furthermore, he could not deduct voluntary payments for the benefit of two other stockholders to the bankruptcy trustee. *Held:* For the IRS. Liabilities paid for the benefit of another cannot be deducted. The partner's share of income from the partnership was fully taxable to the partner whether or not he received the full amount. Finally, adequate records must be kept to establish reasonable and necessary business expense deductions. Busby, 77-2 USTC ¶ 9652, 40 AFTR2d 77-5871 (ND Tex. 1977), aff'd in unpublished opinion (5th Cir. 1980).

Taxpayer stockholder obtained business bad debt deduction. Taxpayer contended that he was entitled to a business bad debt deduction when a loan he made to a corporation in which he had a controlling interest became worthless. *Held:* For taxpayer. The dominant motive for the loan was to obtain an executive position with the corporation so as to enable taxpayer to obtain compensation for his personal services. Kelson, 73-2 USTC ¶ 9565 (D. Utah 1973).

Uncollected debt did not give rise to ordinary loss. Electronics, a partnership, acquired a $200,000 note of Gibraltar Corporation, and in the same transaction acquired shares of stock and warrants of Gibraltar. The objective of Electronics was to have the principal on the note repaid so that the money could be invested elsewhere and to profit from the anticipated appreciation of its entity interest in Gibraltar. Gibraltar went into receivership; no money was received by Electronics, and the partnership contended that the partners were entitled to an ordinary deduction for a business bad debt. The IRS determined that this was a nonbusiness bad debt, subject to capital loss treatment. *Held:* For the IRS. The debt was not created or acquired in connection with a trade or business of the partnership. The purpose of the partnership was to participate in the development of certain companies by means of lending monies to such companies and investing in them; thus the worthless debt did not give rise to a loss deduction under Section 165. Betts, 62 TC 536 (1974).

Deduction for guarantor's payment of his corporation's debt denied; worthlessness not proved. Taxpayer was a coffee broker who acted largely for one importer. He also was manager and principal stockholder of a corporation in the coffee business. Taxpayer's corporation borrowed from the importer, taxpayer personally guaranteeing the loans. When his corporation subsequently became insolvent, taxpayer paid the importer on the guarantee. The corporation continued in business under an agreement that the debt due taxpayer (arising from his payment of the guarantee) would be subordinated to claims of other creditors. The IRS disallowed a deduction for the amount paid. *Held:* For the IRS, in part. Since the corporation was solvent when the loan was guaranteed and taxpayer had not legally precluded himself from being reimbursed, there was a true debtor-creditor relationship here and not merely a contribution to capital as contended by the IRS. The Tax Court held further that taxpayer was not entitled to deduct the guarantor's payment, since he did not prove that the debt was worthless. Whether the debt was business or nonbusiness was not discussed, since the taxpayer had not proved its worthlessness. Merely showing that the corporation was hopelessly insolvent was not, of itself, sufficient. Roussel, 36 TC 235 (1962).

Deductibility of bad debts determined. Taxpayer corporation claimed bad debt deductions for its advances to a 50-percent-owned corporation. The IRS disallowed the bad debt deduction. *Held:* For the IRS. The amounts given were necessary to start the corporation in business, and thus they constituted contributions to capital and were not deductible as bad debts. Since taxpayer only owned 50 percent of the corporate stock, under Section 165(g)(3) it was subject to a capital loss rather than an ordinary loss on the worthlessness of the corporation's securities. Finally, the 50 percent ownership did not entitle taxpayer to file consolidated returns with its subsidiary. Merlite Indus., 34 TCM 1361, ¶ 75,312 P-H Memo. TC (1975).

Deductibility of bad debt determined. Taxpayer advanced $70,000 to a corporation, received back $32,000, and claimed a $38,000 loss deduction that the IRS disallowed. *Held:* For the IRS. No debtor-creditor relationship had been established. There was no instrument, no interest, and the loan was subordinated to other debts. Since no enforceable obligation existed, no capital or ordinary loss deduction was allowed. Furthermore, since no money was paid in the year in question, no business expense deduction was allowed. Jove, 34 TCM 710, ¶ 75,155 P-H Memo. TC (1975).

Deductibility of business bad debt determined. Taxpayers, stockholders of a closely held family corporation, claimed bad debt loss deductions, which the IRS disallowed. *Held:* For the IRS. Loans made by taxpayers to provide operating funds for the corporation

BAD DEBTS: *Reserves For*

were contributions to capital and not loans. There was no evidence of indebtedness and no interest was paid. Also, the loss actually occurred in an earlier year when an assignment of all the corporation's assets was made for the benefit of creditors. Furthermore, finance charges on the purchase of a car, and depreciation on the car used in business were deductible on the basis of taxpayer's unimpeached testimony and the court's computation of the correct amounts. Gilmore, 33 TCM 196, ¶ 74,041 P-H Memo. TC (1974).

Reserves For

Transfer of reserve for bad debts under Section 351 not allowed; reserve is ordinary income to extent of tax benefit. The IRS ruled that where a sole proprietorship or partnership incorporates under Section 351, the accumulated reserve for bad debts on the books prior to the transfer is not transferable. Further, this reserve represents ordinary income to taxpayer in the year the accounts receivable are transferred to the extent that tax benefits were derived in prior years. Rev. Rul. 62-128, 1962-2 CB 139.

Transfer to controlled corporation did not generate income on predecessor's bad debt reserve. Prior to April 1, 1963, taxpayer and his wife had been the sole partners in L.M. Scofield Company. On that date, the partnership had accounts receivable of $54,000 and a bad debt reserve of $7,000. On that same date, partnership assets were transferred to a corporation in exchange for stock and corporate assumption of liabilities. The corporation thereafter continued the business without change in management, line of business, or ownership. The IRS conceded that the transfer qualified as a nontaxable exchange, but assessed a deficiency based on the transfer of the receivables and reserve. *Held:* For taxpayer. The court said that the value of receivables transferred to the corporation was their face amount reduced by the bad debt reserve. Since the fair market value of the stock received equaled the net amount of the receivables, no income was realized. Only if the consideration received had exceeded the net value of the receivables would income be realized. Scofield, 70-2 USTC ¶ 9609, 25 AFTR2d 1434 (9th Cir. 1970).

Bad debt reserve is not added, but is income on Section 351 transfer. Taxpayer operated as a proprietorship and used the reserve method of accounting for bad debts. Taxpayer transferred the property of the proprietorship, including accounts receivable (subject to a reserve for bad debts), to a corporation solely in exchange for its stock. The IRS contended that the reserve should be restored to income at the time of transfer. *Held:* For taxpayer. The value of the securities received by taxpayer with respect to the accounts receivable was limited to the face value less the amount of the reserve for bad debts; therefore, taxpayer did not have to add back to income unused amounts in his bad debt reserve. Erlich, 34 TC 1231 (1970).

Additions to reserve for bad debts disallowed. Taxpayer maintained a substantial bad debt reserve but had relatively small bad debt charges against the reserve for the years in question. Taxpayer increased the reserve during these years because taxpayer's business was with private contractors, not with the government, as it had been previously. Subsequent to the years involved, taxpayer had a large bad debt loss. *Held:* For the IRS. The court held that taxpayer had not met the burden of showing that the additions to the reserve were reasonable, since the reserve maintained was far in excess of the bad debts incurred. West Va. Steel Corp., 34 TC 851 (1960).

Affiliated group filing a consolidated return cannot include intergroup loans in computing bad debt reserve. *P*, a bank, and *S*, engaged in a separate business, were members of an affiliated group filing a consolidated return. *P* made cash loans to *S* during 1974. The IRS ruled that *P* may not include such loans in its base for computing the addition to its reserve for bad debts under Section 585. The amount of the Section 585 bad debt addition attributable to the loans to *S* were treated as a deferred loss on the disposition of the loan under Regulation § 1.1502-14(d)(1). Rev. Rul. 76-430, 1976-2 CB 183.

No carry-over of bad debt reserve under Section 334(b)(2) liquidation. Section 381 covers carry-over provisions in corporate liquidations and mergers. Section 381 (a) makes the carry-over provisions inapplicable in liquidations under Section 334(b)(2). The IRS ruled that since the bad debt reserve did not carry over under Section 381, the reserve must be returned to the income of the liquidating corporation to the extent of the tax benefit derived. Rev. Rul. 65-258, 1965-2 CB 94.

BARGAIN PURCHASES

(*See* Compensation for Personal Services; Dividends and Distributions—Bargain Purchases and Sales)

BARGAIN SALES

(*See* Compensation for Personal Services; Dividends and Distributions—Bargain Purchases and Sales)

BASIS OF PROPERTY

(*See also* Liquidations—Basis of Property Received; Reorganizations; Tax-Free Exchanges; Tax-Free Incorporations)

Sidewise attribution rules properly applied to pre-1964 transaction. In 1961 and 1962, taxpayer purchased the stock of corporations owned in part by its stockholders. The corporations were then liquidated, and a stepped-up basis was claimed pursuant to Section 334(b)(2). The IRS disallowed the stepped-up basis on the ground that, by applying sidewise attribution rules, there was no purchase as defined by Section 334(b)(3). Taxpayer contended that by amending Section 318 in 1964, Congress evidenced an intention that sidewise attribution should never be applied. The Tax Court held for the IRS. *Held:* Affirmed. The elimination of sidewise attribution in 1964 was prospective only. Baker Commodities, Inc., 415 F2d 519, 69-2 USTC ¶ 9589, 24 AFTR2d 69-5516 (9th Cir. 1969), cert. denied, 397 US 988 (1970).

Taxpayer's basis in corporate stock at time of a Subchapter S election in his adjusted cost basis and not fair market value. Taxpayer, in 1940, purchased the outstanding stock of a corporation for $13,000. In 1958, he caused the corporation to make a Subchapter S election. In the years 1958, 1959, and 1960, the corporation suffered net operating losses totaling in excess of $40,000. Evidence showed that the value of taxpayer's stock in 1958 was approximately $130,000 as a result of accumulated profits. The IRS disallowed taxpayer's deduction of the corporation's net operating losses to the extent that they exceeded his cost basis. *Held:* For the IRS. Taxpayer's deduction for his corporation's losses were limited to the basis of his stock. Such basis was initially equal to his basis in the stock at the time of the Subchapter S election, not the stock's current fair market value. Byrne, 361 F2d 939, 66-2 USTC ¶ 9483, 17 AFTR2d 1272 (7th Cir. 1966).

Parent company's basis for subsidiary reduced by subsidiary's capital losses used on consolidated return. The IRS reduced taxpayer's basis for its wholly owned subsidiary by the amount of capital losses that the subsidiary applied against capital gains of taxpayer in consolidated returns. The district court conceded that literal application of the regulations would not require a reduction in basis. However, the court held that the basis must be adjusted to prevent a double deduction. *Held:* Affirmed. The rule that a general provision (the prohibition of double deductions) must give way to a specific one was held not applicable since there was no specific allowance of this double deduction. Associated Tel. & Tel. Co., 306 F2d 824, 62-2 USTC ¶ 9659, 10 AFTR2d 5414 (2d Cir. 1962), cert. denied, 371 US 950 (1962).

Corporation does not increase asset base by distributing them to redeem stock and later repurchasing assets. Taxpayer, *X* Corporation, transferred depreciable assets having a tax basis of approximately $169,000 and a market value of approximately $746,000 to two of its major stockholders in redemption of their stock. On the same day, taxpayer required the same assets from the former stockholders in exchange for corporate notes in the amount of the fair market value. The court, in reversing the district court below, had held that the transaction did not create an interruption in the ownership of the corporation sufficient to produce a new basis. In order to acquire a stepped-up basis, X would have to make a clear and distinct severance of its ownership prior to the reacquisition. Taxpayer requested a rehearing. *Held:* Rehearing denied. In denying a request for a rehearing to give taxpayer the opportunity to stress the bona fides of the transaction, the court pointed out that it did not question the good faith of the parties or of the business purpose of the redemption and purchase. There was not, however, a sufficient severance of the corporate ownership for tax purposes. General Geophysical Co., 296 F2d 86, 61-2 USTC ¶ 9698, 8 AFTR2d (5th Cir. 1961), cert. denied, 369 US 849 (1961).

IRS allocation of basis upheld. Taxpayer, as part of a corporate reorganization, exchanged old bonds for new bonds and corporate common stock. Taxpayer subsequently sold the common stock and allocated the entire cost basis of the old bonds to the stock. The IRS determined that a portion of the cost was properly allocable to the new bonds. *Held:* For the IRS. It was not shown that the IRS' allocation was erroneous. Elward, 420 F. Supp. 840, 76-2 USTC ¶ 9745 (ND Ill. 1976).

Parent determined basis for gain on sale of consolidated subsidiaries' stock with reference to subsidiaries' earnings and profits that did not reflect its deduction of accelerated depreciation. Taxpayer owned all of the stock of four subsidiaries with which it filed consolidated returns. The subsidiaries used accelerated methods of depreciation for computing taxable income, although as per Section 312, straight-line depreciation for computing earnings and profits was used. Taxpayer sold all of the subsidiaries' stock and, in computing gain on the sale, determined its basis in such stock by reference to the subsidiaries' earnings and profits pursuant to Regulation § 1.1502-32. The IRS asserted that taxpayer must further reduce its basis for determining its gain by the excess of accelerated over straight-line depreciation, since the subsidiaries' earnings and profits only reflected use of straight-line depreciation. *Held:* For taxpayer. Computation of basis was proper without adjustment for excess of accelerated over straight-line depreciation. If this permits a double deduction, then the regulation should be amended. Woods Inv. Co., 85 TC No. 14 (1985).

Novation of corporate debt increased stockholder's stock basis. Taxpayer and the three other stockholders of a Subchapter S corporation were guarantors of a $450,000 bank loan to their corporation. Later, the stockholders gave the bank their personal note for $450,000 and canceled the corporate note. In 1976, taxpayer reported his share of a net operating loss. The IRS disallowed the deduction to the extent that it exceeded the sum of taxpayer's original contributions plus some direct loans. *Held:* For taxpayer. The substitution of the Stockholders' note to the bank for the corporate note created a genuine debt from the corporation to the stockholders, thus increasing their bases in the corporation within the meaning of Section 1374(c)(2)(B). Therefore, taxpayer was permitted to deduct his share of net operating losses up to an adjusted basis, which included his share of the note. Gilday, 43 TCM 1295, ¶ 82,242 P-H Memo. TC (1982).

Basis of property exchanged determined. Taxpayer partner received property from the partnership in a sale. The partnership books had a $19,500 value, while the IRS determined a higher value so that there was a $57,000 dividend. *Held:* For the IRS, in major part. The fair market value was $192,000, based on comparable property values. The city assessment of $24,000 that taxpayer relied on was not reliable as property values were increasing significantly in the area. Thus, the deficiency was upheld. Victor Constr. Inc., 33 TCM 1136, ¶ 74,256 P-H Memo. TC (1974).

Basis of herd received in tax-free exchange was zero, the same as in hands of transferor. An individual transferred the assets of his ranch, including a breeding herd, to taxpayer corporation in a tax-free exchange under Section 351. Taxpayer later liquidated the herd and claimed a basis to the transferor of $13,800. The IRS, however, determined that the corporation had no basis, since the individual transferor had been reporting his income on a cash basis without the use of inventories and had a zero basis at the time of the transfer. *Held:* For the IRS. From the available evidence, the transferor reported on the cash basis. There was nothing on his individual returns to suggest the use of an inventory of cattle. In fact, he had claimed depreciation on the breeding herd and must have recovered his total cost long before the transfer to taxpayer. Thus, his basis in the herd must have been zero, which carried over to taxpayer in determining the amount of gain on the sale of her herd. Kittitas Ranch Inc., 26 TCM 640, ¶ 67,141 P-H Memo. TC (1967).

BONDS AND DEBENTURES

In General	107
Bond Discount and Premiums	108
Deduction of Interest Paid	111
Equity Investments Distinguished	115

In General

After weighing all factors under an "objective test of economic reality," interest in bonds held by sole stockholder was held to be preferential dividend. Taxpayer was authorized to issue 50,000 shares of common stock and 50,000 shares of preferred. The preferred stockholders, although generally not possessing any voting rights, were entitled to vote if taxpayer failed to pay dividends for a specified period of time. Taxpayer also issued $50,000 worth of debentures bearing a 6 percent interest rate and due in 10 years. Additionally, if taxpayer defaulted on interest payments on the debentures for two consecutive years, each holder was entitled to cast 100 votes per $1,000 note on all matters upon which stockholders voted. Upon dissolution, the rights of the debentures were superior to the stock but subordinate to general creditors. *W* owned all of taxpayer's stock and 467 of the $1,000 debt instruments. In exchange for the stock, *W* gave taxpayer stock in his other corporations. *W* received interest on the bonds, which the IRS determined to constitute a nondeductible preferential dividend paid to *W*. *Held:* For the IRS. Deduction was denied for interest payments on the debentures where payments were in reality nondeductible preferential dividends. The bonds were deemed capital because of the risk involved, the subordination of the bonds to the general creditors, the lack of a maturity date to allow holders to force redemption, and the identity between the stockholders and the bondholders. Weighing all factors, under an "objective test of economic reality," no outside lender would have assented to the terms. M.W. Wood Enters., 538 F. Supp. 974, 82-2 USTC ¶ 9425 (ED Pa. 1982).

Bonds issued by redevelopment authority qualified as "small issue." The IRS argued that bonds issued by the Redevelopment Authority of Philadelphia to taxpayer bank did not qualify for the "small issue" exemption and therefore taxpayer was required to include the interest on th obligation as income. *Held:* For the taxpayer. Substantially all of the proceeds of the bond issue were used for the acquisition, construction, reconstruction, or improvement of land or property that qualified for the depreciation allowance under Section 103(b)(6)(A). However, a subsequent second issue did not qualify since no part of the proceeds were used for qualified expenditures. Continental Bank, 517 F. Supp. 918, 81-2 USTC ¶ 9570, 48 AFTR2d 81-5206 (ED Pa. 1981), aff'd in an unpublished opinion (3d Cir. 1982).

Sale of notes not disguised sale of stock. Taxpayer sold stock in their corporation. At the same time, they also sold notes due them from the corporation. The IRS contended that the notes were equity, and payments received were additional consideration for the stock. *Held:* For taxpayer. Even if the notes

Bonds and Debentures: *Bond Discount and Premiums*

were a class of stock, their bases would be equal to their face amount, and no gain would be realized. Rushing, 52 TC 888 (1969).

Exchange of unregistered stock. Taxpayer received a corporate purchaser's interest-bearing note for an amount greater than the value of 51 percent of the unregistered common stock of a public corporation. The note was treated as issued for stock or securities traded in an established securities market for the purposes of Section 1232(b)(2)(B). Any difference between the issue price of the promissory note received by the taxpayer, (fair market value of the shares at the time of acquisition) and the face amount of such promissory note represented the original issue discount that must be reported as ordinary income by the taxpayer over the life of the promissory note pursuant to Section 1232(a)(3)(A) and Regulation § 1.12323A. Rev. Rul. 75-117, 1975-1 CB 273.

Bond Discount and Premiums

Repurchase of hybrid securities does not, under facts, result in amortizable bond discount. Taxpayer had outstanding stock called "guaranteed stock." This stock: (1) had a face value which became due six months after payment of the 7 percent "guaranteed dividend" was in arrears, (2) paid dividends regardless of earnings, and (3) was secured by taxpayer's property. Holders of "guaranteed stock" can vote their shares and can participate in liquidation proceeds after the common stockholders. Holders of such stock were entitled to dividends in excess of the guaranteed amount if more than that was paid on the common stock. Taxpayer repurchased some of the "guaranteed stock" for a price far in excess of the face value of such stock. Taxpayer claimed a deduction for the excess of the purchase price over the stock's par value. *Held:* For the IRS. The "guaranteed stock" is a hybrid security which may be treated as debt for some purposes and as equity for others. For purposes of determining whether repurchase resulted in amortizable discount, the "guaranteed stock" is more like stock than debt. Thus, no discount arises.

Further, taxpayer made no attempt to allocate between equity and debt characteristics of stock. Richmond, Fredericksburg & Potomac RR Co., 528 F2d 917, 76-1 USTC ¶ 9101, 37 AFTR2d 76-424 (4th Cir. 1976).

Amortizable bond discount found to exist on bonds exchanged for preferred (and preferred-like) stock that had stated value less than the face amount of the bonds. In 1941, the SEC required taxpayer to simplify its capital structure. Taxpayer, in exchange for all its preferred and "preference" stock, issued 30-year 3 percent sinking fund debentures. The face amount of the debentures was equal to the stated value of the exchanged stock plus call premiums and 14-year's worth of dividend arrearages. The IRS argued that no amortizable discount existed with respect to the debentures. Taxpayer claimed that the face amount of the debentures exceeded the value of the stock for which they were exchanged, and thus the debentures were issued at a discount. *Held:* For taxpayer, in part, and IRS, in part. Taxpayer incurred additional "costs" in substituting its debentures for the stock; namely, the face amount of the debentures exceeded the stated value of the preferred and the original consideration paid at the time of its issuance. To retain the use of the capital represented by the preferred and preference stock, taxpayer incurred an additional cost by replacing an uncertain stock obligation with a fixed one of greater value. Accordingly, debt discount arose. Cities Serv. Co., 522 F2d 1281, 75-1 USTC ¶ 9107, 35 AFTR2d 75-462 (2d Cir. 1974).

Conversion features of debentures not amortizable as bond discount. On March 1, 1961, taxpayer sold, at par, an amount of convertible debentures which were convertible into taxpayer's common stock. Taxpayer alleged a certain value for the conversion right and the value of the debt. The IRS accepted the values, but disagreed with taxpayer's assertion that the value of the conversion rights measured or reflected a debt discount amortizable over certain years after the sale. *Held:* For the IRS. For there to be a discount, there must be an added cost to the issuer over and above the stated interest for the use of the

BONDS AND DEBENTURES: *Bond Discount and Premiums*

payee's capital. In the case of the debenture issued with a conversion feature, the holder may either convert his debenture into stock or redeem the debenture at the end of the prescribed period; he may do one or the other, but not both. In any event, the issuer does not incur costs above the debentures stated value plus the stated interest. There may be economic consequences to the issuer for choosing not to sell the conversion feature separately, but this "loss" will be reflected, as here, in a lower interest rate on the debenture. Taxpayer failed to carry the burden by showing that the amount allocable to the conversion feature represented a cost of borrowing money that must without qualification be paid. Chock Full O'Nuts, 453 F2d 300, 72-1 USTC ¶ 9146, 29 AFTR2d 72-305 (2d Cir. 1971).

Bond discount must be reasonable. Upon incorporation of a partnership business, $22,000 of par value of stock was issued for most of the fixed assets, goodwill, and prepaid items; $64,000 of debentures were issued for inventories, receivables, furniture, and fixtures. The debentures bore interest at 4 percent and matured in 20 years, but could be redeemed earlier at a premium. The district court held that the interest on the debentures was deductible, that there was a business purpose for their issuance, and that they had the characteristics of debt instruments. The court also allowed a deduction for a 32 percent premium paid on the retirement of certain of the debentures. *Held:* Affirmed only as to the deductibility of the bond interest. Merely because the bonds were issued to the stockholders in proportion to their stock interests did not mean the bonds should be considered capital. Premiums paid on retirement of the bonds, constituting approximately 32 percent of their face value, were deductible only to the extent they were reasonable. Haskel Eng'g & Supply Co., 380 F2d 786, 67-2 USTC ¶ 9534, 20 AFTR2d 5077 (9th Cir. 1967).

Conversion feature of debentures explained. On or about March 1, 1961, taxpayer sold, at par, convertible debentures having a face amount of $100 each. They were due on March 1, 1981, and bore interest at the rate of 4.25 percent per annum. They were convertible into taxpayer's common stock at the rate of five-sixths of one share for each $100 debenture through March 1, 1971, and at a somewhat lesser rate thereafter. Taxpayer asserted that the value of the conversion rights measured or reflected a debt discount amortizable for the years 1961, 1962 and 1963. *Held:* For the IRS. In its review, the Courts Claims noted that in order for there to be a discount, there must be an added cost to the issuer over and above the stated interest for the use of the payee's capital. In the case of the debentures issued with a conversion feature, the holder may either convert his debenture into stock or redeem the debenture at the end of the prescribed period. In any event, the court observed that the issuer does not incur costs over and above the face value of the debenture plus the stated interest. Hence, the interest deduction was disallowed for original issue discount on convertible debentures. The issue price of the convertible debentures was held to include any amount attributable to the conversion feature. AMF, Inc., cert. denied, 476 F2d 1351, 73-1 USTC ¶ 9353, 31 AFTR2d 73-1136 (Ct. Cl. 1973).

No bond discount incurred in an exchange of debentures for common stock. The IRS asked the court to reconsider its original opinion as to whether bond discount was incurred on the exchange of taxpayer corporation's debentures for its common stock. *Held:* Prior decision was modified to the extent that no bond discount was deemed incurred on the exchange, as the value of the common stock on the date of exchange exceeded the maturity value of the debentures. Missouri Pac. RR Co., 433 F2d 1324, 70-2 USTC ¶ 9698, 26 AFTR2d 70-5812 (Ct. Cl. 1970), cert. denied, 402 US 904 (1971).

Premium paid to stockholder for debt retirement deductible. Taxpayer's 50 percent stockholder owned its entire issue of 6 percent bonds. The other stockholders desired to retire the bonds, but the 50 percent stockholder was reluctant to permit this because the bonds were thought to be an attractive investment. After negotiations, a 7 percent premi-

BONDS AND DEBENTURES: *Bond Discount and Premiums*

um was paid to retire the bonds. The IRS disallowed the premium as a deductible expense in the year of retirement. *Held:* For taxpayer. Although the parties were related, the dealing here was at arm's length. Thus, the premium was deductible. Baltimore Steam Packet Co., 180 F. Supp. 347, 60-1 USTC ¶ 9231 (Ct. Cl. 1960).

Interest and premium paid to foreign parent upon converted debentures held not deductible. Taxpayer and its subsidiaries operated an integrated oil and gas business in the United States and abroad. *H*, its parent, was similarly engaged in Canada. In 1972, taxpayer issued debentures which were convertible into the common stock of its parent. Upon redemption, 100 percent of principal plus accrued interest to redemption was paid, with an additional premium tacked on for redemptions prior to June 15, 1972. In 1977, taxpayer called the debentures for redemption. They were redeemed from the parent by the issuance of two interest-bearing promissory notes for approximately $23 million. Taxpayer computed the interest and premium due on $23 million. On its 1977 return, taxpayer deducted various related items that the IRS disallowed, including the unamortized premium and interest paid to *H* upon the converted debentures. *Held:* For the IRS. In *H*'s hands, the converted debentures represented merely the right to the underlying principal amount. Therefore, taxpayer could not deduct the amounts paid as "interest" on the converted debentures or premium. The election by the holder of a convertible debenture called for redemption to convert such debentures into common stock and extinguished the issuer's obligation to pay those components of the redemption price, which consisted of accrued interest and premiums. Husky Oil Co., 83 TC 717 (1984), appealed (10th Cir. 1985).

Premium paid on redemption of convertible notes not deductible. Taxpayer issued to one of its principal stockholders notes with a face value of $40,000, which were convertible into stock. Taxpayer had an agreement with that stockholder to purchase his shares at book value on his death or retirement. The stockholder died, and taxpayer paid $117,000 for his notes, the book value of the stock into which the notes were convertible. Taxpayer claimed a loss of $77,000 as incurred in retirement of debt. The IRS disallowed the deduction. *Held:* For the IRS. Regulation § 1.61-12(c)(1) allows a deduction for the excess of the purchase price of a bond over its face, but that deduction must be limited here to the redemption price (106 percent of face plus accrued interest). Otherwise, Section 311, which disallows any corporate loss on a distribution with respect to its stock, would be circumvented. This security had elements of both a bond and a stock, and these must be separated to avoid form controlling substance. In substance, taxpayer purchased its stock, a practice in line with its established policy of allowing only active employees to be stockholders. Roberts & Porter Inc., 37 TC 23 (1961).

Amortization of discount on debentures issued to sole stockholder disallowed. An individual transferred all the assets of his proprietorship to taxpayer, a newly formed corporation, for all of its stock and debentures, which were to mature in 10 years. He claimed that a portion of the inventory was the consideration for the debentures, which were valued in the transfer at $1,000 each and had a face value at maturity of $1,500. Taxpayer sought to amortize this discount over the 10-year period; the IRS disallowed the deduction. *Held:* For the IRS. The court held that the issuance of the notes was merely part of a more comprehensive transaction. Consequently, it could not be said that the debentures were issued for assets worth less than their face amount. The claimed discount was completely artificial. The court did not decide whether to follow the rule in Montana Power Co., 232 F2d 541 (1956), which holds that, where there is no arm's-length dealing between the seller and the purchasing corporation, no deduction is available in respect of discount allegedly inhering in the obligation of the purchasing corporation issued for assets transferred to it. Nassau Lens Co., 35 TC 268 (1960).

**Discount purchase of notes, and subsequent merger with debtor corporation give rise to or-

BONDS AND DEBENTURES: *Deduction of Interest Paid*

dinary income equal to discount. In a prior transaction unrelated to a subsequent statutory merger, a corporation purchased notes of the merged corporation from certain banks at a discount. IRS ruled that no gain or loss would be recognized on the satisfaction of the indebtedness. However, ordinary income would be recognized to the extent of the market discount originating when the notes were purchased. Rev. Rul. 72-464, 1972-2 CB 214.

IRS determines amount deductible on call premium paid on repurchase of corporation's debentures. On March 24, 1964, a corporation issued, at par, 5 percent subordinated convertible debentures, each in the face amount of $100, due on March 17, 1974. The debentures were convertible, at the holder's option, at any time on or before the date fixed for redemption, into two shares of the common stock of the corporation. Under the terms of the bond, the corporation reserved the right to call the debentures at decreasing prices beginning at 105 percent of face value up to March 17, 1969, and diminishing to 100 percent after September 17, 1973. On December 18, 1968, the corporation repurchased all of the debentures of $167 each. On that date, each share of the common stock of the corporation had a fair market value of $83.50. In determining the deductibility of the call premium under Section 163, the IRS noted that since the corporation obligated itself prior to September 5, 1968 to repurchase its convertible bonds at a specified price, after call, the deductibility of the premium paid on repurchase must be tested under the provisions of Regulation § 1.163-3(c)(1), which provides that the allowable deduction may not exceed an amount equal to one year's interest at the rate specified in the bond, except to the extent that the corporation can demonstrate to the satisfaction of the IRS that an amount in excess of one year's interest does not include any amount attributable to the conversion feature. Accordingly, the IRS held that the amount deductible by the corporation under these facts would be limited to $5, the amount of the call premium specified in each debenture related to the cost of borrowing. The excess amount paid on repurchase of each debenture, $62 (i.e., $67 minus $5) is not deductible, since the corporation was under no legal obligation to pay such amount, and it does not relate to the cost of borrowing money, but represents an expenditure by the corporation to preclude conversion of the bonds into its common stock. Rev. Rul. 69-243, 1969-1 CB 56.

Discount interest on bonds carries over to new bonds in nontaxable exchange. Taxpayer, who was not a broker, trader, or dealer in securities, exchanged certain nondefaulted, noninterest-bearing debentures that had been issued at a discount for new ten-year debentures pursuant to a tax-free reorganization of the debtor. When new debentures are redeemed prior to, or at maturity, that part of the redemption value that represents original issue discount will constitute interest and will be taxable as ordinary income. Rev. Rul. 60-37, 1960-1 CB 307.

Deduction of Interest Paid

Interest deduction allowed where intention was to create a debt. Taxpayer was incorporated to construct and operate an office building. Although some outside loans were obtained, they were insufficient for all of taxpayer's needs. Consequently, taxpayer issued 7 percent, 19-year debentures purchased by its stockholders. The IRS, pointing to a four-to-one debt-equity ratio, contended that the debentures were equity certificates and denied an interest deduction. *Held:* The interest was deductible. Thin capitalization is only one consideration in determining whether an issue is debt or stock. After looking at other criteria, the court found it obvious that the intention was to create a debt instrument. 1661 Corp., 377 F2d 291, 67-1 USTC ¶ 9438 (5th Cir. 1967).

Interest deduction denied absent true indebtedness. Two partnerships, composed entirely of members of one family, acquired a parcel of real estate. After deciding to construct a building thereon, they formed taxpayer corporation, to which the property was "sold" in exchange for mortgages and notes. Taxpayer

Bonds and Debentures: *Deduction of Interest Paid*

then obtained a construction loan to which the partnership notes were subordinated. The District court held that interest deductions on the loans from the partnerships were denied for lack of a true indebtedness. *Held:* Affirmed. The transaction was merely a capital transfer because (1) the repayment schedule on the loans was ignored; (2) no dividends were paid by taxpayer; (3) the partnerships subordinated their interests to the bank loan; (4) the corporation was thinly capitalized; and (5) there was complete identity of interest between taxpayer's stockholders and the "creditors." Aronov Constr. Co., 338 F2d 337, 64-2 USTC ¶ 9837 (5th Cir. 1964).

Payments to holders of debenture bonds considered interest. Taxpayer corporation was expanding, and in order to acquire new assets at a cost of about 2.5 times the amount of its capital represented by stock, it retired its preferred stock and simultaneously authorized the issuance of debenture bonds. These bonds were purchased by the stockholders or members of their families in proportion to their stockholdings. Although the debenture bonds satisfied all the formal requirements to make them effective as debt obligations, the Tax Court found that they in fact were nothing more than a continuation of the risk represented by the stock. *Held:* Reversed. Some of the bonds were held by nonstockholders. There was no reason to believe that the debentures could not be enforced as debt instruments. Payments to the debenture bondholders were, therefore, deductible as interest. Gloucester Ice & Cold Storage Co., 298 F2d 183, 62-1 USTC ¶ 9212 (1st Cir. 1962).

Bonds without fixed interest obligation held to be equity capital. Seven individuals incorporated taxpayer and transferred their real estate holdings to taxpayer in exchange for stock and registered gold bonds. The bonds were unsecured and provided that interest would be paid only at the discretion of the board of directors and were in no event to exceed 7 percent. Interest payments were not cumulative, and there was no provision for maturity in case of default. Each stockholder held one-seventh of the stock and one-seventh of the bonds. The amount of interest to be paid each year was determined by the board of directors at a meeting held at the end of the year. No dividends were ever declared by taxpayer. The IRS argued that the bonds represented equity. *Held:* For the IRS. The Tax Court held, and the appellate court affirmed, that the bonds were no genuine indebtedness, but rather equity capital; therefore, the payments thereon were not deductible as interest. Gokey Properties, Inc., 290 F2d 870, 61-2 USTC ¶ 9493 (2d Cir. 1961).

Deduction for interest denied on debentures that were in substance equity. Taxpayer was organized in 1957. An individual transferred to it land and $12 in cash in exchange for all taxpayer's stock plus $89,000 in five percent, 20-year, unsecured debentures. The debentures were subordinated to all obligations except stockholder's. No dividends on stock were to be paid until the debentures were retired. Despite this, dividends on preferred stock were paid in 1966 through 1968. No provision was made for retirement through a sinking fund. No interest was paid on the debentures until 1962, when $22,500 was paid for 1957 through 1962. Although the land was originally transferred to taxpayer for development and rent, it was clear in 1957 that taxpayer's principal source of income would be from the sale of the land. The debentures were never retired. The IRS argued that the debentures were equity, not debt, and that the 1962 "interest" payment of $22,500 was not deductible. *Held:* For IRS. The only purpose of the debentures was to reduce corporate taxes, and were not treated as debts. Ram Corp., 305 F. Supp. 831, 69-2 USTC ¶ 9708 (WDNC 1969).

Debentures transferred to trust for children held bona fide obligations. The assets of a proprietorship business had a fair market value of $200,000. Taxpayer corporation was organiaed to acquire the business with $150,000 of 5 percent debentures and 5,000 shares of two different classes of stock. The debentures were then given to trusts for the benefit of the sole stockholder's children. The IRS denied an interest deduction on the bonds. *Held:* For taxpayer. Interest on the

BONDS AND DEBENTURES: *Deduction of Interest Paid*

debentures was deductible. It was intended that a bona fide indebtedness be created. The debentures were not subordinated to the claims of other creditors. Air-Vent Aluminum Awning Mfg. Co., 66-1 USTC ¶ 9115 (SD Cal. 1965).

Interest deductible on debentures issued on parent company. Taxpayer was formerly a division of an investment company and became a subsidiary to make operations more efficient. The parent transferred all the assets of the business to taxpayer in exchange for $1 million in stock and $3 million in debentures. The IRS contended that the debentures did not constitute debt. *Held:* For taxpayer. Although the debentures gave the holder certain voting rights in cases of default and were held exclusively by the sole stockholder, the court found that they should be recognized as debt instruments for tax purposes. The interest was therefore deductible. Luden's Inc., 196 F. Supp. 526, 61-2 USTC ¶ 9595 (ED Pa. 1961).

Debentures issued to stockholders recognized as debt. Upon incorporation of a partnership, stock and debenture bonds were issued to stockholders. The bonds were in the ratio of 4 to 1 to the stock. They provided for a fixed maturity and a fixed interest. Taxpayer corporation claimed a deduction for the amount of interest paid to the stockholders. The IRS disallowed the deduction on the grounds that the bonds did not represent true debt. *Held:* For taxpayer. The court found that there was an intention to create true indebtedness, and that interest on the debentures was deductible. Daytona Mach. Supply Co., 61-2 USTC ¶ 9523 (SD Fla. 1961).

Debentures were real debt; interest allowed. The IRS contended that the interest paid by the taxpayer corporation on debenture bonds issued by it was dividends paid on the equivalent of stock. *Held:* For taxpayer. The district court stated: "The interest paid on the debentures had all of the characteristics of interest and none of dividends unless inferred. The dentures had no provision whereby they could profit or increase in amount of return through the prosperity of the corporation or by the increase in value of the common stock.

The owners of the debenture had the right to receive interest semi-annually, regardless of profits or losses, and had to be paid in full at maturity regardless of whether or not the assets of the corporation were sufficient to pay the general creditors or whether the common stockholders received anything. At maturity, the debenture owners were entitled to receive only the face value of the debentures plus accrued interest, if any, even though all common and secured creditors had been paid and the common stock was worth many times its face value." Burke Golf Equip. Corp., 193 F. Supp. 615, 61-1 USTC ¶ 9229, 7 AFTR2d 652 (ND Ill. 1961).

Corporation allowed interest deduction because it was subject to demands of bondholders although not timely paid. Taxpayer, an accrual basis corporation, had debenture bonds outstanding. Its bookkeeper computed the interest thereon at year end and notified the bondholders. She had the authority to write checks and to pay the interest at any time after it became due. Sufficient funds were readily available. The interest was not paid within two and a half months after the close of the taxpayer's fiscal year, but was claimed by the the taxpayer as a deduction. *Held:* For taxpayer. The only question was whether the bondholders were in constructive receipt of the interest. The bookkeeper could draw checks and pay the interest at any time after it became due, and the bondholders could demand it after such time. The interest income was unqualifiedly subject to their demands. Furthermore, no additional corporate action was necessary to bind it to pay the interest. It was therefore concluded that the interest income was constructively received by the bondholders; accordingly, the interest deductions were not disallowed under Section 267(a)(2). F.D. Bissett & Son, Inc., 56 TC 453 (1971), acq. 1971-2 CB 2.

Notes were bona fide debt. Taxpayer corporation was organized to rescue and financially rehabilitate a partnership and eventually allow the partners to reaquire the business. The initial capital structure was in a bank loan and a three-to-one ratio of subordinated notes to stock. Taxpayer claimed an interest

Bonds and Debentures: Deduction of Interest Paid

deduction on the subordinated notes. *Held:* For taxpayer. The notes represented bona fide indebtedness, not contributions to capital. The intent of the parties was evidenced by a debt instrument that provided for a fixed maturity date and a fixed rate of interest. A continued pro rata securities holding did not exist, and a business purpose was established for the initial capital structure. Taxpayer also had the ability to obtain outside funds. Based on the facts, the payments were deductible as interest. Green Bay Structural Steel, Inc., 53 TC 451 (1969).

Deductibility of interest determined. Taxpayer corporation, organized to acquire the assets of a division in financial trouble, obtained funds by issuing common stock, selling debentures to a stockholder, and obtaining bank loans and stockholder advances in the form of unsecured notes. The IRS disallowed taxpayer's deductions for interest paid on the debentures and notes. *Held:* For the IRS. The advances did not constitute valid debts, and note and bond interest was not deductible. Despite the fact that the debentures had a fixed maturity date, such date had been extended three times. The debentures were subordinated to the bank loan, and thus their holder's rights to share in liquidation and to demand payment on the maturity date were invalidated. The subordination agreement and the poor financial condition of taxpayer's business indicated that the notes would not be repaid. Thus, the payments by taxpayer constituted dividends, not deductible interest payments. Killhour Sons, Inc., 32 TCM 855, ¶ 73,183 P-H Memo. TC (1973).

Corporate instruments were debentures, and interest payments were deductible. Taxpayer corporation issued debentures upon incorporation and reorganization and subsequently claimed interest deductions. The IRS disallowed the deductions, claiming that the debentures were really equity investments. *Held:* For taxpayer. The corporate instruments were true debentures as they had debt-related characteristics: fixed maturity date, certainty of payment of interest and principal, the absence of voting rights, as well as the right to share in profits of the business. Therefore, taxpayer was entitled to the interest deductions. Weaver Popcorn Co., 30 TCM 1204, ¶ 71, 281 P-H Memo. TC (1971).

Interest deduction disallowed where corporate note did not create a bona fide indebtedness. Taxpayer corporation agreed to repurchase 240 shares of its stock for a $70,000 note at a 5 percent interest rate and took deductions for the payment of interest. The IRS disallowed the deductions. *Held:* For the IRS. The facts determined that there was not an unconditional intent to repay the demand note; therefore, it was not a bona fide indebtedness for tax purposes. Also, the payments were in the nature of dividends. The note could not have been paid on demand without impairing taxpayer's ability to operate. No principal payments were demanded by or paid to the initial noteholder or her estate. This was a family corporation, and no payments would have been made unless the noteholder needed funds and the corporation could afford to pay them. W.O. Covey, Inc., 28 TCM 1379, ¶ 69,273 P-H Memo. TC (1969).

Interest allowed on debentures owned by stockholders in proportion to stockholdings. X Corporation organized to construct a ski lift issued $94,200 of 7 percent debentures to its stockholders in proportion to their stockholdings in exchange for the advancement of funds. The debentures were issued after the corporate tried unsuccessfully to secure outside loans. The stockholders had originally invested $20,000 in stock. The IRS contended that the debentures were not true debt and disallowed the deduction of interest thereon paid. *Held:* For taxpayer. Even though the debentures were subordinated to the debts of the general creditors and provided that interest thereon could be postponed for up to three years, the court found that the debentures constituted a genuine debt; hence, interest payments on the debentures were properly deducted. Brighton Recreations, Inc., 20 TCM 127, ¶ 61,029 P-H Memo. TC (1961).

IRS ruled on deductibility of interest accrued on convertible debentures. Taxpayer, a domestic corporation, issued 20-year debenture

BONDS AND DEBENTURES: *Equity Investments Distinguished*

bonds convertible into its own capital stock. Interest was payable on April 1 and October 1 of each year. The debentures provided that upon conversion of the debenture between interest payment dates, no interest would be payable for such period. Taxpayer computes its income under an accrual method of accounting on the fiscal year ending August 31. The IRS, citing Section 461 and related regulations, held that the corporation could not accrue and deduct at the end of its taxable year the interest attributable to the period from the most recent interest payment date. The IRS reasoned that all of the events had not occurred by August 31 and that Regulation § 1.461-1(a)(2) would allow taxpayer to deduct the interest on the convertible bonds. That is, between August 31 and the following September 30 of each year, there exists the possibility of all debenture holders converting their debentures into taxpayer's capital stock, thus eliminating all liability of taxpayer to pay interest on the debentures for April-September 30 interest period. It is irrelevant for the purpose of the "all events test" that it is unlikely that all debenture holders will convert during that period. Rev. Rul. 74-127, 1974-1 CB 47.

Equity Investments Distinguished

Debentures were valid debt instruments. The district court held that payments on certain debentures issued by taxpayer corporation to its stockholders were deductible interest, not non-deductible dividends. *Held:* Affirmed. The debentures were debt instruments because they contained a fixed payment date, provided for a commercially reasonable rate of return, contained an unconditional promise to repay, and the right to force complete payment in the event of default of interest or principal, and were not automatically subordinated to the claims of tradesmen or vendors. In terms of economic reality, a debtor-creditor relationship existed. Scriptomatic, Inc., 555 F2d 364, 77-1 USTC ¶ 9428, 40 AFTR2d 77-5059 (3d Cir. 1977).

Indebtedness constituted capital contributions; interest disallowed. Taxpayer corporation issued bonds and notes to its stockholders and deducted interest on such indebtedness. The IRS disallowed the deduction and was upheld by the Tax Court. Although interest was regularly paid and the debt equity ratio was quite low, it was ascertained that taxpayer never paid cash. The advances were found to be of an investment nature in that they were unsecured, no demand for payment was ever made, the maturity date of bonds not redeemed was extended, and they were subordinate to the issuer of a line of credit. Thus the payments more resembled nondeductible dividends. *Held:* Affirmed. Taxpayer failed to meet its burden of proving that the bonds were debt in substance as well as form. Trans-Atlantic Co., 469 F2d 1189, 72-2 USTC ¶ 9758, 31 AFTR2d 73-322 (3d Cir. 1972).

Interest on subsidiary's bonds held by parent not deductible where repayment not expected. During 1960 through 1964, taxpayer was a wholly owned subsidiary indebted to its parent, which held two bond issues. The bonds were issued in 1913 and 1928. No payment of interest had been made since 1930, and no payment of principal was ever made. Taxpayer was insolvent, but had rental income from its parent. A deduction was claimed for accrued interest expense on the bonds. The Tax Court held against the taxpayer. *Held:* Affirmed. The bonds in substance represented equity capital rather than debt. A parent's failure to enforce its rights as a creditor belies the existence of true debt. Taxpayer was insolvent and could not meet its interest obligation. Accordingly, the interest deduction was improper. Tampa & Gulf Coast RR Co., 469 F2d 263, 72-2 USTC ¶ 9746, 30 AFTR2d 72-5723 (5th Cir. 1972).

Assignment to corporation of option rights held by stockholders in return for cash and notes was a sale. Taxpayer corporation was dormant until another corporation owned by the same stockholder acquired a tract of land and gave the stockholder and another party an option to purchase the land. Shortly thereafter, the remainder of taxpayer's outstanding stock was acquired by the two aforementioned parties. At the same time, taxpayer acquired the options held by the stockholders,

Bonds and Debentures: *Equity Investments Distinguished*

paying therefor with unsecured promissory notes, exercising the options, and selling the acquired lots to outside purchasers. The considerations given by taxpayer to the stockholders for each option received was equivalent to or less than the fair market value thereof, and, until the IRS questioned whether the purported sales were bona fide, taxpayer paid interest on the notes and current payments of principal. At no time did it pay dividends or salaries. The IRS determined that the sales were not bona fide, but constituted contributions of the options to the corporation's capital. Therefore, the claimed interest deductions were disallowed, and the cost basis of the property to taxpayer were adjusted. The Tax Court upheld the IRS, finding that although there was evidence of sales, the transfers of options were contributions to capital, and the promissory notes were to be regarded as equity investments with the interest paid thereon constituting dividends. *Held:* Reversed. As factors indicating sales, the Tax Court found that the notes were unconditional promises to pay with fixed maturity dates, that they bore reasonable intent, and conferred no voting rights. The Tax Court found significant the fact that the notes were issued proportionately to the two stockholders and concluded that this was consistent with the conclusion that the notes represented an equity interest in the corporation. However, while a proportionate relationship might have been consistent with the conclusion that notes represented equity, such a relationship standing alone did not constitute evidence of that conclusion. The only substantial factor supporting the determination that the transfers were not sales was taxpayer's undercapitalization. The Tax Court relied on Burr Oaks, 365 F2d 24 (7th Cir. 1966), and Aqualane, 269 F2d 116 (1959), distinguishing the present case from Sun Properties, 220 F2d 171 (1955). In the latter case, notwithstanding a thin capitalization, the transfer of income-producing properties in exchange for an unsecured promise to pay was deemed a sale and not a contribution to capital. The court thus concluded that the Burr Oaks and Aqualane cases were clearly distinguishable from the instant case and that Sun Properties should be followed. Negotiations here had begun before taxpayer had acquired title to any land, thus giving some degree of certainty to the financial success of the venture, and thereby refuting the contention that the properties for which the notes were issued were placed as equity at the risk of the corporation. Piedmont Corp., 388 F2d 886, 68-1 USTC ¶ 9189, 21 AFTR2d 534 (4th Cir. 1968).

Notes treated as equity capital. The stockholders of taxpayer corporation lent it $365,000 on interest-bearing notes in proportion to their stockholdings. The notes provided that if any notes were paid, the others had to be paid proportionately. Interest on the notes was waived from time to time. In the taxable years at issue, interest was paid. The IRS denied the interest deduction. *Held:* For the IRS. The court held that the notes represented equity capital. The interest was not deductible. Covey Inv. Co., 377 F2d 403, 67-1 USTC ¶ 9471 (10th Cir. 1967).

Subordinated debentures did not create a bona fide indebtedness. Taxpayer corporation was formed to acquire the assets and assume the liabilities of a business previously operated by two brothers as equal partners. Each brother received half of the capital stock and half of the subordinated debentures of the corporation. The debentures were payable in 20 years with interest at 6 percent payable semiannually. They were subordinated to the claims of general creditors and transferable by written assignments on the books of the corporation. The IRS determined that the interest payments constituted dividends and denied the deduction, contending that the debentures created rights not dissimilar to preferred stock. Taxpayer contended that the intent of the parties was to create an obligation. The district court directed a verdict in favor of the taxpayer. *Held:* Reversed. The questions were whether the debentures constituted an indebtedness or a contribution to capital, and whether the intent of the parties should be disregarded in this transaction. Here, the issue was not *merely* one of attempting to create a debt relationship, nor *merely* the subordination of debt, but both. In addition, the debentures were long term and unsecured, lacking in limitations on payment of dividends, and without provision for a sinking fund. Furthermore, the subordination provisions made practically ineffectual what otherwise appeared to be an absolute obligation to pay interest regularly and principal when due. To construe the document as an "indebtedness" would be to give substance to a transaction that, on its face, lies outside the plain interest of the statute. Snyder Bros., 367 F2d 980, 66-2 USTC ¶ 9573, 18 AFTR2d 5316 (5th Cir. 1966), cert. denied, 386 US 956 (1967).

Debentures held to be stock; thin capitalization not in issue. Taxpayers purchased ten-year 4 percent debentures and Class A stock in a real estate corporation. The IRS contended that the repayments of principal on the debentures were dividends, and that the provisions of the debentures applied more to a stockholder than a creditor. In support of this argument, the IRS cited the following debenture provisions: (1) a moratorium on default if 75 percent of holders agreed, (2) 75 percent of holders could alter the agreement, and (3) the formula for repayment of principal would not require a sinking fund, but would depend on working capital ratios. The corporation appealed the IRS' determination to the Tax Court, while the stockholders sued for a refund in the district court. In the district court, taxpayer-stockholders refuted the IRS' position by pointing out that the debentures were adequately secured, and that this was not a thin capitalization situation. The district court sustained the IRS, stating that a number of factors must exist in order for a debtor-creditor relationship to be bona fide. An examination of the provisions of the debenture agreement, together with testimony of various purchasers, including taxpayers, showed that the 4 percent interest paid on the bonds, which were subordinate to first and second mortgages, did not make an attractive investment. The investors were looking for principal repayment within five or six years, as well as appreciation in the common stock. The Tax Court likewise found for IRS, holding that the debentures did not represent bona fide indebtedness. The petition to the Sixth Court for review of the Tax Court decision was consolidated with the appeal from the district court judgment for hearing in the appellate court. *Held:* Affirmed. The question of whether the debentures represented bona fide indebtedness was one of facts for the Tax Court and the district court. Since these findings were not clearly erroneous, the appellate court could not set them aside. Fellinger, 363 F2d 826, 66-2 USTC ¶ 9586 (6th Cir. 1966).

Notes of stockholder incorporators held equity capital. The two stockholder incorporators of taxpayer contracted to purchase assets of existing businesses in order to activate taxpayer. The price was over $425,000. To finance the purchase, taxpayer obtained a bank loan of $300,000, which the incorporators guaranteed. Each incorporator transferred $100,000 to the corporation, with $75,000 designated as a loan and $25,000 as equity capital. The stockholders' loans, which were represented by two $75,000 demand notes, were subordinated to the bank loan. The Tax Court sustained the IRS' disallowance of interest deductions on the notes. *Held:* Affirmed. The court found that the notes represented equity capital rather than bona fide debt, and that the use of the funds to purchase the necessary assets of the business indicated a permanent investment at the risk of the business. Even though the notes were in demand form, they were in fact subordinated to the bank's loan and in effect could not be deemed to have a maturity date prior to the obligations of the bank. General Alloy Casting Co., 345 F2d 794, 65-2 USTC ¶ 9462 (3d Cir. 1965).

"Debentures" issued on transfer of intangibles upon incorporation treated as equity capital. Taxpayers, equal partners in business, transferred certain of the partnership assets to X Corporation for $150,000 par value of stock and $166,000 face value of debentures. The debentures were issued in direct proportion to stock ownership in exchange for goodwill and other intangibles. In order to provide X with working capital, the stockholders in a separate transaction loaned X $20,000, evidenced by notes. The Tax Court held that the debentures represented an equity interest in X Corporation rather than indebtedness, and hence were the equivalent of stock. *Held:* Af-

BONDS AND DEBENTURES: *Equity Investments Distinguished*

firmed. There was no new capital or money transferred to the corporation for the debentures when there was a need for operating capital, and the assets which were transferred for the debentures were a part of *X* Corporation's permanent capital structure. Therefore, amounts paid as "interest" were in reality dividends, and amounts received upon retirement of the debentures were also essentially equivalent to dividends. Moughon, 329 F2d 399, 64-1 USTC ¶ 9345 (6th Cir. 1964).

Interest deduction disallowed on debt-heavy capital structure. An accrual-basis taxpayer, engaged in the business of construction and renting apartments, sought to deduct interest accrued on its outstanding debenture notes. *Held:* The disctrict court's disallowance of the deduction was affirmed, since: (1) the notes were held only by stockholders and in the same proportion as their stock ownership; (2) the debt-to-equity ratio was 4 to 1; (3) the notes were substantiated to all other corporate indebtedness; (4) corporate income was not enough to pay expenses; and (5) there was no funding provision to pay the notes at maturity. McSorley's, Inc., 323 F2d 900, 63-2 USTC ¶ 9797, 12 AFTR2d 5874 (10th Cir. 1963).

Indefinitely subordinated debentures held equity capital. Taxpayer, a finance company, required substantial amounts of additional money that were not available through ordinary channels. It therefore issued 7 percent, five year, registered debenture bonds to its sole stockholder and his wife, who supplied the additional funds. Although the instruments bore a maturity date, they were not paid. Due to bank agreements subordinating these debentures, payment thereon had, in effect, been extended indefinitely. The IRS determined that the investment in the debentures was one that was intended to ride with the ups and downs of the venture, and was not a bona fide debt payable in any event. *Held:* For the IRS. Interest payments on the debentures were nondeductible dividends. The court, however, rejected the Tax Court's reasoning that taxpayer was thinly capitalized, since finance companies customarily operate on large amounts of borrowed capital. P.M. Fin. Corp., 302 F2d 786, 62-1 USTC ¶ 9465, 9 AFTR2d 1454 (3d Cir. 1962).

Advances held loans as the notes evidencing the loans had stated maturity dates, and reasonable and fixed interest rates. Taxpayer corporation had four stockholders who were also officers. The stockholders each contributed a certain amount of capital to the corporation, partially in return for common stock, and the remainder as loans evidenced by promissory notes. There was no specific collateral for these notes and repayment depended on taxpayer's ability to make good its obligations. During the years in question, taxpayer made payments to stockholders that it characterized as interest payments due on the notes held by the respective stockholders, and the corporation claimed a deduction for these payments on its tax returns. The IRS disallowed the deductions. *Held:* For taxpayer. The notes evidencing the loans had stated maturity dates, reasonable stated interest rates, and a fixed interest rate that did not vary from year to year. There was a clear identity of ownership between the stockholders and the holders of these notes; however, the notes themselves conferred no rights of management in the corporation. Since the notes were transferable, it was possible to remove identity and proportionality of ownership. Additionally, the noteholders' rights were those of general creditors of the corporation, and the notes had never been subordinated to other creditors. Furthermore, the corporation never failed to pay interest due the noteholders. Lastly, the financial structure of the corporation was sound. Flomaton Wholesale Co., 74-2 USTC ¶ 9704, 34 AFTR2d 74-5875 (SD Ala. 1974).

Mortgage bonds in substance equity. The IRS determined that mortgage bonds issued by taxpayer corporation in exchange for its preferred stock were equity; therefore, interest deductions were disallowed. *Held:* For the IRS. Among the factors supporting the IRS' determination was a debt-equity ratio of twenty to one. This ratio became even more relevant in view of the fact that the bondholder also owned 75 percent of taxpayer's stock. It was also significant that no new cap-

Bonds and Debentures: *Equity Investments Distinguished*

ital was introduced into taxpayer as a result of the exchange of preferred stock for bonds. Finally, taxpayer had additional rights to subordinate the bond interest if it became necessary to do so. Rialto Realty Co., 366 F. Supp. 253, 73-2 USTC ¶ 9791 (ED Pa. 1973).

Objective factors considered in debt vs. equity situation. The IRS disallowed accrued interest on bonds held by taxpayer corporation's stockholders. *Held:* For the IRS. The court determined that there was an absence of the usual objective characteristics of a valid loan, such as an unconditional promise to repay, a fixed maturity date, a fixed interest rate, a repayment schedule and a provision for a sinking fund. Champaign Realty Co., 324 F. Supp. 922, 71-1 USTC ¶ 9205 (SD Ohio 1971).

Analysis of evidence determined existence of bona fide debt obligation. Taxpayer corporation had capital of $9,500 and debentures of $86,500. The IRS determined that the latter were not true debt instruments, but were a substitute for equity, and accordingly treated the interest paid as nondeductible. *Held:* For taxpayer. The debentures represented a bona fide debt obligation of the corporation, and the questioned payments were interest rather than dividends. This was evidenced by (1) intent, (2) receipt of new corporate funds, (3) a definite, ascertainable, fixed maturity date, (4) reasonable subordination provisions, (5) a realistic and fixed interest rate, and (6) an unconditional obligation to pay. In addition, the debentures were not held pro rata by the corporate stockholders. In the remaining issue of the case, compensation of a corporate officer was deemed to be unreasonable based on services rendered. Weylin Corp., 312 F. Supp. 400, 70-1 USTC ¶ 9392 (WD Mo. 1970).

Amounts paid on debentures owned by stockholders were interest. Taxpayer was formed by a group of doctors and dentists to build and operate a professional office building. Stock and debentures were purchased in proportion to the office space to be occupied. The IRS disallowed interest on the debentures. *Held:* For taxpayer. After applying 16 tests as to the true nature of an instrument, the court concluded that the debentures were bona fide. The pro rata holding of stock and debentures indicating that the latter were really equity was overcome by the fact that the debentures, unlike the stock, were not a risk, and that the stock was of limited negotiability (it could only be sold to other doctors). There were no such restrictions on the debentures. Medical Tower, Inc., 69-1 USTC ¶ 9305 (ED Va. 1969).

Bonds issued to stockholders were bona fide debt despite loose arrangements. Taxpayer issued to its stockholders 6 percent unsecured, negotiable bonds. The bonds did not contain any subordination provisions. Only 10 of the 18 semiannual interest payments were made on time; the rest were delayed for two weeks to ten months. The stockholders also extended the maturity date of the bonds. Taxpayer had never paid a cash dividend, although it issued a stock dividend at a time when its surplus was $180,000. The IRS contended that the bonds were equity instruments and that the interest rate was in reality dividends, and was therefore not deductible. Pointing to the stockholders' indifference to regular interest payments, the security for the payment of principal, the lack of agreement on and the extension of the maturity date, and the delay in issuing the bonds, the IRS argued that the transaction was in true substance a "loose intra-family" arrangement for distributing earnings in the form of deductible interest. *Held:* For taxpayer. There was a valid consideration for issuing the bonds, and there remained with the company a surplus of $181,000. Stone Mountain Grit Co., 65-2 USTC ¶ 9702, 16 AFTR2d 5959 (ND Ga. 1965).

Debenture bonds deemed loans, not capital. Partly in exchange for notes held by taxpayer and partly for cash, taxpayer's controlled corporation issued $50,000 of debenture bonds, $18,000 in the names of his children. The bonds had all the features of a true indebtedness such as fixed interest maturity. *Held:* For taxpayer. The court found that the loans were not considered capital for tax purposes. Principal payments are not taxable. The

Bonds and Debentures: *Equity Investments Distinguished*

court found, however, that there was no real gift to the children. Taxpayer was taxable on all of the interest. Certain reimbursements made by the corporation were also found to be dividends. Little, 191 F. Supp. 12, 61-1 USTC ¶ 9154 (ED Tex. 1960).

Indebtedness deemed repayable from operating revenues, not stock; deductions for interest allowed. To finance the construction of a parking garage, taxpayer corporation issued discount bonds and debentures. The interest rate was fixed, but the bonds and debentures were to be retired from a fund consisting of 20 percent of gross receipts each year or $20,000, whichever was greater. Nevertheless, the bonds and debentures represented a fixed obligation due at maturity. The principal amount of the indebtedness was $600,000; only $6,000 was paid in for stock, but stockholders held only 21 percent of the indebtedness. *Held:* For taxpayer. The court held that the bonds and debentures represented actual debt and not equity, as the IRS contended. Deductions for interest and discount amortization were allowed. Blaise, Inc., 59-2 USTC ¶ 9725 (ED La. 1959).

Interest deduction denied in 1955 through 1957 for bonds issued in early 1930s. As a result of a series of transactions in the early 1930s, taxpayer succeeded to the operation of a textile finishing business. The stockholders of taxpayer's predecessor emerged from the transactions in 1934 holding all taxpayer's stock and $7,050,000 of its five-year, 6 percent registered bonds. In 1935, and then again with respect to $6,050,000 of the bonds in 1939, when all the bonds fell due, the stockholders and taxpayer agreed that interest on the bonds would be payable on an annual basis from net income only, and would not be cumulative. Taxpayer never made any payments on the principal of the bonds. The IRS denied taxpayer any deductions for alleged interest payments in the years 1955 through 1957 on the grounds that the payments were dividends. *Held:* For the IRS. The bonds were merely a continuation without change of the equity interests of the bondholder-stockholders. There had been no new money contributed to the business and no change in its method of operation; the only benefit was the tax deductibility of interest paid on the bonds. Even if the bonds were a valid indebtedness when issued, the subsequent conduct of the parties belied their status as a debt in 1955 through 1957. Sayles Finishing Plants, Inc., 399 F2d 214, 68-2 USTC ¶ 9474, 22 AFTR2d 5173 (Ct. Cl. 1968).

Debentures deemed stock, not equity, in thin corporation. Upon incorporation of a partnership, *X* Corporation issued $35,000 of capital stock and $800,000 of debentures. The debentures were issued in the same proportion as the stock. They were subordinated to other debts and had certain voting rights in case of default. The IRS contended that the debentures were in fact stock and disallowed the interest deductions. *Held:* For the IRS. Due to the thinness of the capital structure, the court found the debentures to be equity capital for tax purposes. Interest was not allowable as a deduction. R.C. Owen Co., 180 F. Supp. 369, 60-1 USTC ¶ 9255 (Ct. Cl. 1960), cert. denied, 363 US 819 (1960).

Payments on purchased corporate notes held to constitute dividends. Taxpayers purchased stock plus some notes held by previous stockholders. Gains resulting from payments on the notes were reported on taxpayer's tax returns as long-term capital gains under Section 1232(a). The IRS determined that the amounts constituted dividends taxable to taxpayer as ordinary income. *Held:* For the IRS. Upon purchase, the notes were transformed for bona fide indebtedness to capital. Therefore, payments received on the notes were dividends. Edwards, 50 TC 220 (1968).

Debentures and mortgage bonds issued at incorporation of partnership found to be true debt rather than equity. Two corporations were formed by two partners who transferred the partnership assets and liabilities to one corporation in return for $55,000 capital and $50,000 debentures, and $86,500 capital and $50,000 mortgage bonds to the other corporation. The IRS disallowed the corporations' deductions for the interest paid on the mortgage bonds and debentures, contending that

BONDS AND DEBENTURES: *Equity Investments Distinguished*

the bonds and debentures constituted equity rather than debt. *Held:* For taxpayers. The partnership assests were transferred to the corporations in exchange in part for the debentures and mortgage bonds with the expectation that these instruments would be repaid regardless of the future success of the corporate businesses. Interest had been paid annually; the instruments were in legally proper form and provided for acceleration of principal in the event of default; the advances were carried on the corporate books as indebtedness. There was no subordination of either the debentures or mortgage bonds to general creditors. The court also noted that the ratio of debt to equity was not excessive for either corporation and there was therefore no problem of thin incorporation. Plastic Toys Inc., 27 TCM 707, ¶ 68,143 P-H Memo. TC (1968).

Debenture bonds treated as equity capital. Taxpayer, unable to borrow $350,000 to buy out a retiring stockholder, issued $350,000 in debentures to a group organized to advance the funds together with a new class of voting stock of nominal par value. The IRS disallowed a deduction for interest on the debentures, and, claiming that the debentures were equity, treated payments of bond principal as dividend income. *Held:* For the IRS. In an earlier district court decision, identical debentures held by two other members of the group had been construed to be an equity investment. Aside from the obvious compulsion of the doctrine of *stare decisis,* the court independently reached a similar conclusion. The debentures represented an advance of necessary working capital that taxpayer was unable to borrow through regular commercial channels, and without which taxpayer could not have continued. Also, the debentures were subordinated to other principal indebtedness and thus granted the holders rights normally enjoyed only by common stockholders. Hippodrome Bldg. Co., 24 TCM 113, ¶ 65,025 P-H Memo. TC (1965).

Bonds issued at incorporation of sole proprietorship for half of total investment held to represent bona fide debt. In 1954, taxpayer converted his sole proprietorship into a corporation and received stock having a total par value of $525,000 plus 6 percent five-year bonds in the face amount of $500,000. Taxpayer took the bonds rather than a corresponding amount of stock because he was not willing to put everything he owned at the permanent risk of the business. In 1956, taxpayer sold the bonds to an investment house for face value plus accrued interest to date of transfer, and six months later the corporation retired the bonds. The IRS alleged that the bonds did not represent a bona fide debt and that when taxpayer sold the bonds and had them renderd in that same year, he in effect received dividend income. *Held:* For taxpayer. The bonds were valid evidence of debt, and their redemption with interest after sale did not result in any income to taxpayer. The court noted the absence of any unbalance in ratio of corporate equity capital to indebtedness and the fact that material amounts of capital were invested in stock. Vantress, 23 TCM 711, ¶ 64,123 P-H Memo. TC (1964).

Bonds issued upon incorporation of partnership in exactly the same proportion as partnership investment were equity capital. Taxpayer corporation took over the business of a family partnership and issued to the partners 20,000 shares of $1 par common stock and $340,000 of 20-year, 3.5 percent debenture bonds. The stock and debentures were issued to the partners in exactly the same proportion as their interests had been in the partnership. The IRS recharacterized the bonds as equity. *Held:* For the IRS. Interest incurred on the bonds was disallowed on the ground that the debentures represented equity capital, not bona fide debt. The fact that the debentures were originally issued for an equity interest, contained subordination features, and substantially exceeded the stock investment designated the existence of a debtor-creditor relationship. R.C. Owen Co., 23 TCM 673, ¶ 64,120 P-H Memo. TC (1964).

Debentures given to sole stockholder upon incorporation represent true debt. Taxpayer transferred assets of a sole proprietorship having a net value of $44,000 to a corporation in exchange for stock valued at $10,000 and 6 percent debentures in the face amount of

BONDS AND DEBENTURES

$34,000. The IRS contended that at least $25,000 of the $34,000 of debentures represented equity capital and denied a deduction for interest payments on such indebtedness. *Held:* For taxpayer. There was no undercapitalization, and the debentures were bona fide and enforced according to their terms. Moreover, they were not subordinated to the claims of other creditors and were intended to be what they purported to be. Esrenco Truck Co., 22 TCM 287, ¶ 63,072 P-H Memo. TC (1963).

"Interest" on gold bonds was dividends where debt-to-equity ratio was 12 to 1. The original issues of the taxpayer's stock in 1928 and 1929 were for land, money, and services furnished to, and rendered for, the corporation. In 1930, all the stock was exchanged for gold bonds, and at the same time a minimal amount of new common stock was issued to the bondholders in proportion to their respective interests in the gold bonds. Prior to the exchange, the stockholders' equity was 99 percent of the total assets; after the exchange, their equity was reduced to 7.6 percent. In 1950, taxpayer retired the gold bonds by exchanging them for debenture bonds. No new capital came into the corporation by the exchange of stock for gold bonds in 1930 or by the exchange of gold bonds for debentures in 1950. No reserve or sinking fund was ever set up on taxpayer's books for the retirement of the gold bond liability or for the debenture liability. The IRS determined that the deduction for interest claimed in 1956, 1957, and 1958 was not allowable because the amounts represented payment of dividends. *Held:* For the IRS. Although the bonds purported to be evidences of indebtedness, the court found that the original stockholders intended their investments to be at risk of the business, and taxpayer failed to establish that the debenture bonds in substance represented a creditor interest and not an equity interest. Louisquisset Golf Club, Inc., 21 TCM 1577, ¶ 62,297 P-H Memo. TC (1962).

High debt-to-equity ratio not controlling; debentures considered debt. A real estate corporation sold its stock in 15-share blocks to purchasers who were required to make a corresponding purchase of six debentures with each block of stock. The debentures had fixed maturities, were noninterest bearing, and were issued at a 5 percent discount. *Held:* For taxpayer. Even though the ratio of debt to equity approximated 15 to 1, the court found on the facts that the debentures evidenced genuine indebtedness and the "debenture discount" thereon was amortizable as interest on indebtedness. Davidson Bldg. Co., 20 TCM 1291, ¶ 61-247 P-H Memo. TC (1961).

BONUSES

(*See* Business Expenses—Bonuses; Compensation for Personal Services—Bonuses; Dividends and Distributions—Bonus Payments)

BOOT

(*See* Reorganizations—Boot)

BRIBES

(*See* Business Expenses—Bribes and Other Illegal Payments)

BURDEN OF PROOF

(*See* Accumulated Earnings Tax—Burden of Proof; Procedure)

BUSINESS EXPENSES

(*See also* Dividends and Distributions)

In General	123
Bonuses	127
Bribes and Other Illegal Expenses	127

BUSINESS EXPENSES: *In General*

Capital Expenditures Distinguished ... 128
Deductible by Whom 130
Interest Expenses 133
Liquidating Expenses 134
Medical Expenses 135
Ordinary and Necessary
   Requirement 136
Organizational Expenses 140
Payment of Claims 140
Payments to Related Taxpayers ... 141
Payments to Stockholders'
   Beneficiaries 141
Profit Motive Requirement 142
Salaries 143
Stockholders' Expenses 144
Substantiation 144
Travel and Entertainment Expenses 144

In General

Payment for purchase of minority stock not deductible by corporation; no part allocable to employment contract. Taxpayer entered into a contract with a minority stockholder officer whereby it purchased his stock ownership for a stated price. The agreement also stated that all respective rights and obligations under the stockholder's employment contract were terminated, but allocated no portion of the contract price to the termination of employment. Taxpayer's board of directors thereupon ratified the agreement and allocated a portion of the purchase price to the employment contract, which had been accrued on the books as an expense. No information return was filed, and the recipient reported the entire amount received as a capital gain. The Tax Court upheld the IRS' determination that the entire consideration was paid for the purchase of the stock and refused to allocate any part to the employment contract. *Held:* Affirmed. The contract was clear and ambiguous on its face. In fact, the negotiations showed that the seller was representing all of the minority stockholders, and that the taxpayer did not alter the terms of the contract for fear that it would not be consummated if any portion were allocated. The decision of the Tax Court was amply supported by the evidence, and its decision was not clearly erroneous. Coca-Cola Co., 369 F2d 913, 67-1 USTC ¶ 9129, 18 AFTR20 6154 (8th Cir. 1966).

Hotel officer taxable on value of meals, lodgings, and servants furnished. The president and majority stockholder of a hotel corporation received meals and a rent-free apartment for herself and her daughter, also an officer, from the corporation. The wages of her personal maid and butler-chauffeur were paid by the hotel. In addition, the corporation paid for landscaping done at her personal residence. *Held:* For the IRS. The Tax Court held that there was no evidence that the convenience of the employer was served by furnishing the meals, the apartment, or the servants. It therefore held the rental value of the apartment, the wages of the servants, and the cost of the landscaping taxable income to the president. It also held the value of the meals as taxable to both the president and her daughter and denied the corporation the deduction for these items. Atlanta Biltmore Hotel Corp., 349 F2d 677, 65-2 USTC ¶ 9573 (5th Cir. 1965).

Corporation's deduction for legal expenses was limited where portion of payments actually constituted nondeductible dividends. Taxpayer corporation deducted legal expenses of $76,000 paid to its controlling stockholder. The IRS contended that $25,000 of the amount was deductible as payment of salary and bonus, but reclassified $51,000 as nondeductible dividend payments. *Held:* For the IRS, in major part. The court held $36,000 constituted nondeductible dividend and $40,000 salary was reasonable in amount. Hamilton Erection, Inc., 71-1 USTC 9334, 27 AFTR2d 71-1129 (DSC 1971).

Stock dividend expenses not deductible. Taxpayer, a public utility, issued nontaxable stock dividends to its stockholders. The expenses included transfer agents' fees, printing expenses, and brokers' fees incurred in connection with the trading and redemption of scrip certificates. *Held:* For the IRS. These expenses constituted capital expenditures and consequently were not deductible. The court followed the decision in General Bancshares Corp., 326 F2d 712 (1968) and similar cases. Southern Gas & Water Co., 64-2 USTC ¶ 9789 (SD W. Va. 1964).

Reimbursed proxy expenses of winners deductible. Taxpayer corporation deducted the expenses of its prior management in defending against a proxy fight. After the insurgents won, the corporation's stockholders ratified the action of the old directors in using corporate funds to pay proxy solicitation expenses. Stockholders then authorized reimbursement of similar expenses of the new management. The IRS disallowed a deduction for the reimbursements. *Held:* For taxpayer. The Tax Court allowed the deduction, reasoning that if the expenses of the incumbent management were deductible, then the proxy expenses of the insurgents should be also. Central Foundry Co., 49 TC 234 (1967), acq. 1968-2 CB 2.

Diverse research costs deductible where company had history of new development. A mechanical engineer who controlled a lock manufacturing company was a prolific inventor. Over a period of years, he obtained many patents that he licensed to the corporation. In 1956, he and the corporation executed an agreement providing that the corporation would pay all the research costs of a new compressor on which the engineer had a patent application. In return, the corporation was to receive a license to produce the device. Subsequently, another agreement between these parties stipulated that the corporation pay the development costs of numerous inventions of the engineer and would receive the right to any licensing. Stating that this research was not related to the lock making business of the corporation, the IRS disallowed the research expenses and determined that they were constructive dividends to the engineer. *Held:* For taxpayer. The Tax Court allowed the deduction. It held that in return for its expenditures, the corporation received full consideration under licensing agreements. This arrangement had existed for many years and was closely related to the activities of the corporation. The corporation had a history of developing new products; the legislative history of Section 174 does not indicate that it does not apply to developing new product lines unrelated to a company's usual product lines. Best Universal Lock Co., 45 TC 1 (1965), acq. 1966-2 CB 4.

Disallowed corporate expenses were dividends to sole stockholder. A corporate taxpayer was denied expense deductions for (1) legal fees, (2) travel expenses of its president, (3) salaries of its president, (4) expense for the upkeep of a lodge, and (5) expenses for factory repairs. *Held:* For taxpayer, in part. The court (1) allowed the deduction for legal fees, finding that the fact that the attorneys (on a retainer basis) who received the fees worked without fee on the estate of the father of taxpayer's president did not mean that the fees were paid with respect to the estate work; (2) allowed the travel expenses (except for $1,000, which the court allocated to taxpayer's president's wife) even though the only record the president kept was to note the difference between the amount of money with which he started his trip and the amount with which he returned; (3) allowed the full deduction for the full salary paid its president, finding that although the salary was increased when the president and his family became sole stockholders and when dividends were reduced and not paid, the president's salary was in line with what other officers of other firms of a comparable nature were receiving, and therefore the salary was reasonable; (4) allowed most of the expenses for the upkeep of the lodge, finding that the lodge was kept for the use of company personnel and business guests; the fact that the president's sons stored their boats at the lodge merely reduced the amount of the deduction by 10 percent; and (5) disallowed expenses for factory repairs, finding that the replacement of a wooden door by a metal one is a capital item since there was no proof that the expenditure did not add to the life of the business. The court also held that disallowed expenses were dividend income to the taxpayer's president. Alabama-Georgia Syrup Co., 36 TC 747 (1961), acq. 1962-2 CB 3.

BUSINESS EXPENSES: *In General*

Expenses of officer's farm not deductible by corporation. Taxpayer's president and majority stockholder owned a farm and leased a portion of it to taxpayer for a five-year term. The lease provided that taxpayer was to make improvements on property to which it would have no claim and no renewal rights at the term's end. To an undetermined extent, taxpayer used the property for entertaining people interested in its products. The IRS disallowed the deductions for rent and amortization of the improvements. *Held:* For the IRS. The Tax Court, noting that the taxpayer had failed to prove substantial use of the property for, or in, its trade or business, disallowed the deductions. The transaction was not at arm's length. Coe Laboratories, Inc., 34 TC 549 (1960).

Preliquidation payments by corporation pursuant to tax avoidance scheme. On the same day that taxpayer purchased all of the stock of a closely held corporation, he caused the corporation to pay $150,000 to his wholly owned partnership for certain lease rights and to pay himself $100,000 in salary. Five weeks later, taxpayer liquidated the corporation. The IRS claimed that the payments were not deductible by the corporation because they were part of taxpayer's overall tax avoidance scheme. *Held:* For the IRS. The payments had no business purpose and were made only as a means to avoid taxes by draining the corporation of its current earnings and profits, and thus its taxable income, prior to liquidation. The corporation could not have benefited from the lease rights acquired only five weeks prior to its liquidation, and since taxpayer performed little or no services for the corporation, the payment to him could not constitute salary. Williams, 47 TCM 846, ¶ 84,011 P-H Memo. TC (1984).

Consultant payments made to retired owner properly deductible. The IRS contended that payments made to a doctor who retired from a professional corporation were consideration for the shares he surrendered, not compensation for future consulting services. *Held:* For taxpayer. The sale agreement provided for adequate compensation for the shares apart from the payments for consulting work. The court held these payments properly deductible under Section 162. Muskogee Radiological Group, Inc., 37 TCM 1851-6, ¶ 78-490 P-H Memo. TC (1978).

Deductibility of various business expenses determined on the basis of negligence and other factors. Taxpayer corporation incurred and deducted various compensation, employee travel, and entertainment expenses, which were additions to bad debt reserves and losses. The IRS disallowed these deductions. *Held:* For the IRS in part. Compensation paid for the services of the principal stockholder was reasonable and deductible to the extent of $1,500 per year, not the $6,000 per year claimed. Although two employees traveled and spent 80 percent of their time on firm business, they did not substantiate their expenses, as required by Section 274, so that expenses were not deductible for years in which Section 274 was applicable. Prior years' expenses were deductible. Similarly, certain expenses for club dues were partially allowed and partially disallowed. A long-term capital loss on country club stock was not deductible. Although taxpayer did not use the facility for the year in which the loss was claimed, it was not shown that the stock had become worthless in that year, and so that fact was irrelevant. A deduction for addition to a bad debt reserve of some $55,000 was allowed, not the $165,000 claimed by a new accountant who was trying to correct account discrepancies. A negligence penalty was proper for a year in which taxpayer claimed a deduction for payments to public officials, since it knew that such payments were nondeductible from a previous audit. The negligence penalty was improper in later years when the evidence did not indicate negligence. The penalty was proper for earlier years because taxpayer did not show that underpayments for those years were not due to negligence. Drew, 31 TCM 143, ¶ 72,040 P-H Memo. TC (1972).

Various deductions as well as income items of taxpayer determined. Taxpayer deducted $56,794 as business expenses paid on behalf of his wholly owned corporation. He also assigned his lessor's interest in property to a

Business Expenses: *In General*

trust, had his debts paid by a corporation, and received bonuses from his corporation. The IRS disallowed the deduction and imputed additional income to taxpayer. *Held:* For the IRS. The taxpayer could not disregard his wholly owned corporate entity and claim that the $56,794 paid on behalf of the corporation for back rentals, withholding taxes, and business operations was at his expense. Therefore, he was not entitled to a deduction for them. His assignment of the income from a lease to a trust for his child's benefit did not prevent taxpayer from being taxable on the income because in order to avoid taxation, he would have had to also assign the underlying corpus, or lease. A corporation's payment of taxpayer's personal obligation is taxable as income to him. The payment of a $25,000 bonus to taxpayer in excess of his $10,550 salary was a deductible bonus only to the extent of $15,000, and the other $10,000 (not the IRS' claimed $22,600) was a distribution of profits. Hudlow, 30 TCM 894, ¶ 71, 218 P-H Memo. TC (1971).

Advances to ensure a source of supply were deductible. Taxpayer, a manufacturer of plywood, advanced funds to World Woods Corporation, which was formed by taxpayer's three major stockholders for the purpose of providing taxpayer with a source of supply. It was understood that the advances would be repaid only in the event of the successful operation of World Woods' business. Due to unforeseen operational difficulties, World Woods became hopelessly insolvent. Taxpayer sought to deduct its advances as either a business debt or a business loss. *Held:* For the IRS, in part. The advances were capital contributions. This conclusion was not precluded by the fact that taxpayer itself did not own stock in World Woods. However, under the "source of supply" theory, taxpayer could deduct as business expenses advances made before March 21, 1966 (the date it was decided to dissolve World Woods). Advances made after that date ($54,000) were made to stave off bankruptcy. This $54,000 was not a dividend to the common stockholders, since no personal obligations of any of taxpayer's stockholders were discharged as a consequence of these advances, and no individual economic benefit was accrued to them thereby. However, a $25,000 advance that the corporation used to pay off a note on which one of the stockholders was personally liable was treated as a dividend to him. Old Dominion Plywood Corp., 25 TCM 678, ¶ 66,135 P-H Memo. TC (1966).

Costs of corporate pamphlet opposing tax legislation held to constitute nondeductible political expense. Taxpayer, a domestic corporation engaged in manufacturing, published a pamphlet in 1973 that it mailed to its stockholders. The pamphlet focused on proposed legislation that would eliminate tax incentives for taxpayers to make capital improvements. In addition, the pamphlet explained why such legislation would be detrimental to the stockholders, and suggested measures that would increase the tax incentives for capital improvements. The pamphlet further suggested that the stockholders make their views known to their congressional representatives. The IRS held that under Section 162(e)(2)(B), the corporation's preparation, printing and distribution costs were nondeductible because the intention was to influence legislation. Rev. Rul. 74-407, 1974-2 CB 45.

Dividends paid to officer through revocable trust held deductible. A corporation created a revocable trust. The corpus consisted solely of its stock. The income was paid to a corporate officer as additional compensation. Assuming the total compensation paid was reasonable, the corporation could deduct the amount of trust income paid to the officer. (IT 2358 superseded.) Rev. Rul. 69-559, 1969-2 CB 25.

Payments for use of charity's name were business expenses. The IRS ruled that payments made by a corporation to a charitable organization for the use of that organization's name in connection with an advertising campaign were not gifts or contributions, but constituted ordinary and necessary business expenses. Accordingly, the limitations imposed by Section 170 were not applicable. Rev. Rul. 63-73, 1963-1 CB 35.

BUSINESS EXPENSES: *Bribes and Other Illegal Expenses*

Bonuses

Contingent bonuses not deductible where they were determined on a contingent basis corresponded proportionally to employee's stock holdings and were not for services rendered. Taxpayer corporations were owned by the same three stockholders in identical proportions. *D* operated four limestone quarries, and *G* sold asphalt. Collectively, the three stockholders managed every phase of the combined operations of the two corporations. No records were kept of the time expended by each director stockholder on behalf of taxpayers, and the individuals involved admitted that they could not determine how much time they spent, or what services they rendered on behalf of each taxpayer. The ratio between salaries paid by each taxpayer was very similar to the ratio of stock held by the three officers and the salaries were contingent on the year's profits. Upon an audit, the IRS determined the salaries to be unreasonable and disallowed a portion of the deductions taken by each taxpayer. *Held:* For the IRS. Where the bonuses were determined on a contingent basis, corresponded proportionally to the employees, stock holdings, and were not actually shown to be for services rendered, they were unreasonable. Accordingly, taxpayers were allowed to deduct only a portion of the amounts paid as were reasonable under the facts and circumstances. Trinity Quarries, Inc., 679 F2d 205, 82-2 USTC ¶ 9436, 50 AFTR2d 82-5151 (11th Cir. 1982).

Deduction allowed for bonuses immediately loaned back to corporation. Taxpayer, a closely held corporation, declared bonuses regularly at year-end to its employee stockholders. These bonuses reduced its net taxable income to below $25,000. The accrued bonuses, although paid within two and a half months after the close of the payer's year, were immediately returned by the recipients as loans to the corporation. The IRS, relying solely on Section 267, argued that the bonuses were not paid within the required two and a half months and that the whole process was nothing more than a paper transaction. *Held:* For taxpayer. The bonuses were compensation and were includable in the gross income of the recipients on the dates that the bonus checks were issued. The recipients' decision to lend their bonuses back to the family business, in which all of them were vitally interested and engaged, was voluntary and not subject to any tacit or implied agreement to return the money. The court noted that the real evil that the IRS saw in this situation was the consistent reduction of corporate income below the $25,000 surtax level. Walsh Food Serv., 25 TCM 318, ¶ 66,057 P-H Memo. TC (1966).

Accrued but unpaid expenses of fiscal year corporation and calendar year stockholder held nondeductible. A corporation on the accrual basis with a taxable year ending on June 30 accrued a bonus payable to its sole stockholder, who then used the cash method of accounting and reported on a calendar year. The bonus was paid on October 1, 1966, more than two and a half months after the close of the year ending on June 30, 1966. The sole stockholder included the bonus in income for 1966. Because the corporation lacked constructive receipt and because payment was not made within two and a half months after the close of its taxable year as required by Section 267(a)(2), the IRS ruled that the corporation was not allowed the deduction. Rev. Rul. 68-114, 1968-1 CB 100.

Bribes and Other Illegal Expenses

Payments to supplier's employee were not illegal kickbacks. Taxpayer was a manufacturer's representative selling the brand name products of various manufacturers to military commissaries. The sales manager of Stokely, a food processing company, was instrumental in causing Stokely to engage taxpayer as its military sales representative. The Stokely product line soon became taxpayer's volume leader. Stokely's sales manager often accompanied taxpayer's salesmen on their calls to the various military installations. Unknown to Stokely, taxpayer paid commissions ranging from $13,000 to $19,000 a year to the sales manager. About a month after Stokely learned about this commission arrangement, the sales manager was retired. However, Stokely continued to do business with taxpayer. The IRS disallowed a deduction for

Business Expenses: *Capital Expenditures Distinguished*

the commissions, claiming that they were in the nature of kickbacks. *Held:* For taxpayer. The payments were not like kickbacks since neither taxpayer nor sales manager had the power to decide whether or not to buy. This choice rested exclusively with the commissary officers, and payments to said officers would be illustrative of kickbacks. Although the sales manager was being paid by two parities, he put forth extra efforts to increase sales of the product and no public policy was violated. V.H. Monette & Co., 45 TC 15 (1965).

Payments to blackmailer by corporation were neither dividends nor deductible. Taxpayer corporation made payments to one of its employees who was blackmailing its sole stockholder. It then deducted the payments as business expenses. The corporation also claimed deductions for the cost of supplies that it transferred for no consideration to another corporation also controlled by its sole stockholder. The IRS claimed that neither payment was deductible and that both resulted in constructive dividends to its sole stockholder. *Held:* For the IRS in part. The blackmail payments were not deductible because they were not ordinary and necessary business expenses. However, because these payments were made to protect the corporation's business, and did not result in a personal economic benefit to the stockholder, they did not result in constructive dividends to the stockholder. The cost of supplies, however, did result in a constructive dividend to the stockholder since he received a direct benefit when the supplies were provided to his other corporation for no consideration; the corporation could not take a deduction for their cost. Wells, 47 TCM 1114, ¶ 84,079 P-H Memo. TC (1984).

Evidence fails to establish that salary paid to sole stockholder of a successful collection business was unreasonably high and therefore nondeductible. During 1971 and 1972, taxpayer, a Maryland corporation, was engaged in the business of collecting delinquent accounts on behalf of hospitals. In 1971 and 1972, taxpayer paid compensation to its sole stockholder in the amounts of $167,916 and $198,908, respectively. The IRS, on audit, determined that these amounts were excessive, and it issued deficiency notices seeking to disallow a portion of taxpayer's expense deduction claimed under Section 162(a)(1). In addition, the IRS asserted that the compensation violated an executive order issued under the 1970 Economic Stabilization Act, and therefore the amount was nondeductible under Section 162(c)(2) as an illegal payment. *Held:* For taxpayer. On the issue of the reasonableness of compensation, the court noted that the sole stockholder worked an inordinate number of hours per week, that he alone was responsible for the startling success of the business, that he was an excellent and innovative salesman, a key factor in obtaining business, and that he possessed excellent managerial skills. On the basis of the stockholder's unique and special performance, the compensation paid could not be said to have been unreasonable. On the second issue, the court ruled that the IRS had failed to carry its burden of proving a willful violation, as its evidence fell short of establishing a violation under Section 162(c)(2) by clear and convincing proof. Medical Collection Corp., 36 TCM 1074, ¶ 77,266 P-H Memo. TC (1977).

Capital Expenditures Distinguished

Appraisal litigation expenses treated as nondeductible capital outlays. Taxpayer corporation (Hilton) owned the majority of shares of a company (Waldorf) with which it planned to merge. The proposal was formally opposed by the holders of 6 percent of Waldorf shares, who rejected a Hilton cash offer and commenced appraisal proceedings to determine the value of their stock. The proceedings were terminated more than a year later upon settlement by the parties. In a refund suit brought in the district court, taxpayer challenged the IRS' characterization of the expenditures it had incurred in connection with the appraisal proceedings as nondeductible capital outlays. Judgment was entered for taxpayer, and the expenditures at issue were deemed deductible as ordinary and necessary business expenses under Section 162. The IRS unsuccessfully appealed to the Seventh Circuit. *Held:* Reversed. The Seventh Circuit's holding was reversed by the Supreme

BUSINESS EXPENSES: *Capital Expenditures Distinguished*

Court, which noted that the appraisal proceedings as well as the passage of title were part of the acquisition process. The fact that title to dissenters' stock had passed before, rather than after, appraisal was of no significance in characterizing the litigation expenditures for tax purposes. As the court held in the companion case of *Woodward*, the expenses of litigation that arose out of the acquisition of a capital asset were nondeductible capital expenses, irrespective of whether the taxpayer's purpose in incurring them was the defense or perfection of title to property. Hilton Hotel Corp., 397 US 580, rev'g 410 F2d 194, 69-1 USTC ¶ 9336, 23 AFTR2d 69-1180 (7th Cir. 1969).

Cost of redeeming stock of dissident stockholder was capital expenditure. Taxpayer was engaged in river construction. Taxpayer's three stockholders entered into a buy-sell agreement that provided that any stockholder who desired to sell his stock must offer it first to the corporation and then to other stockholders for the adjusted book value of the shares as defined in the agreement. Taxpayer sought a tax refund on taxes paid for 1973 through 1975, claiming that it was entitled to deduct, as an ordinary and necessary business expense under Section 162, the price paid for the purchase of a stockholder's stock, the legal and appraisal fees connected with it, and the amounts unilaterally allocated by taxpayer to covenants not to compete included in agreements with two former stockholders. The IRS disallowed the deductions. *Held*: For the IRS. Where the evidence indicated petty friction and discord among stockholders, taxpayer's existence was not threatened. Accordingly, taxpayer could not deduct the cost of redeeming shares as ordinary and necessary business expenditures under Section 162. Legal and appraisal fees were not deductible where the purchase price was not deductible. Taxpayer could not deduct for the covenants not to compete because taxpayer had not met the burden of proving that, if anything, it was required to pay. Markham & Brown, Inc., 648 F2d 1043, 81-2 USTC ¶ 9518, 48 AFTR2d 81-5349 (5th Cir. 1981).

Expenses incurred in bringing shareholder derivative actions held current, not capital, items under "origin and nature" test. In 1960, taxpayer, a corporation engaged in the newspaper publishing business, purchased a controlling interest in the stock of a daily newspaper located in another city. The managing officers of the acquired company, who held their positions through the exercise of a voting trust stock, bitterly resisted the take-over. In response, taxpayer filed six lawsuits in both state and federal court alleging mismanagement, breaches of fiduciary duties and diversion of corporate assets. The various actions were consolidated as stockholder derivative suits in state court; during 1966, the matter was settled and a final judgment entered. The terms of the settlement did not provide for payment of taxpayer's costs and legal fees, which totalled $478,472 from 1963 through 1967. In each of those years, taxpayer claimed deductions on its corporate returns. The IRS, however, asserted that since the original suits were initiated as stockholder derivative actions, the claimed deductions were for the benefit of the acquired company, not for taxpayer corporation. On this ground, the IRS determined that the claimed expenses were nondeductible under Section 162, and that, alternatively, that they were capital expenditures incurred in connection with taxpayer's acquisition of stock. *Held*: For taxpayer. The Third Circuit noted that there is no rule of law denying expenses of a stockholder derivative suit per se. Such items of expense are allowed if taxpayer, as here, is able to demonstrate that the expense was undertaken to protect or promote its business, rather than merely to pay the expenses of another taxpayer. At the same time, the court rejected the government's alternative argument on the basis of the "origin and nature" test announced by the Supreme Court in Woodward, 397 US 572 (1970). Since the origin and nature of taxpayer's expenses related to the operations of the acquired company and not the actual purchase of stock, there was no doubt that these were not capital expenses incurred in the acquisition. Newark Morning Ledger Co., 539 F2d 929, 39 AFTR2d 76-5366, 76-2 USTC ¶ 9523 (3d Cir. 1976).

Business Expenses: *Deductible by Whom*

Interest payments not cost of goods sold. Taxpayer operated a finance business and a real estate business as one corporation. In computing gross income, it deducted interest payments made in connection with its finance business as part of its cost of goods sold. The Tax Court held that the payment was only deductible from gross income. *Held*: Affirmed. The payment was a business expense and not a repayment of capital as contemplated by Regulation § 1.61-3(a), on which taxpayer mistakenly relied. Hilldun Corp., 408 F2d 1117, 69-1 USTC ¶ 9319, 23 AFTR2d 69-1090 (2d Cir. 1969).

Investment banker's fee for standby agreement held nondeductible as business expense. In order to obtain additional capital to expand, taxpayer formulated a plan to restructure its capital account whereby preferred stock was converted into common. Taxpayer paid an investment banker's fee for a standby agreement that would facilitate the conversion. Taxpayer deducted the fee on its federal income tax return as a business expense for professional services rendered. The IRS disallowed the deduction. *Held*: For the IRS. The underlying transaction was in fact a recapitalization, so the fee was not deductible. Nor was it deductible as a premium paid for debt retirement, since the preferred stock was converted and not retired. The fee was a capital expenditure that was not amortizable because (1) the preferred stock had an indeterminable life, (2) the fee was incurred to raise capital by issuing more common stock and was unrelated to the preferred stock, and (3) the capital so acquired was not an exhaustible asset. Skaggs Cos., 59 TC 201 (1972).

Company disallowed business deduction for amount paid in settlement of suit instituted by estate of former stockholder. A 50 percent stockholder of taxpayer died. As a result, the decedent's estate received $160,000, believed to be full market value. Thereafter, taxpayer arranged a sale for $1,100,000, in 1974. The decedent's estate brought suit to obtain the fair market value of its interest, which had previously been surrendered, according to taxpayer's estimate of the value of decedent's assets. The parties settled the matter for $190,000. In its 1966 return, taxpayer deducted the $190,000 as a business expense. *Held*: For the IRS. Application of the origin-of-the-claim test led to a conclusion that the expenditure was a nondeductible capital expense. The origin of the claim was in the sale of the stock. Thus, the additional amount paid constituted an additional portion of the purchased price. Taxpayer failed to show that any portion of the amount paid constituted a deductible business expense. DuGrenier, 58 TC 931 (1972).

Legal advice on merger, stock split and partial redemption represented capital expenditure. Legal fees were incurred in connection with the merger of one corporation into another, followed by a split of the stock of the surviving corporation. The surviving corporation also planned to redeem a portion of its outstanding stock. The redemption did not materialize, but no final plans were made to abandon the redemption. The IRS ruled that the legal fees incurred in connection with the merger, stock split and proposed redemption were capital expenditures, since they affected the capital structure of the corporation and were therefore nondeductible under Section 263. In the year in which the corporation could show it had abandoned plans to affect a redemption of a part of the corporate stock, the amount of legal fees attributable to such advice was deductible under Section 162(a). Rev. Rul. 67-125, 1967-1 CB 31.

Deductible by Whom

Corporation cannot deduct compensation for services rendered to prior proprietorship. The Tax Court held that a corporation could not deduct compensation paid to its president for his services to a sole proprietorship that operated the business (a vineyard) before the corporation was formed. The proprietorship continued to own the land, which it leased to the corporation. *Held:* Affirmed. The corporation was a separate entity that did not succeed to all of the proprietorship's assets. Young, 650 F2d 1083, 81-2 USTC ¶ 9501, 48 AFTR2d 81-5602 (9th Cir. 1981).

BUSINESS EXPENSES: *Deductible by Whom*

Parent may not deduct indemnification for which subsidiary should be responsible. Taxpayer was the U.S. parent corporation of a Swiss subsidiary that made a loan to a British corporation in which taxpayer had a 49 percent interest. Taxpayer indemnified its Swiss subsidiary against a foreign currency loss that resulted when the British pound fell against the Swiss franc. Taxpayer deducted the indemnification payments as a business expense. The IRS disallowed the deduction. *Held*: For the IRS. The payments were a nondeductible capital contribution to its British affiliate. The debtor was the party that normally would insure the Swiss lender against foreign exchange loss. Nalco Chem. Co., 561 F. Supp. 1274, 83-1 USTC ¶ 9287, 52 AFTR2d 83-5177 (ND Ill. 1983).

Jury determined that business expenses were deductible by corporation and not its stockholders. Taxpayers, husband and wife, took various deductions, including certain business expenses that the IRS maintained were corporate expenses that were not properly deductible on taxpayers' individual income tax return. *Held*: For the IRS. Where a taxpayer did not establish that an expense was incurred by him personally, and the facts as determined by a jury indicated they were corporate expenses, an individual taxpayer can not deduct the expenses. Phillips, Jr., 72-1 USTC ¶ 9358, 29 AFTR2d 72-944 (SD Fla. 1972).

Parent allowed to deduct expenses incurred for subsidiary. In 1965, a corporation organized a subsidiary and paid the expenses incurred for the subsidiary directly during the start-up period. The IRS denied the parent the deduction on the grounds that it had paid the subsidiary's expenses rather than its own. *Held*: For taxpayer. In substance, if not in form, the new organization was a branch rather than a subsidiary, and therefore its expenses were the parent's expenses. Baltimore Aircoil Co., 333 F. Supp. 705, 71-2 USTC ¶ 9579, 28 AFTR2d 71-5427 (D. Md. 1971).

Parent corporation entitled to deduct certain compensation and expenses paid by it to its employees for services rendered abroad for foreign subsidiaries. Taxpayer had foreign subsidiaries located all over the world. From time to time, taxpayer sent its employees abroad to advise and assist its foreign subsidiaries. Taxpayer compensated its employees and paid their expenses while they were abroad. The IRS disallowed all such expenses as payments made on behalf of another taxpayer. *Held*: For taxpayer, in part. Expenses that could be shown to be for taxpayer's direct benefit were allowed; expenses for both taxpayer's direct benefit and the direct benefit of a subsidiary were allocated. Expenses relative to the day-to-day operations of its subsidiaries were disallowed. Also, the overall supervision of affairs of subsidiaries did not justify a Section 482 allocation of income to taxpayer. Young & Rubicam, 410 F2d 1233, 69-1 USTC ¶ 9404, 23 AFTR2d 69-1385 (Ct. Cl. 1969).

Stockholder cannot deduct expenditures made for corporation. Taxpayer was a 95 percent stockholder of a corporation. He paid personal property taxes and filing fees on behalf of the corporation and deducted such payments on his personal income tax return. The amount of damage to corporate property was likewise deducted *Held*: For the IRS. Corporate expenses and losses are deductible only by the corporation. Having chosen to avail himself of the non-Subchapter S corporate form, taxpayer was not allowed to disregard it in order to reduce his taxes. The corporation carried on continuous research and perfected its mining claims annually. Such activity was sufficent to qualify for treatment as a separate taxable entity. Rink, 51 TC 746 (1969).

Payment by stockholders of expense of liquidated corporation deductible by corporation. Pursuant to a plan of liquidation under Section 337, a corporation sold its assets and paid out all of its funds as liquidating distributions. Shortly thereafter, the state notified the corporation that the gain on liquidation was taxable for state tax purposes and refused to permit surrender of the charter until payment had been made. Since the corporation no longer had any funds, the stockholders paid the tax. The corporation deducted this tax and carried back the resultant loss to

BUSINESS EXPENSES: *Deductible by Whom*

a previous year. The IRS objected, stating that the expense was not paid by taxpayer and that at the time of the payment, taxpayer was no longer in existence. *Held*: For taxpayer. The Tax Court held that the tax was deductible. Local laws created a liability from stockholder to corporation for the corporation's debts that could not be paid because of excessive liquidating distributions. As the corporation had the right of recovery, it indirectly made the payment. The corporation continued to exist until the state permitted the surrender of the charter to appropriate authorities. Royal Oak Apartments, Inc., 43 TC 243 (1964).

Expenses of subsidiary paid by parent company allowed. A wholly owned subsidiary of a gas company that furnished service to consumers sold and leased hot water heaters and conversion burners. While leases of these appliances were for an indefinite period subject to termination by the customer, such leases on the whole tended to remain in effect for extended periods. The costs of delivery and installation of leased appliances were shared by the parent company and the subsidiary and were deducted by both in the year incurred. The lease of applicances had the effect of increasing the gas sales of the parent. *Held*: The installation costs of the subsidiary were in the nature of capital expenditures and had to be amortized over the composite life of the leases. The same result was applied to the costs paid by the parent company. Although the general rule is that the separate corporate entities preclude a parent from deducting expenses of the subsidiary's business, the parent in this case had a substantial interest in increasing its own sales by promoting the leasing of gas appliances. The court found that the composite life determined by the IRS was unreasonable and made its own determination. Indicating the possibility that the parent's costs might be capitalizable to its investment in the subsidiary, the court stated that it would not resolve that issue, since it had not been raised by the IRS. Fall River Gas Co., 42 TC 850 (1964).

Stockholder's expenses not deductible by corporation and dividend to stockholder. Taxpayer manufactured concrete mixers. Its sole stockholder was a yacht fancier, and the corporation owned a yacht that was docked in front of the stockholder's home and was available to him at all times. This yacht was one of a series owned by either the stockholder or taxpayer each succeeding boat being more luxurious as the taxpayer's business increased. The IRS disallowed part of the yacht expense, depreciation, travel expense of the stockholder's wife, and other similar items, and assessed the stockholder for constructive dividends. *Held*: For the IRS. The yacht was acquired primarily for the personal gratification of the stockholder, and any business use was distinctly secondary. The relation to business of the other expenses was also not shown. Challenge Mfg. Co., 37 TC 650 (1962), acq. 1962-2 CB 4.

Legal expenses disallowed to subsidiary. Taxpayer, a wholly owned subsidiary, was liquidated and dissolved as one step in a partial liquidation of its parent. Legal expenses of $3,000 deducted by taxpayer were disallowed. *Held*: For the IRS. Taxpayer failed to prove that no part of the expenses were incurred on behalf of its parent. Standard Linen Serv., Inc., 33 TC 1 (1959), acq. 1960-2 CB 7.

Obligation to purchase stockholder's stock pursuant to a buy-out agreement was corporation's, not that of stockholder acting for corporation. Taxpayer corporation paid principal and interest on an installment note that was part of an agreement to purchase a stockholder's stock. The purchase agreement was entered into by another stockholder. The IRS argued that because the obligation to purchase was the latter stockholder's, the amounts paid by the corporation were constructive dividends to trust stockholder, and that the corporation was therefore not entitled to deduct the interest. *Held*: For taxpayer. The second stockholder entered into the purchase agreement on behalf of the corporation and not in a personal capacity. Therefore, the obligation was the corporation's, and it was entitled to deduct the interest. State Pipe & Nipple Corp., 46 TCM 415, ¶ 83,339 P-H Memo. TC (1983).

BUSINESS EXPENSES: *Interest Expenses*

Individual not permitted to deduct losses from corporate-owned entity. Taxpayer deducted an operating loss and a loss from the sale of the assets of his restaurant in his individual return. The IRS argued that only the corporation that owned the restaurant was entitled to the deductions. *Held:* For the IRS. Evidence showed that an earlier purported bill of sale transferring the restaurant from the corporation to taxpayer had not been executed on the date alleged. Therefor, the restaurant continued to be owned by the corporation, which was entitled to the deductions. Haynes, 43 TCM 99, ¶ 81,709 P-H Memo. TC (1981).

An individual's losses could not be attributed to family corporations. Taxpayer developed various industrial machines in a sole proprietorship and planned to have a corporation owned by himself and his sons take over manufacturing and sales. The corporation and his sole proprietorship had the same name, business address, and shared the same bank account. The IRS attributed losses on his developmental activities, which taxpayer deducted on his own returns, to the corporation. *Held:* For taxpayer. The expenses in developing the machines were borne by him personally, and his intent was to operate as a proprietorship. Lumb, 37 TCM 1052, ¶ 78,245 P-H Memo. TC (1978).

Parent may not deduct bonuses paid to employees of his subsidiary, but subsidiary can. Cash bonuses paid by a parent corporation to the employees of its wholly owned subsidiary are treated as a contribution to the subsidiary's capital and may not be deducted as a Section 162 business expense by the parent. However, if the bonuses do not exceed reasonable compensation for its employees' services, the subsidiary may deduct then under Section 162. Rev. Rul. 84-68, 1984-1 CB 31.

Corporation that succeeded partnership may deduct payments to retired partner. Pursuant to the partnership agreement a partnership made Section 736(a)(2) guaranteed payments to a retired partner. This partnership was then incorporated under Section 351 and continued to make the guaranteed payments. The IRS ruled that the payments were deductible by the corporation as a Section 162 expense. Rev. Rul. 83-155, 1983-2 CB 38.

Interest Expenses

Interest paid on loan to pay insurance premiums was deductible. Taxpayer was a Tennessee corporation in the business of operating analytical laboratories. During the years in question, Edgar Tenent, Sr. and his son were the principal stockholders. The corporation borrowed money from Franklin Life Company to purchase "key man" life insurance policies from that company on both Mr. Tenent and his son. The corporation deducted the amount it paid for interest on these loans. The IRS disallowed this deduction, claiming the transaction was a sham. On summary judgment, the district court held that the interest was deductible. *Held:* Affirmed. The purchase of the policies was found to be for a legitimate business reason. The court also found it necessary for the corporation to make regular and substantial loans from banks to finance its operation. The rate of interest paid on these loans was less than any banks would charge. This was found to be a true loan, and the interest deduction was allowed. Woodson-Tenent Laboratories, Inc., 27 AFTR2d 417 (WD Tenn. 1970), aff'd, 454 F2d 637, 72-1 USTC ¶ 9222, 29 AFTR2d 72-531 (6th Cir. 1972).

Interest and loan premium deductible, although proceeds reloaned interest-free to affiliate. A corporation borrowed $875,000 and executed various 6 percent notes evidencing this indebtedness. The loan, secured by a mortgage, included a premium of $175,000, leaving a $700,000 in net proceeds. The corporation made the proceeds available free of interest charges to related companies and claimed deductions for loan interest and amortization of the discount in the year in issue. The IRS contended that the loan was a sham and disallowed the deduction. *Held:* For taxpayer. The court held that the premium properly constituted interest, and since the corporation made payments as interest on a genuine indebtedness for which it was primarily liable, it was entitled to the deductions claimed. Meridian Inc, 322 F2d 198, 63-2

BUSINESS EXPENSES: *Liquidating Expenses*

USTC ¶ 9691 (1963), cert denied, 375 US 992 (1963).

No interest allowed; transaction was sale of stock. Taxpayer corporation needed $50,000 to repurchase a franchise granted to a third party. The stock of the corporation was then selling at $3 per share. Two individuals purchased 16,666 shares from taxpayer at that price, pursuant to a contract under which they could, at their option, cause the corporation to repurchase the 16,666 shares by a certain time at $4.50 per share. Upon repurchase of the stock, the corporation claimed an interest deduction for an amount greater than the difference between the sale price of $3 per share and the purchase price of $4.50 per share. The IRS disallowed the deduction. *Held:* For the IRS. The court ruled that evidence that the transaction was a loan was not convincing in view of specific statements in the depositions of the parties and specific recitals in the instrument. Accordingly, the court held that no interest deduction was allowable. Pigeon-Hole Parking, Inc, 194 F. Supp. 591, 61-1 USTC ¶ 9295 (ED Wash. 1961).

Interest deductible as Section 162 trade or business expenses. Taxpayer finance company's business expenses consisted of interest (65 percent of gross income) and other expenses (2 percent of gross income). Under Section 542, a finance company is not a personal holding company if its deductions under Section 162 (trade and business expenses) are at least 15 percent of gross income. The IRS argued that taxpayer was a personal holding company, since interest, being specifically deductible under Section 163, left taxpayer with Section 162 expenses under the 15 percent requirement. *Held:* For taxpayer. The Tax Court, after construing the statutes, regulations, and congressional intent, held that Sections 162 and 163 merely overlap and are not repugnant to each other. Although Section 163 left provides for the deduction of interest, this does no prevent the deduction under Section 162 for interest incurred in trade or business. McNutt-Boyce Co., 38 TC 462 (1962).

Interest was deductible, although borrowing was for another. Taxpayer, a corporation engaged in the real estate business, obtained several mortgage loans from a related mortgage and loan corporation. Part of the loan proceeds was lent to a stockholder. The IRS disallowed an interest deduction to taxpayer on the grounds that the interest payments could not qualify as business expenses, since the proceeds were used personally by the stockholder. *Held:* For taxpayer. Under the Code, all interest paid on genuine indebtedness is deductible whether or not it qualifies as ordinary and necessary business expenses. Here, the loans were made to taxpayer in its corporate capacity using corporate assets as security for the borrowed funds. Accordingly, these were legitimate, enforceable loans, and the fact that the proceeds were loaned to a stockholder was immaterial. Arcade Realty Co., 35 TC 256 (1960), acq. 1961-2 CB 3.

Liquidating Expenses

Business expense deduction denied for the sale of assets in 12-month liquidation. Taxpayer, pursuant to a plan of complete liquidation qualifying under Section 337, sold all of its assets at a gain in excess of $1 million and distributed the proceeds less amounts required to meet claims to its stockholders. By virtue of Section 337, none of the gain was recognized; therefore, there were no taxes. However, taxpayer filed a tax return deducting expenses incurred in the sale of the assets. The IRS disallowed the deductions, but the district court held the selling expenses to be ordinary business expenses under Section 162(a) and allowed the deduction. *Held:* Reversed. Under Section 337, where capital gain is given no recognition and has no tax incidence to the corporation, the costs of producing that gain are to be ignored. Alphaco, Inc., 385 F2d 244, 67-2 USTC ¶ 9700, 20 AFTR2d 5660 (7th Cir. 1967).

Court permits business expense deduction of attorney fees incurred during course of liquidation even though a portion of such fees attributable to Section 337 sale of assets. Taxpayer adopted a plan of liquidation and sold all of its assets pursuant to Section 337. In

BUSINESS EXPENSES: Medical Expenses

the course of liquidating, it incurred attorney's fees, which it deducted as a business expense on its final return. The IRS asserted that a portion of such fees were allocable to the asset sale, and were thus nondeductible. *Held:* For taxpayer. Even if a portion of such fees are attributable to the asset sale, they are still deductible in their entirety as a business expense arising in the liquidation of a corporation. Mountain States Mixed Feed Co., 365 F2d 244, 66-2 USTC ¶ 9604, 18 AFTR2d 5488 (10th Cir. 1966).

Distinction between costs for dissolution and liquidation rejected by district court. Prior to its dissolution, taxpayer was a Delaware corporation involved in the oil business. On June 21, 1965, its stockholders adopted a plan of complete liquidation and dissolution in conformity with Section 337. On July 1, 1965, the corporation sold all of its assets except certain oil and gas properties and cash for $10.5 million and the assumption by the purchasing corporation of certain liabilities and obligations amounting to $3.54 million for a gross sale price of $14 million. The liquidation and dissolution was in compliance with Section 337. The corporation incurred and paid expenses in the aggregate amount of $260,635 in connection with these transactions. Of this amount, $25,000 was paid to an individual for financial and accounting consultation, of which $2,500 was attributable to the sale of assets and $22,500 was not attributable to such sale; $210,000 was paid to another party for brokerage in connection with the sale of assets to the purchaser; and $25,635 was paid to a law firm for legal services, of which $12,817 was attributable to the sale of assets and $12,817 was not attributable to such sale. On these facts, the IRS disallowed the deduction as not ordinary and necessary. *Held:* For taxpayer. Citing Mountain States Mixed Feed Co., 365 F2d 244 (10th Cir. 1966), the court, in its terse opinion, found that the costs of liquidating a business are necessarily "interwoven" with the dissolution of the company, and that therefore the IRS cannot make a distinction between the two in applying Section 162. Benedict Oil Co., 76-2 USTC ¶ 9559, 38 AFTR2d 76-5486 (ND Okla. 1976).

Expenses incurred in connection with a partial liquidation held deductible. Taxpayer divested itself of its bank stock by organizing a new corporation to which it transferred the stock. It then spun off the new corporation's stock to its stockholders. The divestiture of bank stock was made under the provisions of a plan of distribution enacted by Congress under which confiscatory tax consequences could be avoided. The spin-off involved the elimination of approximately three fourths of taxpayer's surplus and a substantial decline in the market value of stock. Taxpayer claimed a deduction for legal fees, transfer agent fees, and other expenses relating to the new stock. The deduction was disallowed. Taxpayer contended that the expenses in connection with the divestiture were ordinary and necessary business expenses. The IRS contended that the expenses were related to a change in the capital structure, not a mere partial liquidation, and were therefore capital expenditures. *Held:* For taxpayer. Because the banking business is the object of government scrutiny, it is constantly subject to expenses necessary to comply with regulations. In this case, the only change in corporate structure was the formation of the banking corporation; there was no change in the structure of taxpayer that would benefit its future existence. Consequently, taxpayer had met the burden of proving that the dominate purpose of the plan of liquidation was the divestiture of the bank stock in the ordinary course of business. Transamerica Corp., 254 F. Supp. 504, 66-2 USTC ¶ 9541, 18 AFTR2d 5226 (ND Cal. 1966).

Medical Expenses

Oral medical reimbursement plan payments deductible. Taxpayers' income was increased when the IRS disallowed their Subchapter S corporation deductions for payments made under a medical reimbursement plan. *Held:* For taxpayers. The plan was not in writing, but it was not required to be. The employees who were covered knew that they were covered and that a plan existed. Furthermore, taxpayers were not only stockholders but also officers and employees, so that a plan existed

BUSINESS EXPENSES: *Ordinary and Necessary Requirement*

for a class of employees. Epstein, 31 TCM 217, ¶ 72,053 P-H Memo. TC (1972).

Employee's medical expenses held to be dividend and not deductible when he owned the business. Taxpayer incorporated his plumbing business, thus becoming the corporation's only full-time salaried employee. The corporation then deducted and paid taxpayer's medical expenses, which he excluded from income under Section 105(b). *Held:* For the IRS. The payments were includable in taxpayer's gross income as dividends and were not deductible to the corporation as a business expense. The purpose of setting up the "plan" was to benefit taxpayer as owner of the business, not as an employee. Smithback, 28 TCM 709, ¶ 69,139 P-H Memo. TC (1969).

Ordinary and Necessary Requirement

Airplane expenses not ordinary and necessary for a professional medical corporation. A corporation bought and maintained an airplane used by its doctor stockholders. The airplane was not used in the daily practice of medicine. The IRS disallowed a deduction for these costs. *Held*: For the IRS. The airplane was used for personal purposes. The doctors received a constructive dividend equal to the fair rental value of the airplane. Harbor Medical Corp., 38 TCM 1144, ¶ 79,291 P-H Memo. TC (1979), aff'd, 676 F2d 708 (9th Cir. 1982).

Payment to widow of corporate officer held not to have been for nonbusiness purposes and therefore was not deductible. Taxpayer, a public corporation, paid the widow of its president the sum of $55,000 as a death benefit. During his life, the president earned about $80,000 annually. The testimony indicated that very slight consideration was given to the business benefits that would accrue from the payment and that there was no corporate policy of paying death benefits to widows of corporate officers. The IRS contended that the payment was not a necessary business expense and therefore not deductible. The Tax Court found for the IRS. *Held*: Affirmed. The payment was made in apprecia-tion for services rendered, and not in order to obtain business benefits. Allen Indus., Inc., 414 F2d 983, 69-2 USTC ¶ 9610 (6th Cir. 1969).

Expense of declaring and paying stock dividends not ordinary and necessary business expenses. Taxpayer incurred certain expenses in declaring and paying stock dividends that had the effect of changing its capital structure. The Tax Court held that such expenses are capital in nature and not deductible business expenses. *Held*: Affirmed. Arkansas La. Gas Co., 331 F2d 850, 64-1 USTC ¶ 9483, 13 AFTR2d 1413 (5th Cir. 1964).

Real estate corporation could not deduct finder's fee paid to principal investors. An arrangement between X Corporation and its principal stockholders whereby X agreed to pay the stockholders a "finder's fee" for locating the principal asset of X was determined not to be a payment in consideration for any services rendered, but rather a nondeductible distribution of corporate profits. *Held*: For the IRS. Since the stockholders were themselves the major investors, the court noted that if it were considered that they rendered any service, such service would be in effect rendered principally to themselves. Thus it was not deemed necessary. for X to agree to pay the stockholders any fee. Darco Realty Corp., 301 F2d 190, 62-1 USTC ¶ 9377 (1962).

Sales of controlled selling corporation reportable by parent, the manufacturer. Taxpayer, as a sole proprietor, manufactured oil-well cementing equipment. Upon receiving an order for over $500,000 of equipment for Venezuelan wells, he formed a Venezuelan corporation to sell and service his products and service other equipment previously exported by him. Taxpayer was the majority stockholder of record of the new corporation, and the Tax Court found as a fact that he controlled and managed its affairs. Although he contracted to sell it equipment at cost plus 10 percent, the prices billed were in fact less than 110 percent of list price. In addition, he claimed a deduction for amounts charged by the subsidiary for technical services to buyers. This

BUSINESS EXPENSES: *Ordinary and Necessary Requirement*

was computed as 90 percent of the sales prior to incorporation. *Held*: Affirmed. The court disallowed all but a small part of this deduction, holding that it was not an ordinary or necessary expense. In addition, to reflect the true income of taxpayer, the court treated all of the sales of the foreign corporation as taxpayer's sales but allowed a reasonable deduction for selling and service expense. Hall, 294 F2d 82, 61-2 USTC ¶ 9582, 8 AFTR2d 5161 (5th Cir. 1961).

Part of corporate rental payments that reduced stockholders' obligations disallowed as ordinary business expense. Stockholders of taxpayer corporation granted an option to a third party for the purchase of all their stock. The option could be exercised by the optionee only if he also exercised an option independently acquired from the same stockholders to lease coal properties that they owned individually. Taxpayer corporation had also been renting diesel locomotives from the stockholders, and in connection with the exercise of the options, the corporation proposed to modify the locomotive lease by shortening its terms and increasing the rate of payment. The optionee agreed to the increased rental payment by the corporation only on the condition that such increase be applied first to reduce his purchase price of the stock and then to any payments due on the coal properties lease. Taxpayer sought to deduct the rental payment as business expenses. The IRS disallowed a portion of the deductions. *Held*: For the IRS. The Tax Court held that the increased rental for the locomotives in effect satisfied the optionee's personal obligation and could not be deducted by the corporation as an ordinary and necessary business expense. West Va. Northern RR Co., 282 F2d 63, 60-2 USTC ¶ 9702, 6 AFTR2d 5557 (4th Cir. 1960), cert. denied, 366 US 929 (1961).

Disallowed corporate expenses were dividend to stockholder. The IRS held that disallowed cash Christmas expenses of a corporation were a dividend to taxpayer individual, who was a majority stockholder. Taxpayer argued that the amounts, deemed to be a preferential dividend, were in fact used as Christmas gifts to business-related individuals and that taxpayer did not derive any personal benefit from the monies involved. *Held*: For the IRS. Substantiation produced by taxpayer was found to be insufficient. Orner, 75-2 USTC ¶ 9763 (ND Ill. 1975).

Sale of stock to employees below value was deductible loss. Taxpayer owned 73 percent of a corporation's stock. At a time when the shares were selling for $28, he sold some of his own stock to key employees for $5 as an inducement to their continuing with the company. *Held*: For the IRS. The $23 difference between the fair market value and the selling price was not an ordinary and necessary business expense of taxpayer, but a loss on a transaction entered into for profit. Taxpayer's motive was to enhance the value of the stock he retained. Berner, 282 F2d 720, 60-2 USTC ¶ 9717, 6 AFTR2d 5603 (Ct. Cl. 1960).

Handling charges of foreign affiliate were proper. Four brothers owned the stock of taxpayer corporation, which imported flower bulbs from Holland. Two of the brothers were American citizens and two were citizens of Holland. The brothers also controlled a Dutch corporation that grew bulbs. This corporation sold to taxpayer at the minimum price under Dutch regulations, but charged taxpayer a six percent handling fee. The IRS disallowed this charge as excessive. It also disallowed travel expenses for the American stockholders' trips to Holland. *Held*: For taxpayer. The handling charge was legal under Dutch law, and compensated the Dutch company at a reasonable rate for packing, freight, and insurance. The court found clear evidence that the trips to Holland were for business rather than personal reasons. Doornbosch Bros., 46 TC 199 (1966).

Payments by corporation to settle claim against controlling stockholder officer for reimbursement were deductible. Individual *A*, before acquiring a controlling interest in *X* Corporation (taxpayer), employed *B*, a management consultant, to study the operations of the corporation. *A* agreed to the employment of *B* as president of *X* if and when the proposed purchase took place. *A* acquired the

BUSINESS EXPENSES: *Ordinary and Necessary Requirement*

majority of the X voting stock on February 10, and B was elected president of X. B was removed from his office on May 25 and brought an action against A and X for fraud and breach of contract. A notified X that he would seek reimbursement for any liability incurred in this action. The corporation's attorneys considered A's claim to be held harmless valid. They also suggested the settlement of B's action. X incurred $117,000 in settlement of the lawsuit, most of which was disallowed by the IRS on the ground that it was for A's benefit and therefore not ordinary and necessary. *Held*: For taxpayer. Taxpayer met the three tests set up in *Levitt*, 142 F2d 795 (1944), to determine whether an expense is necessary. These are: (1) taxpayer was not entirely confident that McGraw's claim would not succeed; (2) payments were made to avoid damages or liability from McGraw's suit; (3) a reasonable person would have thought the settlement necessary. Taxpayer relied on counsel and acted reasonably. The payment was held also to be ordinary since it is the accepted defense against such lawsuits. Old Town Corp., 37 TC 845 (1962).

Parent can deduct payments to manufacturing subsidiary to cover operating losses. A corporation distributing sport-fishing equipment owned all the stock of a manufacturing subsidiary, which was its sole source of patented metal and glass fishing rods. Without this source, the parent would have been unable to meet the demands of customers for these rods, and both its sales and its position in the industry would have suffered. The parent reimbursed the subsidiary for operating losses and deducted such payments as business expenses. The IRS disallowed the deductions, claiming that they were not ordinary and necessary. *Held*: For taxpayer. Amounts paid to the subsidiary to reimburse it for operating losses were held deductible by the parent as a necessary business expense. Fishing Tackle Prods. Co., 27 TC 638 (1957), acq. in result only, 1964-1 CB 4.

Travel expenses incurred by principal stockholder to assist his mother in operating family business and to sell operating assets of such corporation not deductible business expenses. Taxpayer, who was not an employee of the family business, was merely an interested stockholder who served without compensation for his assistance. Taxpayer claimed travel expenses incurred while assisting in the operation of the business. The IRS disallowed the deduction. *Held*: For the IRS. The absence of salary or other compensation prevented the court from finding that his activities rose to the level of an independent trade or business. Further, taxpayer's failure to seek reimbursement for such expenses, despite the poor financial condition of the family business, caused the expenses to be characterized as not ordinary and necessary, and thus not deductible under either Section 162 or 212. Meyer, 45 TCM 1337, ¶ 83,208 P-H Memo. TC (1983).

Rental payments to principal stockholders held reasonable. Taxpayer, a closely held corporation, leased a building owned by its principal stockholders. The IRS had looked into stockholders' compensation and questioned whether the rent was deductible under Section 162 (a)(3). *Held*: For taxpayer. The rental rate was reasonable and was required to be paid for the use of the property. The rental terms, although based on a percentage of taxpayer's gross sales, were found to be customary in that business. Phillips Co., 36 TCM 638, ¶ 77,150 P-H Memo. TC (1977).

Deferred compensation payments were reasonable and deductible. Taxpayer corporation made deferred compensation payments to the widow of its founder and majority stockholder. The IRS disallowed the deductions as unreasonable compensation and claimed that they were dividends. *Held*: For taxpayer. Taxpayer and the founder had a properly authorized deferred compensation agreement. The founder was inadequately paid during the corporation's earlier years, and the taxpayer's profits were due to his ability and reduced salaries. Although no dividends had been paid, the widow did not have sufficient control over the corporation to receive dividends disguised as deferred compensation. Therefore, the payments to the widow were properly deductible as deferred compensa-

BUSINESS EXPENSES: *Ordinary and Necessary Requirement*

tion. Andrews Distrib. Co., 31 TCM 732, ¶ 72,146 P-H Memo. TC (1972).

Section 482 used to deny deductions for work in excess of cash amounts actually paid. Taxpayer corporation gave out work to a subcontractor that was owned by the same party that owned taxpayer. Taxpayer deducted $62,000 and $71,000 for subcontractor fees. The IRS disallowed part of these deductions. *Held*: For the IRS, in part. Taxpayer paid the subcontractor $58,350 and $59,000 only for the years in question. In absence of any evidence to the contrary, the IRS' disallowance under Section 482 of the unpaid subcontract expense was correct. Furthermore, a consulting expense of $6,666 per year over a three-year contractual period was deductible even though few services were performed, and taxpayer obtained little benefit from the payments. Taxpayer had a reasonable expectation of receiving benefits, so the payments were deductible as ordinary and necessary business expenses. Fumigators, Inc., 31 TCM 29, ¶ 72,013 P-H Memo. TC (1972).

Taxpayer denied deduction for stockholder's sporting expenses where no proximate relationship to business was shown. Taxpayer's major stockholder, besides being an active general manager, was an avid tennis and golf player. Taxpayer deducted many of his tennis and other expenses, claiming them as promotional activites. The IRS denied the deduction, stating that there existed no proximate relationship between the expenditures and the hotel business. *Held*: For IRS, in part. The court felt that although the activities were predominantly motivated by personal reasons, one third of the expense actually served to promote the hotel's business. Other less-related costs were totally disallowed. Taxpayer's claims that the expenses should be characterized as additional compensation and allowed as a deduction were also denied because the manager was adequately paid and there was no intent to additionally compensate him. Cambridge Hotels, Inc., 27 TCM 1411, ¶ 68,263 P-H Memo. TC (1968).

IRS payments by public trucker to related entities deductible as reasonable expenses. Taxpayer was the successor by merger to another motor freight company, IFC. For the years 1953 through 1957, IFC paid a related corporation brokerage commissions averaging 7.25 percent of its gross revenues for its services in procuring freight hauling contracts. IFC also paid 2.25 percent as compensation for the services of its chief executive officer, who was never an elected officer or employee of the company, although he was its de facto head. As a result of the deductions, IFC claimed a net operating loss carry-over to its return for 1958. The IRS disallowed the so-called compensation, which was paid to a partnership consisting of the executive officer and his wife, because it was found to be excessive, or alternately a distribution of profits. The brokerage commissions in excess of 4 percent of IFS's gross revenues were held to be unreasonable and were disallowed. *Held*: For taxpayer. Payment of the brokerage commissions was the common practice of the motor freight industry. The payments that IFC paid the related corporation were, on the average, less than those paid by other carriers, and less than those charged to other carriers for like services. Also, the payments to the partnership were reasonable compensation for services performed and were fully deductible. Thus the deductions were properly taken in computing the net operating loss carryover to 1958. Hoover Motor Express Co., 25 TCM 1359, ¶ 66,267 P-H Memo. TC (1966).

Loan fee charged to related borrower held bona fide. Taxpayer corporation and a savings and loan association were owned by the same individual. So that the association would meet reserve requirements, it was decided that the development of a certain tract controlled by the association would be handled through taxpayer. It was also decided to have the common owner sever his control of taxpayer by selling his stock in the latter to two employees. Taxpayer then acquired the track (after the association completed the preliminary work) and borrowed the funds from the association for development of the property. It paid the association a substantial loan fee geared to a sharing of profits. *Held*: The loan fee was deductible by taxpayer. The sum was ordinary and necessary and reasona-

BUSINESS EXPENSES: *Organizational Expenses*

ble in amount when compared to similar fees charged other experienced builders in fully negotiated arm's-length transactions. Furthermore, the arrangement between taxpayer and the association, considering their respective contributions to the venture, resulted in a fair division of profits from the subdivision development. Martell Builders, Inc., 23 TCM 1501, ¶ 64,250 P-H Memo. TC (1964).

Payments for use of molds made to controlling stockholder denied; obligation to pay not shown. The controlling stockholder of taxpayer held a patent on and molds for a laundry tray. The patent expired in 1951. Rental payments by the corporation to the controlling stockholder in 1953, 1954, and 1955 for continued use or possession of the molds were denied as ordinary and necessary business expenses where there was no evidence of any contract or agreement or other proof that the payments were required to be made. *Held*: For the IRS. The court noted that the payments could just as easily have been dividends in the guise of rent. There was no evidence that the payments were made for good will acquired by taxpayer from the stockholder upon its incorporation. Burman Co., 20 TCM 1524, ¶ 61,293 P-H Memo. TC (1961).

Organizational Expenses

Merged corporation's pre-1954 organizational expenses not deductible by either merged or surviving corporation. Taxpayer acquired the assets and liabilities of another corporation through a merger. When the acquired corporation was formed in 1936, it incurred organizational expenses that remained on its books at the time of the merger. Taxpayer sought to deduct these expenses as a loss incurred in the merger. The district court held for the IRS on the ground that, while pre-1954 organizational expenses may be deducted as a loss upon liquidation, a merger provides no such opportunity because such expenses result in assets that continue beyond the existence of the acquired corporaion into the business of the surviving corporation. *Held*: Affirmed. Canal-Randolph Corp., 568 F2d 28, 78-1 USTC ¶ 9131, 41 AFTR2d 78-362 (7th Cir. 1977).

Payment of Claims

Indemnity payments nondeductible constructive dividends. Taxpayer corporpation gave wrong tax advice to two of its stockholders about certain distributions it had made, as a result of which the stockholders were assessed additional taxes and penalties. Taxpayer agreed to indemnify its stockholders for the additions and sought to deduct the payments as Section 162 busines expenses. The IRS disallowed such deductions. *Held*: For the IRS. The stockholders had never considered filing a lawsuit against taxpayer. The corporation gratuitously made payments based solely on the personal liability of its stockholders. As such, these payments were not deductible. Furthermore, the payments constituted constructive dividends to the stockholders. Inland Asphalt, 756 F2d 1425, 85-1 USTC ¶ 9293, 55 AFTR2d 85-1 1264 (9th Cir. 1985).

Payment of a liquidated corporation's depts are ordinary and necessary. Taxpayer paid off a liquidated corporation's debts in order to get credit from the corporation's former suppliers. The IRS claimed that the expenses were not ordinary and necessary. *Held*: For taxpayer. These payments were helpful in promoting taxpayer's business and were of a type "known" in the community. Furthermore, these were not capital expenditures in the formation of a new business but were made to protect and promote a continuing business. M.L. Eakes Co., 686 F2d 217, 82-2 USTC ¶ 9550, 50 AFTR2d 82-5582 (4th Cir. 1982).

Deduction allowed for settlement payment to victim injured by taxpayer's car while driven for personal purposes by sole stockholders' son. The son of taxpayer's sole stockholder seriously injured another person while using one of taxpayer's cars for personal purposes. The victim of the accident filed a $4.2 million suit against taxpayer and the individual members of the stockholder's family. The existence of the suit caused concern among taxpayer's creditors and caused the taxpayer's bank to freeze its line of credit. Taxpayer's contingent liability as a result of this suit was noted on its financial statements. To relieve

BUSINESS EXPENSES: *Payments to Stockholders' Beneficiaries*

its financial stress, taxpayer settled the suit with the victim. Taxpayer deducted the amount paid to the victim and attorney fees incurred due to the accident. The IRS disallowed the deductions. Taxpayer justified the deductions on the ground that the settlement was made to protect its "credit standing and financial durability." *Held*: For taxpayer. The court determined that because taxpayer was named a party defendant and was therefore exposed to a direct threat of a monetary judgment, the law suit was not merely tangentially threatening to taxpayer's assets. Accordingly, under the "origin of the claim" analysis, the settlement payment was a deductible business expense made to protect corporate assets. Kopp's Co., 636 F2d 59, 79-2 USTC ¶ 9430, 46 AFTR2d 80-6018 (4th Cir. 1980).

Deduction for disputed liability of accrual basis taxpayer limited to amount of judgments. Taxpayer, a construction company on the accrual basis, defaulted on a performance bond and was eventually liable for a $186,000 judgment. When taxpayer deducted $258,000 as an operating loss on the basis of the judgment, the IRS partially disallowed the loss. *Held*: For the IRS. Taxpayer's liability was accruable and deductible only when the liability was established and settled by the entry of a judgment, and his deduction was limited to the amount of that judgment, $186,000. Gould, 30 TCM 365, ¶ 71,090 P-H Memo. TC (1971).

Payments to Related Taxpayers

Financing fee to related savings and loan association disallowed. Three brothers owned the stock of taxpayer corporation and of a savings and loan association. The corporation developed a tract of land and claimed $5,000 per house as the cost of some 90 houses. The Tax Court found no proof that the cost was more than $4,000, and if the additional $1,000 were paid as claimed to the savings and loan association as a financing fee, it was not allowable. *Held*: Affirmed. The brothers were merely attempting to obtain a deduction for the taxpaying construction corporation by diverting funds to the exempt savings and loan association, from which they hoped to recover the funds at capital-gain rates. Biltmore Homes, Inc., 228 F2d 336, 61-1 USTC ¶ 9344, 7 AFTR2d 1035 (4th Cir. 1961).

Section 267 does not bar accrual of deduction for bonus and rent paid to "related" stockholders. Taxpayer, an accrual basis taxpayer, was owned by Leonard and his sister, both cash basis taxpayers. Immediately before the end of taxpayer's fiscal year, its board approved a bonus payable to Leonard, which was paid in two equal installments: one before the end of the fiscal year and one six months later. Leonard and his sister were also taxpayer's landlords. Rent due for the year in excess of expenses paid on behalf of its landlords was paid to them after the close of the fiscal year. The IRS challenged, under Section 267, the deduction of the bonus and rent for the year in question because such payments were made to "related" cash basis taxpayers. *Held:* For taxpayer. Section 267 is applied only when the deductible payment was received by a person who, under his method of accounting, is required to include it in income. W.C. Leonard & Co., 324 F. Supp. 422, 71-1 USTC ¶ 9290, 27 AFTR2d 71-964 (ND Miss. 1971).

Payments to Stockholders' Beneficiaries

Payments to officer's widow not deductible. Taxpayer claimed a deduction for payments to the widow of one of its founders under an agreement between the taxpayer and its officer stockholders. The agreement provided that the corporation, upon the death of either stockholder, would continue to pay to stockholder's widow and/or children an amount equal to 50 percent of the salary paid to the surviving officer stockholder. The IRS disallowed the deduction. The taxpayer contended that the amounts paid were deductible under Section 404 as payments to a deferred compensation plan, or under Section 162 as ordinary and neccessary business expenses. The Tax Court found that the payments did not represent deferred compensation and that even if they did, they would not have qualified as reasonable for salary. *Held*: Affirmed.

BUSINESS EXPENSES: *Profit Motive Requirement*

In addition, the original agreement that gave rise to the payment was not an arm's-length transaction. Willmark Serv. Sys., Inc., 368 F2d 359, 66-2 USTC ¶ 9719 (2d Cir. 1966).

Court found payments to widow not deductible and taxed them as dividend to remaining stockholder. Decedent, who owned almost 50 percent of taxpayer's stock, was estranged from his wife and family and did not provide for them in his will. His principal beneficiary was the other stockholder of the corporation. The corporation had no established plan to pay benefits to widows of employees, but resolved to pay the widow an amount in recognition of decedent's past services. *Held*: For the IRS. The payments were not deductible. They were made because the surviving stockholder (and principal beneficiary) felt that he had a moral duty to do so. Since the payments were made for the surviving stockholder's benefits and personal gratification, they constitute a constructive dividend. Montgomery Eng'g Co., 344 F2d 996, 65-1 USTC 9368, 15 AFTR2d 746 (3d Cir. 1965).

Payments pursuant to informal death benefit plan are deductible by corporation. A stockholder was the executive of taxpayer corporation. He was a bachelor who resided with and supported his three sisters, who were also stockholders. After the death of the executive it was voted at two meetings of the board of directors of taxpayer to make payments to the three sisters in consideration of their brother's past services. Although taxpayer had no formal plan for paying retirement or death benefits, it had always made some voluntary payment in connection with an employee's retirement or death. This policy was well known to its employees. Taxpayer deducted the payments as an employee benefit. Construing the payments as dividends the IRS disallowed the deduction. *Held*: For taxpayer. The payments were deductible as death benefits to beneficiaries of a deceased employee. As for the $5,000 death benefit exclusion under Section 101(b), the sisters had to apply this to the first amounts received. Since more than $5,000 was received in 1960,, nothing received in 1961 was excludable. John C. Nordt Co., 46 TC 431 (1966).

Payments to widow of deceased officer not deductible as they served the personal needs of stockholders. The stockholder officers of a Subchapter S corporation had entered into an agreement with their corporation, providing that, upon the death of any of them, the widow was to receive one half of her husband's salary at the time of his death for the rest of her life. The corporation made the required payments to an officer's widow and deducted them as deferred compensation under Section 404(a). *Held*: Deduction was denied. The agreement did not provide an economic benefit to the corporation, but rather served the personal needs of the stockholders. Payments under such an agreement were clearly not ordinary and necessary expenses of the corporation and thus could not qualify as a deduction under Section 404(a). Furthermore, there was absolutely no proof that the payments to the widow, even if deferred compensation, represented reasonable additional compensation for her husband's services. Wallace, 26 TCM 76, ¶ 67,011 P-H Memo. TC (1967).

Profit Motive Requirement

Lack of profit motive prevents deduction of business expense. Taxpayer, an unincorporated, nonprofit association, operated a game preserve and related activities. The profits it obtained from rental property were used to offset losses from club activities, and thus reduce membership dues. The district court held that the club's activities constituted "ordinary and necessary expenses in carrying on a trade or business," and therefore were fully deductible against taxpayer's gross income. *Held*: Reversed. Where the activities did not have a profit motive, the expenses were not ordinary and necessary expenses of carrying on a trade or business. Therefore, the expenses could not be offset against profits from the club's nonrecreational profit-making endeavors. Five Lakes Club, 468 F2d 443, 72-2 USTC ¶ 9716, 30 AFTR2d 72-5663 (8th Cir. 1982).

Taxpayer denied business bad debt deduction for amounts paid under his guarantee of notes issued by a corporation in which he held a 70 percent interest and was principal officer. Tax-

BUSINESS EXPENSES: *Salaries*

payer owned significant stock interests and was a principal officer in three corporations. With respect to one corporation, taxpayer was instrumental in promoting its formation and devoted a substantial amount of time and effort to it. It was regarding this corporation that taxpayer guaranteed notes when unforeseen circumstances rendered its original capital insufficient. Taxpayer's involvement with the remaining two corporations was insubstantial and he was not instrumental in their formation. Further, taxpayer was not in the business of lending money. Taxpayer was required to make good under his guarantee when his principal corporation became insolvent and failed to pay principal and interest on the notes. Taxpayer claimed a business bad debt deduction for amounts paid under his guarantee. *Held*: For the IRS. Taxpayer failed to show that the guarantee arose in the course of taxpayer's separate business activities, nor did the enactment of Section 166(f) affect the rationale and holding of Putnam, 352 US 82 (1956), which would have made losses of this character deductible under Section 165. Campbell, 19 TCM 207, ¶ 60,039 P-H Memo. TC (1960).

Salaries

Distributions to stockholder employee not salary payments. Taxpayer corporation entered into an agreement providing the terms and conditions under which it was obligated to purchase the stock of departing stockholders. Subsequently, one of the stockholders departed and received payment for the surrender of his stock, the amount being based in part on the valuation of the accounts receivable. Taxpayer deducted the payment as a salary expense, and the IRS disallowed the deduction. *Held*: For the IRS. The payment represented a redemption of stock, since it was paid to the stockholder in his capacity as a stockholder, not as an employee. The stockholder's only interest in the accounts receivable was as they affected the value of his stock. Steffen, 69 TC 1049 (1978).

Constructive receipt of accrued salaries by stockholders prevented disallowance of deduction to corporation. Taxpayer was owned by three individuals who were also partners. For the years in question, taxpayer accrued salaries for its officer-stockholders, but did not pay them within two and a half months of the close of the taxable year of the respective accrual. The accrued salaries were not reported by the stockholders until actually received, as they were on the cash basis method of accounting. The IRS contended that the deduction for the accured salaries should be barred by virtue of Section 267(a)(2). *Held*: For taxpayer. The only issue was whether there had been constructive receipt of the salaries so as to preclude the application of Section 267(a)(2). Where a corporation is able to borrow an amount that would enable it to pay accrued salaries, the doctrine of constructive receipt is applicable. Salary accruals in accordance with an accountant's recommendation are not a restriction on the payment of salaries. Nor are the conditions voiced by an officer to the taking of accrued salaries restrictive enough to prevent the salaries from being constructively received by the stockholders. Since the doctrine of constuctive receipt applied to the salary accruals, the deduction was not barred. Hyplains Dressed Beef, Inc., 56 TC 119 (1971).

Bargain stock sale to employees of closely related corporation not deductible as compensation. Taxpayer claimed a deduction for compensation paid to two alleged employees based on a sale of its stock to them at a price of $10 less per share than market value. The recipients of the stock were in fact stockholders of taxpayer but were employees of a closely related corporation. The IRS denied the deduction. *Held*: For the IRS. Taxpayer did not prove (1) that the employees were its employees, (2) that the alleged compensation in the form of bargain sales of stock was reasonable in amount for any work that they performed, and (3) that the market value of the stock was actually $15 per share as contended by taxpayer. Danskin, Inc., 40 TC 318 (1963).

Corporate payments on behalf of sole stockholder held not compensation. Taxpayer, the sole stockholder, had the corporation pay a note, interest and legal fees on his behalf. The corporation deducted the payments as Sec-

Business Expenses: *Stockholders' Expenses*

tion 162 expenses. The IRS determined that those payments were not deductable as business expenses. *Held*: For the IRS. The court concluded that the payments were not made with compensatory intent, disallowed the deduction, and treated them as constructive dividends. Russos, 36 TCM 1222, ¶ 77,309 P-H Memo. TC (1977).

Stockholders' Expenses

Corporation's payment of personal entertainment expenses held constructive dividend. The Tax Court held that taxpayer stockholder realized constructive dividends by charging personal entertainment expenses to the corporation. *Held*: Affirmed. The lower court's decision was not clearly erroneous. Also, errors in the treatment of debt forgiveness resulted in the realization of taxable income. Negligence penalties were sustained. Magill, 651 F2d 1233, 81-1 USTC ¶ 9437, 47 AFTR2d 81-1483 (6th Cir. 1981).

Constructive dividends realized on luncheon expenses reimbursements. Taxpayer, a doctor, incurred expenses in taking his nurses and other physicians to lunch approximately four times a week for the purpose of obtaining referrals. Taxpayer's professional corporation reimbursed him for these lunch expenses and claimed a business expense deduction for the amount reimbursed. The IRS determined that the lunch expenses were taxpayer's personal nondeductible expenses and that he realized constructive dividends to the extent he was reimbursed by his corporation. *Held*: For the IRS. The luncheon expenses constituted nondeductible personal expenses, and taxpayer realized a constructive dividend to the extent his corporation reimbursed him. The fact that taxpayer may have discussed general business matters or obtained patient referrals from his colleagues was not sufficient to convert those personal expenses into deductible business expenses. Hankenson, 47 TCM 1567, ¶ 84,200 P-H Memo. TC (1984).

Stockholder's expenses not deductible by corporation and were dividend to stockholder. Taxpayer corporation manufactured concrete mixers. Its sole stockholder was a yacht fancier, and taxpayer owned a yacht that was docked in front of the stockholder's home and was available to him at all times. This yacht was one of a series owned by either the stockholder or taxpayer, each succeeding boat being more luxurious as taxpayer's business increased. The IRS disallowed part of the yacht expense, depreciation, travel expense of the stockholder's wife, and other similar items, and assessed the stockholder for constructive dividends. *Held*: For the IRS. The yacht was acquired primarily for the personal gratification of the stockholder and any business use was distinctly secondary. The relation to business of the other expenses was also not shown. Challenge Mfg. Co., 37 TC 650 (1962), acq. 1962-2 CB 4.

Substantiation

Deductions disallowed when taxpayer failed to substantiate business expenses. Taxpayer corporation filed tax returns on a consolidated basis with various other corporations claiming they were affiliated. The IRS disallowed certain business expenses and determined that taxpayer had not established that two of the corporations were members of the affiliated group. *Held*: For the IRS. Taxpayer bears the burden of proving that the IRS' notice of deficiency is incorrect. At trial taxpayer's controlling stockholder made a minimal effort to substantiate the amounts claimed to have been expended. Furthermore, a witness' testimony that he had directed an unnamed person to complete incorporation of the various companies claimed to be affiliated with taxpayer was not an adequate record. Franke Exploration Corp., 48 TCM 1202, ¶ 84,508 P-H Memo. TC (1984).

Travel and Entertainment Expenses

Corporation denied deductions on resort property used by stockholders. Taxpayer corporation spent about $370,000 to acquire and furnish a country home. The Tax Court found that during the years at issue, the country home was not used for entertaining customers or other business purposes. Its function

BUSINESS EXPENSES: *Travel and Entertainment Expenses*

then was as a vacation home for the stockholders and their families. *Held*: Affirmed. The court allowed the corporation no deductions for depreciation or maintenance in excess of the amount of rent paid by the stockholders. However, the value of the use was not a dividend; the rent the stockholders paid (about $1,200 a month for the summer months) was fair. International Trading Co., 275 F2d 578, 60-1 USTC ¶ 9335, 5 AFTR2d 970 (7th Cir. 1960).

Bank could deduct cost of parties cohosted by its president. Taxpayer, a bank, paid the costs of two parties cohosted by its president. A vice-president of the bank cohosted the second party, the same annual social event as the party a year earlier. The guest of honor of the first party was a significant client of taxpayer and a longtime personal friend of the president; the guest of honor of the second party was a mutual friend of the hosts. The IRS contended that the costs of the parties were not deductible business expenses. *Held*: For taxpayer. The parties were an effective way for taxpayer to reach its top clients and prospective clients in the upper echelon of the local financial community. The fact that people were present who did not fall into these categories did not establish that the parties were purely for entertainment purposes; labeling a party celebrating a social event as a business function would have frustrated taxpayer's purposes. Whether the entertainment costs were ordinary and necessary expenses was left to the discretion of taxpayer. It was his decision what kinds of advertising and promotion were needed to obtain and hold business. First Nat'l Bank of Omaha, 20 AFTR2d 5751 (D. Neb. 1967).

Excess travel allowances to stockholders were dividends. Taxpayer corporation paid travel allowances in excess of actual expenses incurred by its two stockholder employees. Taxpayer claimed the excess allowances as salary, deductible under Section 162(a). The IRS treated them as constructive dividends. *Held*: For the IRS. A salary deduction is allowed only if payments are actually intended to be paid for services. No such intent existed here. Lubbock United Gen. Agency, Inc., 44 TCM 273, ¶ 82,359 P-H Memo. TC (1982).

Reimbursement of auto expenses were constructive dividends. A professional corporation claimed a business deduction for reimbursing its officer stockholders for their automobile expenses. The IRS disallowed the deductions and charged that the reimbursements were constructive dividends. *Held*: For the IRS. Most of the automobile expenses were the doctors' personal commuting expenses. Home office deductions, and travel deductions for the wife of one doctor on a business trip were also disallowed. ON-RI-GA Medical Professional Ass'n, 37 TCM 786, ¶ 78,183 P-H Memo. TC (1978).

Travel expense allowance for officers disallowed as unreasonable compensation. Taxpayer, a corporation in the wholesale grocery business, paid its three officers a prearranged sum each year for travel expenses. This was done pursuant to a resolution of the board of directors authorizing the payment of an amount not to exceed $100 per week for general promotion of the business. A portion of the travel expenses was shown to have been used for hunting trips, weekend trips, and other social activities. To qualify the expenses as deductions, taxpayer alleged that they were intended as compensation to the officers. *Held*: For the IRS. Even if the amounts had been intended as compensation, taxpayer failed to present credible evidence of reasonableness. Further, the fact that salaries of the officers were increased several times in prior years rebutted taxpayer's argument that the allowances were in lieu of salary increases. P.F. Scheidelman & Sons, Inc., 24 TCM 168, ¶ 65,031 P-H Memo. TC (1965).

Corporation can deduct unexpended travel and entertainment allowances paid to officers. Two officers were each granted as compensation $52,000 for the year, plus any unexpended travel and entertainment allowances. In the taxable years 1956 and 1957, they each received $5,400 and $7,800 respectively as travel and entertainment allowances, of which they actually expended only $3,100 each year. Neither of the officers included the unexpended portion of the allowance in his own income. *Held*: The court held that such unexpended portions of the allowances constituted additional compensation, not dividends to the recipients. The court noted that (1) the unexpended portions were comparatively minor in amount, being less than 10 percent of the fixed annual salaries on one year and less than 5 percent in the other; (2) the corporate minutes early in 1956 explicitly provided that any such unexpended portions of the allowances were to be treated as compensation; and (3) the parties stipulated that the amounts did "not constitute excessive and unreasonable compensation." The court thus approved a method of avoiding dividend treatment resulting from a disallowance of expense at the corporate level. Bell Oldsmobile, 22 TCM 330, ¶ 63,076 P-H Memo. TC (1963).

BUSINESS NEEDS

(*See* Accumulated Earnings Tax—Reasonable Business Needs)

BUSINESS, SALE OR PURCHASE OF

(*See* Acquisitions to Avoid Tax; Reorganizations)

BUSINESS PURPOSE

(*See* Redemptions; Reorganizations)

CANCELLATION OF INDEBTEDNESS

Court denies taxpayer's deduction of failing subsidiary's losses on ground that such losses were already deducted when taxpayer made additions to its bad debt reserves for loans to the subsidiary. Taxpayer formed a subsidiary for a special enterprise and dissolved it five years later. The subsidiary was never successful and existed on loans from taxpayer. Immediately before its dissolution, taxpayer forgave its loans to the subsidiary. Taxpayer deducted the subsidiary's net operating losses. Also, during the years that the subsidiary was in business, taxpayer deducted under its bad debt reserve amounts lent to the subsidiary. The IRS disallowed the loss deductions. *Held:* For the IRS. The court held that the deductions were properly disallowed on the ground that such amounts were already deducted when added to taxpayer's bad debt reserves. Marwais Steel Co., 354 F2d 997, 66-1 USTC ¶ 9138, 17 AFTR2d 11 (9th Cir. 1965).

No corporate gain where own installment obligation acquired in return for stock and then cancelled. Taxpayer was created to acquire A, an existing business. A contributed $100,000 in cash in exchange for 78 percent of taxpayer's stock. Thereafter, taxpayer executed a contract to buy the business and paid $100,000 in cash, $90,000 for accounts receivable valued at $90,000, and $10,000 as a down payment on the remainder of the purchase price of $817,031, which was to be paid in installments. Two years later, A transferred the remaining indebtedness to taxpayer for 120,050 shares of stock. Taxpayer contended that the transfer was tax free under Section 351. The Tax Court and the IRS determined that the cancellation of the installment obligation amounted to a "disposition" of the obligation, which under Section 453(d)(1) resulted in gain to taxpayer. *Held:* Reversed. There was no gain to taxpayer where there was a cancellation of the obligation by the "buyer" of the property. The transaction was not a "disposition." Jack Ammann Photogrammetric Eng'rs., 341 F2d 466, 65-1 USTC ¶ 9251 (5th Cir. 1965).

"Forgiven" corporate debt owed to stockholders was ordinary income on liquidation. Taxpayers were the sole stockholders in B Corporation. B periodically accrued and deducted salaries and interest due to the taxpayers that were not paid. Following the adoption of a plan of liquidation under Section 337, the debts were forgiven by the stockholders. Upon liquidation, taxpayers reported the entire distribution as capital gain. *Held:* For the IRS. The forgiveness of the amounts owed the taxpayers was a sham because it would be difficult to believe that the corporation's liabilities to outside creditors would exceed the amount of cash it had on hand. The cancellation of the debt was not designed to aid the corporation financially, to increase its ability to borrow money, or to facilitate the continuation of its business, and the corporation was not insolvent. Braddock Land Co., 75 TC 324 (1980).

Forgiveness of prior year's indebtedness of subsidiary a nondeductible contribution to capital, not a deductible business expense. Taxpayer, a real estate corporation, rented property to its three subsidiaries. It accrued the rents charged as income for 1958, although no cash was received that year. The subsidiaries suffered losses; in 1960, taxpayer reduced its rents by 50 percent retroactive to 1958. Taxpayer claimed a deduction in 1960 for the difference between the amount previously reported as income in 1958 and the "adjusted" rent for that year. *Held:* For the IRS. The deduction was denied. A forgiveness of the prior year's liability without consideration was not a deductible business expense, but constituted a nondeductible gift or contribution to the capital of the subsidiaries. Noll's Food Co., 23 TCM 456, ¶ 64,069 P-H Memo. TC (1964).

Cancellation of debt used to buy out "silent" stockholder does not constitute a dividend to sole remaining stockholder. Taxpayer and Thompson were equal partners in a transportation company; Thompson was a "silent" partner. The partners agreed to incorporate the partnership with all shares of stock to be issued to taxpayer in his own right and as nominee of Thompson so as not to disclose Thompson's relationship to the business. Later, the relationship between taxpayer and Thompson deteriorated seriously, and Thompson demanded his stock, which taxpayer declined to transfer to him. The parties then agreed that the corporation was to pay Thompson $40,000 in cash, with taxpayer as guarantor, to buy out his 50 percent interest.

In form, the transaction was made to appear that taxpayer purchased the stock from money loaned to him by the corporation. This was done because it was erroneously believed by the parties that the corporation could not at that time purchase its own shares. When it was learned that the corporation could purchase its own shares, the books were corrected to show that the shares were purchased from Thompson by the corporation and were held as treasury stock. The "accounts receivable" due from taxpayer was cancelled. *Held:* The court held that in substance the corporation redeemed Thompson's shares so that taxpayer was not really indebted to the corporation. Accordingly, the cancellation of the purported indebtedness did not constitute a taxable dividend to the taxpayer. Beggs, 20 TCM 626, ¶ 61,127 P-H Memo. TC (1961).

Corporation's forgiveness of interest on subsidiary's debt yields income to subsidiary under tax benefit rule. *P*, an accrual basis corporation, forgave interest on a loan to its subsidiary, *S*, when *S* was solvent. *S* had accrued and deducted interest on prior year's returns. The IRS ruled that *S* received income to the extent of any tax benefit resulting from its prior deductions. Rev. Rul. 73-432, 1973-2 CB 17 superseded. Rev. Rul. 76-316, 1976-2 CB 22.

Cancellation of indebtedness was considered payment in the year of cancellation for the 30 percent test. When a corporation redeemed stock for cash and cancelled an unrelated debt and promissory note payable over a period of years, the cancellation of indebtedness was treated as payment in the year of redemption for the 30 percent test of Section 453(b)(2)(A)(ii). If the amount of debt cancelled and the cash payment exceeded 30 percent of the contract price, the transaction gain could not be reported on the installment method. Rev. Rul. 76-398, 1976-2 CB 130.

Distributed note is not income from discharge of indebtedness. Where a subsidiary that is being liquidated distributes to the parent the parent's note, which it acquired as security for a loan, the amount of the note is not in-

CANCELLATION OF INDEBTEDNESS: *In General*

come to the parent from the discharge of indebtedness. Rev. Rul. 74-54, 1974-1 CB 76.

CAPITAL ASSETS

(*See* Capital Gains and Losses—Capital Asset Defined)

CAPITAL CONTRIBUTIONS

(*See* Contributions to Capital)

CAPITAL EXPENDITURES

(*See* Business Expenses—Capital Expenditure Distinguished)

CAPITAL GAINS AND LOSSES

In General 148
Assignment of Income 149
Capital Asset Defined 149
Holding Period 151
Ordinary Gains/Losses Distinguished 151

In General

Payment by wholly owned subsidiary to its parent prior to the latter's sale of the stock was part of purchase price. Taxpayer, a publicly held corporation, was the stockholder of several wholly owned subsidiaries. An outside party offered to sell all of the stock of two of the subsidiaries for $3,500,000. Taxpayer had for several years considered the payment of dividends by the subsidiaries, and counteroffered to sell the stock for $700,000 after payment of dividends in the total amount of $2,800,000. Said dividends were declared, and one of the subsidiaries issued its promissory note for that amount, due in one month with interest. Shortly thereafter, and according to negotiations that had been conducted by the various interests, taxpayer sold the stock of the two subsidiaries for $700,000. The purchaser guaranteed all liabilities. The new stockholders then borrowed $2,800,000 to satisfy the note to taxpayer. Taxpayer treated the receipt of the $2,800,000 as a dividend, and did not include the receipt in the consolidated return that it filed with its subsidiaries. The IRS determined that the payment represented capital gain on the sale of the stock of the subsidiaries. The Tax Court held for the taxpayer, stating that the note reflected a true dividend and was therefore not part of the purchase price. *Held:* Reversed. The dividend and sale were one transaction. The note was a transitory step in a prearranged sale of the stock. In substance, the subsidiary neither declared nor paid a dividend to taxpayer, but acted as a mere conduit for payment of $2,800,000 by the purchaser to taxpayer. Waterman Steamship Corp., 430 F2d 1185, 70-2 USTC ¶ 9514, 26 AFTR2d 70-5185 (5th Cir. 1970), cert. denied, 401 US 939 (1971).

Corporate distribution of stock of a wholly owned subsidiary and subsequent sale to an unrelated corporation was a sale on the corporate rather than the shareholder level. Taxpayer was an affiliate of a corporate group and owned stock in another affiliate the only asset of which was a parcel of unimproved real estate that was purchased for the construction of a drive-in theater. That project never materialized. The parcel was put up for sale; later, taxpayer's parent corporation needed cash. Pursuant to an oral agreement, taxpayer cancelled an outstanding indebtedness of its subsidiary and distributed to its parent-stockholder the stock of the subsidiary as a dividend in-kind. The distributees of the stock then sold said stock to the unrelated purchaser, thus completing the transaction at a price for the stock equal to the agreed-upon price for the plan. Taxpayer reported no gain on the sale, contending that the sale was by the stockholders. The Tax Court upheld the IRS in rejecting that contention. *Held:* Affirmed. The appellate court stated that its function was to review the record of the Tax Court to see if there was sufficient evidence to warrant its findings. In this case, the Tax

Court found that the initial objective of the transaction was to sell the land owned by the subsidiary. The negotiations were all carried out in that context. Their ultimate finding was not clearly erroneous. Waltham Netoco Theatres, Inc., 401 F2d 333, 68-2 USTC ¶ 9614, 23 AFTR2d 69-416 (1st Cir. 1968).

Corporate distributions constituted long-term capital gain. Taxpayer's corporation ran a shoe business and transferred materials to a Florida corporation. Taxpayer received the stock of the Floirda corporation and payments for the materials. The IRS characterized the payments as income to taxpayer. *Held:* For the IRS. The payments constituted distributions to taxpayer in liquidation of her corporations. Furthermore, since she could not establish any basis for the stock, the entire distribution was a long-term capital gain. Finally, taxpayer was liable for a 25 percent penalty for failure to file a return. Calderazzo, 34 TCM 1, ¶ 75,001 P-H Memo. TC (1975).

Loss on employer's shares was capital. A capital loss resulted from the worthlessness of shares purchased voluntarily by an officer stockholder from his brokerage firm. The purchase was made during a time of prosperity and rapid growth when the stock appeared to be a good investment. Rev. Rul. 75-13, 1975-1 CB 67.

Gain and loss on different blocks of stock may not be offset in C reorganization. Taxpayer corporation acquired substantially all of the assets of another corporation in exchange for taxpayer's stock in a transaction qualifying under Section 368(a)(1)(C). The acquired corporation distributed to its stockholders one share of taxpayer stock having a value of $500 per share plus property having a value of $5 per share. A stockholder transferred two blocks of stock with different bases to taxpayer in exchange for taxpayer's stock and other property. If each block of stock were considered separately, the shareholder would realize a gain on one block and a loss on the other block. The IRS ruled that the gain or loss must be considered separately; thus the loss on one block could not offset the gain recognized under Section 356(a) on the other block. Further, under Section 356(c), no loss would be recognized. Rev. Rul. 68-23, 1968-1 CB 144.

Assignment of Income

"Locked in" profits on contracts taxable to former stockholders following liquidation. Taxpayers were sole stockholders in a corporation that liquidated pursuant to Section 337. As part of the plan, all its assets and property were sold to another company. A significant portion of the business concerned futures contracts. Taxpayers claimed that the corporation did not realize income on the sale of the contract, since they were too speculative to value. The IRS maintained that, although income had not accrued to the company on the date of sale, a substantial profit was "locked in." The company, therefore, realized income on the sale of the contracts. *Held:* For the IRS. The value of the futures contracts would be discounted 25 percent for uncertainties and administrative costs. As transferees of the company, the former stockholders were responsible for reporting such income under the assignment of income doctrine. Peterson, 723 F2d 43, 84-1 USTC ¶ 9103, 53 AFTR2d 84-398 (8th Cir. 1983).

Capital Asset Defined

Sale of rights to unpatented invention produced capital gain due to delay in patent approval. Taxpayer acquired rights to an invention and applied for a patent while marketing the invention. He sold the rights to his corporation in March 1966 and reported the proceeds as capital gain before the patent was granted in April 1967. The IRS claimed that the proceeds were taxable as ordinary income. The Tax Court held for taxpayer. *Held:* Affirmed. The appellate court, following Estate of Stahl, 442 F2d 324 (7th Cir. 1971) and Chee, 486 F2d 696 (1st Cir. 1973), held that the patent applications were not depreciable property at the time of the transfer because it was not until over a year later that the applications were approved. The fact that the invention was marketed successfully did not

Sale of renegotiated franchise was really sale of two franchises when early contract not terminated. Taxpayer, sole proprietor of a binding business, acquired a franchise that bound books by using a special spiral process. In order to give his manager an interest in the business, taxpayer organized a corporation to take over the proprietorship business, and took back 60 percent of the stock. His manager acquired the other 40 percent. Shortly before the incorporation, taxpayer renegotiated the old franchise, which as a result had 15 more years to run. Taxpayer then transferred the new franchise to his corporation for $600,000, to be paid at the rate of $40,000 per year. Over the IRS' argument that the transfer was in substance a contribution to capital and that the $40,000 payments constituted dividends, the Tax Court held that the transfer was a sale in an arm's-length transaction and that the franchise was not a mere license but represented a capital asset. The court also found, however, that the renegotiation had resulted in a cancellation of the old franchise and the creation of a new one, so that the taypayer's gain was short-term. Furthermore, the corporation was formed for a valid business reason other than tax avoidance and was entitled to amortize the cost of the franchise over its 15-year life. *Held:* Reversed and remanded. Although the renegotiated agreement created significant new rights, it left some others untouched and neither terminated nor replaced the earlier contract. Thus, in reality, two contracts were sold. The court remanded the case to the Tax Court for an allocation of the gains between the original franchise. On remand, the Tax Court also would have to determine the amount of depreciation taxpayer could claim for the year in issue, as this depended on the basis of the renegotiated franchise. Brook, 360 F2d 1011, 66-1 USTC ¶ 9422, 17 AFTR2d 1009 (2d Cir. 1966).

Payment for rights to condemnation award deemed capital in nature. Taxpayer entered into a lease with K whereby K removed an old building on taxpayer's lot and replaced it with a new one. Before the building was destroyed, the city proposed to widen the street on which the building stood. Since taxpayer was entitled to a larger award if the building existed at the time of the condemnation, taxpayer sought to delay K. When K sought to build a smaller building to accommodate a widened street, taxpayer obtained a restraining order prohibiting the building's destruction. Thereafter, K purchased taxpayer's right to a condemnation award for $80,000. The sum was not reported on taxpayer's return as income. The IRS determined that it should have been reported as ordinary income. *Held:* For taxpayer. Rights to a condemnation award were property rights and were capital in nature. Hence, there was capital gain to the extent that payment exceeded basis. Where the basis was impossible to ascertain, the sum was applied to reduce the cost basis of the entire property. Trunk, 32 TC 1127 (1959).

Stockholdings and cash advances were capital investments; resulting losses were capital. In 1969, D, a computer programming firm, acquired C, which operated computer training schools. During 1969 through 1970, D made cash advances and guarantees of loans to C to provide working capital. D had to make good on some guarantees, and in 1970 sold C at a loss. D claimed an ordinary loss, while the IRS contended that the loss was capital. *Held:* For the IRS. The stock of C was a capital asset obtained by D for an investment, not to ensure a supply of computer programmers for D's own operations. The stock did not become wholly worthless prior to the sale in 1970; thus Section 165(g)(3) was unavailable. Advances and payments on guarantees were contributions to capital and were added to stock basis, not debts. Thus, all losses were capital, subject to the limitations thereon. Datamation Servs. Inc., 35 TCM 1092, ¶ 76,252 P-H Memo. TC (1976).

Employee homes purchased by employer corporation held to constitute capital assets. Ap-

Capital Gains and Losses: Ordinary Gains/Losses Distinguished

plying the venerable *Corn Products* doctrine, the IRS held that homes purchased under a home-buying plan by a corporation to assist relocating employees in the sale of their personal residences, when sold by the corporation, are capital assets within the meaning of Section 1221. Rev. Rul. 82-204, 1982-2 CB 192.

All of subsidiary's gross receipts considered in determining whether shares were a capital asset. To determine whether a parent's subsidiary's shares were a capital asset, the gross receipts for the entire period of existence for a subsidiary that became insolvent within five years of its formation should be considered when using the 90 percent test of Section 165(g)(3)(B). Rev. Rul. 75-186, 1975-1 CB 72.

Holding Period

Assignment of patent rights to secure loan was a complete transfer of rights. Taxpayer, the originator and developer of the paint roller and tray, organized E-Z, Inc. to develop his business. In order to obtain loans from a "Chicago interest," taxpayer assigned patent rights and applications to E-Z. Later, the rights were reconveyed to taxpayer in exchange for granting E-Z an exclusive licensing agreement. The IRS determined that the royalties received under the agreement with the "Chicago interest" did not qualify as long-term capital gain. *Held:* For the IRS. Taxpayer's assignment of his patent rights constituted a complete transfer of those rights. Accordingly, the period of time during which the rights were assigned could not be included in taxpayer's holding period. Hence, taxpayer was not entitled to long-term capital gain treatment. Touchett, 19 TCM 403, ¶ 60,076 P-H Memo. TC (1960).

Section 1223(2) applied to distribution of stock to parent. A subsidiary corporation distributed appreciated portfolio stock to its parent. The IRS ruled that the holding period of such securities would carry over to the parent pursuant to the provisions of Section 1223(2). Rev. Rul. 70-6, 1970-1 CB 172.

Ordinary Gains/Losses Distinguished

Gain on bootstrap sale determined. The Tax Court held that the decision in Clay Brown, 380 US 563 (1965) that a bootstrap sale was a sale and that the gain was a capital gain, applies only if the purchase price is reasonable for a nonexempt purchaser. Since the price in issue was unreasonably high, more than twice what a nonexempt taxpayer would have paid, the transaction was not a sale, and taxpayer's entire gain was ordinary income. *Held:* Reversed, in part. Taxpayer was entitled to capital gain treatment to the extent that the reasonable price for a nonexempt purchaser exceeds taxpayer's basis in the property. The balance of the purchase price was an ordinary income. Berenson, 507 F2d 262, 74-2 USTC ¶ 9806, 34 AFTR2d 74-6181 (2d Cir. 1974).

Guarantee of part of purchase price in merger resulted in capitalized loss. Taxpayer sold his majority interest in *A* corporation to *B* corporation for 62 percent of *B*'s outstanding stock. Taxpayer guaranteed the market value of certain assets to consummate the exchange. He had to indemnify *B* after the assets upon sale brought less than guaranteed. The Tax Court sustained the IRS determination that loss was a capital expenditure. *Held:* Affirmed. The guarantee was part of the purchase price, since it was required as a condition for completion of the exchange. The claimed loss was not allowable since it was incident to a tax-free reorganization. McGlothlin, 370 F2d 729, 67-1 USTC ¶ 9166 (5th Cir. 1967).

Bargain option price on real estate deemed ordinary income to stockholder. Taxpayer owned real estate that he leased for many years to a corporation in which he was a 40 percent stockholder. The corporation needed funds, and the Reconstruction Finance Corporation agreed to make a loan if the corporation would take title to the property and use part of the loan to improve it. Since the corporation had no cash and the Reconstruction Finance Corporation would not agree to a purchase for notes, taxpayer sold the property, worth $72,000, to the corporation for preferred stock and the assumption of the mortgage. Taxpayer was given the option to repurchase the property for $72,000 after the loan was paid. He exercised his option when the property was worth $150,000 due to the improvements made by the corporation with the loan proceeds. The Tax Court held that taxpayer received taxable income of $78,000 on his bargain repurchase. *Held:* Affirmed. There could be no explanation of the low option price except compensation to taxpayer for the rent income he was losing when title to the property was in the corporation. The court also rejected taxpayer's alternative argument that the option was a compensatory option, therefore taxable in 1952 (the year received) and not in 1957 (the year of the repurchase). The option was not immediately exercisable, and it was doubtful whether any one other than taxpayer would have been interested in buying it. Haag, 334 F2d 351, 64-2 USTC ¶ 9634 (8th Cir. 1964).

Sale to corporation at inflated price did not produce ordinary income where corporation had no earnings or profits. Before going into bankruptcy, taxpayer sold a mailing list to his corporation at an inflated price of $150,000. At that time, the corporation had no earnings or profits. Taxpayer claimed that the mailing list was a capital asset, and accordingly reported his $135,000 profit on the sale as capital gain. The $135,000 was equal in amount to the inflation in the purchase price and to taxpayer's debt to the corporation. The sale satisfied the debt. The IRS contended that taxpayer's point was ordinary income. *Held:* For taxpayer. Unlike the IRS, taxpayer may not now recharacterize the sale as a corporate distribution taxable under Section 301(c) as a capital transaction, since the corporation had no earnings or profits. That did not mean, however, that in the absence of a Code provision to such effect, that the IRS may treat the gain as ordinary income. It could do so only if it could be shown that by casting the transaction as a sale, taxpayer's tax liability was less than it should have been. In re Margulies, 271 F. Supp. 50, 67-2 USTC ¶ 9688 (DNJ 1967).

Loss of sale of stock qualified as a business capital loss. Taxpayer was engaged in the acquisition, development, and sale of real estate, and in the business of buying and selling stock on a large scale. He obtained financing from three lenders, and after one of the lenders purchased a large block of stock in an insurance company, the taxpayer did likewise. However, after a contemplated merger fell through, both the lender and the taxpayer sold their stock in the insurance company, the taxpayer sustaining a loss on the sale. At this time, one of the lenders informed the taxpayer that a large quantity of its stock would become available. In order to prevent the purchase of the stock by investors unfriendly to the taxpayer, the taxpayer purchased the shares and ultimately sold a substantial amount of the stock at a loss. The taxpayer treated both losses as business capital losses. The IRS determined that the losses were nonbusiness capital losses because there was no actual nexus between the acquisition and sale of the stock and the taxpayer's real estate business. *Held:* For taxpayer, in part. The losses incurred on the sale of the insurance company stock were nonbusiness capital losses because there was no direct connection between the purchase of the stock and the conduct of the taxpayer's business. In fact, investment considerations motivated the purchase. However, for one of the lenders, the losses incurred on the sale of stock were capital business losses because the acquisition of the stock in the insurance company was directly related to retaining that company as a source of borrowed funds. Crow, 79 TC 541 (1982).

Corn Products **doctrine allows ordinary loss for unreimbursed capital contributions.** Taxpayer was engaged in research and development. Taxpayer, with another, formed a separate corporation to engage in a specific research and development project. Taxpayer made cash advances to this corporation. When the project failed, taxpayer gave up its stock interest in the corporation and claimed an ordinary loss for the unreimbursed amounts. The IRS challenged taxpayer's deduction of an ordinary loss for the advances, claiming that taxpayer's loss was capital in nature. *Held:* For taxpayer. The court reasoned, citing Schlumberger Tech. Corp., 443 F2d 1115 (5th Cir. 1971), that where a loss arises with respect to capital contributions made for business (as opposed to investment) purposes, that loss should be treated as an ordinary loss under the *Corn Products* doctrine. Chemplast, Inc., 60 TC 623 (1973).

Liquidation converts ordinary income into capital gain. Taxpayer *T*, a closely held corporation, and several other corporations entered into a joint venture agreement for the purpose of constructing a tunnel. *T* was the "sponsoring joint venturer" of the tunnel and, as such, accounted to the other members of the joint venture. *J*, director of *T*, was the project manager and signed all receipts. *T* adopted a plan of liquidation and therein distributed its 30 percent interest in the former assets of the joint venture. The former assets included two contested claims against the Bureau of Reclamation and the Industrial Indemnity Company. The IRS determined that the income realized on the settlement of the claims should be included in *T*'s income for its final short period. It would be taxed as ordinary income, regardless of the fact that *T* had been liquidated and discolved under state law before receiving the payments. *Held:* For taxpayer. Once a corporation adopts a plan of liquidation and is dissolved under state law, it ceases to exist for tax purposes, and it has no tax liability for income accruing thereafter. Contested claims that are part of the payment in exchange for stock in the liquidation result in capital gain or loss. Where contested claims that can't be valued are received in corporate liquidation, computation of capital gain with respect to these claims is held open until they are settled, collected, or otherwise reduced to ascertainable value. The Shea Co., 53 TC 135 (1969).

Postdissolution recovery held not taxable to corporation; capital gain allowed. Taxpayers, husband and wife, were the sole stockholders of a corporation that for many years had operated a motion picture theatre. The corporation was dissolved in 1949, and all its assets were distributed to taxpayers. In 1953, a suit was instituted by the corporation against Loew's Inc. and other film distributors for alleged violation of antitrust laws, loss of profits, and damages incurred by the corporation, for the years 1932 through 1948. The case was settled in 1956, and taxpayers received a net settlement of $32,000. Taxpayers treated this as long-term capital gain taxable to them; the IRS asserted that the award was taxable to the corporation and that taxpayers were liable as transferees. The IRS' case was based on a state statute under which a corporation's existence is deemed to continue for the purpose of winding up its affairs. *Held:* For taxpayer. The court found that this provision would help the IRS only if the claim against Loew's were retained by the corporation. The parties stipulated, however, that *all* assets had been distributed. There were no unpaid liabilities and no affairs to wind up, and the evidence indicated that the corporation was "dead" after 1949. The fact that the suit was brought in the name of the corporation, and taxpayers as "trustees in dissolution" was merely a matter of form. Poro, 39 TC 641 (1963), acq. 1963-2 CB 5.

Stockholder allowed ordinary loss deduction on payment for release of guarantee of corporation's debts. Taxpayer purchased an interest in a new corporation under an agreement that the other stockholders would buy him out at his request. To establish credit for the new business, taxpayer and the other stockholders jointly guaranteed the corporation's loans. Taxpayer's liability would not exceed $166,666 if the coguarantors remained solvent. Taxpayer later requested that his stock be purchased and that he be released on his guarantee, but the other stockholders did not agree to the latter condition. Eventually, taxpayer sold the stock and had to pay the others $26,000 for his release. He deducted the payment as an ordinary loss. The IRS treated the payment as a reduction of the sales price and allowed the loss as capital. *Held:* For taxpayer. Since taxpayer could have sold his stock, the payment for the release was separate from the sale. Taxpayer's liability under the guarantee was not a capital asset. The payment was incurred in a transaction entered into for profit under Section 165(c)(2). The court distinguished Putnam, 352 US 82 (1956), which treated a stockholder-guarantor's payment as a nonbusiness bad debt by pointing out that the payment by tax-

Capital Gains and Losses: *Ordinary Gains/Losses Distinguished*

payer was to coguarantors, not to creditors. The payment created no debt. Shea, 36 TC 577 (1961).

Sole stockholder suffered capital and not ordinary loss on termination of corporation due to loan that was really a capital contribution. When taxpayer's wholly owned corporation was terminated, he claimed an ordinary loss of $39,000, which included his original $25,000 investment and two transfers of $2,000 and $12,000. The IRS determined that a capital loss was suffered. *Held:* For the IRS. The corporate entity could not be disregarded because business had actually been carried on. Therefore, the $25,000 was not an expense of a business conducted by taxpayer, but a capital loss. The $12,000 transfer did not create a loan, which would result in a business bad debt, because there was no instrument or bookkeeping entry denominating the transfer as a loan. There was also little hope of repayment. This transfer was thus a contribution to capital. The $2,000 transfer was a loan resulting in a business bad debt because it was entered on the books as such. There was an intent to make a loan rather than a contribution to capital. Faucher, 29 TCM 950, ¶ 70,217 P-H Memo. TC (1970).

Payments under an indemnification agreement were capital loss and not bad debt. An attorney, *P*, acquired all the stock of *X* Corporation. *P* later transferred one-half of the corporate stock to the taxpayer in consideration of taxpayer's agreement to indemnify *P* to the extent of one-half of any losses *P* might suffer by reason of advances made to *X* Corporation. When the company went into bankruptcy in 1956, *P*'s unrepaid advances totaled $37,000; taxpayer, in accordance with his agreement, paid *P* $18,500 that year. *Held:* For the IRS. The court held that these payments could not be deducted as a bad debt or business loss since the amount that taxpayer paid was the consideration and basis for his stock. Taxpayer was therefore held entitled only to a capital loss in the amount of $18,500 that resulted from worthless stock in that year. Lockwood, 21 TCM 1470, ¶ 62,278 P-H Memo. TC (1962).

Stockholder allowed ordinary loss deduction on surrendering preferred stock, despite retaining common stock. Taxpayer was one of several stockholders of a corporation that had operated at substantial losses. To improve the financial position of the corporation, taxpayer surrendered his preferred stock for cancellation, retaining his interest as a principal common stockholder. No contribution was made by the other stockholders. The IRS argued that the taxpayer had made a capital contribution. *Held:* For taxpayer. The court held that taxpayer sustained a deductible loss as a result of the surrender and cancellation of the stock that was equal to the difference between the cost basis to him of the stock surrendered and the stipulated increase in value of his remaining shares. Since the surrender for no consideration was neither a sale nor an exchange of a capital asset, the loss was deductible in full as an ordinary loss. Duell, 19 TCM 1381, ¶ 60,248 P-H Memo. TC (1960).

Gain realized on purchase and retirement of corporate bonds ordinary income. A corporation purchased its own bonds on the open market and proceeded to retire the obligations. The corporation also sustained capital losses during the year. There is no sale or exchange by a corporation that purchases and retires its own obligations within the meaning of Section 1232. Such gain is ordinary income and may not be offset against capital losses. (IT 2846 superseded.) Rev. Rul. 69-613, 1969-2 CB 163.

CARRY-BACK AND CARRY-OVER

(*See* Consolidated Returns—Net Operating Loss Carry-Overs; Net Operating Losses—Carry-Back; Net Operating Losses—Carry-Forward; Reorganizations—Carry-Over of Net Operating Losses and Other Tax Attributes)

CHANGE OF ACCOUNTING METHODS

(*See* Accounting Methods—Change of Methods)

CHARACTER OF GAIN OR LOSS

(*See* Capital Gains and Losses)

CHARITABLE CONTRIBUTIONS

Charitable deductions denied for gifts to tax-exempt parent organization. Three wholly owned subsidiaries each paid 5 percent of their taxable income as a donation to their tax-exempt parent. The IRS disallowed the charitable contribution deductions taken by the subsidiaries. The Tax Court upheld the IRS on the basis of Crosby Valve & Gage Co., 380 F2d 146 (1967). *Held:* Affirmed. The parent foundation's control over the subsidiaries was such that the stockholders' will dominated. This was not a charitable donation, but actually a dividend. Dave Inv. Co., 462 F2d 1373, 72-2 USTC ¶ 9619 (9th Cir. 1972).

Charitable deduction denied for transfer of land where intent was to gain a direct economic advantage. Taxpayer entered into a contract to purchase land that was contingent to property being rezoned to accommodate a trailer park and a shopping center. A plot presented by taxpayer to the zoning commission described a strip of property to be dedicated to the city. This strip would provide access to the trailer park. The zoning commission rezoned the area, and taxpayer purchased the property. Taxpayer deducted the value of the dedicated strip as a charitable donation. The IRS argued that this transfer was intended to benefit taxpayer directly, and thus was not a charitable donation. *Held:* For the IRS. The mere fact that dedication was not coerced was irrelevant. To be deductible, such a transfer must be a gift (out of donative intent) without expectation of personal economic gain. The fact that it did not turn out to be financially advantageous to taxpayer was irrelevant. Stubbs, 428 F2d 885, 70-2 USTC ¶ 9468, 26 AFTR2d 70-5010 (9th Cir. 1970).

Payment by corporation to charity that owned 75 percent of its stock was a dividend. Taxpayer's stock was owned 75 percent by individual *A* and 25 percent by individual *B*. *A* devised his 75 percent stock interest foundation, which was transferred to his foundation upon his death. Taxpayer then paid $100,000 to the foundation and claimed a charitable deduction. The IRS disallowed the charitable deduction and contended that the payment was a dividend. The district court found for the taxpayer. *Held:* Reversed. The manner in which the charity acquired the stock was irrelevant. Since the charity owned 75 percent of taxpayer's stock, it controlled taxpayer; therefore, a distribution to the charity was a dividend and not a charitable contribution. Richardson Carbon & Gasoline Co., 416 F2d 867, 69-2 USTC ¶ 9635 (5th Cir. 1969).

Contribution of stock followed by redemption did not result in tax liability. Palmer College was owned by a profit-making corporation. The assets of the college comprised approximately 80 percent of the assets of the corporation. Seventy percent of the corporation's stock was owned by taxpayer's trust, and the remaining shares were owned outright by the taxpayer. In 1966, a charitable organization, of which taxpayer was controlling trustee, purchased the shares owned by the trust. On the same day, the taxpayer contributed enough shares to the foundation so that it thereafter owned 80 percent of the outstanding shares. On the following day, the corporation redeemed all the shares held by the foundation in return for the college assets. The IRS determined that this transaction constituted a taxable event. *Held:* For taxpayer. This was a valid contribution of stock in the corporation to the charitable foundation, as opposed to an assignment of the proceeds from the redemption of the stock. There was an actual gift and an absence of an obligation to have the stock redeemed. The foundation was not a sham, and although the stockholder was the controlling trustee, the foundation had dominion and control over the stock received as a gift from the taxpayer stockholder, and thus he incurred no tax liability on the redemption. Palmer, 62 TC 684 (1974).

Failure to timely file corporate resolution concerning postyear and charitable contributions with return does not prevent deductions under two and a half month rule. Taxpayer, an accrual-basis taxpayer, made a charitable contribution within two and a half months after its 1969 tax year ended. Taxpayer complied with all of the requirements of Section 170 (a)(2), which would allow the deduction for this charitable contribution in 1969, except that the corporate minutes authorizing the contribution and corresponding verified statement of a corporate officer were filed after (and not with) its 1969 return. *Held:* For taxpayer. All essential requirements of Section 170(a)(2) were met within time limit. Accordingly, the deduction was allowed for 1969. Columbia Iron & Metal Co., 61 TC 5 (1973), acq. 1978-2 CB 1.

Donation of real property with retained mineral or lease rights did not qualify under Section 170. Two taxpayers donated real property to a charitable organization. In the first situation, taxpayer corporation retained all mineral rights, including the sole right to exploit and sell any minerals. In the second situation, taxpayer individual donated real property, subject to a lease, and retained the right to receive lease payments until his death. The IRS stated that neither of these qualified for the Section 170 deduction. Neither contribution was of the taxpayer's entire interest, or of an undivided interest. Rev. Rul. 76-331, 1976-2 CB 52.

Charitable contribution by closely held corporation is not a dividend to its stockholders. Where a closely held corporation donated some of its debentures to a private foundation run by the corporation's shareholders and employees, and the foundation used the income to provide scholarships to students located within the corporation's business territory, the corporation's contribution was not a dividend to the stockholders because it did not serve only a personal objective of a stockholder. Rev. Rul. 75-335, 1975-2 CB 107.

Contribution by domestic corporation to domestic charitable corporation would qualify even though contribution was to be used in foreign country. A domestic commercial corporation was entitled to a charitable contribution deduction for a contribution to a domestic charitable corporation even though the contribution was to be used in a foreign country. Section 170(c)(2) denies a deduction for a charitable contribution by a corporation to a trust, chest, fund, or foundation if it is used outside the United States. There is no limitation on a gift to a domestic corporation. Rev. Rul. 69-80, 1969-1 CB 65.

Corporate payments to educational institutions from which many employees were hired were deductible as contributions. A corporation made contributions to exempt educational foundations from whom the corporation drew a number of its employees. The educational institutions involved selected the recipients of the scholarships. For the purpose of determining whether a contribution is made to or for the use of an organization described in Section 170, not to a particular individual who ultimately benefits from the contribution, the organization must have full control of the use of the donated funds. Also, the contributor's intent in making the payment must have been to benefit the charitable organization itself and not the individual recipient. Accordingly, the payment of scholarship grants under the facts given were deductible contributions. Rev. Rul. 68-484, 1968-2 CB 105.

Contribution deduction denied for payments to a sole stockholder that was an exempt organization. In 1966, a taxable corporation paid dividends to its sole stockholder, an exempt charitable organization. In addition, the corporation made a contribution to its sole stockholder and claimed a deduction. The corporation had sufficient earnings and profits from which to pay both the dividends and the contribution. The IRS, relying on Crosby Valve & Gage Co., 380 F2d 146 (1st Cir. 1967), and Knapp Brothers Shoe Mfg. Corp.,

384 F2d 692 (1st Cir. 1967), ruled that the corporation was not entitled to a charitable contribution deduction for amounts contributed to its exempt organization-sole stockholder. Rev. Rul. 68-296, 1968-1 CB 105.

Contributions for Vocational Guidance Program of Plans for Progress deductible. Plans for Progress was founded in 1961 by a group of government and industry officials to assist the President's Committee on Equal Employment Opportunity. Its method was to adopt programs to provide equal employment opportunity within the government and private industry. The organization conducted the Vocational Guidance Program to acquaint high school educational guidance counselors with business needs and methods to improve preparation of minority youth for jobs in industry. The IRS ruled that contributions made to Plans for Progress for use exclusively in advancing its Vocational Guidance Program were deductible under Section 170, subject to the limitations of that Section, as contributions for the use of the United States for exclusively public purposes. Rev. Rul. 67-298, 1967-2 CB 111.

CLASSIFICATION OF ENTITIES FOR TAX PURPOSES

(*See* Associations Taxable as Corporations; Corporations as Taxable Entities)

CLEARLY REFLECTING INCOME

(*See* Allocation Among Related Taxpayers)

CLOSELY HELD CORPORATIONS

(*See* Affiliated Corporations; Allocation Among Related Taxpayers; Consolidated Returns; Compensation for Personal Services; Dividends and Distributions; Related Taxpayers)

COLLAPSIBLE CORPORATIONS

Definition 157
Liquidation Of 163
Realization of Substantial Part of
  Income Exception 166
Three-Year Holding Period Exception   169

Definition

Corporation purchased land with intent to rezone and then sell was not "collapsible." Two individuals purchased agricultural land expecting that it could be rezoned for residential use and resold at a profit. They then incorporated. Upon later sale, the taxpayers sought to take advantage of Section 337, but the IRS claimed that the corporation was collapsible. *Held:* For taxpayer. This property was not held for sale in the ordinary course of business to customers, nor did the rezoning constitute construction for purposes of Section 341. Thomas, ¶ 81,387 P-H Memo. TC (1981), aff'd, Cates, 716 F2d 1387, 52 AFTR2d 83-6099 (6th Cir. 1983).

Corporation that owned apartment house was collapsible. Taxpayers formed a corporation and transferred to it a newly purchased apartment house. Approximately one year later, the corporate stock was sold to a nonprofit corporation set up to operate the building. The IRS held that taxpayers' gain on the stock sale was ordinary since the corporation was collapsible. A jury found for the IRS, but the district court overturned the jury verdict. *Held:* Reversed. Taxpayers were in the business of selling the apartment units individually, an ordinary income-producing activity. Just before realizing the income, they transferred the corporate property in a manner that sought to recover the fruits of taxpayer's labor at capital gain rates. The jury finding was correct. Combs II, 655 F2d 90, 81-2 USTC ¶ 9577, 48 AFTR2d 81-5625 (6th Cir. 1981).

Gain from distribution of excess borrowed construction funds held wholly attributable to collapsible assets constructed with those funds. Taxpayer, with others, owned a realty corporation. This corporation leased unimproved

COLLAPSIBLE CORPORATIONS: *Definition*

land under 99-year leases to other corporations owned by taxpayer and his fellow stockholders. These other corporations constructed apartment buildings on this land, and then distributed the excess mortgage money to its stockholders. These development companies had no earnings at the time of the distribution, and in fact sustained operating losses for that year. Taxpayer reported capital gains from the distribution to the extent that it exceeded the bases in his interests in the development corporations. The IRS asserted that this gain should be reported as ordinary income from "collapsible" assets. Taxpayer conceded that the development corporations were collapsible, but argued that, under a Code exception, he was not subject to collapsible treatment because more than 30 percent of the gain arising from distribution was attributable to the now-enhanced value of the leaseholds (i.e., noncollapsible assets). *Held:* For the IRS. The distribution was made out of excess mortgage monies. Since the mortgage monies were lent to construct the collapsible assets (i.e., the building), the distribution was directly attributable to those assets, and not the leases. Thus, all of taxpayer's gain was attributable to the collapsible assets. Benedek, 429 F2d 41, 70-2 USTC ¶ 9500, 26 AFTR2d 70-5049 (2d Cir.), cert. denied, 400 US 992 (1970).

Corporation collapsible; ordinary income distributions allowed. Taxpayer and another contributed $500 each to the capital of X Corporation. X Corporation purchased a parcel of land and proceeded to construct rental housing units. By using the declining balance method of depreciation, X showed a loss for the year 1949 that offset the small operating income in the years 1950, 1951, and 1952. X Corporation distributed $100,000 to its stockholders in 1949, $65,500 in 1950, $46,900 in 1951, and $46,800 in 1952. The distributed cash was generated by borrowed funds and rental receipts. The mortgage exceeded the total cost of the land, improvements, buildings, equipment, and furnishings by approximately $100,000. The IRS contended that X was a collapsible corporation and affirmed the distributions of ordinary income to taxpayer. *Held:* For the IRS. Although taxpayers did not actually surrender any of their stock upon each distribution, the surrender would have been meaningless. The effect of the transaction was the same as if they had. Pomponio, 288 F2d 827, 61-1 USTC ¶ 9363 (4th Cir. 1961).

Where, due to unforseen events, stockholders sold their stock in a newly formed real estate development corporation that had recently completed construction of a housing project, court determined that corporation was not collapsible. Taxpayer, a builder, bought land on which to build a housing project. He and other investors formed a corporation to construct and operate the housing project. Construction was completed in June 1950, and the apartments were quickly rented. Evidence indicated that the corporation's stockholders viewed their involvement as a long-term investment (i.e., requests to sell the project were refused). In September 1950, structural defects began to appear, and taxpayer advised the other stockholders to sell their interest; they, however, countered with a proposal to buy his interest. At a later meeting, the stockholders decided to sell all their interests. In November, they authorized a sale of their stock, which was consummated in February 1951. The IRS asserted that taxpayer's gain on this sale was ordinary income from the sale of stock in a collapsible corporation. The Tax Court agreed. *Held:* Reversed. A necessary prerequisite to collapsible corporation status is that the corporation was "formed or availed of principally for construction of property with a view to a sale of stock by its stockholders prior to a realization by the corporation of a substantial part of the net income to be derived from such property. Here, the intent to sell the corporation's stock clearly did not arise until after the corporation was formed and construction completed. Jacobson, 281 F2d 703, 60-2 USTC ¶ 9612, 6 AFTR2d 5205 (3d Cir. 1960).

Collapsible corporation treatment not applicable to forced sale of stock. Taxpayer sold all of his stock in X Corporation at a gain of $56,000, which he reported as long-term capital gain. The IRS determined the gain to be taxable as ordinary income on the theory that the company was a collapsible corporation under Section 341. Taxpayer paid the assessment and sought a refund. *Held:* For taxpayer.

COLLAPSIBLE CORPORATIONS: *Definition*

Where a jury found that a taxpayer was compelled to sell his stock due to circumstances beyond his control and which he could not have reasonably anticipated when he went into the business venture, taxpayer did not have the requisite "view" under Section 341. Specifically, Section 341 requires that for a corporation to be collapsible, it must be formed or availed of for the construction of property "with a view to" (1) the sale or exchange of stock by its owners prior to the realization by the corporation of a substantial part of the net income to be derived from such property, and (2) the realization by such stockholders of gains attributable to such property. Theilen, Jr., 68-1 USTC ¶ 9202, 21 AFTR2d 399 (SD Tex. 1967).

Stock sale motivated by heart attack does not render corporation collapsible. Taxpayer, an architect, formed two corporations with a builder for the purpose of constructing an apartment house project. During the construction, taxpayer suffered a heart attack, and his doctor ordered him to "immediately retire from active practice." The joint venture needed additional financing, but the builder was unwilling to provide money and supervision of the construction while the project remained a joint venture. He offered to buy out taxpayer and continue alone. Taxpayer was in no condition to object, and a sale of his stock was effected. The IRS contended that the corporations were collapsible. *Held:* For taxpayer. The court found no evidence that the sale was motivated by any circumstance other than the heart attack. Since the decision to sell was not a matter of deliberate choice in furtherance of a previously formed or considered plan, the proscribed statutory view was not present. Shilowitz, 221 F. Supp. 179, 63-2 USTC ¶ 9690 (DNJ 1963).

Jury, instructed that collapsibility requires existence of view to sale during construction, finds corporations not collapsible. The stockholders sold their stock in three apartment corporations. The IRS contended that the stockholders had ordinary income, not capital gain on the sales because each of the corporations was collapsible. After paying the deficiency and filing claim for refund, taxpayers brought this suit in which they asked for a jury trial. The court instructed the jury that the requisite view to the sale or exchange of the stock by the stockholders must exist at some time during construction if the corporations are to be considered collapsible. If a sale, exchange, or distribution is attributable solely to circumstances that arose after the completion of construction, the corporation is, in the absence of compelling facts to the contrary, considered not to have been formed or availed of with a view to the sale or exchange of the stock by the stockholders. *Held:* For taxpayers. Upon these instructions, the jury found that none of the three corporations was collapsible as that term had been defined to them. Coates, 60-2 USTC ¶ 9673 (D. Or. 1960).

Jury found corporation collapsible; corporation's intent to dissolve before realizing substantial income present. Taxpayer completed construction of an apartment building in October, rented most of the units, and sold the building the following May. A few months later, taxpayer corporation dissolved, and its assets were distributed to its stockholders. The IRS asserted that the corporation was collapsible. *Held:* For the IRS. A jury found that the intent to dissolve before realizing substantial income was present and that taxpayer was a collapsible corporation. The jury also found the value of a second mortgage that taxpayer received on the sale of the business. 688 E. Ave., 59-2 USTC ¶ 9704 (WDNY 1959).

Gain on disposition of stock in collapsible corporation entitled to capital gain treatment. Taxpayer decedent owned 20 percent of the stock of a corporation formed to operate a community antenna system for cable television. Before the corporation reported any taxable income, the stockholders sold their stock and reported the gain as a capital gain. The IRS determined that the corporation was collapsible and that the gain was reportable as ordinary income. *Held:* For taxpayer. Although the corporation was collapsible, there was no net unrealized appreciation in its "subsection (e) assets," since the net unrealized appreciation in these assets was less than 15 percent of net worth. The only subsection (e) assets were current subscription contracts, which represented the right to earn income for services rendered. Since their renewal was uncertain, their fair market value was limited. Further, investment credit claimed by taxpayer with respect to the corporation was to be recaptured on the sale of stock. Estate of Diecks, 65 TC 117 (1975), acq. 1978-1 CB 1.

Collapsible status of computer tax return corporation determined. Taxpayer was formed to design computer programs for specific customers. A program developed for processing tax returns was in use from 1963 through 1965. Taxpayer was subsequently purchased by another company. The IRS determined that taxpayer was a collapsible corporation, and hence the stockholders' gain on the sale should be treated as ordinary income. *Held:* For taxpayer. Production of the computer program for preparation of income tax returns was completed by April 1965, the earliest time at which a view was formed to sell an interest in the corporation's program. For the purposes of Section 341, the production stage of a process that changes and develops as it is used ends when it is ready to produce income on a commercial basis. Computer Sciences Corp., 63 TC 327 (1974).

Exercise of option to purchase stock does not make corporation collapsible. Taxpayer purchased one half of the stock of Rayburn Land Company. As a condition to this purchase, taxpayer was required by the other stockholder to grant that stockholder a unilateral option for five years whereby the other stockholder could reacquire taxpayer's stock interest. Prior to completion of construction and after disagreements over development policy, the stockholder exercised his option and purchased taxpayer's stock interest. The IRS determined that because the corporation was collapsible, the gain was ordinary income. *Held:* For taxpayer. The corporation was not collapsible because the view proscribed by Section 341 was not present. Taxpayer's sale of stock did not occur with the freedom of choice contemplated in that statute, but was compelled by circumstances beyond his control. Crowe, 62 TC 121 (1974).

Limited real estate activities did not render corporation collapsible. Taxpayers, individually and through a corporation, purchased two parcels of unimproved land and within two years sold both parcels. Taxpayers had no intention of developing the properties or of subdividing to sell piecemeal; they intended only to sell the land as it was. Their only significant activity was to have one parcel rezoned from agricultural to residential use. *Held:* For taxpayer. The court held that neither parcel was held for sale in the ordinary course of business and that the corporation was not collapsible. The very limited activities of taxpayers, amounting to no more than any landowner would have done, did not put them in the real estate business and did not constitute "construction" under Section 341(b). Cohen, 39 TC 886 (1963).

Collapsibility found despite stockholders' capital gain status; *Ivey* **again overturned.** Taxpayer corporation, formed to construct a shopping center, purchased land, arranged for zoning, retained an architect, negotiated for permits and performance bonds, and obtained two tenants before it found itself unable to obtain mortgage financing. Before any construction had begun, it sold the center, pursuant to Section 337, and liquidated. The IRS determined that Section 337 was not available because taxpayer was collapsible. *Held:* For the IRS. Taxpayer's activities before the sale constituted "construction" within the definition of collapsible corporations, the requisite "view" was present at the time of these activities, and taxpayer would have been collapsible if it had first liquidated its assets in kind to its stockholders instead of selling the assets under Section 337 and distributing the cash. Taxpayer's argument that it was not collapsible because its stockholders would have realized capital gain if the corporate form were not used was rejected on the basis of Braunstein, 305 F2d 949 (2d Cir. 1962). The rule established by Ivey, 294 F2d 799 (5th Cir. 1961), was disregarded. The court also held that the sale resulted in capital gain to taxpayer because Section 341 applied only to treatment of gain by the stockholders; the property had not been held primarily for sale to customers in the ordinary course of taxpayer's business. Sproul Realty Co., 38 TC 844 (1962).

Corporation held collapsible; stock was held after preliminary construction. Taxpayer entered into a contract for the purchase of land for the purpose of constructing and selling houses; he assigned this contract to his wholly owned corporation, which took title and performed some of the preliminary steps. It hired an architect, made arrangements for street improvements and filed an application with the FHA. Taxpayer then sold his stock to a new corporation of which he was half owner. The new corporation carried out the physical construction. The IRS contended that taxpayer realized ordinary income because he sold stock of a collapsible corporation. *Held:* For the IRS. The corporation was formed primarily for the construction of property with a view by taxpayer to sell its stock prior to its realization of a substantial part of the income to be derived from the property. The court rejected taxpayer's argument that (1) the corporation had not engaged in construction, and even if it had, no gain could be distributed to such construction, and (2) that in no event could 70 percent of the gain be attributed to such construction as required by the Code. The court held that the corporation's preliminary activities constituted "construction," that gain was attributable to such construction, and that such gain met the 70 percent requirement. Farber, 36 TC 1142 (1961).

Real estate corporation held collapsible after distribution of excess mortgage proceeds and stock sale deemed ordinary income. Taxpayer's corporations constructed apartment house projects with FHA mortgages. In the year after completion of construction, the corporations distributed the excess of the mortgage proceeds to the stockholders. Later in that same year, the stock of the corporations was sold. Taxpayer claimed that unexpectedly high costs and a higher than estimated vacancy rate provoked the sale. The IRS argued that the receipts from both transactions were ordinary income from a collapsible corporation. *Held:* For the IRS. The requisite "view" existed prior to completion. The transactions were not attributable solely to circumstances arising after construction that could not have been reasonably anticipated. The court stressed the lack of stockholder-risk capital, the fact that the land for the projects was leased to the corporation by the wives of the stockholders (so as to return their investment in five years), and the personal use of corporate funds. Braunstein, 36 TC 22 (1961).

Distribution of excess mortgage proceeds is gain from collapsible corporation. Taxpayer's corporation, with bank financing, constructed an apartment house. Based on an appraisal immediately after completion of the building, a revaluation surplus was created from which a distribution was to be made. Bank loans to the corporation endorsed by the stockholders were obtained to pay the surplus distribution. Shortly thereafter, an FHA-insured mortgage was secured, and the proceeds were used to pay off the building and the other bank loans. Taxpayers reported the surplus distribution as long-term capital gain. The IRS contended that the distribution was ordinary income from a collapsible corporation. *Held:* For the IRS. Cases taxing distributions of surplus mortgage proceeds as ordinary income are controlling. It makes no difference that the distribution was made from the bank loan first and then the surplus mortgage proceeds were acquired through FHA-insured loans. Braude, 35 TC 1158 (1961).

Gain realized on redemption of stock below par from collapsible property. Taxpayers transferred land to one of their corporations in exchange for common stock having a par value equal to their cost and transferred other land costing $16,000 to another corporation for $40,000 par value common stock. Apartments were constructed by both corporations. The architects in both cases received stock, in addition to cash, for their fees. Within three months after insurance, the architects sold the stock to taxpayers at considerably below par. A year later, the corporations redeemed the stock at greater than par. Taxpayers claimed that the gain on the redemption was not taxable under the collapsible corporation provisions, since more than 30 percent was not attributable to the statutory property. *Held:* For the IRS. Finding that the value of the stock issued to the architects was the price at which they sold it to taxpayers and not the par value, the Tax Court held that the 70-30 rule did not apply. Taxpayers' gain was ordinary income. The contention that the source of taxpayers' gain was the advantageous purchase from the architects was specious. Reliance on director's resolutions and state laws concerning prime face value of stock was not sufficient to overcome taxpayers' burden of proof. These reasons also apply to the argument that the source of part of taxpayers' gain was transfer of the land to the second corporation. Short, 35 TC 922 (1961).

Corporation not collapsible; sale due to doctor's advice to owner. Taxpayer, a real estate developer, acquired land on which to construct an apartment house project. To obtain FHA mortgage insurance, the property was transferred to X Corporation, of which the taxpayer owned all the common stock. Taxpayer, individually, was the contractor and manager of the apartments. Based on his doctor's advice that he needed more physical activity than managing the apartments afforded, and in order to return to the construction business, in the year after the project was completed, taxpayer began a new development. In the following year, because of his increased involvement in the new project, taxpayer sold his stock in the corporation. The IRS asserted that the corporation was collapsible. *Held:* For taxpayer. The Tax Court found that the corporation was not collapsible as it was not formed or availed of with the proscribed "view." Taxpayer's sale of stock was attributable solely to circumstances that arose after construction of the project was completed. Riley, 35 TC 848 (1961).

Diner corporation collapsible. Taxpayer sold his stock in two recently constructed diner corporations. The IRS claimed that both corporations were collapsible. *Held:* For the IRS, in part. One diner corporation was not collapsible since taxpayer sold his stock due to unforeseen family problems that occurred after the diner had opened for business. The other, however, was collapsible since the sale of taxpayer's stock was a recognized possibility from the outset. Felix, 41 TCM 1040, ¶ 81,099 P-H Memo. TC (1981).

Taxpayer sold stock because of co-owner's actions; corporation not collapsible. Taxpayer and a friend organized a corporation to develop a shopping center. The friend's construction company was to construct the building. In order to get a bank loan, the friend's family guaranteed the loan for a fee. Taxpayer's lawyer advised him that the fees were excessive, as were the charges being made by the construction company. Taxpayer was further advised that these potentially fraudulent charges might render him personally liable to the other creditors. In view of this, taxpayer sold his stock to his friend while the center was still being built. The IRS contended that the gain was ordinary income, since the corporation was collapsible. *Held:* For taxpayer. Taxpayer acquired his stock as a long-term investment, which purpose never changed. He sold his stock only after the potentially fraudulent actions of his copromoter left him with no freedom of choice. These were unforeseeable circumstances beyond his control. Stahl, 25 TCM 505, ¶ 66,094 P-H Memo. TC (1966).

Corporation collapsible; ordinary income arose on stock redemption. A builder and real estate operator organized five corporations to construct housing for rent or sale with FHA financing. After construction was completed and stock was held for more than six months, the builder redeemed most of the stock and sold the balance to outsiders. The redemption violated his FHA commitments. The IRS contended that the corporation was collapsible. *Held:* For the IRS. The court found the corporation collapsible and held that the gains from the redemptions and sales of stock were taxable as ordinary income. Taxpayer also contested the year in which the gains should be reported because the monies were received illegally and improperly. On this point, the court held that the funds were received under a claim of right, and even if the distribution amounted to embezzlement, it would still be income when received. Estate of Louis Alper, 20 TCM 1626, ¶ 61,316 P-H Memo. TC (1961).

COLLAPSIBLE CORPORATIONS: *Liquidation Of*

Owner-lessor of shopping center not engaged in construction. An owner-lessor's leasing of additional land to a department store tenant, on which tenant constructed an addition, would not be deemed the lessor's construction under Section 341(b). The IRS ruled that Section 341(a) would not apply where the lessee provided its own financing, and the useful life of the addition was less than that of the leasehold. Rev. Rul. 77-306, 1977-2 CB 103.

Tax-free exchange possible with collapsible corporation. The IRS ruled that the gain or loss on the exchange of shares in a collapsible corporation for those in a noncollapsible corporation under a C reorganization would not be recognized. The provisions of Section 354(a)(1) supersede those of Section 341(a) inasmuch as Regulation § 1.341-4(a) requires that the gain be "recognized gain." Moreover, the gain realized on the subsequent sale of stock would not be subject to the collapsible rules because the noncollapsible corporation was not subject to Section 341 at the time of sale, and the taxpayer was able to show that the exchange had not been made to avoid the payment of income taxes. Rev. Rul. 73-378, 1973-2 CB 113.

Leasing land, approving plans, sharing rents, and subordinating title was construction for Section 341 purposes. A lessor corporation leased land, approved the lessee's construction plans, shared rents, and subordinated title to the land to the mortgage of the lessee. Such activities were deemed "construction" for purposes of Section 341. Completion of construction for purposes of Section 341(d)(3) was the date following the actual full physical construction. Rev. Rul. 69-378, 1969-2 CB 49.

Restoration of building to original condition not "construction" within the meaning of Section 341. A corporation owned a building that was damaged by fire. Insurance proceeds were used to repair and restore the building to its former condition. There was no change in structural character or appreciable increase in fair market value of the net income realizable therefrom. There was no increase in rental space, fair market value of the structure, or the net income that could be realized by the liquidation of the corporation. Accordingly, the restoration was not "construction" within the meaning of Section 341 and specifically the three-year limitation of Section 341(d)(3). Rev. Rul. 68-472, 1968-2 CB 138.

Liquidation Of

Oil and gas corporation after sale of leases and liquidation held not collapsible. After the principal partner in a family partnership had an operation for cancer, he set about to put his affairs in order. Among other things, the oil- and gas-producing business operated by the family partnership was transferred to a corporation. About one and one-half years later, after the corporation had acquired new leases and made new discoveries, it sold all its oil and gas leases at a substantial profit. The sale was made pursuant to a plan of complete liquidation within 12 months under Section 337. The corporation, therefore, reported no gain or loss on the sale. The IRS determined that the corporation was collapsible and therefore not entitled to benefit from the nonrecognition provisions of Section 337. *Held:* For taxpayer. The court found that there was no intent to liquidate the corporation before a substantial part of the taxable income from the leases had been realized and that there was no intent to convert ordinary income into capital gain through use of a corporation. There had been no need to utilize the corporate form to realize a capital gain. The primary view in incorporating had been to provide for the stockholder's family; taxes were not thought of until later. Honaker Drilling, Inc., 190 F. Supp. 287, 61-1 USTC ¶ 9168 (D. Kan. 1960).

Gain on sale realized upon liquidation because corporation collapsible. Taxpayer, a corporation, entered into a contract for the lease and sale of swim club facilities that it constructed. After three years from the date of construction, the swim club was sold. Taxpayer was dissolved soon after. The IRS contended that the gain realized by taxpayer was not eligible for nonrecognition under Section 337 because taxpayer was a collapsible corporation as defined in Section 341(b). *Held:* For the IRS. Although Section 341(d)(3) provides that gain realized by a stockholder may escape ordinary

COLLAPSIBLE CORPORATIONS: *Liquidation Of*

income treatment if realized more than three years after construction is completed, it is irrelevant to the applicability of Section 337. Nonrecognition under Section 337 is denied to a collapsible corporation as defined by Section 341(b), nor does it depend on the treatment given to gains of certain stockholders. Accordingly, taxpayer was taxable on the sale. Leisure Time Enters., Inc., 56 TC 1180 (1971).

Nonrecognition of gain in liquidation defeated by collapsibility. A space engineer working in the area of Cape Kennedy became interested in the real estate development of the area. After buying and selling several parcels profitably, he purchased a newly subdivided 760-acre plot. When he executed the purchase contract with a local brokerage firm, he orally agreed to pay the broker 5 percent of the proceeds and 5 percent of the profit on any resale. Three weeks after this purchase, the broker began negotiations for a resale. The resale being assured, taxpayer consulted his tax attorney. On the advice of counsel, taxpayer formed a corporation and assigned the purchase contract to the corporation. The corporation then resold the property to the buyers with whom taxpayer had previously negotiated. Liquidating pursuant to Section 337, the corporation distributed the net proceeds of sale to taxpayer. Contending that the corporation was collapsible, the IRS disapproved the nonrecognition of gain under Section 337. *Held:* For the IRS. The corporation was collapsible as defined by Section 341(b). Taxpayer formed the corporation with the intention of purchasing the property for sale to customers and distributing the proceeds to the stockholder before realization of gain by the corporation. A letter from his tax counsel demonstrated that the intent to liquidate existed before the formation of the corporation. Taxpayer also argued that the court should ignore the corporate existence and tax the gain directly to taxpayer. The court rejected this argument. Van Heusden, 44 TC 491 (1965).

Corporation not collapsible; view toward sale arose too late. In October 1954, taxpayer was incorporated for the purpose of purchasing an office building. The three major stockholders were Black, Margolis, and Sutherland. A suitable building was purchased in November 1954 together with parking lots. During 1954 and 1955, taxpayer and its stockholders received several feelers and offers by prospective purchasers, all of which were turned down. Sutherland was president and director of Security Bank, located a short distance from the office building; Black was also a director of the same bank. Margolis, Black, and Sutherland were all stockholders of the bank. Due to increased business, Security found its physical plant inadequate, and in September 1955 began a search for a new location. After considering various sites, the bank decided that taxpayer's building best met its needs. Black, Sutherland, and Margolis resisted the efforts of Security's board of directors to arrange a sale, but finally gave in and granted the bank an option to purchase on April 4, 1956. On July 23, 1956, taxpayer adopted a plan of complete liquidation under Section 337. The sale took place on October 1, 1956, and the assets were distributed thereafter. The IRS contended that taxpayer was collapsible and therefore not entitled to the use of Section 337. It further contended that the bank's need for space was known to Sutherland, Black, and Margolis at the time taxpayer purchased the office building, and that therefore taxpayer was formed with a view toward a distribution to its shareholders before the realization of a substantial part of its taxable income. *Held:* For taxpayer. The Tax Court failed to find the requisite view toward collapsibility at the time of the purchase and found that the view arose a year or more thereafter when the bank began to consider a new location. The court also held that the useful life of the building at the time it as acquired was 30 years, and that Black was not a transferee of taxpayer's unpaid taxes. Southwest Properties, Inc., 38 TC 97 (1962), acq. 1966-2 CB 7.

Corporation not collapsible. Taxpayers owned a corporation that had a tract of land. They built small houses on part of it. After they had trouble selling the homes, they liquidated the corporation, sold the realty, and reported gain from the liquidation as capital gain. The IRS claimed that the proceeds were ordinary income from a collapsible corporation. *Held:* For taxpayer. The corporation was not collapsible, as the view to collapsing did not exist at the time the property was acquired or when the houses were built; the gain from the liquidation was a capital gain. No negligence penalty was imposed where the taxpayers reported the gain in the year after the distribution, mistakenly relying on Section 333 to defer the gain. Kellner, 30 TCM 1240, ¶ 71,293 P-H Memo. TC (1971).

Presumption of corporate collapsibility rebutted by proof of lack of requisite "view." Taxpayer, through a wholly owned corporation, purchased an apartment building in 1956. Until that time, taxpayer had never engaged in real estate activities other than those relating to his electrical supply business. In 1958, the corporation sold the apartment building at a $57,000 profit and liquidated, pursuant to Section 337. The IRS alleged that the corporation was collapsible and that sales made by a collapsible corporation are excluded from the operation of Section 337. Taxpayer, however, contended that he had no view to selling the building when his corporation acquired it, but it was his subsequent entry into the electrical business in New York and Florida, with the resultant need for cash, that caused his "view" to change. *Held:* For taxpayer. Although the IRS' determination was aided by a presumption of collapsibility created by Section 341(c), the court found the evidence sufficient to overcome the presumption. It held that the corporation was not collapsible. The gain realized by the corporation on the sale of the property was therefore not recognized under Section 337. Saltzman, 22 TCM 336, ¶ 63,080 P-H Memo. TC (1963).

Corporation that acquired tract of land and liquidated before starting construction considered not collapsible. *X* Corporation was formed to acquire a tract of land, subdivide it into lots, and build houses thereon for sale to the public. *X* acquired the land but was liquidated before any construction began. At liquidation, the land was in the same condition as when it was purchased. The IRS asserted that the corporation was collapsible. *Held:* For taxpayer. The court held that the corporation was not collapsible since at the time it was formed and the land was acquired, the incorporators entertained no thought of its liquidation prior to its realization of a substantial part of income from the property acquired. The intent to liquidate first came when the corporation was pressed for funds to commence building. The court also noted that in fact no construction ever occurred prior to liquidation, so that the requisite view to liquidate could not be said to have existed during construction. Gain on the liquidation was therefore properly reported as capital gain. McPherson, 21 TCM 583, ¶ 62,106 P-H Memo. TC (1962).

IRS examines effect of like-kind exchange in collapsible corporation context. In January 1971, *X* Corporation was formed to construct and operate a commercial shopping center. Construction of shopping center *A* was completed in March 1972. In November 1977, *A* was exchanged for shopping center *B*, a property owned by an unrelated corporation on which construction was completed in May 1976, and on which no further construction was performed. That transaction qualified as a tax-free exchange under Section 1031(a). In December 1978, *X* adopted a plan of liquidation and completely liquidated. Upon the liquidation, the stockholders of *X* received *B*, the fair market value of which exceeded the adjusted basis of the *X* stock held by the stockholders. The IRS held on these facts that *B* had to take the date of completion of construction of *A* for purposes of applying Section 341(d)(3). Therefore, Section 341(d)(3) was satisfied and the gain realized by the *X* stockholders was not subject to Section 341(a). Rev. Rul. 79-235, 1979-2 CB 135.

Disposal of asset prior to liquidation falls outside taint of Section 341. In May 1972, *X* Corporation was formed to construct and operate commercial shopping centers. In June 1973, construction of shopping center *A* was completed. In January 1974, construction of shopping center *B* was completed. Construction of shopping center *C* was completed in August 1976. Each shopping center was operated separately and located on separate parcels of land not contiguous to each other. In December 1976, *X* sold *C* to unrelated purchasers. On March 1, 1977, a plan of liquidation was adopted, and *X* was completely liquidated. Upon the liquidation, the stockholders of X received all of X's property, including A and B, the fair market value of which exceeded the adjusted basis of the X stock held by the stockholders. At the time of the liquidation, more than 70 percent of the gain realized by the stockholders of X was attributable to A and B. The IRS held that under the facts described, construction of C was not to be considered in determining whether Section 341(d)(3) applied to the liquidation of X, and no part of the gain realized by the stockholders of X was to be considered attributable to property for which the manufacture, construction, production or purchase occurred or was completed within three years before the date of liquidation. Rev. Rul. 79-226, 1979-2 CB 134.

Parent of collapsible subsidiary not necessarily collapsible. If a parent corporation sells its stock in a collapsible subsidiary and realizes ordinary income, the stockholders of the parent, upon liquidation of the parent, will not realize ordinary income with respect to the same underlying collapsible property. Rev. Rul. 56-50, 1956-1 CB 174.

Realization of Substantial Part of Income Exception

Collapsible corporation's gain on Section 337 liquidation subject to tax. Taxpayer purchased farmland and buildings that it held primarily for sale to customers in the ordinary course of business. In January 1968, the corporation contracted to sell one parcel of the land, and incurred expenses for the construction of an access road thereon, which was completed in 1972. In March, 1968, taxpayer contemplated liquidation. On August 16, 1968, the corporation adopted a plan of liquidation and sold substantially all the remaining acreage. The IRS determined that gains on the sales were includable in taxpayer's income because taxpayer was a collapsible corporation. The Tax Court found for the IRS. *Held:* Affirmed. The facts showed that taxpayer was availed of principally for the construction of property with a simultaneous view toward liquidation. Taxpayer realized only an insubstantial amount (9.3 percent) of its total taxable income from the property prior to forming the intent to liquidate. Manassas Airport Indus. Park, Inc., 557 F2d 1113, 77-2 USTC ¶ 9494 (4th Cir. 1977).

Corporation collapsible; distribution to stockholders allowed as ordinary income. Two corporations, wholly owned by taxpayer, were formed to construct and operate housing projects. The proceeds of FHA insured mortgages exceeded construction costs. Part of this excess was distributed to taxpayer before the corporations realized a substantial part of the net income to be derived from the properties. The Tax Court ruled that the corporations were collapsible; accordingly, the distribution to taxpayer was ordinary income. *Held:* Affirmed. The requisite "view" to make the distribution was deemed to have existed prior to the completion of construction, since taxpayer knew in advance that the mortgage proceeds would exceed construction costs. Hartman, 296 F2d 726, 62-1 USTC ¶ 9145, 9 AFTR2d 342 (2d Cir. 1961).

Construction corporation deemed collapsible; taxpayer's gain as allowed ordinary income. Taxpayer was the sole stockholder of X Corporation, which was organized to purchase unimproved lots and construct houses on them. X Corporation, when it made a distribution in partial liquidation, had realized less than 17 percent of its combined expected income from sales and rents. Before liquidation was completed, X had realized over 50 percent of its total income. The Tax Court ruled that X was collapsible and that taxpayer's gain on the liquidation was ordinary income. *Held:* Affirmed. The distribution to taxpayer was made before the corporation realized a substantial part of the net income to be derived from the property. Its collapsible status had to be determined at that time. Heft, 294 F2d 795, 61-2 USTC ¶ 9655, 8 AFTR2d 5465 (5th Cir. 1961).

Gain realized by excess mortgage and stock sale proceeds taxed as ordinary income because corporation held collapsible. Taxpayers were stockholders in X Corporation, which fi-

COLLAPSIBLE CORPORATIONS: *Substantial Part of Income Exception*

nanced construction of apartment houses with FHA-guaranteed mortgages. Shortly after the completion of construction, the excess of the mortgage over the construction costs was distributed to the stockholders. Shortly thereafter, the stockholders sold their stock. The IRS determined that the gain realized by the distribution of the excess mortgage proceeds and the proceeds received from the sale of stock should be taxed as ordinary income because X was a collapsible corporation. The Tax Court agreed with the IRS. The issues raised by taxpayers on this appeal were (1) whether there was sufficient evidence from which the Tax Court could find that X was availed of by taxpayers "with a view to ... the sale or exchange of the stock by its shareholders ... prior to the realization by the corporation ... constructing ... the property of a substantial part of the net income to be derived from such property"; (2) whether the distribution and sale took place prior to the realization of the substantial part of the net income to be derived from the property; and (3) whether more than 70 percent of the gain to petitioners was attributable to the constructed property. *Held:* Affirmed. According to the court, the taxpayers' attempt to separate the gain on the land, which was owned before X was formed, from the gain on construction was a distinction of form only, and there was no proof of substantial increase in value in the land before it was transferred to the corporation. Mintz, 284 F2d 554, 60-2 USTC ¶ 9803, 6 AFTR2d 5894 (2d Cir. 1960).

Wherry Act housing corporation held collapsible; gain derived from stock redemption deemed ordinary income. Gain derived by taxpayers upon the redemption of part of their stock in rental housing projects was found to be ordinary income. The corporations were collapsible. The corporations built rental housing under the Wherry Act at Fort Bragg. The redeemed stock, Class B Stock, had originally been issued to an architect but was later acquired by taxpayers, whose Class A Stock was not redeemed. The Tax Court considered it immaterial whether the distributions in redemption of the stock were paid out of mortgage loans or whether they were made out of rents received by the corporations. *Held:* Affirmed. In either event, the gain was attributable entirely to the properties constructed and was distributed before the corporations realized a substantial part of the total net income to be derived from them. Bryan, 281 F2d 238, 60-2 USTC ¶ 9603, 6 AFTR2d 5191 (4th Cir.), cert. denied, 364 US 931 (1960).

Two rental housing corporations found collapsible; taxpayer realized ordinary income on stock redemption. Preliminary to construction on land he owned, taxpayer made improvements, including curbs, gutters, and sewers. He then formed two corporations that leased the land for 99 years and engaged taxpayer's construction firm to erect rental housing projects. FHA-insured mortgages exceeded construction costs by about $330,000. Taxpayer's stock in each of the corporations was redeemed a few months after completion of construction, when the corporations had already realized some rental income. Taxpayer received about $216,000 in excess of the basis of his stock. The IRS contended that the two corporations were collapsible and that taxpayer realized ordinary income upon the redemption. *Held:* For the IRS. The court found that both corporations were formed for the construction of properties with a view of a redemption to taxpayer's stock before the corporations were to realize substantial income from the properties. Taxpayer argued that more than 30 percent of his gain was paid out of rentals; therefore, since less than 70 percent of the gain was attributable to constructed property, the corporations were not collapsible. But taxpayer had not established that the distribution was not made out of the excess of the FHA mortgage over construction costs. However, even if the distribution were out of rents, it would still be attributable to constructed property. The court also rejected taxpayer's argument that part of the gain was attributable to the land improvements, since taxpayer, not the corporations, had paid for them. They were added to his basis of the land, not of the stock. Spangler, 278 F2d 665, 60-1 USTC ¶ 9424, 5 AFTR2d 1336 (4th Cir.), cert. denied, 364 US 825 (1960).

Jury found that stock sold before corporation realized income from sale of real estate was not sold to collapse corporation. Taxpayer was a stockholder in a corporation that purchased and developed real estate. Before the corporation realized any income from the sale of properties, taxpayer sold his stock. The IRS contended that the gain was ordinary income under the collapsible corporation provisions of Section 341. Taxpayer contended that he sold the stock because of his worsening health and the fact that the City Planning Commission refused to approve plans for the corporation. He contended that neither of these circumstances could have been reasonably anticipated when the corporation was formed or when the property was acquired. *Held:* The taxpayer. A jury found that taxpayer was entitled to capital gain treatment. Steves, III, 66-1 USTC ¶ 9214 (WD Tex. 1966).

Corporation not collapsible where 40 percent of income realized. Taxpayers incorporated Interstate in April 1952 and became its first stockholders. In 1952, Interstate purchased 82 homes in one subdivision, acquiring all but one home for the same contractor, a corporation in which some of taxpayers owned stock. In 1953, Interstate purchased nine additional homes in the same subdivision from a different contractor. Interstate first leased each of the homes to individual tenants but sold 61 of them by November 1954. In 1954, Interstate had the first contractor build 153 additional homes, which were completed in May 1954, in another subdivision. Under a separate agreement with the FHA, Interstate agreed to hold these latter homes for at least two years and rent them to defense workers. Taxpayers sold their stock in Interstate in November 1954. The IRS treated the gain as ordinary income on the theory that Interstate was a collapsible corporation. *Held:* For taxpayers. The evidence established that Interstate had realized 40 percent of the income to be derived from its property at the time of sale. The court followed Kelley, 293 F2d 904 (5th Cir. 1961) and Zongker, 334 F2d 44 (10th Cir. 1964), to determine that this was a substantial part. The evidence further established that taxpayers did not form or employ Interstate with the intention of selling or exchanging its stock prior to the realization of a substantial part of its income. The court found, however, that more than 70 percent of the gain on the sale of the stock was attributable to collapsible assets. For this purpose, the 91 homes acquired in the first subdivision were not viewed as an integrated unit. This finding was not controlling, however, in light of the conclusions drawn from the other evidence. Winn, 243 F. Supp. 282, 65-2 USTC ¶ 9521 (WD Mo. 1965).

Corporation not collapsible due to realization of substantial part of income. A corporation was organized for the development of real estate subdivisions and the construction and sale of houses. It was liquidated in 1963 after it had realized 100 percent, 93 percent, and 56 percent, respectively, of the taxable income to be derived from its three projects. The IRS contended that the corporation was collapsible and distributions in liquidation were ordinary income to taxpayer. *Held:* For taxpayer. The controversy centers on the meaning of "substantial part" as used in Section 341(b). The test of the statute is whether a corporation has realized a substantial part of the taxable income to be derived from the property. Based on the facts, the corporation was not a collapsible corporation and gain was taxable at capital gain rates. Day, 55 TC 257 (1971).

Corporation collapsible if its stock sold prior to the realization of a substantial part of its income. A newly formed corporation purchased property that it leased to a race track corporation at a substantial rent. At the same time, its stockholders, including taxpayer, gave the race track corporation an option to purchase their stock in the lessor corporation. The following year, the race track corporation exercised its option and purchased taxpayer's stock. The IRS contended that the lessor corporation was collapsible. *Held:* For the IRS. The corporation was availed of with a view to selling the stock before it realized a substantial part of its rental income. The result was not changed by the fact that taxpayer would have realized capital gain if he had owned the property personally. Tobias, 40 TC 84 (1963).

Tax Court found corporation collapsible. Taxpayers formed a corporation to acquire land and to construct, own, and operate an apartment development. The IRS contended that it was a collapsible corporation. *Held:* For the

IRS. On the record, the court found that various distributions made to the stockholders prior to the corporation's realization of a substantial amount of the income to be derived from the property had been contemplated prior to the completion of construction. Zorn, 35 TCM 1048, ¶ 76,241 P-H Memo. TC (1976).

What is "substantially all of the properties?" The IRS stated, in determining whether a corporation is a collapsible corporation, that a sale of substantially all of the properties occurs if, during the liquidation, one acre of undeveloped land, representing 4 percent of all preliquidation assets, and an installment obligation from a previous sales of land were both retained. Rev. Rul. 73-500, 1973-2 CB 113.

Corporation that realized one-third of its income from property it produced not collapsible. A corporation that realized one third of the taxable income to be derived from property it produced or purchased is not collapsible within the meaning of Section 341(b). Rev. Rul. 62-12 revoked. Rev. Rul. 72-48, 1972-1 CB 102.

70-30 rule and three-year rule operate independently. Section 341(d) provides three limitations on the application of the collapsible corporation rules. One of these, Section 341(d)(2), often called the 70-30 rule, provides that collapsible treatment (viz, ordinary income) does not apply unless more than 70 percent of the stockholder's gain is attributable to Section 341 assets. A second limitation, Section 341(d)(3), known as the three-year rule, in substance makes the collapsible treatment inapplicable to gain realized after the Section 341 assets have been held for at least three years. The IRS ruled that the 70 percent limitation is not automatically applicable if a corporation assumed to be collapsible distributes appreciated assets in complete liquidation and at least 30 percent of the gain on liquidation is attributable to assets on which the three-year limitation of Section 341(d)(3) has run. The 70-30 rule is applied to the total gain *including* gain on assets held for more than three years. Thus, the three-year-old assets fall on the 70 percent side, not the 30 percent side of the limitation. The three-year rule does not change the character of the gain assets held for that period; such assets retain their character as gains on Section 341 property. The two limitations operate independently. Rev. Rul. 65-184, 1965-2 CB 91.

Three-Year Holding Period Exception

Income from sale of utility corporation stock was income from collapsible corporation. Taxpayers owned material interests in corporations engaged in the construction of utility systems. The IRS argued that gain from the sale of stock of such corporations was ordinary, since the corporations were collapsible corporations, and that the gain was attributable to tainted property under Section 341(d)(2). The lower court upheld the IRS. *Held:* Affirmed. Construction of the utility systems was crucial to the operation of the utility franchises. Therefore, the corporations were formed, or at least availed of, principally for the construction of property. The sales took place within three years of completion of construction. Moreover, the development of utility franchises was the production of intangible property within the meaning of Section 341(b)(1). Income from the sale of stock of a real estate development corporation was also found to be ordinary income from a collapsible corporation. King, 641 F2d 253, 81-1 USTC ¶ 9307, 47 AFTR2d 81-1330 (5th Cir. 1981).

Taxpayer's completion date for building accepted; three-year rule rendered corporation not collapsible. Taxpayer was a stockholder in a corporation organized to build an apartment house. The building was 9 percent completed by April 1, 1955, and a contractor's requisition dated May 31, 1955 certified that the building was then fully completed, although partitions for commercial tenants had not been installed. By the next month, the apartments were fully rented. A dispute with the FHA over commercial space was resolved in August 1955, at which time the FHA reported the job as 100 percent completed. The stock of the corporation was sold in June 1958. The IRS contended that the corporation was collapsible; therefore, taxpayer's gain was ordinary income. *Held:* For taxpayer. The corporation was not collapsible. The building was completed by April 1955, three years before the stock was sold. In addition, the prohibited view was not formed until long after the apartment building was completed. Freitas, 25 TCM 545, ¶ 66,105 P-H Memo. TC (1966).

Regulation § 1.341-4(c)(2) was used to compute gain on distribution from collapsible corporation where certain property was constructed more than three years before realization. Taxpayer formed a corporation that proceeded to construct a number of apartment buildings. One of the buildings was completed more than three years from liquidation of the corporation, and the other property was completed within the three-year period. Regulation § 1.341-4(c)(2) was used to compute the portion of the gain subject to the provisions of Section 341(a). Rev. Rul. 70-93, 1970-1 CB 71.

Alterations and corrections on newly completed office building held not to constitute part of the original "construction." Taxpayer, a corporation, was organized in 1957; shortly thereafter, it began construction of a multistory office building. The total cost of erecting the building, including the cost of making all installations required by the original tenants, was $9,000. These expenditures were incurred prior to December 31, 1958, and all construction described in the plans and specifications was completed by that date. The building constituted the corporation's principal asset and was totally leased and occupied by December 31, 1958. After the last tenant had secured occupancy, the corporation spent $30, $40, and $45 respectively in 1959, 1960, and 1961 on minor alterations and corrections in the existing structure. The minor alterations and corrections included a change in the decor of the interior of the building, the removal of an obstruction for the convenience of the tenants, and the installation of additional rest room facilities. As a result of these alterations and corrections, there were no structural changes in any respect. Moreover, there was no appreciable change in the fair market value of the building. In 1962, the corporation sought advice as to whether a liquidation would receive favorable tax treatment under Section 333 or whether it would be treated as a Section 341 collapsible corporation. The IRS noted that under Section 341(d), in the case of constructed property, there is a presumption that gain realized by the stockholders after the expiration of three years following completion of construction is taxed under the collapsible corporation rules. Under these facts, the IRS held that such minor alterations and corrections as those made from 1959 through 1961 would not be considered "construction" for purposes of the three-year rule. Rev. Rul. 63-114, 1963-1 CB 74.

Realization of gain on collapsible stock unaffected by installment election. The collapsibility rules of Section 341 do not apply to gain realized after the three years of the property's completion. The question here ruled upon is whether an election to report a sale of stock in a corporation deemed collapsible under the installment method has an effect on that three-year rule. The IRS says it does not. The installment method defers payment of tax; it does not defer realization of gain, the criterion under Section 341. Rev. Rul. 60-68, 1960-1 CB 151.

Date rezoning becomes final starts three-year period to determine collapsibility. Taxpayer had to have land rezoned from residential to commercial in order to construct a shopping center. This was contested over a period of years. For purposes of applying Section 341 relating to collapsible corporations, the rezoning is an integral step in the construction of the center. The three-year holding period is held to begin on the day following the date that the rezoning becomes final if the corporation has no other construction activity with relation to the land after the date that the rezoning becomes final. Rev. Rul. 56-137, 1956-1 CB 178.

COLLECTION OF TAXES

(*See* Assessment and Collection)

COMPENSATION FOR PERSONAL SERVICES

In General	171
Bonuses	173
Dividend Equivalence	179
Held Reasonable	181
Held Unreasonable	194
Loans Distinguished	204
Past Services	204

In General

Compensation payment recharacterized as stock redemption. Taxpayer, a corporation engaged in the coal brokerage business, had two equal stockholders, one of whom managed the business and received a salary. During the first nine months of operation, taxpayer earned a profit of $100,000, at the end of which time the managing stockholder was taken into protective custody and had to liquidate his interest. Under an agreement with taxpayer, he received $50,000 in compensation for past services and $1,000 in redemption of his stock. Subsequently, the remaining stockholder continued to operate the business successfully. The IRS denied taxpayer's claimed deduction under Section 162 for the $50,000, arguing that it was part of the consideration for the redemption. *Held:* For the IRS. At the time of the sale, the retiring stockholder had already been adequately compensated, and the business had a substantial going-concern value that was not dependent on the retiring stockholder's continued services. American Int'l Coal Co., 43 TCM 1097, ¶ 82,204 P-H Memo. TC (1982), aff'd, 709 F2d 1490 (3d Cir.), cert. denied, 464 US 6 (1983).

Excess compensation paid to husband could not be deducted as salary for his wife. The IRS asserted that taxpayer's use of a company car for personal commuting resulted in income to him equal to the car's fair rental value and that taxpayer had received a salary in excess of reasonable compensation for his services to the corporation of which he was the majority stockholder. *Held:* For the IRS, in major part. The IRS was upheld on the first issue. The court determined the amount of taxpayer's salary that was reasonable compensation and held that the excess could not be deducted as a salary to his wife, also an employee. There was no evidence that taxpayer was receiving income for his wife or that they were to be paid as a unit. C.A. White Trucking Co., 601 F2d 867, 44 AFTR2d 79-5513 (5th Cir. 1979).

Tax Court's determination of reasonable salary upheld. Taxpayer corporation deducted a $9,000 salary paid to its vice-president. After review, the Tax Court determined that reasonable compensation for the employment was $5,000; accordingly, it denied the deduction of the remainder of the salary. *Held:* Affirmed. The determination of what is reasonable is a question of fact. Where the evidence supports the Tax Court's conclusion that a reasonable salary is a lesser amount, the decision will be upheld. Cozart Packing Co., 475 F2d 1399, 73-1 USTC ¶ 9366, 31 AFTR2d 73–1142 (4th Cir. 1973).

"Cavalier" salary overruled in light to prior year's compromise. A corporation owned real property that it rented to three tenants, two of which were related corporations. Rental income from the latter was never actually collected, but was shown as an intercompany accounts receivable. For 1950 through 1954, of the $12,000 salary paid to taxpayer's three officer stockholders, $9,400 was allowed by the IRS. When taxpayer deducted $9,400 in 1955, the IRS allowed only $1,500 as reasonable. The Tax Court found that the total time actually required to perform all of the corporate duties did not exceed 15 to 20 hours a week. It concluded that a reasonable allowance for compensation for all the personal services actually rendered by the the officers was not in excess of $5,200. *Held:* Remanded. Although the burden of proof remained with taxpayer, when taxpayer showed that some services were performed and *that the compensation had been accepted as reasonable in prior years,* there was some obligation on the part of the IRS to offer proof that the salaries were excessive. Seven Canal Place Corp., 332 F2d 899, 64-2 USTC ¶ 9516, 13 AFTR2d 1568 (2d Cir. 1964).

COMPENSATION FOR PERSONAL SERVICES: *In General*

Salaries in excess of $100,000 found reasonable for part-time services. Under a plan adopted in 1933, taxpayer paid its two controlling stockholder officers compensation calculated on a base salary, a guaranteed minimum salary, and a percentage of net profits. In 1956 and 1957, each officer received salaries in excess of $100,000. The IRS contended that reasonable salaries were $65,000 for one officer and $60,000 for the other and that payments in excess of these amounts constituted disguised dividends. The trial court listed the factors that the jury was to consider and refused to admit into evidence the amount of salary paid by a subsidiary that the IRS wished to use as an index of the time spent in taxpayer's business. The jury found the salaries reasonable. *Held:* Affirmed. The jury was aware that the officers devoted only part of their time to the taxpayer's affairs. The officers' compensation from other sources was not relevant to the reasonableness of the compensation here at issue. McWane Cast Iron Pipe Co., 331 F2d 921, 64-1 USTC ¶ 9490 (5th Cir. 1964).

Salary deduction reduced corporate resolution called for smaller salary. Taxpayer was a family farm corporation. The board of directors passed a resolution increasing the president's and vice-president's salaries. The IRS denied the taxpayer's deductions in excess of certain amounts that it considered reasonable salaries for the two officers. *Held:* For the IRS. There was an inference that the compensation was unreasonable where there was a sudden increase in compensation coincidental with the increase in profits from the Soviet grain sale and a lack of arm's-length dealing. M&K Farms, Inc., 556 F. Supp. 50, 82-2 USTC ¶ 9671, 51 AFTR2d 83-478 (D. Mont. 1982), aff'd in unpub. opin. (9th Cir. 1984).

Jury determined that payments to stockholders were salaries, not dividends, and that the IRS's reallocation of corporate expenses was unreasonable and arbitrary. In 1962 and 1963, taxpayer corporation paid certain amounts as salaries to its two executive officer-owners that the IRS disallowed in part as unreasonable. The IRS also reallocated administrative expenses from the taxpayer to a commonly owned corporation. *Held:* For taxpayer. After reviewing the evidence, the jury determined that the salaries paid to the corporate officers were reasonable and resulted in no dividends to the stockholder-employees. It also determined that the IRS abused its discretion in reallocating administrative expenses from taxpayer to a commonly owned corporation. Home Improvement Co., 67-2 USTC ¶ 9702 (ND Ala. 1972).

Jury determined reasonable compensation. During an audit of taxpayer corporation's 1959 and 1960 tax returns, the IRS assessed a deficiency each year based on improper treatment of some expenses. These items were improperly deducted in the year paid and had to be capitalized over a number of years. A settlement agreement entitled taxpayer to refunds in various amounts for fiscal years ending in 1958, 1961, 1962, and 1963. In 1963, the corporation deducted $124,000 as compensation paid to the president of the corporation. The IRS challenged this deduction as an unreasonable amount for compensation for the services performed. *Held:* For taxpayer, in part. The jury found $100,000 to be reasonable and allowed the deductions for that amount. The extra tax due on the disallowed portion was offset against the refunds due to taxpayer. Jaybee Mfg. Corp., 70-2 USTC ¶ 9618, 26 AFTR2d 5584 (CD Cal. 1970).

Pension plan contribution constituted unreasonable compensation. Taxpayer dentist formed a professional corporation and elected Subchapter S status. The initial fiscal year covered 14 days. The taxpayer deducted $24,000 on that return as an expense attributable to the pension plan contribution from funds borrowed from the taxpayer. The pension plan deduction produced a net operating loss, and the IRS disallowed a part of the claimed pension plan deduction that represented an amount that was not reasonable compensation for services rendered by taxpayer professional. *Held:* For the IRS. The pension plan contribution constituted, to the extent of $19,000, unreasonable compensation to the taxpayer. LaMastro, 72 TC 377 (1979).

Repayment of excess part of prior year's salaries did not reduce current year's salaries; claim

COMPENSATION FOR PERSONAL SERVICES: *Bonuses*

of right inapplicable. Taxpayers were officers, directors, and stockholders of a closely held corporation. In 1956, the IRS disallowed part of the officers' salaries for 1953 and 1954 as excessive. The day after the disallowance was imposed, the directors demanded the return of the excess amounts. This was done, and taxpayers deducted the returned amounts from their 1956 salaries. The IRS then determined that taxpayers should report their full salaries. *Held:* For the IRS. The claim of right doctrine did not apply. The corporation could not have compelled the return of excess salaries. The court rejected the taxpayers' argument that they made the repayments involuntarily based on the IRS' representation that the repayments would be deductible. Berger, 37 TC 1026 (1962).

IRS announces policy on deduction of compensation where dividends have historically been insubstantial. The IRS held that the failure of a closely held corporation to pay more than an insubstantial portion of its earnings as dividends on its stock is a significant factor to be taken into account in determining the deductibility of compensation paid by the corporation to its stockholder-employees. Conversely, after an examination of all of the facts and circumstances (including the corporation's dividend history), where compensation paid to stockholder-employees is found to be reasonable in amount and paid for services rendered, deductions for such compensation under Section 162(a) will not be denied on the sole ground that the corporation has not paid more than an insubstantial portion of its earnings as dividends on its outstanding stock. Rev. Rul. 79-8, 1979-1 CB 92.

Control by stockholder-president of January 31 fiscal year triggered constructive receipt of past year's unpaid salary. Taxpayer was the president of an accrual basis corporation that filed its return for the fiscal year ending January 31, 1971. During 1970, taxpayer was in control of the corporation by owning one third of the corporation's capital stock and by being the trustee for the remaining capital stock, which was placed in irrevocable trusts for the benefit of his wife and two children. Taxpayer also kept the books of the corporation and was its active manager. Under a corporate resolution of 1962, the taxpayer's salary of $2x$ per month accrued to him monthly. On January 31, 1971, the end of the corporation's fiscal year, the corporation credited taxpayer's account with the amount of $22x$, which represented 11 months of undrawn salary for 1970. Taxpayer's monthly salary could have been paid or credited to his account monthly during 1970 without financial embarrassment to the corporation. Taxpayer merely had to make the necessary monthly book entries reflecting the accrual of his undrawn salary or the actual payment of his salary. The IRS reviewed the case-law treatment of the constructive receipt issue raised in these facts, and, consistent with its previous litigating position, it held that the authorized but undrawn 1970 salary was includible in taxpayer's income for 1970. Rev. Rul. 72-317, 1972-1 CB 128.

Bonuses

Reasonable compensation determined with regard to bonuses. Taxpayer and his father owned all the stock of a soda bottling company. An arrangement was entered into between taxpayer and the corporation, giving him a base salary plus a bonus as high as 33 percent of corporate profits. The IRS claimed this salary to be unreasonable and recharacterized a portion as dividends. *Held:* For the IRS. Reasonable compensation was set at the same base salary, but bonuses were not to exceed 15 percent of corporate profits. The court held that the excess represented dividends. Royal Crown Bottling Co. of Winchester, 46 TCM 1570, ¶ 83,611 P-H Memo. TC (1983), aff'd, 760 F2d 265 (4th Cir. 1985).

Compensation of officer reasonable. Pursant to a corporate resolution, taxpayer officer received an annual salary of $6,000 plus a bonus based on a percentage of corporate net income before taxes. Taxpayer worked 50 to 70 hours per week, and six or even seven days a week, if necessary. For 1968, his salary was $67,200, for 1969 it was $88,500, and for 1970, it was $97,600. The IRS allowed a salary of $40,000 for each of those years. The Tax Court held for taxpayer, in part. *Held:* Affirmed. Although the formula used by the taxpayer to determine the executive's salary was unrealistic and excessive when compared with that of other officers in similar businesses, taxpayer was entitled to salaries exceeding those allowed by the IRS, to wit: $50,000 for 1968, $54,500 for 1969 and $57,500 for the year of 1970. Pepsi-Cola Bottling Co. of Salina, 528 F2d 176, 76-1 USTC ¶ 9107, 37 AFTR2d 76-369 (10th Cir. 1975).

Year-end bonuses to corporate officers in excess of annual salary were reasonable. The president and vice-president of taxpayer corporation received bonus payments at the end of each year that exceeded their annual salaries. The IRS alleged that the total amount of salaries and bonuses claimed as deductions exceeded the reasonable compensation for services rendered and that the bonuses were not authorized by the board of directors in the year of accrual. *Held:* For taxpayer. Considering the unique skills of the officers and the extra services they performed, the total paid did not exceed reasonable compensation. Furthermore, the fact that the bonuses were paid only after each year's profits were ascertainable and that no corporate dividends were paid was of no consequence, since the bonuses were intended to compensate the officers for the extra work they did in rendering consulting services, the value of which could not be calculated until the year's end. The IRS was, however, correct in postponing the deduction for the bonuses from the year during which the services were rendered to the year they were authorized by the board of directors. The deduction allowed for the bonuses was the amount shown to have been actually authorized in the minutes in each of the years in question, not the bonuses actually paid. The court also disallowed a corporate deduction allocable to personal use by the officers of a company car, a deduction of country club dues paid for its president, claimed Christmas gifts and bonuses, and travel and entertainment expenses arising out of attendance of the president's wife at trade association conventions. The court increased the corporate income due to discharge of a corporate note by a creditor with whom taxpayer continued to do business, and for roofing materials and other supplies sent by corporate suppliers direct to the vice-president for his personal use. The latter not only constituted income to the corporation, but also constructive dividends to the vice-president. L.R. Schmaus Co., 406 F2d 1044, 69-1 USTC ¶ 9211, 23 AFTR2d 69-602 (7th Cir. 1969).

Bonus paid after corporation decided to stop its business held unreasonable. Taxpayer corporation paid large bonuses to its two stockholders after they decided to discountinue the corporation's business. The IRS denied a deduction for the bonuses. *Held:* For the IRS. The bonuses were contingent on profits and were paid because the profits were not to be used in the business. Also, the corporation had never paid a dividend. Joseph P. Kropf, Inc., 534 F. Supp. 581, 82-1 USTC ¶ 9379, 50 AFTR2d 82-5164 (D. Colo. 1982).

Salaries and bonuses to executive officers who were principal stockholders held reasonable. The two executive officers of taxpayer were husband and wife. The former was continually employed in the woodworking industry and the latter in office management for 30 years prior to their acquisition and control of taxpayer corporation. Prior to their acquisition, the business and net worth of taxpayer had continually declined, but as a result of the management of the two executives and the establishment of their basic salaries at minimum levels, net worth increased from $62,000 when they acquired control to $236,000 seven years thereafter. The corporation had no patents, franchises, or distributorships, and the evidence clearly disclosed that its success in a competitive market was due to the hard work and abilities of the officer stockholders, for which they received $59,000, $77,000, and $99,000 in the years in issue. The IRS disallowed $15,000, $35,000, and $47,000 in these years. *Held:* For taxpayer. The officers worked long hours without vacations and performed all the duties involved in the operation of a manufacturing plant whose sales rose from $438,000 to $966,000 in six years. In addition, the wife designed the company's products, which gained wide public acceptance, and the husband designed the machinery by which these products were mass produced. W.R.

Vermillion Co., 283 F. Supp. 350, 68-1 USTC ¶ 9252 (WD Mo. 1968).

Bonuses paid to officer-stockholders deemed reasonable compensation. Taxpayer corporation was owned by four officers and their wives. The officers received annual salaries of $20,000 each plus bonuses of $3,000 in 1954 and $6,000 in 1955 and 1956. In those years, sales were $885,000, $982,000 and $1,005,000, and net income after bonuses was $2,300, $25,000, and $39,000, respectively. Taxpayer sued to recover taxes paid on the disallowance of the bonuses as unreasonable compensation. The judge charged the jury that it could consider the fact that taxpayer had not declared dividends on its common stock and that the corporation had accumulated earnings and profits. He also charged that the size alone of the amount received, although substantially increased over previous years, did not make the total compensation unreasonable and that the jury should consider the fact that a revenue agent had allowed total compensation of $93,000 as reasonable in 1951, when gross sales were smaller than in 1954. The judge further charged that the corporation had the right to reward the officers for sacrifices made by them in earlier years when funds were not available. *Held:* For taxpayer. The jury found that the bonuses paid were reasonable compensation. C&E Canners, 59-2 USTC ¶ 9684 (DNJ 1959).

Inflation plays role in determination of reasonable compensation. The IRS questioned the reasonableness of compensation paid to executives of a mobile home corporation. The same question for earlier tax years was litigated for the same executives in Giles Indus., Inc., 496 F2d 556 (Ct. Cl. 1974). *Held:* The court allowed a larger deduction for compensation than the IRS allowed. It used the prior decision as a basis, but adjusted the salaries for inflation and reduced one executive's salary to reflect a drop in responsibilities. Giles Indus., Inc., 650 F2d 274, 81-1 USTC ¶ 9178, 48 AFTR2d 81-5032 (Ct. Cl. 1981).

Unreasonable compensation determination sustained in part. The IRS contended that part of the salaries, bonuses, and profit-sharing plan contributions that taxpayer paid to three of its executives were dividends. *Held:* For taxpayer, in part. The fact that the company declared no dividends and paid larger bonuses than salaries showed that part of the payments were profit distributions. The court held that the salaries were excessive but increased the salaries for two of the executives over what the IRS allowed. Petro-Chem Mktg. Corp., 602 F2d 959, 79-2 USTC ¶ 9484, 44 AFTR2d 79-6087 (Ct. Cl. 1979).

Bonus from controlled corporation payable after year-end not constructively received. Taxpayer, on the cash basis and using the calendar year, was president of his controlled corporation, which was on the accrual basis and had a fiscal year ending October 31. Taxpayer's employment contract called for a nominal weekly salary and a bonus of 45 percent of the company's net earnings, payable 65 days after the end of the fiscal year. During the year in question, taxpayer received advances on his bonus, and on January 3 of the following year received the balance of his bonus less an amount withheld sufficient to cover his tax for the earlier year. *Held:* For taxpayer. The Tax Court held that the balance of the bonus and the entire amount of the withholding were not constructively received in the earlier year. These amounts were not unconditionally set apart for taxpayer, as per his contract, until the next year. The fact that taxpayer, as dominant stockholder, could have caused the corporation to make payment earlier did not control. He did not do so and did not have the right to do so. While he may have had the power to do it, a substantial minority interest might have prevented such action. However, that portion of the amount withheld attributable to the advance payment of the bonus was, as a practical matter, considered constructively received in the earlier year. Basila, 36 TC 111 (1961), acq. 1962-2 CB 4.

Compensation paid to sole stockholder and president of corporation unreasonable. Taxpayer, the sole stockholder and president of a corporation, received $27,000 plus 20 percent of net profits and a Christmas bonus as compensation. The IRS determined that part of this compensation was unreasonable. *Held:* For the IRS. In view of the size and nature of the corporation, and the taxpayer's responsibilities, his compensation was clearly excessive. Clymer, Jr., 47 TCM 1576, ¶ 84,203 P-H Memo. TC (1984).

Bonuses to corporate president reasonable compensation. Taxpayer corporation entered into an employment contract with its president under which taxpayer agreed to pay the president a salary and bonus at the end of each fiscal year. Subsequently, taxpayer implemented a recapitalization that the IRS had approved as a Section 368(a)(1)(E) reorganization. The recapitalization allowed taxpayer to give its lender-stockholder a return on its investment via priority dividends and give the president his bonuses without making substantial cash outlays. The IRS disallowed taxpayer's deductions for a portion of the bonuses paid to the president on the ground that they were disguised dividends. *Held:* For taxpayer. The entire amount of the bonuses was part of the reasonable compensation paid to president for his services and was deductible as such. The taxpayer's payment of priority dividends pursuant to the corporation's recapitalization was independent of the bonuses, and it was not intended that any part of the bonuses constituted a dividend. Railroad Dynamics, Inc., 47 TCM 957, ¶ 84,040 P-H Memo. TC (1984).

Bonus based on corporation's profit reasonable. The employee joined the taxpayer corporation as a salesman in 1960 and by 1963 became its president. The company became extremely successful primarily because of the employee's unique capabilities and outstanding performance. The company adopted a policy of compensating the employee with both an annual salary and a bonus equal to a percentage of the company's net profits before taxes. During the years in question, the employee owned 53 percent of taxpayer's stock. The IRS determined the bonus to be unreasonable compensation and disallowed the deductions. *Held:* For taxpayer. Bonuses to an employee based on corporate profits were reasonable where the employee demonstrated special skills that resulted in significant corporate profits. The fact that the payments were not pro rata to other employee-stockholders tended to support the position that the amounts were intended as compensation for services rendered and not dividend distributions. Georgia Crown Distrib. Co., 46 TCM 959, ¶ 83,459 P-H Memo. TC (1983).

Bonus paid to corporate president reasonable. Taxpayer was president and sole stockholder of a corporation that operated a GM diesel engine distributorship. The corporation was set up in 1967 under a contract whereby GM provided the initial financing and taxpayer received as compensation a salary plus a bonus based on a percentage of earnings. For 1974 through 1977, taxpayer received compensation in excess of $100,000–$100,000, $115,000, and $143,250, respectively, of which no more than $50,000 per year represented salary. The corporation paid no dividends during this period, in which the corporation's operations greatly expanded. The IRS attached the compensation as excessive. *Held:* For taxpayer. The original bonus arrangement was the result of an arm's-length transaction designed to motivate GM's distributors. The taxpayer's increased compensation during the years in question was the result of taxpayer's efforts, not fortuitous market forces. The failure to pay dividends was justified by expense of corporate expansion. Neils, 43 TCM 982, ¶ 82,173 P-H Memo. TC (1982).

Compensation unreasonable for passive corporate officer. Taxpayer was a subcontractor for insulation, roofing, waterproofing, and dampproofing jobs. *R*, the majority stockholder, became the president of taxpayer after her husband died. *R* seldom worked at taxpayer's office or plant but occasionally contacted taxpayer by telephone. During 1974 through 1976, *R* was paid a salary and bonuses. Taxpayer paid no dividends during this period. The IRS determined that the amounts in excess of the salary were unreasonable compensation and disallowed the deductions taken by taxpayer in excess of that amount, pursuant to Section 162(a). *Held:* For the IRS. Because the officer took no active part in running the business, the corporation was not justified in issuing bonuses to her. The "bonuses" paid to the officer were actually a return on her investment. Because the excess compensation was unreasonable, taxpayer was not allowed a deduction for those amounts. General Roofing & Insulation Co., 42 TCM 1697, ¶ 81,667 P-H Memo. TC (1981).

Compensation paid under bonus plan covering principal stockholder employees adopted immediately before sale of substantial block of stock to an unrelated third party subject to scrutiny on question of reasonableness. Taxpayer, immediately prior to 1970, was essentially a family-owned business. Its principal officers and directors were members of this family and held part-time positions with taxpayer. Prior to 1970, taxpayer had a bonus plan that did not include its officers. While negotiations arose involving the purchase by International Harvester Co. of a 35 percent stock interest in taxpayer, taxpayer amended its bonus plan to include its officers. International Harvester acquired its interest with full knowledge of the amended plan. The IRS challenged the compensation (including bonuses) paid to taxpayer's principal officers in 1973 and 1974 as unreasonable. *Held:* For the IRS. Where a corporation adopts a bonus plan that favors its principal stockholder-employees, it invites scrutiny by the courts. While the acceptance by International Harvester of the bonus plan was some evidence of its reasonableness, the circumstances of this case do not indicate that the plan was freely bargained at arm's length between the employee and employer. Under the facts, it was not shown that the compensation paid was reasonable in light of the services rendered. Kewavnee Eng'g Corp., 38 TCM 672, ¶ 79,154 P-H Memo. TC (1979).

Court upholds deduction of bonus that was 300 percent of base salary. In 1969 taxpayer entered into a contract with a key employee whereunder the employee would be paid, in addition to salary, a bonus equal to 50 percent of all profits and permitted him to acquire 60 percent of taxpayer. Subsequent to this agreement, taxpayer's success was to a large extent attributable to the efforts of this employee. Ultimately, this bonus provision accounted for 75 percent of the employee's salary. Taxpayer did not pay dividends because it was for the most part illiquid due its investment in operating assets and because of its potential liability in a major construction accident. The IRS asserted that a portion of the bonus was unreasonable compensation and disallowed a portion of taxpayer's deduction for compensation paid to this employee-stockholder. *Held:* For taxpayer. Although the employee ultimately acquired control of taxpayer, he was only an employee at the time the agreement was executed. Accordingly, the bonus provision was not the product of his proprietary control over the corporation. The evidence indicated that such bonus provisions were common in the industry and, in this instance, clearly bore a direct relationship to the services rendered as an employee. Finally, the bonus was not a disguised dividend because taxpayer was in no position to pay dividends. Steel Constructors, Inc., 37 TCM 1851, ¶ 78,489 P-H Memo. TC (1978).

Compensation held reasonable although based on a percentage of profits. In 1971 and 1972, *B* and *S*, who were principal officers and sole stockholders of taxpayer, received compensation consisting of modest salaries and substantial bonuses which constituted a predetermined percentage of the profits. Taxpayer, a car dealership, paid no dividends but, in 1971 and 1972, made substantial additions to a working capital account maintained in accordance with the requirements of the auto company. The IRS disallowed the compensation in part, and determined the excess amounts to be dividends. *Held:* For taxpayer. Compensation was deemed reasonable where (1) the business had extraordinary success; (2) the percentage of profits was decided by a board of directors, or where the individual did not control the business; (3) the percentage of profits was actually less than the percentage used by other businesses; (4) a predetermined formula was followed, and taxpayer paid substantial taxes. Good Chevrolet, 36 TCM 1157, ¶ 77,291 P-H Memo. TC (1977).

Compensation held unreasonable. Taxpayer, a successful corporation, never paid a dividend. Taxpayer paid large bonuses to its two principal officers. The size of the bonus was determined on an ad hoc basis, not by means of a formula. Taxpayer contended that compensation was reasonable, since it maintained a generous bonus policy and the compensation paid to nonstockholder salesmen was about the same as that paid to the officers. *Held:* For the IRS. Taxpayer failed to carry its burden of proof because it failed to present expert testimony and evidence of compensation ordinarily paid for like services under like circumstances. Southwestern Rubber & Packing Co., 36 TCM 716, ¶ 77,173 P-H Memo. TC (1977).

Bonus paid pursuant to an IRS agent's suggested formula for close corporations held reasonable. Taxpayer, a very successful McDonald's restaurant, paid its two equal stockholder-employees bonuses computed in accordance with a formula for close corporations suggested to taxpayer's accountant by an IRS agent with regard to a different client. The formula established a base salary and permitted a bonus based on a decreasing percentage of profits as reduced by base salaries and a reserve for future growth. The IRS challenged the bonuses as unreasonable compensation. *Held:* For taxpayer. The evidence presented showed that taxpayer's success was largely due to the efforts of these stockholder-employees and that, after the operation became successful, they continued to be involved with its operations. While taxpayer paid an inconsequential amount of dividends, the facts indicated that earnings were consistently invested in capital improvements. Schanchrist Foods, Inc., 36 TCM 555, ¶ 77,129 P-H Memo. TC (1977).

Salaries and bonuses found deductible by corporation as reasonable compensation. The IRS assessed a deficiency in taxpayer corporation's taxes, claiming that certain salaries and bonuses were excessive and, therefore, not deductible under Section 162(a). *Held:* For taxpayer. The salaries and the bonuses, based on a percentage of net profits were found to be reasonable compensation for the services. Osborne Motors, Inc., 35 TCM 691, ¶ 76,153 P-H Memo. TC (1976).

Reasonableness of salaries determined. The IRS claimed that the salaries paid to officer stockholders were unreasonable and constituted dividends. *Held:* For the IRS, in major part. Taxpayer corporation never paid any dividends. At the end of the year, after salaries were paid, bonuses were distributed based on what the corporation could afford. The high salaries of officer stockholders were unreasonable and, along with a portion of the bonuses, constituted nondeductible dividends. Carole Accessories, Inc., 32 TCM 1285, ¶ 73,273 P-H Memo. TC (1973).

Bonuses and unreasonable compensation not deductible. In a prior case, it was determined that bonuses paid to stockholder officers for 1962 through 1964 that were returned to the corporation and recorded as loans payable were in fact not deductible, since no funds actually left the corporation. The IRS currently disallowed deductions for bonuses for 1965 through 1967 paid by a successor corporation. *Held:* For the IRS, in major part. The corporation failed to show that the bonuses constituted reasonable compensation; thus, their deduction was disallowed. Furthermore, amounts paid to taxpayers out of the loan accounts were taxable corporate distributions to taxpayers. The bonuses accrued and credited to the loan accounts in earlier years were not includable in taxpayer's income when the loan account was closed out a later year. Finally, taxpayers were responsible for unpaid federal income tax liabilities of the transferor corporation for bonuses paid in 1967. The successor corporation also was liable for uncollected taxes of the transferor, as goodwill and inventory were transferred without consideration. Sanders, 32 TCM 332, ¶ 73,075 P-H Memo. TC (1973).

Compensation in excess of reasonable amounts not allowed as a deduction to a corporation. Taxpayer corporation paid bonuses of up to 90 percent of its net profits to its major stockholder-manager and its two key employees. It deducted the amounts as compensation. The IRS disallowed part of the deduction as excessive of reasonable salary. *Held:* For the IRS. Although the amounts were paid pursuant to contracts, the employees were the sole stockholders and controlled the corporation. Ninety percent of the profits was paid in bonuses, in proportion to stockholdings. No dividends were paid, and the bonuses represented almost two thirds of the total amount paid as compensation. The IRS concluded that the compensation was excessive; compensation was merely a mechanism for distribution of profits, and no deduction was allowed. Craigs Drug Store, Inc., 28 TCM 1104, ¶ 69,208 P-H Memo. TC (1969).

Increased compensation to sole stockholder unreasonable. Taxpayer corporation, engaged in trading in grass seeds and grains, paid its sole stockholder and dominant officer a base salary of $25,200 for the years 1963 and 1964, plus a bonus of $16,050 for 1963 and $30,000 for 1964, paid near the end of each year. For the two previous years, his compensation had been $22,000 and $29,000. The IRS disallowed as unreasonable the payments in 1963 and 1964 that exceeded $30,000. *Held:* For the IRS. The sudden increases in compensation for the taxable years were not justified in the light of the fact that the officer's activities were essentially unchanged from the prior years. Some portion of the total payments made to the officer in 1963 and 1964 was intended as a distribution of earnings, not as compensation for services currently rendered. Pacific Grains, Inc., 26 TCM 46, ¶ 67,007 P-H Memo. TC (1967).

Bonuses paid to officer-stockholders not disguised dividends and therefore represented reasonable compensation. Taxpayer corporation was organized by three individuals, its stockholders and officers, to engage in the highly specialized field of dealing in municipal securities. It paid two of the officers a bonus of $12,500 and the third a bonus of $7,500. In each instance, the bonus was 50 percent of the officer's regular annual salary. The IRS contended that the bonuses were unreasonable compensation. *Held:* For taxpayer. In determining that the bonuses represented reasonable compensation, not dividends, the court noted that the success or failure of taxpayer depended to a large extent on the three officers and their abilities. It found not only was taxpayer's payment of bonuses to its three officers in line with established practice in the area, but it was consistent with taxpayer's general policy of paying substantial bonuses to employees other than the officers. King, Quirk & Co., 20 TCM 1429, ¶ 61,274 P-H Memo. TC (1961).

Dividend Equivalence

Excessive compensation disallowance upheld. The Tax Court upheld the IRS' disallowance of a portion of the compensation of officer stockholders of taxpayer corporation as excessive and unreasonable. *Held:* Affirmed. No dividends were ever paid, and the amounts distributed to officer-stockholders were almost identical to the percentage of stock held by each of them. Paul E. Kummer Realty Co., 511 F2d 313, 75-1 USTC ¶ 9262, 35 AFTR2d 75-772 (8th Cir. 1975).

Wages to stockholder's children unreasonable; withdrawals treated as disguised dividends. The son and daughter of the majority stockholder served as officers of taxpayer, a hotel corporation. They received salaries of $8,000 and $3,100 a year, but had no regular duties to perform. The majority stockholder made numerous substantial withdrawals from the corporation; these withdrawals were carried on the corporate books in an open account. The corporation also claimed a shortened useful life for the hotel and the adjoining convention hall because of extraordinary obsolescence caused by the competition of nearby motels. The Tax Court held that the salaries paid to stockholder's children were unreasonable and disallowed them in part. It considered the withdrawals to be dividends in the year withdrawn rather than true loans. It also denied the claim for the shortened life for the buildings. *Held:* Affirmed in part and reversed in part. The evidence supported the findings regarding the salaries and withdrawals, and the Tax Court decision on these matters was affirmed. As the convention hall could be operated only in conjunction with the hotel, however, it could be depreciated over the shorter period terminating with the end of the useful life of the hotel. Atlanta Biltmore Hotel Corp., 349 F2d 677, 65-2 USTC ¶ 9573 (5th Cir. 1965).

Payments on reservation of interest in business that is subsequently incorporated are not dividends. Decedent left his business to his widow, but expressed the wish in his will that the business be operated by his sons with 5 percent of the gross receipts being paid to the widow for life. The sons formed a partnership and delivered a written promise to the mother that the 5 percent of gross would be paid during her lifetime. Subsequently the partnership was incorporated. During the period of the partnership, the sum paid to the mother was reported as her share of business income under the title of "commissions paid." After incorporation, the sum was taken as a deduction under "salaries and wages." The IRS contended that the payment to the widow was really a dividend to the sons, which they gave her. *Held:* For taxpayer. The court disagreed, holding that the mother, as owner of the business by virtue of her husband's will, had reserved an interest when she transferred it to the sons. Consequently, the sons, as partners, and their corporate successor were acting as trustees to collect and pay over the 5 percent purchase price to the mother. Fellows Sales Co., 200 F. Supp. 347, 62-1 USTC ¶ 9204 (DSD 1961).

Stockholders' salaries unreasonable on basis of competitor's pay scale. Taxpayer was a mechanical contractor. The controlling stockholder, his son, and a third stockholder were its three executive officers; these three and the wife of the controlling stockholder were taxpayer's directors. As president, the controlling stockholder received an annual salary of $15,000 in 1960 and 1961; his son, the secretary-treasurer, received salaries of $8,400 and $8,850; the vice-president received a salary of $9,600. In addition, each man received a $25,000 bonus in 1960 and a $27,500 bonus in 1961. The IRS determined that reasonable compensation for the vice-president was $27,500 a year and $20,000 for the secretary-treasurer. *Held:* For the IRS. There is no definite formula for determining reasonable compensation for employees for income tax purposes; each case rests on its particular facts. When the employees are also stockholders, they must introduce clear and convincing evidence that the payments to them are salaries and not dividends. The most significant factor in this regard is the compensation paid to similar employees by similar concerns in similar industries. Taxpayer offered no such evidence. The IRS, however, was able to offer evidence in support of its determination. The fact that the vice-president's salary increased while his responsibilities remained the same further supported the IRS' determination, as did the fact that the secretary-treasurer, who was less experienced than the vice-president and performed less responsible functions, received approximately the same salary. Griffin & Co., 389 F2d 802, 68-1 USTC ¶ 9172, 21 AFTR2d 460 (Ct. Cl. 1968).

Salaries having characteristics of dividends held unreasonable. Taxpayer, a corporation, paid its officer-stockholders compensation pursuant to a profit-sharing arrangement that provided for payments in the amount of 90 percent of net profits. Taxpayer was further required to make payment of such amounts to the heir or estate of each stockholder in the event of his death prior to the end of the fiscal year. The IRS contended that the salaries were unreasonable and denied the deduction. *Held:* For the IRS, in part. That which constitutes reasonable compensation is especially a question of fact that must be determined from the circumstances of each individual case. The provision for payment of profits to the heirs or estate of each stockholder was characteristic of distributions of earnings rather than compensation for services. Based on the facts, taxpayer was denied a deduction for the unreasonable salaries paid. This amount was less than that disallowed by the IRS. Boyle Fuel Co., 53 TC 162 (1969).

Employment contract to selling stockholder not part of stock sale; no constructive dividend to remaining stockholder. A 50 percent stockholder of a corporation disagreed on management and was bought out by taxpayer, the other stockholder, in 1952. On the same day, the selling stockholder entered into a five-year employment contract with the corporation. He performed some services in 1952 and 1953. However, he performed no services from 1954 through 1956. The IRS argued that the payments were dividends to taxpayer. *Held:* For taxpayer, in part. The court held that although the payments for the latter three years were not deductible by the corporation, they were not constructive dividends to taxpayer. On the facts, the employment contract was not part of

COMPENSATION FOR PERSONAL SERVICES: *Held Reasonable*

the purchase price for the stock. The contract was given to effectuate the selling stockholder's removal as an officer, to compensate him for past services, and to prevent competition. The payments during the first two years of the contract compensated the recipient not only for his services in those years, but for services rendered in earlier years during which he was underpaid. Therefore, the payments for 1954 through 1956 were not deductible as past compensation. Glasgow Village Dev. Corp., 36 TC 691 (1961), acq. 1962-2 CB 4.

Taxpayer could not recharacterize compensation as a nontaxable dividend. Taxpayer's wholly owned corporation deducted $34,000 it paid to taxpayer as compensation for his services. However, taxpayer reported only $24,000 as taxable income on its return. Taxpayer claimed the $10,000 balance constituted unreasonable compensation. Since the corporation had no current or accumulated earnings and profits, the balance resulted in taxpayer's nontaxable dividend. *Held:* For the IRS. The entire $34,000 was compensation to taxpayer and was deductible by the corporation. The IRS never raised the issue of reasonable compensation and taxpayer did not sustain his burden of proving that the compensation was unreasonable. Mosby, 47 TCM 1154, ¶ 89,090 P-H Memo. TC (1984).

Portion of executive salaries found to be excessive under Section 162. Substantially all the stock of a corporation was owned by three officers. In addition to salaries, the officers split 40 percent of the net profits before taxes between themselves as bonuses. No dividend was ever declared. The IRS assessed a deficiency and disallowed a portion of the salary deductions as excessive compensation. *Held:* For the IRS. A portion of the salaries was in effect distribution of earnings and profits equivalent to a dividend. Reppel Steel & Supply Co., 35 TCM 368, ¶ 76,086 P-H Memo. TC (1976).

Compensation disguised as dividends denied in part. Taxpayer corporation claimed a $155,000 salary deduction in 1970 for its president. The IRS allowed only a $70,000 deduction, claiming that the rest was unreasonable compensation. *Held:* For taxpayer, in part. Taxpayer was a family business that was later incorporated. The company prospered because of the president's connections. He was a major stockholder and paid no dividend until 1970. Part of the compensation was actually disguised dividends. The court thus determined that a salary of $120,000 was deductible by taxpayer. Way Eng'g Co., 34 TCM 210, ¶ 75,032 P-H Memo. TC (1975).

Lack of evidence as to 50 percent stockholder's duties rendered salary nondeductible dividends. Taxpayer corporation paid a relatively high salary to a 50 percent stockholder whose duties were undefined and limited. The IRS deemed the compensation to be a nondeductible constructive dividend and added a negligence penalty. *Held:* For the IRS. Taxpayer failed to prove that the salary was reasonable or that the stockholder actually performed services. Also, taxpayer did not disprove negligence. Ruth, 28 TCM 262, ¶ 69,047 P-H Memo. TC (1969).

Held Reasonable

Family trucking company paid reasonable compensation. Taxpayer was a family owned corporation founded by *L* and operated by *L* and his children. *L* and his children worked extremely long hours and were extremely dedicated and well qualified to perform their executive positions. *L* and his children each received a salary but no bonuses, and the compensation was not directly proportional to the percentage of stock they owned. The business was extremely successful and paid a high rate of return on invested capital in the years in question. The parties produced evidence showing that their salaries conformed with others in the industry. *Held:* For taxpayer. Compensation was found reasonable in light of the employee-stockholders' qualifications, experience, and the business' success. Trucks, Inc., 763 F2d 339, 85-2 USTC ¶ 9461, 56 AFTR2d 85-5209 (8th Cir. 1985).

Reasonable compensation determined. At the district court level, a jury determined that salaries totaling $1,143,041 over a two-year period paid to the general manager of two box manufacturing corporations completely controlled

Compensation for Personal Services: *Held Reasonable*

by his brother, in addition to a salary of $24,000 paid to him as manager of a partnership box manufacturing company, were reasonable and thus deductible by the corporate taxpayer as an operating expense. The IRS appealed, arguing that the trial court erred in not ordering a directed verdict or entering a judgment N.O.V. in its favor. *Held:* Reversed. The Fifth Circuit reversed the trial court and held the compensation payments to be unreasonably high because even though the employee worked long hours, there was no justification for the corporation's percentage of profits payment. The court also compared salaries of other executives in the same business. Miller Box, Inc., 488 F2d 695, 74-1 USTC ¶ 9195, 33 AFTR2d 74-602 (5th Cir.), cert. denied, 417 US 945 (1974).

Corporation's compensation deduction limited where amount determined to be unreasonable. Taxpayer corporation took a deduction for the $80,000 that it paid its president and major stockholder. The IRS disallowed $20,000 of the deduction. The Tax Court held for the IRS. *Held:* Affirmed. Since the corporation failed to show that the IRS' determination was not reasonable in light of the services rendered by the president, the deduction was limited to $60,000. Lakewood Mfg. Co., 453 F2d 451, 72-1 USTC ¶ 9157, 29 AFTR2d 72-341 (6th Cir. 1972).

Officer's compensation allowed as a deduction despite payment in proportion to stockholdings and a poor cash position. The IRS disallowed deductions for officers' salaries, contending that the amounts paid constituted constructive dividends. There was evidence that the bonuses paid bore the same ratio as stockholdings and that the corporation had a low cash position. The district court found for the taxpayer. *Held:* Affirmed. The appellate court upheld the lower court's holding that the amounts were reasonable and were not paid for any reason other than compensation. Safety Eng'g & Supply Co., 374 F2d 885, 67-1 USTC ¶ 9331, 19 AFTR2d 1028 (5th Cir. 1967).

Reasonable salaries of officer stockholders determined. A corporation in the excavation and concrete construction business paid each of its two executive officers and sole stockholders $31,250 for 1957, $24,500 for 1958, and $26,000 for 1959. The IRS determined that each was entitled to $13,000 per year as reasonable compensation and disallowed the remainder. *Held:* For taxpayer. Considering the evidence with respect to the duties, responsibilities, and activities of the officers, which clearly indicated that the success or failure of taxpayer's business depended almost entirely on the efforts and abilities of these two men, the court found that $24,500 each was reasonable compensation for the services rendered for 1957 and 1958 while $26,000 each was reasonable for 1959. Savko Bros., 338 F2d 956, 64-2 USTC ¶ 9851 (6th Cir. 1964).

IRS failed to rebut showing of reasonable compensation. Taxpayer, a resident of Texas, was the sole stockholder of a real estate corporation that owned and operated an apartment building in Kansas City, Mo. The corporation engaged a local real estate manager at an annual fee of $1,700 and employed a janitor at a salary of $1,700. Taxpayer made two trips to Kansas City during the year. She was paid an annual salary of $7,200. The evidence introduced by taxpayer showed that she had substantial business experience and made significant decisions on the modernization of the building, purchase of equipment, and other operating problems. The IRS introduced no evidence. *Held:* For taxpayer. The Tax Court's finding that the compensation was unreasonable was clearly erroneous. Taxpayer's evidence rebutted the presumption of correctness of the IRS' determination. Robert Louis Stevenson Apartments, Inc., 337 F2d 681, 64-2 USTC ¶ 9818 (8th Cir. 1964).

Reasonableness of salary affirmed by Tax Court. A corporation paid salaries to its officers (who were also stockholders and directors) on the basis of a fixed amount plus a percentage of the profits. The corporation had exceptional years in 1952 and 1953, resulting in large salaries to these officers. The Tax Court determined lower salaries as reasonable. *Held:* Affirmed. In failing to introduce any evidence of salaries to officers in similar companies, taxpayer corporation could not use the facts

Compensation for Personal Services: *Held Reasonable*

appearing in two prior decisions of the Tax Court because the court had no original jurisdiction and had no right to give original considerations to matters that were not urged upon the tribunal whose order was under review. Ernest, Holdeman & Collett, Inc., 290 F2d 3, 61-1 USTC ¶ 9398, 7 AFTR2d 1231 (7th Cir. 1961).

Compensation to principal stockholder and president found reasonable. The IRS contended that compensation paid to the principal stockholder and president of a close corporation was excessive. *Held:* For taxpayer. Although the remuneration was in excess of the usual amount for such a position, the stockholder, in his capacity as president of the corporation, was primarily responsible for the business' success and worked long hours. Furthermore, the salary arrangement was entered into prior to the corporation's profit-making years. Denison Poultry & Egg Co., 83-1 USTC ¶ 9360, 52 AFTR2d 83-5148 (ND Tex. 1982).

Court holds salary to president equal to 7 percent of gross sales reasonable, but disallows salary paid to institutionalized 89-year-old stroke victim. Taxpayer corporation was established by its president, who owned 60 percent of the outstanding stock. The remainder was owned by his brother and father in equal shares. In 1970 and 1971, taxpayer paid salaries to its president of $49,200 and $56,700, respectively. In addition, it contributed a total of $3,917 to his account in the company's profit-sharing plan for the two years. At the same time, his father, who had served as office manager until suffering a permanently disabling stroke in 1969, was paid $9,600 in salary for each of the two years. The IRS conducted an audit of taxpayer and concluded that the salaries paid to both men were unreasonable and nondeductible under Section 162(a)(1). *Held:* For taxpayer. Because taxpayer was a closely held family business, the payment of salary to its president equal to between six and seven percent of gross sales was not unreasonable. The evidence showed that he was the predominant force behind the development and success of the business and that the steady growth of his salary was consistent with that of the corporation as a whole. In the case of the father, however, the court reached a contrary result. An 89-year-old invalid confined to a nursing home by a paralyzing stroke cannot be said to provide services that would merit the level of salary paid to him. Consequently, the court held that his salary constituted an unreasonable and nondeductible salary. Quinn, 40 AFTR2d 77-5097, 77-1 USTC ¶ 9369 (D. Md. 1976).

Contributions to profits, volume of work, comparison to predecessor cited as grounds for finding salary reasonable. From 1970 through 1974, taxpayer corporation paid to its president annual compensation averaging approximately $106,000. The corporation was among the world's four largest manufacturers of hair coloring products, and had gross sales during the respective taxable years of $11.97 million, $9.04 million and $12.88 million. The IRS determined that the compensation was unreasonable and, therefore, nondeductible under Section 162. *Held:* For taxpayer. The district court rejected the IRS' contention that only half of the salary paid was reasonable on the grounds that the large volume of business, coupled with the president's direct contribution to corporate profits, demonstrated the reasonableness of his compensation. The court also noted that the salary was "not markedly out of line" with what was paid to his predecessor. Roux Laboratories, Inc., 76-2 USTC ¶ 9751, 38 AFTR2d 76-6051 (MD Fla. 1976).

Salaries, bonuses, and contributions to pensions reasonable compensation for business expense deduction. Taxpayer corporation claimed a business expense deduction for salaries, bonuses, and pension plan contributions to owner-employees. The IRS disallowed the deduction on the grounds that the total compensation was unreasonable. *Held:* For taxpayer. Salaries and bonuses were reasonable as compared with those of similar businesses in the area. The plan payments still resulted in sums that were reasonable compensation for the services performed. The court refused to rule that salaries and bonuses alone represented the maximum sums within a reasonable range. Edwin's, Inc., 77-1 USTC ¶ 9265, 39 AFTR2d 77-1161 (WD Wis. 1977).

Compensation for Personal Services: *Held Reasonable*

Salaries paid to stockholder-employees were reasonable. Taxpayer was a worker-owned plywood plant. During the years in question, the stockholder-employees were paid for work in the mill at the rate of $3.50 per hour. The actual amount was based on the number of hours worked. The union employees were paid pursuant to an industrywide collective bargaining agreement at a rate of less than $3.50 per hour. The IRS contended that the amounts paid to stockholder-employees were unreasonable and so disallowed portions of taxpayer's deduction for the salaries. *Held:* For taxpayer. The wages paid were reasonable for the quantity and quality of work rendered. This was logical because the stockholder-employees were more experienced and had less turnover than did the union employees. Additional benefits stemming from the employment of stockholder-employees included fewer foremen and an overall greater productivity. Multnomah Plywood Corp., 72-2 USTC ¶ 9677, 30 AFTR2d 72-5273 (D. Or. 1972).

Jury determined compensation reasonable. Taxpayer paid its president and sole stockholder a salary that the IRS contended was not reasonable and that represented, in part, a distribution of profits as a nondeductible dividend. *Held:* For taxpayer. Because the circumstances existing when the compensation was fixed indicated that the amount paid was reasonable, taxpayer could deduct the corresponding amount as an expense. Evidence considered by the jury in making its decision included the size, nature, and complexity of taxpayer's business, the quality and quantity of services rendered by the stockholder-employee, their skills and experience, the amount of time they worked, the success of the taxpayer's business, comparable salaries to such employees, whether the proportion of the salary paid to sales and the profits of the business was reasonable, and whether taxpayer was setting the salary to avoid taxes. Dietrich Mfg. Co., 72-1 USTC ¶ 9124, 24 AFTR2d 72-548 (SD Ill. 1971).

Jury determined reasonable compensation. Taxpayer corporation took deductions on its 1965, 1966, and 1967 federal income tax returns for salaries and other compensation paid to its president. The IRS disallowed the deductions in part and assessed deficiencies against taxpayer. Taxpayer paid the deficiencies and filed for a refund, which was denied. *Held:* For taxpayer, in part. Whether compensation paid to an employee is reasonable in a particular year is determined under the particular facts and circumstances of the year in question. Factors reviewed by the jury included the size and nature of the business, dividend history, whether the amount paid was set at a time when profits for the year were known, and whether the officer-employee or a member of his family owned a substantial stock interest in the taxpayer. Strickland Paper Co., 71-1 USTC ¶ 9105, 26 AFTR2d 70-5919 (ND Ala. 1970).

Salary plus 5 percent of gross rental income reasonable compensation to president of real estate corporation. Taxpayer, a real estate corporation, paid its president a salary of $200 a month plus 5 percent of its gross rental income. The IRS contended that the compensation paid the corporation's president was excessive. *Held:* For taxpayer. A salary of $200 a month plus 5 percent of gross rental income was reasonable compensation to the taxpayer's president. Bunton Inv. Co., 69-2 USTC ¶ 9645 (WD Ky. 1969).

Salary and pension fund contributions for two corporate officers were reasonable. The IRS claimed that the amount of salary and pension fund contributions for two corporate stockholder-officers was excessive and therefore disallowed a portion of the deduction. *Held:* For taxpayer. The jury found that the value of the services to the corporation was at least reasonably equal to the amounts paid as salary and pension fund contributions. Bellamy, 69-1 USTC ¶ 9284 (SD Fla. 1968).

Compensation paid to corporate officers reasonable under the circumstances. Taxpayer was engaged in the wood-working business. The IRS claimed that excessive compensation was paid to corporate officers. *Held:* For taxpayer. The compensation was reasonable considering the amount of the corporation's income derived from personal services as opposed to capital, the nature and amount of

Compensation for Personal Services: *Held Reasonable*

services performed, and a comparison with salaries paid by companies engaged in similar businesses. Modern Woodworking, Inc., 69-1 USTC ¶ 9256 (D. Colo. 1968).

Salary paid to secretary-treasurer, wife of corporate president, was reasonable. Taxpayer bore the last name of its president and his wife, taxpayer's secretary-treasurer. It paid the latter a salary of $12,500 and its president a salary approximately 50 percent more. The ratio of the husband's salary to that of his wife was approximately the same in the preceding year, although both salaries were smaller by approximately two thirds. In the current year, taxpayer's gross sales were $1.4 million; its net income after taxes was $18,500. The latter represented a 19 percent return on capital. Both husband and wife testified that the wife's salary was reasonable. The IRS disagreed, disallowing one-half as an ordinary and necessary business expense. *Held:* For taxpayer. The amount paid taxpayer's secretary-treasurer constituted a reasonable salary for her services. In earlier years, the salaries paid her and her husband were inadequate. Lohoefer, Inc., 68-1 USTC ¶ 9148 (ED Wash. 1967).

Salary of taxpayer's son-in-law held reasonable. Taxpayer's declining health led him to hire his son-in-law in 1949 to assist in the management of the family's school for retarded children and to place increasing reliance on him thereafter. As his son-in-law's duties and responsibilities increased, so did his salary, generally reflecting the increase in business profits. In the years 1959 through 1961, the son-in-law's salary was $400 a month plus 25 percent of the net profits before taxes. Taxpayer's son, who had joined the school as resident physician in 1956, was then receiving a like amount. The IRS contended the portion of the son-in-law's salary in excess of $12,000 annually was excessive compensation and not deductible. *Held:* For taxpayer. Taxpayer's determination to bring his son and son-in-law into the family business, in which continuity of management was so important, was a sound business decision. The increase in his son-in-law's salary in the years in issue was proportionate to the son-in-law's former compensation and consistent with taxpayer's policy of rewarding an employee in relationship to the success of the business and the increased responsibility of the employee. The compensation paid to the son-in-law did not exceed the fair and reasonable value of his services. Liberty Nat'l Bank & Trust Co., 67-1 USTC ¶ 9361, 19 AFTR2d 1164 (WD Ky. 1967).

Salary paid to widow who managed business was reasonable. The widow of the founder of taxpayer corporation assumed active management of the business shortly after her husband's death. The corporation manufactured chemicals that had dental applications. Her husband had been a dentist and she had assisted him in the formulation of the products and had been in charge of the administrative aspects of the business. His salary had been $27,000 to $37,000 a year. Her salary was set from about $18,000 to $25,000 each year. *Held:* For taxpayer. An analysis of the facts convinced the court that the salary was reasonable in relation to her responsibility and knowledge of the business. Num Specialty, Inc., 257 F. Supp. 1, 66-1 USTC ¶ 9454 (WD Pa. 1966).

Salary of president of pet food manufacturer held reasonable in light of services performed. Taxpayer, a manufacturer of pet foods, paid its president and 95-percent-stockholder $80,000 a year. Taxpayer's president, a consulting engineer, had personally developed taxpayer's very successful pet food line. He performed many valuable services for the taxpayer, including many not usually performed by most chief executives. Among other things, he personally set up procedures for taxpayers' purchases, managed its fleet of trucks, directed its advertising program, and supervised its plant maintenance. Taxpayer's sales exceeded the combined sales of all its competitors. It gross income for 1956 through 1958 averaged about $9.5 million, and its profits were about average for the industry. The IRS disallowed $40,000 of the $80,000 paid to the president for these years. *Held:* For taxpayer. The compensation was reasonable in comparison to all of the services performed. The success of taxpayer, in comparison with other comparable companies, was indicative of excellent management, and was regarded by management

Compensation for Personal Services: *Held Reasonable*

consultants as a strong indicator of proper compensation for taxpayer's president. Lewis Food Co., 64-1 USTC ¶ 9386 (SD Cal. 1964).

Jury finds compensation reasonable. Taxpayer, a closely held corporation, paid its officer-stockholders salaries plus bonuses. The bonuses to the three stockholders were in the same proportion as their respective percentages of stockholdings. The IRS disallowed the deduction of the compensation by taxpayer, in part, as unreasonable. *Held:* For taxpayer. A jury found the compensation reasonable. It was instructed to consider the nature of the services rendered, the time devoted by the stockholder-employees, the qualifications and previous experience of the parties, taxpayer's dividend history, salaries of comparable jobs in other corporations, and whether taxpayer recognized and rewarded its employees' sacrifices that had been made in the hard, formative years of the corporate existence by granting more generous compensation when earnings were better. Patten Seed Co., 63-1 USTC ¶ 9491, 11 AFTR2d 1585 (MD Ga. 1963).

Compensation of officers of training school reasonable. A family that operated business schools acquired the assets of a school for the training of airline employees. The family organized a corporation and hired an outsider to run the school. The outsider's contract provided for a commission on all receipts and the right to purchase 50 percent of the stock. He and a member of the family worked full time on the business, and it prospered through their efforts. The compensation of each exceeded $90,000 in some years, based on the commission rate originally agreed upon. *Held:* For taxpayer. The court held that the compensation basis was arrived at by arm's-length bargaining and that the resulting compensation was reasonable. Weaver Airline Personnel School, Inc., 218 F. Supp. 599, 63-1 USTC ¶ 9488 (WD Mo. 1963).

Jury determines reasonable salary for corporate officers. Taxpayer, a closely held corporation, paid certain amounts as salaries to its managing officer-stockholders. The IRS determined the amounts to be unreasonable and disallowed their deduction, in part. *Held:* For taxpayer. The jury found the salaries to be reasonable where it was instructed to examine the quality and quantity of services rendered, the amount of time devoted by the employees to their work, the professional and business qualifications of employees, the profits earned by the business, the salaries for employees of like businesses, the relationship of payments to stockholdings, the corporate dividend history, the general economic conditions of the industry, and the amount of compensation paid. Childers & Venters Motors, Inc., 62-2 USTC ¶ 9825, 11 AFTR2d 731 (ED Ky. 1962).

Officers' salaries were reasonable. M and S each owned 50 percent of the taxpayer corporation and served as president and vice-president-treasurer, respectively. Each received $9,600 per year for their corporate services. The IRS disallowed $4,600 of the deduction claimed for each by taxpayer as unreasonable. *Held:* For taxpayer. The officers were responsible for the success of the business, had superior qualifications, and devoted substantial time to the business; thus, the compensation was found to be reasonable. Although dividends had not been paid, the court found no attempt to evade taxes; instead, it found a justifiable need to build up assets for expected growth and an informal agreement with a mortgagee to pay off a loan before dividends were distributed. Capitol Market, Ltd., 207 F. Supp. 376, 62-2 USTC ¶ 9678, 10 AFTR2d 5388 (D. Hawaii 1962).

Salary of corporation's prime mover and manager held reasonable. Taxpayer, a closely held corporation, paid S a yearly salary of $9,000 for services rendered as president, including originating of taxpayer's motel business venture, executive management of that phase of taxpayer's business, and sole management of an extensive portfolio of securities. The services performed required a high degree of executive and managerial ability and S's special knowledge and experience. S's salary was established by minority stockholders and was not demanded by him. The IRS determined the salary to be unreasonable and disallowed taxpayer's deductions in part. *Held:* For taxpayer. Taxpayer was entitled to deduct S's entire salary as an ordinary and necessary ex-

Compensation for Personal Services: *Held Reasonable*

pense incurred in carrying on business, as the salary was a reasonable and necessary expense for services actually rendered by *S* to taxpayer. Rawlins Bucking House Lodge, 62-1 USTC ¶ 9459, 9 AFTR2d 1467 (D. Wyo. 1962).

Officers' salaries redetermined in proportion to gross earnings of taxpayer. Taxpayer paid $7,200 to its president and $13,600 to its secretary-treasurer in 1956. Both officers were the taxpayer's sole stockholders. The president was an experienced attorney who, for 10 months, worked full time, and frequently overtime, on taxpayer's business. The secretary-treasurer worked full time throughout the year. Both officers were experienced individuals whose services were apparently beneficial to taxpayer. *Held:* The court found that the salaries increased from 1955 to 1956 proportionately more than the taxpayer's gross earnings. Accordingly, the reasonable salary of the president was determined to be $4,500 and that of the secretary-treasurer to be $11,000. J.E. Craig Fin. Co., 200 F. Supp. 554, 62-1 USTC ¶ 9275 (WDSC 1962).

Salary paid to executive's wife for social duties sustained as ordinary and necessary business expense. Taxpayer owned and operated a horse farm as a subsidiary business. It paid $2,500 as an annual salary in 1954 to the president's wife for services rendered in contacts with an entertainment of prospective purchasers of race horses. Taxpayer took the position that it benefited from these services, which were over and above what might be expected from the wife of an executive in a business organization. *Held:* For taxpayer. The court held the salary payments to be reasonable and deductible as ordinary and necessary business expenses. Journal Box Servicing Corp., 62-1 USTC ¶ 9258 (SD Ind. 1962).

Compensation of officers for personal services found reasonable. The IRS determined that the compensation paid to the three principal officers of X Corporation for personal services was excessive and disallowed a portion of their salaries. *Held:* For taxpayer. The jury found that the compensation paid to each of the three officers was reasonable in light of the court's instruction that the jury could consider (1) the experience, training, and other qualifications of each officer and his business acumen; (2) the kind and extent of services rendered by each, including the difficulties, if any, the work load, and responsibilities assumed; (3) the results produced by the efforts of each of the officers and their contributions to the business enterprise from its inception in 1937 through 1955; (4) the relative size of the business and its ratio of earnings to sales, officers' salaries, and total assets in previous years and during the two years in question; (5) the general economic and business conditions, including competitive conditions, that existed in 1954 and 1955 and the years in which the company was doing business; (6) the stock holdings of the executive officers in question and the amounts paid to them as salaries and bonuses in the years in question and in prior years; (7) the amount of surplus accumulations in 1954 and 1955 as compared with the surplus accumulations in prior years; (8) the policies of the corporation concerning payment of dividends and the circumstances under which such policies were determined; and (9) the evidence, if any, as to salaries customarily paid by like companies under comparable circumstances. Miller Chem. Corp., 60-2 USTC ¶ 9766 (ND W. Va. 1960).

Jury finds salaries of printing/publishing stockholders reasonable. Taxpayer corporation, engaged in the newspaper, printing, and publishing business, paid to its three principal stockholders salaries of $40,000 each. The IRS contended that reasonable salaries for the three men would have been $30,000, $20,000, and $20,000, respectively. *Held:* For taxpayer. The jury found that $40,000 paid to each of the three men was reasonable compensation for their respective services during 1955. Natrona County Tribune, 60-2 USTC ¶ 9620 (D. Wyo. 1960).

Sound business judgment and direct responsibility for profits held to justify executive's compensation. The taxpayer corporation was directed by the same individual who also served as president, board chairman, and in other capacities. Later, his son entered the business, and together they operated the company for 30 years without employing other executive

COMPENSATION FOR PERSONAL SERVICES: *Held Reasonable*

personnel. From 1963 through 1966, the board of directors determined that the father would receive compensation of $1,000 per week, plus 20 percent of net profits, and the son would receive $700 per week and 20 percent of profits. Their combined salaries for the taxable years at issue ranged from $187,801 to $213,500. The IRS, on audit, determined that such salaries were unreasonable and denied the corresponding deductions claimed by taxpayer corporation. *Held*: For taxpayer. After a thorough review of the facts and applicable law, the court concluded that the compensation paid was "reasonable" within the meaning of Section 162(a)(1). The court noted that taxpayer enjoyed a level of profitability that was considerably higher than that of similar businesses and that its performance was largely due to the skill of the father and son in submitting competitive bids for government printing work. They wisely chose to concentrate the company's business on specialty printing, and they were particularly adept at keeping overhead and production costs low. Because they were directly and jointly responsible for the high rate of profit, the court was constrained to hold that the IRS disallowance was unjustified. Federal Lithograph Co., 37 AFTR2d 76-997, 76-1 USTC ¶ 9281 (Ct. Cl. 1976).

Court of claims allows salaries that taxpayer claimed. Taxpayer's president, who, with his wife, owned all of taxpayer's stock, received a salary and bonus of $40,000 in 1954 and $50,000 in 1955. The IRS reduced these to $18,000 for each year, and the trial commissioner appointed by the court of claims found the reasonable salary to be $35,000. *Held*: For taxpayer. The court allowed the full amount claimed. It stressed the taxpayer's honesty, the fact that he knew his business better than anyone else, the growth of the company under his direction, the fact that his salesmen got up to $24,000, and the testimony of a banker and businessmen. Cordy Tire Co., 296 F2d 476, 62-1 USTC ¶ 9119, 8 AFTR2d 5876 (Ct. Cl. 1961).

Reasonableness of officers' compensation upheld. During the years 1971 through 1975, individual taxpayers *X*, *Y*, and *Z* received very substantial compensation from the corporate taxpayer, consisting of salaries, bonuses, and commissions, based on a percentage of the corporation's sales. In some years, compensation was over $1 million. *X* and *Y*, who were related, owned actually and constructively more than 50 percent of the stock of the corporation. *Z*, unrelated, owned a negligible amount of stock. During the years 1971 through 1975, the corporation's sales and profits increased substantially and the corporation paid high dividends. The IRS determined that the salaries were excessive and reduced the deduction the corporation could claim for salaries paid during 1971 through 1975. *Held*: For taxpayers. The compensation was reasonable, despite the fact that it was abnormally high, and it was justified by the value of the services provided. Home Interiors & Gifts, Inc., 73 TC 1142 (1980).

Officer's compensation reasonable. Taxpayer's stock was owned entirely by *L* and his family. L, the president and chairman of the board, was responsible for credit, collection, written credit and financial policies, and warehouse operations. *L* attended weekly staff meetings and performed other duties. The corporation paid *L* $59,000, $63,000, and $64,000 during three years, pursuant to an agreement whereby he was to receive an annual salary of $55,000 or the amount paid to his son, whichever was greater. The IRS disallowed his compensation to the extent it exceeded $27,000 in each year. *Held*: For taxpayer. *L* had 50 years experience in the business, the credit and collection function accounted for 40 percent of the total corporate operation, and *L* was excluded from the pension plan and other corporate benefit plans. The court further held that rent paid by the company on one of its stores was an ordinary and necessary business expense, and held legal and professional expenses deductible. Levenson Klein, Inc., 67 TC 694 (1977).

Compensation from seven corporations reasonable. Taxpayer controlled seven corporations engaged in similar business activities. All the corporations received income in the form of commissions. From 1956 through 1959 taxpayer received total salaries of $91,375, $100,000, $105,400, and $78,400 from the seven corporations. Limiting taxpayers's total

Compensation for Personal Services: *Held Reasonable*

compensation to $75,000, the IRS allocated this figure among the corporations in proportion to commissions received. *Held*: For taxpayer. The salaries were reasonable, since taxpayer was personally responsible for the success of the corporations. In the years under consideration, sales increased substantially as a result of taxpayer's efforts. V.H. Monette & Co., 45 TC 15 (1965).

Salary to majority stockholder reasonable in light of services and expertise. The IRS argued that the salary taxpayer corporation paid to its majority stockholder was not reasonable. *Held:* For taxpayer. The employee brought with her 25 years of solid business experience, she performed extensive services, and she was responsible for the financial success of the corporation. A comparison of salaries paid with gross and net incomes shows that the salary was not set to drain off taxpayer's profits to avoid tax. Medina, 46 TCM 76, ¶ 83,253 P-H Memo. TC (1983).

Reasonable compensation determined. Amounts paid by a corporation to its vice-president were considered excessive by the IRS. The excess was determined not to constitute earned income for purposes of Section 1348. *Held*: For taxpayer, in part. The court determined that compensation was greater than that allowed by the IRS based on traditional indicia of reasonableness, not from the conflicting expert testimonies of both parties. Walsh, 42 TCM 267, ¶ 81,336 P-H Memo. TC (1981).

Salaries to stockholder employees reasonable. Taxpayer, a closely held corporation engaged in the sale of insurance, claimed business expense deductions for salaries paid to its two 50 percent stockholders who were also its principal employees. The IRS challenged these deductions in part as either unreasonable compensation or disguised distribution of profits. *Held*: For taxpayer. The employees were directly responsible for generating taxpayer's income and ensuring its profitability. Thus, compensation was reasonable. Old Colony Ins. Serv., Inc., 41 TCM 1258, ¶ 81,177 P-H Memo. TC (1981).

Compensation determined to be reasonable in light of stockholder's contribution to company. Taxpayer corporation deducted amounts paid as compensation for services to its sole stockholder and president. The IRS argued that the amounts were unreasonable because the employee was away in Florida for lengthy periods. *Held*: For taxpayer. Despite the trips and an absence of dividend declarations, the salary was reasonable in light of the employee's experience and contributions to the company. Shotmeyer, 40 TCM 589, ¶ 80,282 P-H Memo. TC (1980).

Salaries to stockholders reasonable. A corporation deducted the compensation paid to three stockholder employees who were compensated on the basis of a salary plus a percentage of profits. The IRS disallowed part of the payments. *Held*: For taxpayer. The compensation was reasonable for services actually rendered. Lundy Packing Co., 39 TCM 541, ¶ 79,472 P-H Memo. TC (1979).

Professional corporation paid architect stockholder reasonable salary. The IRS charged that the professional corporation wholly owned by a prominent architect paid him an unreasonable salary. *Held*: For taxpayer. The ratio of salary to gross income for the years involved differed little from that of earlier years. It was not clear that a hypothetical outside investor would have demanded a dividend. Eduardo Catalano Inc., 38 TCM 763, ¶ 79,183 P-H Memo. TC (1979).

Reasonable salaries for husband and wife determined. The IRS ruled that part of the salaries paid to a husband and wife who owned all the stock of a food freezing corporation was unreasonable and so not deductible. *Held*: For taxpayer, in part. The husband's salary for one year was fully reasonable, but part of the salary for another year in issue was unreasonable. His wife's salary in both years was too high, but the disallowed amount was smaller than the IRS contended. Rich Plan of N. New England, Inc., 37 TCM 1853-8, ¶ 78,514 P-H Memo. TC (1978).

Part of stockholder president's compensation unreasonable. Taxpayer paid its president and

Compensation for Personal Services: Held Reasonable

sole stockholder $330,000 in salary and bonuses over two years. The IRS considered all but $100,080 of it to be unreasonable compensation. *Held*: For the taxpayer, in part. The court allowed a deduction of $230,000. Although the president performed unique and valuable services his compensation was unreasonable compared with that of other employees. Ken Miller Supply, Inc., ¶ 78,228 P-H Memo. TC (1978).

Reasonableness of salary upheld. Amount of compensation paid to taxpayer's founder and chief executive officer was found reasonable in amount in view of the executive's contribution to the growth of taxpayer. *Held*: For taxpayer. The business expense deduction was allowed. Ledford, 36 TCM 858, ¶ 77,204 P-H Memo. TC (1977).

Officer's salary not deductible. Taxpayer was a part-time vice-president of a corporation that was almost wholly owned by her husband. Taxpayer's husband exchanged oil and gas leases for cancellation of indebtedness with the corporation. The IRS determined that the taxpayer's salary was excessive and that the value of the oil and gas leases was insufficient for cancellation of the indebtedness. *Held*: Taxpayer, in part. Taxpayer was overpaid as vice-president. She was paid twice the salary of the full-time vice-president. The excess of her salary over the reasonable value of her services was nondeductible to the corporation. The IRS erred in its determination of the value of the oil and gas leases. Oil companies offered to purchase those leases at an amount very close to the value claimed by the taxpayer about the time of the transfer to the corporation. Graham, 35 TCM 1315, ¶ 76,295 P-H Memo. TC (1976).

Compensation to officer upheld where financial skills were key to success in "erratic business climate." Taxpayer was a Texas corporation engaged in the wholesale grocery business along the Mexican border. From 1967 through 1970, the corporation paid total compensation of $123,900 to Dipp, who served as its secretary-treasurer and owned 57.8 percent of the outstanding stock. The IRS, on audit, determined that the salary and bonus payments were unreasonable and that not more than $10,000 for each of the four taxable years was allowable. *Held:* For taxpayer. The evidence presented to the Tax Court showed that Dipp was "a man of substantial financial means with over 40 years of experience in the grocery business." He functioned as the company's chief executive officer with authority over all financial matters. His primary contribution was the daily management of short-term financing that enabled the corporation to maximize the utility of its available cash and also buy goods at full discount. The court found that Dipp's "hard work and constant vigilance" were "clearly responsible" for taxpayer's success in the "erratic business climate" in Mexico. Accordingly, the claimed deductions were permitted in full. Economy Cash & Carry, Inc., 35 TCM 1253, ¶ 76,280 P-H Memo. TC (1976).

Contingent compensation plan payments employee-stockholder were reasonable. Taxpayer corporation deducted payments made to an employee-stockholder paid under a contingent compensation plan. The IRS disallowed this deduction. *Held:* For taxpayer. The amounts paid were justified by the services received by the corporation and were directly related to operational success. Central Freight Lines, Inc., 35 TCM 85, ¶ 76,025 P-H Memo. TC (1976).

Reasonableness of compensation determined. The IRS disallowed taxpayer corporation's deduction for a part of the salary paid to its chief executive officer (the majority stockholder) as excessive compensation. *Held:* For taxpayer. The IRS' expert witness was not familiar with the wall-covering industry or the officer's ability. The salaries of chief officers of other less successful companies were not comparable. Finally, the officer had much experience and ability, and devoted a great deal of time to all aspects of the business. His contingent salary portion was based on a long-standing company policy and was negotiated at arm's length with an independent board of directors. Therefore, the compensation was reasonable, and the court upheld the deduction. Albert Van Luit Co., 34 TCM 321, ¶ 75,056 P-H Memo. TC (1975).

Compensation for Personal Services: *Held Reasonable*

Salary held reasonable and deductible in major part due to owner's effort and experience. Taxpayer corporation operated an auto agency and claimed deductions for compensation paid to the agency's sole owner and an officer. The IRS claimed that a part of the payments represented unreasonable compensation. *Held:* For taxpayer, in major part. The success of the agency was due mainly to the efforts of the owner who had a great deal of experience in the car selling business. It was also the general practice of this type of business to pay owners in the form of compensation and salary. Taxpayer paid the owner some $110,000 in 1969 and $140,000 in 1970. The IRS disallowed deductions for payments in excess of $78,000 in 1969 and $90,000 in 1970. Based on all the evidence, it was determined that the salaries were reasonable and deductible to the extent of $89,000 in 1969 and $117,000 in 1970. Superior Motors Inc., 33 TCM 805, ¶ 74,187 P-H Memo. TC (1974).

Compensation deemed reasonable as commissions did not represent compensation paid by taxpayer and salaries were not excessive. An individual who was a buyer and seller of tools, as well as a sales representative for tool manufacturers, established taxpayer corporation, which then took over the tool buying and selling business. Taxpayer's gross recorded sales included its tool sales and the individual's commissions from sales. The IRS determined that the payments of the commissions to the individual in the amount of about $33,000, and the payment of salaries which amounted to about $45,000, constituted unreasonable compensation. *Held:* For taxpayer. Regardless of what the books showed, taxpayer could still show the true facts. Taxpayer never received an assignment of the sales agency contracts; taxpayer also was a conduit for the individual's commission income. Thus, the commissions did not represent compensation paid by taxpayer. Furthermore, the salaries were reasonable in light of the hard work performed by the employee. He devoted a great deal of time and energy to the company, and as a result the company grew rapidly. Plimpton Tool Co., 31 TCM 612, ¶ 72,134 P-H Memo. TC (1972).

President's salary deemed reasonable due to his skill and effort. The IRS claimed that the salaries paid to the president and sole owner of an automobile agency were unreasonable. *Held:* For taxpayer. Before the president took over, the profits and sales were poor. He spent 70 hours a week correcting procedures. The agency then began showing a good profit as gross sales doubled. Such increase resulted from his managerial abilities and advertising, promotional, and organizational skills. The salaries paid were reasonable and were deductible by the corporation. Skyland Oldsmobile, Inc., 31 TCM 47, ¶ 72,017 P-H Memo. TC (1972).

Compensation deemed reasonable due to comparative compensation of other franchise owner-managers. Taxpayer corporation's franchise restaurants paid salary and bonuses to their sole stockholder owner-managers and deducted the amounts as compensation. The IRS disallowed part of the deduction. *Held:* For taxpayer. Based on taxpayer's evidence and the evidence of an expert witness who testified with respect to compensation paid to other franchise owner-managers, it was determined that the compensation paid was reasonable and that the corporation was entitled to business expense deductions for such amounts. Ehrlich, 30 TCM 317, ¶ 71,076 P-H Memo. TC (1971).

Corporation allowed deductions for officer's salaries, which were proved reasonable based on the value of their work. Taxpayer corporation took deductions for salaries paid to its officers. The IRS reduced the amount of deductions allowed to two of the officers, claiming that they were unreasonable. *Held:* For taxpayer, in part. The salaries of these officers were reasonable in light of their lengthy service, their valuable technical know-how, their customer contacts, and their full working efforts for the business. One salary deduction was allowed in full and another was partially reduced, although the amount was still greater than the IRS' allowance. Hammond Lead Prods. Inc., 28 TCM 54, ¶ 69,014 P-H Memo. TC (1969).

COMPENSATION FOR PERSONAL SERVICES: *Held Reasonable*

Reasonableness of compensation determined for family members who rendered part-time services for corporation. Taxpayer corporation carried on a wholesale meat business that formerly had been conducted as a partnership. The widow of one partner had been receiving $75 a week from the partnership profits under a trust created by her late husband. When the widow remarried, the trust was terminated, and the successor corporation, now owned by her sons-in-law, paid her a salary of $75 a week and later $100 a week. The IRS disallowed the corporate deduction for her salary as unreasonable and also disallowed a salary deduction of $175 a week paid to the daughter of the majority stockholder. *Held:* For taxpayer, in part. The two individuals performed some services for which they could reasonably be compensated. The court applied the *Cohan* rule and found that $25 a week was reasonable compensation for the former widow, and $35 a week was reasonable for the majority stockholder's daughter. Irving Levitt Co., 27 TCM 551, ¶ 68,115 P-H Memo. TC (1968).

Annual payment of over $289,000 to chief executive officer who was also an inventor deemed reasonable compensation. Taxpayer's chief executive officer and major stockholder was also an inventor of great ability. He obtained numerous valuable patents, some of which covered the most profitable products manufactured by taxpayer. He was paid $289,800 in 1956 and $261,800 in 1958. The IRS disallowed payments in excess of $100,000 as unreasonable compensation. *Held:* For taxpayer. Although a salary of $100,000 would have been adequate compensation for his executive and administrative duties, the officer's greatest service to taxpayer was as an inventor. The officer's salary was justified if a comparison was made between his salary and a reasonable projected royalty payment for his inventions. His services to taxpayer as an inventor were invaluable. Appleton Elec. Co., 26 TCM 1043, ¶ 67,211 P-H Memo. TC (1967).

Compensation of auto agency president found reasonable on basis of successful operation. Taxpayer was president and sole stockholder of an auto agency. In 1961 and 1962 he withdrew $49,000 and $75,000 respectively as his annual compensation. For 1960 his compensation had been fixed at $24,000. The IRS determined that all amounts paid in excess of $25,000 in 1961 and 1962 were unreasonable and nondeductible. *Held:* For taxpayer. His tireless efforts on behalf of the agency were primarily responsible for the success of the business, whose progress and success exceeded considerably that of any other agency in his area. Taxpayer's salary per car sold was lower than the average salaries per car sold paid to other owners of similar agencies, and the net profits per car sold were higher than the average for the area. However, the court held that the 1962 salary of $75,000 was excessive to the extent of $15,000. This was based on the fact that the percentage of taxpayer's compensation to gross sales and net profits increased in 1962 over prior years, despite the fact that he did not appear to have rendered any more valuable services. Van's Chevrolet, Inc., 26 TCM 809, ¶ 67,172 P-H Memo. TC (1967).

Compensation paid to officer-stockholders on basis of a profit-sharing plan deemed reasonable. Two individuals, each a specialist in his field, acquired the assets of a bankrupt corporation and formed a new corporation for the purpose of operating a plastic manufacturing business. The corporation paid each of the two officer-stockholders salaries of $36,000, plus 25 percent of the net profits. This resulted in total salaries of $84,700 each in 1953 and $58,200 each in 1954. The IRS disallowed the salaries in excess of $36,000 each as unreasonable. *Held:* For taxpayer. The business was very large and complex, and the expertise of the officers was highly valued; the salaries were based on an arm's-length profit-sharing arrangement and thus were not unreasonable. Smith, 24 TCM 899, ¶ 65,169 P-H Memo. TC (1965).

Compensation paid officers of family corporation deemed reasonable. Taxpayer, a motor freight corporation, paid its executive vice-president and its secretary-treasurer, sons of the founder, $22,000 each in 1959 and $23,500 each in 1960. The IRS disallowed $4,000 for each in the first year, and $5,000 for each in the second. Both employees had extensive ed-

Compensation for Personal Services: *Held Reasonable*

ucational and business experience in the freight field. *Held:* For taxpayer. Based on expert testimony supported by the record, the compensation for both years was fair and reasonable. Ward Trucking Corp., 24 TCM 217, ¶ 65,040 P-H Memo. TC (1965).

Five officers' salaries deemed reasonable due to their qualifications, their scope of duties, their time commitments, and the relationship of compensation to sales. Taxpayer paid its five officer-stockholders salaries ranging from $33,000 to $69,000 in one year, and from $30,000 to $60,000 in the second year. The IRS determined that the salaries were unreasonable. *Held:* For taxpayer. The compensation for all five officers was reasonable. In reaching its decision, the court considered the qualifications of the officers, the nature and scope of their duties, the amount of time they devoted to the business, and the relation of the compensation to the corporation's sales, income, profits, invested capital, and dividends. Griswold Rubber Co., 24 TCM 184, ¶ 65,033 P-H Memo. TC (1965).

Commissions paid to a related sales corporation were reasonable. Taxpayer and Sterno Sales Corp. were wholly owned subsidiaries of Sterno Corp., a holding company. Taxpayer was engaged in the business of marketing and distributing Sterno canned heat and related products. Sterno Sales was incorporated to limit multiple state problems, as well as to limit legal liability in connection with salesmen traveling in cars. Incorporation also took place to departmentalize and dissociate sales activities from taxpayer's general operations. Sterno Sales acted as taxpayer's sales representative and charged taxpayer a commission of 1.5 percent of sales plus reimbursement for all operating expenses. The IRS contended that the commissions were unreasonable. *Held:* For taxpayer. The commissions constituted reasonable compensation for services rendered, based on the evidence as to what unrelated sales representatives charge. A prior Tax Court decision (decided on the basis of the burden of proof) that held that commissions payable for a prior year were excessive to the extent of Sterno Sales' net income for that year did not constitute validation of the IRS' method. Sterno, Inc., 24 TCM 94, ¶ 65,023 P-H Memo. TC (1965).

Salaries paid to officers of real estate corporation partly disallowed due to minimal services performed. Taxpayer corporation owned two parcels of improved real property, one of which was occupied by corporations controlled by a common stockholder. Taxpayer's three officers, all related, were its sole stockholders and employees. They drew salaries aggregating $9,400 for the taxable year. The IRS argued that the salaries were unreasonable. *Held:* For taxpayer, in part. The salary of $5,200 paid to the corporate president was reasonable. In addition to routine administrative work, he also conducted special negotiations and investigations. A salary of $1,800 paid to his wife who served primarily as his administrative assistant was also upheld as reasonable. But an annual salary of $2,400 paid to the vice-president was found excessive to the extent of $1,800, based on the fact that the services performed were minimal. Seven Canal Place Corp., 23 TCM 1643, ¶ 64,270 P-H Memo. TC (1964).

Salary of $12,000 allowed to wife of taxpayer's president. The stock of taxpayer was owned by its president, the president's wife, and a third party. The wife was instrumental in the affairs of the corporation and participated in policy decisions, and financial, promotional, and personnel work. She worked over 100 hours per month. Before her marriage, she had held various supervisory positions in a department store. The IRS allowed only $600 of a $12,000 salary paid to her. *Held:* For taxpayer. The full salary was reasonable. The wife's services exceeded the usual endeavors of the so-called "good wife." Scott Krauss News Agency, Inc., 23 TCM 1007, ¶ 64,171 P-H Memo. TC (1964).

Salaries to father and son paid for 10 years and never geared to income or profits deemed fully deductible. A closely held corporation paid annual salaries of $11,000 and $9,000 to two officer-stockholders who were father and son. The IRS determined that a reasonable salary was $3,000 to each. *Held:* For taxpayer. The same salaries had been paid for 10 years and

Compensation for Personal Services: *Held Unreasonable*

had never been geared to income or profits. Although the number of hours the officers worked was not known, their activities were corroborated by evidence of valuable sales activities and capable managerial services. Failure to pay dividends was due to the fact that capital was being accumulated to build a plant. Pennsylvania Containers, Inc., 22 TCM 1235, ¶ 63,246 P-H Memo. TC (1963).

Compensation of $162,000 for two corporate executives allowed in full without reduction. Taxpayer's business was the designing, styling, manufacturing under contract, and selling of women's dresses. It sold during the taxable year one general price line of cotton dresses, i.e., $45 per dozen, and sold about one million such dresses in the taxable year. Taxpayer claimed a total deduction of $163,000 for compensation of its two executives. The IRS disallowed $38,000, the excess paid in the taxable year over the amount paid the same two men in the prior year, as unreasonable compensation. *Held:* For taxpayer. The court found that the services of the executives in the success of their business, in which fixed assets played such a minor part, justified the payment to them of the large part of the gross income that those services produced, and the IRS erred in disallowing the deduction of a part of the compensation paid to them. Gladstone-Arcuni, Inc., 21 TCM 1016, ¶ 62,185 P-H Memo. TC (1962).

President's compensation, based on prior arm's-length agreement, deemed reasonable. Taxpayer corporation was engaged in the warehouse steel business. Salary payments to its president, a 50 percent stockholder, pursuant to an earlier agreement, amounted to $131,000 and $115,000 for fiscal years ending in 1956 and 1957 and represented 20 percent of the taxpayer's net profits before taxes. The IRS disallowed as unreasonable 50 percent of such salaries. *Held:* For taxpayer. The court concluded that while the amount of compensation was large, it was paid in accordance with an agreement entered into prior to the years in controversy and in arm's-length negotiations. Accordingly, it constituted reasonable compensation. Nothing in the evidence indicated that the rate of compensation was fixed with an eye to the distribution of earnings, and it appeared that by any test the president's contribution to taxpayer's success was unquestionable. Ziegler Steel Serv. Corp., 21 TCM 311, ¶ 62,057 P-H Memo. TC (1962).

Compensation to officer-stockholder considered reasonable because of unique services provided. Taxpayer was engaged in photofinishing. E, who owned 99 percent of taxpayer's stock, had for many years served taxpayer in numerous capacities and functions. Taxpayer's success was attributable to E's innovations and inventions. The IRS determined E's compensation to be unreasonable. *Held:* For Taxpayer. A salary, including a bonus, is not unreasonable when the employee-stockholder's services throughout taxpayer's history are unique and when his functions are more numerous and varied than those of other executives in the industry. Fotocrafters, Inc., 19 TCM 1401, ¶ 60,254 P-H Memo. TC (1960).

Officers responsible for corporation's success were paid reasonable salary. O and T each held approximately 43 percent of taxpayer's stock, either personally or jointly with others. O was president; I was vice-president; T was secretary; and the three were directors of taxpayer. In the early years their salaries were low or nonexistent, but later O received a substantial salary plus contributions to a pension and profit-sharing plan, and his wife T received a similar, although lower, compensation package. The IRS determined O's and I's compensation to be unreasonable and disallowed the deduction in part. *Held:* For taxpayer, in part. The record disclosed that the corporation's growth and success were a direct result of the stockholder-employee's business talents and acumen, and that the corporation had a history of paying dividends. The compensation was, therefore, held to be reasonable. Bardahl Mfg. Corp., 19 TCM 1245, ¶ 60,223 P-H Memo. TC (1960).

Held Unreasonable

Reasonableness of incentive compensation agreement judged by circumstances when agreement was made. The Tax Court held that a portion of the compensation paid to taxpay-

Compensation for Personal Services: *Held Unreasonable*

er by his corporate employer in 1973 and 1974, pursuant to a 1950 incentive compensation agreement, was unreasonable. Taxpayer's father owned the bulk of the corporate stock. Furthermore, such disallowed compensation did not qualify as earned income for the maximum tax. *Held:* Reversed. Regulation § 1.162-7(b)(2) states that an incentive compensation agreement is to be judged by the facts existing at the time the agreement was made, not at the time it is questioned. In this case, the agreement was fair when entered into. Since taxpayer became general manager, corporate income increased nearly elevenfold. Furthermore, taxpayer's compensation was more reasonable due to the absence of such fringe benefits as pension plans and stock options. As the entire amount of compensation was reasonable, it followed that it was all subject to maximum tax treatment. Kennedy, Jr., 671 F2d 167, 49 AFTR2d 82-628 (6th Cir. 1982).

Salaries were unreasonable based on the amounts that the competitor paid. Taxpayer was a wholesale distributor of appliances and floor coverings and also carried products from certain major manufacturers. All of the company stock was owned by three individuals. On its tax return, the company deducted certain amounts of compensation to its employees, which the IRS determined were unreasonable in part. The district court reviewed all the facts surrounding the bonuses that were paid to the major stockholders and found that they represented nearly one-half of the company's net income before taxes and compensation to the officers. The district court concluded that the bonus payments of 68 percent of the pretax income in excess of $250,000 to the two men that owned 79 percent of the outstanding stock of the company were more characteristic of dividends than of compensation for services and that the IRS's determination had not been overcome. *Held:* Affirmed. When a taxpayer fails to establish the reasonableness of compensation paid to an employee by a preponderance of the evidence, it has failed to meet its burden of proof. Citing Patton, 168 F2d 28 (6th Cir. 1948), the court noted that the reasonableness of an employee's compensation is determined according to (1) the nature of the services performed and the responsibilities they entail. (2) the amounts of compensation paid in proportion to the net profits, (3) comparison of salaries paid with the distributions to stockholders, and (4) the compensation paid to similar employees by similar concerns engaged in similar industries. Knodel-Tygrett Co., 80-2 USTC ¶ 9702, 46 AFTR2d 80-5676 (6th Cir. 1980).

Evidence supports disallowance of excessive compensation. Taxpayer paid salaries to its officer-stockholders based on contingency of profit. The IRS contended that these salaries were unreasonable and disallowed the deductions. The Tax Court upheld disallowance for excessive compensation of salaries paid to the officer-stockholders. *Held:* Affirmed. The fact that the compensation was based on contingency of profits does not necessarily mean it will be reasonable where, as here, there was evidence of lack of arm's-length bargaining. Furthermore, no dividends were paid during the period in question even though profits were good. Lastly, the compensation paid was grossly disproportionate in comparison to compensation paid those in comparable companies within the same industry. Schneider & Co., 500 F2d 148, 74-2 USTC ¶ 9563, 34 AFTR2d 74-5422 (8th Cir. 1974).

Sole stockholder's compensation held to be unreasonable. Barton-Gillet Company was a corporation organized in Maryland that originally was in the printing business. During the late 1950s and early 1960s, Barton transformed the business into one that served as a public relations firm for colleges and other eductional institutions. Barton was the majority stockholder through 1964, at which point he became the sole stockholder. For his duties as president, Barton was paid $15,000 per year. In addition, his income included a commission for his work on accounts and contributions by the corporation for his benefit to a deferred compensation plan. The total compensation for 1964 was $96,000, and for 1965 it was $101,000. For 1966, the total was $128,000. The IRS claimed that these amounts were unreasonable compensation and allowed the corporation a deduction for the first two years of $60,000 per year. For the third year, the IRS allowed a deduction of $75,000. The Tax

Compensation for Personal Services: *Held Unreasonable*

Court agreed with the IRS that the amounts claimed by the corporation were unreasonable but disagreed as to the exact amounts that were excessive. *Held:* Affirmed. The court felt that Barton was entitled to high compensation because his work was responsible for the success of the business. However, no evidence was produced showing the amount of compensation paid to executives in similar businesses. In addition, the fact that he was the sole or primary stockholder negated the need for him to receive incentive compensation. The court also found the fact that no dividends were paid during this period to be important. This showed that a portion of the compensation was really a dividend, for which no deduction was allowed. For the three years in question, the court found the reasonable compensation amounts to be $80,000, $83,000, and $108,000, respectively. Barton-Gillet Co., 442 F2d 1343, 71-1 USTC ¶ 9480, 27 AFTR2d 71-1550 (4th Cir. 1971).

Determination by a jury of reasonable compensation for six officer-stockholders affirmed. Taxpayer corporation deducted certain amounts that it paid its officers as salaries and bonuses. The IRS determined the amounts to be unreasonable and disallowed the deduction of amounts in excess of what it considered reasonable. A jury in a district court reviewed all the facts and found the compensation to be unreasonable. Specifically, the jury considered the history of the business; the personal qualifications of the stockholders, including their background in the work; and the nature and amount of work that each of them did and the manner in which compensation was determined. *Held:* Affirmed. The jury reviewed all the facts, was given proper instructions, and thereafter found a portion of the compensation paid by a corporation to its employee-stockholders to be unreasonable. East Tenn. Motor Co., 453 F2d 494, 72-1 USTC ¶ 9150, 29 AFTR2d 72-313 (6th Cir. 1971).

Increased compensation to sole stockholder unreasonable since no significant change in his duties. Taxpayer corporation, engaged in trading in grass seeds and grains, paid its sole stockholder and dominant officer a base salary of $25,200 for each of the years 1963 and 1964, plus a bonus of $16,050 for 1963 and $30,000 for 1964, paid near the end of each year. For the two prior years, his compensation had been $22,000 and $29,000. The IRS disallowed as unreasonable the payments in 1963 and 1964 that exceeded $30,000. The Tax Court sustained the IRS' determination. It found that the sudden increases in compensation in the taxable years were not justified in light of the fact that the officer's activities were essentially unchanged from the prior years. The court concluded that some portion of the total payments to the officer in 1963 and 1964 was intended as a distribution of earnings rather than as compensation for services currently rendered. *Held:* Affirmed. Reasonable compensation to a corporate officer is to be determined in light of all the evidence. Here, the failure of taxpayer to pay any dividends while radically increasing the compensation of its sole stockholder, the lack of any showing of a significant change in the duties of the stockholder all supported the Tax Court's determination. The determination was not clearly erroneous. Pacific Grains, Inc., 399 F2d 603, 68-2 USTC ¶ 9536, 22 AFTR2d 5413 (9th Cir. 1968).

Salary of inactive officers held excessive. Taxpayer corporation owned one section of a ten-section apartment complex containing 1,520 apartments. A real estate management firm collected all rents, executed all leases, and supervised all regular maintenance. Drawing cash from the corporation during the year, the stockholders, husband and wife charged the drawings to officers' loan accounts. At the end of the year, they allocated these accounts between officers' compensation and dividends. The minutes of the corporation authorized a total combined maximum salary of $15,000, but the stockholders determined the exact amount when the net income of the corporation became known at the end of the year. The IRS allowed only $1,500 as officers' compensation; the Tax Court sustained the IRS' position. In view of the lack of services performed by the stockholders, the court found the salary to be obviously excessive. *Held:* Affirmed. The court could not say that the limitation of the corporate salary deduction to $1,500 a year was unreasonable or that the findings of the

COMPENSATION FOR PERSONAL SERVICES: *Held Unreasonable*

Tax Court were clearly erroneous. Langley Park Apartments, Sec. C., Inc., 359 F2d 427, 66-1 USTC ¶ 9368 (7th Cir. 1966).

Percentage salary arrangement upset. A husband and wife were stockholders in a corporation that paid them salaries equal to 7.5 percent of gross annual sales. For 1960 and 1961, the corporation paid them $32,000 and $34,000, respectively. *Held:* For the IRS. The court found that the salary arrangement was unreasonable and held that $25,000 for each of the stockholders was reasonable. A percentage of sales compensation for the officer-stockholders suggested that the receipt of reasonable compensation for their services was not the sole objective, and that they were not overlooking the possibility that by this arrangement they could drain off some of the corporate profit in the guise of salaries. There was no attempt to show that the salaries were in line with salaries paid to officers of comparable corporations, nor did taxpayers prove that the salaries were not excessive. Hampton Corp., 65-2 USTC ¶ 9611 (9th Cir. 1965).

Part of officer's salaries disallowed as excessive and unreasonable. Salaries paid in 1951 to 1953 to the three officer-stockholders of a corporation engaged in the tool and die business consisted of a base salary plus a bonus geared to profits. Two officers received a base salary of $25,000 and bonuses of $18,000 to $27,000; the president received a base of $36,000 and bonuses of $28,000 to $41,000. Although the Tax Court concluded that the executives were thoroughly trained and experienced, possessed a high degree of intelligence and technical knowledge, worked skillfully and efficiently for long hours, rendered very valuable services, and were entitled to substantial compensation, it determined that a portion of the compensation actually paid was excessive and unreasonable. *Held:* Affirmed. A good deal of the profit, it was determined, was due to the Korean War and not to the officer's ability. Thus, part of the officers' salaries was disallowed. Huckins Tool & Die, Inc., 289 F2d 549, 61-1 USTC ¶ 9384, 7 AFTR2d 1142 (7th Cir. 1961).

Salary of family corporation's president deemed unreasonable since substantial year end dividends were waived. A salary payment of $250,000 to the president, who was the son of the founder of a closely held family corporation engaged in the paper industry, was deemed unreasonable to the extent it exceeded $110,000. The Tax Court commented that no evidence was presented to show that the son possessed special qualifications, either with respect to the paper industry generally or the corporation's operations in particular. The fact that he waived substantial dividends in the years at issue indicated that the payment was intended as a dividend. *Held:* Affirmed, on basis of Tax Court's holding. Gilman Paper Co., 284 F2d 697, 61-1 USTC ¶ 9152, 6 AFTR2d 6063 (2d Cir. 1960).

IRS' determination of officer's salaries upheld in part. The IRS determined the salary of an officer and 10 percent stockholder and assessed deficiencies, basing its determination of the compensation paid to another of the company's employees. *Held:* For the IRS, in part. It was not logical to compare the salary paid the officer to that of another employee. The officer was a registered engineer, performed supervisory functions, and had responsibility in the financial and sales fields in addition to his engineering duties. The other employee to whom he was compared performed none of these additional functions. A partial disallowance was warranted, however. Despite the record year of the corporation and the officer's contribution toward its volume, the amount paid was disproportionate to amounts paid in earlier years. Taxpayer was only in his early thirties and had returned from the service just four years earlier. Dahlem Constr. Co., 268 F. Supp. 103, 66-2 USTC ¶ 9772 (WD Ky. 1966).

Corporate president's salary deemed excessive for services rendered. Taxpayer, a corporation engaged in the manufacture and distribution of dog and cat food, paid its president and sole stockholder a salary of $120,000 each year for the taxable years 1952 through 1954, and $80,000 for 1955. It deducted these amounts as salary expenses. The IRS determined that $30,000 per year was a reasonable salary and that payments in excess thereof were not deductible as ordinary and necessary business expenses. The company paid no dividends on its rather substantial earnings. *Held:* The court found that $40,000 per year for each of the taxable years 1952 through 1955 was fair and reasonable compensation to the president for the services rendered by him. Lewis Food Co., 193 F. Supp. 611, 61-1 USTC ¶ 9434 (SD Cal. 1961).

Excessive salary determined on basis of comparability. In earlier years, taxpayer established and its board ratified salaries for certain key employees. As the years passed, the nature of these employees' activities became more limited. For example, one officer's salary was established when he was head of the entire organization. But during the year in question, he was merely a part-time consultant. *Held:* For the IRS. The salaries paid to the key employees were excessive when compared with the salaries paid for similar services in the industry. Accordingly, salaries once reasonable became unreasonable as the nature or extent of the employee's work changed. Gay Gibson, Inc., 75-1 USTC ¶ 9460, 35 AFTR2d 75-1487 (Ct. Cl. 1975).

Salary based on profits found unreasonable in part. As part of a plan of compensating executives, including stockholder-officers, taxpayer set aside 60 percent of its profits after a return on invested capital. The IRS contended that the compensation was unreasonable. *Held:* For the IRS, in part. Weighing all of the elements, including compensation paid by taxpayer's competitors in the construction business, the court found that the compensation paid to the officer-stockholders under this formula was in part unreasonable. It allowed about two-thirds of the claimed deductions. Irby Constr. Co., 290 F2d 824, 61-2 USTC ¶ 9497, 7 AFTR2d 1573 (Ct. Cl. 1961).

Compensation unreasonable where not paid for services rendered to the payor. Taxpayer and another corporation formed a joint venture to acquire, produce, and sell agricultural products. The taxpayer's president and sole stockholders entered into an employment contact with the joint venture under which he was to be compensated for services rendered thereto. The compensation was to be 40 percent of the taxpayer's net profits before taxes and deferred compensation. The taxpayer deducted the amounts as compensation paid for services rendered. The IRS determined that a substantial portion of the compensation was unreasonable and constituted dividends to the recipients. *Held:* For the IRS. The services were performed on behalf of the joint venture, not of the taxpayer. A portion of the payments, however, was deductible as compensation for seeing to the taxpayer's corporate affairs and for representing the taxpayer in its activities as a joint venturer. Cropland Chem. Corp., 75 TC 288 (1980), aff'd, 665 F2d 1050 (7th Cir. 1981).

Unreasonable compensation determined (TC). C, a closely held warehousing corporation, paid its general manager, the taxpayer, under an incentive compensation arrangement since the corporation's inception in 1951. Taxpayer and his family owned all of C's stock. From 1951 to 1954, taxpayer received approximately 26 percent of C's net profits, 34 percent thereafter. From 1951 to the year in issue, the corporation grew from two employees to more than 200. Part of taxpayer's compensation was disallowed. *Held:* For the IRS. The high percentage of taxpayer's contingent compensation arrangement did not represent his worth to the corporation during the years in issue. The corporation's growth and success was not attributed solely to taxpayer, and the corporation was not dependent on his services during the years in issue as it was during the formative years. The corporation also was not rewarding the taxpayer for his previous services, since he had already been rewarded for his earlier accomplishments. Kennedy, Jr., 72 TC 793 (1979).

Reasonable compensation determined. Taxpayer corporation paid $45,000 and $40,000 in salary for 1965 and 1966, respectively, to its sole stockholder and president. The IRS only allowed $15,800, which was the salary paid him in 1964. *Held:* For the IRS, in part. The court allowed $35,000 for each year, based on the president's services to taxpayer and on comparative salaries paid elsewhere. Salem

Compensation for Personal Services: *Held Unreasonable*

Packing Co., 56 TC 131 (1971), acq. 1971-2 CB 3.

Officer's compensation excessive. A corporation engaged in construction and land development increased the salary of its sole stockholder from $13,000 to $53,901 over a four-year period. The IRS determined that $53,901 was excessive and that a $34,900 salary was reasonable. *Held:* For the IRS. The IRS' determination carried the presumption of correctness. Taxpayer failed to rebut this presumption by introducing evidence as to salaries paid to executives in similar positions. Perlmutter, 44 TC 382 (1965).

Salary paid to son of taxpayer's president held unreasonable, in part. Taxpayer corporation was a family controlled printing press manufacturing corporation. The son of the president of taxpayer corporation was elected secretary-treasurer and shortly thereafter was inducted into the army. While in the army, the son did some work for taxpayer and had business telephone conversations with his father. Taxpayer deducted the amounts paid to the son as salary. The IRS determined the salary to be unreasonable. *Held:* For the IRS, in part. The court held that the salary paid to the son was unreasonable but, in view of the fact that some services were rendered, determined a smaller reasonable salary. Brandtjen-Kluge Inc., 34 TC 416 (1960).

Amount of conpensation paid to sole stockholder found to be unreasonable. The taxpayer corporation sought to deduct compensation paid to its sole stockholder. The IRS disallowed part of the deduction and was sustained by the Tax Court. The Ninth Circuit reversed and remanded in Elliotts, Inc., 716 F2d 1241 (9th Cir. 1983). *Held:* For the IRS. After considering the factors set forth in the Ninth Circuit opinion, the amount of the sole stockholder's compensation was found to be unreasonably high. The factors considered were the role of the stockholder in the taxpayer corporation, a comparison of the stockholder's salary with those paid by similar companies for similar services, the character and condition of the taxpayer corporation, any conflict of interest between the taxpayer and the stockholder that would permit a disguise of corporate distributions as salary expenses, and any internal inconsistency in the taxpayer's treatment of payments to employees. Elliotts, Inc., 48 TCM 1245, ¶ 84,516 P-H Memo. TC (1984).

Compensation paid to chairman of board unreasonable. Taxpayer, a closely held corporation, claimed a deduction for the fees paid to its chairman of the board. The IRS determined that the amount paid was unreasonable compensation. *Held:* For the IRS. Taxpayer failed to establish the nature and extent of services rendered by the chairman and to establish that the value of the services actually rendered was in excess of the amount determined by the IRS to be reasonable. Woesner Abstract & Title Co., 47 TCM 722, ¶ 83,764 P-H Memo. TC (1983).

Compensation to principal stockholders and officers unreasonable. The IRS determined that the amount of compensation paid by taxpayer to its two principal stockholders and officers was unreasonable. Accordingly, the IRS redetermined the amount of taxpayer's allowable deduction. *Held:* For the IRS, in part. The court found from all the facts (including a comparison of the amount of compensation paid with the amount of the distributions to stockholders) that the compensation paid was unreasonable, but not to the extent disallowed by the IRS. Estate of Shantz, 47 TCM 614, ¶ 3743 P-H Memo. TC (1983), aff'd (7th Cir. 1985).

Part of compensation determined to be dividend. *D* formed taxpayer, a closely held corporation, to import and wholesale leather jackets. *D*, as the president, was engaged in all phases of the business operations. *D* worked 6 days a week and 12 hours a day under an employment contract with taxpayer that provided for a fixed salary plus bonuses. On its federal income tax return, taxpayer deducted certain amounts for salary and contributions paid on behalf of corporate officers to taxpayer's qualified pension and profit-sharing plan. The IRS determined that the compensation was unreasonable and disallowed the amount in part. *Held:* For the IRS, in part. When the compensation fluctuated in response to taxpayer's

Compensation for Personal Services: *Held Unreasonable*

earnings, a certain portion of the compensation was attributed to dividend distributions rather than compensation for services rendered. The portion that was allowed as reasonable compensation was determined by factors such as long hours, multiple duties, and varied responsibilities. Demian, Ltd., 47 TCM 311, ¶ 83,683 P-H Memo. TC (1983).

Unreasonable salary not deductible. The IRS disallowed the deduction by taxpayer corporation of salary paid to its sole stockholder on the grounds that it was unreasonable. *Held:* For the IRS, in part. While the business was growing and highly profitable during the years in question, the rapid increase in the employee's salary was due to his becoming a sole stockholder of taxpayer. Taxpayer never paid dividends and failed to show that it needed to accumulate funds for specific corporate purposes. The salary deduction was, however, greater than that allowed by the IRS. Lefkowitz, 46 TCM 485, ¶ 83,356 P-H Memo. TC (1983).

"Percentage of net profit" compensation held unreasonable in part. Taxpayers, mother and son, sole stockholders of a coal brokerage Subchapter S corporation, annually drew 90 percent of net profits as compensation. The business was extremely profitable due entirely to the taxpayers' efforts, and resulted in multimillion dollar salaries. The IRS charged that the salaries were unreasonable and that a portion was dividends. *Held:* For the IRS, in part. Although percentage of profit compensation formulas are authorized, the reasonable percentage in this instance was lower than that used by taxpayers. Foos, 41 TCM 863, ¶ 81,061 P-H Memo. TC (1981).

Pharmacist's compensation determined. *C* acquired *D* pharmaceutical corporation at a time when its gross sales were approximately $70,000. In addition to working as a pharmacist, *C* took on all types of responsibilities at *D*, including those of manager. He did a number of things to increase *D*'s business, such as installing a postal substation. As a result, the gross sales increased to over $600,000 a year. During this period few dividends were paid. The IRS determined that the salary paid by *D* to *C* was unreasonable and that in the absence of significant dividend payments, the salary was a disguised nondeductible dividend. *Held:* For the IRS. Under Regulation 1.162-7(a), the test of deductibility in the case of compensation required the amounts to be reasonable and in fact payments purely for services. Determining whether a salary was reasonable was a factual issue. Because the corporation failed to distribute significant dividends, this factor weighed heavily against the positive factors for receiving a high salary, such as the individual's special attributes. As the dividends distributed did not represent a reasonable return on the investment, the inference was that the salaried owner was receiving dividends in the form of salary compensation. Although the owner was being paid a salary as an employee, the risk factors in running the business were not among those that were to be considered in deciding whether the salary was in fact reasonable. Drexel Park Pharmacy, Inc., 39 TCM 788, ¶ 79,518 P-H Memo. TC (1979).

Salary payments found to be unreasonable. Taxpayer, a bus company, greatly increased the salary of its president and sole stockholder. The IRS contended that a portion was not deductible as reasonable compensation for services performed. *Held:* For the IRS. Taxpayer failed to carry its burden of proof. Also, taxpayer failed to pay any dividends during the years in question even though it was expanding rapidly. Niagara Falls, 36 TCM 1088, ¶ 77,269 P-H Memo. TC (1977).

Compensation unreasonable when compared to other executives. Taxpayer corporation claimed a $300,000 salary deduction in 1969 for its president, founder, and major stockholder. The IRS allowed only a $100,000 deduction. *Held:* For the IRS, in part. The court found that $175,000 was a reasonable salary. Several factors were used to determine the reasonableness of the compensation. The salary, tied to profits, rose from $6,500 in 1961. Only small cash dividends were paid. The president was in control, but his value to the corporation decreased as the corporation expanded. His salary was much larger than other executives. Finally, an addendum to his employment con-

COMPENSATION FOR PERSONAL SERVICES: *Held Unreasonable*

tract, which required that he repay salaries determined excessive, indicated a pre-existing knowledge of the problem. Saia Elec., Inc., 33 TCM 1357, ¶ 74,290 P-H Memo. TC (1974).

Salary determined not commensurate with services performed. Taxpayer pharmacist and an associate operated an incorporated pharmacy. The IRS disallowed a deduction for the associate's salary. *Held:* For taxpayer, in part. The associate had and performed actual duties and functions. Even though the corporation was liquidated shortly after the salary payment, such salary had no connection with the liquidation. While the associate was entitled to a salary, the $16,100 payment was unreasonable in relation to his services. Only a $4,000 salary was reasonable and deductible. Lombardo, 33 TCM 1114, ¶ 74,250 P-H Memo. TC (1974).

Salary deduction denied due to excessive salaries for president, vice-president, and other officers. Taxpayer corporation claimed deductions for salaries paid to its officers. The IRS disallowed part of the deduction. *Held:* For the IRS. Taxpayer's president was an officer of a bank and loan company. The law could require these loans to be insured. Taxpayer corporation's underwriting was done in conjunction with the bank and loan company, and since few claims were processed, taxpayer had little but administrative work to do. Taxpayer's president's salaries of $18,000 and $23,000 were unreasonable in excess of $8,000. The vice-president's salaries of $18,000 and $23,000 for supervisory work were unreasonable and excessive in the amount in excess of $9,000. Other officer's salaries were also found to be unreasonable in part and therefore not deductible. National Underwriters, Inc., 33 TCM 49, ¶ 74,014 P-H Memo. TC (1974).

Salary deductions held unreasonable in part due to excessive percentage of manager's compensation to taxpayer's net income when compared with other companies. The IRS determined that salaries paid by taxpayer, a small loan office, to its manager and sole stockholder in excess of $25,000 constituted unreasonable compensation. *Held:* For taxpayer, in part. Based on a variety of factors, it was determined that for 1967, 1968, and 1969, $40,000 was a reasonable salary and neither the $25,000 allowed nor the actual salary range of $38,600 to $58,000 from 1961 through 1969 was reasonable. The manager was mainly responsible for taxpayer's successful operation. The fact that he spent some time on outside interests was not relevant in light of his devotion of whatever time was necessary to make the business operate successfully. Comparisons revealed that statistically, the percentage of the manager's compensation to taxpayer's net income was substantially in excess of the comparable percentage for similar companies. Taxpayer's net taxable income rose from $63,500 to $88,500 while the manager's salary rose from $38,600 to $58,000. The manager's salary absorbed the increase in profits despite the fact that his services did not increase. Only minor dividends were paid in two years. Finally, taxpayer's taxable income level always hovered around $25,000; thus the surtax rate was generally inapplicable. All of these factors pointed to the unreasonableness of the salary. Capitol Fin. Co., 31 TCM 1021, ¶ 72,206 P-H Memo. TC (1972).

Compensation deemed reasonable in part, due to effort and functions of vice-president. Taxpayer corporation's vice-president and major stockholder received $9,000 in compensation. The IRS determined that only $2,400 was reasonable compensation. *Held:* For the IRS, in part. The vice-president lived out of state and operated his own separate business. However, he followed taxpayer's operations closely; he studied sales and profit reports; he made suggestions which increased production and profits; and he traveled to the company every two to three months. An annual salary of $5,000 was determined to be reasonable. Cozart Packing Co., 31 TCM 867, ¶ 72,175 P-H Memo. TC (1972).

Deductibility of officer's salary disallowed due to undocumented "unusual" services. Taxpayer was president, sole stockholder and supervisor of a telephone answering service business. He received $18,000 as compensation for 1966 and 1967, a part of which the IRS disallowed. *Held:* For the IRS. Taxpayer broke down his compensation as follows: $12,000 was regular salary and $6,000 was for unusual legal and

Compensation for Personal Services: *Held Unreasonable*

accounting services. However, the performance of the unusual services was not completely documented. In spite of the taxpayer's diligent efforts to make the business profitable, a reasonable compensation would have been only $13,000, and that was held to be the limit on the amount deductible by the corporation. Furthermore, taxpayer was entitled to a deduction for legal fees incurred in a tax investigation. The fees did not constitute a personal nondeductible item and were partly spent for preparation of taxpayer's individual case, which was distinguished from the corporation's tax investigation. Office Communications Co., 31 TCM 33, ¶ 72,014 P-H Memo. TC (1972).

Salary paid to corporate president was unreasonable as president had another full-time job. Taxpayer corporation received between $8,000 and $17,000 of receipts by acquiring and renting real estate, and then claimed salary deductions for its president, ranging from $4,800 to $7,800 over three years. The IRS disallowed the deductions as unreasonable for salary in excess of $4,800 a year. *Held:* For the IRS. The president had another full-time government job and presented no evidence to show that he spent more than three hours a week on corporate business. Thus, salary in excess of $4,800 was unreasonable and not deductible by the taxpayer corporation. Ettle Co., 30 TCM 351, ¶ 71,086 P-H Memo. TC (1971).

Stockholder-officer's salaries held reasonable and sufficient for greater deductions than allowed. Taxpayer corporation took deductions for the compensation—salary, pension, and director's fees—paid to its owner-officers. Two officers also excluded the value of lodging provided by the corporation from their gross income. The IRS reduced the salary deductions and included the lodging value in gross income. *Held:* For the IRS, in part. Taxpayer showed services actually rendered by the officers and thus proved the reasonableness of their salaries and therefore, a larger deduction than the IRS had previously allowed. Ruck, Inc., 28 TCM 63, ¶ 69,016 P-H Memo. TC (1969).

Reasonableness of compensation paid to officers of closely held corporation determined on the basis of their value to the company. Taxpayer, a family corporation, manufactured a line of detergents and other chemical specialties for the dry-cleaning industry. The IRS contended that corporate payments to its president and vice-president, a father and son, during 1962 through 1964, were unreasonable and excessive, and that salary payments in 1964 to the president's son-in-law, an attorney who was employed by the corporation, were unreasonable. Both the president and vice-president worked long hours without any significant vacation time and were experienced in the business. Both also made special contributions to the corporation. They received relatively small salaries during the early years and their salary increases for 1962 and 1963 were modest and relatively closely in line with taxpayer's sales. In 1964 the vice-president's salary was nearly doubled and the president's was increased by 30 percent, while corporate sales increased only 20 percent. *Held:* For the IRS, in part. Although the salaries for the president and vice-president for 1962 and 1963 appeared reasonable, the court did not feel that their service in 1964 supported the increase in salary for that year. Hence part of their salaries for 1964 were disallowed and deemed unreasonable. The court also found $12,500 of the $24,800 paid to the son-in-law as reasonable, taking into account his legal training and the time he devoted to the legal matters of the corporation. The court upheld the IRS' disallowance of the corporate deduction for reimbursement of expenses incurred by the president in excess of $20 per week. The disallowed portion was includible in the income of the president. Dixo Co., 27 TCM 644, ¶ 68,133 P-H Memo. TC (1968).

Salary paid a president of television antenna system corporation for his part-time services held excessive. Taxpayer corporation maintained and sold the services of a community television antenna system. It paid its controlling stockholder, who was also its president, an annual salary of $20,000 for 1957 and 1958, and $12,000 for 1959. He was not compensated for the years prior to 1957. The IRS disallowed the deductions claimed for 1957 through 1959 to the extent that they exceeded $10,000 in each year. *Held:* For the IRS. Taxpayer offered no evidence as to the salaries paid by other companies engaged in similar enterprises and did not show that its president had any special skills or qualifications for the job. Moreover, during most of the period in question, the officer was employed on a fulltime basis by the federal government in Washington, and spent little time on taxpayer's business. Although he received daily reports from taxpayer's manager, and communicated with him by long distance telephone approximately once a week, the evidence presented was far from persuasive that the services rendered were sufficient to justify the salaries paid. Tele-ception of Winchester, Inc., 26 TCM 1208, ¶ 67,238 P-H Memo. TC (1967).

Compensation of $7,800 paid to officer-stockholder of real estate corporation deemed unreasonable due to minimal amount of time and effort. Taxpayer corporation was originally organized to operate an automobile agency. On the death of the owner of the corporation, the franchise was terminated, and his widow, who became the sole stockholder, continued the corporation solely to lease corporate real estate to an unrelated tenant at a net rental of $25,000 per annum. Taxpayer had no office or place of business other than the taxpayers' home during the years in issue. The IRS determined that compensation of $7,800 paid to taxpayer as officer was excessive to the extent of $2,800 for 1962 and $6,451 for 1963. *Held:* For the IRS. Taxpayer's services to the corporation in both years were minimal, and required only a comparatively small amount of time and effort. Bev Andersen Chevrolet, Inc., 26 TCM 388, ¶ 67,064 P-H Memo. TC (1967).

Reasonableness of compensation paid to ill officer of family corporation determined. Taxpayer corporation paid its president, major stockholder, and founder, Chism, a salary of $24,000 for each of the years 1953 through 1956. Chism was physically incapacitated and was confined almost entirely to his home as the result of a heart ailment. Thereafter, he continued as taxpayer's president, but his activities were confined principally to occasional visits of one-half hour or so to taxpayer's office, accompanied by a nurse. After 1953, he was confined entirely to his home, where from time to time he had conferences regarding business matters with taxpayer's general manager, up until his death in 1956. The IRS determined that the compensation was unreasonable. *Held:* For the IRS. The court found the reasonable salary for Chism to be $20,000 in 1953, $15,000 in 1954, and $12,000 for 1955 and 1956. It rejected taxpayer's alternative argument that the excess payments should be allowed as health insurance payments, since taxpayer did not have any plan or health insurance in effect during any of the years involved. Taxpayer also took out a retirement income policy on the life of its general manager, under which the insurance company was to provide taxpayer with future funds that it might use thereafter to provide the manager with retirement payments. Since taxpayer was directly the beneficiary under the policy, the court held that the insurance premiums were not deductible. The court also upheld the IRS' determination that informal withdrawals by Chism and his wife from the corporation, totaling $78,000 at the time of his death, were not true loans, but informal dividends, and includible in the recipients' income. Chism Ice Cream Co., 21 TCM 25, ¶ 62,006 P-H Memo. TC (1962).

Reasonableness of salaries paid by family corporation determined based on services performed. Taxpayer was in the business of jobbing nonfood items such as plastic and metal housewares and toys through a chain outlet. Its stock was held by a husband and wife, both of whom devoted their full efforts to the business. After the contract with the chain outlet was canceled in 1957, taxpayer's business dropped off, and the husband devoted his efforts to obtaining a new distribution source. The IRS determined deficiencies of 1955 and 1956 by reducing the wife's salary from $11,800 and $15,000 respectively to $9,300 and $10,500. For 1959, the IRS reduced the salary of the husband from $15,800 to $7,500. *Held*: For taxpayer, in part. The court, considering the wife's long hours of valuable clerical services rendered in 1955 and 1956, held $11,000 to be a reasonable salary for both years. It also sustained $7,500 as a reasonable salary for the husband in 1959, when his main activities consisted of trying to get a new disbribution source. Ryanco Sales Co., 20 TCM 1689, ¶ 61,327 P-H Memo. TC (1961).

Compensation paid founder and nominal head of hospital held unreasonable. The salary paid to an elderly practicing physician who was the nominal head and founder of a family-owned hospital was determined by the IRS to have been unreasonable where the services performed in fact were occasional, irregular, and ill-defined. *Held*: For the IRS, in part. The court found that the value of the physician's services did not exceed the $100 per week allowed by the IRS. However, salaries paid to his two sons, also physicians and stockholders, whose services in operating and administering the hospital, together with their professional services to patients, which were substantial and on a full-time basis, were deemed reasonable. McClung Hosp., Inc., 19 TCM 449, ¶ 60,086 P-H Memo. TC (1960).

Officers' salaries paid by real estate corporation deemed unreasonable. The IRS disallowed officers' in excess of $2,500 a year for a family held corporation that owned a single piece of rental property. *Held*: For the IRS. The actual management of the rental property was conducted by a rental agent, and the services of the officer-stockholders on the facts were "rather inconsiderable." Akten Realty Corp., 19 TCM 150, ¶ 60,027 P-H Memo. TC (1960).

Loans Distinguished

Receipts were salary, not loan repayment. Taxpayer was a majority stockholder of a corporation and an officer of it and its subsidiary, both of which encountered financial difficulties. Taxpayer advanced funds to both. The subsidiary deposited funds in taxpayer's personal bank account, which taxpayer claimed were repayment of loans. The Tax Court found that the deposits preceded the loans and were salary income, which taxpayer then lent to one or both of the corporations. *Held*: Affirmed without opinion. Creswell, 278 F2d 722, 60-2 USTC ¶ 9511 (5th Cir. 1960).

Advances from corporation are salary, not loans. Taxpayer, stockholder-employees of their corporation, received regular advances from the corporation, that were characterized as loans. The IRS recharacterized them as compensation for services. *Held*: For the IRS. An intention on the stockholders' part to repay and a corresponding intention on the corporation's part to enforce the obligation is required at the time the advances are made to validate the characterization as a loan. Evidence of these intentions did not exist in this case. Nix, 44 TCM 105, ¶ 82,330 P-H Memo. TC (1982).

Corporate withdrawals not intended as bona fide loans; increase in officers' salaries deemed unreasonable. "Informal" withdrawals by a husband and wife from their family-owned real estate corporation, although recorded on the corporate books as loans, were treated as dividends by the IRS. *Held*: For the IRS. The evidence did not indicate any intention to repay the so-called "loans" until after the IRS questioned their bona fides. Salaries paid to the husband and wife, which were increased in the taxable year to $10,000 and $3,000, respectively, were reduced to $8,000 and $2,500 on the ground that there was no evidence to justify such increase. Isaac Engel Realty Co., 22 TCM 1372, ¶ 63,273 P-H Memo. TC (1963).

Past Services

Corporation allowed compensation deduction to estate of deceased stockholder. Taxpayer corporation paid $10,000 to the estate of a deceased stockholders-executive in redemption of stock and also paid $7,500 to the same estate for deferred compensation, which it claimed as a deduction. The IRS disallowed the deduction, claiming that $7,500 was an additional payment for the stock. The Tax Court upheld the IRS. *Held*: Reversed. The IRS did not prove that the value of the redeemed stock exceeded $10,000. Lewis & Taylor, Inc., 447 F2d 1074, 71-2 USTC ¶ 9616, 28 AFTR2d 71-5550 (9th Cir. 1971).

Compensation for services allowed in part. Ivers Department Stores, Inc., a corporation formed in 1954, operated retail department stores in California. From 1954 through 1960, Jesse Ivers served as president and general merchandise manager of the corporation, for which he was paid $18,000 per year. In 1960, Ivers stepped down from these positions for health reasons. During that year, the corporation resolved to pay him $9,000 per year for the rest of his life as compensation for past services and for keeping himself available as a consultant. In 1963, Ivers was elected president and a director of the corporation. For the fiscal year that ended in 1963, the corporation paid him $9,000. For the next two fiscal years, he was paid $9,900 each year. These amounts represented payments for his consulting services. The IRS disallowed the deduction for all amounts in excess of $1,200 per year, claiming that the excess amounts were unreasonable compensation for the services performed during those years. *Held*: For taxpayer, in part. The court found that the major portion of each payment was for services actually rendered as a consultant during the three years in question. The court found that $1,000 each year was in recognition of services performed before 1954 and disallowed the deduction for that portion. The balance of each payment was held to be reasonable compensation, and the deduction was allowed for that amount. Ivers Dep't Store, Inc., 71-2 USTC ¶ 9611, 28 AFTR2d 5716 (CD Cal. 1971).

Jury determined reasonable compensation of stockholder-manager of closely held corporation. Taxpayer corporation paid its manager, a 50 percent stockholder, a salary of $60,000 and contributed 15 percent of that amount to its profit-sharing plan in each of the two years in issue. The IRS determined that the salary was in excess of reasonable compensation and disallowed the excess above $40,000. Taxpayer contended that the growth of the company was due to the efforts of the manager, and that the salary was not only for services performed in the years in issue, but for the previous four years when it was not as high as it should have been. Taxpayer also introduced testimony of outsiders concerning the value of the manager's services. The IRS answered that the payments should be carefully scrutinized because the manager and his wife were in control of the corporation and because the corporation had not paid any dividends since inception. *Held*: The jury determined that the reasonable compensation for services for the years in issue were $45,000 and $55,000 respectively. Midwest Mobile Home Supply Co., 67-1 USTC ¶ 9414 (D. Minn. 1967).

A jury found salary reasonable for past services. The reasonableness of the salary paid by taxpayer to its president and controlling stockholder might depend on whether he was inadequately compensated for prior years. A salary of $36,000 had been paid during the year at issue, and the IRS allowed $20,000. There is no indication of the salary paid in prior years. *Held*: For taxpayer. The jury found that the entire $36,000 was reasonable compensation to the president. Hyneman Gin, Inc., 65-1 USTC ¶ 9146 (ED Ark. 1964).

Officer's salaries deemed reasonable due to past, loyal services, and knowledge of company. Two officers had served taxpayer corporation for over 50 years, but in the taxable year involved they were devoting no more than 2 days a week to company affairs. One of the officers, who was chairman of the board, was concerned with personnel, inventory, and general operations, and the other, also a director, with payroll and confidential recordkeeping. The IRS asserted that the salaries were unreasonable. *Held*: For taxpayer. Finding that the salaries were determined with regard to long and loyal past services and wide knowledge of company operations, the court allowed their deduction as reasonable compensation. The opinion did not disclose the amounts involved. Hammond Sheet Metal Co., 60-1 USTC ¶ 9412 (ED Mo. 1960).

Compensation for previous undercompensated years held reasonable. Taxpayer, sole stockholder of a gasoline distributor, was paid minimal salaries in order to maintain a healthy financial position in the corporation. After the gasoline distributor was split into two new corporations, the new companies paid taxpayer compensation that was deemed excessive by the IRS. *Held*: For taxpayer. Although the services performed during the years in question were minimal, the compensation was paid for services that were performed for predecessor corporations in prior years, for which taxpayer had been underpaid. Evidence was introduced to show that there had always been an intent to make up the inadequate compensation. R.J. Nicoll Co., 59 TC 37 (1972).

Salary of a stockholder-employee not justified by past services. Taxpayer was the founder and sole stockholder of *V*. During the years in question, he was the chief operating officer and decision maker for all business aspects of *V*. Taxpayer had unusual qualities as an inventor and businessman. *V* used taxpayer's inventions and was profitable but never paid dividends. The IRS determined the salaries paid by *V* to taxpayer were not reasonable and disallowed part of *V*'s deductions. *Held*: For the IRS. The compensation in the years in question could not be justified in part as compensation for services in previous years. Taxpayer's other business interests plus the fact that he had received royalties from the use of his patents by *V* were also considered. Dockery, 44 TCM 1044, ¶ 82,599 P-H Memo. TC (1982).

Excessive salaries not considered late payments for earlier years. The IRS determined that over half of the salaries paid by a corporation to its sole stockholders were unreasonable. The taxpayers argued that the "excessive" salaries were actually late payments of salaries for earlier years that the corporation authorized but did not pay. *Held:* For the IRS. The corporation was not legally bound to pay the maximum shares authorized in prior years. If additional salaries had been paid in those years, they would probably have been unreasonable. Harry Fox, Inc., 37 TCM 1847-53, ¶ 78,453 P-H Memo. TC (1978).

Compensation paid to employee-stockholders was reasonable. Taxpayer, a closely held corporation, claimed $62,800 in salary deductions in both 1972 and 1973 for amounts paid to an employee owning preferred stock. The employee performed valuable services for the corporation as director, officer, guarantor of loans, and key executive. This employee had successfully encouraged the corporation to expand into the highly profitable automobile accessories industry. In past years, the employee, a founder of the corporation and wife of the former president, had worked gratuitously.

The taxpayer argued that no dividends had been paid despite considerable earnings because working capital was needed for expansion. *Held:* For taxpayer. The salary, which was paid purely for services, was reasonable considering the corporate profits and the value of the services performed. Allison Corp., 36 TCM 689, ¶ 77,166 P-H Memo. TC (1977).

Payment of $12,500 to corporate president reasonable compensation even though he was not present at corporate plant during entire year. Taxpayer corporation was engaged in bottling and marketing a soft drink in the Louisville area. Its president, who had a thorough background in soft drink marketing, lived in Texas but nevertheless presided over taxpayer's affairs, leaving routine daily operations in the hands of a resident vice-president. In order to improve taxpayer's position as much as possible, the president agreed not to take salary although he continued to perform services for the corporation. In fiscal 1963, he was paid a corporate salary of $12,500; the IRS allowed taxpayer only $3,000, contending that the balance was unreasonable. *Held:* For taxpayer. The president was the dominant executive of taxpayer even though he was only present in Louisville on occasion over the years, and not present at all during fiscal 1963. He rendered extensive and valuable executive direction and services to taxpayer. Because he had not received any compensation during many earlier years, and because the two prior years had been eminently successful, his salary was deemed reasonable, although the monies were solely for services rendered during fiscal 1963. Dr. Pepper Bottling Co., 27 TCM 73, ¶ 68,013 P-H Memo. TC (1968).

Accrual-basis taxpayer may deduct in year paid compensation for services for prior years. The predecessor of taxpayer corporation was purchased in 1945 and operated since that date as a bookbindery. In the early years, the owner spent a considerable amount of time and effort in improving the company. He engineered a merger with another company that caused taxpayer to be better organized. He attracted and trained younger men to handle the everyday operation of taxpayer and provided the necessary managerial and technical advice.

From the merger until 1959, the owner received an average annual salary of approximately $5,350. For 1960 through 1963, taxpayer paid him $21,000, $24,000, $26,800, and $27,127. The IRS allowed only $8,000 annually as reasonable compensation. *Held:* For taxpayer. The amounts paid in 1960 through 1963 were reasonable in that they included compensation for services performed in previous years when the owner had been inadequately compensated. If the amounts that the IRS found to be unreasonable were added to the total compensation paid during 1948 through 1959, his average annual salary would only be approximately $10,900, an amount considered reasonable. The court disallowed the corporation an accrual salary deduction under Section 267, which states that such a deduction may be accrual only if a payee who owns more than 50 percent of the stock of a payor receives the unpaid salary actually or constructively within two and a half months after the close of the payor's year. Weise-Winckler Bindery Inc., 26 TCM 1336, ¶ 67,259 P-H Memo. TC (1967).

Compensation paid by bottling company to its stockholder-officers is fully deductible. Taxpayer corporation was engaged in the business of bottling and merchandising soft drinks. It paid its president $32,000 in 1957 and $35,000 in 1958, and it paid its vice president $30,000 for each of these years. Because these salaries constituted a substantial increase over what the officers had received during prior years, the IRS reduced the claimed salaries as being excessive. *Held:* For taxpayer. Considering the complexity of the business, the unusual qualification of the officers, their long hours of work, their performance of both managerial and executive duties, the fact that they were underpaid in prior years, and the growth of the company, the court found the salaries claimed by taxpayer were justified. Mahaska Bottling Co., 21 TCM 1530, ¶ 62,289 P-H Memo. TC (1962).

Reasonableness of compensation to stockholder-officers for services rendered in taxable year and in prior years determined. Two real estate corporations, owned by the same three stockholders in equal shares, paid salaries to each of the three men based on earnings. No dividends had ever been paid. One corporation claimed a deduction of $2,400. The IRS reduced the deductions to $3,000 and $500 respectively. *Held:* For the IRS, in part. The court found that the salaries paid by the first corporation to the officer-stockholders were intended to compensate them not only for the services rendered by them in the taxable year but for the uncompensated or inadequately compensated services rendered in prior years. It found as a fact that the reasonable compensation for the services so rendered by the three officers was $10,500. As to the second corporation, the evidence showed that the services rendered by the officers were minimal. The court sustained the IRS' disallowance of $1,900 out of the $2,400 paid as excessive and unreasonable. Penley Realty Corp., 19 TCM 1005, ¶ 60,193 P-H Memo. TC (1960).

COMPLETE LIQUIDATIONS

(*See* Liquidations)

COMPLIANCE

(*See* Assessment and Collection; Procedure; Tax Avoidance)

CONSENT DIVIDENDS

(*See* Accumulated Earnings Tax; Personal Holding Companies)

CONSOLIDATED RETURNS

(*See also* Affiliated Corporations)

In General	208
Control Defined	211
Elections	213
Excess Loss Account	216
Intercorporate Transactions	216
Net Operating Loss Carry-Overs	218

207

CONSOLIDATED RETURNS: *In General*

In General

Consolidated return filed two years late was invalid. Taxpayers, related corporations, filed their first consolidated return for 1972 in 1975. The Tax Court held the return was filed too late to consolidate their income and deductions and imposed a late filing penalty. *Held:* Affirmed. A consolidated return must be timely filed. No reasonable cause excused them from the penalty. Millette & Assoc., 594 F2d 121, 79-1 USTC ¶ 9349, 43 AFTR2d 79-1109 (5th Cir.), cert. denied, 444 US 899 (1979).

Parent and subsidiary allowed to use different accounting methods when filing consolidated returns. Taxpayer was in the business of buying, slaughtering, processing, and selling beef and cattle products, and operating on an accrual basis. Its subsidiary, *B*, which was engaged in buying, feeding, and selling cattle, operated on a cash basis. On the fiscal year-end income tax returns for 1965 and 1966, consolidated returns were filed. The IRS recast the returns, placing *B* on an accrual basis, which resulted in a substantial amount of tax liability. *Held*: For taxpayer. The corporations did not need pre-return filing permission for the farmer-child and processor-parent to file a consolidated return using two different accounting methods because initial elections did not require IRS approval. Gold-Pak Meat Co., 522 F2d 1055, 75-2 USTC ¶ 9693, 36 AFTR2d 75-5664 (9th Cir. 1975).

Parent not entitled to keep refund of bankrupt subsidiary. A bankrupt subsidiary filed a consolidated federal income tax with its parent, who was an unsecured creditor, and another wholly owned corporation. The return indicated that the consolidated group was entitled to a refund resulting from a net operating loss which could be carried back for a refund of taxes paid by members of the group in prior tax years. The entire refund was due to the earnings history of the bankrupt subsidiary. The referee in bankruptcy determined that the parent could retain the refund and use it as a set-off against an unsecured lien. The district court determined that the trustee was entitled to the refund. *Held*: Affirmed. Generally, as a matter of state corporate law, and absent an agreement to the contrary, a tax refund resulting solely from offsetting losses of one member of a consolidated group against the income of that same member in a prior, or subsequent, year should inure to the benefit of that member. The only reason tax refunds were not paid directly to the subsidiary was because the income tax regulations required the parent to act as the sole agent, when duly authorized by the subsidiary, in handling all matters relating to the tax return. Since there was no express or implied agreement that the parent-agent had the right to keep the refund, the parent's position was that of a trustee for the bankrupt subsidiary and this placed the parent under a duty to return the tax refund to the subsidiary's estate. In re Richards Chrysler Plymouth Corp., 473 F2d 262, 73-2 USTC ¶ 9482, 31 AFTR2d 73-1222 (9th Cir. 1973).

Consolidated return rules override the allowance of a bad debt deduction under Sections 166 and 595. Taxpayer entered into a transaction resulting in its wholly owned affiliate partially defaulting on an obligation issued to taxpayer. Taxpayer and affiliate filed a consolidated tax return for the year. The IRS argued that the deduction had to be deferred under Regulation 1.1502-14(d), which provides that to the extent gain or loss is recognized to a one member of an affiliated group because of a disposition of an obligation of another, such gain or loss shall be deferred. *Held*: For the IRS. The validity of the consolidated return regulations have for 50 years never been in doubt. The enactment of intervening bad debt or other loss deduction provisions of the Code does not supersede them. Sooner Fed. Sav. & Loan Ass'n, 84-1 USTC ¶ 9296, 53 AFTR2d 84-974 (Cl. Ct. 1984).

Court upholds negative basis adjustment required under consolidated return regulations. Taxpayer filed consolidated returns with its subsidiary for years 1967 and 1968. The subsidiary sustained large net operating losses each year, which either reduced consolidated income or were carried back to offset income in prior years. The aggregate amount of these losses exceeded taxpayer's basis in the subsidiary's stock. The subsidiary became insolvent by the end of 1968. The IRS claimed that when the subsidiary became insolvent, taxpayer realized income equal to the excess of the subsidiary's net operating losses in 1967 and 1968 over its basis in the subsidiary's stock. Taxpayer argued that under general tax principles, basis in an asset cannot be reduced below zero. *Held*: For the IRS. The regulations requiring that under certain circumstances, a consolidated parent's basis in its subsidiary's stock must be reduced below zero were held to be valid. Covil Insulation Co., 65 TC 364 (1976).

Consolidated return filed without consent was invalid but started period of limitations for separate return. Taxpayer, a subsidiary of a long-established parent, obtained two extensions for its fiscal year ended October 31, 1957. A request for a third extension to October 15, 1958 was denied. The parent corporation, on a calendar-year basis, had a history of consistent losses. In 1956, it joined taxpayer in a Chapter XI bankruptcy proceeding. An arrangement with the creditors was eventually worked out. In 1959, a consolidated return was filed for the fiscal year ended October 31, 1957. On this return, taxpayer's net income of $97,000 was offset against the parent's loss of almost $2 million. The IRS rejected the return as invalid and asserted a deficiency against taxpayer. *Held*: For the IRS. The consent on Form 1122 was not filed by the due date of the return. No extension of time for the consolidated return was ever sought. In fact, taxpayer sought extensions for filing its separate return. Moreover, Regulation § 1.1502-14(a) requires that each subsidiary's taxable year be the same as the parent's. The parent never sought permission to change a calandar to a fiscal year. However, the deficiency was barred by the statute of limitations. Although the consolidated return was rejected as a consolidated return, it disclosed the income of each of the corporations and should be treated as taxpayer's separate return to start the running of the three-year period for assessment. The court rejected the IRS' argument that the return was never *intended* as a separate return and that taxpayer failed to sign it. (It was signed by the parent's president.) Substantial compliance was sufficient to start the running of the assessment period. The information on the return was sufficient to fully apprise the IRS of taxpayer's income and deductions, and the assessment was in fact based on the information contained in the return. General Mfg. Corp., 44 TC 513 (1965).

Corporation filing for short year prior to consolidation with new parent need not annualize income. Taxpayer, a corporation on a calendar-year basis, was acquired by another corporation, which had a fiscal year that ended April 30. In order to file a consolidated return with its new parent, taxpayer changed its tax year and filed a return for a short year beginning January 1 and ending April 30. Although the IRS had consented to the change, it contended that Section 443(b)(1) required taxpayer to annualize its income for the short period. *Held*: For taxpayer. The Tax Court held that taxpayer need not annualize its income. Regulation § 1.1502, which governs the mechanics of adding a corporation to an affiliated group, required the filing of a short period return but does not require annualization. Erwin Properties Inc., 43 TC 888 (1965), acq. 1967-1 CB 2.

Normal operating expenses constitute a "built in" deduction on consolidated return. A bank holding company acquired the stock of a cash-basis bank, which had an accrued operating loss recognized after it became part of the affiliated group. The normal operating expenses constituted a "built in" deduction, but are limited to consolidated return income attributable to the acquired bank. Rev. Rul. 79-279, 1979-CB 316.

New subsidiary's unused investment credit. The portion of consolidated unused investment credit of an affiliated group filing a consolidated return, attributable to the common parent's two new wholly owned subsidiaries, may be carried back to the parent's separate return for a year in which the subsidiaries were not in existence, but may not be carried back to any other member of the group. Rev. Rul. 75-54, 1975-1 CB 293.

Permission to change tax allocation method denied. No permission will be granted to an affiliated group that includes an insurance company to change its method of allocating consolidated tax liability to either the method in Reg-

CONSOLIDATED RETURNS: *In General*

ulation § 1.5521-1(a)(2) or to the combined method. Rev. Rul. 75-80, 1975-1 CB 292.

IRS provides example of deemed dividend election computation for consolidated returns. When an affiliated group consists of a parent corporation, *P*, and its wholly owned subsidiary, *S-1*, and that subsidiary's wholly owned subsidiary, *S-2*, the deemed dividend election of Regulation § 1.1502-32(f)(2) operates first to decrease the accumulated earnings and profits of *S-1* to zero and to increase the accumulated earnings and profits of *P* in the same amount. It then reduces the accumulated earnings and profits of *S-2* to zero and increases the accumulated earnings and profits of *S-1* in the same amount. Thus, a deemed dividend in any given year is passed only to a corporation's immediate parent in the chain of affiliation because only the amount of accumulated earnings and profits in a corporation's account at the end of the previous year is deemed distributed. Rev. Rul. 75-212, 1975-1 CB 107.

Subsidiary's year change was group's year change. A subsidiary that joined an affiliated group in the preceding year changed its taxable year to that of the group, as required by the consolidated return regulations. The group was considered to have made a change within the prior 10-year period and the IRS' consent was required to make another change. Rev. Rul. 74-326, 1974-2 CB 142.

Permission to break consolidation denied. The IRS ruled that no permission to discontinue filing consolidated returns will be granted where a common parent's home state imposed a tax on a corporation's net worth, and its wholly owned subsidiary in another state is subject to a capital stock tax that is declared unconstitutional and replaced with a similar tax. Rev. Rul. 74-378, 1974-2 CB 287.

Accounting period for member leaving the group. A corporation that was a member of an affiliated group that was acquired during the group's calendar year may change its accounting period to a fiscal year, and the income of the part of the year during which it was a group member is reported in the consolidated return. Rev. Rul. 74-585, 1974-2 CB 143.

Subsidiary amending its tax return in order to file a consolidated return with parent did not have to annualize its income. A fiscal year subsidiary had filed its tax return prior to its parent's election to file consolidated returns. The subsidiary was required to amend its tax return to reflect the consolidation. The income reflected in the short year amended return of the subsidiary did not have to be annualized. Rev. Rul. 70-378, 1970-2 CB 178.

Mexican subsidiary could be included in consolidated return. A domestic parent could elect to file a consolidated return with a wholly owned Mexican subsidiary that was organized solely to comply with Mexican law as to title and operation of property in Mexico. The domestic parent could not have acquired the land directly. Thus, the requirements of Section 1504(d) were met. Rev. Rul. 70-379, 1970-2 CB 179.

Corporations organized under the laws of Mexico by a domestic parent may file consolidated returns. Corporations organized under the laws of Mexico by a domestic parent that owns 100 percent of their capital stock and otherwise meets the requirements of Section 1504(d) may file consolidated returns with their domestic parent. Rev. Rul. 69-182, 1969-1 CB 218.

Separate or consolidated declarations of estimated tax may be filed for the first two consecutive consolidated return years. The IRS ruled that an affiliated group may file either separate or consolidated declarations of estimated tax for the first two consecutive consolidated return years. Thereafter, Regulation § 1.1502-5(a)(1) requires the filing of a consolidated declaration of estimated tax. Rev. Rul. 69-622, 1969-2 CB 169.

Short period return of corporation joining a consolidated group need not be annualized. The IRS ruled that where a corporation becomes a member of an affiliated group of corporations and the corporation joins the group in the filing of a consolidated return under Section 1501, the corporation is not required under Section 443(b) to annualize its income on a

CONSOLIDATED RETURNS: *Control Defined*

separate short period return. (Rev. Rul. 57-602 revoked.) Rev. Rul. 67-189, 1967-1 CB 255.

Consolidated estimated tax required where consolidated income tax returns filed for two previous years. A parent corporation and its subsidiaries filed consolidated income tax returns for 1965 and 1966. Separate estimated returns were filed for 1965 and 1966 by each member. The IRS ruled that under Regulation § 1.1502-5, the affiliated group was required to file its declaration of estimated tax on a consolidated basis for 1967. Rev. Rul. 67-334, 1967-2 CB 316.

Bankruptcy of a member of an affiliated group does not negate requirement that consolidated returns be filed. After filing consolidated returns for a number of years, one of the members of an affiliated group filed a voluntary petition in bankruptcy and was adjudicated a bankrupt. The trustee in bankruptcy failed to file Form 1122 (consent and authorization to common parent to file on a consolidated basis). Regulation § 1.1502-11(a) requires, with certain exceptions, that if a consolidated return is made for any year, consolidated returns must be made for every subsequent year during which the affiliated group remains in existence. Since the bankruptcy of a member corporation is not one of the exceptions, the IRS ruled that the affiliated group must continue to file their returns on a consolidated basis. Rev. Rul. 63-104, 1963-1 CB 172.

Validity of a subsidiary's short period return depends on whether consolidated return is filed. If an election is made to file a consolidated return, each subsidiary must adopt an annual accounting period in conformity with that of the common parent not later than the close of the first consolidated year ending thereafter. The IRS ruled that if a subsidiary, in anticipation that it will be included in a consolidated return with its acquiring parent, files a timely short period return to conform its accounting period to that of the parent, the short period return will have no validity if a consolidated return is not filed. Rev. Rul. 56-360, 1956-2 CB 595.

Control Defined

Taxpayer had less than 80 percent control; consolidated returns not permitted. Taxpayer owned directly 62 percent and trustees, under a voting trust, held 25 percent of the stock of a corporation. Taxpayer filed a consolidated return with the corporation in the year 1954. The voting trust was created in 1952 and was to continue for 20 years. In 1953, the legislature enacted a provision that a voting trust can be created for a period not exceeding 10 years. Taxpayer argued that the result of this enactment was to render the voting trust invalid and that, therefore, it really owned "at least 80 percent" of the voting power of all classes of stock, which would entitle it to file consolidated returns. *Held:* For the IRS. The court held that the taxpayer could not file consolidated returns. Even if the voting trust were invalid, the beneficial owners would have the right to vote the stock. Taxpayer would still have less than 80 percent of voting control. Standard Lumber Co., 299 F2d 382, 62-1 USTC ¶ 9200 (9th Cir. 1962).

Eligibility to file consolidated return upheld. *C*, the owner of 80 percent of the oustanding stock of *P*, transferred his ownership in *P* to a broker to be held in a subordinated securities account. Under the terms of the account, *C* retained some of the incidents of ownership, including the right to dividends and the right to vote the stock, but the broker acquired legal title to the stock, and the stock could be sold to satisfy claims of the broker's creditor. While this account was in effect, *C* (and other stockholders of *P*) sold their stock in *P* to *DL*. *DL* filed a consolidated return with *P*, and the IRS determined that *DL* had not acquired more than 80 percent control of *P* due to the nature of *C*'s account with the broker. *Held:* For taxpayer. During the period that the *P* stock was held in the broker account, the monthly statements sent to *C* by the broker indicated the stock was held "long," thus signifying that the parties thought of *C* as the owner throughout the period. The agreement with the broker created a bailment. Therefore *C* was the beneficial owner of the stock; after the sale *DL* directly owned at least 80 percent of the stock of *P* within the meaning of Section 1504(a). Miami Nat'l Bank, 67 TC 793 (1977).

CONSOLIDATED RETURNS: *Control Defined*

Common ownership required for 80 percent of Section 1563. Sirkel owned 100 percent of the outstanding stock of *O* and 69.4 percent of the outstanding stock of *W*. The other 30.6 percent of *W*'s stock was owned by an unrelated party. The IRS determined that *O* and *W* were members of a controlled group of brother-sister corporations, and assessed deficiencies. Its contention was based on the premise that the stock of a 50 percent stockholder could be included in computing the 80 percent test of Section 1563. *Held:* For taxpayer. Under Vogel Fertilizer Co., 455 US 16 (1982), each stockholder must own stock in each brother-sister corporation for purposes of the 80 percent test of Section 1563. As Sirkel owned only 69.4 percent of *W*'s stock, *W* and *O* were not part of a controlled group. Overhead Door Co. of Albuquerque, 43 TCM 406, ¶ 82,039 P-H Memo. TC (1982).

Consolidated returns and direct ownership requirement under the consolidated returns provisions explained. The IRS ruled that a domestic parent corporation that is the grantor and sole beneficiary of a revocable voting trust be treated as directly owning the stock that it transferred to that voting trust for purposes of Section 1504(a). The direct ownership requirement of Section 1504(a) means beneficial ownership, and where a parent corporation retains dominion and control over the stock it transfers to a revocable voting trust for its own benefit, it is treated as the direct owner of that stock. Rev. Rul. 84-79, 1984-1 CB 190.

Participating preferred stock not exempt from 80 percent test for eligibility to file consolidated return. Under the 80 percent test of Section 1504 for determining eligibility to file a consolidated return, the parent of the group need not count stock that is "limited and preferred as to dividends." Nonvoting preferred stock that may participate in corporate earnings beyond its fixed preferred dividend is not "limited and preferred" stock. If the parent owns less than 80 percent of that class of stock, the group cannot file a consolidated return. Rev. Rul. 79-21, 1979-1 CB 290.

Fifty percent test in Section 1502 for determining reverse acquisitions does not include stock acquired in a prior unrelated transaction. *P* Corporation and *T* Corporation, common parents of affiliated groups, effected a merger of *T* into *P*, with each share of *T* being exchanged for a share of *P*. After the merger, former *T* stockholders owned more than 50 percent of the value of *P* stock. However, this figure included *P* stock acquired by a former *T* stockholder in a prior transaction unrelated to the merger. The IRS held that this stock did not have to be counted for purposes of the 50 percent test in Regulation § 1.1502-75(d)(3)(i), which is used in determining whether a reverse acquisition had accurred. Rev. Rul. 76-164, 1976-1 CB 270.

Nonvoting convertible preferred stock not stock. Nonvoting convertible preferred stock does not constitute stock in determining the voting power of all classes of stock owned by a parent corporation under Section 1504(a). Rev. Rul. 71-83, 1971-1 CB 268.

Preferred stock entitled to elect some directors is voting stock. Preferred stock of a subsidiary that may be voted to elect three directors out of eight is voting stock. The voting power requirements of Section 1504(a) is met if all the common and one half of the preferred stock is owned by the parent. Rev. Rul. 69-126, 1969-1 CB 218.

Common parent not affiliated with an unrelated corporation whose stock was included as leased property from another unrelated corporation. For consolidated return purposes, a common parent of an affiliated group is not affiliated with an unrelated corporation whose stock was included with certain properties leased from another unrelated corporation. Under the terms of the lease, the common parent is not the owner of the stock of the unrelated corporation within the meaning of Section 1504(a). Rev. Rul. 68-623, 1968-2 CB 404.

Unexercised warrants do not affect 80 percent stock requirement for filing consolidated returns. *Z* owned more than 80 percent of *Y* stock. *Y* issued to investors warrants exercisable within five years. These warrants conferred no rights prior to exercise. If the stock represented by the warrants were added to *Y* outstanding stock, *Z* would not have the required 80 percent needed to file a consolidated return. The IRS ruled that the unexercised warrants were not to be taken into account in determining qualification. These warrants did not confer any rights prior to their exercise and consequently did not constitute stock ownership. Rev. Rul. 64-251, 1964-2 CB 338.

Elections

Consolidated regulations prohibiting breaking of election found valid. Taxpayer argued that Regulation § 1.1502-11A(a) was invalid. Regulation 1.1502-11A(a) provides that a corporation that files a consolidated return for any taxable year must continue to file consolidated returns for subsequent years unless certain conditions are met. The district court held for the IRS. *Held:* Affirmed. The regulation is a reasonable exercise of the discretion conferred on the Secretary of the Treasury by Congress when it enacted Sections 1501 and 1502. Orgill Bros. & Co., 508 F2d 1219, 75-1 USTC ¶ 9196, 35 AFTR2d 75-600 (6th Cir. 1975).

Consolidated return regulations valid. Taxpayer and its 19 wholly owned subsidiary corporations elected to file a consolidated income tax return. In the subsequent year, taxpayer and its subsidiaries filed separate returns. The IRS contended that they were required to file a consolidated return. The Tax Court held for the IRS. *Held:* Affirmed. Regulation § 1.1502-11A(a) provides that if an affiliated group of corporations elect to file a consolidated return, they must file a consolidated return in each subsequent year during which the consolidated group remains in existence. The regulations accurately reflect the clearly expressed will of Congress; therefore, taxpayer was required to file a consolidated return with its subsidiaries. Regal, Inc., 435 F2d 922, 70-2 USTC ¶ 9703, 26 AFTR2d 70-5806 (2d Cir. 1970).

Filing consolidated returns constitutes election; failure to file Form 1122 not fatal. Petitioners became affiliated on February 1, 1954 and filed consolidated returns for 1954 through 1956. The subsidiaries failed to file Form 1122 (consent and authorization to file on a consolidated basis). They contended that this rendered their election to file consolidated returns void and that their income must be computed on a separate basis under Regulation § 1.1502-18(a). The Tax Court held that the filing of a consolidated return constitutes the election and consent to have the tax computed on a consolidated basis. Form 1122 may be filed after an effective election has been made (Regulation § 1.1502-18(a)). *Held:* Affirmed. The requirement that Form 1122 be filed is merely an administrative provision for the protection of the IRS. Regulation § 1.1502-18(a) is not intended to provide taxpayers with the means of repudiating their election by some omission, but was designed to provide a means of curing defects. Nor does it require the IRS to notify the taxpayer of the defects; failure to so notify results in acceptance of the return and ends the matter. The 1954 consolidated return should have included the income of the subsidiaries from February 1, 1954, the date of affiliation. Landy Towel & Linen Serv., Inc., 317 F2d 362, 63-2 USTC ¶ 9513 (3d Cir. 1963).

Corporation elected consolidated return too late. Taxpayer believed that it could have avoided the personal holding company tax by filing a consolidated return with its subsidiaries, and sought consolidated treatment of its prior year's returns. The IRS rejected this request on the grounds that it was not timely. *Held:* For the IRS. Consolidated returns should be filed by the date of the corporate returns for the year. An exception in the regulations permitting late filing by some members of the group applies only if other members joined in a consolidated return. The IRS did not abuse its discretion. Lion Assocs., 515 F. Supp. 550, 81-2 USTC ¶ 9505, 48 AFTR2d 81-5276 (ED Pa. 1981).

Subsidiary obtaining no benefits from Section 931 was allowed to file consolidated return with its parent. Taxpayer, together with its three wholly owned domestic subsidiaries,

CONSOLIDATED RETURNS: *Elections*

filed a consolidated return for the year in question. One of taxpayer's subsidiaries did its entire business in Puerto Rico and thereby qualified under Section 931. Due to a net operating loss, the subsidiary was not able to avail itself of the benefits of Section 931. The IRS contended that the subsidiary was ineligible to join in a consolidated return with taxpayer pursuant to Section 1504(b)(4). *Held:* For taxpayer. The literal wording of Section 1504(b)(4) indicates that the existence of a benefit under Section 931 is a prerequisite to its operative significance. An examination of Section 931 points in the same direction. To argue, as the IRS implicitly did, that the "benefit" is the exclusion from gross income, without regard to the economic effect of such an exclusion, would be to give the statute a strange interpretation, inconsistent with its objective. Since the subsidiary had a loss, it could not obtain the benefits of Section 931. Within the meaning of the statute, accordingly, the subsidiary was eligible to file a consolidated return with taxpayer. In the light of the foregoing, Rev. Rul. 65-293, 1965-2 CB 323, was held invalid. Burke Concrete Accessories, Inc., 56 TC 588 (1971).

Election to file separate returns is proper after significant change in tax law. Taxpayer and its subsidiaries filed consolidated returns for the calendar years 1961 through 1963. The return for 1963 was filed pursuant to an extension for filing on June 16, 1964. For the calendar years 1964 and 1965, taxpayer and its subsidiaries filed separate returns. The IRS contended that taxpayer improperly filed separate returns for 1964 and 1965 because a consolidated return was filed for 1963. *Held:* For taxpayer. The enactment of the Revenue Act of 1964 constituted a significant change in the tax laws within the meaning of Regulation § 1.1502-11A. Therefore, a new election was authorized. There was no basis for limiting the exercise of a new election to the return filed for 1963, as that year was entirely unaffected by any change in law. The election to file separate returns made in the 1964 return was therefore proper. Robbins Door & Sash Co., 55 TC 313 (1970).

Ambiguous revenue ruling makes election to file a separate return valid. Shortly after the enactment of the Revenue Act of 1962, taxpayer filed its first consolidated return for its 1962 fiscal year. In its 1963 fiscal year, taxpayer elected to file a separate return. *Held:* For taxpayer. The interpretation of Rev. Rul. 62-204 by taxpayer was entirely reasonable because it was ambiguous. The IRS' later attempts to clarify its meaning reflected its ambiguous nature. Taxpayer was therefore entitled to file a separate return, not withstanding the prohibition of the ruling. Corn Belt Hatcheries of Ark., 52 TC 636 (1969), acq. (in result only) 1970-1 CB xv.

Affiliated group's allocation of consolidated tax liability did not invalidate its election. An affiliated group allocated consolidated tax liability among its members for nontax purposes using a method different from that provided in the group's election under Regulation § 1.1502-33(d)(3). The IRS stated that this different allocation would not invalidate the group's election. However, for tax purposes, earnings and profits of group members must be determined in accordance with the election. Rev. Rul. 76-302, 1976-2 CB 257.

Affiliated group waived consolidated return provisions. The parent of a group of affiliated corporations filed an individual return on the return's due date. Subsequently, it realized that it had done so inadvertently, and all three members of the group had intended to file a consolidated return. The IRS ruled that a consolidated return could not be filed, since by filing an individual return, the parent waived its right to file as a consolidated group. Rev. Rul. 76-393, 1976-2 CB 255.

Controlled group of corporations may amend election under Regulation § 1.1564-1(b) provided that at least one year remains in the statutory period of assessment. The IRS ruled that a controlled group of corporations may amend an election under Regulation § 1.1564-1(b) at any time prior to one year remaining on the statutory period of assessment, provided the corporations file necessary claims for refund and/or amended returns. Rev. Rul. 72-603, 1972-2 CB 517.

CONSOLIDATED RETURNS: *Elections*

Consolidated return election not adversely affected by members' failure to change accounting period or file separate return. The IRS stated that an affiliated group's election to file a consolidated tax return is not adversely affected where one member of the group fails to obtain permission to change its accounting period or fails to file a timely amended separate return to exclude items included in the consolidated return. Rev. Rul. 72-258, 1972-1 CB 283.

Member of affiliated group for 30 days or less may elect to not be considered as member of group. The IRS ruled that a corporation that had been a member of an affiliated group for 30 days or less could, at its option and during a consolidated return year, be considered as not having been a member of the group during such year. Rev. Rul. 71-440, 1971-2 CB 326.

Treatment of intangible drilling costs of consolidated group. Where a common parent has elected to capitalize intangible drilling costs and a member of the group has elected to expense them, each must follow the previously elected method. When properties are transferred between the group and the common parent, the prior election for such costs remains in effect. If operating properties are acquired by a member who did not make an election, they may be expensed or capitalized even if they were acquired from a member of the consolidated group. (IT 3763 superseded.) Rev. Rul. 69-590, 1969-2 CB 170.

When new common parent acquires stock of existing common parent, old group may not file consolidated return. A new group came into existence during the year as a result of a new common parent acquiring the stock of an existing common parent. The new common parent could not make an election not to be a member of the new group. Accordingly, the old group ceased to exist and could not file a consolidated return for the entire year. Rev. Rul. 69-163, 1969-1 CB 217.

Domestic member of consolidated group may elect with respect to foreign corporation when common parent does not. Regulation § 1.1502-77(a) provides that a common parent shall, in all matters relating to the tax liability for the consolidated return year, be sole agent for each subsidiary in its group. On the other hand, Regulation § 1.963-1(a)(4) provides that, if the common parent filing a consolidated return under Section 1501 makes no election as to treatment of the group as a single U.S. stockholder, then any member of such group may make such election. Because of the need for consistent treatment under Sections 963 and 964, a domestic corporation that is a member of an affiliated group filing consolidated returns may make an election under Regulation § 1.964-1(c)(3) if the election is not made by a controlling U.S. stockholder, as required. Rev. Rul. 68-641, 1968-2 CB 325.

IRS rules on deemed consents by members of affiliated groups. In response to inquiries, the IRS has clarified the method to be used by members of an affiliated group in consenting to the filing of a consolidated return. As stated in Regulation § 1.1502-75(b), the consent of a corporation is made by such corporation joining in the making of a consolidated return. A corporation is deemed to have joined in the making of a consolidated return if it files a Form 1122 in the manner specified in Regulation § 1.1502-75(h)(2). If a member fails to file a Form 1122, Regulation § 1.1502-75(b)(2) authorizes the IRS to determine, under the facts and circumstances, that such member has joined in the making of a consolidated return. Rev. Rul. 67-146, 1967-1 CB 254.

New corporation was organized indirectly by parent; no new consolidated return election. The regulations provide that an affiliated group that has elected to file consolidated returns does not have the usual right of a new election because a new corporation joins the group, if the new member was created or organized directly or indirectly by a member of the group. In the situation here ruled on, a parent of an affiliated group acquired the stock of a new corporation one month after its organization by the wives of two of the three controlling stockholders of the parent. The IRS held that the acquired corporation

CONSOLIDATED RETURNS: *Excess Loss Account*

was indirectly organized by the acquiring corporation. Accordingly, it denied the affiliated group the right to file separate returns for the taxable year of the acquisition. Rev Rul. 59-326, 1959-2 CB 197.

Excess Loss Account

Excess loss account reduces aggregate basis. Taxpayer filed consolidated returns with its subsidiary. It owned assets with adjusted bases exceeding their fair market value and had an excess loss account. The group was acquired by another corporation, and the new group elected to file consolidated returns. During the first consolidated year of the new group, taxpayer sold one of the assets at a loss. The IRS ruled that in determining whether the built-in loss deduction was subject to the Regulation 1.1502-15(a)(1) limit on deductibility, the loss account reduced the aggregate adjusted bases of taxpayer's assets for the purpose of computing its aggregate bases to fair market value ratio under Regulation 1.1502-15(a)(4)(i)(b). If the excess of the loss account over the aggregate adjusted bases does not exceed 15 percent, the built-in deduction is considered de minimis and the limit on deductibility of the loss does not apply. Rev. Rul. 83-14, 1983-1 CB 199.

Intercorporate Transactions

No deferral on gain from intercompany sale of timber. The IRS held that gains realized on intercompany sales, involving a parent and its subsidiaries, were taxable as ordinary income on a 1978 consolidated return. The lower court upheld the IRS. *Held:* Affirmed. Although gain or loss on intercompany transactions is generally deferred when a consolidated return is filed, Regulation §1.1502-13 provides, in part, that where depletable property is acquired by an affiliated corporation in a deferred intercompany transaction, the gain is immediately taxable as ordinary income. Georgia Pac. Corp., 648 F2d 653, 81-2 USTC ¶ 9515, 48 AFTR2d 81-5484 (9th Cir. 1981).

Amounts paid by subsidiary to parent of consolidated group were dividends as controlling parent demonstrated both the intention and the ability to have its subsidiary pay the parent an amount equal to the savings contemplated from filing consolidated returns. *CW* paid certain amounts to *P*, the parent of its consolidated group. *P* then made distributions to taxpayer. The payment from *CW* to *P* was characterized as an advance of the allocable amount of *CW*'s tax liability. Therefore, amounts received by taxpayer and *P* were not treated as distributions of earnings and profits, although *CW* had sufficient earnings and profits to characterize the distributions as such. The Tax Court agreed with the taxpayer. *Held:* Reversed. Substance over form indicated both intent and ability by a controlling parent to have its subsidiary pay the parent an amount equal to the savings contemplated from filing consolidated returns. Therefore, that amount is a dividend unless it was shown that the subsidiary had insufficient earnings and profits to permit it to pay the amounts without impairing its capital. Hence, the distributions were dividends in this instance. Singleton, Jr., 569 F2d 863, 78-1 USTC ¶ 9301, 41 AFTR2d 78-952 (5th Cir.), cert. denied, 439 US 940 (1978).

Basis of property acquired from member of affiliated group through mortgage foreclosure is not stepped up. Over the years, the taxpayer had advanced over $500,000 to a wholly owned subsidiary. These advances were secured by mortgages. In an effort to collect this debt, a judgment was obtained against the subsidiary late in 1955, and court foreclosure action was initiated. At the foreclosure sale in 1956, good faith attempts to obtain a buyer failed, and the taxpayer, the only bidder, bid in all of the subsidiary's assets for the amount of its judgment ($517,000). Of this amount, $476,000 was set up as depreciable assets, although the subsidiary's basis for these same assets was $200,000 less. Taxpayer and the subsidiary filed a consolidated return for 1956. The IRS determined that the basis should be the same as it was in the subsidiary's hands, since Regulation § 1.1502-38(c) provides that the basis of depreciable property is not affected by a transfer during a consolidated return period. *Held:* For the IRS. The court, after finding a lack of judicial precedent, construed that regulation to apply to a court-ordered, court-conducted mortgage foreclosure as well as to a voluntary transfer. Southern Silk Mill, 220 F. Supp. 437, 63-2 USTC ¶ 9592 (ED Tenn. 1963).

Deficiency assessed under sharing agreement not deductible. Taxpayer, a former member of an affiliated group of corporations that filed consolidated returns, entered into an agreement to share the payment of potential federal income tax liabilities that might subsequently be owed by the affiliated group for prior consolidated return years. Following an assessment against the group, taxpayer made a payment and deducted its portion under the sharing agreement. The IRS determined that the payment represented Federal income taxes and was not deductible. *Held:* For the IRS. When taxpayer filed a consolidated return, it consented to being taxable on the entire income of the group and was severally liable for payment of the tax. Accordingly, since the tax may be collected from any one of the members of the group, it was not deductible under Section 275. Globe Prod. Corp., 72 TC 609 (1979), acq. 1980-1 CB 1.

Intercorporate profit of parent company eliminated in consolidated return was not deemed ordinary income in year stock of subsidiary was sold to outsider; Rev. Rul. 60-245 overturned. Taxpayer constructed a housing project for its controlled subsidiary. Taxpayer's profit on the operation was eliminated on the consolidated return filed with the subsidiary. In a later year, the taxpayer sold all the stock of the subsidiary to an unrelated corporation. The IRS contended that the taxpayer's profit on the construction was ordinary income to it in the year of sale. *Held:* For taxpayer. There is no authority in the statute or regulations for taxing the previously eliminated profit. The consolidated return regulations provide only that the eliminated profit is to reduce the subsidiary's basis for depreciation on the project, and this was done. The transaction in all respects was bona fide and was not to be considered an "open" transaction until some disposition was made to an outside party.

Rev. Rul. 60-245, which supports the IRS' position, cites no authority and does not justify a judicial interpretation to protect the revenue. That ruling was in fact issued two months before the deficiency notice in this case. Henry C. Beck Builders, Inc., 41 TC 616 (1964).

Elimination of intercompany profits on consolidated return does not constitute an accounting method. In a prior opinion in this case (TCM 1964-145), the Tax Court held on the authority of Henry C. Beck Builders, Inc., 41 TC 616 (1963), that a parent corporation's intercompany profits from contracts with subsidiaries, which were properly eliminated from consolidated returns filed for the years 1955 through 1957, did not constitute income taxable to the parent in 1958, when all the stock of the subsidiaries was sold to an unrelated party. The court agreed to reconsider its prior opinion after the IRS contended that the instant case was distinguishable from *Beck*, since it involved post-1954 years whereas *Beck* involved pre-1954 years, and that Section 481 of the 1954 Code mandated the income adjustment because of a change in the accounting method. *Held:* For taxpayer. Elimination of intercompany profits under the consolidated return regulations did not constitute an accounting method, and the termination of an affiliation did not change the accounting method. Thus the IRS' inclusion of the eliminated intercompany profits in the parent's income is neither authorized nor required by Section 481. Vernon C. Neal, Inc., 23 TCM 1338, ¶ 64,220 P-H Memo. TC (1964).

Prepaid rent between members of affiliated group. Rent prepaid by a cash method corporation to its wholly owned accrual method subsidiary, both part of a consolidated return, is a defined intercompany transaction. The expense is not deductible in the income includable until the year to which the rent applies. Rev. Rul. 74-589, 1974-2 CB 286.

Deferred intercompany inventory gain recognized in short taxable year when stock of subsidiary was sold to an unrelated corporation. An affiliated group filed consolidated tax re-

Consolidated Returns: *Net Operating Loss Carry-Overs*

turns for a number of years during which intercompany inventory gains were deferred. The stock of the subsidiary that realized the gains was sold to an unrelated corporation. The deferred gain was taken into account by the subsidiary during the taxable period for final consolidation with the old parent. The subsidiary was not required to reflect an adjustment for initial inventory amount in its taxable income for the period affiliated with the new parent. Rev. Rul. 72-321, 1972-1 CB 285.

Net Operating Loss Carry-Overs

Deduction for carry-over of preaffiliation losses not permitted. Beginning in 1970, *W* owned 80 percent of *R*'s outstanding common stock, and subsequently filed consolidated returns with *R,* using *R's* pre-acquisition net operating losses to offet its profits. The IRS determined that those carry-over losses could not be deducted. *Held:* For the IRS. Regulation §1.1502-21(c) applied, limiting the net operating loss carry-overs to the portion of the group's consolidated taxable income attributable to the single member. Since *R* generated no income in the year of consolidation, its preacquisition carry-over losses could not be used to offset its parent corporation's postacquisition profits. Wolter Constr. Co., 634 F2d 1029, 80-2 USTC ¶ 9799, 46 AFTR2d 80-6089 (6th Cir. 1980).

Insolvent member of affiliated group not entitled to full refund received by its parents. *M* Corporation, one of an affiliated group of insurance companies that filed consolidated returns, became insolvent, and came into the hands of a state insurance superintendent. The group parent received a net operating loss carry-back refund for *M*'s losses, and the superintendent sued to have the refund turned over to *M*. The district court held that *M* was entitled only to part of the refund equal to its own tax payments; the superintendent appealed. *Held:* Affirmed. The remainder of the net operating loss was not *M*'s asset, since it could not carry forward the loss (it had already received a refund for the carry-back). Also, *M* could not bargain with the parent for the use of the loss, since *M* could not withdraw its consent to a consolidated return without the IRS' consent. Jump v. Manchester Life & Casualty Management Corp., 579 F2d 449, 78-2 USTC ¶ 9557, 42 AFTR2d 78-5275 (8th Cir. 1978).

Portion of consolidated net operating loss for 1962 attributable to subsidiary could be carried back to offset income of parent in a separate return year prior to incorporation of the subsidiary. Taxpayer organized a wholly owned subsidiary and filed a consolidated return for 1962. The consolidated return resulted in a net operating loss, which taxpayer carried back to 1959 and 1960, when it filed separate returns. The Tax Court allowed a carry-back only for taxpayer's portion of the consolidated loss. *Held:* Reversed. Citing Rev. Rul. 64-93, the court held that the operating loss attributable to the subsidiary could be offset against taxpayer's income in a separate return prior to incorporation of the subsidiary. Nibur Building Corp., 444 F2d 1020, 71-1 USTC ¶ 9474, 28 AFTR2d 71-5030 (7th Cir. 1971).

Carry-back of net operating losses allowed to year corporation was not a member of affiliated group, or not in existence. Taxpayer, in its consolidated return, sought to carry-back from 1957 to 1955 its losses and losses of 12 affiliated corporations to offset its taxable income and that of only 6 of the 12 for 1955, the year at issue. The members of the group sustaining losses in 1957 were not members of the affiliated group or were not in existence in 1955. The Tax Court agreed with the IRS that the taxable income or loss of each member of the group must, before consolidation, be computed individually. *Held:* Reversed, in part, and remanded. Where losses were incurred by newly created members of an affiliated group, a carry-back of a net operating loss to offset an existing member's income was permissible to a year in which the new corporation did not yet exist. Midland Management Co., 316 F2d 190, 63-1 USTC ¶ 9432 (5th Cir. 1963).

Consolidated regulation could not be applied retroactively. Taxpayer parent filed a consolidated return in 1965 with a subsidiary that came into existence in 1963. The IRS determined that taxpayer could not carry back the 1965 loss, attributable to the subsidiary, to its separate 1962 return. *Held:* For the IRS. Current Regulation § 1.1502-31A(d) permits a parent to carry back a subsidiary's loss to a year when the subsidiary was not in existence, but is only applicable for years after 1975 and is not to be applied retroactively. F.D. Rich Co., 79-1 USTC ¶ 9385, 44 AFTR2d 79-5032 (D. Conn. 1979).

Parent's waiver of loss deduction binding on subsidiaries. Taxpayer was a member of an affiliated group of corporations that filed consolidated returns for several taxable years. The IRS disallowed a loss deduction claimed on the consolidated return for 1973, and the parent consented to the disallowance. Subsequently, the taxpayer, no longer affiliated with the group, claimed a carry-forward deduction for its share of the 1973 loss. The IRS disallowed the loss on the grounds that the parent acted as agent for the entire group when it agreed to the disallowance. *Held:* For the IRS. The parent corporation had the authority to agree for the group that the loss was not allowable. That the taxpayer left the affiliation does not terminate the agency relationship regarding tax matters arising from a consolidated return. Once a group of corporations files consolidated returns, each agrees to be bound by regulations governing such matters, particularly the parent's right to act for the subsidiaries in tax matters. Craigie, Inc., 84 TC 466 (1985).

Loss carry-overs from pre-consolidation years could not offset minimum tax. In 1972, the shareholders of *A* and *B* Corporations contributed all of their stock in those corporations in exchange for the stock of a new company, *C* Corporation. In 1970 and 1971, *A* and *B* filed separate corporate income tax returns. *A* had tax-preference items in 1971 and generated tax carry-overs in both 1970 and 1971. *A*, *B*, and *C* filed consolidated returns for 1972 and 1973, and attempted to offset *A*'s carry-overs from 1970 and 1971 against the preference items *B* generated in 1972 and 1973. The IRS determined that the loss carry-overs could not be used to offset the minimum tax. *Held:* For the IRS. No regulations authorize one corporation to use the tax carry-overs of another in computing minimum tax liability, and no authority permits the carry-overs of one corporation to be used in computing the minimum tax liability of another on a consolidated return. Wegman's Properties, Inc., 78 TC 786 (1982).

Net operating loss could not be carried back to preconsolidation year because of delay. On January 30, 1976, a corporation was organized, and on March 31, 1976, taxpayer acquired all of its stock. Taxpayer filed a consolidated return with its subsidiary for 1976 and 1977 and incurred losses entirely attributable to the operations of the subsidiary. Taxpayer carried those losses back to 1974, and the IRS disallowed the carry-back. *Held:* For the IRS. The regulations permit the carry-back of a subsidiary's loss to a preconsolidation year if the loss corporation becomes a member of the group immediately after it is organized. In this case, the subsidiary did not become a member of the group immediately after its organization. There was a two month delay between incorporation and conveyance of the stock to taxpayer by the original stockholders, and those two months constituted a short taxable year of the subsidiary. Jim Burch & Assocs., 76 TC 202 (1980).

Filing of separate return by subsidiary prevents net operating loss carry-back. Taxpayer organized two subsidiaries, including *H*, on October 6, 1972. *H* filed a short tax return for the taxable year ended October 31, 1972. Taxpayer filed a separate return for the taxable year ended October 31, 1972, reflecting taxable income in excess of $2 million, excluding net operating loss carry-overs and carry-backs. For the taxable year ended October 31, 1973, taxpayer filed a consolidated return with its subsidiaries in which it carried back net operating losses from *H*. The effect was to offset taxpayer's income for the taxable year ended October 31, 1972 with *H*'s net operating losses. The IRS disallowed the carry-back to the taxable year ended October 31, 1972. *Held:* For the IRS. Although Regulation § 1.502-79(a)(2) created an exception that allowed the carry-back of consolidated

Consolidated Returns: *Net Operating Loss Carry-Overs*

losses attributable to a subsidiary to the separate year of the parent, it did not apply where the subsidiary had been in existence and had filed a separate return in the previous year. Accordingly, that portion of the consolidated net operating loss attributable to H for the taxable year ended October 31, 1973 could not be carried back and applied against taxpayer's separate return income for the taxable year ended October 31, 1972. Electronic Sensing Prods., Inc., 69 TC 276 (1977).

Effect of late filing on validity of consolidated return and extent of consolidated net operating loss carry-back. Taxpayer and its newly formed subsidiaries filed a consolidated income tax return for 1964, six days after the extended due date. This return reflected substantial taxable income. Subsequent consolidated returns reported losses, and taxpayer attempted to carry back the 1966 consolidated loss to a 1963 return of the parent. The IRS determined that the late-filed consolidated return resulted in denial of the consolidation privilege and that the carry-back of the entire loss to the parent's 1963 year was an error. *Held:* For the IRS, in part. The late filing did not invalidate the election to file consolidated returns (pre-1966 regulations). However, the carry-back of the 1966 loss was limited in that only the parent's portion of the loss could be carried back to its separate 1963 return. Daron Indus. Inc., 62 TC 847 (1974).

Net operating losses of subsidiary were deductible on consolidated return. Taxpayer's activities included ownership and operation of a motel. Taxpayer purchased 56 percent of the stock of X Corporation, which owned and operated a hotel that sustained operating losses. X then sold the hotel to one of taxpayer's subsidiaries at a loss and leased back the property. Subsequently, and over a period of two years, taxpayer acquired additional stock of X to bring its ownership to 80 percent of X's outstanding stock. X was liquidated, and taxpayer claimed the X net operating losses, including the loss on the sale of the hotel building, on its consolidated return with X. The IRS disallowed the loss deduction. *Held:* For taxpayer. The principal purpose of taxpayer's acquisition of control of X was not tax avoidance as stipulated in Section 269, but sound business reasons. Nor did X's business change sufficiently after its acquisition to preclude the loss carry-overs under Section 382(a). Further, the sale of the hotel to taxpayer's subsidiary was recognized, and the loss sustained by X was allowable. Capri Inc., 65 TC 162 (1973).

Carry-back of consolidated group loss to year in which member did not file a return disallowed. In 1969, taxpayer organized a wholly owned subsidiary that did not file a return for that year or authorize taxpayer to file a consolidated return on its behalf. Consolidated returns were filed in subsequent years. In 1972, the consolidated group realized a net loss, and taxpayer claimed a carry-back against its 1969 taxable income. The IRS disallowed a portion of the deductions. *Held:* For the IRS. Under Regulation § 1.1502-79(a)(1)(i), only the portion of the group's 1972 loss attributable to taxpayer's operations can be carried back to a year in which it filed a separate return. It was immaterial that the subsidiary did not file a separate return for that year. Luna Indus., Inc., 43 TCM 963, ¶ 82,168 P-H Memo. TC (1982).

Acquisition of tax losses by brother corporation allowed. A sole stockholder sold 100 percent of stock of one corporation to his wholly owned second corporation so that on a consolidated return, the first corporation's losses could offset the second corporation's income. The IRS claimed that the transfer was not effective to pass title to the stock from the stockholder to the profitable corporation. *Held:* For taxpayer. The sale was valid for the purpose of creating an affiliated group, despite the lack of business purpose, the contingent nature of the sales price (the amount was never paid), and the fact that the transfer was voidable under California law. Gunlock Corp., 43 TCM 687, ¶ 82,105 P-H Memo. TC (1982).

If acquisition of subsidiary lacks business purpose, loss is not deductible on consolidated returns. One affiliated group acquired a loss subsidiary from another affiliated group controlled by the same individual and sought to utilize the net operating loss of the acquired subsidiary in the consolidated return. The IRS disallowed the net operating loss carry-over. *Held:* For the IRS. The subsidiary's loss was not allowable for determining consolidated taxable income because of the lack of the requisite business purpose for affiliation. Even though a proper connection through stock ownership existed, a business purpose must be shown for an affiliation before the acquired corporation can be treated as a member of the affiliated group. The court also noted that a primary motive for transferring the subsidiary was to permit the old group to claim a bad debt for the large advances made to the transferred subsidiary, which the parent could not claim as long as the subsidiary remained a member of the group. Book Prod. Indus., 24 TCM 339, ¶ 65,065 P-H Memo. TC (1965).

Consolidated net operating loss of affiliated group may not be carried back 10 years. Taxpayer was an affiliated group of corporations that filed consolidated returns. Its common parent was not a financial institution under Sections 585, 586, or 593. However, another member of the group was a financial institution. The IRS ruled that a net operating loss completely attributable to the common parent may not be carried back 10 years under Section 172(b)(1)(F), despite the fact that another member of the group is a financial institution. Rev. Rul. 84-136, 1984-1 CB 193.

Carry-back of a consolidated subsidiary organized in a loss year. The portion of a loss attributable to a newly organized subsidiary not included as part of the consolidated group in prior years may be included in the current year's consolidated net operating loss carry-back. The resulting tax refunds may be allocated to members who generated the tax liability in prior years. Rev. Rul. 74-423, 1974-2 CB 289.

Consolidated net operating loss, attributable to subsidiary not in existence prior to the loss may be carried back to parent's separate return year. A corporation was formed in 1965 and filed a separate return for the year ended December 31, 1965. The following year, the corporation created a subsidiary that sustained a net operating loss. A consolidated tax return was filed reflecting a net operating loss. Such loss could be carried back to the separate return year of the parent pursuant to Regulation § 1.1502-79. Rev. Rul. 69-623, 1969-2 CB 171.

Net operating loss allowable on separate return basis to member of consolidated group to compute "hypothetical" tax for earnings and profits. In computing the earnings and profits of each member of a consolidated group, Section 1552(a)(2) provides for the allocation of the consolidated tax on the basis of the percentage that the member's hypothetical tax bears to the tax of all members of the group. The IRS ruled that, in computing the hypothetical tax, a net operating loss deduction is computed as if the member had filed a separate return for that year. A net operating loss absorbed in prior years by the group does not enter into the hypothetical computation. Rev. Rul. 66-374, 1966-2 CB 427.

Net operating loss from separate return is not carried back to consolidated loss year. The IRS ruled that a net operating loss sustained by a corporation for a year after it left an affiliated group was not reduced by its taxable income for a prior period that was included in a consolidated return that reflected a consolidated net operating loss. Rev. Rul. 66-91, 1966-1 CB 54.

Affiliate's first year net operating loss may be carried back and applied against affiliated group's consolidated income from prior years. Three corporations, formed in 1961, filed a consolidated return for that year with each corporation reflecting taxable income. A new corporation was formed in 1962 and immediately joined in the filing of a consolidated return for that year with the other three corporations. The portion of the consolidated net operating loss for 1962 attributable to this new corporation may be carried back and applied against the affiliated group's consolidated taxable income for 1961, although the new corporation was not in existence in 1961. Regulation § 1.1502-31(a)(4) prohibits a car-

CONTRIBUTIONS TO CAPITAL: *In General*

ry-back to the extent attributable to a corporation making a separate return or filing as a member of another affiliated group in the carry-back year. Since the new corporation was not formed until 1962 and immediately became an affiliate, it never filed a separate return in any preceding taxable year, nor was it ever a member of any other affiliated group. The contrary decisions in Houston Oil Field Material Co., 252 F2d 357 (5th Cir. 1958), and Midland Management Co., 38 TC 211 (1962), will not be relied on by the Service. Rev. Rul. 64-93, 1964-1 CB 325.

IRS discusses consolidated net operating loss carry-over of affiliated group terminated prior to tax year's close. *X* Corporation was the common parent of an affiliated group of corporations that filed consolidated returns on a calendar-year basis. On December 31, 1956, the group had a consolidated net operating loss carry-over, and on March 1, 1957, *Y* Corporation purchased *X*'s stock and did not elect to file a consolidated return. During 1957, *X* had taxable income, while its subsidiaries had losses until March 1, 1957. Without accounting for any consolidated net operating loss carry-over, the final return of the group reflected taxable income, all of which was attributable to *X*. The IRS ruled that the consolidated net operating loss attributable to all members of the group is applicable in full against the consolidated income for the taxable year of termination, even though that income is entirely attributable to the parent. The IRS decided not to limit the carry-over to that portion of the consolidated net operating loss carry-over attributable to *X*. Rev. Rul. 61-224, 1961-2 CB 145.

CONTINUITY OF INTEREST

(*See* Reorganizations–Continuity of Interest)

CONTRIBUTIONS

(*See* Charitable Contributions; Contributions to Capital)

CONTRIBUTIONS TO CAPITAL

(*See also* Bad Debts; Debt vs. Equity)

In General	222
Distinguished From Debt	226
Preferred Stock	248

In General

Surrender of small portion of stock interest held by majority stockholder as part of settlement between corporation and creditors is a capital contribution. Taxpayer and another person were the officers, directors, and owners of 70 percent of C&S, Inc. In order to settle a dispute between C&S, Inc. and its convertible noteholders, its directors agreed to change the conversion rate of the notes. To facilitate the settlement of this dispute and thereby preserve C&S, Inc.'s business, taxpayer and the other majority stockholder-director-officer agreed to surrender to C&S, Inc. stock amounting to a 5 percent interest in the corporation. Taxpayer treated the surrender of stock as a transaction giving rise to long-term capital gain (equal to the excess of the value of the surrender stock over his basis in such stock) and claimed an ordinary loss equal to the value of such stock. The IRS rejected taxpayer's treatment and treated the surrender as a capital contribution to C&S, Inc. The Tax Court held for taxpayer, but limited his loss to the basis of the surrendered shares. *Held:* Reversed. The surrender of stock constituting such a small portion of his holdings and resulting in a negligible diminution in the value of such holdings is not a loss transaction, but is a capital contribution. Accordingly, no deduction is allowed; however, the basis of the surrendered stock is to be added to the basis of the stock retained by taxpayer. Schleppy, 601 F2d 196, 79-2 USTC ¶ 9551, 44 AFTR2d 79-5505 (5th Cir. 1979).

Land transferred to taxpayer as inducement to locate in shopping center is a nontaxable contribution to capital. A shopping center developer transferred land to taxpayer to induce it to locate in his shopping center. On this land taxpayer was to construct and operate its store; if taxpayer did not, the land would be forfeited. The facts indicated that the success of the shopping center was dependent on popular retailers, like taxpayer, locating in the center. The IRS argued that the transfer of land was not an "indirect and intangible" benefit within the meaning of Section 118(a), and thus taxpayer was taxable on receipt of the land. *Held:* For taxpayer. The court found too restrictive the IRS argument that "indirect and intangible benefits" for Section 118(a) are limited to contributions that can be enjoyed as a member of the community at large. The relationship between the enhanced value of the shopping center (due to taxpayer's presence) and the contribution of land was not sufficiently direct to make the transfer of land taxable. May Dep't Stores, 519 F2d 1154, 75-2 USTC ¶ 9628, 36 AFTR2d 75-5503 (8th Cir. 1975).

Land transfers were capital contributions. The Tax Court held that land transfers to taxpayers' corporation were capital contributions, not a sale, and that taxpayers' receipts relating to the land transfer contracts were dividend income. Also, the corporation's claims for interest deductions relating to the land transfer contracts were disallowed. *Held:* Affirmed. The capital contributions finding was supported by the degree of control taxpayers exercised over the corporation and the fact that the land contracts did not appear to contain late payment or default provisions. On another issue, no offsetting cost deductions from prior years could be applied against additional corporate income. Hayutin, 508 F2d 462, 75-1 USTC ¶ 9108, 35 AFTR2d 75-428 (10th Cir. 1974).

Sale by nonstockholder was contribution to capital. A nonstockholder sold property to taxpayer corporation for a cash down payment and a note secured by a mortgage. Since taxpayer had to borrow from a bank to make the down payment, the note was subordinated to the bank loan. The bank loan was paid off, but no principal payments were made on the note, and the due date was extended. The Tax Court held that the interest paid on the note was not deductible. It reasoned that the seller was, in effect, a preferred stockholder, not a creditor. From the facts, it concluded that there was no intent to create a debtor-creditor relationship. *Held:* Affirmed in part and reversed in part. The Tax Court's findings of fact and the inferences drawn therefrom were conclusive unless clearly erroneous. However, the failure of the Tax Court to allow taxpayer to step up its carry-over basis in the contributed property by the amount taxpayer paid the nonstockholder was error. Foresun, Inc., 348 F2d 1006, 65-2 USTC ¶ 9572, 16 AFTR2d 5282 (6th Cir. 1965).

Sale of contributed stock by corporation treated as sale by contributing stockholder. Taxpayer and another each owned 50 percent of the stock of four corporations, *A*, *B*, *C*, and *D*. Taxpayer managed *A* and *B* while the other stockholder managed *C* and *D*. Pursuant to agreement, when the other stockholder refused to contribute additional capital to *B*, they broke up the partnership by having the other stockholder transfer his *A* stock to *A* and his *B* stock to taxpayer for a stipulated consideration. At the same time, taxpayer contributed his *C* and *D* stock to *B*'s capital. *B* then sold its *C* stock to *C* and the *D* stock to *D* for cash. *B* reported a capital gain on the sale. After this transaction, taxpayer owned all the outstanding stock of *A* and *B*, and the other individual owned all the stock of *C* and *D*. *Held:* For the IRS. The court held that the gain from the sale by *B* was taxable to taxpayer. *B* corporation was a mere conduit of the stock, and the proceeds of sale actually represented a cash contribution by taxpayer to *B*. Abbott, Jr., 342 F2d 997, 65-1 USTC ¶ 9331, 15 AFTR2d 678 (5th Cir. 1965).

Stockholder's advances are contributions to capital; guarantor's loss deductible as business expense. Taxpayer formed *X* Corporation with only $4,000 cash paid in for capital stock, for the specific purpose of having *X* enter into a $700,000 contract for the building of 100 houses and a plant. Most of operating funds were obtained from (1) cash advances from its stockholders (including taxpayer), (2) taxpayer's payment of certain corporate expenses, and (3) bank loans obtained on the personal credit of taxpayer. *X* Corporation became insolvent in the second year of operations and was liquidated. The Tax Court held that the stock loss, as well as all payments and advances that taxpayer made to or on behalf of X, represented capital contributions deductible only as capital losses. However, the Tax Court also held that the final advance that taxpayer made for the specific purpose of enabling X to pay off its bank loan on which taxpayer gave his personal guarantee constituted a guarantor's loss deductible as a nonbusiness bad debt. *Held:* Reversed on latter issue. The payment was made primarily to preserve taxpayer's business reputation and credit. It was a business expense. Allen, 283 F2d 785, 60-2 USTC ¶ 9759, 6 AFTR2d 5840 (7th Cir. 1960).

The transfer of land to a controlled corporation was a capital contribution, not a sale. In 1956, the two taxpayer corporations were formed to develop farmland. The majority stockholder's husband, Sansberry, "contributed" the land to the corporations in exchange for an open account payable. He claimed that the land was sold to the corporation, but the IRS argued that it really was a contribution to capital. In addition, the IRS argued that the only purpose for using the different corporations for the development was tax avoidance. *Held:* For the IRS. Even though Sansberry received an open account payable, the transaction was a capital contribution. No notes were issued indicating an obligation to repay, and no interest was ever paid. The repayment date was left open pending sale of the lots, and the amount to be repaid was conditioned on the corporation's profitability. In addition, the small cash contributions were insufficient to run the business, and the land was essential. These factors were used by the court to find an equity interest. The court also found that because Sansberry was actually in control of the corporations, the contribution was tax-free, and the corporations took a carry-over basis. Because the operations of the corporations were virtually identical, the court agreed with the tax-motivation argument of the IRS and disallowed two surtax exemptions. Western Hills, Inc., 71-1 USTC ¶ 9410, 27 AFTR2d 1345 (SD Ind. 1971).

Transfer to controlled corporation was contribution, not sale. After forming X Corporation with a capital stock of $11,000, the taxpayer sold land to X for $198,000. The down payment was $10,000, and the balance was payable over about five years. The IRS argued that despite the form of a sale, the transaction should be considered a contribution to capital for tax purposes. *Held:* For the IRS. The thinness of the corporation's capital suggested that this was not a true indebtedness. Accordingly, payments of principal and interest on the obligation were treated as dividends. Bruce, 180 F. Supp. 907, 60-1 USTC ¶ 9249 (D. Minn. 1960).

Transfer of assets to corporation was sale, not contribution of capital. Taxpayer was a partner in a logging business with a net worth of about $60,000. The partnership was offered a promising, but hazardous, logging contract. A new corporation was formed with a capitalization of $3,000 to take over this contract. The partnership sold its net assets to the corporation, accepting the capital stock in part payment. Stock was divided among taxpayer and his three partners in the same proportion as their partnership interests. Upon its organization, the corporation was indebted to taxpayer and another partner for $50,000. The corporation was able to obtain all necessary credit from banks and suppliers on the basis of its own financial condition, without the personal guarantees of the principal stockholder-creditors, and without subordination of their claims. The IRS treated subsequent payments of $7,000 to taxpayer as a dividend, rather than as a reduction of debt. *Held:* For taxpayer. On the facts the court found that the initial capitalization of the corporation was adequate, and that payments to taxpayer were reductions of debt to him, not taxable dividends. Kinsel, 60-1 USTC ¶ 9197 (D. Ore. 1960).

Property transfer to subsidiary was capital contribution, not a sale; property had substituted basis. Taxpayer, an inactive corporation with no assets or outstanding stock, purchased, under an installment agreement, trucks and equipment worth $221,000 from a corporation controlled by its incorporators. Subsequently, the taxpayer became a subsidiary of that corporation, selling its stock to it

Contributions to Capital: *In General*

for $5,000. Payments were made irregularly on the installment agreement, and finally, the unpaid balance was transferred on the taxpayer's books to a simple open account payable and consolidated with other advances by the parent. Subsequently, stock was issued to the parent in cancellation of the account payable. Taxpayer claimed that its basis for the trucks was the price specified in the installment sales agreement. *Held:* For the IRS. Looking at the entire transaction, the court concluded that there was no bona fide sale, merely a capital contribution. Since gain on the transfer of property to a controlled corporation in exchange for its stock was not recognized, the taxpayer took it with a substituted basis. Accordingly, the taxpayer's basis for the trucks was the same as the basis of the trucks in the hands of the parent. Truck Terminals, Inc., 314 F2d 449, 63-1 USTC ¶ 9317, 11 AFTR2d 901 (9th Cir. 1963).

Cost depletion disallowed for transactions undertaken to step up basis of oil interests. Quantities of wheat were contributed to taxpayer, a controlled real estate corporation, taxpayer in a Section 351 transaction. The corporation used the proceeds to purchase farmland. The farmland was then exchanged with its stockholders for fractional oil royalty interests in which they had, prior to the transfer, recovered their full cost basis through cost depletion. Taxpayer claimed cost depletion with respect to the royalties received, contending it had acquired the interests by purchase in exchange for farmland. However, the IRS alleged that in substance the royalty interest, rather than the wheat, constituted a contribution to the corporation's capital so that it had no cost basis, and it limited the corporation to percentage depletion. *Held:* For the IRS. The principal purpose of the formation of taxpayer corporation was to enable the stockholders to transfer oil interests to it to permit taxpayer to obtain cost depletion deductions. The oil interests were thus in substance contributed to taxpayer, and it too was entitled to take only percentage depletion. The court also expressed doubt about the substance of a retransfer of farmland back to taxpayer for a two-year period for $1,600 to enable taxpayer to obtain better wheat allotments. Accordingly, taxpayer was denied a deduction for the $1,600. Kimball Farms Inc., 26 TCM 1180, ¶ 67,231 P-H Memo. TC (1967).

Cancellation of debt owed by wholly owned subsidiary to parent constituted a contribution to capital. Taxpayer corporation advanced funds to its wholly owned subsidiary, which was insolvent at the time, expecting payment only out of future earnings and profits, if any. In a later year, when the subsidiary was still insolvent, taxpayer canceled the debt in exchange for newly issued common stock of the subsidiary. Taxpayer claimed a bad debt deduction to the extent that the amount of the indebtedness exceeded the value of the shares received. The IRS disallowed the deductions. *Held:* For the IRS. Taxpayer's gratuitous cancellation of the indebtedness to buoy the subsidiary's weak financial condition constituted a capital contribution. W.A. Krueger Co., 26 TCM 946, ¶ 67,192 P-H Memo. TC (1967).

Conveyance by sole stockholder to corporation treated as a sale rather than a capital contribution. The IRS contended that a conveyance by a husband and wife of 47.17 acres of land to the taxpayer, their controlled corporation, in return for a note and mortgage, was a contribution to capital. *Held:* For taxpayer. The court held it to be a sale in substance as well as in form, and not a contribution to the capital of the corporation. Accordingly, the basis to the taxpayer of the property was its purchase cost. The court noted that (1) the sale occurred approximately 14 months after the taxpayer was incorporated; (2) the note was payable in yearly installments, without reference to corporate earnings, and bore interest; (3) the original capital of the taxpayer, though not large, was suggested by the accountant at incorporation as sufficent to commence operations; and (4) there existed a reasonable probability of repayment of the note from outside financing and from proceeds of sales of other developed lots held by the taxpayer. Gain from the later sale of the acreage by the taxpayer was treated as ordinary income on the ground that it was holding the land for sale, although, generally, the

Contributions to Capital: *Distinguished From Debt*

taxpayer did not offer a specific piece of property for sale to customers in the ordinary course of its trade or business until such property had been developed into building lots. Evwalt Dev. Corp., 22 TCM 220, ¶ 63,056 P-H Memo. TC (1963).

Property transfer to foreign subsidiary by domestic subsidiary with 80 percent ownership required favorable letter ruling to be treated as contribution of capital. *P*, a domestic corporation, owned all of *S-1*, a domestic corporation. *S-1* owned 40 percent of *S-2*, a foreign corporation, with *P* owning the remaining 60 percent. *S-1* proposed to transfer property to *S-2* without consideration. Since *P* owned 100 percent of *S-1*, under Section 318(a)(3)(C), *S-1* was considered to own *P's* stock in *S-2*. Therefore, immediately after the transfer, *S-1* would own at least 80 percent of the voting power of *S-2* and, under Section 367(d), a prior favorable letter ruling had to be obtained in order to have the transfer treated as a contribution to capital. Rev. Rul. 76-240, 1976-1 CB 101.

Cash given to donee to buy property from donor was a contribution. A corporation furnished lodging for its employees in a facility it owned that was run by an exempt organization to which it paid a specified sum each year for the availability of the facility. The corporation wished to transfer ownership of the facility to the organization and to otherwise continue the arrangement. Because of the mortgage, it was necessary for the corporation to give cash to the organization in an amount equal to the fair market value of the property and for the organization to immediately pay this amount to the corporation for the purchase of the property. The transaction was a contribution of land, not cash, and the corporation was entitled to a deduction, equal to the fair market value of the property, reduced by the amount that would have been treated as gain to which Sections 1245 and 1250 would have applied had the property been sold at its fair market value. In addition, the corporation could deduct the sum it paid each year to the organization as a business expense. Rev. Rul. 76-151, 1976-1 CB 59.

Gain or loss recognized on a contribution to capital made before a merger. The majority stockholder of an acquired corporation contributed a portion of his shares to capital as an inducement to minority stockholders to vote in favor of a proposed merger. Gain or loss was recognized to the majority stockholder to the extent of the difference between the fair market value of the shares and their adjusted basis at the time of the transfer. However, the minority stockholders were treated as having received the transferred shares after the merger, thus realizing income. Rev. Rul. 73-233, 1973-1 CB 179.

Distinguished From Debt

Bad debt deductions denied because advances to corporation were equity. Taxpayer advanced funds to three corporations he controlled that operated hotels. He also guaranteed the corporations' loans from outside lenders. The hotels failed, and taxpayer claimed bad debt deductions. The IRS denied the deductions. *Held:* For the IRS. The facts showed that taxpayer did not expect repayment unless the corporations' financial status improved. This and other factors showed the "loans" were contributions to capital, not debt. The guarantees by taxpayer were also capital contributions. Lane, 742 F2d 1311, 84-2 USTC ¶ 9817, 54 AFTR2d 84-6098 (11th Cir. 1984).

Cash advances to sister corporation held contributions to capital. Taxpayer, a domestic automobile dealership, advanced cash and other property to a Bahamian fishing corporation that had a common stockholder. Taxpayer sought a bad debt deduction for a portion of these funds. *Held:* For the IRS. The advances were not a bona fide loan, but were a contribution to capital. There was no provision for specific repayment; no repayment was ever requested; and the notes were unsecured and subordinated to other creditors. Furthermore, the contributions to capital constituted constructive dividends to the stockholder. Stinnett's Pontiac Serv., Inc., 730 F2d 634, 84-1 USTC ¶ 9406, 53 AFTR2d 84-1197 (11th Cir. 1984).

Contributions to Capital: *Distinguished From Debt*

Section 482 allocation rejected because interest was collectible. Taxpayer corporation made interest-free loans to a related corporation and the IRS allocated interest income to it under Section 482. *Held:* For taxpayer. In the years at issue the related corporation's income was less than the allocated interest and it eventually went into receivership. Taxpayer had in effect made a contribution to capital and could not reasonably expect repayment. Johnson, 44 TCM 1076, ¶ 82,517 P-H Memo. TC (1982), aff'd, 729 F2d 1447 (3d Cir. 1984).

Bad debt deduction denied as capital contribution. Taxpayer personally secured a debt of his wholly owned corporation. When the corporation failed to repay the debt, the creditor foreclosed on the security. Taxpayer deducted that amount as a business bad debt, which the IRS disallowed. *Held:* For the IRS. Taxpayer's motivation was to protect his investment in the corporation, not his employment. The corporation never paid him a salary, and he received compensation from another employer. He was not entitled to a nonbusiness bad debt deduction because he failed to show that the debt became wholly worthless in the year at issue. Holland, Jr., 728 F2d 360, 84-1 USTC ¶ 9260, 53 AFTR2d 84-880 (6th Cir. 1984).

Advances to affiliated corporation were equity contributions, not loans. Taxpayer, a nonprofit corporation, made loans over 10 years to an affiliated corporation. Taxpayer later claimed a bad debt deduction, eliminating its liability for unrelated business income under Section 511. A jury found that the advances were loans and allowed most of the claimed bad debt. *Held:* Reversed. The advances were clearly equity contributions. No interest was paid, there were few repayments of principal, and the same board of directors controlled both corporations. Texas Farm Bureau, 725 F2d 307, 84-1 USTC ¶ 9502, 53 AFTR2d 84-856 (5th Cir. 1984).

Funds transferred to corporation were contribution to capital. Taxpayer claimed a bad debt deduction on account of loans to his wholly owned corporation that he personally guaranteed and repaid. *Held:* For the IRS. Taxpayer offered no evidence to support his claim that loans were intended. Therefore, the funds were proceeds of personal loans that were contributed to the corporation's capital; taxpayer was entitled only to a Section 165(g) deduction for worthless securities. Sankary, 44 TCM 414, ¶ 82,387 P-H Memo. TC (1982), aff'd, 722 F2d 747 (9th Cir. 1983), cert. denied, 466 US 905 (1984).

Advance determined to be capital contribution. The IRS held that amounts taxpayers advanced to a Mexican farming association that failed were capital contributions. Taxpayer contended such amounts were debt and that they are subject to a bad debt deduction rather than a capital loss. *Held:* For the IRS. The underlying notes specified no maturity date or provision for interest. The facts indicated that a capital investment was intended. Rolwing-Moxley Co., 589 F2d 353, 79-1 USTC ¶ 9116, 43 AFTR2d 79-445 (8th Cir. 1978).

Property exchanged for notes was capital contribution. Taxpayer stockholders' transfer of property to their closely held corporations in exchange for notes was determined by the IRS to be a contribution to capital. The lower court also found that the notes were equity, not debt. *Held:* Affirmed. The facts indicated that decisions on whether to make payments on the notes were based on the criteria usually associated with dividend decisions, and this favors equity classification. Also there existed an absence of timely interest payments. On another matter, sale of three parcels of land was in the ordinary course of business and therefore generated ordinary income. Drive Indus. Park, 561 F2d 572, 77-2 USTC ¶ 9696, 40 AFTR2d 77-5940 (5th Cir. 1977).

A jury's verdict that advances to a corporation were loans was overruled by the court on an IRS motion as advances were necessary to secure bonds required in the course of business. Although the jury found that taxpayer's advances to his nearly wholly owned corporation were loans, the district court ruled that such finding was unreasonable and entered judgment for the IRS that advances were

Contributions to Capital: *Distinguished From Debt*

contributions to capital. In this case, there were (1) no notes or evidences of indebtedness, (2) no security or collateral, (3) no interest charged on outstanding amounts, and (4) no attempt to repay advances. Furthermore, the corporation making the advances was "grossly undercapitalized" and repayment was clearly dependent on the success of the business. *Held:* For the IRS. The court of appeals also determined that on the basis of the facts the advances were necessary for the corporation to secure bonds required in the course of its business and, under the circumstances, no third party would have made similar advances to the corporation at the time that taxpayer's advances were made. Casco Bank & Trust Co., 544 F2d 528, 76-2 USTC ¶ 9722, 38 AFTR2d 76-5943 (1st Cir. 1976), cert. denied, 430 US 907 (1977).

Advances to affiliates determined to be capital contributions. The lower court held that advances by taxpayer corporation to three affiliates, formed to diversify taxpayer's business interests, were true loans on which additions to taxpayer's bad debt reserve could be based. *Held:* Reversed. The transactions with the affiliates were found to be contributions to capital, as opposed to debts. Factors supporting this determination included absence of a fixed rate of interest, lack of a specified repayment date, and the fact that the three affiliates were undercapitalized with high debt-equity ratios. In re Uneco, Inc., 532 F2d 1204, 76-1 USTC ¶ 9326, 37 AFTR2d 76-1119 (8th Cir. 1976).

Advances to corporation held capital contribution. The Tax Court held advances by taxpayers' partnership to a corporation wholly owned by one of the partners were capital contributions, rather than loans, and deductible only as capital losses when the advances became worthless. *Held:* Affirmed. The capital contribution of $10,000 initially was inadequate for even the day-to-day operations of the business. Therefore, the purported loans were really capital contributions and the loss was capital. Astleford, 516 F2d 1394, 75-1 USTC ¶ 9490, 36 AFTR2d 75-5063 (8th Cir. 1975).

Lost advances not ordinary deductions. The district court held that cotton production and other farm operations conducted by taxpayer corporation's Mexican corporation was a mere extension of taxpayer's domestic activities, and therefore taxpayer was entitled to ordinary deductions for lost advances made to the Mexican entity. *Held:* Reversed. The corporation was found to be a separate and distinct entity whose agricultural operations had no relationship with taxpayer's own farming activities. Therefore, the advances and other related items were capital in nature and could only be deducted under the provisions of Sections 1211 and 1212. Eliott H. Raffety Farms, Inc., 511 F2d 1234, 75-1 USTC ¶ 9271, 35 AFTR2d 75-811 (8th Cir. 1975).

Stockholder's advances to corporation were determined, as a matter of law, to be capital contributions. To obtain an automobile dealership, taxpayer's corporation had to be capitalized with an additional $20,000. Taxpayer advanced this money to the corporation and made additional advances (including direct payments to the corporation's creditors). These advances were never made the subject of notes or other evidences of indebtedness, nor was there any agreement on the payment of interest, the provision of collateral, or the existence of maturity dates. The only corporate recognition of these advances was in the corporate ledger under the heading "notes payable." Furthermore, taxpayer never received a salary while he worked for the corporation. When the corporation became insolvent, taxpayer claimed a bad debt deduction for these advances. The IRS challenged these deductions on the ground that taxpayer's advances were capital contributions. *Held:* For the IRS. No reasonable person could have expected that these advances would be repaid in the absence of corporate profits. Furthermore, the evidence clearly indicated that the corporation was inadequately capitalized. Raymond, 511 F2d 185, 75-1 USTC ¶ 9289, 35 AFTR2d 75-921 (6th Cir. 1975).

Loans to two companies were actually capital contributions. Taxpayer, a building materials firm, set up two subsidiaries and advanced each $20,000. The parent and both subsidiaries treated the advance as loans. Taxpayer claimed a bad debt deduction when the subsidiaries went out of business. The IRS contended the advances were capital contributions and the district court held for the IRS. *Held:* Affirmed. The court noted that at least one of the advances was not backed by any enforceable obligation to repay. Midland Distribs., Inc., 481 F2d 730, 73-2 USTC ¶ 9543, 32 AFTR2d 73-5390 (5th Cir. 1973).

Husband's corporation's guarantee of notes of wife's corporation was contribution to capital by husband. Husband's corporation guaranteed a debt of a second corporation in which his wife was the sole stockholder. The IRS claimed that the notes represented a contribution to the second corporation's capital. The Tax Court held for the IRS. *Held:* Affirmed. The deduction was disallowed because the guaranteed debt did not represent an indirect contribution to capital. The notes were subordinate to other indebtedness, the corporate assets were inadequate to sustain the high amount of indebtedness, and most of the funds were used to start the operation. Plantation Patterns, Inc., 462 F2d 712, 72-2 USTC ¶ 9494, 29 AFTR2d 72-1408 (5th Cir. 1972).

Corporation denied interest deductions for interest paid on stockholder advances that the court determined were capital contributions. Taxpayer was formed in 1955 for the purpose of acquiring a tract of land and immediately reselling it. After acquiring the tract, it could not find a buyer and its stockholders decided that the tract would be used to develop a shopping center. Conventional financing was not readily available, and the stockholders were required to advance funds to taxpayer to sustain the project. In return for the initial advances, the stockholders received interest-bearing notes. Taxpayer's board declared, at the end of 1955, that all advances thus far received would be carried on taxpayer's books as paid in surplus and all notes would be canceled. In 1956 and 1957, additional funds were advanced. These amounts were noted in taxpayer's books as surplus, but were given the designation "shareholder's cash and notes receivable capital contributions, subordinated to creditors' accounts, not subject to withdrawal without Board of Directors' sanction." In 1957, taxpayer was reorganized. Its old stock and debt was canceled and new stock and debt was issued in a 1-to-3 ratio: Each share of common stock (valued at $1,000) was obtainable if accompanied by a loan of $3,000. The new notes were subordinated to creditors and would not be payable during "the period of two years or after, unless it was the unanimous decision of the Board . . . [to] reduce the time limit of [the] notes." After the reorganization, additional amounts were advanced to taxpayer using this 1-to-3 ratio of stock to debt. In 1958, taxpayer first received outside financing. Also, in 1958, new stockholders invested in taxpayer. Upon their entry, the old stockholders' notes were canceled and new 6 percent notes, due on September 1, 1963, were issued to all stockholders. The payment of principal and interest on these new notes could be postponed by unanimous approval of all parties. Taxpayer claimed interest deductions for amounts accruing on these notes. The IRS challenged the deductibility of these amounts on the ground that the advances were in truth capital contributions. The district court held for taxpayer based on the interest of the parties as documented by the notes and the business purpose of the advances. *Held:* Reversed. The district court should have given greater weight to evidence indicating that the "maturity dates and interest rates . . . were, at best, illusory and [that] in fact no interest payments or payments of principal were made at the time this litigation commenced." The power vested in taxpayer's board concerning the time of payment rendered the maturity dates on the notes meaningless. Further, the notes were subordinated and unsecured, were issued in a fixed ratio to equity, and were obtained because conventional financing was unavailable. Austin Village, Inc., 432 F2d 741, 70-2 USTC ¶ 9620, 26 AFTR2d 70-5550 (6th Cir. 1970).

Loans from stockholder incorporators were contributions to capital. Taxpayer was formed to incorporate a partnership to which one of

Contributions to Capital: *Distinguished From Debt*

the partners had contributed funds in anticipation of incorporation. At the time of incorporation, the equity of the partnership of $75,000 was settled by the issuance of $45,000 in capital stock and loans for the balance. During the first years of corporate operation, the stockholders made additional advances so that two years thereafter, each stockholder held $15,000 in capital stock and was owed $36,000 by taxpayer. The next year, two of the stockholders agreed to buy out the third and made additional advances to taxpayer to enable it to redeem his stock. Interest was paid on the notes, but not always on time or at the stipulated rate. None of the principal had been repaid, the notes were subordinated to bank borrowing and were not protected by collateral, an acceleration clause or a sinking fund. *Held:* For the IRS. There was no dispute that the parties generally designated the advances as loans and that there were notes in existence. In addition, there was originally a fixed maturity date, although the parties were not fully conscious of the dates and probably would not have made a demand for payment. Although taxpayer contended that repayments were made, the amounts were minor. Although it further contended that new business developments caused postponements in payment beyond the maturity dates, the IRS was correct in asserting that when payments were made, they were only for the purpose of equalizing the positions of the three individuals with respect to the corporation. No dividends were paid during the relevant period of time during which interest deductions were claimed and operations were admittedly profitable. Probably the strongest of the IRS' arguments was that once the loans were equal, there was no variation. The above factors indicated that the individuals intended to treat their advances to the corporation essentially as contributions to capital. As a result, the deductions claimed for interest were properly disallowed. A.R. Lantz Co., 424 F2d 1330, 70-1 USTC ¶ 9308 (9th Cir. 1970).

Stockholder advances were equity not debt. Taxpayer and his brother transferred their partnership business to a new corporation for all the latter's stock and unsecured, demand, interest-bearing notes. The IRS disallowed interest deductions claimed by the corporation on the notes, and was granted a directed verdict by the district court. *Held:* Affirmed. (1) The notes represented equity not debt: The corporation was thinly capitalized (an initial debt-equity ratio of 7 to 1) and the advances were used to acquire capital assets; the notes contained no creditor safeguards; they were first subordinated to a bank loan and later to all corporate creditors; interest payments were irregular and the notes were held by the stockholders pro rata. (2) Since none of the relevant circumstances were in dispute, there was no jury question. Tyler, 414 F2d 844, 69-2 USTC ¶ 9559, 24 AFTR2d 69-5426 (5th Cir. 1969).

Despite the jury's decision on the question of debt versus equity, the facts justified a finding in favor of the IRS. At formation, the stockholders of taxpayer each paid $5,000 for their stock. They then advanced $83,000, for which each was given promissory notes. Later they advanced another $10,000, and more notes were issued. On its income tax return for each fiscal year involved, taxpayer claimed deductions for the interest paid on these notes. The IRS disallowed the deductions, contending that the amounts advanced were contributions to capital and that the money paid as interest was, in substance, a dividend. A jury reviewing all the evidence found the advances to be loans. However, the trial judge issued a judgment N.O.V. for the IRS. *Held:* Affirmed. Because the debt-equity ratio of the corporation was found to be 21 to 1, without including institutional indebtedness, the stockholders' advances were equity and not loans. The issue of whether the operative facts add up to debt or equity is a question of law and not fact and therefore was correctly decided by the trial judge in favor of the IRS. Berkowitz, 411 F2d 818, 69-1 USTC ¶ 9398, 23 AFTR2d 69-1582 (5th Cir. 1969).

Advances by a parent corporation to its subsidiary constituted capital, not debt. Taxpayer, a construction corporation, and another company were principally owned by the same individual. In order to retain the services of a valued employee, he was given a stock inter-

Contributions to Capital: *Distinguished From Debt*

est in the company. However, since the employee did not have the funds to obtain a significant investment either in the taxpayer or in the affiliated company, a new corporation was formed with a capital of $10,000. The employee acquired a 35 percent interest in the new company. It was proposed that the new company enter into joint ventures with taxpayer, but, because of the employee's illness and other factors, the new corporation went bankrupt. Prior thereto, taxpayer had advanced to the new company approximately $500,000, which was recorded on the books of both companies as a loan. The Tax Court held that the advances were capital and not loans, and therefore not deductible as bad debts, since there was no fixed repayment date, no interest, and no firm expectation of repayment. *Held:* Affirmed. However, the case was remanded to the Tax Court to decide whether the advances were deductible as worthless securities, a question raised on appeal. Road Materials, Inc., 407 F2d 1121, 69-1 USTC ¶ 9259, 23 AFTR2d 68-859 (4th Cir. 1969).

Fourth mortgage note was equity rather than indebtedness. A husband and wife acquired an apartment house by paying cash, giving the seller a purchase money note and third mortgage, and taking the property subject to first and second mortgages. They operated the property as individuals for one year and then transferred it to a newly formed corporation, in exchange for all of the issued and outstanding stock at a stated value of $5,000 and a note of the corporation in the amount of $193,000, secured by a fourth mortgage payable in monthly installments and bearing interest on the unpaid balance. The note and capital stock were equal to their equity in the property and approximately equal to the cash they had paid on purchase of the property. The next year, the stockholders advanced money so that the corporation could discharge the second mortgage. During the two years following the transfer, the corporation made 12 of the 15 required monthly payments on the fourth mortgage and reduced the principal thereby to $180,000. At this stage, the parties altered the terms of the mortgage to provide that no further installments would be paid, but the entire balance would be discharged at the end of approximately five years with monthly interest payments to continue. Taxpayer made the required interest payments and took deductions therefor but, although the time for payment of the principal had expired, the indebtedness remained and the stockholders took no action to enforce payment. The IRS then determined that both the interest payments and the payments on account of principal made before the modification were distributions with respect to stock. The Tax Court agreed. *Held:* Affirmed. The court agreed for the following reasons: (1) On the transfer of property to the corporation, the corporation's debt-equity ratio was 123 to 1; (2) as subsequent evidence showed, the parties did not treat the notes as a debt, (3) the stockholders held the notes in the same proportion that they held their stock; and (4) the property was in such need of modernization, and so overburdened with mortgages, that no reasonable person would have expected the notes to be discharged in accordance with the terms stated. Ambassador Apartments, Inc., 406 F2d 288, 69-1 USTC ¶ 9164, 23 AFTR2d 69-401 (2d Cir. 1968).

Advances to sister corporation were capital contributions, not loans due to preponderance of debt to equity capital as well as lack of interest and security provisions. Taxpayer was engaged primarily in the construction of gas distribution facilities. From the end of 1954 to March 1956, it advanced over $300,000 on open account to a sister corporation that taxpayer's stockholders had organized to do electrical construction work for one of taxpayer's most important customers. The sister corporation had an initial capital of $12,000. In 1956, taxpayer consolidated with its sister corporation; subsequently, however, taxpayer deducted a portion of the latter's net operating loss carry-over against its own income. In 1956, taxpayer claimed a business bad debt deduction for the unpaid advances it had made to its sister corporation. Alternatively, taxpayer claimed the unpaid amount as an ordinary and necessary business expense or as a deductible loss. The IRS contended that the advances were capital contributions. The

Contributions to Capital: *Distinguished From Debt*

district court agreed. It reasoned that whether advances to a closely held corporation are loans or capital contributions depends on the facts of the particular case. Here, according to the court, the heavy preponderance of debt to equity capital, and the absence of any provision for interest, for a fixed maturity for repayment, or for security, all established that the advances were capital contributions. Other facts that supported this conclusion were that repayment depended solely on the success of the sister corporation's venture, which taxpayer considered as its own, and that the sister corporation could not have obtained the advances from an outside party on the same terms. *Held:* Affirmed over dissent. The district court correctly concluded that the advances to the sister corporation were capital contributions. Taxpayer failed to establish either that it made the contributions in the ordinary course of business or that its loss came within the provisions of Section 165(g)(3), which deals with worthless securities of affiliated corporations. Northeastern Consol. Co., 406 F2d 76, 69-1 USTC ¶ 9153, 23 AFTR2d 69-412 (7th Cir.), cert. denied, 396 US 819 (1969).

Advances by sole stockholder to his corporation deemed an equity investment rather than indebtedness. Taxpayer was sole stockholder of a corporation that he incorporated with a $25,000 capital account. Over the years, taxpayer made substantial advances to and expenditures for the benefit of the corporation, which were evidenced on the corporate books by an account payable to taxpayer. Withdrawals were charged to the same account. The corporation claimed a deduction for alleged interest paid taxpayer on the amount it owed him. *Held:* Deduction denied. On the totality of the evidence, the advances and expenditures by taxpayer to his corporation were held to be in the nature of "equity," rather than indebtedness, with the result that the so-called "interest" was not deductible by the corporation and the net amount of repayments constituted dividends. Donisi, 405 F2d 481, 69-1 USTC ¶ 9119 (6th Cir. 1969).

Advances from 1934 through 1940 held to be risk capital, not loans from 1959 through 1960. Taxpayer's two 50 percent stockholders made pro rata advances to it at various dates during six years beginning with its incorporation in 1934. Shortly after taxpayer received the advances, it either acquired or improved the rental properties comprising its principal assets. The notes that taxpayer issued to evidence the stockholders' advances were unsecured demand notes, secondary to mortgages placed on the property. The executor of the estates of one of taxpayer's two original stockholders demanded payment of his note in 1951 and at the same time requested redemption of the estate's stock. Taxpayer honored the demand and request, refinancing its properties to raise the necessary cash. In 1962, the IRS for the first time denied taxpayer any interest deduction for interest payments on the notes in 1959 and 1960. The district court upheld the denial of the deduction. It considered significant the absence of any evidence that the stockholders expected their advances to be repaid. It also believed that there was a basis for inferring, from the fact that the stockholders paid in only $10,000 apiece in equity capital while arbitrarily designating $53,000 apiece as loans, that the stockholders placed all their money at the risk of the business. The court also considered numerous other criteria in reaching its decision. *Held:* Affirmed over dissent. In the case of a closely held corporation, a useful criterion in determining whether alleged loans are capital contributions is to determine if the stockholders' loans are far more speculative than what an outsider would make. Here, in 1934, it was impossible to obtain any outside mortgage financing for real estate except through a purchase money mortgage. An outside businessman would not have risked his capital in the manner of taxpayer's stockholders. Moreover, there was nothing to indicate that these loans, which in fact were capital contributions when made, ever lost their status as such. Fin Hay Realty Co., 398 F2d 694, 68-2 USTC ¶ 9438, 22 AFTR2d 5004 (3d Cir. 1968).

Auto dealer's advances to his controlled corporations were capital contributions and were not made in his trade or business. Taxpayer, an automobile dealer for approximately 50

Contributions to Capital: Distinguished From Debt

years, bought into a chain of rental and sales dealerships in the late 1950s, and eventually increased his interest from 50 percent to 100 percent. When taxpayer first acquired his stock interest, the corporations needed funds, which taxpayer provided by personal loans and guarantees of corporate loans. Taxpayer had to make good on some of the latter when two of the corporations were unable to pay their debts. He deducted these guarantee payments and his loans as business bad debts. The IRS denied the deductions on the grounds that the advances and payments were capital contributions and that they were not made in taxpayer's trade or business. The district court upheld the denial, finding that taxpayer had made the loans and guarantees to provide operating capital necessary for the continued operations of the corporate activities. Thus, the court concluded that they were capital contributions, not loans. Moreover, the court held the loans were nonbusiness bad debts made for the principal purpose of protecting taxpayer's reputation, investment, portfolio and only indirectly meant to secure his job or commissions through saving his investments. *Held:* Affirmed. Each case involving the capital versus debt distinction must be judged on its own merits. Based on the entire record, his loans and guarantees were a capital contribution. Curry, 396 F2d 630, 68-2 USTC ¶ 9439, 22 AFTR2d 5039 (5th Cir.), cert. denied, 393 US 967 (1968).

Cemetery corporation denied deduction for payments on "certificates of indebtedness" issued for burial land. Taxpayer, a cemetery corporation that was incorporated with the minimum paid-in capital required by law, issued "certificates of indebtedness" to its promoters in return for burial land. Amounts to be paid to the certificate holders were based on a percentage of the base sales price of burial space sold. The corporation deducted the amounts paid under the certificates as the cost of burial spaces. *Held:* For the IRS. The deduction was denied. None of the certificates represented true indebtedness but rather evidenced equity interests. Hence distributions on such equity interests could not be deducted as land costs. Jefferson Memorial Gardens, Inc., 390 F2d 161, 68-1 USTC ¶ 9194 (5th Cir. 1968).

Thin corporation bars Section 337 benefits, since notes were equity capital invested at the risk of the business. Three stockholders owned all the stock of a perfume company. One bought out the other two and gave the sellers notes for most of the purchase price. The purchaser liquidated the corporation and took over the assets personally (at a stepped-up basis); he then "sold" them to taxpayer, a newly formed corporation that also used the stepped-up basis, in exchange for stock ($100,000) and notes ($5.1 million). These notes were part of the collateral for the purchaser's debt to his two co-stockholders. Some 10 years later, when another individual offered to buy taxpayer's assets, taxpayer adopted a plan of complete liquidation pursuant to Section 337. When the 12-month period expired, taxpayer retained sufficient assets to pay various items, including $1.8 million still due on the note to its principal stockholder. The Tax Court agreed with the IRS in stating that the notes were equity capital invested at the risk of the business. This being the case, the court denied taxpayer the benefits of Section 337 on the authority of Regulation § 1.337-2, which forbids a corporation to set aside any amount designed to meet the claims of its stockholders with respect to their stock. *Held:* Affirmed. Whether advances to a corporation create a debtor-creditor relationship or are contributions to capital is a question of fact. In this case, the finding of the Tax Court was not clearly erroneous. John Town, Inc., 67-1 USTC ¶ 9462, 19 AFTR2d 1389 (7th Cir. 1967).

Advances to a closely held corporation were contributions to capital. Taxpayer, his son-in-law, and his grandson-in-law started a new business and took varying proportions of the capital stock along with other people. During a period of 10 years, the corporation borrowed from a bank on the endorsement of taxpayer, who also made advances directly to the corporation. There was no security for the advances; it was generally understood that they would not be paid back until the enterprise showed a profit. The corporation con-

Contributions to Capital: *Distinguished From Debt*

tinued to lose money, but taxpayer continued to advance money and guarantee loans. When the corporation terminated operations, taxpayer deducted as an ordinary bad debt the total of the advances. The IRS disallowed the loss on the grounds that the advances constituted capital investments, and the loss was deductible only as a capital loss. The IRS contended that even if the advances constituted an indebtedness, the loss resulting from their worthlessness was still only a capital loss because they were not business bad debts. The district court held that the advances constituted indebtedness and that during the years of the advances, taxpayer was in the business of lending money. *Held:* Reversed. No valid debt exists unless there is an unconditional obligation to repay. In this case, although taxpayer alluded to the nomenclature and form of the notes and the intent of the parties, these factors were not controlling. The facts and circumstances did not support the conclusion that there was any genuine intent to repay the sums advanced on the dates fixed in the notes. It was generally understood that payment would be contingent on the success of the business. In addition, the advances were substantiated to the claims of other creditors who were paid in full upon the cessation of operations, although no payments were made on the notes to the taxpayer. Even if the notes did create an indebtedness, the evidence was overwhelming that taxpayer was not in the business of lending money. Such activities did not occupy a substantial amount of taxpayer's time or effort, and the only return suggested was that of an investor. Henderson, 375 F2d 36, 67-1 USTC ¶ 9330 (5th Cir. 1967).

Advances to dissolved corporation constituted equity capital; bad debt deduction denied. Taxpayer claimed a deduction for a business bad debt resulting from loans to his wholly owned corporation that were not satisfied when the corporation was dissolved. The corporation had tried unsuccessfully to borrow money directly, whereupon taxpayer borrowed the funds that were deposited in the corporate account. The Tax Court held that it was necessary for the taxpayer to establish that the advances were true loans and not contributions to capital. It found further that the advances were placed at the risk of the business and constituted equity capital. *Held:* Affirmed. Sufficient evidence was present in the record to form a basis for the determination, which was here found not to be erroneous. Smith, 370 F2d 178, 67-1 USTC ¶ 9109 (6th Cir. 1966).

Loans by stockholders were additional contributions to capital. Taxpayer was formed in 1956 with a capitalization of $30,000. Within two weeks thereafter, each of its five stockholders lent to taxpayer three times the amount of his contribution to capital. The court instructed the jury that the three-to-one ratio was not abnormally high. The loans to taxpayer were evidenced by 5.5 percent debentures subordinated to all present and future indebtedness, and were payable in 10 years. The debentures had no acceleration clause. Taxpayer invested approximately $29,000 in fixed assets and employed the $90,000 of borrowed funds in working capital. Taxpayer recorded the loans as indebtedness and deducted the payments thereon as interest. It declared no dividends, although during the three years in question, from 1959 to 1961, its accumulated earnings rose by $96,000 to $121,000. The jury in the lower court case found for the IRS. *Held:* Affirmed. Based on the evidence presented, the jury's finding that the payments on the debentures were not deductible interest because debentures were capital contributions was not clearly erroneous. Coleman Good, Inc., 359 F2d 434, 66-1 USTC ¶ 9402 (3d Cir. 1966).

Advances to loss corporation pending sale are treated as capital contributions. Taxpayer was a 50 percent stockholder in a Ford agency and was also engaged in the construction business as a sole proprietorship. In 1956, when the automobile agency became unprofitable, the taxpayer began devoting more time to his construction business, which he felt had a greater profit potential. From 1956 through 1960, taxpayer tried unsuccessfully to sell the agency. From 1954 through 1961, taxpayer made advances to the corporation, usually to prevent a particular creditor from bringing a collection suit. The corporation's

CONTRIBUTIONS TO CAPITAL: *Distinguished From Debt*

poor financial condition made outside borrowing impossible. Notes were issued by the corporation to cover taxpayer's advances, but these were often issued after the particular advances had been made, were unsecured, and had no maturity date. Only one of the notes bore interest, and no interest was ever paid. The notes were subordianted to all other corporation debts. When the agency was finally sold in 1961, taxpayer claimed a business bad debt deduction for partial worthlessness of his advances. *Held:* The deduction was disallowed, since the advances were contributions to capital, not loans. Taxpayer did not expect to be repaid but made the advances to keep the corporation in operation so that it would continue to be "a saleable piece of merchandise." Jones, Jr., 357 F2d 644, 66-1 USTC ¶ 9272 (6th Cir. 1966).

Corporation is thin where debt to equity ratio is 60 to 1. Taxpayer, a cemetery corporation "purchased" $60,000 of money and property from nonstockholders in exchange for certificates of indebtedness which bore no fixed obligation to pay and no maturity date, and which paid no interest. Taxpayer's initial capital was $1,000 the minimum required by state law. The Tax Court held that the certificates were not debt. *Held:* Affirmed. The following factors indicate that the certificates were not debt: (1) taxpayer's thin capitalization, (2) the speculative nature of the enterprise and the anticipated returns based on the sales of lots, (3) the difficulty in preceiving any reason other than tax avoidance for the method of obtaining capital, and (4) the obvious opportunity for tax avoidance in the method used. Sherwood Memorial Gardens, Inc., 350 F2d 225, 65-2 USTC ¶ 9537, 16 AFTR2d 5111 (7th Cir. 1965).

Advances to corporation were capital, not loans. Smith caused taxpayer corporation to be organized and purchased all its stock for $25,000. Taxpayer then purchased a wood-treatment plant, which cost $74,000. Although Smith originally thought he would have to advance about $40,000 to get the plant in operation, he actually advanced $132,000 in the first two years. The district court held that of the $132,000 in advances, $129,000 was a capital contribution and interest thereon was disallowed. *Held:* Affirmed. The $129,000 was not evidenced by notes and had no fixed maturity date; further, taxpayer was thinly capitalized. No banker or businessman would have made such a loan without additional security and the interest payments were not authorized in the corporate minutes. Wood Preserving Corp. of Baltimore, Inc., 347 F2d 117, 65-2 USTC ¶ 9509 (4th Cir. 1965).

Loan at incorporation represents risk capital rather than indebtedness. Taxpayer corporation was organized with $10,000 capital to acquire and operate a motel. Four days later, the father of the sole stockholder advanced $100,000 to the corporation. This sum represented more than one third of the amount required to purchase the motel, and was evidenced by a 10 percent promissory note secured by a third mortgage. At some later time, the corporation, having failed to raise funds for construction purposes, issued a demand note to the father for a further advance of $236,000. *Held:* For the IRS, in part. Considering the relatively large amounts of money that the father advanced to the corporation, the close family group that he and the officers and directors constituted and the fact that no steps were taken to foreclose although the mortgage note was in default, the Tax Court held that the father's initial advance of $100,000 was a contribution of risk capital notwithstanding his not being a stockholder of record. However, as to the later advances of $236,000, the court found that both taxpayer and the father intended this amount to be temporary financing only, to be repaid when an anticipated bank loan was consummated. Interest was therefore allowed from the date the loans were converted to permanent notes. The Motel Co., 340 F2d 445, 65-1 USTC ¶ 9183, 15 AFTR2d 199 (2d Cir. 1965).

Advances to an undercapitalized corporation held to be contributions of risk capital; bad debt deduction is denied. Taxpayer acquired a controlling interest in a newly organized radio broadcasting company and was required to advance to the company substantial sums

Contributions to Capital: *Distinguished From Debt*

for working capital purposes. These advances were not made in proportion to the stockholdings and were represented by demand interest notes. Their purpose was to enable the company to become established in a business and to keep the business in operation. The company was unable to make any repayments to taxpayer during the years in issue, nor did it pay any interest. The record also showed that taxpayer did not make any real attempt to finance loans by outside lenders or lending institutions. The Tax Court denied taxpayer a deduction for part of the advances as partially worthless debts. *Held:* Affirmed. Taxpayer did not advance the funds "with reasonable expectations of repayment regardless of the success of the venture." The funds were definitely "placed at the risk of the business" of the broadcasting company. Schine Chain Theatres, Inc., 331 F2d 849, 64-1 USTC ¶ 9478 (2d Cir. 1964).

Advances by stockholder were equity; bad debt deduction disallowed. To induce taxpayer to "stand behind" a failing company, taxpayer was given a 50 percent stock interest in the company at a time when the company desperately needed working capital. Taxpayer made advances on open account and received repayments from time to time. The Tax Court denied taxpayer a bad debt deduction for the advances upon a finding that the advances did not qualify as a debt, even though they were designated as such on the books, because in economic reality the money advanced was placed at the risk of the business in the same manner as would be equity capital; the only prospect for repayment was in the event the company was operated at a profit. *Held:* Affirmed. The fact that taxpayer, an East Coast furniture manufacturer, saw this as an opportunity to develop the company's West Coast business did not make the loss an ordinary deduction. Diamond Bros. Co., 322 F2d 725, 63-2 USTC ¶ 9717, 12 AFTR2d 5632 (3d Cir. 1963).

Loans and advances to railroad treated as capital investment. A coal mining company acquired ownership of a railroad and adjacent coal land. It paid $17,500 for the land and $132,500 for the railroad. The latter transaction was cast in the form of the purchase of $127,500 of the railroad's indebtedness and the payment of $5,000 for its stock. The Tax Court held that the purchase of the indebtedness should be disregarded in considering the realities of the situation for tax purposes, since the form of the transaction resulted in an obviously thin capitalization. *Held:* Affirmed. The indebtedness purchased, plus later advances to the railroad, constituted part of the equity investment and not true loans. On final sale of the railroad assets and the railroad corporation's dissolution in 1954, taxpayer incurred a capital loss. Jewell Ridge Coal Corp., 318 F2d 695, 63-2 USTC ¶ 9545, AFTR2d 1663 (4th Cir. 1963).

Advances to corporation constituted capital contributions; no interest deduction allowed on notes held by stockholders. Taxpayers transferred partnership assets to *X* Corporation in exchange for notes and stock. The partnership had a book net worth of $66,805, but its market value as a going concern was $240,000. Taxpayer partners received notes in the principal amount of $66,805, plus capital stock having a par value of $680. Taxpayers owned the notes in the same percentage as the capital stock. At a later time, the taxpayers sold some of their stock in order to employ a new man for *X* Corporation. It was suggested that this new man loan to *X* additional monies as well as purchase stock. The IRS argued that the advances constituted contributions to capital. *Held:* For the IRS. The monies loaned by the new man bore the exact same proportion as his proportionate ownership of the corporate stock. Furthermore, at one time, taxpayers voluntarily subordinated their notes to the loans of a bank in order to obtain additional capital for the corporation and waived the payment of interest at a time when *X* was short of cash and striving to meet current obligations. The rate of return was in excess of the interest rate that *X* would have had to pay if it had borrowed money from other lenders, and taxpayers extended the maturity date of the notes and lowered the interest rate when *X* needed cash in 1954. Thus, the court concluded that the advances to the corporation constituted capital contributions, not loans. Charter Wire,

CONTRIBUTIONS TO CAPITAL: *Distinguished From Debt*

Inc., 309 F2d 878, 62-2 USTC ¶ 9845, 10 AFTR2d 6030 (7th Cir. 1962), cert. denied, 372 US 965 (1963).

Locked-in 5 percent income notes held equity capital. Taxpayer corporation issued new 20-year, 5 percent income notes in exchange for old notes, and sought interest deduction on the new notes for the years 1953 through 1955. The old notes had been acquired by taxpayer's stockholders together with all taxpayer's stock as a package by a group of purchasers. The new notes (all in the hands of stockholders) were "locked in"—that is, they could not be sold unless all the notes together with all of the stock held by the stockholder were sold and then only after first offering the notes and stock to taxpayer. Interest was, in effect, payable at the discretion of the directors and was not cumulative. The IRS recharacterized the notes as equity. *Held:* For the IRS. The court found, based on these facts, that the notes were equity capital, not debt, and that therefore taxpayer could not deduct its payments as interest. Universal Castings Corp., 303 F2d 620, 62-1 USTC ¶ 9499 (7th Cir. 1962).

Advances to corporation considered capital contributions. Taxpayer had been engaged as a sole proprietor in selling certain equipment. He took on the sale of new products through a new corporation, which was undercapitalized. The sole proprietorship and the corporate business were conducted from the same address and had substantially the same customers and the same employees. Taxpayer made several advances to the corporation, which the IRS characterized as contributions to capital. *Held:* For the IRS. Advances that taxpayer was required to make to the corporation to keep it going were held to constitute capital contributions rather than debts. The court also held that they were not expenditures made to protect existing good will or to prevent loss of earnings by taxpayer's sole proprietorship, since they were never intended as such. Dodd, 298 F2d 570, 62-1 USTC ¶ 9223, 9 AFTR2d 528 (4th Cir. 1962).

Alleged interest payments were dividends. The assets of a sole proprietorship were transferred to a new corporation in exchange for 200 shares of $100 par value common stock and a promissory note for $90,000 due in five years. At the end of the five-year period, the note was extended for an additional five-year term. Interest on the notes was paid regularly when due and the corporation claimed a deduction for it. The district court concluded that the "notes" were an equity investment in the corporation, subject to the risk of the corporate venture, that the notes were never intended to be enforced according to their terms, and that the interest payments were not true interest payments deductible under the Code, but rather payments in the nature of dividends. Although the factor of "thin incorporation" was absent in this case, the other factors cited by the district court were relevant considerations in determining reality of the situation, for example, that the notes were extended when due in spite of the great prosperity of the corporation. The combination of evidentiary facts pointing toward risk capital was strong enough that the court not say that the finding of the district court was clearly erroneous. Brake & Elec. Corp., 287 F2d 426, 61-1 USTC ¶ 9291, 7 AFTR2d 921 (1st Cir. 1961).

Funds advanced by taxpayer to grossly undercapitalized corporation held to be capital contributions. In 1947, taxpayer acquired a controlling interest in IMI, which had been formed in 1941 to exploit a two-headed parking meter. Taxpayer entered into an agreement with IMI under which taxpayer would manufacture and IMI would act as the selling agent for the meters. The venture was not financially successful, and IMI, initially having no funds of its own, relied on taxpayer's advances to survive. Although these advances were entered on the books of both corporations as loans, no notes were given, no interest was charged, and no maturity dates were set. In 1951, IMI was liquidated and its assets distributed, but taxpayer did not fully recover the advances made. Taxpayer claimed a bad debt loss. The IRS asserted, and the Tax Court held, that only a capital loss was available. *Held:* For the IRS. Although the advances were not made in proportion to stockholdings in IMI, because of the facts and because repayment of the advances was clearly dependent on the success of IMI's business, the advances were capital contributions. American-La France-Foamite Corp., 284 F2d 723, 61-1 USTC ¶ 9153, 6 AFTR2d 6056 (2d Cir.), cert. denied, 365 US 881 (1960).

According to the facts, the credit balances owed to stockholders in the corporation's bills payable account were held to represent an equity investment. When taxpayer's stockholders originally formed taxpayer in 1915, the initial capitalization was not paid in. However, $200,000, an amount approximately equal to the initial capitalization requirements, was placed in a special account by the stockholders in proportion to their stock interests. Taxpayer used its initial earnings to satisfy its stockholders' paid-in capital commitment. In 1939, the special account was converted to a bills payable account from which taxpayer would pay interest to its creditors annually but which required no specific times for the amortization of principal. Notes were issued to persons with credit balances in this account. The rate of interest was established annually by taxpayer's board, with reference to taxpayer's earnings for the year. The IRS disallowed taxpayer's deductions for interest payable on amounts outstanding under this account. *Held:* For the IRS. The amounts in the bills payable account represented, according to the facts, an equity investment. Any amounts denominated as interest were really dividends. Wilbur Sec. Co., 279 F2d 657, 60-2 USTC ¶ 9596, 5 AFTR2d 1553 (9th Cir. 1960).

Loans to close corporation from family trust were capital contributions; interest deductions disallowed. Taxpayer corporation began business with minimum capital. As the business grew (its annual cost of goods sold approached $1 million), the need for equity capital increased. The corporation borrowed over $257,000 from certain trusts set up by the sole stockholder for the benefit of herself and her children. The trustee was the husband of the grantor and also the corporation's chief executive officer. Although the advances made by the trust were ostensibly repayable on demand, no payments were made to reduce the balance of $257,000, and no demand was made for repayment. The advances were never collateralized and were subordinated to bank loans. The IRS contended that the advances were capital contributions. *Held:* For the IRS. On the facts the court found that the advances were not bona fide indebtedness but constituted capital contributions. Accordingly, deductions for "interest" paid on the advances were denied. Zephyr Mills, Inc., 279 F2d 494, 60-1 USTC ¶ 9469 (3d Cir. 1960).

Note given sole stockholder on incorporation not intended to be debt. Taxpayer corporation, which took over a sole proprietorship from its stockholder, issued to him a demand note for $200,000 in payment for certain of the assets transferred. The Tax Court found that, at the time the note was issued, the stockholder did not intend to enforce payment by his corporation if by so doing the corporation would be at all inconvenienced. It held no valid indebtedness existed, and that taxpayer was, therefore, not entitled to deduct accrued interest on the notes. *Held:* Affirmed. There was no business reason for a note rather than stock when the corporation was first organized. Very few financial institutions would lend $200,000 to any corporation for six and a half months on an unsecured note without interest or fail to require interest payments for over three years. The court also noted the disparity between the interest deduction taken by the corporation and the interest income reported by the sole stockholder. Kruse Grain Co., 279 F2d 123, 60-2 USTC ¶ 9490, 5 AFTR2d 1544 (9th Cir. 1960).

Note to owners on incorporation of partnership held really capital. The Tax Court found that no real creditor-debtor relationship was established between a corporation and a husband and wife, its chief officers and stockholders. On formation, the corporation had issued stock of $49,000 and notes to stockholders of about $232,000 for partnership assets worth $281,000. All other corporate debts were given preference by subordination of stockholder loans. Some of the stockholder loans were not paid at maturity. The Tax

Court disallowed the interest deduction: Payments to stockholders were, it held, distributions of corporate profits taxable as dividend income. *Held:* Affirmed. The court found that the question was one of fact and stated that the Tax Court decision was supported by the evidence. Gooding Amusement Co., 236 F2d 159, 56-2 USTC ¶ 9808, 49 AFTR2d 1973 (6th Cir.), cert. denied, 352 US 1031 (1956).

Advances to corporations that were never repaid were capital contributions and therefore not deductible as business bad debts. Taxpayer advanced funds to his corporation, which could not obtain financing from commercial lending institutions. The loans were evidenced by a promissory note and stated an interest rate of 7.5 percent. The money advanced was used to pay the corporation's general day-to-day operating expenses, and was not used for capital investment. In 1968 and 1969, taxpayer sold corporate stock, thereby recognizing a capital gain. No demand for repayment was ever made on the notes, and no repayment of principal or interest was made. The notes were not accompanied by any security, and were not listed as business bad debts on tax returns. Taxpayer first filed for an arrangement under Chapter XI. This was followed three years later by a straight bankruptcy, which was granted. Later taxpayer filed for tax refunds based on deductions for bad debt losses on the advances made to the corporation. The IRS disallowed the refunds. *Held:* For the IRS. Where the evidence indicated that advances to a corporation were not bona fide business loans, but instead contributions to capital, a business bad debt deduction was denied. This followed because the corporation was undercapitalized, there had been no demand for repayment, the notes were unsecured, and taxpayer was the president and principal stockholder of the corporation. In re Mindheim, 80-1 USTC ¶ 9271, 45 AFTR2d 80-1183 (D. Nev. 1980).

Advances were capital contributions and not deductible bad debts as they were not made with a reasonable expectation of repayment. Taxpayer was 50 percent stockholder, general manager, and executive vice-president of a car dealership. The business had a history of financial losses and taxpayer obtained funds from third parties. The funds were either paid directly to the dealership or transferred to it through taxpayer. The dealership was eventually placed in receivership with a large amount advanced left unreturned. Taxpayer claimed a business bad debt deduction based on the amounts advanced. *Held:* For the IRS. Taxpayer failed to prove that his advances created a debtor-creditor relationship. A three-point test applies to such situations, consisting of form, intent and economic reality. First and foremost, there was no written document and therefore no provisions for interest, no enforceable obligation, no maturity date, and no provision for repayment. The intent of the parties showed the advances to be equity investments. Prolonged defaults were tolerated, which evidenced placement of stockholder interests ahead of creditor interests. Under the economic reality test, no unrelated party would have advanced funds under like circumstances. The court thus held that the advances were not made with a reasonable expectations of repayment. Fischer, 441 F. Supp. 32, 77-2 USTC ¶ 9722, 40 AFTR2d 77-5755 (ED Pa. 1977), aff'd (3d Cir. 1978).

Advances from stockholders were capital contributions. The IRS held that advances made by stockholders to taxpayer, a closely held corporation, were not in fact loans and therefore no interest deductions were allowed on repayment. *Held:* For the IRS. The IRS' position was supported by the corporation's capital insufficiency, the advances being proportionate to stock ownership, lack of creditor's safeguards, and unobserved maturity dates. Du Gro Frozen Foods, Inc., 73-1 USTC ¶ 9164 (ND Ga. 1973).

Advances to controlled corporation were capital contributions and not loans. Taxpayer was the sole stockholder and president of *E*, a corporation that sold and leased carbonated beverage–dispensing equipment and related items. During its four years of existence, *E* continually operated at a net operating loss. Each of these years, taxpayer advanced sub-

Contributions to Capital: *Distinguished From Debt*

stantial sums of cash to *E*, which the corporate records showed as loans. However, *E* did not give taxpayer a promissory note or collateral for the advances. *E* paid no interest, and there was no definite repayment schedule. The IRS determined that the advances were contributions to capital and not loans to *E*. *Held:* For the IRS. When there were advances because of taxpayer's activities as an investor trying to save his investment, the amounts were contributions to capital and created a nonbusiness bad debt on their becoming worthless. Commercial Bank at Daytona Beach, 71-2 USTC ¶ 9668, 28 AFTR2d 71-5719 (MD Fla. 1971).

Advances deemed capital contribution. The IRS held that advances by taxpayer, a stockholder and officer of corporations acting as manufacturers' agents for the distribution of industrial equipment, were in fact contributions to capital. *Held:* For the IRS. The factors supporting a capital finding included (1) the debt-equity ratio was as high as 300 to 1 in one of the years affected, and (2) the notes supporting the advances did not have a maturity date or enforcement provisions. Lynch, 337 F. Supp. 1297, 72-1 USTC ¶ 9166 (ND Ga. 1971).

Corporation's distribution to 60 percent stockholder was a dividend, not a loan repayment. From 1954 through 1955, taxpayer advanced money to a corporation in which he was a 60 percent stockholder, to be used for land development costs. The advance was carried on the corporation's books as open account indebtedness. In 1962, the corporation made a final repayment of the loan of $23,000 to the taxpayer. The IRS argued that the distribution was a dividend under Section 302(b)(1). *Held:* For the IRS. (1) The advance was equity, not debt: There was no note, security, interest, or maturity date, and repayment was contingent on sale of the land. The loan was subordinated in fact, other financing was unavailable, the debt-equity ratio was eight to one, and the advance was used to purchase fixed assets, not to provide working capital. (2) The loan was, in substance, preferred stock and the "repayment" was a redemption essentially equivalent to a dividend. Sansberry, 70-1 USTC ¶ 9216 (SD Ind. 1970).

Pro rata advances to corporation were capital contributions. Taxpayer and another person each paid $5,000 for 50 shares of stock of a newly formed corporation that had no other stockholders. At various times thereafter, they each advanced additional amounts to the corporation on a pro rata basis. The total amount of their advances was $25,500. In exchange for their advances, the corporation issued taxpayer and the other stockholder the corporation's unsecured subordinated promissory notes, payable on demand, with interest at 6 percent after maturity. No interest or principal payments were ever made on the notes; in fact, repayment of the first three advances was expected to come only out of profits. Taxpayer made the last advance to the corporation to protect the good name of another corporation in which he owned all the stock. When the corporate notes became worthless, taxpayer deducted the amount of the advances as a business bad debt. The IRS denied the deduction, contending that the advances were contributions to capital. *Held:* For the IRS. The advances did not fall within the definition of "classic debt." The absence of a fixed maturity date also was a significant factor. It was clear that in making the advances, taxpayer intended to incur the risks of a corporate venture. Obermeyer, 262 F. Supp. 421, 66-2 USTC ¶ 9728, 18 AFTR2d 5936 (SD Ohio 1966).

Advances were capital contributions and not loans. Taxpayer corporation deducted interest paid on $50,000 given it by a stockholder. The corporation failed in attempts to get bank loans, and the equity investment in the corporation was $10,000. The IRS contended that the loans by the stockholder were capital contributions and denied the deduction for interest paid on the loans. *Held:* For the IRS. Applying pertinent tests, the advance was a capital contribution. The jury considered the degree of risk, the parties' intent and motives, the form of the obligation, and the debt-equity relationship. Herculoc Corp., 66-2 USTC ¶ 9662, 18 AFTR2d 5703 (EDNY 1966).

Contributions to Capital: *Distinguished From Debt*

Purported sale of land to controlled corporation was capital contribution. After organizing a corporation with $1,000 capital stock, taxpayer sold a tract of farm land to it for $80,000. The corporation paid the purchase price by issuing its interest-bearing notes to taxpayer. The corporation then subdivided the land. The IRS asserted that the transaction was a Section 351 tax-free exchange and disallowed interest on the notes. *Held:* For the IRS. The transaction was a contribution to capital, and the corporation did not have a stepped-up basis for the land. The ratio of indebtedness to equity capital was 80 to 1; aside from the land, taxpayer's only asset was the $1,000 cash paid for the stock, an amount insufficient to develop the land. The notes therefore represented equity capital and the interest payments were not deductible. Castle Heights, Inc., 242 F. Supp. 350, 65-2 USTC ¶ 9483 (ED Tenn. 1965).

Stockholder advances to thin corporation treated as equity. During construction of a drive-in movie theatre, taxpayer corporation obtained outside mortgages of $150,000 and advances from stockholders of $43,000. The amount paid in for stock was only $500. The IRS determined the advances to be equity. *Held:* For the IRS. Considering that the notes to stockholders were substantially proportionate to stockholding and were obviously part of the permanent capital, the court held that the notes really constituted equity. Interest was therefore disallowed. Broadway Drive-In Theatre, Inc., 220 F. Supp. 707, 63-2 USTC ¶ 9578, 12 AFTR2d 5195 (ED Mo. 1963).

Section 482 allocation of imputed interest struck down; "loans" were capital contributions. Taxpayer corporation acquired control of another corporation in a series of transactions, some of which were listed on the taxpayer's books as loans to the acquired corporation. The IRS, noting that no interest was charged on the "loans," imputed interest income to taxpayer under Section 482. *Held:* For taxpayer. The "loans" were actually capital contributions; their treatment as loans was an accounting error. Post Corp., 640 F2d 1296, 81-1 USTC ¶ 9197, 47 AFTR2d 81-659 (Cl. Ct. 1981).

Advances from parent to subsidiary did not remain a valid indebtedness because the subsidiary remained insolvent for many years. Taxpayer was organized by its parent corporation to become the recipient of some of the latter's real property. To finance taxpayer's operations, the parent either loaned money directly or purchased its promissory notes from other parties. Over a 40-year period from inception, such indebtedness and accured interest totaled $3,600,000. The parent forgave the indebtedness on the grounds that taxpayer was and always had been hopelessly insolvent. Taxpayer had accured interest on the indebtedness, giving rise to net operating loss carryover. This was disallowed. *Held:* For the IRS. To satisfy the requirements of Section 163, there must be a debt and interest thereon accrued during the taxable year. The important underlying principle is that no valid debt exists unless there is an unconditional obligation to repay. The transaction merits particular scrutiny in parent-subsidiary relationships. Here, it was likely that the parent's advances to taxpayer in exchange for the latter's notes were intended to create a debtor-creditor relationship when they were made 40 years earlier. It was apparent that the parties had no intention of continuing the debtor-creditor relatonship long before the year in question. All of the facts of this case led to the conclusion that the advances were intended as a contribution to capital rather than an indebtness. Cuyuna Realty Co. & Misabe Realty Co., 382 F2d 298, 67-2 USTC ¶ 9571, 20 AFTR2d 5172 (Ct. Cl. 1967).

Proportionate advances to corporation equity, not loans. To induce the only other stockholder of Consolidated Corporation to vote with them when they acquired Consolidated stock, the stockholders of taxpayer, a family corporation, had taxpayer, instead of stockholders, buy the Consolidated stock. Taxpayer financed 40 percent of the $500,000 purchase with a 5-percent bank loan secured by (1) the personal guarantees of its stockholders, (2) a collateral pledge of the Consolidated stock, and (3) a promise by taxpayer's stockholders to subordinate to the bank loans that they would make towards the purchase price. In accordance with the bank agreement, taxpayer's stockholders, individually and as executors and trustees, advanced the balance of the purchase price under subordinated loans at 4 percent interest. Loans on the estate made by taxpayer's stockholders on the basis of their beneficial interests in the estate were evidenced by demand notes and were substantially in proportion to stockholdings in taxpayer. Prior to the purchase of the Consolidated stock, taxpayer's equity was $4,000. The IRS denied taxpayer any deductions for interest paid on the stockholder loans. *Held:* For the IRS. Form does not control substance. Contrasting the bank loans to the stockholders' loans evidences that the latter were in reality contributions to capital. Only the stockholders' loans were dependent upon taxpayer's earnings; the bank loans were secured by the stockholder guarantees and the collateral pledge. The demand feature of the stockholder loans were meaningless because the loans were subordinate to the bank debt. No outsider would have made loans on similar terms. The fact that the advances by the stockholders were substantially in proportion to their stockholdings and to the 131-to-1 debt-equity ratio was further evidence that the loans were capital contributions. Affiliated Research, Inc., 351 F2d 646, 65-2 USTC ¶ 9684, 16 AFTR2d 5752 (Ct. Cl. 1965).

Payments by seller to purchaser to secure release of liability as guarantor held deductible as an ordinary loss. Taxpayer was interested in developing POP, a family amusement park in the nature of Disneyland. On the basis of its research, taxpayer concluded that such a park could be built for $3 million. On the basis of the reports, taxpayer entered into a pre-incorporation agreement with CBS whereby it would purchase the stock of the newly incorporated POP for $400,000 each and guarantee loans from banks or other financing institutions in amounts in the aggregate of $2.2 million. After the incorporation of POP and the start of the construction, completion of the project required expenditure of amounts far in excess of those originally foreseen, although periodic reports and surveys indicated that the enterprise could be made profitable. Consequently, both taxpayer and CBS invested an additional $500,000 in the capital of POP. In addition, taxpayer became unconditional guarantor of loans in the amount of $4.396 million, while CBS guaranteed approximately the same amount. After the park opened, closed for changes, and reopened again, it became apparent that POP could not operate it at a profit. In addition, POP had incurred commitments to advertisers, concessionaires and lessees. Several methods of terminating taxpayer's and CBS' interest in POP were presented, but the only feasible alternative was the transfer of the stock to a third-party purchaser accompanied by the payment of cash to such party. The transaction was consummated with taxpayer paying $4,396,000 to the purchaser, which amount was used to secure the release of its liability as guarantor of bank notes. On its return, taxpayer claimed an ordinary loss deduction for the payment and long-term capital loss of $900,000 on the worthlessness of the stock of POP. The IRS disallowed the loss deduction on the grounds that the unconditional guarantees constituted borrowings of taxpayer that were contributions to the capital of POP. *Held:* For taxpayer. The payment for release from the guarantee was irretrievably lost in a transaction in which taxpayer had no right to compensation for its loss through compensation, subrogation, or otherwise. The transaction thus met the requirements of Section 165(a). The agreements showed that the primary debtor was POP, and that taxpayer and CBS were guarantors. The loans by the bank to POP, guaranteed by taxpayer and CBS, were valid loans and not contributions to capital. From the outset, it was anticipated that a substantial portion of the financing would come from borrowings, and the additional contributions to capital in excess of the original $800,000 negated the argument of thin capitalization. Although the IRS argued that it was unreasonable to expect that the loans could be satisfied by POP according to the terms, the periodic reports prepared for POP, taxpayer, and CBS all indicated that POP would be able to pay the loans. For the advance to be a loan, it was not necessary for

Contributions to Capital: *Distinguished From Debt*

there to be an unqualified expectation of repayment. The court also did not accept the argument that the third-party purchaser was used as a conduit for payment directly to the bank, partly because there was arm's-length dealing with a third party in which taxpayer sought to limit the amount that it was ultimately required to pay. Santa Anita Consol., Inc., 50 TC 536 (1968).

Thin capitalization of realty corporation resulted in loss of interest deductions. Taxpayer corporation was formed with a capitalization of $1,000 to take title to two apartment buildings costing $205,000. The properties were taken subject to an existing first mortgage and a purchase money mortgage, totalling $155,000. The $50,000 required to close the transaction was loaned to taxpayer by the stockholders, and ten-year, 10 percent promissory notes secured by a third mortgage on the buildings were issued in return. The notes made no provision for amortization, although $4,000 was paid off four years after issuance. *Held:* For the IRS. Despite the fact that regular payments were made and the notes were in proper form with the outward appearance of a "classic debt," interest deductions were disallowed. In economic reality, the loans represented equity investment. They were made in ratio to stockholdings, the corporation was thinly capitalized (205 to 1), and the evidence did not indicate that an outsider would have made a loan on the same terms. There was no intent to repay the loans, and they were placed at the risk of the business. 2554-58 Creston Corp., 40 TC 932 (1963).

Subsequent acts converted loans into capital contributions; interest was not deductible. A stockholder and members of taxpayer's board of directors advanced a total of $40,000 to taxpayer. Each loan was evidenced by 6 percent demand notes. In order to increase taxpayer's line of credit with a bank, the individuals agreed to subordinate their loans to any bank loans, provided that the interest on the demand notes was increased to 12 percent. A corporate resolution recited the fact that the individuals agreed to leave the $40,000 "as permanent working capital for the company." *Held:* For the IRS. In agreeing with the IRS that the interest on the loans should be disallowed in full, the court noted that (1) the statement quoted above in the minutes and subsequent actions were consistent with the proposition that the loans were converted to capital contributions, (2) the directors were either direct or beneficial owners of the stock of taxpayer's parent, (3) the loans were roughly in proportion to these stock interests, (4) taxpayer failed to establish that its capitalization was adequate, (5) by subordinating their loans to the bank's loans, the noteholders in effect placed their money at the risk of the business, since no repayment was ever made, and (6) the 12 percent interest rate was unlawful under state law. Oak Hill Fin. Co., 40 TC 419 (1963).

Payments to bondholders not deductible as interest; loans really capital contributions. Taxpayer, a corporation, was formed to construct a 237-house housing development. It was capitalized with $4,500 of common stock, $300,000 of bonds and notes and $2.8 million in construction loans. The bondholders were to receive 50 percent of the profits from the venture on the form of bond premiums and interest. The IRS determined that the bond premiums and interest were not deductible. *Held:* For the IRS. In view of taxpayer's thin capitalization and the profit-sharing agreement, the court found that the $300,000 was risk capital. Aldon Homes, Inc., 33 TC 582 (1960).

Stockholder's advances to insolvent corporation were capital contributions; bad debt deduction disallowed. Taxpayer, in the construction, real estate, mortgage, and insurance brokerage businesses, was also a stockholder of a financially distressed corporation. To prevent the corporation from going bankrupt, taxpayer advanced substantial sums to its president for use by the corporation. The president, who was also the principal stockholder, assigned one-half of the outstanding shares to taxpayer. Advances were, for the most part, not evidenced by promissory notes, and no date was stipulated for repayment. The corporation and its president later went bankrupt, and taxpayer claimed a business bad debt deduction. The IRS denied the

CONTRIBUTIONS TO CAPITAL: *Distinguished From Debt*

deduction and argued that the advances were merely additional capital contributions. *Held:* For the IRS. The evidence indicated that once the president turned the funds over to the corporation, he was no longer liable to taxpayer. Even if the advances had been loans, the court would have denied a business bad debt deduction, since taxpayer was not in the business of lending money for profit. Zivnuska, 33 TC 226 (1959).

Advances to corporation by stockholder held contributions to capital rather than loans. Taxpayer was a 10 percent owner and manager of a car leasing corporation. He effectively controlled all aspects of the business and made day-to-day decisions. Taxpayer made a series of advances to the corporation to keep it financially viable. Generally, the advances were not evidenced by notes, except for a promissory note for $10,000, which taxpayer, as secretary-treasurer of the corporation, signed. The note was unsecured and unrecorded, and only $5,000 was deposited into the corporate account. Taxpayer filed suit against the corporation for collection of the promissory note plus interest. Later, the note was purchased by his mother's investment corporation. At this time, no interest was paid on the note. After a series of events and legal actions, and after not receiving payment on the note, taxpayer claimed a business bad debt deduction in the amount of $10,000 on his federal income tax return. The IRS disallowed the claimed deduction. *Held:* For the IRS. Advances made to a thinly capitalized corporation by a 10 percent stockholder were capital contributions, not loans, to the corporation. This followed where the evidence indicated that the note was unsecured and unrecorded and that no interest was paid or could be expected to be paid on the note. Since only $5,000 was deposited in the corporate account at the time the unsecured note was drawn, the note was but a mere formality to cover taxpayer's earlier advances without notes. Accordingly, the conclusion was that taxpayer did not intend to create a debt relationship with the corporation when he made the advances. Farkas, 50 TCM 1085, ¶ 85,488 P-H Memo. TC (1985).

Taxpayer's advances to his closely held corporation were equity. Taxpayer claimed a $75,000 business bad debt deduction for the amount for which he was liable under the personal guarantee of loans he made to his corporation. In fact, he had only paid $23,000 pursuant to his guarantee. The IRS determined that taxpayer, not the corporation, was the true borrower of the funds, and that taxpayer was entitled only to a capital loss deduction for $23,000. *Held:* For the IRS. The taxpayer was the true borrower of the funds from the bank since the bank made the loan based totally on taxpayer's credit history and personal guarantee. Atkinson, 48 TCM 577, ¶ 84,378 P-H Memo. TC (1984).

Property transferred to wholly owned subsidiary was equity, not debt. Taxpayer corporation transferred cash and merchandise to its wholly owned subsidiary. Taxpayer contended that these transfers of property were advances or loans and claimed a bad debt deduction when no repayment was made. The IRS determined that the transfers were contributions to capital. *Held:* For the IRS. The subsidiary was undercapitalized, did not execute any notes or other documents evidencing debt, did not pay any interest on the purported advances, and never repaid any portion of the amount transferred to it by taxpayer. Accordingly, the transfers were capital contributions and no bad debt deduction under Section 166 was allowed. Further, because under Section 267 the taxpayer and its controlling stockholder were related parties, no capital loss deduction was allowed on the sale of the subsidiary's stock to taxpayer's controlling stockholder. Smithco Eng'g, Inc., 47 TCM 966, ¶ 84,043 P-H Memo. TC (1984).

Advances to a corporation were capital contributions. During periods of financial difficulty, taxpayer corporation's stockholders advanced money to it in exchange for interest-bearing notes. When taxpayer obtained cash, it made payments to the stockholders and deducted the payments as interest on the notes. The IRS claimed that the advances were not loans and disallowed the interest deductions. *Held:* For the IRS. The advances were indispensible to taxpayer's financial survival, re-

Contributions to Capital: *Distinguished From Debt*

payment of principal and interest was uncertain, the notes were subordinated to taxpayer's other indebtedness, and the stockholders intended to subject the advances to taxpayer's economic fortunes. Thus, the advances were contributions to capital and not genuine indebtedness. Accordingly, interest was not deductible. Towne Square, Inc., 45 TCM 478, ¶ 83,010 P-H Memo. TC (1983).

Advances by stockholder were contributions to capital. Taxpayer advanced funds to an insolvent close corporation of which he was a substantial stockholder. The advances were not evidenced by promissory notes, were subordinated to unsecured general creditors, and repayment effectively depended on the company's future performance. Taxpayer deducted them as business bad debts, which the IRS disallowed. *Held:* For the IRS. The Tax Court held that the advances were nondeductible contributions to capital. It based its decision on grounds that the normal indicia of a loan were lacking. Steiner, 41 TCM 1392, ¶ 81,212 P-H Memo. TC (1981).

Transfer of assets to corporation was a capital contribution, not a loan. Taxpayer transferred the assets of a sole proprietorship to a new wholly owned corporation. The value of the assets was $32,000, of which only $500 was assigned to the stock issued; the balance was treated as a loan. Taxpayer treated withdrawals as loan repayments. The IRS contended that the transfer resulted in a contribution to capital, not a loan. *Held:* For the IRS. The assets were placed at the risk of the business, and repayment was dependent upon its financial success. Hutchins Standard Serv., 41 TCM 777, ¶ 81,033 P-H Memo. TC (1981).

Advances to company not loans, since evidence of indebtedness was lacking. Taxpayers were stockholders in a failing business. They advanced funds that they later deducted as business bad debts. The IRS claimed that the advances were contributions to capital and were thus nondeductible. *Held:* For the IRS. Evidence of indebtedness was never drawn up, and taxpayers never filed claims in bankruptcy for the amounts advanced. Outside financing was unobtainable and the transaction was not made at arm's length. Sekulow, 41 TCM 582, ¶ 80,564 P-H Memo. TC (1980).

Loans to closely held corporation not deductible. Taxpayer made loans to pay his closely held corporation's debts. The IRS denied the deductions, arguing that the payments represented contribution to capital. *Held:* For the IRS. The payments were loans, but they could not be deducted as a business bad debt because the taxpayer's primary motive was investment. Thus the loans were a nonbusiness bad debt. Estate of Ripson, 39 TCM 224, ¶ 79,394 P-H Memo. TC (1979).

No bad debt deduction allowed for advances, which were capital contributions. Taxpayer operated a sole proprietorship and organized a corporation that did not issue stock. Taxpayer received loans, which he deposited in the corporation's account. The proprietorship filed for bankruptcy, and claimed a business bad debt deduction for the advances, which it claimed were loans. The IRS disallowed the deduction. *Held:* For the IRS. Taxpayer could substantiate only one advance to the corporation: a contribution to capital. Based on the totality of facts, the advance did not give rise to a bona fide deductible debt, evidenced by the lack of an instrument of indebtedness, by the fact that the corporation gave no security and there was no reasonable expectation of repayment, among other factors. Taxpayer could at most contend that he suffered a capital loss on worthless securities. Taxpayer could not, however, establish worthlessness, since he could not make it clear when business operations ceased, if at all. He did not produce corporate records to prove the year of insolvency, and he did not show that the corporation dissolved or filed for bankruptcy. McHenry, 37 TCM 1254, ¶ 78,300 P-H Memo. TC (1978).

Advance to corporation held contribution to capital. Taxpayer advanced $530 to a corporation in which he was a stockholder. The corporation subsequently went out of business. The taxpayer claimed that the advance was a loan. *Held:* For the IRS. Evidence suggested that the advance was a contribution to capital. No interest was provided for on the advance. No note was given, nor was any collateral offered. Moreover, it appeared that the corporation was undercapitalized. Freer, 37 TCM 1193, ¶ 78,282 P-H Memo. TC (1978).

Advances to stockholders' inadequately capitalized corporation were contributions to capital. Taxpayers advanced money to a pharmacy corporation in which they were stockholders. The corporation was dissolved and no payment was made to taxpayers. Taxpayers deducted the advances as business bad debts. *Held:* For the IRS. Since the corporation was in poor financial condition, and there were no creditor safeguards when the money was advanced, the advances were contributions to capital and not loans. Even if the advances had been debts, they would be nonbusiness bad debts because taxpayers were not in the business of making loans. Thaler, 37 TCM 147, ¶ 78,024 P-H Memo. TC (1978).

Corporation's sale of real estate attributed to sole stockholder. Taxpayer, active in the real estate industry, owned 100 percent of two real estate development corporations that were experiencing financial difficulties. In August 1969, taxpayer transferred his interest in certain real estate to these corporations, and in October 1969, this real estate was sold. Proceeds from the sale were principally used to pay off outstanding liabilities to the purchaser of the land, a lumber supplier. Later in 1969, taxpayer liquidated both corporations. The IRS argued that under Section 482, taxpayer should be deemed to have sold real estate to the corporations. *Held:* For the IRS. Taxpayer should be viewed as selling real estate to the supplier and then having made a capital contribution of the sales proceeds to the corporations. Also, unsecured advances to the corporations, although initially viewable as debt, later became capital contributions when taxpayer subordinated them to the claims of other creditors; therefore, taxpayer was not entitled to a bad debt deduction for advances. Frazier, 34 TCM 951, ¶ 75,220 P-H Memo. TC (1975).

Capital loss sustained on worthlessness of advance to corporation. Taxpayers advanced funds to their 100 percent owned corporation, sold the stock, and accepted a note for the balance of the purchase price due. When the note became worthless they claimed a business bad debt loss, which the IRS disallowed. *Held:* For the IRS. As to the advances, taxpayers were still creditors of the corporation, and no debtor-creditor relationship existed between taxpayers and purchaser. The note received was for the unpaid purchase price, not for the advances, and there was no substitution of obligors, so that the loss on the note was of the same capital nature as the original advance to the corporation and was not a deductible business bad debt. Ritsos, 30 TCM 495, ¶ 71,116 P-H Memo. TC (1971).

Taxpayer's advances to his controlled corporation were capital contributions, not loans; therefore bad debt deductions were disallowed. With a limited capital, taxpayer created a corporation to sell and service garbage disposal units. He immediately advanced funds to the corporation for its operating expenses. Later, he took bad debt deductions for the unpaid loans, but the IRS disallowed them. *Held:* For the IRS. The advances were contributions to capital, not loans, as evidenced by (1) the minimal expectation of repayment, as the business was continually unsuccessful; (2) the inadequacy of original capital; (3) the immediate need for operating capital; (4) the lack of outside sources of capital due to the firm's poor financial position; (5) the lack of loan security; (6) the lack of notes evidencing the debts; (7) the absence of a schedule of repayments or interest payments; and (8) minimal repayments of principal. Thus, taxpayer was not entitled to bad debt deductions for the nonexistent loans. Nystrom, Jr., 28 TCM 1050, ¶ 69,201 P-H Memo. TC (1969).

Transfer under subordination agreement was equity, not debt. Taxpayer was one of the incorporators of a brokerage business. The company was required to close its doors until additional funds were contributed. To reinstate the business, taxpayer transferred securities to the company under two subordination

Contributions to Capital: Distinguished From Debt

agreements. After the company went into bankruptcy, taxpayer deducted the cost of the transferred shares as a business bad debt. *Held:* For the IRS. The subordination agreement reflected an equity rather than debt transaction despite references to "loan" and "indebtedness" therein. Copley, 27 TCM 383, ¶ 68,077 P-H Memo. TC (1968).

Advances by stockholders to family corporation to cover initial construction costs of apartment building were capital. A father and son organized a real estate company on a fifty-fifty basis to take over an apartment building under construction. At the time of incorporation, both father and son listed capital contributions of $10,000, and each advanced $20,072, evidenced by one-year promissory notes, which were extendable by the corporation for up to 20 years with interest payable at 4 percent. The advances were originally made before the incorporation in order to cover initial construction costs of the apartment building. The corporation deducted "interest" payments on the advances. *Held:* For the IRS. The deductions were denied. The advances were in the nature of equity capital at risk in the family business and could not be treated as true debt. When the organizers of a new enterprise designate as loans a substantial amount of money that they lay out in order to get the business established and under way, it is often inferred that such sums are contributions to the corporation's capital. In addition, the advances were called debts so that the corporation could borrow money from other sources. Peco Co., 26 TCM 207, ¶ 67,041 P-H Memo. TC (1967).

Loans to brother corporation were contributions to capital. Taxpayer advanced funds to an affiliated corporation that was unable to secure outside financing. The advances were made without the normal creditor safeguards, and security for the loan was of almost negligible value. No effort was made to enforce payment because to do so would have forced the debtor into bankruptcy. *Held:* For the IRS. A bad debt deduction was denied. The advances were capital contributions, since a true debtor-creditor relationship did not exist. Williams Contracting Co., 25 TCM 500, ¶ 66,093 P-H Memo. TC (1966).

No valid debt found for advances made to joint venture. Taxpayer, a successful real estate operator, advanced $12,000 to his brother's company to permit the latter to exercise options to acquire certain building lots. The advances were represented by subordinated non-interest-bearing notes. Taxpayer became an officer in his brother's company, participated with his brother in the construction, and guaranteed invoices for materials. Subsequently, a land developer participating in the venture defaulted, and taxpayer paid an attorney $400 to enable the company to bring suit against the developer. On completion of the project (at a loss) taxpayer advanced the company $28,000 to pay off the materialmen and subcontractors. The advances were claimed as a business bad debt deduction in 1956. The IRS disallowed the deductions. *Held:* For the IRS. No valid indebtedness existed and the deduction was denied. The $12,000 advanced to enable the company to acquire the option represented a capital contribution. The subordination of the advances to the debts owed to outsiders, the lack of a relatively fixed date on which taxpayer could have demanded a definite sum regardless of profits earned, and the fact that outside investors would not have made similar advances, strongly indicated lack of true debt. The $400 and $28,000 advances were made without expectation of repayment and could not be considered a loan. Regarding taxpayer's argument that the $28,000 was paid under a guarantee and that taxpayer thereby became subrogated to the materialmen's claims against the company, the court noted that the advances were not to creditors but to the debtor so that it could itself pay creditors. Thus there were no rights of subrogation. Rouse, 23 TCM 1823, ¶ 64,297 P-H Memo. TC (1964).

Realty corporation thinly capitalized where ratio of capital is 1 to 25; "advances" held to be equity capital, not loans. Taxpayer and others organized *X* Corporation to acquire, develop, subdivide, and sell real estate lots. The authorized capital was $1,000. A few days later,

Contributions to Capital: *Preferred Stock*

the stockholders advanced $25,000 as "loans" evidenced by notes and made in direct proportion to stockholdings. The money thus "advanced" enabled *X* Corporation to acquire a tract of land. Proceeds from the subdivision and sale of the tract were used first to pay off the seller and then to pay off the stockholders' notes. *Held:* For the IRS. The payments by the corporation on the stockholders' notes constituted dividends. The advances were, in effect, equity capital, not bona fide loans. Lancaster, 23 TCM 631, ¶ 64,108 P-H Memo. TC (1964).

Advances of nonstockholder not obtainable from other sources treated as equity capital. Taxpayer corporations were each capitalized with an investment of $1,000. Each corporation shortly thereafter borrowed $50,000 in cash from an unrelated nonstockholder, and each delivered therefor its unsecured promissory notes. The funds alleged to have been loaned could not have been borrowed from any other source. The corporations claimed deductions for interest expense. *Held:* For the IRS. The deductions were denied. No debtor-creditor relationship existed as the advances represented capital equity placed at the risk of the business to get it started. The "borrowed" funds could not have been borrowed from any other source, and the ratio of risk capital to debt was unrealistic. Moreover, no attempt was made to enforce payment when the original maturity date passed. Merlo Builders, Inc., 23 TCM 185, ¶ 64,034 P-H Memo. TC (1964).

Corporate advances were for capital contributions, not loans; investment deduction allowed as capital loss. Taxpayer advanced more than $50,000 over a two-year period to a corporation in which he acquired a 50 percent stock interest. Through an agent, taxpayer took over the management of the business and changed the name of the corporation to improve its credit. No notes or other evidences of indebtedness were given in return for the advances. *Held:* The court found that the advances were contributions to capital and not loans. Accordingly, the deduction for worthlessness of the investment could be taken only as a capital loss. Mangrum, 19 TCM 700, ¶ 60,136 P-H Memo. TC (1960).

Preferred Stock

Payments were dividends, not interest. The corporate taxpayer issued securities, which it denominated as preferred stock, as part of the purchase price for the assets of a public passenger transportation system. The terms of the preferred stock required a 5 percent cumulative dividend per annum and a sinking fund for the retirement of the preferred stock. The taxpayer sought to deduct the dividend payments as interest on its federal income tax returns. The Tax Court held that the payments were dividends, not interest. *Held:* Affirmed. Despite a definite maturity date for redemption of the stock, the maturity date was contingent to a certain degree on prior retirement of the bonds and notes. Further, the stock was subordinate to the debt represented by bonds and notes and general creditors. In proceedings before the Public Service Commission of Wisconsin and the SEC, taxpayer represented that the securities were preferred stock. Thus, the court stated that the preferred stock was an equity investment in the corporation. Payments on it were dividends, not deductible interest. Milwaukee & Suburban Transp. Corp., 283 F2d 279, 60-2 USTC ¶ 9741, 6 AFTR2d 5719 (7th Cir. 1960), cert. denied, 368 US 976 (1961).

Payments were dividends on preferred stock, not interest. Taxpayer made distributions on certain securities. It deducted the distributions as interest payments on indebtedness. The documents and references to the securities referred to them as preferred stock. On tax returns and corporate records, the securities were treated as preferred stock. The securities were entitled to receive dividends, but only out of surplus on net profits, and the holders were entitled to participate in management on an equal footing with the common stockholders. The IRS determined the securities to be preferred stock and the distributions to be dividends. *Held:* For the IRS. Because the facts evidenced no debtor-creditor relationship, the securities were preferred stock. Accordingly, the distributions were

CONTRIBUTIONS TO CAPITAL: *Preferred Stock*

dividends on the preferred stock, and not deductible payments of interest. Sunny Isles Ocean Beach Co., 62-1 USTC ¶ 9151, 9 AFTR2d 388 (WDNY 1961).

Sale to controlled corporation was equity contribution; payments resulted in dividend. Taxpayer acquired a 30-day option to purchase farm acreage but failed to give the grantor the required written notice of his intention to exercise it. Eight months later, he purchased two parcels of the land and sold them a month later, claiming long-term capital gain. Taxpayer argued that he actually sold the *option*, not the land, and that the option had been orally extended and held for more than six months. Taxpayer also sold other land to a controlled corporation at a greatly inflated price and received payments therefor on the installment basis. *Held:* For the IRS. Nothing in the transaction suggested that an option was sold. Since the land itself was sold, the gain was short-term. The sale to the controlled corporation was not bona fide, but was actually a contribution of equity capital. Since the installment notes were not true indebtednesses, but a form of "preferred stock," payments on the notes were dividends. Fleming, 25 TCM 1284, ¶ 66,251 P-H Memo. TC (1966).

Preferred stock issued in exchange for debt was stock, not debt. A development company purchased from individual sellers undeveloped vacant land. As part of the purchase price, the company gave the sellers a $50,000 5 percent promissory note. In 1947, the note was in default, and the company offered the sellers 5 percent preferred stock with a par value of $150,000 in payment of the note. In 1957 and 1958, the company made payments of $10,000 and $5,000 on the preferred stock and sought to deduct them as interest. The IRS contended that the payments constituted nondeductible dividends. *Held:* For the IRS. The court found nothing in the evidence to disprove that what was denominated and recorded on the company's books and documents as preferred stock, represented to prospective purchasers of the company as such, and treated as preferred stock by its holder on her tax returns was actually preferred stock. The basic element of debt, the right to enforce payment on a fixed date, was extinguished with the issuance of the stock. Marin Canalways & Dev. Co., 20 TCM 1705, ¶ 61,333 P-H Memo. TC (1961).

CONTROLLED CORPORATIONS

(*See* Affiliated Corporations; Consolidated Returns; Transfers to Controlled Corporations)

CORPORATE DIVISIONS

(*See* Reorganizations—Spin-Offs and Other Divisive Reorganizations)

CORPORATE ENTITIES

(*See* Associations Taxable as Corporations; Corporations as Taxable Entities)

CORPORATE INCOME

(*See* Taxable Income of Corporations)

CORPORATE LIQUIDATIONS

(*See* Liquidations)

CORPORATE REDEMPTIONS

(*See* Redemptions)

CORPORATE REORGANIZATIONS

(*See* Reorganizations)

CORPORATE SEPARATIONS

(*See* Reorganizations—Spin-Offs and Other Divisive Reorganizations)

CORPORATIONS AS TAXABLE ENTITIES

Corporations used by partnerships to avoid state usury laws held to be taxable entities. Taxpayers were partners in two real estate partnerships that could not obtain financing at prevailing interest rates because of a state usury law. Since the law did not apply to corporate borrowers, taxpayers set up corporations to hold part of the property and to borrow funds. The IRS disallowed taxpayers' distributive shares of partnership losses on the ground that the losses belonged to the corporations. *Held:* For the IRS, in part. Taxpayers could not disregard the corporations as taxable entities, since they received economic benefits from the corporate form. The court did allow the partnerships to deduct expenses not attributable to property transferred to the corporations. Ogiony, 617 F2d 14, 80-1 USTC ¶ 9265, 45 AFTR2d 80-884 (2d Cir.), cert. denied, 449 US 900 (1980).

Because of activities beyond mere title holding, corporation, not partnership, held to be true owner of real property. For the purpose of obtaining a bank loan, taxpayer and his partners formed a corporation and transferred title to certain real estate to it. After the loan was obtained, the corporation executed various documents as owner of the mortgaged property concerning financing and related considerations. The IRS asserted that the corporation was the true owner of the property and redetermined the partnership's and the partners' income accordingly. *Held:* For the IRS. The courts do not ignore a corporation where its activities go beyond the mere holding of title. Strong, 66 TC 12 (1976), aff'd, 553 F2d 94 (2d Cir. 1977).

Corporation formed to hold and sell land was too active to be ignored. Taxpayer and his partner owned land that they wanted to sell. As a condition of sale, a potential buyer requested that the land be rezoned. Because taxpayer's partner was reluctant to seek rezoning openly, they formed a corporation to seek rezoning and sell the land. Title to the land was transferred to the corporation, and the corporation sold the land. A bank account was opened for the corporation. Before the sale was consummated, income from the land was collected by the corporation, and the corporation borrowed money to finance an acquisition of land. The proceeds from the sale of land were used by the corporation to pay off the amount borrowed and the balance distributed. The corporation held the mortgage on the land sold. Taxpayer reported income from the sale of land as capital gain. The IRS asserted that the corporation realized income from the sale and from the interim operation of the land, and that the distribution of sales proceeds to taxpayer was a dividend. *Held:* For the IRS. The corporation went well beyond the level of activity necessary to hold and transfer title. Taylor, 445 F2d 455, 71-2 USTC ¶ 9521, 28 AFTR2d 71-5102 (1st Cir. 1971).

Retention of assets by dissolving corporation continues its tax life. Under a liquidation plan, taxpayer corporation assigned all its assets (including an undetermined amount due on a condemnation award, but excluding $2,400 to pay liabilities) to a bank. When the balance of the award was received in December 1956, it was endorsed over to the bank. Taxpayer contested the validity of a 1956 assessment based on this award, since the corporation's legal existence had ended prior to the receipt of the balance of the award. *Held:* For the IRS. The court held that the existence of a dissolving corporation continues for tax purposes during the period of its retention of assets. As of January 1, 1957, taxpayer still maintained a bank balance in excess of $1,000. Wood Harmon, 311 F2d 918, 63-1 USTC ¶ 9182 (2d Cir. 1963).

Corporation recognized as entity separate from its stockholders. A bankrupt died testate owning an interest in 20,000 acres of Texas land. The executor formed *X* Corporation to administer the estate. The preferred stock, which was made redeemable from the corporate income, was given to the creditors, while the common stock was eventually given to the legatees. The IRS sought to have the corporation disregarded. *Held:* For taxpayer. The Tax Court held that *X* should be recognized as a taxable entity separate from its stockholders. Its activities exceeded the mere holding of bare legal title. X actively carried on business, issued annual reports, incurred expenses, and paid taxes. Hagist Ranch, Inc., 295 F2d 351, 61-2 USTC ¶ 9704, 8 AFTR2d 5617 (7th Cir. 1961).

Corporate entity engaged in business activity subsequent to incorporation could not be disregarded by stockholder. Taxpayer claimed that a corporation that he organized to conduct timber milling operations was never really a corporate entity for tax purposes because it failed to comply with all state requirements. Accordingly, taxpayer argued that "advances" to the "corporation" were in reality to his own business venture, so that subsequent losses were recognizable to him individually. *Held:* For the IRS. The court disagreed with taxpayer, maintaining that if a corporation engages in business activity subsequent to its incorporation, its entity will not be disregarded for tax purposes. O'Neill, 271 F2d 44, 59-2 USTC ¶ 9717, 4 AFTR2d 5686 (9th Cir. 1959).

Corporation formed to obtain financing for real estate development ignored, thus permitting partnership to deduct interest and expenses associated with operating the property. Taxpayer was a member of a partnership engaged in real estate development. To develop an apartment building, the partnership sought financing from a bank. The bank made the loan commitment to the partnership and, to avoid usury laws applicable to individuals, required that the loan documents be executed by a corporation that held legal title to the mortgaged property. The partnership formed a corporation solely for the purpose of obtaining the bank loans. Although there was no commitment to do so, after the loan was obtained, the property was reconveyed to the partnership. A similar conveyance and reconveyance occurred when the partnership later needed additional financing. The partnership constructed and operated the apartment building. The corporation engaged in no activity except with respect to the conveyances required to obtain financing. The IRS, alleging that the corporation owned the property, challenged the partnership's deduction of interest on the loans and expenses associated with operating the apartment building. *Held:* For taxpayer. The evidence indicated that the partnership, and not the corporation, legally and beneficially owned the apartment building, and thus had "actual command" over the income and benefits of such property. Schlosberg, 81-1 USTC ¶ 9272, 47 AFTR2d 81-1208 (ED Va. 1981).

Corporation and stockholder not separate entities. The IRS made assessments against a corporation for taxes owed by taxpayer, who was the sole stockholder and president. *Held:* For the IRS. Taxpayer failed to observe corporate formalities and used the corporation for his own purposes. The corporation was taxpayer's alter ego, and to treat the two as independent entities would be to ignore reality. Pacific Dev., Inc., 79-1 USTC ¶ 9138, 43 AFTR2d 79-421 (DDC 1979).

Separate entity of subsidiary could not be ignored. A parent corporation transferred certain real estate to a subsidiary in exchange for all of the subsidiary's capital stock. The subsidiary then proceeded to sell the land and report capital gains on the sale. The IRS endeavored to ignore the separate status of the subsidiary and to tax the gain to the parent. *Held:* For taxpayer. The record indicated that the subsidiary functioned as a separate corporation in the management, control, and sale of the land, apart from the activities of the parent. The separate corporate entity of the subsidiary could not be ignored. Loans & Serv., Inc., 193 F. Supp. 683, 61-1 USTC ¶ 9356 (ND Ohio 1961).

Corporation maintained its taxable corporate entity despite charter cancellation. A corporation's charter was cancelled for nonpayment of franchise tax, but the corporation continued to conduct the business in which it was then engaged. Taxpayer stockholder sought to deduct the losses in his individual return, and the IRS argued that the losses were property deductible by the corporation. *Held:* For the IRS. The court held that the cancellation of its charter did not, under applicable state law, end the existence of the corporation. It was still a taxable entity. Hvidsten, 185 F. Supp. 856, 60-2 USTC ¶ 9656 (DND 1960).

Channeling income to previously dormant subsidiary not successful. Taxpayer was a mechanical contractor who did most of its installation work at its customers' sites. Before April 1960, taxpayer also manufactured and sold some sheet metal. After April 1960, taxpayer took the orders for the latter item in the name of a wholly owned subsidiary. Taxpayer then manufactured the items to the subsidiary's order and sold them through the subsidiary. The subsidiary had been dormant before April 1960; it had incurred losses in a venture joined in by taxpayer and another. Taxpayer had become the subsidiary's sole stockholder as a result of the redemption of the other venturer's shares. The IRS contended that the sales made in the subsidiary's name were in fact made by taxpayer; he therefore denied the subsidiary's existence for tax purposes and allocated its income and expenses to taxpayer. The subsidiary's officers and its principal office were the same as taxpayer's; it had no employees and only a modest bank account. Taxpayer justified the subsidiary's existence on the grounds that it allowed taxpayer to enter into a favorable union contract, thus permitting taxpayer to employ lower-paid workers to manufacture the sheet metal. *Held:* For the IRS. The subsidiary was a mere shell corporation; the fact that it kept its own books and records did not require a different conclusion. Contrary to taxpayer's contention, there was nothing to establish that the subsidiary's existence enabled taxpayer to enter into a better union contract. Griffin & Co., 389 F2d 802, 68-1 USTC ¶ 9172, 21 AFTR2d 460 (Ct. Cl. 1968).

Corporate form ignored because business purpose not shown. Taxpayers wholly owned two corporations each. In two partnerships that were formed, each of the four corporations held a 23 percent interest. The corporations received income from the partnerships that they reported on their individual corporate returns. The IRS contended that the income should be taxable to taxpayers, the individual stockholders. *Held:* For the IRS. Generally, a corporate entity is respected. In this case, however, there was no evidence that the corporations engaged in any substantive activity. They were mere paper corporations that existed for the sole purpose of obtaining the tax benefits available through splitting the income of the partnerships. The only reason for the corporations' existence was to achieve tax savings; therefore, they were ignored, and the income of the partnerships was taxable to the individual stockholders. Noonan, 52 TC 907 (1969).

Corporation not disregarded for tax purposes. Taxpayer owned a corporation that operated retail liquor stores. When the corporation began encountering financial difficulties, taxpayer paid numerous expenses of the corporation including rentals, accounts with liquor wholesalers, and repayments of loans. Taxpayer also made payments settling lawsuits that had been instituted against the corporation. Both taxpayer and corporation claimed the corporation's net operating losses on their returns. The IRS disallowed the losses claimed on the taxpayer's individual returns. The taxpayer claimed that the corporation was merely its agent or alter ego and should be disregarded for tax purposes. *Held:* For the IRS. The corporation was properly formed for a bona fide business purpose and actually carried on substantial business after its incorporation. It was not acting as an agent of taxpayer and was a separate taxable entity. Accordingly, the expenditures made by taxpayer on behalf of the corporation were deemed contributions of capital and loans, and the corporation's net operating losses may be claimed only on the corporate returns. Betson, Jr., 48 TCM 113, ¶ 84,264 P-H Memo. TC (1984).

Real estate holding company held a taxable entity. The IRS disallowed a deduction for net operating losses incurred in connection with a partnership's management of real property. A corporation formed to obtain loans to circumvent state usury laws held title to the real property, but had no other assets. *Held:* For the IRS. The corporation was formed for a business purpose and its separate existence would not be disregarded for tax purposes. Taxpayers also failed to show that the corporation was acting as agent for the partnership. Sarkisian, 43 TCM 1074, ¶ 82,199 P-H Memo. TC (1982).

One-man business purporting to be corporation not taxable as an association. GIC claimed to be a corporation, although its sole stockholder operated the business as if he were the true owner after its state charter was cancelled in 1967. After a 1976 reincorporation, the stockholder and his wife were each issued half of the stock. *Held:* For the IRS, in part. GIC was not taxable as a corporation before the reincorporation, but was taxable as such afterward. Proceeds from the sale of corporate real estate that the wife received were taxable as a dividend. Garriss Inv. Corp., 43 TCM 396, ¶ 82,038 P-H Memo. TC (1982).

Losses were sustained by corporation, not individual owner. Taxpayer deducted on his individual tax return losses sustained by his four wholly owned real estate corporations. The IRS denied the deductions. *Held:* For the IRS. The corporations were organized for valid business purposes and were not merely dummies. Linczer, 40 TCM 253, ¶ 80,139 P-H Memo. TC (1980).

Taxpayer could not report income and deductions of his businesses after incorporating them. Taxpayer, REM Corporation, held legal title to various rental properties. It deposited rental receipts from these properties into its own checking account and paid most expenses on the rental properties by checks drawn on the account. In a similar fashion, taxpayer *M* incorporated an experimental aircraft business, Aero, and a TV and appliance business, Appliances. The reasons that *M* formed the corporations were to segregate his businesses, to limit his personal liability, and to facilitate obtaining financing. Taxpayer *M* reported losses from REM's rental properties, business expenses from Aero, and some of the income and deductions of Appliances on Schedule C of his individual income tax returns. After auditing *M*'s federal income tax returns for several years, the IRS determined that the corporations should be respected as separate entities, and as a result, individual taxpayer *M* did not have a right to include the corporations' income and deductions on his individual return. *Held:* For the IRS. Because the evidence indicated that the businesses functioned as corporations with regard to their activities, they were to be treated as separate entities for tax purposes. REM Enter., Inc., 39 TCM 672, ¶ 79,494 P-H Memo. TC (1979).

Recognition of corporation for tax purposes produces capital loss to investors when business fails. Taxpayer, with others, formed *F* Corporation to hold weekly dances. Stock was authorized, but never issued. The charter named the incorporators as directors, but no meetings were ever held. The corporation contracted to rent a nightclub. Later, the group orally extended the lease, and made improvements to the rented property, hoping to expand the business to a full-time nightclub. The group contributed money to this venture and considered forming a new corporation, but never did. Little attention was paid to corporate formalities, but the group often described itself as *F* Corporation. The corporate charter was later annulled for nonpayment of state taxes, and shortly thereafter, the business failed. Taxpayer sought to ignore *F*, and claimed an ordinary loss on his return as a member of a partnership. *Held:* For the IRS. *F* was validly incorporated, engaged in substantial business activity, and described itself as a corporation. It could not be ignored. Taxpayer's loss was limited to his investment in *F*. Schuerholz, 35 TCM 726, ¶ 76,163 P-H Memo. TC (1976).

No Section 482 allocation among 10 related real estate corporations formed to fragment integrated business. Two partners engaged in the real estate business formed a corporation for purpose of insuring limited liability. They later formed 10 additional corporations to fragment the business pertaining to buying and developing land and constructing and selling houses thereon. The IRS determined that the additional corporations were shams and attributed their income to the original corporation under either Section 61 or Section 482. *Held:* For taxpayer, on the issues raised under Sections 61 and 482. The multiple corporations were not shams or mere paper corporations, since each conducted an active business. The fact that they did not have employees or own equipment was immaterial in light of their specialized function in the integrated business organization. Their existences were not limited to a short life terminated upon reporting $25,000 of taxable income, or upon selling all houses in a single subdivision. A Section 482 allocation must be based on a determination that there was an actual shifting of income and deductions. The mere finding that the common owners have the power to shift income is not enough. There was insufficient evidence of an actual shifting of income, as the corporations dealt with each other at arm's length. The IRS therefore acted arbitrarily and unreasonably in applying Section 482. However, the ostensible purpose for the formation of 7 of the 11 corporations was to acquire the benefit of extra surtax exemptions; accordingly, those exemptions were denied under Section 269. Dorba Homes, 26 TCM 693, ¶ 67,150 P-H Memo. TC (1967).

Income of wholly owned foreign subsidiary not attributed to parent. Taxpayer, a manufacturing corporation, formed a wholly owned foreign sales subsidiary to insulate itself from potential liability to foreign customers, to arrange shipment and insurance, and to bear the burden of the risk of loss and credit. The subsidiary took over taxpayer's foreign customers and greatly expanded the business. It did not maintain an inventory of the parent's products, but filled its sales orders by purchasing the needed items from the parent. The parent supplied its subsidiary with facilities, know-how, and employees. The parent was compensated by specific allocations or adjustment of the price paid by the subsidiary for its products. The IRS contended that the subsidiary was not a viable entity for tax purposes, or alternatively, that its income and deductions belonged to the parent as principal. *Held:* For taxpayer. The subsidiary was a viable entity. It served the bona fide purpose of insulating taxpayer from the various risks of foreign operation. Accordingly, allocation by the IRS of 100 percent of its sales to the parent under either Section 61 or 482 was a clear abuse of discretion. The court also determined the arm's-length price on each of the various products sold to the subsidiary, and on that basis redetermined the allocation of income between the two corporations. Johnson Bronze Co., 24 TCM 1452, ¶ 65,281 P-H Memo. TC (1965).

Sole stockholder could not disregard corporate entity as a straw man. Taxpayer sought to deduct from his individual gross income certain expenses pertaining to the real estate and business of a wholly owned corporation engaged in the restaurant business. He contended that the corporation was merely a straw man that held only the naked title to the premises on which it operated the restaurant business and that the beneficial ownership of the real estate was in him individually. *Held:* For the IRS. The court found such contention not supported by, and contrary to, the evidence, since the corporation as a separate taxable entity employed a manager, kept separate books of account, and filed corporate income tax returns on which it claimed deductions for certain business expenses. The court also noted that a payment of over $800 by taxpayer to the restaurant manager represented compensation and was thus deductible only by the corporation, not by taxpayer. It also sustained the IRS' use of an eight-year remaining useful life for certain tenement buildings and a $1,000 salvage value (instead of $1,800, as claimed by the IRS) in computing depreciation on taxpayer's automobile. Strasburger, 21 TCM 1351, ¶ 62,255 P-H Memo. TC (1962).

Landholding corporation disregarded for tax purposes. Taxpayer corporation was organized primarily as a convenience to receive, hold, and transfer title to properties in which several joint venturers were interested. No money was paid for taxpayer's stock, and shares were issued for qualifying purposes. After agreeing on certain purchases, the venturers furnished the funds. For convenience, bank accounts were opened in the name of the corporation, and the money advanced was deposited and used for the purchases agreed upon. When properties were sold, the proceeds were deposited, expenses paid, and net profits distributed to the joint venturers according to their interests. The IRS determined that the income from the sale of the properties should be taxed to the joint venturers, and not to the corporation. *Held:* For the IRS. Because the corporation had no beneficial interests in the property and engaged in no substantial business activities, the income from the sale of properties held was taxable to the joint venturers and not the corporation. K-C Land Co., 19 TCM 183, ¶ 60,035 P-H Memo. TC (1960).

DEATH TAXES, REDEMPTION OF STOCK TO PAY

(*See* Redemptions—Redemptions to Pay Death Taxes)

DEBENTURES

(*See* Bonds and Debentures)

DEBTS

(*See* Bad Debts)

DEBT VS. EQUITY

(*See also* Bad Debts; Bonds and Debentures—Equity Investments Distinguished; Contributions to Capital)

In General	255
Bona Fide Indebtedness	257
Intent of Parties	266
Thin Capitalization	268

In General

Notes conceded by IRS to be debt when held by transferor did not become equity when acquired for de minimus consideration where the purchasers expected corporate debtors to develop profitable operations and no significant event occurred to change the character of the notes from debt to equity. In 1953, Hambro Automobile Corp. acquired all of taxpayer's stock. Hambro's operation of taxpayer was unsuccessful and, in 1955, taxpayer's directors voted to liquidate and dissolve. Before these plans were effected, a group of four investors acquired taxpayer in 1957. Taxpayer's unpaid notes to Hambro (totaling $129,000) were purchased by the investors for $2,000, and new notes were issued by taxpayer in proportionate amounts to each of the investors. After acquisition, taxpayer's financial picture improved significantly, and it began to make interest payments and retire some of the notes. The IRS challenged the deduction of that portion of these payments designated by taxpayer as interest on the ground that such notes were not valid indebtedness for tax purposes. Even though the Tax Court found, based on the IRS' stipulation, that the notes were debt while held by Hambro, it held in favor of the IRS. *Held:* Reversed. The IRS did not show any significant event from which it could be held that debt in the hands of Hambro changed to equity when purchased by the investors. Taxpayer was not defunct or inactive when acquired and obviously retained the potential for profitable operation. Imperial Car Distribs. Inc., 427 F2d 1334, 70-2 USTC ¶ 9477, 26 AFTR2d 70-5004 (3d Cir. 1970).

Advances determined to be loans. Taxpayer stockholder argued that advances to his controlled corporation were loans, not capital contributions. Therefore, when the loans were not repaid he claimed a business bad debt deduction. *Held:* For taxpayer. After considering such factors as intent, "thinness" of capital structure, and risk, the advances were determined to be loans. However, advances made after the corporation became financially unsound were capital contributions. Newman, 558 F. Supp. 1035, 83-2 USTC ¶ 9549, 52 AFTR2d 83-5570 (DVI 1983).

Advances to wholly owned corporation were held loans. The IRS contended that taxpayer's advances to his wholly owned corporation, *X*, were not loans but contributions to capital. *Held:* For taxpayer. On the evidence, the advances were loans. Moreover, taxpayer did not subordinate his rights to those of two

Debt vs. Equity: *In General*

other wholly owned corporations *Y* and *Z*, that also made loans to *X*. When *X* liquidated, all available funds were distributed to taxpayer. The repayment schedule did not cause taxpayer to receive constructive dividends. In a related issue, the court held *Y* and *Z* did not distribute constructive dividends to taxpayer and were entitled to claim bad debt losses for advances to *X*. Turner Tire Co., 344 F. Supp. 634, 72-2 USTC ¶ 9570 (MD La. 1972).

Payment on retirement of corporate indebtedness not a dividend. The IRS held that payments which taxpayer individuals received on the retirement of notes from a related corporation were dividend income. *Held:* For taxpayer. The notes were valid corporate indebtedness from the time they were first issued. The loans were not made to get the corporation started, nor were the advances made for the purchase of capital assets or expansion, but were used exclusively for operating funds during slack years long after the corporation commenced operation. Hutton, 499 F2d 527, 74-2 USTC ¶ 9545 (6th Cir. 1974).

Loans by stockholders were debt, not capital. Taxpayer corporation was organized to buy conditional sales contracts from an auto dealer owned by related interests. It was originally intended that taxpayer would resell the paper to a bank. However, the bank's credit policies were so stringent that sales were being lost. It was therefore decided that taxpayer would retain the contracts. To supply funds, members of the stockholding family advanced money, and taxpayer issued its promissory notes. The IRS contended that the notes represented capital and that repayments were taxable as dividends. *Held:* For taxpayer. The court found that the loans should be treated as such for tax purposes. The contracts were security for the notes. The stockholders merely advanced money to the corporation on the same terms as would the bank. The repayments were not dividends. Jaeger Auto Fin. Co., 61-1 USTC ¶ 9465 (ED Wis. 1961).

Interest accrued before issue date deductible. Taxpayer, a publicly held corporation, issued 50-year 6 percent income debentures in exchange for most of its outstanding stock of one class. Interest on the debentures was accrued and paid for a period of 15 months prior to their issuance. The IRS contended that the instruments represented equity and payments thereon were not deductible as interest. *Held:* For taxpayer. The debt-equity question must be resolved based on the facts and circumstances. The terms of the debenture, in this case, showed a closer relationship to debt than to equity. The debentures contained a definite maturity date, they could be redeemed, and holders could not vote for management. The fact that the interest was denominated as attributable to a period prior to the issuance of the obligations was immaterial. The interest was therefore properly deductible on the debentures. Monon R.R., 55 TC 345 (1970).

Debt had some characteristics of equity. Taxpayer was a mutual insurance company dealing in all types of commercial insurance. To conform with the laws of the some 30 states in which it operated, taxpayer maintained a guaranty fund derived from the sale of certificates. These were issued in denominations of $1,000 and paid interest at the rate of 7 percent. About half of the certificates were owned by persons who were neither policyholders nor directors. Certificate holders had the right to elect 50 percent of taxpayer's directors. During the years involved, all directors were, however, policy owners. Certificates had no date of maturity. Arguing that the certificates were not a debt, the IRS disallowed the interest deduction. *Held:* For taxpayer. The interest was deductible. Since no tax-avoidance scheme was involved, there was no reason to disregard the form of the transaction. The right to elect directors was a device to protect the rights of the creditors. Union Mut. Ins. Co. of Providence, 46 TC 842 (1966).

Stockholder's advances to adequately capitalized new corporation were valid debts. Retaining the accounts receivable and a portion of the inventory, taxpayer incorporated his prosperous chemical supply business. Thereafter, he advanced additional inventory and funds to the corporation. On its books, the corporation recorded the advances as an open account payable. The IRS contended that the repayment of this account was a dividend to taxpayer. *Held:* For taxpayer. A corporation may incur a valid indebtedness to a major stockholder. Since this corporation had adequate capitalization, the open account represented a bona fide indebtedness. Petersen, 24 TCM 752, ¶ 65,145 P-H Memo. TC (1965).

Stockholder's advances to corporation with borrowed funds resulted in bona fide debt. Taxpayer, a franchised dealer in Ford automobiles, had borrowed money from a bank to buy out a controlling stockholder and to pay off an indebtedness to the stockholder's related corporation. This indebtedness had to be rearranged prior to the close of that year to comply with the minimum net worth requirements that the Ford Motor Company imposed on its dealers. To accomplish this, the bank suggested that taxpayer's remaining stockholder, Boyte, be interposed between the taxpayer and the bank, and that part of the loan run through Boyte as a conduit. Boyte thus became the bank's creditor and, in turn, loaned the money to taxpayer. Taxpayer thereafter showed its loan from Boyte as subordinated. The IRS denied taxpayer a deduction for interest paid on the loan, contending Boyte's advances constituted a contribution to capital. *Held:* For taxpayer. A bona fide indebtedness continued to exist on the part of taxpayer through Boyte to the bank. Payments to Boyte represented deductible interest on that indebtedness. Oak Motors, Inc., 23 TCM 520, ¶ 64,086 P-H Memo. TC (1964).

Bona Fide Indebtedness

Advance by stockholder taxpayer was loan where evidence indicated that corporation was financially sound, and where stockholder's debt was evidenced by demand notes. Taxpayers made cash advances to their wholly owned corporation. The payments were reflected on the corporate books as loans, and the periodic payments by the corporation as principal and interest payments to taxpayers.

The corporation deducted the interest payments and taxpayers declared the interest as income and treated the principal payments as a return on capital. The Tax Court agreed with the IRS' determination that the advances were capital contributions, and disallowed the interest deductions. Accordingly, taxpayers were held to have received taxable dividends. *Held:* Reversed. Since evidence indicated that the corporation was not thinly capitalized but financially sound and that the stockholder's debt was evidenced by demand notes, the advances were loans and not equity. Bauer, 748 F2d 1365, 84-2 USTC ¶ 9996, 55 AFTR2d 85-433 (9th Cir. 1984).

Stockholder's advance was loan in form and substance. Taxpayer, a builder, transferred his business assets to a corporation in 1954 in return for stock of $10,000 and an unsecured interest-bearing note of $20,600. The major asset was land that required substantial development before it could be used for constructing homes. The company had no working capital and no source of obtaining it except from taxpayer or from mortgaging the land. The corporation claimed interest deductions on the note for each of the fiscal years 1959 and 1960. In 1960, the corporation paid off the loan in full. The IRS disallowed the deductions, treating the payments as dividends to taxpayer. The Tax Court upheld the IRS' determination, concluding that the entire properties transferred to the corporation were in the nature of a contribution to the corporate equity capital. *Held:* Reversed. Whether advances to a corporation are a loan or an equity investment is a mixed question of law and fact. Thus, the appellate court did not have to determine that the Tax Court decision was clearly erroneous in order to reverse it. Here, the transaction in form and in substance was a loan, and not a tax-avoidance scheme. The debt-equity ratio was 2 to 1, and taxpayer was not thinly capitalized. A taxpayer may commit only so much of his assets to the equity of a corporation as he desires, and his actions will be respected, absent a mere subterfuge or sham. Nothing in the law prohibits a sole stockholder from lending funds to his corporation. J.S. Biritz

DEBT VS. EQUITY: *Bona Fide Indebtedness*

Constr. Co., 387 F2d 451, 68-1 USTC ¶ 9118, 20 AFTR2d 5891 (8th Cir. 1967).

Notes issued to charitable foundations not equity. Taxpayer, *X* Company, purchased *Y* Company's stock from two charitable foundations. The foundations received interest-bearing notes, which they then donated to various charities. The IRS disallowed *X*'s interest deductions on some notes. *Held:* For taxpayer. This case does not involve an attempt to give the foundations or the charities disguised equity interests. The notes were bona fide. *X*'s high debt-equity ratio and its failure to issue dividends did not alone justify equity treatment. The Lansall Co., 81-1 USTC ¶ 9418, 48 AFTR2d 81-5175 (SDNY 1981).

Interest deduction allowed controlled subsidiary on demand loans from parent corporation used to finance acquisition of a business. The parent corporation held a 50 percent stock interest in taxpayer (but voted 100 percent of taxpayer's stock). The parent guaranteed the bank loans made to taxpayer to finance the acquisition of a business. The parent lent funds to taxpayer to make payments on these bank loans. Taxpayer claimed a deduction for the interest paid on these loans. The IRS disallowed the deductions, contending that the loans were in fact contributions to capital. *Held:* For taxpayer. The evidence supported the treatment of the parent's advances as loans: (1) the advances were reflected in promissory notes; (2) the notes bore interest; (3) the notes were not subordinated and were recorded as liabilities on both the parent's and taxpayer's books; and (4) the advances were not made pro rata by taxpayer's stockholders, nor did they increase any stockholder's interest in taxpayer. Coast Sash & Door Co., 75-2 USTC ¶ 9680, 36 AFTR2d 75-5741 (WD Wash. 1975).

Advances to oil drilling company by its controlling stockholder were bona fide loans. Taxpayer was the managing officer and 20 percent owner of a family corporation as well as the majority stockholder of two other corporations in the oil business. The family corporation, a drilling company, borrowed from banks to finance its early operations. Taxpayer would guarantee payment of the loans as well as make his own advances evidenced by demand, interest-bearing promissory notes. The drilling company drilled a series of wells for one customer, which defaulted due to financial difficulties and taxpayer purchased the account so that the company could discharge its obligations to the banks to which the account had previously been assigned. Taxpayer shortly before had sold his stock to the remaining stockholders and released the drilling company from its liability to him. Taxpayer claimed a deduction for a business bad debt. *Held:* For taxpayer. The history of the loans and the prior dealings between taxpayer and the corporation did not disclose anything other than a bona fide debt at the time the advances were made. The undisputed evidence indicated that the company was unable to pay the debt and that the transfer of the stock to the remaining stockholders would not have transpired without the relinquishment of the debt. Full deductibility of the debt turned on its proximate connection with activities that must be found to constitute a trade or business. The trade or business of taxpayer was the "oil business" in its various facets. He conducted it as an individual, promoter, partner, venturer, and stockholder in controlled corporations. It was an inescapable conclusion that in a substantial degree the common purpose of taxpayer and the corporation was the attempted profitable operation of the common interests with which they both dealt. Schafer, 68-1 USTC ¶ 9306 (WD Okla. 1968).

After examining transaction as opposed to intention or form used by the parties, advances were held to be loans, not equity. Through a bank, four investors decided to advance certain sums of money to taxpayer. Each individual advanced $85,000 to taxpayer in exchange for a six-year, 6 percent, $100,000 bond. The funds were used to liquidate some of taxpayer's indebtedness and to pay its operating costs. To secure the funds, taxpayer executed a deed of trust to the bank in the amount of all the properties it owned. The accompanying contract for the advances contained a provision placing the individuals on

Debt vs. Equity: Bona Fide Indebtedness

the board of directors, and they also acquired a small amount of taxpayer's stock. The IRS disallowed the deduction of the accumulated interest on the advances because it deemed the advances to be equity and not loans. *Held:* For taxpayer. The jury was told to examine the transaction and not what was intended or the form that the parties used. Thereafter, it concluded the advances were loans. Browning Turkey Farms, Inc., 68-1 USTC ¶ 9239, 21 AFTR2d 877 (ED Ky. 1968).

Loans from stockholders were bona fide indebtedness. At various times, beginning with the time of its incorporation, taxpayer borrowed funds from its stockholders, issuing its 8 percent promissory notes bearing a stated maturity date not conditioned on corporate earnings. Approximately 60 percent of taxpayer's original capitalization was represented by promissory notes payable to its stockholders. The notes were not convertible and carried no rights relating to voting power or to participation in the profits of taxpayer. Taxpayer made all payments of principal and interest as they came due. The IRS claimed that the the interest payments were not deductible, but was overruled by the district court. On appeal, the IRS claimed that the district court erred in imposing on the IRS the burden of proving that the arrangement and notes were "phony" or "fraudulent" by clear and convincing evidence. The Tenth Circuit agreed, holding the burden of proving the specific amount of a claimed deduction was on the taxpayer. In remanding the case, the court stated the issue was whether the substance of the arrangement as revealed by the entire transaction created a real indebtedness or was an investment in the equity of the enterprise. The IRS could not, however, dictate the proportion of debt to equity. *Held:* For taxpayer. The notes were negotiable and unrelated to stockholdings. The amounts of the loans were dictated by the needs of the business, not the investment needs of the stockholders. Repayments were not conditioned on earnings. Under these circumstances, the notes represented true and genuine indebtedness. Intermountain Furniture & Mfg. Co., 67-2 USTC ¶ 9735 (D. Utah 1967).

Signatures of stockholders on loan as cosignors did not prevent valid loan from being created. Taxpayer family members desired to create an "integrated" poultry business. After establishing taxpayer corporations, they arranged to borrow $130,000 from a bank in order to purchase a mill. As security for the loan, taxpayer corporations signed the note as principals, and each individual taxpayer co-signed the note as a principal. The entire proceeds of the loan were used by one taxpayer corporation for the acquisition and improvement of the mill. Taxpayer corporation accordingly made payments on the loan and deducted the interest payments. The IRS determined the $130,000 to be a contribution to capital and not a loan, and disallowed the interest deductions. *Held:* For taxpayers. A valid loan existed where (1) there was intent to create a bona fide indebtedness; (2) the entire proceeds were used by the corporation; (3) it was the custom to require principals of closely held corporations to co-sign, (4) payments were made and carried on its books as long-term debt; (5) there was no subordination; and (6) the bank did not participate in corporate management. Fors Farm, Inc., 66-1 USTC ¶ 9206 (WD Wash. 1966).

Loans to corporation set up to give creditor greater participation in venture were bona fide. Taxpayer agreed to advance funds to finance two real estate promoters in the development of land they had contracted to buy. Taxpayer paid $1,000 for one-third of the stock of the newly incorporated Furlands, Inc. He had the option to buy the remaining two-thirds from the promoters, the option being security for the loans taxpayer agreed to make. On incorporation, taxpayer loaned Furlands the funds, which the corporation used to buy some of the land the promoters previously had contracted to purchase. Furlands then sold the land to a development corporation controlled by the promoters. All the parties contemplated that taxpayer's loans would be repaid out of the proceeds on the sales to the development corporation. However, the lot sales by the latter fell behind the scheduled timetable and taxpayer finally exercised his option and then sold all the stock of Furlands to outsiders. Taxpayers

DEBT VS. EQUITY: *Bona Fide Indebtedness*

reported the interest he received on the loans as income but did not report payments received on principal. The IRS contended that the loans were contributions to capital and that, therefore, the payments received thereon were taxable dividends to taxpayer. The IRS also contended that Furlands could not deduct the interest payments. *Held:* For taxpayer. The facts supported the conclusion that the advances were bona fide loans. There was no agreement for stockholders to make loans in proportion to stock ownership. Hirs, 243 F. Supp. 910, 65-2 USTC ¶ 9590 (SD Ala. 1965).

Stockholders' advances to loan company were not capital contributions; interest deduction allowed. It was the practice of the taxpayer (a small loan company) to accept loans from its stockholders, their relatives, and others. These were evidenced by interest-bearing demand notes. The IRS disallowed the interest deductions on loans from stockholders and their relatives on the ground that these advances were capital investments. *Held:* For taxpayer. The court found that (1) the thin capitalization test has little application to loan companies; (2) although the notes had no maturity dates, they were fixed obligations; (3) the subordination of some of the advances to a bank loan did not render them capital. Security Fin. & Loan Co., 210 F. Supp. 603, 62-2 USTC ¶ 9759 (D. Kan. 1962).

Parent corporation's cash advances and open accounts receivable for sales of materials and know-how to its subsidiary were loans and not capital contributions. Taxpayer, a U.S. corporation, formed a Canadian subsidiary to do business in Canada. When forming the subsidiary, taxpayer committed itself to transfer special equipment and make cash advances to its subsidiary. This equipment and cash were necessary for the subsidiary to commence operations. The cash advances were made according to notes that, although unsecured, stated a market rate of interest. The transfer of goods and services was treated as non-interest-bearing open account liabilities to taxpayer. Taxpayer argued that both the notes and the open account liabilities should be treated as liabilities of the subsidiary to taxpayer. The IRS argued, on the basis of the subsidiary's failure to repay or satisfy such liabilities, that the transactions were capital contributions, not loans. *Held:* For taxpayer. The evidence supported the treatment of the liabilities as a debt for tax purposes: (1) Both corporations treated the advances and open accounts receivable on their books as liabilities; (2) the subsidiary made interest payments regularly; and (3) the subsidiary's inability to repay its liabilities to taxpayer was due to events unforseen at the time such liabilities arose. Wagner Elec. Corp., 76-1 USTC ¶ 9209, 37 AFTR2d 76-694 (Ct. Cl. 1976).

Corporation organized to acquire going business held not thinly capitalized in light of liquid assets of acquired business. Taxpayer was organized to buy all the stock of Jack Daniel Corporation. Its initial capital consisted of $2 million of stock and $3.5 million of debt due to its parent corporation. The parent had borrowed from a bank the money it loaned to taxpayer. Taxpayer acquired the Jack Daniel stock for $18 million, paying $5.4 million down and the balance in negotiable promissory notes. The notes were paid prior to the debt to taxpayer's parent. Shortly after acquiring Jack Daniel, taxpayer liquidated the corporation and received liquid assets of $2.8 million in cash, $500,000 in accounts receivable, and $11.5 million in inventory. Taxpayer used these assets and the profits from the operation of the liquor business to pay off the loan from its parent. The IRS contended that the loan was a capital contribution and denied taxpayer a deduction for that portion of the payments representing "interest." *Held:* For taxpayer. The following factors support the conclusion that the loan was legitimate: (1) the parties clearly intended to create a debt; (2) at the time of the loan, there was a reasonable expectation that the loan would be repaid and it was repaid; (3) when considered with respect to taxpayer's capital structure, especially as it existed after the liquidation, the amount of the loan was not excessive; (4) there was a business purpose for arranging the Jack Daniel corporate acquisition in the form it took; (5) the bank loan was

DEBT VS. EQUITY: *Bona Fide Indebtedness*

made to taxpayer's parent in the expectation that taxpayer could, and would, pay the debt to its parent. Factors that indicated that the loan was not what it purported to be were not persuasive in light of the listed factors. Jack Daniel Distillery, Inc., 379 F2d 569, 67-2 USTC ¶ 9499, 19 AFTR2d 1027 (Ct. Cl. 1967).

Reasonable assurance of repayment of advances made advances bona fide loans and not contributions to capital. A corporation was initially capitalized with $25,000 by its five equal stockholders. A cash requirement and profit projection showed a need for an additional $75,000, which was advanced by the stockholders at 6 percent interest and due in five years. Production problems resulted in the need for $55,000 more. This was advanced under the same terms as the original advance. The IRS contended that the repayment of the advances resulted in dividend income to taxpayer. *Held:* For taxpayer. The initial prospects of the business were bright, lending support to the conclusion that there was clearly a reasonable expectation of repayment. Moreover, the initial debt-equity ratio was low and the notes had a fixed maturity date and a fixed date of interest. Based on the facts, the advances were bona fide indebtedness and the repayment was tax free. Mennuto, 56 TC 910 (1971).

Investment in stock of corporation with no earnings and profits deemed equity, not debt. Taxpayer invested in cumulative preferred stock of a corporation that had no earnings and profits. On receiving distributions, taxpayer excluded the amounts received from income as return of capital. *Held:* For taxpayer. The investment was in form and substance an acquisition of stock, and the payments were distributions with respect to the stock, not a loan with payments taxable as interest income. There was no maturity for the stock, since there was no guarantee that it would be redeemed, and the payment of dividends was not assured. Although there were tax advantages to this arrangement, there was no reason to call the transaction a loan. Zilkha & Sons, Inc., 52 TC 607 (1969).

Fourth mortgage note was equity, not indebtedness. A husband and wife acquired an apartment house by paying cash, giving the seller a purchase money note and third mortgage, and taking the property subject to first and second mortgages. They operated the property as individuals for one year and then transferred it to a newly formed corporation in exchange for all of the issued and outstanding stock at a stated value of $5,000 and a note of the corporation in the amount of $193,000, secured by a fourth mortgage payable in monthly installments and bearing interest on the unpaid balance. The note and capital stock were equal to their equity in the property and approximately equal to the cash that they had paid on purchase of the property. The next year, the stockholders advanced money so that the corporation could discharge the second mortgage. During the two years following the transfer, the corporation made 12 out of the 15 required monthly payments on the fourth mortgage and reduced the principal thereby to $180,000. At this stage, the parties altered the terms of the mortgage to provide that no further installments would be paid, but that the entire balance would be discharged at the end of approximately five years with monthly interest payments to continue. Taxpayer made the required interest payments and took deductions therefor but, although the time for payment of the principal had expired, the indebtedness remained and the stockholders took no action to enforce payment. The IRS determined that both the interest payments and the payments on account of principal made before the modification were distributions with respect to stock. *Held:* For the IRS. This case raised once again the question of whether a stockholder's investment in his corporation, although in form a debt, is a debt in substance. The court's primary concern was with the situation at the time the "debt" was incurred, although the parties' subsequent treatment was relevant in determining substance. The IRS' argument was based on the theory that on transfer of the property, the corporation was thinly capitalized with a debt-equity ratio of 123 to 1 and that the parties did not treat the note as debt. Although the note contained all the formal indicia of a

DEBT VS. EQUITY: *Bona Fide Indebtedness*

debt, it was held by the stockholders in the same proportion as their stock and was approximately 40 times the stated value of their stock. Furthermore, the property was already subject to three prior liens and was so old as to require the investment of still more capital for required modernization and improvement. The property was so burdened with mortgages that no reasonable person would have expected the note to be discharged in accordance with its terms. In addition, the stockholders made no efforts to enforce the obligation and modified the amortization requirement. Ambassador Apartments, Inc., 50 TC 236 (1968).

Advances from parent to newly organized subsidiary to cover inventory requirements represented bona fide indebtedness. Taxpayer corporation was organized by its parent corporation to carry on in Missouri the business formerly conducted by its parent based in Tennessee. The parent paid $50,000 for all taxpayer's issued and outstanding stock and also advanced $400,000 in the form of cash and inventory. The allocation was made after careful consideration of all anticipated factors as envisioned by the competent management of the parent. The parent continued to make advances and taxpayer made some repayments. All advances were carried on open account and no notes or other formal evidence of indebtedness was given, nor were the advances secured in any fasion. No maturity date or rate of interest was specified although such was later charged at a flat rate per four-week period. The parent and taxpayer at all times expected that the advances would be repaid. The IRS disallowed the interest deductions on the grounds that the advances to taxpayer were contributions to capital. *Held:* For taxpayer. In the final analysis the issue was one of fact. The parent corporation was engaged in the grocery business and taxpayer took over a nucleus of that business. The great bulk of the advances were for current assets, which at all times exceeded the total of the advances. The inventory was highly liquid, reflected a full market value, and turned over quickly. Under such circumstances there was not doubt that the indebtedness could have been paid off in full at any time. That it was not so liquidated was the result of a rapid expansion of business which required a constantly increasing inventory. Malone & Hyde, Inc. of Mo., 49 TC 575 (1968), acq. 1968-2 CB 2.

Monies advanced to corporation by its principal stockholder to finance development of real estate subdivision held to be loans rather than capital contributions. Taxpayer held acreage and entered into an agreement with three other parties whereby they would all form a corporation to develop the property. Taxpayer paid cash for his 52 percent of the outstanding stock as did the other parties for their respective interests. Thereafter, he transferred the acreage to the corporation in three separate parcels. The corporation paid for the first parcel, obtaining the funds from a bank on a promissory note endorsed by taxpayer. It gave taxpayer promissory notes for the other parcels. In addition, taxpayer advanced money to finance the development, taking back interest-bearing promissory notes. During the tax years, the market for real estate subsided and the corporation, in order to satisfy its indebtedness to taxpayer, transferred the remaining unsold lots to him for an amount in excess of the indebtedness. The IRS, relying on Burr Oaks Corp., 365 F2d 24 (7th Cir. 1966), determined that the advances to the corporation were capital contributions rather than loans and that the distributions to taxpayer were dividends rather than repayments. *Held:* For taxpayer. In form, the advances to the corporation were loans bearing definite due dates and interest at a specified rate. Although the IRS argued that substance should prevail over form, the contention was not applicable to the facts here. It did not appear that taxpayer intended to finance the development with capital contributions rather than loans. The argument that the only source of repayment was earnings and profits was likewise unsound, since there was evidence that the corporation could have borrowed on its own security to obtain the funds for repayment. The case was distinguishable from *Burr Oaks* in that there was no attempt to transfer the land to the corporation at an inflated value and because of the presence of substantial ownership of the stock by unrelated parties. Taxpayer's transfers of the land to the corporation were reported as sales at a price that reflected the actual value. Although the corporation was thinly capitalized, it had assets in excess of its indebtedness to taxpayer, whose notes were not subordinated to the claims of general creditors. Lots, Inc., 49 TC 541 (1967).

Loan by corporation to taxpayer was bona fide although simultaneous with capital contribution. The Taxpayer was loaned money by a corporation in which he was a 51 percent stockholder. At the same time, he transferred business assets to the corporation for common stock. The IRS argued that the loan was not a separate transaction, but part of the consideration for the transfer of assets, thus increasing taxpayer's gain on the transfer. *Held:* For taxpayer. The loan was a bona fide transaction relating to earlier transactions involving taxpayer and other corporations. Spain, 37 TCM 1158, ¶ 78,270 P-H Memo. TC (1978).

Startup "loan" by stockholder was a capital contribution, but others were true loans. Taxpayer contributed cash to a new closely held corporation for stock and then "loaned" more cash to the corporation that was used as the down payment to acquire vital manufacturing assets. He also made "loans" after the business was under way. The IRS argued that these "loans" were capital contributions that did not give rise to a bad debt deduction when the corporation later became insolvent. *Held:* For taxpayer, in part. The initial "loan," since it was used to acquire vital assets and occurred at the start of the venture, was actually a capital contribution. The later loans were true loans, since the business had operating experience that showed they could be repaid; the majority were in fact repaid. The court also held that the bad debts were business debts producing ordinary losses. Gilboy, 37 TCM 510, ¶ 78,114 P-H Memo. TC (1978).

Some loans to corporation were bona fide debt. Taxpayer corporation made interest payments to its stockholders on their loans to the corporation. The IRS disallowed the interest deductions, claiming that the loans actually constituted contributions to capital. *Held:* For the IRS, in major part. The payments were evidenced by non-interest-bearing unsecured notes and were listed on the corporation's books as noncurrent liabilities. Thus, certain payments were not loans but contributions to capital; the interest payments on them were not deductible. Two advances that were repaid shortly thereafter constituted loans, and interest payments on those advances were deductible. Waste Disposal, Inc., 34 TCM 1118, ¶ 75,261 P-H Memo. TC (1975).

Bona fide indebtedness entitled corporations to interest expense deductions. Taxpayer corporations made interest payments to their two sole stockholders and took deductions for the payments. The IRS disallowed the deductions. *Held:* For taxpayer. The sole stockholders had transferred valuable assets to the corporations for which they received notes. The notes were determined to represent bona fide corporate indebtedness as they were not subordinated to the claims of other creditors, the corporations were not undercapitalized, and there was a fixed maturity date, a fixed interest rate, and regular interest payments. Thus, the interest payments were deductible expenses. Fischer Bros. Aviation, 30 TCM 1351, ¶ 71,315 P-H Memo. TC (1971).

Corporation denied deductions for purported interest paid on stockholders' advances. Taxpayer, a real estate corporation, was organized by its three stockholders who initially advanced it $60,000 as loans. At the end of taxpayer's first fiscal year, its accountant established a capital account by transferring $4,000 from the stockholders' loan account to the newly created capital account. The capital account was later increased to $20,000 by cash contributions and partly by debiting the officers' loan accounts. The IRS disallowed interest deductions on the stockholders' loans, contending they constituted contributions to capital. *Held:* For the IRS. The court noted the following reasons for its conclusion: The corporation failed to issue any formal evidence of indebtedness; the purported debts were held by the three stockholders in the same proportions as their stock; The stockholders arbitrarily designated as loans the major portion of the initial capital; the corporation was thinly incorporated, since the ratio of debt to equity, excluding a mortgage indebtedness of $65,000, was 26.5 to 1; taxpayer was unable to obtain needed funds from outside sources on comparable terms; no payments on the principal of the alleged loans were made until their authenticity was questioned; and taxpayer had not shown that the advances were made with the expectation of repayment regardless of the success of the venture. S.P. Realty Co., 27 TCM 764, ¶ 68,156 P-H Memo. TC (1968).

Advances were bona fide loans as repayment occurred within a reasonable time and the advances were at all times treated as debts. Taxpayer, a shipping magnate, advanced $240,000 to his controlled corporation, T, which was repaid by the end of the year. Other sums were advanced to T by taxpayer or another controlled corporation. None of the advances were evidenced by notes or security, but they were treated as genuine debts. To satisfy the debts, T transferred funds from its account to taxpayer's account, both of which were maintained by the same firm. The IRS determined that almost one third of the transfer was a distribution of accumulated earnings subject to taxation as a dividend. *Held:* For taxpayer. Where repayment occurred within a reasonable time, the lack of formality between taxpayer and his controlled corporation was not significant. Since the advances were at all times treated as debts, the repayments were not distributions with respect to T's stock. Ravano, 26 TCM 793, ¶ 67,170 P-H Memo. TC (1967).

Unsecured advances by an investment partnership to an unrelated real estate developing company were bona fide loans. Taxpayer corporation, formed to develop a tract of land and build houses, worked out an arrangement with an unrelated partnership to borrow $300,000 for construction purposes. The IRS denied the corporation interest deductions on the loans, contending that the $300,000 advance represented an equity interest in the corporation. The advances were evidenced by promissory notes, which bore no fixed maturity date, and were unsecured but guaranteed by five persons who had a combined net worth of $2 million. The source of payments was to be proceeds from the sale of each house constructed. Neither the partnership nor any of its members had rights of any nature to participate in the corporate management. *Held:* For taxpayer. The advances were bona fide loans and were obtained in an arm's length transaction from an outside source that was otherwise unconnected with the partnership. No stockholder of the corporation was a partner in the lending partnership and no partner was a stockholder of the corporation. Winnefield Heights, Inc., ¶ 66,185 P-H Memo. TC (1966).

Stockholder's advances were contributions to capital. Taxpayers, husband and wife, conducted a general insurance agency business. In 1960, they formed a corporation with an initial capital contribution of $500 to process special insurance risks that the agency could not handle. The corporation used the physical facilities and personnel of the agency business. During 1960 and 1961, the corporation suffered losses, and taxpayers made numerous advances to it to help meet its operating expenses. No corporate notes, certificates, or other evidences of indebtedness were given taxpayers for these advances; no interest was charged; no definite time was set for repayment; and no repayments were in fact made. At no time did the corporation make any effort to borrow money from sources other than taxpayer. On dissolution of the corporation, taxpayer claimed a loss from worthlessness of the advances as a business bad debt. The IRS disallowed the deductions, arguing that the advances were contributions to capital. *Held:* For the IRS. The advances constituted contributions to capital rather than bona fide loans. Consequently, taxpayer was entitled only to a capital loss arising from the worthlessness of stock. Frank, 24 TCM 979, ¶ 65,187 P-H Memo. TC (1965).

Stockholders' loans and notes given in exchange for preferred stock were valid debts. In 1954, 4.5 percent demand notes were issued by taxpayer corporation in redemption of its

DEBT VS. EQUITY: *Bona Fide Indebtedness*

7 percent cumulative preferred stock. Contending that the exchange did not create an indebtedness, the IRS denied a deduction for interest paid on the notes. *Held:* For taxpayer. The notes represented valid debts based on the following factors: (1) The notes contained an unconditional promise to pay a fixed sum; (2) there was a fixed rate of interest that was payable regardless of the corporation's financial position; (3) the notes were not subordinated to other unsecured claims; (4) the corporation treated the notes as debts on its books; and (5) the notes contained an ascertainable maturity date. The court also held that advances from stockholders and related parties were a valid indebtedness. The factors that convinced the court of this were: (1) The advances were recorded as indebtedness; (2) a reasonable rate of interest was paid; (3) all advances were repaid and all interest was paid; (4) the ratio of taxpayer's equity to stockholder debt was reasonable; (5) the advances were not subordinated to other creditors; (6) the ratio of each stockholder's advances was disproportionate to stock ownership; (7) the advances though having no fixed maturity date were payable on demand and were actually repaid; and (8) the advances were required for ordinary operating expenses. P.F. Scheidelman & Sons, 24 TCM 168, ¶ 65,031 P-H Memo. TC (1965).

Advances by incorporators created bona fide indebtedness. The incorporators of taxpayer transferred to the corporation a tract containing sand and gravel deposits valued in excess of $255,000 in return for its capital stock. They also advanced to the corporation $128,000 for operating funds. Promissory notes due in one year, with interest at 6 percent were executed for the advances. The notes were all paid in full, with interest, and were at all times treated as indebtedness on the corporate books. *Held:* For taxpayer. The court noted that this was not a case of thin capitalization, as the ratio of indebtedness to equity capital was about 1 to 2. It concluded that the corporate notes evidenced valid indebtedness giving rise to a bona fide debtor-creditor relationship. The interest paid on the notes was therefore deductible, and the repayments thereof did not constitute dividend distributions with respect to the stock. Mason-Dixon Sand & Gravel Co., 20 TCM 1351, ¶ 61,259 P-H Memo. TC (1961).

Corporate promissory note represented bona fide debtor-creditor relationship. In 1953 a corporation issued a promissory note for $47,800 to taxpayer in consideration for the transfer to it of assets that taxpayer and his son had purchased from a predecessor partnership. The corporation had capital stock of $2,000 owned in equal amounts by taxpayer's son and a friend. In 1956 the corporation paid taxpayer $10,000 on the note, which the IRS treated as a corporate dividend. *Held:* For taxpayer. From a consideration of all the facts the court concluded that the note represented an actual debt of the corporation to taxpayer, that the note was in substance what it appeared to be on its face, and that the payment by the corporation of $10,000 to taxpayer in 1956 constituted a partial retirement of an actual note indebtedness and was not income to taxpayer. McGah, 20 TCM 783, ¶ 61,157 P-H Memo. TC (1961).

A $500,000 note to principal stockholder was true indebtedness; thus interest deduction was allowed. In the incorporation of a partnership, one of the partners, *B*, took back a $500,000 note on the transfer of the partnership assets to the corporation. This was done because the other two partners were unable to contribute more than $30,000 each to taxpayer's capital, and *B* wanted to maintain proportionate contributions according to profit interests. The note bore interest, unconditionally obligated taxpayer to pay the face value at maturity, provided for mandatory payment whenever taxpayer's net earnings exceeded $50,000, and so on. In order to secure refinancing for expansion, the note was subordinated to certain bank loans. The IRS determined that the issuance of the note was for tax avoidance and was not a true debt; accordingly, the IRS disallowed the interest deduction. *Held:* For taxpayer. Because the evidence indicated no tax avoidance, and subordination and nonenforcement of payment were necessary to secure refinancing for expansion, there was a true indebtedness, and so the interest was deductible. Bulkley Dun-

Debt vs. Equity: *Intent of Parties*

ton & Co., 20 TCM 660, ¶ 61,133 P-H Memo. TC (1961).

Notes issued by corporation to its stockholders for cash found to be bona fide. Taxpayer corporation issued notes to its principal stockholders in consideration for a $200,000 loan. The notes were negotiable, bore interest at 6 percent, and had a fixed maturity date. *Held:* For taxpayer. Even though no security was given by the corporation, or insisted on by the stockholders, the court deemed that fact immaterial, since the notes represented in substance as well as in form a bona fide indebtedness. Interest paid on the notes was allowed as a deduction. There was no question of thin capitalization because material amounts of capital were invested in stock. M&M Corp., 18 TCM 1051, ¶ 59,217 P-H Memo. TC (1959).

Intent of Parties

Advances made to client companies were bona fide debt. Taxpayer, a financial consultant, often made loans to new companies in return for long-term consulting contracts. The IRS argued these loans were capital contributions, not bona fide loans. *Held:* For taxpayer. The intent was to treat the advances as loans, there was a reasonable expectation of repayment, taxpayer's equity interests were minor, and the advances were not made in proportion to stockholdings. Adelson, 737 F2d 1569, 84-2 USTC ¶ 9599, 54 AFTR2d 84-5428 (Fed. Cir. 1984).

Notes issued by insurance companies under Arizona law payable only after surplus exceeds a certain amount constitute indebtedness. Taxpayer purchased from three stockholders all of the capital stock and outstanding "surplus notes" of a life insurance company organized under the laws of Arizona. These notes were later discharged with accrued interest. The surplus notes were issued under a statute that provides that the insurer may borrow to defray the expenses of organization of provide funds for surplus or for the business on a written agreement with the lender that such money may only be repaid out of surplus in an amount stipulated in the agreement with a stipulated maximum interest rate. The statute also provides that the money borrowed and accrued and accrued interest shall not form a part of legal liabilities except as to the excess over the stipulated surplus. The corporations were adequately capitalized and the debt-equity ratios were 1 to 2. The surplus notes conferred no voting or management rights, were superior to stockholders' claims on liquidation, and were freely transferable. The district court held that the surplus notes were genuine debts, not capital investments, and this result was not altered by the stipulation that they were repayable only after surplus exceeded a specified amount. The fact that they were not shown on the corporate balance sheet as a liability was not controlling, particularly since this treatment was in accord with Arizona law. *Held:* Affirmed. Because of the ambiguity of the notes, the district court properly considered the intent of the parties and there was no error in concluding that a genuine debt was intended. No significant importance was placed on the identity of ownership between the stockholders and the note holders. Consideration of all the factors point to debt rather than stock. Harlan, 409 F2d 904, 69-1 USTC ¶ 9321, 23 AFTR2d 69-1102 (5th Cir. 1969).

Advances held to constitute debt, not equity. The United States filed a tax claim in taxpayer's bankruptcy proceeding. The claim was based on the disallowance of worthless debt losses. The IRS contended that the "debt" constituted equity. *Held:* For taxpayer. The debt-equity issue turns on the intent of the parties as shown by objective manifestations. The court found that the taxpayer presented evidence that overcame the initial presumption of correctness in favor of tax claims and that the burden of proof was then placed on the IRS. In re Koscot Interplanetary, Inc., 77-2 USTC ¶ 9497 (MD Fla. 1977).

A jury determined advances to be valid indebtedness. Taxpayer corporation received advances from its stockholders. The IRS determined the advances to be contributions to capital, and therefore the interest payments were not deductible. *Held:* For taxpayer. Because the jury determined that the advances were made to others who intended to take the risk and the parties themselves were not the risk takers, the advances were loans. The guidelines used to determine intent included (1) the names given to certificates evidencing indebtedness; (2) bookkeeping entries; (3) whether the corporation was undercapitalized, and whether repayment depended on the success of the business; (4) subordination to other creditors; (5) whether a prudent lender would make advances under the same terms and circumstances; (6) the source of corporate repayment and interest; and (7) the expectation of repayment. Hearn & Curran, Inc., 71-2 USTC ¶ 9720, 28 AFTR2d 71-5618 (ND Fla. 1971).

Repayment of advances by taxpayer to his wholly owned corporation represented return of loans and not distributions of dividends. Taxpayer was president and sole stockholder of a corporation in which his initial capital investment was $100,000. Prior to the years in issue, he had made periodic advances that had totaled $228,000 but had been reduced to $105,000. The corporation repaid that entire amount during a three-year period. The IRS determined that the advances from taxpayer constituted contributions to capital so that, on repayment, taxpayer received distributions essentially equivalent to dividends. *Held:* For taxpayer. Both taxpayer and the corporation intended that the sums advanced from him would constitute loans rather than contributions to capital. Furthermore, they intended that the loans thus created be repaid by use of the corporate bank account. Rosenberg, 68-1 USTC ¶ 9229 (CD Cal. 1968).

Incorporation of partnership followed by corporation's note-financed purchase of partnership's assets was respected; payment to stockholder, who acquired rights in a note on partnership's liquidation, was not a dividend. For limited liability purposes, taxpayer and his partners incorporated their partnership and its business. To allow key employees to acquire stock without a large cash investment, the corporation purchased the partnership's assets. A portion of the purchase price was represented by a note in which taxpayer acquired an interest on liquidation of the partnership. Because both the key employees and the partners received stock in the corporation, the corporation's debt (arising from the purchase of the assets) was not held pro rata by the corporation's stockholders. The evidence indicated that all of the stockholders considered the corporation's note to be a corporate debt obligation and that although the corporation's capitalization was thin, third parties would have made loans to the corporation. The IRS treated the payments to taxpayer made by the corporation under the note as dividends. *Held:* For taxpayer. The corporation's note represented a debt, not an equity investment. Haley, 60-1 USTC ¶ 9169, 5 AFTR2d 365 (D. Ore. 1959).

Record of loans to controlling stockholder indicated genuine debt. The wholly owned subsidiary of taxpayer's wholly owned corporation made numerous cash advances to taxpayer that were reflected as loans in the corporate records and evidenced by interest-bearing promissory notes. The subsidiary also purchased land and constructed buildings on it, including taxpayer's eventual residence. The IRS determined that the loans and the costs of the purchase of and construction on the property were constructive dividends. *Held:* For taxpayer. There was a genuine intent on both the subsidiary's and the taxpayer's parts to create a genuine debt that would be repaid. Corporate personnel, independently of taxpayer, kept track of amounts advanced. The arrangement was not used as a method of siphoning off the subsidiary's earnings, since the property was purchased and constructed for almost daily use connected with significant corporate activities. Turner, 49 TCM 1107, ¶ 85,159 P-H Memo. TC (1985).

Stockholder advances were debt. Taxpayer, a close corporation, characterized advances from its stockholders as loans rather than equity, and deducted payments to the stockholders as interest. *Held:* For taxpayer. The intent was to create debt; the stockholders could reasonably expect to be repaid; and economic reality suggested a debtor-creditor relationship. R-W Specialties, Inc., ¶ 81,697 P-H Memo. TC (1981).

Advances deemed loans entitling corporation to bad debt deduction. Taxpayer owned 30 percent of the stock of Lumber Co. and *H* owned 70 percent. Taxpayer and *H* each owned 24.5 percent of the stock of Fireless. *B*, an unrelated third party, owned the remaining shares. By agreement between *H*, *B*, and others, Lumber Co. agreed to advance working capital to Fireless, as needed, for the manufacture of shingles. The IRS determined that Lumber Co. was not entitled to a bad debt deduction for the advances (which were unrecoverable), since such advances were in the nature of capital contributions. *Held:* For taxpayer, in part. Although the companies were engaged in a common profit-making plan, the evidence indicates that the advances were intended to be loans. However, advances made after 1971 were contributions to capital. Johnson, 36 TCM 1780, ¶ 77,436 P-H Memo. TC (1977).

Thin Capitalization

Debentures were debt, not stock where corporation was not thinly capitalized. During 1965 and 1966, taxpayer claimed certain interest expenses paid on 5 percent debentures held by its stockholders. Taxpayer made payments constituting only 96 percent and 84 percent of the total amount due to the debenture holders in the respective years and fell behind in the payments because of its finances. The debentures were subordinated to the claims of general creditors in the event of taxpayer's liquidation or dissolution. The debentures were not held in proportion to the stockholders' equity holdings. The IRS determined that the debentures were not loans. *Held:* For taxpayer. Because the corporation was not thinly capitalized, 90 percent of its issued debentures were secured, and there was a valid business reason for issuing the debentures, they were considered debt and not stock. Barton Theatre Co., 701 F2d 126, 83-1 USTC ¶ 9226 (10th Cir. 1983).

Ratio of stockholder notes to capital of 9 to 1 was not too thin; interest was deductible. In organizing taxpayer corporation, which was to develop a residential tract, the promoters raised the capital from a group of individuals. In each case, the investor was issued notes in the ratio of 9 to 1 for the stock. After several years of operation, the ratio of debt to net worth changed to about 5 to 4. The notes bore all of the usual indicia of debt instruments. *Held:* The notes were recognized as such for tax purposes, and the interest was deductible. Sherry Park, Inc., 64-2 USTC ¶ 9681 (SD Fla. 1964).

Interest allowed on stockholders' loans to "thin" corporation. Taxpayer corporation was in the retail lumber and hardware business. Although the initial capitalization indicated a "thin" corporate capital structure, it was done so that each of its two stockholders could own approximately 50 percent of its equity and for bona fide and legitimate business purposes. After the incorporation, the principal stockholder, in good faith and for valid and sufficient business reasons, made certain advances to taxpayer. They were evidenced by promissory notes and provided for the payment of interest. The IRS determined the notes to be capital contributions and disallowed the deductions claimed for interest payments. *Held:* For taxpayer. The loans were clearly in the form of debt instruments, and the intent clearly indicated that the advances were loans and not capital contributions. Thus the interest payments on the advances were deductible. Iron County Lumber Co., 63-2 USTC ¶ 9613 (D. Utah 1963).

Corporation not thin although debt to stock ratio was 30,000 to 1; interest payments were not dividends. Taxpayer corporation was organized to operate oil and gas leases. Its authorized capital was $400,000 but only $3 was paid in. At the same time, one of the incorporators and a nonstockholder lent the corporation a total of $150,000 on notes to purchase leases. Interest was paid on the notes during the seven-year period in which they were being paid off, about one third in cash and two thirds in stock. Within five years from organization, the debt to stock ratio was reduced to 1 to 1. The IRS argued that the notes represented equity capital and that the interest payments were dividends. *Held:* For taxpayer. The court held that the corporation was not thin and that the interest payments were not dividends in disguise. There was a bona fide business purpose in issuing notes, since, as creditors, the lenders would have been in a better position to recover their funds in the event of failure. The notes bore interest at a fixed reasonable rate (5 percent) and had a reasonably close fixed maturity date (three years). The debt was not subordinated and interest was regularly paid when due. One of the noteholders had no voting stock at any time, and the stock was not held in ratio to loans. A business purpose other than tax reduction was served and the parties intended to create a debtor-creditor relationship. The fact that payment of interest and principal were expected to be made, and actually were made, out of profits, did not convert the loans into stock investments. Payment of indebtedness to creditors usually depends on profits. Royalty Serv. Corp., 178 F. Supp. 216, 59-2 USTC ¶ 9791 (D. Mont. 1959).

Advances to subsidiary held to be loans. Taxpayer parent contended that loans and not capital contributions were made to its foreign subsidiary in connection with advances and intercompany accounts receivable for materials shipped and personnel lent by taxpayer to subsidiary. *Held:* For taxpayer. Since the subsidiary was organized with an adequate capital structure and the advances were evidenced by unsecured interest-bearing notes, bad debt treatment was appropriate. Wagner Elec. Corp., 76-1 USTC ¶ 9209, 37 AFTR2d 76-694 (Ct. Cl. 1976).

Thin incorporation theory did not apply due to reasonable debt-equity ratio, regularly paid interest, and substantial repayment of principal. Four brothers owned the stock of taxpayer corporation. Two of the brothers were citizens of Holland and two were U.S. citizens. At the inception of the corporation, the brothers paid in $50,000 and received $25,000 in capital stock and $25,000 in demand notes. A restrictive agreement, similar to a restrictive stock agreement, governed the transfer of the notes. Alleging that the notes were equity capital, the IRS asserted that a withholding tax on dividends applied to the interest and amortization paid to the Dutch stockholders. The IRS also stated that fees received by the Dutch brothers were dividends. In addition, it denied an interest deduction on the notes. *Held:* For taxpayer. The debt-equity ratio of taxpayer was reasonable. The notes were never subordinated. Interest was paid regularly, and a substantial repayment of principal was also made. Furthermore, the restriction on transfer of the notes had terminated. The weight of evidence indicated that the notes were bona fide indebtedness. Since the fees paid to the Dutch stockholders were in payment of substantial services, the fees were not dividends. Doornbosch Bros., 46 TC 199 (1966).

No thin incorporation where ownership of stock was different from ownership of debt. A real estate operator owned 60 percent of an office building in Kansas City, and his adult son and daughter owned the remaining 40 percent. Although interested in selling the property, the family had not received an acceptable offer. However, the daughter's husband, also a realtor, thought that the property was a good investment. In cooperation with the son, he offered to buy the father's interest. The two formed a corporation and contributed $50,000 to its capital. The corporation purchased the property, giving a $50,000 down payment and an installment obligation. Viewing the transfer as a contribution to capital under Section 351, and the installment obligation as equity, the IRS disallowed the interest expense, lowered the basis of the building, and treated the payments of interest and principal as dividends. *Held:* For taxpayer. The court treated the installment obligations as debts and not equity. A decisive factor in this determination was the disparity in ratio of ownership between the capital stock and the installment notes. While the children had a 40 percent interest in the notes and a 100 percent interest in the stock, the father had a 60 percent interest in the notes and no interest in the stock. The sales price was fair and the terms of the mortgage were not unreasonable. Curry, 43 TC 667 (1965), non acq. 1968-2 CB 3.

Debt vs. Equity: *Thin Capitalization*

Payment of incorporator's loan was not a dividend. Taxpayer, one of three partners, transferred his partnership interest, represented by a capital account of $26,000, to a corporation. The corporation in return issued stock with a stated value of $2,500 and set up a loan payable of $23,500. From inception of the corporation, the loan account, although not represented by any notes, appeared on the balance sheets and financial statements of the corporation as "Notes Payable—Officers." The loan account had never been subordinated to any other indebtedness of the corporation. In 1958, the corporation paid taxpayer $10,500, which was charged against the loan account. *Held*: For taxpayer. The payment was not a dividend. The record clearly established that at the time of the corporation's formation it was the desire and intent of the partners to lend it a part of their undistributed profits; the subsequent actions of the parties were clearly consistent with such intent. The court also rejected the IRS' claim that the corporation was "thinly capitalized." Nominally the ratio of capital to debt was 1 to 4.5. Considering the unlisted contributed assets, it was probably closer to 1 to 2. Salvadore, 22 TCM 1718, ¶ 63,327 P-H Memo. TC (1963).

Real estate venture with debt-to-capital ratio of 2.6 to 1 not undercapitalized; genuine debt affirmed. Taxpayer acquired a one-half interest in a medical-dental building by buying half of the stock of the corporation that owned the building and then liquidating the corporation. Later, the taxpayer transferred his equity in the building, which had a fair market value of $225,000 (building value of $625,000 less mortgage of $400,000), to a new corporation in return for a $50,000 promissory note and all of the corporation in return for a $50,000 promissory note and all of the corporation's capital stock. The new corporation repaid the note with interest within three years. The IRS contended that payments on the notes were dividends and not payments on a debt. *Held*: For taxpayer. The note was a bona fide debt: The corporation was not undercapitalized, having a debt-to-capital ratio of 2.6 to 1 even when including the obligation on the mortgage in the debt figure. Furthermore, the existence of a business purpose was also evidence that a genuine debt was intended; the taxpayer owed money on loans made to finance the original stock acquisition and wanted to be in a position whereby he could extract money from the new corporation to pay that debt, even though the latter's earnings and profits did not justify payment of a dividend. Murphy, 21 TCM 1161, ¶ 62,219 P-H Memo. TC (1962).

Alleged loan of $100,000 to thinly captialized corporation was a bona fide indebtedness. Taxpayer corporation was capitalized with a paid in capital of $1,000. It acquired an option to purchase building lots and when it applied for a bank loan of $1.35 million, the bank insisted that the stockholders lend the corporation $100,000, which they did. Taxpayer excuted its promissory notes evidencing the loans, interest was charged, and the amount of the notes was paid to the lenders. The IRS claimed that the loans were in fact contribution to capital. *Held*: For taxpayer. The mere fact that the stockholders might have contributed the amount of $100,000 to capital did not mean that they actually did so, and the court's recognition of the thin capitalization of the corporation did not of itself require a contrary conclusion. From the evidence, the court was satisfied that the alleged loan was in fact a loan, and that the interest paid thereon was a properly allowable deduction. Daro Corp., 20 TCM 1588, ¶ 61,309 P-H Memo. TC (1961).

Advance rulings may be issued on loans versus equity in thin capitalization cases. Ordinarily, the IRS will not issue advance rulings on the question of whether advances to thin corporations constitute loans or equity investments. This is a slight change from the position the IRS took in Rev. Proc. 64-31, where the IRS classified this area as one where rulings would not be issued at all. Rev. Proc. 67-29, 1967-2 CB 642.

DEDUCTIONS

(*See particular items, such as* Business Expenses; Charitable Contributions)

DEPRECIATION AND AMORTIZATION

In General 271
Recapture Of 272

In General

Sale of subsidiary did not make taxable previously eliminated intercorporate profit. Taxpayer corporation constructed an apartment house for a wholly owned subsidiary. It filed a consolidated return with the subsidiary for that year, and eliminated the intercompany profit on this transaction. In computing depreciation for the property, the subsidiary reduced its cost basis by this eliminated intercompany profit. The Tax Court held that on a subsequent sale of the subsidiary stock to a third party, the parent was not required to include in income the previously eliminated profit. *Held*: Affirmed per curiam. United Contractors, Inc., 344 F2d 123, 65-1 USTC ¶ 9347 (4th Cir. 1965).

Pipeline right of way held depreciable over useful life of pipe. Taxpayer was a common carrier of petroleum products by pipeline. Taxpayer's investment in its right of way consisted of easements over tracts of land in 10 states. In addition to the costs related to the pipe and its construction, taxpayer made various payments for easements and roadage to landowners, as well as payments for abstract and title guarantees, and so forth. Taxpayer deducted annual depreciation on the entire investment. The IRS disallowed the depreciation deduction for the right-of-way costs. *Held*: For taxpayer. The cost of acquiring an easement was depreciable over the useful life that was established for the pipeline. It was an intangible asset with a life expectancy equal to that of the pipe. Great Lakes Pipe-Line Co., 293 F. Supp. 1073, 68-2 USTC ¶ 9578, 22 AFTR2d 5594 (WD Mo. 1972).

Franchise purchase payments held amortizable over owner's life expectancy. Taxpayer corporation, a distributor of automobiles, induced a competitor to surrender his Pontiac franchise by agreeing to pay $15,000 to the dealership over a three-year period and to pay a percentage of its profits directly to the previous owner, M, for five years. Thereafter, taxpayer was awarded a franchise. The franchise agreement included a right to terminate in the event of death or withdrawal of the taxpayer's controlling stockholder and manager, J. During 1962, taxpayer paid the agreed sums and deducted the corresponding amounts on its tax return. The IRS disallowed the deduction of the payments to M as the ordinary and necessary business expense of M's salary. In the alternative, taxpayer maintained that if the amounts were not deductible, they were amortizable over the life of the franchise. *Held*: For the IRS, in part. Where payments were directly related to the acquisition of the franchise, they were capital investments, and not deductible as "ordinary and necessary business expenses." Taxpayer was entitled to amortize the payments over the life expectancy of its owner J. This followed from the terms of the franchise agreement, which provided for the termination of the agreement on J's death, and from evidence that the termination agreement was strictly enforced. Hampton Pontiac, Inc., 294 F. Supp. 1073, 69-1 USTC ¶ 9200, 23 AFTR2d 69-624 (DSC 1969).

Leasehold improvements amortized over useful life. Taxpayer rented its business premises from a corporation whose principal stockholders were the same, although not in the same proportions, as the stockholders of taxpayer. It also leased a portion of the premises from a partnership composed of its principal stockholders. *Held:* For taxpayer. The court found that despite the nominal five year lease, taxpayer could renew the leases indefinitely. Therefore, leasehold improvements should be written-off over their useful life. The court also found that executive automobiles were not held by taxpayer as a dealer but were subject to depreciation and capital gain treatment on sale. Finally, the court applied Hansen, 360 US 446 (1959) to tax dealers reserves of installment paper. Bruce-Flournoy Motor Corp., 62-2 USTC ¶ 9695 (ED Va. 1962).

DISCHARGE OF DEBT: *Recapture Of*

Payment for alleged leasehold services merely a distribution of corporate profits. A corporation set up on its books an account in the amount of $468,000 due to stockholders as "deferred leasehold expenses" and amortized a proportionate part of this account as part of its leasehold expense deduction. The IRS denied the amortization deduction. *Held:* For the IRS. The liability was created merely to distribute corporate funds to those who controlled its affairs, in proportions to their corporate interests, and was never intended as bona fide payment for leasehold services. Wilson, 20 TCM 676, ¶ 61,135 P-H Memo. TC (1961).

Corporation must use straight-line depreciation in determining earnings and profits even when its partnership income uses accelerated method. Two corporations formed a partnership that took accelerated depreciation on property in its business. In computing their earnings and profits, each corporation could only take into account straight-line depreciation on the partnership property. Section 312(k), in imposing this limitation, was not restricted to property owned directly by a corporation. Rev. Rul. 79-20, 1979-1 CB 137.

Recapture Of

Nonapplicability of depreciation recapture to Section 351 transaction leads to recapture on later liquidation. Taxpayer corporation (the successor in interest) acquired the stock of the target corporation in 1965. The target business had for years been operated as a sole proprietorship and a corporation had been recently formed by its sole stockholder in anticipation of the acquisition. Two months later, the target, then a wholly owned subsidiary of taxpayer, was liquidated. The IRS assessed a deficiency based on taxpayer's failure to report depreciation recapture. *Held:* For the IRS. The court found that the transfer of assets to the target qualified as a tax-free transaction under Section 351, and therefore Section 1245 recapture was not applicable. As a result, depreciation recapture was triggered on the later liquidation, and taxpayer was required to report it in the year of the liquidation. Culligan Water Conditioning, Inc., 567 F2d 867, 78-1 USTC ¶ 9228, 41 AFTR2d 78-715 (9th Cir. 1978).

Depreciation recapture applicable where basis determined under Section 334(b)(2). Taxpayer subsidiary was liquidated into its parent and the parent determined its basis in taxpayer's assets pursuant to Section 334(b)(2). The IRS held that taxpayer subsidiary was subject to the recapture provisions of Section 1245 to the extent that the parent's basis for the assets acquired in liquidation exceeded taxpayer subsidiary's adjusted basis for such assets. *Held*: For the IRS. This transaction did not fall into one of the exceptions to depreciation recapture provided in Section 1245(b). Lucar-Naylor Egg Ranches, 75-1 USTC ¶ 9329 (CD Cal. 1975).

No Section 1245 gain recognized on transfer of Puerto Rican property to domestic corporation. A domestic corporation owned Puerto Rican property that was subject to the provisions of Section 1245. The property was transferred to a corporation that met the requirements of Section 931 in a Section 351 transaction. No gain was recognized on the transaction. However, gain would be recognized on a subsequent disposition of the property. Rev. Rul. 71-569, 1971-2 CB 314.

DISCHARGE OF DEBT

(*See* Cancellation of Indebtedness)

DISCOUNT BONDS

(*See* Bonds and Debentures—Bond Discount and Premium)

DISCs

(*See* Domestic International Sales Corporations)

DIVIDENDS AND DISTRIBUTIONS: *In General*

DISGUISED DIVIDENDS

(*See* Dividends and Distributions)

DISTRIBUTIONS

(*See* Dividends and Distributions)

DISTRIBUTIONS IN KIND

(*See* Dividends and Distributions—Dividends in Kind)

DISTRIBUTIONS OF STOCK AND RIGHTS THERETO

(*See* Dividends and Distributions—Stock Dividends and Rights; Reorganizations)

DIVIDEND EQUIVALENCE

(*See* Compensation for Personal Services—Dividend Equivalence; Dividends and Distributions; Redemptions—Dividend Equivalence; Reorganizations)

DIVIDENDS AND DISTRIBUTIONS

(*See also* Compensation for Personal Services—Dividend Equivalence; Earnings and Profits; Redemptions—Dividend Equivalence; Reorganizations)

In General	273
Bargain Purchases and Sales	277
Bonus Payments	282
Cancellation of Indebtedness	282
Capital Gains Distinguished	288
Disallowed Corporate Expenses	285
Disguised and Constructive—Generally	287
Distribution of Stock of Controlled Corporation	291
Diverted Funds	292
Dividends in Kind	293
Earnings and Profits	293
Excessive Salaries	295
Guarantor Fees	296
Intercorporate Transfers	296
Life Insurance Premiums	298
Loans Distinguished	299
Payments Benefiting Stockholders	304
Payments to Stockholders' Beneficiaries	309
Satisfaction of Stockholder Obligations	312
Stock Dividends and Rights	316
Stockholder Use of Corporate Property	320
Taxable Party	322
Withdrawals by Stockholders Treated as Dividends	323

In General

Distribution by corporation to partnership owner, treated by owner as debt repayment and return of capital, was not dividend. Taxpayer was the beneficial owner of a 2.5 percent interest in a partnership, *H*, which had acquired all the outstanding stock of several corporations, including *C*, together with promissory notes for each. *H* then contributed the notes and stock to *C*. Thereafter, *C* organized *E* Corporation, to which it contributed certain real estate. The real estate was sold for $12 million, the proceeds of which were indirectly used to pay off *H*'s indebtedness to *B*. Specifically, the $15.5 million indebtedness of *H* to *B* was repaid in advance of the sale from the proceeds of a loan of $18 million by *B* to *C*. Thereafter, the new loan was repaid, in part, through funds obtained from *C* and its subsidiaries, including *E*. Taxpayer maintained that the distribution from *C* to *H* was a debt repayment to the extent of $7.5 million and a return on capital to the extent of $10 million. The Tax Court agreed with the IRS that *H* had received a taxable dividend from *C*. *Held:* Reversed. A corporation without accrued or present earnings and profits borrowed against its own appreciated assets and made a distribution in anticipation of future profits; the distribution did not result in taxable income to the stockholder. Falkoff, 604 F2d 1045, 79-2 USTC ¶ 9569, 44 AFTR2d 79-5627 (7th Cir. 1979).

Corporation's repayment of advance not taxable as dividend due to valid debtor-creditor relationship between bank and taxpayer. Taxpayer, who owned 15 percent of the stock of a bank, advanced $140,000 to the bank to help cover losses resulting from an embezzlement. The IRS contended that repayment of the $140,000 constituted a dividend to taxpayer. The district court held for taxpayer. *Held:* Affirmed. Repayment was not a taxable event. The bank and taxpayer intended to create a debtor-creditor relationship. Neither taxpayer nor the other stockholders who made similar advances received any of the usual benefits of an equity investor. Estate of Mixon, 469 F2d 394, 72-2 USTC ¶ 9537, 30 AFTR2d 72-5094 (5th Cir. 1972).

Payment of call premiums on public utility's preferred stock was not a dividend. In connection with a new issue of 4.75 percent preferred stock, taxpayer, a public utility, called for redemption of prior issues of 6 percent and 7 percent preferred stock. Taxpayer treated the payment of call premiums as a dividend and claimed a tax credit under Section 26(h) of the 1939 Code. *Held:* For the IRS. Payment of call premiums on preferred utilities stock is not a voluntary payment. Accordingly, such payments were not dividends. Kentucky Utils. Co., 394 F2d 631, 68-1 USTC ¶ 9361, 21 AFTR2d 1262 (6th Cir. 1968).

Temporary transfer of corporate assets to stockholders to secure sale of stock was not a dividend. Taxpayers owned stock in a bank which they agreed to sell. To accommodate the financing of the buyer, the sale took these steps: (1) The bank "sold" its building to taxpayers for an amount that was actually paid to the bank by the buyer of the stock; (2) taxpayers leased the building to the bank and then deeded the building to the buyer; (3) the buyer borrowed to pay taxpayers for the stock, using the building as collateral for the loan; (4) the buyer later deeded the building back to the bank for cash. The IRS assessed to taxpayers as a dividend the value of the building gratuitously transferred to them under step 1. *Held:* For taxpayer. The court held that there was no taxable dividend. The net effect of the transaction was a mere sale of the taxpayer's stock in the bank corporation. The transfer giving rise to the alleged dividend was simply a security device. Cuckler, 341 F2d 54, 65-1 USTC ¶ 9205, 15 AFTR2d 286 (10th Cir. 1965)

Gallonage payments paid to transferor of a franchise were dividends. Taxpayers held several Dairy Queen franchises, which they transferred to a wholly owned corporation in consideration for payment of a stated amount per gallon of mix used. They reported the income received as a long-term capital gain. The IRS asserted that the gallonage payments constituted dividends, not payments for a franchise. *Held:* For the IRS. Whether the payments to taxpayers constituted payment or distributions of corporate dividends was a question of fact; the burden lay with taxpayers to prove the former. After showing that the corporation would sustain losses on deduction of the payments, whereas taxpayers previously showed profits from operations, and after considering the perpetual term of the payment, the court concluded that the payments constituted a means to distribute corporate earnings in such a manner as to produce more beneficial tax consequences. Accordingly, they were treated as dividends. Dunn, 259 F. Supp. 828, 66-2 USTC ¶ 9627 (WD Okla. 1966).

Corporate dividend of subsidiary stock ignored where immediately followed by sale. Taxpayer parent, *P*, owned all the stock of *S-1*, which in turn owned all the stock of *S-2*. On November 24, 1964, *S-1* distributed all of its stock in *S-2* to *P*, and on November 25, 1964, *P* sold the stock of both *S-1* and *S-2* to an unrelated third party. *P* reported dividend income of $501,870 with respect to the receipt of *S-2* stock and claimed a dividends received deduction on 85 percent of this amount. The stock sales generated a $2,310,218 long-term capital gain. The IRS determined that there was in effect no dividend, eliminated all dividend aspects of the transaction, and in-

Dividends and Distributions: *In General*

creased the reported gain from the stock sales by $501,870, the amount of the dividend eliminated. *Held:* For the IRS. *S-2* distribution, which was followed by a sale, was not a dividend within the meaning of Section 316(a)(1) but a device to reduce tax by allowing *P* to obtain *S-1*'s basis in *S-2* practically tax-free by virtue of the dividend received deduction. Basic Inc., 549 F2d 740, 77-1 USTC ¶ 9161, 39 AFTR2d 77-823 (Ct. Cl. 1977).

Valid business purpose for transfer of corporate assets prevents dividend to stockholder. Taxpayer was the sole stockholder of a building corporation which would buy unimproved land, build houses on it, and sell the houses on the open market. In order to obtain financing, adequate sewer facilities had to be provided. The corporation built its own sewer system for the houses. Since the sewers were expensive to maintain and repair, they were transferred to a public utility in return for the utility's agreement to maintain and service the system. The IRS contended that taxpayer received a constructive dividend. *Held:* For taxpayer. It is a common practice for land developers to construct sewer facilities and then transfer them without consideration to a utility in return for a maintenance agreement. There was no showing that the utility was not a viable corporate entity independent of taxpayer, even though the utility's stockholders were members of taxpayer's family. The transfer was for bona fide business reasons and therefore was not a taxable distribution to taxpayer. Dean, 57 TC 32 (1971).

Payment by a wholly owned subsidiary to its parent prior to the latter's sale of the stock held a dividend and not part of the purchase price of the stock. Taxpayer, a publicly held corporation, was the stockholder of several wholly owned subsidiaries and received an offer from an outside party to sell all of the stock of two of them for $3.5 million. Taxpayer had for several years considered the payment of dividends by the subsidiaries and therefore made a counter offer to sell the stock for $700,000 after payment of dividends in the total amount of $2.8 million. Said dividends were declared and one of the subsidiaries issued its promissory note for that amount due in one month with interest. Shortly thereafter and according to negotiations that had been conducted by the various interests, taxpayer sold the stock in the two subsidiaries for $700,000 with the purchaser guaranteeing all liabilities. The new stockholders then borrowed $2.8 million to satisfy the note to taxpayer. Taxpayer treated the receipt of the $2.8 million as a dividend and eliminated it in the consolidated return that it filed with its subsidiaries. The IRS determined that the payment represented capital gain on the sale of the stock of the subsidiaries. Taxpayer contended that it was the equitable and legal owner of the stock on which the dividend was declared and paid "in property." The IRS argued that irrespective of the form of the transaction, it was in substance a sale of the stock of the subsidiaries for a total consideration of $3.5 million. *Held:* For taxpayer. It was apparent that when taxpayer made its counteroffer for the proposed sale, taxpayer intended to receive the total consideration from the purchaser in such a manner as to have $2.8 million designated as a dividend. It was also plain, however, that there were compelling business reasons for casting the transaction in the form of a sale of stock and not of individual assets. For this reason, no firm commitments were entered into and there was no legal acceptance of the offer and no legally binding contract of sale of the stock until after the dividend was declared and the note delivered. The court did not agree with the IRS, which stated that the substance of the transaction was a transfer of equitable title in the stock followed by the declaration of a dividend. Although both parties cited cases relating to the declaration of dividends prior to the closing of a sale, most of the cases cited turned on the precise provisions of the agreement. In negotiating contracts of this sort, the parties have the right to cast the transaction in terms most beneficial to them and may arrange the form of the transaction to reduce or eliminate the taxable income resulting therefrom. Where such form is neither a sham nor a subterfuge, its substance should not be considered to differ therefrom merely because the same result could have been ac-

Dividends and Distributions: *In General*

complished in a different manner. Waterman S.S. Corp., 50 TC 650 (1968).

Distribution by corporation to purchasing stockholder was dividend; no estoppel. Taxpayer was a corporation wholly owned by an individual who had obtained an option to buy the stock of another corporation. He then borrowed a large sum in the name of that corporation; it received the money and distributed it to taxpayer. Taxpayer used that money to pay the owners of the first corporation for their stock. The IRS at first treated the distribution of the loan proceeds to taxpayer as a loan, reallocated the interest deduction between the corporations involved, and asserted and collected additional taxes from the individual as a transferee, since the taxpayer corporation had been dissolved. The IRS then contended that the distribution to taxpayer was a taxable dividend and asserted liability against taxpayer as transferee. *Held:* For the IRS. The court found (1) that the distribution was a taxable dividend, notwithstanding that technically the taxpayer did not own stock of the distributing corporation at the time of the distribution; (2) that there was no estoppel, laches, or election against the IRS, rejecting taxpayers' argument that the IRS, by treating the transaction as a loan and collecting taxes on that basis, could not now change its theory; and (3) that interest was to be charged against taxpayers from the date they received the assets, providing that they had notice of the debtor-creditor relationship between themselves and the IRS at that time. Saigh, 36 TC 395 (1961).

"Paper transaction" may not be "erased." On an accountant's faulty advice, taxpayer, a majority stockholder of a corporation, caused the corporation to declare dividends and then apply the amount of dividends against his debt to the corporation. When he learned about the tax results, he "erased" the dividends and restored the debt to its predividend balance. *Held:* For the IRS. Taxpayer chose to operate the business in corporate form and must accept the risks of corporate existence. Taxpayer had an income when he received the dividends even if no cash changed hands and even if he had effectively returned the money to the corporation by changing the book entries. A dividend is income when it is declared and paid, even if it is immediately restored. Chapman, 44 TCM 35, ¶ 82,307 P-H Memo. TC (1982).

Long-term buy-out of controlling stockholder deemed a dividend distribution. Decedent owned the majority of the stock of a family corporation, and his wife and sons owned the remainder. In 1955 decedent and the corporation entered into an agreement for the purchase of decedent's stock with payments to be made over a period of years. Simultaneously, the same parties entered into an escrow agreement (no details given) and an employment contract. Decedent was given the right to receive dividends on and vote as much of the stock transferred to the escrowees as had not been paid for. Decedent's son understood the contract to mean that decedent "still owned the stock which was not paid for in toto." Decedent was elected president and chairman of the board for 1955 through 1958 by unanimous vote of his sons. He continued to remain active in the business and spent half his time on the business premises. No dividends were paid during the period 1954 through 1958, and the payments under the contract continued until decedent's death. *Held:* For the IRS. Applying the "net result" test, the court found that no redemption or sale had taken place, but that the essential equivalent of a distribution of a large amount of accumulated corporate profits to an individual, who was in effect the dominant stockholder, had taken place. Hence, the distributions were taxable as ordinary dividends. Estate of Silverman, 22 TCM 694, ¶ 63,146 P-H Memo. TC (1963).

Distribution in proportion to amount of business found to be a dividend. A corporation's distribution to its stockholders in proportion to the amount of business each stockholder conducted with the distributing corporation, rather than on the basis of the stock held by each stockholder, is still a dividend under Section 316. Rev. Rul. 83-141, 1983-2 CB 65.

Regulated investment company's first-year dividend paid after year end. A dividend may

Dividends and Distributions: Bargain Purchases and Sales

be treated as paid during the first taxable year if it is declared and paid by a regulated investment company after the close of its first taxable year and before the due date of the return; it must be declared and paid after the close of a subsequent short taxable year during which other dividends were declared as well, and paid for the first year and short taxable year. Rev. Rul. 75-183, 1975-1 CB 193.

Life insurance proceeds distributed to stockholders are taxable as dividends. The IRS updated and restated its position that life insurance proceeds received by a corporate beneficiary are taxable to stockholders when distributed to the extent of earnings and profits. IT 2131 superseded. Rev. Rul. 71-79, 1971-1 CB 112.

Rights to acquire new membership in a taxable membership association was not a distribution. A taxable voluntary membership association amended its constitution, thereby increasing its authorized shares and granting present members the right to acquire the new memberships. There was no distribution within the meaning of Section 305(a). However, a distribution of funds to its members attributable to a sale of "rights" on behalf of its members would be a dividend. Rev. Rul. 70-432, 1970-2 CB 75.

Distribution of subscriber's stock and the restructuring of the parent into an exempt organization gave rise to dividend, as the continuity of interest requirements were not met. Parent corporation and its subsidiary were both in the active conduct, for profit, of a college and trade school. The parent corporation was closely held by two individuals. The parent corporation distributed the stock of the subsidiary to its stockholders. The parent was then restructured as a Section 501(c)(3) organization so that students could be placed on the government list for financial aid. The IRS ruled that the distribution of the subsidiary's stock to the stockholders of the parent corporation was taxable as a dividend because the continuity of interest requirements of Regulation § 1.355-2(c) were not met. The stockholders of the parent corporation held no proprietary interest in the parent after the restructuring. Rev. Rul. 69-293, 1969-1 CB 102.

Rate of payment determines date of dividend distribution. The IRS ruled that the date of payment, not the date of declaration, constitutes the date of distribution of a dividend. Accordingly, where a dividend is paid from current earnings and profits, its taxable status will be determined by reference to the corporation's earnings and profits for the taxable year of payment. Where dividends are paid from accumulated earnings and profits, taxability will be determined by reference to earnings and profits on the date of payment. Rev. Rul. 62-131, 1962-2 CB 94.

Bargain Purchases and Sales

Bargain sale to taxpayer resulted in constructive dividend. Taxpayers, husband and wife, owned E Corporation, which rented sandblasting, corrosion protection, and painting equipment. The husband developed a porta-shot blast machine for use in a painting business service that he ran as a sole proprietor. Taxpayer was the sole owner of the patent rights of his machine but had a family owned corporation, N—in which he and his wife owned the majority of stock—that manufactured the machines and sold them to him and others. At the time taxpayer made purchases from N, some of the machines were sold to a major corporation at a higher price. The IRS determined that the sales of porta-shot blast machines by N to taxpayer were not at arm's length and that the difference between the fair market value of the equipment at the time and price paid by taxpayer represented a constructive dividend to the taxpayer by N. On taxpayer's federal income tax return, he treated all the income from his painting business as earned income. However, the IRS determined that only 30 percent was earned income and that capital was the material income-producing factor for the other 70 percent. The Tax Court agreed with the IRS. *Held:* Affirmed. Because the sale at the same time of similar new machines to an unrelated corporation established a significantly higher fair market value, the stockholder received a constructive dividend from his bargain sales of equipment from his controlled manufacturing corporation. Although his capital investments and expenses were extensive and large portions of income were derived directly from the use of machinery, capital was a material income-producing factor in taxpayer's business. Hence, only 30 percent of the income from taxpayer's painting proprietorship was eligible for maximum tax benefits. Nelson, 767 F2d 667, 85-2 USTC ¶ 9504, 56 AFTR2d 85-5334 (10th Cir. 1985).

Sale of works of art to closely held corporation resulted in dividend. Taxpayer sold 33 works of art from his own collection to his wholly owned corporation; 27 of the items were retained in taxpayer's home. The IRS argued that the taxpayer had received a dividend equivalent to the sales price allocated to those 27 pieces of art. *Held:* for the IRS. The distribution made by the corporation was for the personal benefit of the stockholder rather than for a valid business purpose and therefore constituted a dividend. Kluge, 41 TCM 690, ¶ 81,005 P-H Memo. TC, aff'd, 671 F2d 492 (2d Cir. 1981).

Stockholder received constructive dividend on bargain purchase among controlled corporations. Taxpayer, as the controlling stockholder of several large corporations, had his corporations purchase a multiwall bag and paper business from *F* Corporation. The complicated sales plan called for the purchase of the business to be split among corporations and required leases between the corporations involved. Later, five of taxpayer's controlled corporations involved in the sales plan sold their *F* stock, at cost, to *I*, another of taxpayer's corporations. Thereafter, the business was sold at a profit to an independent third party, *W*. The district court agreed with the IRS and found that when the taxpayer caused the stock to be transferred out of his five controlled corporations to *I*, *I* received a bargain purchase. The court concluded that this savings of $500,000 was a constructive dividend to taxpayer and that because this amount exceeded 25 percent of the gross income reported by taxpayer, the six-year limitation period was applicable. *Held:* Affirmed. A taxpayer need not personally receive money from the transaction, for it is the power to dispose of income and the exercise of that power that determine whether taxable income has been received. Where taxpayer moved a business between wholly owned or controlled corporate entities at a bargain price, the taxpayer in fact exercised such power. Sammons, 433 F2d 728, 70-2 USTC ¶ 9678, 26 AFTR2d 70-5746 (5th Cir. 1970), cert. denied, 402 US 945 (1971).

Bargain purchase from corporation was dividend income to stockholder. Taxpayer sought to buy all the stock of a bank corporation for $475,000. The bank owned a building that was worth $133,000, but was recorded on its books at only $33,000. In order to raise $100,000 of the purchase price, paxpayer, in a complicated transaction that used the sellers as dummies, purchased the building for $33,000. The IRS sought to add $100,000 to taxpayer's income, claiming that the purchase was a bargain purchase resulting in dividend income. The Tax Court agreed after analyzing the complex transaction, and concluded that the sellers of the stock were mere dummies in receiving the bank building. *Held:* Affirmed. Parol evidence admitted by the Tax Court was proper to explain intent and motive. Lacy, 341 F2d 54, 65-1 USTC ¶ 9205, 15 AFTR2d 286 (10th Cir. 1965).

Resale of property by stockholder to corporation at profit was a disguised dividend. A controlling stockholder of a family corporation purchased for $35,000 a building under lease to the corporation and immediately resold it to the corporation for $75,000. The Tax Court found as a fact that only $35,000 of the $75,000 paid by the corporation to the stockholder was consideration for the property and that the remaining $40,000 was a disguised dividend. *Held:* Affirmed. The stockholder's attempt to show that the property itself was worth $75,000 at the time was unconvincing, in view of the corporation's long-term lease at low rental. Goldstein, 298 F2d 562, 62-1 USTC ¶ 9304, 9 AFTR2d 752 (9th Cir. 1962).

Bargain sale of land was dividend. The IRS determined that taxpayer stockholders re-

Dividends and Distributions: *Bargain Purchases and Sales*

ceived constructive dividends from their corporation when it sold land to them at less than fair market value. *Held:* For the IRS.The fact that a stockholder's wife took title as a tenant by the entirety did not preclude a constructive dividend. Fausek, Jr., 81-1 USTC ¶ 9243, 47 AFTR2d 81-1306 (ED Mo. 1981).

A jury determined that stockholders received dividend in regard to a bargain purchase. On December 1, 1965, taxpayer corporation sold its interests in mineral properties, including machinery and equipment at two drilling fields. The property was first offered to the stockholders only but was eventually sold to both stockholders and nonstockholders. The total price paid for the property was $210,000. The IRS determined that the property had a total value of $1.4 million on the date of the sale and therefore was sold at a price substantially less than its fair market value. For the stockholder purchasers, this created a taxable constructive dividend. *Held:* For the IRS, in part. The district court jury found that the fair market value was in excess of the price paid but held it to be less than what the IRS claimed. They found that the fair market value exceeded the purchase price by a total of $375,000. Central Oil Co., 71-1 USTC ¶ 9257, 27 AFTR2d 410 (SD Miss. 1970).

Sale of property by corporation to stockholder at less than fair market value was a dividend. Taxpayer and her family owned approximately 35 percent of the stock of a corporation that engaged in the ownership and operation of commercial real estate. A hotel property owned by the corporation was sold to taxpayer for an amount substantially less than the adjusted basis of the corporation. The IRS contended that taxpayer realized dividend income as a result of the transaction. *Held:* For the IRS. Expert witnesses gave evidence concerning the fair market value of the hotel on the date of sale to taxpayer. Based on all the facts, it was determined that the value of the hotel on that date was in excess of the amount paid by taxpayer. Taxpayer was in receipt of a distribution, to the extent of this excess, out of the earnings and profits of the corporation and, consequently, said amount was dividend income. It was further held that the corporation could deduct the loss on the sale to the extent that its adjusted basis exceeded the fair market value of the property. Honigman, 55 TC 1067 (1971).

Payment of excessive price to stockholders for merchandise was a dividend. Taxpayers were partners who owned standing timber, which they contracted to sell to their corporation. In the contract of the sale, the parties set forth a schedule of prices, and provided that if the IRS adjusted these prices, the parties would recompute any amounts due. Taxpayers reported the proceeds of the sale as capital gain in 1959 and 1960. In 1963, the IRS determined that the fair market value of certain of the timber was substantially less than the sales price. Agreeing to this finding (and the resulting deficiency), the corporation set up an account receivable from the sellers and increased its retained earnings. There was, however, no evidence that taxpayers were refunded this amount, although the partnership made a contra journal entry reflecting a liability to the corporation for the excessive amounts. The IRS sought to treat the excess over fair market value as a dividend from the corporation. Taxpayers contended that the excess was not a dividend but a reduction of their capital gain and should be treated as such (viz., a capital loss). *Held:* For the IRS. The payment in excess of fair market value constituted a dividend. The substance of this transaction overcame the formal relationship between buyer and seller. Emmerson, 44 TC 86 (1965).

Bargain sale to stockholder was dividend. Taxpayer was a one-third stockholder in a corporation that sold him six lots for a total consideration of $4,100. The IRS determined that the fair market value of the lots at the time of the sale was $17,100 and assessed a deficiency on the $13,000 excess. Taxpayer conceded that any excess of fair market value over cost would constitute a dividend to him, but he disputed the IRS' valuation. *Held:* The court, after weighing the expert testimony, determined the fair market value to be

Dividends and Distributions: *Bargain Purchases and Sales*

$12,000, with a resultant dividend to the taxpayer on the $7,900 excess. Estate of Mundy, 36 TC 703 (1961), acq. 1962-2 CB 5.

Dividend in stockholder's bargain purchase of land parcels determined as difference between fair market value and price paid. Taxpayer, a dentist, owned one third of the shares in a land development corporation. An arrangement existed wherein the stockholders could buy individual lots of land from the corporation at about cost. Whenever a lot was sold to a stockholder, the other stockholders could make a similar purchase. Taxpayer purchased three vacant lots at less than their fair market value. The IRS contended that taxpayer received a dividend to the extent of the difference between the fair market value and the price that he paid. *Held:* For the IRS. The fact that another stockholder purchased five lots was irrelevant; dividends need not be in proportion to stock holdings. The court ruled that the fair market value of the lots to be used was the price that any willing buyer would pay and not the generally lower price that would be paid by a dealer who intended to resell at a profit. Finally, the court held that when these inventory assets were distributed to the stockholders, the corporations earnings and profits were increased to the extent of the difference between their fair market value and basis of the assets. Dellinger, 32 TC 1178 (1959).

Undercharge by corporation not constructive dividend to stockholder. Taxpayer corporation constructed an addition to a building owned by its stockholder, but did not charge the stockholder for the full cost of the addition. The corporation had constructed projects for stockholder in the past and always charged the full cost, which the stockholder always paid. The IRS determined that the stockholder received a constructive dividend in the amount of the undercharge, and that taxpayer had understated its gross receipts and overstated its operating loss as a result. *Held:* For taxpayer, in part. The stockholder established that he could pay and intended to pay for the full cost of the addition, and that his failure to do so was because of a mistake by the bookkeeper of the corporation. Because the undercharge was inadvertent, no constructive dividend was found. However, since the corporation did include the full cost in computing its loss but included only the amount charged to the stockholder in gross receipts, the IRS' determination that the corporation overstated its operating loss and understated its gross receipts was sustained. Helgesen Properties, Inc., 47 TCM 751, ¶ 83,771 P-H Memo. TC (1983).

Sale of property to and payment of stockholder's expenses were constructive dividends. Taxpayer borrowed money from a bank, securing it with insurance policies he owned on his life. In order to repay the loan, he bought property for less than its fair market value from his controlled corporation, leased it, and used the rent payments to repay the loan. His corporation also paid the legal fees for securing the loan and the premiums on the insurance policies. The IRS determined that the sale and payments constituted dividends to the taxpayer. *Held:* For the IRS. Since the transaction was for the stockholder's benefit, the insurance premiums, the legal fees, and the difference between the fair market value of the property and its sale price were all constructive dividends. Lynch, 45 TCM 1125, ¶ 83,173 P-H Memo. TC (1983), aff'd (5th Cir. 1985)

Stockholder's bargain purchase of residence from his closely held corporation constituted a dividend in an amount equal to the bargain element. Taxpayer and his father owned 100 percent of the stock of a corporation that constructed houses. Taxpayer purchased a house constructed by the corporation for an amount that was less than the price that an unrelated third party would have paid for a similar residence. *Held:* For the IRS. The court held that a stockholder's below-fair-market-value purchase of a house from his corporation was a dividend to the stockholder in an amount equal to the excess of fair market value (not the corporation's costs) over the purchase price paid. Terris, 45 TCM 530, ¶ 83,029 P-H Memo. TC (1983).

No constructive dividend when subsidiary's stock purchased at fair market value. Taxpayers spun off the manufacturing business of their close corporation. They formed a new corporation which then merged into the spun-off corporation. The IRS argued that the price taxpayers paid for the subsidiary's stock was below fair market value; therefore, taxpayers received a constructive dividend. *Held:* For taxpayers. Taxpayers' valuation of the stock was correct, since a pending damage claim reduced its value. Sackett, 42 TCM 1666, ¶ 81,661 P-H Memo. TC (1981).

Sale of timber from stockholders to their corporation was bona fide and not a constructive dividend. Under a long-term agreement, *K* Corporation cut and removed timber from land owned jointly by *K*'s stockholders. The price *K* paid was set by an independent appraiser each year. The IRS considered part of the price a constructive dividend to the stockholders. *Held*: For taxpayers. The agreement and its pricing provision was fair when judged by the standard of an arms-length agreement. There was no need to inquire further into the correctness of the appraisal. Stuchell, 37 TCM 1017, ¶ 78,236 P-H Memo. TC (1978).

Bargain sale of stock to stockholder results in dividend. Taxpayer purchased stock in a small corporation from a corporation that he controlled. The IRS determined that taxpayer received a dividend, asserting that the sale was at a bargain price. *Held*: For the IRS, in part. The court determined the value of the purchased stock to be between the values claimed by the IRS and the taxpayer. Miller, 36 TCM 169, ¶ 77,039 P-H Memo. TC (1977).

Bargain sale to stockholder resulted in constructive dividend. A corporation in which taxpayer was the sole stockholder conveyed to him commercial real estate which the parties valued at $120,000. The IRS claimed that the property was worth in excess of that amount and set up a constructive dividend for the difference between the price and the alleged value. *Held*: For the IRS. The court determined that the fair market value of the property at the date of the sale was $55,000 more than the sale price. This difference in value was to the extent of the corporation's earnings and profits treated as an ordinary dividend to taxpayer. Wojciechowski, 24 TCM 726, ¶ 65,135 P-H Memo. TC (1965).

Sale to controlled corporation at inflated price was partly a dividend. Taxpayers sold their personal residence to a controlled corporation for $100,000. No income was reported from the sale, since taxpayers reinvested the full proceeds in a new home within a year. The IRS determined that taxpayers received a dividend from their corporation because the amount paid by the corporation for the home was in excess of the fair market value of the property at the date of sale. *Held*: For the IRS. Considering the testimony of expert witnesses as to sales of similar property in the area, the court concluded that the fair market value of the residence was $85,000, and that taxpayers therefore received a $15,000 dividend. Bardahl, 24 TCM 613, ¶ 65,116 P-H Memo. TC (1965).

Corporation's bargain sale of assets to seller of its stock was a dividend to the buyer. As part of the consideration for taxpayers purchase of stock in a company, the corporation transferred to the selling stockholder (taxpayers' uncle) insurance policies having a cash surrender value of $24,000 for only $12,000. The IRS determined that taxpayers received a dividend from the corporation to the extent of $12,000, in that the corporation, by the bargain sale, in effect, paid part of the cost of the stock that taxpayers bought. Taxpayers argued that the satisfaction by the corporation of their obligation created a bona fide indebtedness and not a dividend. *Held*: For the IRS. Since the alleged indebtedness was never recorded, no notes were executed, and no payments were made, the court sustained the dividend determination made by the IRS. O'Keefe, 20 TCM 310, ¶ 61,059 P-H Memo. TC (1961).

Resale of property by stockholder to corporation at a profit was a disguised dividend. A controlling stockholder of a family corporation purchased for $35,000, a building under lease to the corporation and immediately resold it to the corporation for $75,000. The

DIVIDENDS AND DISTRIBUTIONS: *Bonus Payments*

IRS claimed that only $35,000 of the $75,000 paid by the corporation to the stockholder was consideration for the property and that the remaining $40,000 was a disguised dividend. *Held*: For the IRS. The stockholder's attempt to show that the property itself was worth $75,000 at the time was unconvincing, in view of the corporation's long-term lease at low rental. Goodstein, ¶ 60,276 P-H Memo. TC (1960).

Bonus Payments

Court determined that bonuses paid to stockholder-employees in proportion to their stockholdings were distribution of earnings. All of taxpayer's stockholders were its employees. Each year, taxpayer paid its stockholder-employees bonuses. These bonuses were paid to each in the same proportion as their stockholdings. Taxpayer did not, however, pay any dividends. Taxpayer deducted these bonuses as compensation. Taxpayer entered into a redemption agreement with one of its stockholder-employees, agreeing to pay him for a five-year period a percentage of after tax profits (increased by bonuses and salaries paid in excess of 60 percent of fee billings). The IRS challenged the bonuses as "excessive compensation", and asserted that they were disguised distributions of corporate earnings. *Held*: For the IRS. Compensation is deductible only if it is reasonable and for personal services actually rendered. The factors considered were as follows: (1) Bonuses were in exact proportion to stockholder-employee's stockholdings; (2) payments were in lump sums rather than as services were rendered; (3) no dividends were paid; (4) bonuses were awarded at various times during the year on no apparent pre-determined basis; (5) taxpayer consistently reported negligble taxable income indicating that the bonus system was based on funds available (and not services rendered); (6) bonus payments were made only to the stockholder-employees; and (7) the redemption agreement took into account bonuses paid. Nor-Cal Adjusters, 503 F2d 359, 74-2 USTC ¶ 9701, 34 AFTR2d 74-5834 (9th Cir. 1974).

Bonus was dividend, not compensation. Three brothers were the sole stockholders and officers of taxpayer. In addition to receiving substantial salaries, each brother received a "bonus" of $10,000 at the end of the taxable year. The IRS determined that in as much as the brothers owned equal amounts of stock, the bonuses were dividends. The jury district court was charged to find that the payments were dividends if the stockholders had received the payments because they were owners of the business. *Held:* Affirmed. Because the stockholders owned all of the stock of a corporation in equal amounts and received considerable compensation for their services, the bonuses paid to the stockholders were in fact dividends. Louisville Chair Co., 297 F2d 621, 61-2 USTC ¶ 9765, 8 AFTR2d 5783 (6th Cir. 1961).

Bonus payments, although not unreasonable, were treated as dividends. Taxpayer deducted bonuses to its officer stockholders that, although not directly proportional to stockholdings, were closely related thereto. The IRS disallowed the deductions, contending that the payments were distributions of profits made in a manner calculated to avoid the income tax. Taxpayer contended that the payments were reasonable in view of the fact that there were no family relationships, services were actually performed, and dividends were paid on both preferred and common stock. *Held*: For the IRS. Despite taxpayer's contentions, the burden of proof that the IRS' determination was incorrect was not discharged. The bonus payments to the officers bore a high proportion to basic salary, where as bonuses to non-stockholding employees averaged only a small percentage of their salaries. Even a payment that is reasonable is not deductible if it is actually a distribution of earnings, as contrasted with compensation for services actually rendered. Northlich, Stolley Inc., 368 F2d 272, 66-2 USTC ¶ 9740, 18 AFTR2d 5937 (Ct. Cl. 1966).

Cancellation of Indebtedness

**Presumption of constructive dividend's correctness overturned; cancellation of debt for benefit of stockholder not deemed construc-

Dividends and Distributions: *Cancellation of Indebtedness*

tive dividend. Taxpayer and two other stockholders were indebted to their corporation in the amount of $35,800, the subscription price of their stock. Book entries showed the corporation's cancellation of this debt, while a second corporation owned by the same stockholders canceled the $35,800 of a debt owed to it from the first corporation for construction work. The Tax Court held for the IRS on the ground that taxpayer had failed to overcome the presumption of correctness of the IRS' finding that a constructive dividend resulted. *Held:* Remanded. Introduction of substantial evidence of book entries by taxpayer dissolved this presumption. On the record, there was no evidence to support a finding by the Tax Court of a constructive dividend. Stout, 273 F2d 345, 60-1 USTC ¶ 9185, 5 AFTR2d 407 (4th Cir. 1959).

Use of corporate assets as part payment of stock purchase was a dividend to purchaser. Taxpayer purchased all the stock of a corporation. He made a down payment, and the balance of the purchase price was payable in monthly installments for 10 years. Pending payment, the sellers would retain legal title to the stock, and taxpayer would have beneficial ownership. Taxpayer, with certain limitations, had the right to vote the stock, control and manage the corporation, and have it pay him dividends provided that they were applied in reduction of his outstanding debt to the sellers. Pursuant to the terms of the agreement, taxpayer caused the corporation to surrender a life insurance policy owned by the corporation on the life of one of the former stockholders. The proceeds were paid to the sellers. Taxpayer also caused the corporation to cancel a debt of a prior stockholder. The IRS contended that taxpayer received a dividend to the extent of the value of the policy and the canceled debt. *Held:* For the IRS. These transactions were part of the purchase agreement, and the payments reduced taxpayer's debt for the stock purchase. Christensen, 33 TC 500 (1960).

Loan to parent from subsidiary held not abandoned although parent intended to liquidate without repaying the loan. Taxpayer corporation borrowed money from its subsidiary. The IRS argued that the fact that the parent intended to liquidate and that it did not have enough funds to repay the loan indicated that the subsidiary had abandoned the loan. Therefore, taxpayer received constructive dividends from this forgiveness of indebtedness. *Held:* For taxpayer. Taxpayer booked the intercompany loan as an open account on its balance sheets and financial statements and treated all intercompany borrowing consistently for many years, even when such loans were occasionally informal. P.J. Anderson & Sons, 46 TCM 382, ¶ 83,323 P-H Memo. TC (1983).

Discharge of debt constructive dividend. Taxpayer, a director of his wholly owned corporation, discharged a debt to his corporation owed by another corporation in which he was a 50 percent stockholder. The IRS contended that the amount discharged was a constructive dividend to him. *Held:* For the IRS. Taxpayer was embroiled in controversy with the other 50 percent stockholder of the debtor corporation, and the release of the claim was part of the consideration in the deal to sell his share in that corporation. Thus, the release was intended primarily to confer an economic benefit on taxpayer, and the amount constituted a constructive dividend to him from his corporation. Kipnis, 44 TCM 849, ¶ 82,471 P-H Memo. TC (1982).

Payments by a corporation in settlement of stockholder's guarantee constituted a dividend. Taxpayer was the sole stockholder and president of *W*, a very unprofitable animal-slaughtering business. *W* borrowed funds from *S*, a real and personal property holding company owned wholly by taxpayer, and in effect maintained a running loan and exchange account with *S*. Taxpayer guaranteed certain notes delivered to creditor *R* for debts incurred by *W*. After paying some of these notes as a guarantor, taxpayer deducted the amounts on his tax return as losses. Later *S* paid *R* certain amounts in settlement of notes on which taxpayer was the guarantor, which were never repaid or claimed as losses or deductions by *S*. The IRS determined that *S* had constructively distributed a dividend to taxpayer, and that taxpayer was not entitled

Dividends and Distributions: *Capital Gains Distinguished*

to a deduction under Section 165 for payment in discharge of his liability as guarantor of the corporate note. *Held:* For the IRS. Because the corporation paid out of its surplus a debt of its sole stockholder with no intention of being repaid, it was a constructive dividend. Furthermore, the stockholder was denied a loss deduction for making good on the guaranty, as he failed to prove his endorsement was with the expectation of repayment by the corporation. Bernstein, 19 TCM 1569, ¶ 60,287 P-H Memo. TC (1960).

Parent company had dividend income from debt discharge on subsidiary's distribution of its bonds. A subsidiary corporation purchased unmatured bonds of its parent corporation. Later the subsidiary distributed these bonds in the face amount of $1,400 to the parent. The subsidiary's adjusted basis for the bonds was $1,200, and the fair market value was $980. The parent was solvent before the distribution, and it did not file a consolidated return with its subsidiary. The subsidiary had adequate earnings and profits available for dividends. The IRS ruled that (1) the parent realized dividend income in the amount of $980 under Section 301(c); (2) the difference between the $980 distribution and the $1,400 face amount of the bonds was income to the parent from the discharge of indebtedness under Section 61(a)(12); (3) the subsidiary's earnings and profits must be reduced by $1,200, its adjusted basis for the bonds under Section 312(a); and (4) the subsidiary realized no gain or loss on the distribution under Section 311(a). Rev. Rul. 61-96, 1961-1 CB 68.

Capital Gains Distinguished

Cash distribution in corporate buy-out deemed part of purchase price of stock. A complex multi-step corporate buy-out involved two groups of taxpayer stockholders; one group bought additional shares and the other sold their shares. Contemporaneous with the buy-out, taxpayer sellers received pro rata cash distributions from the paid-in capital surplus accounts of the corporations involved; taxpayer buyers also received such distributions. The IRS and the Tax Court held that these distributions constituted ordinary dividend income to both taxpayer buyers and taxpayer sellers. *Held:* Reversed in part. As to taxpayer sellers, the economic substance of the transaction indicated that the cash received was part of the purchase price of their stock and thus subject to capital gains taxation. Since the distribution to taxpayer sellers were part of the purchase price for their stock, such distributions resulted in an economic benefit to taxpayer buyers. Consequently, these same distributions, although not directly received by taxpayer buyers, resulted in ordinary dividend income to them. Finally, the cash distributions received directly by taxpayer buyers were also deemed to be ordinary dividend income, even though they were made from the paid-in capital surplus accounts. Casner, 450 F2d 379, 71-2 USTC ¶ 9651, 28 AFTR2d 71-5676 (5th Cir. 1971).

Corporate distribution constituted a dividend, not capital gain. Taxpayers and others formed a medical and surgical corporation which subsequently became the owner of a hospital. After gifts of the capital stock were made to the owners' children, the donees transferred their shares back to the parents in order to facilitate a transfer of the stock to local governmental agencies. On November 30, the corporation declared a dividend and on December 1 the stock was transferred to the local county and city. Taxpayers reported the distributions from the corporation as long-term capital gain, and the IRS determined that the distribution was a taxable dividend. *Held:* For the IRS. The files of the taxpayers' counsel indicated that the intent of the parties was to declare a dividend of all cash and receivables as of November 30. The distribution was a dividend in substance as well as form and could not be treated either as the proceeds of a sale, as a redemption and gift, or as a partial liquidation and gift. The taxpayers proposed to make a gift of the stock to the governmental agencies, and this in fact occurred. When the dividend was declared, the taxpayers alone had the beneficial ownership. Reitz, 61 TC 443 (1973).

DIVIDENDS AND DISTRIBUTIONS: *Disallowed Corporate Expenses*

Disallowed Corporate Expenses

Constructive dividend treatment of nondeductible corporate expense could not be imposed without proof of economic benefit to stockholder-officer. Taxpayer was a California corporation engaged in residential real estate leasing activities. On its income tax returns for 1963 through 1965, taxpayer deducted travel and entertainment expenses amounting to $7,653, $5,078, and $5,979, respectively. The IRS disallowed the deduction as claimed and argued in Tax Court that the entire amount represented constructive dividends to the corporation's officers. The Tax Court ruled for the IRS. *Held:* Reversed. The Ninth Circuit held that the Tax Court erred in finding that disallowed corporate expenses "automatically" became constructive dividends to the owners. The test for imposing constructive dividends is twofold: The expenses must be nondeductible to the corporation and they must represent some economic gain or benefit to the owner sought to be taxed. The Ninth Court chided the Tax Court for failing to apply the second of the two tests and reversed for further proceedings. Palo Alto Town & Country Village, Inc., 565 F2d 1388, 78-1 USTC ¶ 9200, 41 AFTR2d 78-517 (9th Cir. 1977).

Corporation's payment of stockholders' personal expenses was a constructive dividend, notwithstanding a subsequent resolution to apply the amounts to their loan. Taxpayers had made a loan to their controlled corporation on which they were paid interest but not principal. As a result of the examination of the corporate returns, certain personal items charged to business expense were disallowed. The taxpayers caused a resolution to be passed by the corporation stating that such disallowances were to be applied against the principal of the loan, and would not constitute dividend income to them. The IRS contended that the disallowances must be treated as constructive dividends despite the indebtedness to the stockholders. Taxpayer contended that the corporation was entitled to treat the disallowances as a repayment of the delinquent indebtedness. The Tax Court held for the IRS. *Held:* For the IRS. The issue addressed by this case was whether the subsequent act of the taxpayers could convert what should have been a taxable constructive dividend into a repayment of a prior indebtedness. The payments here were clearly constructive dividends; this fact was not altered by the subsequent expression of intent by the taxpayers. One year's income could not be changed by events occuring in subsequent years. Noble, 368 F2d 439, 66-2 USTC ¶ 9743, 18 AFTR2d 5982 (9th Cir. 1966).

Controlling stockholders operated yacht leased to their corporation for personal purposes; corporate deductions disallowed and held dividend to taxpayers. Taxpayers purchased a 161 foot ocean-going schooner and claimed business deductions for the expenses of running the ship for four years until they leased it to their newly incorporated proprietorship. When the corporation was organized, they leased the ship to the corporation, which was required to pay for the maintenance and upkeep of the yacht. Thereafter, the corporation, which was engaged in the heavy industrial machine contracting business, paid the expenses of operating the yacht and claimed them as business deductions. Taxpayers were concerned with the operation of the corporate office and the formulation of policy decisions. They no longer maintained contacts with customers of the corporation or performed contract negotiations, and customer's employees who were responsible for placing contracts were not entertained aboard the yacht. The yacht's log showed many guests who were social friends of taxpayers but who had no business connection with the corporation. The IRS disallowed the deductions to the corporation and taxed them as dividend income to taxpayers. *Held:* For the IRS. The yacht was used primarily for the personal recreation and enjoyment of taxpayers, who failed to show any substantial proximate relationship between the expenditures for the maintenance of the yacht and the business of the corporation. The expenses disallowed were to be included in taxpayers' income as a constructive dividend. In addition, the corporation claimed an eight-year useful life and no salvage value. This was also totally unrealistic. Taxpayers had offered the yacht for sale through brokers at three times its original purchase price, and at one time had refused an offer equal in amount to the price that they had paid for it some 10 years prior thereto. In addition, they had taken the yacht on an ocean voyage some 17 years after the date of acquisition and had testified in an earlier case that with proper maintenance, it could last "forever." Larrabee, 68-2 USTC ¶ 9442 (CD Cal. 1968).

Rental value of corporate yacht was constructive dividend to controlling stockholder. Taxpayer was the majority stockholder of a family held corporation. The corporation purchased a yacht and a resolution was passed by its board of directors stating that any expenses incurred in the personal use of the boat were to be borne by taxpayer, and that an accurate log was to be kept of all business use. The IRS disallowed all expenses connected with the operation of the boat and charged taxpayer with a constructive dividend based on the cost of the yacht. *Held:* For the IRS, in part. Taxpayer's evidence was insufficient and based on highly conjectural testimony; thus the corporation was not permitted to claim the expenses of operation. The expenses in question were for the personal benefit of the stockholders of the corporation and were taxable as dividend income constructively received. Taxpayer made the boat available and was in complete control of the events; therefore, he was in receipt of the constructive dividend, despite the fact his son, also a stockholder, was the principal user of the boat. The amount of the dividend, however, was not the cost of the boat but instead its fair rental value. Nicholls, North, Buse Co., 56 TC 1225 (1971).

Nondeductible expenses benefiting officer-stockholders constituted dividends to them. Corporation made various promotional and entertainment expenses and gifts, many of which were of marginal or little business value. The corporation took them as business deductions, while the individuals did not report them as income. The IRS eliminated some of the deductions entirely and included the amounts in the individual officer's income. *Held:* For the IRS, in part. Although some of the expenses, such as wedding presents, were unrelated to the business, others were partially related and half were allowed. Also, the individuals failed to sustain the burden of proof that the IRS' determination of underpayment was due to negligence. Berkley Mach. Works, 27 TCM 1487, ¶ 68,278 P-H Memo. TC (1968), aff'd, 422 F2d 362, 70-1 USTC ¶ 9261 (4th Cir. 1970).

Legal costs paid by corporation in defense of speeding ticket received by sole stockholder was a constructive dividend. Taxpayer was the president and sole stockholder of a corporation. While proceeding in a company car from his home to his golf course to keep an appointment with a substantial customer of the corporation, he was arrested for speeding. In successfully defending the charge, he incurred legal costs of $450, which were paid by the corporation. The corporation claimed the costs as a business expense but the IRS disallowed the deduction. *Held:* For the IRS. The legal defense was personal to taxpayer, since his activities that day were not connected with business. Accordingly, the costs were not deductible by the corporation but resulted in a constructive dividend to him. Weil, 26 TCM 388, ¶ 67,078 P-H Memo. TC (1967).

Corporation's payment of president's expenses was constructive dividend. A corporation paid legal fees in connection with a suit between its president and his wife for separate maintenance, a divorce, and a division of the community property. The corporation deducted these fees as ordinary and necessary expenses, claiming that they were incurred to protect the corporate business by preventing the wife from assuming any control over the corporation. The IRS disallowed the deduction. *Held:* For the IRS. The legal services were incurred for the benefit of the taxpayer *individually* and not for the benefit of the corporation. Furthermore, the legal fees constituted the payment of a constructive dividend to the president to the extent of the available earnings. On another issue, the fair market values of various items of property and paintings were determined by the court on the basis of available testimony. Hartwell, 24 TCM 278, ¶ 65,049 P-H Memo. TC (1965).

Dividends and Distributions: *Disguised and Constructive—Generally*

Disallowed corporate expenditures treated as constructive dividend to sole stockholder. Cash was withdrawn by taxpayer from his controlled corporation for alleged corporate expenses. *Held:* For the IRS. The IRS' determination that disallowed corporate expenses (other than strike payments to union truckmen and payoffs to police, which payments could not be deducted by the corporation) constituted income to taxpayer in the form of constructive dividends was sustained. Taxpayer also failed to prove that he incurred business expenses on behalf of the corporation for which he was not reimbursed. Marks, 22 TCM 1600, ¶ 63,304 P-H Memo. TC (1963).

Disguised and Constructive—Generally

"Surplus capital notes" from insurance company not equity interests. Taxpayers, two stockholders of insurance company *A*, advanced funds to *A* in return for "surplus capital notes." The funds were borrowed from another insurance company, *B*. *B* later purchased part of the business of *A* in return for payments to *A* that were distributed to taxpayers as repayment of the notes and ultimately applied to repay taxpayers' liability to *B*. The IRS argued that the transactions were equivalent to a dividend from *A* to the taxpayers (treating the "surplus capital notes" as disguised equity interests). The district court upheld the IRS. *Held:* Reversed. The transactions were designed to inject capital into *A* without violating state insurance regulations banning regular financing. The payments produced a nontaxable repayment of *A*'s notes to taxpayers. Jones, 659 F2d 1311, 81-2 USTC ¶ 9276, 48 AFTR2d 81-6034 (5th Cir. 1981).

Constructive dividend disguised as inflated royalty payment. Taxpayer was controlling stockholder in *S*, a coal brokerage company. Taxpayer leased mining property for a royalty of $0.25 per ton and then subleased the property to *R* for $0.50 per ton. *S* then bought coal from *R* at a higher than normal price intended to cover the extra royalty that *R* paid. The IRS charged that the $0.25 per ton profit to taxpayer was a constructive dividend from *S*. *Held:* For the IRS. Taxpayer failed to justify the extra royalty that *R* paid him. The facts showed that the arrangement was a sham. Estate of Lucas, 71 TC 838 (1979), aff'd, 657 F2d 841, 81-2 USTC ¶ 9782, 48 AFTR2d 81-5836 (6th Cir. 1981).

Payments not intended as compensation were dividends. Taxpayer had its election as a Subchapter S corporation involuntarily terminated, without its knowledge. Subsequent thereto, it made distributions to its stockholders who performed substantial and valuable services, but these amounts were treated as dividends, and no reference was made to salaries in the corporate records. The IRS disallowed a deduction for these distributions of salaries claimed by taxpayer on learning of its conventional corporate status. The Tax Court held for the IRS. *Held:* Affirmed. There was no intent on the part of the corporation to compensate its officers, and intent at the time of the distributions is controlling. Both the corporation and the stockholders treated the amounts received as dividends, and the payments were in proportion to the stock held by the recipients. Paula Constr. Co., 474 F2d 1345, 73-1 USTC ¶ 9283, 31 AFTR2d 73-926 (5th Cir. 1973).

Purchase of stock of sister corporation from controlling stockholder was constructive dividend. Taxpayer, on the cash basis, owned all the stock of Industrial and Southern. The former operated at a profit and the latter at a loss. In order to offset Southern's losses against Industrial's profits on a consolidated tax return, taxpayer sold his stock in Southern to Industrial. The sale was made in 1961 on credit, although an anticipated corporate note was never issued. In 1962, Industrial issued more stock to taxpayer in satisfaction of its new debt to him. Taxpayer conceded to the IRS that the 1961 sale was within the ambit of Section 304 and, hence, Section 302 as well, but disputed that there was either (1) a distribution within the meaning of that section or (2) a distribution that was essentially equivalent to a dividend. The district court held for the IRS, however. It reasoned that under the doctrine of constructive receipt, a distribution within the meaning of Section

Dividends and Distributions: *Disguised and Constructive—Generally*

302 does not require an actual segregation or transfer of funds. In the case of a corporation with sufficient accumulated earnings, the creation of a new indebtedness is sufficient, regardless of whether the debt is evidenced by a note or whether the corporation has the funds on hand to make payment. Any other result would allow a cash-basis taxpayer to recognize income by choosing the year of distribution. Since there was no basic change in taxpayer's ownership or control of either Industrial or Southern, the distribution in this case was essentially equivalent to a dividend. The fact that there may have been a corporate business purpose for the transaction, which in any event was difficult to distinguish from taxpayer's own purpose, was not considered to be controlling. Taxpayer argued that he could have achieved the same result by employing another method, such as by donating his Southern stock to Industrial. This argument similarly was not considered to be any reason for not taxing him on the method he employed. *Held:* Affirmed. In the instant case, all the conditions necessary to constitute a dividend were fulfilled, and none of "conspicuously countervailing" considerations the court alluded to in Bradbury, 298 F2d 111 (1962), which might otherwise dispel the aura of "dividend equivalence" were present. Where the taxpayer is the sole or dominant stockholder of the distributing corporation, the presence of a business purpose is irrelevant. The controlling fact was that taxpayer received an unfettered indebtedness which, at least to the extent that profits were available, was equivalent to a dividend. The fact that taxpayer could have achieved the same result by a different procedure, without incurring the tax consequences of the procedure he elected was no reason for not taxing him on the basis of the method he employed. Wiseman, 371 F2d 816, 19 AFTR2d 580 (1st Cir. 1967).

No dividend to 40 percent stockholder where development corporation transfers utility assets to stockholder's wholly owned, related utility corporation. Taxpayer owned 40 percent of the stock of a land development corporation. After installing water and sewer facilities in certain lots, the development corporations transferred such facilities to a utility corporation wholly owned by taxpayer. The only consideration for this transfer was the utility company's assumption of the obligation to furnish continuous services at reasonable rates to purchasers of houses in the development. The IRS determined that this transfer resulted in a constructive dividend to taxpayer. The Tax Court held that no dividend resulted, since such transfers were a common practice among real estate developers to make land saleable, and that there was no evidence that the transaction was a device to siphon off corporate profits. Furthermore, the cost of constructing the transferred facilities was held to be properly included in the basis of the lots. *Held:* Affirmed. The Fourth Circuit agreed with the Tax Court's conclusions, which were more than adequately supported by the record and were in accord with earlier cases. Offutt, 336 F2d 483, 64-2 USTC ¶ 9757 (4th Cir. 1964).

Purchase by corporation from one who previously sold property to corporation's sole stockholder was not a constructive dividend to the stockholder. Taxpayer bought a house and 10 acres of property from S for $40,000. Taxpayer then traded to S two properties for another 200 acres of land. Shortly thereafter, S conveyed a certain tract of land to B Corporation for $35,000 cash and a promissory note in the amount of $150,000 payable in five equal installments. The IRS determined that the $35,000 was paid on behalf of taxpayer and therefore was a constructive dividend to taxpayer, who was the sole stockholder and manager of B. *Held:* For taxpayer. There was no constructive dividend to the sole stockholder of the corporation, since the end result of the purchase of real estate by the corporation from a third party resulted in no reduction in the value of the corporation. Blackmon, Jr., 68-2 USTC ¶ 9655, 22 AFTR2d 5860 (ND Tex. 1968).

Exchange of assets for preferred stock by controlled corporation was not a dividend to stockholders. Taxpayers, who owned the controlling interests in a domestic corporation and a Canadian corporation, caused the Canadian corporation to transfer all of its oper-

Dividends and Distributions: *Disguised and Constructive—Generally*

ating assets to a newly formed wholly owned Canadian subsidiary of the domestic corporation. In exchange for these assets, the Canadian corporation received preferred stock of the subsidiary as well as the assumption of its liabilities and cash. The IRS contended that the fair market value of the assets received by the subsidiary exceeded the value of the preferred stock transferred in exchange, and that such excess was a constructive dividend to taxpayers. *Held:* For taxpayers. The IRS' use of the capitalization of earnings method was deficient in this case. The domestic corporation supplied solicitation of export sales, corporate organization, research and development, advertising, and training for the Canadian corporation. The domestic corporation could also terminate a license for the right to use a trademark. This would diminish the purchase price that an unrelated purchaser would pay. Accordingly, no excess existed on the exchange and taxpayers did not receive a constructive dividend. Gray, 56 TC 1032 (1971).

Employment contract to selling stockholder not part of stock sale; no constructive dividend to remaining stockholder. A 50 percent stockholder of a corporation disagreed on management and was bought out by taxpayer, the other stockholder, in 1952. On the same day, the first stockholder entered into a five-year employment contract with the corporation. In 1952 and 1953 he performed some services but he performed no services in the last three years of the contract. The IRS argued that the payments for 1954, 1955, and 1956 were not deductible by the corporation but constructive dividends to taxpayer. *Held:* For taxpayer, in part. The court ruled that while the payments were not deductible, they were not constructive dividends to taxpayer. On the facts, the employment contract was not part of the purchase price for the stock. The contract was given to effectuate the other's removal as an officer, to compensate him for past service, and to prevent competition. The payments during the first two years of the contract compensated the recipient not only for the services rendered in those years but for services in prior years when he was underpaid. Therefore, the payments for 1954 through 1956 were not deductible as past compensation. Glasgow Village Dev. Corp., 36 TC 691 (1961), acq. 1962-1 CB 4.

Stockholders received dividend on sale by corporation. Taxpayer was a family corporation whose voting stock was owned entirely by S and his wife. S was the president and chairman of the board of directors of taxpayer. S conveyed certain real estate holdings to taxpayer but retained a lifetime lease for himself or his wife, whoever lived longer. Thereafter, he built a home on the leased property. Taxpayer sold the real estate to the U.S. government, subject to a reservation by the grantor for 30 years. On closing, the $262,500 purchase price was transferred to taxpayer, which paid S $99,347, an amount equal to 70 percent of the building costs of the house. At the time, taxpayer had accumulated earnings and profits in excess of $100,000. On its federal income tax return, taxpayer reported the amount realized on the sale as $150,653, which was calculated by subtracting the $99,347 paid to S and certain legal fees. The IRS disallowed the deduction on taxpayer's return and determined that S had received a dividend in the amount of $99,347. *Held*: For the IRS. The entire proceeds were realized gain and includible by taxpayer on its return because that portion of the proceeds attributable to S's leasehold was negligible, because of his age. Accordingly, S was not entitled to a portion of the proceeds; the payment to him was a dividend from taxpayer. Frank Spenger Co., 41 TCM 1210, ¶ 81,156 P-H Memo. TC (1981).

Dividend income from controlled development corporation. Taxpayer formed a corporation, D, to develop cooperative and condominium apartment complexes on land he owned. He leased to D all the land under the co-ops and the land under the condominium's recreational facilities. The land for the condominiums was sold to D. The leases were later assumed by the owners of the apartments. The IRS argued that the assumption of the lease obligations by the owners produced added income to D and a constructive dividend to taxpayer. The IRS also argued that the price received by taxpayer for the sale of the condominium land was a dividend. *Held*: For taxpayer, in part. The owners' assumption of the ground leases was not added consideration for the sale of their units and produced no dividend. But the sales proceeds for the land duplicated the rent received under the recreational lease, which was too high for the leased land alone, and the sales proceeds were dividends. Mangurian, 38 TCM 366, ¶ 79,091 P-H Memo. TC (1979).

Sale of land by stockholder not attributable to corporation and did not produce constructive dividend. In 1968, a corporation transferred land to its sole stockholder in exchange for other land. The deed from the corporation mistakenly omitted 82 acres that were intended to be part of the transfer. In 1973, when stockholder sold the land, corporation deeded the 82 acres to stockholder so that the buyer would have clear title. The IRS argued that the 82 acres were actually sold by the corporation in 1973 and the sale proceeds were a dividend to the stockholder. Held: For taxpayer. In 1968, stockholder assumed the benefits and the burdens of ownership of the 82 acres, including the payment of real estate taxes. The land was, in substance, owned by him. Cashion, Inc., 37 TCM 1847-96, ¶ 78,466 P-H Memo. TC (1978).

Amounts received as partial reimbursement for expenses paid by stockholder not dividends. Taxpayer shareholder paid corporate expenses and kept the rents he collected on the corporation's behalf. The IRS found that taxpayer realized dividend income from the corporation. Held: For taxpayer. Amounts collected as rents by taxpayer were reimbursements for advancements made to pay corporate expenses and were not dividends. However, expenses paid in excess of rents collected were not deductible. Klausner, 37 TCM 1688, ¶ 78,405 P-H Memo. TC (1978).

Increase in rentals paid by a corporation to a seller of stock were dividends. Taxpayer purchased the stock of Railroad Company from the Jenkins family for $500,000, represented by a note payable over a period of years, with the stock held as collateral. Prior to the sale the Jenkins family had a right as lessors of two locomotives to receive 7.5 cents for each ton of freight hauled by Railroad Company. Concurrent with the sale, the locomotive rental was increased by 5 cents, with the increase to be applied against taxpayer's note due the Jenkins family. Held: For the IRS. The amounts paid by Railroad Company which were credited by the Jenkins family against installments on taxpayer's note, represented dividend income to taxpayer. As the 5 cent portion of the locomotive rental was the device used to pay the Jenkins family for their stock, such payments could not be excluded from Railroad Company's income nor deducted by Railroad Company as additional locomotive rental. Lewis, 27 TCM 292, ¶ 68,056 P-H Memo. TC (1968).

Purchase of 50 percent stock interest by corporate joint venture not a constructive dividend to remaining stockholder. Taxpayer, an incorporated beauty salon, was owned equally by two stockholders. It agreed to transfer all of its assets to a joint venture in which it was to have a 50 percent interest, for a sales price of $40,000 to be paid by the other joint venturer. At the same time, one of its stockholders in a separate agreement agreed to purchase the other's stock interest for $30,000. In consummation of the transactions, the other joint venturer paid $10,000 directly to taxpayer and $30,000 to the selling stockholder for cancellation of her stock interest. The IRS held that taxpayer had a long-term gain of $40,000 and that the purchasing stockholder received a constructive dividend of $30,000 from taxpayer. Held: Taxpayer received a long-term gain on the sale of half the operating assets to the venture, no basis having been established for such assets. The purchasing stockholder, however, did not receive a constructive dividend. After the transaction was completed, she was no richer than she was before. Before the transaction she indirectly owned 50 percent of the assets of taxpayer through her 50 percent ownership. After the transaction she still owned indirectly 50 percent of the assets of the business because of the joint venture, although she was then owner of 100 percent of taxpayer. Estelle Wyler, Inc., 26 TCM 678, ¶ 67,147 P-H Memo. TC (1967).

DIVIDENDS AND DISTRIBUTIONS: *Distribution of Stock*

Payments in proportion to stockholdings were dividends. Under a plan formulated by his attorney, a successful physician assigned his office lease to a newly formed corporation of which he eventually became a 60 percent stockholder. The corporation also purchased his accounts receivable at a discount, as well as his office furniture and equipment. The physician then formed a medical partnership which paid the corporation a higher rent under the office lease and also rented from the corporation all the office furniture and equipment it had previously sold. The corporation made payments for services to each of its stockholders in proportion to their holdings. *Held*: The payments were dividends and therefore not deductible by the corporation. There was no proof that any amounts were due for services rendered. Medical & Professional Servs., Inc., 24 TCM 1211, ¶ 65,238 P-H Memo. TC (1965).

Payment for stock could not be disguised as deductible retirement pay. Three stockholders of a clothing business entered into a contract with their corporation calling for the sale of the stock by one of them to the remaining two stockholders. Under the same contract the corporation obligated itself to pay the selling stockholder and his son $20,000 as "retirement pay." The IRS argued that the payment was not a reasonable allowance for services actually rendered to the corporation but was realized by the selling stockholder for the sale of his stock to the other two. *Held*: For the IRS. Since the corporation paid the $20,000 out of earnings and profits on behalf of the two buying stockholders, the payment constituted a constructive dividend to them. Glenn-Minnich Clothing Co., 19 TCM 1131, ¶ 60,207 P-H Memo. TC (1960).

No constructive dividend when subsidiary purchases parent's stock. The IRS ruled that when a subsidiary purchases its parent's stock from the parent's sole stockholder, there is no constructive dividend to the parent. Rev. Rul. 69-261, 1969-1 CB 94, was modified to the extent that it held that the parent is in receipt of a constructive dividend pursuant to Section 304(b)(2)(B). Rev. Rul. 80-189, 1980-2 CB 106.

Money received in exchange of stock was a dividend. X owned the stock of A, which had accumulated earnings and profits. X transferred the A stock to newly created B Corporation in exchange for B stock and cash borrowed by B from a bank. A guaranteed B's repayment. Later, A transferred funds to B, which were then used to repay the loan. The IRS ruled that, in substance, B was a mere conduit for the passage of the cash dividend from A to X. Rev. Rul. 80-239, 1980-2 CB 103.

Subsidiary's purchase of parent's stock results in constructive dividend to both parent and stockholder. A wholly owned subsidiary purchased a portion of its parent's stock from the sole stockholder of the parent for cash. Section 304(b)(2)(B) provides that if a subsidiary corporation purchases outstanding stock of its parent the proceeds of such sale shall be considered first a distribution by the subsidiary to the parent corporation and then immediately thereafter a distribution by the parent in redemption of its own stock. Accordingly, the parent corporation received a constructive dividend even though no distribution was actually made to it. The sole stockholder received a dividend to the extent of the actual money received. Rev. Rul. 69-261, 1969-1 CB 94.

Distribution of Stock of Controlled Corporation

Transferor corporation continued in active business. The IRS contended that the distribution of stock of a newly formed corporation to the stockholders of the transferor corporation failed to meet the requirements of Section 355 because the transferor was not, immediately after the distribution, engaged in the auto business which it had conducted for more than five years prior to the distribution and there was no business purpose for such distribution. *Held*: For the taxpayer. Although transferor did not remain in the auto business after the distribution, the fact that transferor financed the transferee corporation's sales satisfied the continuity of business requirement under Section 355. The business reasons for the transaction were to add depth to management and promote permanence in employees by bringing in additional stockholders and to obtain a new franchise agreement with a different cancellation cause. The fact that the same purposes could have been obtained by another route was irrelevant. Hanson, 338 F. Supp. 602, 72-1 USTC ¶ 9171, 29 AFTR2d 72-514 (D. Mont. 1971).

Nonrecognition under Section 355 allowed where distribution and contribution had valid business reasons. As a result of a federal antitrust decree, P was required to divest itself of any interest in subsidiary S. P canceled a bona fide debt that S owed P in order to make S a more attractive investment and to expand its operations. Thereafter, P distributed all S stock pro rata to its stockholders. At the time of the cancellation of the debt, P anticipated that an unrelated corporation, Z, would merge into S under Section 368(a)(1)(A). There was no plan by P's stockholders at the time of the distribution to liquidate P or S; to redeem or dispose of their stock in either corporation; or to sell any of the assets of P or S, outside of the ordinary course of business. The nonrecognition provision of Section 355 applied to the receipt of S stock by P's stockholders. Where the distribution and debt cancellation were for valid business reasons, the transaction was not principally a device for the distribution of earnings and profits. Rev. Rul. 83-114, 1983-2 CB 67, revoking Rev. Rul. 58-68, 1958-1 CB 183.

Distribution qualifies under Section 355(b)(2)(D). The IRS ruled that a distribution by an acquired corporation of its shares in a wholly owned subsidiary corporation falls within Section 355(b)(2)(D); however, a distribution by the acquiring corporation of these shares to its stockholders does not. Rev. Rul. 74-5, 1974-1 CB 416.

Meeting active business test of Section 355(b). The active trade or business requirement is met where a holding company distributes, for valid business reasons, the shares of a subsidiary that operates a manufacturing business and owns all the shares of other corporations engaged in trade or business and that has as its only remaining asset shares of a nonactive business corporation which owns shares of other corporations actively doing business. Rev. Rul. 74-382, 1974-2 CB 120.

Active business requirements of Section 355(b) explained. A farm corporation satisfies the active business requirements of Section 355(b) even though some of its farming activities are performed by tenant farmers acting as independent agents if it performs substantial management and operational functions. Rev. Rul. 73-234, 1973-1 CB 180. Similarly, a construction contractor's performance of substantial management and operational activities, apart from those activities performed by subcontractor, satisfies the active business requirement of Section 355(b). Rev. Rul. 73-237, 1973-1 CB 184. Not so, however, for a trust that conducts its real estate leasing activities through independent contractors in accordance with the real estate investment trust provisions of Section 856. Rev. Rul. 73-236, 1973-1 CB 183.

Business purpose test of Section 355 was met when distribution was necessary to acquire another corporation. A corporation, engaged in the warehousing business, owned all the outstanding stock of a transportation business. A proposal was put forth in which the parent would merge with another warehousing company of equal size. However, the stockholders of the other corporation did not want a one-third interest in the parent, but an equal representation because of equal size. Therefore, it was necessary to distribute the stock of the transportation company to the stockholders of the parent corporation in order to permit a merger in which both companies would participate equally. The IRS ruled that the business purpose test of Regulation § 1.355-2(c) was met. Rev. Rul. 72-530, 1972-2 CB 212.

Diverted Funds

Diverted corporate funds were dividends to guilty stockholders. Taxpayers were the owners of five sixths of the stock of a corporation.

DIVIDENDS AND DISTRIBUTIONS: Earnings and Profits

In order to avoid the payment of taxes, they personally pocketed a substantial amount of the corporate income. They argued that this was an embezzlement, and the funds were, therefore, not taxable income. *Held:* For the IRS. The Tax Court held that taxpayers, as the entire board of directors, in effect, paid themselves a dividend. The court distinguished Wilcox, 327 US 404 (1945), which involved a mere salaried employee, and J.J. Dix, Inc., 223 F2d 436 (1955), where the diverting officer, although having the voting rights to and a life interest in one fourth of the stock, did not own any stock outright. Federbush, 34 TC 740 (1960).

Corporate funds diverted by sole stockholder constituted dividend. Taxpayers were a corporation and its sole stockholder. The corporation's unreported receipts were deposited in bank accounts under the stockholder's name. The stockholder withdrew funds from the corporation's bank accounts purportedly for repayment of loans, which did not actually exist. The stockholder did not file income tax returns. *Held:* For the IRS. The evidence supported the IRS' computation of the amount of unreported income. The funds the individual taxpayer fraudulently diverted from the corporation to avoid tax constituted dividends received. The repeated failure to report income justified imposition of additions to tax. Blue Creek Coal, Inc., 48 TCM 1504, ¶ 84,579 P-H Memo. TC (1984).

Dividends in Kind

Dividends in kind generate income to distributing corporation. The Tax Court held that a family corporation's distribution of dividends in kind, represented by bills of sale for quantities of navy beans, resulted in income to the corporation and its stockholders. The stockholders immediately sold back the property to the supplier at a higher price than the original open contract price. *Held:* Affirmed. The dividends in kind were primarily a tax-avoidance device and not distributed for any substantive business reason. Because the corporation participated sufficiently in the sale back to the supplier, profits should be attributed to the corporation. Bush Bros. & Co., 668 F2d 252, 82-1 USTC ¶ 9129, 49 AFTR2d 82-481 (6th Cir. 1982).

Distribution in kind by corporation treated as taxable gain. Taxpayer received the use of a house owned by a corporation, which also forgave a debt he owed it. The corporation had no earnings and profits allocable to the distributions. *Held:* For the IRS. Since taxpayer did not establish his basis in the stock, the entire distribution was capital gain. Robins, 39 TCM 470, ¶ 79,451 P-H Memo. TC (1979).

Earnings and Profits

Distribution fully taxable as a dividend. Taxpayer contended that a 1969 distribution from a controlled corporation was partially nontaxable as a return of capital pursuant to Section 301(c). The IRS and the Tax Court found that the distribution was a fully taxable dividend under Section 316(a). *Held:* Affirmed. A 1962 redemption of the interest of minority stockholders did not reduce earnings and profits, since it was paid from funds obtained by borrowing against the capital appreciation of a building owned by the corporation. The borrowing created a voluntary deficit, not an operating deficit that could offset future earnings and profits. Estate of Uris, 605 F2d 1258, 79-2 USTC ¶ 9547, 44 AFTR2d 79-5493 (2d Cir. 1979).

Distributions by reorganized corporation were taxable dividends where deficit was eliminated in reorganization. Taxpayer received distributions in 1956 and 1959 as a stockholder of a railway company that was completely reorganized by 1947. Pursuant to the reorganization, new stock and securities were issued to creditors of the railway company in satisfaction of their claims. The railway company reported aggregate net losses of upwards of $50 million during the 14-year period of reorganization (1933 through 1947), resulting in a sizable deficit prior to 1947. The distributions in 1956 and 1959 exceeded the corporation's earnings and profits for those years, but the corporation's post-1946 accumulated profits were in excess of the distributions. *Held:* The distributions were taxable as dividends, since the reorganization eliminated the pre-1947 deficit by discharging the corporation's outstanding liabilities, thus leaving the corporation with sufficient accumulated profits to cover the distributions. Banister, 236 F. Supp. 972, 65-1 USTC ¶ 9114, 15 AFTR2d 271 (ED Mo. 1964).

The "hypothetical dividend" of Section 304(b)(2)(B) is merely a mechanism to adjust earnings and profits and does not result in an intercorporate taxable dividend between the purchasing subsidiary and the issuing parent. Taxpayer owned all of TIDC's stock. TIDC redeemed taxpayer's stock from two of taxpayer's three principal stockholders. Under Section 304, this transaction was treated as a redemption by taxpayer of its own stock from such stockholders. As affected by Section 304, the redemptions were treated as sales by such stockholders under Section 302. The sole issue before the court was whether the "hypothetical dividend" prescribed by Section 304(b)(2)(B) should be treated as a taxable dividend. *Held:* For taxpayer. The "hypothetical dividend" section operates solely to adjust the redeeming corporation's (i.e., parent's) earnings and profits to determine the amount that is a dividend to the stockholder selling the parent's stock to the subsidiary. Virginia Materials Corp., 67 TC 372 (1976).

Entire dividend paid by reorganized railroad is ordinary income. Taxpayer received a dividend distribution of $11,500 from a railroad that had reorganized in bankruptcy. Taxpayer argued that since prior to reorganization the railroad had a large deficit, the portion of the dividend not out of current earnings was a return of capital. The IRS maintained that the reorganization wiped out the deficit. *Held:* For the IRS. The entire distribution was ordinary income. The payer corporation's deficit was eliminated when the bankruptcy court approved the recapitalization. Caspers, 44 TC 411 (1965).

Dividends on common stock (to corporate owner) reduced earnings; payments on preferred stock (to individuals) not taxable. Taxpayer was an individual preferred stockholder of a corporation, the common stock of which was owned practically 100 percent by a corporation. In 1946 a dividend on common stock had wiped out surplus, which had never been rebuilt. However the corporate parent had, following the receipt of the dividend, purchased additional common stock for an equivalent amount of cash. The corporation continued to pay dividends on the preferred. The IRS asserted the dividends were taxable in that the 1946 transaction was a mere wash. *Held:* For taxpayer. Although that common stock dividend might have contravened state law, it did reduce accumulated earnings and profits to zero. Consequently the distributions on the preferred were not dividends for tax purposes. Lundeen, 33 TC 19 (1959).

Distributions taxable even though current earnings were less than prior deficit. At the beginning of the year, a corporation had a deficit in its accumulated earnings and profits. The corporation distributed most of its current earnings and profits to taxpayer, its sole stockholder. Taxpayer contended that since the current earnings and profits were less than the accumulated deficit, the distribution was not taxable as a dividend. *Held:* For the IRS. The distributions were taxable dividends. They were less than current year's earnings and profits. The fact that there was a deficit at the beginning of the year larger than the distributions was immaterial. Mollath, 24 TCM 1621, ¶ 65,290 P-H Memo. TC (1965).

Dividend treatment given first to priority stock, then to other classes, where total distributions exceed available earnings and profits. During the taxable year, the subject corporation had outstanding common stock, prior preferred cumulative stock entitled under the corporate charter to dividends at the rate of $6 per share before the payment of any dividend on any other class, and cumulative convertible stock entitled to cumulative dividends at the rate of $2 per share. During the year the corporation made distributions on the prior preferred stock in the total amount of $6 per share and on the cumulative convertible stock in the total amount of $2 per share. The total amount distributed in 1968 was $35x$ but the corporation had earnings

DIVIDENDS AND DISTRIBUTIONS: *Excessive Salaries*

and profits for the taxable year of only $24x$ and had no accumulated earnings and profits. The earnings and profits of the corporation were sufficient to cover the dividend requirements on the prior preferred stock, and if applied first to the dividends on that stock, would leave earnings and profits to be applied to the dividends paid on the cumulative convertible stock equal to 12 percent of the amount distributed to holders of such stock. On the other hand, if the earnings and profits were prorated as to all the dividends paid, 68.57 percent of the amount received by the holders of each class of stock would be regarded as a distribution of earnings and profits and the remainder would constitute a distribution of capital. Applying Section 316, the IRS held that the earnings and profits must be regarded as having been first used for the payment of the dividends on the prior preferred stock as required by the charter of the corporation and the contract with the prior preferred stockholders, and only the earnings and profits remaining after such dividend requirements had been met could be regarded as having been paid to the junior stockholders. In other words, the earnings and profits of the corporation for the year must be regarded as having been distributed in accordance with the provisions of the corporate charter, giving the prior preferred stockholders the right to dividends before any earnings and profits can be distributed to the other stockholders. Rev. Rul. 69-440, 1969-2 CB 46.

Excessive Salaries

Fifty percent stockholder's salary was a constructive dividend. IRS determined that salaries paid by taxpayer corporation, a retail shop, for 1962 through 1964 to a 50 percent stockholder for alleged promotional services were nondeductible constructive dividends. The Tax Court agreed, on the basis of taxpayer's failure to prove that the value of the alleged services equaled the claimed compensation. Negligence penalties under Section 6653(a) were also imposed for failure of proof. *Held:* Affirmed. No employment relationship was established and all witnesses were financially interested in the outcome of the case. Alicia Ruth, Inc., 421 F2d 1393, 70-1 USTC ¶ 9185, 25 AFTR2d 70-481 (5th Cir. 1970).

Excessive compensation was dividend to president and sole stockholder. Taxpayer was the president and sole stockholder of eight corporations, each of which paid him a salary for his services. In addition to the salary, each corporation paid him a substantial bonus at the end of each year and certain of his travel and entertainment expenses. The IRS determined that the total compensation paid to taxpayer by each corporation was unreasonable and that the excess compensation and travel and entertainment expenses were dividends. *Held:* For the IRS. Although the taxpayer did perform substantial services over the years for each corporation, he did not run the day-to-day business of each and the total compensation paid him was clearly excessive. In addition, as none of the corporations ever paid dividends, the bonuses paid to the taxpayer more closely resembled a distribution of net profits than compensation. Accordingly, the excessive amount of compensation constituted dividends to the sole stockholder taxpayer. Bruce Oil Co., 47 TCM 1728, ¶ 84,230 P-H Memo. TC (1984).

Principal stockholder charged with dividend on excessive salaries paid to his sons. Each of two sons of the principal stockholder received from the corporation a monthly salary of $400, in addition to amounts designated as "officers' salaries" which ranged from $6,000 to $17,500. The sons paid over to their father a substantial portion of the amounts received as "officers' salaries," purportedly for the father's promise to transfer to the sons shares of stock in the corporation and other related businesses at some undisclosed future time. The IRS contended that the excess distribution over reasonable compensation for the sons constituted dividend income to the father. *Held:* For the IRS. The court noted that the corporation never declared a dividend: that the sons in fact received more for their services than their father, who had the full responsibility as manager of the entire operation and had more than 30 years of experience in the business; and that there was no

Dividends and Distributions: *Guarantor Fees*

written evidence that any enforceable rights to stock were ever acquired by the sons through the payments to the father. The substance of the transactions was that the surplus earnings found their way into the possession and control of the principal stockholder, as would a dividend. Quarrier Diner Inc., 22 TCM 276, ¶ 63,069 P-H Memo. TC (1963).

Guarantor Fees

Guarantor fee payments were dividends. The IRS determined and the lower court held that guarantor fee payments made by taxpayer corporation to its stockholders were not deductible because such payments were dividends. *Held:* Affirmed. The evidence indicated that the stockholders had signed the guarantees to protect and enhance their corporate investment. Furthermore, the corporation had never paid dividends, and the payments were in proportion to the stockholders' stock ownerships. Olton Feed Yard, Inc., 592 F2d 272, 79-1 USTC ¶ 9299, 43 AFTR2d 79-973 (5th Cir. 1979).

Dividend treatment accorded guarantee fees paid by taxpayer to stockholders in proportion to their stockholdings. Taxpayer was principally owned by 13 individuals. Taxpayer engaged in two businesses: feeding its customers' cattle and, when its pens were not filled to capacity, purchasing and feeding cattle for its own account. Taxpayer generally financed about 70 percent of the purchase of its cattle. To obtain financing for this purpose, its principal stockholders guaranteed loans to taxpayer in proportion to their stockholdings. In 1970, taxpayer's board voted to pay to each of its stockholder-guarantors a fee equal to 3 percent of the amount guaranteed by him. No evidence was presented to show that such fee bore any relationship to the risks involved with the guarantees. Until 1972, taxpayer had not declared a dividend. Taxpayer deducted the fees. The IRS treated the fees as dividend distributions. *Held:* For the IRS. In addition to the evidence, taxpayer failed to show that it is customary in the feedlot business to pay stockholder-guarantors a 3 percent guarantee fee or to show that such amount was reasonable. Tulia Feedlot, Inc., 513 F2d 800, 75-2 USTC ¶ 9522, 36 AFTR2d 75-5078 (5th Cir.), cert. denied, 423 US 947 (1975).

Court distinguishes *Tulia Feedlot I* and permits deduction of stockholder guarantee fees not paid in proportion to stockholdings. Taxpayer, in the course of operating a feedlot, purchased cattle for its own account. Lenders of the funds necessary to acquire the cattle required personal guarantees. The only persons willing to guarantee such loans were taxpayer's stockholders. These loan guarantees were not made in proportion to the stockholders' stock interests. The stockholders were paid annually a fee of 3 percent of the amount that remained open under their guarantees. The IRS asserted that taxpayer was not entitled to deduct these fees. *Held:* For taxpayer. Unlike Tulia Feedlot, Inc., 513 F2d 800 (5th Cir. 1975), taxpayer here showed that (1) guarantees were not made in proportion to the stockholders' interests; (2) unrelated parties would not have lent money to taxpayer without a guarantee; (3) no unrelated parties would guarantee loans to taxpayer; and (4) 3 to 5 percent guarantee fee was customary under the circumstances. Tulia Feedlot, Inc., 83-2 USTC ¶ 9516, 52 AFTR2d 83-5702 (Cl. Ct. 1983).

Intercorporate Transfers

Transfers between brother-sister corporations were constructive dividends. A corporation, in which one stockholder owned 74 percent of the stock, agreed to furnish whatever funds were necessary to keep in business another corporation, in which the same stockholder owned 43 percent. The IRS argued that the transfers were distributions by the first corporation to the stockholder, followed by contributions by him to the second corporation. *Held:* For the IRS. The test is (1) did the transfer cause funds to leave the transferor and allow stockholder to exercise control over them through an instrumentality other than the transferor, and (2) did the transferor objectively intend the primary benefit of the transfer to go to the stockholder? In this case both parts of the test were satisfied. Stinnett's Pontiac Serv. Inc., 730 F2d 634, 84-1 USTC ¶ 9406, 53 AFTR2d 84-1197 (11th Cir. 1984).

DIVIDENDS AND DISTRIBUTIONS: *Intercorporate Transfers*

Intercorporate transfer held a dividend to controlling stockholder. Taxpayer was the sole stockholder of *M* and *R*. *R* owned the building in which *M* operated its automobile sales business, and *M* was *R*'s sole tenant until its business ceased. Because of *M*'s financial situation, taxpayer advanced money to *M*. Taxpayer borrowed $60,000 from First National and endorsed it over to *M* in exchange for *M*'s 90-day note. *M* used the funds to pay First National monies due under individual notes executed on receipt by *M* for each automobile and truck in its inventory. *R* borrowed $100,000 from Clark County Bank and advanced $60,000 to *M* in exchange for *M*'s demand note; the amount was never repaid. In turn, *M* transferred the $60,000 to taxpayer to pay *M*'s debts to taxpayer, which taxpayer used to pay off his personal debt of $60,000 to First National. *R* advanced $33,000 to taxpayer in exchange for a demand note. Taxpayer repaid $1,000 of the amount in order that *R* could satisfy a tax assessment but made no other efforts to repay the advance. The Tax Court held for the IRS. *Held:* Affirmed. *R*'s transfer of $60,000 to *M* was merely an attempted device to enable taxpayer to extract $60,000 from *R* at no tax cost to taxpayer, in order to pay taxpayer's $60,000 obligation to First National. Therefore, the intercorporate transfer, being for taxpayer's benefit, was a constructive dividend to taxpayer. Second, the advance of money to taxpayer was not bona fide indebtedness, as taxpayer intended to repay it only at his convenience or if the corporation needed it, and the demand note contained no interest payment provision and was unsecured. Therefore, the advance was a constructive dividend to taxpayer. McLemore, 494 F2d 1350, 74-1 USTC ¶ 9411, 33 AFTR2d 74-1239 (6th Cir. 1974).

Jury finds payments by insurance company not to be dividends. Taxpayer, a credit corporation, received certain amounts of money from a life insurance company that taxpayer contended were intercorporate dividends entitled to a credit of 85 percent, pursuant to Section 243(a). The IRS determined the distributions to be a division of premiums subject to treatment as ordinary income. *Held:* For the IRS. A jury determined, based on the evidence presented, that the distributions in dispute were not dividends but in fact were a division of premiums with or commissions to taxpayer. Steadman Credit Co., 62-1 USTC ¶ 9396, 9 AFTR2d 1746 (WD Tex. 1962).

Transfers between related corporations not constructive dividends: Six corporations controlled by taxpayer filed separate petitions for arrangement under the Bankruptcy Act, and the proceedings were consolidated. The debtor corporations sold their assets to an unrelated party, and their assets, as well as the proceeds from the sale, were distributed to satisfy creditors' claims, including those claims personally guaranteed by taxpayer. The IRS determined that taxpayer had received constructive dividends from intercompany transfers regarding the proceeds from the sale of the assets of the corporations, and these proceeds were used to pay off the liabilities, some of which he had guaranteed. *Held:* For taxpayer. The intercompany transfers had a substantial business purpose, and any resulting benefit for the stockholder was merely incidental. Accordingly, he did not receive a constructive dividend. Schwartz, 69 TC 877 (1978).

No constructive dividend on intercorporate transfer. Taxpayer received a 75 percent interest in *A* Corporation under an agreement that provided that he would arrange a transfer of inventory to it from *B* Corporation, which he controlled. On the transfer, the inventory was not applied to reduce taxpayer's liability. Instead, he eventually paid cash for the obligation. The IRS claimed the inventory transfer was a constructive dividend to taxpayer from *B*. *Held:* For taxpayer. Despite the original arrangement, the inventory transfer did not reduce taxpayer's debt and thus did not benefit him. Siff, 41 TCM 587, ¶ 80,566 P-H Memo. TC (1980).

Taxpayers realized constructive dividends on transfers of corporate funds. Taxpayers, who controlled several corporations, were charged with constructive dividends on account of intercorporate transfers of funds. *Held:* For the IRS. The method was used to siphon the earnings of profitable entities into other entities to provide start-up capital or operating funds. There was no corporate business purpose for the transfers. Freidus, 39 TCM 740, ¶ 79,507 P-H Memo. TC (1979).

Intercorporate transfer of management fees held constructive dividends. Taxpayer, a controlling stockholder in A Corporation, caused a transfer of funds to B Corporation, of which he was president and one-third owner. The IRS determined that the amounts transferred were for the benefit of taxpayer stockholder and accordingly constituted constructive dividends. *Held:* For the IRS. Although the funds never passed through taxpayer's hands, he was in control of the transferor corporation. There was no valid business purpose for this transfer, and taxpayer benefited as both president and stockholder of floundering B Corporation. Carter, 36 TCM 1295, ¶ 77,322 P-H Memo. TC (1977).

Transfer of funds between controlled corporations was constructive dividend to stockholders. Taxpayer and Duncan each owned 50 percent of the stock of Westley, an operator of chartered vessels and a freight agent. In 1956 they formed two new foreign corporations, West Line and Guatemala Line. In 1957 a third corporation was formed, Caribbean Line, and West Line and Guatemala Line each subscriped to 50 percent of the stock ($60,000 total subscription). Westley then advanced $60,000 to Caribbean Line to enable the latter to purchase a ship. The IRS asserted that the $60,000 advance by Westley to Caribbean Line was a constructive dividend to taxpayer and Duncan, rather than a loan. *Held:* For the IRS. There was no record of West Line or Guatemala Line actually paying for or acquiring the stock of Caribbean Line. There was also a total lack of evidence that the advance was intended as a bona fide indebtedness. There was no indication that any note or instrument was executed, or that a repayment date was fixed, or that interest or security was provided for. Caribbean Line's sole capital came from Westley's $60,000 "advance" and since this discharged the $60,000 obligation of West Line and Guatemala Line to purchase the stock of Caribbean Line, constructive dividends inured to taxpayer. In substance, it was as if taxpayer withdrew the funds from Westley for investment in Caribbean Line. Since Westley had earnings and profits of only $38,000, the excess was capital gain. Aylsworth, 22 TCM 1111, ¶ 63,221 P-H Memo. TC (1963).

Life Insurance Premiums

Split-dollar insurance premiums paid by corporation were dividends. In 1970, a wife created a life insurance trust funded with policies that covered her husband's life. The policy was to benefit the wife, her son, and her grandchildren. In 1973 and 1974, X, a bank, 31 percent owned by taxpayers, purchased two split-dollar life insurance policies on the husband's life and paid the entire premiums on both policies. On the death of the husband, X was entitled to the cash surrender value of the policies, and the trust established by the wife was entitled to the remainder of the proceeds. Taxpayers reported no income from the payments of premiums by X, and IRS determined that taxpayers received dividends from the premium payments. *Held:* For the IRS. Taxpayers received economic benefit from the premium payments because they received the insurance portion of the policies, i.e., the portion of the policies' proceeds not payable to X. Even though X owned the policies, the premium payments were made on policies that were for the benefit of the taxpayers' family, and the fact that the proceeds were payable to an irrevocable trust made no difference. Johnson, 74 TC 1316 (1980).

Corporation's payment of insurance premiums resulted in constructive dividend. Under its supplemental group life insurance plan, a corporation paid the annual premiums on a $200,000 life insurance policy on its principal stockholder and executive officer, the decedent. The IRS claimed that the payment of the premiums by the corporation resulted in a constructive dividend taxable to decedent. *Held:* For the IRS. The premiums resulted in a constructive dividend because it was not shown that the payments were intended as compensation for the decedent's services. Furthermore, even if intended as compensation, it was not established that such compensation was reasonable. Estate of Worster, 47 TCM 1266, ¶ 84,123 P-H Memo. TC (1984).

Life insurance premiums on sole stockholder's life were constructive dividends. A corporation paid premiums on its sole stockholder's life insurance policies payable to his wife. The IRS disallowed a deduction for the premium payments. *Held:* For the IRS. Under the insurance agreement, the corporation was allowed to draw against the proceeds of the policies in order to maintain solvency. This beneficial interest was sufficient to bring the corporation within Section 264(a)(1).The payment of premiums did not constitute compensation to the stockholder because it was not established that the payments were intended as compensation. Because the expenditure conferred an economic benefit on the stockholder and did not further the corporation's interest, it therefore constituted a constructive distribution to the stockholder. Such a distribution was not excludable under Section 79, since it was not a group-term life insurance policy. Additions to tax pertaining to the distributions were also upheld. Brock, 35 TCM 1541, ¶ 82,335 P-H Memo. TC (1982).

Insurance proceeds paid by corporation constituted a distribution. A corporation owned two insurance policies on its sole stockholder's life. On his death, the proceeds were taken by taxpayer, who was his widow and corporate president, on her own account. As the corporation needed money, taxpayer repaid a portion of the proceeds. The IRS claimed that taxpayer received the funds as distributions from the corporation, not as a loan. *Held:* For the IRS, in part. The proceeds from only one of the policies were treated as a loan, i.e., recorded on the books as such and invested so as to be available for repayment. Estate of Lear, 42 TCM 667, ¶ 81,432 P-H Memo. TC (1981).

Value of split-dollar life insurance included in stockholder's income. Corporation procured a split-dollar life insurance policy for one of its principal stockholders and agreed to pay the premiums to the extent of the yearly increase in the case surrender value of the policy, with the stockholder paying the remainder. The stockholder's designated beneficiary would receive the proceeds less the premiums paid by the corporation. This arrangement constituted a distribution under Section 301(c), and the stockholder had to include in income the value of the insurance protection in excess of the premiums he paid. Rev. Rul. 79-50, 1979-2 CB 138.

Loans Distinguished

Loans to stockholders that produced business not a dividend. Taxpayer's wholly owned plumbing and heating corporation loaned money to taxpayer to help finance construction of buildings for his other businesses. The company loaned funds to related corporations and taxpayer's brother. The IRS asserted that all the loans were constructive dividends to taxpayer. *Held:* For taxpayer, in part. The loans to taxpayer resulted in business for the corporation and were bona fide, so they did not result in dividends. But the other loans served no corporate business purpose, and were thus dividends. Johnson, 652 F2d 615, 81-1 USTC ¶ 9414, 47 ATFR2d 81-1460 (6th Cir. 1981).

Corporate advances were loans and not constructive dividends. Taxpayer was a stockholder in a corporation that advanced him money. The advances were characterized as loans. The IRS contended that the advances were dividends. *Held:* For taxpayer. Money advanced to taxpayer for payment of interest on a bank note and for miscellaneous personal items was a loan. There were records, an expectation of repayment, and an account maintained to cover the amount of the loans. Simpson, 74-2 USTC ¶ 9722, 34 AFTR2d 74-5902 (ED Va. 1974).

Court acknowledged that stockholders' assignment of improved land to their corporation was merely a loan to enable the corporation to acquire a line of credit. Taxpayer and two other stockholders held equal interest in Cap-

Dividends and Distributions: *Loans Distinguished*

ital Lumber Co. Before the formation of Capital Lumber, taxpayer and his fellow stockholders improved real estate in an installment purchase in which the seller retained title until the last of the installments were paid. The land was leased to Capital Lumber, which assumed and paid as rent all payments due under the land sales contract. At the bank's suggestion, the land was assigned to Capital Lumber to enable it to obtain a line of credit. The Tax Court found that this assignment was merely a loan of the land for the purpose of obtaining a line of credit. When all installment payments had been made, the deed to the land was delivered to taxpayer and his fellow stockholders. They then renewed Capital Lumber's lease of the land. The IRS asserted that the assignment transferred ownership of the land to Capital Lumber, and thus the acceptance of the deed by its stockholders constituted a dividend to them. *Held:* Affirmed. The purpose and effect of assignment were to loan the land to Capital Lumber, and not to convey title. Therefore, the receipt of the deed was not a dividend. The court viewed as nondispositive the fact that the corporation's accountant treated, without the stockholders' knowledge, the corporation as owner of the land for tax and book purposes. Callner, 287 F2d 642, 61-1 USTC ¶ 9313, 7 AFTR2d 850 (7th Cir. 1961).

Loans to stockholders were not dividends. The IRS argued that loans a food supply corporation made to its president and his wife were constructive dividends. *Held:* For taxpayer. The payments were, in fact, loans. Taxpayers made partial repayments of the loans, which were evidenced by promissory notes. The amounts of the loans did not correspond to the corporation's earnings. Turner, 85-1 USTC ¶ 9440, 56-1 AFTR2d 85-5186 (D. Wyo. 1985).

Loan to stockholder not a dividend when he began to repay it in the same year. Taxpayer was the vice-president of a corporation and a 50 percent stockholder. In 1977, taxpayer withdrew over $14,000 from the corporation, with the approval of the other 50 percent stockholder. The books of the corporation reflected that the withdrawals were accounts receivable in the form of loans, and other financial statements for banks similarly noted the amounts. No promissory notes were executed. During 1977, $3,737 of the amount was repaid to the corporation, primarily through payroll deductions from taxpayer's salary. The IRS determined the amounts to be constructive dividends from the corporation to taxpayer. *Held:* For taxpayer. Because taxpayer needed the authority of the other 50 percent stockholder to obtain an advance from the corporation and had repaid over one fourth of the loan in the year he borrowed it, the advances were loans and not constructive dividends. Shea, 83-1 USTC ¶ 9115, 51 AFTR2d 83-658 (ND Ala. 1982).

Advances from sole stockholder to corporation pass muster as loans. Taxpayer made advances to *C* Corporation, of which he was sole stockholder. The corporation made regular interest payments and repaid part of the principal. The IRS considered the advances as equity investments and taxed the repayments as dividends. *Held:* For taxpayer. The advances were valid loans. The business had performed well enough before incorporation to make repayment a reasonable prospect. *C*'s failure to pay dividends did not change this conclusion. Culberson's, Inc., 79-2 USTC ¶ 9694, 45 AFTR2d 80-313 (ND Tex. 1979).

Jury finds that stockholder withdrawals were loans. Taxpayer stockholders withdrew funds from a corporation as loans. The IRS determined the withdrawals to be taxable dividends. *Held:* For taxpayers. The jury found the corporate payments to its stockholders to be valid loans and not taxable dividends. In so deciding, the jury was instructed to examine whether the withdrawals were evidenced by promissory notes executed in good faith with an intent to repay; the actual loan terms, the absence or presence of bona fide business purpose for the loans, and the corporate book treatment; whether the sums were repaid; the amount of surplus and accumulated earnings at the time of the loans; and whether the loans were proportional to the corporate stock holdings of the taxpayers. Soden, 63-1 USTC ¶ 9329, 11 AFTR2d 1004 (WD Mo. 1963).

DIVIDENDS AND DISTRIBUTIONS: *Loans Distinguished*

Loans between a corporation and a stockholder were not dividends. In the first of two separate transactions, taxpayer loaned cash to his wholly owned corporation. The loan was evidenced by a note and was fully repaid. Thereafter, taxpayer borrowed from his corporation. Evidence indicated that the transaction was a bona fide loan. The IRS determined the transaction to be a distribution of corporate profits. *Held:* For taxpayer. The court found that the transactions were honestly made and were bona fide loans; thus, dividend treatment was not imposed. Marsden, 62-1 USTC ¶ 9140, 9 AFTR2d 301 (DND 1961).

Advances to stockholder were loans, not dividends. Taxpayer, a 50 percent stockholder in a California corporation, withdrew monies in the form of loans, executing non-interest-bearing notes. Subsequently, taxpayer repaid some of the loans by transferring stockholdings in a branch corporation and conveying his residence to the corporation. Taxpayer's loans were substantially more than loans made to the other 50 percent stockholder of the company, and the corporation maintained a deficit surplus and subsequently filed a petition in bankruptcy. The IRS contended the withdrawals by the taxpayer represented dividends. *Held:* For taxpayer. The advances were bona fide loans because taxpayer always intended to repay the advances; the advances were recorded as accounts receivable and some of them were collateralized; and taxpayer made three substantial repayments by conveying property to the company. The loans made to taxpayer far exceeded the loans made to the other 50 percent stockholder and, therefore, there was no relationship between loans and capital investment. The corporation maintained a deficit in retained earnings. Pierce, 61 TC 424 (1974).

Bona fide loans not constructive dividend. Taxpayers' wholly owned companies made loans to a company owned by taxpayers and their children. Although the companies recorded the transfers as loans on their books, they did not record interest charges. The IRS determined that taxpayers received constructive dividends as a result of the transfers. *Held:* For taxpayers. The companies' directors intended that the transfers constitute bona fide loans. Furthermore, both creditor corporations benefited from the transfers. Although insufficient to explain contributions to captial, such benefits were sufficient to explain the short-term loans extended here. Allen, 49 TCM 677, ¶ 85,054 P-H Memo. TC (1985).

Distribution from taxpayer's wholly owned corporation was loan. Taxpayer had his wholly owned corporation distribute $20,000 to each of his two minor children. Each child signed an unsecured, non-interest-bearing promissory note for $20,000 payable to the corporation. Taxpayer then put the loan proceeds into CDs in trust for each child. The IRS contended that the distribution was a dividend to taxpayer. *Held:* For taxpayer, in part. The distribution was clearly a loan according to the form of the transaction and taxpayer's credible testimony regarding his intent to repay the loan. Furthermore, the CDs provided a means for repayment and collateral for the notes executed by the children. However, because taxpayer maintained complete control over the proceeds, the loans were made to him, and the interest earned thereon was taxable to him under the grantor trust rules. Parfrey, 47 TCM 689, ¶ 83,756 P-H Memo. TC (1983).

Advances to a related corporation not constructive dividends. Taxpayer's corporation loaned money to a corporation owned by taxpayer's children. The IRS argued that the amounts were constructive dividends to taxpayer. *Held:* For taxpayer. At the time the loan was made, there was a business reason for making the loan and a reasonable expectation that the second corporation would be profitable. Furthermore, any benefit accruing to taxpayer from the transfer of funds was too remote to suggest a dividend. Simmons, 46 TCM 458, ¶ 83,349 P-H Memo. TC (1983).

Loans to stockholder were not disguised dividend. Taxpayer purchased the stock of a corporation using funds provided by the corporation in the form of loans for which taxpayer

Dividends and Distributions: *Loans Distinguished*

gave one-year interest-bearing promissory notes. Before repayment came due, the corporation was liquidated. The canceled loans were treated as a liquidating distribution for which taxpayer claimed capital gain treatment. The IRS treated them as dividends to the extent of earnings and profits. *Held:* For taxpayer. The liquidation was due to business circumstances unforeseen at the time of the acquisition. Taxpayer presented credible evidence of his intent and ability to repay the loans. Baird, 43 TCM 1173, ¶ 82,220 P-H Memo. TC (1982).

Corporate transfers to stockholders owning 100 percent of stock were loans. Taxpayers, officers of a corporation and owners of all of its shares, received transfers from the corporation and executed non-interest-bearing unsecured demand notes. The Corporation did not pay any formal dividends to taxpayers, nor did taxpayers receive any compensation. Taxpayers treated the amounts transferred to them as loans. The IRS argued that the net transfers constituted dividend income to taxpayers. *Held:* For taxpayer. Taxpayers intended to repay all the transfers. Miller, 41 TCM 139, ¶ 80,445 P-H Memo. TC (1980).

Evidence favors taxpayer in the treatment of distributions as loans. Before 1973, taxpayer received money from and advanced money to various corporations in which he was the sole or substantial majority stockholder. All the advances were reflected as "loans" on the corporate books, and all financial statements prepared for book loans treated all advances other than salary as existing debts or assets. Taxpayer let his accountant set a fair and reasonable interest rate for each loan, and the corporations reported their interest income. The taxpayer received certain advances for the purchase of real estate that he could not repay because of conditions in the real estate market. The corporation holding the loan made no effort to collect the advances. The IRS determined the advances to be dividend income. *Held:* For taxpayer. Because the evidence clearly showed that taxpayer had requisite intent to repay advances at the time they were made, such advances were loans and not dividends. Faist, 40 TCM 1128, ¶ 80,354 P-H Memo. TC (1980).

Bona fide loan between controlled corporations was not a constructive dividend to taxpayers. Taxpayers, in control of one corporation, advanced funds from that corporation to another controlled corporation in the form of a loan, but the IRS claimed that the transfer was a constructive dividend to taxpayers. *Held:* For taxpayers. The transfers were loans. There was a reasonable expectation that the advance would be repaid with appropriate interest in a reasonable time. Payments of interest and principal had been made when due and other investors were willing to make the same loan. Taxpayers were not in receipt of constructive dividends. Stirling, 29 TCM 215, ¶ 70,049 P-H Memo. TC (1970).

Withdrawals from family corporations were loans. Taxpayers borrowed money from their controlled family corporations for current expenses and investments in anticipation of repaying from future income from the corporations. The IRS treated the withdrawals as the equivalent of dividend distributions. *Held:* For taxpayers. In analyzing the various objective manifestations of taxpayers' intent, the court noted the following: (1) the withdrawals were reflected as loans on the corporate books and all corporate statements; (2) interest-bearing notes were given with a specified maturity date, although they had been issued a number of years after the withdrawals had begun, and substantial interest was actually paid thereon; (3) although the annual net withdrawals varied greatly in amount, in some of the years preceding the IRS' investigation repayments exceeded the withdrawals. Withdrawals from a closely held corporation, carefully scrutinized, should not be considered the equivalent of dividends if the preponderance of the evidence establishes that the funds were intended to be repaid. Thus the form of the withdrawals or the intended use were not determinative and the corporation could be used as a private bank for the stockholder's benefit under the present statutory scheme without the withdrawals being invariably considered taxable dividends.

DIVIDENDS AND DISTRIBUTIONS: *Loans Distinguished*

Hoffman, 26 TCM 737, ¶ 67,158 P-H Memo. TC (1967).

Withdrawals from a controlled corporation were bona fide loans rather than dividends. Taxpayer was in the real estate business, which he operated through various corporations. During the taxable years in question, he was also the sole proprietor of two businesses that developed and sold an automatic garage door. Taxpayer arranged for a series of bank loans to one of his corporations, which he personally guaranteed, and then withdrew such funds to cover expenses incurred in his proprietorships. The IRS contended the withdrawals were taxable dividends to him, while taxpayer claimed the withdrawals were bona fide loans, which he fully intended to repay. *Held:* For taxpayer. Weight was given to the following factors: (1) the loans or receivables were so treated on the corporate books and financial statements; (2) the advances were evidenced by regular demand interest-bearing notes; (3) the intent to repay at the time of each withdrawal was evidenced by actual repayments during and after the years in issue; (4) taxpayer was a wealthy man who was able at any time to repay his borrowings and did in fact do so; (5) taxpayer personally guaranteed and collateralized the corporation's loans from the bank. Taxpayer was also allowed deductions for large losses from the operation of his two sole proprietorships. They were not hobby losses but viable businesses conducted for profit. Purdy, 26 TCM 409, ¶ 67,082 P-H Memo. TC (1967).

Withdrawals by corporate officer were loans for personal expenses, and not dividends. Taxpayer, president and minority stockholder of a closely held corporation, withdrew money from the corporation primarily for personal living expenses. The withdrawals were charged to a loan account, although no interest was ever paid on the withdrawals and no security given. Repayments were made but the withdrawal account was never reduced to zero. Dividends were declared and paid consistently to the stockholders and taxpayer was compensated at a level that would have allowed total repayment of the withdrawn amounts within a reasonable time. The IRS contended that the net withdrawals constituted taxable distributions of corporate funds to the officer who borrowed them. *Held:* For taxpayer. The net amounts withdrawn were intended as loans. The withdrawal account was consistently treated as an accounts receivable on the books and financial statements, and to secure a bank loan. Furthermore, taxpayer was not in a position to control corporate policy whereby he could have withdrawn corporate funds solely at his discretion. The withdrawals were loans, intended as such, and so recognized by all stockholders. Wentworth, 25 TCM 869, ¶ 66,167 P-H Memo. TC (1966).

Key executive's withdrawals from corporation were true loans. Taxpayer withdrew money from a newspaper publishing company in which he was the majority stockholder and its key executive. His principal reason for the withdrawals was to aid in the liquidation of an indebtedness orginally incurred to purchase the corporate stock. Taxpayer considered the withdrawals as loans, periodically made cash repayments, and applied his bonus and automobile expense allowance against the withdrawals. He also had a separate estate at all times from which the debt could be repaid, and in a later year, when requested by the corporation, gave the latter a note and mortgage to secure the unpaid balance. The IRS attempted to treat the net withdrawals as dividends. *Held:* For taxpayer. The amounts withdrawn were in fact loans at the time paid out, and not taxable dividends. Taxpayer made systematic repayments of the loans. He had a good reason for borrowing the money and maintained a separate estate from which the debt could be paid. Thistlethwaite, 25 TCM 193, ¶ 66,030 P-H Memo. TC (1966).

Advances from subsidiary to parent created bona fide debt; advances from the parent's stockholders did not. Advances by a wholly owned subsidiary to its parent corporation were alleged by the IRS to have been in fact dividend distributions. The IRS pointed to the facts that the parent did not execute any promissory notes, gave no security, and was not required to pay any interest on the advances. *Held:* For taxpayer, in part. The absence of notes, security, and interest did not destroy the fundamental character of the advances as genuine loans. It is not unusual for a corporation to lend money to its sole stockholder without demanding security, or interest, or notes. In view of the minutes and book entries of the subsidiary and parent, the consistently substantial dividend payments made by the subsidiary, the pattern of short-term advances made by the subsidiary to its parent, which consistently had been repaid, an obvious corporate purpose for the advances in issue, and the complete satisfaction thereof at a later date by the parent pursuant to a downstream merger, the court found that the advances represented bona fide loan obligations. However, advances to the parent by the common stockholders of the parent in proportion to their stock ownership, which were represented by subordinated 5 percent notes, were held to be equity investment. Purported interest accrued by the parent on such notes was not deductible. Edwards Motor Transit Co., 23 TCM 1968, ¶ 64,317 P-H Memo. TC (1964).

Withdrawals by husband from wife's corporation treated as loans. Taxpayer and his wife owned nine corporations which operated hotels and motels. The wife was sole owner of eight of these and taxpayer was sole owner of one. Taxpayer had accounts with several of his wife's corporations reflecting money and property withdrawals. These were recorded in the respective corporate books as accounts receivable. One of the wife's corporations had paid $800 of her travel expenses for a goodwill trip. The corporation also paid her club dues and furnished the husband with the use of an auto. The IRS contended that the advances and payments by the corporation were constructive dividends. *Held:* The club dues and $800 in travel expense were not made for the corporation's benefit and hence constituted a constructive dividend to the wife. However, no part of the auto expenses were considered as a constructive dividend, since the auto was used almost entirely in the operation of the corporate business. As to the withdrawals by the husband, the court found that they were bona fide loans. The husband was not a stockholder, he was permitted to make withdrawals only after he had established his own financial responsibility, his repayments on account were regular and substantial, and he testified convincingly concerning his intention of repayment. Roschuni, 23 TCM 1984, ¶ 64,321 P-H Memo. TC (1964).

Withdrawals from controlled corporations were recognized as loans, but bargain purchases and inflated sales were dividends. Taxpayer, the sole stockholder of several corporations, withdrew funds from his corporations. The books and financial statements treated the withdrawals as loans and interest was accrued on the principal amounts, but there was no security on the withdrawals. Taxpayer purchased five lots from one of his corporations for one third of their fair market value and later conveyed two of the lots to a second corporation in order to discharge a debt of greater value owed to the second corporation. The IRS determined that the withdrawals constituted dividends, not loans, and that the taxpayer had received dividends from his bargain purchases of the five lots and his later conveyance at inflated prices of two of the lots to discharge a debt. *Held:* For taxpayer, in part. Because the evidence indicated the withdrawals were treated as loans on corporate books and financial statements, they were in fact loans. The purchases by a controlling stockholder of property at a bargain price from his corporation and the later conveyance of two lots to discharge a debt of significantly more value were dividends to the stockholder. Binda, 22 TCM 1195, ¶ 63,236 P-H Memo. TC (1963).

Payments Benefiting Stockholders

Payments made from corporate bank account for stockholder's benefit were dividends. Taxpayers, a corporation and its stockholder, were assessed deficiencies. The IRS found that certain payments the corporation made to its sole stockholder, his wholly owned corporation, and other parties were dividends. *Held:* For the IRS, in part. Payments made from the corporation's bank account to satisfy the personal obligations of the stockholder and his sole proprietorships constituted constructive dividend income to the extent that the stockholder received economic benefit. The payment the corporation made to the stockholder's wholly owned corporation was also a dividend to the stockholder because there was no proof that it was for repayment of a loan. However, some of the payments were made for the corporation's expenses; those deductions were allowed. Amis, Jr., 49 TCM 281, ¶ 84,642 P-H Memo. TC (1984), appeal filed (11th Cir. 1985).

Payments by corporation to improve sole stockholder's land were dividends. Taxpayer, who owned all of the stock of X and Y Corporations purchased real estate in his own name; X and Y then used their funds to renovate the property. Later, taxpayer deeded the property to Y. The IRS determined that expenditures by X and Y were constructive dividends to taxpayer. *Held:* For the IRS, in part. Taxpayer treated the property as his own and was not a nominee for X or Y until he transferred the realty to Y. Corporate expenditures before the transfer were dividends, but payments made by Y after the transfer were not. Bihlmire, 38 TCM 68, ¶ 79,021 P-H Memo. TC (1979), aff'd (7th Cir. 1980).

Whether payment of stockholders' expenses was constructive dividend remanded for proper determination. The district court found that costs incurred by a corporation in improving its shareholders' land were taxable as dividends to the stockholders to the extent that they failed to reimburse the corporation for such costs. *Held:* Reversed. The holding was not based on appropriate findings, and, if such dividends were realized, they were improperly computed. Loftin & Woodward, Inc., 577 F2d 1206, 78-2 USTC ¶ 9645, 42 AFTR2d 78-5637 (5th Cir. 1978).

Constructive dividend determination upheld. The Tax Court upheld the IRS and found that taxpayer had received constructive dividends due to payments to or for the benefit of taxpayer by three solely owned corporations. *Held:* Affirmed. No evidence was presented to contradict the IRS' position. Linsker, 75-1 USTC ¶ 9225 (DC Cir. 1975).

Corporate costs of operating speedboats were income of controlling officer-stockholder. Taxpayer, a family corporation, was in the electrical contracting business and incurred expenses for maintaining and operating racing boats. Taxpayer deducted the expenses, alleging that the boats were used for advertising to promote business. The Tax Court held that the use of the corporate funds were nondeductible expenses and a dividend to the stockholder-president and his family. *Held:* Affirmed. Nondeductible advertising expenses were incurred by taxpayer in the operation and maintenance of racing boats. The funds expended were for the personal pleasure of the stockholder-president and his family and represented a constructive dividend to him. W.D. Gale, Inc., 297 F2d 270, 62-1 USTC ¶ 9168, 9 AFTR2d 344 (6th Cir. 1961).

Corporate improvements to lessor-stockholder's property a dividend. J was the president and majority stockholder of taxpayer, a motor car company. Taxpayer leased J's property and made and paid for various improvements on it. The parties had a 30-day notice agreement whereby J could take possession of the property at any time, including the improvements. No dividends were paid by taxpayer, although it had substantial earnings. J formed a finance corporation for selling taxpayer's autos. The finance company accrued the interest payable on obligations to J. J and other employees of taxpayer sold insurance policies and assigned the commission rights to taxpayer and J. Under state law, the corporation could not sell the insurance directly. The Tax Court held that the improvements paid for by taxpayer constituted dividend income to J; the accrued interest was constructively received by J; and there was an anticipatory assignment of income to taxpayer and the finance company by J from the insurance sales. *Held:* Affirmed. The improvements constituted dividends, although the disbursement was not proportional to the stockholders' holdings. The insurance commissions were taxable to the stockholder, even though he made an anticipatory transfer of income to the corporations, which could not, under state law, act as insurance agents. Evidence supported the Tax Court's finding that the accrued interest was constructively received from the finance company by the stockholders. Jaeger Motor Car Co., 284 F2d 127, 60-2 USTC ¶ 9793, 6 AFTR2d 5874 (7th Cir.), cert. denied, 365 US 860 (1960).

Fee to analyze feasibility of public offering was not for benefit of majority stockholder. Taxpayer, who was chief executive and majority stockholder of a corporation, was contemplating retirement. He engaged a financial consultant to study the feasibility of a public offering. The study indicated that a public offering was not immediately feasible. A short time later, the stock was sold in a private transaction. The IRS contended that the study was for taxpayer's benefit and that the corporate payment for the study was income to him. *Held:* For taxpayer. The cost of the study, paid by the corporation, was not taxable to taxpayer. Other stockholders and employees benefited from the study. The IRS also contended that the gain on the sale of the stock was taxable to taxpayer, even though he had given the stock to his charitable foundation before the sale. This contention was rejected. At the time of the gift, the sale had been negotiated but not completed. Martin, 251 F. Supp. 381, 66-1 USTC ¶ 9338 (D. Md. 1966).

Improvements to taxpayer's property by controlled corporation resulted in constructive dividend. Taxpayer, his son, and Gateway, a controlled corporation, owned certain real property adjacent to a shipyard owned by Gibbs. Taxpayer had been one of the organizers of Gibbs and had transferred most of his Gibbs stock to his family, making his son the principal stockholder. To induce Erie, an unrelated corporation, to become a long-term tenant of the real property, extensive alterations and improvements to the property were made. Gibbs paid for these improvements, which cost $345,000. The initial rents under the lease were not paid to Gibbs. However, when it became apparent that Erie would not be able to carry out its obligations as tenant, Gibbs' records were charged retroactively to show that the landowners had contracted to repay the $345,000 to Gibbs only out of the rents paid by Erie. *Held:* For the IRS. Taxpayer received a constructive dividend to the extent of one third of $345,000. There was no intention to repay the monies expended by Gibbs. Even if there had been, the cancellation of the debt brought about a dividend. An abandonment loss for the improvements was also denied for failure to prove worthlessness and actual abandonment. A negligence penalty, but not a fraud penalty, was upheld. Gibbs, 64-2 USTC ¶ 9672, 14 AFTR2d 5374 (MD Fla. 1964).

Boat expenses incurred by corporation not income to controlling stockholder. Taxpayer owned a controlling interest in a corporate automobile dealership that acquired and used two motorboats for entertaining customers and prospective customers. The corporation paid for the maintenance of the boats: primarily salaries, insurance, major repairs, and depreciation. Taxpayer himself paid for all fuel, food, refreshments, and minor repairs to the boats. Less than 10 percent of the use of the boats was by taxpayer and his family; over 90 percent of the use of the boats was in furtherance of the business of the corporation. *Held:* For taxpayer. The court found that the expenses incurred by the corporation in maintaining the boats were not income to the controlling stockholder. Gottlieb, 61-2 USTC ¶ 9638 (ED La. 1961).

Corporation's assumption of principal stockholder's buy-out obligation did not result in a dividend to stockholder when the value of the property received under the budget was greater than the amount paid for such property. Taxpayer entered into a buy-out arrangement with his fellow stockholder in X Corporation. Under the buy-out agreement, the shares of X were to be purchased from the deceased stockholder's estate for an amount not in excess of $200,000. When his fellow stockholder died, his shares of X stock were worth more than $200,000. Taxpayer caused his wholly owned Y Corporation to purchase the X stock from the estate. The IRS asserted that Y's satisfaction of taxpayer's obligation

Dividends and Distributions: *Payments Benefiting Stockholders*

under the buy-out agreement constituted a dividend to him in the amount equal to the price of the stock. *Held:* For taxpayer. A dividend necessitates a distribution of corporate earnings measured by the corresponding reduction to the corporation's net worth. Here, Y received property worth more than the amount it paid. Accordingly, there was no dividend. Citizens Bank & Trust Co., 580 F2d 442, 78-2 USTC ¶ 9568, 42 AFTR2d 78-5429 (Ct. Cl. 1978).

Value of work performed by a corporation on stockholders' properties was dividend income to them. Taxpayer formed two corporations to carry out its electrical contracting business. Taxpayer and his wife were the president and sole stockholder of the two corporations. Taxpayer had several separate developments, which he conducted either by himself or with partners. In order to complete the buildings he was constructing on land he owned, taxpayer entered an agreement with one of his corporations to have it do the electrical contracting work on the structures. On all these jobs, taxpayer acted as a general contractor and personally supervised the corporation's work. Under the agreement, taxpayer was obligated to pay the corporation's overhead and direct construction costs on work done. The corporation performed work for taxpayer in 1970 and 1971, but no payments were made during the years in which the costs were incurred. In the years following, taxpayer did make payments, but the record was unclear as to how and when the amounts were repaid. The corporation deducted all of the job costs spent on taxpayer's projects as ordinary and necessary business expenses on its tax return for the year ended April 30, 1971 and as part of an adjustment to earnings on the corporate income tax return ended April 30, 1972. The IRS asserted deficiencies, contending that taxpayers had received constructive dividends for the work completed on the property in 1970 and 1971. *Held:* For the IRS. Because the corporation conferred an economic benefit on a stockholder without the expectation of repayment, that benefit became a constructive dividend, taxable to the stockholder. Lack of intent to repay was evidenced by the failure to make repayments during the years that those job costs were incurred or when the work was completed. Evidence such as the corporation's accounting entries on costs indicated that the corporation did not expect repayment in the year of the work and, furthermore, that the corporation did not intend to take steps to enforce payment at that time. Magnon, 73 TC 980 (1980), acq. 1981-1 CB 1.

No constructive dividend to common sole stockholder of two corporations based on extension of credit between the corporations where no direct or tangible benefit resulted to stockholder. A, an individual, owned all of the stock of X and Y corporations. X manufactured electrical parts, and Y supplied X with housings for those parts. Y was formed to be X's supplier. During the years involved, X accounted for approximately 90 percent of Y's business. Y set up accounts receivable for housings sold to X in the same manner as with its unrelated customers. However, X paid these receivables both with cash and the raw materials it purchased from which Y made its housings. X developed financial difficulties and paid Y whatever it could without jeopardizing its business and financial position. Between 1964 and 1969, the opening accounts receivable balance due to Y rose from approximately $185,000 to $740,000. No notes were given by X to Y with respect to these balances. The additional capital that became available to X from this extension of credit was principally used to build up its inventory. During the years involved, Y had accumulated and current earnings. Neither corporation paid any dividends, made use of or disposed of their individual capital, assets or profits in a way that was unrelated to their businesses. The IRS asserted that the net increases in Y's accounts receivable from X were constructive dividends to A. *Held:* For taxpayer. Net increases were not, under facts, made primarily for conferring a direct or tangible benefit to A. Rapid Elec. Co., 61 TC 232 (1973).

No constructive dividend where controlled corporations built 40-year buildings on land leased for 12 years from stockholder. Taxpayer bought two pieces of land and leased them to controlled corporations for 12 years. The corporations then constructed factory buildings that had useful lives of 40 years on the land. The IRS first assessed taxpayer for the total cost of the improvements but later abandoned this because of Section 109. The IRS then claimed that, because the transactions were not bona fide and taxpayer obtained a substantial economic benefit, taxpayer was taxable on constructive dividends. *Held:* For taxpayer. The Tax Court disagreed with the IRS and found from the evidence that the corporations were bona fide business entities and that if the transactions had been with strangers, there would not have been substantially different results. While it was conceded that taxpayer received economic benefit from the corporate expenditures, this did not result in the realization of gain within the meaning of the law. Bardes, 37 TC 1134 (1962), nonacq. 1964-1 CB 6.

Transfers to Swiss bank account were constructive dividends. Taxpayers controlled two corporations. After receiving money from the first corporation for labor and materials, the second corporation routinely remitted part of it to the contractor as payment for the labor. The second corporation would then pay a Swiss entity the balance. The entity, after deducting a certain percentage as compensation for participation in the transaction would deposit the balance in a Swiss bank account controlled by the taxpayers. The IRS determined that the amount in the account was a constructive dividend to IRS taxpayers. *Held:* For the IRS. Taxpayers controlled the amount and accumulation in the account for their personal benefit, not for the corporations'. Rosenbaum, 45 TCM 825, ¶ 83,113 P-H Memo. TC (1983).

Building erected by corporation on stockholder's land was dividend. A corporation erected a warehouse on its sole stockholder's property. The corporation did not have a lease on the land and did not use the warehouse. The IRS determined that this resulted in a dividend. *Held:* For the IRS. There was no arm's-length agreement concerning the corporation's use of the warehouse. The corporation's cost in constructing the warehouse was a Section 301 distribution. Cash & Lincoln Fence, 44 TCM 110, ¶ 82,331 P-H Memo. TC (1982).

Reimbursed airfares constructive dividends Taxpayer was reimbursed for several round-trip airfares during the winter from Florida to Wisconsin by his 85 percent owned corporation. *Held:* For the IRS. The airfares were personal commuting expenses. The reimbursements were constructive dividends from the corporation. Munson, 40 TCM 173, ¶ 80,121 P-H Memo. TC (1980).

Payment of medical expenses by corporation to sole stockholder was constructive dividend. Taxpayer's medical expenses were paid by a professional corporation of which he was the president and sole shareholder. Taxpayer contended the amounts were excludable from gross income under Section 105. *Held:* For the IRS. Even if the expenses were made pursuant to a plan, the purpose of the plan was to benefit the taxpayer as stockholder and not as employee. Accordingly, the payments constituted a constructive dividend and were includable in income. Kennedy, 36 TCM 878, ¶ 77,210 P-H Memo. TC (1977).

Payment of controlling stockholder's expenses were dividends. Taxpayer was reimbursed by his controlled corporation for travel, entertainment, and club expenses. He kept no record of these expenses and did not submit itemized statements to the corporation. The corporation also deducted depreciation and paid and deducted maintenance costs of three residences rented to taxpayer's family. It also transferred to the stockholders at a bargain price certain land that it was obligated to sell to an optionee at a fixed price so as to enable the stockholders to make the sale. *Held:* For the IRS. In the absence of any evidence to the contrary, the IRS's disallowance of about 75 percent of the claimed travel, entertainment, and club expenses had to stand, and these disallowed amounts were constructive dividends to the stockholder. Similarly, the excess of the maintenance and depreciation deductions on the residences over the rents received were not deductible and were constructive dividends to the stockholder.

Dividends and Distributions: *Payments to Stockholders' Beneficiaries*

Finally, the gain on the sale of the land was attributable to the corporation. Riss & Co., 23 TCM 1113, ¶ 64,190 P-H Memo. TC (1964).

Corporation's payments on behalf of sole stockholder dividends. Taxpayer was the president and sole stockholder of a corporation. During 1957 and 1958, the corporation made payments of premiums totaling over $13,000 on taxpayer's personal life insurance policies. These premium payments were not charged to the officer's loans receivable account. In 1959, after an audit by the corporation's accountants, a transfer entry was made as of October 31, 1959 placing the total of the premium payments to taxpayer's loan account. The IRS contended that the payments constituted dividends to taxpayer. *Held:* For the IRS. The insurance premium payments were dividends to taxpayer. The corporate records failed to indicate that at the time of the corporate payments for taxpayer's benefit, there was any intent by taxpayer to repay such sums. The court also held that payment by the corporation of taxpayer's indebtedness to a former stockholder likewise constituted a dividend distribution. Schwartz, 22 TCM 1786, ¶ 63,340 P-H Memo. TC (1963).

Corporate purchase of yacht for principal stockholder a dividend. The purchase by a corporation, with corporate funds, of a yacht for the use of its principal stockholder, title to which was taken in the stockholder's name, was determined by the IRS to result in the payment of a dividend to him. *Held:* For the IRS. The court also denied the corporation a depreciation deduction, even though the yacht was shown on the corporate books as an asset. The corporation was, however, permitted a deduction for a portion of the amounts expended in operating the yacht on the grounds that it was used sometimes for business entertainment. The disallowed portion of the expenses was considered a dividend to the stockholder. Von Hessert, 20 TCM 1119, ¶ 61,226 P-H Memo. TC (1961).

Corporate payments of stockholders' liabilities treated as constructive dividends. After agreeing to buy out a 50 percent stockholder for $45,000, taxpayer had the corporation pay $10,000 of the stipulated price purportedly for an assignment to it of a lease held by the selling stockholder. *Held:* For the IRS. The court found that the lease had little or no value, and the parties in fact assigned no value to the lease in their bargaining. Accordingly, the payment of $10,000 by the corporation was part of the consideration of taxpayer's purchase of the other stockholder's shares and constituted a constructive dividend. Taxpayer had borrowed funds, evidenced by notes, with which to make his payments. The corporate repayment of such loans was also held to constitute a constructive dividend to the extent of the principal and interest paid. Taxpayer's contention that the corporation made an investment rather than paid a dividend when it paid off taxpayer's notes was found not to conform to the intent as evidenced by the corporate charge of the payments to taxpayer's personal account. Berlin, 20 TCM 969, ¶ 61,194 P-H Memo. TC (1961).

Payments to Stockholders' Beneficiaries

Disallowed corporate payments were constructive dividend. The district court held that payments made by taxpayer's wholly owned corporation to taxpayer's sister-in-law were not deductible by the corporation as an ordinary and necessary business expense but were not a constructive dividend. *Held:* Reversed. The lower court's disallowance of the deduction of the payments as an ordinary and necessary business expense conclusively established that they served no conceivable corporate purpose. Absent such justification, the court found the payments to be constructive dividends that were paid at taxpayer's direction to a relation by marriage for reasons wholly personal to taxpayer. Hardin, 461 F2d 865, 72-1 USTC ¶ 9464, 29 AFTR2d 72-1446 (5th Cir. 1972).

Pension payments by family corporation to widow of stockholder officer treated as dividends. A family corporation voted to pay the widow of its officer-stockholder $200 per month for the remainder of her life as pension payments for the past services of her de-

Dividends and Distributions: *Payments to Stockholders' Beneficiaries*

ceased husband. The corporation sought to deduct the pension payments as a business expense. The IRS disallowed the deductions and contended that the payments were dividends. *Held:* For the IRS. The corporation had in fact no pension or death benefit plan for such payments to widows of deceased employees. It had never declared a dividend throughout its corporate existence, and the widow had at no time performed any services for the corporation. The court ruled that no deduction was available to the corporation for the "pension" payments and that they were dividends. Schner-Block Co., 329 F2d 875, 64-1 USTC ¶ 9363 (2d Cir. 1964).

Pension to widow to discourage stock sale a dividend. A stockholders' agreement among family members provided that, if any of them died, the remaining stockholders would cause the corporation to pay the surviving widow a pension, but only as long as she held the stock. The Tax Court found the amounts paid under the agreement to represent a corporate distribution of profit, and as such were taxable to the widow and were not deductible by the corporation. The fact that the corporation was not a party to the agreement and that the carrying out of its provisions was procured by the stockholder who wanted the stock to remain in the family was considered by the Tax Court as negating any intent to make a gift or pay a pension. *Held:* Affirmed. If payment was for the purpose of assuring control over the stock, then this payment was not a deductible business expense. Standard Asbestos Mfg. & Insulating Co., 276 F2d 289, 60-1 USTC ¶ 9370 (8th Cir. 1960), cert. denied, 364 US 826 (1960).

Constructive dividend received by majority stockholder who waived dividend payment for himself and increased dividend was payment to children. Fifty percent of the stock of *B* was owned by taxpayer, 11 percent by taxpayer's second wife, and 11 percent by his sister. Twenty percent was set up as a trust for the children of his first marriage, and 8 percent to the four children of his second marriage. *B* paid a dividend to all its stockholders except for taxpayer and his wife, who waived their dividends. The IRS contended that taxpayer received a constructive dividend equal to 50 percent of the total dividend. *Held:* For the IRS. Even though taxpayer received no economic benefit from the distribution, he did receive a constructive dividend. In essence, taxpayer's share of the dividends was given as a gift to his children and sister. Bagley, 348 F. Supp. 418, 72-2 USTC ¶ 9518 (DSD 1972).

Payments to stockholder's sister dividends to stockholder. A husband and wife owned nearly all the stock of taxpayer, a corporation engaged in the paper business. The wife was an officer and was familiar with the paper industry and taxpayer's customers. She entertained the wives of customers, arranged for gifts to customers, and spent about 25 hours a week on corporate business. The husband's sister, who lived out of state, was claimed to be used as a contact to expedite orders from suppliers. The corporation sought to deduct payments made to both women as ordinary and necessary business expenses. The IRS determined that the payments were dividends. *Held:* For taxpayer, in part. The court found that the payments to the wife officer were deductible business expenses, but the amounts paid to the husband's sister were dividends to the husband and wife, and thus not deductible by the corporation. Duffey, 63-1 USTC ¶ 9442 (D. Minn. 1963).

Payments to children of deceased director were dividends. A corporation, after the death of its founder, voted that payments be made to the founder's five surviving children, who were also the beneficial owners of all the corporate stock. Payment to the children was continued for about two and a half years after the death of their father. The corporation sought to deduct the amounts paid as business expenses. *Held:* For the IRS. The court denied the deduction. The payments were dividends, notwithstanding that the amounts were not pro rata to the stock holdings. Nickerson Lumber Co., 214 F. Supp. 87, 63-1 USTC ¶ 9316, 11 AFTR2d 1094 (D. Mass. 1963).

Constructive dividend found when controlling stockholder's family members were benefited. Taxpayers were a corporation and its control-

DIVIDENDS AND DISTRIBUTIONS: *Payments to Stockholders' Beneficiaries*

ling stockholder. The corporation received income in the year goods were sold by a third party acting as its agent, although it did not receive the proceeds until the following year. The IRS determined that the corporation had unreported income and that the individual taxpayer had received a constructive dividend. *Held:* For the IRS. Since the individual taxpayer controlled the corporation and his children benefited from the transactions involving the corporation, he received a constructive dividend. P.R. Farms, Inc., ¶ 84,549 P-H Memo. TC (1984).

Payments by family corporation to or for benefit of controlling stockholder were dividend income. Taxpayer was the president and principal stockholder of a family-owned trucking company and also had interests in other family businesses. In 1956, he organized a corporation, Auto, with a friend, Wills, for the sale of auto and truck parts. They purchased a racing car for $12,000, and financed the purchase with funds paid by the trucking company to Auto on fictitious invoices. The IRS determined that the payments made by the trucking company to Auto were dividends to the taxpayer. *Held:* For the IRS. Taxpayer realized income to the extent of the money advanced to Auto for the racing car operations. The car racing constituted a personal interest and hobby of taxpayer, and the payments were for taxpayer's personal benefit except to the limited extent that the trucking company could show it derived some advertising benefits from its name displayed on the racing car. Hoover, 27 TCM 226, ¶ 68,049 P-H Memo. TC (1968).

Death-payments to stockholders' widows were dividends. Taxpayer, since its inception, was owned and controlled by four related family groups. As each of the three original founders died, the corporation began monthly payments of $370 to the stockholder widows. One widow had been receiving benefits for over 30 years, another for over 20 years, and a third for a much shorter time. There was no evidence that the payments were made pursuant to any contractual obligation or established plan for payment to families of deceased employees. The widows argued that the payments were excludable gifts and that if the payments were found to be compensatory and taxable to them, they should be deductible by the corporation. *Held:* For the IRS. The payments constituted dividends; thus, they were taxable income to the recipients and not deductible by the corporation. The corporate resolution made no reference to past services, and there was no evidence that the payments reflected any reasonable benefit to the corporation. The payments could not be considered gifts, as the chief executive officer was unfamiliar with the financial needs of each of the three widows and continued the same payments to each for indefinite periods. Furthermore, the fact that the payments were originally recorded on the corporate books in a loan account negated any donative intent. Jordano's, Inc., 25 TCM 1127, ¶ 66,218 P-H Memo. TC (1966).

Corporate advances for controlling stockholder's personal benefit were constructive dividends, although indirectly made through a related corporation. Taxpayer controlled X Corporation, and his father controlled Y Corporation. Both companies were in the business of renting real estate. X Corporation borrowed funds on a mortgage and then used such funds for the construction of a personal residence for taxpayer, title to which was taken in Y. Taxpayer moved into the house in 1954, but no lease was entered into between taxpayer and Y until two years later. Taxpayer contended that he personally received no money from X in 1954 that could constitute a dividend, since the funds were actually advances to Y, which constructed and held title to his house. Y's books, however, did not show any account due or other evidence of indebtedness to X until some time after 1956. The IRS argued that the advances were dividends. *Held:* For the IRS. On the facts, the court found no business season for the arrangement other than to accommodate taxpayer, who planned to occupy the house to be built by Y. Irrespective of the fact that Y held title to the house, the payments made by X were for taxpayer's personal benefit and constituted dividends to him to the extent of X's earnings and profits. Greenthal, 21 TCM 659, ¶ 62,126 P-H Memo. TC (1962).

Dividends and Distributions: *Satisfaction of Stockholder Obligations*

Satisfaction of Stockholder Obligations

Corporation's payment of stockholder's tax liability nondeductible and a constructive dividend. Stockholders of an S corporation, pursuant to the corporate accountant's advice, did not include certain corporate distributions in their taxable income. The IRS determined a deficiency that the corporation paid to settle the stockholders' claim of misrepresentation arising out of the erroneous tax advice. The Tax Court held these payments to be nondeductible to the corporation and a constructive dividend to the stockholders. *Held:* Affirmed. There was no evidence that the corporation's payments were necessary, as nothing suggested that the corporation reasonably believed in the potential merits of a misrepresentation claim. As an unnecessary expenditure of corporate funds, the payments were constructive dividends. Inland Asphalt Co., 756 F2d 1425, 85-1 USTC ¶ 9293, 55 AFTR2d 85-1264 (9th Cir. 1985).

Divorce decree ordering corporation to redeem shares does not give rise to constructive dividend. Taxpayer and his wife in a community property state, owned 100 percent of a close corporation. The couple subsequently divorced. The interlocutory judgment provided that taxpayer buy out his wife's shares in the corporation. This judgment was subsequently modified to require the corporation to redeem the shares. The court ruled that taxpayer's obligation under the interlocutory judgment was void. The IRS contended that the corporation's payment for the stock was a constructive dividend to taxpayer. *Held:* For taxpayer. No constructive dividend existed because the modified divorce decree imposed no obligation on taxpayer. Edler, Jr., 727 F2d 857, 84-1 USTC ¶ 9285, 53 AFTR2d 84-916 (9th Cir. 1984).

Repayment of stockholder's loan was a dividend. Taxpayer secured a loan from a creditor through his brother to purchase an automobile operation. He agreed to pay the said note when it became due in shares of stock of the automobile business once the agency commenced business and the book value of the shares determined. There was also an accompanying promissory note that was made out to taxpayer's brother and immediately assigned to a third party. On its corporate income tax return, taxpayer treated the amount paid to the creditor as a purchase of treasury stock. Taxpayer and his wife, as employees of their corporation, were furnished with automobiles for the year. The Tax Court, agreeing with the IRS, determined that taxpayer, as the controlling stockholder of the corporation, (1) had a constructive dividend when the dealership corporation paid the debt to the creditor and that (2) it was not redeeming the creditor's interests as a stockholder, as the preincorporation agreement did not refer to stock subscriptions, was not ratified by the corporation, and said that the payment was a loan to the stockholder. Similarly, the personal use of the dealership corporation's demonstrator car was a constructive dividend. *Held:* Affirmed. The creditor advanced funds so that taxpayer could buy into a dealership. The creditor also considered the stockholder personally liable to him. Thus, repayment by the corporation was a constructive dividend. Personal use of a corporate automobile was not incidental to the business and therefore represented a constructive dividend. Gardner, 613 F2d 160, 80-1 USTC ¶ 9179, 45 AFTR2d 80-570 (6th Cir. 1980).

Wholly owned corporation's repayment of stockholder's debt constituted a dividend and not a loan. Taxpayer borrowed money from his wholly owned corporation, *A*. Taxpayer was advised to repay this loan and did so by having his wholly owned corporation, *B*, transfer funds to *A*. The district court held for the IRS. *Held:* Affirmed. Even though *B*'s transfer of funds to *A* was labeled by taxpayer and *B* as a loan to taxpayer, the court found that there was no intent to repay the loan. Therefore, the transfer of funds from *B* to *A* was a dividend to the taxpayer stockholder. Factors considered material by the court were (1) the note merely required repayment on demand; (2) no payments on the note were ever made; and (3) *B* never sought to collect all or a portion of the funds lent to taxpayer. Miller, 538 F2d 511, 76-1 USTC ¶ 9424, 88 AFTR2d 76-6101 (2d Cir. 1976).

DIVIDENDS AND DISTRIBUTIONS: *Satisfaction of Stockholder Obligations*

Constructive dividend resulted when corporation fulfills personal obligations of its stockholders. A dispute arose between the two major stockholders of a corporation. One of the stockholders personally offered to purchase the stock of the other. His offer was accepted. Thereafter, the purchasing stockholder formed a corporation, had the corporation borrow the purchase price, acquired the stock of the selling stockholder, and merged the acquiring and acquired corporations. The assets of the acquired corporation were then used to repay the loan. The IRS contended that the repayment of the loan was a dividend to the stockholder, since the stockholder was personally obliged to acquire the stock. The district court granted the IRS' motion for a directed verdict. *Held:* Affirmed. The obligation to acquire the stock was a personal obligation. Thus, the satisfaction of that obligation by the acquired corporation repaying the loan made to acquire the stock was a constructive dividend to the stockholder. Apschinkat, 421 F2d 910, 70-1 USTC ¶ 9228, 25 AFTR2d 70-612 (6th Cir. 1970).

Payment of claims against stockholders was constructive dividend. Taxpayers *A* and *B*, stockholders of *X* Corporation, were sued by former stockholder *C*. *X* was later added as a defendant. The suit was settled by payments from *X* to *C*. The IRS claimed that *A* and *B* realized constructive dividend income from *X*'s payments. *Held:* For the IRS. *C*'s suit was against *A* and *B* personally; the later addition of *X* as a defendant had little substance. The corporation's payments discharged legal liabilities of the stockholders and so were dividends to them. Iron Range Plastics, Inc., 82-1 USTC ¶ 9107, 49 AFTR2d 82-612 (D. Minn. 1981).

Purchase of parent corporation's outstanding shares resulted in constructive dividend. Taxpayer subsidiary, as part of a plan to avoid gain on an involuntary conversion, purchased the outstanding shares of its parent, which had assets similar to those that were destroyed. The IRS argued that, under Section 304(a)(2), such purchase had to be treated as a constructive dividend to the parent, and was subject to the 85 percent intercorporate dividends received deduction. *Held:* For the IRS. The purchase was found to have discharged an obligation of the parent that directly benefited the parent; this fact supported the imposition of a constructive dividend to the parent. Broadview Lumber Co., 75-2 USTC ¶ 9832, 36 AFTR2d 75-6367 (ND Ind. 1975).

In absence of corporation's potential liability or damage to its business reputation, corporation's payment to principal stockholder's wife to settle claim against the stockholder was a dividend to him, and not a deductible expense. Taxpayer deducted a $10,000 payment made to its principal stockholder's wife to avoid a lawsuit, alleging that the payment was necessary to protect its business reputation. Evidence presented showed that the stockholder and his wife were in the process of getting a divorce and that the wife's complaint (settled by the payment) related to certain acts the stockholder committed while acting in his personal capacity, and not as an agent of taxpayer. The IRS asserted that the payment was not made to avoid any potential liability of taxpayer, and thus the payment was a dividend to the stockholder. *Held:* For the IRS. Settlement payment was a dividend to taxpayer's principal stockholder and thus was nondeductible. Mobile Beverage Co., 60-1 USTC ¶ 9403, 5 AFTR2d 1280 (ND Ala. 1960).

Corporate discharge of stockholder's personal liability resulted in dividend income. Taxpayer was a majority stockholder in an investment company and a sales-finance company. The sales-finance company obtained a bank loan, which taxpayer personally endorsed, for the purpose of purchasing two third-party notes from the investment company. The two notes purchased became worthless, and the sales-finance company was insolvent. In order for the sales-finance company to meet its obligations on its bank loan, the investment company repurchased the notes. The IRS contended that the repurchase payment was a constructive dividend to taxpayer. *Held:* For the IRS. The corporate discharge of a stockholder's personal liability was a dividend. Since the sales-finance company was unable to pay its

Dividends and Distributions: *Satisfaction of Stockholder Obligations*

debt to the bank and would have been forced to default, the transfer was caused by taxpayer to avoid liability on his endorsement. Accordingly, taxpayer was in receipt of dividend income. Other stockholders, not being personally liable on the note, received no dividend income. Cox, 56 TC 1270 (1971).

No constructive dividend in payment by corporation of loans made to permit its purchase. Taxpayers desired to purchase Reiner's Inc., a department store. The owners demanded $475,000 in cash, rejecting taxpayer's offer of $125,000 in cash and the balance in notes given by Reiner's in redemption of its stock. Subsequently, taxpayers contracted to purchase all of the outstanding stock of Reiner's. They and their relatives then formed a corporation, Alfred, Inc., to which they transferred $477,500 in return for stock, debentures, and a promissory note that was issued to Jerome Kobacker, not a taxpayer here. Taxpayers assigned to Alfred their contract to purchase Reiner's. Alfred then purchased the entire stock of Reiner's. After a period of operation as parent and subsidiary, Alfred was merged into Reiner's, with Reiner's assuming the debts of Alfred. The IRS contended that the payment by a corporation of a liability representing part of the consideration for the purchase of its stock constituted constructive receipt of dividends by the purchasing stockholders, taxpayers here. *Held:* For taxpayer. The Tax Court held that because taxpayers were not personally liable on the promissory note, they were not the "purchasing shareholder" on whose behalf the corporate payment was made. This was not a sham or subterfuge entered into merely to avoid taxes. There was no constructive dividend to taxpayers. Kobacker, 37 TC 882 (1962), acq. 1964-2 CB 6.

Taxpayer's use of corporate funds to purchase corporate stock constituted dividend. A corporation borrowed against land it owned. All the corporation's stock was then sold to taxpayer, an individual, who used the proceeds of the corporate loan to pay for the stock. The IRS contended that a distribution and dividend resulted. *Held:* For the IRS. Since the corporation paid taxpayer's obligation, the purchase price of the stock constituted a corporate distribution and dividend to the extent of corporate earnings and profits. Clements, 42 TCM 1144, ¶ 81,530 P-H Memo. TC (1981).

Payment of taxpayer's personal obligations by corporation was constructive dividend. Taxpayer was the president and sole stockholder of two corporations. Taxpayer purchased business *T* and assigned his interest in *T* to *E* Corporation, which had been incorporated to hold *T's* title. In order to finance the purchase of *T*, taxpayer had his other corporations issue checks to *E*. Taxpayer transferred his interest in the purchase contract to *E*, which issued stock in exchange for a cash payment. *E* executed notes to the other corporations to cover the amounts of the payment to the seller. Other advances were made by the corporations to cover the taxpayer's various debts and personal obligations. The payments were listed in the corporate books as advances. The corporations did not distribute dividends during this time, even though they had high earnings. The IRS determined the advances to be constructive dividends to taxpayer. *Held:* For the IRS. Evidence indicated that the advances were not loans, as (1) no notes were actually executed covering the advances; (2) taxpayer's debit balance kept increasing without repayment; (3) the account dealings between taxpayer and his corporations were open; (4) taxpayer's attitude was that the corporate assets were his personal assets; and (5) the corporations failed to declare dividends despite substantial earnings during the period in question. Estate of Colley, 40 TCM 81, ¶ 80,107 P-H Memo. TC (1980).

Loan payments by corporation constructive dividends. A married couple obtained a loan to purchase the remaining stock in a corporation and signed as primary obligors. The IRS contended that payments of principal and interest on the loan by the corporation were dividends. *Held:* For the IRS. The couple personally incurred the liability and made no attempt to structure the transaction as a redemption until after it was completed. Mc-

314

DIVIDENDS AND DISTRIBUTIONS: *Satisfaction of Stockholder Obligations*

Keown, 39 TCM 917, ¶ 80,018 P-H Memo. TC (1980).

No constructive dividend to sole stockholder of brother-sister corporations when currency exchange laws blocked payment of fee by one corporation to the other. Taxpayer's corporation designed and constructed golf courses. The corporation was requested to design a golf course for a customer who was located in a blocked currency area. Taxpayer formed a new corporation, which could receive such currency to construct the golf course. This new corporation agreed with its sister corporation to pay the standard 10 percent fee for golf course designs. Taxpayer owned all of the stock of both corporations. Total payment for the golf course was received by the new corporation. Despite attempts to pay the design fee to its sister corporation, the new corporation was unable to do so because of currency control laws. The IRS asserted that the failure to pay the fee constituted a constructive dividend to taxpayer on the theory that taxpayer was relieved of financing a portion of the new corporation's activities through use of his own personal funds. *Held:* For taxpayer. Before a constructive dividend may be found to exist, there must be some evidence that the stockholder received a personal benefit and not merely some indirect or derivative benefit. Since there was insufficient proof that taxpayer would be required to contribute additional capital to the new corporation, it could not be said that the failure to pay the fee resulted in any direct benefit to taxpayer. Robert Trent Jones, 34 TCM 488, ¶ 75,101 P-H Memo. TC (1975).

Corporate payment of debts constructive dividends. Taxpayer, pursuant to a marital settlement, was to buy out his wife's stock interest in their corporation. The corporation redeemed the stock, and the IRS determined that taxpayer was in receipt of constructive dividends. *Held:* For the IRS. The obligation to purchase the wife's stock interest was solely the taxpayer's. The corporation had no obligation to redeem the stock. Therefore, the corporation's redemption of the stock relieved taxpayer of his obligation and constituted a constructive and taxable dividend to taxpayer. Berger, 33 TCM 737, ¶ 74,172 P-H Memo. TC (1974).

Payment by corporation of minority stockholder's obligation to buy out majority stockholder was a dividend. Taxpayer, a minority stockholder, personally agreed to acquire the stock of the majority stockholder for $120,000. The corporation made all the payments, including expenses for interest, legal fees, and title insurance. Taxpayer did not sign any note to the corporation for these advances, and did not repay any of them. The IRS contended that the payments made by the corporation were constructive dividends. Taxpayer contended that the transaction, in substance, was a complete redemption by the corporation of the majority stockholder's shares, and that taxpayer was merely acting as agent of the corporation in purchasing the stock. *Held:* For the IRS. The form of the transaction compelled the conclusion that payments, including interest on a loan obtained by the corporation to pay part of the purchase price, relieved taxpayer of his contractual obligation, and thus constituted a constructive dividend to him. There was no plan at the time for a corporate redemption of the stock. Further, the interest that the corporation paid on the loan was not deductible. Miles, 25 TCM 1278, ¶ 66,250 P-H Memo. TC (1966).

Proceeds of redemption of donated stock used to pay off former stockholder's indebtedness held to be a dividend. Taxpayer, a trustee of a museum, owed $13,500 to a taxidermist for mounting an elephant that taxpayer had been commissioned by the museum to procure. Taxpayer formed a tax-exempt foundation to which he transferred some stock he held in a closely held corporation. The stock was then redeemed by the corporation for $16,000. At the same time, the foundation sent a donation of $13,500 to the museum with a letter advising the museum to use the funds to discharge the balance of taxpayer's indebtedness to the taxidermist. The IRS determined that taxpayer received a dividend. *Held:* For the IRS. Taxpayer received a constructive dividend from the corporation to the extent that his indebtedness was satisfied from the redemption proceeds. The intended result was to enable the closely held company to satisfy a personal indebtedness of taxpayer from corporate surplus, with the same net effect as if that corporation had first paid a dividend to taxpayer, and taxpayer had then utilized the dividend to satisfy his debt. Neither the foundation nor the museum retained the redemption proceeds, nor was it intended that they retain them. Phelon, 25 TCM 1024, ¶ 66,199 P-H Memo. TC (1966).

Corporation's advances to partnership were an investment, not a dividend. Taxpayers each owned 50 percent of the stock of a corporation engaged in the truck leasing business. They were also partners with another individual in a firm that leased terminals. The corporation advanced funds to the partnership for the acquisition of a new terminal. It was orginally agreed that the terminal would be owned by a newly formed corporation whose stock would be two thirds held by taxpayer's corporation and one third held by the outside partner. The IRS contended that the advances were for the benefit of taxpayers and were therefore taxable to them as dividends. *Held:* For taxpayers. The IRS failed to establish that the advances were to pay an obligation of the taxpayers, or were for their direct benefit; thus, the advances could not be considered dividends to them. The advances were intended as an investment in which taxpayers' corporation, and not taxpayers, was the two-thirds owner. Casali, 25 TCM 720, ¶ 66,139 P-H Memo. TC (1966).

Payment of debts of sister corporation not a dividend to stockholders. Taxpayer owned the stock of four corporations, each engaged in retail sales of shoes in different cities. When the Cincinnati store became insolvent, the Lexington store paid off the former's suppliers by giving them notes signed by taxpayer as president. The IRS contended that the payments of the notes by the Lexington store were dividends to taxpayer. *Held:* For taxpayer. No dividend resulted. The notes to the suppliers covering the liability of the Cincinnati store were notes of the Lexington store signed by taxpayer in his capacity as president. Their payment was not a payment of taxpayer's personal debt. The Lexington store received a benefit from the payments, since it was desirable to retain the good will of these suppliers for its own business in the future. Estate of Baynham, 25 TCM 310, ¶ 66,054 P-H Memo. TC (1966).

Stock Dividends and Rights

No right to receive cash in lieu of stock renders stock dividend nontaxable. Taxpayer received a stock dividend pursuant to a directors' resolution that stated that "said dividends may be cashed at the request of the stockholders at a value per share yet to be determined." Taxpayer owned only a very small fraction of the outstanding stock of the corporation, 50 percent of which was owned by his brother and the remainder by other members of the family, employees and friends. Taxpayer excluded the dividend from income, but the IRS determined that the dividend was taxable based on the selling prices of some shares of the dividend sold by others. *Held:* For taxpayer. As a matter of corporate policy of prior years, any stockholder who wished to sell stock to the company had to obtain the approval of the 50 percent stockholder. He generally declined such approval but personally loaned money to stockholder-employees who desired to sell. The resolution merely reduced to writing the corporate policy and was not intended to alter the rights of the corporation or any stockholder. The permissiveness implied by the language of the resolution made it clear that it did not give the stockholders rights to receive cash in lieu of stock or to convert stock into cash. Furthermore, taxpayer had clearly established that there was no attempt to effect a distribution of corporate earnings through the guise of a stock dividend. Rinker, 297 F. Supp. 370, 68-2 USTC ¶ 9625 (SD Fla. 1968).

Valuation of stock dividend determined. Taxpayer received a stock dividend of all the stock of a wholly owned subsidiary of a scrap metal corporation. Taxpayer argued that the stock had no value because it was of a closely held corporation in financial difficulty, and the industry was volatile. The IRS determined that the stock had value based on underlying corporate assets less liabilities. *Held:* For the IRS. The IRS determination was not clearly erroneous. Taxpayer was, however, allowed a 15 percent across-the-board discount to reflect subsequent costs of liquidating the subsidiary. Rosenberg, 83-2 USTC ¶ 9591, 52 AFTR2d 83-6003 (Cl. Ct. 1983).

Distribution taxable to stockholder. Taxpayer entered into an agreement with General Motors to establish an automobile dealership. He was required to finance his operations through the "Dealer Investment Plan," a standard plan used for new dealerships. In accordance with this plan, taxpayer made an initial investment in exchange for nonvoting stock. General Motors' holding division provided the remaining capitalization in 6 percent long-term notes and through the purchase of voting stock. Taxpayer had the right to purchase all the shares held by the holding company but "only from funds received . . . or dividends on a bonus from the dealer." The option agreement required that upon taxpayer's receipt of his dividend check, he endorse it and mail it to the holding company, which in turn would mail him the voting stock. Next, taxpayer had to convert the stock to nonvoting stock. Taxpayer contended that in fact he received a nontaxable stock dividend under Section 305(a). *Held:* For the IRS. Where the purpose of a dividend is a distribution of earnings as opposed to financing the purchase of the stockholder's stock, it was a taxable distribution to the stockholder. In sum, the transaction was not regarded for tax purposes as a stock dividend or as a redemption of the holding company's stock because it lacked the substance of either transaction. Dietzsch, 498 F2d 1344, 74-2 USTC ¶ 9517, 34 AFTR2d 74-5241 (Ct. Cl. 1974).

Distribution of subsidiaries' stock by parent to stockholders is taxable dividend. Taxpayers were stockholders in a corporation engaged in the freight business. This corporation in turn was the sole stockholder of three corporations that were engaged in the real estate business. The only income of the subsidiaries was derived from the rent of motor freight terminals to their parent on a net lease basis. Distribution of the shares of the subsidiaries was made to taxpayers by the parent. Taxpayers did not report gain on said distribution. *Held:* For the IRS. Based on the facts and circumstances, the distribution constituted a taxable dividend because the subsidiaries were not engaged in the active conduct of a trade or business during the five-year period prior to the date of distribution. In accordance with Section 355, gain is recognized and taxable as a dividend if the "active conduct of a trade or business" requirement is not satisfied. King, 55 TC 677 (1971).

No dividend in transfer of subsidiary stock in trust for stockholders. A national bank owned all the stock of a subsidiary that performed functions that the bank itself was not permitted to perform. To meet the requirement of the Comptroller of the Currency that it divest itself of the subsidiary, the bank transferred the subsidiary stock to its directors as trustees, with the beneficial interest in the bank stockholders. The IRS contended that the transfer was a dividend to the stockholders. *Held:* For taxpayer. Since this beneficial interest could not be transferred separately and was automatically transferred with the transfer of the bank stock, the court held that the bank stockholders did not receive a dividend distribution upon transfer by the bank of the subsidiary stock to the trustees. Wilkinson, 29 TC 421 (1957), nonacq. 1960-2 CB 8.

Reduction of par value of stock accompanied by reduction in stock subscription price equivalent to nontaxable stock dividend. Taxpayers each subscribed for 1,000 shares of stock with a par value of $1 each. Subsequently, the par value of the stock was reduced to one cent each. The IRS claimed that taxpayers realized a discharge of indebtedness income when the corporation reduced the par value of the stock, and regarded the issued stock as fully paid for when taxpayers tendered the one cent per share. Taxpayers claimed that the reduction of par value and reduction of their subscription price did not result in taxable income. *Held:* For taxpayers, in part. The reductions of par value and reductions in the amounts due on the taxpayers' subscriptions were equivalent to nontaxable stock dividends and did not result in discharge-of-indebtedness income to taxpayers. Whiting, 47 TCM 1334, ¶ 84,142 P-H Memo. TC (1984).

Right to receive common stock constituted constructive receipt of distribution. Taxpayers received cumulative preferred stock that provided for crediting of accrued but unpaid dividends for taxpayers' benefit. Taxpayers whose preferred shares had dividends past due for two or more successive quarters had the option of electing to receive an amount of common stock equal in value to the credit balance of the accrued dividend account. The IRS ruled that when such unrestrictive right to receive common stock arises, taxpayers are in constructive receipt of the common stock under Section 305(b)(4). Accordingly, such distributions are treated as distributions of property, to which Section 301 applies. Furthermore, interest credited at the end of the second quarter in which the preferred dividend was not distributed is treated as an additional distribution. Rev. Rul. 84-141, 1984-2 CB 80.

Recapitalization resulted in constructive stock dividend where corporation issued stock with a redemption value in excess of issue price. A was the president of X and held 80 of its 100 shares of outstanding common stock. B, his son, was a key employee of X and held the other 20 shares of X common stock. Pursuant to a recapitalization plan designed to transfer control and ownership to B in conjunction with A's retirement, a single class of nonvoting, dividend-paying preferred stock was authorized. Thereafter, A exchanged 80 shares of common stock for 80 shares of preferred stock, giving B all of the common stock. At the time of the exchange, the common stock had a fair market value of $1,000x$ per share, and the preferred had a fair market value of $600x$ per share. Furthermore, on A's death, X was required to redeem the preferred stock from A's estate at its par value of $1,000 per share. According to the actuarial tables, A had a life expectancy of 24 years at the time of recapitalization. *Held:* For the IRS. A was deemed to have constructively received a Section 301 stock distribution with respect to the preferred stock within the meaning of Section 305(b)(4) by reason of Section 305(c). The distribution was in the amount of $340x$ ($400x$ less a deemed reasonable redemption premium of $60x$) on each share of preferred stock constructively over A's expected life of 24 years. Upon A's death, any part not yet constructively received would be deemed then received. The difference between the issue price and the redemption price and the fact that the stock could not be redeemed for a specific period of time were factors that combined to produce a deemed distribution. Rev. Rul. 83-119, 1983-2 CB 57.

Dilution of conversion rights cannot be remedied by common stock distribution. Under Section 305(b)(4), a stock dividend with respect to preferred stock is taxable unless it takes the form of an increase in the conversion ratio of convertible preferred stock made solely to take account of a dilution in conversion rights due to a stock dividend or split. Taxpayer, in lieu of increasing the conversion ratio, distributed common stock to the holders of the preferred stock. The IRS ruled that Section 305(b)(4) does not permit such distribution; therefore, the common stock is taxable to the preferred stockholders under Section 301. Rev. Rul. 83-42, 1983-1 CB 76.

Preferred stock issued to target corporation's stockholders was not Section 305 distribution. The IRS ruled that preferred stock in a taxpayer corporation was not a Section 305(a) stock distribution where it was issued to the stockholders of a target corporation that merged with taxpayer's subsidiary in exchange for the target corporation's old stock. This was because the preferred stock was not made to taxpayer's stockholders with respect to their stock. However, subsequent changes in redemption premiums, redemption prices, or conversion ratios of the preferred stock may be treated as Section 305(b) or 305(c) distributions. Rev. Rul. 82-158, 1982-2 CB 77.

Subsidiary's stock rights to parent's stockholders held not taxable. A subsidiary issued nontransferable rights to acquire its stock to the stockholders of its parent corporation. The transaction was a nontaxable distribution of stock rights from the subsidiary to the parent within the meaning of Section 305(d)(1), followed by a distribution of property of the parent within the meaning of Section 317(a), subject to the provisions of Section 301. Its value was fair market value on the date of distribution. Rev. Rul. 80-292, 1980-2 CB 104.

Distribution by corporation excludable stock dividend. The two stockholders of a foreign corporation directed it to pay a cash dividend and increase their capital investment by that amount, which was then carried out on the corporation's books. The stockholders did not have an election to be paid in stock or property within the meaning of Section 305(b)(1), so the distribution was not includable in the stockholders' gross income under Section 305(a). Rev. Rul. 80-154, 1980-1 CB 68.

Stock acquired in dividend reinvestment plan was taxable. X Corporation adopted a dividend reinvestment plan in which the stockholders could elect to purchase X stock at 95 percent of the stock market price with the proceeds of their dividend payment. Stockholders who elected this plan received a taxable stock dividend under Section 305(b)(1) in the amount of the fair market value of the stock. It was irrelevant that X paid cash to an agent who then used the cash to purchase stock from X. Rev. Rul. 79-42, 1979-2 CB 130.

Dividend reinvestment plan and stock bargain purchase plan resulted in taxable dividends. Stockholders of X Corporation could elect either to receive cash dividends or to reinvest the dividends in X common stock. Those who chose to reinvest their dividends could also purchase additional shares of X common at 95 percent of fair market value. The stock received as a dividend reinvestment was taxable under Section 305(b)(1) in the amount of its fair market value. The purchase of additional stock resulted in a taxable dividend under Section 305(b)(2) in the amount of the 5 percent discount. Rev. Rul. 78-375, 1978-2 CB 130.

Reinvested dividends were Section 301(a) distributions. Stockholders of X Corporation could participate in a dividend reinvestment plan. Under the plan, cash dividends were paid to an agent who purchased shares on the open market. The IRS ruled that these were Section 301(a) distributions and that Section 305 was not applicable because X was not distributing any stock. Rev. Rul. 77-149, 1977-1 CB 82.

Distribution of preferred stock, immediately redeemable for cash at stockholders' option, was treated as a Section 301 distribution. Corporation made a pro rata distribution of preferred stock to holders of common stock. The stock was immediately redeemable at par for money. The IRS ruled that the redeemability feature gave the stockholder an election to receive either stock or property within the meaning of Section 305(b)(1)(A), and, thus, the distribution was treated under Section 301. Rev. Rul. 76-258, 1976-2 CB 95.

Nonconvertible preferred stock redemption premium was a distribution of stock includable in gross income. A corporation, authorized by its charter to issue 500 shares of nonconvertible preferred stock by January 10, 1969, issued 200 shares for $100 per share, redeemable by the corporation in 1978 and thereafter for $150. In 1974, the corporation issued an additional 100 shares at $100 per share as consideration for the common stock of a corporation acquired in a reorganization. Under Section 305, a difference between redemption price and issue price is treated as a distribution includable in gross income unless the stock was issued before January 10, 1969 or the redemption premium is reasonable. A redemption price not in excess of $10 is considered reasonable. Since there were no facts in this case to indicate that a larger premium was reasonable, and the stock was not issued before January 10, 1969, the redemption premium was considered a distribution of additional stock on the preferred stock issued in the 1974 reorganization and was includable in gross income. However, distributions on preferred stock issued as of January 10, 1969 were not includable. Rev. Rul. 76-107, 1976-1 CB 89.

Dividends and Distributions: *Stockholder Use of Corporate Property*

No basis adjustment where rights declined in value. Where a coporation distributes transferable subscription rights to stockholders of its common shares and the rights declined in value from more than 15 percent of the common shares' value to no value and the subscriptions received were refunded, stockholders who failed to sell, exercise, or surrender their rights, surrendered the rights, or exercised the rights and received a refund in the same taxable year need not make an adjustment to basis. Rev. Rul. 74-501, 1974-2 CB 98.

Distribution of a subsidiary's shares is tax-free. The distribution of all a subsidiary's stock to its parent's sole stockholder qualifies under Section 355(a)(1). No gain or loss is recognized to the stockholder even though immediately after the distribution, the stockholder transferred, as part of the plan, all of the stock of an unrelated corporation to the subsidiary for new shares of the subsidiary in an exchange under Section 351(a). Rev. Rul. 73-246, 1973-1 CB 181.

Gain or loss recognized on sale of fractional shares issued as part of stock dividend. The proceeds from the sale of fractional shares resulting from a stock dividend declaration, which stockholders authorized to be united and sold on their behalf, were treated as part of a nontaxable stock dividend distribution. The transaction was treated as though the fractional shares were distributed as part of the stock dividend that was nontaxable as provided by Section 305. Gain or loss was recognized to the stockholders entitled to the fractional shares on the sale of the fractional shares measured by the basis allocated to such fractional share and their share of the proceeds of the sale. Rev. Rul. 69-15, 1969-1 CB 95.

Stock rights received from unrelated corporation not taxable on receipt. Pursuant to a plan of liquidation, X Corporation sold certain of its assets to Y, an unrelated corporation, and its other assets to Z Corporation. Neither X nor Y held any stock interest in Z. In order to raise funds to purchase X's assets, Z made a public offering of its debentures and stock and issued rights to Y's stockholders. Each right entitled the holder to purchase one unit of Z's debentures and stock at a specified price. There was no obligation on Z's part to issue such rights to Y's stockholders. The number of rights issued to each stockholder of Y was proportionate to his holdings of Y stock. The situation was thus distinguishable from a distribution by a corporation to its own stockholders and was not governed by the rules relating to stock rights and dividends, Sections 305 and 301, respectively. Y stockholders realized no taxable income on the distribution, and the basis of the rights was zero. Since the Y stockholders were not dealers and the debentures and stock would have been capital assets if the rights had been exercised, gain on the sale of the rights was capital gain in accordance with Section 1234. The entire proceeds on an immediate sale of the rights were a short-term capital gain. Rev. Rul. 63-225, 1963-2 CB 339.

Stockholder Use of Corporate Property

No constructive dividend where taxpayer lived rent free on property where he retained a life interest. Taxpayers were stockholders in a family-owned corporation. After residing in an estate for many years, taxpayers sold the property to the corporation but reserved the full, complete, and unqualified right to the exclusive use, occupancy, and possession of the property for themselves or their heirs as long as the property was owned by the corporation. Taxpayers lived on the property but paid no rent. The corporation expended funds landscaping and maintaining the surrounding property, paid the salaries of a chauffeur and cook, and paid the cost of the residents' utilities and the operating expenses of the automobiles. The IRS contended that the amounts corresponding to the value of these items and the fair market value of the rent of the property represented constructive dividends to taxpayer. *Held:* For taxpayer. By reserving the right to occupy said premises rent-free for the remainder of their lives, taxpayers had the right to rent-free occupancy. Even if this were not so, the requirement by the corporation that taxpayers be constantly and immediately available for duty at

Dividends and Distributions: *Stockholder Use of Corporate Property*

the plant site made taxpayer's occupancy a convenience for the employer; under the three-part test of Regulation § 1.119-1(b), the value of such lodging was excludable from the taxpayer employees' income. The amounts incurred for landscaping and maintaining the land constituted expenditures for the maintenance of a corporate investment from which the taxpayers received no economic benefit and so were not constructive dividends to taxpayer. Because the evidence indicated no suitable motel or restaurant accommodations nearby, the amounts paid to the cook were valid corporate expenditures. Similarly, chauffeur and automobile costs were not constructive dividends to the extent that their use was for corporate business. Crosby, 496 F2d 1384, 72-2 USTC ¶ 9550, 34 AFTR2d 74-5371 (5th Cir. 1974).

Operation of lodge for stockholder's benefit brings constructive dividend. Taxpayer, a common carrier of automobiles for Studebaker, constructed and equipped an expensive lakefront lodge. In addition to its use as a summer home for taxpayer's sole stockholder, the lodge was used to entertain the stockholder's friends and Studebaker executives. From 1957 through 1961, taxpayer deducted $100,000 for upkeep of the lodge and also claimed a deduction for depreciation. The stockholder reimbursed taxpayer at the rate of $10 per person for each day that a member of his family was present at the lodge. *Held:* The court held that the expenses in excess of the reimbursements were not ordinary and necessary corporate business expenses and resulted in constructive dividends to the stockholder, except to the extent of $2,100 per year. Robert R. Walker, Inc., 362 F2d 140, 66-1 USTC ¶ 9426 (7th Cir. 1966).

Furnishing automobiles to stockholders was dividend. Taxpayer was owned equally by two stockholders, both of whom served as officers and directors of taxpayer. Taxpayer purchased two automobiles for the personal use of the stockholders and deducted the full cost of the vehicles as part of its officers' salaries expense. The IRS determined the costs to be dividend distributions and disallowed the deductions. *Held:* For the IRS. Because the evidence failed to show that taxpayer purchased the automobiles with the intent of paying its officers added compensation, the costs were dividend distributions and thus nondeductible. Annabelle Candy Co., ¶ 61,170 P-H Memo. TC (1961), aff'd, 314 F2d 1, 62-2 USTC ¶ 9707, 10 AFTR2d 5380 (9th Cir. 1962).

Plane purchased by professional corporation was a constructive dividend to stockholder. Taxpayer, a professional dental corporation, claimed business deductions for an airplane it purchased to transport dentists from another city to taxpayer's clinic. The plane was never used for this purpose, but instead was used by taxpayer's principal stockholder for a vacation. The IRS disallowed the deductions and asserted that the stockholder received a constructive dividend from the corporation's purchase of the plane. *Held:* For the IRS. The plane was purchased primarily for personal, not business reasons. A.S. Barber, Inc., 85-1 USTC ¶ 9183, 55 AFTR2d 85-765 (ED Mo. 1984).

Cost of yacht built by corporation not a constructive dividend. A construction corporation paid the cost of building a yacht. The IRS asserted that these payments constituted constructive dividends to its controlling shareholder. *Held:* For taxpayer. The yacht was primarily a place to conduct discussions with customers leading to construction contracts. Some features of the yacht were unique. When the stockholder used it for his personal use, he paid the company a fair rent. Accordingly, the stockholder was not in receipt of a constructive dividend. Krapf, 37 TCM 594, ¶ 78,138 P-H Memo. TC (1978).

Stockholder received constructive dividend when title to real estate purchased with corporate funds was held in his name. Taxpayer and his wife were sole stockholders of *X* Corporation. They purchased real estate in a wooded vacation area in Vermont with corporate funds. Title was held in taxpayer's name. The IRS determined that taxpayer received a constructive dividend in the amount of the value of the real estate. *Held:* For the IRS. The real estate was purchased with corporate funds

Dividends and Distributions: *Taxable Party*

and held in taxpayer's name. There was no corporate investment purpose and the property was used personally by taxpayer. Daly, 37 TCM 15. ¶ 78,005 P-H Memo. TC, aff'd (1st Cir. 1978).

Use of car by stockholder employee was dividend. Taxpayer allowed a stockholder employee to use one of its cars for commuting to and from work and deducted the full amount of the expenses incurred in connection with the car. The IRS disallowed a portion of the expense. *Held:* For the IRS. The use gave rise to a constructive dividend to the stockholder employee. Perrotto, 36 TCM 464, ¶ 77,099 P-H Memo. TC (1977).

Taxable Party

Record date determines whether seller or buyer earns dividend for tax purposes. Taxpayer corporation purchased a corporation's preferred stock after a dividend's record date (the date the corporation uses in determining to whom the dividend should be paid), but before the ex-dividend date determined by the New York Stock Exchange. The Exchange requires the seller to pay over the dividend to the taxpayer when the seller receives it. Taxpayer considered itself the recipient of the dividend, included it in income minus the 85 percent dividends received deduction, and later claimed a capital loss when it sold the stock. The IRS considered the seller the recipient of the dividend, holding that part of taxpayer's purported payment for the stock was not actually for the stock, but for an account receivable from the seller. Accordingly, the IRS reduced taxpayer's basis in the stock. *Held:* For the IRS. The seller received the dividend for tax purposes. The record date determines who receives the dividend because it determines who receives the dividend check and who can sue the corporation if it fails to pay. This view is consistent with the rule that the record date determines whether a decedent's final income tax return or his estate tax return includes a dividend. Silco, Inc., 591 F. Supp. 480, 84-2 USTC ¶ 9716, 54 AFTR2d 84-5680 (ND Tex. 1984).

Buyer of all corporate stock could not say dividend he took immediately after acquisition should be taxed to sellers. Taxpayer corporation, wholly owned by one individual, was formed to purchase the stock of a piston company. Taxpayer borrowed the money to effect the purchase, and the piston company transferred to taxpayer funds to repay the loans. The transaction took this form because the sellers refused to pay dividends to themselves prior to sale. Taxpayer reported the transaction as a dividend and took the 85 percent dividend credit. On its return, taxpayer denied that it was a personal holding company although it showed thereon that it had only one stockholder and that over 85 percent of its income was from dividends. The taxpayer argued that since the payment to it by the newly purchased piston company was for the benefit of the sellers, they, not it, should be regarded as receiving dividend income. *Held:* For the IRS, in part. The court held the taxpayer to the form of the transaction it carried out: The receipt was a dividend to it. But taxpayer was not liable for penalty to file a personal holding company return; all the data necessary to show that it did qualify was shown on its return. McKinley Corp. of Ohio, 36 TC 1182 (1961).

Buyer of stock held to receive constructive dividend. Taxpayer seller sold stock in *B* Corporation to taxpayer buyer for cash, and then *B* transferred real estate to the seller for a price less than fair market value. Both sides agreed with the IRS that the transaction produced a constructive dividend to one of the parties in the sale, but each argued that the dividend was taxable to the other party. *Held:* For taxpayer seller. The court viewed the transaction as a sale of *B* stock to the buyer, followed by a constructive distribution of *B*'s realty to the buyer, who then transferred it to the seller as part of the purchase price. The dividend was thus taxable to the buyer. Missimer, 38 TCM 192, ¶ 79,048 P-H Memo. TC (1979).

Withdrawals by Stockholders Treated as Dividends

Advances to stockholder were dividends despite stockholder's repayment after IRS audit had begun. Taxpayer was the sole stockholder and employee of a professional corporation. During the tax years 1973, 1974, and 1975, taxpayer withdrew from the corporation sums of money that he used primarily to pay construction and mortgage expenses for a new building to house the corporation. Taxpayer and his wife held title to the building and reported rent from other tenants in the building on their personal income tax return. Taxpayer issued a series of non-interest-bearing promissory notes to the corporation. There was no repayment schedule, and the loans were unsecured. After being contacted regarding an audit, taxpayer fully repaid the withdrawn funds. The Tax Court agreed with the IRS and found that the net amounts withdrawn each year were constructive dividends includible in taxpayer's income, and not loans. *Held:* Affirmed. Advances to a stockholder were dividends despite the stockholder's repayment of the withdrawals from the corporation. The Seventh Circuit observed that the factors considered by the Tax Court were consistent with the advances' being classified as constructive dividends and not loans, and therefore the Tax Court was not clearly erroneous. Specific factors were that the corporation's retained earnings increased substantially over the period in question, even though the corporation declared no dividends; the promissory notes did not cover the full amount of the withdrawals and had no maturity date or interest to be paid; some of the payments were for personal use; the rental income was reported as personal income; and most important, taxpayer did not demonstrate an intent to repay at the time the withdrawals were made. Busch, 728 F2d 945, 84-1 USTC ¶ 9266, 53 AFTR2d 84-930 (7th Cir. 1984).

Advances were constructive distributions, not loans. Taxpayer received various advances from his wholly owned professional corporation that he did not include in gross income, claiming they were loans. The IRS determined that these advances were constructive dividends. *Held:* For the IRS. There was no corporate resolution authorizing advances and establishing limits on them, no repayment schedules and security arrangements were established, and no interest rate was set. Thus, at the time of withdrawal there was no repayment intent and the amounts were not bona fide loans. Busch, Jr., T.C. Memo. 1983-98. Discharge of individual obligations by corporation was also held to be a constructive dividend. Jacobs, 698 F2d 850, 83-1 USTC ¶ 9193, 51 AFTR2d 83-627 (6th Cir. 1983).

"Loans" between commonly controlled corporations produced constructive dividends. Taxpayers wholly owned each of two corporations. One corporation made a series of "loans" to the other, which were unsecured and non-interest-bearing. The IRS argued that the advances were not true loans and that the stockholders had received a constructive dividend from the transaction. *Held:* For the IRS. The advances lacked the indicia of loans. They enhanced the value of the recipient corporation's stock and helped that company to discharge bank loans that the stockholders had guaranteed. These benefits justified imposition of constructive dividends on the stockholders. Wilkof, 37 TCM 1851-31, ¶ 78,496 P-H Memo. TC (1978), aff'd, 636 F2d 1139, 81-1 USTC ¶ 9155, 47 AFTR2d 81-593 (6th Cir. 1981).

Advances held to be dividend instead of loan. The sole stockholder of three corporations was involved in several suits stemming from a divorce action. Taxpayer corporations paid most of its stockholder's personal living expenses and treated the advances as loans and accounts receivable on the corporate books. The charges were offset from time to time by payments, but no interest was paid on the balances owed for about five years after the separation agreement. Interest, but no principal, was paid after that time. Instead, new notes were issues covering new advances. The advances covered such expenses as child support, improvements on the home, legal expenses and taxes. The IRS contended that the advances treated as accounts receivable were constructive dividends and not loans. At all times, the corporation had sufficient earnings and profits to cover the amounts. The district court agreed and found the net advances exceeded what was permissible as a corporate loan to a controlling stockholder. *Held:* Affirmed. The summary judgment was properly granted on the issue of loans versus dividends. The record showed no evidence from which an inference of intent to repay or expectation of repayment could be drawn. Dolese, 605 F2d 1146, 79-2 USTC ¶ 9540, 44 AFTR2d 79-5724 (10th Cir.), rehearing denied per curiam in 605 F2d 1146 (10th Cir. 1979).

Where taxpayer's regular and continuous withdrawals of its subsidiaries' receipts were dividends and not loans, the court did not need to put to the jury the question of intent to repay. Taxpayer regularly caused its 52 wholly owned subsidiaries to transfer to it all receipts from their operations in excess of immediate operating expenses. Taxpayer used these funds to pay its operating expenses. The district court determined that even though these transfers were reflected as loans on the corporations' books, they were actually dividends because (1) under the facts, taxpayer had no indefinite intention to repay these transfers; (2) no notes or other evidences of indebtedness were executed; (3) no interest accrued on the outstanding amounts; (4) no collateral was given as security for repayment; (5) no repayment dates were established; and (6) no effort was made to pay or force repayment of the purported loans. *Held:* For the IRS. The question of intent to repay need not be put to the jury if the evidence overwhelmingly establishes taxpayer's lack of any genuine intention to repay. Furthermore, mere declarations of such intent are subject to more intensive scrutiny when made by a debtor who has total control over its lender. Alterman Foods, 505 F2d 873, 75-1 USTC ¶ 9151, 35 AFTR2d 75-518 (5th Cir. 1974).

Withdrawals by sole stockholder deemed dividends. The IRS and district court held that withdrawals made by taxpayer in his capacity as president and sole stockholder of a small loan corporation were dividends rather than loans even though demand notes were given by taxpayer to corporation. *Held:* Affirmed. The court found support for its holdings in the fact that the amounts had never been repaid aside from a small amount, and withdrawals had been made at will. Estate of Taschler, 440 F2d 72, 71-1 USTC ¶ 9298, 27 AFTR2d 71-960 (3d Cir. 1971).

Loans taken over by family members deemed dividends upon repayment. A personal holding company used bank loans to purchase additional shares of stock of a related corporation for family members. Subsequently, the loans were taken over by another family member who distributed the obligation to the family stockholders involved. Later, loan repayments were held by a district court jury to be taxable dividends. *Held:* Affirmed. The obligation in substance lacked a definite maturity date and an obligation to repay. An additional factor supporting dividend treatment was the waiving of interest payments by the stockholders. Dillin, 433 F2d 1097, 70-2 USTC ¶ 9647, 26 AFTR2d 70-5649 (5th Cir. 1970).

Advances to trust deemed dividends. Taxpayer corporation advanced funds to a trust that owned stock in taxpayer. The Tax Court held that the loans were, in substance, dividends. *Held:* Affirmed. The facts indicated no intention or expectation of repayment of principal. Furthermore, although interest was specified, there was no indication that such interest had been paid. Livernois, 433 F2d 879, 70-2 USTC ¶ 9642, 26 AFTR2d 70-5632 (6th Cir. 1970).

Purchase of sister corporation's stock was a dividend, not a loan repayment. Taxpayer's controlled corporation, S, purchased his stock in another controlled corporation, C. The IRS contended that the purchase was substantially equivalent to a dividend under Section 304. Taxpayer contended that the purchase was really a repayment of his loan to C on behalf of S. The Tax Court held that taxpayer received dividend income on the transaction. *Held:* Affirmed. The facts did not support taxpayer's contention of a loan by the purchasing corporation. The evidence showed that the loans were made by taxpayer

Dividends and Distributions: *Withdrawals by Stockholders*

himself. Swan, 355 F2d 795, 66-1 USTC ¶ 9224 (6th Cir. 1966).

Stockholder's loans taxable as dividends. Taxpayer was the sole stockholder of a real estate corporation. In 1957 and 1958, he withdrew $7,500 and $1,000, respectively, from the corporation in the form of loans. No notes were executed by taxpayer to the corporation, and no interest was charged on the loans. Taxpayer's withdrawals from 1948 through 1961 amounted to almost $49,000, whereas repayments were only $13,700. The corporate financial statement generally did not reveal the withdrawals or loans. The district court held that the withdrawals were taxable dividends. It concluded from the facts that taxpayer did not treat the withdrawals as taxable loans. *Held:* Affirmed. There was no dispute about the legal concept of a loan. The appellate court was satisfied that the facts justified the conclusion of the district court. Gurtman, 353 F2d 212, 66-1 USTC ¶ 9107 (3d Cir. 1965).

Drawing accounts on corporate books treated as informal dividends. Three brothers, the sole stockholders of taxpayer, made it a policy to have their personal expenses paid by taxpayer, which charged such expenses to their individual drawing accounts. The withdrawals were not represented by notes, bore no interest, and were not repayable at any given time. When one of the brothers became incapacitated in an auto accident, the local court, in a nonadversary proceeding, approved a plan whereby taxpayer purchased the stock of that brother, applying the balance in the drawing account against the purchase price of the stock. Taxpayer had adequate earnings and profits at all times and never formally declared any dividends. *Held:* For the IRS. The court held that the net withdrawals on taxpayer's books were not true loans but constituted informal dividends. It also held that payments made to the disabled brother when he was no longer able to render services to taxpayer could not be deducted as salary because they were disguised dividends. Chesapeake Mfg. Co., 347 F2d 507, 65-2 USTC ¶ 9523 (4th Cir. 1965).

Payments by thin cemetery corporation are dividends. Individual taxpayers organized the corporate taxpayer, a cemetery organization, and took back certificates of indebtedness in exchange for their investment. The certificates, of indeterminate amounts, required the corporation to pay to the certificate holders 25 percent of the base sales price of every lot sold by the corporation for 50 years. *Held:* For the IRS. In a per curiam opinion, the Fourth Circuit affirmed the Tax Court decision that payments under the certificates were dividends to the holders and not deductible by the corporation as land costs. The corporation had limited capital and the certificates were not bona fide evidences of debt, but constituted equity capital. Gardens of Faith, Inc., 345 F2d 180, 65-1 USTC ¶ 9324, 15 AFTR2d 646 (4th Cir.), cert. denied, 382 US 927 (1965).

Funds received from corporation and reinvested in another corporation were dividends to receiving corporation. W owned most of taxpayer and half of H Corporation. W decided to establish M Corporation, a restaurant. Interest-free funds were advanced to M by taxpayer from funds received from H, and by W from moneys paid to him and charged to his account. The Tax Court agreed with the IRS determination that every payment originating from H was a dividend to taxpayer. *Held:* Set aside and remanded. Where the evidence indicated that the payments were not meant as gifts as opposed to loans, the court's treatment of these payments as dividends constructively received by taxpayer in their entirety was necessarily wrong. Accordingly, the payments from W to M for labor and materials were loans, not dividends. However, the evidence failed to show that the payments from H to M were bona fide loans. General Aggregates Corp., 313 F2d 25, 63-1 USTC ¶ 9237 (5th Cir.), cert. denied, 375 US 815 (1962).

Withdrawals from family corporation treated as dividends, not loans. Taxpayer and his family were in complete control of a corporation that had a large amount of cash in its bank account, apparently far in excess of its needs. Because of litigation then pending involving ownership of some of the stock, dividends could not be declared. Taxpayer and his family, however, withdrew large sums from the corporation for their own use and for the use of other corporations in which they were interested, without any of the usual formalities followed in making bona fide loans. The IRS contended that the withdrawals were dividends. *Held:* For the IRS. Under the circumstances, the withdrawals were not loans, but dividends. Spheeris, 284 F2d 928, 61-1 USTC ¶ 9143, 6 AFTR2d 6066 (7th Cir. 1960), cert. denied, 366 US 944 (1961).

Withdrawals, if from earnings, taxed as dividends. Taxpayer withdrew money from a corporation that she controlled as administratrix and sole heir of her father. The money was entered on the books as open account loans and was in excess of the earnings and profits of the corporation. The Tax Court held that the withdrawals were not loans, but were dividends to the extent of earnings and profits. The court found that the stockholder had no intention of repaying the withdrawals. *Held:* Affirmed. That the withdrawals were disproportionate to taxpayer's personal interest in the corporation was unimportant because she controlled the corporation. The fact that the sum of the withdrawals exceeded the earnings and profits also did not preclude treatment of the payments as dividends to the extent of earnings. Roschuni, 271 F2d 267, 59-2 USTC ¶ 9748, 4 AFTR2d 5759 (5th Cir. 1959), cert. denied, 362 US 988 (1960).

"Loans" to stockholder were dividends. Taxpayer owned a tool and die machinery company. In order to fulfill two major government contracts, taxpayer had to move his personal residence away from the business. To finance his residence, taxpayer received four payments from the corporation from 1967 through 1970 that he called loans and that were denominated on the books of the corporation as either due from the officers or loans receivable officer. No notes were given to evidence these loans, no security was given, no interest was provided for or paid and no date was specified for repayment. During the years at issue, the corporation had sufficient earned surplus to cover the amounts.

No loan payments were made in 1971 or 1972. After 1972, taxpayer obtained a bank loan and repaid the advances. Through a statistical study, the IRS issued a deficiency assessment. *Held:* For the IRS. In applying the "economic reality of the marketplace" test, the advances were not debts, but dividends. No outsider dealing at arm's length would consider lending the taxpayer sums where there was no real intent to repay. Taxpayer's intent was evidenced by the absence of a note or future payment date, his control over the corporation, and the lack of security. Other evidence considered was taxpayer's failure to mention his indebtedness when he applied for a bank loan. Genito, 80-2 USTC ¶ 9771 (DNJ 1980), aff'd in unpublished opinion, 659 F2d 1066 (3d Cir. 1981).

Advances from wholly owned corporation were dividends. The IRS determined that monies advanced by *X* Corporation, which was wholly owned by taxpayer, to taxpayer, and to corporations controlled by taxpayer constituted constructive dividends to taxpayer. The facts indicated that taxpayer lacked liquidity to pay back the advances. *Held:* For the IRS. The substance of the transactions indicated that the advances were in fact dividends and that taxpayer failed to prove otherwise. In re Wrenn, Jr., 78-1 USTC ¶ 9424, 41 AFTR2d 78-1372 (WD Tenn. 1978).

Repayment of loan to stockholder made by one related corporation to another treated as constructive dividend. During taxable year 1957, taxpayer was the sole stockholder of two corporations, *R* and *S* companies. Before 1957, taxpayer developed an interest in investing in a certain real estate partnership. Toward this end, he caused *S* to issue a $65,000 check to him personally. At the same time he executed a $65,000 promissory note payable to *S* on demand. At the suggestion of his financial adviser, taxpayer replaced the loan by issuing a $65,000 check from *R* payable to taxpayer that was endorsed and deposited in the account of *S* Company. On its books, *S* recorded this payment under an account entitled "exchanges," rather than as a repayment of the loan. *S* therefore continued to show a $65,000 amount receivable as a

DIVIDENDS AND DISTRIBUTIONS: *Withdrawals by Stockholders*

loan to officers. The IRS, on an audit of *R*, treated the $65,000 item as a constructive dividend reportable as income by taxpayer. *Held:* For the IRS. Taxpayer argued unsuccessfully that the transactions constituted a bona fide loan and that the discrepancies in bookkeeping were irrelevant to establishing his true intent. The trial court took the contrary view and held that taxpayer had no intention of repaying the $65,000 advance made by *R*. The court noted that the promissory instrument made no provision for scheduled repayments. A later audit by a CPA revealed the state of facts, but nothing was done to correct the books. The taxpayer expressed to the CPA his intention of repaying the loan only on the dissolution of the real estate partnership. Even though such a liquidation later took place, the loan remained unpaid. Miller, 404 F. Supp. 284, 37 AFTR2d 76-426, 76-1 USTC ¶ 9193 (EDNY 1975), aff'd without opinion, 500 F2d 1007 (2d Cir. 1976).

Withdrawals dividends, not loans. The IRS contended that taxpayer's withdrawals from his wholly owned corporation constituted taxable dividends, not nontaxable loans. *Held:* For the IRS. The withdrawals were not backed up by notes, no interest was charged, there was no definite repayment date and there was no security given. Thus, the prerequisites for a loan were not established. Wheeler, 75-1 USTC ¶ 9170, 35 AFTR2d 75-604 (WD Tex. 1974).

Jury finds withdrawals from corporation not loans. Taxpayer was the organizer, sole stockholder, president, managing officer, and director of *E*, a corporation deriving its income from the rents of a certain office building. During 1967, 1968, and 1969, taxpayer personally withdrew certain amounts from the corporate funds. The IRS determined the withdrawals to be dividends. *Held:* For the IRS. Whether a withdrawal of corporate funds by a stockholder was a loan or dividend was a question to be determined by a jury. The jury reviewed the stockholder's intent at the time of the withdrawals, bookkeeping entries, the existence or lack thereof of an agreement to repay, collateral for the advances, interest charged, and the corporation's financial condition, including its earnings and profits, and found that the evidence tended to indicate the advances were in fact mere devices to obtain a distribution from the corporation. Oxenhandler, 74-1 USTC ¶ 9482, 34 AFTR2d 74-5076 (ED Mo. 1974).

Interest deductions lacking enforceable debt were disguised dividends. In 1916, taxpayer corporation leased land for 99 years and erected a building. The lease called for monthly payments of rent, but did not require payments of interest on unpaid rents. In 1942, taxpayer's stockholders formed a trust and, in proportions corresponding to their stock ownership, paid $2,000 for a "claim for rent past due" of $127,000. The IRS disallowed interest payments made by taxpayer to the trust. *Held:* For the IRS. There was no enforceable debt. The payments were disguised dividends. Metropolitan Inv. Co., 72-2 USTC ¶ 9761 (D. Ohio 1972).

Funds withdrawn by sole stockholder were intended for corporate investment, not dividends. Taxpayer, sole stockholder of a corporation, withdrew $80,000 from the corporate bank account for the purchase of a parcel of real estate. Taxpayer contended that the withdrawals were for a corporate investment that he took in his own name as nominee. The IRS contended that this was a dividend distribution. *Held:* For taxpayer. At all times, taxpayer had ample funds of his own to make the investment if he had really intended it to be a personal investment. The separate accounting for the income from this property also confirmed the intent not to treat it as a personal investment. Nasser, 257 F. Supp. 443, 66-1 USTC ¶ 9438, 18 AFTR2d 5083 (ND Cal. 1966).

Jury found that withdrawals from corporation resulted in dividends. Taxpayer and his family owned all the stock of a corporation. Taxpayer, who managed and controlled the corporate business, gave the corporation unsecured demand promissory notes for money advances to him. Taxpayer paid interest on the notes. *Held:* For the IRS. The court advised the jury to consider whether a valid corporate purpose was being served and stated factors that would tend to establish either bona fide loans or dividends. The jury found that the advances were dividends, not loans. Case, Jr., 64-2 USTC ¶ 9673 (DNJ 1964).

"Loan" to controlling stockholder was taxable dividend. Taxpayer and a family trust he controlled owned 99 percent of the capital stock of an automobile agency. The corporation gave him a check for $10,000 charged to a loan account. At the time of the withdrawal, the corporation had a surplus in excess of $10,000. Taxpayer contended that he intended to repay the money whenever the corporation needed it, but the IRS determined the payment to be a taxable dividend. *Held:* For the IRS. There was no note or security given and no provision for interest agreed to or paid. Taxpayer had withdrawn $7,500 in a prior year and, although he had ample funds to repay both items, never did so except for two $500 payments made on advice of counsel after taxpayer brought this refund suit. Hamer, 60-2 USTC ¶ 9489 (ND Ill. 1960).

Transfer of funds to redeem stock was a constructive dividend. Taxpayer was the sole stockholder of *A* Corporation and a 50 percent stockholder of *B*. *A* borrowed $20,000 and transferred it to *B* to enable *B* to redeem the 50 percent ownership of the other stockholder (taxpayer's brother). The IRS determined that the transaction resulted in a constructive dividend to taxpayer in the amount of the loan. *Held:* For the IRS. The taxpayer was able to obtain a sole interest in *B* without reducing the value of his interest, since the funds used to redeem his brother's stock were obtained from *A*. Therefore, the taxpayer realized economic benefit by using the funds of *A* to obtain personal control of *B*. Gilbert, 74 TC 60 (1980).

Corporate distributions were dividends, not return of capital. The directors of a Subchapter S corporation desired to pay dividends to stockholders from undistributed income accounts and adopted a resolution to issue promissory notes on October 1 to stockholders of record on September 30. The corporation then revoked its Subchapter S election effective October 1, and the stockholders excluded these distributions as return of capital. The IRS determined that they were dividends. *Held:* For the IRS. There was no legal obligation to pay the notes before October 1, and there was no evidence that the corporation carried a dividend liability as accounts payable on its books commencing September 30. Futhermore, the doctrine of constructive receipt was not applicable. Estate of McWhorter, 69 TC 650, aff'd (8th Cir. 1978).

Lack of intent to repay makes withdrawn funds dividends. Taxpayer owned all of the stock in a corporation that in turn was the sole stockholder of another corporation. The subsidiary sold all of its assets to an unrelated party and became inactive. Taxpayer made cash withdrawals that were evidenced by non-interest-bearing notes. The IRS argued that the withdrawals were dividends. *Held:* For the IRS. Although the advances were evidenced by notes, no repayment was ever made, and there was no evidence of any plan of repayment or of any intention to repay. The withdrawn funds were therefore distributions to the parent corporation and taxable dividends to taxpayer. The IRS was not estopped from claiming that the withdrawals were dividends even though it previously allowed similar withdrawals as loans. Tollefsen, 52 TC 671 (1969).

Payment of parent's bank note by newly acquired subsidiary a dividend rather than a loan. Taxpayer corporation acquired all of the outstanding stock of another corporation. To finance the acquisition, taxpayer borrowed from a bank and from two other corporations. Shortly after the acquisition, the acquired corporation advanced sums of money to taxpayer that the latter used to discharge the indebtedness. Simultaneously, the acquired corporation incurred an indebtedness to the bank secured by Treasury bills acquired with taxpayer's repayment of the advance. Several days after the end of the taxable year, the acquired corporation entered into the reverse of this transaction. The purpose of the transaction was to show a bank loan from taxpayer rather than a liability to the

DIVIDENDS AND DISTRIBUTIONS: *Withdrawals by Stockholders*

subsidiary. The IRS determined that the advances from the newly acquired subsidiary to taxpayer constituted a dividend. *Held:* For the IRS. Although taxpayer contended that the transaction was a bona fide loan, the facts indicated that the advances resulted in distributions essentially equivalent to a dividend and that the series of transactions was to improve the appearance of taxpayer's balance sheet but was otherwise without legal significance. No other purpose for the advance was suggested other than to pay for the acquisition of the stock, and taxpayer had no income from which to pay the advances unless it subsequently engaged in income-producing activities or later sold the stock. The Ogden Co., 50 TC 1000 (1968).

Loans by subsidiary to stockholder of parent corporation treated as dividends out of parent's surplus. Taxpayer, the principal stockholder of a family corporation, received large sums of money from the corporation on open account. He did not treat these amounts as dividends, and the IRS did not compel him to do so. Later, the corporation formed a subsidiary to specialize in short-term investments. It advanced $2.86 million on open account to the new subsidiary. In turn, the subsidiary advanced $968,000 to taxpayer. Taxpayer never repaid these loans, but explained that upon his death the corporation was to transfer its claim against him to a charitable foundation. The IRS treated the loans as a dividend distribution from the parent, charging that the parent corporation was the source of the funds. *Held:* For the IRS. Taxpayer intended to retain the funds for his own use. Because his control of both corporations was unfettered, he was able to use the subsidiary as a conduit. The court determined that the parent had sufficient earnings and profits to pay dividends. Kaplan, 43 TC 580 (1965).

Distributions to taxpayers treated as dividends during partnership incorporation. Taxpayers' partnership reorganized into a corporation to increase a line of credit with a financial institution. Subsequently, partnership capital accounts, renamed "stockholder advances," were distributed to the stockholders. Taxpayers argued that the distribution was repayment of a loan made upon incorporation. The IRS determined that the distributions were dividends. *Held:* For the IRS. Although Section 351 provides for nonrecognition, the distributions were dividends, as they were not in satisfaction of a liability owed to taxpayers by the corporation. Property transferred pursuant to Section 351 that is subsequently distributed to the stockholders is subject to normal corporate distribution rules. Furthermore, the distributions were from corporate earnings. Guyer, 49 TCM 1376, ¶ 85,210 P-H Memo. TC (1985).

Cash distribution is dividend, not loan. Taxpayer, a lawyer, owned a real estate development corporation. Transfers of cash between taxpayer and the corporation were common. The IRS determined that a $15,000 payment from the corporation to taxpayer, which was characterized as a loan, was actually a dividend. *Held:* For the IRS. No written unconditional obligation to pay existed, the ratio of debt to equity was extreme, and taxpayer expected repayment only if its business were successful. As such, the funds were never absolutely to be repaid by him at any time, and thus constituted a dividend. Rapoport, 47 TCM 205, ¶ 83,657 P-H Memo. TC (1983), aff'd (2d Cir. 1984).

Loans taken by corporation were constructive dividends. A corporation partly owned by taxpayer took a bank loan and used its proceeds to buy its shares held by another stockholder. The shares were transferred to taxpayer (held by his wife as nominee). Taxpayer claimed that the parties intended a redemption, not a stock sale. *Held:* For the IRS. Taxpayer may have intended to create a redemption, but the seller structured the transaction as a stock transfer, therefore it was a sale. Thus, the amount of the loans the corporation used to pay for the shares constitutes a constructive dividend to taxpayer in the year the stock was transferred. Montpetit, 45 TCM 304, ¶ 82,715 P-H Memo. TC (1982).

Distributions to stockholder were dividends, not loans. Taxpayer corporation's former

Dividends and Distributions: *Withdrawals by Stockholders*

stockholders sold all its stock to another corporation. Taxpayer participated in financing the transaction by taking certain loans and paying the new stockholder's debts to the sellers. The buyer corporation's stockholder never repaid the debts. Taxpayer claimed that the amount of loans was a bad debt from the new stockholder; the IRS said that it was a dividend distribution to it. *Held:* For the IRS. No bona fide loan existed because the common stockholder never intended to repay taxpayer for the loans. Since he controlled both corporations, his intent was attributed to both. The amounts distributed to the buyer corporation were dividends. Brown Corp. of Ionia, 45 TCM 200, ¶ 82,683 P-H Memo. TC (1982).

Payments from corporation were dividends. Taxpayer advanced funds characterized as a loan to a family corporation. The corporation's payments to him were characterized as repayment of the loan. The IRS contended that the advances were a contribution to capital and the payments were dividends. *Held:* For the IRS. There were no formal indicia of the corporation's repayment obligation, fixed maturity dates, or interest payment. Taxpayer failed to meet his burden of proving the nature of the payments. Finley & Co., 44 TCM 225, ¶ 82,345 P-H Memo. TC (1982).

Cash withdrawals were dividends, not loans. Taxpayers withdrew cash for personal use from a corporation they controlled. After an IRS audit, they executed promissory notes to the corporation. The IRS treated the withdrawals as dividends. *Held:* For the IRS. The evidence showed that there was no intent to repay the withdrawals. Hardy, 43 TCM 1210, ¶ 82,225 P-H Memo. TC (1982), aff'd, 709 F2d 1515 (9th Cir. 1983).

Corporate funds used for personal use constituted dividends. Taxpayers, sole owners and officers of a family corporation, withdrew funds from the corporation for their personal use. The IRS argued that the amounts were dividends and assessed the fraud penalty. *Held:* For the IRS. Taxpayers received dividend income to the extent that corporate earnings were not shown to be retained by the corporation or used for corporate purposes. Bourque, 40 TCM 824, ¶ 80,286 P-H Memo. TC (1980).

Withdrawals were dividends, not loans. Taxpayer was the president and sole stockholder of *F* Corporation, which sold insurance. Taxpayer's son was the president and sole stockholder of *C* Corporation. Over the years, taxpayer made certain withdrawals and listed them on *F*'s books as loans receivable, including withdrawals for the purchase of *C*'s automobile and taxpayer's son's down payment for a home. Taxpayer maintained the books and tax returns of both *C* and *F*. His treatment of these payments as loans from the stockholder on *C*'s tax return was inconsistent with the treatment of these payments on *F*'s tax return as loans receivable. No fixed repayment schedule was established regarding the withdrawals, no security or notes were executed, and no interest was charged on the loans. *F* at no time made dividend distributions to its stockholder taxpayer but had sufficient earnings and profits to cover the amounts in dispute. The IRS determined the withdrawals to be dividends. *Held:* For the IRS. The withdrawals were taxable dividends and not loans where the evidence did not establish bona fide loans. The failure to pay interest, to secure the loans, or to draw up promissory notes, and the inconsistent treatment of the withdrawals showed a lack of intent to repay the withdrawals when they were made. Fenn Jr., 40 TCM 559, ¶ 80,229 P-H Memo. TC (1980).

Constructive dividends found in absence of evidence of loans. Taxpayers' wholly owned corporation and subsidiary made payments to and on behalf of taxpayers, who characterized them as repayments of loans. The IRS disallowed the deductions claimed and recharacterized the payments as constructive dividends. *Held:* For the IRS. Taxpayers failed to introduce notes or other evidence of the alleged loans and thus the payments were constructive dividends. A determination of unreported income from sums deposited into bank accounts was also upheld. Additions to tax were sustained because there was no adequate explanation for taxpayers' failure to

Dividends and Distributions: *Withdrawals by Stockholders*

maintain or provide records. Hedrick, 39 TCM 1111, ¶ 80,054 P-H Memo. TC (1980).

Stockholder loans actually dividends. Taxpayers, sole stockholders of a corporation, characterized disbursements to themselves as loans. The IRS contended that these distributions were dividends. *Held:* For the IRS. The distributions were not consistently treated as loans in the corporate books and records; no notes were executed; no interest was paid; and no collateral was pledged. Smith, 39 TCM 900, ¶ 80,015 P-H Memo. TC (1980).

Stockholder's "loans" from wholly owned corporation were distribution. Taxpayer withdrew money from a corporation of which he was the sole stockholder and reported it as loans on the corporation's books. He executed no notes, paid no interest, and followed no repayment schedule. The corporation declared no dividends. The IRS treated these "loans" as corporate distributions taxable under Section 301. *Held:* For the IRS. The withdrawals lacked the indicia of true loans. The fact that they could have been proceeds of loans the corporation made with outside lenders did not show the stockholder's intent to repay his "loans" because the corporation itself could repay its loans. Whitaker, 37 TCM 310, ¶ 78,061 P-H Memo. TC (1978).

Payments were dividends, not loans. Taxpayer made payments to its parent without a formal declaration of dividends. The IRS contended that the payments were loans, and that taxpayer was not entitled to a dividends paid deduction. *Held:* For taxpayer. The evidence showed that there was never an intent to repay the amounts transferred to the parent. Further, taxpayer was not estopped from claiming that the payments were dividends by past treatment of the payments as loans, since taxpayer received no tax benefit from so claiming. Deviney Constr. Co., 36 TCM 413, ¶ 77,092 P-H Memo. TC (1977).

Advances to controlling stockholder were dividends, not loans. Taxpayer, 60 percent stockholder of a corporation, made certain withdrawals from the corporation. The IRS contended that the amounts were dividends, not bona fide loans. *Held:* For the IRS. No collateral was given, no maturity date or payment schedule was fixed, no payments of interest or principal were ever made or sought by the corporation. The taxpayer was found liable under state law as a transferee for tax deficiencies of the company to the extent of the withdrawals. Fugate, 36 TCM 85, ¶ 77,018 P-H Memo. TC (1977).

"Loans" were constructive dividends. Taxpayers received "loans" from three corporations that they controlled. Taxpayers delayed in issuing notes for the "loans." Even after the notes were issued, no interest or principal was paid. The IRS argued they were constructive dividends. *Held:* For the IRS. The facts show the advances were not bona fide loans. Williams, 35 TCM 1672, ¶ 76,306 P-H Memo. TC (1976).

Advances to stockholder were dividends. Taxpayer owned all of the stock of a realty company and a car dealership that leased the realty. While the car dealership incurred losses, the realty company obtained a $100,000 loan and advanced $60,000 to the dealership for a note. The dealership then paid off a $60,000 debt to taxpayer. The realty company also directly loaned taxpayer $33,000. The IRS determined that both payments were dividends to taxpayer. *Held:* For the IRS. The loans were primarily for the benefit of taxpayer. The realty company had no valid business reason to make a loan to the car dealership, especially when it was losing money. Also, the direct loan to taxpayer was evidenced by an unsecured and non-interest-bearing demand note indicating a questionable intent to repay. Thus, both loans constituted dividends to the taxpayer and were taxable as such. McLemore, 32 TCM 259, ¶ 73,059 P-H Memo. TC (1973).

Amounts loaned to officer-stockholders constituted dividend income. Taxpayer corporation transferred $14,500 to each of its officer-stockholders in return for notes agreeing to repay the amounts. The IRS determined that the amounts were really dividends, and taxpayer was not entitled to a deduction. *Held:* For the IRS. The transfers were dividends to

DIVIDENDS AND DISTRIBUTIONS: *Withdrawals by Stockholders*

the extent of taxpayer's earnings and profits, and no deduction was allowable. Taxpayer failed to show that the amounts were intended as compensation, the transfers were carried on its books as notes receivable, and the distribution had been made pro rata to the two stockholders of the close corporation, indicating a dividend. Savage, 29 TCM 690, ¶ 70,158 P-H Memo. TC (1970).

Withdrawals represented dividends, return of capital and capital gains; on sale, corporation property's basis was zero. Taxpayer owned a corporation that, after several withdrawals, was liquidated. Taxpayer sold the assets. The character of the withdrawals, amount of capital gain on asset sale, and several penalties were in dispute. *Held:* For the IRS. Taxpayer received dividends to the extent of earnings and profits; he received return of capital to the extent of adjusted basis under Section 301 (c)(2); and, as he was unable to show otherwise, he received capital gains on the remainder of the withdrawals from the corporation. On the sale of the assets, their basis was zero, since the return of capital had exhausted all basis. When income was properly reconstructed, taxpayer could not prove that bank deposits, which spanned a six-year period, as well as unreported rents, which were adjusted downward slightly under the *Cohan* rule, were not additional income. The benefit of joint rates was denied when taxpayers failed to file returns. The IRS was not barred from determining transferee liability against taxpayer, as the period of limitation had an extra year to run under Section 6901(c)(1). Penalties for late filing and for failure to file, for which no reasonable cause was shown, and penalties for negligent underpayment of tax, were upheld. Dritz, 28 TCM 874, ¶ 69,175 P-H Memo. TC (1969).

Thin capitalization caused corporate payments to be constructive dividends, not loan repayments. Taxpayer incorporated his business with $5,000 cash and $120,000 of equipment, which was subject to a $47,000 loan. The $73,000 difference was classified as a loan from taxpayer that was gradually repaid. The IRS declared the repayments to be constructive dividends, along with certain personal expenses of taxpayer for which the corporation paid. *Held:* For the IRS. Since the corporation was so thinly capitalized and the purported loan was without interest, security or maturity date, it was in reality a contribution to capital, and the repayments were not loans, but taxable dividends. The corporation's payments for some of taxpayer's personal living expenses were also constructive dividends to him and were not deductible by the corporation when taxpayer failed to sufficiently substantiate the deductions. Lizak, Inc., 28 TCM 804, ¶ 69,163 P-H Memo. TC (1969).

Absent intention or expectation of repayment, advances were deemed dividends rather than loans. Taxpayer trust controlled several corporations. Their stock had been contributed by the settlor who, after his death, was held to owe large amounts of income taxes. To meet such payments, the related corporations, threatened with seizure of assets by the IRS, contributed funds to the trust that paid the income tax. The trustee and the corporations recorded the amounts as interest-bearing notes, but the IRS held them to be dividends to the trust. *Held:* For the IRS. Although the amounts were recorded as loans, no interest was ever paid, and, most important, there was no intention or expectation of repayment. Furthermore, the trust was taxable on part of the payments, receiving a distributions deduction, and the beneficiary, settlor's wife, was taxable on the remaining part. Livernois Trust, 28 TCM 583, ¶ 69,111 P-H Memo. TC (1969), aff'd, 433 F2d 879, 70-2 USTC ¶ 9642.

Advances to sole stockholder for construction of factory deemed dividends rather than loans. Taxpayer was the sole stockholder of a corporation engaged in the electrical business. The corporation advanced him sums of money on open account for the construction of a factory-office building that he later transferred to the corporation. The IRS treated the advances as dividends to the extent of the corporation's earnings and profits, and as long-term capital gain to the extent the excess exceeded his basis in the stock. *Held:* For the IRS. The construction funds were advanced without evidence of any indebtedness and without a lien on the building to secure repayment. No interest was ever accrued by the corporation on the advances, no repayment was made on the alleged initial repayment date, and no corporate action had been taken to extend that original due date. Berthold, 26 TCM 483, ¶ 67,102 P-H Memo. TC (1967).

Distributions by corporation constituted dividends rather than loan repayments. Taxpayer, a real estate broker, was president and stockholder of a corporation that acquired from him for $5,000 a purchase contract to acquire real property. In the following years, taxpayer received further sums from the corporation and alleged that all sums received, including the $5,000, constituted repayment of moneys previously advanced to the corporation. *Held:* For the IRS. The $5,000 constituted a fee, and the sums allegedly previously advanced to the corporation were in the nature of equity. Thus, regarding the earnings and profits, the corporate distributions in the taxable years were taxable dividends rather than loan repayments. Ogier, 26 TCM 448, ¶ 67,093 P-H Memo. TC (1967).

Corporate loans to controlling stockholder considered dividends. Taxpayer withdrew funds from two corporations controlled by him. The withdrawals were recorded in various open accounts on the books of the corporations. None of the withdrawals was evidenced by notes, no collateral security was ever furnished to the corporations, and no interest was ever paid. The net withdrawals were practically equivalent to the accumulated earnings, and neither corporation paid any formal dividends during the years in question. Taxpayer used a substantial portion of the amounts withdrawn for personal investments. *Held:* For the IRS. The corporate withdrawals constituted an advancement in lieu of dividends rather than true loans and were considered taxable to taxpayer as constructive dividends. Tarrson, 25 TCM 671, ¶ 66,133 P-H Memo. TC (1966).

Corporate withdrawals were dividends, not loans. Taxpayer was secretary-treasurer of a family corporation. For several years, he withdrew funds that were charged to various accounts on the company's books. He used the funds for personal expenses, and over a period of years made no payment of any kind to reduce the balance. In 1963, after the IRS asserted that the withdrawals constituted dividends rather than loans, taxpayer assigned stock and insurance policies to the corporation to secure the so-called loans. *Held:* For the IRS. The withdrawals were taxable as dividends. There was no evidence of any agreement concerning a maturity date for repayment or payment of any interest. No repayments were made by taxpayer, and the corporation declared no dividends despite the fact that it had an adequate earned surplus. The assignment of the securities subsequent to the deficiency notice was insufficient to establish the intention of the parties at the time the withdrawals were made. Bibb, 24 TCM 1640; ¶ 65,296 P-H Memo. TC (1965).

Withdrawals of corporate funds for officer's personal use were disguised dividends. Taxpayer and his wife owned a controlling interest in *W* Corporation, which was engaged in the performance of architectural and engineering services and in construction work. He was also a partner in *R* Company and the owner of *S* Corporation. The proceeds of checks paid by *W* to taxpayer, *R*, *S*, and taxpayer's partner eventually were turned over to taxpayer and were charged on the corporate books as purported selling, engineering, and reimbursed travel expenses. The IRS recharacterized these payments as constructive dividends to taxpayer. *Held:* For the IRS. The various amounts received, either from the payees of the corporate checks or as purported reimbursements of travel expenses, were properly included in taxpayer's income as disguised dividends. Thomas Worcester, Inc., 24 TCM 1021, ¶ 65,199 P-H Memo. TC (1965).

Corporate withdrawals by officer taxed to him as dividends. Taxpayer, president and principal stockholder of a corporation, made substantial withdrawals from his corporation in addition to his salary for payments to his personal creditor. Although the withdrawals were charged on the corporate records to taxpayer's loan account, the IRS determined that the payments were dividends. *Held:* For the IRS. Taxpayer failed to meet his burden of proving that the IRS' determination was incorrect. Taxpayer executed no evidence of indebtedness to the corporation for the withdrawals, pledged no security as collateral, and paid no interest on the alleged loans. The corporation had earnings and profits in excess of the withdrawals and had outstanding loans from commercial sources on which it paid interest. Blinsinger, 23 TCM 2054, ¶ 64,331 P-H Memo. TC (1964).

Withdrawals of corporate funds by sole stockholder taxable as dividends. The IRS determined that withdrawals by taxpayer from his wholly owned corporation that were charged on the corporate books to a receivable account were disguised dividends rather than loans. *Held:* For the IRS. The court considered the following facts as controlling: Taxpayer gave no notes or any other instrument to evidence his indebtedness; there was no fixed or systematic plan for the repayment of the claimed "loans;" taxpayer did not pay, nor did the corporation demand, any interest on the purported "loans;" the net withdrawals approximated the accumulated earned surplus; the funds withdrawn were used for recurring personal items; withdrawals were made over a span of years with increasingly larger "loan" balances and only negligible repayments; and the corporation never paid a formal dividend. Cohen, 22 TCM 1189, ¶ 63,234 P-H Memo. TC (1963).

Repayment of loans after transfer to capital surplus deemed a dividend. From time to time, taxpayer found it necessary to advance funds to his corporation and to leave his salary with the corporation. These amounts were reflected on the corporate books as loans payable. Finding that he was running into difficulty whenever he borrowed money for the corporation because of the loans due him, taxpayer decided to cancel the obligations by transferring them on the corporate books to capital surplus. The amounts so transferred were later paid out to taxpayer. *Held:* For the IRS. The court held that no true debtor-creditor relationship existed between the corporation and taxpayer with respect to the funds shown on the corporate books as capital surplus. The advances made by taxpayer in that amount represented, as a matter of substantial reality, investments of equity capital put at the risk of the business. Accordingly, the payments to taxpayer did not constitute repayments of loans but were essentially equivalent to dividends, and were taxable as such. McMinn, Jr., 21 TCM 913, ¶ 62,165 P-H Memo. TC (1962).

Stockholders' withdrawals from controlled corporation for personal use were dividends. Taxpayers, husband and wife, were the sole stockholders of a corporation. During the years in issue, they did not draw from the corporation regular salary checks as did the other employees, but instead made corporate withdrawals that were charged to a loan account. This account was credited each year with taxpayers' salaries. No note or security was given for any of the advances, and no interest was provided for. The withdrawals were for living and other personal expenses of taxpayers. *Held:* For the IRS. The court found that the conduct of the parties with respect to the drawing accounts, considered in conjunction with all other facts of record, supported an inference that the withdrawals involved here were not loans, but were permanent distributions by the corporation to taxpayers for their personal use. Accordingly, it upheld the IRS' determination that taxpayers received dividend income in amounts slightly less than their net withdrawals. Kountz, 21 TCM 131, ¶ 62,029 P-H Memo. TC (1962).

Withdrawals from corporation taxable as dividends even though recorded as loans. Substantial increases in the personal account of a stockholder who owned all but one share of stock in a company, and representing payments of personal indebtedness of the stockholder and withdrawals of cash were determined by the IRS to constitute informal dividends, not loans. *Held:* For the IRS. Although recorded on the books as loans, there were no notes, no interest payments, no definite dates of repayment, and no security ar-

DIVIDENDS RECEIVED DEDUCTION

rangement. Cruser, 20 TCM 313, ¶ 61,060 P-H Memo. TC (1961).

Monthly withdrawals from corporation disguised dividends rather than loans. Taxpayers, two stockholders of a corporate auto dealership, took monthly withdrawals from their corporation. They claimed that these withdrawals were loans. The IRS contended that they were dividends. *Held:* For the IRS. The court found the withdrawals to represent corporate distributions with no intention of repayment and with no restriction concerning the use of the funds. They therefore constituted dividends rather than loans. The payments were not treated as salaries because the corporation did not characterize or claim them as such. The court also found that weekly payments of $100 to each of the stockholders reflected on the corporate books as travel and entertaining expenses were intended to be and were in fact payments of salaries. Carter, 19 TCM 1090, ¶ 60,205 P-H Memo. TC (1960).

Corporate withdrawals for personal use treated as dividends and not as loans. Funds withdrawn from a corporation for investments in numerous speculative ventures of the two stockholders or their partnership for a personal residence for the stockholders and other personal expenditures were determined by the IRS to be, in part, dividends and not loans. *Held:* For the IRS. The advances were upon open account, were not evidenced by notes, and no interest was paid. Lowes Lumber Co., 19 TCM 727, ¶ 60,141 P-H Memo. TC (1960).

DIVIDENDS PAID DEDUCTION

(*See* Accumulated Earnings Tax; Personal Holding Companies)

DIVIDENDS RECEIVED DEDUCTION

Corporate owner of stock leased to another for 99 years not entitled to dividends received deductions. Prior to March 1, 1913, taxpayer had acquired various railroad properties, including the capital stock of certain railroads. It leased the stock and properties to others for 99 years. The stock certificates representing the leased stock were registered in the names of one of the lessees as "trustee." The district court held that taxpayer, as lessor, was the true owner of the securities and entitled to the 85 percent dividends received deduction. In addition, the district court held that taxpayer could amortize that portion of its stock basis allocable to the interest it retained when it distributed its reversion interest in the lease to its stockholders over the remaining term of the lease. *Held:* Reversed. The lessees had virtually all the indicia of present ownership of the stock. They, if any one, were its beneficial owners. The holding of the stock in trust for their benefit, and their unrestricted use of the dividends, bolstered this conclusion. The fact that taxpayer distributed its reversion interest was further support for the conclusion that taxpayer was not entitled to the credit. Moreover, taxpayer could not amortize its basis in the stock, since the leasehold, not the stock, was the wasting asset, and taxpayer had no basis in the leasehold. Georgia R.R. & Banking Co., 348 F2d 278, 65-2 USTC ¶ 9525, 16 AFTR2d 5061 (5th Cir. 1965), cert. denied, 382 US 973 (1966).

Cemetery perpetual care funds not held in trust; 85 percent dividends received deduction available. To provide for the maintenance of lots, a cemetery association entered into perpetual care agreements with lot owners. Segregating the funds received on account of these agreements, the association did not report the funds as taxable income. The association, however, invested the funds in securities, mingled the dividends with the rest of its funds, and reported the dividends as taxable income. The only issue was whether the association could claim the 85 percent dividends received deduction. Arguing that the perpetual care agreements set up an express trust, the IRS contended that the trust, not the association, owned the dividends and had the right to the deduction. The IRS further argued that the association was estopped from claiming the funds as its own because it had not reported the original "corpus" as income. The district court agreed with the IRS. *Held:* Reversed. The segregation of the funds was merely careful financial management and did not create a trust. Furthermore, a taxpayer is not estopped from correcting the manner in which it reports income. Oak Woods Cemetery Ass'n, 345 F2d 361, 65-1 USTC ¶ 9277 (7th Cir. 1965).

Dividends received deduction disallowed; sale of stock to corporation delayed until after record date. A calendar year corporation contracted on December 7, 1954 to purchase certain corporate stock. The contract was conditioned upon the seller receiving a no-action letter from the SEC before the end of the year. The contract provided that all dividends paid or payable on the stock after December 7 would be the property of the buying corporation. A dividend was declared to stockholders of record on December 20 and was paid on December 31. The no-action letter was received early in January 1955, and the sale was consummated later that month, with the dividends being used to reduce the purchase price. The buyer corporation claimed a dividends received deduction for 1955. The Tax Court disallowed the deduction, since the buyer was not a stockholder on the record date. *Held:* Affirmed. At that date, the contract was executory only. The condition was not fulfilled until after the record date, so taxpayer was not a stockholder within the meaning of Section 316(a) and thus had not received a dividend. Joseph L. O'Brien Co., 301 F2d 813, 62-1 USTC ¶ 9393 (3d Cir. 1962), cert. denied, 371 US 820 (1962).

Dividends paid pursuant to contract denied 85 percent credit. Taxpayer was a finance company. The unpaid balances of its loans were insured under credit insurance issued by an insurance company. Taxpayer bought all the preferred stock of the insurance company under a plan that required the insurance company to pay 90 percent of the net profit on this credit insurance as dividends on the preferred stock. The district court denied the 85 percent intercorporate dividend credit on these dividends. *Held:* Affirmed. While avoiding the characterization of the transaction as a sham that could be ignored for tax purposes, the court held that the profits on these policies never became part of the surplus of the insurance company from which dividends were paid but were merely a refund of premium. Liston Zander Credit Co., 276 F2d 417, 60-1 USTC ¶ 9329 (5th Cir. 1960).

Distribution received by new parent corporation from old qualified for dividend received deduction. P Corporation and its subsidiaries, S-1, S-2, and S-3, were engaged in manufacturing. P created holding company H, which in turn created subsidiary S. Before H or S had conducted any business, S was merged into P in a reorganization plan that qualified under Sections 368(a)(1)(A) and 368(a)(2)(E). As a result of the merger, H owned all of the stock of P, which in turn owned all of the stock of S-1, S-2, and S-3. Later, P declared and distributed all of the outstanding stock of S-1, S-2, and S-3 to its sole stockholder, H, making H the common parent of P, S-1, S-2, and S-3. P retained more than 90 percent of the fair market value of its net assets and more than 70 percent of the gross assets it held immediately before the transfer. In accordance with Regulation § 1.243-4(c), P elected on behalf of the affiliated group to qualify for the 100 percent dividends received deduction under Section 243(a)(3). The group had never elected the Section 1562 multiple surtax exemption. The IRS ruled that, since P and H were members of an affiliated group when the qualifying dividends were distributed, the distribution of S-1, S-2, and S-3 stock by P to H qualified for the 100 percent dividends received deduction. Rev. Rul. 84-154, 1984-2 CB 61.

Record date owner entitled to Section 243 deduction. Y Corporation sold shares of stock to Z Corporation after the record date but before the ex-dividend date. Y signed an agreement that Z was entitled to the dividends pursuant to stock exchange rules. The dividends were taxable to Y because Y was the record date owner. Stock exchange rules were not controlling for income tax purposes. Thus, Y, not Z, was entitled to the Section 243 dividends received deduction. Rev. Rul. 82-11, 1982-1 CB 51.

Grant of call does not reduce holding period for purposes of limit on dividends received deduction. *X* Corporation wrote call options on stock that it owned in domestic corporations. Its holding period in the stock was not reduced under Section 246(c) by the period during which the call was outstanding for the purpose of the dividends received deduction. Rev. Rul. 80-238, 1980-2 CB 96.

DIVISIVE REORGANIZATIONS

(*See* Reorganizations—Spin-Offs and Other Divisive Reorganizations)

DOMESTIC INTERNATIONAL SALES CORPORATIONS

Section 337 sale involving DISC stock no longer tax free after 1976. If stock of a DISC subsidiary is among the assets sold in a Section 337 sale occurring before 1977, no income or gain should be recognized in relation to DISC stock. However, after 1976, the selling corporation must include as a dividend the gain on the sale to the extent of the accumulated DISC income attributable to the seller under Section 995(c)(2). Rev. Rul. 79-104, 1979-1 CB 263.

Commissions received by DISC from its parent's foreign subsidiary included in its gross receipts. Taxpayer DISC received commissions from its parent's foreign subsidiary for making purchases of U.S.-manufactured components for the foreign subsidiary's manufacturing operations. The IRS ruled that for purposes of the 95 percent gross receipts test of Section 992(a)(1)(A), the DISC includes commissions from the foreign subsidiary that are not qualified receipts under Section 993(a)(1). Rev. Rul. 76-338, 1976-2 CB 233.

DUMMY CORPORATIONS

(*See* Associations Taxable as Corporations; Corporations as Taxable Entities)

EARNINGS AND PROFITS

EARNED SURPLUS

(*See* Earnings and Profits)

EARNINGS AND PROFITS

(*See also* Dividends and Distributions)

Only subsidiary, and not parent, adjusts its earnings when its employee exercises qualified stock option on parent corporation's stock. In determining whether a parent corporation had sufficient earnings to cause distributions to taxpayer to be taxed as a dividend, the Tax Court examined whether distributions from subsidiaries to the parent were dividends. In the course of this examination, the Tax Court determined that: (1) The Jarvis method (discussed in William D.P. Jarvis, 43 BTA 439 (1941), aff'd, 123 F2d 742 (4th Cir. 1941)) was appropriate for computing the adjustment to a subsidiary's earnings upon a redemption of its stock; (2) upon such a redemption, only that portion of the capital account attributable to the class of stock redeemed should be charged; and (3) upon an exercise of a qualified stock option in the parent's stock by a subsidiary's employee, only the subsidiary adjusts its earnings for the difference between the option price and the value of the stock received. *Held:* Affirmed. Anderson, 583 F2d 953, 78-2 USTC ¶ 9707, 42 AFTR2d 78-5876 (7th Cir. 1978).

Earnings and profits reduced by bargain spread upon exercise of qualified stock option. Under the exercise of certain qualified stock options, taxpayer sold stock at bargain prices. Corresponding to the sales, earnings and profits were reduced by the difference between the fair market value of the stock and its purchase price. As a result, earnings and profits were reduced so that later distributions to stockholders were tax free. The Tax Court agreed with the IRS that earnings and profits should not be reduced by such amounts that they result in tax-free distributions to stockholders. The Seventh Circuit reversed and remanded the case, allowing the reduction in earnings and profits. *Held:* Affirmed. Where the corporate taxpayer was required to sell stock at bargain prices under the exercise of certain stock options, the earnings and profits were properly reduced by the bargain spread. Divine, 500 F2d 1041, 74-2 USTC ¶ 9527, 34 AFTR2d 74-533 (2d Cir. 1974).

Earnings and profits reduced by the difference between the exercise price and the fair market value of restricted stock options. In 1961, taxpayer received a cash distribution in connection with Rapid American stock and was advised that the distribution was a return of capital because the company did not have earnings and profits. The IRS contended that the company did have earnings and profits; therefore, the distribution was a dividend. Whether the company had earnings and profits depended upon if earnings and profits were reduced by the difference between the exercise price and the fair market value of stock that employees purchased pursuant to restricted stock options. The Tax Court held that since the company did not receive a deduction on the exercise of restricted stock options, there was no reduction in earnings and profits. *Held:* Reversed. The difference between the exercise price and the fair market value of a restricted stock option was compensation and reduced earnings and profits regardless of when the company was permitted to deduct such compensation from income. Luckman, 418 F2d 381, 70-1 USTC ¶ 9101 (7th Cir. 1969).

Adjustment in Chapter 11 bankruptcy proceeding did not give rise to earnings and profits. Taxpayer and his wife were stockholders of a closely held corporation. After the corporation suffered financial reverses, creditors filed a petition for involuntary bankruptcy. In the ensuing arrangement, the corporation received a discharge of indebtness. Pursuant to Section 1016, the corporation wrote down the value of its assets. The corporation credited this devaluation to contributed capital. The arrangement also required taxpayer to provide the corporation with additional working capital. In order to do this, taxpayer transferred 700 shares of a listed stock to his broker with instructions to sell them and give proceeds to his corporation. Due to a rise in price, it was only necessary to sell 638 shares. The remaining 62 shares were returned to taxpayer. The corporation used part of the proceeds to redeem the stock of taxpayer's wife. The IRS contended that the value of the 62 shares returned to taxpayer was a dividend distribution, as was the redemption of his wife's shares. The Tax Court agreed. It held that the cancellation of indebtedness over the amount that reduced the asset's bases increased earnings and profits out of which dividends could be paid. All the circumstances indicated that taxpayer transferred 700 shares to the corporation. The return of the 62 was a dividend. The redemption of the wife's shares was essentially equivalent to a dividend, since the wife's ownership changed only slightly, and there was no corporate reason for making the redemption. Only taxpayer's wife appealed. *Held:* Reversed and remanded. Section 395 of the Bankruptcy Act provides that no income or profit shall be deemed to have accrued or been realized from an adjustment under Chapter 11. This case, therefore, was distinguishable from those involving realized income that was not recognized. The purpose of the Bankruptcy Act—to preserve a going business—controls, and it requires providing not only tax relief to the corporate debtor's own income tax situation but to its accounting for all tax purposes. To the extent of the corporation's earnings in the year of the redemption, however, profits were available for distribution as a dividend. Meyer, 383 F2d 883, 67-2 USTC ¶ 9671, 20 AFTR2d 5603 (8th Cir. 1967).

Cash basis corporation could accrue federal income and excess profits taxes in computing earnings and profits, thereby making distributions nontaxable return of capital to the extent of such taxes. Land Trust, of which taxpayers were stockholders, was found to be an association taxable at corporate rates. It was required to pay substantial additional taxes from 1949 through 1955. During this time, the Trust made distributions to taxpayers. Taxpayers paid taxes on the distributions and filed a timely claim for a refund. Taxpayers contended that the Trust's earnings and profits should be reduced by the taxes paid, making distributions a return on capital and not a taxable distribution from earnings and profits. The IRS' motion for summary judgment was granted with judgment. Taxpayers appealed. *Held:* For taxpayers. Regardless of whether the accrual or cash basis method of accounting was used, the corporation was allowed to accrue corporate taxes in corporate income, thus reducing earnings and profits. Since the earnings and profits were reduced, part of the distribution was a return of capital. Demmon, 321 F2d 203, 63-2 USTC ¶ 9660, 12 AFTR2d 5371 (7th Cir. 1963).

Nondepreciable asset did not reduce undistributed earnings and profits in Section 333 election. In 1929, Lexington Holding Company purchased a contractual right to a determined amount of electricity to be supplied annually. The purchase price was $75,000, and the contract term was perpetual. On liquidation in 1955, when accumulated earnings and profits were $178,159, taxpayer, a stockholder, sought to deduct the cost of this contract in computing her ratable share to be reported as ordinary income. The IRS disallowed the deduction, and taxpayer obtained a judgment for refund in the district court. *Held:* Reversed. The Fourth Circuit held the deduction to be improper. In distinguishing Burnet V. Logan, 283 US 404 (1931), the court noted that this was not a case of an asset whose useful life was impossible to evaluate. Here, the asset would last forever and would not be depleted. There was no evidence that the supplier of electricity would be unable to perform either through instability of the business or failure of the natural resources. Since the asset would not be consumed, there could be no deduction for depreciation. Curry, 298 F2d 273, 62-1 USTC ¶ 9201 (4th Cir. 1962).

Allocation of earnings to new corporation resulting from spin-off determined under Regulation § 1.312-10(a). Taxpayers were stockholders in Canal, a corporation, who in 1960 received cash distributions with respect to their stock. Taxpayers argued that only a portion of the distributions were taxable as dividends, while the IRS argued all were. The dispute involved Canal's post-1913 earnings and profits as affected by (1) its formation in a tax-free spin-off, and (2) a 1957 redemption of part of its stock treated as an exchange under Section 302(a). As to its formation, Canal was organized in 1955 as the result of a transfer to it of property by another corporation in a spin-off under Sections 355 and 368(a)(1)(D). The transferors had both pre- and post-1913 earnings and profits. Taxpayer argued that Canal's initial earnings and profits were to be determined by allocating to it a portion of the transferors earnings on the basis of the relative tax bases of the assets held by each corporation after the spin-off. The IRS argued that the allocation was to be made on the basis of the relative fair market value of the businesses of each. As to the 1957 redemption, the IRS argued that the redemption distribution was first to be applied against pre-1913 earnings and profits (allocated to Canal as described previously) until they were fully exhausted, and only then against post-1913 earnings. *Held:* For the IRS. (1) In cases like this, involving D reorganizations, the allocation of earnings is, under Section 312(i) and Regulation § 1.312-10(a), to be made on the basis of the fair market value of the businesses, unless the "net basis" method is shown to be proper one in the particular case. This taxpayers failed to do. The regulation was upheld as valid, even though another part of it (Regulation § 1.312-10(b)) might not have been. Thus, $289,810 of the transferor's pre-1913 earnings and $1,844,913 of its post-1913 earnings were allocable to Canal. (2) As to the 1957 redemption distribution after a portion was properly charged to capital account under Section 312(c), the rest was first applied against pre-1913 earnings (i.e., $289,810) until they were fully exhausted. See Foster, 303 US 118 (1938); Jervis, 123 F2d 742 (Ct. Cl. 1957); Bennett, 427 F2d 1202, 70-1 USTC ¶ 9458 (Ct. Cl. 1970).

Redemption of preferred stock affected earnings and profits. In an exchange under Section 302(a), a cash basis corporation redeemed preferred stock at less than its issuance price, giving the seller a promissory note. No adjustment was made to earnings and profits. The IRS determined that in computing the amount taxable as a dividend, the redemption of preferred stock at less than issue price caused the full amount of the redemption distribution to be chargeable to the capital account of that stock. *Held*: For the IRS. The capital account of the preferred stock was clearly distinguishable from that of the common. Under Section 312(e), the full amount of the redemption distribution is properly chargeable to the capital account of the preferred stock. The court further held that in computing the corporation's earnings and profits, no reduction was allowed for unpaid but accrued taxes. Webb, 67 TC 1008 (1977).

IRS clarifies position on method to be used in adjusting earnings and profits following stock redemption. On the basis of the court's decision in Jarvis, 43 BTA 439 (1941), nonacq. 1970-2 CB xxii, aff'd, 123 F2d 742 (4th Cir. 1941), the IRS announced that it would follow the court's formula to determine the portion of a redemption distribution in exchange for common stock, pursuant to Section 302(a), that is properly chargeable to the capital account of a corporation incorporated subsequent to March 1, 1913. The correct formula is that in which the ratio between the charge to capital and the capital prior to retirement is the same as the ratio between the number of shares retired and the number of shares outstanding prior to retirement. The balance of the redemption distribution is charged to earnings and profits. Rev. Rul. 79-376, 1979-2 CB 133.

Charitable gift of appreciated property reduces corporation's earnings and profits by adjusted basis only. The IRS ruled that a corporation that donated appreciated real estate to a city could reduce its earnings and profits only by the adjusted basis of the propery despite the fact that it could deduct its full fair market value as a charitable contribution. The IRS stated that it would not follow Kaplan, 43 TC 580 (1965), to the contrary. Rev. Rul. 78-123, 1978-1 CB 87.

Unrecognized gain from liquidation sale under Section 337 does not increase corporate earnings and profits. The IRS held that realized but unrecognized gain from a corporation's sale of its assets pursuant to a Section 337 liquidation does not increase earnings and profits for the year. Section 312(f)(1) controls the result. Rev. Rul. 76-239, 1976-1 CB 90.

Deemed stock distribution under Section 305(c) decreases corporation's earnings and profits and increases debenture-holders' basis. X Corporation, with a single class of stock outstanding, plus convertible debentures, increased the conversion ratio to reflect cash dividends paid on the stock. The IRS held that this adjustment produces a deemed distribution of stock to the debenture-holders under Section 305(c). This, coupled with the cash dividend on the stock, causes the deemed distribution to be treated under Section 301, pursuant to Section 305(b)(2). Since the corporation's earnings and profits exceed the value of the deemed distribution, the entire amount is a dividend under Section 316, and is includible in income of the debenture-holders under Section 301(c). Under Section 301(d)(1), the basis of the debentures will be increased by the value of the distribution. Under Section 312(d)(1)(B) and Regulation 1.312-1(d), the corporation's earnings and profits will be reduced by the value of the distribution included in the debenture-holders' income. Rev. Rul. 76-186, 1976-1 CB 86.

Deficit in earnings and profits reduced by debt cancellation exceeding reduction in basis. The IRS ruled that where there is an arrangement under a Chapter 11 bankruptcy to cancel an indebtedness, where such cancellation exceeds the reduction of the basis of the retained assets, the deficit in earnings and profits will be reduced. The IRS will not follow the *Meyer* decision, which held otherwise. Rev. Rul. 75-515, 1975-2 CB 117.

Ordinary dividend precedes redemption distribution. The IRS ruled that ordinary distributions take priority in determining current earnings and profits available for dividends when both an ordinary distribution and a redemption distribution are made in the same year. Rev. Rul. 74-339, 1974-2 CB 103.

Dividend arrearages charged to earnings and profits. The IRS ruled that dividend arrearages paid on the redemption of preferred stock are charges to earnings and profits; redemption costs are chargeable to the capital account. Rev. Rul. 74-266, 1974-1 CB 73.

Amortizable bond premium on tax-exempt bonds reduces earnings and profits. The IRS restated its position that amortizable bond premium on tax-exempt bonds held by a corporation that is not a dealer in securities is an expense of the year to which attributable and must be reflected in earnings and profits. (IT 3764 superseded.) Rev. Rul. 71-165, 1971-1 CB 111.

Prior years' taxes are deductible in year of payment for computing earnings and profits available for dividends of cash-basis corporation. The IRS restated under current law and regulations its earlier decision that when computing earnings and profits available for dividends, additional federal income taxes paid by a cash-basis corporation for a prior year are deductible in the year of payment. (GCM 2951 superseded.) Rev. Rul. 70-609, 1970-2 CB 78.

IRS sets forth method for determining portion of redemption properly chargeable to capital account versus distribution of earnings and profits. The subject calendar year corporation had 10 shares of common stock outstanding that had each been issued for $8x$ cash. At the end of the taxable year, when stockholders A and B each held $5x$ shares (50 percent) of the stock, the corporation redeemed for cash the 50 percent held by A at its fair market value of $225x$ in circumstances that permitted the redemption to be treated by A as a distribution in full payment in exchange for the stock under Section 302. No other distribution was made with respect to its stock during the taxable year. At the time, the corporation's balance sheet showed the amount properly chargeable to capital account was $40x$ plus $125. The $40x$ represented paid-in capital ratably attributable to the shares redeemed (half of $80x$). The $125x$ was the amount of other attributes, including unrealized appreciation surplus attributable to the shares redeemed and the total earnings and profits ($120) ratably attributable to the shares redeemed, i.e., half of $200x$. The part of the distribution properly chargeable to earnings and profits was $60x$, A's pro rata share. Rev. Rul. 70-531, 1970-2 CB 76.

Guidelines modified on determination of taxable status of corporate distributions. Rev. Proc. 65-10 provides instructions for determining and reporting the taxable status of corporate distributions on Form 1096. For 1966, the lower portion of Form 1096 was to be filed only by those corporations claiming part of the distribution to be nontaxable and by corporations liquidating under Section 333. The revenue procedure requires a computation of current year earnings and profits as well as the tax-basis surplus (Rev. Proc. 65-10 modified). Rev. Proc. 67-12, 1967-1 CB 589.

Contributions by customers of public utility to aid construction not part of earnings and profits. The IRS ruled that earnings and profits available for dividends do not include amounts contributed to a public utility by customers or prospective customers. Such receipts not to be included in gross income. In computing earnings and profits, the corporation may not claim depreciation on facilities purchased with such construction aid receipts. On disposition of such facilities, any gain includible in taxable income of the corporation will become part of earnings and profits at that time. Rev. Rul. 66-353, 1966-2 CB 111.

Effect of investment credit on earnings and profits. The IRS has amplified Rev. Rul. 63-63 dealing with the effect of the investment credit on earnings and profits. The IRS ruled that (1) federal income tax reduced by the current taxable year investment credit, plus any prior year unused credit used in the current year, reduces earnings and profits; (2) a tax refund resulting from a carry-back of an unused credit increases earnings and profits for the unused credit year to the extent of the refund; (3) a basis adjustment under Section 48(g) has no effect on earnings and profits; (4) the restoration of basis after repeal of Section 48(g) has no effect on earnings and profits; (5) depreciation allowed on Section 38 property reduces earnings and profits. Rev. Rul. 66-336, 1966-2 CB 110.

Unamortized bond premium or discount does not affect earnings and profits. The IRS ruled that the amortization of either bond premium or discount affects earnings and profits only in the year and in the amount that the write-off is credited to or charged against income. In computing earnings and profits available for dividends no adjustment is made for the unamortized premium or discount. Rev. Rul. 66-35, 1966-1 CB 63.

Income tax refund increases earnings and profits for dividends. An accrual-basis corporation sustained a net operating loss in 1960 that it carried back to 1958 and 1959. It filed timely claims for refunds of taxes paid based on the carry-back. These refunds of taxes for 1958 and 1959 were reflected in the earnings and profits for 1960 for dividend purposes. The event that fixed the right to a refund for 1958 and 1959 occurred at the close of 1960, when the amount of the net operating loss for that year became definite and certain. Rev. Rul. 64-146, 1964-1 CB 129.

ENTERTAINMENT EXPENSES

(*See* Business Expenses—Travel and Entertainment Expenses)

ESSENTIALLY EQUIVALENT TO A DIVIDEND

(*See* Compensation for Personal Services—Dividend Equivalence; Dividends and Distributions; Redemptions—Dividend Equivalence; Reorganizations)

EXCHANGES—TAX-FREE

(*See* Reorganizations; Tax-Free Exchanges; Tax-Free Incorporations)

EXPENSES

(*See* Business Expenses)

FAIR MARKET VALUE

(*See* Valuation of Property)

FAMILY TRANSACTIONS

(*See* Related Taxpayers)

FOREIGN CORPORATIONS

Payment by Canadian subsidiary was partial liquidation, not a dividend. Taxpayer had seven subsidiaries, including one Canadian corporation. These corporations sold all their current assets to an unrelated corporation and then leased their fixed assets to the purchaser for a term of five years. Upon termination of the lease, the lessee was to purchase the assets. After the sale, the Canadian subsidiary distributed to taxpayer 1.5 million which it reported as a dividend. Taxpayer claimed a foreign tax credit under Section 902. The IRS contended that the distribution was in partial liquidation under Section 346 and that taxpayer was therefore not entitled to the foreign tax credit and should have reported capital gain rather than dividend income. *Held*: For the IRS. The court held that it is not necessary to have a formal plan of complete liquidation in order to have a distribution under Section 346. It made no difference that the stock was not actually redeemed, since taxpayer owned all the stock. The contraction of the subsidiary's operations and the need for capital constituted a valid business purpose for redeeming its stock. Since the payment was not a dividend, it did not entitle taxpayer to a foreign tax credit. Section 902 applies only to ordinary dividends, not to distributions in partial liquidation. Fowler Hosiery Co., 301 F2d 394, 62-1 USTC ¶ 9407, 9 AFTR2d 1252 (7th Cir. 1962).

Income from foreign corporations retained its character. A domestic corporation owned all of the stock in three foreign corporations. The foreign corporations increased their earnings in the United States. The income of the foreign corporations retained its character when passed through to the parent corporation for the purpose of determining if the domestic corporation was a personal holding company. Rev. Rul. 76-403, 1976-2 CB 229.

IRS set forth proper method of accruing Swiss National Defense Tax. For purposes of a domestic corporation claiming a foreign tax credit involving taxes paid by a Swiss subsidiary, the IRS set forth the proper method of accrual of the Swiss National Defense Tax. The tax is assessed on corporate net profits for the two-year period preceding the first year of a biennial assessment period. The computation is shown for the first five years of existence of the Swiss subsidiary. Rev. Rul. 76-39, 1976-1 CB 206.

Foreign corporation holding securities in domestic corporations must file Form 1120NB with Schedule PH. A Netherland corporation, the majority of whose stock was owned by five aliens and whose capital was invested in stocks and bonds of domestic corporations, was classifiable as a personal holding company, even though the alien stockholders were not subject to a surtax on distributed corporate earnings. As a personal holding company, the corporation was entitled to a deduction for dividends paid, including consent dividends. Even though its U.S. income tax on dividends received from sources within the United States was fully satisfied at the source, the corporation was required to file a Form 1120NB together with Schedule PH. Rev. Rul. 60-34, 1960-1 CB 203.

FOREIGN TAX CREDIT

(*See* Foreign Corporations)

FORGIVENESS OF DEBTS

(*See* Cancellation of Indebtedness)

GOODWILL

Goodwill had no basis where taxpayer did not transfer business with goodwill. In 1950, taxpayer purchased all the stock of P, paying approximately $200,000 in excess of the fair market value of the underlying assets. Although P's balance sheet after the purchase did not reflect goodwill as an asset, a year later, the consolidated balance sheet of taxpayer and P attributed the $200,000 differential to goodwill. Subsequently, P was merged into taxpayer, and taxpayer debited goodwill at approximately $200,000, and on its tax return listed goodwill in the same amount on Schedule L. In 1966, taxpayer sold the assets and deducted a loss from goodwill equal to the differential of $200,000. On its 1966 federal income tax return, taxpayer included goodwill with a basis of $200,000 as an asset it had sold and claimed a loss on the sale. The IRS determined that the goodwill had no basis for federal income tax purposes, and reduced taxpayer's net operating loss carry-back to 1965. *Held:* For the IRS. Where a corporation continues its business, goodwill remains its asset, because goodwill is incident to an ongoing business and cannot be transferred unless the business itself is transferred. Accordingly, no goodwill was transferred in 1950, and taxpayer had no basis in goodwill for federal income tax purposes in 1966. Peerless Inv. Co., 58 TC 892 (1972).

Corporation's goodwill not part of stockholder's stock basis. Taxpayer, husband and wife, owned all but one share of the outstanding stock of a corporation that sold all its assets and liquidated pursuant to Section 337. In computing their gain on the liquidation, taxpayers increased the basis of their stock by the goodwill that the liquidating corporation transferred to the buying corporation. The IRS disallowed this addition to basis. *Held*: For the IRS. The court held that the goodwill was part of the liquidating corporation's basis and not part of the basis of the stockholder's stock. Any cost basis of such goodwill would be material to the selling corporation's computation of gain or loss if gain or loss had

GOODWILL

been determined and recognized in the sale. Philbrick, 38 TC 666 (1962).

Customer card file, a major factor in production of income, is separate from goodwill. Taxpayer liquidated its subsidiary and allocated the basis of its stock among the assets acquired in the liquidation. The IRS determined that amounts allocated for the leasehold interest and the customer card file should be allocated instead to goodwill. *Held:* For taxpayer, in part. Although the files were not the primary productive asset of taxpayer's business, the information they contained was a significant productive asset. However, since one third of taxpayer's customers would have returned without the use of the file, taxpayer may amortize only two thirds of the file. Metro Auto Auction of Kansas City, Inc., 48 TCM 894, ¶ 84,440 P-H Memo. TC (1984).

HOLDING COMPANIES

(*See* Affiliated Corporations; Consolidated Returns; Personal Holding Companies)

HOLDING PERIOD

(*See* Capital Gains and Losses—Holding Period)

ILLEGAL INCOME AND TRANSACTIONS

(*See* Business Expenses—Bribes and Other Illegal Expenses)

INCOME

(*See* Taxable Income of Corporations; Taxable Income of Stockholders)

INCOME SPLITTING

(*See* Affiliated Corporations; Allocation Among Related Taxpayers)

INCORPORATIONS

(*See* Reorganizations; Transfers to Controlled Corporations)

INDEBTEDNESS

(*See* Bad Debts; Cancellation of Indebtedness)

INSTALLMENT OBLIGATIONS

(*See* Accounting Methods—Installment Sales)

INSTALLMENT REPORTING

(*See* Accounting Methods—Installment Sales)

INSTALLMENT SALES

(*See* Accounting Methods—Installment Sales)

INTERCOMPANY TRANSACTIONS

(*See* Affiliated Corporations; Allocations Among Related Taxpayers; Dividends and Distributions—Intercorporate Transfers)

INTEREST EXPENSE

(*See* Business Expenses—Interest Expense)

INTEREST INCOME

Section 483 may be applied to impute interest income with respect to stock received pursuant to a contingent stock right acquired in a nontaxable reorganization. In a nontaxable reorganization, taxpayer exchanged his stock in *A* Corporation for stock in another corporation. Under the exchange agreement, the taxpayer was to receive a specified number of shares in the year of the exchange and additional shares in three years, if at that time he still held the stock received in the exchange and the value of such stock did not reach a certain amount. The stock's value did not increase sufficiently, and taxpayer received additional stock. The IRS assessed taxpayers, asserting that a portion of the additional stock's value should have been reported as interest income by reason of Section 483. *Held:* Affirmed. First, the Code's nontaxable reorganization provisions do not, as a general matter, override application of Section 483. Second, "payment" for purposes of Section 483 includes transfers of property such as stock. Third, the receipt of the contingent stock rights was not receipt of the stock transferred later because such rights did not give taxpayer, in the year of exchange, the right to vote or any other rights attributable to the additional shares (e.g., dividends). Sidney R. Solomon, 570 F2d 28, 78-1 USTC ¶ 9140, AFTR2d 78-411 (2d Cir. 1977).

Interest imputed on shares issued pursuant to contingent stock rights received in a nontaxable reorganization. Taxpayer owned stock in *A* Corporation. *A* was merged into *B* Corporation. However, since the parties could not agree upon the value of *A*'s assets, stockholders in *A* received stock in *B* plus the right to receive additional *B* stock if *A* (while operated as a subsidiary of *B*) achieved earnings over a certain amount. The maximum number of *B* shares that would be issued in this event was set out in the merger agreement. This condition was satisfied after five years, and taxpayer received additional *B* stock. *Held:* For the IRS. Although a valid nontaxable reorganization occurred and the contingent stock right was not boot, Section 483 could be applied to impute an interest element in the value of the additional shares received. Jeffers, 556 F2d 986, 77-1 USTC ¶ 9421, 40 AFTR2d 77-5026 (Ct. Cl. 1977).

Interest income accrued despite forgiveness later in year. An accrual basis calendar year taxpayer held a demand note of its subsidiary and each month accrued the interest due on the note. In December, taxpayer forgave by corporate resolution the interest on the note; the subsidiary was not insolvent or unable to pay the interest. The subsidiary was subsequently liquidated, and the subsidiary never paid the principal or interest on the note. The IRS included in taxpayer's income the monthly interest accrued up to the date of the corporate resolution waiving the interest. *Held:* For the IRS. The court agreed with the IRS as to this treatment of the interest, holding that interest began to run automatically from the date of the note, that taxpayer accrued the interest monthly, and that, therefore, taxpayer must include interest in income up to the date of the corporate resolution waiving the interest on the notes. Oregon Pulp & Paper Co., 34 TC 624 (1960).

Corporation did not have interest income on noninterest bearing loan to its president. Taxpayer corporation made noninterest bearing loans to its officers and employees. Although the borrower signed a standard note form with provision for interest, no interest was charged on taxpayer's books on these loans. Taxpayer, in accordance with this practice, made a loan to its president. The IRS contended that taxpayer, in using a net loss carry-back, failed to report an amount representing accrued interest on this loan. *Held:* For taxpayer. There was no intention to charge interest, and in fact, no interest was charged or collected from the president on this loan. Brandtjen-Kluge Inc., 34 TC 416 (1960).

INVENTORIES

(*See also* Accounting Methods)

INVENTORIES

Basis of inventory received in Section 334(b)(2) liquidation was adjusted replacement cost. Taxpayer purchased stock in another corporation and liquidated this corporation pursuant to Section 334(b)(2). Taxpayer argued that its basis in the inventory received as a liquidating distribution was the catalog price of the inventory. *Held:* For the IRS. The imputed cost of the inventory was its replacement cost, not the catalog price to the public, adjusted for various items, including deemed profit on a sale to a willing buyer. Knapp King-Size Corp., 527 F2d 1392, 76-1 USTC ¶ 9128, 37 AFTR2d 76-501 (Ct. Cl. 1976), withdrawing 36 AFTR2d 75-5591 (Ct. Cl. 1975).

Transferee corporation's inventory need not reflect transferor's errors. The assets of two partnerships engaged in selling petroleum were transferred to taxpayer in a Section 351 transaction. The final tax returns of the transferors erroneously omitted portions of their closing inventory, and taxpayer used the actual amount of inventory transferred by the partnerships. The IRS contended that taxpayer was required to use the lower (erroneous) figure. *Held:* For taxpayer. Under Section 362(a)(1), the transferee was entitled to use as its basis for its opening inventory the actual amounts of inventory on hand, unadjusted for errors in the transferor's basis, even though the curative adjustments for prior years were barred as to the predecessor transferor. Las Cruces Oil Co., 62 TC 764 (1974).

Noninventoried supplies deductible despite subsequent year's sale pursuant to Section 337. On January 2, 1958, a partnership engaged in the truck leasing business transferred its assets to taxpayer corporation, which continued the business. Taxpayer was on the accrual basis but kept no inventory of supplies (e.g., tires, tubes, parts, gas). Such items were expensed in full when acquired. On January 2, 1959, taxpayer's stockholders adopted a plan of complete liquidation pursuant to Section 337 and arranged for the sale of the corporate assets. The contract of sale specifically set forth prices for gasoline, tires, and supplies. The IRS set up a closing inventory for these items in its audit of 1958, offsetting deductions taken for them. *Held:* For taxpayer. No inventory of supplies was necessary. The regulations provide that inventories are necessary if merchandise is an income-producing factor. As taxpayer did not purchase the supplies for resale or in abnormal quantity, the regulations did not apply. The IRS could not upset taxpayer's method of accounting, which clearly reflected income for 1958, merely because taxpayer would have an advantage from it in 1959. The IRS' attack should have been directed at 1959. Smith Leasing Co., 43 TC 37 (1964), acq. 1965-2 CB 6.

Ending inventory sold under Section 337 must be considered in cost of goods sold. Taxpayer adopted a plan of complete liquidation under Section 337 in November 1959 and sold all its assets a few days later. The inventory was sold in bulk to one customer for $55,000, and using a zero basis, the entire $55,000 was reported as nontaxable profit under Section 337. Taxpayer claimed a cost of goods sold of $136,000 on its final return by using a zero closing inventory. The IRS asserted that the cost of goods sold figure should have been reduced by the $55,000 received on the later sale of the inventory in bulk, since that was its cost. *Held:* For the IRS. Taxpayer failed to meet the burden of proof to overcome the IRS' determination. The cost of goods sold erroneously included the basis of inventory still on hand at the time the gross profit was determined. Winer Enters., Inc., 25 TCM 525, ¶ 66,099 P-H Memo. TC (1966).

Bulk sale of LIFO valued inventory. A corporation selling appreciated inventory accounted for under the LIFO method is not required to include the appreciation in income where the sale is in bulk to one person pursuant to a plan of complete liquidation. Rev. Rul. 74-431, 1974-2 CB 107.

Inventory transferred under Section 351 has a zero basis where cost previously deducted. The IRS ruled that the basis of inventory of supplies and parts transferred to a controlled corporation under Section 351 is zero where the cost thereof has been previously deducted by the cash-method proprietorship. (IT 2562 superseded.) Rev. Rul. 69-117, 1969-1 CB 103.

Gain or loss on sales of inventoried breeding animals not recognized under Section 337. Taxpayer, a ranching corporation, elected to value its livestock, including breeding animals, under the unit-livestock-price method. Taxpayer adopted a plan of liquidation under Section 337 under which it sold its breeding animals at substantial gains. The IRS ruled that the gains realized were not recognized under Section 337. Under Regulation § 1.471-6(g), a rancher using the unit-livestock-price method may elect to include in inventory animals used for draft, breeding, and dairy purposes. Under Section 1231, breeding animals are considered as property used in trade or business, notwithstanding that they are inventoried. Consequently, breeding animals are not treated as property that would properly be included in inventory for Section 337 purposes where they are not held for sale to customers in ordinary course of business. Rev. Rul. 64-239, 1964-2 CB 93.

INVESTMENT TAX CREDIT

Section 331 liquidation triggers investment tax credit recapture. Taxpayer liquidated his Subchapter S corporation in a Section 331 liquidation and transferred the corporate property into his own partnership. The IRS determined that the property was subject to recapture of the investment tax credit. Taxpayer argued that the property was not subject to investment tax credit recapture because the liquidation and subsequent transfer were mere changes in form. *Held:* For the IRS. Since at liquidation, the property took a fair market value basis and not a carry-over basis, the "mere change in form" exception to investment tax credit recapture did not apply. Sexton, 42 TCM 1030, ¶ 81,494 P-H Memo. TC (1981).

IRS abandons strict application of recapture rules in respect of incorporating going concerns. Following the issuance of Rev. Rul. 76-514, 1976-2 CB 11, the Tax Court decided the case of Loewen, 76 TC 90 (1981), in which taxpayers, as a part of the incorporation of their farming and cattle-feeding business, transferred most of their operating assets except for real estate to the new corporation. The Tax Court held that taxpayers' lease of the land to the corporation, along with the transfer of the other assets necessary to operate the farm, was "a mere change in form" and that, therefore, investment credit recapture was not required on the machinery and equipment. The IRS revoked Rev. Rul. 76-514 and adopted the substance of the *Loewen* decision. Rev. Rul. 83-65, 1983-1 CB 10.

Section 351 transfer triggers recapture on Section 38 property. In a Section 351 transaction, taxpayer, a dentist, transferred to a new corporation certain equipment used in his practice on which he had claimed an investment credit. The transfer occurred prior to the expiration of the equipment's useful life upon which the credit was based. Taxpayer retained ownership of a building also used in his practice and leased it to the corporation. The building comprised 30 percent of the assets of the practice. The IRS ruled that the credit on the transferred equipment was subject to recapture, since the failure to transfer substantially all the assets of the practice resulted in more than a mere change in the form of doing business. Rev. Rul. 76-514, 1976-2 CB 11.

Investment credit carry-over may be disallowed even if original year is closed. A taxpayer claimed an investment credit in 1965 that resulted in a carry-over. After 1965 was closed, the IRS determined that the property did not qualify for the investment credit. The IRS could have assessed a deficiency based on the carry-over of the 1965 credit even though 1965 itself was closed. Rev. Rul. 69-543, 1969-2 CB 1.

INVOLUNTARY CONVERSIONS

(*See also* Liquidations—Involuntary Conversions)

Exchange of stock effected by a business maneuver not an involuntary conversion. In the course of a dispute between two insurance groups, a settlement was effected whereby stock in one corporation was exchanged for stock in another, both corporations having been formed by the two groups to provide insurance for substandard business. The Tax Court held that the exchanges did not add up to a statutory involuntary conversion but were a business maneuver. *Held:* Affirmed. The court ruled that the facts fell far short of establishing that any property was the subject of "destruction," "theft," "seizure," or "requisition or condemnation, or the threat or imminence" of requisition or condemnation. Accordingly, gain was recognized on the exchange. In computing the amount received on the exchange by one of the transferors, the court used as such value the book value of the stock transferred. Hitke, 296 F2d 639, 62-1 USTC ¶ 9114, 8 AFTR2d 5886 (7th Cir. 1961).

Sale of stock pursuant to SEC order not an involuntary conversion. In accordance with an SEC order, taxpayer sold its large holdings of Detroit Edison Co. and realized a substantial loss. The order was issued to compel taxpayers to comply with the Public Utility Holding Company Act. Taxpayer contended that this was an involuntary conversion, entitling it to a deduction for an ordinary loss. *Held:* For the IRS. The court held that taxpayer suffered a capital loss only. This was not condemnation, requisition, or the exercise of the power of eminent domain; it was an order requiring taxpayer to dispose of property that it was prohibited to own under the Public Utility Holding Company Act. The court observed that there was no evidence that the sale of stock was below market value. The Code provides for nonrecognition of gain or loss on certain transactions ordered by the SEC, but the section applies to exchanges, not sales. American Natural Gas Co., 279 F2d 220, 60-2 USTC ¶ 9507, 5 AFTR2d 1590 (Ct. Cl.), cert. denied, 364 US 900 (1960).

Exchange of stock authorized by FCC involuntary conversion eligible for nonrecognition. A corporation exchanged its stock in a newspaper for the newspaper's stock in a television station pursuant to a certification by the FCC that the divestiture was necessary to effectuate FCC rules and policies. The IRS ruled that the corporation could elect, under Section 1071, to have the exchange treated as an involuntary conversion. Further, the corporation could elect under Section 1033, and no gain would be recognized. Rev. Rul. 78-269, 1978-2 CB 209.

Involuntarily converted garage could not be replaced with a retail store building. Taxpayer owned property that it leased out for a garage and service station. The city condemned the property, and the owner used the proceeds from rents to purchase other rental property used by other types of businesses. The IRS ruled that the involuntary conversion provisions of the Code would be available only if the replacement property could be used for servicing, storing, or parking cars. Property adaptable to use only as a retail store building would not be "similar or related in service or use" to a garage. Rev. Rul. 56-347, 1956-2 CB 517.

JUDICIAL DOCTRINES

(*See* Redemptions—Business Purpose)

KICKBACKS

(*See* Business Expenses—Bribes and Other Illegal Expenses)

LIABILITIES, ASSUMPTION OF

(*See also* Cancellation of Indebtedness)

Section 357 held to apply to "tax" liabilities and not accounting liabilities. Taxpayer operated a masonry contracting business that he decided to incorporate. Pursuant to Section 351 the business assets, including trade accounts payable, were transferred to the corporation in exchange for stock and a promissory note. Taxpayer tried to change to the accrual method but was required to keep the cash-basis method. The Tax Court and IRS determined that, since taxpayer was on a cash basis, the trade accounts payable were liabilities for purposes of Section 357(c). As a result the liabilities assumed by taxpayer's wholly owned corporation exceeded the adjusted basis of the transferred assets, thereby creating a taxable gain to taxpayer. *Held:* Reversed. The payables of a cash-basis taxpayer were liabilities for accounting purposes but not for tax purposes under Section 357(c) until they were paid. As a result, the total amount of liabilities to which the property was subject did not exceed the adjusted basis of the transferred property. Accordingly, there was no taxable gain. Bongiovanni, 470 F2d 921, 73-1 USTC ¶ 9133 (2d Cir. 1972).

No deduction for partnership debt paid by corporation. Taxpayers owned a partnership. A discharged employee brought suit claiming he was a 25 percent partner. In 1956, while the suit was pending, the partnership was incorporated. The new corporation acquired all the partnership assets except land and buildings, which it leased. In 1957, the discharged employee received a judgment (against taxpayers and the partnership, but not the corporation) that appointed a receiver to take possession of all assets owned by the partnership as of 1955. In 1957, the corporation paid the employee $23,971 in settlement, which it deducted as a business expense. The IRS denied the deduction and argued the payment was a constructive dividend. Taxpayers originally argued the corporation had to make the payment to save its business. During the trial of the refund suits, however, they argued that the corporation had assumed all the liabilities of the partnership. The district court held for taxpayers on both issues on the ground that the corporation assumed the partnership's liabilities. *Held:* Reversed and remanded. If there was assumption of liabilities, there was no constructive dividend. The evidence, however, was scanty and the appellate court held that the trial court must make full findings of the facts surrounding the incorporation. If there was no assumption of liabilities, the gratuitous payment was a constructive dividend. This would be so even if there was a corporate business purpose for the payment. Reade Mfg. Co., 301 F2d 803 (3rd Cir. 1962). If liabilities were not assumed, the business expense deduction was, of course, improper. If they were assumed, the issue depended on why the assumption was made. If it was made for a purpose other than acquisition of property, a Section 162 deduction could be allowable. Smith, 69-2 USTC ¶ 9640 (5th Cir. 1969).

Assumption of liability destroyed tax-free exchange. One day before transferring securities and other assets to a newly formed investment company, taxpayer placed a large loan, using the assets as collateral. The new corporation assumed the loan and issued stock and securities to taxpayer for the assets. The district court held that the exchange was not tax free. *Held:* Affirmed per curiam. A transfer to a controlled corporation under Section 351 is not tax free if there is an assumption of liabilities unless the taxpayer establishes there was not tax-avoidance purpose. In this case, taxpayer failed to establish the absence of tax avoidance. Thompson, 353 F2d 787, 65-2 USTC ¶ 9766 (5th Cir. 1965).

Incorporation was taxable where liabilities exceed assets. Taxpayer transferred all the assets and liabilities of his sole proprietorship to a wholly controlled corporation. The liabilities exceeded taxpayer's basis for the assets by almost $200,000. The Tax Court held that under Section 357(c) taxpayer had income in that amount. Taxpayer reasoned that since Section 357(c) by its language becomes operative where "the *sum* of the amount of the liabilities assumed *plus* the amount of the liabilities to which the property is subject exceeds the total of the adjusted basis of property transferred" [emphasis supplied], this required that *both* types of liabilities be present for the section to apply. The Tax Court rejected this argument, noting that the Committee Reports used the disjunctive rather than the conjunctive and, in fact, gave an illustration where only one type of liability was involved. On appeal, taxpayer contested this statutory construction and also complained that the Tax Court had erred in entering its decision seven days after its opinion was rendered, since this did not permit taxpayer and the IRS to submit computations pursuant to Tax Court Rule 50. *Held:* Affirmed. Taxpayer was taxable on the excess of the liabilities assumed by the corporation over taxpayer's adjusted basis of the property transferred. Section 357(c) was applicable, even though there was no encumbered property existing on the date of the transfer. The Tax Court determination under Rule 50 was proper; the withholding of a decision pending computations by the parties was discretionary. Even if the seven-day period might be considered short, taxpayer gave no notice, made no motion for an extension of time, and in no way indicated his intention of contesting the court's computation. Testor, 327 F2d 788, 64-1 USTC ¶ 9252 (7th Cir. 1964).

Obligation assumed deductible in full despite reimbursement from owners of transferor corporation. Taxpayer corporation acquired X and Y Corporations in a tax-free merger. Taxpayer subsequently deducted $234,297 in connection with the settlement of a contract claim from a former officer of X. However, the IRS stated that X was not entitled to such deduction to the extent of $171,512, such amount having been reimbursed to taxpayer by previous owners of X and Y under an indemnification agreement executed prior to the effective date of the merger. *Held:* For taxpayer. The deduction was allowable under Section 381(c)(4). The findings and conclusions of the trial judge were adopted, but not as a precedent, because of the complexity of the issues involved. VCA Corp., 77-2 USTC ¶ 9736, 40 AFTR2d 77-6047 (Ct. Cl. 1977).

Assumption of deductible obligation was nonrealizable event where taxpayer was on a cash basis. Taxpayer formed a wholly owned corporation to which he transferred all the assets and liabilities of his proprietorship. Taxpayer, who was on a cash basis, did not report any income from the assumption of the liabilities. The IRS determined that taxpayer had recognized ordinary income to the extent that the liabilities exceeded the adjusted basis of the assets under Section 357(c). *Held:* For taxpayer. Citing Crane, 331 US 1 (1947), the court noted that where taxpayer was on a cash basis, the assumption of a deductible obligation was a nonrealizable event. A finding to the contrary would deny taxpayer the otherwise deductible expense at the time of payment. Focht, 68 TC 223 (1977), acq. 1980-2 CB 1.

Assumption by corporation of sole proprietorship liability owed to it did not disqualify Section 351 transaction. Taxpayer, a sole proprietor, transferred his assets and liabilities to a pre-existing controlled corporation. One of the proprietorship's liabilities assumed by the corporation was a debt owed the corporation. Taxpayer's basis for the assets was exceeded by the liabilities. Taxpayer contended that the transaction qualified under Section 351, with the liability assumption resulting in partial taxation under Section 357(c)(1). The IRS argued that because the debt became discharged in the transaction, taxpayer received "other property or money" under Section 351(b), and gain should be recognized to that extent. *Held:* For taxpayer. Assumption of a liability must be distinguished from its discharge. Here, the discharge took place by operation of law upon the assumption, and only because of it. Sections 351 and 357 look to the assumption of a liability; subsequent discharge is immaterial. Nor was it important to whom the liability was owed. Since Section 357(c)(1) applied, taxpayer was taxable only to the extent the liabilities transferred exceeded his basis for the assets. Knifflen, 39 TC 553 (1963), acq. 1965-2 CB 5.

Capital gain recognized when newly formed corporation assumed liabilities of sole proprietorship. Taxpayer's sole proprietorship had liabilities in excess of its assets at the time taxpayer incorporated. One of the liabilities was a note for a loan for which taxpayer was personally liable. Taxpayer claimed that the note was not assumed and that he had had the corporation execute a note to him for the original amount of the loan. The IRS contended that the corporation had assumed all the liabilities of the sole proprietorship, resulting in gain to taxpayer. *Held:* For the IRS. The books and records of both the proprietorship and corporation show the same outstanding liabilities; payments on the note were made from the same account both before and after incorporation; and the bank's record of interest shows no change at the time of incorporation. Taxpayer thus failed to disprove a state law presumption that the proprietorship's debts were assumed by its successor corporation. Taxpayer realized a capital gain from this assumption of the liabilities. Christopher, Jr., 48 TCM 663, ¶ 84,394 P-H Memo. TC (1984).

Assumption of liabilities triggered recognition of gain under Section 357(c). Taxpayers obtained three loans, two of which were secured by the assets of two proprietorships operated by taxpayers. They transferred the assets of both proprietorships to two new corporations in exchange for stock. The IRS argued that taxpayers must recognize gain, since the liabilities exceeded the value of the assets they received in exchange. *Held:* For the IRS. The loans secured by proprietorship assets fell within Section 357(c). Beaver, 41 TCM 52, ¶ 80,429 P-H Memo. TC (1980).

Offset to liability held constructive income. Taxpayer, a hospital, purchased assets from and assumed liabilities of a proprietorship. Later, an accounting of medicare payments offset amounts due taxpayer against amounts previously owed by the proprietorship. It was argued that liabilities were never assumed; thus, when credit was made, taxpayer received nothing. *Held:* For the IRS. The court found that the liabilities were assumed and, as a result, the offset constituted constructive income to taxpayer. A secondary argument for a corresponding Section 162 deduction was also denied. Intermed, Inc., 36 TCM 1209, ¶ 77,306 P-H Memo. TC (1977).

Income not realized where liabilities were not in excess of basis of property transferred. Taxpayer transferred his individually owned insurance business to a new wholly owned corporation. The IRS determined that taxpayer realized $33,318 because the liabilities assumed by the corporation exceeded the basis of the property transferred. *Held:* For taxpayer. Based on taxpayer's testimony and prior business purchases, it was determined that the adjusted basis of insurance renewals,

$17,500, exceeded the liabilities assumed by some $10,000. Not all of the liabilities were assumed by the corporation. Taxpayer later consolidated unassumed liabilities and executed a personal note, which he paid from his own funds. Therefore, Section 357(c) was inapplicable and no income was realized. However, taxpayer did realize a constructive dividend because of the corporation's payment of part of his personal liability of the notes. Parsons, ¶ 72,072 P-H Memo. TC (1972).

Assumption of liability for valid business purpose avoided recognition of income. Taxpayer borrowed funds from his finance company and purchased over half the stock of another company. The latter company was then merged into his company, and its assets were mortgaged and then transferred to a wholly owned subsidiary. The mortgage proceeds were then used in the finance business. The IRS claimed that the assumption of the indebtedness by the subsidiary caused a gain to be recognized on the exchange. *Held:* For taxpayer. The mortgaging of the acquired property and the transfer of the business to the subsidiary had a valid business purpose: the protection of taxpayer's line of credit with banks objecting to the investment of the finance company's funds in an unrelated business. There was no tax-avoidance purpose under Section 357(b) in the subsidiary's assumption of the liability and no gain was taxable on the transfer. ISC Indus., Inc., 30 TCM 1216, ¶ 71,283 P-H Memo. TC (1971).

Assumption of indebtedness ignored in Section 351 transaction. An individual used funds borrowed from a bank to purchase 90 percent of the stock of X Corporation which he then transferred to Y Corporation in a Section 351 exchange, with Y assuming the liability incurred. The individual was treated as a mere intermediate agent employed to satisfy banking rules and regulations; the assumption of the indebtedness was ignored for purposes of Sections 357(a) and 304(a)(1). Rev. Rul. 80-240, 1980-2 CB 116.

Section 357(c) not applicable to F reorganizations. Section 357(c) does not apply to cause recognition of gain on an assumption of liabilities in excess of adjusted basis in an *F* reorganization even though the reorganization may also be described as a D reorganization. Rev. Rul. 79-289, 1979-2 CB 145.

No gain to parent where subsidiary assumed substituted debt. Taxpayer corporation conducted two separate businesses. It transferred the assets of one to a newly formed subsidiary solely in exchange for stock and the assumption of liabilities related to the transferred assets. One liability was a debt incurred on a new loan replacing one that could not be transferred. No gain was recognized on the assumption of the debt under Section 357(b). Rev. Rul. 79-258, 1979-2 CB 143.

Section 304(a)(1) prevails over Section 357(a) where both apply. The IRS ruled that in a transaction where both Sections 304(a)(1) and 357(a) apply, Section 304(a)(1) prevails as to the assumption that a liability is "property" for purposes of Sections 304 and 317. Further, Section 351(a) applies to the portion of the transaction in which stock of the acquiring corporation is received. Rev. Rul. 78-422, 1978-2 CB 129.

Acquired corporation recognizes gain or loss when stockholders assume liability. Where the acquired corporation's stockholders in a reorganization under Section 368(a)(1)(C) assume the liability of the acquired corporation to pay a finder's fee to an unrelated party, which liability could only be satisfied with stock of the acquiring corporation received by the acquired corporation as consideration for the reorganization, the gain or loss on the transfer must be recognized pursuant to Sections 1001 and 1002, because the acquired corporation is deemed to have transferred the stock directly to the finder in satisfaction of its liability. Rev. Rul. 70-271 is distinguished. Rev. Rul. 75-450, 1975-2 CB 328.

Trade accounts receivable have a zero basis for cash-basis taxpayer for Section 357(c) purpose. The IRS reaffirmed the position taken by the Tax Court in Raich, 46 TC 604 (1966), which held that trade accounts receivable would be given a zero basis for purposes of computing gains under Section 357(c). The IRS stated that it will apply this theory under similar facts. However, trade accounts receivable will not have a zero basis for accrual-basis taxpayers. Rev. Rul. 69-442, 1969-2 CB 53.

LIKE-KIND EXCHANGES

Loan between parties did not destroy tax-free exchange. Taxpayer received an assignment of an option to purchase certain property. Firemen's Insurance Company agreed to assist taxpayer in the purchase and placed $425,000 in escrow for this purpose. Taxpayer used the escrow fund to purchase the property, and then exchanged it for a building owned by Firemen's plus $45,000. On his return, taxpayer treated the transaction as a like-kind exchange under Section 1031; the IRS contended that it was a purchase. *Held:* For taxpayer. The $425,000 advanced to taxpayer was a loan, and not part of the consideration received by taxpayer for the exchange. There was a valid like-kind exchange of property, with the $45,000 paid by Firemen's representing "boot." 124 Front St., Inc., 65 TC 6 (1975).

Like-kind exchange of property not taxable. A corporation purchased property from taxpayer parent corporation and then transferred it to taxpayer subsidiary corporation in exchange for similar property. The IRS disallowed the Section 1031(a) nonrecognition of gain claimed on the exchange. *Held:* For taxpayers. The third-party corporation actually wanted the subsidiary's property. Although the parent retained certain rights, leases, and option privileges in the property it sold, the independent purchaser obtained a fee interest. Both properties exchanged were held for use in trade or business. Therefore, the exchange of the properties qualified for section 1031 treatment and no gain was recognized on the exchange. Boise Cascade Corp., 33 TCM 1443, ¶ 74,315 P-H Memo. TC (1974).

Gain recognized on failure to prove exchange of like properties. Taxpayer's father had left his farm, consisting of 94.5 acres, to his wife and two daughters, giving each a one-third undivided interest. The heirs sold off a 91-acre tract of the farm. The IRS assessed tax on the exchange. Taxpayer, one of the daughters, alleged that she had traded her interest in the larger tract for her mother's and sister's interest in the remaining 3.5 acres, which contained a rented dwelling, and that accordingly she effected a like-kind exchange on which no gain or loss was recognized. *Held:* For the IRS. The court noted that had the heirs exchanged deeds to accomplish such a transfer of interests before the contract for sale of the other tract was made, there could be no question of this. However, as there was no proof that the alleged transfer occured prior to the sale, the daughter was taxable on one third of the gain on the 91-acre tract. Estill, 19 TCM 334, ¶ 60,064 P-H Memo. TC (1960).

LIQUIDATING TRUSTS

Qualifying liquidating trust subjects stockholders to tax. A corporation adopted a plan of complete liquidation, but was unable within 12 months to sell land, the location of a heating plant, and a related right of way. A trust to which those assets were distributed qualified as a liquidating trust for tax purposes. The corporation's stockholders, as owners of the trust, would be taxed on the income therefrom. Rev. Rul. 80-150, 1980-1 CB 316.

Trust classified as a liquidating trust. A trust established under state law for the purpose of liquidating, for the benefit of stockholders, a corporation's assets not distributable in kind, including two notes from an unrelated corporation that were due in ten years and were not salable at or near face value, was classified as a liquidating trust under Regulation § 301.7701-4(d). Rev. Rul. 75-379, 1975-2 CB 505.

LIQUIDATIONS

In General	353
Assignment of Income Doctrine	357
Basis of Property Received	360
Expenses Incurred in Liquidation	363
Involuntary Conversions	365
Liquidating Corporation's Gain or Loss	368
Liquidating Distributions	371
Liquidation of Subsidiaries	373
One-Month Liquidations	375
Partial Liquidations	379
Reincorporations	385
Stockholders' Gain or Loss	389
Twelve-Month Liquidations—In General	392
Twelve-Month Liquidations—Sale of Assets	399
Twelve-Month Liquidations—Sale of Contracts	403
Twelve-Month Liquidations—Sale of Inventory	403
Twelve-Month Liquidations—Sale of Receivables	405
Unused Bad Debt Reserve	406

In General

Section 1361 termination generated a corporate liquidation. Individual taxpayers *A* and *B* operated different unincorporated businesses and elected, pursuant to the now defunct Section 1361, to have such business taxed at corporate rates. All such elections were automatically terminated as of January 1, 1969. The IRS held that since there was no actual incorporation of these businesses as of January 1, 1969, the "Section 1361 corporations" and taxpayers would be treated as if a complete liquidation, pursuant to Section 331(a), had occurred as of such date. The Tax Court, in *A*'s case, found for the IRS; the district court, in *B*'s case, found for taxpayer. *Held:* The Tax Court affirmed. The district court reversed. A Reading of the Committee Reports indicated that Congress intended that a termination of a Section 1361 election, without

LIQUIDATIONS: *In General*

a transfer to an actual corporation, would serve to treat such termination as a corporate liquidation. Prescott, 561 F2d 1287, 77-2 USTC ¶ 9639, 40 AFTR2d 77-5716 (8th Cir. 1977).

Liquidation section takes precedence over reorganization section. The Tax Court held that a purchase and subsequent merger, three months later, of a subsidiary corporation into taxpayer parent, with cancellation of the subsidiary's stock and retention of the subsidiary's employees, was in fact a Section 332 liquidation with basis being determined under Section 334(b)(2). *Held:* Affirmed. Although the transaction qualified as an A reorganization, it also qualified as a liquidation under Section 332, which takes precedence over 368. Furthermore, basis should be determined under Section 334(b)(2). Kansas Sand & Concrete, Inc., 462 F2d 805, 72-2 USTC ¶ 9590, 30 AFTR2d 72-5275 (10th Cir. 1972).

Expenses of selling assets pursuant to plan of tax-free liquidation were offsets of gain on sale and were not deductible. Taxpayer corporation adopted a plan of complete liquidation under Section 337 and then sold all its assets. On its final return taxpayer deducted the expenditures it incurred directly in connection with the sale. The IRS denied the deduction, holding that the expenditures offset the gain that taxpayer realized (but did not recognize) on the sale. *Held:* For the IRS. The legislative history of Section 337 and the authorities support the IRS's position. The purpose of Section 337 is to remove the specter of double taxation assessed on technicalities in corporate liquidations. Treating the expenses of selling the corporate assets as offsets of the capital gain achieves this result, that is, it achieves the same result as would result if the corporation first liquidated and its shareholders then sold the assets received on the liquidation. Lanrao, Inc., 422 F2d 481, 70-1 USTC ¶ 9223 (6th Cir.), cert. denied, 398 US 928 (1970).

Marketable securities and other current assets not entitled to treatment as cash or equivalent when acquired in a Kimbell-Diamond transaction. Taxpayer acquired the stock of another corporation and liquidated it in a transaction that met the requirements of Sections 332 and 334(b)(2). Taxpayer took the position that the marketable securities, inventory, accounts receivable and supplies received were included in the phrase "cash and its equivalent" in Regulation § 1.334-1(c)(4) and deducted these items from the adjusted purchase price, allocating the remainder to the remaining assets. Since it used the fair market value of the aforementioned current assets at the date of acquisition, it reported no gain when the assets were sold. The IRS determined that the basis was to be determined by allocating the purchase price of the stock to all assets except cash and accounts receivable and, since the total to be allocated was less than the fair market value, held that a taxable gain to that extent resulted from the transaction. The district court held for the IRS. *Held:* Affirmed. The phrase "cash and its equivalent" as used in the regulations does not include marketable securities, supplies, and inventories. The phrase is intended to encompass money, that is, items that do not logically have a basis. Section 334(b)(2) was enacted to eliminate the subjective intent test in *Kimbell-Diamond,* thus negating taxpayer's argument that the subsidiary was acquired in order to pay full cash value for the money, supplies, inventory, and receivables. In addition, the method of allocation prescribed by the regulations was fair and equitable. Although taxpayer may have preferred to purchase the individual assets, it did not do so and was therefore bound by the regulations applicable to a stock acquisition and liquidation situation. Boise Cascade Corp., 429 F2d 426, 70-2 USTC ¶ 9595, 26 AFTR2d 70-5532 (9th Cir. 1970).

Character of assets acquired in tax-free liquidation must be redetermined in distributee's hands. Taxpayer acquired solely in exchange for its own stock of *X* Corporation, engaged in a dissimilar business. About six months later, *X* was liquidated under Section 332, and on the same day its assets were sold by taxpayer to an unrelated corporation. Among the assets sold were accounts receivable, inventory, land, and depreciable property, upon which taxpayer claimed an ordinary loss.

Taxpayer's theory was that the character of the assets passing in the tax-free liquidation retained their nature, and that if X had first sold the assets at a loss before being liquidated, it would have had an ordinary loss. *Held:* The Tax Court's finding that the loss was a capital loss was affirmed. The subsidiary's assets were not used in the ordinary course of *taxpayer's* business and thus did not fall within the class of assets that are excepted from the definition of "capital assets." The "use" of X's assets for a short time on the day the liquidation took place (before the closing of the sale took place) was not enough to establish "use" nor was taxpayer in the business of selling such assets. Acro Mfg. Co., 334 F2d 40, 64-2 USTC ¶ 9604, 14 AFTR2d 5106 (6th Cir.), cert. denied, 379 US 887 (1964).

Mortgage received in corporate liquidation had ascertainable value. On liquidation of a corporation of which he was sole stockholder, taxpayer took over a second mortgage that the corporation had received as part of the sale of the property four years earlier. In reporting capital gain on this sale, the corporation had valued the mortgage at 20 percent of face. In the liquidation, however, taxpayer took the position that the mortgage had no ascertainable value and reported the collections as received capital gain. *Held:* For the IRS. The court found that the obligation was not merely contingent and that the mortgage had a value of 20 percent at time of liquidation. Collections in excess of that value were ordinary income. Campagna, 290 F2d 682, 61-1 USTC ¶ 9458 (2d Cir. 1961).

Distribution was not from corporate liquidation and was taxable as ordinary income. Taxpayer individual owned 100 percent of the stock of X Corporation, which in turn owned five sevenths (71.4 percent) of the stock of Y Corporation. The other two sevenths of Y Corporation was owned by a trust of which taxpayer was a 50 percent beneficiary. Taxpayer subsequently purchased the trust's interest for $108,000. Taxpayer then caused X Corporation to acquire an additional 400 shares of treasury stock of Y, which increased X's ownership to 81.8 percent. Y was then liquidated and taxpayer received $108,000 from such liquidation. Taxpayer reported no gain or loss, as it was argued that this was a capital transaction with the proceeds received being equal to taxpayer's basis in Y stock. X Corporation treated the Y assets it received as being received in a nontaxable liquidation of a wholly owned subsidiary. The IRS determined that the proceeds taxpayer received were ordinary dividend income. *Held:* For the IRS. There was no intention to give up the corporate form of doing business, since all that happened was that Y's operating assets were transferred to X, and therefore there was no liquidation within the meaning of Section 331. The distribution was a dividend. Massell, Jr., 76-2 USTC ¶ 9619 (ND Ga. 1976).

Corporate dissolution was not a reorganization. Taxpayer reported distributions from a dissolved corporation as long-term capital gain. The IRS, however, held that in substance a reorganization into another corporation had occurred and, therefore, the distributions to taxpayer, to the extent of earnings and profits, represented dividends reportable as ordinary income. *Held:* For taxpayer. The facts indicated that the dissolved corporation completely terminated its business at the time of dissolution and, thus, the court held that there was a genuine liquidation. Mitchell, 451 F2d 1395, 72-1 USTC ¶ 9115, 28 AFTR2d 71-6163 (Ct. Cl. 1971).

"Control" defined for purposes of Section 334(b)(2). Following taxpayer's acquisition of controlling interest in another entity, the latter redeemed sufficient stock to reduce taxpayer's ownership to 79 percent. Taxpayer then purchased additional stock to obtain more than 80 percent ownership, and liquidated the subsidiary under Section 332, claiming the basis for the assets received should be the same as the adjusted basis for the stock. *Held:* For taxpayer. The determination of control within the meaning of the statute is at the time of liquidation, not at the time the purchase begins. Therefore, this transaction constituted a "purchase." Madison Square Garden Corp., 58 TC 619 (1972).

LIQUIDATIONS: *In General*

Liquidation qualified under Section 337 despite retention of cash to pay unlocated stockholders. Taxpayer was an exempt mutual water company whose assets were condemned by a new state agency. Taxpayer claimed that it liquidated within a 12-month period as required by Section 337, and so gain on the condemnation sale was tax free. The IRS said that taxpayer did not qualify because: (1) a small amount of cash was retained to pay off stockholders who had not been located; and (2) the date of adoption of the plan of liquidation did not meet statutory tests. *Held*: For taxpayer. The Tax Court, examining the corporate record on meetings, concluded that the date on which the directors decided not to appeal the condemnation award was the date of the adoption of the plan of liquidation, and this date met the tests of Section 337. As to the retention of cash, the court found that there was a good-faith attempt to liquidate, and the minor deviation should not bar the benefits of Section 337. Mountain Water Co. of La Crescenta, 35 TC 418 (1960), acq. 1961-2 CB 5.

Distribution of assets followed by transfer to grantor trust constituted Section 336 liquidation. Taxpayers operated a chicken farm as an S corporation, and decided to run the business through a grantor trust in order to conserve the assets of the ranch for estate planning purposes. The business assets were distributed to the taxpayers who subsequently contributed them to a trust. Taxpayers treated the exchanges as tax free. The IRS determined the distribution to be in fact a liquidation with capital gains from the asset distributions, recapture of investment tax credit and depreciation, and ordinary income from the distribution of inventory. Furthermore, the IRS considered the taxpayers to be actual or constructive owners of 100 percent of the trust, and therefore all the income and deductions claimed by the trust in its tax return were adjusted to taxpayer's return. *Held*: For taxpayers, in part. Uncontradicted evidence indicated that the distribution was a liquidation under Section 336, resulting in recapture of investment tax credit and depreciation, and capital gains treatment on the asset distributions except for inventory, which received ordinary income treatment. Where the IRS failed to show that taxpayers owned more than 73 percent of the trust, reallocations of income and deductions were denied. Gorton, 49 TCM 612, ¶ 84,045 P-H Memo. TC (1985).

Dividends received pursuant to long-term liquidation plan treated as exchange for basis in stock. Taxpayers received corporate distributions. They classified them as liquidating dividends and treated them as reducing their basis in stock. The IRS argued that the distributions should be treated as ordinary income. *Held*: For taxpayer. Although the liquidation plan the corporation adopted required several years for implementation, legitimate business reasons existed for the liquidation and the length of time needed to accomplish it. The corporation undertook the elimination of long-term obligations, the sale or alienation of corporate assets, and the payment of liquidating distributions. The corporation thus satisfied the three-pronged test. Olmsted, 48 TCM 594, ¶ 84,381 P-H Memo. TC (1984).

Liquidation not disqualified because of transfer of nominal assets to new subsidiary. The IRS ruled that a transaction involving a statutory merger of a wholly owned subsidiary into its parent qualifies as a Section 332 complete liquidation of the subsidiary even when the parent transfers a portion of the subsidiary's assets to its newly formed subsidiary, since the assets transferred were nominal and the purpose of the transfer was to protect the liquidated subsidiary's corporate name. Rev. Rul. 84-2, 1984-1 CB 92.

"Taxable year" in Sections 332(b)(2) and 332(b)(3) refers to the distributing corporation. Sections 332(b)(2) and 332(b)(3) provide for nonrecognition of gain or loss when liquidating distributions are made within a certain time after the close of the "taxable year." The IRS stated that these references are to the taxable year of the corporation making the liquidating distribution. Rev. Rul. 76-317, 1976-2 CB 98.

Liquidation following purchase of controlling interest qualifies for nonrecognition. Where a

LIQUIDATIONS: *Assignment of Income Doctrine*

corporate stockholder owning 50 percent of a corporation purchases all the remaining stock and immediately thereafter adopts a plan for complete liquidation, the 80 percent control test of Section 332(b)(1) is met. Rev. Rul. 70-106 distinguished. Rev. Rul. 75-521, 1975-2 CB 120.

Active trade or business requirement met. A corporation can meet the active trade or business requirements of Section 355(b) by liquidating a wholly owned subsidiary that meets those requirements and acquiring the subsidiary's business in a tax-free transaction. Rev. Rul. 74-79, 1974-1 CB 81.

Period between sale on termination of business and final distribution cannot be considered in computing active business test. The IRS ruled that the period between the date of sale of assets on termination of a business and the date that proceeds are distributed cannot be included in determining the five-year active business test of Section 346(b)(1). Rev. Rul. 71-473, 1971-2 CB 179.

Credit on partnership books equivalent to distribution. A corporation was liquidated and operated as a partnership. Each partner was credited with his share of equity of the corporation although no amounts were actually distributed. The IRS held that the crediting on the partnership books was equivalent to the distribution of the assets and gain or loss was recognized under Section 331. (IT 1323 and SR 1240 superseded.) Rev. Rul. 69-534, 1969-2 CB 48.

Assignment of Income Doctrine

Locked-in profit from sale of futures by liquidating corporation is taxable despite Section 337. Taxpayers controlled a corporation that sold its assets under Section 337 and liquidated. The assets sold included offsetting futures contracts in which the contracts to sell had a higher price than the contracts to buy. The district court held that the corporation's locked-in profit on these transactions was taxable to the corporation under the assignment-of-income doctrine, which overrides Section 337. *Held*: Affirmed. Because of the certainty of this profit, selling it was an assignment of future income. Peterson, 723 F2d 43, 84-1 USTC ¶ 9103, 53 AFTR2d 84-398 (8th Cir. 1983).

Assignment of income doctrine applied in context of Section 337 sale to make taxable gain realized from contracts under which income was earned but had not yet accrued. Storz-Wachob-Bender Co. (SWB), wholly owned by taxpayer, was in the business of underwriting securities. SWB, an accrual basis taxpayer, recognized income only on successfully completing underwriting (i.e., when the securities are sold to the public), since contingencies on payment exist until that time. SWB adopted a plan of liquidation and sold its assets and business as a "going concern" to another securities company. The assets sold included partially performed underwriting contracts, some of which were substantially completed. The purchaser determined that approximately $230,000 of income would be received under these contracts. SWB did not, by reason of Section 337, report any gain or loss from the sale of its assets. The IRS allocated a portion of the sales proceeds, under the assignment of income doctrine, to the partially performed underwriting contracts, and assessed SWB for tax on this income. *Held*: Reversed. Although income under the contracts had not yet accrued due to contingencies that could prevent payment, they had a definite value to SWB which was reflected in the purchase price. Income that has not yet accrued may yet be earned, and thus is reachable under the assignment of income doctrine. Accordingly, this income may be taxed irrespective of the application of Section 337 to gain realized on the sale of SWB's other assets. Storz, 583 F2d 972, 78-2 USTC ¶ 9597, 42 AFTR2d 78-5024 (8th Cir. 1978).

Donation of stock held to be anticipatory assignment of liquidation proceeds. Taxpayer owned approximately 10 percent of the outstanding stock of *B*, a business that owned two insurance companies. A plan of liquidation was adopted for all three corporations. After taxpayer was informed that she would receive a liquidating distribution, taxpayer donated her stock to various public charities. Thereafter, the liquidation was completed. Taxpayer claimed a charitable deduction for the donated stock on her tax return. Although the charitable deduction was allowed, the IRS viewed the transaction as an anticipatory assignment of liquidation proceeds, and determined that taxpayer was subject to a capital gains tax. The district court, relying on Jacobs, 280 F. Supp. 437 (SD Ohio 1960), aff'd, 390 F2d 877 (6th Cir. 1968), found for taxpayer. *Held:* Reversed and remanded. Where the realities and substance of the events indicated that a liquidation was certain to be completed, the donation of stock prior to completion of the liquidation was an anticipatory assignment of liquidating proceeds. Jones, 531 F2d 1343, 76-1 USTC ¶ 9247, 37 AFTR2d 76-885 (6th Cir. 1976).

Donation of stock in liquidating corporation held to be anticipatory assignment of liquidation proceeds even though the liquidation plan could have been rescinded. Taxpayer and his wife owned over 80 percent of Container Properties, Inc. (Container). Container owned 100 percent of the stock of X and Y Corporations. On April 26, 1985, Container adopted a plan of complete liquidation and, as a first step, distributed to its stockholders the stock in X and Y. Furthermore, pursuant to a 1963 agreement, Container sold some real estate to an unrelated third party on September 15, 1965. On July 7, 1965, taxpayer transferred a 56.8 percent stock interest in Container to a charitable donee. Taxpayer claimed a charitable deduction for the Container stock donated. The IRS challenged taxpayer's deduction and required that taxpayer report again on the contribution of liquidation proceeds to the charitable donee. The IRS and the Tax Court agreed that taxpayer did not donate stock, but, under the facts, merely made an anticipatory assignment of liquidation proceeds. *Held:* Affirmed. The answer to the question of whether an anticipatory assignment occurred depends on whether the liquidation had, at the time of the donation, proceeded to a stage where the plan of liquidation was irreversible. While under state law it was possible for Container to rescind its plan to liquidate, a rescission would require a favorable vote by two thirds of the stockholders. The charitable donee only had a 56.8 percent interest and it was highly unlikely that any other stockholder would vote in favor of rescission. Specifically, a rescission would require that the stockholders receiving stock in X and Y treat such distribution as a dividend. Kinsey, 477 F2d 1058, 73-1 USTC ¶ 9429, 31 AFTR2d 73-1262 (2d Cir. 1973).

Assignment of income doctrine overrides Section 337 nonrecognition of gain on sale of uncompleted but partially performed contracts where net profit attributable to partial performance is ascertainable. Taxpayer was the transferee of Surface Combustion Corp. Surface was a corporation engaged in the manufacture and installation of certain equipment. Because its contracts with customers required performance generally extending beyond one year, it used the completed-contract method to report income and expenses arising from its business. In 1959, Surface sold all of its assets to taxpayer, with taxpayer assuming all of Surface's liabilities. Among the assets sold were certain uncompleted, but partially performed, contracts between Surface and its customers. Under Surface's method of accounting, the income and expense associated with these contracts had not been reported. Nevertheless, the net profits earned by Surface's partial performance were sufficiently ascertainable that an agreed on value was placed on them by Surface and taxpayer. By reason of Section 337, Surface reported no gain or loss on the sale to taxpayer. The IRS asserted and the District Court held that Section 337 did not avoid Surface's recognition of ordinary income with respect to these contracts. *Held:* For the IRS. The contracts are property that may be sold without recognition of gain or loss under Section 337; however, in the first instance, gain qualifying for nonrecognition under Section 337 is still subject to analysis under the assignment of income doctrine. Under the facts, this doctrine required Surface to report income on the sale notwithstanding Section 337, equal to the net profit attributable to its partial performance. Midland-Ross Corp., 485 F2d 110,

73-2 USTC ¶ 9678, 32 AFTR2d 73-5850 (6th Cir. 1973).

Gift of stock after liquidation proceedings commenced was assignment of income. The IRS held that taxpayer was not entitled to exclude from his gross income liquidation dividends on stock of a closely held corporation that taxpayer had donated to various tax-exempt organizations. Such stock donation occurred before actual payments of proceeds were received but after the stockholders had fully adopted a plan of complete liquidation and the corporation had sold its principal assets. The district court held for taxpayer. *Held:* Reversed. Under state law the dissolution steps are considered started at the time the stockholders approve the plan of complete liquidation. As a result, the plan was considered to have been irreversible at the time of the gifts. Thus, there was an anticipatory assignment of income. Hudspeth, 471 F2d 275, 73-1 USTC ¶ 9136, 31 AFTR2d 73-488 (8th Cir. 1972).

Sale of installment accounts receivable pursuant to Section 337 liquidation was anticipatory assignment. All the stock of taxpayer, a cash-basis corporation, was sold to another corporation that purchased taxpayer for the purpose of dissolving it and acquiring its assets. After the sale, a plan of complete liquidation was adopted. Taxpayer sold all its installment accounts receivable to unrelated persons and was liquidated. Taxpayer contended that the nonrecognition provisions of Section 337 applied. The Tax Court held that, despite the fact that taxpayer had not elected to report on the installment basis, these accounts receivable were installment obligations within the meaning of the provision of Section 337 (making installment obligations ineligible for nonrecognition of gain on sale of assets in such a liquidation). *Held:* Affirmed. The court, in affirming, expressly left undecided the question of whether the installment obligations constituted "property" within the meaning of Section 337. Instead, the court used the rationale of its decision in Kuckenberg, 309 F2d 202 (9th Cir. 1962), and held that the IRS had the authority under Section 446 to disregard taxpayer's cash basis of accounting and to require a recomputation that would clearly reflect income. Taxpayer here sold a right to receive income and nothing more. It was never contemplated in Section 337 that a cash-basis taxpayer should get advantageous treatment over an accrual-basis taxpayer through its ability to avoid the consequences of an anticipatory assignment of income. Family Record Plan, Inc., 309 F2d 208, 62-2 USTC ¶ 978, 10 AFTR2d 5794 (9th Cir. 1962), cert. denied, 373 US 910 (1963).

Corporate liquidating distribution of rights under a contract was an anticipatory assignment of income. Taxpayers were transferees of the assets of a dissolved corporation. The corporation was the assignee of a contract calling for the construction of a city water system. The contract provided that if the system were completed in its entirety, it would be conveyed to the water district at cost plus a specified profit to the assignee corporation. If, however, the system were only partially completed, conveyance would be provided at a price per water tap connection, which would also yield a profit. At the time the corporation was dissolved, it was evident that the conveyance would take place in accordance with the latter option. This was accomplished, and payments were made over a period of years to the transferees. The IRS assessed deficiencies against the stockholders as transferees, contending that the profit was taxable as ordinary income to the corporation. Taxpayers contended the Section 336 precluded the assessment, since it provided that no gain or loss would be recognized to a corporation on the distribution of property in complete or partial liquidation. *Held:* For the IRS. The job on which the income was based was completed long before the date of dissolution, and the rights of the corporation had ripened. Section 336 was not intended to abrogate the doctrine of anticipatory assignment as set forth in *Horst*. All the elements of anticipatory assignment were present here; that is, the property was completely under the control of the corporation, it brought about the enjoyment of the income by the sole stockholders, and the payment of the income was not remote in time from the assignment. Cummins Diesel Sales of Colo. Co.,

LIQUIDATIONS: *Basis of Property Received*

263 F. Supp. 677, 67-1 USTC ¶ 9265 (D. Colo. 1967).

Basis of Property Received

Stepped-up basis denied to subsidiary that liquidated corporations received from parent in a Section 351 exchange. Parent corporation purchased stock of a group of corporations. Parent immediately contributed this stock to its subsidiary in an exchange pursuant to Section 351. The group was liquidated and the assets were distributed to the subsidiary. Under Section 334(b)(2), the subsidiary claimed a basis in assets determined with respect to parent's cost basis in the group's stock. The IRS claimed that the subsidiary's basis in these assets was a carry-over basis from the liquidated group. The district court held for the IRS. *Held:* Affirmed. Section 334(b)(2) does not permit a stepped-up basis because the subsidiary did not acquire the stock by "purchase." Further, the *Kimbell-Diamond* doctrine does not apply because it was supplanted by Section 334(b)(2) when enacted. In re Chrome Plate, 614 F2d 990, 80-1 USTC ¶ 9332, 45 AFTR2d 80-1241 (5th Cir.), cert. denied, 449 US 842 (1980).

Subsidy payment by Virgin Islands did not cause decrease in basis. Taxpayer corporation had a Virgin Islands subsidiary, which it liquidated under Section 332. Under Section 334(b)(1), the basis of the subsidiary's assets in taxpayer's hands remained the same as the subsidiary's basis before liquidation. Relying on this carry-over basis, taxpayer computed its income tax liability. The IRS assessed a deficiency based on the contention that subsidies received by the subsidiary were nonstockholder contributions to capital, reducing the subsidiary's basis in its inventory, and therefore taxpayer's opening carry-over inventory basis as well. This reduction had the effect of decreasing taxpayer's cost of goods sold, thereby increasing its taxable income for the year in question. *Held:* For taxpayer. The parent corporation's basis in the liquidated subsidiary's assets were not reduced by the subsidies paid to the subsidiary under the Virgin Islands' industrial incentive law. The clear intention of the legislature and the understanding of the corporations induced to establish businesses in the Virgin Islands was that this "subsidy" was to be a reduction of income taxes. This intention would be frustrated by a ruling that payments constituted nonstockholder contributions to capital, reducing the basis of the grantee's assets and, in many cases, causing an immediate increase in taxable income in the amount of the subsidy. HMW Indus., 504 F2d 146, 74-2 USTC ¶ 9726, 34 AFTR2d 74-5921 (3d Cir. 1974).

Rehearing states that the basis of assets is determined under Section 334(b)(2). Taxpayer was the president and sole stockholder of *F* Corporation, which was engaged in the life insurance business. According to a plan, *U*, another insurance company, reinsured all of *F*'s policies, purchased many of *F*'s assets, and assumed *F*'s liabilities. Taxpayer sold 250 shares of *F* to his attorney, and *F* redeemed 750 shares. Six months later, the attorney sold his 250 shares to *U*, and thereafter *U* liquidated *F*. The IRS determined that *F* recognized a gain on the sale of its business and included certain amounts in *F*'s income. The Tax Court held that the reissuance agreement constituted a sale of *F*'s business, that Sections 332 and 381 were not applicable, and that taxpayer was liable as a transferee in equity of *F*. The Fifth Circuit affirmed. *Held:* Rehearing denied. Because *F*'s stock was acquired within 12 months and the liquidation occurred within the prescribed time, the basis of the assets was determined under Section 334(b)(2). Sections 381(c)(1) and 381(c)(22) were inapplicable because the basis of assets received in a Section 332 liquidation was so determined. Estate of Glass, Jr., 453 F2d 1375, 72-1 USTC ¶ 9244, 29 AFTR2d 72-565, reh'g denied, 460 F2d 321, 72-1 USTC ¶ 9408, 29 AFTR2d 72-1092 (5th Cir. 1972).

Contracts received in liquidation. The taxpayer acquired 98 percent of the stock of Snellstrom in April 1964. The company was liquidated in April 1965 and the taxpayer received in liquidation certain timber-cutting contracts that had been held by the company prior to April 1964. Taxpayer cut timber under those contracts from May to December 1965 and reported the profits as long-term capital gain under Section 631(a). *Held:* For taxpayer. The Tax Court held that the taxpayer had acquired the Snellstrom stock and timber-cutting contracts under circumstances provided in Section 334(b)(2) and was entitled to use, as its basis in the assets received on liquidation of the company, its adjusted basis in the stock of Snellstrom. Under Section 1223(1), it was held that taxpayer was also entitled to tack its holding period of the Snellstrom stock onto its holding period of the timber-cutting contracts. Taxpayer could also make the election provided in Section 631(a) and was entitled to its benefits. Cabax Mills, 59 TC 401 (1972), acq. 1973-2 CB 1.

Tax Court refused to extend ambit of Section 351. Taxpayer corporation purchased all of the stock of *O* by issuing cash and debentures to its stockholders in exchange for their stock. Afterwards, *O* was liquidated pursuant to Section 332, and the assets subject to the liabilities were transferred to taxpayer. Taxpayer computed a basis for the assets by totaling the cost of the stock and the assumed liabilities pursuant to Section 334(b)(2). Taxpayer allocated the step-up in basis to the assets. The IRS determined that Section 334(b)(2) was inapplicable, that Section 351 applied, and that Section 334(b)(1) should be used to determine the basis of the assets. *Held:* For taxpayer. Where the stockholders in taxpayer were in a different proportion than in the subsidiary, where one subsidiary stockholder did not own shares in taxpayer, and where over 50 percent of taxpayer's stockholders had no interest in the subsidiary, the control requirement of Section 351 was not met. Accordingly, taxpayer properly computed the basis of the assets under Section 334(b)(2). Stevens Pass, Inc., 48 TC 532 (1967).

Attribution rules applied to deny stepped-up basis in liquidation. Taxpayer corporation owned installment contracts on the sale of land. Its principal stockholder accepted an offer from his son and son-in-law to purchase taxpayer. A new corporation was organized by them for that purpose. Each received 99 shares, and an employee was "named" as the owner of the other two. The new corporation purchased taxpayer and liquidated it. Taxpayer claimed that this was not a disposition of installment obligations requiring recognition of gain. The new corporation contended that it was entitled to a stepped-up basis under Section 334(b)(2). *Held:* For taxpayer, in part. No gain was recognized on the transfer of the installment obligations. There was a completed liquidation of taxpayer corporation into the new corporation, and nothing in Section 334 required a contrary conclusion; but the new corporation did not get a stepped-up basis. The employee was only a nominal owner of the stock. The son, as a 50 percent stockholder, constructively owned the stock his father owned in the liquidated corporation. Therefore, the attribution rules of Section 318 applied and Section 334(b)(2) did not apply. The new corporation took over the same basis as taxpayer corporation. Bijou Park Properties, Inc., 47 TC 207 (1966).

Collection files had value in liquidation. A commercial collection agency, in which taxpayer was a stockholder, maintained a group of records containing materials relating to delinquent accounts. The corporation was liquidated, and these files were distributed to taxpayer, who assigned a value to the files and reported a capital gain on the liquidation. He later received fees for collections of these accounts and treated the fees as a recoupment of his basis. The IRS contended that the fees were ordinary income. *Held:* For taxpayer. As a principal asset of a collection business, the files had value at the time of liquidation. Taxpayer was correct in treating the fees as a return of basis for which he had paid a tax. Drybrough, 42 TC 1029 (1964).

Carry-over basis applied to stock attributed to taxpayer more than 12 months before liquidation. Taxpayer corporation acquired all the stock of X, which owned all the stock of Y. X's ownership of the Y stock was attributable to taxpayer under Section 318(a). Fifteen months later, taxpayer liquidated X under Section 332 and thus "purchased" all of Y's stock. Taxpayer's basis in the Y stock was on a carry-over basis, not an adjusted basis, since its "purchase" of more than 80 percent of Y's stock did not occur within the 12-

month period specified by Section 334(b)(2)(B). Rev. Rul. 80-358, 1980-2 CB 110.

Allocation of basis of subsidiary's stock to its assets in a liquidation explained. Parent, P, purchased all of the stock of subsidiary, S, for $480,000, the fair market value of S's assets. Six months later, P liquidated S pursuant to Section 332 in a transaction in which the basis of the assets was determined under Section 334(b)(2). The IRS ruled that the adjusted basis of the stock in S would be allocated proportionally among the various assets except cash or its equivalent. However, where the allocation would give the accounts receivable (a non-cash asset) a basis in the hands of P greater than its fair market value, the allocation to such receivables would be limited to fair market value, and the basis of the remainder of the non-cash assets would be increased accordingly. Rev. Rul. 77-456, 1977-2 CB 102.

IRS examines basis of assets and stock in aftermath of liquidation. All the outstanding stock of X Corporation (voting common stock) was owned by individuals A (40 percent), B (20 percent), and C (40 percent). All the outstanding stock of Y Corporation (voting common stock) was owned by individuals B (45 percent), D (30 percent), and E (25 percent). A and B were father and son, and C and D were father and son. Otherwise, the stockholders of X and Y were not related to each other. The stockholders of X sold all of their X stock to Y for cash. Immediately thereafter, X was completely liquidated into Y. The IRS was asked to rule on the question of whether the basis of assets received on the complete liquidation of a subsidiary under Section 332 is determined by reference to Section 334(b)(1) or Section 334(b)(2). The IRS found initially that, by force of Section 318(a)(1)(A), the three stockholders A, B, and C were deemed to own 100 percent of the stock of X and 75 percent of Y before the transaction. Accordingly, since Y acquired the stock of X for cash from a person or persons A, B and C in control of both the issuing corporation (X) and the acquiring corporation (Y), the transaction must be treated as an acquisition of stock by a related corporation within the meaning of Section 304(a)(1) and thus a redemption of the stock of Y, the acquiring corporation. By a similar analysis, the sale was treated as a Section 302(a) redemption, so that the basis of the X stock in the hands of Y was the same as it would be in the hands of the X stockholders, increased in the amount of gain recognized to the X stockholders as provided in Section 362(a) and Regulation § 1.304-2(a). Consequently, the basis of the X stock in the hands of Y had to be determined in part by reference to the adjusted basis of the X stock in the hands of the former X stockholders. The acquisition of the X stock, therefore, was not a "purchase" within the meaning of Section 334(b)(3) because it comes within the exception of Section 334(b)(3)(A). Accordingly, the basis to Y of the assets of X received on the complete liquidation of X must be determined under Section 334(b)(1). Rev. Rul. 77-427, 1977-2 CB 100.

Basis of assets received in a liquidation of a subsidiary's subsidiary. A stock distribution was considered a purchase where a wholly owned subsidiary's distribution to its parent of all of its wholly owned subsidiary's stock, the basis of which was greater than the fair market value, was followed by a complete liquidation within 12 months. Rev. Rul. 74-211, 1974-1 CB 76.

Subsidiary's basis carried over to parent on liquidation in satisfaction of an indebtedness. A parent corporation completely liquidated a subsidiary in satisfaction of indebtedness owed to the parent. The parent corporation's basis would be the same as the subsidiary's basis pursuant to Section 334(b)(1), which deals with the satisfaction of an indebtedness. Rev. Rul. 69-426, 1969-2 CB 48.

On liquidation of newly purchased subsidiary, assets take stock basis regardless of intent. Section 334(b), the codification of the Kimbell-Diamond rule, 187 F2d 718 (5th Cir. 1951), provides an exception to the general rule that on the liquidation of a subsidiary the parent takes the assets at the basis the subsidiary had for them. The special rule is

LIQUIDATIONS: *Expenses Incurred in Liquidation*

that if liquidation occurs within two years of acquiring control, the parent takes the assets at the basis it had for the stock. The IRS ruled that the intent of the parent in acquiring the stock is, under the Code, irrelevant. It may or may not have purchased the stock only as a means of securing the assets. Rev. Rul. 60-262, 1960-2 CB 114.

Cost of stock held in subsidiary at time of liquidation determines stepped-up basis of assets received by parent. Pursuant to Section 334(b)(2), a parent corporation can get a stepped-up basis on liquidation of a subsidiary where it acquires 80 percent control of the stock by purchase within a two-year period. Only the adjusted basis of the stock held by the parent immediately prior to the liquidation is includible in determining the basis of the property. However, amounts paid by the parent to the minority stockholders after the liquidation are treated as the release of a liability assumed by the parent with respect to the minority stockholders, and the amounts so paid are also included as part of the overall basis of the assets acquired. Rev. Rul. 59-412, 1959-2 CB 108.

Expenses Incurred in Liquidation

Commissions paid in sale of capital assets, as part of a Section 337 liquidation, held not to be deductible. In the course of a Section 337 liquidation, a corporation incurred brokerage commissions on the sale of real estate held as a capital asset. The corporation deducted these commissions as business expenses. *Held:* For the IRS. The general rule that costs incurred in the disposition of a capital asset are to be capitalized applies to expenses incurred in a sale accorded nonrecognition under Section 337. The court recognized that its holding could result in a disparity of tax treatment with respect to property distributed to the stockholders before a sale but did not feel that this consequence violated the policy of Section 337. George Page, 524 F2d 1149, 75-2 USTC ¶ 9731, 36 AFTR2d 75-5945 (9th Cir. 1975).

Fourth Circuit reversed itself in *Pridemark, Inc.* and held that legal fees incurred in course of Section 337 sale of assets were nondeductible. Taxpayer sold its assets and liquidated pursuant to Section 337. On its return for the year of liquidation, it deducted as a business expense legal fees incurred in connection with the sale of its assets. The IRS denied the deduction and the Tax Court decided in favor of the IRS. *Held:* Affirmed. Attorney fees incurred in connection with the sale of corporate assets pursuant to Section 337 are not deductible as a liquidation expense. Of Course, Inc., 499 F2d 754, 74-2 USTC ¶ 9546, 34 AFTR2d 74-5348 (4th Cir. 1974).

Selling expenses of Section 337 liquidation were nondeductible capital expenditures. Taxpayer corporation sold all its assets in connection with a Section 337 liquidation. On its 1963 return, taxpayer sought to deduct selling expenses incurred in disposing of its assets. The IRS argued that the expenses were nondeductible capital expenditures that offset the realized but unrecognized capital gain on the asset sale. The district court upheld the IRS. *Held:* Affirmed. Section 337's purpose was to prevent double taxation, not to convert capital expenditures into deductible business expenses. Lanrao, Inc., 422 F2d 481, 70-1 USTC ¶ 9223, 25 AFTR2d 70-568 (6th Cir. 1970).

Attorney fees for dissolution on liquidation were deductible, but fees for collection of insurance were not. A fire severely damaged taxpayer corporation's property. As a result, taxpayer decided to liquidate. Taxpayer deducted its expenses on liquidation, including appraisal and legal fees in connection with its insurance recovery. The IRS contended that the liquidation expenses were not deductible, but conceded the deductibility of legal fees on appeal except as to those fees incurred in collecting the insurance, which, it argued, were capital costs. The district court disagreed with the IRS, holding for taxpayer. *Held:* Reversed as to the deductibility of the legal and appraisal fees. To allow what ordinarily is considered a capital expenditure as an ordinary business expense is overextending the congressional purpose in enacting Section 337. The case was remanded to the district court to determine what portion of

LIQUIDATIONS: *Expenses Incurred in Liquidation*

the legal fee was allocable to the recovery of the insurance claim and what portion allocable to the other activities incident to the liquidation. Morton, Sr., 387 F2d 441, 68-1 USTC ¶ 9143, 21 AFTR2d 368 (8th Cir. 1967).

Eighth Circuit rejected the IRS' waiver of the basis of its argument before the Tax Court, which the Tax Court found valid. Taxpayer *B* held 50 percent of the stock of taxpayer, a closely held corporation. In order to allow *B* to retire yet keep taxpayer in the hands of its former stockholders, an agreement was reached whereby taxpayer purchased 175 of *B*'s 200 shares, and a second stockholder purchased the remainder. Not having sufficient cash to cover the entire purchase, taxpayer transferred to *B* land and improvements and an insurance policy in lieu of cash. After *B* formally transferred the 175 shares to taxpayer, the stock was canceled on the corporate records. The IRS took the position before the Tax Court that the transaction was in part a liquidation and in part a recapitalization, and the court found a partial liquidation. On appeal, the IRS sought to deny its previous arguments regarding a partial liquidation and to establish the transaction as only a reorganization. *Held:* For taxpayer. Because the Tax Court concluded, from all the facts, that a partial liquidation had been effected, the decision was proper and was not to be denied by the IRS on appeal. As the dominant aspect of the transaction was the partial liquidation and not the recapitalization, the legal fees and expenses were attributable to the partial liquidation and hence deductible as ordinary and necessary business expenses in carrying on the business. Gravois Planning Mill Co., 299 F2d 199, 62-1 USTC ¶ 9271, 9 AFTR2d 733 (8th Cir. 1962).

Selling expenses of real property were not ordinary expenses in one-year liquidation. Taxpayer corporation liquidated under the one-year provision of Section 337 and deducted as ordinary business expenses the amounts incurred in selling real property. The IRS disallowed the item as an ordinary deduction. *Held:* For the IRS. The fact that the liquidation qualified under Section 337 did not convert the real property selling expenses from capital expenditures into ordinary business expenses. Washington Trust Bank, 70-2 USTC ¶ 9688 (ED Wash. 1970).

State taxes and other expenses were deductible in a Section 337 liquidation. Under a Section 337 plan of liquidation, taxpayer's lumber corporation sold its land, timber, milling plant, inventories, accounts receivable, and cash to several corporations, realizing a substantial gain. Although the corporation recognized no gain for federal income tax purposes, state taxes were imposed. The corporation incurred accounting expenses plus interest on the state taxes in the year in question, which were assessed against taxpayer because the corporation was dissolved. The IRS disallowed deductions for the state taxes plus interest thereon and the accounting expenses. *Held:* For taxpayer. The state income taxes plus interest thereon and accounting expenses in connection with a Section 337 liquidation were deductible. Section 265, which disallowed expenses attributable to wholly exempt income, was inapplicable because the gains were not wholly exempt. Rushton, 63-2 USTC ¶ 9647, 12 AFTR2d 5443 (ND Ala. 1963).

State taxes on Section 337 liquidation gains were deductible. Taxpayer liquidated under Section 337, and although it was not subject to federal taxation on the profits realized from the sale of its property, taxpayer was subject to state taxation. Taxpayer deducted the state taxes from the corporation's other income on its federal tax return. The IRS determined that because no federal tax was due on account of the profits, the corporation was not allowed to deduct the state income tax attributable to them. *Held:* For taxpayer. Gains that were not recognized were not the same as wholly exempt income. Therefore, Section 265 was not applicable, and the state income taxes were deductible. Tovrea Land & Cattle Co., 63-1 USTC ¶ 9430, 11 AFTR2d 1374 (D. Ariz. 1963).

Expenses associated with the settlement of antitrust claims were deductible under Section 212(1). When *T* Corporation was liquidated, taxpayer and another stockholder received, as a portion of the proceeds from the liquidation, the potential claim of the corporation against Kaiser Aluminum for treble damages resulting from possible violations of federal antitrust laws. The potential claim had no ascertainable fair market value at the time of distribution. Taxpayer deducted the legal fees and expenses for the settlement as miscellaneous deductions on his tax return. The IRS determined that the legal fees and expenses should be disallowed under Section 212, but allowed offsets to long-term capital gains to be reported as a result of the claim's settlement. *Held*: For taxpayer. Because the claim was the collection of income, the tax treatment of the realization on the claim did not change from ordinary income to capital gain by the corporate liquidation. Therefore, the legal fees and expenses were deductible under Section 212(1). Estate of Mead, 31 TCM 935, ¶ 72,190 P-H Memo. TC (1972).

Expenses of sale cannot be deducted under Section 337. In 1956, taxpayer corporation, which was engaged in holding and renting real property, adopted a plan of complete liquidation within 12 months and authorized the officers to sell its real estate within that period. The corporation incurred expenses of $3,000 for broker's commissions and $350 for legal fees in effecting the sale. It sought to deduct these expenses as ordinary and necessary business expenses, although it did not report any gain on the sale of the property because of the nonrecognition provisions of Section 337. *Held*: For the IRS. The court held that the expenses involved were chargeable to capital account as an offset against the sales price in the computation of the unrecognized gain: These items were not deductible from the current income of the corporation. Ruprecht, 20 TCM 618, ¶ 61,125 P-H Memo. TC (1961).

Involuntary Conversions

Early title passing in condemnation upset tax-free liquidation. Taxpayer corporation was notified that condemnation proceedings were instituted against its property by the United States and that a deposit was made in the district court in the amount of $200,000. Taxpayer, in its response, contested only the amount of the award and, six months thereafter, adopted a plan of complete liquidation intended to qualify for the benefits of Section 337. Thereafter, the deposit was paid to the taxpayer, and the balance of the award was paid in the following year in the amount of $105,000 plus interest. Although a resolution authorizing the transfer of the assets of the corporation to a trustee was passed within the 12-month period, the steps taken to carry out the liquidation were not timely completed. Nevertheless, the corporation excluded from income the gains on the condemnation and on the sales of its real and personal property. The Tax Court upheld the IRS' determinations that the real estate had been "sold" when the condemnation proceedings were instituted prior to the adoption of the plan of liquidation, and that the gains on sales of assets were to be recognized inasmuch as the corporation failed to distribute substantially all of its assets within the 12-month period as required under Section 337. *Held*: Affirmed. The court was correct in its finding that title vested on the filing of the declaration of taking and the deposit of the amount of estimated compensation, and that such an involuntary conversion is deemed a sale or exchange for purposes of Section 337. Since the "sale" took place prior to the adoption of the plan, the gain thereon did not qualify for nonrecognition. In other issues, the court correctly found that the distribution of assets in complete redemption of stock did not take place within the 12-month period as required. There were sales of corporate property after the period had elapsed and substantial activity in the corporate bank account for a period of two years thereafter. Its finding that the gain on the condemnation proceeding was taxable in the year when the entire amount was paid over was, however, erroneous and not in agreement with the finding that title passed and the right to compensation vested when the deposit was paid into the district court. The deposit to which the taxpayer had an absolute right was taxable in the earlier year, with the remainder taxable in the later year by virtue of the jury determination at that time. Covered Wagon, Inc., 369 F2d 629, 67-1 USTC ¶ 9117 (8th Cir. 1966).

LIQUIDATIONS: *Involuntary Conversions*

Section 337 benefits lost owing to prior title passage under local law. Under New York State law, title passes on a condemnation of property when the condemning authority files a map in the county clerk's office. After this date but before receipt of the proceeds, taxpayer corporation adopted a plan of complete liquidation. The IRS denied taxpayer the benefits of Section 337. *Held*: For the IRS. The district court held that the gain on the condemnation was not within the nonrecognition provisions of Section 337 because title passed, and thus the sale took place before the plan of liquidation was adopted. The court also held that the gain was not realized until the subsequent year because the price was not finally determined until then. Dwight, 328 F2d 973, 64-1 USTC ¶ 9305 (2d Cir. 1964).

New York City condemnation law upset Section 337 liquidation. Pursuant to its condemnation law, New York City took title to taxpayer's property on August 5, 1955. On January 28, 1956, the corporation adopted a plan of dissolution and distributed its assets within one year of that date. The final decree fixing the amount of the condemnation award was entered on September 25, 1956 and paid on November 5, 1956. Taxpayer contended that no gain was recognized under Section 337. The Tax Court held that although a condemnation is a sale, the gain must be recognized. The date of a condemnation sale depends on local law, which in this case was the vesting of title in the city on August 5, 1955, *before* the adoption of the plan of liquidation. On appeal, taxpayer urged that the condemnation law made it difficult to take advantage of Section 337. *Held*: Affirmed. The position of the IRS is an eminently reasonable one; a taxpayer who acts with "sufficient celerity and acuity" can utilize Section 337. 44 West 3rd St. Corp. sub nom. Wendell, 326 F2d 600, 64-1 USTC ¶ 9193 (2d Cir. 1964).

Gain from receipt of insurance proceeds nonrecognizable as Section 392 applies regardless of whether a plan of liquidation had previously been adopted. Taxpayer's plant and equipment were destroyed in an explosion. The destroyed assets were insured for an amount that exceeded their cost reduced by tax-allowed depreciation. After receiving the insurance proceeds, taxpayer was liquidated. The Tax Court agreed with the IRS that the phrase "sale or exchange" as used in Section 392(b) does not include involuntary conversion. As a result the gain realized from receipt of the insurance proceeds before adoption of the plan of liquidation pursuant to Section 337 was recognized. *Held*: Reversed and remanded. Section 392 extends nonrecognition to gains from an involuntary conversion, and applies regardless of whether a plan of liquidation had previously been adopted. Kent Mfg. Corp., 288 F2d 812, 61-1 USTC ¶ 9308 (4th Cir. 1961).

Section 337 applicable where assets destroyed by fire before liquidation plan adopted. After suffering a fire loss, taxpayer corporation adopted a plan of liquidation and then submitted proof of loss to its insurer. Taxpayer contended it qualified under Section 337 for nonrecognition of gain because it was not entitled to the insurance proceeds until after adopting the plan. *Held*: For taxpayer. The district court, following Morton, 387 F2d 441 (8th Cir. 1967), held that the sale took place when the proceeds were received, not when the fire occurred. Kinney, 73-1 USTC ¶ 9140 (ND Cal. 1972).

Insurance proceeds not recognized where liquidation occurred after involuntary conversion. Taxpayer corporation's plant, machinery, and inventory were destroyed by fire. Later, but before taxpayer had settled any of its claims or received any insurance funds, a formal plan of liquidation under Section 337 was adopted. As taxpayer was on the accrual basis, the IRS argued that the right to receive insurance proceeds became fixed before taxpayer's plan of liquidation was adopted, i.e., approximately at the time of the fire. *Held*: For taxpayer. In insurance accrual cases, it has been held that the right to proceeds does not become fixed until there is an unqualified recognition of liability by the obligor (the insurance company). The court found that such recognition did not occur at the date of adoption of a formal liquidation plan. Thus, subsequent receipt of insurance proceeds fell under the nonrecognition of gain provision of Section 337. Also, recognition of gain under Section 1245 accrued in the year of settlement and legal fees attributable to negotiation and settlement of the insurance loss were a capital expenditure. Central Tablet Mfg. Co., 339 F. Supp. 1134, 72-1 USTC ¶ 9324, 37 AFTR2d 72-388 (SD Ohio 1972).

Gain recognized; liquidation not completed in 12 months. Anticipating condemnation of its property, taxpayer corporation's stockholders adopted a plan of liquidation. The property was held in the name of a nominee of the corporation who refused to make the conveyance to the corporation. After extended litigation it was held that the corporation was entitled to the condemnation award. Although the stockholders surrendered their stock in taxpayer corporation before the expiration of the 12-month period in which liquidation must be completed to avoid recognition of gain under Section 337, other corporate activities continued. *Held*: For the IRS. The court held that liquidation was not completed in the required period, no assets having been distributed. The court also held, without discussion, that the legal fees incurred to establish taxpayer's right to the property were deductible as ordinary business expenses. Best Realty Co., 62-2 USTC ¶ 9588, 10 AFTR2d 5222 (ND Tex. 1962).

Fire insurance proceeds nontaxable under Section 337. After adopting a plan of liquidation, taxpayer suffered a fire loss. The insurance proceeds exceeded the basis for the property. Taxpayer claimed the gain was not taxable under Section 337. That section provides for nonrecognition of gain or loss on sale of corporate assets during a 12-month liquidation. The IRS argued that Section 337 was not applicable because there was no sale or exchange. *Held*: For taxpayer. An involuntary conversion is treated as a sale for purposes of Section 337, as for other purposes. The legal and adjuster fees were not deductible, however; they had to be applied to reduce the proceeds. Towanda Textiles, Inc., 180 F. Supp. 373, 60-1 USTC ¶ 9258, 5 AFTR2d 702 (Ct. Cl. 1960).

Condemnation prior to adoption of plan resulted in gain. Taxpayer was in the real estate business. Its property was condemned by the authorities. Based on state law, the filing of the declaration of taking resulted in a sale of the property. This preceded the adoption of a plan of liquidation. Taxpayer did not report the gain. *Held*: For the IRS. In determining the effective date of a sale of condemned property, the date title passes is controlling. Since title passed based on state law as of the declaration of taking, taxpayer was taxable on its realized gain. Gallina, 53 TC 130 (1969).

Condemnation of property predated and nullified Section 337 election. Taxpayer's corporation owned property that was condemned by the United States in 1957. At that time, the mortgage exceeded the basis. In June 1958, the United States deposited $171,000 for the property. Taxpayer sued for a larger award (which it got in 1962), but was authorized to withdraw the deposited amount, which it did in August 1958, shortly after it adopted a plan of liquidation. Taxpayer excluded the gain, treating the condemnation as a sale covered by Section 337. *Held*: For the IRS. Gain was realized in 1957 to the extent of the excess of the mortgage over the basis. Further gain was realized at the time of withdrawal. Since, in condemnation proceedings, title passes when the proceedings are begun, the nonrecognition provisions of Section 337 were not applicable. Foster, ¶ 66,273 P-H Memo. TC (1966).

Section 337 liquidation upset by New York City condemnation law. On August 7, 1957, New York City acquired title to taxpayer corporation's property upon a condemnation order by the Supreme Court of New York. On February 24, 1958, taxpayer adopted a plan of complete liquidation pursuant to Section 337. On April 14, 1958, the Supreme Court, after trial, rendered its final decree fixing the amount of the condemnation award, which was actually paid on July 8, 1958. Taxpayer claimed that the "sale or exchange" of its property did not occur until the Supreme Court fixed the amount of the award in April 1958, while the IRS contended the sale oc-

LIQUIDATIONS: *Liquidating Corporation's Gain or Loss*

curred on August 7, 1957, prior to the date taxpayer adopted a plan of complete liquidation. *Held*: For the IRS. An involuntary sale of condemned property takes place at the time title vests in the public authority acquiring the property. Since the sale occurred prior to February 24, 1958, it could not qualify under Section 337 for nonrecognition of the gain realized. Nor did the payment of the condemnation award qualify for capital gain benefits as a "retirement" of an "evidence of indebtedness," since the obligation to pay for the condemnation did not constitute a bond, debenture, note, certificate, or other evidence of indebtedness. 84 Woodbine St. Realty Corp., 22 TCM 1324, ¶ 63,262 P-H Memo. TC (1963).

IRS rules on effect of involuntary conversion occurring during liquidation. The IRS has announced that, consistent with court decisions on the question, involuntary conversions of property of the type described in Section 337 by reason of destruction by fire will be treated as sales or exchanges for purposes of that section where such conversions result in loss as well as gain, regardless of whether such property is the type described in Section 1231 and regardless of whether such property has been held for more or less then six months. Rev. Rul. 64-100, 1964-1 (Part 1) CB 130.

Court order vesting title in condemned property was sale for 12-month liquidation. The condemnation of real estate held by a corporation and the vesting of title in the condemning authority pursuant to court order constituted a sale of property on the order date within the meaning of Section 337, even though payment of the award did not occur until a later year. Therefore, since the corporation had a plan of complete liquidation on the date of the order, and it completely liquidated within the 12-month period beginning with the date of adoption of the plan, the taxpayer qualified under Section 337, and no gain or loss was recognized on the condemnation. Rev. Rul. 59-108, 1959-1 CB 72.

Fire insurance not proceeds of sale of destroyed property. The receipt of fire insurance after the complete destruction of a building by fire was not a sale. Taxpayer corporation adopted a plan to sell assets and liquidate within 12 months, tax-free to the corporation under Section 337. The conversion was not a tax-free sale under this section. Rev. Rul. 56-372, 1956-2 CB 187.

Liquidating Corporation's Gain or Loss

Section 336 does not permit a liquidating corporation to avoid the tax-benefit rule. Taxpayer was a closely held corporation engaged in the dairy operation business. Taxpayer deducted on purchase the full cost of the cattle feed purchased for use in its operations, as permitted by Section 162. At the close of the taxable year a substantial portion of the feed was still on hand. Two days into the next taxable year, taxpayer adopted a plan of liquidation and distributed its assets, including the remaining cattle feed, to its stockholders. Taxpayer reported no income on the transaction, relying on Section 336, which shields a corporation from the recognition of gain on the distribution of property to its stockholders on liquidation. The IRS contended that taxpayer should have included the value of the distributed feed in income, and assessed a penalty. The District Court held for taxpayer and the Ninth Circuit affirmed. Taxpayer's case was consolidated with *Hillsboro Nat'l Bank* for review before the Supreme Court. *Held:* For the IRS. Section 336 does not prevent the application of the tax-benefit rule. The court began its analysis by noting that Section 162(a) requires that business expenses be deducted only in the amount that they are actually consumed and used in operation in the taxable year. Although Section 336 specifically shields a taxpayer from the recognition of gain in the context of liquidation, courts generally held that exceptions do apply. The court noted the striking similarity in language between Section 336 and Section 337, a provision that governs sales of assets followed by distribution of the proceeds in liquidation. The Court further stated that it is well established that the tax-benefit rule overrides Section 337. Finding that the function of Sections 336 and 337 require that they be construed in tandem, the Court was compelled to subordinate Section 336 to the tax-

LIQUIDATIONS: *Liquidating Corporation's Gain or Loss*

benefit rule. Hillsboro Nat'l Bank, 460 US 370 (1983).

Loss on liquidation sale of accounts receivable deductible despite Section 337. Taxpayer corporation sold its assets under a Section 337 liquidation plan. The accounts receivable were sold at a discount. To resolve a dispute about the collectibility of some of the accounts, taxpayer reacquired the more doubtful accounts. Taxpayer deducted the discount as a loss on the sale of installment obligations under Section 337(b)(1)(B), and also deducted bad debt losses on the accounts reacquired from the buyer. *Held:* For taxpayer. The accounts receivable were "installment obligations" under Section 337, although no Section 453 election was made; thus, taxpayer could recognize the loss. The later reacquisition of the doubtful accounts was deemed a partial rescission of the original sales, so taxpayer could deduct the bad debts as if the accounts had never been sold. Liberty Nat'l Bank & Trust Co., 650 F2d 1174, 81-2 USTC ¶ 9487, 48 AFTR2d 81-5239 (10th Cir. 1981).

Tax-benefit principles apply to Section 337 transaction. Taxpayer corporation sold its entire assets and business pursuant to a plan of liquidation under Section 337. As part of the liquidating sale, taxpayer was reimbursed for advertising. The IRS held that since such advertising had been recovered in full through ordinary business deductions in a prior year and in the year of sale, (1) the portion allocable to the prior year constituted ordinary income to the extent of the tax benefit secured and (2) the portion allocable to the year of sale had to be treated as taxable income or as offset to the advertising expense deduction taken for such year. The district court found for the IRS. *Held:* Affirmed. The court found that Congress did not intend to eliminate tax-benefit principles from application in a Section 337 transaction. Connery, 460 F2d 1130, 72-1 USTC ¶ 9441, 29 AFTR2d 72-1188 (3d Cir. 1972).

Nonrecognition of gain under Section 337 not applicable to a tax benefit that distorted income. Taxpayer, a corporation in the cattle feeding business, had elected not to report inventories. Instead, it deducted from gross income the cost of feed and supplies purchased during the year pursuant to Regulation § 1.162-12. During the year, taxpayer was liquidated under Section 337 and did not report any income from the lump-sum sale of the feed and supplies. The IRS disallowed the expense deduction to the extent of the sale price in order to prevent distortion of income; the district court ruled against the IRS. *Held:* Reversed. When costs are recovered in the taxable year in which they were incurred, the extent of deductible costs is accordingly reduced. On the related matter of basis, the case was remanded so that the transferees of the corporation could be given an opportunity to establish cost. Spitalny, 430 F2d 195, 70-2 USTC ¶ 9545, 26 AFTR2d 70-5351 (9th Cir. 1970).

Deductions attributable to production of an unharvested crop not deductible when crop was sold with the land in a Section 337 liquidation. Taxpayer, a dissolved corporation, sold its orange grove at a substantial gain, which was not recognized under Section 337. Prior to the liquidation, it expended sums of money to grow oranges with the unharvested crop sold with the land. The deduction of these expenses resulted in a net operating loss that was carried back to the two years prior to liquidation and resulted in refunds that the IRS contested successfully in the Tax Court. The IRS contended that the expenses were not allowable by reason of Section 268, which denies the deduction when an unharvested crop is sold as Section 1231 property. The taxpayer contended that the unharvested crop was not property used in trade or business under Section 1231. *Held:* Affirmed. Section 1231 specifically includes an unharvested crop in the definition of property used in trade or business. Beauchamp & Brown Groves Co., 371 F2d 942, 67-1 USTC ¶ 9200, 19 AFTR2d 588 (9th Cir. 1967).

Claim with no ascertainable value need not be included in gain in year of corporate liquidation. On liquidation of a corporation that they controlled, taxpayers received as a liquidating distribution a small amount of cash and other assets and a claim that the corpora-

LIQUIDATIONS: *Liquidating Corporation's Gain or Loss*

tion had against the United States. The claim was for compensation on contracts that the corporation had performed, and was settled three years later for nearly $1 million. Taxpayers considered the claim to have no ascertainable value and they did not include it in computing the gain on liquidation in their tax return. *Held:* For taxpayers. The court found that since the claim had no ascertainable value in the year of liquidation, the taxpayers' treatment was proper. Henderson, 64-2 USTC ¶ 9799, 14 AFTR2d 5858 (WD Wash. 1964).

Allocation of income on liquidation was determined. Taxpayers, stockholders in a production company, received, on liquidation of the corporation, its contract rights to payments for a motion picture and a TV program. The liquidation occurred on May 23, at which time the company had not received payments under either contract. The taxpayers did not include the payments receivable in the corporation's final return. The IRS contended that all of the payments due from the picture were includible, and a proportionate part of the payments for the TV program were includible in the corporate income, since the company had earned these amounts. *Held:* For the IRS, in part (as to the motion picture contract). A corporation is taxable on income earned, accrued, or realized prior to liquidation. It must have fixed and determinable rights in a certain amount of income. Here, only the payment under the motion picture contract right for April was subject to accurate computation, because the other payments were for periods ending after the date of liquidation. Further, taxpayers' taxable income, which included gain on the corporation's liquidation distribution, could not be adjusted for their liability as transferees of the corporation's assets. In addition, taxpayers were not entitled to recover their basis in the assets received on the liquidation before recognition of any income. Schneider, 65 TC 18 (1975).

Liquidating corporation's noncompetition covenant had economic reality. A corporation that operated beauty salons sold its assets for $100,000 after adopting a liquidation plan pursuant to Section 337. The IRS claimed that the corporation realized ordinary income of $30,000, the amount allocated to a noncompetition covenant under the sales agreement. *Held:* For the IRS. That taxpayer had adopted a liquidation plan prior to signing the agreement and that this had been communicated to the buyer did not deprive the covenant of economic reality, since taxpayer could invest the sales proceeds in new beauty salons in the same neighborhoods as its former shops. MacDonald, 43 TCM 1381, ¶ 82,270 P-H Memo. TC (1982).

Loss on liquidation was unsubstantiated. Taxpayer claimed that the fair market value of cash and stock proceeds received in a liquidating distribution from a corporation in which he held shares was less than his basis. *Held:* For the IRS. A Form 1099-L information return was insufficient to establish the fair market value of the property received except for cash. Russell, 41 TCM 954, ¶ 81,082 P-H Memo. TC (1981).

Tax-benefit rule applied to Section 337 liquidation. Taxpayer, Altec, was the transferee of assets of ARC. On the liquidation of ARC, under Section 337, certain previously expensed property was transferred to Delaware (a subsidiary of taxpayer). The IRS determined that ARC received ordinary income to the extent of the previously expensed items. *Held:* For the IRS. The court held that the tax-benefit rule applied to Section 337 liquidations. The previously expensed items were treated as if reconverted to property. Altec Corp., 36 TCM 1795, ¶ 77,438 P-H Memo. TC (1977).

Loss disallowed on Section 337 liquidation. Taxpayer, a nursing home corporation, sold all of its assets pursuant to a plan of liquidation. The IRS disallowed a $36,000 loss deduction. *Held:* For the IRS. The transaction fit within the requirements of Section 337 and that section must apply. Therefore, the loss was not recognized. Anchorage Nursing Home, Inc., 33 TCM 1372, ¶ 74,295 P-H Memo. TC (1974).

LIQUIDATIONS: *Liquidating Distributions*

Gain not recognized when property was sold under Section 337 six and one-half months after acquisition. A corporation acquired real property and six and one-half months later sold the property, not recognizing the gain under a Section 337 liquidation. The IRS disallowed the nonrecognition of gain. *Held:* For taxpayer. The property was not inventory held primarily for sale to customers. It was acquired as an investment asset, no other sales were made, no efforts to sell were made, and it was sold on a broker's solicitation, which overcame the factor of the short holding period of the property. The requirements of Section 337 were met and therefore, the gain on the sale was not recognized. Furthermore, no loss deduction was allowed on mining stock when there was no proof of loss or identifiable event, no insolvency, and the company had valuable assets. Ginsburg, 33 TCM 814, ¶ 74,191 P-H Memo. TC (1974).

Nonrecognition of gain was allowed on corporate liquidation. Taxpayers formed a corporation and transferred land to it, later sold the property and treated the sale as an individual event, reporting gain on the installment method. The IRS determined that the corporation sold the property and that taxpayers received partially dividends and partially a return of capital. *Held:* For taxpayer. The corporate liquidation qualified under Section 337. An informal but proper plan of complete liquidation was adopted; all property was sold within 12 months; all assets (an installment note payable to the taxpayers individually) were distributed, except those retained to meet claims; and the corporation discontinued operations. Section 337 does not require a formal plan or resolution of liquidation on the part of the stockholders and directors of the corporation. Here, the facts showed that the assets were sold as part of a plan to liquidate. Therefore no dividends were received. Mitchell, 31 TCM 1077, ¶ 72,219 P-H Memo. TC (1972).

Liquidating Distributions

Termination of valid Section 1361 election resulted in liquidating distribution to owners. Taxpayer operated a water company. He and his wife owned a 70 percent community interest, and their daughter owned the remaining 30 percent. In 1962, by a letter to the IRS that only he signed, taxpayer elected Section 1361. Subsequently, corporate returns were filed consistent with the election. Following repeal of Section 1361, the IRS treated the owners as receiving a liquidation distribution. *Held:* For the IRS. The requirement in the regulations that all owners sign the election was merely directory. There was substantial compliance: All parties knew of and consented to the election, and the husband had the power to manage the community property. Further, liquidation treatment was sustained in Prescott, 66 TC 128 (1976). The court also redetermined the value of the liquidation distribution, and upheld the IRS' determination of the value and useful life of various depreciable assets. O'Dowd, 595 F2d 262, 79-1 USTC ¶ 9383, 43 AFTR2d 79-1242 (5th Cir. 1979).

Loans were liquidating distributions; capital gains allowed. A group of Americans and Cubans formed a steamship company to act as a carrier of automobiles under the Gulf-Havana Steamship Conference, which set forth and supervised transportation rates. The company accumulated substantial earnings, which the Cubans wished to realize but which the Americans did not want distributed to them because of the taxation of dividend income. At the suggestion of a Cuban lawyer, the corporation adopted a plan to make loans to each stockholder in proportion to his stockholdings, pending liquidation of the corporation. The corporation adopted no formal plan of liquidation because Cuban law required completion and report of liquidation within 30 days. Within six months, the American group sold its stock to the corporation for $38,000 cash and the simultaneous credit on the corporate books of $150,000 against the prior loans for a like amount. The IRS and the Tax Court recognized the final cash payment as a liquidating dividend to be treated as capital gain, but held that the $150,000 received via loans was ordinary income. *Held:* Reversed. Viewing the transactions as a whole, the court ruled that there was an attempt to liquidate the corporation,

LIQUIDATIONS: *Liquidating Distributions*

the first step of which was the issuance of the loans. The absence of formal corporate resolutions adopting a fixed plan of liquidation was not fatal because of an intent to liquidate the corporation—to wind up its affairs, gather its resources, settle its liabilities, cease taking on new business, and then distribute to its stockholders all that was left. Shore, 286 F2d 742, 61-1 USTC ¶ 9230, 7 AFTR2d 653 (5th Cir. 1961).

Liquidating distribution of patent license agreement ascertainable value. The fair market value of three patent license agreements received by a decedent on liquidation of a corporation was found by the Tax Court to be ascertainable, since the decedent himself had valued them at $22,500 in his income tax return in the year of liquidation. Accordingly, the liquidation was a closed transaction, and all royalties received in pursuance of the agreements subsequent to the date of liquidation were ordinary income. *Held:* Affirmed. Whether the contract had an ascertainable value was entirely a question of fact, and the Tax Court's finding was supportable. Marsack Estate, 288 F2d 533, 61-1 USTC ¶ 9340, 7 AFTR2d 1047 (7th Cir. 1961).

Corporation was in liquidation; distributions were return of capital, not dividends. The IRS asserted that distributions made to taxpayer by a closely held corporation of which her deceased husband had been an active officer were ordinary dividends. The corporation had regarded them as distributions in liquidation. *Held:* For the IRS. The distributions were a return of capital; the excess over taxpayer's basis was capital gain. The minutes showed a decision to liquidate in 1953 because of the age of the operating owners. Sales of various lumber yards, out of which the distributions at issue were made, occurred in 1954 and 1955. Additional yards were sold in subsequent years, and the business was completely dissolved by 1959. The special distributions were treated on the books as in liquidation and reported on Form 1099L, the information return for distributions in liquidations. Apparently the only formal step the corporation omitted was filing of the notice with the IRS within 30 days of adoption of a plan of complete liquidation. This was omitted because the corporate officers were acting without legal advice and were unaware of the requirement. McGregor, 60-1 USTC ¶ 9298 (D. Kan. 1960).

Cash-basis corporation taxed on receivables distributed to stockholders on liquidation. Taxpayer was the sole stockholder of a dissolved corporation that had always used cash-basis accounting. After dissolution, taxpayer collected the receivables that had been earned before dissolution but that had not been reported by the corporation on the cash basis. The IRS asserted that the corporation realized income by distributing the receivables as a liquidating dividend to the taxpayer. *Held:* For the IRS. The court pointed out that its determination did not put the corporation on an accrual basis but merely adjusted one item so as to clearly reflect the realization of income by the corporation. Williamson, 292 F2d 524, 61-2 USTC ¶ 9583, 8 AFTR2d 5172 (Ct. Cl. 1961).

Due to informal plan of liquidation, corporate distributions after certain date were liquidation proceeds. Taxpayer made open account "loans" to X, a corporation he controlled. X's business was unsuccessful, so over a period of months X's assets were sold to pay creditors. X never adopted a formal plan of liquidation. During this period, X made distributions to taxpayer that he contended were nontaxable loan repayments or liquidating distributions taxable as capital gain under Section 331. The IRS argued that the payments were dividends. *Held:* For taxpayer, in part. The loans to X were really capital contributions. The court found that an informal plan of liquidation was made as of a certain date and that distributions after this date were taxable under Section 331. Those made before it were dividends. Pitts, 37 TCM 1849-3, ¶ 78,469 P-H Memo. TC (1978).

Stockholders' private auction fixed fair market value of liquidating distribution. Taxpayer held 50 percent of the stock of a corporation that owned a building. Two other individuals held the remaining 50 percent. The three decided to liquidate the corporation, and it was agreed that the other two stockholders would either purchase taxpayer's interest in the building or sell their interest in the building to taxpayer. The three stockholders agreed to sell to the interest making the highest bid. Taxpayer bid $100,250, and then acquired the interest of the other two on dissolution of the corporation by paying them $50,125. Taxpayer valued her liquidating dividend, however, by using an appraiser's valuation of $80,000, claiming that the auction bids were inflated because the other stockholders knew of her determination to acquire the property for sentimental reasons. *Held:* For the IRS. The fair market value of taxpayer's 50 percent interest in the building received on dissolution was $50,000. The court found that the bid of $100,000 by the other two stockholders constituted a proper measure of fair market value, since it was made as a willing offer to purchase without compulsion. Moore, 18 TCM 1119, ¶ 59,233 P-H Memo. TC (1959).

Non-pro rata liquidating distribution deemed pro rata distribution. If a liquidating corporation's distributions to stockholders are not pro rata, the distribution will be treated as pro rata for determining the stockholders' taxable gains under Section 331. Stockholders who received less than their pro rata share are deemed to have made transfers to stockholders receiving more than their pro rata share. These implied transfers may be treated as taxable gifts of the transferors, as compensation, or as other income to the transferees, depending on the facts and circumstances. Rev. Rul. 79-10, 1979-1 CB 140.

Cash transfer by liquidating corporation to independent trustee to meet claims is a distribution under Section 337. A corporation adopted a plan of liquidation pursuant to Section 337. Within the 12-month period, the corporation distributed to its stockholders all of its assets except for an amount of cash and real property. This property was transferred to an independent trustee within the 12-month period. The property was transferred to the trustee to meet contingent liabilities and to sell the real property, which, because of its uniqueness could not be sold within the 12-month period. The transfer constituted a distribution under Section 337. Rev. Rul. 72-137, 1972-1 CB 101.

Liquidation of Subsidiaries

Tax-benefit rule overrides nonrecognition. Taxpayer corporation was in the business of extracting, processing, and selling sand. It incurred substantial expenditures in the initial stage of mining, which it deducted. It then liquidated under Section 332 and distributed all of its assets. The transferee corporation took a stepped-up basis in the sand. The IRS determined that the liquidating corporation had realized income in the amount of the costs it had previously deducted in the initial stage of mining. *Held:* For the IRS. This case is controlled by Bliss Dairy, 460 US 370 (1983), which requires the tax-benefit rule to be applied to override the nonrecognition provisions. Ballou Constr. Co., 611 F. Supp. 375, 85-1 USTC ¶ 9418, 56 AFTR2d 85-5277 (D. Kan. 1985).

Holding period in subsidiary liquidation determined. Taxpayer, a corporation engaged in the logging business, acquired 98 percent of another corporation in a similar business, which included cutting rights to timber, and established the acquired entity as a subsidiary. Subsequently, the subsidiary was liquidated and taxpayer received the cutting contracts. Taxpayer reported income from these contracts as long-term capital gain, but the IRS contended that the date of acquisition was not the date the subsidiary's stock was acquired but rather the liquidation date; hence the income was ordinary. *Held:* For taxpayer. Inasmuch as taxpayer acquired and liquidated the subsidiary within the provisions of Section 334(b)(2), it was entitled to use as its basis in the assets received on liquidation its basis in the subsidiary's stock, and thus was entitled to tack on its holding period of the stock to the timber-cutting contracts. Therefore, taxpayer could elect to treat the cutting as a sale or exchange and was entitled to long-term capital gain. Cabax Mills, 59 TC 401 (1972).

LIQUIDATIONS: *Liquidation of Subsidiaries*

Subsidiary's losses in liquidation were recognizable but gains were not. Taxpayer purchased more than 80 percent of the stock of a bank. The net assets were sold at a gain and the bank was liquidated in the same year. Certain securities were sold separately at a loss, as a result of a sudden market decline. In reporting the liquidating sale, the bank reflected only the losses and excluded the gains. The IRS argued that (1) Section 337 does not permit recognition of losses in this type of liquidation and (2) losses must be netted with the gain from the sale of the other assets. *Held:* For taxpayer. The Tax Court held that the losses were deductible. In Section 334, Congress codified the *Kimbell-Diamond* rule, which allows an acquiring corporation a stepped-up basis for assets of a subsidiary liquidated within two years. To conform with this rule, Section 337(c)(2)(B) provides, in effect, that only gain attributable to the appreciation of assets occurring after the stock purchase will be recognized. Since the losses in issue resulted from a market decline occurring after the stock acquisition, taxpayer could deduct the losses. Nothing in the statutory scheme compelled taxpayer to net losses against gains. United States Holding Co., 44 TC 323 (1965), acq. 1966-2 CB 7.

Parent must have owned 80 percent of subsidiary when liquidation plan was adopted. Taxpayer, a closely held corporation, was engaged in a variety of business activities. It owned 69.4 percent of Y Corporation that it wanted to change from a subsidiary to a corporate division. It also owned 17.4 percent of a gas company. In order to obtain the assets of Y, negotiations were begun that resulted in the approval and adoption of a plan of reorganization whereby each holder of Y stock exchanged his stock for common stock of the gas company, and the assets and goodwill of Y were transferred to taxpayer. At the same time, taxpayer's chief operating officer and sole stockholder mailed out a letter and proxy statements to Y's minority stockholders to obtain their interests. Taxpayer contended that the transfer of Y's assets to taxpayer was in fact a tax-free Section 332 liquidation, as it equitably, through the proxies and letter, owned 80 percent of the subsidiary at the time of the merger. The IRS determined that there was a taxable exchange of the gas company stock for Y's assets followed by a taxable liquidation of Y with a liquidating distribution to Y's stockholders of the gas company's stock, which resulted in an increase in taxpayer's taxable income in 1972. *Held:* For the IRS. Because the record clearly indicated that taxpayer owned less than 80 percent of the subsidiary's stock before the adoption of a plan of liquidation, Section 332 was not applicable to the liquidation of the subsidiary, and Section 331 governed the tax aspects of the liquidation. Crescent Oil, Inc., 38 TCM 97, ¶ 79,026 P-H Memo. TC (1979).

Liquidation of acquired corporation was not a reorganization. Taxpayer corporation acquired the stock of a corporation engaged in outdoor advertising that was owned by two stockholders who also owned 49 percent of taxpayer. Taxpayer was formed shortly before the sale. The selling price was $400,000, to be paid in negotiable notes of $380,000 plus $20,000 in cash. On acquisition of the stock, taxpayer immediately dissolved the corporation. It carried on the outdoor advertising business with the same location, assets, employees, and customers of the predecessor. Taxpayer contended that its basis in the advertising structures it acquired when it liquidated the corporation was the same as its basis in the stock under Section 334(b)(2). The IRS maintained that the steps taken (formation of the corporation by the mutual stockholders and its dissolution) represented either a D, E, or F reorganization and that consequently, taxpayer's basis in the advertising structures should be the same as the adjusted basis of the predecessor corporation. *Held:* For taxpayer. The absence of 80 percent control of taxpayer by the stockholders of the old corporation prevented the transaction from qualifying as a D reorganization. Also, the substantial shift in the proprietary interest of the two corporations precluded an E or F reorganization. The acquisition of the advertising structures was a transaction falling under Section 334(b)(2), and the basis of such assets was to be determined under the provisions of that section. Turner Advertising of Ky., Inc., 25 TCM 532, ¶ 66,101 P-H Memo. TC (1966).

Domestic subsidiary recognized gain on sale of asset in liquidation despite parent's failure to secure an advance ruling under Section 367. Where a foreign corporation, parent of a wholly owned domestic subsidiary, failed to secure an advance ruling under Section 367, this failure could not be used by the subsidiary to consider the parent as not a corporation in order to obtain nonrecognition of gain on the sale of an asset pursuant to a plan of complete liquidation of the subsidiary. Section 332 therefore applied to the liquidation, thus resulting in the recognition of gain under Section 337(c)(2)(A). Rev. Rul. 76-90, 1976-1 CB 101.

Transaction did not qualify as liquidation where parent continued subsidiary's business. A transaction did not qualify as a complete liquidation under Section 337 where the parent sold all of its operating assets for cash and within 12 months after adoption of the plan paid its liabilities and distributed no cash to its stockholders in exchange for nearly all of its stock, when immediately afterward the parent's wholly owned subsidiary was liquidated into the parent, which continued the subsidiary's business. Rev. Rul. 74-544, 1974-2 CB 108.

Liquidated subsidiary taxable on supplies distributed to its parent. Where a subsidiary was liquidated tax-free into its parent under Sections 332 and 334(b)(2) in a transaction to which Section 336 also applied, the IRS ruled that the subsidiary had to include in its gross income the allocated value of incidental supplies it distributed to its parent for which a deduction had been taken in a previous year resulting in a full tax benefit. Rev. Rul. 74-396, 1974-2 CB 106.

Liquidation of subsidiary qualified under Section 334(b)(2) even though distribution delayed three years. A subsidiary adopted a resolution providing for the complete liquidation of the subsidiary into its parent corporation. Because of a financing arrangement that prohibited the liquidation of the subsidiary until certain outstanding obligations were paid, the liquidating distribution was not made until the third year after the adoption of the plan of liquidation. Because of the compelling business reasons and the fact that all other requirements of Sections 332 and 334(b)(2) were met, the IRS held that the liquidation of the subsidiary qualified under both Sections 332 and 334(b)(2). Rev. Rul. 71-326, 1971-2 CB 177.

"Cash and equivalent" under Section 334(b)(2) defined. Where the necessary holding period is met, Section 334(b)(2) provides that the basis of property received by a parent corporation on the complete liquidation of a subsidiary will be the adjusted basis of the subsidiary corporation's stock as provided in Regulation § 1.334-1(c). One of the required adjustments is a decrease in basis by cash and its equivalent received by the parent; as required by Regulation § 1.334-1(c)(4)(v)(b)(1). The IRS ruled that "cash and its equivalent," as used in these regulations, includes cash, currency, bank deposits (including time deposits) whether or not interest-bearing, savings and loan accounts, checks, drafts, money orders, and similar items. The term does not include accounts receivable, inventories, marketable securities, and similar current assets. Rev. Rul. 66-290, 1966-2 CB 112.

Subsidiary must distribute all its property to qualify under Section 332. The retention by a subsidiary of any property, no matter how small in amount, for the purpose of continuing the operation of its present business or for the purpose of engaging in a new business, will prevent the distribution of its remaining property to its parent from qualifying as a distribution in complete liquidation under Section 332. Rev. Rul. 66-186, 1966-2 CB 112.

One-Month Liquidations

Nonrecognition benefits of Section 333 forfeited due to failure to file Form 964. The IRS and the district court held that taxpayer stockholders forfeited the nonrecognition benefits of a one-month liquidation under

LIQUIDATIONS: *One-Month Liquidations*

Section 333 due to failure to file Form 964, even though they complied with all other requirements of the section. *Held:* Affirmed. The Code and regulations, when read together, specifically require that such form shall be filed within 30 days after the adoption of the plan of liquidation. Posey, 449 F2d 228, 71-2 USTC ¶ 9659, 28 AFTR2d 71-5666 (5th Cir. 1971).

Distribution of building in a Section 333 liquidation constitutes a "purchase," thus denying distributee-stockholder a loss deduction on demolition of the distributed building where intent to demolish was evident prior to receipt. In 1959, taxpayer and another person formed a corporation to purchase land and a building. The building was operated through 1963 and served as a source of income. Consistent with plans made in 1960, taxpayer dissolved the corporation and distributed the land and the building. These plans involved demolition of the building followed by construction of a new building involving the corporation's land and adjoining lots owned by its stockholders. The liquidation qualified as a Section 333 liquidation. In the year the old building was demolished, taxpayer claimed a demolition loss. The IRS denied the loss on grounds that the Section 333 liquidation distribution constituted a purchase with a view toward demolition nondeductible under Section 165. Taxpayer argued that a Section 333 liquidation was not a purchase. *Held:* Affirmed for the IRS. Receipt of the building in a Section 333 liquidation was equivalent to a purchase because "the basis in assets acquired was not carried over from the corporation but rather was derived from the stock surrendered" (i.e., a substituted basis). Ivey, 423 F2d 862, 70-1 USTC ¶ 9313, 25 AFTR2d 70-892 (2d Cir. 1970).

Basis of assets received in Section 333 liquidation allocated by reference to the fair market value of all assets distributed, including receivables. Taxpayer received receivables with a face value of $26,600 and land and other assets that had appreciated almost $75,000 on the liquidation of his wholly owned corporation. He elected to have his gain taxed under Section 333. In allocating the basis of his stock among the assets received, however, he contended that he was entitled to assign a basis to the receivables that was equal to their book value in the hands of the corporation. In the alternative, he argued that the basis of the assets he received was allocable in proportion to the respective corporate book values of all the assets. Taxpayer concluded by arguing that if he was required to recognize any gain on the subsequent collection of the receivables, it was taxable as long-term taxable gain and not as ordinary income. The Tax Court denied each of his contentions, sustaining the regulations under Section 334(c). *Held:* Affirmed. The regulations require an allocation on the basis of the net fair market values of all the assets distributed. Garrow, 368 F2d 809, 66-2 USTC ¶ 9761 (9th Cir. 1966).

Failure to file stockholders' election voided Section 333 benefits. All the stockholders of a corporation voted to liquidate the corporation within one calendar month under the provisions of Section 333. Although they filed Form 966, they failed to file the stockholders' election required by Section 333(c) (Form 964). The IRS contended that Section 333 was not applicable. *Held:* For the IRS. Since none of the stockholders filed anything purporting to be an election under Section 333, and since the corporate notice on Form 966 does not constitute a proper election, the benefits of Section 333 were not available. Accordingly, the entire gain on liquidation was taxable as capital gain. Lambert, 338 F2d 4, 64-2 USTC ¶ 9816 (2d Cir. 1964).

Failure to file written election precluded use of Section 333. The IRS contended that taxpayers, with respect to the liquidation of their corporation, could not avail themselves of Section 333 because of failure to file the written election required by Section 333(d). *Held:* For the IRS. The court held that there was no nonrecognition of gain and 1964 was the year that assets were transferred and gain realized. Bachman, 1974-2 USTC ¶ 9763 (D. Idaho 1974).

Distribution of securities in liquidation subject to taxation. In 1978, *D* Corporation was liquidated pursuant to Section 333. The taxpayers, stockholders in *D*, received General Motors stock as a part of the liquidating distribution. *D* had received the GM stock after 1953 as a result of the court-ordered divestiture by duPont of its interest in General Motors. The taxpayers did not report a capital gain on this distribution on the ground that the shares had been acquired by duPont, and thus by *D*, before 1954. The IRS determined that the distribution of the GM stock constituted a distribution of securities acquired after 1953. *Held:* For the IRS. The requirement that the stock distributed in liquidation must be "acquired" after 1953 does not relate to whether it was received in a taxable or a nontaxable transaction. Nor is there a "voluntariness" test in Section 333, and the fact that the GM stock was received involuntarily had no bearing. Knowlton, 84 TC 160 (1985).

Failure to file Form 964 voided Section 333 liquidation. Taxpayers were the sole officers, directors, and stockholders of their controlled corporation. On November 28, 1969, the corporation adopted a plan of liquidation pursuant to Section 333, and all of its properties were distributed on December 21, 1969. The corporation filed Form 966 within the prescribed time, with a copy of the minutes of the stockholders' meeting authorizing the liquidation, but the taxpayers did not file Form 964. The IRS determined the liquidation pursuant to Section 333 was defective. *Held:* For the IRS. Failure to file Form 964 precluded the taxpayers from being "qualified electing shareholders," and thus they were not entitled to nonrecognition of their gain, even though Form 966 provided all the information that Form 964 would have contained. Dunavant, 63 TC 316 (1974).

Filing of dissolution papers in compliance with state law held tantamount to adoption of plan of liquidation. Taxpayers, the owners of a grain storage and merchandising corporation, filed for a voluntary dissolution under state law on November 18, 1960. On March 17, 1961, taxpayers filed Form 966 with the IRS, in which February 16, 1961 was listed as the date that the corporation had adopted a plan for a Section 333 liquidation. Taxpayers reported long-term capital gains from the liquidation on their 1961 income tax returns, which the IRS determined were ordinary income under Section 333(e). *Held:* For the IRS. The filing for voluntary dissolution was tantamount to the adoption of a plan of liquidation by the corporation within the meaning of Section 333. Since an election to liquidate under Section 333 was not timely filed within 30 days of that date, taxpayers' election to liquidate under Section 333 was invalid. Wales, 50 TC 399 (1968).

Stockholders not bound by Section 333 election based on mistake of fact. Taxpayer corporation negotiated the sale of its assets to a third party. The assets were then transferred to its stockholders, who consummated the sale. The stockholders then elected to liquidate the corporation under Section 333 with the understanding that they would be treated as having made the sale. The IRS contended that the corporation had recognizable gain under Section 333, since it must be treated as having made the sale of its assets. Taxpayer contended that if the sale was imputed to it, then the stockholders' election to liquidate under Section 333 was not binding, since it was based on a mistake of fact. Accordingly, no gain would be recognizable by the corporation under Section 337. *Held:* For the IRS, in part. The sale of the assets must be attributed to taxpayer corporation. However, because the stockholders based their Section 333 election to liquidate on the mistaken idea that they would be treated as the sellers of the assets, their election was not binding. Thus, under Section 337, the gain was not recognizable by taxpayer corporation. DiAndrea, Inc., 47 TCM 731, ¶ 83,768 P-H Memo. TC (1983).

Section 333 gain on distribution in kind determined. A corporation made a liquidation distribution of assets to stockholders who made a valid Section 333 election. An individual stockholder received real estate, which is not taxable under Section 333. Another stockholder, a tax-exempt organization, received cash, which would have resulted in recognition of gain to a nonexempt stockholder. The IRS had previously ruled, in the context of a distribution of trust corpus, that a non-pro rata distribution in kind is a pro rata distribution of all assets, followed by an exchange of part of the assets between recipients. The IRS has now ruled that the application of that rule to Section 333 liquidations is not warranted and that Section 333 will be applied with reference to assets actually received. Rev. Rul. 83-61, 1983-1 CB 78.

Section 333 election made by partnership had varied consequences for partners. A partnership owned all the stock of X Corporation, which was to be liquidated within one month under Section 333. The partners were an individual and Y and Z Corporations; Z owned a 60 percent interest in partnership property. The Section 333 election was made by the partnership, not the partners. The individual treated his distribution under Section 333(e), and Y treated its distribution under Section 333(f). But Z, which was treated as if it owned 60 percent of X's stock directly, was an "excluded corporation" ineligible for Section 333's benefits. Rev. Rul. 79-82, 1979-1 CB 141.

Holding period not "tacked" for Section 333 purposes. A corporation that had received stock in its capacity as a stockholder of another corporation and was allowed to "tack" its holding period for Section 1223(2) purposes was not allowed to refer to the transferor's holding period when its own holding period became relevant in a Section 333 liquidation. Rev. Rul. 78-350, 1978-2 CB 135.

Prearranged immediate transfer of property received in a Section 333 liquidation did not qualify for Section 1031. Taxpayer was sole owner of a corporation that was liquidated under Section 333. The only asset (which was distributed in the liquidation) of the corporation was a shopping center. Immediately following the liquidation, according to a prearranged plan, the shopping center was exchanged for like-kind property owned by an unrelated third party. The IRS ruled that the exchange did not qualify for nonrecognition under Section 1031. The taxpayer did not hold the property for productive use in trade or business or for investment. Rev. Rul. 77-337, 1977-2 CB 305.

IRS recasts form of transfer of corporate assets and Section 333 liquidation. X Corporation held post-1953 money or securities with no accumulated or current earnings and profits. X transferred all of its assets to a partnership in exchange for an interest in the partnership, then distributed the partnership interest in complete liquidation to its sole stockholder, who elected to be governed by Section 333. The IRS ruled that the holding of the partnership interest by the corporation was a transitory step and that the transfer served no corporate purpose other than avoiding stockholder taxes. The IRS ruled that the corporation had distributed its assets to the stockholder, who was deemed to have transferred these assets to the partnership. The stockholder therefore had to recognize gain under Section 333(e)(2). Rev. Rul. 77-321, 1977-2 CB 98.

Section 333 liquidation distribution to sole stockholder produced gain to corporation where part of distribution satisfied corporation's debt to the stockholder. Taxpayer, sole owner of a corporation, elected a one-month liquidation. The corporation had no accumulated earnings and profits, but owed a bona fide debt to the stockholder. It made a liquidation distribution of one appreciated asset and one loss asset. The IRS held that a pro rata portion of the fair market value of each asset would be applied to satisfy the debt, and treated it as a sale or exchange by the corporation on which it would realize gain and loss. The gain would be recognized notwithstanding Section 336, but the loss would be disallowed by Section 267. The recognized gain (less the loss and taxes) would generate corporate earnings and profits, which would, in turn, force the stockholder to recognize dividend income under Section 333(c)(1). The ruling sets forth a sample computation of the gain and loss realized by the corporation. Rev. Rul. 76-175, 1976-1 CB 92.

Corporation existing solely to collect tax refunds could use Section 333. A corporation that distributed to its stockholders within one month all of its property including the rights to income tax refunds and remained in existence solely in order to collect such refunds met the requirements of Section 333. Rev. Rul. 74-476, 1974-2 CB 104.

Stock distributed under Section 333 treated as cash where originally acquired from a foreign corporation. Taxpayer corporation, newly organized in 1957, received investment stock pursuant to a nontaxable reorganization with a foreign corporation, which had acquired such stock prior to January 1, 1954. Taxpayer adopted a plan of liquidation and distributed all its property under Section 333. The IRS ruled that the investment stock was acquired by taxpayer after December 31, 1953 and was the equivalent of cash for computing recognized gain. Taxpayer was not in existence on December 31, 1953 and therefore could not exchange an asset owned on such date for the investment stock. The fact that the foreign corporation owned the stock on December 31, 1953 was not controlling as a foreign corporation cannot qualify under Section 333. Consequently, the investment stock was held to have been acquired on the reorganization date. Rev. Rul. 64-257, 1964-2 CB 91.

Transfer is "within one month" if certificates are given to transfer agent. A personal holding company with a large portfolio of stocks was fearful that it would be physically unable to complete the transfer of certificates to stockholders within one month. The IRS held that liquidation would be within one month if during that one month certificates were sent to transfer agents, the rights to fractional shares assigned to a nominee for stockholders, and dividends whose record date was later were assigned to stockholders. Rev. Rul. 56-286, 1956-1 CB 172.

Partial Liquidations

Reduction of construction activity not a partial liquidation. Taxpayer corporation's subsidiary was engaged in construction, including pipeline construction. Subsidiary stopped building pipelines and distributed assets related to that activity to the parent. The Tax Court held that taxpayer could not treat the distribution as a partial liquidation of the subsidiary under pre-TEFRA Section 346(b). *Held:* Affirmed. The pipeline-laying was not a separately managed trade or business from the subsidiary's other construction business, so there was no "termination of a business" as is required under pre-TEFRA Section 346(b). Kenton Meadows Co., 766 F2d 142, 56 AFTR2d 85-5350 (4th Cir. 1985).

Court combined the businesses of several corporations in determining whether there was a sufficient reduction in business activity to justify partial liquidation treatment. Taxpayer owned three corporations engaged in one or more aspects of the traveling carnival business. Taxpayer, however, conducted the separate activities of each corporation as if they were parts of a single business enterprise. When taxpayer became ill, he decided to sell the assets of two of his corporations and caused the corporations to adopt plans of liquidation. Proceeds from these sales were distributed to taxpayer and were, in part, used to acquire additional business assets. Taxpayer treated these distributions as amounts received in partial liquidation of two of his corporations. The IRS argued that the distributions were dividends. *Held*: For the IRS. The amounts received by taxpayer were not received as a result of a partial liquidation and were therefore taxed as a dividend. The activities of all of taxpayer's corporations were viewed as a single business enterprise because that was the manner in which taxpayer viewed his corporation's activities, and some of the corporations did not alone have all the functions necessary for a complete business activity. When the activities and assets of all three corporations were combined, the sales of the assets and the distribution of proceeds resulted in a mere 5 percent reduction of the corporations' combined net worth. Accordingly, there was no meaningful reduction in the corporations' combined business activities. Furthermore, the corporations' failure to seek purchasers of their other assets indicated that the initial sales were not intended to be part of the plan to liquidate taxpayer's corporations. Donald L. Mains, 508 F2d 1251, 35 AFTR2d 75-541 (6th Cir. 1975), on remand, Gooding, 38 AFTR2d 76-5336 (SD Ohio

1976), aff'd, 78-1 USTC ¶ 9414, 42 AFTR2d 78-6026 (6th Cir.), cert. denied, 439 US 981 (1978).

Corporate distribution was a fair dividend, not capital gain on partial liquidation. Taxpayer was the sole stockholder of a trucking corporation and was approached to sell all of his stock. At the time of the negotiations, the corporation leased some of its trucks from another of the taxpayer's wholly owned corporations, but the purchaser required that the trucking corporation own all of the units. To accomplish this, the taxpayer gave his note to purchase the equipment at its adjusted basis and immediately transferred the units to the trucking company as a capital contribution. The IRS determined that taxpayer had received a dividend of the difference between the fair market value of the trucks and the adjusted basis. The district court held for the IRS. *Held*: Affirmed. The IRS was entirely justified in establishing the fair market value of the trucks on the basis of subsequent sales, since the transactions between the taxpayer and his corporations were not at arm's length. The route followed by the taxpayer resulted in a dividend and not a partial redemption of stock under Section 346(a)(2), as contended by the taxpayer. Under a partial liquidation, the stockholder does not give up cash or notes; instead, the redeemed stock is the consideration. Goodling, 395 F2d 938, 68-1 USTC ¶ 9399 (5th Cir. 1968).

Sale of property immediately after distribution in partial liquidation upheld. Three members of a family owned substantially all of the outstanding stock of taxpayer, a corporation holding improved real estate. After one of the stockholders expressed a desire to withdraw for personal reasons, the corporation transferred to him by warranty deed, in full liquidation of his stock, a 64 percent interest in a building whose sale previously had been negotiated by a related family partnership, without definite commitment. The distribution in partial liquidation and the sale of the real estate to the buyer occurred on the same day. The IRS sought to tax the corporation as if it had sold the property and had in turn distributed a part of the cash to the stockholder whose interest was redeemed. The district court held that the corporation was taxable only on the gain on its 36 percent interest in the property; the transfer to the stockholder of a 64 percent interest in the property was a "genuine liquidation." *Held*: Affirmed. The issue was factual, and the appellate court stated that it would not review the lower court's weighting of the evidence. McNair Realty, 298 F2d 35, 62-1 USTC ¶ 9158 (9th Cir. 1961).

A corporation must recognize gain on proceeds distribution under partial liquidation plan. Under a partial liquidation plan, a corporation sold a building that it held as rental property. The proceeds from the sale were later paid to the three stockholders when each surrendered a proportionate share of his stock to the corporation. Each stockholder reported capital gains on his return, based on the difference between the amount received from the sale and the basis of the stock he surrendered. The corporation did not include or recognize any of the gain on its return. The corporation argued that the sale and, later, the distribution of cash in partial liquidation should be treated as one integrated transaction because that was the obvious intent of the parties. *Held*: For the IRS. The court held that whether it was part of one integrated transaction was of no consequence. The issue was the taxability of the sale proceeds, not the taxability of the distribution. There is no provision in Section 336 for nonrecognition of gain when a corporation sells corporate property and later distributes the proceeds to its stockholders. If the corporation had distributed the building to the stockholders under a partial liquidation plan, no tax or gain would have resulted to the corporation. The stockholders could have sold the building and reported the gain as a capital gain. This transaction was mishandled and resulted in double taxation. However, the plain wording of the statute prevailed over the intent of the parties. Midwest Inv. Co., 386 F. Supp. 847, 75-1 USTC ¶ 9181, 35 AFTR2d 75-607 (DND 1975).

Distribution of race car treated as ordinary dividend, not liquidation. An insurance company that sold racing insurance also participated in stock car racing. The company's name was displayed prominently on the sides of its cars. Taxpayer, an officer of the company, received a famous car when the company's racing activities wound down. He subsequently restored the car and gave it to a museum. Taxpayer sought to have the distribution treated as a partial liquidation subject to capital gains tax. *Held*: For the IRS. The racing activities were not a separate business, but advertised the insurance business to the racing public. In addition, the distribution did not result in any genuine corporate contraction. Krauskopf, 48 TCM 620, ¶ 84,386 P-H Memo. TC (1984).

PreTEFRA partial liquidation disqualifies stock disposition. In a prior case the court held a 1977 distribution in partial liquidation to be an exchange under Section 331(a)(2), which constituted a nonqualifying disposition under Sections 442(a)(1) and 442(c)(1), resulting in ordinary income. Taxpayer argued that since TEFRA deleted Section 331(a)(2), partial liquidations were no longer stock exchanges and therefore the prior decision should not stand. *Held:* For the IRS. TEFRA Section 222(f) provides that, with some exceptions, the Section 331 amendment applies after August 31, 1982. It thus had no retroactive effect to 1977. Schumann, 45 TCM 550, ¶ 83,035 P-H Memo. TC (1983).

Corporate distributions were dividends, not partial liquidation. Taxpayers, doctors holding all the stock of a corporation owning their medical building, claimed capital gains treatment for a distribution in partial liquidation of their corporation. The IRS determined that it was a dividend. *Held:* For the IRS. While initially there was a resolution for a partial liquidation under which the distribution was made, and later a supplemental plan of complete liquidation, there was no evidence that there was a plan of complete liquidation as of the date of the initial plan and distribution. The distribution was therefore a dividend. A casualty loss was not deductible for purposes of determining earnings and profits in the year of the dividend. There was a reasonable prospect of recovery, which was in fact received in large part in a subsequent year. Jones, 31 TCM 724, ¶ 72,145 P-H Memo. TC (1972).

Partial liquidation qualifies although not pro rata. A corporation distributed the net proceeds of a corporate contraction to its 90 percent stockholder in redemption of one third of his stock. The 10 percent stockholder did not receive anything. The distribution did not qualify as a Section 302(b) redemption. The transaction was to be characterized, for partial liquidation purposes, solely at the corporation's level. Because that transaction otherwise qualified as a distribution in partial liquidation under Section 346(a)(2), it was not disqualified because it was made non-pro rata. TEFRA amended the partial liquidation provisions, which are now contained in Sections 302(b)(4) and 302(e)(1). Rev. Rul. 82-187, 1982-2 CB 80.

Actual surrender of stock not required in partial liquidation. A pro rata distribution of property to stockholders qualifies under Section 346(a)(2) as a partial liquidation where there is a genuine contraction of business, even if there is no actual redemption of stock, where the surrender of stock by the stockholders would be a meaningless gesture. The requirement of a redemption would be satisfied by constructive exchanges deemed to have occurred. Rev. Rul. 81-3, 1981-1 CB 125.

Substituted assets disqualified as a distribution of proceeds for a partial liquidation. A corporation sold a portion of its business for a note and a mortgage. It distributed appreciated securities to its stockholders pro rata. The distribution of securities in substitution for the notes was not a distribution in partial liquidation. The distribution also did not qualify under Section 302(a) as a payment in exchange for the stock redeemed. Thus, the corporation had to recognize gain. Rev. Rul. 79-275, 1979-2 CB 137.

Distribution was partial liquidation without surrender of stock. A subsidiary distributed its assets and working capital to its parent, which continued operating the business. No

LIQUIDATIONS: *Partial Liquidations*

stock was exchanged. Since there was a genuine contraction of the business, the surrender of stock by the parent, the sole stockholder, was meaningless. Thus, the distribution of property was a partial liquidation. Rev. Rul. 79-257, 1979-2 CB 136.

IRS strikes down partial liquidation characterization in sale of all subsidiary stock. *P* Corporation owned all of the single class of outstanding stock of *S* Corporation for many years, during which time each had been engaged in the active conduct of a trade or business. Pursuant to a plan, *P* sold all of the stock of *S* to an unrelated party for cash and distributed the proceeds of the sale pro rata to its stockholders in redemption of part of their *P* stock. On these facts, the IRS concluded that the distribution by *P* to its stockholders of the proceeds of the sale of the *S* stock would not qualify as a distribution in partial liquidation within the meaning of Section 346(a)(2), and the distribution would be treated as a distribution by *P* of property taxable to the *P* stockholders under Section 301 by reason of Section 302(d). Rev. Rul. 79-184, 1979-1 CB 143.

Intentional delay could prevent a distribution from qualifying as a partial liquidation. The IRS has ruled that in order for a distribution to receive tax treatment as a partial liquidation, three requisites must be met: (1) It must not be essentially equivalent to a dividend; (2) it must be in a redemption of part of the stock pursuant to a plan; and (3) it must occur within the taxable year or within the succeeding taxable year. Failure to comply with any of the above provisions will lead to a loss of the benefits of Section 346(a)(2). Rev. Rul. 77-468, 1977-2 CB 109.

Size of the discontinued business irrelevant in partial liquidation. *P* desired to discontinue the business of a wholly owned subsidiary, *S*. Under a plan, *P* sold *S's* assets, liquidated *S* under Section 332 and 381, and distributed the proceeds to its stockholders as a partial liquidation under Section 346. The IRS ruled that Section 381 treats *P* as having operated the business of its subsidiary. For the purpose of determining whether the active conduct requirements of Section 346(b) were met, the size of the discontinued business is immaterial. Consequently, the distribution qualified under Section 346. Rev. Rul. 77-376, 1977-2 CB 107.

Cancellation of liquidated subsidiary's indebtedness to parent is not a distribution in partial liquidation of parent. *S*, a wholly owned subsidiary of *P* had bona fide indebtedness to *P* for several years. *S* then sold all its assets for cash and was liquidated in a transaction to which Sections 332 and 381 applied. *S's* debt to *P* was canceled. The proceeds of the liquidation were distributed to *P's* stockholders in exchange for a portion of their stock. The IRS ruled that the amount of the distribution in partial liquidation by *P* to its stockholders that resulted from the complete liquidation of *S* did not include the portion of distribution attributable to the cancellation of *S's* debt to *P*. This held true despite Section 332(c). Rev. Rul. 75-223 was distinguished. Rev. Rul. 77-375, 1977-2 CB 106.

Working capital qualified as a partial liquidation distribution when taxpayer shut down unprofitable retail operation. Taxpayer corporation operated a profitable wholesale appliance distributorship and maintained a retail outlet that had incurred operating losses over a period of years. Taxpayer had gradually committed funds derived from the wholesale division's profits to the retail division. The retail division was closed, and a building that housed its operation, together with the working capital, was distributed to the stockholders as a Section 346(a)(2) partial liquidation. The IRS ruled that the working capital qualified as part of the distribution, since the funds were supplied by the wholesale division over a period of years. Rev. Rul. 76-289, 1976-2 CB 100.

Parent's distribution of proceeds of sale of subsidiary's assets is partial liquidation. Where a parent corporation has a wholly owned subsidiary and distributes to its stockholders either the assets or proceeds from the sale of the assets of the subsidiary, a partial liquidation under Section 346(a)(2) from a contraction of the corporate business results. A distribution of the subsidiary's stock does not, however, qualify as a partial liquidation but must satisfy the requirements of Section 355. Rev. Rul. 75-223, 1975-1 CB 109.

Distribution of cash, on termination of 95 percent of corporation's business, was a partial liquidation. The termination of a contract that represented 95 percent of the gross income of a corporation resulted in a genuine contraction of the corporation's business and the distribution of cash, made available by the release of restricted funds representing the working capital attributable to the terminated business in redemption of part of the corporation's stock, was a partial liquidation. Rev. Rul. 75-3, 1975-1 CB 108.

Distributions to minority stockholder under Section 346(a)(2) partial liquidation are governed by Sections 346, 331(a)(2), and 302. Distributions to a minority stockholder in a Section 346(a)(2) partial liquidation of cash and appreciated property and of cash in redemption of his remaining shares are governed by Sections 346 and 331(a)(2) to the extent of the property and Section 302 with respect to cash. Rev. Rul. 74-465, 1974-2 CB 114.

Conversion of department store to discount store was a contraction of business. A contraction of business includes a situation in which a full-time department store converted to a discount apparel store by eliminating departments and most forms of credit; changing the types of merchandise sold; and reducing space, employees, inventory, fixed assets, etc. A pro rata distribution by the corporation to its stockholders in redemption of part of their shares qualified as a partial liquidation. Rev. Rul. 74-296, 1974-1 CB 80.

Temporary investment of corporate assets qualified as a liquidating distribution. A corporation that engaged in the ownership and operation of television stations sold one of its stations at a profit. Proceeds of the sale were placed in a temporary investment account trusteed by a bank in order to preserve the assets. At a later date, it was decided to distribute the proceeds in partial liquidation. Such distribution qualified as a partial liquidation under Section 346, since the distribution was attributable to the contraction of the corporate business and not essentially equivalent to a dividend. Rev. Rul. 71-250, 1971-1 CB 112.

Partial liquidation denied where proceeds of sale of assets used to remodel remaining property. A real estate corporation adopted a plan of partial liquidation. It sold one of its parcels of real estate and used the sales proceeds to renovate some of its remaining property. Shortly thereafter, it distributed an amount equal to the sales proceeds to redeem some of its stock. The IRS ruled that while the sale of one parcel was a potential contraction of the business, the remodeling of other property was an expansion of the business. Therefore, the real estate sale did not result in a genuine contraction of the corporate business and the distribution did not qualify for capital gain treatment to the stockholders under Regulation § 1.346-1(a)(2). Rev. Rul. 67-299, 1967-2 CB 138.

Partial liquidation denied on distribution of condemnation proceeds. A corporation that had been in the business of mining limestone and manufacturing various lime products had about half of its proven limestone reserves condemned by a state agency in 1962. The remaining reserves, normally adequate for 18 to 27 years, were used from 1963 through 1965 to meet increased production requirements. In 1965, taxpayer received the condemnation award. After setting aside sums to be invested in facilities for manufacturing new limestone products and to diversify further, the balance was distributed pro rata to stockholders in redemption of the only class of stock outstanding. Section 346(a)(2) permits capital gain treatment for a partial liquidation if the distribution is not essentially equivalent to a dividend, is in redemption of part of the corporate stock, and occurs within the taxable year when the plan is adopted or in the succeeding taxable year. Regulation § 1.346-1(a) provides that there must also be a genuine contraction of the corporate business. On the above facts, the IRS ruled that the condemnation did not cause any current cessation of

LIQUIDATIONS: *Partial Liquidations*

business activity, since the corporation could continue its operations to the same extent as prior to the condemnation for a considerable time; and there were no plans to contract the business. The distribution did not, therefore, qualify as a partial liquidation under Section 346(a)(2). Since earnings and profits were available, the distribution was taxable under Section 301. Rev. Rul. 67-16, 1967-1 CB 77.

IRS rules on liquidation in partial sale of business operations. Taxpayer corporation was principally engaged in the business of repairing contractors' equipment. The corporation also bought, sold, and traded used contractors' equipment. It had an inventory of such equipment that it rented to contractors. The corporation owned the building in which the business was conducted. During the taxable year, the corporation entered into an arm's-length sale of part of its assets, consisting of rental equipment, all miscellaneous inventory, all work in process, and a service truck. The buyer leased the real estate of the corporation and also other property, consisting of shop equipment, machines, tools, office furniture and fixtures, and storage equipment. The corporation thereafter was engaged only in the business of leasing such property to the buyer. Pursuant to a plan of partial liquidation, the corporation distributed an amount in cash and securities equal to the net proceeds from the sale of the business assets plus that portion of the working capital (cash, accounts receivable, etc.) attributable to the business activity terminated by the sale. This distribution was pro rata to the stockholders and each stockholder turned in for cancellation and redemption a portion of his stock in the corporation. On these facts, the IRS held that in any case where the termination of all or part of one business of a corporation results in a genuine contraction of the corporate business, a distribution by the corporation in redemption of a portion of its capital stock constitutes a distribution in partial liquidation within the meaning of Section 346(a) to the extent that the distribution does not exceed the net proceeds from the sale of the business assets plus that portion of the working capital reasonably attributable to the terminated business activities and no longer required in the operation of the continuing business activities. Rev. Rul. 60-232, 1960-2 CB 115.

Business not being contracted; distribution not in partial liquidation. Taxpayer, a leather tanner, bought and treated skins and then sold the leather. It had large accumulated earnings despite losses in recent years. Attempting to stop the losses, it switched from one type of skins to another and moved into a different segment of the leather trade. Prospects still being poor, it decided to curtail purchases and reduce inventories. It asked whether a distribution of unneeded cash and government bonds would be a partial liquidation (taxable like a sale). The IRS pointed out that if a corporation has available earnings, there is no partial liquidation unless there is a contraction of the business. This corporation in prior years retained earnings and built up inventory and investments in government bonds. Their liquidation would not be a genuine contraction of the business, and the distribution would be taxed as a dividend. Rev. Rul. 60-322, 1960-2 CB 118.

Changing plan of complete liquidation to partial did not make distributions dividends. The management of a publicly held corporation sold all its assets and adopted a plan of complete liquidation. It characterized the first distribution as a liquidating dividend. After the initial distribution a new board of directors was elected, and it voted not to liquidate completely. It modified the plan to provide for partial liquidation instead. Under the modified plan, one thirtieth of the former capital was retained to be used in the purchase of a new business. The initial distribution and those distributions made pursuant to the modified plan were held to qualify as distributions in partial liquidation. For the purpose of determining whether the distributions were essentially equivalent to a dividend, the original plan to liquidate completely was irrelevant. Rev. Rul. 59-240, 1959-2 CB 112.

Reincorporations

Transaction was liquidation-reincorporation where 15 percent of assets transferred to related corporation. Taxpayer individuals owned 100 percent of the stock of X and Y Corporations. Taxpayers caused X to be liquidated, with 15 percent of its assets sold to Y and the remaining assets distributed to taxpayers. The IRS held that the transaction was not a liquidation but a D reorganization. Therefore, the distributions to taxpayers were ordinary income instead of capital gain. *Held:* For the IRS. This was a liquidation-reincorporation, since the transfer of 15 percent of X's assets to Y was a transfer of substantially all of the former's assets. Although the percentage was small, it constituted all of X's operating assets. Smothers, 642 F2d 894, 81-1 USTC ¶ 9368, 47 AFTR2d 81-1372 (5th Cir. 1981).

Liquidation-reincorporation deemed a D reorganization. The district court held that the liquidation of a corporation and the subsequent reincorporation of its assets and liabilities into two new structures was in substance a tax-free reorganization as opposed to a taxable liquidation. *Held:* Affirmed. Although the transferee corporations were subsequently sold, such sale was deemed to be secondary and not interdependent with the reorganization of the one corporation into two. Thus, the reorganization was deemed to be a tax-free D reorganization. Stephens, Inc., 464 F2d 53, 72-2 USTC ¶ 9547, 30 AFTR2d 72-5128 (8th Cir. 1972).

The dissolution of one corporation and incorporation of another was a liquidation and not a reorganization. Taxpayers owned 25 percent of the shares of V and B Corporations. After V purchased the assets of B Corporation, B was liquidated and dissolved under state law. After the sale, one or more of the B stockholders did not possess at least 80 percent of the voting power of V. Taxpayers reported long-term capital gains from the sale or exchange of their B stock. The operations of B and V differed substantially with respect to their corporate management, sales, service, credit policies and procedures, banking arrangements, and business location. V was an 80 percent-owned subsidiary of F Corporation. The sale by B to V was motivated by genuine business reasons; for example, the general economic conditions were better in V's area. The IRS determined the sale and liquidation to be a reorganization. *Held:* For taxpayer. There was a bona fide liquidation under Section 331(a)(1) motivated by genuine business considerations, and therefore, taxpayers realized long-term capital gains and not dividends. There was no D reorganization because the "control" element did not exist, and hence there was no "boot" taxable as a dividend to taxpayers. Similarly, there was more than a mere change in identity, form, or place of organization, and hence no F reorganization, and therefore no boot taxable as a dividend to taxpayers as a result thereof. Haensli, 68-2 USTC ¶ 9582, 22 AFTR2d 5663 (CD Cal. 1968), aff'd sub nom. Breech, Jr., 439 F2d 409, 71-1 USTC ¶ 9273, 27 AFTR2d 71-950 (9th Cir. 1971).

Liquidation-reincorporation to let employee buy stock interest not a bail-out. Taxpayer owned all the shares of his corporation. In order to let one of his employees obtain a proprietory interest in the business, taxpayer agreed to have the corporation sell its assets to a new corporation and to liquidate under Section 337. The employee bought half of the new corporation's stock, giving taxpayer an option to repurchase it if taxpayer became dissatisfied with the employee's services. The IRS contended that the transaction lacked economic substance, that it was in effect a reorganization with taxpayer receiving a dividend, and that the liquidation was not bona fide. The Tax Court rejected all three arguments. *Held:* Affirmed. The appellate court agreed with the Tax Court's conclusion that the transaction was bona fide in every respect, was motivated by business considerations, and that any purpose to minimize income tax liability, if present at all, played only a minor role. The IRS' argument that, if the business of a liquidated corporation was continued by a new corporation, there was no "complete liquidation" within the meaning of Sections 331 and 337, was rejected by Congress at the time of the 1954 Internal Revenue Code and did violence to the plain mean-

LIQUIDATIONS: *Reincorporations*

ing of the statute. Berghash, 361 F2d 257, 66-1 USTC ¶ 9446, 17 AFTR2d 1163 (2d Cir. 1966).

Reincorporation not treated as reorganization where business was substantially changed. Taxpayer was an executive representative of a manufacturer of prefabricated homes. Although taxpayer was financially successful, friction with the manufacturer prompted it to seek a new brand. A plan was adopted to sell uncompleted sales contracts to the manufacturer under a Section 337 plan and then to liquidate the corporation. The sale was made and the remaining assets were distributed to an assignee for the stockholders. The assignee promptly turned the assets over to a new corporation, which operated as an agent for another maker of prefabricated homes. The stockholders of the old corporation owned about 90 percent of the stock of the new corporation, but in somewhat different proportions. *Held:* The gain on liquidation was capital gain and not boot received in a reorganization. The Tax Court was reversed on this issue. The new corporation's business could not be considered a continuation of the old. On other related issues the Tax Court was affirmed. The sale of the uncompleted contracts had to be treated as ordinary income and the cash distributions were dividends. Customers' deposits retained by taxpayer when the contracts were sold became taxable in the year of such sales. Legal fees in connection with the sale of certain assets had to be deducted from the capital gain on the sales. Finally, the court made an adjustment to the salary of one of taxpayer's officers. Pridemark, Inc., 345 F2d 35, 65-1 USTC ¶ 9388, 15 AFTR2d 853 (4th Cir. 1965).

Liquidation and sale effected a reorganization. Wellington Funds, Inc., a mutual fund, had separate contracts with Wellington Corporation for investment and advisory services and with W.L. Morgan & Co. for the national promotion and distribution of the Fund's securities. These contracts constituted the principal, if not the exclusive, business of the investment adviser and distributor. Taxpayer was the sole stockholder of both the adviser and the distributor. In 1952, the Fund canceled its contract with adviser and immediately thereafter entered into a contract with Morgan, the distributor, for advisory services. The advisory corporation sold furniture and equipment to Morgan and also transferred its research data to it. The adviser distributed to its sole stockholder (taxpayer here) all its assets, cash, and U.S. Treasury bonds. He treated this as a distribution in liquidation of the adviser and reported long-term capital gain. The IRS, however, determined a deficiency on the ground that the distribution was taxable as a dividend. The Tax Court held that even assuming all the other conditions had been met, the distribution could not qualify as dividend income because the taxpayer had not exchanged his stock in the liquidated adviser for stock in Morgan. *Held:* Reversed. The distribution was made pursuant to a plan of reorganization. The majority opinion stated that if the assets of the transferor (the advisory firm) had been transferred to a newly formed corporation in exchange for stock, there would be no question that boot would have been received and taxed as dividend income, and the fact that an existing corporation (Morgan) in which taxpayer was the sole stockholder was the transferee did not alter the true nature of the transaction. The dissenting opinion said that it would agree if additional worth had been added to the transferee corporation through the corporate transfer of valuable assets of the liquidating corporation, but where, as in this case, there was a sale at fair value, the transfer of office furniture and equipment did not enrich the transferee. Morgan, 288 F2d 676, 61-1 USTC ¶ 9317, 7 AFTR2d 909 (3d Cir.), cert. denied, 368 US 836 (1961).

Liquidation-reincorporation was a reorganization with ordinary income to taxpayer stockholder. *A* Corporation and new *B* Corporation were both in substance controlled by taxpayer individual. The IRS held that the distribution by *A* to taxpayer of the proceeds from the sale of stock of related companies (but not including *B*) after *A* had liquidated and transferred its assets to new *B* resulted in ordinary income. *Held:* For the IRS. This case was in substance a reorganization and evidenced little business purpose aside from avoidance of taxes. It made no difference that taxpayer held stock in *A* under a Clifford trust and in new *B* under his name. Ringwalt, 75-2 USTC ¶ 9864 (D. Neb. 1975).

Liquidation deemed genuine, although later followed by reincorporation. The IRS held that distributions from a corporation on liquidation were ordinary dividends due to the fact that the corporation was later reincorporated. *Held:* For taxpayer. The distributions were capital gain, as there was no evidence of any preliquidation plan to reincorporate. Also, the IRS failed to establish a D, E, or F reorganization because the corporation failed to meet the respective requirements of each type. Swanson, 319 F. Supp. 959, 70-2 USTC ¶ 9624, 26 AFTR2d 70-5593 (ED Cal. 1970).

Liquidation followed by transfer of assets to new corporation not a reorganization. Taxpayer owned 50 percent of the stock of two corporations. One of the corporations granted taxpayer an option to purchase some of its land. That corporation's stock was transferred to the other corporation. The land was sold to a third party, subject to the option, which was subsequently transferred to a new corporation. This new corporation was formed after the original two corporations had been liquidated. Taxpayer reported his gain (consisting of cash and corporate assets) on the liquidation of the corporations as capital gain. The IRS contended that the whole arrangement added up to a reorganization and that taxpayer received dividend income. *Held:* For taxpayer. Taxpayer's expectation of buying the land in the future was subject to too many uncertainties to amount to a plan. In addition, the requirement that a corporation in a D reorganization acquire substantially all of the assets of the transferee corporation was not met here. The corporations were liquidated for valid business reasons (the stockholders were in financial difficulty), and not for tax-avoidance purposes. Sharp, 263 F. Supp. 884, 66-2 USTC ¶ 9723 (SD Tex. 1966).

Liquidation-reincorporation really D reorganization. Taxpayer was the sole stockholder of a corporation engaged in the florist business. He desired to retire from the business and in order to make his business salable, he had to remove two pieces of real estate owned by the corporation. He did this by liquidating the corporation and then transferring the operating assets, but not the real estate, to a new corporation. Taxpayer took capital gain treatment on the transaction. The IRS argued that it was a D reorganization, leaving dividend treatment of the boot. *Held:* For the IRS. Although taxpayer retained the two pieces of real estate, substantially all the operating assets of the first corporation were transferred to the second one. This is due to the fact that the "substantially all" test looks to the beneficial use, not to who has title. The real estate constitutes boot taxable as a dividend. Viereck, 83-2 USTC ¶ 9664, 52 AFTR2d 83-6350 (Cl. Ct. 1983).

Liquidation and subsequent reincorporation resulted in capital gains. Taxpayer liquidated his wholly owned corporation and thereafter operated its business as a sole proprietorship. For reasons arising subsequent to the liquidation, taxpayer created a new corporation transferring the operating assets of the proprietorship. Taxpayer reported the amounts received on liquidation as capital gain. *Held:* For taxpayer. This was not a formal liquidation followed by a prearranged reincorporation. The corporation was liquidated both in form and substance and the new corporation was created for reasons that did not exist on the liquidation date. There was ample uncontradicted evidence that taxpayer had no intention to reincorporate after liquidation; therefore, the distribution was in complete liquidation and was not taxable as a dividend or as boot arising out of a reorganization. Kind, 54 TC 600 (1970), acq. 1970-2 CB xx.

Transfer of assets through sole stockholder was a reorganization, not liquidation. Taxpayer, a U.S. corporation, was liquidated under Section 337 and claimed nonrecognition of gains realized on the sale of securities. The proceeds of the sale and other assets were distributed to the sole stockholder. During the period of the liquidation, the stockholder transferred cash and securities, some of which had been received from the liquidated

LIQUIDATIONS: *Reincorporations*

U.S. corporation, to a wholly owned Panamanian corporation in exchange for stock. He also transferred to the Panamanian corporation shares representing his 50 percent ownership in another U.S. corporation actively engaged in manufacturing in the United States. After it changed its name, the Panamanian corporation qualified to do business in New York, and, shortly thereafter, the sole stockholder transferred to it additional securities but not in exchange for stock or securities. The IRS determined that the transfer of assets of taxpayer in liquidation constituted a reorganization and that the gain realized on the sales of assets was therefore to be recognized. Taxpayer contended that the corporation was completely liquidated and was not reorganized, and that the transferee's business consisted of the management of a subsidiary and the search for new businesses, activities completely different from those conducted before liquidation. *Held:* For the IRS. Although taxpayer was liquidated according to the formalities of Section 337(a), the transferee was in effect a continuation of that business, since the liquidation could not be considered an isolated transaction but had to be viewed together with the related transfer from the sole stockholder to the transferee. Under Section 368(a)(1)(D), reorganization includes a transfer by a corporation of all or part of its assets to another corporation controlled by the same stockholders. In addition, the transferee received all of the stocks and properties and an amount of cash equal to that held by taxpayer in exchange for stock that was distributed to the stockholder according to a plan, which was not required to be in writing. The transferee also contended that it was not liable for the deficiency as a transferee because the stockholder was willing and able to pay the taxpayer's deficiency. However, the IRS had a choice of proceeding against the assets in the hands of the transferee corporation or the stock in the hands of the stockholder or both. Abegg, 50 TC 145 (1968).

Liquidation-reincorporation taxable only as capital gain. Taxpayers' corporation operated a general stevedoring and terminal business in West Coast ports, principally in California. In 10 years of operation it had an accumulated earnings and profits of more than $800,000 and had paid dividends in two years totaling $100,000. A new (California) corporation was formed by the active stockholders of the old corporation (taxpayers here) and certain key employees of the business, capitalized at $300,000. The new corporation bought the operating assets of the old for $100,000 and continued the business. The old corporation was liquidated in two years, and the stockholders reported the $1 million so received as long-term capital gain. The transactions were made to: (1) eliminate estates and widows of formerly active stockholders from the business (they held 38 percent); (2) permit one stockholder to acquire more stock; (3) allow key executives to become stockholders; and (4) reduce one stockholder's ownership because he intended to compete with the corporation. The active stockholders (62 percent owners) received $670,000 on the liquidation and invested $220,000 for a 73 percent interest in the new corporation. The remaining $80,000 was contributed to the key employees. *Held:* For taxpayer. The Tax Court held that there had been a distribution in partial liquidation of the old corporation, which was bona fide and precisely within the language of Sections 346(a)(1) and 331(a)(2). Therefore, capital gains treatment must apply unless, under the step transaction doctrine, a reorganization has taken place so that Section 356 comes into play. Regulation § 1.331-1(c), warning of possible dividend treatment in liquidation-reincorporation cases, does not apply without a reorganization. There was no reorganization here under Section 368(a)(1)(C) (not solely for voting stock) or 368(a)(1)(D) (no 80 percent control). Gallagher, 39 TC 144 (1963), acq. and nonacq. 1964-2 CB 5.

Liquidation-reincorporation treated as reorganization separate from earlier stock purchase. Individual taxpayers purchased the stock of a corporation that operated a ski lodge. The corporation had difficulty obtaining financing due to the low book value of the assets. Seven months after the purchase, the corporation was liquidated, and its assets transferred to a newly formed corporation that assumed and made payments on taxpayers' indebtedness to the original sellers. Taxpayers treated the stock purchase and the liquidation-reincorporation as a purchase of assets by the successor corporation under the step-transaction doctrine, giving the corporation a cost basis in its assets and a deduction for the interest payments. The IRS determined that the liquidation-reincorporation was a separate transaction, constituting a reorganization. As a result, the corporation took a carry-over basis in the assets, and the corporation could not deduct the interest payments, which constituted constructive dividends to the individual taxpayers. *Held:* For the IRS. The step-transaction doctrine did not apply because at the time of the stock purchase, the taxpayers did not intend to liquidate the corporation in order to obtain its assets. Lang, 43 TCM 874, ¶ 82,149 P-H Memo. TC (1982).

The IRS recast liquidation of subsidiary followed by reincorporation as a partial liquidation. *P* Corporation was the 100 percent owner of *S*, which engaged in two businesses with approximately equal assets and working capital. *S* sold the assets of one of its businesses to an unrelated party, and shortly thereafter was liquidated into *P*. Two weeks later, *P* reincorporated the assets of *S*'s remaining business in a new subsidiary, *N*. The IRS stated that the liquidation of *S* was not covered by Section 332, because it was in substance a partial liquidation of *S*. *S* and *N* would be considered the same corporation for tax purposes, with part of *S*'s stock considered redeemed in a Section 346 partial liquidation. Rev. Rul. 76-429, 1976-2 CB 97.

Section 337 is inapplicable to liquidation followed by reincorporation. A disposition within a 12-month period of all the assets of a corporation that retains its corporate charter, followed by the immediate reactivation of the corporation in another business by its former stockholder, was not a complete liquidation for purposes of Section 337. Consequently, gain or loss was recognized to the corporation on sales within the 12 months following adoption of the plan. Rev. Rul. 60-50, 1960-1 CB 150.

Stockholders' Gain or Loss

Liquidation of four corporations resulted in ordinary income where stockholder owned fifth corporation, which continued the business. The Tax Court held that taxpayer stockholder received ordinary income as opposed to capital gain from the liquidation of four corporations when he retained ownership of stock in a fifth corporation, which continued the business. *Held:* Affirmed. The evidence indicated that the five corporations were really one business entity and therefore distributions of the earnings and profits of the four liquidated corporations were substantially equivalent to a dividend. Greenberg, 75-2 USTC ¶ 9624, 36 AFTR2d 75-5479 (4th Cir. 1975).

Stockholder recognized capital gain on receipt of damage award resulting from lawsuit initiated by liquidated corporation. Upon liquidation of a corporation in which he owned stock, taxpayer received the right to share in any damage award arising from prosecution by the corporation at the time of its liquidation. The action, which survived the liquidation, was one for lost profits resulting from the landlord's wrongful possession of the premises at which the corporation carried on its business. Upon receipt of such right, taxpayer and his fellow stockholders were obligated to continue this litigation and pay additional costs associated with it. Although the corporation's right to damages were certain, at the time of liquidation, the landlord still vigorously contested the action and the amount of damages. When, after many years, taxpayer received payment of his share of the damages, he reported the amount as capital gain. The IRS asserted that this amount should have been reported as ordinary income. *Held:* For taxpayer. On the date of the corporation's liquidation, the rights received by taxpayer had no reasonably ascertainable fair market value. Therefore, amounts received several years later by reason of these rights related back to the liquidation as an amount received upon such liquidation. Nakatani, 60-1 USTC ¶ 9213, 5 AFTR2d 519 (ND Cal. 1959).

LIQUIDATIONS: *Stockholders' Gain or Loss*

Gain or loss of stockholder determined following liquidation. Taxpayer's corporation liquidated its assets pursuant to Section 333, and taxpayer received cash, securities, cancellation of a loan, and a one-third interest in real property. He also assumed his portion of the mortgage liability on the property and other corporate liabilities. Taxpayer contended that he was entitled to a capital loss, since the liabilities assumed exceeded the distributed property's book value. The IRS disallowed the loss and determined that taxpayer had realized a gain under Section 1001. *Held:* For the IRS. Taxpayer's gain or loss on the disposition of his stock was computed under Section 1001, which defines the realized gain or loss as the difference between the fair market value of the property distributed and the stockholder's basis in the stock. Section 333 merely governs the recognition of gain or loss realized under Section 1001. Shereff, 77 TC 1140 (1981).

Liquidation did not result in gain to stockholder. Taxpayer was the major stockholder of Perma-Line. The corporation sold its assets, including an account receivable from the taxpayer on open account to an unrelated partnership. The receivable from taxpayer was to be paid by him from excess sales commissions as outlined under the purchase agreement. The IRS determined that the agreement and liquidation of Perma-Line resulted in a cancellation of his debt to the corporation and thus was a liquidating distribution. *Held:* For taxpayer. The purchase agreement was legally sufficient to transfer the account to the buyer. Furthermore, at the time of the purchase, there was a reasonable chance that taxpayer could receive sufficient commissions to repay the debt, and subsequent decline in business was due to unforeseeable conditions. Further, as distributee of the corporate assets, taxpayer was liable as a transferee for income taxes owing at the time of the corporate liquidation, and this assessment was not barred by the statute of limitations prescribed by Section 6901(c)(1). Alexander, 61 TC 278 (1973).

Loans could not be withdrawn tax free on liquidation. Taxpayer was the sole stockholder of a corporation that was liquidated. Among the corporate assets distributed to him was an account reflecting funds disbursed to him that were treated as loans by the corporation. Taxpayer contended that the distributions were compensation or dividends and not taxable on liquidation. *Held:* For the IRS. The distributions were clearly treated as loans at the times that they were made as shown by the manner in which they were reflected on the books and records of the taxpayer and the corporation. The duty of consistency was owned by taxpayer, and he could not avoid paying any taxes on the withdrawals from the corporation. Bartel, 54 TC 25 (1970).

Excessive bonus resulted in a capital gain distribution. A bonus was authorized and paid after a corporation liquidated, ceased doing business, and sold its operating assets. On audit of the corporation's return, $15,000 of the bonus was disallowed as excessive compensation. Taxpayer claimed that the excessive compensation should be a liquidating dividend and taxable as capital gain. *Held:* For taxpayer. Any determination regarding the nature of the payment was to be based on all of the circumstances. The payment was a liquidating distribution because it was made to taxpayer in his status as controlling stockholder after a sequence of events that left no doubt that the corporation was liquidating. Consequently, this amount was taxable as capital gain. Garrison, 52 TC 281 (1969).

Liquidation gain on restricted stock valued on transfer date. Taxpayers, sole stockholders of a liquidating corporation, contended that for purposes of determining the amount of gain on liquidation, the proper valuation date was the date the liquidating corporation exchanged its equipment and inventory for the stock of another corporation. *Held:* For the IRS. The proper date was the date the stock of the liquidating corporation was transferred to the taxpayer. The stock was discounted from the selling price to accommodate its restrictions, but a barter-equation method of valuation was rejected. Stroupe, 37 TCM 280, ¶ 78,055 P-H Memo. TC (1978).

LIQUIDATIONS: *Stockholders' Gain or Loss*

Capital gain recognized on corporate liquidation. Taxpayers liquidated their corporation, received property, and did not recognize gain. The IRS claimed that income must be recognized. *Held:* For the IRS. No Section 333 liquidation election was made. Under Section 331, gain is recognized to the extent of the excess of the distributed property's fair market value over the adjusted bases of taxpayers' stock. Barlow, 34 TCM 1373, ¶ 75,316 P-H Memo. TC (1975).

Sale and liquidation of corporations were reorganizations resulting in dividend distributions. Taxpayer owned three corporations, two of which sold their assets to the third, liquidated, and made distributions to taxpayer for which he claimed capital gain treatment. The IRS treated the distributions as dividends. *Held:* For the IRS. Although the liquidations were proper in form and there might have been business reasons for the actions, the transactions were D reorganizations as the businesses were carried on in substantially the same form by another corporation wholly owned by the same stockholder. Therefore, the distributions were taxable as dividends. The amount of the dividend was measured, under Section 356, by the undistributed earnings of the liquidating corporations and not, as the IRS contended, by the earnings of all three companies. Estate of Bell, 30 TCM 1221, ¶ 71,285 P-H Memo. TC (1971).

Contract based on future sales had no ascertainable market value. Taxpayer was a major stockholder of a manufacturer of a synthetic starch. The corporation's directors and stockholders adopted a plan of liquidation under which the corporate assets were sold to another corporation. Payment was in installments and based on a percentage of sales of the product purchased. If there was a default, the seller could reacquire the assets and treat any payments as liquidated damages. The corporation assigned the contract to taxpayer and its other stockholders as a liquidating distribution. *Held:* For the taxpayer. On the facts, the court found that the rights to the future installments had no ascertainable fair market value on the date of distribution and that no value need be included for the rights in computing gain on liquidation. Altorfer, 20 TCM 266, ¶ 61,048 P-H Memo. TC (1961).

Court valued real estate received on corporate liquidation. A corporation owned a building used in part as a car showroom and in part for offices. Upon dissolution and complete liquidation, all of its net assets were distributed to *W* and *D*, brothers, in equal one-half, undivided shares in redemption of their stock. Each stockholder reported gains from the liquidation on the difference between the assets received, the stock basis, and expense; however, each one-half interest in the building was valued below 50 percent of its fair market value. The brothers continued to operate the building as a business after the liquidation. The IRS determined deficiencies in the amounts reported, and in particular in the value attributed to the building. *Held:* For the IRS. The circumstances indicated that a one-half undivided interest in real property was worth 50 percent of the full market value; thus, taxpayers were not entitled to use a lower figure in computing the value of their interests for tax purposes. Coddington, 19 TCM 498, ¶ 60,095 P-H Memo. TC (1960).

Distributions in complete liquidation to stockholders proportionate to blocks of shares in multistockholder corporation. The IRS calculated the gain to be reported by a stockholder of a multistockholder corporation who owned more than one block of shares having different adjusted bases and who received a series of distributions during the complete liquidation of the corporation. Each distribution to such stockholder must be allocated among the different blocks of shares in the proportion that the number of shares in a particular block bears to the total number of shares owned by the stockholder. Rev. Rul. 68-348, 1968-2 CB 141, is amplified. Rev. Rul. 85-48, 1985-1 CB 126.

Cancellation of receivable stockholder loans in liquidation treated as the receipt of money by stockholders. The cancellation of valid loans receivable from stockholders as part of a liquidation of the corporation constitutes the receipt of cash by the stockholders involved under Sections 333(c)(2) and 333(f)(1). Rev. Rul. 70-409, 1970-2 CB 79.

A series of corporate liquidation distributions must be prorated among a stockholder's separate blocks of stock. The IRS ruled that where a stockholder owns more than one block of stock and receives a series of distributions in complete liquidation of the corporation, each distribution must be allocated ratably among the several blocks of stock in the proportion that the number of shares in a particular block bears to the total number of shares outstanding. Gain or loss must be computed separately with respect to each block of stock, and gains will be recognized only after the adjusted basis of each block has been recovered. Once the adjusted basis of each block has been recovered, all subsequent distributions allocable to that block are recognized as a gain in their entirety. Any losses resulting from a complete liquidation are recognized only after the corporation makes its final distribution. Rev. Rul. 68-348, 1968-2 CB 141.

Twelve-Month Liquidations—In General

Section 337 applied to preliquidation sale of stock received in reorganization. *O* Corporation exchanged all of its assets for 0.96 percent of the stock of *U* Corporation in a C reorganization. *O* then sold some of its *U* stock in order to pay creditors, then distributed the remaining *U* stock to its stockholders in liquidation. The IRS argued that the stock sale was not exempt from gain under Section 337 and that the liquidation distribution was not tax-free under Section 354. *Held:* For taxpayer. Reorganization and liquidation are not mutually exclusive. The court refused to follow FEC Liquidating Corp., 548 F2d 924 (Ct. Cl. 1977), which held Section 337 inapplicable under similar facts. General Housewares Corp., 488 F. Supp. 926, 78-2 USTC ¶ 9693, 42 AFTR2d 78-6047, modified, 615 F2d 1056, 80-1 USTC ¶ 9384, 45 AFTR2d 80-1518 (5th Cir. 1980).

Failure to distribute assets within year of sale was untimely even though proceeds of sale were deposited within a year. Taxpayer adopted a plan of liquidation pursuant to Section 337 and, within one year after the sale of its principal asset, deposited the proceeds in the corporate checking account. More than one year after the adoption of the plan, the proceeds were distributed to the stockholders. The IRS held that the distribution was not timely. The Tax Court held for the IRS. *Held:* Affirmed. Placing the proceeds in the checking account did not constitute distribution, nor did this constitute constructive receipt to the stockholders. Further, the retention of a building with a value approximately equal to a mortgage against it plus a debt to one of the stockholders was fatal, as nothing was done to set this building apart for the payments of claims until subsequent to the one-year period. Vern Realty, Inc., 73-1 USTC ¶ 9455 (1st Cir. 1973), aff'g 58 TC 1005 (1972).

Payment of 5 percent of total distributions after 12 months did not disqualify Section 337 liquidation. Taxpayer corporation and its subsidiary sold their assets for slightly more than $1 million, elected Section 337, and distributed virtually all assets during the 12-month period. Taxpayer retained certain minor assets and certain legal claims in order to satisfy certain contingent liabilities. Because taxpayer realized more on its retained claims than anticipated and settled its contingent liabilities for less than anticipated, there was distributed an additional $50,000 to its stockholders. The IRS contended that there was no complete liquidation within 12 months and disallowed Section 337 treatment. The Tax Court held for the IRS. *Held:* Reversed. There was a good faith attempt to estimate the potential liabilities. Therefore, there was a valid Section 337 liquidation. O.B.M. Inc., 427 F2d 661, 70-1 USTC ¶ 9437, 25 AFTR2d 70-1291 (2d Cir. 1970).

"Gain on sale" interest income taxable in Section 337 liquidation. Zeckendorf Hotels Corporation, a subsidiary of Webb & Knapp, Inc., offered to buy stock of Commodore Hotel, Inc. To secure financing, Zeckendorf approached a number of New York financing institutions. Although refusing credit to Zeckendorf, the financiers were willing to supply the funds to a new corporation created expressly for acquiring the stock of Commodore. Accordingly, Zeckendorf purchased the shares of Commodore and transferred them to the new corporation, taxpayer. Taxpayer concurrently granted Zeckendorf an option to buy back the shares at a higher price. Zeckendorf owned one third of taxpayer; the financiers owned two thirds. Some months later, Zeckendorf obtained sufficient funds to exercise the option. Taxpayer adopted a plan of liquidation pursuant to Section 337 and sold the Commodore shares to Zeckendorf. It excluded the gain from the sale under Section 337. The Tax Court, however, held that the difference between the "purchase" price and the "selling" price of the shares was interest income and taxable as such. It concluded that, in reality, the whole arrangement was a plan to make the money available to Zeckendorf at a prearranged price. The object of forming taxpayer corporation was not to embark on a new hotel operation but rather to procure for the participating financiers practically risk-proof security for their advances plus a handsome profit from the overall arrangement. Webb & Knapp had agreed to indemnify taxpayer's stockholders against any loss by guaranteeing them a 6 percent return plus recovery of expenses. While taxpayer held the shares, it could not sell, pledge, or otherwise dispose of them. Its position was that of a mortgagor. *Held:* Affirmed. In looking through the form to the substance of the transaction, the Tax Court was not wrong in characterizing the transaction as a short-term financing scheme in which taxpayer received ordinary income, and not a sale. Comtel Corp., 376 F2d 791, 67-1 USTC ¶ 9433, 19 AFTR2d 1425 (2d Cir. 1967).

Failure to make distribution within requisite time bars use of Section 337. Taxpayers each owned 50 percent of two corporations. Each corporation adopted a resolution for a complete liquidation under Section 337. Within 12 months after the plan was adopted, each corporation had sold substantial assets and had distributed the proceeds from the sales to its stockholders. Neither corporation was ever legally dissolved under state law, and both corporations retained title to their assets after the one-year liquidation period. On audit, the IRS disallowed Section 337 treatment and assessed taxes against taxpayers as transferees of the corporation. Taxpayers paid the assessments and sued for a refund. *Held:* For the IRS. Where stockholders held title to assets and continued operating the corporate business after the 12-month liquidation period, Section 337 was disallowed. Section 337 was narrowly drawn with precise conditions to be fulfilled if a corporation were to receive its preferred treatment. Owings, 83-2 USTC ¶ 9618, 52 AFTR2d 83-5982 (WD Tenn. 1983).

Rescission and adoption of new plan of liquidation on same day started one-year period for purposes of Section 337. Taxpayer owned the fee to one parcel of real estate and a one-third beneficial interest in an adjoining parcel. Upon learning that the state was considering condemning the parcels, taxpayer adopted a plan of liquidation under Section 337 on January 7, 1960. On December 1, 1960, the state condemned the parcel in which taxpayer held a beneficial interest; it did not condemn the second parcel. Taxpayer revoked its January 7 plan of liquidation on December 27, 1960, and adopted a new plan on the same day. The state condemned taxpayer's second parcel of real estate on June 21, 1961, and agreed to reimburse taxpayer for the taking on December 2. Taxpayer completed its liquidation on December 22, 1961. It did not include in income its profit on the condemnation of its second parcel of real estate. The IRS contended that taxpayer never rescinded, but merely extended, its first plan of liquidation, and that, therefore, the condemnation did not occur during a one-year period of liquidation as required by Section 337 for nonrecognition of gain. Taxpayer had not taken any steps to liquidate between the date of adopting its first plan of liquidation and the date of adopting its second plan. *Held:* For taxpayer. Taxpayer originally decided to liquidate because it had no purpose in continuing after the state taking. The failure of the state to effect the taking in 1960, however, led taxpayer to abandon its earlier plan. It adopted a new plan because it knew funds would be available after the taking for distribution on liquidation. West St.-Erie

LIQUIDATIONS: *Twelve-Month Liquidations—In General*

Boulevard Corp., 294 F. Supp. 145, 68-2 USTC ¶ 9491 (NDNY 1968).

Nonrecognition held to result from Section 337 liquidation; transaction distinguished from a *D* reorganization. Taxpayer was a transferee of *X* Corporation, which had acquired and operated a luxury apartment building. He and the other stockholders were preoccupied with their other unrelated professional activities and wished to sell the building. Efforts to sell the property failed due to the large cash outlay required; consequently the corporation entered into an agreement to accept cash and a tenement property in exchange therefor. The transaction was consummated after *X* Corporation adopted a plan of liquidation under Section 337. The stockholders, however, did not want to be associated with the operation of the tenement. They formed *Y* Corporation and had the tenement property transferred to it. *X* Corporation was liquidated and dissolved and the cash distributed to the stockholders within the 12-month period. The IRS assessed deficiencies against the taxpayer as transferee of *X* Corporation on the theory that the transactions constituted a reorganization of *X* Corporation under Section 368(a)(1)(D). Taxpayer contended that he was not subject to tax on the ground that gain was not recognized to the corporation under Section 337. *Held:* For taxpayer. The sole operating asset of *X* Corporation was sold to an independent entity pursuant to a Section 337 liquidation. The asset that it acquired in exchange therefor was accepted on the representation that it was readily saleable, and it was in fact held for only five days. Section 368 was not applicable, since it applies only if, under Section 354, the transferee acquires substantially all the assets of the transferor corporation. The IRS' contention that *Y* Corporation received substantially all of the assets was not valid, since the tenement property constituted only about 9 percent of the consideration for the apartment building, and during the time it was held by *X* Corporation it could hardly have been considered an operating asset. The court was satisfied that the officers and stockholders of *X* Corporation adopted a plan of liquidation under Section 337 and complied fully therewith. Rommer, 268 F. Supp. 740, 67-2 USTC ¶ 9481 (DNJ 1966).

Plan of liquidation preceded sale. The evening before completing a contract to sell its franchise and assets, taxpayer's stockholders determined to wind up its affairs. The actual sale of the assets took place two months later, and the formal steps toward dissolution of taxpayer corporation were completed seven months after that. The IRS contended that the sale preceded the adoption of the plan of liquidation, rendering the nonrecognition provisions of Section 337 inapplicable. *Held:* For taxpayer. The court found that taxpayer had adopted a plan of dissolution prior to the sale. The gain was not recognized under Section 337. As required by that section, taxpayer had adopted a liquidation plan and distributed all its assets within 12 months. No gain was recognized on its sales within the 12 months. Powell's Pontiac-Cadillac, Inc., 60-1 USTC ¶ 9317, 5 AFTR2d 977 (DNJ 1960).

No plan of liquidation existed when stockholders intended to liquidate corporation only if the property were sold. Evidence produced at trial indicated that the corporation's stockholders intended to liquidate their corporation only if a major asset of the corporation were sold. Accordingly, it was only after this asset was sold that an unconditional plan to liquidate the corporation was put into effect. The IRS asserted that because the sale of this asset occurred before the plan was adopted, Section 337 did not apply, and the corporation was thus required to recognize gain on the sale. *Held:* For the IRS. Although a plan of liquidation or a result of formal action need not be in writing, such a plan does not exist if it is subject to a condition precedent (here, the sale of a particular corporate asset). Whitson, 190 F. Supp. 478, 61-1 USTC ¶ 9144, 7 AFTR2d 301 (DND 1960).

Liquidation tax free because control acquired before formal plan adopted. On December 27, 1967, taxpayer notified minority stockholders of its subsidiary corporations that it proposed to sell the assets and liquidate, and also that it was contemplating an offer to purchase their shares. On April 17, 1968, the directors voted to liquidate the subsidiaries and to make an offer to purchase all the outstanding stock held by the minority stockholders. On May 9, 1968, taxpayer acquired at least 80 percent of the outstanding stock of its subsidiaries, and on June 20, 1968, a plan of liquidation was adopted. Taxpayer contended that the liquidation was not subject to taxation pursuant to Section 332. The IRS determined that the gain was recognizable, since the plan of liquidation was adopted prior to the acquisition of the requisite 80 percent control. *Held:* For taxpayer. The taxpayer was the owner of at least 80 percent of the stock of the liquidated subsidiaries on the date that the liquidation plan was adopted; hence, gain did not have to be recognized on the liquidation. The notice to the stockholders merely indicated that the company was contemplating liquidation and acquisition of the minority interests. A mere intent to liquidate cannot be equated with the adoption of a plan of complete liquidation. Riggs, Inc., 64 TC 474 (1975).

Complete liquidation resulting in continuation of liquidated corporation's business in corporate form with continuity of proprietary interest in excess of 84 percent did not constitute a complete liquidation under Section 337. Taxpayer, in addition to carrying on its own business activities, owned 100 percent of the stock of *X* and *Y* Corporations, each actively engaged in business. Taxpayer, after having adopted a plan of complete liquidation, sold the stock of *X* to an unrelated third party for cash. Taxpayer transferred all of its assets and liabilities to newly formed *Z* Corporation in exchange for 100 percent of its stock, and distributed in liquidation all of its cash, *Y* and *Z* stock to its stockholders. In the course of these transactions, taxpayer redeemed approximately 15 percent of its stock from a single stockholder. *Z* Corporation changed its name to taxpayer's and continued its business uninterrupted, using the same office, telephone numbers, and stationery. Taxpayer reported no gain from the sale of *X* stock by reason of Section 337. *Held:* For the IRS. Section 337 requires that the corporation distribute all of its unsold assets in complete liquidation. A complete liquidation requires a bona fide elimination of the corporate entity and does not include "a transaction in which substantially the same shareholders continue to utilize a substantial part of the directly-owned assets of the same enterprise in uninterrupted *corporate* form." Telephone Answering Serv. Co., 63 TC 423 (1974).

Section 1245 overrides Section 337, so gain had to be recognized. A corporation sold all of its assets, including Section 1245 property, pursuant to a plan of liquidation. The gain on the sale of its assets qualified for nonrecognition under Section 337. The IRS contended that the gain on the sale of the Section 1245 property had to be realized by taxpayer as transferee. Taxpayer contended that the net result would be to nullify the benefits of Section 337 and was not intended by Congress. *Held:* For the IRS. The plain words of the statute sustained the IRS' contention. The regulations and the legislative history provided the same. Section 1245 overrides Section 337 with the consequence that the gain involved had to be recognized as ordinary income. Clayton, 52 TC 911 (1969).

Court prevented taxpayer from reversing its claim to Section 337 nonrecognition to recognize the loss on sale of assets. On June 26, 1961, taxpayer's board adopted a plan of liquidation and authorized the taxpayer's assets to be sold. Any unsold assets and cash were to be distributed no later than 12 months from June 26, 1961. Taxpayer's assets were sold or distributed within the 12-month period, after which taxpayer received a tax refund that was deposited into taxpayer's sole stockholder's bank account. Realizing that by completing the sale and liquidation within the 12-month period, Section 337 would prevent the deduction of taxpayer's loss on the sale of its assets, taxpayer urged that the unforeseen receipt of the tax refund caused the liquidation to fail the Section 337 requirements. *Held:* For the IRS. Taxpayer presented no proof that the liquidating distribution did not transfer to taxpayer's sole stockholder rights to all unknown, contingent, or unmatured claims (e.g., the tax refund) within the prescribed 12-month period. All evidence

LIQUIDATIONS: *Twelve-Month Liquidations—In General*

indicated that taxpayer, who had advice of tax counsel, intended to and did comply with Section 337. Failure to follow procedure described in Rev. Rul. 63-215, 1963-2 CB 144, was immaterial because such procedure is not exclusive or mandatory. Bird Management, Inc., 48 TC 586 (1967).

Second plan of liquidation adopted 12 years after the first did not fall within Section 337. In 1946, taxpayer's corporation adopted a plan of liquidation. Over a 10-year period, it sold less than half its assets and made distributions to stockholders as liquidating dividends. In 1958, the corporation adopted another liquidation plan and then sold its remaining assets. Gain on the 1958 sale was not reported on the theory that Section 337 applied. The IRS contended that the gain was taxable to the corporation. *Held:* For the IRS. The plan under which the assets were sold was adopted *before* June 22, 1954, so Section 337 could not apply. The new plan could not extend the 12-month period of the statute. All the steps taken after 1946 were consistent with the plan adopted that year, even though it finally took 13 years to liquidate. Howell, 40 TC 940 (1963).

Court holds that liquidation plan adopted at stockholder meeting notwithstanding prior agreement to liquidate. In May 1977, stockholders entered into an agreement for the complete liquidation of their corporation. At a stockholders' meeting on June 22, 1977, the corporation formally adopted a liquidation resolution. On July 22, 1977, stockholders filed their Section 333 elections. The IRS claimed that the May 1977 agreement constituted the adoption of the liquidation plan and that the June 22, 1977 corporate resolution merely ratified that adoption. Since stockholders' elections had not been filed within 30 days of the May agreement, their distributions did not qualify for nonrecognition treatment. *Held:* For taxpayer. The stockholders' intent that the corporation adopt the liquidation plan at the June 22, 1977 stockholders' meeting was found to be controlling despite contradictory language in the May 1977 agreement. Accordingly, the stockholders' elections were timely filed. Lake Iola Groves, Inc., 47 TCM 880, ¶ 84,018 P-H Memo. TC (1984).

Distributions timely under Section 337 even though title to abandoned property retained. On December 26, 1973, X Corporation distributed parcels of land to taxpayer, its sole shareholder, under a plan of liquidation adopted on December 26, 1972. X retained title to another parcel, which it had abandoned. The IRS asserted deficiencies against taxpayer as transferee of X's assets, arguing that the land distribution was untimely and that retention of the abandoned parcel defeated Section 337. *Held:* For taxpayer. The land distribution was timely under Section 7503. Retention of bare title to the abandoned property did not defeat Section 337. Snyder, 41 TCM 1416, ¶ 81,216 P-H Memo. TC (1981).

Section 337 treatment denied on account of retained assets. A corporation adopted a plan of liquidation under Section 337 after real property it owned was condemned. It distributed the condemnation award within the 12-month period, but retained other assets. The IRS denied nonrecognition treatment. *Held:* For the IRS. The retention of receivables and claims precluded Section 337 treatment. There was no established relation of these assets to the payment of claims. Casa Loma, Inc., 39 TCM 1251, ¶ 80,078 P-H Memo. TC (1980).

Lack of formal dissolution was no bar to nonrecognition of gain on sale under Section 337. Taxpayer corporation sold its licenses to another company subject to a federal regulatory agency's approval. Under a Section 337 plan adopted in August, 1964, it reported a nonrecognized gain from the sale of the licenses. The IRS claimed that the sale proceeds were not entitled to nonrecognition treatment. *Held:* For taxpayer. Although the corporation could not formally dissolve until final approval of the transaction, it ceased doing business by selling its equipment, discharging its employees, and closing its bank accounts, all within 12 months of the adoption of the Section 337 plan. The sale was completed concerning rights and obligations of the parties thereto becoming fixed, and a proper Section 337 liquidation had taken place, so that taxpayer did not have to recognize gain on the transaction. Male, 30 TCM 1282, ¶ 71,301 P-H Memo. TC (1971).

Assignment of corporate assets to stockholders beyond 12-month period fatal to a Section 337 liquidation. Taxpayers were transferees of a real estate corporation. The corporation adopted a plan of dissolution and liquidation on January 26, 1956, and sold its real property on February 1, 1956, receiving cash and a purchase money mortgage. Through January 1957, payments of interest and principal on the mortgage were made by checks payable to the corporation and deposited in the corporation's bank account. From and after the sale of February 1, 1956, the sole assets of the corporation consisted of cash and the purchase money mortgage, and the corporation engaged in no business activity other than payment of debts and the collection of payments on the mortgage. Although the corporation filed its certificate of dissolution with the Secretary of State of New York on January 24, 1957, it did not execute an assignment of the mortgage to its stockholders until February 28, 1957, and did not close out its bank account until November 7, 1958. The IRS alleged that the corporation did not comply with the 12-month requirement of Section 337 and accordingly was taxable on the gain from the sale of its property. *Held:* For the IRS. The corporation was not completely liquidated within the 12-month period. Not only did it continue to maintain a bank account and make payments therefrom well beyond the 12 months, it also remained the record owner of the mortgage at least until February 28, 1957. Taxpayers' contention that, under New York law, the corporation was dissolved on January 24, 1957, and that the directors thereafter became trustees of the corporate assets for the benefit of the stockholders was rejected on the ground that a dissolution of a corporation under New York law does not ipso facto constitute a liquidation for purposes of Section 337. Also, an alternative argument that the delay in liquidation was caused by a difficulty in deciding to which stockholder (husband or wife) the corporation should distribute interests, represented by shares issued in the husband's name, was also rejected, since, in such a predicament, the interest could have been assigned in escrow. Since the officers of the corporation in good faith believed that a purchase money mortgage had, for tax purposes, been constructively distributed to stockholders immediately after the sale of the assets and, on that basis, concluded that the corporation's income for 1956 was more than offset by allowable deductions, and that it had no income for 1957, the negligence penalty and a penalty for failure to file were not sustained. Yeckes, 25 TCM 924, ¶ 66,178 P-H Memo. TC (1966).

Section 337 not applicable where liquidation did not occur within 12-month period. Taxpayer adopted a plan of complete liquidation on August 25, 1957 but did not distribute the assets to its stockholders until 14 months later. Taxpayer contended that the date in the written minutes (August 25, 1957) was wrong and that the plan of dissolution was actually adopted two months later. *Held:* On the record, a plan of dissolution was adopted on August 25, 1957. Taxpayer was not entitled to the benefits of Section 337(a), since it had not only failed to show that it had made any distribution of assets within the requisite 12-month period but had also failed to show a complete liquidation of all its assets. Maxine Dev. Co., 22 TCM 1579, ¶ 63,300 P-H Memo. TC (1963).

Failure to prove compliance with Section 337 made gain taxable. A corporation sold land at a gain in the year of its liquidation, and on its final return the corporation stated that the gain was not recognized pursuant to Section 337. *Held:* For the IRS. The court found the statement on the tax return insufficient. There was no evidence that information return Form 966, which is required to be filed within 30 days after adoption of the plan of liquidation, was ever filed or that the corporation ever adopted a resolution or plan to liquidate its assets. The court also denied the corporation a claimed $1,500 bad debt deduction on account of an advance to a hired employee who left without ever performing any work. There was no evidence indicating when the money was advanced or when the so-called debt became worthless, and no evidence was presented that a bona fide indebtedness in fact existed. Intercounty Dev. Corp., 20 TCM 1071, ¶ 61,217 P-H Memo. TC (1961).

Twelve-month period of Section 337 defined. The 12-month period of Section 337 for nonrecognition sale of corporate assets begins on the date the plan of liquidation is adopted and ends at midnight of the day before the corresponding date of the following year. Rev. Rul. 79-3, 1979-1 CB 143.

Deliberate delay beyond 12-month period doomed Section 337 plan. On January 1, 1975, the stockholders of a domestic corporation adopted a plan of complete liquidation as described in Section 337. In connection with this plan of liquidation, the corporation sold its assets on February 1, 1975, to an unrelated third party and realized a loss upon the sale. In order to avail itself of the use of this loss, the corporation intentionally waited until April 1, 1976, a period in excess of 12 months from the date of adoption of the plan of liquidation, before distributing all of the proceeds from the sale of its assets to its stockholders in liquidation. The IRS held that Section 337 does not apply to a transaction in which a corporation sells its assets at a loss and deliberately delays the liquidation distribution beyond 12 months from the date of adoption of the plan of liquidation. Consequently, the loss was realized and recognized by the corporation. Rev. Rul. 77-150, 1977-1 CB 88.

No Section 337 treatment for noncompetition covenant. The amount received in a liquidation allocable to a covenant not to compete, that is separately bargained for, and that is not part of good will does not qualify for the nonrecognition provisions of Section 337. Rev. Rul. 74-29, 1974-1 CB 79.

Second plan of liquidation qualified under Section 337 following bona fide cancellation of original plan. On January 1, 1965, a corporation contracted to sell all its assets to an unrelated purchaser and the shareholders approved a plan for a Section 337 liquidation. On June 30, 1965, when the assets were to be transferred, the purchaser defaulted. On July 2, 1965, the plan of liquidation was rescinded. Normal operations were carried on until March 1, 1966 when another purchase offer was received. Another plan of liquidation was approved, the assets were sold, and the proceeds distributed within the required 12-month period. The IRS ruled that under the facts, there was no extension of the original plan as prohibited by Regulation 1.337-1. Here, the original plan had been rescinded and normal operations continued without disposition of corporate assets. Therefore, the liquidation plan of March 1, 1966 qualified under Section 337. Rev. Rul. 67-273, 1967-2 CB 137.

Transfer of tax claims to trustee within 12-month period satisfied Section 337. Following the approval of a plan of complete liquidation by the stockholders, a corporation sold all its assets except a claim for refund of federal taxes that was not reasonably susceptible to sale or division among the stockholders. Within the 12-month period specified in Section 337, the proceeds from the sale of the assets were distributed to the stockholders. Also during this period, the corporation's affairs were wound up, and the tax refund claim was transferred pursuant to the plan of liquidation to an independent trustee for the benefit of the stockholders. The applicable local law authorizes a trustee so appointed to receive a liquidating distribution for the benefit of stockholders and, when reduced to cash, pay it over to the shareholders. On these facts, the IRS held that the liquidation had been accomplished as provided in Section 337. The IRS stated that when the only unsold or uncollected asset of a corporation in the process of liquidation consists of a claim for refund of federal taxes, the corporation will be considered to have distributed all of its assets in complete liquidation within the meaning of Section 337 if, within the 12-month period specified therein, it is finally divested of such claim by a complete transfer of it to an independent trustee selected by the stockholders pursuant to the plan of liquidation. Rev. Rul. 63-245, 1963-2 CB 144.

Twelve-Month Liquidations—Sale of Assets

Stockholders' meeting adopted liquidation plan before sale; Section 337 applied. Taxpayer alleged that a stockholders' meeting at which a plan of liquidation was adopted was held before the sale of its assets. If so, the gain on the sale would not be taxed under Section 337. The court charged the jury that such a meeting could be held by the principal stockholders even if the other stockholders were not present. *Held:* For taxpayer. The jury found that the meeting was actually held, and the gain was not recognized. Republic Nat'l Bank of Dallas, 64-1 USTC ¶ 9157, 13 AFTR2d 522 (ND Tex. 1963).

Insurance agency expirations was property; sale tax-free under Section 337. Insurance agency expirations are the records of the agency as to the policyholders. They permit the agency to contact the policyholders before the expiration date and to obtain renewal business. Taxpayer corporation sold these expirations after adopting a plan of liquidation and claimed that the gain was tax-free under Section 337. The IRS contended that the sale was of a right to future income. *Held:* For taxpayer. The expirations were a property right in the nature of good will. The gain was not recognized. Calley & Clark Co., 220 F. Supp. 111, 63-2 USTC ¶ 9764 (SD W. Va. 1963).

Both parent and subsidiary in chain liquidation can claim benefits of Section 337. Taxpayer and its parent, both operating companies, simultaneously adopted plans of complete liquidation. Both sold their assets to an unrelated third party. Taxpayer was wholly owned by its parent. Following the sale of assets, the sales proceeds were distributed to the parent's stockholders, none of which were corporations. By reason of Section 337, neither reported gain from the sale of their assets. The IRS asserted that taxpayer's liquidation was governed by Section 332, and thus Section 337 did not apply because of Section 337(c)(2). *Held:* For taxpayer. The purpose of Section 337(c)(2) was to prevent the avoidance of tax upon a corporation's liquidation, both at the liquidated corporation's level and its nonliquidated corporate parent's level. Here, the simultaneous chain liquidation of parent and subsidiary into the hands of noncorporate stockholders resulted in a tax at the stockholder level. Accordingly, to avoid payment of a double tax by reason of Section 337(c)(2), the court held that Section 332 does not apply where simultaneous liquidations of both parent and subsidiary are involved. Kamis Eng'g Co., 60 TC 763 (1973).

Sale of minks qualified for nonrecognition while pelts were taxable. Taxpayer, a corporation in the business of producing and selling mink pelts, liquidated pursuant to Section 337. Pelts and live minks were sold. The final distribution was made, but taxpayer did not have sufficient funds in its checking account to pay the distribution. Consequently, actual payment was made outside the requisite 12-month period. The IRS denied the nonrecognition of the gain on the sale of the minks and pelts. *Held:* For taxpayer, in part. To require formal legal steps to be taken would defeat the purpose of the statute. Taxpayer had sufficient funds and merely had to deposit them into its checking account. The final distribution was therefore completed within the required time and nonrecognition of gain was approved. However, the gain on the sale of the pelts was taxable because they were inventory and were not sold in bulk. Pastene, 52 TC 647 (1969).

Prolonged liquidating distributions forfeited Section 337 treatment. As its primary asset, a corporation owned a parcel of real property that was subject to condemnation proceedings by New York City. Shortly before the city took title, the corporation adopted a plan of liquidation pursuant to Section 337. Within one year, the president of the corporation executed an assignment of the condemnation proceeds in favor of the stockholders. He failed to record the assignment in the minutes or on the books and neglected to notify the city or a creditor bank. To aid the stockholders in spreading the gain in liquidation over

LIQUIDATIONS: *Twelve-Month Liquidations—Sale of Assets*

two years, the corporation distributed a portion of the condemnation proceeds more than a year after the adoption of the plan. Because of this delayed payment, the IRS argued that Section 337 was inapplicable and sought to hold the stockholders liable as transferees of the corporate tax. Taxpayers replied that the assignment effected a timely distribution. *Held:* For the IRS. Taxpayers were liable for the tax. Since taxpayers and the corporation made no effort to record the assignment or to notify the city that it was ever made, the assignment was ineffective. Section 337 was, therefore, inapplicable to the condemnation gain. Taxpayers were liable as transferees because the distributions rendered the corporation insolvent. Fibel, 44 TC 647 (1965).

Recognition of loss allowed on sale of government securities in anticipation of the adoption of a plan of liquidation. On May 26, 1959, taxpayer sold certain government securities at a loss, anticipating that a plan of liquidation would soon be adopted. On May 29, 1959, taxpayer's stockholders adopted a plan of liquidation and a resolution approving the sale of taxpayer's assets. The adoption of such plan was the goal of several months of activity and negotiations between taxpayer and the purchaser of its stock (another bank that waited to acquire the taxpayer's assets by purchase). These purchasers intended to liquidate taxpayer as soon as they had sufficient stock interest in taxpayer. The IRS asserted that the plan of liquidation was adopted both before the sale of such securities and before the plan was formally adopted by taxpayer's stockholders. Thus, the loss on the sale of securities was not recognized under Section 337. *Held:* For taxpayer. The general intent to liquidate does not constitute the adoption of a plan of liquidation. Accordingly, sales in anticipation that a plan of liquidation would be adopted, even if made to avoid falling within Section 337's "liquidation period," are not sales pursuant to a plan of liquidation. Further, where a plan of liquidation is formally adopted, the court is reluctant to examine the facts and circumstances to determine if such a plan had been informally adopted earlier. City Bank of Washington, 38 TC 713 (1962).

Section 337 applied to sale of assets preceding adoption of a plan of complete liquidation when both events occurred on the same day. On October 10, 1957, at an informal meeting, the corporation's stockholders executed documents with respect to a proposed sale of its assets; (1) a memorandum indicating buyer's offer was conditional to, among other things, the termination of a testamentary trust holding a majority interest in the corporation and liquidation of the corporation; (2) an agreement by all of the trust beneficiaries assenting to sale of the trust assets, liquidation of the corporation, and termination of the trust; and (3) an agreement by the trust's trustees agreeing to termination of the trust. On October 21, 1957, at a special stockholder's meeting, the buyer's offer was accepted. The buyer paid for the assets, the corporation executed a bill of sale, and, finally, the corporation adopted a plan of liquidation. The corporation suffered a loss on the sale of its assets and claimed the loss on its final return. The IRS claimed that, under Section 337, the loss should not have been recognized. *Held:* For the IRS. The sale of assets occurred on October 21st, since the sale was conditioned upon events that did not occur until that date. Even though the sale of assets preceded adoption of the liquidation plan, both occurred on the same day. Under Section 337, it is not necessary to consider the exact time of day on which such events occur. Accordingly, Section 337 applies to a sale that precedes adoption of a liquidation plan when both occur on the same day. Adams, 38 TC 549 (1962).

Stockholders held to be selling parties of corporate assets. Taxpayers, sole stockholders of a corporation, received assets distributed in liquidation and sold them in an installment sale. Taxpayers reported capital gain and interest income from the payments in the first year after the sale, but not in subsequent years. The IRS assessed deficiencies for the unreported amounts. Taxpayers argued that the corporation was the seller and that the corporation's net operating losses offset the income from the sale. *Held:* For the IRS. The form of the transaction identifies taxpayers as the sellers of the assets. Furthermore, the cor-

LIQUIDATIONS: *Twelve-Month Liquidations—Sale of Assets*

poration was not a sham. Taxpayers may not offset the income from the installment sale by the corporation's net operating losses. Stamler, 49 TCM 972, ¶ 85,119 P-H Memo. TC (1985).

Sale and liquidation qualify for nonrecognition of gain. W owned two thirds of A Corporation (taxpayer) and B Corporation. M owned the other third of each corporation. A leased land, buildings, and fixtures to B. In June 1959, W exchanged his interest in B for M's interest in A. Then A sold all its assets to B for promissory notes in the amount of $167,000. Some time prior to August 1959, A was liquidated, and its assets were distributed to W, who transferred these assets (the notes) to newly formed C Corporation. The IRS determined a deficiency in A's return based on its failure to recognize gain on the sale of all of its assets. *Held:* For taxpayer. The transaction was not a Section 368 reorganization as the IRS asserted, but a sale and liquidation within 12 months of the adoption of a plan under Section 337. The mere fact that the proceeds of the sale of the assets of A found their way into C, which was owned by the same stockholder, did not deprive A of the nonrecognition benefits of Section 337. Workman, 36 TCM 1534, ¶ 77,378 P-H Memo. TC (1977).

Section 337 complied with by informal plan and equitable assignment of note. Taxpayer sold all of its assets, except cash, in return for a note. Taxpayer's president and sole stockholder directed that payments on the note be made to him. He subsequently received all of the taxpayer's cash within 12 months of the liquidation. The IRS contended that Section 337 was not available, either because there was no plan of liquidation or because all assets were not distributed within 12 months, as the note was never formally assigned to taxpayer's president. *Held:* For taxpayer. There was an informal plan to liquidate and an equitable assignment of the note under state law. Since all assets were sold or distributed and there was no intention of using taxpayer's corporate form in the future, Section 337 applied. Badias & Seijas, 36 TCM 518, ¶ 77,118 P-H Memo. TC (1977).

Sale of assets followed by liquidation within 12 months was not an F reorganization. Taxpayer corporation was controlled by the Cuneo family. Both Cuneo and taxpayer controlled Middle States, which was completely liquidated pursuant to Section 337. In the course of the liquidation, Middle States sold some of its improved realty to a third corporation, Milwaukee, which was owned by Cuneo's wife and two family trusts and was engaged in a shopping center development. The IRS contended that the gain realized by Middle States did not qualify under the nonrecognition provisions of Section 337, and that the "liquidating" distributions by Middle States to its stockholders had to be treated as taxable "boot" received in an F reorganization (a mere change in form or identity). *Held:* For taxpayers. The sale of assets of Milwaukee and the liquidation of Middle States did not constitute an F reorganization. The requisite continuity of ownership and business activity was absent. After the liquidation, Milwaukee was no longer chiefly engaged in the shopping center business. Assets amounting to less than one-half the value of Middle State's operating assets were transferred to the new corporation. Book Prod. Ind., Inc., 24 TCM 339, ¶ 65,065 P-H Memo. TC (1965).

Advance royalty payment treated as a sale or exchange under Section 337. After adopting a plan of complete liquidation under Section 337, taxpayer received an advance royalty for coal to be mined. For tax years beginning in 1977, Section 671(c) treats such royalties as received in payment for the sale of coal. Therefore, the IRS ruled that such royalties are protected from recognition of gain under Section 337(a). Rev. Rul. 77-109, 1977-1 CB 87.

Sale to a 50 percent stockholder qualified under Section 337. No gain or loss was recognized in an arm's-length sale of a corporation's assets to a corporate stockholder who owned 50 percent of the shares, as provided for in a liquidation plan adopted because of irreconcilable differences between the purchasing and other stockholders, followed by a pro rata distribution of the sale proceeds to

LIQUIDATIONS: *Twelve-Month Liquidations—Sale of Assets*

all stockholders. Rev. Rul. 73-551, 1973-2 CB 112.

IRS modifies ruling that implied nonapplicability of Section 337 where stockholders would have nontaxable distributions. Following the enactment of Section 337, the IRS held in Rev. Rul. 56-387, 1956-2 CB 189, that the new statute did not apply where the entire proceeds from the sale of a bankrupt corporation's assets were distributed to creditors. That position was modified to remove any implication that nonrecognition of gain or loss to the corporation applies only if the liquidating distribution results in a tax at the stockholder level. Rev. Rul. 73-264, 1973-1 CB 178.

Stockholders' retention of interest in assets sold to new corporation by liquidating corporation made transactions taxable. A corporation sold within a 12-month period following the adoption of a complete liquidation plan sold substantially all of its assets to a new corporation formed by the management of the seller. The new corporation paid $18,000, consisting of $2,025 of its own stock (equal to 45 percent of issued stock), $4,975 in long-term notes, and $11,000 in cash. The new company immediately sold its remaining shares (55 percent) to the public through underwriters. The old company then completely liquidated, distributing its assets (the proceeds of the sale to the new corporation) to its stockholders after paying certain liabilities. The IRS disregarded the issuance to new investors of 55 percent of the new company's stock and considered it as a separate transaction from what was essentially a reorganization. It reasoned that the transaction was a device to withdraw corporate earnings at capital gain rates by distributing all of the old company's assets in complete liquidation and promptly re-incorporating them. There was no reality to the Section 337 "sale" of assets or to the "liquidation," since each was a step in reorganizing the old company. The new company was utilized to effect, in substance, a recapitalization and change in identity simultaneous with a withdrawal of the old company's accumulated earnings for the benefit of its stockholders, who maintained a substantial and continuing equity interest. Consequently, there was no Section 337 liquidation and sale of assets. There was a tax-free reorganization, and the new corporation took over the "purchased" assets at their basis to the old. The stockholders received a dividend in the amount of the assets distributed to them in liquidation. The IRS concluded that this ruling would not be applied retroactively to transactions consummated prior to August 21, 1961. Rev. Rul. 61-156, 1961-2 CB 62.

No gain recognized on sale of emergency facility during 12-month liquidation. The Code permits a taxpayer to amortize emergency facilities through deductions over a 60-month period. In case of a sale of such facilities, it provides that to the extent the adjusted basis is less than it would have been if only depreciation deductions had been taken, any gain is ordinary income. The IRS here considered the case of a sale of such property by a corporation that had elected to liquidate within 12 months under Section 337. That section excludes from tax any gain on the sale of corporate property during that period. The IRS ruled that there would be no recognition of any gain even on emergency facilities since the facility qualifies as property under that section. Rev. Rul. 59-308, 1959-2 CB 110.

Income realized on sale of discounted notes despite Section 337 election. A cash-basis corporation adopted a plan of complete liquidation under Section 337 (no gain on sale of assets within 12 months of liquidation) and sold all of its assets, including discounted notes. It was ruled to have realized ordinary income on gain from the sale of the notes; the gain represented interest income earned but not received by the corporation at the time of the sale. The IRS pointed out that if taxpayer did not report this income, it would escape tax in the hands of the buyer, who would report only that accrued after purchase. Section 337 was intended to defer tax on appreciation, not on ordinary accruals. Rev. Rul. 59-120, 1959-1 CB 74.

Liquidation occurred within 12 months despite prior sale of assets. A publicly owned corporation sold a separate business division in

1954 at a time when liquidation was not contemplated. During 1955, the officers and directors decided to dispose of the remaining assets and business and liquidate the corporation completely. The stockholders adopted a resolution to that effect on December 15, 1955. For purposes of Section 337, the IRS ruled that the corporation could liquidate within 12 months after December 5, 1955, the date on which the stockholders adopted the plan of liquidation, without realizing any gain or loss on the subsequent sale. The sales in 1954 were not in accord with any formal or informal plan of liquidation; therefore the 12-month period was measured from the date of adoption of the plan. Rev. Rul. 57-140, 1957-1 CB 118.

Gain recognized on sale of bankrupt's assets. The IRS ruled that Section 337, relating to nonrecognition of gain to a corporation upon a sale of its assets followed by a complete liquidation within 12 months, would not be applicable to the gain from the sale of a bankrupt's assets ordered by a court. All the assets would be distributed to creditors, and the stockholders would receive nothing in the liquidation. Rev. Rul. 56-387, 1956-2 CB 189.

Twelve-Month Liquidations—Sale of Contracts

Contract income taxable despite Section 337 sale. Taxpayer was a cash-basis construction company. It decided to liquidate under Section 337 and sold a particular contract to a real estate agent. All the work was done, but $327,000 was unpaid. The IRS argued that the proceeds of the sale of the contract must be treated as ordinary income to clearly reflect taxpayer's income in the year of liquidation. The Tax Court held that the contract was property, that it qualified under the provisions of Section 337 as a sale of an asset in complete liquidation within a 12-month period, and that therefore the gain should not be recognized. *Held:* Reversed. The appellate court agreed with the IRS' contention that income was not clearly reflected. The allocation of income to partially completed contracts assigned to stockholders was also approved, and the stockholders were held liable as transferees. Kuckenberg, 309 F2d 202, 62-2 USTC ¶ 9768, 10 AFTR2d 5758 (9th Cir. 1962), cert. denied, 373 US 909 (1963).

IRS ruled on liquidations involving transfer of unperformed service contracts. A corporation engaged in the mortgage banking business that was not a collapsible corporation as defined in Section 341(b) sold all of its assets to a commercial banking corporation for $400x and distributed the entire proceeds to its stockholders in complete liquidation pursuant to the terms of Section 337. In connection with and as part of the sale, the purchasing corporation paid $47x for the right to service real estate mortgage contracts. At the time of the sale, no services had been performed by the selling corporation, and thus no income had been earned by it with respect to these contracts. In response to an inquiry as to whether the selling corporation qualified under Section 337, the IRS held that mortgage servicing rights were property under Section 337. In so holding, the IRS indicated that only those types of property expressly excluded by Section 337(b) would fall outside of the definition of "property" as used therein. The IRS specifically renounced its previous contention that the term "property" was synonymous with the term "capital asset" contained in Section 1221. Rev. Rul. 77-190, 1977-1 CB 88.

Twelve-Month Liquidations—Sale of Inventory

Liquidating corporation had to recognize gain on inventory, since disposition did not occur in one transaction. Taxpayer corporation, engaged in real estate development, adopted a plan of liquidation. Three days later, it entered into an agreement with X to purchase its inventory of 38 lots. Taxpayer argued that pursuant to Section 337(a)(2), no gain should be recognized on such a disposition. The IRS and the Tax Court held that gain should be recognized, since this transaction constituted a piecemeal disposition of inventory. *Held:* Affirmed. The agreement with X did not qualify as a disposition of inventory to one purchaser in one transaction as required by Section 337(b)(2). The agreement was merely

LIQUIDATIONS: *Twelve-Month Liquidations—Sale of Inventory*

on executory contract, since legal title to a given lot was not transferred until it was selected and paid for. Bear, 650 F2d 1167, 81-2 USTC ¶ 9489, 48 AFTR2d 81-5236 (10th Cir. 1981).

Section 337 applied although part of inventory unsold to meet claims. Sales of inventory do not qualify for nonrecognition of gain under Section 337 unless the sale is in bulk. At the time of entering into a plan of liquidation, taxpayer corporation had two parcels of land for development. A purchaser had placed a deposit on one parcel. The other parcel was sold in a single transaction. After first finding that the corporation was a dealer in real estate and held both parcels as inventory, the district court considered whether the sale of the lots was a sale in bulk of substantially all of its inventory. It concluded that it was not but was subject to a contract to sell. *Held:* Reversed. The parcel subject to a contract to sell was property subject to claims. Section 337 permits the retention of property to pay claims. The court read this as an exception to the rule that substantially all inventory must be sold in bulk, permitting nonrecognition where inventory is retained to meet claims. Jeanese, Inc., 341 F2d 502, 65-1 USTC ¶ 9259, 15 AFTR2d 429 (9th Cir. 1965).

Jury found liquidation plan preceded sale. At issue in this case was the factual question of whether a plan of liquidation was adopted before the sale of assets so that gain on the sale would not be recognized under Section 337. The stockholder resolution apparently was passed after the sale. The court instructed the jury that it could consider that fact, but could also conclude, if it found that stockholders owning two thirds of the stock had previously formed the intent to liquidate and had a plan to that effect, that the plan was adopted when the intent was formed. *Held:* For taxpayer. The jury found that the plan of liquidation preceded the sale. Bloomington Hotel Co., 65-1 USTC ¶ 9283, 15 AFTR2d 741 (SD Ill. 1965).

Recognition of loss allowed on accrual basis taxpayer's sale of accounts receivable within 12-month period following adoption of Section 337 liquidation plan. Taxpayer adopted a plan of liquidation and sold its assets and distributed the proceeds within 12 months of the adoption of the plan. Among the assets sold were accounts receivable for the sale of inventory, which taxpayer, under the accrual method, included in income at face value. In the sale of its assets, the negotiated price of the receivables was less than their face value. Taxpayer claimed that the loss on the receivables should be recognized notwithstanding the application of Section 337 to its liquidation. The IRS disagreed. *Held:* For taxpayer. Section 337 does not apply to installment obligations arising from the sale of inventory. Installment obligations for this purpose include accounts receivable, and are not, as the IRS argued, limited solely to obligations under Section 453. Further, Section 337 was not intended to apply to income or loss arising from sales made in the ordinary course of business. The sales of these receivables came within this rule. Coast Coil Co., 50 TC 528 (1968).

Sale of work-in-process inventory in Section 337 liquidation qualified for nonrecognition. Taxpayer, engaged in the custom manufacture of tools, adopted a plan of liquidation pursuant to Section 337. One of taxpayer's employees promoted a new corporation to acquire the assets of taxpayer. The sale contract provided that the buyer would complete all orders in process. Upon completion of the orders, the buyer was to divide the proceeds between taxpayer and buyer in proportion to relative costs incurred. Many of the orders required four to five months for completion. Taxpayer excluded the proceeds from these orders under Section 337(b)(2) as a sale in a single transaction with one person. The IRS determined that a joint venture existed and that the proceeds were income to taxpayer. *Held:* For taxpayer. The sale qualified for nonrecognition. Taxpayer intended to sell the work-in-process inventory to the new corporation. Since this buyer needed its remaining funds for operations, taxpayer was willing to wait for payment until the buyer completed the orders. Luff Co., 44 TC 532 (1965).

LIQUIDATIONS: *Twelve-Month Liquidations—Sale of Receivables*

Noninventoried supplies deductible despite subsequent year's sale pursuant to Section 337. On January 2, 1958, a partnership engaged in the truck leasing business transferred its assets to taxpayer corporation, which continued the business. Taxpayer was on the accrual basis but kept no inventory of supplies (e.g., tires, tubes, parts, gas). Such items were expensed in full when acquired. On January 2, 1959, taxpayer's stockholders adopted a plan of complete liquidation pursuant to Section 337 and arranged for the sale of the corporate assets. The contract of sale specifically set forth prices for gasoline, tires, and supplies. The IRS set up a closing inventory for these items in its 1958 audit, offsetting deductions taken for them. *Held:* For taxpayer. The Tax Court held that no inventory of supplies was necessary. The regulations provide that inventories are necessary if merchandise is an income-producing factor. As taxpayer did not purchase the supplies for resale or in abnormal quantity, the regulations did not apply. The IRS could not upset taxpayer's method of accounting, which clearly reflected income for 1958, merely because taxpayer would have an advantage from it in 1959. The IRS' attack should have been directed at 1959. The court also allowed 95 percent of the cost of operating a car used by taxpayer's president in furthering taxpayer's business. Smith Leasing Co., 43 TC 37 (1964), acq. 1965-2 CB 6.

Lower price for a portion of inventory did not constitute second sale. Taxpayer corporation entered into an agreement to sell its entire inventory, claiming the sale was not taxable under Section 337(b)(2). The IRS argued that more than one sale took place since the buyer paid a lower price for some of the items. *Held:* For taxpayer. Since those items were produced between the signing and closing of the agreement, they could not be inspected for price determination. The later price determined for them later was adequately explained. Stokes, 45 TCM 1415, ¶ 83,229 P-H Memo. TC (1983).

Twelve-Month Liquidations—Sale of Receivables

Loss on accounts receivable allowed to a corporation liquidating under Section 337. Taxpayer corporation adopted a plan of liquidation pursuant to Section 337. It sold its trade accounts and notes receivable within the 12-month period. It sustained and claimed a loss on the sale. The IRS disallowed the loss, and the Tax Court held for taxpayer. *Held:* Affirmed. The sale of the receivables amounted to a loss on an installment obligation; hence, it qualified for loss recognition under Section 337(b)(1)(B). Although a taxpayer does not report by the installment method, this does not imply that the trade accounts and notes receivable are not "installment obligations" as that term is used in Section 337(b)(1)(B). The latter section's intent is much broader than that of Section 453. Liberty Nat'l Bank & Trust Co., 650 F2d 1174, 81-2 USTC ¶ 9487, 48 AFTR2d 81-5239 (10th Cir. 1981).

Receivables sold under Section 337 result in recognition of gain. A cash-basis corporation adopted a plan of complete liquidation. It sold its assets, including notes and accounts receivable, receiving therefore two promissory notes of the buyer. It then distributed the notes to its stockholders in complete liquidation within 12 months after adoption of the plan. The IRS contended that the corporation realized ordinary income in conveying the accounts and notes receivable to the buyer in return for the promissory notes. *Held:* For the IRS. Such income is not non-recognizable under Section 337, since accounts and notes receivable are considered "installment obligations" and not "property" within the meaning of Section 337(b)(1). Wimp, 20 TCM 1790, ¶ 61,342 P-H Memo. TC (1961).

IRS ruled on tax results where liquidation involved receivables. The IRS held that pursuant to a plan of complete liquidation under Section 337, the sale of accounts receivable by a corporation that had used the accrual method of accounting and the reserve method of treating bad debts from which it had received a tax benefit results in income to the extent that the amount received exceeds the face amount of the receivables less the

LIQUIDATIONS: *Unused Bad Debt Reserve*

amount of the reserve for bad debts. The IRS noted that the burden is on taxpayer to show that the amount received in excess of the net value of the accounts receivable is not a recovery of a tax benefit, but is attributable to economic factors such as appreciation in value of interest-bearing accounts receivable resulting from changes in prevailing interest rates. Rev. Rul. 78-279, 1978-2 CB 135.

IRS examined tax results from bad debt reserve adjustments necessitated by transfer of receivables in complete liquidations. The IRS ruled that a complete liquidation, to which Sections 332(a) and 336 apply, of a subsidiary that used the accrual method of accounting and the reserve method of treating bad debts results in income to the liquidating corporation. The amount to be recognized is equal to the extent that the fair market value of accounts receivable, the basis of which exceeds the face amount of the receivables less the amount of the reserve for bad debts, additions to which had resulted in tax benefits in prior years. This is so where the basis of accounts receivable in the hands of the transferee determined under Section 334(b)(2) is equal to its fair market value. Rev. Rul. 78-278, 1978-2 CB 134.

Unused Bad Debt Reserve

Entire bad debt reserve includible in income in year of sale. Taxpayer corporation, which was on the accrual basis, pursuant to a plan of liquidation under Section 337 sold its installment loan receivables. Of the $164,311 in the bad debt reserve, taxpayer contended that it had recovered only $64,777 and that only this amount should be included in income in the year of the sale. Taxpayer argued that the remaining $99,534 was not recovered because the selling price had been reduced by this amount, and therefore no tax benefit was received. The district court held that only $64,777 was recovered. *Held:* Reversed. Unlike the fact situation of Nash, 398 US 1 (1970), taxpayer did not receive consideration equal to the net amount of the receivables transferred. In this case, taxpayer received $4,648,523 for its receivables, an amount which was $435,260 more than what taxpayer conceded to be their net value. Thus, the entire reserve of $164,311 was included. Citizens Acceptance Corp., 462 F2d 751, 72-2 USTC ¶ 9510, 29 AFTR2d 72-1441 (3d Cir. 1972).

Unused reserve for bad debts is income at liquidation. Taxpayer, a banking corporation, sold its assets and liquidated within one year under Section 337. The Tax Court ruled that taxpayer must report income of $19,000, representing the balance of its bad debt reserve. *Held:* Affirmed. The court noted the general rule that the balance of a bad debt reserve is taxable in the year in which the need for the reserve ceases. Taxpayer's argument that Section 337 prevents taxation of the reserve was rejected. The court ruled that Section 337 merely precludes taxing to a liquidating corporation the gain on the sale of its assets. The reserve was not transferred to the purchasing bank, and none of the consideration received was attributable to the reserve. West Seattle Nat'l Bank, 288 F2d 47, 61-1 USTC ¶ 9281, 7 AFTR2d 790 (9th Cir. 1961).

The Tax Court upheld IRS' characterization of balance in reserve for bad debts when the taxpayer sold its assets as ordinary income. Taxpayer was a corporation that manufactured and distributed shade cloth products. Under a plan of complete liquidation, taxpayer sold substantially all of its assets (notes and accounts receivable) for a price equal to the face value less the balance contained in its reserve for bad debts. The IRS determined that the balance in the reserve for bad debts at the time of the sale constituted ordinary income, arguing that taxpayer's need for maintaining the reserve had ceased upon disposition of the accounts receivable. *Held:* For the IRS. The court stated that any balance in a reserve for bad debts existing when the reserve becomes unnecessary must be included in taxable income because the balance represents amounts that had already been deducted. The court rejected taxpayer's contention that the amount of the reserve to income could be restored only if the amount that was previously deducted was recovered and only to the extent that the receivables were sold at a sum above the face value less the amount of the reserve. J.E. Hawes Corp., 44 TC 705 (1965).

LOANS

(*See* Bad Debts; Bonds and Debentures; Cancellation of Indebtedness; Dividends and Distributions—Loans Distinguished)

LOSS CORPORATIONS

(*See* Acquisitions to Avoid Tax; Consolidated Returns; Net Operating Losses)

LOSSES

(*See also* Bad Debts; Business Expenses; Capital Gains and Losses; Net Operating Losses)

Parent permitted deduction for worthlessness of subsidiary whose only asset was tax losses. Taxpayer's wholly owned subsidiary incurred very large losses. Finally, the creditors foreclosed, leaving taxpayer with a corporate shell whose only "asset" was its huge tax losses. In the year of foreclosure (1959), neither taxpayer nor the subsidiary had plans to start, acquire, or merge with a profitable business whose income could be offset by these losses. In 1960, the subsidiary was merged with a profitable corporation, and its losses were used to offset the income from the merged enterprise. For the tax year 1959, taxpayer claimed a loss for its worthless stock and debt in the subsidiary. The IRS disallowed this loss. *Held:* For taxpayer. The value of the shell's tax losses was too tenuous to prevent a deduction for the worthlessness of its stock. Textron, Inc., 561 F2d 1023, 77-2 USTC ¶ 9539, 40 AFTR2d 77-5452 (1st Cir. 1977).

Ordinary loss allowed on securities loaned to bankrupt firm. Taxpayer claimed ordinary loss on securities loaned to an investment corporation to help it meet its capital requirements. The corporation had sold the securities and gone into bankruptcy; taxpayer was not a stockholder of such firm. The district court found for taxpayer. *Held:* Affirmed. The agreement between taxpayer and the securities firm was not a debtor-creditor relationship, but a bailment; it allowed the loss as one incurred in a transaction entered into for profit. Stahl, 441 F2d 999, 70-2 USTC ¶ 9714, 26 AFTR2d 70-5823 (DC Cir. 1970).

Case remanded to determine if worthless stock resulted in ordinary loss as affiliated corporation securities. The Tax Court decided that net advances made by taxpayers to a corporation were capital contributions, not loans. Thus, when the advances became worthless in 1962, capital losses (Section 165(g)(1)), not business bad debts (Section 166(a)), resulted. *Held:* Remanded to determine if the advances resulted in an ordinary loss under Section 165(g)(3) (securities in affiliated corporation). Inness, 413 F2d 290, 69-2 USTC ¶ 9472 (5th Cir. 1969).

Year of loss determined to be year in which no further payments could be expected. Taxpayers were stockholders in an unsuccessful business corporation. At the end of 1954, the corporation ceased business activity. In 1955, most of the assets were sold, and $12,000 was distributed to taxpayers as liquidating payments. In early 1956, payments of $2,700 were made, and in December of that year, an additional $400 was distributed. The corporation was dissolved in 1958. *Held:* Affirmed. The court affirmed the Tax Court's holding that the loss was not sustained in 1954 when business ceased but in 1956 when no further payments could be expected. Bodzy, 321 F2d 331, 63-2 USTC ¶ 9599, 12 AFTR2d 5166 (5th Cir. 1963).

Arms-length transaction with subsidiary produced allowable loss. Taxpayer, a building contractor, agreed to build an apartment house for its subsidiary at a price that was fair at the time of the contract. Subsequently, after performance, taxpayer discovered that the intervention of the Korean War, bad weather, and increased costs plus the addition of "extras" to the building caused actual construction cost to exceed the contract price. Taxpayer claimed a loss for the excessive cost. The IRS disallowed the loss. *Held:* For taxpayer, in part. The court found that the claimed loss was allowable, except for the extras, which were contributions to the capital of the subsidiary. Since the original price was equivalent to the existing market price at the time of the contract, any loss caused by intervening factors had to be allowed. Long Corp., 298 F2d 450, 62-1 USTC ¶ 9191 (Ct. Cl. 1962).

Stockholder's payment to other stockholder for share of losses of their corporation was deductible in full. Taxpayer was a stockholder in two corporations. He made a loan to one corporation and took notes of the other corporation. In connection with the liquidation of the first corporation, which was insolvent, taxpayer transferred part of the notes to the other stockholder and was released from further liability. *Held:* For taxpayer. The court held that this loss was incurred in a transaction entered into for profit and was deductible in full. The transfer was not in payment of taxpayer's liability as guarantor of the corporation's debts, but was in satisfaction of his own liability to the other stockholder for the losses of the corporation. Condit, 40 TC 24 (1963).

Stockholder was joint venturer with corporation; could deduct loss in paying for goods it used. Taxpayer obtained from a manufacturer a franchise to assemble and distribute merchandise. Taxpayer organized a corporation with two other individuals to conduct this business, was an officer and director, and devoted a substantial portion of his time to the corporation. The manufacturer invoiced the merchandise to taxpayer as an individual, but the corporation paid the amount of the invoice and conducted the business. Taxpayer sought to have the corporation billed directly, but the manufacturer would not consent. The corporation, which ultimately became insolvent, sued taxpayer and collected the balance due for merchandise invoiced to him. Taxpayer sought to deduct this amount in full as a loss under Section 165(c). The IRS contended that taxpayer suffered a nonbusiness bad debt, and that under Section 166(d)(1) he was limited to short-term capital loss treatment. *Held:* For taxpayer. The court held that taxpayer was the primary debtor of the manufacturer and that taxpayer and his corporation were, in a sense, joint venturers. Since the transaction was entered into for profit, the loss was deductible in full under Section 165(c). Horner, 35 TC 231 (1961), acq. 1961-2 CB 4.

Diversion of corporate funds by major stockholders not embezzlement. Five brothers were the officers and owners of five sixths of the stock of taxpayer corporation. Over a period of years, they diverted to themselves a substantial amount of corporate income and also charged taxpayer for fictitious purchases. Taxpayer, resisting income tax on the diverted income, argued that is was entitled to an embezzlement-loss deduction. *Held:* For the IRS. The Tax Court disallowed the deduction on the ground that the officer-stockholders did not have the requisite intent to steal from the corporation. Rather, they were interested primarily in reducing their taxes by diverting corporate income directly and secretly into their hands. The fact that the diversions may have constituted embezzlement under local law was immaterial; otherwise, stockholders could avoid corporate and individual taxes by diverting corporate funds and then claiming embezzlement if discovered. The fact that not all the stockholders participated was immaterial. Federbush, 34 TC 740 (1960).

Stockholder failed to establish loss on his contribution of stock to new management. Taxpayer was the principal stockholder in a closely held corporation that had been suffering losses. He contributed some of his stock to new managers who themselves donated $12,000 to the corporation as surplus. Taxpayer claimed a loss in the amount of the difference between his basis for the stock he gave to the new management and the proportionate interest of his remaining shares in the $12,000 donated surplus. *Held:* For the IRS. The Tax Court agreed that the case was similar to Wright, 47 F2d 871 (7th Cir. 1931), in which a loss was allowed on such a transaction. There, the basis of the stock surrendered was measured against its fair market value on the theory that the continuing stockholder believed that the benefits he would realize were at least equal to the value of the stock he surrendered. However, the court stated that the record here was barren of any showing of the value of the stock, and so it was unable to allow any loss. Sack, 33 TC 805 (1960).

Losses of corporation operating properties for partnership not attributed to stockholder-partners. As joint venturers, taxpayers owned mining subleases. They organized a financing corporation, United, and an operating corporation, Oscura. United acquired all of the stock of Oscura and advanced funds to the operating corporation that were used to construct a mill and to operate the mine. The amounts Oscura expended were transferred by journal entry to the books of the joint venture, which then claimed these expenditures as its own on the theory that Oscura was acting solely as agent for the joint venture. *Held:* For the IRS. The court found that no agency relationship could be established from the evidence, since United and Oscura engaged in carrying on business, but for tax purposes the corporations were separate entities from their incorporators. The court also found that checks drawn to the account of Oscura and deposited to the joint venture were payments to the venturers as stockholders. But since neither Oscura nor its parent, United, had any accumulated or current earnings and profits, the distribution was held applicable against the capital investment, which the court found to include alleged advances. The capital investment exceeded the amounts received, and thus no gain resulted from the distribution. Greer, 21 TCM 998, ¶ 62,182 P-H Memo. TC (1962).

MARKET VALUE

(*See* Valuation of Property)

MERGERS

(*See* Reorganizations)

MITIGATION

(*See* Procedure)

MULTIPLE CORPORATIONS

(*See* Affiliated Corporations)

NET OPERATING LOSSES

(*See also* Affiliated Corporations—Net Operating Loss Carry-Overs; Consolidated Returns—Net Operating Loss Carry-Overs; Reorganizations—Carry-Over of Net Operating Losses and Other Tax Attributes)

Carry-Back of Net Operating Loss 409
Carry-Forward of Net Operating
Loss 411
Loss Limitations 416

Carry-Back of Net Operating Loss

Court determined treatment of net operating loss carry-back to year in which alternative loss computation method was used. Taxpayer sought to carry back a net operating loss to a year in which it used the alternative method for determining its net operating loss. *Held:* For taxpayer. The excess of taxpayer's net operating loss for the later year over ordinary income in the earlier year may be carried forward, even though the earlier year's net operating loss was less than taxpayer's ordinary income and capital gain in the earlier year. Olympic Foundry Co., 493 F2d 1247, 74-1 USTC ¶ 9230, 33 AFTR2d 74-700 (9th Cir. 1984).

Net operating loss carry-back from year under audit could be offset against earlier year's deficiency. Taxpayer petitioned the Tax Court to review deficiencies assessed by the IRS for 1958 and 1959. When the case was called to trial in the Tax Court, taxpayer consented in a stipulation that the deficiencies were correct, but that a net operating loss incurred in 1962 should be used to offset the deficiency of 1959. The IRS indicated that the 1962 return was currently under examination, and

Net Operating Losses: *Carry-Back of Net Operating Loss*

that therefore the net operating loss could not be properly placed before the court. The Tax Court held that it could not consider a matter on which the IRS had not made a determination. The court reasoned that it was established to provide a tribunal in which taxpayers could contest a final adverse action of the IRS. *Held:* Reversed. The decision of the Tax Court was reversed on the uncontested motion of taxpayer that the decision was not in accordance with the law. Yellow Cab Co., 65-2 USTC ¶ 9568, 16 AFTR2d 5457 (7th Cir. 1965).

Taxpayer was not permitted to carry over net operating loss resulting from payment of unreasonable salary. A corporation was operating at a net operating loss when it paid sums to its officers. The IRS disallowed the carry-back of the net operating loss to the corporation. At issue was the reasonableness of the salaries paid to the officers and the corresponding deduction of a net operating loss. *Held:* For the IRS. The net operating loss carry-back was denied to the corporation because it resulted from deductions for unreasonable compensation paid to officers. The determination that the amounts were unreasonable was an issue to be decided by the jury. Equipment Rental Co., 70-2 USTC ¶ 9542, 25 AFTR2d 70-1077 (WD Ky. 1970).

Loss carry-back not barred by statute of limitations. Taxpayer was the transferee of the assets of a corporation. In 1970, the corporation realized a net operating loss that was carried back to 1968. The corporation received a refund. The IRS subsequently disallowed the loss carry-back. The taxpayer transferee repaid all but $9,349 of the erroneous refund and claimed that the corporation was entitled to a loss carry-back from 1971 to 1968, and that $9,349 represented the amount of taxes saved by such a carry-back. The IRS determined that the 1971 loss carry-back was not available since it was barred by the statute of limitations. *Held:* For taxpayer. The 1971 loss carry-back was admissible because it did not result in an overpayment by the corporation, but replaced the disallowed 1970 loss carry-back. Jones, 71 TC 391 (1978).

Net operating loss carry-back period computed. Taxpayer corporation carried back its 1970 calendar year net operating loss to its 1967 calendar year. The IRS disallowed the carry-back deduction in 1967. *Held:* For the IRS. Taxpayer filed a separate return for the period January 1, 1968 to June 30, 1968, and a consolidated return for the remainder of the 1968 calendar year with its acquiring parent. These two periods and the 1969 taxable year represented three taxable years. Since net operating loss carry-backs can only be applied against the three years preceeding the year of the loss, the 1970 net operating loss could not be carried back to 1967, the fourth preceeding year. Valley Paperback Mfrs., Inc., 34 TCM 1359, ¶ 75,311 P-H Memo. TC (1975).

Net operating loss carry-back disallowed where loss not established. Taxpayer transferred assets from two of his corporations to a third corporation and claimed operating losses on the transfer. The IRS disallowed the losses. *Held:* For the IRS. Since taxpayer's contention that the excess of liabilities over assets should be considered a loss was denied, and there was no determination of a loss either in a tax sense or in an economic sense, the loss deduction was properly disallowed. Petersen, 30 TCM 95, ¶ 71,021 P-H Memo. TC (1971).

Time-barred adjustments may be taken into account in determining overpayment from net operating loss carry-back. A corporation carried back its net operating loss to a year in which an unclaimed deduction was time-barred. In determining the amount of overpayment in the carry-back year, any barred adjustments decreasing taxable income are allowed only as counteradjustments to normally barred adjustments that increase taxable income. For purposes of a net operating loss carry-over from the first carry-over year, all adjustments to taxable income, whether time-barred or not, are considered. Rev. Rul. 81-88, 1981-1 CB 585.

Consolidated net operating loss and unused credit may not be carried back to newly formed corporation's subsidiaries. *P* Corporation was formed by unrelated interests for the purpose of acquiring two separate corporations, X and Y. P and its subsidiaries filed consolidated returns for subsequent years. A consolidated net operating loss and consolidated unused investment credit attributable to P and not to any assets or operations of X and Y could not be carried back to the separate return years of X and Y. Rev. Rul. 80-79, 1980-1 CB 191.

IRS ruled on tentative carry-back adjustments in the face of future deficiencies. In 1977, taxpayer had a net operating loss of $50x$ that was carried back to 1974. Taxpayer timely filed a complete Form 1139 (Corporation Application for Tentative Refund from Carry-back of Net Operating Loss) that contained no omissions or errors of computation. Tax of $100x$ was shown on the 1974 income tax return, but the IRS examined the 1974 return and determined a proposed deficiency of $200x$ that had not been assessed at the time the Form 1139 was filed. In addition, the 1974 return was under criminal investigation. It was also anticipated that a later examination of the 1977 return would eliminate the net operating loss. On these facts, the IRS held that where, as here, an application for a tentative refund from the carry-back of a net operating loss is timely filed on Form 1139 or Form 1045, it must be allowed, provided that the application contains no omissions or errors of computation, even though, in the year to which the loss was carried, a deficiency exceeding the amount of the tax plus the amount of the loss had been proposed. The taxpayer was therefore entitled to a credit or refund of the decrease in tax shown on the application even though the 90-day period described in Section 6411(b) had lapsed. Rev. Rul. 78-369, 1978-2 CB 324.

Carry-Forward of Net Operating Loss

Net operating loss carry-over denied where business inactive. The lower court upheld the IRS' determination that taxpayer corporation's 1960 net operating loss was not allowable as a carry-over deduction to 1963 because of Section 382(a). *Held:* Affirmed. Although taxpayer had mining income in the carry-over year (1963), at the time the change in ownership took place in May 1961, taxpayer had suspended its active business activities. Therefore, the carry-over was disallowed pursuant to Regulation § 1.382(a)-1(h)(6). On a related matter, depreciation taken on property prior to its transfer to taxpayer in a Section 351 transaction was to be recaptured by taxpayer on a subsequent sale pursuant to Section 1245. Six Seam Co., 524 F2d 347, 75-2 USTC ¶ 9765, 36 AFTR2d 75-6101 (6th Cir. 1975).

Net operating loss carry-overs of liquidated corporations limited by Section 382(b). The Tax Court held that reorganizations under Section 368 involving the acquisition of two corporations by taxpayer and the subsequent liquidation of those corporations under Section 332 were part of a serial set of transactions; therefore, net operating loss carry-forwards of the liquidated corporations were limited under Section 382. *Held:* Affirmed. The records indicated that the decision to liquidate could not be shown to have been made entirely apart from the initial decision to enter into statutory mergers. Resorts Int'l Inc., 511 F2d 107, 75-1 USTC ¶ 9405, 35 AFTR2d 75-1337 (5th Cir. 1975).

No disallowance of net operating loss carry-forwards where corporation was in substantially the same business. The district court held that taxpayer corporation, a real estate developer, continued to carry on the trade or business in substantially the same way as before a change in ownership; therefore, net operating loss carry-forwards were not subject to disallowance under Section 382(a). *Held:* Affirmed. Although there was a transfer of certain assets, the transfer was deemed to have merely reduced the corporation's operations rather than to have changed them; thus, there was no discontinuance within the meaning of Regulation § 1.382-1(h)(7). The court also stated that the principles of *Libson Shops* did not govern the continuance of business requirements of Section 382(a)(1)(C). Coast Quality Constr. Corp., 463 F2d 503, 72-2 USTC ¶ 9548, 30 AFTR2d 72-5144 (5th Cir. 1972).

Net Operating Losses: *Carry-Forward of Net Operating Loss*

Loss carry-forward disallowed where business and ownership changed. Taxpayer corporation terminated its lumber business and invested the proceeds from the sale of lumber assets in securities. A short time later, more than 50 percent of ownership changed. The year in which the operating assets were sold produced a loss. After carrying back a portion of the loss, taxpayer carried forward the balance to years after which the change in ownership had occurred and in which taxpayer corporation was engaged in investment activities. The district court allowed these carry-forwards, contending that the income tax regulations under Section 382, dealing with a change in business and change in ownership, were not applicable because they were not in effect either at the time of taxpayer's change in business or change in ownership. *Held:* Reversed. Section 7805 gives the Secretary of the Treasury the right to determine when regulations shall be applied retroactively. Therefore, since Regulation § 1.382(a)(1)-1(h)(4) was deemed valid, in order to be allowed the loss carry-forward, taxpayer corporation would have had to continue a trade or business that was substantially the same as the one conducted before the change. Such business did not have to be the one which produced the loss. Exel Corp., 451 F2d 80, 71-2 USTC ¶ 9731, 28 AFTR2d 71-5992 (8th Cir. 1971).

Net operating loss denied to discontinued business. Taxpayer corporation was engaged in the retail furniture business and sustained a net operating loss. All of its stock was sold to *X* Corporation, which also purchased control of another corporation, *Y*. Taxpayer sold all of its assets to *Y*, including its installment basis accounts receivable. Thereafter, taxpayer carried on no trade or business. Taxpayer claimed a net operating loss deduction, which it offset against income realized on the disposition of its installment receivables. The Tax Court held for the IRS. *Held:* Affirmed. Congress stated in Section 382(a) that a corporation that experiences a substantial change in its stock ownership may enjoy the benefit of its net operating loss carry-overs only if it continues to carry on substantially the same trade or business as that conducted before the change in ownership. When a corporation ceases business operations, it has not continued to carry on the same business; therefore, it is not entitled to deduct the net operating loss carry-over. SFH Inc., 444 F2d 139, 71-1 USTC ¶ 9454 (3d Cir.), cert. denied, 404 US 913 (1971).

Net operating loss carry-over of liquidated corporation deductible from profits earned after recapitalization. John Williams Buick Company was a corporate Buick dealer in Colorado that sustained net operating losses in 1953 and 1954. During those years, more than 50 percent of its outstanding stock was owned by a division of General Motors. The company was relatively inactive and in the process of liquidation from 1953 through 1955. In 1955, General Motors, then the sole stockholder, decided to continue as an investor instead of dissolving the corporation. It changed the name of the corporation to Jackson Oldsmobile, relocated it in Macon, Ga., and recapitalized it by selling a 40 percent stock interest to a new operator who was to operate the Oldsmobile dealership. In 1957, the outstanding stock ownership changed to 51 percent for General Motors and 49 percent for Jackson. In 1956 and 1957, Jackson Oldsmobile sought to deduct the net operating loss carry-over of the corporation from when it was a Buick dealership. The IRS relied on Sections 269 and 382 and *Libson Shops* to deny the deduction of the net operating loss carry-over. The district court allowed the carry-over. *Held:* Affirmed. Sections 269 and 382 were inapplicable, since General Motors owned more than 50% of the outstanding stock. Thus, there was no acquisition of control over taxpayer, and there had not been a change in the ownership of taxpayer's stock of at least 50 percentage points. The court distinguished *Libson Shops*, since the instant case concerned a single corporate taxpayer with continuity of majority stock ownership, which did not change the character of its business to a distinctly new and different endeavor. The court also held that there was no de facto liquidation. Jackson Oldsmobile, Inc., 371 F2d 808, 67-1 USTC ¶ 9231 (5th Cir. 1967).

NET OPERATING LOSSES: Carry-Forward of Net Operating Loss

Corporate entity denied net operating loss carry-over against income of new business. Taxpayer corporation was engaged in the business of mining and selling coal. After a change in stock ownership in 1951, it disposed of the operating assets of the coal mining business at a loss. It remained inactive until early 1953, when it acquired a business of manufacturing electric components. Taxpayer sought to carry over and deduct against its 1954 income the 1951 net operating loss. The Tax Court denied the carry-over. *Held:* Affirmed. In the interval between 1951 and 1954, there were radical changes in the business enterprise, including changes in the capital structure, location, management, type of stock ownership, and products, and even the name of the business. It therefore concluded that the 1954 income was not produced from substantially the same business as that that produced the 1951 loss; hence, there was no "continuity of business enterprise" as that phrase is used in the *Libson Shops* case. Norden-Ketay Corp., 319 F2d 902, 63-2 USTC ¶ 9575, 12 AFTR2d 5093 (2d Cir.), cert. denied, 375 US 953 (1963).

Loss carry-forward denied because of lack of continuity of business of single corporate taxpayer. A corporation in the hosiery business that suffered substantial losses in 1950, 1951, and 1952 ceased operations early in 1953 and for all practical purposes liquidated. It bought 348 of its 350 shares, which had been owned by its deceased manager, leaving control in the hands of one stockholder. Early in 1954, the sole stockholder amended the corporate charter and changed the corporation's name so that it could conduct an electrical heating and plumbing business that he had formerly conducted as a sole proprietorship. In 1954 and 1955, the new business prospered, and the corporation sought to deduct the losses of the hosiery business in prior years from the profits of the plumbing business. The IRS disallowed the claimed net operating loss carry-over. *Held:* For the IRS. Whether or not the sole stockholder acquired control of the corporation for the purpose of avoiding income tax by securing the benefit of a loss deduction he would not otherwise enjoy, the corporation was denied the deduction on the ground that the business that produced the income was not the same business that incurred the losses. The court cited Libson Shops, 353 US 382 (1943). Dudley Co., aff'd, 298 F2d 750, 62-1 USTC ¶ 9224 (4th Cir. 1962).

Net operating loss deduction that did not benefit current year could be carried over to subsequent year. Taxpayer corporation had net operating loss carry-overs and net operating loss carry-back in 1962. Although taxpayer's net long-term capital gain exceeded its taxable income for 1962, taxpayer still arrived at a lower tax liability by calculating its tax under the alternative method (Section 1201) instead of under the normal method, Section 11. Taxpayer contended that since its net operating loss carry-back and carry-overs were not used to reduce the income on which its 1962 tax was based, it should be permitted a loss carry-forward to 1963. *Held:* For taxpayer. Taxpayer received no benefit from the net operating loss carry-back and carry-forwards in 1962, since there was no ordinary income in the 1962 tax calculation. See Chartier Real Estate Co., 428 F2d 474 (1st Cir. 1970). Naegele, 383 F. Supp. 1041, 73-2 USTC ¶ 9696 (D. Minn. 1973).

Tax scheme barred net operating loss deduction upon subsidiary's liquidation. Taxpayer corporation sold over 70 percent of its subsidiary's stock under contracts, authorizing transfer of the stock back to taxpayer if the purchasers defaulted. All of the purchasers defaulted within one year, and taxpayer repossessed all of the stock. At the same time, taxpayer purchased other outstanding stock in order to acquire 80 percent control of the subsidiary. After liquidation of the subsidiary, taxpayer deducted the subsidiary's net operating loss carry-over. *Held:* For the IRS. Notwithstanding the applicability of Section 381, the net operating loss deduction had to be disallowed pursuant to Section 269. The repossession and the purchase of stock were not independent transactions, but were essentially unitary in concept and impact. Both transactions were part of a single plan that was intended to achieve 80 percent control. Taxpayer did not show that tax-avoidance

Net Operating Losses: *Carry-Forward of Net Operating Loss*

was not the principal purpose of the acquisition. Although the acquisition entitled taxpayer to the subsidiary's loss carry-over, the purpose of the acquisition barred the deduction. Swiss Colony, Inc., 52 TC 25 (1969), aff'd, 428 F2d 49, 70-1 USTC ¶ 9439 (7th Cir. 1970).

Two years of dormancy did not destroy net operating loss carry-over. Taxpayer corporation liquidated the assets it had used in an unprofitable enterprise and remained dormant for two years. It then embarked on a new, successful venture. The IRS argued that the corporation had in fact dissolved and thus could not use its net operating loss carry-overs. *Held:* For taxpayer. The Tax Court allowed the carry-overs on the ground that the corporation that incurred the losses and the one that earned the profits were the same. Rev. Rul. 63-40 specifically approves the use of a net operating loss carry-over by a corporation that has started a new business venture without a substantial change in ownership. Anbaco-Emig, 49 TC 100 (1968), acq. 1968-2 CB 1.

Revived tire company allowed net operating loss carry-forward. Taxpayer, a corporation manufacturing rubber tires, suspended operations after suffering financial setbacks. Taxpayer leased its plant to another large tire company and used the rents to improve credit conditions. The lease included an option to purchase taxpayer's capital stock. The lessee exercised this option. Under new ownership, taxpayer resumed production of rubber tires. The IRS denied the net operating loss carry-forward from the years that the plant was leased. *Held:* For taxpayer. The net operating loss deduction was allowable. Section 269 provides that a deduction is not allowable if the principal purpose of an acquisition is tax-avoidance. The principal purpose of the acquisition was market expansion. The transaction did not violate Section 382 because the same business continued. The time during which taxpayer leased its assets was not a period of inactivity. Since the transaction fell within the scope of Section 382, the *Libson Shops* doctrine was inapplicable. Clarksdale Rubber Co., 45 TC 234 (1965).

No deduction for subsidiary's net operating loss that accrued prior to its acquisition. Shortly after taxpayer's predecessor acquired the stock of a subsidiary that had substantial net operating loss carry-overs, the subsidiary filed for bankruptcy. When the subsidiary's reorganization plan was confirmed, taxpayer and its predecessor advanced funds to it, and kept it in business for approximately two years. Taxpayer then liquidated the subsidiary into itself and claimed deductions for the subsidiary's net operating loss carry-overs. The IRS determined that taxpayer was not entitled to claim any portion of the net operating losses because the subsidiary was not solvent on the date of its liquidation and the purchase of the subsidiary's stock by taxpayer's predecessor was motivated by tax-avoidance considerations. *Held:* For the IRS, in part. Taxpayer's and its predecessor's advances to the subsidiary constituted equity, not debt, because neither taxpayer nor its predecessor intended to form a true debtor-creditor relationship with the subsidiary. Because of these advances, the court found that the subsidiary was solvent on the date of its liquidation. Accordingly, the liquidation qualified under Sections 332 and 334(b)(1). Therefore, taxpayer was not precluded by Section 381(a) from claiming the subsidiary's net operating losses. However, because it was clear that the acquisition of the subsidiary's stock by taxpayer's predecessor was principally motivated by tax-avoidance considerations, Section 269 precluded taxpayer from deducting any losses that accrued to the subsidiary prior to the acquisition. Only the losses that were economically sustained by the subsidiary after its acquisition were deductible by taxpayer. Inductotherm Indus., Inc., 48 TCM 167, ¶ 84,281 P-H Memo. TC (1984), aff'd (3d Cir. 1985).

Net operating loss carry-over and loss on sale of stock disallowed. Taxpayer, president of a sales company, also owned stock in his family's department store. The store went out of business, and taxpayer decided to merge it into the sales company to take advantage of the store's net operating loss. At this time, he sold his shares in the store to the sales company for a loss. The IRS disallowed the net operating loss carry-over. *Held:* For the IRS. Section 269 disallows the use of the net operating loss carry-over. Taxpayer didn't attempt to revitalize the department store, so tax avoidance was the principal purpose of acquiring control of the store. Section 267 denies the loss on the sale of stock on the grounds of taxpayer's 100 percent ownership of the purchaser. In addition, the IRS found constructive dividends for corporate payments of individual expenses, and deductions were disallowed for lack of substantiation. Snyder, 47 TCM 355, ¶ 83,692 P-H Memo. TC (1983).

Acceleration of income to offset net operating loss carry-over disallowed. Taxpayer corporation had a large net operating loss carry-over that was about to expire in 1966. On the last day of 1966, it entered into an agreement to sell certain future revenues to tax-exempt organizations for some $1.3 million and reported the amount as income in 1966. The IRS claimed that the payments should have been included in income in 1967. *Held:* For the IRS. No sale of future revenues had taken place and the attempt to assign future income was ineffective. Therefore, the $1.3 million was income to taxpayer in 1967. Hydrometals, Inc., 31 TCM 1260, ¶ 72,254 P-H Memo. TC (1972).

Net operating loss carry-overs denied where nature of business changed. Taxpayer corporation had been engaged in the construction business. As a natural accompanying activity, it rented out unused equipment. In 1960, it sold the equipment, acquired river barges, and rented them. During 1959 and 1960, certain individuals had acquired more than 50 percentage points of the fair market value of taxpayer's outstanding stock. The IRS disallowed the carry-over of earlier net operating losses to 1960 and 1961. *Held:* For the IRS. There was nothing to show that taxpayer ever intended to be in the rental business when it was formed, and its rental activities were only an offshoot of its construction business. In 1960, taxpayer was no longer in the construction line, but in a different business. Rentals and the carry-over deductions were disallowed under Section 382(a)(1)(C). The Clare Co., 28 TCM 1348, ¶ 69,264 P-H Memo. TC (1969).

Charitable contributions carry-over increased net operating loss and could not be carried over. In 1972, taxpayer corporation had excess contributions and a net operating loss. In 1973, the corporation had taxable income without regard to charitable contributions or the net operating loss deduction, which was less than the net operating loss carry-over from 1972, and, therefore, had no taxable income. As a result, no contribution deduction was allowed in 1973, since such a deduction is limited to 5 percent of taxable income. In order to compute its net operating loss carry-over to 1974, the corporation had to take into account contributions actually made in 1973 and the carry-over from 1972. Accordingly, those amounts were subtracted from taxable income in 1973 without regard to net operating loss or any other such contributions to arrive at a taxable income that was subtracted from the net operating loss carry-over from 1972. The result was a net operating loss carry-over to 1974 that had been increased by the contributions taken into account. Rev. Rul. 76-145, 1976-1 CB 68.

Net operating loss carry-over permitted where stock ownership increased. Where a corporation purchased 25 percent of a second corporation's stock over a four-year period and then acquired from the second corporation enough stock to increase its ownership to 85 percent by exchanging property for the stock, the later stock acquisition was a Section 351 transaction and was not a purchase for the purposes of Section 382(a)(4). Therefore, the net operating loss of the second corporation could be carried over to the first corporation. Rev. Rul. 75-248, 1975-1 CB 125.

Corporation could not offset net operating loss against income of acquired sole proprietorship. A corporation acquired a sole proprietorship and assumed its income tax liability. The new corporation suffered a net operating loss during its first year of operation. The corporation could not carry back its loss against the net income of the sole proprietor-

Net Operating Losses: *Loss Limitations*

ship. (ARR 1597 superseded.) Rev. Rul. 69-515, 1969-2 CB 38.

Parent could not carry over subsidiary's net operating loss accumulated prior to distribution of subsidiary's assets to parent. Pursuant to a plan of liquidation and within the taxable year of adoption, a parent corporation caused its wholly owned, insolvent subsidiary to distribute all of its assets subject to its liabilities to the parent. The subsidiary corporation had sustained operating losses in prior years that resulted in a net operating loss carry-over as of the date of distribution, and its liabilities exceeded the fair market value of the assets transferred. The transaction did not qualify as a distribution under Section 332 because the parent received no payment for the stock of the subsidiary. Under Section 381(c), the net operating losses of a subsidiary may be carried over to a parent corporation only if the liquidation of the subsidiary qualifies under Section 332. Accordingly, no carry-over losses were permitted. Rev. Rul. 68-359, 1968-2 CB 161.

Parent could not succeed to net operating loss of liquidated subsidiary whose liabilities exceeded the fair market value of its assets. A wholly owned subsidiary had sustained net operating losses in prior years that resulted in a carry-over. The subsidiary was indebted to the parent in an amount greater than the fair market value of its assets. The parent corporation cancelled the indebtedness owed to it by the subsidiary and immediately thereafter transferred all of the assets subject to liabilities of the subsidiary to the parent pursuant to a plan of complete liquidation. Since the step involving the cancellation of the indebtedness from the subsidiary to the parent was an integral part of the liquidation and had no independent significance other than to secure the tax benefits of Section 381, it was disregarded. Accordingly, the parent was considered to have received nothing in payment of its stock interest, and no liquidation transpired within the meaning of Section 332. Rev. Rul. 68-602, 1968-2 CB 135.

Net operating loss carry-over denied where corporation held investments at the time a change of ownership occurred. A corporation engaged in the lumber business sold its operating assets and incurred a net operating loss in 1959. In subsequent years, the sole income was from investments. At the end of 1962, stockholders held at least 50 percentage points more of stock than they held at the beginning of the fiscal year or the prior taxable year within the meaning of Section 382(a). Under Regulation § 1.382(a)-1(h)(4), investments in securities is not a trade or business unless it has historically been the corporation's principal activity. Therefore, under Regulation § 1.382(a)-1(h)(6), the corporation was not carrying on an active trade or business at the time of the change of ownership. The IRS held that the corporation was not entitled to avail itself of the net operating loss carry-over from taxable years prior to the change of ownership. Rev. Rul. 67-186, 1967-1 CB 81.

Loss Limitations

No attribution rules apply in determining change of ownership under Section 382(b)'s loss limitation rules. *X, Y,* and *Z* corporations were each 50 percent owned by two families. The corporations were not equal in net worth, nor did the individual family members hold the same percentage of interest in each of the three corporations. *X* and *Y* were merged into *Z,* a loss corporation, in a "tax-free" reorganization. The IRS sought to reduce, under Section 382(b), the amount of premerger net operating loss that *Z* could use to offset future income. *Held:* For the IRS. Section 382(b) reduced the amount of *Z*'s usable net operating losses because no attribution rules apply under Section 382(b). It is the change in percentage held by the individual family members that is relevant, not the percentages held by the family as a group. In this case, the change was sufficiently large to trigger a loss limitation under Section 382(b). Kern's Bakery of Virginia, Inc., 68 TC 517 (1977).

Net operating loss deduction was limited to taxpayers' adjusted basis in their stock. Taxpayers, a husband and wife, incorporated their business in 1963. In 1964, they deducted

PERSONAL HOLDING COMPANIES: *In General*

$12,000 as their pro rata share of the net operating loss sustained by the corporation. The IRS disallowed the major part of the deduction. *Held:* For the IRS. Since it was determined that taxpayers had a basis of $4,777 in the assets transferred, liabilities assumed upon transfer amounted to $4,757, and no additional contributions to capital were made, the loss deduction was limited to the adjusted basis of stock, or $20, under Sections 1374(c)(2)(A) and 1374(c)(2)(B). No increase in basis was allowed for the purposes of net operating loss computations where salary indebtedness owed to cash-basis taxpayer-wife by the corporation had not been reported as income. Deductions for automobile depreciation, $748, and operating expenses, $584, were disallowed to taxpayer-husband for lack of proof and records sustaining the depreciation and expenses. Finally, an addition to tax for delinquent filing was sustained, since no reasonable cause for delay was shown. Wise, 30 TCM 169, ¶ 71,038 P-H Memo. TC (1971).

Loss carry-over limited by deductions even though such losses were barred by statute of limitations. A net operating loss that is carried back to the third preceding taxable year will be applied against the net income of the third preceding taxable year including allowable but unclaimed deductions even though such deductions are barred by the statute of limitations. Only the excess is available as a carry-back to the second preceding taxable year. Rev. Rul. 65-96, 1965-1 CB 126.

NONTAXABLE EXCHANGES

(*See* Like-Kind Exchanges; Reorganizations; Transfers to Controlled Corporations)

OPERATING LOSSES

(*See* Net Operating Losses)

ORDINARY AND NECESSARY

(*See* Business Expenses—Ordinary and Necessary Requirement)

PARENT CORPORATION

(*See* Affiliated Corporations)

PARTIAL LIQUIDATIONS

(*See* Liquidations—Partial Liquidations; Redemptions—Partial Liquidations)

PARTY TO A REORGANIZATION

(*See* Reorganizations)

PAYMENT OF TAX

(*See* Assessment and Collection)

PERSONAL COMPENSATION

(*See* Compensation for Personal Services)

PERSONAL HOLDING COMPANIES

In General	417
Deficiency Dividends	420
Dividends Paid Deduction	422
Exemptions From Personal Holding Company Status	423
Personal Holding Company Defined	426
Personal Holding Company Income	431

In General

Tax attributable to capital gain of personal holding company was determined without changing dividends-received credit. In computing undistributed personal holding company income, a deduction is allowed for federal income taxes paid (including the tax on capital gains), long-term capital gains, and various other items. In order to prevent a double deduction, the long-term capital gains deduction must be reduced by any tax attributable to such gain. Taxpayer contended that in computing "tax attributable to capital gain," the entire corporate tax must be recomputed without including capital gains, and that the resultant difference in taxes would be the tax attributable to capital gain. Under this method, taxpayer would have taken a reduced dividends-received credit, since the exclusion of the large capital gain would have brought into play the limitation on the dividends-received credit to the extent of 85 percent of now-reduced taxable income. This would result in a smaller figure than that obtained by merely reducing taxable income by the long-term capital gain without changing the dividends-received credit (the IRS' method). Thus, a correspondingly larger deduction could be taken. *Held:* Affirmed. The court found that Section 545(b) clearly indicated that the IRS' method was the correct one. Litchfield Securities Corp., 325 F2d 667, 64-1 USTC ¶ 9106, 12 AFTR2d 6042 (2d Cir. 1964), cert. denied, 377 US 931 (1963).

Interest on personal holding company tax accrues from return due date. The IRS held that interest on a personal holding company tax deficiency accrued from the due date of the return and not the date of notice and demand by the IRS. *Held:* For the IRS. The personal holding company tax is meant to be reported on the return and is treated as selfassessable. Hart Metal Prods. Corp., 76-2 USTC ¶ 9781, 38 AFTR2d 76-6118 (Ct. Cl. 1976).

Taxable year of includability determined. Calendar year taxpayers owned all the outstanding stock of *Y*, a foreign personal holding company, which in turn owned 90 percent of *O*, also a foreign corporation. Both *Y* and *O* used a taxable year ending June 30. In September 1962, *O* redeemed all of its preferred stock held by *Y*. At the same time, the taxpayers sold all their stock in *Y* to independent third parties. The IRS determined that the transaction constituted a taxable redemption by *O*, followed by taxpayers' sale of that stock. Therefore, *Y* had received a dividend. Accordingly, taxpayers had to report undistributed foreign personal holding company income for calendar year 1963. *Held:* For the IRS. Taxpayers were taxable on their respective pro rata shares of *Y*'s undistributed foreign personal holding company income for the fiscal year 1963, as was includable in their income under Section 551(b). Since the redemption occurred in September 1962, it had occurred during *Y*'s tax year ended June 30, 1963. Gray, 71 TC 719 (1979), acq. 1979-2 CB 1.

Reliance on accountant was good reason not to file separate Form 1120PH. Taxpayer corporation did not file a separate Form 1120PH because its accountant was under the impression that the personal holding company tax only related to "individuals in the motion picture industry and individuals with large incomes who wanted to incorporate." *Held:* For taxpayer. The court held that the corporation was entitled to rely on the accountant because, despite his misconception about the form, he was experienced in tax matters. West Coast Ice Co., 49 TC 345 (1968), acq. 1968-1 CB 2.

Transfer to 90 percent stockholder was loan. *Y* corporation transferred funds to *X*, a 90 percent stockholder, that were used to pay off *Y*'s former stockholders for the purchase of *Y* stock by *X*. *Held:* For taxpayer. The transfer constituted a bona fide loan, since many of the indicia of indebtedness were present. In addition, *X* had the ability to, and did, pay off the loans. Since the transfers were not dividends, *Y* was not subject to the personal holding company tax. Gamble Constr. Co., 37 TCM 1675, ¶ 78,404 P-H Memo. TC (1978).

Personal holding company deficiency dividend payments determined premature. Taxpayer was determined to have been liable for the personal holding company tax and decided to pay deficiency dividends to reduce the tax. The IRS claimed that the dividend payments were premature. *Held:* For the IRS. The deduction for deficiency dividends is permitted only within 90 days of a determination that a

PERSONAL HOLDING COMPANIES: *In General*

taxpayer is liable for the personal holding company tax. The Tax Court's decision of liability was not such a determination until the time for the appeal of that decision had expired. Since that time had not expired, the question of whether taxpayer may pay deficiency dividends was not properly before the court. Marshall Inv. Co., 32 TCM 382, ¶ 73,087 P-H Memo. TC (1973).

Net operating loss used in computing personal holding company tax although carried back in computing regular tax. A personal holding company can use a net operating loss of the preceding year in computing the personal holding company tax, although the prior year's loss is carried back to an earlier year for purposes of the regular corporate income tax. Rev. Rul. 79-59, 1979-1 CB 209.

Taxpayer's notification of appeal to district conference constituted a "contest" for purposes of accruing personal holding company deduction for accumulated earnings and personal holding company tax. Upon examination of taxpayer's 1968 tax return, it was determined that the accumulated earnings tax was applicable as well as certain other adjustments. Taxpayer disagreed with the proposed adjustments and requested a district conference. Proposed tax deficiency could not be carried back to 1968 to be used in computing the tax applicable to the accumulated earnings of the corporation or, where applicable, the pesonal holding company tax. Rev. Rul. 72-306, 1972-1 CB 165.

Stock attribution rules of Section 544(a)(1) do not apply to stockholders of small business investment companies. The IRS illustrated that a small business investment company cannot, through the attribution rules of Section 544(a)(1), be classified as a personal holding company when the attribution to the stockholders flows through the personal holding company. However, when the stock can be attributed to the stockholders through a business concern that is not a small business investment company, personal holding company status can be applied. Rev. Rul. 70-551, 1970-2 CB 130.

Contracts may be oral or written for personal holding company purposes. The IRS ruled that the term "contract" as used in Section 543(a)(7) includes oral as well as written contracts. Rev. Rul. 69-299, 1969-1 CB 165.

IRS ruled on stockholder use of property leased by corporate lessee. As part of its acquiescence in the courts decision in 320 East 47th St. Corp., 243 F2d 894 (2d Cir. 1957), the IRS agreed with the holding that where rental income is derived from a corporate lessee, the stockholders of the lessee corporation indirectly have the right to use the leased property. Such indirect right is obtained by means of an "other arrangement" within the meaning of Section 543 (a)(6) of the personal holding company provisions. Accordingly, the IRS' position is that rental income derived from a corporate lessee, any one of whose stockholders directly or indirectly owns 25 percent or more in value of the outstanding stock of the lessor corporation, constitutes income from the use of corporation property described in Section 543(a)(6). Rev. Rul. 65-259, 1965-2 CB 259.

Procedure modified for personal holding company informal agreements. Where a personal holding company deficiency is determined, a corporation has 90 days to distribute "deficiency dividends" to reduce or eliminate the proposed deficiency. Form 2198 is the agreement form designed to be used in such cases. Rev. Proc. 59-1 requires that this form be filed concurrently with waiver Form 870 or 870-AD and that the waiver from contain four specified conditions. This procedure has been modified somewhat so that: (1) The four conditions need no longer be set forth in Form 870-AD (but are still required for Form 870), and (2) one of the conditions has been modified, making Form 2198 subject to approval by authorized officials as well as the district director. Rev. Proc. 63-1, 1963-1 CB 471.

No personal holding company tax due for period after corporation's status changes. For the first nine months of its taxable year, a corporation qualified as a personal holding company; for its last three months, it qualified as a

PERSONAL HOLDING COMPANIES: *Deficiency Dividends*

bank (exempted from the personal holding company provisions under Section 581). The IRS ruled that the corporation was subject to the personal holding company tax for the period during which it operated as a personal holding company but *not* for the period when it operated as a bank. Rev. Rul. 63-103, 1963-1 CB 116.

Lifting costs are a cost of oil and gas sold. A company is a personal holding company if, among other tests, 80 percent of its total gross income is from specified sources. The IRS ruled that lifting costs must be deducted from gross sales in computing the total gross sales in computing the total gross income of the owner of oil and gas wells. Lifting costs are the costs incurred after drilling but before production; they are a cost of production. Rev. Rul. 60-344, 1960-2 CB 186.

No personal holding company tax on retained capital gain. A domestic personal holding company may retain in the corporation without penalty the net long-term gain derived from the sale of securities, less the amount of tax applicable to such gain. Rev. Rul. 55-702, 1955-2 CB 272.

Deficiency Dividends

Liquidation distribution did not qualify as deficiency dividend. The district court agreed with the IRS that a liquidating distribution made by taxpayer corporation before it had been designated a personal holding company by the IRS did not qualify as a deficiency dividend. *Held:* Affirmed. The distribution was not made within 90 days of a determination of the deficiency, as required by Section 547. The relief provisions of Section 316(b)(2) didn't apply due to the timing of the distribution. Fletcher, 674 F2d 1308, 82-1 USTC ¶ 9347, 49 AFTR2d 82-1401 (9th Cir. 1982).

Property dividend limited to adjusted basis. There was a determination, within the meaning of Section 547(c), that taxpayer was liable for personal holdings tax in 1972 and 1973. Pursuant to a board of director's resolution, timely deficiency dividends were paid to stockholders in cash and property that had a fair market value in excess of its adjusted basis in taxpayer's hands. The Tax Court found Regulation § 1.562-1(a) to be valid but yielded to the decision in H. Wetter Manufacturing Co., 458 F2d 1033 (6th Cir. 1972), which held the regulation to be invalid and stated that the amount of claimed deduction should be based on fair market value rather than on the adjusted basis at the time of distribution. The Sixth Circuit ordered that the judgment of the Tax Court be vacated and that the action be remanded to the Tax Court for further proceeding in light of Fulman, 434 US 528 (1978). Therein, the Supreme Court upheld the validity of Regulation § 1.562-1(a), which limits the dividends paid deduction for personal holding companies that make deficiency distributions of appreciated property to the adjusted basis of the property distributed. The Tax Court held that the subsequent decision in *Fulman* should be given retroactive effect and that taxpayer was therefore limited to a claimed dedution based on the adjusted basis of the distributed property. *Held:* Affirmed. Because appreciated property was distributed, the deficiency dividend deduction was limited to the property's adjusted basis. Taxpayer's reliance on the lower court's holding that Regulation § 1.562-1 was invalid was not enough to avoid retroactive application of the Supreme Court's decision holding the regulation valid. C. Blake McDowell, Inc., 81-1 USTC ¶ 9150, 47 AFTR2d 81-567 (6th Cir. 1980).

"Dividends" three years after liquidation not deficiency dividends. Taxpayers were 50 percent stockholders in a corporation that made liquidating distributions of all its assets to taxpayers in exchange for all of their stock. When the plan of liquidation was established, the corporation filed for dissolution under state law. The corporation conducted no business in the ensuing years but existed under state law to perform such functions as settling claims and filing suits. Three years later, the IRS determined that the corporation was liable for personal holding company tax for the taxable years because its liquidation plan had been drawn up. As a result of the transfers of its assets in the liquidating distributions, the corporation was rendered insolvent and lacked the assets necessary to pay the deficiencies in the personal holding company taxes plus the accompanying interest. To avoid the tax liability, taxpayers opened a bank account in the corporate name, deposited their own funds into the account, and had the corporation's board of directors declare and distribute to taxpayers "deficiency dividends" in an aggregate amount substantially equal to the total amount deposited in the corporate account by taxpayers. The Tax Court, upholding the IRS, held that the purported distribution was not a genuine distribution for purposes of Section 316(b)(2) and therefore did not qualify for the deficiency dividends deduction under Section 547 or that even if the distribution were genuine, it did not qualify for the deficiency dividends deduction under Section 547. *Held:* Affirmed. Section 316(b)(2)(A) did not govern distributions from a personal holding company. However, a distribution from a personal holding company was classifiable as a "dividend" for purposes of Section 316, providing that the procedure in Section 316(b) were followed. The provision required that such distributions be made within 24 months after a plan of liquidation was adopted, but this requirement had not been met. Thus, the distributions failed to qualify as deficiency dividends. Callan, 476 F2d 509, 73-1 USTC ¶ 9332, 31 AFTR2d 73-1056 (9th Cir. 1973).

Liquidating distributions not deficiency dividends. Taxpayers liquidated a corporation that they owned. The IRS then told them that the corporation was a personal holding company and imposed the personal holding company tax. Taxpayers argued that the personal holding company income should be reduced by the liquidating distributions, and that those distributions were deficiency dividends. *Held:* For the IRS, in part. Only the personal holding company income for its last tax year is exempt from the personal holding company tax because of the liquidation. The distributions were not deficiency dividends because they were made before a "determination" (as defined in Section 547(c)) that the corporation was a personal holding company.

Fletcher, 674 F2d 1308, 82-1 USTC ¶ 9347, 49 AFTR2d 82-1401 (9th Cir. 1982).

Premature deficiency dividend did not qualify for deduction and thus could not avoid assessment of personal holding company tax. Taxpayer conceded its liability for personal holding company tax and executed both a Form 870 Waiver and a Form 2198 Determination of Personal Holding Company Liability. Before the district director signed the Form 2198, taxpayer declared and paid a deficiency dividend in sufficient amount to avoid any such tax liability. Under Section 547 and its regulations, a deficiency dividend deduction is authorized for deficiency dividends paid within 90 days after the IRS signs Form 2198. *Held:* For the IRS. Even though the IRS was not prejudiced in any manner by taxpayer's early payment of the dividend, the statute and regulations were clear. No deficiency dividend deduction is allowed except for dividends paid within the prescribed 90-day period. Furthermore, because the IRS did not intentionally mislead the taxpayer or negligently induce it to pay a premature deficiency dividend, taxpayer cannot successfully assert the doctrine of waiver or equitable estoppel. Leck Co., 73-2 USTC ¶ 9694, 32 AFTR2d 73-5891 (D. Minn. 1973).

Corporation allowed deficiency dividend deduction, even though dividend, although sufficient in total amount, was paid in wrong proportions to stockholders. Taxpayer paid a deficiency dividend that, although correct in total amount, was paid disproportionately to its stockholders. This was a result of a clerical error made by the corporation's accountant. The IRS disallowed the deduction on the ground that each stockholder was not paid the proper amount. *Held:* For taxpayer. The court held that the stockholder who was overpaid in the deficiency dividend must hold the excess payment as a constructive trustee for the other stockholders. Hanco Distrib. Co., 73-2 USTC ¶ 9632, 32 AFTR2d 73-5485 (D. Utah 1973).

IRS not estopped from amending tax on deficiency dividends paid to taxpayers. Taxpayers, stockholders in a personal holding company, stated that the IRS was collaterally estopped from holding that taxpayers received income from deficiency dividends due to an erroneous statement in an earlier suit that taxpayers would not be taxed on such dividends. *Held:* For the IRS. The court found that there was no evidence to indicate that the tax consequences of the deficiency dividends to taxpayers were considered in the prior suit. Buder, Jr., 322 F. Supp. 345, 71-2 USTC ¶ 9683 (ED Mo. 1971).

Deficiency dividend deduction measured by fair market value of property distributed. Taxpayer, a personal holding company, paid deficiency dividends in cash and property. The dividend had a fair market value of $102,000 on the date of distribution and a basis of $1,000. Taxpayer claimed a deficiency dividend deduction measured by the fair market value of the property distributed, and the IRS determined that the deduction was limited to the basis of the property. *Held:* For taxpayer. Although the regulations under Section 562 limit the deduction for dividends paid to the adjusted basis of the property, the court must follow a controlling circuit court decision. Here, the Sixth Circuit declared the regulation invalid. The appeal would lie to that court. McDowell, Inc., 67 TC 1043 (1977), nonacq. 1978-2 CB 4.

For purposes of personal holding company deficiency dividend deduction, Tax Court decision becomes final 90 days after entry. The IRS stated that for purposes of the defiency dividend deduction afforded a personal holding company, a decision of the Tax Court becomes final 90 days after entry provided no notice of appeal has been duly filed within that time. Rev. Rul. 72-251, 1972-1 CB 172.

Stockholders of personal holding company constructively received dividend despite stock transfer. After the IRS proposed an assessment of personal holding company tax, the stockholders transferred their shares to a wholly owned corporation. The personal holding company then issued a deficiency dividend to avert the personal holding company tax as provided for by Section 547. The corporation claimed an 85 percent dividends received credit against the deficiency dividend. The IRS ruled that allowing this scheme would frustrate the purpose of the dividend deficiency provisions of the Code that are intended to permit an escape from the personal holding company tax when the stockholders themselves pay tax. The transfer to the corporation was regarded as having no business purpose; it was undertaken solely to avoid tax. Hence, the stockholders were considered as constructively receiving the deficiency dividend. Rev. Rul. 60-331, 1960-2 CB 189.

Dividends Paid Deduction

A personal holding company's dividends paid deduction determined with reference to the adjusted basis, not fair market value, of the appreciated property distributed to its stockholders as a dividend. Taxpayer argued that the amount of a personal holding company's dividends paid deduction for a distribution of appreciated property should be determined in the same manner as the amount of dividend realized by its stockholders upon such distribution (with reference to the fair market value and not the adjusted basis of such property). The IRS argued that pursuant to Regulation § 1.562-1(a), the amount of such deduction is determined by the adjusted basis of such property. Both the district court and the court of appeals held for the IRS. *Held:* Affirmed. The Supreme Court stated that although taxpayer's argument was logical and not inconsistent with the personal holding company rules, the IRS' argument was similarly not inconsistent with such rules. Accordingly, the court, invoking the "rule of deference," namely, that treasury regulations must be sustained unless unreasonable and plainly inconsistent with the Code, held that Regulation § 1.562-1(a) was valid. Fulman, 434 US 528, 78-1 USTC ¶ 9247, 41 AFTR2d 78-698 (1978).

Property dividend deduction limited to adjusted basis. The IRS determined that pursuant to Regulation § 1.562-1(a), a dividends paid deduction involving a property distribution was limited to adjusted basis, not fair market value, for personal holding company tax pur-

PERSONAL HOLDING COMPANIES: *Exemptions*

poses. The district court found for taxpayer. *Held:* Reversed. The Supreme Court's decision in Fulman, 434 US 528 (1978), was found to have retroactive application. Gulf Inland Corp., 570 F2d 1277, 78-1 USTC ¶ 9351, 41 AFTR2d 78-1163 (5th Cir. 1978).

Requirement of timely designation of personal holding company distribution as a dividend upheld. Taxpayer adopted a plan of liquidation in which all of its assets would be distributed to the sole stockholder within 24 months thereafter. It did not designate any part of the distribution as a dividend, nor did it identify itself as a personal holding company on its final return. Subsequently, the IRS determined that taxpayer was a personal holding company and had undistributed personal holding company income subject to tax. Taxpayer filed an amended return with a Schedule PH attached, claiming a dividends paid deduction in an amount equal to its undistributed personal holding company income. The IRS determined that taxpayer had failed to designate the distribution as a dividend within the time provided by the regulations and held that the distribution could not qualify as dividends paid. *Held:* For the IRS. The regulations were valid in requiring distributions timely reported to be treated as a dividend. To permit a later correction would permit corporations to gamble on not filing a personal holding company return, and then to file the PH Schedule only upon an adverse determination following an examination. L.C. Bohart Plumbing & Heating Co., 64 TC 602 (1975).

Carry-back of dividends for personal holding company was limited. Taxpayer claimed that dividends paid within two and a half months after the close of its taxable year were to be included in that year, thus taking it out of the personal holding company category. *Held:* For the IRS. Section 563(b) limits the amount of carry-back dividends to either the undistributed personal holding company income in the year in question or 20 percent of the dividends actually paid in that year. Jacqueline Sundstrom Trust, 42 TCM 358, ¶ 81,356 P-H Memo. TC (1981).

"Business expenses" held constructive dividends, eliminating personal holding company tax liability. A corporation sold its business but remained in existence while its main stockholder searched for a new business. The IRS disallowed some business deductions relating to a search for another business, disallowed other business deductions as being constructive dividends, and imposed personal holding company tax. *Held:* For the IRS, in part. The business deductions were properly disallowed. Also, taxpayer was the personal holding company, but the dividends paid deduction from the constructive dividends eliminated its undistributed personal holding company income. Heim, 37 TCM 584, ¶ 78,137 P-H Memo. TC (1978).

Exemptions From Personal Holding Company Status

Lending company not exempt from personal holding company status. Taxpayer, a finance company, was originally formed for the purpose of providing financing for customers of one of its sister organizations. From 1973 through 1975, its sole lending activities and income were loans to various sister corporations. Taxpayer maintained no employees of its own, but utilized one of its sister corporation's personnel and facilities in exchange for a percentage of gross income. The IRS determined that taxpayer was subject to the personal holding company tax, and taxpayer contended that it was exempt from that tax as a "lending or finance company." *Held:* For the IRS. Taxpayer's lending and finance activities were not conducted on an active and regular basis during the years in issue, since all of its loans were made to its sister corporations. The loans had been standing since 1973, their servicing required little or no expense, and two of the debtor corporations were permitted to postpone paying substantial portions of interest. Omaha Aircraft Leasing Co., 646 F2d 341, 81-1 USTC 9392, 47 AFTR2d 81-1453 (8th Cir. 1981).

Industrial loan company not exempt from personal holding company tax because its interest expense was not a Section 542(c)(6)(C) deduction. Taxpayer, an industrial loan company, was engaged in a high-risk lending business (e.g., second mortgages). From 1964 through 1965, it argued that it was exempt from personal holding company tax as a bank or finance company under Sections 542(c)(2) and 542(c)(6). About half of taxpayer's expenses for 1964 through 1965 were interest payments. *Held*: For the IRS because (1) legislative history shows that Section 542(c)(2), applying to banks was not intended to apply to industrial loan companies and (2) taxpayer was also not exempt under Section 542(c)(6), since it failed to satisfy the 15 to 5 percentage deduction test of Section 542(c)(6)(C), and its interest expense was not a Section 542(c)(6)(C) deduction. Norfolk Indus. Loan Ass'n, 70-2 USTC ¶ 9527, 26 AFTR2d 70-5296 (ED Va. 1970).

Corporation that did not derive more than 60 percent of ordinary gross income from lending or financing was a personal holding company. Taxpayer was engaged in general financing, making loans, factoring receivables, discounting sales contracts, and entering into chattel leasing agreements. It claimed that it was not subject to classification as a personal holding company because it was a "lending or financing company" under Section 542(d)(1). *Held:* For the IRS. Taxpayer's ordinary gross income from chattel lease agreements was not derived from a lending or financing business. Therefore, it did not derive more than 60 percent of its ordinary gross income from a lending or financing business and did not qualify for exclusion from the personal holding company classification. Pacific Sec. Cos., 59 TC 744 (1973).

Amount of deposits or loans did not determine bank status. Taxpayer, a bank, had two full-time employees, was open for business six days a week, and offered banking services to the public. Its deposits and loans were not large and were attributable in part to a related corporation. The IRS contended that taxpayer was a personal holding company because it did not qualify for exclusion as a bank. *Held:* For taxpayer. Section 581 does not set forth the minimum number of deposits that an institution must receive and the minimum number of loans it must make to qualify as a bank. Taxpayer was subject to supervision and inspection by state banking authorities and conducted itself as a bank. Accordingly, taxpayer was a bank and as a result, not a personal holding company. Austin State Bank, 57 TC 180 (1971).

Taxpayer was a personal holding company and not a loan or investment company. Taxpayer was a wholly owned corporation whose stockholder was the managing and controlling stockholder of a real estate loan business. Before his retirement, the stockholder had set up corporations to engage in that business. Taxpayer made real estate loans, mainly to business acquaintances of the stockholder, and operated out of the same office and with the same employees as the other corporations. Most of its resources were supplied by the stockholder in the form of borrowings evidenced by unsecured interest-bearing demand promissory notes. Its gross income consisted almost entirely of interest and loan fees. Some of taxpayer's borrowings from its stockholder were repaid, but additional amounts were borrowed to finance the lending operations. Taxpayer was liquidated after four years under Section 331, and the stockholder reported capital gain on the liquidating distribution, taking all the assets in exchange satisfaction of the corporation's debt to him and in exchange for his stock. The IRS determined that taxpayer was a personal holding company. Taxpayer contended that it was exempt as a loan or investment company or, alternatively, that it was entitled to a dividends paid deduction by carry-back of the liquidating distribution to the earlier years. *Held:* For the IRS. Taxpayer met some of the requirements of a loan or investment company but did not meet the requirement that a substantial part of the business consist of receiving funds that were not subject to check and which were evidenced by installment or fully paid certificates of indebtedness or investment. In addition, the certificate of incorporation did not indicate that taxpayer was incorporated to operate a business to receive funds or deposits from the general public. The method chosen by the stockholder to finance operations did not convert the business itself into one of receiving funds, as the term is used in the statute. The exception to personal holding company treatment was intended to apply to "near banks." Taxpayer's alternative argument of a carry-back of the liquidating distribution was also not contemplated by statute, since, in this case, the dividends paid deduction was limited to dividends paid during the taxable year. Jos. K., Inc., 51 TC 584 (1969).

Taxpayer engaged in a loan business was a personal holding company because it was precluded from deducting interest. Taxpayer conducted a loan business. Its loans were secured by mortgages on real estate. It borrowed money from banks in order to make the loans and paid interest on the bank loans. The IRS determined that the interest paid was not deductible for the purpose of determining whether business deductions exceeded 15 percent of ordinary gross income, and that taxpayer was therefore a personal holding company. Taxpayer relied entirely on McNutt-Boyce Co., 38 TC 462(1962), in which it was held that the interest paid was deductible. *Held:* For the IRS. The taxpayer's argument was not accepted by the court because Section 542, as interpreted by the case on which taxpayer relied, was amended by the Revenue Act of 1964, which applied to the taxable year. Section 542(d)(2)(A), as amended, expressly limits business deductions for the purpose of determining status as a personal holding company to those allowable under Section 162 or Section 404. Interest is specifically allowable under Section 163 and does not therefore fall within either category. In view of these statutory changes, *McNutt-Boyce Co.* no longer applied. Audrey Realty, Inc., 50 TC 583 (1968).

Finance company status not lost where excessive advances to majority stockholder were not true loans. Because it was unable to borrow funds for its working capital requirements, taxpayer, a small loan company, had an arrangement with Grable Finance Co., its principal stockholder, whereby the latter borrowed funds from a bank and then turned them over to taxpayer. Because of delays and recordkeeping problems, this arrangement was later simplified so that the bank transferred the funds directly to taxpayer but held Grable as primary obligor on the loans. Using these bank funds, taxpayer paid off its obligations to Grable due under the old arrangement, and when Grable opened a new loan office, began to advance substantial sums to Grable. The IRS determined that taxpayer had lost its status as a personal finance company and had become a personal holding company by reason of its loans to 10 percent or more stockholders in excess of the $5,000 limit prescribed in Section 542(c)(6). *Held:* For taxpayer. After construing that section, the court found it inapplicable, since the "loans" to Grable were not genuine loans, but merely inter-company transfers of corporate funds. Grable was primarily liable on the bank loans from which the funds emanated. Despite the fact that the loans were recorded on taxpayer's books as notes receivable, were evidenced by interest-bearing demand notes, and the minutes of a meeting of Grable's directors described the advances as having been "borrowed," these were mere formalities which, due to Grable's control of taxpayer, lacked substance. The court concluded that taxpayer was a mere conduit for the channeling of borrowed funds. Oak Hill Fin. Co., 40 TC 419 (1963).

Home rental corporation subject to personal holding company tax. The IRS determined that taxpayer corporation, a home rental corporation, was subject to the personal holding company tax. *Held:* For the IRS. Taxpayer did not meet the conditions set forth in Section 542(c)(6) for the exemption from the tax as a lending and financing institution. Since its rental and interest income constituted more than 60 percent of its adjusted ordinary gross income, the personal holding company tax applied. Karon Corp., 34 TCM 1230, ¶ 75,283 P-H Memo. TC (1975).

Industrial loan company failed to qualify for personal holding company exemption. An industrial loan company failed to qualify for exemption from personal holding company status provided by Section 542(c)(6) for lending or finance companies since it made a loan of more than $5,000 to a more than 10 percent stockholder. The IRS concluded that it could not then qualify for exemption under the more general Section 542(c)(2) provision for banks. Rev. Rul. 81-37, 1981-1 CB 368.

Finance company's loan to stockholder's partnership jeopardized exemption from personal holding company tax. Under Section 542(c)(6)(D), a finance company is exempt from personal holding company status if, among other things, it loans no more than $5,000 to a person who owns 10 percent or more of its stock. If the finance company makes a loan to a partnership in which a 10 percent or more stockholder is a partner, the company will be a personal holding company if that stockholder's pro rata share of the partnership loan exceeds $5,000. Rev. Rul. 79-156, 1979-1 CB 210.

A corporation not exempt from personal holding company tax merely because its sole stockholder was exempt. The IRS ruled that a domestic corporation was not exempt from the personal holding company tax merely because its sole stockholder was exempt from such tax as a licensed small business investment company operating under the Small Business Investment Act of 1958. Rev. Rul. 73-179, 1973-1 CB 296.

Parent corporation engaged in the lending or finance business was personal holding company. A parent corporation was engaged in the lending and finance business as defined by Section 542(d)(1)(A)(iv). However, the corporation, in attempting to meet the exclusionary provisions of Section 542(c)(6), could not meet the third test, a requirement that the company have deductions in excess of certain amounts. Because the statute contains no provisions under which a parent corporation may be excluded from any of the provisions of Section 542(c)(6), the company qualified as a personal holding company. Rev. Rul. 70-612, 1970-2 CB 129.

Personal Holding Company Defined

Personal holding company tax applied. Taxpayer corporations were major stockholders of a foreign corporation. The IRS determined that the foreign corporation was a foreign personal holding company, and thus the constructive distribution to the domestic corporations resulted in their classification as domestic personal holding companies. The Tax Court upheld the IRS. *Held:* Affirmed. The Tax Court correctly determined the corporations to be personal holding companies. Melinda L. Gee Trust, 761 F2d 1410, 85-1 USTC ¶ 9428, 56 AFTR2d 85-5110 (9th Cir. 1985).

Bottling company that leased assets to partnerships was not personal holding company. Taxpayer owned soft drink bottling equipment that it leased to two partnerships. The partnerships held the rights to bottle and sell the soft drink in a certain area. The IRS claimed that part of the "rent" taxpayer received constituted franchise royalties, not rent for the equipment, and that taxpayer was therefore a personal holding company. *Held:* For taxpayer. The franchises had little value, and the lease, which followed the purchase of equipment from the partnerships, was a financing transaction. Taxpayer was not a personal holding company. Dothan Coca-Cola Bottling Co., 745 F2d 1400, 84-2 USTC ¶ 19910, 54 AFTR2d 84-6402 (11th Cir. 1984).

No dividend received by parent on subsidiary's purchase of parent's stock from stockholder's estate. A controlled subsidiary purchased a portion of its parent's stock from a stockholder's estate. The parent was later liquidated and dissolved. The IRS argued that the stock's selling price was a constructive dividend to the parent and that the parent's receipt of the dividend caused it to be a personal holding company subject to the personal holding company tax. *Held:* For taxpayer. Under Section 304, property received by the parent's stockholder in exchange for stock provides no basis for taxing the parent corporation on a dividend from its subsidiary. Payment of the selling price is treated as a distribution by the subsidiary to the parent, followed by a redemption by the parent of its own shares. This legal fiction does not mean that the stock is actually redeemed, rather that it becomes an asset of the subsidiary. The parent is not taxed on the fictional distribution from the subsidiary because the parent received nothing in the transaction. Because the parent did not receive a dividend, it was not a personal holding company, and the stockholders were not liable as transferees. Webb, 572 F2d 135, 78-1 USTC ¶ 9406, 41 AFTR2d 78-1264 (5th Cir. 1978).

Penalty tax imposed on corporation that sold its business. Taxpayer, a clothing business, reported on a fiscal year ending May 31. In December 1968, taxpayer sold all its assets and invested part of the proceeds in securities. During the remainder of its fiscal year, taxpayer had no plans to enter a new business. The Tax Court held for the IRS. *Held:* Affirmed. The court agreed with the Tax Court's finding that the taxpayer became a mere holding and investment company as of December and was subject to a penalty tax for its fiscal year ending May 31, 1969, since under the circumstances, five months was sufficient to develop plans. Alex Brown, Inc., 496 F2d 621, 74-1 USTC ¶ 9405, 33 AFTR2d 74-1226 (6th Cir. 1974).

Financing conduit could not characterize interest as rent to avoid being personal holding company. Taxpayer formed a corporation to facilitate the sale of residential housing of a related corporation by providing financing. The corporation purchased houses and resold them to the purchaser under a conditional sales contract. Each payment received consisted of principal, interest, and tax escrow. The IRS contended that the interest received was personal holding company income during 1959 and 1960 and that a subchapter S election had terminated. The Tax Court held for the IRS. *Held:* Affirmed. For interest to qualify as rent under former Section 543(a)(7), it has to be interest on debts owed to the corporation, attributable to the sale of real property held primarily for sale to customers in the ordinary course of business. Based on the facts, the corporation was a financing company and not in the real estate business. It was merely a conduit for the related corporation, the true seller. Accordingly, the corporation was a personal holding company. Moreover, the interest received exceeded 20 percent of gross receipts, calculated by including only the partial principal received on property sold; therefore the subchapter S election was terminated. It was further held that a distribution to taxpayer was a dividend and taxable accordingly. Sich, 73-1 USTC ¶ 9281, 31 AFTR2d 73-694 (8th Cir. 1973).

Personal holding company resulted from loans to stockholder. Taxpayer made advances to its major stockholder and to business entities in which stockholder had interests. Notwithstanding the advances, taxpayer sought to exclude itself from classification as a personal holding company on the ground that it was a lending and finance company that satisfied all of the requirements of Section 542(c)(6). The Tax Court held for the IRS. *Held:* Affirmed. The substance of the transactions, evidenced by the interest payments, proved that the withdrawals were loans. Since the advances were loans and they were made to a major stockholder, taxpayer was a personal holding company and not a lending or finance company within the meaning of the statute. Fidelity Commercial Co., 71-2 USTC ¶ 9667, 28 AFTR2d 71-5751 (4th Cir. 1971).

Personal services of officer stockholder subjected corporation to personal holding company tax. Taxpayer was a corporation providing management services to entertainers. All the stock of the corporation was owned by the president. The clients of the agency were provided with a standard contract that required the president of the agency to be available to personally supervise their business. A number of subagents were employed, but their activities were incidental to the president's. Taxpayer contended that it was not subject to personal holding company tax because less than 80 percent of the income was derived from the services of the stockholder after allocation of the services of the subagents. *Held:* For the IRS. The corporation was a personal holding company; the stockholder's personal services were the only services required by the contract. Based on the facts, no income could be found that was attributable to the subagents. The reputation and know-how of the stockholder were the services the artists sought to obtain. Kurt

PERSONAL HOLDING COMPANIES: *Personal Holding Company Defined*

Frings Agency, Inc., 351 F2d 951, 65-2 USTC ¶ 9719, 16 AFTR2d 5853 (9th Cir. 1965).

Loan company charges were interest; personal holding company tax imposed. Taxpayer was an unregulated small-loan company. It added a "contract charge" to loans. The income from these charges, together with interest income, was greater than 80 percent of gross income. Taxpayer claimed that it was not a personal holding company because the charges were not "interest." *Held:* Affirmed. Affirming the Tax Court, the appellate court ruled that taxpayer was a personal holding company whose contract fees, charged to defray the expenses of a small loan business, were not truly separable from interest. The borrower was interested only in obtaining a loan and paid whatever was required, however denominated, to obtain it. The fact that the charges were authorized by local law in addition to the legal interest rate did not mean that they were not interest under the revenue laws. Western Credit Co., 325 F2d 1022, 64-1 USTC ¶ 9207, 13 AFTR2d 431 (9th Cir. 1963).

District court, applying *Bardahl* test, ruled personal holding company tax inapplicable. Taxpayer, a Louisiana corporation, was formed in 1958 to engage in the grocery business. Its stock was owned by members of the same family. The IRS, on audit of taxpayer's 1972 taxable year, assessed a deficiency on the ground that the corporation was liable under the personal holding company tax rules. The IRS noted that at the end of fiscal year 1972, the corporation had $226,934 that was retained instead of distributed as a dividend. In the IRS' view, the corporation had no demonstrated business need to retain its earnings, so the personal holding company tax was assessable on the entire amount. *Held:* For taxpayer. Applying the *Bardahl* formula, the district court concluded that the corporation proved that it had specific and definite plans for future expansion when it decided to retain the 1972 earnings, and that the full $226,934 was needed to effectuate such plans. The court examined the corporation's operating needs under the *Bardahl* formula and concluded that well over $1 million was needed to accomplish its expansion and to have adequate liquid assets for operations. James W. Salley, Inc., 76-2 USTC ¶ 9739, 38 AFTR2d 76-5306 (WD La. 1976).

Taxpayer was personal holding company in last partial year so that part of liquidation distribution was ordinary income. Taxpayer corporation was an operating company prior to its last partial year. Taxpayer had adopted a plan of liquidation under Section 337. However, the IRS argued that part of the liquidation distribution to the individual stockholder was ordinary income because taxpayer was a personal holding company during its last period. The personal holding company's income for this period was all interest income, and the stock ownership requirements under Section 542 were met. *Held:* For the IRS. The fact that taxpayer was an operating company prior to the last partial year did not alter its status as a personal holding company in the period. Therefore, upon liquidation, Section 337 did not shield the personal holding company income from dividend treatment under Sections 301 and 316(b)(2)(B). Weiss, 75-2 USTC ¶ 9538, 36 AFTR2d 75-5186 (ND Ohio 1975).

Personal holding company tax imposed on holder of bottling franchise. Taxpayer, *M* Company, held a franchise to bottle Coca-Cola. *M* did not actively perform any business, but received payments from partnerships that bottled the soft drink. The IRS sought to impose the personal holding company tax on *M*. *Held:* For the IRS. The payments were not compensation for the use of *M*'s facilities but for the use of its franchise. Montgomery Coca-Cola Bottling Co., 615 F2d 1318, 80-1 USTC ¶ 9230, 45 AFTR2d 80-795 (Ct. Cl. 1980).

Imposition of personal holding company tax upheld for corporations liquidated after January 1, 1966. Upon the imposition of personal holding company tax on two corporations, taxpayers contended that they were entitled to relief by virtue of the Revenue Act of 1964, which provides relief for corporations liquidated prior to 1966, and for stockholders who liquidated such corporations prior to 1967.

Taxpayers resolved to liquidate the corporations on November 30, 1966, filing appropriate forms on December 1, 1966. Taxpayers contended that both relief provisions should be read as requiring liquidation before 1967. *Held:* For the IRS. Taxpayers' reliance on the stockholder relief provision was misplaced. The pertinent provisions deal with corporate relief, and the applicable date was January 1, 1966. Since neither corporation liquidated prior to this date, both were liable as personal holding companies. Hirshfield, 64 TC 103 (1975).

Corporate partner not a personal holding company. A construction company entered into a partnership arrangement with a valued employee, Sam. To limit his liability and to round out fluctuations in his annual earnings, Sam organized taxpayer corporation. Taxpayer was substituted for Sam as a partner. The IRS contended that the corporation was a personal holding company under Section 543(a)(7), which provides that amounts received by a corporation under a personal service contract constitute personal holding company income if a person, other than the corporation, can designate who is to perform services or if the individual who is to perform the services is designated in the contract. The IRS argued that the partnership arrangement was actually an agreement to employ Sam as an independent contractor (therefore a personal service contract), and that if a partnership did exist, the partnership agreement designated Sam as the person to perform the services. *Held:* For taxpayer. A partnership did exist, and taxpayer's income was actually a distributive share of partnership income rather than personal service income. Moreover, the partnership agreement did not give a person other than taxpayer the right to designate the individual to perform the services, nor did it itself designate such a person. Claggett, 44 TC 503 (1965).

Finance company properly accrued and reported interest income on notes executed by a principal stockholder and was subject to the personal holding company tax. Taxpayer corporation, a finance company reporting on the accrual basis, regularly accrued interest on two large notes executed in 1955 by its principal stockholder. The accrual interest was charged against her account on the corporate books. The stockholder died in 1958; her estate, reporting on a cash basis, deducted the interest. No interest was ever actually paid by the stockholder or her estate. Taxpayer was dissolved in 1962 in conjunction with the administration of the estate. The IRS sought to hold the corporate transferees (the executor of the estate, who was a corporate stockholder, and the estate beneficiaries) liable for the personal holding company tax assessed against taxpayer. *Held:* For the IRS. The notes held by taxpayer were executed as valid debts on behalf of the stockholder by her co-stockholder, the present executor. The interest thereon was properly reported as interest income by taxpayer. Considering such interest income, taxpayer satisfied the gross income test for classification as a personal holding company for 1956 through 1961. It was not entitled to a dividends-paid deduction in computing its personal holding company taxable income because it paid no dividends except for the liquidating distributions in 1962, a year not in issue. Assessment of the personal holding company tax against the transferees was not barred. The six-year statute applied to taxpayer, and the deficiency notices were sent to the transferees of both the corporation and the estate within one year of the expiration of the limitation period against each transferor. Commercial Fin. Co., 27 TCM 1114, ¶ 68,229 P-H Memo. TC (1968).

Payments received were interest and not rents for determining personal holding company status. Taxpayer transferred a parcel of real estate to a corporation, Terminal, in exchange for its common stock. It also loaned Terminal substantial sums of money on 7 percent notes. Through the taxable year, more than 50 percent of value of taxpayer's stock was owned by or for not more than five individuals. The IRS contended that taxpayer was a personal holding company, since 80 percent of its income was from interest and rents, and the rents constituted less than 50 percent of the gross income. Taxpayer argued that the so-called interest payments received from

Personal Holding Companies: *Personal Holding Company Defined*

Terminal were paid on a debt owed to taxpayer upon the sale of real property it held for sale to customers in the ordinary course of its trade or business; therefore, the payments constituted "rent" as defined by Section 543(a)(7). *Held*: For the IRS. The court held that it was clear from the facts that the real estate had been exchanged for stock and that the loans to taxpayer had given rise to the interest payments at issue. Since the payments were true interest, the rents did not comprise 50 percent of the gross income, and taxpayer was held subject to the personal holding company tax. Producers Realty Corp., 21 TCM 900, ¶ 62,162 P-H Memo. TC (1962).

Dividends of bank holding company affiliate eliminated. For the purpose of determining its separate personal holding company income for a consolidated return year, a parent corporation could eliminate dividends it received from a 90 percent owned holding company that owned 100 percent of a bank and whose only income was dividends from the bank. Rev. Rul. 74-432, 1974-2 CB 175.

Personal holding tax not applicable despite relationship and nature of brokerage services. The IRS held that an individual who owns a stock exchange membership and works as a broker on the exchange floor may organize a member corporation and not be subject to the provisions of Section 543(a)(7) relating to personal service contracts. Under the facts presented, the personal services rendered were not unique and could be substituted. Thus, other brokers could be brought into the member corporation. Also, individuals selected to perform the personal services would not be named or designated in the contracts entered into and third parties would not have the right to name or designate the individuals who were to perform such services. Accordingly, commissions that earned by the member corporation as a broker on the exchange floor as a result of the individual's efforts would not be considered income from personal service contracts within the meaning of Section 543 (a) (7). Rev. Rul. 71-372, 1971-2 CB 241.

Small loan company does not become personal holding company by precomputing interest. The state of Illinois permits small loan companies to precompute interest by determining the amount of interest that would be due on each scheduled installment date; these amounts are totaled and added to the principal of the loan. The aggregate of the principal and total precomputed interest is then divided by the number of scheduled installments to yield the amount of each scheduled installment. State-regulated finance and lending companies are excluded from the definition of personal holding companies if, among other conditions, specified percentages of gross income are compounded or derived from lawful interest not payable in advance and are computed only on unpaid balances. The precomputation of interest under Illinois law is not identical with the computation of the unpaid balance required by the regulations governing personal holding companies. Therefore, although the adoption of the precomputation of interest method will not cause a small loan company to lose its exemption from the personal holding company definition, any excess interest charged under the precomputation method that would not be charged under the unpaid balance method must not be taken into account in determining whether the loan company satisfies the percentage of gross income requirement prescribed for that exemption. Rev. Rul. 60-194, 1960-1 CB 206.

Insurance agency not personal holding company although only stockholders were licensed to perform services for which company received commissions. In 1954, the IRS ruled in Rev. Rul. 54-34 that income received by a fire insurance agency was personal service income; thus, the company was subject to the personal holding company tax. The corporation received commissions from insurance companies, but the contracts with the agency specified that only named persons, who were stockholders, were authorized to accept risks (i.e., to perform the service for which the commission was paid). The IRS ruled that an agency whose contracts with the insurance companies did not specifically name the persons authorized to accept risks. However,

PERSONAL HOLDING COMPANIES: *Personal Holding Company Income*

only persons licensed by the state could sell insurance, and the only licensed persons in the agency were stockholders who met the other personal holding company tests. The IRS ruled that commissions earned were not personal service income because specific individual stockholders were not designated by the contracts as persons who could perform the services. Licensed employees could be taken into the agency without violating the contract with the insurance company. Rev. Rul. 59-172, 1959-1 CB 144.

Personal Holding Company Income

Receipt of interest triggered personal holding company tax. Taxpayer corporation entered into a joint venture with another corporation. The stockholders of the other company agreed to repay taxpayer the amount of its investment plus 6 percent "interest" if the joint venture did not distribute profits by a certain date. The venture failed to distribute profits, so taxpayer received the interest. The Tax Court held that the interest triggered the personal holding company tax. *Held*: Affirmed. The 6 percent payment was interest, not a return of capital. The parties labeled it interest and intended it as such. Investors Ins. Agency, 677 F2d 1328, 82-1 USTC ¶ 9404, 50 AFTR2d 82-5104 (9th Cir. 1982).

Personal holding company income did not arise from lease of trucks. Taxpayer, whose principal business was leasing trucks and real estate, leased trucks and real estate to its sister corporation. Both taxpayer and its sister corporation were wholly owned by the same individual. The IRS treated the rents paid under this lease as personal holding company income on the theory that the sister corporation's use of the trucks was imputed to the common individual stockholder for purposes of Section 543(a)(6). The Tax Court held for taxpayer on the ground that the use of the leased property could not be attributed to the common stockholder as long as there was a business nexus for the lease. *Held*: Affirmed. Evidence showed that the common stockholder did not use, and had no right to use, the leased property for personal purposes. Allied Indus. Cartage Co., 647 F2d 713, 81-1 USTC ¶ 9425, 47 AFTR2d 81-1460 (6th Cir. 1981).

Contested tax deficiencies not allowed in personal holding company computation. The IRS held that taxpayer, in computing its personal holding company tax, could not deduct contested income tax deficiencies. The district court found for the IRS. *Held*: Affirmed. The appellate court held that for the personal holding company computation, income taxes were deductible only in the years in which they accrued. When a liability is contested, accrual occurs in the year of payment under Section 461(f). Also, certain deductions allowed in a prior year could not be taken again. LX Cattle Co., 629 F2d 1096, 46 AFTR2d 80-6050 (5th Cir. 1980).

Rental income from related corporation not personal holding company income. Taxpayer corporation received rental income from a corporate lessee. The IRS asserted that the rent was personal holding company income to the taxpayer. *Held*: For taxpayer. The income was not personal holding company income because the controlling stockholders of the lessor were also substantial stockholders of the lessee. Silverman & Sons Realty Trust, 620 F2d 314, 80-1 USTC ¶ 9439, 45 AFTR2d 80-1604 (1st Cir. 1980).

Interest received on land sale was rent and not personal holding company income. P and B, two family corporations, had assets consisting primarily of duplex homes. For financial reasons, it was decided that the duplexes should be sold and not rented. The units were sold, and the taxpayer stockholders received principal and interest payments from the purchasers and made payments on the existing mortgages for which they were liable. The Tax Court agreed with the IRS that the interest on the debts was personal holding company income because the realty was not held primarily for sale in the ordinary course of business. As a result, a personal holding company tax was imposed. *Held*: Reversed. Because the evidence indicated that the land was held primarily for sale to customers, the interest received on the debt from the sale of the land was rent and excluded from personal holding company income. Parkside Inc., 571 F2d 1092, 78-1 USTC ¶ 9147, 41 AFTR2d 78-451 (9th Cir. 1977).

Advances between controlled corporations did not create personal holding income. Taxpayer was a closely held corporation, the voting stock of which was equally held by four related individuals. While planning the construction and operation of a new apartment building, the stockholders created a second corporation in order to limit their liability. There were frequent transfers of money between the two brother-sister corporations. Taxpayer consented to proposed IRS adjustments on the accrual of interest on the monies transferred. As a result, taxpayer received interest from its brother corporation; and in turn, the sister corporation was permitted to deduct interest. The IRS determined that for the years in question, taxpayer's interest income exceeded 10 percent of its ordinary gross income. Because no dividends were paid, the rents otherwise received by taxpayer became personal holding company income. In reviewing the IRS' contention, the Tax Court held that the monies transferred from taxpayer to its brother corporation were loans producing interest income. In addition, bona fide interest-free loans by a corporation did not give rise to constructive dividends to the stockholders who owned both corporations. *Held*: Reversed, in part. Because the evidence indicated that the advances were capital contributions, there could be no finding that the monies transferred were interest-producing loans unless the following factors are considered: the equal ownership of the stock, the inability of the debtor corporation to repay the notes for a number of years, the impossibility of the debtor corporation to raise other funds, and the fact that a prudent businessman would not have invested in the unsecured demand notes at their specified rate of interest. Because the advances between the corporations were bona fide obligations, although interest free, there were no constructive dividends to the stockholders. The transferred funds were not siphoned off to or for the benefit of the stockholders but, instead, benefited only the corporation. Lupowitz Sons, Inc., 497 F2d 862, 74-1 USTC ¶ 9485, 34 AFTR2d 74-5054 (3d Cir. 1974).

Bonuses were royalties and personal holding company income. From 1959 through 1963, taxpayer received bonuses upon the execution of oil and gas leases and claimed percentage depletion thereon. In each of the succeeding years, 1960 through 1964, respectively, the lease of the immediately preceding year was terminated without production, and taxpayer returned as income a sum equal to the depletion deduction claimed for the immediately preceding year. The IRS held that taxpayer was subject to the personal holding company tax for certain years. The Tax Court held for the IRS, in part. *Held:* Affirmed. The bonuses only, and not the sums corresponding to amounts previously deducted as depletion and reported as income in the succeeding year, were royalties within the meaning of Section 543(a) and therefore personal holding company income. The depletion deduction was not allowable in computing the 15 percent requirement of pre-1964 Section 543(a)(8)(B). Taxpayer was, therefore, a personal holding company in 1959, 1960, and 1963. Bayou Verret Land Co., 450 F2d 850, 71-2 USTC ¶ 9713, 28 AFTR2d 71-5961 (5th Cir. 1971).

Tax attributable to capital gain of personal holding company determined without complete recomputation of corporation's tax. In computing personal holding company income, a deduction is allowed for income taxes paid (including the tax on capital gains), long-term capital gain, and various other items. To prevent a double deduction, the long-term capital gain deduction must be reduced by any tax "attributable to capital gain." The IRS computed the "tax attributable to capital gain" by applying the tax rate to the capital gain. Taxpayer contended that the tax attributable to capital gain should be determined by comparing the tax paid with the tax that would have resulted if the capital gain were not part of taxable income. This produced a smaller adjustment because of the interplay with the dividends received deduction. The district court agreed with the IRS. *Held:* Affirmed per curiam. The court relied on the similar decision of the Second Circuit in Litchfield Secs., 325 F2d 667 (1964). Delk Inv. Co., 344 F2d 696, 65-1 USTC ¶ 9393 (8th Cir. 1965).

Copyright royalties for purposes of the personal holding company tax include those amounts paid to persons without a proprietary interest in a copyright if they are determined as a percentage of actual copyright royalties. Taxpayer was formed by its sole stockholder, the composer Irving Berlin. Taxpayer and its sole stockholder entered into a publishing arrangement under which taxpayer, in addition to being its stockholder's publisher, became his exclusive agent for licensing the use of his compositions. Berlin, however, retained ownership of the copyrights to his songs. The IRS asserted that taxpayer's share of amounts paid to it under performing rights licenses were copyright royalties and not amounts rendered for services as an agent and therefore constituted personal holding company income. *Held:* For the IRS. The amounts paid to taxpayer were copyright royalties under the personal holding company rules, even though taxpayer did not hold a proprietary interest in the copyrights. Copyright royalties for this purpose include compensation measured as a percentage of the royalties paid for the use or right to use copyrights. Irving Berlin Music Corp., 487 F2d 540, 73-2 USTC ¶ 9786, 32 AFTR2d 73-6147 (Ct. Cl. 1973), cert. denied, 419 US 832 (1974).

Interest allocated under Section 482 was personal holding company income. Taxpayer corporation made interest-free loans to related corporations. The IRS allocated interest income to the taxpayer under Section 482, and by so doing increased the taxpayer's undistributed personal holding company income, which in turn increased its personal holding company tax for the years in question. The IRS assessed the personal holding company tax. The taxpayer contended that although the allocation was valid for income tax purposes, the allocated interest was fictional income that did not constitute personal holding company income. *Held:* For the IRS. The purpose of Section 482 is to cancel any advantages that commonly controlled corporations may obtain by artificially shifting income among themselves and to place them on a parity with uncontrolled corporations. The allocated interest was part of the taxpayer's adjusted ordinary income and was thus interest income for purposes of the personal holding company provisions. The Krueger Co. & Merri Mac Corp., 79 TC 65 (1982).

Rents from shopping center and mobile home park deemed personal holding company income. Taxpayer corporation received income from the operation of a shopping center and a mobile home park. Although taxpayer had income from sales, a significant portion of its income was from rents. The IRS determined that taxpayer was subject to personal holding company income tax. *Held:* For the IRS. Income received from the operation of a trailer park and commercial shopping center constituted rents within the meaning of Section 543(a)(2). Taxpayer was subject to personal holding company income tax because 60 percent of its adjusted ordinary gross income consisted of rents, and the nonrent income was 10 percent or less of its ordinary gross income. Eller, 77 TC 934 (1981).

Unique but replaceable services under service contract did not result in personal holding company income where without a provision designating service performed. Taxpayer received commission income under sales contracts governing machine parts negotiated by its president and principal stockholder on behalf of a machine part manufacturer. The commission contract with the manufacturer did not designate taxpayer's president as the person required to perform, according to the contract. The IRS argued that under Section 543(a)(7), these commissions constituted personal holding company income. *Held:* For taxpayer. Although the president's abilities were unique and the parties involved anticipated that he would be rendering services under the commission contract, he was not designated thereunder by name or description, nor were his services irreplaceable. Accordingly, because his services were not and could not be required under the contract, Section 543(a)(7) was inapplicable. Thomas P. Byrnes, Inc., 73 TC 416 (1979).

Personal Holding Companies: *Personal Holding Company Income*

Interest from purchase money mortgage is personal holding company income. Taxpayer corporation sold realty and elected installment reporting. The interest received on the notes constituted over 60 percent of taxpayer's income for the year, and the IRS determined that taxpayer was a personal holding company. Taxpayer contended that the interest received was not personal holding company income, since no money was loaned, and the term "interest," as used in Section 543, means amounts received for the use of money loaned. *Held:* For the IRS. The definition of "interest" as used in Section 543 is not limited strictly to amounts received for the use of money loaned. The fact that the transaction in question was a purchase money mortgage was not sufficient to bar the application of Section 543 to the interest received. Lake Gerar Dev. Co., 71 TC 887 (1979).

Payments measured by amount of a property's use (e.g., extraction of minerals), as opposed to a period or term of use, were royalties for personal holding tax purposes, regardless of the parties' intent or their character under state law. Taxpayer received rental income from certain properties and received amounts designated as rents under a mineral lease covering a stone quarry. Rent was .05 cents per ton of rock sold under the mineral lease. The IRS assessed taxpayer for the personal holding company tax. If the amounts received under the mineral lease were rental income, under Section 543(a), taxpayer's rental income would exceed 50 percent or more of his adjusted ordinary gross income, and its personal holding company income (excluding rents and royalties) would be 10 percent or less of its ordinary gross income. As a consequence, the rents would not be personal holding company income. If, however, the mineral lease yielded royalties, rents and royalties would be personal holding company income under Section 543(a), and taxpayer would thus be subject to personal holding company tax on this income. *Held:* For the IRS. Payments measured by and dependent on the quantity of minerals extracted (i.e., amount of use) rather than the period of use are royalties, under the personal holding company tax, regardless of their characterization by the parties involved or for state law purposes. Johnson Inv. & Rental Co., 70 TC 895 (1978).

Payment of qualified indebtedness by personal holding company defined. Taxpayers owned all the stock in a personal holding company that was liquidated and dissolved. All assets were distributed to the stockholders. Upon liquidation, the corporation's liabilities included a "qualified indebtedness," and the corporation deducted this indebtedness against its personal holding company income on its final income tax return. The IRS disallowed the deduction. *Held:* For the IRS. The mere distribution of assets in liquidation, and the assumption by the distributee-stockholders of the distributor's liabilities, did not meet the requirement of Section 545 that the qualified indebtedness be paid. Julio, 69 TC 1 (1977).

Imposition of personal holding company tax was proper. Taxpayer, a business trust engaged in renting real estate, obtained bank loans. It lent these funds to two sister corporations. Upon receipt of the interest and principal from these companies, in the same ratio as its obligation to the bank, taxpayer treated itself as a conduit, and did not report the interest income on its tax returns. The IRS imposed the personal holding company tax, determining that the interest received from the sister corporations was reportable as interest income. *Held:* For the IRS. Taxpayer was not a mere conduit that transferred the interest received to the lending bank. Such payments were its own gross income, regardless of the fact that it was under a separate obligation to pay interest (in larger amounts) to its creditor, the bank, in respect of its own borrowed funds, which, in part, were lent to the sister corporations. Bell Realty Trust, 65 TC 766 (1976).

Unaccrued taxes attributable to capital gains reduced deductible gains for personal holding company purposes. Taxpayer was a personal holding company. The IRS computed its net taxable income for personal holding company tax by deducting taxes due on net long-term capital gains included in income that were deductible in computing undistributed personal holding company income. Taxpayer argued that the taxes should not be subtracted, because the taxes did not accrue as a result of a dispute. *Held:* For the IRS. Under Section 545(b)(5), the adjustment for capital gains was expressed in terms of the amount of gains less taxes imposed thereon. It was the amount of the tax "imposed" and attributable that made up the adjustment. It was immaterial when such taxes accrued. Ellis Corp., 57 TC 520 (1972).

Bonuses were royalties and personal holding company income. From 1959 through 1963, taxpayer received bonuses from the execution of oil and gas leases, and claimed percentage depletion thereon. In each year from 1960 through 1964, the lease of the immediately preceeding year was terminated without any oil or gas having been extracted, and taxpayer returned as income a sum equal to the depletion deduction claimed for the immediately preceeding year. The IRS held that taxpayer was subject to the personal holding company tax for certain years. *Held:* For the IRS, in part. Only the bonuses, and not the sums corresponding to amounts previously deducted as depletion and reported as income in the succeeding year, were royalties within the meaning of Section 543(a) and were therefore personal holding company income. The depletion deduction was not allowable in computing the 15 percent requirement of pre-1964 Section 543(a)(8)(B). Taxpayer was therefore a personal holding company in 1959, 1960, and 1963. Bayou Verret Land Co., Inc., 52 TC 971 (1969).

Interest income yields personal holding company tax. The IRS claimed that a corporation was subject to the personal holding company tax because interest received on loans to a related corporation caused its income to meet the requirements of Section 542(a). *Held:* For the IRS. Taxpayer received the interest under a claim of right and not as a mere conduit. Blair Holding Co., 39 TCM 1255, ¶ 80,079 P-H Memo. TC (1980).

Interest accrued on advances by stockholder to corporation determined to be personal holding company income. Taxpayer corporation made loans to a second corporation. The IRS determined that interest should have been accrued and that taxpayer was subject to personal holding company tax. *Held:* For the IRS. The advances made by taxpayer were not contributions to capital. Although there was no formal instrument, substantial repayments were made, and after previous IRS audits, interest income and expense was accounted for by both companies. Therefore, the advances represented a loan. Interest had to be accrued, and such interest was subject to the personal holding tax. Furthermore, stockholders did not receive a constructive dividend when a third company transferred funds to taxpayer pursuant to a bona fide debt obligation. Joseph Lupowitz Sons, Inc., 31 TCM 1169, ¶ 72,238 P-H Memo. TC (1972).

Rental income received by a corporation from a related lessee was not personal holding company income under Section 543(a)(6). A was the sole stockholder of X and Y. X's primary business activity was leasing realty and tangible personal property to Y. A made no personal use of X's leased assets. X received $\$100x$ in rental income from Y and $\$12x$ in interest income from bank deposits. The IRS ruled that the rental income received by X was not compensation for the use of or the right to the use of corporate property by a stockholder under Section 543(a)(6) for purposes of the personal holding company tax provisions. Between brother and sister corporations, unless a corporate lessee can be shown to be a vehicle for facilitating the individual or personal use of leased property by its stockholders, its separate status should not be disregarded so as to impose the personal holding company tax upon the lessor corporation. Rev. Rul. 84-137, 1984-2 CB 116, revoking Rev. Rul. 65-259, 1965-2 CB 174.

Dividend from personal holding company to parent may be personal holding company income. P Corporation and its first- and second-tier subsidiaries, $S1$ and $S2$, filed a consolidated return for computing regular income tax. Since $S2$ was a personal holding company under Section 542(b)(2), the group was not eligible to compute its personal holding company tax on a group basis. *S2* distributed a dividend to *S1*, claiming a dividends paid deduction to avoid personal holding company tax. The dividend was included in *S1*'s personal holding company income, since *S2* took a dividends paid deduction. However, a dividend from *S1* to *P* would not produce personal holding company income to *P* if *S1* did not claim a dividends paid deduction. Rev. Rul. 79-60, 1979-1 CB 211.

Insurance commissions assigned to wholly owned corporation not personal holding company income. Taxpayer earned commissions from the sale of life insurance policies. The insurer had a policy against assigning such rights to corporations. Taxpayer's wholly owned corporation designed and administered pension- and profit-sharing plans that were funded by the commissions. The IRS ruled that such commissions were not personal holding company income. The taxpayer was required to include, but could deduct, the portion paid to the corporation for services performed. Rev. Rul. 77-336, 1977-2 CB 202.

Working mineral interest ruled not to be personal holding company income. Taxpayer was a corporation whose sole purpose was the exploitation of certain working interests in oil and gas properties. If income derived from such interests constitutes a royalty, then it is personal holding company income under Section 543(b)(2). The IRS ruled that the interest was analogous to an operating interest, and, accordingly, was not personal holding company income. Rev. Rul. 77-127, 1977-1 CB 158.

Proceeds of copyright sale not personal holding company income. An author's personal holding company was the transferee of one of his copyrights and had a 15-year exclusive employment contract with him. It did not receive personal holding company income from copyright royalties when it sold the copyright to an unrelated corporation for a substantial lump sum, even though it retained a reversionary interest if the buyer failed to publish or exploit the manuscript within a specified time. It could then keep the lump sum as liquidated damages. Rev. Rul. 75-202, 1975-1 CB 170.

Payment in "output" was royalty to personal holding company lessor. The IRS ruled that a personal holding company that leased oil and gas properties to a drilling company in return for a percentage of the production and a guaranteed sale to the lessee at a stipulated price received royalties for the purpose of computing personal holding company income. Rev. Rul. 73-332, 1973-2 CB 195.

Mortgage servicing fees were not personal holding company income. A lending institution derived fees from servicing mortgages guaranteed by the Government National Mortgage Association and sold to various investors. Fees were customary service fees as specified under a servicing agreement with GNMA and were not personal holding company income. The principal and interest payments collected on the warehoused mortgages were not included in the institution's gross income. Rev. Rul. 72-278, 1972-1 CB 171.

Depletion deduction taken on a bonus but required to be restored to income was not personal holding company income. An individual received bonuses upon being granted an economic interest in a mineral deposit. A depletion deduction was allowed on bonuses but was required to be restored to income upon the expiration, termination, or abandonment of the interest. It was held that the amounts to be restored to income did not constitute royalty or rental income under Section 543. Rev. Rul. 72-148, 1972-1 CB 170.

Payments received under subprocessing contract were royalties. A corporation owned the right to manufacture and distribute a product. By way of a subprocessing contract, it contracted with a partnership for the continued processing of the product. The partners of the partnership were also the stockholders of the corporation. The IRS ruled that the amounts received from the partnership for the right to manufacture the product were royalty payments includable as personal holding company income. Rev. Rul. 71-596, 1971-2 CB 242.

Dividends received from a bank member of an affiliated group were eliminated in computing parent's personal holding company income. A common parent of an affiliated group received a dividend from a bank member of the group. The group filed a consolidated return for the year in question. For the purpose of computing the personal holding company income of the parent, the dividend received from the bank member was eliminated. Rev. Rul. 71-531, 1971-2 CB 242.

Intercorporate interest and managerial fees from subsidiaries were personal holding company income. Taxpayer was engaged in the lending and finance business. In addition to making loans, it managed its subsidiaries and loaned money to them. For purposes of determining ordinary gross income, the intercorporate interest and management fees from the subsidiary had to be included in taxpayer's gross income. Rev. Rul. 69-588, 1969-2 CB 137.

Contested federal income tax deficiency deductible for computing personal holding company income in year paid if provision of Section 461(f) were met. A personal holding company contested but paid a federal income tax deficiency. The amount paid qualified as an adjustment to taxable income under Section 545(b) in determining undistributed personal holding company income. Provisions of Regulation § 1.545-2(a)(1)(i) were to be disregarded if provisions of Section 461(f) were met. Amounts recovered were included as adjustment to personal holding company income in year of receipt unless excludable under Section 111(c)(2). Rev. Rul. 69-620, 1969-2 CB 137.

Subsidy payments were not "rents" for personal holding company purposes. Personal holding company leased farmland to a corporation on a cropsharing basis. The personal holding company participated in the management of the farm. By agreement with the Secretary of Agriculture, the lessor and lessee received farm subsidy payments for withholding acreage from production. The IRS ruled that since the personal holding company participated materially in the management of the farm production, the payments it received under this program were not "rents" for personal holding company purposes. Rev. Rul. 67-423, 1967-2 CB 221.

Procedure set to make election to eliminate lease rents from personal holding company income. Public Law 89-809 amended Section 543(b)(3) to eliminate from the term "rent" for personal holding company purposes any compensation received for the use of tangible personal property manufactured or produced by the taxpayer if, during the taxable year, taxpayer was engaged in substantial manufacture or production of tangible personal property of the same type. Taxpayers can elect to have the amendment made retroactive. The IRS established a procedure for taxpayer to follow if he wishes the benefits made retroactive. To be effective, the election must be made within the period allowed for filing a claim for refund and must be filed with the director of the district in which the return was filed. Rev. Proc. 67-16, 1967-1 CB 593.

PREMIUM, BOND

(*See* Bonds and Debentures—Bond Discount and Premiums)

PROCEDURE

(*See also* Assessment and Collection)

In General	437
Mitigation	439
Penalties and Interest	439
Refunds	440
Returns	441

In General

Prior decision holding debentures to be equity barred current interest deduction. Taxpayer corporation, organized to acquire a family partnership in 1946, originally issued $35,000 in stock and $800,000 in debentures. In a prior adjudication for 1953 through 1955, the Court of Claims denied the corporation an

PROCEDURE: *In General*

interest deduction on the debentures, ruling that they constituted equity capital, not debt. Taxpayer again sought to deduct interest on the debentures for 1961 and 1962. *Held:* For the IRS. The doctrine of collateral estoppel applied to deny the deduction because the controlling facts and applicable legal rules upon which the Court of Claims based its decision in the earlier case remained unchanged. The Court of Appeals also found that it would reach the same conclusion on the merits as did the Court of Claims, and this court affirmed the decision. R.C. Owen Co., 351 F2d 410, 65-2 USTC ¶ 9673 (6th Cir. 1965), cert. denied, 383 US 967 (1966).

Corporation was denied refund of disallowed exemption, although regulation on which the IRS relied had been invalidated. An Arkansas corporation's stock was held in part by individuals who owned stock in an Oklahoma corporation of the same name. Both corporations filed returns each claiming a $25,000 surtax exemption. The lower court held that the corporations had to share one exemption because they were part of a controlled "brother-sister" group under Section 1563(a)(2). The corporations met the 80 percent stock ownership test, although the stockholders each did not own stock in each corporation. They also met the 50 percent test because under attribution rules, one stockholder owned 50 percent of the total value of all shares in each corporation. It did not matter that the stockholder did not control over 50 percent of the total outstanding stock voting rights because of a voting agreement, as the total value ownership test had been met. *Held:* For the IRS. The Arkansas corporation was still denied a refund, even though the Regulation § 1.1563-1(a)(3), on which the IRS relied, was invalidated by the Supreme Court in Vogel, 455 US 16 (1982). Res judicata barred relitigation. Vogel was not intended to apply retroactively. The Arkansas corporation litigated the case before the regulation was invalidated. The Oklahoma corporation litigated after the invalidation and was granted a refund. This unequal treatment afforded a sister corporation did not justify granting equitable relief. Yaffee Iron & Metal Corp., 84-1 USTC ¶ 9299, 53 AFTR2d 84-1064 (WD Ark. 1984).

Settlement did not bar net operating loss carry-back. In 1971, taxpayer and the IRS reached a compromise on taxpayers liability for a late-filing penalty for its 1969-1970 fiscal year. When taxpayer tried to carry back a later net operating loss to its 1969-1970 year, the IRS claimed that the settlement closed that year and barred a refund, even though, as the IRS also claimed, that year's income used up the loss in any event. *Held:* For taxpayer. The settlement stated that only the amount by which the potential tax exceeded the settlement amount was not refundable. A net operating loss carry-back does not "reopen" the prior year. A&A Distribs., 81-1 USTC ¶ 9136, 47 AFTR2d 81-922 (D. Mass. 1980).

Taxpayer can waive error in deficiency notice. The IRS, intending to assert deficiencies from 1956 through 1958, mailed a notice of deficiency based on the years from 1952 through 1954 "as shown in the attached statement." The statement attached to the notice referred to the correct years, 1956 through 1958. The IRS subsequently mailed a second correct notice of deficiency. Taxpayer filed a petition in the Tax Court based on the first notice, alleging that the IRS determined deficiencies from 1956 through 1958; the IRS moved to dismiss on the ground that the deficiency notice upon which the petition was based asserted deficiencies for the years from 1952 to 1954. *Held:* For taxpayer. The court denied the IRS' motion and held that under the circumstances, it was proper to ignore the error and to recognize the notice of deficiency as a proper notice for the years from 1956 to 1958. The court did not declare the second notice null and void, since the court lacked such jurisdiction. Saint Paul Bottling Co., 34 TC 1137 (1960).

Long-term purchaser agreement and sale of stock were unrelated. One of two stockholders of a corporation that manufactured paper sold his stock to four publishers. To assure the purchasers of a supply of newsprint, the corporation contracted to supply it for three

PROCEDURE: *Penalties and Interest*

years at a stated price. The IRS alleged that that price was less than the fair market value of the newsprint, that the price the publishers paid for the stock exceeded its fair market value, and that such excess was additional income to the corporation for the newsprint. *Held:* For taxpayer. The court found that the transactions were independent. It also held that the IRS had failed to sustain the burden of proving that the fair market value of the stock was sufficiently below its sale price to result in the overage constituting more than 25 percent of taxpayer's reported gross income. Accordingly, the five-year statute of limitations was inapplicable, and the three-year statute barred any assessment in the year of the sale of the paper manufacturer's corporate stock. Peavey Paper Mills, Inc., 19 TCM 1325, ¶ 60,237 P-H Memo. TC (1960).

The IRS may issue rulings on certain corporate liquidations. The IRS removed certain corporate liquidations from the list of areas in which it will not issue rulings or determination letters and placed them on the list of areas in which rulings or determination letters will not ordinarily be issued. The affected areas include Sections 302(b)(4), 302(e), 331, 332, 333, 337, and 346(a). Rev. Proc. 84-75, 1984-2 CB 751.

Mitigation

Renegotiation repayment by successor corporation required recomputation under mitigation provisions; not deductible when paid. Taxpayer was the surviving corporation in a statutory merger. The merged corporation had completed contracts with the U.S. government that were subject to renegotiation at the time of the merger. Under Section 381, taxpayer steps into the tax shoes of its predecessor. The district court held that taxpayer could deduct the excess profits to be refunded in the year in which the determination was made. *Held:* Reversed. Under the mitigation provisions, the renegotiation repayment requires a tax recomputation, not a deduction in the later year. Lodge & Shipley Co., 305 F2d 643, 62-2 USTC ¶ 9646 (6th Cir. 1962).

Penalties and Interest

IRS fails to prove amount of nontax payments in Section 6672 case. Taxpayer admitted that he was the responsible person under Section 6672 to collect withholding taxes and that he had signed checks to other creditors after the date that the tax liabilities were incurred. The IRS maintained that taxpayer acted willfully in not paying the taxes and therefore was subject to a penalty. *Held:* For taxpayer. By failing to produce acceptable evidence that the payments that taxpayer made to other creditors exceeded the tax liability, the IRS did not establish that the taxpayer acted willfully. Because the IRS did not prove the facts necessary to establish taxpayer's willfulness, the IRS's motion for summary judgment was denied. Davies, 85-2 USTC ¶ 9687, 56 AFTR2d 85-6176 (DC Mass. 1985).

Taxpayer president was a responsible person who willfully failed to pay withholding taxes. The IRS assessed a penalty against taxpayer for his failure to pay withholding taxes. Taxpayer filed for a Chapter 7 bankruptcy and filed against the IRS. The bankruptcy court granted a summary judgment in favor of the IRS that the district court affirmed. On appeal, the Eighth Circuit remanded the case for a determination of whether taxpayer, as president of the corporation, was a "responsible person" within the meaning of Section 6672 and whether his failure to pay withholding taxes was willful. *Held:* Affirmed. Taxpayer controlled the corporate finances and management and was a responsible person who knew of the delinquency of tax payments and yet signed checks to pay other obligations. Thus, taxpayer's failure to pay withholding taxes was willful. Accordingly, a 100 percent penalty was imposed on taxpayer as the president of the corporation for nonpayment of withholding taxes. In re Turner, 85-2 USTC ¶ 9561, 56 AFTR2d 85-5588 (DND 1985).

In determining a prior year's tax for purposes of the corporate estimated income tax, any tax liability resulting from the recapture of investment tax credits was ignored. In 1975, taxpayer operated at a loss but had an income tax liability as a result of investment tax credit recapture. In 1976, taxpayer did earn taxable

PROCEDURE: *Refunds*

income. Taxpayer made no estimated tax payments for 1976, relying on Section 6655(d)(2). This section provides that taxpayer need pay only estimated tax for the current year based on tax for the prior year. Taxpayer's position was that investment tax credit recapture should be ignored in determining the prior year's tax. The IRS disagreed. *Held:* For the taxpayer. Investment tax credit recapture is an addition to the Section 11 tax, not part of it. Berkshire Hathaway, Inc., 85-2 USTC ¶ 9713, 56 AFTR2d 85-5964 (Ct. Cl. 1985).

Current investment tax credit limitation applicable to corporate estimated tax penalty exception. A corporation that underpaid its estimated tax for 1980 invoked Section 6655(d)(2), which provides that the penalty for underpayment imposed by Section 6655(a) cannot be imposed where the corporation's estimated tax payments equal the amount that would have been required to be paid if the estimated tax had been computed on the basis of facts shown on the corporation's return for, and the law applicable to, the preceding taxable year but at the current taxable year's rates. The IRS ruled that for the purpose of computing this amount, taxpayer's investment credit should be computed on the basis of the increased percentage limitation for 1980. Rev. Rul. 82-65, 1982-1 CB 213.

IRS illustrates how year-end estimated tax payment can be used to avoid penalty. Taxpayer corporation filed its income tax returns on a calendar year basis. Due to the seasonal nature of its business, most of the corporation's income was earned during the last six months of the year. The corporation did not make any installment payments of estimated tax during 1975 until December 15. On December 15, 1975, it paid an amount equal to 25 percent of 80 percent (i.e., 20 percent) of the tax liability that was ultimately reflected on its federal income tax return for the calendar year. The IRS held that in this case, the corporation was required under Section 6154 to make installment payments of estimated tax for each installment period of its tax year. Its fourth installment of estimated tax was required to be 25 percent of the total estimated tax for the year. Under Section 6655(c), the IRS held that because the corporation's estimated tax payment for the fourth period was equal to the amount required for that period (25 percent of the 80 percent of the tax liability for the year), there was no underpayment of estimated tax for the fourth period. Rev. Rul. 76-563, 1976-2 CB 445.

Estimated tax penalty computed without income of subsidiary corporations merged into parent. Section 6655(a) provides for an addition to the tax of 6 percent of any underpayment of estimated tax by a corporation. Section 6655(d)(1) provides for an exception to this penalty based on the tax paid in the previous year. The IRS ruled that when subsidiary corporations previously filing separate income tax returns merge into their parent corporation, the words "tax shown on the return of the corporation for the preceding taxable year" appearing in Section 6655(d)(1) refer only to the tax shown on the return of the parent corporation. Rev. Rul. 68-9, 1968-1 CB 566.

Computation of interest on corporation filing estimated tax discussed. A corporation filed for an automatic extension on Form 7004 before the due date of its return. At the same time, it elected to pay its estimated tax liability of $100,000 in two installments under Section 6152. When filed, the return showed a liability of $80,000, with $30,000 paid as the last installment. A subsequent audit resulted in a deficiency of $10,000. The IRS ruled that since the $50,000 paid as the first installment exceeded by $10,000 the proper first installment determined from the filed return and exceeded the tax on the return plus the deficiency by $5,000, interest on the deficiency was not prorated to the first installment. The interest on the $10,000 deficiency was computed from the due date of the second installment to the date paid. Rev. Rul. 68-258, 1968-1 CB 541.

Refunds

**Two-year-from-payment period for seeking refund based on loss carry-backs was inapplica-

PROCEDURE: *Returns*

ble where income in carry-back year was determined in settlement approved by Tax Court. Taxpayer timely filed its 1959 return in August 1960, reflecting income solely from capital gains. Taxpayer incurred losses in each of the years from 1960 through 1963. The IRS determined a deficiency against taxpayer for 1959. On June 8, 1966, taxpayer and the IRS made a Tax Court approved settlement on this issue according to which taxpayer agreed that its ordinary income was higher than reported. Taxpayer sought to carry back its 1960 through 1963 losses to its 1959 ordinary income as adjusted and thereby obtain a refund. The IRS claimed that taxpayer's suit for a refund was barred by the statute of limitations. Taxpayer relied on the "two-year-from-payment" rule. *Held:* For the IRS. The "two-year-from-payment" rule does not apply where the Tax Court has already made a determination regarding the year involved. Therefore, taxpayer could rely only on the "38.5-month rule" (replacing the "three-year-from-filing rule" in the case of net operating loss). This period had expired before taxpayer sought the refund. Mar Monte Corp., 503 F2d 254, 74-2 USTC ¶ 9707, 34 AFTR2d 74-5856 (9th Cir. 1974).

Suit for refund of Section 6672 penalty dismissed. Taxpayer paid 50 percent of a Section 6672 payroll tax penalty relating to one employee. He then sued for a refund. *Held:* Suit dismissed. Although payment of the penalty relating to one employee is sufficient payment for a refund suit, it must be a full payment. Pritchett, 85-1 USTC ¶ 9430, 56 AFTR2d 85-5410 (MD Ala. 1985).

Returns

Corporate application for extension denied because not accompanied by partial payment of tentative tax. Taxpayer applied for an automatic extension of time to file. On Form 7004, it set forth the unpaid balance of its tentative tax liability but did not make a payment thereon. The IRS then informed taxpayer that the extension could not be granted without payment of at least one-half of the tentative tax, but taxpayer made no payment and mailed the return on what would have been the extended due date. The IRS assessed the penalty for interest plus failure to file a timely return. Prior to the end of the taxable year, taxpayer had paid taxes estimated equal to at least one-half of its eventual tax liability. It contended that pursuant Section 6081(b) it had paid one-half of the "amount properly estimated as its tax" on or before the due date of the return. The IRS contended that Section 6152 applied and that it provides for payment of one-half of the unpaid amount on the date prescribed for payment of the tax. The district court upheld the IRS. *Held:* Affirmed. The appellate court held that the key premise in distinguishing between the seemingly differing sections is that the plain wording of Section 6081(b) requires payment of the proper amount of estimated tax "or the first installment thereof required under section 6152." Therefore, the section taxpayer relied on requires reference to the section the IRS relied on to determine the unpaid amount of income tax, one-half of which must have been paid in order for the automatic extension to be granted. Custom Component Switches, Inc., 396 F2d 514, 68-1 USTC ¶ 9422, 21 AFTR2d 1567 (9th Cir. 1968).

Completely liquidated corporation must file its return on or before the fifteenth day of the third month following dissolution. A corporation that has completely liquidated is considered dissolved. The corporation must file its return and pay the tax due for the short period on or before the fifteenth day of the third month following the dissolution. (Rev. Rul. 215, 1953-2 CB 149 superseded.) Rev. Rul. 71-129, 1971-1 CB 397.

PROFESSIONAL SERVICE CORPORATIONS

(*See* Associations Taxable as Corporations—Professional Associations)

PROOF OF EXPENDITURES

(*See* Business Expenses—Substantiation)

REDEMPTIONS: *In General*

REASONABLE SALARIES

(*See* Compensation for Personal Services)

RECAPITALIZATIONS

(*See* Reorganizations—Recapitalizations)

RECAPTURE OF DEPRECIATION

(*See* Depreciation and Amortization—Recapture Of)

RECOGNITION OF GAIN OR LOSS

(*See* Capital Gains and Losses; Liquidations; Redemptions; Reorganizations; Transfers to Controlled Corporations)

REDEMPTIONS

(*See also* Dividends and Distributions; Liquidations; Reorganizations)

In General	442
Attribution Rules	445
Business Purpose	452
Dividend Equivalence	454
Effect on Redeeming Corporation	462
Effect on Remaining Stockholders	463
Gift Consequences	463
Meaningful Reduction of Stockholder's Interest	464
Partial Liquidations	469
Redemptions by Affiliated Corporations	470
Redemptions of Preferred Stock	474
Redemptions to Pay Death Taxes	477
Satisfaction of Stockholder Obligations	479
Substantially Disproportionate Redemptions	483
Termination of Stockholder's Interest	487

In General

Parties intended a stock redemption for 1966, although documents were executed and assets transferred in 1967. *B* Corporation agreed with *A* Corporation to surrender its stock in *A*, partially assign a lease, and assume a note owed by *A* in return for stock from *A*. Formal agreements were dated January 1, 1966. Notarization, accounting entries, and other records also referred to 1966. *B* did not report the transaction on its 1966 return, believing no capital gain was involved. *B* argued that the written agreements were not signed until 1967 and that the asset transfer did not take place until 1967. The IRS contended that the redemption took place in 1966. *Held:* For the IRS. The evidence showed that the redemption took place in 1966. The court held that the question of when a redemption was consummated is a practical one to be decided by the weight of evidence. Factors considered included whether legal title passed, whether the transferee obtained possession, whether the sale price was fixed, and whether a significant amount of the agreed price was paid. Also considered were the parties' intent and the effective dates and terms in the agreement. Even though the written documents were not executed until 1967 and the testimony showed that the assets were not transferred until 1967, the court found that the evidence supported a finding that the effective date of the redemption was 1966. Barton Theatre Co., 701 F2d 126, 83-1 USTC ¶ 9226, 51 AFTR2d 83-901 (10th Cir. 1983).

Regulation § 1.61-5 did not require ordinary income treatment of gain recognized on a 1962 redemption of agricultural cooperative stock. An agricultural cooperative issued stock to taxpayer in 1960. This stock was redeemed in 1962. The IRS argued that Regulation § 1.61-5 required the gain recognized by taxpayer on this redemption to be taxed as ordinary income. Taxpayer argued and the Claims Court held that this regulation was inapplicable to a 1962 redemption of agricultural cooperative stock and that this redemption was "not essentially equivalent to a dividend" within the meaning of Section 302. *Held:* The appellate court held that the Claims Court correctly determined that application of the regulation to a 1962 redemption of agricultural cooperative stock, otherwise treated as a redemption under Section 302, would be improper. Accordingly, taxpayer realized a long-term capital gain, not ordinary income, on the recemption. Agway, Inc., 696 F2d 1367, 83-1 USTC ¶ 9128, 51 AFTR2d 83-624 (Fed. Cir. 1982).

Sale of assets not taxable to corporation due to redemption. Taxpayer corporation was controlled by four individuals. In November 1965, taxpayer's treasury stock was sold to a second corporation for $40,000. Next, taxpayer's plant and equipment and the $40,000 were distributed to its stockholders in exchange for their outstanding stock. Finally, in that month, taxpayer's stockholders sold the plant and equipment to the second corporation for $100,000. Thus, the stockholders received $140,000. The IRS held that the transaction constituted a taxable sale of assets to taxpayer corporation. Taxpayer argued that it was not taxable under Section 311(a). *Held:* For taxpayer. Although taxpayer was not formally dissolved until 1973, it ceased to be a going concern after the November 1965 transactions. The transactions constituted a stock redemption and a sale of assets by the stockholders. Master Eagle Assocs., 508 F. Supp. 129, 81-1 USTC ¶ 9171, 47 AFTR2d 81-1066 (SDNY 1981).

"Bootstrap purchase" constituted partial redemption of seller's stock. Taxpayer purchased all the outstanding stock of Pacific from the corporation's sole stockholder by depositing the purchase price in escrow. Part of the purchase price had been supplied by Crown Chemical, which was to acquire certain nickel anodes owned by Pacific if the sale went through. At or about the same time that taxpayer made his deposit, the seller caused Pacific to deposit certain of its assets in the escrow. When the escrow was closed, the seller withdrew these assets and the purchase price, and taxpayer withdrew the outstanding stock. Similarly, Crown Chemical received the anodes from Pacific. Subsequently, taxpayer transferred some of the shares he acquired to Pacific as shares in substance redeemed by Pacific from the seller. The shares transferred were equal in value to both the Pacific assets deposited in escrow and withdrawn by the seller and the anodes received by Crown Chemical. The IRS contended that to this extent, taxpayer received a distribution substantially equivalent to, and taxable as, a dividend, arguing that the funds supplied by Crown Chemical and the Pacific assets deposited in the escrow constituted loans to taxpayers that they satisfied by the stock redemption. *Held:* For taxpayer. The net effect of the transaction was that taxpayer acquired all the outstanding stock of a corporation whose assets did not include those deposited in the escrow or the anodes transferred to Crown Chemical. The assets deposited in escrow were, in substance, transferred in redemption of stock from the seller; the anodes transferred to Crown Chemical were sold. Tracy, 66-2 USTC ¶ 9780 (CD Cal. 1966).

Sale and subsequent redemption was a redemption from seller. A majority stockholder wished to liquidate his interest in the corporation. However, the corporation did not have sufficient funds for a redemption, and the minority did not have sufficient funds to buy him out. The majority stockholder was averse to corporate borrowing to fund the redemption for fear that he would be liable as a director for impairment of capital. To avoid this problem, the corporation borrowed funds that it loaned to the minority buyer to complete the purchase. At the same time, the corporation retired the purchased shares and wiped out the loan. The IRS taxed the buyer with a constructive dividend on the redemption. *Held:* For taxpayer. Although in form a sale was followed by a redemption from the buyer, in substance it was simply a complete redemption from the seller. The whole purpose of the series of steps was to protect the outgoing stockholder from liability by showing on the books that his shares were sold rather than redeemed. Bennett, 58 TC 381 (1972).

Merger solely for purpose of "squeezing out" a 9 percent minority interest in transferor corporation for cash treated as a redemption, and thus no question arose over the carry-back of

postmerger net operating losses. Standard Kollsman Industries, Inc. sought to acquire 100 percent of the stock of Old Casco, but it was able to acquire through a public purchase offer only 91 percent of Old Casco's stock. For the sole purpose of acquiring the remaining 9 percent, Standard Kollsman formed New Casco, taking back 100 percent of its stock and, through its control over Old Casco, caused Old Casco to merge into New Casco. On this merger, the receipt of cash was the sole right of the minority stockholders of Old Casco. New Casco sought to carry back a net operating loss to offset Old Casco's premerger income. The IRS denied the carryback on the ground that the merger was not a valid F reorganization because of the 9 percent proprietary shift. *Held:* For taxpayer. Without discussing whether the merger qualified as an F reorganization, the court held that, under the facts, the merger should be viewed as a mere redemption of the 9 percent minority interest. Casco Prods. Corp., 49 TC 32 (1967).

Stock purchase and redemption was not disguised loan. A corporation was formed to acquire a business and needed additional equity capital to obtain required performance bonds. Decedent agreed with the organizers to purchase $500,000 of common stock at $30 per share, with an option to require the corporation to redeem the shares after 18 months at $78 per share. The IRS treated the gain on the redemption as ordinary income, arguing that the transaction was in substance a loan. *Held:* For taxpayer. Decedent had an equity investment that, under state law, would not rate a high priority on liquidation and that was subject to genuine risk. Estate of Schott, 43 TCM 1188, ¶ 82,222 P-H Memo. TC (1982).

Redemption did not occur in taxable year. The IRS contended that the redemption of stock by an estate took place in 1956, the year in issue, and was essentially equivalent to a dividend. *Held:* For taxpayer. The court found that the redemption did not occur until January 1957, a year not before the court. In 1957, the shares were tendered to the corporation and accepted by the corporation. The estate's participation in the redemption had been approved by the probate court in 1955, and the corporation's participation was authorized by its board in 1956. Neither of these unilateral, preparatory actions by the parties to the redemption constituted the redemption. Since the year 1957 was not in issue, the court found it unnecessary to decide whether the redemption was essentially equivalent to a dividend. Estate of Moore, 20 TCM 1346, ¶ 61,257 P-H Memo. TC (1961).

Unanticipated market fluctuation does not affect reasonableness of redemption premium. When a redemption premium of preferred stock was reasonable when the terms of a tender offer became final, but a subsequent event caused the fair market value of the preferred stock of the widely held companies to drop, thereby increasing the premium, the premium was still found to be reasonable. Thus, no taxable distribution resulted. Rev. Rul. 81-190, 1981-2 CB 84.

IRS reverses its position on treatment of prearranged redemption involving a private foundation. Having unsuccessfully contested the issue before the Tax Court, the IRS changed its position on the tax consequences following a stock redemption by a private foundation. The IRS now recognizes that a taxpayer with voting control of a corporation and an exempt private foundation who donates shares of the corporation's stock to the foundation and, pursuant to a prearranged plan, causes the corporation to redeem the shares from the foundation, does not realize income as a result of the redemption. Rev. Rul. 78-197, 1978-1 CB 83.

Redemption of nonvoting stock actually owned and voting stock constructively owned is a redemption of both voting and nonvoting stock. A and B owned all of the voting shares of X. C, A's father, owned all of nonvoting preferred stock. X redeemed a substantially disproportionate amount of A's voting stock and all of C's nonvoting stock. The IRS ruled that C constructively owned all of A's shares and that the redemption of C's stock was a redemption of both voting and nonvoting shares. Since the requirements of Section

302(b)(2) were met, the redemption of C's shares were treated as a distribution in full payment in exchange for the stock. Rev. Rul. 77-238, 1977-2 CB 115.

Sale of stock by a trust recast as a redemption. W was the beneficiary of a trust that owned shares in X and Y corporations. W's children, their spouses, W's grandchildren, and an unrelated party owned the remaining shares of X and Y. The trust sold its X stock to Y because X did not possess sufficient cash to redeem these shares. The IRS ruled that this sale would be recast as a redemption that would give rise to dividend income. The IRS reasoned that under the constructive ownership rules, the trust owned over 50 percent of the shares of both X and Y, bringing Section 304 into play. It further stated that the redemption was to be treated as a dividend and found that there was no complete termination of the trust's interest in X, that the redemption was not substantially disproportionate, and that the redemption did not constitute a meaningful reduction of the trust's interest in X because it retained an indirect interest in excess of 50 percent of X's stock. Rev. Rul. 77-218, 1977-1 CB 81.

Section 302 applies to withdrawals of investment units. Stock in a regulated investment company includes investment units that determine the number of votes of each investor, his ratable share of the fund's profits, and his ratable share of the fund's assets on liquidation. Withdrawals are treated as redemptions of shares to which Section 302 applies. Rev. Rul. 74-463, 1974-2 CB 96.

Gain recognized on redemption. A transfer by three stockholders of their combined 10 percent interest in a corporation to a partnership formed by them will be disregarded where the partnership was formed as part of a plan to have the corporation transfer appreciated assets to the partnership in redemption of stockholders' interests. Rev. Rul. 74-87, 1974-1 CB 72.

Distribution of appreciated property a redemption, not a sale to stockholders. Taxpayer corporation's business consisted of acquiring control in other corporations. Its own stock was publicly held. A related corporation, in which taxpayer owned 20 percent of the stock, planned to merge with an unrelated corporation. Since taxpayer's ownership would be reduced below the level of effective control, it decided to dispose of the related corporation's stock. Taxpayer offered shares of the stock to its own stockholders in redemption for part of their stock in taxpayer. The offer was made on a pro rata basis. Thirty-five per cent of taxpayer's stockholders accepted the offer. The IRS ruled that since the distribution was made because of the corporation-stockholder relationship and not because of a vendor-vendee relationship, no gain was recognized to taxpayer for the appreciation in value of the distributed stock. Rev. Rul. 68-21, 1968-1 CB 104.

Attribution Rules

"Family discord" not a factor in determining tax treatment of redemptions. Trusts cannot execute the waiver capable of arresting application of attribution rules in the case of complete redemption. After the death of David Metzger, the David Metzger Trust, his wife, his three children (Jacob, Catherine, and Cecelia), and trusts for his three children owned the stock of Metzger Dairies. His wife was the life income beneficiary of the David Metzger Trust, and his children were remaindermen. After Metzger Dairies had been operated by his children for several years, extreme open hostility among them prevented the viable functioning of the business. It was decided that Metzger Dairies would redeem all of the stock owned by the David Metzger Trust and his two daughters, including the individual trusts established for their benefit. The IRS treated the amounts received by the David Metzger Trust on redemption of all of its stock as dividends because the trust retained a significant interest in Metzger Dairies by attribution from Jacob Metzger. *Held:* For the IRS. There is no "family discord" exception to attribution, nor does family discord enter into the determination of whether there is a "meaningful reduction" in a stockholder's stock interest in a corporation. Proof of no intent to bail out earnings does not avoid application of the rules concerning the tax treatment of redemptions. In addition, trusts cannot execute the waiver agreement described in Section 302(c)(2)(A) (concerning redemption of a stockholder's entire interest), thereby avoiding the attribution rules. David Metzger Trust, 693 F2d 459, 82-2 USTC ¶ 9718, 51 AFTR2d 82-376 (5th Cir. 1982), cert. denied, 463 US 1207 (1983).

Family attribution rules could not be waived where prohibited interest acquired. Taxpayer and his father, sole stockholders in a real estate company, agreed to have the corporation redeem taxpayer's stock. Following the redemption, taxpayer retained no interest in the company in any capacity. Because of the father's ill health, taxpayer's own corporation entered into a very broad contract to manage all the property held by the real estate company. The IRS determined that this contract represented the acquisition of a prohibited interest, thus preventing the waiver of family attribution rules and preventing a complete termination of taxpayer's interest. *Held:* For the IRS. The distribution did not qualify as a complete termination because of the management agreement. Capital gain treatment is available in situations where family attribution rules apply only when a complete termination occurs and the stockholder retains no interest in the company. Here, the broad powers contained in the contract constituted retention of a prohibited interest. Chertkof, 649 F2d 264, 81-1 USTC ¶ 9462, 48 AFTR2d 81-5194 (4th Cir. 1981).

Estate attribution rules waived, and purchase qualified as Section 302(b)(3) redemption. Taxpayer estate succeeded to decedent's majority interest in a closely held corporation. The corporation then bought all of its shares, which were owned by taxpayer estate. Taxpayer, pursuant to Section 302(b)(3), considered the purchase to be a complete redemption subject to capital gain treatment. The IRS determined that the redemption was essentially equivalent to a dividend, since under Section 318(a)(3), taxpayer estate was deemed to constructively own the shares that its beneficiaries owned. The IRS argued that the Code provides for a waiver of the family attribution rules of Section 318(a)(1) and not the estate attribution rules of Section 318(a)(3). The lower court held against the IRS. *Held:* Affirmed. The IRS' "slavish" interpretation of the attribution rules was rejected, and the court waived the estate attribution rules. This result was found to be more in line with congressional intent. The decedent's death was not a device to bleed out corporate profits at capital gain rates. Finally, the waiver filed by taxpayer estate was timely. Rickey, Jr., 592 F2d 1251, 79-1 USTC ¶ 9323, 43 AFTR2d 79-1023 (5th Cir. 1979).

Redemption denied capital gains treatment. A couple owned 100 percent of X Corporation and transferred 45 percent of their shares to three trusts for the benefit of their children. X subsequently redeemed the trust shares. The IRS and the district court held that the redemption was essentially equivalent to a dividend, not an exchange. Taxpayer appealed. *Held:* For the IRS. By virtue of the Section 318 attribution rules, the preredemption ownership of each trust was 70 percent (15 percent actually and 55 percent constructively, the amount owned by the parents of the trust beneficiary) and the postredemption ownership was 100 percent constructively, the amount owned by the parents when trust shares had been redeemed. Title Ins. & Trust Co., 484 F2d 402, 73-2 USTC ¶ 9630, 32 AFTR2d 73-5691 (9th Cir. 1973).

Payments in redemption of stock of family corporation were a dividend under attribution rules. Taxpayer and her brother each owned 50 percent of a family corporation until her son, who had been employed full time, became the owner of 25 percent of the stock by transfers in equal amounts from each of them. Three years later, a plan was devised whereby the son was to become the sole stockholder. Pursuant to this plan, the corporation was to redeem taxpayer's and her brother's stock by payment of a fixed price per share. She and her brother were to remain as directors and officers at an annual salary of $1,200, the maximum permitted to be earned without reduction in Social Security benefits. The IRS determined that the payments constituted distributions essentially equivalent to dividends under Section 302(b) and was sustained in the Tax Court. On appeal, taxpayer argued that although she failed to meet the requirements of Sections 302(b)(2) and 302(b)(3), Section 302(b)(1) was applicable, since the distribution was not essentially equivalent to a dividend, and that the family attribution rules in Section 318 should not be determinative. *Held:* Affirmed. The "not essentially equivalent to a dividend" test cannot be applied in a vacuum but must be interpreted in the entire statutory scheme of Section 302, which restricts the instances in which stock redemptions qualify for capital gains. In connection therewith, the attribution rules of Section 318(a) were enacted in an attempt to make the law more predictable. Taxpayer must be deemed the owner of her son's shares. Although she contended that the attribution rules should not be determinative, the language of the statute is clear. Accordingly, the son's stock must be attributed to taxpayer, and as a result, she constructively owned 63 percent of the outstanding stock before the redemption and 100 percent after the redemption. Levin, 385 F2d 521, 67-2 USTC ¶ 9687, 20 AFTR2d 5619 (2d Cir. 1967).

Trust can waive family attribution in a redemption. Taxpayer, a trust, filed an agreement under Section 302(c)(2)(A)(iii) to waive family attribution in a redemption under Section 318 so that the proceeds would be capital gain. The IRS argued that a trust cannot waive the family attribution rules. *Held:* For taxpayer. The court followed Rickey, 592 F2d 1251 (5th Cir. 1979), allowing trusts to waive family attribution. The agreement, although filed five years after the return was filed, was timely because previously there was no authority that a trust could file the agreement. Cruvant, 82-1 USTC ¶ 9354, 50 AFTR2d 82-5058 (WD La. 1982).

Section 302(c)(2)(A) agreement filing permitted seven years after redemption of stock. Taxpayer, the sole stockholder of Rental, gave 241 of the 1,380 outstanding shares of stock to his wife, son-in-law, two daughters, and grandchildren. Thereafter, his daughters formed Finance for the purpose of purchasing the commercial paper generated by Rental. Afterwards, taxpayer and his wife transferred all of their remaining stock to Finance in return for Finance's promise to pay them perpetual annuities of $70,000 a year. On the same day, Finance sold the stock back to Rental in exchange for $100,000 and an unsecured promissory note for $625,000. Taxpayer reported the annuity as a long-term capital gain. The IRS disagreed, contending that the annuity was a dividend and that the Finance transaction was a sham that was in fact a redemption by Rental that gave Finance a zero basis in the Rental stock. The IRS taxed the entire sales proceeds as capital gain received by Finance. In a related case cited by the court, the Eighth Circuit affirmed the Tax Court's holding against Finance, holding in part that taxpayer could not qualify under Section 302(c)(2)(A) because he had not timely filed the required agreement. Two years after this decision, taxpayer and his wife, who had not been parties to the previous suit, filed for a refund. Taxpayer had filed the required agreement, two years prior to this action. The IRS maintained that taxpayer had not complied with the filing requirement. *Held:* For taxpayer, in part. Taxpayer had complied with the filing requirement, as he had filed an agreement as soon as he had notice or knowledge sufficient to form a reasonable belief that a filing was necessary. To hold otherwise would in effect force taxpayer to file the agreement any time a transaction might conceivably be ruled a redemption by the IRS, whether or not taxpayer had reasonable grounds for believing that a redemption had occurred. Fehrs, 77-1 USTC ¶ 9423, 40 AFTR2d 77-5040 (Ct. Cl. 1977).

Trusts' ownership of stock not attributable to estate. Decedent owned stock in five corporations. His stock in one was transferred to trusts for his grandchildren, and the estate redeemed stock in the other corporations. The IRS determined that the stock transferred to the trusts was constructively owned by the estate and, therefore, the redemption of the estate's stock did not terminate its interest and resulted in ordinary income. The estate contended that a tax-apportionment agreement

REDEMPTIONS: *Attribution Rules*

between itself and the trusts that was approved by the New York Surrogate's Court determined that the trusts were no longer beneficiaries of the estate and, accordingly, the gain was capital gain. *Held:* For taxpayer. An agreement among the beneficiaries that was sanctioned by the Surrogate's Court irrevocably and permanently determined the trusts' liability to the estate for their share of estate taxes. Accordingly, the trusts were not beneficiaries of the estate at the time of the stock redemptions. Therefore, there was no attribution of stock ownership from the trusts to the estate. Estate of Weiskopf, 77 TC 135 (1981).

Agreements under Section 302(c)(2)(A) were untimely. In 1973, the Tax Court found that distributions in redemption of taxpayer's stock were essentially equivalent to a dividend and taxable as ordinary income. Taxpayer then filed agreements pursuant to Section 302(c)(2)(A) in an attempt to prevent the attribution rules of Section 318 from applying. The IRS contended the agreements were untimely and thus invalid to prevent attribution. *Held:* For the IRS. The agreements were untimely because they were filed six years after the time they should have been filed and no satisfactory excuse was given for the long delay. Therefore, there was no substantial compliance with the statute. Robin Haft Trust, 62 TC 145 (1974).

Independent contractor did not retain interest. Five years before his death, the decedent had his one-third interest in a corporation redeemed, and he resigned as an officer and director of the corporation. Before the redemption, he joined an accounting firm of which he later became a 48 percent owner. As the managing partner in charge of the corporate account, he continued to render accounting services to the corporation after the redemption. Through a recapitalization and purchase from the remaining stockholders, his son increased his holdings in the corporation to two thirds of the outstanding stock. The corporation established a pension plan and designated the decedent as trustee of the plan. He served in this capacity until his death but never was a beneficiary of the plan. The decedent represented the corporation in a federal tax examination and, with an independent accountant, established an accounting procedure designed to prevent the theft or loss of corporate inventories. The IRS determined that the amounts that the decedent received for redeeming his one-third interest were in fact dividends. *Held:* For taxpayer. Because the redemption was a complete redemption of all of the stockholder's stock and the rules of attribution did not apply, the distribution was considered full payment for the stock. There was no attribution from the son where the decedent's services consisted of accounting duties performed as the partner of an independent accounting firm; that is, the services as an independent contractor did not constitute a prohibitive interest under Section 302(c)(2)(A)(i). Estate of Lennard, 61 TC 554 (1974).

Estate could execute and file valid Section 302(c)(2) waiver agreement. Taxpayers, husband and wife, owned as community property one third of the stock of two corporations; the balance of such corporations' stock was held by taxpayers' sons. A stock purchase agreement provided for redemption of taxpayers' stock upon the death of the husband. The husband died, and the corporations redeemed taxpayers' stock. After the redemption, the wife and her husband's estate held interests only as creditors in the corporations. Section 302(c)(2) waiver agreements were filed. The IRS argued that an estate agreement, and thus amounts received from the redemption, would be treated as a dividend according to the application of the attribution rules. *Held:* For taxpayers. An estate can file a valid 302(c)(2) waiver agreement. Crawford, 59 TC 830 (1973), acq. 1984-1 CB 1.

Redemption held essentially equivalent to dividend. Trusts for children were established by parents who owned more than 80 percent of a corporation's common stock. The trusts invested in the company's preferred stock, which was subsequently redeemed. The proceeds were reported as a capital transaction. *Held:* For the IRS. The parents' ownership was attributed to the children and then to the trusts under Section 318. The agreement with the IRS, which was necessary to suspend the operation of the attribution rules, had never been signed. Accordingly, the redemption did not reduce the trust's constructive interest in the corporation and was essentially equivalent to a dividend. Grabowski Trust, 58 TC 650 (1972).

Presence of minority interest makes redemption not essentially equivalent to a dividend. Decedent owned slightly more than 50 percent of the stock of a corporation, and another person, unrelated, owned about 37 percent. The other 13 percent was owned by decedent's family. Pursuant to a stock retirement agreement between decedent and the other principal stockholder, the corporation redeemed some of decedent's stock after his death. As a result, the estate's ownership dropped to 41 percent, the other stockholder's interest rose to 43 percent, and decedent's family then owned 16 percent. The IRS allowed part of the proceeds to qualify under Section 303 and treated the balance as a dividend. *Held:* For taxpayer. Without the attribution rules, the redemption was not essentially equivalent to a dividend. The same result followed even after applying attribution because of the substantial minority interest present and because of the friction between the executor and decedent's family. There was a substantial dislocation of relative stockholdings and a significant change in control. Lewis, 35 TC 71 (1960) distinguished. Estate of Squier, 35 TC 950 (1961), nonacq. 1978-2 CB 4.

Double attribution of stock ownership makes redemption equivalent to a dividend. A decedent had owned 156 of 283 shares of a corporation, the remaining shares having been owned in unequal amounts by her three daughters or their husbands. The decedent, formerly president of the corporation, had received no salary since 1943, but had paid her living expenses from loans received from the corporation totaling about $20,000. Upon the decedent's death in 1954, the corporation redeemed 51 of her shares in satisfaction of her indebtedness; the remaining 105 shares were distributed in equal amounts to her three daughters, pursuant to her will. At this point, the daughters and their husbands owned stock in varying amounts, and the relative interest of each had been changed by the redemption and distribution. The IRS determined that the redemption was essentially equivalent to a dividend and allocated the dividend income to each of the daughters in equal shares. *Held:* For the IRS. Applying Section 318(a), the court attributed the husbands' stock to their wives and then attributed the wives' stock and the attributed stock to the estate. Accordingly, the estate constructively owned 100 percent of the stock, and the redemption from the estate could not qualify as a substantially disproportionate redemption, generally capital gain under Sections 301 and 302. The court was also influenced by the fact that the corporation had never paid a dividend, although it had accumulated earnings, and that the redemption served no business purpose. Lewis, 35 TC 71 (1960).

Pro rata redemption of stock was essentially equivalent to a dividend. An advertising agency was formed with 80 shares of common and 150 shares of preferred stock. All the stock was issued and sold to taxpayer and his wife for $100 per share. Taxpayer acquired 50 shares of the common stock, and his wife acquired all the preferred (for $15,000) and 30 shares of the common. The reason the wife took back preferred stock instead of merely lending the corporation $15,000 was to help the corporation attain a top credit rating. Later, when the preferred was no longer needed to ensure the rating, it was redeemed. The IRS contended that the redemption was essentially equivalent to a dividend. *Held:* For the IRS. By application of the attribution rule, it was as if the sole stockholder received the corporate earnings in return for part of her stock. Levy, 23 TCM 803, ¶ 64-131 P-H Memo. TC (1964).

Partition of community property stock not a Section 302(c)(2)(B) acquisition. A couple partitioned their community property stock in their wholly owned corporation. Following the partition, the corporation redeemed all the wife's stock, so she no longer held any interest, except indirectly through her husband. The IRS ruled that a partition of community

REDEMPTIONS: *Attribution Rules*

property stock does not result in an acquisition from a related person under Sections 302(c)(2)(B)(i) and 302(c)(2)(B)(ii). Therefore, the redemption may qualify for capital gain treatment under Sections 302(b)(3) and 302(c)(2)(A). Rev. Rul. 82-129, 1982-2 CB 76.

Capital gain treatment of redemption lost by appointing former stockholder as stock custodian. A former stockholder whose stock was redeemed was appointed custodian under the Uniform Gifts to Minors Act of the stock of the distributing corporation. The appointment, which took place within 10 years of the redemption distributing, violated the requirements of Section 302. Ownership of the stock was attributed to the custodian, whose parents owned the remainder of the voting stock, causing the distribution to be treated as ordinary income. Rev. Rul. 81-233, 1981-2 CB 83.

Trusteeship acquired through a will does not disqualify redemption. Six years after completely redeeming her stock in *X* Corporation and filing an agreement specified in Section 302(c)(2)(A)(iii), *D* acquired by will the trusteeship in a trust holding voting stock in *X*. Taxpayer was not in violation of the agreement. Rev. Rul. 79-334, 1979-2 CB 127.

Applicability of constructive stock ownership rules to retiring corporate officer. The IRS ruled that taxpayer, a retiring corporate officer, would not be considered a constructive owner of stock in a family corporation when he redeemed his stock but continued to receive payments representing an arm's-length charge for the corporation's use of a building owned by taxpayer. The interest, which was not dependent on the corporation's future earnings or subordinate to the corporation's general creditors, did not represent the prohibited interest referred to in Section 302(c)(2)(A)(i). Rev. Rul. 77-467, 1977-2 CB 92.

Corporation not successor corporation. *A*, *A*'s son, and *B* were the only stockholders of *X* Corporation. *A* redeemed his stock and filed the agreement required by Section 302(c)(2)(A)(iii) for waiving constructive ownership of his son's stock. Two years later, *X* advertised the sale of assets of one of its divisions, representing about 15 percent of *X* assets. *A* and unrelated parties formed a corporation that purchased the assets for cash. The new corporation was not a successor corporation to *X*. It had none of the tax attributes of *X*, *X*'s remaining assets were substantial compared to the assets sold, and the assets were sold for valid business reasons. Rev. Rul. 76-496, 1976-2 CB 93.

IRS illustrates attribution where stock in family owned corporation redeemed by a trust. The subject corporation had 1,000 shares of common stock outstanding, the grandfather owning 675 shares and the balance held by his wife and their lineal descendants, together with a trust, in equal portions. Based on an analysis of the relationship between the parties and the trust, the IRS held that a not substantially disproportionate redemption of the stock held by the trust, which continued to own stock in the corporation through the application of Section 318(a)(3)(B), constituted a meaningful reduction of the trust's interest in the corporation. The redemption was not essentially equivalent to a dividend within the meaning of Section 302(b)(1) and qualified as an exchange under Section 302(a). Rev. Rul. 75-512, 1975-2 CB 112.

IRS rules in estate redemption case involving attribution rules. Applying the constructive ownership rules to an estate situation, the IRS held that the redemption of an estate's 250 shares of common stock by a corporation whose remaining 1,500 shares of such stock were equally divided between the estate's sole beneficiary and an unrelated individual constituted a meaningful reduction of the estate's interest and was not essentially equivalent to a dividend under Section 302(b)(1). Rev. Rul. 75-502, 1975-2 CB 111.

IRS amplifies Rev. Rul. 72-380 dealing with attribution rules. In a ruling concerning the requirements of Section 302(c)(2)(A)(ii) and the holding in Rev. Rul. 72-380, 1972-C CB 201, the IRS stated that statutory requirements were violated where one of two brothers who, within 10 years of the date all of his stock in a family corporation was redeemed and after the required agreement was filed, became president of the corporation while also the executor of the estate of his sole stockholder father. Rev. Rul. 75-2, 1975-1 CB 99.

Renunciation by trust beneficiary avoids attribution. A renunciation of all interest in a trust by a trust beneficiary prior to his redemption of stock in a corporation, which stock was also held by the trust, will be effective in avoiding the attribution of the corporation's stock held by the trust under Section 318(a)(2)(B)(i). Rev. Rul. 71-211, 1971-1 CB 112.

Holder of voting trust certificates was redeeming stockholder for Section 302 purposes. A father and son each owned 50 percent of the stock of a corporation. An independent trustee was appointed to manage a voting trust that acquired all of the corporation's outstanding stock in exchange for voting trust certificates. The corporation redeemed all of the stock represented by the father's voting trust certificates for cash. The IRS ruled that the holder of the voting trust certificates would be deemed the owner of the shares of stock held by the voting trust, so that the transaction would qualify as a redemption under Section 302. Rev. Rul. 71-262, 1971-1 CB 110.

Nonqualifying portion of Section 303 redemption did not qualify under Section 302. An estate redeemed the stock of a deceased stockholder in a transaction that was intended to qualify under Section 303. Only a portion of the redeemed stock qualified under Section 303. The remaining outstanding stock of the corporation not owned by the estate was owned by the deceased's wife and children. Because attribution rules of Section 318 applied, there was no meaningful reduction of the estate's proportionate interest in the corporation. Accordingly, the balance of the stock redeemed that did not qualify under Section 303 also did not qualify under Section 302. Rev. Rul. 71-261, 1971-1 CB 108.

Attribution rules could not be avoided by sale of stock to beneficiary whose own stock was redeemed. An estate that desired to have a corporation redeem all of the stock presently held by it sold all of the stock to its sole beneficiary, who was the mother of the only other stockholder. The beneficiary paid for the stock with the proceeds of a simultaneous redemption by the corporation of her stock. The purpose of the transaction was to have the mother file the agreement specified in Section 302(c)(2)(A)(iii) so as to qualify for waiver of attribution to her of the stock held by her son. Otherwise, the estate, which could not avail itself of the waiver, would be considered to own 100 percent of the outstanding stock of the corporation. The IRS ruled that the corporation was considered to have redeemed the stock from the estate, and since the estate owned, directly and indirectly, 100 percent of the stock of the corporation both before and after the transaction, the redemption did not qualify as a complete redemption of a stockholder's interest under Section 302(b)(3). Rev. Rul. 68-388, 1968-2 CB 122.

Family trust not within family exemption from attribution in stock redemption. In describing redemptions not taxed as dividends, Section 302 requires application of constructive ownership rules. The family-attribution rules are not, however, to be applied in the case of a redemption that is a complete termination. The IRS ruled that attribution of stock held by a family trust must be made because it comes within the section dealing with trusts (for which no exemption is provided), not under the rules applicable to ownership by members of the family of the holder of the stock being redeemed. Rev. Rul. 59-233, 1959-2 CB 106.

Capital gain realized on redemption of stock of son of major stockholder. A son acquired 7 percent stock interest in his employer-corporation by gift from his father, who was a major stockholder and president of the firm. Five years later, the son left the employ of the corporation and engaged in an unrelated business. A complete redemption of the son's stock at his request was held to qualify for capital gain treatment under Section 302 provided that he does not reacquire an interest within 10 years. The son's acquisition by gift within 10 years of the redemption was for a good business purpose; to interest him in the firm. The IRS ruled that the 10-year condition being met, the family-attribution rules did not apply, and the redemption being a complete termination of the son's interest, the gain was deemed capital. Rev. Rul. 56-584, 1956-2 CB 179.

Termination of parent's interest in corporation qualified for capital gain. A husband and wife who held a majority stock interest in a corporation retired completely from the business and sold their shares back to the corporation, leaving their son as sole stockholder. The IRS ruled that the redemption was a complete termination of stock interest subject to capital gain treatment under Section 302, provided neither parent reacquired an interest in the business or rendered services to the corporation within 10 years of the transfer. If this condition had been met, the family-attribution-of-ownership rules would not be applicable, and since parents were not treated as owning the son's stock, the termination of interest would be complete. Rev. Rul. 56-556, 1956-2 CB 177.

Redemption of all of father's stock from estate a dividend; estate indirectly owned stock of beneficiary son. Decedent owned 27 percent of the stock of a corporation; 48 percent was owned by his son, the sole beneficiary of his estate. The corporation was required by contract to buy 13 percent of the estate stock. It bought all. This could not, however, be treated as a complete redemption; under the Code, the estate was considered the owner of the stock owned by the beneficiary (the son), and that stock was not redeemed. Further, the redemption could not escape tax as "not essentially equivalent to a dividend." The relative interest of the principal stockholders was not changed. Rev. Rul. 56-103, 1956-1 CB 159.

Business Purpose

Pro rata redemption of preferred stock was dividend income notwithstanding business purpose. A corporation engaged in the business of operating a seagoing barge decided to purchase a new barge. In order to obtain the necessary financing, additional capital from private sources was required. The board of directors issued preferred stock to secure such financing. Taxpayer and the other stockholders invested in the newly created preferred stock in proportion to their common stock holdings. Approximately six years later, the preferred stock was redeemed. The IRS contended that the amount received on redemption was a dividend. The Tax Court found for the IRS. *Held:* Affirmed. The issue was determined by Davis, 397 U.S. 301 (1969), which held that a redemption without a change in the relative economic interest or rights of the stockholders is always essentially equivalent to a dividend under Section 302(b)(1). The fact that the redemption was consistent with the business purpose for which the stock was issued was immaterial. The amount received by taxpayer was therefore dividend income. Miele, 474 F2d 1338, 73-1 USTC ¶ 9379, 31 AFTR2d 73-1310 (3d Cir.), cert. denied, 414 US 982 (1973).

Distribution was deemed dividend to sole stockholder. Taxpayer, who after application of the stock attribution rules, was the sole stockholder of a corporation, received a corporate distribution in redemption of 70 shares of stock. The IRS held that such distribution was in fact an ordinary dividend, but the district court held for the taxpayer. *Held:* Reversed and remanded. Under Davis, 397 US 301 (1970), the redemption of stock of a sole stockholder is considered a pro rata distribution. Therefore, the court held that such redemption was essentially equivalent to a dividend under the Code. The presence or lack of a valid business purpose was not considered relevant in a sole stockholder situation. Johnson, 434 F2d 340, 70-2 USTC ¶ 9696 (8th Cir. 1970).

Redemption of stock essentially equivalent to a dividend. Taxpayer owned in excess of 55 percent of the outstanding stock of a corporation. Without the approval of the company's directors, taxpayer purchased the stock of the second and third largest stockholders. The former was becoming a competitor of the corporation while the latter was a valued customer who needed cash. Thereafter, over a period of years, the corporation redeemed the shares taxpayer had purchased. The Tax Court ruled that the redemption was essentially equivalent to a dividend. *Held:* Affirmed. Taxpayer's contention that the redemption served a business purpose of the corporation was considered without merit. The business purpose goal, even under the taxpayer's argument, was to accomplish the withdrawal of the two stockholders. This goal was obtained by taxpayer's acquisition of the stock. The later redemption of the stock, at a profit to taxpayer, was not essential to the effectuation of the planned withdrawal. Gloninger, 339 F2d 211, 64-2 USTC ¶ 9882 (3d Cir. 1964).

Net effect test used in holding that stock redemption was equivalent to dividend. Taxpayers, owners of all the stock of Permar Corporation and of a controlling interest in R.P. Collins & Co., Inc., transferred all their stock in Permar to Collins for $15,000 in cash. Since taxpayers had paid $15,000 for the stock in Permar, the transaction was treated by taxpayers as a sale at cost, giving rise to no taxable income. The IRS determined that the redemption was essentially equivalent to a dividend; the district court disagreed. *Held:* Reversed. The court, in overruling the district court, felt that the emphasis should not be placed on the fair market value of the transferred stock or on whether the transfer reduced the surplus of the acquiring corporation. Instead, the net effect after the transfer should be considered. Here, after the dust had settled, taxpayers retained the same proportionate interest in the assets as they had held prior to the transfer, and the consolidated assets of the two corporations had been reduced by $15,000. The situation was no different than if the acquiring corporation had distributed the property to taxpayers without requiring the surrender of stock, except for the fact that the acquiring corporation, instead of taxpayers, held the stock in Permar. This was exactly the situation that Sections 304 and 302 were designed to reach. The questions of business purpose and past dividend record used by the lower court in support of its conclusion bore only limited relevance. The distribution was therefore essentially equivalent to a dividend and was taxable as ordinary income. Collins, 303 F2d 142, 62-1 USTC ¶ 9472 (1st Cir. 1962).

Preferred stock redemption equivalent to dividend. After redemption of other interests, taxpayer held all of the preferred and common stock of a corporation. The stock had originally been issued in the incorporation of a partnership. Taxpayer then had the corporation redeem all of his preferred shares. There was no contraction of the corporate business. The IRS and the district court found that the net effect of the redemption was essentially equivalent to a dividend. *Held:* Affirmed. Any business justification argued by the taxpayer must be compelling to avoid the "net effect test," which points to a tax-avoidance scheme. Ballenger, 301 F2d 192, 62-1 USTC ¶ 9362, 9 AFTR2d 1245 (4th Cir. 1962).

Redemption of sister corporation's stock not a dividend because compelling business purpose existed. Taxpayer owned 65 percent of an American corporation and 74 percent of a Canadian corporation engaged in the same business. A plan was adopted whereby the outstanding stock of the Canadian corporation was purchased from the stockholders by the U.S. corporation. Among the reasons for the purchase was the desire to eliminate minority stockholdings in the Canadian corporation as the first step in a contemplated merger with a public corporation. Upon adoption of the plan, taxpayer sold his Canadian shares to the American corporation, reporting a long-term capital gain. His constructive ownership of the Canadian corporation decreased to 55 percent. The IRS determined that the payment to taxpayer was essentially equivalent to a dividend and taxable as ordinary income. *Held:* For taxpayer. Redemption of the Canadian shares was not essentially equivalent to a dividend. It was motivated by compelling business reasons, not for tax avoidance. The elimination of minority interests could not have been accomplished except by this method. The net effect of the redemption was not the same as if the American corporation had paid a dividend to

REDEMPTIONS: *Dividend Equivalence*

taxpayer. Salvatori, 66-2 USTC ¶ 9670 (SD Cal. 1966).

Business purpose immaterial in determination of dividend equivalency. Taxpayers were the sole stockholders of two corporations. One corporation purchased from taxpayers all their shares in the other corporation through cancellation of taxpayers' indebtedness. The IRS determined that taxpayers had dividend income. *Held:* For the IRS. This transaction is a classical example of the application of Section 304(a). The existence of a business purpose for combining the corporations is immaterial in determining dividend equivalency. Since the purchasing corporation had retained earnings sufficient to pay dividends in the amount of the stock purchase, taxpayers could not escape dividend treatment. Schaefers, 49 TCM 228, ¶ 84,627 P-H Memo. TC (1984).

Redemption of all preferred stock not essentially equivalent to a dividend where only 20 percent of preferred stock held by common stockholders. Taxpayers owned all the common and 20 percent of the preferred stock of a corporation. The remaining 80 percent of the preferred stock was held by an individual who had received it as an inheritance. The preferred stock, which had received a regular 6 percent dividend, was completely redeemed at $100 par in 1959. That same year, the common, for the first time, received a substantial dividend. The IRS attempted to treat the preferred redemption as essentially equivalent to a dividend. *Held:* For taxpayer. The redemption was not essentially equivalent to a dividend under Section 302(b)(1) but was motivated by bona fide legitimate business purposes (i.e., to remove a large block of stock that was inherited by someone not active in the business, and to remove the financial burden of a 6 percent preferred cumulative dividend). Estate of Antrim, Jr., 26 TCM 320, ¶ 67,060 P-M Memo. TC (1967).

Partial redemption of stock essentially equivalent to a taxable dividend. A corporation in the retail shoe business redeemed part of the preferred stock held by the sole stockholder by crediting $5,000 to the stockholder's personal loan account. There were sufficient earnings and profits to cover the redemption. The IRS argued that the redemption was essentially equivalent to a dividend. *Held:* For the IRS. The court noted that even though at the time of the redemption the company had decided to discontinue its men's shoe department, it needed more operating funds than previously as shown by its increase in long-term indebtedness. Since no business purpose had been shown for the redemption, that transaction was held to be essentially equivalent to the distribution of a dividend. Pliner, 20 TCM 1073, ¶ 61,218 P-H Memo. TC (1961).

Dividend Equivalence

Stockholder not taxed on corporation's payment to ex-wife. Taxpayer was originally required by a divorce decree to make payments to his former wife in exchange for her interest in a family corporation. Later, the divorce decree was modified to allow the corporation to redeem the former wife's stock for cash in place of the payments from her ex-husband. The IRS argued that the redemption resulted in a constructive dividend to taxpayer. The Tax Court held for taxpayer. *Held:* Affirmed. The new decree replaced the earlier one and so eliminated any liability of taxpayer to his former wife. The redemption did not discharge a liability of taxpayer and so produced no dividend. Edler, Jr., 727 F2d 856, 84-1 USTC ¶ 9285, 53 AFTR2d 84-916 (9th Cir. 1984).

Redemption proceeds were dividends. Taxpayers purchased the stock of a bank from an estate and then had 217 shares of the stock redeemed. The bank then reissued the same number of shares to taxpayers as a stock dividend. The Tax Court held that the redemption proceeds had to be treated as dividends under Section 316(a). Taxpayers argued on appeal that the redemption was actually from the selling stockholders. *Held:* Affirmed. There was no change in the capital and surplus accounts, and taxpayers owned or controlled all of the stock at the time of redemption. Thus, taxpayers received a dividend.

REDEMPTIONS: *Dividend Equivalence*

Adams, 594 F2d 657, 79-1 USTC ¶ 9234, 43 AFTR2d 79-752 (8th Cir. 1979).

Need well-defined plan to avoid dividend equivalency in serial redemption. Taxpayer, a majority stockholder who needed cash, agreed to restructure the corporation. In 1964, part of taxpayer's stock was redeemed and, in 1968, taxpayer's interest in the corporation was terminated when his remaining stock was redeemed. The IRS and Tax Court held that the 1964 redemption was essentially equivalent to a dividend. *Held:* Affirmed. The court stated that dividend equivalency was avoided in a serial redemption where the redemptions were part of a fixed plan. In the instant case, there was a total absence of a time frame for the redemption plus wide discretion in determining when the redemption was possible. Therefore, the plan was found to be an afterthought rather than a prearranged series of stock redemptions. Benjamin, 592 F2d 1259, 79-1 USTC ¶ 9319, 43 AFTR2d 79-995 (5th Cir. 1979).

Reduction of stock's stated value to compensate for error upon formation of corporation held to be a dividend to stockholders. A partnership in which taxpayer was a member formed a corporation to take over a portion of its operations. The stated value of the stock issued upon its formation was listed as $50,000 when it should have been listed as only $5,000. In a later year, the corporation reduced the stated value of its stock to account for this error and treated this adjustment as a redemption of 90 percent of its shares. Also, at this time, the corporation cancelled certain accounts receivable for merchandise purchased by the partnership. The IRS claimed that this reduction amounted to a dividend distribution. *Held:* For the IRS. The court rejected taxpayer's argument that the reduction was merely meant to correct the error in establishing the stock's initial stated value. Cancellation of the accounts receivable was determined to compensate for the redeemed stock and therefore gave the transaction tax substance. Because the redemption did not affect any stockholder's proportionate interest in the corporation, it was essentially equivalent to a dividend. Maloney, 521 F2d 491, 75-2 USTC ¶ 9608, 36 AFTR2d 75-5458 (6th Cir.), cert. denied, 423 US 1017 (1975).

Section 304 took precedence over Section 351. *A* and *B* corporations were wholly owned by the same group of individuals. To combine the two corporations, this group sold all of the *B* stock to *A* under an installment sales agreement. The individuals reported the sale as a capital gains transaction. The IRS, under Section 304, treated the sales as redemptions that resulted in taxable dividends to the individuals. Taxpayer argued that the installment sales contract was a security within the meaning of Section 351, and thus the sale did not give rise to taxable gain or ordinary income. The Tax Court, in Coates Trust, 55 TC 501 (1970), held for the IRS on the ground that Section 351 did not apply because an installment sales contract is not a security for purposes of that section. *Held:* For the IRS. Section 304 overrides Section 351 where both apply. The Court of Appeals did not rule on whether installment sales agreements can be securities under Section 351. Coates Trust, 480 F2d 468, 73-2 USTC ¶ 9492, 32 AFTR2d 73-5251 (9th Cir.), cert. denied, 414 US 1045 (1973).

Payment of accumulated dividends in connection with redemption treated as a distribution in exchange for stock rather than dividends distribution. Taxpayer held preferred cumulative stock in corporations that served as sales outlets. The corporations redeemed taxpayer's preferred stock for an amount equivalent to par value (the cost basis) plus accrued dividends. Taxpayer reported the transaction as a return of capital to the extent of par value and the excess as an intercorporate dividend subject to the 85 percent deduction under Section 243. The IRS contended that the entire payment was governed by Section 302 and treated the excess over basis as a long-term capital gain, not a dividend. The district court held for the IRS. *Held:* Affirmed. The court stated that accumulated dividends paid to a holder of preferred stock at the time it is called for redemption must be considered an indivisible part of the total amount paid on redemption within the meaning of Section

REDEMPTIONS: *Dividend Equivalence*

302. Cummins Diesel Sales Corp., 459 F2d 668, 72-1 USTC ¶ 9378 (7th Cir. 1972).

Redemption of stock held to be a dividend. Taxpayer purchased 900 of 1,000 outstanding shares of Nedicks, Inc., for $3.6 million. It paid $2 million down, and the balance was payable within six months. To help finance this transaction, taxpayer borrowed $1 million from a bank. Subsequently, taxpayer surrendered 260 shares to Nedicks, Inc. for about $1 million and used the money to pay off its bank loan. The Tax Court, following Wall, 164 F2d 462 (1948) agreed with the IRS that the redemption was a dividend. *Held:* Affirmed. The court rejected taxpayer's argument that in substance, the transaction was a purchase by taxpayer of 640 shares and a redemption from the former stockholders of 260 shares. The court ruled that taxpayer was bound by the form of the transaction it had adopted wherein Nedicks, Inc. did not deal with the former stockholders. Television Indus., 284 F2d 322, 60-2 USTC ¶ 9795, 6 AFTR2d 5864 (2d Cir. 1960).

Court rejected form-over-substance argument in finding dividend equivalency. During 1961, taxpayer and his wife entered into a contract whereby they obligated themselves to purchase all of the stock of a family corporation owned by the wife's parents. The corporation, which was in the laundry and dry cleaning business, had 157 shares of stock outstanding at the time, all owned by the taxpayer's in-laws. It was agreed that taxpayer and his wife would pay $100 per share for the stock, or $15,700. On the day that the contract was signed, the in-laws endorsed their stock, and the corporation reissued certificates in the amounts of 147 and 10 shares to the taxpayer and his wife. The corporation then issued a check in the amount of $14,700 to taxpayer in payment for the 147 shares. This money was then used to pay the contractual obligation to the in-laws for the purchase of their stock. Taxpayer retained the shares of the stock and paid the purchase price of $1,000 from a bonus given him by the corporation for services rendered. The corporate income tax return indicated that it had surplus earnings in the amount of $25,785 for the 1961 tax year. Accordingly, the IRS determined that the distribution of the $14,700 was taxable as a dividend pursuant to Sections 301(c) and 316 and included that amount in taxpayer's income. *Held:* For the IRS. Rejecting taxpayer's substance-over-form argument, the district court noted that the in-laws could have accomplished the same end result by selling 10 shares of stock directly to taxpayer and 147 shares directly to the corporation. Instead, they chose to sell all 157 shares to taxpayer with the understanding that he would sell 147 shares to the corporation and purchase 10 shares for himself. The in-laws' accountant testified that he suggested the stock be sold to taxpayer so that he could serve as a nonconsenting stockholder, thereby insuring the termination of the Subchapter S election and avoiding an increase of taxable income by the corporation's profits. The accountant further testified that he thought it was necessary to maintain the corporate viability that some stock remain outstanding. Despite this argument, the court found that the parties could not ignore their agreement and the method used to accomplish it, and, further, that the court was not in a position to correct it for them. Santulli, 76-2 USTC ¶ 9677, 38 AFTR2d 76-5869 (D. Md. 1976).

Jury found distribution not essentially equivalent to a dividend after determining that it more closely resembled a sale. Taxpayer received a distribution from a corporation in exchange for a portion of its outstanding stock. The IRS determined that the distribution gave rise to dividend income rather than capital gain to taxpayers. *Held:* For taxpayer. The jury found a redemption entitled to long-term capital gains treatment after being instructed to examine the essential attributes of the transaction to see whether it more closely resembled a sale than a distribution of a dividend. Cohron, 62-1 USTC ¶ 9398, 9 AFTR2d 1434 (SD Ala. 1962).

No constructive dividend on redemption splitting jointly owned business. Taxpayer and his brother each owned one-half of the stock of a Missouri corporation and of a Tennessee corporation. The brothers disagreed with respect to the operating policies to be pursued by the corporations and agreed that the Missouri corporation would redeem taxpayer's stock at its fair market value of $136,000 and that the Tennessee corporation would redeem the brother's stock at its fair market value of $170,000. The IRS contended that the redemption by the Tennessee corporation of the brother's stock resulted in a constructive dividend to taxpayer. Alternatively, the IRS argued that the $136,000 that taxpayer received in redemption of his stock by the Missouri corporation should be treated as a dividend and taxed as ordinary income rather than capital gain. *Held:* For taxpayer. The court concluded that the separate identity of the two corporate entities could not be ignored. Accordingly, taxpayer was permitted capital gain on the redemption of his stock in the Missouri corporation. Ward, 193 F. Supp. 154, 61-1 USTC ¶ 9390 (MD Tenn. 1961).

Purchase of stock of sister corporation from individual stockholder taxable dividend. Taxpayer and her husband respectively owned 92.3 percent and 7.7 percent of the outstanding stock of a corporation, which owned a Canadian subsidiary also in the wholesale glove business. Following the death of two key employees in 1958, the corporation sold its U.S. glove business to unrelated third parties for $650,000. It then purchased from taxpayer for $115,000 all the outstanding stock of another corporation from which it leased a warehouse. The IRS contended that the acquisition of the stock from taxpayer was a dividend taxable to her. Taxpayer contended that the purchase was a partial liquidation. *Held:* For the IRS. Whether the redemption of stock of a sister corporation is essentially equivalent to a dividend or is a liquidation under Section 346 is tested by the effect of the redemption on the acquiring corporation. Here, the redemption was not one in a series pursuant to a complete liquidation. Nor was it pursuant to a plan, formal or informal, of partial liquidation. The redemption also was not a distribution in partial liquidation under Section 346(b), since the corporation was engaged in the active conduct of only one business in 1959: the management of its Canadian subsidiary, for which it received only a small portion of its total income and which did not constitute a separate trade or business. The distribution here was essentially equivalent to a dividend because there was no contraction of the corporation's business. Blaschka, 393 F2d 983, 68-1 USTC ¶ 9367, 21 AFTR2d 1294 (Ct. Cl. 1968).

Corporation's purchase of some of sole stockholder's shares held equivalent to a dividend. Taxpayer and his wife owned 99 of a corporation's 100 outstanding shares. In order to raise additional capital for a more profitable manufacturing operation, the corporation purchased 47 of the taxpayer's shares at about half their book value and resold, at a substantial profit, 38 of these shares over a nine- to twelve-month period. The IRS viewed that transaction as a distribution essentially equivalent to a dividend and assessed a deficiency, which the taxpayer paid. Held: For the IRS. There was no change in taxpayer's interest in the corporation immediately after the redemption; the change occurred only *after* the redeemed shares were sold by the corporation. The presence of a valid business purpose is not per se dispositive. Here, the corporation could have raised the required capital by selling authorized but unissued shares. As a result of the method used here, the taxpayer was enriched to the extent of the amount he received for his shares with a resulting depletion of the corporation's earnings and profits. In addition, the value of the taxpayer's remaining 52 shares was substantially greater than the original 99 shares, and he was still in control of the corporation. The redemption was therefore essentially equivalent to a dividend. Neff, 305 F2d 455, 62-2 USTC ¶ 9620 (Ct. Cl. 1962).

Steps toward redemption of stock of controlling stockholder not essentially equivalent to dividend. Decedent had left his one-half of the stock of a closely held corporation to a testamentary trust. The corporate trustee believed that the trust should not have its funds tied up in a small corporation with new and untested management when the purpose of the trust was to provide income to the widow. After extended negotiations, a plan for the purchase of the trust's shares was adopted. The first step was the redemption and cancel-

REDEMPTIONS: *Dividend Equivalence*

lation of one third of the outstanding stock of the corporation pro rata among the three stockholders. The second step was the sale of one-half of the remaining shares held by the trust to members of the family of the other stockholders, and the third step contemplated the sale of the remaining shares as soon as the monetary resources of the other stockholders enable them to complete the purchase. The IRS contended that the first step, a pro rata redemption among the three stockholders, was taxable as a dividend. *Held:* For taxpayer. The Court of Claims held that the transaction, viewed as a whole, meant that the corporation would have new owners and new management upon completion of all three steps, and therefore, the redemption was not essentially equivalent to a dividend. Bains, 289 F2d 644, 61-1 USTC ¶ 9425 (Ct. Cl. 1961).

Sale of corporate stock was actually liquidation, and redemption equivalent to dividend. Taxpayer owned the stock of a Canadian corporation, which in turn owned the preferred stock of a foreign subsidiary of a domestic corporation that was also owned by taxpayer. Taxpayers intended to operate the Canadian corporation as a real estate investment company, but changes in the tax law made dissolution or sale desirable. Investment bankers agreed to buy all the stock for net book value of the assets, less 4.5 percent provided that all of the assets were converted to cash. To accomplish this, taxpayer bought stock and loan investments from the corporation for cash. The sale of stock was then consummated but was subject to the redemption of the preferred stock from the corporation by the related subsidiary. The redemption took place, and the arrangements were thereby completed. Taxpayer claimed the sale and redemption were separate and complete transactions. *Held:* For the IRS. The investment bankers were merely conduits. They never actually spent any money as their checks were in escrow until they received the money from the redemption. The substance of the transaction was a distribution in liquidation followed by a redemption of the preferred stock from taxpayer. Moreover, the redemption was essentially equivalent to a dividend. Gray, 56 TC 1032 (1971).

Assignment of stockholder's liability to corporation resulted in dividend distribution. Taxpayer, by agreement, paid part cash and executed notes for all of the stock of four corporations. The stock was placed in escrow to secure payment. Thereafter, taxpayer assigned his rights, title, and interest in the stock of one of the corporations to one of the other corporations. Taxpayer remained liable for the note. After the assignment, the corporation made payments of principal and interest on the note. The IRS contended that the transaction was a redemption, and the distribution was essentially equivalent to a dividend. *Held*: for the IRS. The assignment of taxpayer's stock interest in a corporation to another controlled corporation was a redemption of stock within the meaning of Section 304. The assumption of liability on the note by the corporation therefore constituted a distribution of property taxable as a dividend under Section 301 to the extent of the corporation's earnings and profits. The corporation had properly deducted interest paid on the notes assigned. Maher, 55 TC 441 (1970).

Redemption of stock resulted in dividend income. Taxpayer owned the stock of two corporations. He sold the stock of one corporation to the other under a contract in which the acquiring corporation agreed to pay taxpayer over a period of ten years. Taxpayer contended that the motivating force for the sale arose from corporate business purposes to obtain credit and improve bonding arrangements. The amount realized was reported as capital gain. *Held:* For the IRS. Based on the evidence, the corporation's credit position and bonding capacity were not materially aided by the sale. The financial position of the corporation had been improved to some extent, but it could not be regarded as the reason for the purchase. There was no real or meaningful shift in the position of taxpayer in relation to the corporation and the other stockholders occasioned by the distribution. Consequently, the distribution was essential-

REDEMPTIONS: *Dividend Equivalence*

ly equivalent to a dividend and was taxable as such. Vinnell, 52 TC 934 (1969).

Redemption of preferred shares not a dividend despite accrued but undeclared dividends. Decedents died owning preferred shares of a corporation to which he was indebted. The estate was unable to pay the debt, and the corporation agreed to redeem its own shares in payment of the debt. The corporation had never paid any dividends on the preferred stock. Although the redemption resulted in a complete termination of the decedent's interest, the IRS contended that part of the redemption represented accrued dividends to be taxed as ordinary income. *Held:* For taxpayer. The Tax Court held that the entire gain on redemption was capital gain. Dividends on stock cannot accrue until there has been a formal declaration of a dividend. The redemption contract could not convert the intangible right to dividends into a fixed liability. Estate of Mathis, 47 TC 248 (1967), acq. 1967-1 CB 2.

Redemption of stock equivalent to dividend. Taxpayer was an officer and stockholder of a corporation that manufactured elevators. Two other stockholders, who controlled a large percentage of stock, wanted to sell their interests. Financially unable to purchase the shares, taxpayer feared for her own position if the stock were acquired by an outside interest. To resolve this difficulty, corporation redeemed taxpayer's stock by transferring to taxpayer certain real property. Mortgaging the property, taxpayer used the proceeds to buy out one stockholder. The corporation redeemed the stock of the second stockholder. Because at the conclusion of the transaction taxpayer owned both stock and real property, the IRS alleged that taxpayer had received a dividend. *Held:* For the IRS. Since the distribution was essentially equivalent to a dividend, Section 302(a) did not apply. Considering the transaction as a whole, taxpayer had received other property in addition to control. Edminster, 46 TC 67 (1966).

Sale of stock, incident to corporate contraction, not a dividend. Taxpayer was the controlling stockholder of a corporation that decided to discontinue one of its two lines of business. A prospective purchaser agreed to first buy out several of the minority stockholders, and the corporation was then to redeem the stock so acquired by turning over one of the businesses. Because the value of the shares held by the selling minority stockholders did not equal the agreed-upon price for the business, taxpayer sold about 2,000 shares to his son, who in turn sold them to the purchaser of the assets. Actually, his son paid taxpayer out of the proceeds of the second sale. The IRS treated taxpayer's sale as a redemption equivalent to a dividend. *Held:* For taxpayer. The Tax Court found there was a bona fide sale by taxpayer and not a dividend. Even if there had been a redemption, the court would have refused to find it equivalent to a dividend. The facts showed it was not. Standard Linen Serv., Inc., 33 TC 1 (1959), acq. 1960-2 CB 7.

Stock redemption not essentially equivalent to a dividend. Surviving stockholders, pursuant to an agreement, upon death of a stockholder, first bought the stock from the deceased's estate and then immediately sold it to their company at the same price. The object of both the stockholders and the corporation was to prevent the stock from falling into the hands of widows, minors, or outsiders. The corporation also desired to acquire treasury stock that could be sold to key employees from time to time as the board of directors deemed it advisable. This objective was carried out. The IRS ruled that the corporation's payments for the deceased stockholders' shares were essentially equivalent to a dividend. *Held:* For taxpayer. On the facts, the Tax Court held that the corporate payments to the surviving stockholders for the deceased stockholder's shares were not distributions essentially equivalent to a dividend. Decker, 32 TC 326 (1959), acq. in result only, 1964-2 CB 5.

Redemption of stock held essentially equivalent to a dividend. Taxpayer obtained a bank loan, and used the funds to purchase stock in a corporation from an estate. The corporation then redeemed some of taxpayer's shares. Taxpayer claimed that there was a

REDEMPTIONS: *Dividend Equivalence*

single, integrated plan of redemption that was not essentially equivalent to a dividend. The IRS treated the redemption as a dividend. *Held:* For the IRS. There was no mutually agreed plan. In the redemption, the corporation assumed taxpayer's liability on the bank loan that financed the stock. The redeemed stock had been collateral for the loan. The redemption was intended by the taxpayer and was essentially equivalent to a dividend. Skyline Memorial Gardens, Inc., 50 TCM 360, ¶ 85,334 P-H Memo. TC (1985).

Redemption of parent's stock equivalent to dividend. Prior to the redemption in issue, the corporate taxpayer held 93 percent of the redeeming corporation's stock. After the redemption, taxpayer held 89 percent of the shares. Taxpayer argued that the redemption was one of six steps undertaken to rearrange the ownership of corporations, which resulted in a tax-free reorganization. *Held:* For the IRS. The court was not convinced that the real purpose of the redemption was not to recoup some of the cash expended in the rearrangement. As a result, the taxpayer was also liable for personal holding company tax. Vahlsing Christina Corp., 50 TCM 75, ¶ 85,273 P-H Memo. TC (1985).

Taxpayer's stock for property exchange was a taxable distribution. Taxpayer exchanged his stock in a corporation for timberland owned by the corporation, but did not report the transaction. The IRS claimed that the transfer of the timberland by the corporation was a taxable distribution resulting in capital gains to taxpayer. *Held:* For the IRS. Taxpayer's trade of his stock for real property was a stock redemption, which does not qualify under the provisions of Section 302(a) or 302(b), and therefore it had to be treated as a distribution of property to which Section 301 applies. Hipp, 47 TCM 623, ¶ 83,746 P-H Memo. TC (1983).

Redemption not dividend. Taxpayer was one of two stockholders in a corporation. The other stockholder wished to dispose of his interest in the business. The corporation redeemed his stock, but made entries on the books that disguised the redemption. The IRS asserted that the payments the corporation made for the stock were constructive dividends. *Held:* For taxpayer. The transaction was intended to be a redemption of stock, not a purchase by taxpayer. Williams, 35 TCM 1672, ¶ 76,368 P-H Memo. TC (1976).

Sale of part of stock to third party and redemption of stock by him was a constructive dividend. Taxpayer and his family owned 37,500 of 50,000 shares of an insurance company. Taxpayer was heavily in debt and sought to raise over by $1 million by selling his stock. His lawyers advised him against the sale of part of his stock to the company, contending that it might be regarded as a dividend distribution. Instead, taxpayer sold 4,167 shares of his stock to a banker at $300 per share with a seven-month option to buy the balance of taxpayer's holdings at the same price. The banker borrowed $1.25 million for the purchase and expected to make a minimum of $30 per share profit by a successful public underwriting of the stock. He also wanted a "vehicle" that would enable him to dispose of the 4,167 shares in the event that he couldn't sell to the public. He was assured by the other stockholder that at the end of the option period the company would, if requested, repurchase the shares at $330 per share. Toward the end of the option period, when the possibility of a successful underwriting became remote, the banker offered the stock to the company, which bought it for $330 per share, and the banker reported the profit of $125,010 as a long-term capital gain. The IRS contended that the intermediate steps involving the banker should be disregarded and that, in effect, the redemption by the company of the 4,167 shares for $330 per share constituted a dividend to taxpayer. *Held:* For the IRS. The banker exacted as a condition precedent to his buying the shares from taxpayer the guarantee that he would be able to dispose of all of them for $330 per share and not suffer any loss. The redemption was in substance from taxpayer, so that taxpayer, in effect, constructively received a dividend. Jaffe, 26 TCM 1110, ¶ 67,223 P-H Memo. TC (1967).

REDEMPTIONS: *Dividend Equivalence*

Redemption of stock to cancel loan was a dividend. Taxpayer owned over 82 percent of the stock of a corporation. He owed the corporation $17,800. In order to improve the corporation's balance sheet by eliminating this receivable, it redeemed 250 of taxpayer's shares for $17,500. After the redemption, taxpayer owned 80 percent of the corporation. Taxpayer did not report any gain because the basis of his redeemed stock was also $17,500. The IRS asserted that the redemption was essentially equivalent to a dividend. *Held:* For the IRS. The court based its holding on the following factors: there was no general contraction of the corporation; the initiative for the cancellation came from taxpayer; there was no substantial change in the proportionate ownership of the stockholders; the corporation had never paid a dividend; and the transaction did not increase the net worth of taxpayer's company. Winnek, 24 TCM 1400, ¶ 65,258 P-H Memo. TC (1965).

Proportionate redemption essentially equivalent to a dividend. Taxpayers were partners in a construction business. They formed two corporations. Each partner received stock in proportion to his interest in the partnership. To satisfy an indebtedness to one corporation, each partner redeemed stock equivalent to his share of the debt. The IRS contended that the redemption was essentially equivalent to a dividend. *Held:* For the IRS. The factor most clearly pointing to a dividend equivalence was that the redemption of the stock was exactly pro rata among the stockholders and left their proportionate interests unchanged. Moore, 23 TCM 103, ¶ 64,020 P-H Memo. TC (1964).

Redemption of another's shares through a continuing stockholder not equivalent to a dividend. Taxpayer was an officer and 25 percent stockholder of a corporation. The balance of the shares were held equally by the manager of the corporation, *M*, and by a trust. Because of *M*'s ill-advised policies and lack of sound business judgment, there was a steady decline in corporate earnings. A conflict between taxpayer and *M* developed, and *M* offered to sell his 375 shares. Taxpayer, acting for a syndicate of purchasers that included the corporation, the trust, members of the family, and himself, accepted the offer. To finance the entire purchase, he obtained a temporary loan of $562,500 from outside sources. The corporation purchased 128 of the 375 shares, for which it paid taxpayer $192,000. The IRS contended that the corporation acquired the shares from taxpayer and paid him $192,000 as a constructive dividend to relieve him from a preexisting debt to *M*. *Held:* For taxpayer. The payment to taxpayer was not essentially equivalent to a dividend, constructive or otherwise. The corporation, as principal, purchased the shares from *M* in redemption of the latter's interest through taxpayer, who merely acted as agent. Taxpayer incurred no personal liability for the $192,000 debt. Peterson, 23 TCM 63, ¶ 64,015 P-H Memo. TC (1964).

No constructive dividend where corporation redeems stock transferred to a creditor of stockholder taxpayer. Taxpayer borrowed money on notes from a third party in order to purchase stock of corporation. When the notes became due, taxpayer was unable to make payment, and was forced to transfer some of the corporate shares to the lender in cancellation of the notes. The corporation then redeemed the shares from the lender at a cost of $91,000. The IRS claimed that the redemption resulted in a constructive dividend. *Held:* For taxpayer. The redemption of the stock of the third party was not a constructive dividend to taxpayer. At the time the stock was redeemed, the third party was a bona fide independent stockholder and not a "straw man" or a mere pawn for a tax-avoidance scheme of the taxpayer. Goss, 22 TCM 1219, ¶ 63,242 P-H Memo. TC (1963).

Distributed cash reserves were Section 302 redemptions. Cash distributed by a mass transit corporation was treated as a redemption subject to Section 302 limitations because the distribution was not a genuine contraction of the corporation's business. The distributions represented reserves no longer needed to purchase replacement buses. Rev. Rul. 78-55, 1978-1 CB 88.

REDEMPTIONS: *Effect on Redeeming Corporation*

Periodic redemptions of preferred stock did not produce constructive stock dividends to stockholders. X Corporation acquired all of the stock of Y Corporation from Y's stockholders in return for 75 percent in cash and 25 percent in a newly issued class of X preferred stock. Each year, 5 percent of this preferred stock was to be redeemed pro rata or by lot over the next 20 years. The preferred stockholders had no control over the redemptions. These periodic redemptions did not produce constructive taxable stock dividends to the common stockholders of X under Section 305 because the plan had the effect of a security or financing arrangement. Rev. Rul. 78-115, 1978-1 CB 85.

Corporation's annual redemption program resulted in dividends to stockholders. A corporation with 24 stockholders adopted a plan in which the corporation would redeem a limited number of shares each year. In 1976, eight stockholders participated in the redemption program. The redemptions were treated as "dividend" distributions under Section 301 rather than "exchange" distributions under Section 302(a). Also, the 16 stockholders who did not have shares redeemed increased their proportionate interests in the corporation and so received taxable stock distributions under Section 305(b)(2). Rev. Rul. 78-60, 1978-1 CB 81.

Redemption not equivalent to dividend. X Corporation owned all of the stock of Y Corporation. X and Y each owned a small number of shares of a large, listed corporation, Z. Z offered to redeem some of its stock for Z assets that were being divested under an antitrust settlement. Y accepted the redemption, but X did not. Applying the attribution rules of Section 318, Y owned 96.7 percent of the Z stock that it owned before the redemption. Since X and Y were minority stockholders in Z and had very little control over the corporate decision to redeem stock, the distribution was not equivalent to a dividend. Rev. Rul. 76-385, 1976-2 CB 92.

Stock redemption price partly a dividend. A corporation had both common and preferred stock outstanding. It was required that quarterly dividends be paid so that the common stockholders would receive no dividend if the preferred stockholders' dividend was not declared and paid or set apart for payment. Contemplating a redemption of the preferred shares at $150, the corporation set aside, but did not pay, a preferred dividend of $5 per share in March, but did pay a dividend of $2 per share on common stock. The corporation redeemed the preferred stock at the end of April for $156, representing the redemption price of $150, the March dividend of $5, and an accrued dividend for April of $1. The amount of $5 was a dividend under Section 301(c)(1), but the accrued dividend of $1 for April was treated as part of the ultimate redemption price of $151 paid for exchange of the stock under Section 302(a), provided that Section 302(b)(1),(2), or (3) applied. Rev. Rul. 75-320, 1975-2 CB 105.

Effect on Redeeming Corporation

Stock sale was completed upon redemption, which was dividend to corporation. Taxpayer wanted to terminate his interest in a wholly owned corporation. A buyer was found to purchase the stock, but he insisted that before the sale, all of the corporate assets be reduced to cash. The assets consisted of a small amount of cash and preferred stock in another corporation that taxpayer controlled. The buyer insisted on redeeming the stock because the redemption price far exceeded the fair market value. The purchase was made subject to a condition subsequent that the stock be redeemed within six days of the purchase. The buyer's checks were placed in escrow, the stock was redeemed, and the escrow was closed. The IRS determined that this was a constructive liquidation followed by the redemption of the stock from taxpayer's hands. *Held:* For the IRS. There was a redemption followed by a sale of the stock. Once the redemption condition subsequent occurred, the sale was completed. The redemption supplied the economic substance needed to complete the sale. It was not a liquidation. The redemption contingency was inconsistent with the premise that a liquidation was completed. Until assets are irrevocably removed from their corporate solution, a complete liquidation cannot occur. The redemption proceeds were received by the corporation as a dividend and included in its personal holding company income. Because the proceeds were undistributed, they were included in taxpayer's gross income. Gray, 561 F2d 753, 77-2 USTC ¶ 9685, 40 AFTR2d 77-5933 (9th Cir. 1977).

Asset-by-asset approach for gain computation on redemption. When a corporation distributes property subject to liabilities in redemption of its stock, the computation of gain under Section 311(c) is made on an asset-by-asset basis. Furthermore, liabilities assumed, but not related to any of the distributed property, are allocated according to the relative fair market value of the assets. Rev. Rul. 80-283, 1980-2 CB 108.

Gain on distributed appreciable property was ordinary to extent not recognized under Section 1250(a). A corporation distributed appreciated depreciable property pursuant to a redemption of stock qualifying under Section 302(b)(2). The gain recognized by the corporation under Section 311(d) as a result of the distribution should be treated as ordinary income under Section 1239 to the extent that such gain was not recognized under Section 1250(a). Rev. Rul. 75-514, 1975-2 CB 116.

Effect on Remaining Stockholders

Corporation's redemption of outsider's stock not a dividend to remaining stockholder. Taxpayer and a corporation in which he was an officer and stockholder agreed to buy the outstanding stock held by outside parties for $85,000, or which $50,000 was to be paid in cash and $35,000 by corporate note. Taxpayer was unable personally to raise more than $32,000 in cash. Accordingly, the corporation borrowed $18,000 from a bank to make up the $50,000 cash payment. The former stockholders transferred $32,000 worth of their shares to taxpayer and the balance to the corporation. It received from the corporation $18,000 in cash plus a note for $35,000. The IRS treated the corporate payments to its former stockholders in redemption of their stock as constructive dividends to taxpayer. *Held:*
For taxpayer. No dividends, either actual or constructive, were distributed to taxpayer. The obligation to repurchase $53,000 of corporate stock was solely that of the corporation, since taxpayer was under no obligation to purchase any of the shares redeemed by the corporation. He was only an accommodation endorser on the corporate note and was never obligated to buy more than $32,000 worth of stock. Gahm, 23 TCM 665, ¶ 64,118 P-H Memo. TC (1964).

Corporation's redemption of stock of majority stockholder did not result in a dividend to minority stockholder. Taxpayer, a minority stockholder, entered into a long-term agreement to buy the stock of the majority stockholder. The agreement was assigned to the corporation, which proceeded to make the required buy-out payments. The IRS contended that the redemption resulted in a constructive dividend to taxpayer. *Held:* For taxpayer. The redemption did not constitute a constructive dividend to taxpayer. Taxpayer was merely acting on behalf of the corporation in negotiating and arranging for the purchase of the stock. He did not incur any personal liability under the contract, nor did he receive any financial or economic benefit other than an increase in his percentage of stock ownership. The IRS' argument that such increased ownership was a taxable benefit to the remaining stockholder was superficial, since it overlooked the fact that the corporation's worth was decreased by the purchase price and that the increased ownership was in a corporation of lesser value. Green, 22 TCM 1241, ¶ 63,248 P-H Memo. TC (1963).

Gift Consequences

Transfer of stock to church was a valid gift; no dividend on subsequent redemption. Taxpayer transferred 51 percent of the shares of his wholly owned corporation to a church. Eight days later, the corporation redeemed the church's stock and conveyed a residence, suitable for a rectory, in exchange for the stock. The redeemed shares were never reissued; therefore, taxpayer regained control of the corporation. The IRS held that the transfer of 51 percent interest to the church was a sham and that, in effect, the transfer of the shares to the rectory was a dividend to taxpayer, the sole stockholder. The Tax Court held for taxpayer. *Held:* Affirmed. There was no evidence to suggest that there was a prior obligation on the part of the church to consent to the redemption in order to enable taxpayer to regain control of the corporation. The gift to the church was complete and effective. Carrington, 476 F2d 704, 73-1 USTC ¶ 9370, 31 AFTR2d 73-1166 (5th Cir. 1973).

IRS charts tax consequences following redemption of family owned stock. As part of the father's plan to retire from the family business and to give ownership of the business to his son, he gave 60 shares of corporate stock to his son as a gift, not as consideration for past, present, or future services. Shorty thereafter, the father resigned and the son assumed the position of chairman of the board and president. The corporation redeemed the remaining 60 shares of stock owned by the father in exchange for property. Immediately after the redemption, the father was not an officer, director, or employee of the corporation, and he no longer had any interest in it. His gift of stock was for the purpose of giving his son complete ownership and control. The corporation's earnings and profits exceeded the amount of the distribution in redemption of the stock. On these facts, the IRS held that the father made a gift of half the stock to the son for tax purposes, and that this gift qualifies for treatment as a distribution in full or part payment in exchange for the stock under Section 302(a). Rev. Rul. 77-293, 1977-2 CB 91.

Meaningful Reduction of Stockholder's Interest

Tax Court affirmed holding that redemption that resulted in loss of control over corporation was a "meaningful reduction" of interest for purposes of Section 302(b)(1), despite the retention of significant interest through constructive ownership. Puritan Corporation's 356 outstanding shares were held as follows: 200 shares by taxpayer, 105 shares by members of the Patterson family (excluding the 40 shares held by Hicks' wife), and 45 shares held by Hicks and his wife. Taxpayer's sole beneficiary was one of the members of the Hicks family. Hicks, in an effort to obtain control over Puritan, caused Puritan to redeem taxpayer's shares. Following the redemption, Hicks exercised his option to purchase 75 shares from Puritan. The IRS asserted that taxpayer should have treated the amount received on redemption as a dividend, and not as a long-term capital gain. *Held:* Affirmed for taxpayer. The sale of taxpayer's entire Puritan stock interest, which gave the taxpayer control over the corporation, resulted in the requisite "meaningful reduction" for Section 302(b)(1). Further, the court found the loss of control to be a meaningful reduction even though its constructive ownership of Puritan stock remained significant. The court also approved the lower court's holding that the shares represented by Hicks' option were to be counted in determining the reduction in taxpayer's actual and constructive Puritan stock interest. Patterson Trust, 729 F2d 1089, 84-1 USTC ¶ 9315, 53 AFTR2d 84-1042 (6th Cir. 1984).

Cash received on redemption of preferred stock taxable as ordinary income. Citing Davis, 397 US 301 (1970), the IRS contended that cash received by taxpayers on redemption of their preferred stock was taxable as ordinary income. The district court held for the IRS. *Held:* Affirmed. The redemption did not meaningfully reduce taxpayers' proportionate corporate interest. Brown, 73-2 USTC ¶ 9640 (6th Cir.), aff'g 345 F. Supp. 241, 72-2 USTC ¶ 9760 (SD Ohio 1972), cert. denied, 414 US 1011 (1973).

Preferred stock redemption essentially equivalent to a dividend in absence of prior dividends, substantial change in control or business purpose. Taxpayer owned 80 percent of the common stock of a closely held family corporation and over 70 percent of the preferred stock. The latter was issued to bring the capitalization up to the minimum needed to qualify as an FHA mortgage company. When the corporate net worth later exceeded the required level, the corporation redeemed a portion of his preferred stock. The IRS asserted a deficiency, contending that the redemption was essentially equivalent to a dividend under Section 302(b)(1). Taxpayer at all times owned 80 percent of the common stock, and the corporation had earnings and profits at all times, but no dividends had ever been paid despite substantial earnings. The Tax Court held that the percentage of ownership of preferred stock was reduced sufficiently to sustain a holding that the distribution was not a dividend. *Held:* Reversed. Applying the standards set forth in Jones, 216 F2d 885 (10th Cir. 1954) to the facts here, it could be seen that the distribution was taxable as a dividend. There had been no distribution of any dividend since the formation of the corporation. It had sufficient accumulated earnings to cover the redemption, and, as a result of the redemption, no substantial change in proportionate ownership or control had occurred. Taxpayer's direct control of the common shares was unaffected, and by application of the attribution rules, he suffered only a slight reduction in his ownership of preferred shares. The corporation did not contract its operations after the redemption, it continued to operate at a profit, and there was no corporate business purpose shown for the redemption. Berenbaum, 369 F2d 337, 67-1 USTC ¶ 9105, 18 AFTR2d 6094 (10th Cir. 1966).

Redemption by controlled corporation was taxable dividend to controlling stockholder. A corporation had 226 shares of common stock outstanding. Taxpayer owned 178 of these shares, and also owned all of the preferred stock. Taxpayer had the corporation redeem 45 shares of the common stock and transferred most of his shares in trust for the benefit of other persons, presumably unrelated. The district court held that taxpayer still controlled the corporation and that the redemption was essentially equivalent to a dividend. The corporation had not paid dividends on its stock for several years, and taxpayer failed to meet the requirements under Section 302. Nor did the transaction qualify as a partial liquidation under Section 346. Furthermore, payments of redemption expenses of the above stock for the benefit of the stockholder were taxable income to taxpayer and were not deductible by him, since the corporation made the payments. *Held:* Affirmed. The sale of the 45 shares reduced taxpayer's control only 7 percent, which was not significant in ascertaining whether the redemption was essentially equivalent to a dividend. The trust agreement never contemplated a definite period within which taxpayer was to dispose of his interest in the corporation. Friend, 345 F2d 761, 65-1 USTC ¶ 9439, 15 AFTR2d 1043 (5th Cir. 1965).

Preferred stock redemption held not substantially equivalent to dividends. Taxpayer owned all the preferred stock of a corporation, and also owned directly and indirectly more than 80 percent of the corporation's voting stock. The corporation redeemed part of the preferred stock during 1957 and 1958. Taxpayer waived accrued but unpaid dividends on this stock. The Tax Court held that the redemption was essentially equivalent to a dividend on the ground that taxpayer's control of the corporation was not diluted by the redemption, his ownership being reduced by less than 5 percent. *Held:* Reversed. If the funds used for redemption had been used to pay a dividend, taxpayer would not have received more than 82 percent, including his indirect ownership. A change of 18 percent in the dividend payment and 5 percent in the equity was a substantial change. The redemption was therefore not equivalent to a dividend. Himmel, 338 F2d 815, 64-2 USTC ¶ 9877, 14 AFTR2d 6009 (2d Cir. 1964).

Loss of guaranteed distribution of earnings following redemption held to constitute "meaningful reduction." In June 1960, taxpayer and his wife divorced. Because it was feared that the business of their two corporations would suffer if the wife continued as a stockholder, non-voting preferred stock was issued to the parties pending the outcome of their divorce proceedings. The stock was entitled to receive dividends. Later, in 1967, the corporations effected a plan of reorganization prior to a public stock offering. In 1969, a merger plan was adopted whereby the two corporations were to become a single unit. Taxpayer surrendered all of his preferred stock in a premerger redemption, and the shares were promptly canceled, with taxpayer receiving cash in exchange. After the merger and redemption, taxpayer was a 50 percent owner of the common stock. For tax reporting purposes, taxpayer treated the redemption as full payment and exchange for his preferred stock, resulting in no gain. On audit, however, the IRS determined that the payments were essentially equivalent to a dividend and, therefore, taxable as ordinary income. *Held:* For taxpayer. Citing Davis, 397 US 301 (1970), for the proposition that courts must ignore the reasons for which stock was issued and redeemed, the district court concluded that the effect of the redemption was not essentially equivalent to a dividend and that taxpayer sustained a meaningful reduction in his proportionate interest in the right to receive corporate earnings. His 50 percent common stock ownership did not guarantee dividend payments as the preferred had, and his 50 percent ownership did not place him in a position to decide whether dividends would be declared. In light of this fact, the court concluded that a significant reduction had taken place, and that Section 302(a) redemption treatment was appropriate. Morris, 441 F. Supp. 76, 77-2 USTC ¶ 9740, 41 AFTR2d 78-335 (ND Tex. 1977).

Redemptions essentially equivalent to dividends. The IRS contended that two redemptions of stock in a close corporation were essentially equivalent to dividends under Section 302(b)(1). *Held:* For the IRS. The court found there had been no meaningful reduction in the interests of the stockholders. Jones, 72-1 USTC ¶ 9349 (DNJ 1972).

Jury found distribution was not essentially equivalent to dividend. Taxpayer received a $25,000 distribution from *M* in exchange for stock. The IRS determined the distribution to be a dividend. *Held:* For taxpayer. A jury reviewed certain factors and concluded that the distribution was for redemption of taxpayer's stock, and that the distribution was not essentially equivalent to a dividend. The factors examined included whether the distribution resulted in a reduction in the amount of taxpayer's relative voting power, whether the corporation went out of business after the distribution, and whether there was a reduction in taxpayer's right to future dividends. Robinson, 71-2 USTC ¶ 9709, 28 AFTR2d 71-5891 (ND Ala. 1971).

Later transaction did not avoid tax consequences of "dividend" redemption. Taxpayer received assets from *C* Corporation, which he controlled, in return for surrendering part of his stock. He was later advised that this redemption would be taxable as a dividend, since his controlling interest was not weakened. He then took back the redeemed shares from *C* and issued a "note" to *C* while retaining the distributed assets. The IRS taxed him on the dividend, and denied a deduction for interest. *Held:* For the IRS. The redemption was not rescinded because taxpayer did not return the assets to *C*. The transaction was not in substance a sale, as taxpayer argued, but was a redemption followed by a futile attempt to escape the redemption's tax consequences. Blanco, 602 F2d 324, 79-2 USTC ¶ 9492, 44 AFTR2d 79-5448 (Ct. Cl. 1979), cert. denied, 444 US 1072 (1980).

Taxpayer's failure to enforce annual redemption right on regular basis led the Tax Court to treat taxpayer's redemption as isolated event, not as an integrated step in a firm and fixed plan to achieve a meaningful reduction of her interest. Under a property settlement agreement arising from a divorce action, taxpayer was entitled to have BSP, Inc. redeem 40 shares of BSP stock each year (if no other BSP stockholder was willing to buy them). While the case was before the court, taxpayer held approximately 19 percent of BSP stock, and her son held approximately 46 percent of BSP stock. In the two years following the divorce, taxpayer did not enforce her redemption rights against BSP. Although BSP redeemed 40 shares in each of the years 1976 through 1978, she did not force a redemption in 1979. The IRS treated the amounts received by taxpayer in redemption of her stock in 1976 as dividends. *Held:* For the IRS. Although the single redemption of 40 shares of BSP stock would not qualify as a "meaningful reduction" of her stock interest so as to achieve "sale" treatment under Section 302, the serial redemption of all her BSP stock at the rate of 40 shares per year might so qualify. However, taxpayer's failure to enforce her redemption was not related to any prior or future redemption as an "integrated step in a firm and fixed plan" to redeem all of her interest in BSP or to achieve a "meaningful reduction" of such interest. Johnston, 77 TC 679 (1981).

Redemption not essentially equivalent to a dividend. Taxpayer owned 45 percent of Trenton's common stock. The public owned the remainder. She also owned 90 percent of Trenton's preferred stock. Trenton's preferred stock A had been issued to a finance corporation as security for loans made in 1934 and 1936. Trenton adopted a plan of recapitalization, which involved retiring all of the preferred stock A, capitalizing dividend arrearages on the preferred stock B, and splitting it two for one and issuing additional common stock. The plan also provided for the periodic retirement of preferred stock B in the amount of $112,000 per year. Under the plan, Trenton redeemed preferred stock held by the taxpayer, who reported the gain as long-term capital gain. The redemption resulted in a decrease in her percentages of total voting stock from 50.54 percent prior to redemption to 43.28 percent after redemption. The IRS determined that the redemptions were essentially equivalent to a dividend. *Held:* For taxpayer. The reduction of the taxpayer's voting rights as a result of the redemption constituted a meaningful reduction in her interest. However, the portion of the par value of the preferred stock B that represented capitalized dividend arrearages was ordinary income. Roebling, 77 TC 30 (1981).

Amounts received in stock redemptions were dividends. Taxpayers owned all the stock of H, and also owned, actually and constructively, 78 percent of N and J, companies that supplied H. Taxpayers, desirous of having H become a public company, were advised by an underwriter that N and J should be combined with H. Taxpayers sold their N and J stock to H for $800,000, financed through stock offerings. The IRS determined that taxpayers were in receipt of dividend income with respect to these sales of stock. *Held:* For the IRS. No overall plan existed to finance the transaction. The redemption was essentially equivalent to a dividend and, although taxpayers' interests were reduced by subsequent public offerings, the reductions were not meaningful. Paparo, 71 TC 692 (1979).

Preferred stock redemption not equivalent to a dividend to owner of most of common stock. Taxpayer owned all of the outstanding nonvoting preferred stock and substantially all of the outstanding common stock of a corporation. He entered into an agreement with Borden under which his corporation would redeem all of his preferred stock at par, and then Borden would exchange with taxpayer its stock for the common stock held by taxpayer. The IRS contended that the redemption was essentially equivalent to a dividend. *Held:* For taxpayer. The purpose of Section 302 is to determine whether the redemption so alters the stockholder's interest as to resemble a sale. When a redemption results in a substantial reduction in the interest of the stockholder in a corporation, it is not a dividend. Here the redemption was a step in Borden's plan to gain control of the corporation. This reorganization radically reduced taxpayer's interest. This was not a redemption arranged by taxpayer to withdraw corporate earnings at capital gains rates. McDonald, 52 TC 82 (1969).

Cash credit received in transaction involving the transfer of stock for stock and cash credit essentially equivalent to a dividend. Taxpayer was the majority stockholder and controller of three corporations: Haserot, H, Northport, N, and Gypsum, G. In 1958, taxpayer transferred to H all of his N and G stock and received a cash credit of $64,850 plus stock of H worth $48,640. At the time of the transaction, H already owned significant amounts of N and G stock. In addition, a majority of H shares were registered in taxpayer's name; he was thus capable of dictating actions to be taken by H with respect to its N and G shares both before and after the transaction. The IRS determined that the cash credited to taxpayer in the exchange constituted dividend income. The Tax Court found that the cash credit was capital gain. The IRS appealed to the Sixth Circuit, which remanded the case to the Tax Court for determination as to whether the transaction at issue was "essentially equivalent to a dividend." The Tax Court vacated its earlier decision, and taxpayer filed a motion to revive it. Subject to its finding on the specific question raised by the remand, the Tax Court granted taxpayer's motion. *Held:* For the IRS. The cash credit was a distribution essentially equivalent to a dividend. The court rejected taxpayer's contention that the transaction produced a substantial change of control at the stockholder level and was thus not essentially equivalent to a dividend within the meaning of Secion 302(b)(1). The court determined that with or without the application of Section 318's attribution rules, both prior to and following the transaction, taxpayer enjoyed majority control of *H,N* and *G* by a wide margin. Haserot, 46 TC 864 (1966).

Stock redemption treated as ordinary income. Taxpayer owned 66 percent of the stock in one corporation, and his son owned 33 percent of the stock of the second corporation. The stock of the second corporation was acquired by the first corporation. The IRS treated the redemption proceeds as a taxable dividend. *Held:* For the IRS. The business purpose behind a redemption is irrelevant in determining whether the redemption is essentially equivalent to a dividend. There was no meaningful reduction of taxpayer's proportionate interests in the first corporation. Estate of Zimmerman, 49 TCM 1616, ¶ 85,259 P-H Memo. TC (1985).

Stock transfer-redemptions result in ordinary income. Taxpayer, owner of 70 percent of the stock of two corporations, transferred stock of one corporation to the other for the cancellation of his indebtedness to the second corporation. The IRS recharacterized his capital gain as ordinary income. *Held:* For the IRS. The distribution was equivalent to a dividend because taxpayer's voting control was unchanged and his net worth and rights to future earnings were only minimally reduced. Therefore, the dividend distribution was ordinary income. Furr, 34 TCM 426, ¶ 75,084 P-H Memo. TC (1975). Similarly, a non-pro rata redemption of taxpayer's stock interest was ordinary dividend income as there was only minimal reduction in his interest and no reduction in voting power. Furr, 34 TCM 433, ¶ 75,085 P-H Memo. TC (1975).

Distribution essentially equivalent to a dividend not a stock redemption. Taxpayer, a majority stockholder, had 300 shares of his stock redeemed so he could repay a loan from a minority stockholder made on behalf of the corporation. The IRS claimed the distribution was a dividend. *Held:* For the IRS. Although the redemption of 300 out of 3,000 preferred shares held was not pro rata because taxpayer received 100 percent of the amount distributed, he still owned 80 percent of the common stock, and redemption of 10 percent was not a meaningful reduction. Taxpayer's claim that it was a meaningful reduction in light of his intention to have a series of redemptions was ignored, as the redemption here had to be tested by the situation existing during the year of distribution. Finally, other factors indicated dividend: the company had sufficient earnings to pay a dividend, taxpayer was in control before and after the distribution, he initiated the distribution, and there was no contraction of the business after the distribution. Hays, 30 TCM 378, ¶ 71,095 P-H Memo. TC (1971).

Redemption of nonvoting preferred stock deemed a dividend when the stockholder retained control and interest. *X* corporation had outstanding voting and nonvoting common stock and nonvoting, cumulative preferred stock. *C,* one of three controlling stockholders, held no nonvoting common or preferred stock directly, but was the beneficiary of trust *T,* which held 18 percent of both stocks. *X* redeemed six of nine shares of the preferred stock held by *T.* Thus *T* was considered to own *C*'s voting stock. The IRS ruled that the lack of any reduction in *T*'s voting power, or a complete termination of *T*'s interest, prevented the redemption from qualifying under Section 302(b)(2) or 302(b)(3), respectively. *T* failed to meet the test laid out in Davis, 397 US 301 (1970), which required a meaningful reduction of *T*'s proportionate interest in *X*. Applying the rules of attribution, *T*'s right to vote and exercise control, to participate in current earnings and accumulate surplus, and to share in net assets on liquidation were not significantly reduced. Because the redemption did not otherwise qualify under Section 302(b), it was not a distribution in part or full payment for stock under Section 302(a). Accordingly, under Section 302(d), the redemption was treated as a distribution of property, to which Section 301 applied. Rev. Rul. 85-106, 1985-30 IRB 14.

Redemption not an exchange where no reduction of stockholder's rights. A redemption in response to a single isolated tender offer did not meet the requirements of the meaningful reduction test, since the stockholder's rights were not diminished. The redemption also failed to qualify for exchange treatment under the "not essentially equivalent to a dividend" provision of Section 302(b)(1). Rev. Rul. 81-289, 1981-2 CB 82.

Redemption reducing stockholder's interest from 90 percent to 60 percent is not a meaningful reduction for Section 302(b)(1) purposes. Notwithstanding that redemption of stockholder's interest reduced his share of voting rights below 66.67 percent, stockholder still had control of day-to-day affairs of the corporation, thus the redemption did not result in a meaningful reduction of his interest under the Davis, 397 US 301 (1970), rehearing denied, 397 US 1071 (1970) rationale. Therefore, the redemption was found to be essentially equivalent to a dividend, and Sections 302(d) and 301 applied. Rev. Rul. 78-401, 1978-2 CB 127.

Partial Liquidations

Redemption of stock constituted a dividend distribution taxable as ordinary income. Taxpayer was the sole stockholder of a corporation that was having difficulty obtaining certain performance bonds. In order to obtain the bonds, taxpayer transferred bank stock he owned to the corporation in exchange for 550 shares of the corporation's stock. When the bonds were no longer needed, the corporation distributed the bank stock to the taxpayer in redemption of 550 shares. Taxpayer claimed that the redemption was pursuant to a partial plan of liquidation under Section 46(b) and therefore was eligible for capital gains treatment. The IRS determined that the redemption resulted in a dividend distribution to taxpayer, ordinary income under Sections 302 and 301, and that the corporation must recognize gain on the distribution under Section 311(d)(1). *Held:* For the IRS. The distribution of the bank stock to taxpayer was not pursuant to a partial plan of liquidation because the corporation did not cease conducting a trade or business when it made the distribution; nor did it distribute all the assets of a terminated business. Thus, under Section 302, the redemption had to be treated as a distribution of property subject to Section 301 and as giving rise to ordinary income. In addition, under Section 311(d), a corporation is required to recognize gain on the distribution in the amount of the excess of the fair market value of the bank stock on the distribution date over its adjusted basis in the stock. Kenton Meadows Co., ¶ 84,379 P-H Memo. TC (1984), 766 F2d 142, 56 AFTR2d 85-5350 (4th Cir. 1985).

Distributions not part of a partial liquidation. Taxpayer stockholders argued that corporate distributions to them were a result of a partial liquidation pursuant to Section 346 and therefore were taxable as capital gains. The IRS held such distributions to be taxable as ordinary dividend income. *Held:* For the IRS. The distributions were found not to be part of a series of distributions in redemption of all of the corporate stock pursuant to a plan within the meaning of Section 346(a)(1).It had previously been decided that the distributions did not qualify under either Section 346(a)(2) or 346(b). Gooding, 38 AFTR2d 76-5336 (D. Ohio 1976), aff'd sub. nom. Mains, 42 AFTR2d 78-6026 (6th Cir. 1978).

Capital gain denied to distribution of stock of subsidiary by parent in partial redemption of its shares. Taxpayer and another individual owned a corporation engaged in the active business of road construction. The corporation organized another corporation to engage in the business of hauling equipment and transferred its hauling equipment to the new corporation in exchange for 67 percent of its common stock. The new corporation operated as a subsidiary for approximately seven years until its shares were transferred to the parent's stockholders in proportionate redemption and cancellation of a portion of the parent's stock. Taxpayer reported the distribution as a capital gain. The IRS ruled that the distribution was taxable as a dividend. *Held:* For the IRS. The statute requires that the distribution be attributable to the ceasing of conduct of an active trade or business by the distributor. In order to qualify under Section 346(b)(1), the business that is terminated must be operated directly by the corporation making the distribution. Since the subsidiary must be viewed as a separate and distinct entity, this transaction did not qualify under Section 346(b) as a partial liquidation and the distribution was taxable as a dividend. Morganstern, 56 TC 44 (1971).

Stockholder buyout followed by redemption was a partial liquidation. Taxpayer corporation owned and operated both a linen supply and a laundry business. Its majority stockholders wanted to sell their shares at a time when taxpayer needed additional capital. An outside firm offered to purchase taxpayer's linen supply business for $2 million. It would not buy stock. A compromise arrangement was devised under which the purchaser first advanced $800,000 to taxpayer in return for the debenture bond, then purchased shares from taxpayer's stockholders for $1.2 million in cash and the debenture bond, and finally surrendered the shares to taxpayer in exchange for the linen supply assets. Taxpayer continued to operate the laundry. The IRS contended that there was a sale of taxpayer's assets and taxed the gain. *Held:* For taxpayer. The Tax Court decided that there was a partial liquidation of taxpayer; therefore no gain was recognized. The court found that the main purpose of this transaction was the buyout of taxpayer's stockholders, not a sale of its assets. The court deemed significant the fact that none of the money paid by the purchaser was retained by taxpayer. Standard Linen Serv., Inc., 33 TC 1 (1959), acq. 1960-2 CB 7.

Proceeds from redemption of stock held for business purposes qualify for partial liquidation. A corporation's distribution of proceeds from the redemption of stock of a co-operative held predominately for business purposes and not investment purposes qualified for a distribution in partial liquidation. Rev. Rul. 60-322, 1960-2 CB 118, distinguished. Rev. Rul. 78-402, 1978-2 CB 138.

Computation of number of shares redeemed in a partial liquidation. Where no shares of stock are actually surrendered but the par value of stock is reduced pursuant to a partial liquidation, the number of shares considered to have been redeemed is determined by dividing the amount of the distribution by the fair market value of one share. The value of widely held stock traded on an exchange is computed as the mean between the highest and lowest selling price on the date of the distribution. See Rev. Rul. 59-240. The valuation of stock "not traded under circumstances necessary to realistically establish its value by the trading price" may be determined by the valuation of the underlying assets. See Rev. Ruls. 59-60 and 56-513. Rev. Rul. 77-245, 1977-2 CB 105.

Assignment of note constituted distribution of the proceeds of a partial liquidation. In a transaction qualifying as a partial liquidation, *X* Corporation received a note from the purchaser of part of its business. Pursuant to a plan of partial liquidation and in redemption of part of its stock, *X* assigned the right to receive all payments on the note to its stockholders. The IRS ruled that the fair market value of the right to receive payments on the note was a Section 346(a)(2) distribution. This irrevocable and complete assignment had the same effect as an actual transfer of the note itself. Rev. Rul. 77-166, 1977-1 CB 90.

Redemptions by Affiliated Corporations

Stock sale was a Section 304 redemption. Taxpayer owned all the stock of two corporations and a minority of the stock in a third with the balance owned by related parties. Taxpayer exchanged all the stock of one of his wholly owned corporations for stock of the third in a B reorganization and simultaneously sold the stock of the other wholly owned corporation to the third for cash. The IRS argued that the sale was a Section 304 transaction and the proceeds were dividends. Taxpayer argued that the sale and B reorganization were one transaction constituting the exchange of stock in the two corporations for stock in the third plus boot, which is governed by Section 351, and that under pre-TEFRA law, Section 351 had priority over Section 304 where both were applicable. *Held:* For the IRS. Although the attribution rules of Section 318 apply in determining the 50 percent applicability test of Section 304, they do not apply in determining the 80 percent control test of Section 351(a) and 368(c). Thus, taxpayer failed the Section 351 test and only Section 304 applied. Brams, 734 F2d 290, 84-1 USTC ¶ 9495, 54 AFTR2d 84-5011 (6th Cir. 1984).

Corporate acquisition did not result in constructive dividend to stockholder. Taxpayer owned 100 percent of the stock of *A* Corporation and 50 percent of the stock of *B* Corporation. The other 50 percent of *B* was owned by taxpayer's brother, *M*. Taxpayer was obligated to purchase *M*'s interest upon the latter's death. When *M* died, *A* purchased the brother's interest in *B* from *M*'s estate for $200,000. The IRS contended that *A* had satisfied taxpayer's obligation. Therefore, the $200,000 payment constituted a dividend to taxpayer. *Held:* For taxpayer. *B*'s stock was found to be worth more than $200,000, and therefore it could not be said that taxpayer stockholder was relieved of a "debt" or "obligation" in the onerous sense that these terms ordinarily connote. *A*'s net worth remained unchanged as cash was merely exchanged for stock. Furthermore, the $200,000 was not a dividend pursuant to Section 304, since a prerequisite for this section is that taxpayer receive the sale proceeds. Here, the proceeds were received by a third party. Also, Section 304 indicates that taxpayer must have owned the additional 50 percent interest in *B* before the transfer, which was not the case here. The court found no basis for imputing ownership to taxpayer. MacArthur, 40 AFTR2d 77-5813 (Ct. Cl. 1977), aff'd sub. nom. Citizens Bank & Trust Co., 580 F2d 442, 42 AFTR2d 78-5429 (1978).

Sale of stock to related company taxed as dividend. Taxpayer owned 22 percent of the common stock of American Timber and 125 shares of the corporate preferred stock. Taxpayers' children owned the remaining common stock. Taxpayers sold their common stock to Lent, a corporation in which they owned no stock but in which their children owned 67 percent of the common stock, and contributed their preferred stock to a tax-exempt foundation. The IRS determined that the transaction generated ordinary income as opposed to a capital gain. The Tax Court agreed with this and found for the IRS. *Held:* Affirmed. The sale was a redemption through the use of a related corporation under Section 304. The distribution was of property to which Section 301 applied, rather than an exchange for redeemed stock. The attribution rules of Section 318 were applicable in determining stock ownership and control, and to determine if the redemption was through the use of a related corporation. Finally, the record did not support consideration of the "bad blood" exception to Section 318(a). Niedermeyer, 535 F2d 500, 76-1 USTC ¶ 9417, 37 AFTR2d 76-1413 (9th Cir. 1976).

Purchase of stock by related corporation treated as dividend. Taxpayer controlled two corporations, although his percentage of ownership in the two was somewhat different. He sold the preferred stock of one to the other, and this stock was used as collateral in a financing transaction. The IRS ruled that the stock purchase was a dividend. *Held:* For the IRS. Under Section 304, the purchase of stock of one corporation by another corporation under common control can be treated the same as a redemption of the stock of the second corporation. The district court held that the stock purchase was a dividend, that the financing could have been effected without the transfer of the stock, that the transfer and payment to taxpayer had no business purpose, and that its net effect was a dividend. Hasbrook, 343 F2d 811, 65-1 USTC ¶ 9351, 15 AFTR2d 736 (2d Cir.), cert. denied, 382 US 834 (1965).

REDEMPTIONS: *Redemptions by Affiliated Corporations*

Redemption of sister corporation's stock not equivalent to a dividend. Taxpayers as individuals owned most of the stock of Supply Co. Their partnership in turn owned all of the stock of four other corporations. Because a shortage of working capital hampered the growth of the partnership and Supply Co., taxpayers, acting on the advice of investment counsel, caused the stock of the four corporations to be transferred to them by the partnership. They in turn sold the stock to Supply Co. for book value. This improvement in Supply Co's balance sheet picture resulted in its securing an adequate line of credit from a bank. The IRS ruled that the distribution was a redemption equivalent to a dividend. A majority of the Tax Court held that the distribution from Supply Co. was a redemption through the use of a related corporation "essentially equivalent to a dividend" under Section 304. The Tax Court majority found that the disproportionate redemption formula under Section 302(b)(2) was inapplicable because the partnership was considered to have remained in existence after the sale of stock as it had collected and paid bills for six months after the transaction. This continued existence resulted in the stock ownership of each partner being attributed to the other so that the 50 percent limitation in Section 302(b)(2) was exceeded. *Held:* Reversed. Looking to the effect of the whole transaction, it was not essentially equivalent to a dividend. There was a business reason for the transaction, and a substantial change in ownership was effected. Sorem, 334 F2d 275, 64-2 USTC ¶ 9610, 14 AFTR2d 5131 (10th Cir. 1964).

Sale of stock to controlled corporation was redemption essentially equivalent to a dividend. Taxpayer owned 100 percent of the stock of Helix, a flour miller, and Kerr, a grain storage and brokerage. In 1955, he sold his Kerr stock to Helix for $50,000, his basis. The IRS determined that the transfer was a redemption through the use of a related corporation under Section 304, and was essentially equivalent to a dividend under Sectio 302. *Held:* Affirmed. The court found that the redemption had the effect of a dividend. It noted that (1) there was no business contraction by either corporation (business in fact increased after the transaction); (2) the initiative for the transaction came from taxpayer; (3) Helix had accumulated earnings and profits and had never paid a dividend; and (4) taxpayer's ownership and control was not changed after the sale. Kerr, 326 F2d 225, 64-1 USTC ¶ 9186, 13 AFTR2d 386 (9th Cir. 1964).

Sale of stock to related corporation taxed as dividend. Taxpayers individually owned 50 percent of the stock of a New Jersey corporation. In approximately the same proportions, they owned stock in a New York corporation, which in turn held the other 50 percent of the New Jersey corporation. The New York corporation also had a wholly owned subsidiary. As individuals, taxpayers sold their 50 percent stock interest in the New Jersey corporation to the subsidiary for cash. This transaction made no difference in their ownership. The IRS and the district court held that the sale had to be treated as a dividend. *Held:* Affirmed. This type of sale is the evil at which Section 304 was aimed. Radnitz, 294 F2d 577, 61-2 USTC ¶ 9672, 8 AFTR2d 5552 (2d Cir. 1961).

"Control" for Section 304 requires that taxpayer hold at least some actual stock interest in both corporations involved. Taxpayer owned a "controlling" interest in X Corporation. Taxpayer sold an approximately 10 percent common stock interest in X to Y, a corporation wholly owned by his sons. After the sale, taxpayer held an approximately 45 percent stock interest in X. The IRs disallowed taxpayer's treatment of gain on this sale as capital gain and treated, under Sections 304 and 302, the amount received by him as a dividend. *Held:* For the taxpayer. For purposes of Section 304, a person can "control" two corporations only if he holds interest in both corporations. Here, taxpayer had an actual stock interest only in X. Accordingly, Section 304 does not apply to taxpayer's sale of X stock to Y. Coyle, 268 F. Supp. 233, 67-1 USTC ¶ 9454, 19 AFTR2d 1525 (SD W. Va. 1967).

Business purpose is irrelevant in determining dividend equivalence under Section 302(b)(1).

The members of a family group controlled *A* and *B*, two corporations conducting related businesses. Inasmuch as they could be managed more efficiently as a single enterprise, the two were combined by having *A* purchase the stock of *B*. The purchase price consisted of cash plus interest to be paid in installments over a period of ten years. the IRS contended that the transaction was a redemption through the use of a related corporation that resulted in a distribution essentially equivalent to a dividend. The taxpayer maintained that the sale to *A* actually represented the transfer of property pursuant to Section 351. It was also argued that the assertion of dividend equivalence was unjustified in view of the business purpose, that the required control was not present under Section 304, and that the alleged dividend distributions were charged to the wrong parties. *Held:* For the IRS. The distribution was in redemption of the stock and was essentially equivalent to a dividend. The fact that a transaction has a business purpose is irrelevant in determining dividend equivalence under Section 302(b)(1). Davis, 397 US 301 (1970). Section 351 was not applicable because the taxpayer did not receive any stock or securities in exchange. The requisite control under Section 304 was present, and the proper parties had been charged. Coates Trust, 55 TC 501 (1971).

Losses of subsidiary deducted from income of parent on consolidated return did not reduce basis of parent's stock in subsidiary. Taxpayer corporation received $53,000 on the redemption of its subsidiary's preferred stock and on the later sale in the same year of the subsidiary's common stock. The two corporations had filed consolidated returns in prior years in which the subsidiary's otherwise unusable losses of $43,000 were offset against taxpayer's income. Taxpayer's combined basis for the subsidiary's common and preferred stock was $25,000, which the IRS contended was to be reduced to zero by the subsidiary's losses. *Held:* For taxpayer. The reduction in basis was limited to the losses in the year "prior" to the redemption and sale. The redemption of the preferred occurred first, and since the taxpayer's receipts therefrom exceeded its basis for both the common and the preferred stock, the common stock had a zero basis when sold. Therefore, even if the sale caused the year of sale to be a "prior" year, there could be no further reduction of the basis. Henry C. Beck Builders, Inc., 41 TC 616 (1964).

Dividend equivalence found for redemption through related corporation. Taxpayer, his brother, and his father each owned one third of the stock of Awnings. After considering stock owned by wives and children, taxpayer and his brother each owned 45 percent of the stock of Products, and their father owned the other 10 percent. The parties each sold all their stock in Awnings to Products for cost ($2,000) at a time when the earnings and profits of both corporations were in excess of $6,000. The IRS ruled that the sale was a redemption essentially equivalent to a dividend. *Held:* For the IRS. The sales constituted redemptions through the use of a related corporation because the parties were in control of both corporations after applying the rules of attribution. Further, since the rules of stock attribution make inapplicable the exceptions under Section 302, the distribution was treated as a redemption of the Products stock, which, in the absence of further evidence, was essentially equivalent to a dividend. Humphrey, 39 TC 199 (1962).

IRS clarifies its position in the McDonald decision. The Tax Court, in McDonald, 52 TC 82 (1969), held that a redemption of stock pursuant to a plan for acquisition of the redeeming corporation by another corporation through an exchange of stock, was not essentially equivalent to a dividend under Section 302(b)(1). The IRS incorrectly treated the redemption and reorganization as separate transactions. Therefore, the redemption issue dealt with by the court in *McDonald* was not the correct one for the decision, and the case was not considered an appropriate precedent. Rev. Rul. 75-360, 1975-2 CB 110.

Redemption using foreign subsidiary's shares. A domestic parent, pursuant to a plan, redeemed all of its shares held by an individual stockholder for shares of its wholly owned foreign subsidiary, which then redeemed all of its shares owned by the individual. The IRS treated the transaction as though the subsidiary made a taxable distribution to the parent in exchange for part of its stock held by the parent and then as a cash redemption of the individual's shares. Rev. Rul. 74-573, 1974-2 CB 95.

Redemption using contributed stock of another corporation held a taxable exchange. Four unrelated individuals each owned 25 percent of the outstanding stock of a corporation. Three of the stockholders also owned 10 percent of the stock of another corporation with 70 percent owned by the fourth stockholder of the first corporation. Pursuant to a prearranged plan, the three 10 percent stockholders transferred their interests to the corporation in which they owned 25 percent. The corporation then redeemed the stock of the fourth 25 percent stockholder issuing the contributed stock of the other corporation. The transaction was a taxable exchange under Section 1001 between groups of stockholders and the use of the corporation as a conduit to accomplish their goals failed. Rev. Rul. 71-336, 1971-2 CB 299.

Tax treatment of sale of stock to a related corporation. An individual owned 100 percent of the stock of a corporation. His son owned all the outstanding stock of another corporation. The father sold 25 shares of stock of his corporation to his son's corporation. The IRS considered the sale an acquisition of stock by a related corporation, and thus a redemption of the stock of the acquiring corporation. Rev. Rul. 71-563, 1971-2 CB 175.

IRS ruled on redemption through the use of related corporations. X Corporation owned 70 percent of Y Corporation and 100 percent of Z Corporation. Y sold all of the stock of its wholly owned subsidiary, S, to Z for cash. The purchase price of the S stock was its fair market value. The inapplicability of Sections 303 and 302(a) resulted in the amount received by Y being treated as a distribution under Section 302(d). The distribution was considered a dividend from Z to Y under Section 301(c)(1) to the extent of Z's earnings and profits. The basis of the S stock in the hands of Z was the same as the basis of the S stock in the hands of Y Rev. Rul. 70-496, 1970-2 CB 74.

Redemptions of Preferred Stock

Preferred stock redemption not a dividend. Taxpayer corporation owned a majority of both the preferred and common stock of a subsidiary corporation. The perferred stock had been received in reorganization of the subsidiary in exchange for bonds and advances. Since the capital had originally been advanced to the subsidiary on a temporary basis, the district court found that its redemption in the taxable year was not substantially equivalent to a dividend. Taxpayer had reported its basis equal to the redemption price, resulting in no gain or loss. *Held:* Affirmed. Upon reviewing the complicated transactions, the court concluded that its basis was only about 90 percent so that a 10 percent capital gain resulted. Since there was no dividend, the asserted personal holding company surtax deficiencies failed, and the tax on the gain was barred by the three-year statute of limitations as there was an omission of less than 25 percent. Further, the distributions by the corporation to its individual stockholders, described as a partial liquidation, were largely nontaxable to the stockholders. The corporation had a deficit at the beginning of its taxable year, and the finding that it did not receive a dividend on the preferred stock redemption limited the taxable ordinary income to the stockholders to the relatively small amount of current year's earnings. The balance of the distribution was a return of capital. Callan Court Co., 274 F2d 532, 60-1 USTC ¶ 9245, 5 AFTR2d 650 (5th Cir. 1960).

Preferred stock issued instead of debt obligations to comply with FHA requirements not debt for tax purposes. A group of individuals in the mortgage loan business formed a corporation to process FHA loans. In order to comply with the FHA regulations, the corporation was required to have capital or surplus of at least $100,000. Initially, the sum of $100,000 was put into the corporation by one individual in exchange for corporate notes.

REDEMPTIONS: *Redemptions of Preferred Stock*

When the FHA informed the company that the $100,000 had to be in the form of stock, the notes were exchanged for preferred stock. Dividends were paid on the preferred stock, and portions of the preferred stock were redeemed whenever the corporation had sufficient capital. The dividends were deducted by the corporation as interest, and no income was reported by the stockholder in redemption of the preferred stock on the theory that the preferred stock was intended as a loan. The IRS denied the corporation an interest deduction and contended that the redemption of the preferred stock was a dividend. *Held:* For the IRS, in part. The corporation was not entitled to an interest deduction, but the redemption of the preferred stock was not essentially equivalent to a dividend. Regardless of the intention of the parties, preferred stock was not debt. However, the background of the FHA requirements resulted in the redemption of the stock not being essentially equivalent to a dividend. Dorsey, 311 F. Supp. 625, 70-1 USTC ¶ 9147 (SD Fla. 1969).

Pro rata redemption was essentially equivalent to a dividend. Taxpayer was a stockholder in Paramount, a corporation. In 1950, Paramount's stockholders, including taxpayer, made advances to the corporation that were designated on the latter's books as open account indebtedness with no maturity date. Later in 1950, Paramount replaced the "indebtedness" with redeemable preferred stock. In 1963, the stockholders preferred stock was redeemed for unsecured, five-year, interest-bearing notes. No change in stockholder relationships resulted from the redemption, which the IRS argued was, regarding taxpayer, essentially equivalent to a dividend under Section 302(b)(1). *Held:* For the IRS. A pro rata redemption effecting no change in stockholder relationships is a dividend under the net effect test. (See Ballenger, 301 F2d 192 (1962)). In the present case, there was no business purpose sufficient to overcome dividend equivalency under the flexible net effect test. (See Bradbury, 298 F2d 111 (1962)). There may be a business purpose where preferred stock is issued to remove debts from the balance sheet and thereby improve credit rating, but that was not the case here. Comess, 309 F. Supp. 1215, 70-1 USTC ¶ 9159 (ED Va. 1969).

Payments for preferred stock not equivalent to a dividend. The IRS contended that the redemption of preferred stock from a decedent's estate was substantially equivalent to a dividend to taxpayer. No other facts were given. *Held:* For taxpayer. The jury found for the taxpayer on receiving the instruction that a finding of the following facts would be persuasive that the redemption was substantially equivalent to a dividend: (1) the redemption was not prompted by a bona fide corporate business purpose; (2) it was initiated by the stockholders; (3) it did not result in a contraction of the business; and (4) it did not effect a substantial change in the proportionate stock ownership of the corporation. Hartman, 67-1 USTC ¶ 9435 (ED Wis. 1966).

Preferred stock redemption was dividend. Two equal partners incorporated the partnership business, taking back both preferred and common stock. Seven years later, a part of the preferred stock was redeemed equally from each stockholder. *Held:* For the IRS. The redemption had the effect of a dividend. The ownership in the corporation was unchanged by the redemption. Cohen, 192 F. Supp. 216, 61-1 USTC ¶ 9252 (EDNY 1961).

Preferred stock redemption not a dividend. The original capitalization of Unitek Corporation consisted of 350 shares of preferred stock, sold at par of $100 per share and 550 shares of common stock sold at $1 per share. For each share of preferred stock purchased, the purchaser was entitled to buy one share of common stock. Thus, holders of the preferred owned 350 shares of common. The balance of the common was owned by three persons who owned no preferred. In 1955, the corporation redeemed 70 shares of preferred by lot. All of taxpayer's five shares were redeemed at par. Taxpayer considered the redemption an exchange on which neither gain nor loss was realized. The IRS treated the redemption as essentially equivalent to a dividend. *Held:* For taxpayer. The court sustained taxpayer for two reasons: (1) The redemption provision had a legitimate business purpose in facilitating the raising of capital. Thus the initiative for the redemption came from the corporation, not from the stockholders; (2) the redemption affected only 20 percent of the preferred stock, thus changing the proportionate stock ownership. The stockholders received a different amount in redemption than if a dividend on all the common stock had been declared. The court also noted that when the remaining preferred stock was redemed in 1959, four years after the taxable year involved, most of that stock was owned by persons who owned no common stock. Thus, viewing the redemption in the aggregate, its effect was also disproportionate. Colvin, 175 F. Supp. 877, 60-1 USTC ¶ 9215 (SD Cal. 1959).

Portion of redemption held to be dividends. A corporation paid a dividend on common stock without paying or setting aside a similiar dividend for its preferred stock. On a subsequent redemption of the preferred stock, the IRS determined that the amount equal to the unpaid dividend should be accorded dividend in lieu of capital gains treatment. *Held:* For the IRS. The certificate of incorporation provided for payment of dividends to preferred stockholders before common stockholders, and the preferred stockholders had a legally enforceable right to compel payment of the dividends. Crown, 58 TC 825 (1972).

Preferred stock redemptions essentially equivalent to dividends. The IRS assessed a deficiency based on the claim that taxpayer received dividend income with respect to the disposition of preferred stock. *Held:* For the IRS. The parties agreed to be bound by the decision in Miele, 56 TC 556 (1971), wherein it was held that the preferred stock redemptions were essentially equivalent to dividends, and did not qualify as a Section 302(a) distribution. Thus, taxpayer was in receipt of taxable income from the transaction. La Fera Contracting Co., 30 TCM 691, ¶ 71,161 P-H Memo. TC (1971).

Redemption of preferred stock is essentially equivalent to a dividend. Taxpayers incorporated their partnership in 1953, at which time each received both common and preferred stock in exchange for the partnership assets. Six years later, the corporation redeemed the preferred at par by issuing to taxpayers 6 percent promissory notes payable in three years. The IRS ruled that the redemption was esentially equivalent to a dividend. *Held:* For the IRS. There was no merit in taxpayers' contention that the notes were not income to cash-basis taxpayers. Terwilliger, 23 TCM 1256, ¶ 64,207 P-H Memo. TC (1964).

Distribution to sole stockholder in redemption of preferred stock issued for genuine business purpose not a dividend. Taxpayer was the principal stockholder of a corporation that was indebted to him in a substantial sum for accumulated salaries and rent. The total debt had been reported as income by taxpayer in the years that the sums were earned. Because of this liability on the books of the corporation, it received a poor credit rating. In order to improve its balance sheet and strengthen its credit position, the corporation issued redeemable preferred stock to taxpayer, thereby removing the obligation from its books. At a time when taxpayer was the sole stockholder, the corporation redeemed the balance of its outstanding preferred stock. The IRS ruled that the distribution constituted a dividend. *Held:* For taxpayer. The distribution to taxpayer in exchange for his preferred did not constitute the distribution of a dividend because of the evident business purpose of the corporation, i.e., the improvement of its credit standing. An additional factor was the corporation's record of liberal dividend payments for several years prior to the preferred stock redemption as well as during the year of redemption. Herzog, 22 TCM 1595, ¶ 63,303 P-H Memo. TC (1963).

Preferred stock redemption of sole owner equivalent to a dividend. A redemption of the preferred stock of a taxpayer who was constructively the sole owner of the corporation was deemed by the IRS to be essentially equivalent to a dividend. *Held:* For the IRS. There was no liquidation or contraction of the corporate business; the corporation accumulated substantial earnings and had never paid any dividends. Simon, 20 TCM 112, ¶ 61,025 P-H Memo. TC (1961).

Preferred stock redemption within Section 302(b)(1). Stockholder owned only nonvoting, nonconvertible, nonparticipating, non-Section 306 preferred stock. The corporation redeemed 5 percent of the preferred stock. The IRS ruled that the rights represented by the redeemed shares could not be recovered through continued stock ownership because no common stock was owned. Thus, the redemption was not essentially equivalent to a dividend and qualifies under Section 302(b)(1). Rev. Rul. 77-426, 1977-2 CB 87.

Redemption of all preferred stock is distribution not equivalent to a dividend when no proportional relationship existed. The redemption by a corporation of all of its preferred stock is a distribution in exchange for the stock pursuant to Section 302, not a dividend where there is no proportional relationship or pattern of stock ownership existing between the holders of preferred stock and the holders of common stock. Rev. Rul. 68-547, 1968-2 CB 123.

Redemption of subsidiary's preferred stock is a dividend eliminated in a consolidated return. The IRS ruled that a corporation that owns 100 percent of the preferred stock and 80 percent of the common stock of a subsidiary receives a dividend when the preferred stock is redeemed, assuming that the earnings and profits of the subsidiary exceed the amount of the redemption. The distribution is essentially equivalent to a dividend, since there is no appreciable change in the position of the subsidiary's stockholders. The IRS further ruled that if a consolidated return is filed, the dividend is eliminated under Regulation § 1.1502-31(b)(1). Under Regulation § 1.302-2(c), the parent's adjusted basis for the preferred stock is allocated to the common stock of the subsidiary owned by the parent. Rev. Rul. 66-37, 1966-1 CB 209.

Redemption of preferred stock essentially equivalent to a dividend. A closely held corporation owned by three families redeemed all of its preferred stock by distributing in exchange therefore stock of another corporation that had been originally contributed by the three families. The redemption was held by the IRS to be essentially equivalent to a dividend, since the proportionate interests of each of the three families were not changed substantially. The distribution of the stock in redemption of the preferred resulted in no gain or loss to the corporation. Rev. Rul. 59-258, 1959-2 CB 105.

Pro rata redemption of part of preferred stock not a dividend. The IRS ruled that a pro rata redemption by a corporation of 20 percent of its preferred stock was not essentially equivalent to a dividend where no single stockholder or family group had more than 25 percent of the voting power. Stockholders who held both preferred and common stock generally did not hold preferred and common in the same proportion. Rev. Rul. 56-485, 1956-2 CB 176.

Redemptions to Pay Death Taxes

Section 303 held applicable to sucessor corporation. A newly created corporation redeemed 180 of 1,409 shares of preferred stock held by taxpayer, a major stockholder. This new corporation held assets which were transferred from a predecessor corporation through taxpayer and her son, another stockholder. Such predecessor corporation had been owned primarily by taxpayer's deceased husband, whose will stipulated that the predecessor corporation be dissolved. The IRS and Tax Court held that the redemption was in fact a dividend to taxpayer. *Held:* Reversed, in part. On appeal, the parties stipulated that Section 303 was applicable. This Section allows capital gains treatment to the extent that such redemption is used to pay estate taxes. Also, on appeal, the parties stipulated that the transfer of the business of the old corporation to the new corporation, through taxpayer and her son, was a D reorganization, so that the boot retained by the stockholders was taxable as ordinary income. Estate of Lammerts, 456 F2d 681, 72-1 USTC ¶ 9328, 29 AFTR2d 72-779 (2d Cir. 1972), aff'g and remanding 54 TC 420 (1970).

REDEMPTIONS: *Redemptions to Pay Death Taxes*

Purchase of stock by beneficiary of estate and subsequent redemption of such stock by corporation to pay estate taxes qualified under Section 303. Decedent devised stock in closely held corporation to trusts for the benefit of his family. Taxpayer, decedent's daughter, purchased the stock from the trust for her benefit primarily to help fix the estate tax value therefor. The corporation then redeemed a portion of such stock. The IRS contended that since taxpayer had purchased the stock, Regulation § 1.303-2(f) precluded Section 303 treatment for the redemption and, therefore, the redemption was a dividend. Taxpayer contended that under Texas law, this was not a purchase, and alternatively attacked the validity of Regulation § 1.303-2(f). The district court allowed capital gain treatment. *Held:* Affirmed. Since the purchase of the stock was by a beneficiary of the decedent who used the redemption proceeds to pay estate taxes, it was not the type of purchase referred to in Regulation § 1.303-2(f) and, therefore, the redemption qualified for capital gains treatment under Section 303. The court expressly avoided passing on the validity of Regulation § 1.303-2(f). Lake, 406 F2d 941, 69-1 USTC ¶ 9195 (5th Cir. 1969).

Section 303 redemption upheld where there were extenuating circumstances delaying actual redemption. Decedent was the sole stockholder of a corporation when he died. Thereafter, decedent's estate became the sole stockholder. The estate elected to use Section 303 to redeem stock to pay his death taxes. Because of a previous escrow agreement between the decedent and his ex-wife and the undetermined valuation of stock, there were delays that led the corporation to make advances to the estate that it carried on its books as dividends. Because of the delays, the IRS assessed a deficiency plus interest for the estate's failure to timely redeem the stock as required by Section 303. *Held:* For taxpayer. Because there was no indication of tax evasion and valid circumstances delayed the stock redemption, Section 303 was liberally construed to allow a delayed redemption. Estate of Cole, 72-1 USTC ¶ 9320, 29 AFTR2d 72-592 (ED Mich. 1971).

Distributions in full payment in exchange for stock redeemed. A distribution in redemption of stock that the decedent had transferred within three years of death will not qualify for capital gains treatment as a distribution in full payment in exchange for stock under Section 303 because the decedent did not actually own the stock at death; and it is not includable in the estate for purposes of Section 303(a). This is so even though the stock is includable in the decedent's estate for purposes of Section 2035 and for determining the percentage requirements of Section 303(b)(2)(A). However, a distribution in redemption of stock actually owned by the decedent at death and that is includable in decedent's gross estate and does not exceed the percentage limitations of Section 303(a) will qualify for treatment as a distribution in full payment in exchange for the redeemed stock. Rev. Rul. 84-76, 1984-1 CB 91.

Redemption of deceased stockholder's shares. The IRS ruled that a distribution by a stock life insurance company to a deceased stockholder's estate that qualified under Section 303 as a redemption was fully includable as to the part made from the policyholder's surplus account in the company's taxable income. Rev. Rul. 74-569, 1974-2 CB 193.

A distribution in redemption is timely even though made within three years and 90 days after an untimely estate tax return. A distribution in redemption of stock to pay death taxes, although made after the untimely filing of a federal estate tax return but within three years and 90 days of the filing of such return meets the requirements of Section 303(b)(1)(A). Rev. Rul. 73-204, 1973-1 CB 170.

Stock convertible into another was still separate for Section 303 purposes. Taxpayer owned 40 percent of the stock of one corporation and 45 percent of the stock of another. Neither block of stock met the percentage requirements for a Section 303 redemption. Within one year of the death of taxpayer, the second corporation acquired the first in a B reorganization. Thus, the estate exchanged the stock of the first corporation for stock of

REDEMPTIONS: *Satisfaction of Stockholder Obligations*

the second corporation. On the alternate valuation date, the percentage requirements were met. For purposes of Section 303, the estate held two blocks of the same corporation's stock, one of which merely represented the other corporation's stock. The two blocks of the same corporation's stock could not be combined to meet the percentage requirements. Rev. Rul. 69-594, 1969-2 CB 44.

Capital gains treatment allowed when decedent's stock is redeemed in a series of distributions. Section 303(a) permits a distribution by a corporation in redemption of stock included in a decedent's estate to be treated as a distribution in full payment for the stock to the extent that the distribution does not exceed estate taxes and funeral and administrative expenses. The distribution must, however, be made not later than 3 years and 90 days after filing of the decedent's federal estate tax return. The IRS ruled that the above requirements were met when the administrator of the estate had the corporation make a series of redemptions of closely held stock within the period. Further, under Rev. Rul. 65-289, the distribution of a note that does not represent an equity interest will satisfy the Code requirement even though the note is paid during this period. Rev. Rul. 67-425, 1967-2 CB 134.

Satisfaction of Stockholder Obligations

Redemption of stock was constructive dividend to other stockholders. Taxpayers, stockholders in a closely held corporation, entered into a written agreement with another stockholder to purchase his shares. Later, sitting as directors, these taxpayers authorized the corporation's redemption of the stock. The shares were subsequently reissued in their names. The IRS claimed that the corporate redemption satisfied taxpayer's obligation under the purchase agreement and was thus a constructive dividend. *Held:* For the IRS. The redemption relieved taxpayers of an obligation to purchase the shares and was thus an economic benefit to them. Jacobs, 698 F2d 850, 83-1 USTC ¶ 9193, 51 AFTR2d 83-627 (6th Cir. 1983).

Stock redemption by corporation resulted in dividend to remaining stockholders. X, a Subchapter S corporation, agreed to redeem the stock of two stockholders, full payment to be made over a period of one year. Taxpayers, who were also stockholders in X, became the high bidders in a contest to acquire the stock of the remaining stockholder. X then purchased the remaining stockholder's stock. The IRS determined that the redemption by X constituted a taxable dividend to taxpayers. The Tax Court held for the IRS, and taxpayer appealed. *Held:* Affirmed. By submitting a high bid for the remaining stockholder's stock, taxpayers became the legally obligated purchasers, and the redemption by X constituted a taxable dividend to them. Taxpayers were acting for themselves, not X Corporation, which relieved them of their personal liability. Stephens, 506 F2d 1400, 74-2 USTC ¶ 9819, 34 AFTR2d 74-6205 (6th Cir. 1974).

Corporation's redemption of minority stock interest in satisfaction of obligation to purchase by sole remaining stockholder was constructive dividend. In 1948, taxpayer, the sole stockholder of an automobile dealership, agreed to sell 40 percent of his stock to an employee of the corporation. The agreement provided that, in the event that the employee terminated his employment, he would resell the stock to taxpayer, who agreed to repurchase same. In 1956, the employee gave taxpayer written notice of his intention to leave the employ of the corporation and of taxpayer's obligation to repurchase his stock. Taxpayer accepted the offer in writing and directed the employee to transfer the stock to the corporation, which then paid the employee the agreed purchase price. The IRS contended that the redemption by the corporation satisfied taxpayer's obligation and resulted in a constructive dividend to him. Taxpayer introduced oral testimony and corporate minutes in an attempt to establish that his right to repurchase was only optional. Invoking the parol evidence rule, the IRS objected to the introduction of oral evidence to construe the 1948 agreement. Taxpayer argued that the parol evidence rule could not be invoked by a stranger to the contract, but was

Redemptions: Satisfaction of Stockholder Obligations

overruled by the district court, which held that the parol evidence rule is a rule of substantive law. Determining that the writings established that taxpayer was primarily obligated to repurchase the employee's stock, the court held that the redemption was a constructive dividend to him. On appeal, taxpayer advanced the additional argument that the lack of mutuality relieved taxpayer of any obligation under the agreement. *Held:* Affirmed.. The agreement was unambiguous, and under it, taxpayer was primarily obligated to repurchase the employee's stock. Hence, whether or not parol evidence would have established that the corporation was also liable was not significant. Taxpayer's argument that the agreement was unenforceable because of lack of mutuality ignored the employee's obligation not to encumber or transfer his stock without taxpayer's consent. The redemption amounted to a constructive dividend to taxpayer because he received an economic benefit in the form of a release from his personal obligations. Sullivan, 363 F2d 724, 66-2 USTC ¶ 9580, 18 AFTR2d 5413 (8th Cir. 1966), cert. denied, 387 US 905 (1967).

Redemption to cancel indebtedness to corporation was dividend equivalent. Taxpayer was indebted to his wholly owned corporation to the extent of $116,000 as a result of renovation work done by the corporation on taxpayer's building. To cancel $112,000 of this debt, taxpayer "transferred" some of his shares to the corporation. Although journal entries to reflect this transfer were made, the stock certificates were never physically delivered to the corporation. When the IRS suggested that the transaction resulted in a dividend rather than capital gains, taxpayer attempted to cancel the transaction by reversing the journal entries and filing an amended return. The Tax Court held that the transfer did take place, and it resulted in a distribution essentially equivalent to a dividend. *Held:* Affirmed. The only purpose of the redemption was to reduce the indebtedness, and the net effect was the same as if taxpayer had received a cash dividend and used the funds to reduce his indebtedness. Tabery, 354 F2d 422, 66-1 USTC ¶ 9135, 17 AFTR2d 001 (9th Cir. 1965).

Redemption of stock essentially equivalent to a dividend. Taxpayer purchased all of the issued and outstanding stock of a family corporation from the widow of taxpayer's deceased brother. Payment for the stock was to be made in installments. Thereafter, over a period of time, taxpayer caused the corporation to redeem all of the preferred stock that he had purchased and to pay the redemption price thereof directly to the widow in discharge of taxpayer's obligations to her under the stock-purchase agreement. The IRS argued that the redemptions were essentially equivalent to a dividend. *Held:* For the IRS. The redemptions represented merely a use of corporate funds to satisfy taxpayer's personal obligation without altering his relationship to the corporation in the slightest. Victorson, 326 F2d 264, 64-1 USTC ¶ 9198 (1964).

Redemption of shares purchased by sole stockholder from former majority stockholder was dividend equivalent. Taxpayer was a minority stockholder in a corporation. The rest of the shares were held by a trust that agreed to sell them to taxpayer for $10,000. The corporation then borrowed $42,000 from a bank and, on the same day, loaned taxpayer's wife $40,000. The wife used the $40,000 to pay for the stock, which was endorsed in taxpayer's name. About four years later, taxpayer surrendered to the corporation the stock he had purchased in exchange for a cancellation of his wife's debt. The IRS ruled that the redemption was essentially equivalent to a dividend under Section 302(b), and was sustained by the Tax Court. *Held:* Affirmed. There was no corporate business purpose for the redemption, which was substantially the same as a cash distribution followed by a repayment of taxpayer's debt. It was immaterial that the same result could have been achieved without adverse tax consequences by having the corporation purchase the stock. That procedure was not followed in this case. McGinty, 325 F2d 820, 64-1 USTC ¶ 9116, 12 AFTR2d 6139 (2d Cir. 1963).

REDEMPTIONS: *Satisfaction of Stockholder Obligations*

Partial redemption of officer's stock essentially equivalent to a dividend. Taxpayer, a major stockholder in a corporation, maintained an open account on the corporate books. The account was charged with withdrawals and was credited with taxpayer's salary and dividends. At the time, the account showed a balance of $21,000, and taxpayer transferred 44 shares of her stock to the corporation for redemption in cancellation of the indebtedness. Applying the attribution of ownership rules of Section 318, taxpayer directly and indirectly owned 91.3 percent of the stock prior to the redemption and 89.7 percent thereafter. There was no plan or policy of contraction prior to the redemption of the stock, and there was no contraction of the corporate business thereafter. The corporation had sufficient earned surplus to cover the distribution. The Tax Court upheld the IRS' determination that the redemption was substantially equivalent to a dividend. *Held:* Affirmed. Although this court, contrary to the Tax Court, found a business purpose for the redemption in that elimination of the indebtedness was necessary for the corporation to obtain a bank loan, it nevertheless concluded the net effect of the redemption to be essentially equivalent to a dividend. Bradbury, 298 F2d 111, 62-1 USTC ¶ 9187, 9 AFTR2d 398 (1st Cir. 1962).

Redemption of stock not equivalent to payment of dividend. In 1954, taxpayer acquired the stock of a deceased stockholder with funds borrowed from a third stockholder. In 1955, a portion of the stock acquired from the deceased stockholder was assigned to the lending stockholder. The assignment and endorsement to the third stockholder cancelled taxpayer's indebtedness. Almost simultaneously with the endorsement to the third stockholder, the corporation redeemed the shares that had previously been acquired from the deceased stockholder. The IRS contended that the redemption through the third stockholder of the shares that taxpayer had owned with the concomitant cancellation of the personal note of taxpayer resulted in a payment to taxpayer that was essentially equivalent to a corporate dividend. Taxpayer, on the other hand, alleged that none of the interested parties in the corporation intended that taxpayer retain the shares of the deceased stockholder and that taxpayer acted only as a conduit for the corporation to facilitate the anticipated redemption of the shares. *Held:* For taxpayer. After finding for the IRS in its first published opinion, the court was persuaded to change its mind. It found the facts to be as taxpayer alleged. Thus, the court concluded that the payment received by taxpayer from the corporation was not essentially equivalent to a dividend. Erickson, 189 F. Supp. 521, 61-1 USTC ¶ 9343, 7 AFTR2d 835 (SD Ill. 1960).

Corporate satisfaction of stockholder's obligation resulted in constructive dividend. Taxpayer was unconditionally obligated to purchase stock held by his father's estate under a stockholders' agreement. The agreement granted options to his sister to sell her stock to him if she so desired. Because taxpayer had insufficient funds to purchase the stock, the corporation redeemed the stock from the estates of his father and sister. The IRS determined that these redemptions resulted in constructive dividends to taxpayer. *Held:* For the IRS, in part. The redemption from the father's estate was a constructive dividend to taxpayer because of his unconditional obligation to purchase the stock. However, redemption of the stock held by his sister's estate did not result in a constructive dividend because taxpayer had no unconditional obligation to purchase. Smith, Jr., 70 TC 651 (1978).

Stock redemption not a constructive dividend. A corporation redeemed the stock of its majority stockholder. The IRS argued that the redemption resulted in a constructive dividend to the corporation's minority stockholder, who was involved in negotiations to purchase the majority stockholder's stock. *Held:* For taxpayer. The corporation did not relieve taxpayer of a legally binding obligation to purchase the majority stockholder's stock. Mozert, 38 TCM 1037, ¶ 79,263 P-H Memo. TC (1979).

Controlling stockholder's donation of corporation's stock to church, followed by purchase of the stock by the corporation, did not produce

REDEMPTIONS: *Satisfaction of Stockholder Obligations*

dividend income. In 1971, taxpayers, sole owners of a bank holding company, transferred stock to a church to satisfy pledges. New certificates were issued in the church's name; then the corporation repurchased the stock from the church. A similar transaction occured in 1972. Taxpayers claimed charitable deductions. The IRS asserted that taxpayer should realize dividend income on the transactions. *Held:* For taxpayers. The court rejected the IRS' argument that these were in reality redemptions of taxpayers' stock, followed by a contribution of the proceeds, or that they were anticipatory assignments of redemption proceeds. There was no obligation to have the stock redeemed, and the gifts were real. Nor did the corporation pay taxpayers' debts, since any debt would be satisfied upon gift of the shares, not upon the latter redemption. Finally, a charitable pledge does not create a debt for tax purposes. Wekesser, 35 TCM 936, ¶ 76,214 P-H Memo. TC (1976).

Reimbursement by corporation to principal stockholders for purchasing stock of other stockholders treated as a redemption not essentially equivalent to a dividend. *B,* a family held corporation, decided to terminate its existing business and become an investment company. Prior to the decision, two stockholders, *Y* and *Z*, requested that they be paid cash for their shares of stock in *B*. Taxpayer, a principal stockholder of *B*, to effectuate *Y*'s and *Z*'s desires, gave them his personal checks for their stock and received their certificates endorsed in blank. *B* then reimbursed taxpayer for the amounts he had personally paid *Y* and *Z* and retired their stock. The certificates formerly owned by *Y* and *Z* were never transferred to the name of taxpayer or any other person, but were cancelled on the stock record book of the corporation. The IRS maintained that the reimbursement to taxpayer was essentially equivalent to a dividend. *Held:* For taxpayer. When taxpayer gave his personal checks to *Y* and *Z* he considered that he was acting for and on behalf of the corporation. He was under no obligation to purchase the shares for himself, and although he used his own funds, he did so as a temporary expedient so that the corporation might acquire and retire the stock in the event that it did not continue in business. Bunton, Sr., 27 TCM 9, ¶ 68,003 P-H Memo. TC (1968).

Partial redemption to allow sole stockholder to satisfy a personal indebtedness held essentially equivalent to a dividend. Taxpayer borrowed funds from a bank on a short-term note to purchase stock in a hotel corporation. Her intent was to liquidate the corporation and to pay off the note with the proceeds. However, when taxpayer found that the hotel liquor license would be lost if the hotel were transferred to her as an individual, she decided to continue operations in corporate form. To retire the indebtedness, she had the corporation redeem part of her stock and pay the sum therefor directly to the bank. The IRS determined that the redemption resulted in a dividend to taxpayer. *Held:* The distribution in redemption was essentially equivalent to a dividend because it resulted in no change in the proportionate ownership of the corporation's stock. Its single purpose was to allow taxpayer, the sole stockholder, to satisfy an indebtedness by means of a direct payment by the corporation to the bank. Estate of Freeman, 23 TCM 1893, ¶ 64,306 P-H Memo. TC (1964).

IRS will follow decision relating to constructive dividends. The IRS will dispose of cases under Section 301 in accordance with the decision in *Maher,* 469 F2d 225 (8th Cir. 1972) when presented with facts substantially identical to those in *Maher,* where taxpayer purchased all the stock in corporations *W, X, Y,* and *Z,* paid cash, and executed two promissory notes. The stock was put in escrow to secure payment of the notes. Subsequently, taxpayer assigned all his "right title and interest" in the stock of *X* in exchange for *W*'s assumption of taxpayer's liability on the notes. Taxpayer remained secondarily liable. *W* made payments of principal and interest for three years, until the notes were fully paid. The accumulated earnings and profits of *W* exceeded payments on the notes for those years. The court determined that the transaction was a distribution by *W* in redemption of its stock under Section 304(a)(1) and a dividend to taxpayer under Section 302(d). Since taxpayer was secondarily liable on the notes, dividends were taxable in the years of payment on the notes by W, instead of when W assumed the liability. Also, interest paid by W was not deductible, but was taxable as additional dividends to taxpayer. Rev. Rul. 77-360, 1977-2 CB 86.

Substantially Disproportionate Redemptions

Section 304 redemption for annuity was a dividend with no stepped-up basis. Taxpayer individuals' stock in A Corporation was transferred by taxpayers to related B Corporation. For this, B agreed to pay taxpayers a lifetime annuity. B immediately resold this stock to A in exchange for cash and unsecured promissory notes. The Tax Court held that this was a redemption through the use of related corporations within the meaning of Section 304. Furthermore, such redemption was a dividend to taxpayer-stockholders, not an exchange by them. *Held:* Affirmed. There was no substantially disproportionate redemption under Section 302(b), and none of the other relief provisions of this section applied. B's basis for the stock was zero because the redemption was a dividend to taxpayers and because there was no property distribution to taxpayers with resulting capital gain and stepped-up basis to B. Basis could be increased by gift taxes paid by taxpayer individuals if not refunded. Fehrs Fin. Co., 487 F2d 184, 73-2 USTC ¶ 9767, 32 AFTR2d 73-6068 (8th Cir. 1973).

Stock redemption plan essentially equivalent to a dividend because it lacked business purpose. Based on a retirement plan agreement, three major stockholders could opt to have the corporation redeem a certain number of shares each year. Taxpayer, having his shares redeemed under this plan, reported the amount as long-term capital gains. The IRS contended the amount was essentially equivalent to a dividend. *Held:* For the IRS. The plan did not exert any compulsion on the stockholders, but permitted each to fit his own redemptions into a pattern set by the others, and thus gave each complete power to prevent any decline in his relative ownership position. The retirement redemption plan was merely an arrangement that allowed the stockholders to withdraw cash while leaving their relative interests unchanged. In addition, a business purpose for the redemptions was not shown. The redemptions were, therefore, essentially equivalent to dividends. Blount, 425 F2d 921, 70-1 USTC ¶ 9132 (2d Cir. 1970).

Stock redemption held to be essentially equivalent to a dividend. Three related individuals and their sons owned the stock of a closely held corporation. The sons were managing the business and desired to own all the stock. The fathers were given options by the corporation to sell to the corporation a certain number of their shares of stock at a certain price each year after they had reached a certain age. Taxpayers reported the sale as a capital gain, and the IRS contended that the sale was equivalent to a dividend. The Tax Court held for the IRS. *Held:* Affirmed. Although the redemptions from each of the stockholders were not exactly proportionate, the difference was not sufficient to sustain capital gains treatment. Blount, 425 F2d 921, 70-1 USTC ¶ 9132 (2d Cir. 1969).

Redemption essentially equivalent to a dividend: options held by partner considered as stock constructively held by taxpayer. As a partner in a partnership, taxpayer received 25 percent of the first $10,000 of profits and 20 percent of the balance. Taxpayer also owned a 45 percent stock interest in a corporation. To induce one of the partners to manage the corporation, taxpayer granted him an option to purchase stock at 85 percent of its value. Taxpayer then turned in the necessary shares to cover the option to the corporation, which gave him a note in exchange. The IRS ruled the redemption was substantially equivalent to a dividend. Treating the option held by the prospective manager as stock held by taxpayer, and treating taxpayer as a 25 percent partner, the Tax Court found that, under the sidewise attribution rules (subsequently repealed), the redemption was not substantially disproportionate. The court then determined that the distribution was essentially equiva-

REDEMPTIONS: *Substantially Disproportionate Redemptions*

lent to a dividend, relying on the fact that the redemption served no corporate purpose. *Held:* Affirmed per curiam. Bloch, 386 F2d 839, 68-1 USTC ¶ 9120 (5th Cir. 1967).

Redemption not essentially equivalent to dividend. Two stockholders owned equally all of the capital stock of a corporation engaged in the automobile business. One, Brown, was not actively engaged in the business, and after discussions with the other, Carey, proposed to sell his stock. The only available buyer was a salesman of the company who did not have sufficient cash to purchase Brown's stock. The company's counsel suggested a plan for acquiring Brown's stock by a pro rata redemption of part of the stock of both Carey and Brown in exchange for the building and other assets, a leasing of the building to the corporation for three years, and the sale of Brown's remaining stock to the salesman. The district court determined that the pro rata redemption did not result in taxable dividends to either Brown or Carey; the IRS appealed from the judgment as to Carey (but not as to Brown). *Held:* Affirmed. The Eighth Circuit affirmed on the basis of fact-findings by the district court that the pro rata redemption was part of an overall plan for the acquisition of one of the stockholder's interest by a third party and was not essentially equivalent to a dividend. The court pointed out that it would be anomalous to consider the pro rata redemption as not essentially equivalent to a dividend regarding one of the two stockholders and not regarding the other. Carey, 289 F2d 531, 61-1 USTC ¶ 9428, 7 AFTR2d 1301 (8th Cir. 1961).

Court of claims ruled for stockholder in a patronage stock redemption challenge. Taxpayer, a Delaware corporation, was organized as a farmers' cooperative doing business in New York. It was also a patron of an Indiana cooperative and received annual patronage dividends at the end of each fiscal year. As a part of its annual dividend, the Indiana co-op distributed 2,193 shares of preferred stock to taxpayer. This brought taxpayer's total stock holdings to about 5,000 shares after 19 years of membership. It represented an ownership interest of 18 percent. During 1960, taxpayer redeemed 1,087 shares that were valued at $60 a share when issued and received $100 per share on the redemption. The IRS treated the $60 per share gain as ordinary income. Taxpayer contended that it was entitled to capital gains treatment under Section 302. *Held:* For taxpayer. Under Section 302(b)(1), a redemption that is essentially equivalent to a dividend is disqualified from treatment as a sale or exchange, and the gain therefrom is to be taxed as ordinary income rather than as a capital gain. Under the long-standing test for determining the application of Section 302(b)(1), there is dividend equivalency if there has been both a pro rata distribution of earnings and no change in the stockholder's ownership. In this case, the redemption shifted taxpayer's ownership from 16 to 18 percent, an insignificant change under these facts. Nevertheless, the court found that there had been no pro rata distribution and that dividend equivalency had not been established by the IRS. Under the terms of the co-op's bylaws, it was provided that "capital advances shall be retired in the order in which they have been received." Thus, all or the same proportion of all shares issued in a single year were required to be redeemed together. The only way a distribution could have been pro rata across the class of stock would have been if each stockholder had received the same number of shares in each year of issue. A subsequent change in governing regulatory law was inapplicable, and therefore judgment was entered for taxpayer. Agway, Inc., 524 F2d 1194, 36 AFTR2d 76-6157, 75-2 USTC ¶ 9777 (Ct. Cl. 1975).

Corporate distribution essentially equivalent to dividend. Taxpayers, a mother and son, owed amounts to their wholly owned corporation substantially in proportion to their stockholdings. The corporation cancelled their indebtedness and redeemed approximately pro rata portions of their stock, effecting no basic change in ownership or control of the corporation. The IRS contended that the redemption was essentially equivalent to a dividend. *Held:* For the IRS. The resolution of this issue depended on the facts. The major factors were whether the distribution was pro

REDEMPTIONS: *Substantially Disproportionate Redemptions*

rata, and whether the transaction affected the relationship of the stockholders to the corporation. This was a classic example of a corporate distribution that was essentially equivalent to a dividend. Estate of Runnels, 54 TC 762 (1970).

Redemption of association interest by installments not a dividend. Taxpayer was a member of an association. He wanted to retire and have the association redeem his entire interest. To avoid a significant financial drain, the association persuaded him to withdraw his interest over several years. The IRS contended that payments in the taxable year were essentially equivalent to a dividend. *Held:* For taxpayer. The Tax Court ruled that taxpayer could not use the substantially disproportionate exception of Section 302(b)(2) because each member of the association had one vote regardless of his interest. Taxpayer received capital gains treatment because the partial liquidation of interest was at the request of the association, not taxpayer. Cornwall, 48 TC 736 (1967), acq. 1968-1 CB 2.

Permanent nonrepayable deposit on product part of sales agreement of stock, not goods. Taxpayer corporation, a seafood processing and sales operation, conducted its foreign sales through the affiliated *S* Corporation. Its principal purchaser, *Y,* wanted to purchase 50 percent of taxpayer's and *S*'s stock, yet avoid a foreign penalty tax imposed in its own country on direct stock purchases. To carry out its plan, *Y* transferred $350,000 to taxpayer and designated the cash a "permanent and not repayable" deposit on product. In conjunction with the transfer, the corporations redeemed their stock, and each reissued 50 percent of its holdings to *Y*. Two taxpayer stockholders, *G* and *T,* received 22.5 percent of the holdings in each corporation plus cash for their 41.5 percent previous holdings of outstanding stock. The IRS determined that the $350,000 transfer was an advance payment for goods subject to taxation as ordinary income. The IRS contended that the transaction was a recapitalization within the meaning of Section 368(a)(1)(E), and that the exchange among *G, T,* and *Y* had the effect of distributing a dividend under Section 356(a)(2). Thus, the cash distributed was taxable as a dividend. The IRS did not include the stock transferred to *Y*. *Held:* For taxpayers. Although the evidence indicated that the deposit was never applied against the price of goods, and that *Y* paid for all goods purchased from taxpayer corporation by letter of credit, there was in fact a sale of stock, regardless of the ambiguities in the terms of the agreement. Within the meaning of Section 302(b)(2), the distributions received by taxpayers *G* and *T* in redemption of their stock were substantially disproportionate with respect to them and therefore were not taxable as dividends. The stock transferred to *Y* was considered in making the determination. Grant, 44 TCM 893, ¶ 82,480 P-H Memo. TC (1982).

Non-pro rata redemption of preferred stock not equivalent to dividend; business purpose established. Taxpayer owned 77 percent of the preferred and 90 percent of the common stock of a corporation. In 1959, the corporation redeemed all of its outstanding preferred stock at par plus a $3 redemption premium called for by the stock. For the 13 years preceding the redemption, the corporation had a history of paying substantial dividends averaging 47 percent of the net profits before taxes. The minutes of the directors' meeting indicated that the action to redeem taxpayer's preferred was taken because the prevailing interest rate on borrowings was lower than the 6 percent dividend rate on the preferred. This action was in line with the corporation's recurring policy to cut expenses in times of declining profits. The IRS held that the redemption of taxpayer's preferred was equivalent to a dividend and taxed the distribution as ordinary income. *Held:* For taxpayer. The distribution was not essentially equivalent to a dividend within the meaning of Section 302(b)(1). The fact that the redemption was not pro rata and that it served a corporate purpose, when considered in the light of the other facts and circumstances, supported taxpayer's contention that there was no tax-avoidance purpose to the redemption. Estate of Hinrichsen, 25 TCM 1383, ¶ 66,271 P-H Memo. TC (1966).

REDEMPTIONS: *Substantially Disproportionate Redemptions*

Redemption through an interim purchase by remaining stockholder not essentially equivalent to a dividend. A public transportation corporation that contemplated converting from trolley cars to buses found that it no longer had any need for a substantial amount of its real estate. It therefore planned to terminate the stock interest of its major stockholder by a redemption of his stock with the excess real estate. Because of an anticipated delay in getting disposable title to the realty, the plan was changed to have the remaining minority stockholder (taxpayer) make an interim purchase of the majority stockholder shares and subsequently have the corporation redeem from taxpayer the purchased shares at the price paid for them. The proceeds from the land sales were used for this redemption. The IRS asserted that the redemption was essentially equivalent to a dividend. *Held:* For taxpayer. The redemption was not essentially equivalent to a dividend. Viewed from the beginning of the plan, which was to effectuate a redemption retirement of the major stockholder, there was a non-pro rata redemption. McShain, 22 TCM 1611, ¶ 63,306 P-H Memo. TC (1963).

Taxpayer's partial redemption held not essentially equivalent to a dividend, despite his continued involvement in the corporation. Because of a long-standing controversy with his son concerning the operation of the corporation he founded in 1926, taxpayer decided in 1955 to sell his stock to his son. Taxpayer (together with his wife) held, before the redemption, a 50.3 percent interest in the corporation; his son held a 47.4 percent interest; and an unrelated person held a 2.3 percent interest. Because neither the corporation nor taxpayer's son could afford to acquire taxpayer's interest all at once, the transaction was structured as a redemption of 60 percent of taxpayer's interest with the corporation's option to purchase the balance later. Apparently, the corporation exercised the option when the 60 percent interest was delivered. It committed itself to make deferred payments for the balance of the stock. The time for making these payments, and thus the tendering of those shares involved, was extended a number of times. Although taxpayer was elected chairman of the board, the evidence indicated that this title was honorary and carried no duties or privileges. Taxpayer regularly visited the corporation's office but had no authority to engage in management functions. Although his name was retained on the corporation's letterhead, this was to retain the goodwill of the business. Furthermore, taxpayer received monthly payments of $6,000. Evidence indicated that this payment was made in respect of past services and that there were similar arrangements for non-stockholder employees. The IRS challenged taxpayer's treatment of the redemption as a sale and asserted a deficiency based on the treatment of the redemption proceeds as a dividend. *Held:* For taxpayer. Despite the attribution rules, the redemption resulted in a "substantial dislocation of stockholdings" and a significant change of control. Accordingly, the redemption was not essentially equivalent to a dividend. Parker, 20 TCM 893, ¶ 61,176 P-H Memo. TC (1961).

Qualification under Section 302(b)(2) for first stockholder measured after redemption of second stockholder's shares. Unrelated parties, A, B, C, and D owned all of X's stock. X had a repurchase agreement with all stockholders except A that if a stockholder ceased to be actively connected with the business of X, such stockholder had to trade his shares of X stock to X for an amount equal to the book value of the stock. On January 1, 1983, B informed A, the founder and majority stockholder in X, of his intention to resign on March 22, 1983. Based on this information, A caused X to redeem 902 out of 1,466 of his shares of X stock on March 15, 1983. Thereafter, B resigned and his shares were redeemed. Examined separately, the transaction on March 15, 1983 met the 50 percent and 80 percent tests of Section 302(b)(2) to qualify as a substantially disproportionate redemption and, accordingly, the exchange treatment pursuant to Section 302(a). However, after the redemption of B's stock, the tests were no longer met by A. The IRS ruled that the redemption did not qualify under Section 302(b)(2). Although the redemptions were causally connected, they were part of a plan for purposes of Section 302(b)(2)(D);

therefore control was measured after the second redemption. Rev. Rul. 85-14, 1985-1 CB 92.

Redemption of voting preferred stock may be substantially disproportionate even though no common stock owned. Taxpayer owned all of the voting preferred stock of X Corporation, which constituted 49 percent of all voting stock and the combined voting power of all classes of stock entitled to vote. After a partial redemption, he owned 36.25 percent. The requirement of Section 302(b)(2)(C) that the stockholder's ownership of common stock also be reduced did not apply where taxpayer owned no common stock at the outset, and hence did not disqualify the redemption from being substantially disproportionate. Rev. Rul. 81-41, 1981-1 CB 121.

IRS to follow *Zenz* decision where reduction of interest is part of an integrated plan. In Zenz, 213 F2d 914 (6th Cir. 1954), a sole stockholder of a corporation, desiring to dispose of her entire interest therein, sold part of her stock to a competitor and shortly thereafter sold the remainder of her stock to the corporation for an amount of cash and property approximately equal to its earned surplus. The IRS contended that the redemption was a dividend. It based its contention on the grounds that the result was the same as if the steps had been reversed, that is, as if the stock had been redeemed first and the sale of stock to the competitor had followed. The court of appeals rejected this contention and held that the purchase of the stock by the corporation (when coupled with the sale of stock to the competitor) was not a dividend to the selling stockholder and that the proceeds should be treated as payment for the stock. The IRS subsequently determined that it would follow the decision in *Zenz* in similar situations. The IRS stated that as a general rule, it would disregard the sequence of events and consider only the overall result in determining whether a distribution is "substantially disproportionate" in plans calling for a stock redemption accompanied either by an issuance of new stock or by a stockholder's sale of stock if the events are clearly part of an overall integrated plan to reduce a stockholder's interest. Rev. Rul. 75-447, 1975-2 CB 113.

Termination of Stockholder's Interest

Conditions limiting payments under redemption agreement do not destroy its capital gains status. Taxpayer treated the redemption of her stock in a GM car dealership as a termination of her interest under Section 302 (b)(3) that produced capital gains. Since some stock was held by other family members, she sought a waiver of family attribution. The IRS charged that provisions in the redemption agreement that limited payments under it if they impaired the dealer's "working capital" gave her an interest other than that of a creditor; waiver was not available, and the payments were ordinary income. *Held:* For taxpayer. The limitation was imposed by GM as a condition to keeping its franchise. Since it was imposed by a third party, it did not, by itself, give taxpayer a continuing proprietary interest. Dunn, 615 F2d 578, 80-1 USTC ¶ 9187, 45 AFTR2d 80-683 (2d Cir. 1980).

Agreement to notify of reacquisition of stock need not be filed with original return. Regulation § 1.302-4(a) requires that for the complete termination provisions on stock redemptions to be fully effective, taxpayer must file with a timely return an agreement to notify the district director of any stock acquisition. Taxpayer inadvertently failed to file this agreement with his return, but filed it about a year later, *before* any proposed assessment. *Held:* Affirmed. Sustaining the district court, the appellate court held the regulation requirement invalid. Taxpayer was entitled to treat the redemption as a capital gain. The IRS was not prejudiced by the failure to file the agreement with the return. The court distinguished the Third Circuit's holding in Archbold, 311 F2d 288 (3d Cir. 1963), which reached the opposite result. *Archbold* did not consider a claim of mistake, and taxpayer there offered to file an amended return with the required agreement *after* the assessment had been made. In the instant case, failure to file the agreement was a mistake, the submission of the agreement preceded the assessment, and the record did not disclose any re-

REDEMPTIONS: *Termination of Stockholder's Interest*

jection of the agreement other than the deficiency assessment. Van Keppel, 321 F2d 717, 63-2 USTC ¶ 9683, 12 AFTR2d 5622 (10th Cir. 1963).

Failure to file agreement showing complete termination in stock redemption rendered redemption a dividend. Taxpayer owned 9 percent of the stock of a corporation and her husband and son owned the balance. The redemption of all of her stock would have been equivalent to a dividend after applying the attribution rules of Section 318 except for the provision of Section 302(c) involving complete termination of a stockholder's interest. However, taxpayer failed to file with her return the required agreement to notify the IRS if she reacquired any shares during a 10-year period. The IRS taxed the redemption as a dividend. *Held:* For the IRS. The court held that the failure to file this agreement with the return rendered the complete termination rule inapplicable. The redemption was properly taxed as a dividend. Archbold, 311 F2d 228, 63-1 USTC ¶ 9171 (3d Cir. 1963).

Son's contingent liability to father's estate for taxes attributable to bequest paid to him prevented estate from completely terminating its interest in corporation upon redemption of father's stock. WSC was owned by Webber, Sr. and his son. A stockholder's agreement between them required the corporation to redeem the stock of a deceased stockholder. The father died, and under this agreement, the corporation redeemed all of his WSC stock from his estate. The redemption occurred before the estate paid estate and death taxes. The estate treated the redemption as a sale of WSC stock. The IRS asserted that the amount received by the estate on redemption was taxable as a dividend. *Held:* For the IRS. The estate did not completely terminate its interest in WSC, as required in Section 302(b)(3). The son was, at the time of redemption, subject to a claim by the estate to return the property bequeathed to him, and, if necessary, to pay the taxes attributable to such property. Because of this contingent liability, the son remained a beneficiary of the estate, and his WSC stock was attributed to the estate at the time of the redemption. Accordingly, the estate did not redeem its entire interest in the estate as required by Section 302(b)(3). Estate of Webber, Sr., 263 F. Supp. 703, 67-1 USTC ¶ 9228, 19 AFTR2d 811 (ED Ky. 1967).

Capital gains treatment allowed on stock redemption even though necessary agreements were filed late. Taxpayer's stock was redeemed by two corporations. He terminated his remaining interest in each by resigning as an officer and director. The necessary agreements required by Section 302(c)(2)(A)(iii) (notification of acquisitions within ten years) were not filed with his return. They were prepared by tax counsel and sent to taxpayer's father by mistake. The father inadvertently placed them in an office file. A copy of the mislaid papers was given to an IRS representative when the return was audited. However, the papers apparently were not technically accepted, and capital gains treatment was denied. *Held:* For taxpayer. Under such circumstances, the refusal of the IRS to accept late filing and to treat the redemption as a complete redemption of all the stock of taxpayer was an abuse of discretion. Taxpayer was entitled to capital gains treatment. Pearce, 226 F. Supp. 702, 64-1 USTC ¶ 9203 (WDNY 1964).

Redemption qualified as complete termination of stockholder's interest. Taxpayer, the sole stockholder of a corporation, transferred some of his stock to his son. Subsequently, the corporation redeemed the balance of taxpayer's stock in exchange for property and a promissory note. Following the redemption, taxpayer performed services for the corporation for which he was compensated, pursuant to a consulting agreement that included a covenant not to compete. The corporation also provided taxpayer with other benefits, including coverage under its medical plan. Taxpayer reported the gain on the transaction as a capital gain. The IRS determined that there had not been a complete termination of his interest and that the gain was an ordinary dividend distribution. *Held:* For taxpayer. Following the redemption, taxpayer was an independent contractor, and he did not retain a prohibited interest in the corporation. The transfer of stock to his son was not for tax avoidance. The payments made to taxpayer and the other benefits he received were not contingent on future profitability and thus did not amount to a substantial interest in the continued success of the business. Futhermore, the fact that taxpayer subordinated the promissory note he received in the redemption in order to enable the corporation to expand did not constitute a prohibited equity interest in the corporation. Lynch, 83 TC 597 (1984).

Capital gains treatment denied to redeeming stockholder who retained position as employee after redemption that left his son the sole stockholder. Taxpayers, Mr. and Mrs. Seda, formed B&B Supply Co. in 1957. In 1959, because of their failing health, they decided to redeem their interests in the corporation and to issue to their son, who was ready to assume ownership and control of the corporation, 1,000 shares of stock. At his son's request, Mr. Seda remained an employee of the corporation after the redemption, receiving a salary of $1,000 per month. Upon learning that his continued employment would cause the amount received upon redemption to be treated as a dividend, taxpayer resigned approximately two years after the redemption. There was no evidence that taxpayer ceased to be involved in management of the corporation during the two years that he continued in the employ of the corporation. *Held:* For the IRS. Although taxpayers completely terminated their actual interest as stockholders in the redemption, their son's stock was attributed to them. Accordingly, their interest was not completely terminated as required under Section 302(b)(3). The rule barring such attribution is not applicable because taxpayers continued to have a financial stake in the corporation. Ignorance of the effect of Mr. Seda's continued employment was "immaterial." Although all continuing employment relationships may not result in the same consequence when there is clearly, as here, a continuing economic stake (e.g., salary) or control (e.g., voice in management) the redeeming stockholder is not considered to have completely terminated his interest as required under Section 302(b)(3). Seda, 82 TC 484 (1984).

Redemption followed by sale qualified for installment reporting and capital gains. Taxpayer owned most of the outstanding shares of a corporation, and his children owned the balance. The corporation redeemed a number of his shares for cash and simultaneously redeemed shares owned by his children. A few days later, taxpayer sold his remaining shares to an unrelated individual for the same price per share as the corporation paid him in redemption, receiving cash and installment notes. The corporate minutes indicated that the redemption and sale were part of the same transaction. Taxpayer reported the gain as capital and claimed installment reporting as to the shares sold. The IRS determined that the redemption proceeds constituted ordinary income and that installment reporting was not available. *Held:* For taxpayer. The redemption was part of an overall plan to terminate taxpayer's interest, and as such it was either (1) a complete termination of interest, since after the transaction the taxpayer did not own any shares in the corporation, or (2) not essentially equivalent to a dividend, since it was so related to the sale of the balance of his shares that it constituted a sale. Monson, 79 TC 827 (1982).

Series of redemptions pursuant to an integrated plan held to result in a complete termination of interest under Section 302(b)(3) despite stockholder's lack of legal obligation. Taxpayer was a land-holding company that owned 30 percent of another corporation. The 70 percent stockholder wanted to own 100 percent of this corporation. Taxpayer and this corporation agreed on an integrated plan to redeem taxpayer's entire 30 percent interest on a monthly basis. Because the corporation did not have sufficient funds on hand, it took 23 weeks to redeem all of taxpayer's stock. During the monthly redemption on its stock, taxpayer was never legally obliged to sell the balance of its shares. *Held:* For taxpayer. Even though taxpayer was at no time legally obliged to sell all of its stock, it was agreed that it would do so, and the parties acted accordingly. The monthly redemptions of taxpayer's stock were a series of redemptions leading to a complete termination of its interest, as prescribed in Section 302(b)(3). Thus, the amounts that taxpayer received arose from a sale or exchange of stock and so were not dividends. Bleily & Collishaw, Inc., 72 TC 732 (1979), aff'd (9th Cir. 1981).

Complete stock redemption permitting others to manage company not equivalent to dividend. Taxpayer conducted an automobile dealership for many years. He owned 49.5 percent of the stock of the dealership. Gradually, he turned the active management of the business over to his sons. One son eventually owned 50 percent of the stock in the dealership corporation. Wishing to devote all his time to farming, taxpayer decided to release his interest in the corporation. He agreed to sell his shares back to the corporation at book value. The corporation agreed to pay in installments and at the end of each year to receive shares of stock equivalent to the amount paid. Taxpayer terminated his active participation in the business. The IRS insisted that the redemption over a five-year period was essentially equivalent to a dividend. *Held:* For taxpayer. The partial redemptions were part of a single redemption. Taxpayer withdrew both from ownership and management except for formal but inactive retention of his position as an officer and director. Not only did his sons succeed to the ownership of the business, but they independently took over active management and clearly were not just fronts for taxpayer. Nor was there any evidence suggesting that the transaction was motivated by reasons of tax avoidance. Lewis, 47 TC 129 (1966).

Requirement of filing agreement on reacquisition within ten years is directory, not mandatory; redemption in complete termination of stockholder's interest was capital gain where agreement filed in later year. Upon the death of her husband, taxpayer owned all but a few shares of stock of a corporation. The other shares were owned by her son. All of taxpayer's stock was redeemed by the corporation, but she failed to file the agreement called for by Section 302(c)(2)(A)(iii) to notify the IRS of reacquisition of stock within ten years. When this failure was pointed out in the audit of her return, taxpayer filed the agreement a year after filing the return. *Held:* For taxpayer. The provision requiring the agreement is directory and not mandatory, so substantial compliance is sufficient. The primary purpose of the requirement is to make records available to the IRS. This is merely a procedural detail. The IRS was not prejudiced by a later filing because the statute of limitations did not begin to run until after notification to the IRS of any reacquisition. Cary, 41 TC 214 (1963).

Cash distribution was in redemption of stock. Taxpayer was a 50 percent stockholder in two corporations. One corporation completley redeemed all his shares and bought most of his shares in the second corporation. The second corporation redeemed the remainder of the stock with a cash distribution of one-half of its undistributed taxable income. The corporation and the redemption agreement treated this distribution as a dividend. Taxpayer treated it as capital gains. The IRS argued that it was a dividend. *Held:* For taxpayer. Viewing the interrelated transactions together, taxpayer terminated all interests in the corporations. A dividend requires a payment to a stockholder in his capacity as stockholder. The taxpayer was no longer a stockholder on receipt of payment, so the distribution represented payment for termination of his stock interest. Roth, 47 TCM 178, ¶ 83,651 P-H Memo. TC (1983).

Amounts received by stockholder were dividends, since no redemption plan resulting in termination of his interest existed. Taxpayer entered into a redemption contract with his wholly owned corporation. During the redemption period, taxpayer was the sole stockholder of the corporation. He later terminated his interests in it. Taxpayer argued for capital gains treatment because the redemption was part of a plan that resulted in the termination of his interest. The IRS contended that the transaction resulted in dividends to the stockholder. *Held:* For the IRS. Taxpayer failed to prove that a firm and fixed plan for total divestment of interest existed.

REDEMPTIONS: *Termination of Stockholder's Interest*

Court upholds redemption under the facts despite continued long-term involvement of redeemed stockholders. Taxpayer purchased all the stock of its two principal stockholders. Under the purchase agreement, the stockholders received a down payment and a note entitling them to deferred payments over a 20-year period. In addition, the stockholders retained the right to vote the stock sold, their membership on taxpayer's board, and their employment as officers. Their stock was turned over without endorsement to an escrow holder. The IRS challenged taxpayer's deduction of interest on the notes given to these stockholders, alleging that no redemption occurred and that the interest payments were thus actually dividends. *Held:* For taxpayer. It was clear from the facts that there existed a firm and fixed plan to eliminate the stockholders' interest in taxpayer. The retention of title and the right to vote were clearly security for taxpayer's obligation under the notes. Although the retention of title to the stock could have resulted in the stockholders' being paid dividends, any amounts so paid would have been credited against the stock's purchase price. Furthermore, although the stockholders retained their positions as directors and officers, the evidence showed that they did not actively participate in management or exert any appreciable influence on corporate affairs after the redemptions. Although the length of the payout period was unusually long and thus weighed heavily against the existence of a sale, under the circumstances, the period did not cause this redemption to fail. The stockholders' right to sell the stock upon the taxpayer's default was similarly dismissed. Lisle, 35 TCM 627, ¶ 76,140 P-H Memo. TC (1976).

Related party's reacquisition of stock within ten years of redemption not for tax-avoidance purpose. Taxpayer held 100 of the total 600 shares of stock in the corporation. His father owned the other 500 shares. Taxpayer received 20 of his shares from his father as a gift and the remainder as an inheritance. Two years after the making of the gift and immediately prior to the corporate redemption of his shares, taxpayer sold the 20 shares acquired from his father back to him at fair market value. Taxpayer had never been involved in the corporation's affairs. The IRS ruled that the father's reacquisition of the shares did not have as one of its principal purposes the avoidance of federal income tax within the meaning of Section 302(a)(2)(B). The redemption qualified as a termination of interest under Section 302(b)(3). Rev. Rul. 85-19, 1985-1 CB 94.

Right to payments under unfunded pension agreement not retention of prohibited interest under Section 302(c)(2)(A)(i). Taxpayer and his children owned all the stock of a corporation that redeemed all of its stock held by taxpayer. Taxpayer filed the agreement provided for in Section 302(c)(2)(A)(iii) to treat the redemption as full payment in exchange for stock under Section 302(b)(3). The sole relationship between taxpayer and the corporation after the redemption was an unfunded written pension agreement under which payments were not dependent upon the corporation's future earnings, and taxpayer's claim was not subordinate to those of the corporation's general creditors. The IRS ruled that taxpayer's right to receive payments under the unfunded pension agreement did not constitute the retention of a prohibited interest under Section 302(c)(2)(A)(i). Rev. Rul. 84-135, 1984-2 CB 80.

Redemption within liquidation prevented recognition of gain. X Corporation, an operating company, held 70 percent of Y Corporation's stock, and A held the rest. Y, which held certain investments, owned 25 percent of X, the value of which constituted half of the net value of all of Y's assets. X and A felt that Y should dispose of its X stock. After a series of negotiations, X and A decided to liquidate Y and have Y distribute its assets, including the X stock, to X and A. To effect the plan of liquidation, Y paid its liabilities and distributed 70 percent of each remaining asset to X and 30 percent to A. As a result, X received X stock at a time when the fair market value of its Y stock was $16x$ and its adjusted basis in the Y stock was $10x$. Therefore, X realized a gain of $6x in the transaction. X did not recognize gain on that part of the Y stock that was exchanged for X stock of equal value because X redeemed its stock from stockholder Y, and under Section 311(a)(2), no gain or loss is recognized to a corporation on a distribution of property with respect to its stock. Because Y completely terminated its interest in X within the meaning of Section 302(b)(3) and because the other requirements of Section 311(d)(2)(A) were met, the provisions of Section 311(d)(1) and any other exceptions to Section 311(a) were not applicable. The IRS noted that Rev. Rul. 79-314, 1979-2 CB 132 held that in similar factual patterns, the nonrecognition provisions of Section 311(a) prevailed over the general recognition provisions of Section 1001. However, gain was recognized under Section 1001 on that part of the Y stock that was exchanged for property other than X stock. Rev. Rul. 80-101, 1980-1 CB 70.

Gain recognized by corporation upon transfer of appreciated property in satisfaction of a note issued in redemption of stock. Upon receipt of a corporation's promissory note in redemption of his entire stock interest, taxpayer ceased to be a stockholder and became a creditor of the corporation. A later transfer of appreciated real property by the corporation as payment due on the note would not qualify for nonrecognition treatment under Section 311(d)(2)(A) as a distribution "with respect to its stock." Gain was recognized to the corporation for the difference between the fair market value of the transferred property and its adjusted basis to the corporation. Rev. Rul. 77-256, 1977-2 CB 96.

Stock redemption did not qualify as a dividend where plan to dispose of entire interest. Corporate taxpayer, a stockholder in X Corporation, sought to have a stock redemption by X characterized as a dividend in order to claim the 85 percent dividends-received deduction of Section 243 and to increase the basis in its remaining X stock by the basis of the stock redeemed under Regulation § 1.302-2(c). Taxpayer purchased 4,000 shares of X stock for $1 million because X, a widely held and publicly traded corporation, offered to redeem shares of its common stock at the rate of $250 a share. Taxpayer planned to redeem 800 shares and then to sell the remaining 3,200 shares at a loss with a stepped-up basis to an unrelated third party. The IRS ruled that taxpayer's integrated plan to dispose of its entire interest in the stock would require the redemption to be treated as a sale under Section 302(b)(3). Rev. Rul. 77-226, 1977-2 CB 90.

Executor may file Section 302 agreement. The IRS ruled that an executor may file an agreement under Section 302(c)(2)(A)(iii) on behalf of the decedent. Rev. Rul. 77-93, 1977-1 CB 80.

Brothers' qualification as executors of father's estate not a "forbidden interest" under Section 302(c)(2)(A)(ii). Two brothers and their father owned all the outstanding stock of a corporation. The brothers' stock was redeemed in total. At a subsequent date, less than 10 years from the date of the redemption, the brothers were named executors of their father's estate. The IRS ruled that the appointment of the brothers was not a "forbidden interest" under Section 302(c)(2)(A)(ii). Rev. Rul. 72-380, 1972-2 CB 201.

Tax treatment of purchase of family stock by one son from another son. A father and son each owned 50 percent of the outstanding stock of a corporation. The corporation redeemed all of the stock of the father. The father severed his relationship with the corporation. The father's other son subsequently purchased some of the first son's stock in the corporation. The purchase by the second son, which was within ten years after the date of redemption, was not an acquisition of an interest by the father within the meaning of Section 302(c)(2)(A)(ii). Rev. Rul. 71-562, 1971-2 CB 173.

Redemption of stock owned by voting trustee not a termination of interest under Section 302(b)(3). All of the stock of a corporation was owned by taxpayer and her four children. The stock was held by a voting trust of which the taxpayer was one of the voting trustees. Taxpayer intended to remain as a voting trustee after a distribution of her stock by the trust and a subsequent redemption by the corporation. The IRS ruled that there was no termination of interest as required by Section 302(b)(3) under the facts stated because taxpayer continued as a trustee of the voting trust that held the corporation's stock. Rev. Rul. 71-426, 1971-2 CB 173.

Interest in subsidiary was terminated by liquidation and distribution of assets of the subsidiary and leaseback arrangement with the parent. A subsidiary corporation was liquidated and all of its assets distributed to the parent. The stock of the parent was held by a number of unrelated individuals. The assets of the subsidiary were then distributed to one of the stockholders in complete redemption of his stock interest in the parent. Thereafter, a leaseback arrangement was entered into between the former stockholder and the parent corporation. There was a complete termination of the former stockholder's interest under Section 302(a). Rev. Rul. 70-639, 1970-2 CB 74.

Stockholder's interest not terminated if he had right to name director. A stockholder, all of whose stock of a corporation had been redeemed, requested a ruling about the effect of an agreement with the remaining stockholders, all of whom were related to him, giving him the right to nominate a member of his law firm as a director of the corporation to protect his interests as a creditor. The IRS ruled that in the event of such an agreement, the stockholder's interest in the corporation would not be considered as terminated, and the redemption would be treated as a distribution taxable as a dividend. The stockholder could, however, designate a representative to attend the board meetings solely to determine whether the terms of the stock redemption agreement were complied with and still qualify under the provisions permitting the redemption to be treated as in full payment for the stock. Rev. Rul. 59-119, 1959-1 CB 68.

REINCORPORATIONS

(*See* Liquidations—Reincorporations; Reorganizations)

RELATED TAXPAYERS

(*See also* Affiliated Corporations; Allocation Among Related Taxpayers; Compensation for Personal Services; Dividends and Distributions—Payments to Stockholders' Beneficiaries; Transfers to Controlled Corporations)

In General	493
Expenses	495
Losses	497
Sales—In General	497
Sales—Depreciable Property	500

In General

Splitting sister corporations between co-owners held taxable stock exchanges. The Tax Court held that there were taxable exchanges of stock on the transfer by three stockholders of X, a realty corporation, of all of their shares to Y, an automobile dealership they controlled where this was followed by a transfer of $43,000 from Y to X and a transfer by Y of the X shares to one of the stockholders in exchange for his one-third interest in Y. *Held:* Affirmed. On a related point, the Tax Court was reversed by the Fifth Circuit, which held that the $43,000 transfer was a dividend to the two remaining stockholders of Y. Kuper, 533 F2d 152, 76-1 USTC ¶ 9467, 38 AFTR2d 76-5162 (5th Cir. 1976).

Attempt to preserve deduction and achieve faster write-off failed in newly purchased property through inactive subsidiary. Taxpayer was a charter corporation in the coal mine business. It leased coal lands under a long-term lease from an unrelated party. One of taxpayer's subsidiaries held title to some reserve coal lands. The subsidiary never had any working capital, liquid assets, or employees. When taxpayer decided to buy the lands it leased, however, taxpayer transferred

Related Taxpayers: *In General*

$741,000 to the subsidiary to enable it to make the purchase; taxpayer did not make the purchase because then its leasehold and fee would have merged. At the time of purchase, taxpayer agreed to pay $744,000 in royalties as the coal was extracted. As a result, taxpayer claimed a royalty deduction, and the subsidiary used cost depletion to offset the royalty income. The Tax Court offset the plan and treated the transaction as if taxpayer had bought the property directly. Relying on Court Holding Co., 324 US 331 (1944), the court concluded that the fact that taxpayer had used a subsidiary to effect the transaction did not control. The court emphasized the fact that having the subsidiary take title served no business purpose. It also noted that it was unlikely that taxpayer would have advanced $741,000 and would have agreed to pay an additional $744,000 in royalties to an unrelated party. *Held:* Affirmed per curiam. The findings of fact and inferences drawn from the findings by the Tax Court were not clearly erroneous. Valley Camp Coal Co., 405 F2d 1208, 69-1 USTC ¶ 9172 (6th Cir. 1969).

Insurance business and bank separate tax entities. Taxpayer, a bank, claimed that an insurance business with which it was connected was a separate tax entity. The IRS contended that the insurance business was part of the bank's operations. The insurance business was run as a partnership, filed partnership tax returns, had a separate bank account, and conducted its correspondence on insurance company stationery. In addition, there was a valid business entity. The IRS argued that there was no written partnership agreement, that the bank and the insurance company had common personnel and occupied common premises, that the bank paid the rent and salaries of personnel who devoted part of their services to the insurance business, and that the distribution of profits from the insurance business to stockholders of the bank was made in proportion to their stockholdings. The court found that the insurance business was a separate tax entity. *Held:* Affirmed. First Sec. Bank, 334 F2d 120, 64-2 USTC ¶ 9544, 13 AFTR2d 1685 (9th Cir. 1964).

Bank and related insurance partnership separate entities. Several stockholders of taxpayer, a bank, were interested in entering the insurance business. Since state law prevented a bank from engaging in the insurance business, taxpayer's stockholders (except one) formed a partnership to engage in the insurance business. The insurance partnership conducted its business on taxpayer's premises and paid no rent; taxpayer paid for the partnership's telephone, advertising, office supplies, and postage. The IRS contended that taxpayer was taxable on the income derived by the partnership from the insurance business, since taxpayer and the partnership were operated as one for all but tax purposes. *Held:* For taxpayer. The Tax Court held that the partnership was a separate entity and that its income could not be imputed to taxpayer. Although there was a close relationship between the partnership and taxpayer, the stockholders in good faith and for a business purpose intended two separate entities, and the two were found to be separate tax entities. Campbell County State Bank, 37 TC 430 (1962), acq. 1966-2 CB 4.

Dividend by subsidiary before sale of its stock by parent not part of purchase price. The stock of taxpayer's wholly owned subsidiary was sold to a corporation that, for its own tax reasons, wanted the subsidiary to pay taxpayer a dividend before the sale closed. The offer to buy permitted, but did not require, the dividend. The purchase price was, in effect, increased to the extent that the dividend was less than $180,000, but the increase was limited to $64,000. The IRS argued that the payment was a dividend and not part of the purchase price. *Held:* For the IRS. The buyer would not purchase the subsidiary's accumulated surplus and would not pay more than a stated figure. If taxpayer wanted the extra money, it had no choice but to have its subsidiary pay the dividend. Steel Improvement & Forge Co., 36 TC 265 (1961).

Receipts from controlled corporation were profit on construction contract. Taxpayer, a building contractor, orally agreed with his corporation to construct an apartment house project. He received more than the contract price and claimed that the excess was not profit on the contract but a partial return of his investment in the corporation. The IRS determined that the entire amount was profit. *Held:* For the IRS. The court included the full amount as profit. Taxpayer was in control of the corporation and the funds. Riley, 35 TC 848 (1961).

Children taxed separately on profits from operations of a cattle business that was related to the business of their father's controlled corporation. Taxpayer was engaged in the cattle raising business through a controlled corporation. His four children, three of whom were minors, borrowed money from a bank to purchase cattle. Taxpayer acted as guarantor. In line with their business operations, the children paid taxpayer's controlled corporation for feeding costs and services rendered. Profit from the sale of the cattle was reported in the children's returns. The IRS contended that the entire income from the cattle should be taxed to the corporation and to taxpayer as a constructive dividend. *Held:* For taxpayer. The children contributed the capital to purchase the cattle and earned the income from the sale of these cattle. The mere fact that taxpayer managed their income-producing property either as an agent of the corporation or as a father who wanted to encourage his children to become farmers and cattle raisers was not sufficient to visit the tax consequences of the transactions upon him. The court also held that the income from a joint potato transaction, which one of taxpayer's sons engaged in in conjunction with the corporation, was taxable to the son rather than to the father; that an amount paid for a weather forecasting service by the corporation for the primary purpose of evaluating its long-range feeder cattle market was a proper corporate deduction even though taxpayer may have used the weather reports in connection with his private investments; and that the value of cattle given by the corporation to employees as bonuses was a proper expense. Jones Livestock Feeding Co., 26 TCM 306, ¶ 67,057 P-H Memo. TC (1967).

Stock transferred to family corporation must be treated on a share-by-share basis. To satisfy debt, taxpayer transferred stock to a family corporation in which he was the majority stockholder. There was a gain on some shares and a loss on others. The IRS ruled that taxpayer could not net his gains and losses. Since Section 267 specifically denies a loss deduction for transactions between a majority stockholder and a corporation, taxpayer could not claim any loss, but was taxable on any gain. Rev. Rul. 76-377, 1976-2 CB 89.

Sale of assets between brother-sister corporations followed by liquidation; distribution of one corporation gives rise to dividend distribution. A brother corporation sold its operating assets to its sister corporation at fair market value. The corporation retained current assets which, after paying off remaining liabilities, were distributed in liquidation to the sole common stockholder of the two corporations. The IRS ruled that the transfer of the assets between the two corporations would be treated as a reorganization under Section 368(a)(1)(D). The sole stockholder would be treated as having received the sister stock in exchange for his stock in the brother plus the liquidating distribution. The gain recognized by the sole stockholder would be recognized under Section 356(a)(1) to the extent of the cash received and treated as a dividend under Section 356(a)(2). Rev. Rul. 70-240, 1970-1 CB 81.

Expenses

Interest paid to exempt parent corporation on unsecured advances not deductible. Taxpayer was an insurance agent and a holding company that owned all of the stock of a life insurance company, over 75 percent of the stock of a casualty company, and 50 percent of a prospecting and resources development corporation. Taxpayer, in turn, was wholly owned by an exempt farm organization and deducted interest on advances from the parent that gave rise to a loss. The interest was paid at 6 percent on unsecured promissory notes that contained no provision for acceleration of principal in event of default. In addition, of the $3.5 million advanced by the parent, $1 million was cancelled. The casualty company owned by taxpayer was operating at a loss, and the life insurance company was limited in the amount of dividends it could pay. Also, advances to the development corporation were exhausted. *Held*: For the IRS. The claimed interest payments were not deductible. The nature of the instrument, the use of the proceeds to finance undercapitalized subsidiaries, the cancellation of some notes, and the small likelihood of payment of the remainder indicated that an unrelated lender dealing at arm's length would not have made these loans. National Farmers Union Serv. Corp., 400 F2d 483, 68-2 USTC ¶ 9653 (10th Cir. 1968).

Commissions to related sales organizations found excessive. Taxpayer, a manufacturing corporation, and a sales company were wholly owned subsidiaries of a parent holding company. The sales company had no office separate and apart from taxpayer and no employees other than salesmen. It employed no clerks, and all accounting records kept for it or in its name were kept by taxpayer's bookkeeping department. Its office costs were also borne entirely by taxpayer. The IRS disallowed a deduction for the commissions. The Tax Court determined that, of the $120,000 commissions paid by taxpayer to the sales corporation, $20,408.49 (an amount equal to sales corporation's net income for the year) was disallowed as a deduction to taxpayer as unreasonable and excessive for the services actually rendered. *Held*: Affirmed. Sterno, Inc., 286 F2d 548, 61-1 USTC ¶ 9250 (2d Cir. 1961).

Entire salary paid to officer who was sole owner of corporation disallowed. Taxpayer, a tenant farmer, incorporated his operations. He was the sole stockholder. He entered into a contract with the corporation whereby he was to receive a percentage of the income on a graduated scale. He had but one attorney, who represented both himself and the corporation. No resolution or action of the board in paying him this salary was made except by himself, his lawyer, and an insurance man. He testified that the incorporation was solely for tax purposes. No other facts were given in the published order and decree. The court charged the jury to render a verdict in favor of the IRS. *Held*: For the IRS. The IRS was correct in disallowing the salary deduction. Since no man can represent both sides in the same transaction, any contract so made is void because no one person can trade with himself. There must be two parties to negotiate a transaction. Inasmuch as nobody determined the amount of taxpayer's salary except himself, there was no legal fixing or paying of his salary. Willie Teeter Farming, Inc., 66-2 USTC ¶ 9768 (ND Tex. 1966).

Taxpayer could not deduct bonuses to family members not paid within two-and-a-half months after close of taxable year. Taxpayer owned, as a sole proprietorship, a saw mill and lumber business, which were managed by his two sons. He had an oral agreement with his two sons whereby each of them was to receive 25 percent of the net profits of the business. Prior to the latter part of February 1956, the books of the company revealed no entry of the bonus or any bonus credited to the sons' accounts. An entry on the work sheets of the company's accountant in the latter part of February 1956 only tentatively established the bonuses, and they were not finally determined until their entry in the books of the company in April, after the inventory of logs had been ascertained and the valuation checked. The IRS disallowed a deduction for the bonuses paid to taxpayer's sons. *Held*: For the IRS. The court held, in accordance with Section 267, that the bonuses of the two sons were not deductible, since they were not paid within 2.5 months after the close of the calendar year of the taxpayer. Bennett, 185 F. Supp. 577, 60-2 USTC ¶ 9618 (ED Wash. 1960).

Error in corporation's minutes resulted in lost deduction. Despite the fact that the controlling stockholders of taxpayer corporation were aware of the statutory requirement that accrued commissions to them had to be paid within 2.5 months after the close of the year under Section 267, the resolution of the board of directors erroneously recorded that payment be made "90 days from year ending." The actual payments were not made within the prescribed 2.5-month period. The IRS claimed that the deduction by the corporation was lost. *Held*: For the IRS. Although taxpayers attempted to avoid the rule of Section 267 by claiming constructive receipt, the court found that the constructive receipt doctrine was "sparingly applied" and that the due date expressed in the corporate records, standing uncorrected, was a substantial restriction on the receipt of the commissions. Young Door Co., 40 TC 890 (1963).

Losses

Loss on sale of future interest in real estate disallowed where transaction was not at arm's length. Taxpayer corporation sold a future interest in real property to another corporation. Both corporations had the same beneficial owners. The sale agreement provided that both the selling and purchasing corporations could not dispose of their respective interests in the premises prior to 1990 without first consulting each other. Taxpayer claimed a loss on the sale, which the IRS disallowed. *Held*: For the IRS. There was no bona fide sale since no business purpose of either the purchaser or taxpayer was served by the transaction. In reaching its conclusion, the court also emphasized that (1) there was no clear evidence that the objective contemplated by the agreement to consult before disposing of any interests was not for reacquisition of the interest conveyed, (2) there was no evidence that taxpayer received a fair value for the conveyance, and (3) there was no evidence of the adjusted basis for the interest conveyed at the time of sale. White-Delafield-Morris Corp., 22 TCM 1700, ¶ 63,325 P-H Memo. TC (1963).

Sales—In General

Sales between related companies were bona fide and should have been recognized. Taxpayer purchased equipment that it leased and later sold to a related company. At the time of sale, the equipment was fully depreciated. The IRS reduced depreciation deductions with a consequent increase in the basis of the equipment sold. Said increases served to change the profit reported on the sale to a loss that was not recognized by the IRS due to the affiliation between taxpayer and vendee. The Tax Court made no findings on the bona fide nature of the sale, but upheld the IRS' depreciation adjustments. Taxpayer contended that the Tax Court was in error in not allowing a deduction for the aforesaid losses. *Held*: Reversed and remanded. There was sufficient evidence to permit a finding on the bona fida nature of the transaction. Such evidence included the allowance of rent paid by the affiliated corporation to the taxpayer in the year in issue, as well as evidence of prior sales of vehicles and substantial differences in stock ownership. The Tax Court was required to resolve all material issues properly raised before it and to make appropriate fact findings. It failed to do so on these issues. Transport Mfg. & Equip. Co., 374 F2d 173, 67-1 USTC ¶ 9293, 19 AFTR2d 889 (8th Cir. 1967).

Corporate gain on the sale of a motion picture to its sole stockholder constituted ordinary income under Section 1239. Taxpayer, a leading motion picture studio, wanted to purchase the motion picture rights to Tennessee Williams' play, *A Streetcar Named Desire*. In order to do so, it was necessary to negotiate for the purchase of all of the assets or outstanding stock of a corporation that had acquired the literary property for use as a motion picture. The transferor's sole stockholder wanted the proceeds from the sale of his stock to be treated as a long-term capital gain. He was notified that a favorable ruling would be issued on the condition that, prior to the sale of his stock, the transferor corporation sell all the rights to *Streetcar*. He thereupon personally purchased the film from his corporation, with the latter paying a capital gains tax on the proceeds, sold all of his stock to taxpayer, and, shortly thereafter, sold all his rights in the film to taxpayer. The IRS contended that taxpayer, the transferee of all of the assets of the transferor corporation, was liable for a tax deficiency against that corporation based on the difference between ordinary income and capital gain on the sale of the film to the stockholder. The IRS relied on Section 1239, which treats as ordinary income the gain on sale of depreciable property by a corporation to an 80 percent or more stockholder. The Tax Court sustained this position. *Held:* Affirmed. The stockholder had purchased the film subject to an agreement under which he could not realize income during the pendency of the agreement. Taxpayer claimed, therefore, that he was not entitled to a depreciation allowance because the film was not property held for the production of income. The fault with this argument was that the aforementioned agreement did not apply to the reissue of the picture, the licensing, or distribution in cities where it had already been shown. There was no doubt that the film was purchased by the stockholder for the ultimate realization or production of income; the failure actually to realize income or take deductions for depreciation was not critical. Twentieth Century-Fox Film Corp., 372 F2d 281, 67-1 USTC ¶ 9203, 19 AFTR2d 602 (2d Cir. 1967).

No loss allowed on transfer of manufactured products between related parties. Taxpayer, who operated a machine shop as a sole proprietor, also owned all the stock of a corporation engaged in the metal stamping business. The corporation received about 80 orders from its customers and farmed out the work to taxpayer's sole proprietorship. The machine shop did the work and billed the corporation. Of the 80 orders filled, 46 resulted in a loss to the machine shop of $11,000; the balance resulted in a gain of $5,000. The IRS applied Section 267 to disallow the $11,000 loss in full without allowing any of the $5,000 gain to be offset against such loss. *Held:* For the IRS. There was no limitation in the statute to support taxpayer's argument that Section 267 applied to sales of capital assets and not to sales made in the ordinary course of a trade or business. Estate of Johnson, 355 F2d 931, 17 AFTR2d 227 (6th Cir. 1965).

Corporation was conduit on sale of property subject to contract. Taxpayer's corporation operated at a loss for some years and owed $177,000 to a bank. After the bank requested further security, taxpayer gave the bank a mortgage on real property that his wife owned. As the prospect of further operating losses appeared imminent, the bank suggested that the corporation needed additional capital. Taxpayer and his wife decided to sell the real property and apply the proceeds to the indebtedness. They contracted to sell the property to a third party for $35,000. Two days after they had signed the contract of sale and received a deposit as earnest money, they transferred the real property to the corporation, which in turn passed title to the purchaser. The corporation reported the gain on the sale, applying its loss carry-over. Taxpayer applied $27,500 to the bank indebtedness and personally retained the balance. *Held*: For the IRS. Taxpayer was required to report the sale. After the execution of the contract, the transfer to the corporation was ineffective. The corporation was merely a conduit for title. Palmer, 354 F2d 974, 66-1 USTC ¶ 9117, 16 AFTR2d 6112 (1st Cir. 1965).

Attribution rules not applicable to sale between estate and a corporation. Decedent owned 25 percent of the stock of a family corporation. The other 75 percent was owned by three revocable trusts whose beneficiaries were decedent's three sisters. The sisters were also the sole legatees of decedent's estate. The corporation redeemed some of the decedent's shares from his estate at a price that resulted in a loss to the estate (it was lower than value at date of death). The Tax Court held that the loss was disallowed under Section 267 as occurring between related taxpayers. The Tax Court's reasoning was as follows: Following Ingalls, 132 F2d 862, property sold by an estate is considered sold by the beneficiaries. Turning to Section 267(c), since the beneficiaries were members of the same family, each was considered the owner of all of the stock of the corporation, and his 50 percent-or-more controlled corporation. *Held:* Reversed. Section 267(b)(2) disallows losses between an individual and his controlled corporation. The attribution of ownership rules determine whether the control exists, but they cannot be applied to bring the transaction within the section. Since the sale was not by an individual, the section cannot apply. Estate of Hanna, 320 F2d 54, 63-2 USTC ¶ 9616 (6th Cir. 1963).

Purported exchange of depreciable for nondepreciable property and simultaneous purchase

back of the depreciable property found to lack substance. Taxpayer, his brother, and his mother were partners in a California farming operation. Taxpayer was the only active partner. In 1959, taxpayer, at the suggestion of his tax adviser, created two wholly owned corporations and dissolved the partnership. Taxpayer then purportedly exchanged his interest in the depreciable farming assets, which were jointly owned with his brother, for the brother's interest in the nondepreciable jointly owned farming assets. Simultaneously, the brother purportedly sold the depreciable assets received in the exchange to taxpayer and his two corporations. The IRS contended that the purported exchange and simultaneous sales constituted a single, unitary transaction whereby taxpayer bought his brother's undivided interest in the jointly owned farming property consisting of both the depreciable and nondepreciable assets. *Held:* For the IRS. In substance, taxpayer bought out his brother's undivided interest in the jointly owned farming property. Thus, taxpayer could not attribute the entire purchase price to the depreciable assets. He had to allocate the total price between the depreciable and nondepreciable assets comprising his brother's undivided interest. Harris, 27 TCM 405, ¶ 68,086 P-H Memo. TC (1968).

Sale of vessel at a loss to a newly formed corporation controlled by stockholders of selling corporation was bona fide. Taxpayer, an operator of freight vessels, sought to dispose of its smaller, unprofitable vessels. It received an offer for one such vessel from a Canadian corporation, and in 1960 agreed to sell it for $40,000. The sale would have resulted in a substantial loss that taxpayer sought as a carry-back to 1957. Under the regulations of the Federal Maritime Commission, prior approval of the Secretary of Commerce is required for any vessel sold to a foreign purchaser, but is not required for a vessel sold to a domestic purchaser. When taxpayer learned that approval of the sale could not be assured in 1960, it rescinded the sale with the Canadian corporation and sold it instead in 1960 for $37,000 to a new domestic corporation, Tower. Tower had been incorporated by taxpayer's officers in their individual capacities.

Tower then applied for permission to sell the vessel to the Canadian corporation for $40,000. On its 1960 return, taxpayer claimed the loss on sale of the vessel. The IRS denied the loss, contending that the sale to Tower was not bona fide since Tower was merely acting as agent for taxpayer in negotiating the later sale to the Canadian corporation. *Held:* For taxpayer. Tower was a separate corporation having substance; its separate corporate entity could not be ignored. It executed a valid contract with taxpayer to purchase a registered vessel, took delivery, possession, and control thereof, and entered into a later valid contract of sale of the vessel with the Canadian corporation. Tomlinson Fleet Corp., 25 TCM 59, ¶ 66,013 P-H Memo. TC (1966).

Sale between two corporations not taxable to controlling partnership. Taxpayer and his brothers were members of a partnership that exported tallow to Japan. It was suggested that the partnership engage in ship chartering ventures to reduce freight costs. For this purpose, Veronica, a Panamanian corporation, was formed, and two ships were chartered. It was then decided that if the ships could bring copra from the Philippines back to the United States, profits would increase enough to permit Veronica to buy ships rather than charter them. To carry out this plan, Veronica built a copra processing plant in the Philippines using funds borrowed from taxpayer's partnership. The partnership then formed a Philippine corporation, which purchased the plant at a large profit to Veronica. The IRS determined that the gain on the sale of the copra plant should be reported by the partnership, since in substance, the partnership used Veronica as a mere conduit for executing the sale. *Held:* For taxpayers. Taxpayers were not taxed on the sale. Veronica was at all times a bona fide entity, separate and apart from the partnership, and acted as a principal rather than as a nominee in the transaction. Jerome, 24 TCM 1763, ¶ 65,316 P-H Memo. TC (1965).

Operating loss on sales to related corporation disallowed under Section 267. Taxpayers, a father and three sons, acquired the timber rights in a certain tract of land. They sold rough timber cut from this tract to a related corporation engaged in the business of purchasing, processing, and finishing rough lumber. Taxpayers claimed a loss on the sale that the IRS disallowed. *Held.* For the IRS. Since taxpayers owned more than 90 percent of the corporate stock, the court disallowed, under Section 267, a loss allocable to the sales to the corporation. It found no merit in taxpayer's argument that the loss involved was not within the contemplation of Section 267 because it was in the nature of an operating loss rather than a loss in a capital transaction. Ferguson, 21 TCM 1587, ¶ 62,298 P-H Memo. TC (1962).

Sales—Depreciable Property

Sale of property by one commonly controlled corporation to the other not imputed to common individual stockholders for purposes of triggering Section 1239. Taxpayer owned more than 80 percent of the stock of two corporations, one of which was a subchapter S corporation. This subchapter S corporation reported a capital gain on a sale of depreciated equipment to the other commonly controlled corporation. The IRS asserted that because of taxpayer's stock interest in both corporations, the sale was, for purposes of Section 1239, indirectly a sale between the taxpayer and the purchasing corporation and thus, under Section 1239, ordinary income was recognized on the sale. *Held:* For taxpayer. Section 1239 does not apply to sales between two corporations controlled by the same individual. The court rejected the IRS' argument that such a sale was an indirect sale involving the common stockholder. Roy Miller, 510 F2d 230, 75-1 USTC ¶ 9236, 35 AFTR2d 75-714 (9th Cir. 1975).

Option to buy minority stockholder's stock not considered actual ownership for Section 1239 purposes. In a newly formed corporation, taxpayer took back 79 percent of the stock, and Kelly, an unrelated person, took back the other 21 percent. Kelly borrowed the necessary funds from taxpayer, giving taxpayer his promissory note secured by a pledge of the stock and an option agreement.

Taxpayer then sold to the corporation depreciable property and reported a capital gain on the transaction. The Tax Court, with one dissent, held that the necessary 80 percent control required under Section 1239 did not exist by virtue of the option agreement. Section 1239 speaks in terms of actual ownership and not ownership "in substance" or "tantamount ownership." *Held:* Remanded. The case was remanded to the Tax Court for a determination of whether taxpayer's stock constituted more than 80 percent in value of the outstanding stock. Trotz, 361 F2d 927, 66-1 USTC ¶ 9466, 17 AFTR2d 1262 (10th Cir. 1966).

Oral agreement did not negate 80 percent control test under Section 1239. Taxpayers, husband and wife, owned 100 percent of the stock of a corporation. Before March 1967, an oral agreement was made to sell one third of the corporate stock to an employee. On June 27, 1967, taxpayers sold depreciable property to the corporation, and on September 29, 1967, the transfer of stock to the employee was finally consummated. The IRS contended that gain on the real estate sale was taxable as ordinary income pursuant to Section 1239. Taxpayers contended that Section 1239 was inapplicable because the pre-March 1967 oral agreement with the employee bought the number of shares under the requisite 80 percent. *Held:* For the IRS. At the time of the realty sale, the employee did not beneficially own one third of the corporate stock. The transfer date was not fixed, the entitlement to dividends was not specified, and the employee had no right to exercise voting rights in the stock. Although there was an oral agreement, the transaction was still in the development stage. Brown, 377 F. Supp. 370, 74-1 USTC ¶ 9314 (WDNC 1974).

Court approves stepped-up (lost) basis on sale of depreciable assets between controlled corporations where substantive nontax business reasons for the sales. Woolley formed Rental Tool Co. with cash used by the corporation to buy depreciable equipment from Woolley. Woolley then formed Tool, Inc., Equipment Co., and Fishing Tool Co. with cash and depreciable assets that he owned. The evidence indicated that he had strong, nontax business purposes for forming each of these corporations. Because the assets transferred to Tool, Inc. had a high fair market value but a low book value, Woolley caused Tool, Inc. to sell these assets to Equipment Co. and Fishing Tool in exchange for a secured installment note providing a fair rate of interest and fixed payment and maturity dates. The IRS challenged the subsidiaries' use of a stepped-up basis from the asset sales to determine their depreciation deductions on the assets, alleging that the notes were not debt for tax purposes and thus the sales were, in fact, capital contributions. *Held:* For taxpayer. The evidence showed that the sales were made to enhance the corporations' financial statements so as to be more appealing to lenders and investors. After these sales, Woolley transferred all of the stock in Rental Tool Co., Equipment Co., and Fishing Tool Co. to Tool, Inc., which thus became a holding company that provided only management and administrative services for its subsidiaries. Woolley Equip. Co., 268 F. Supp. 358, 67-1 USTC ¶ 9281, 19 AFTR2d 1116 (ED Tex. 1966).

Gain on sale to controlled corporation was ordinary income. In exchange for a mortgage and the cancellation of an indebtedness, taxpayers transferred a theatre property they owned to a corporation in which they held 90 percent of the stock. The IRS contended that under Section 1239, the gain on the transfer of the depreciable property was ordinary income. *Held:* For the IRS. Although taxpayers and the corporation were willing to reduce the price, there was no actual recision. The gain could not be reduced, since the proceeds were received under a claim of right. Ainsworth, 60-2 USTC ¶ 9595 (ED Wis. 1960).

The appropriate time to measure value for the "80 percent in value" test under Section 1239 was before the sale to which Section 1239 would otherwise apply. For a 7.5 percent royalty, taxpayer granted *M* Corporation the exclusive right to "make, use, sell, and rent throughout the world" devices utilizing certain patents owned by taxpayer. Taxpayer held a 79.64 percent stock interest in *M*, whose sole business was manufacturing devices using taxpayer's patents. Taxpayer treated the royalty payments as long-term capital gain. The IRS asserted that these payments should, by reason of Section 1239, be treated as ordinary income. The issue before the court was whether taxpayer owned more than 80 percent in value of the outstanding stock in *M*. *Held:* For taxpayer. The facts indicated that the value of taxpayer's interest in *M* before the exclusive license was equal to his stockholding percentage (i.e., 79.64 percent). However, once he executed the exclusive license, *M* developed a going concern value that enhanced its value and the value of a controlling interest in *M* and thus gave taxpayer greater than an 80 percent in value interest. Nevertheless, the appropriate time to measure the value of an interest for purposes of Section 1239 is before the transfer. Because taxpayer's interest at that time was not more than 80 percent, Section 1239 does not apply. Robishaw, 616 F2d 507, 80-1 USTC ¶ 9232, 45 AFTR2d 80-817 (Ct. Cl. 1980).

Gain on sale of leasehold to family corporation was ordinary income under Section 1239. In 1955, taxpayers became lessees of a farm under a 10-year lease that called for an annual rent of $7,000. In 1956, they sold the lease to Trailback Plantation, Inc., a family-controlled corporation, for $30,000. They reported this amount as a long-term capital gain on their joint return. Trailback claimed a deduction for lease amortization on its return. The IRS determined that the gain on the sale was ordinary income under Section 1239. Taxpayers conceded that all of the requisite provisions of Section 1239 were present except those stipulated in Subsection 1239(b), which requires the property in the hands of the transferee to be of a character subject to the allowance for depreciation under Section 167. Since a leasehold is property subject to an allowance for amortization under Section 162, taxpayers argued that Section 1239 was not applicable. *Held:* For the IRS. The court held that taxpayers' argument had merit only on the surface. It construed the intention of Congress to cover situations such as this, citing Fackler, 45 BTA 708 (1941), which held a leasehold to be of a character subject to the allowance for depreciation. Baker, 38 TC 9 (1962).

Sale of patent to family corporation resulted in ordinary income. In 1952, taxpayer sold his patent on a ballast spreader to his family corporation, which agreed to pay 5 percent of the retail price received from sales. In 1956, taxpayer received $62,500 from the corporation and reported it as gain realized on the sale of a capital asset held for more than six months. The IRS contended that the sale resulted in ordinary income. *Held:* For the IRS. The court held that the gain was ordinary income under Section 1239, which provides for ordinary income on the sale of depreciable property to a controlled corporation, since a patent in the hands of the corporation is considered property subject to an allowance for depreciation within the meaning of that section. Kershaw, 34 TC 453 (1960).

Tax consequences of a sale of partnership interests to a controlled corporation by a husband and wife discussed. A husband and wife owned all the interests in a partnership whose sole assets were land and an apartment building. The individuals sold their partnership interests to a controlled corporation in which they owned all the outstanding stock. The IRS ruled that the provisions of Section 1239 would apply in the instant case. Accordingly, any gain realized on the sale of the partnership interests that was attributable to the depreciable property would be taxable as ordinary income as required by Section 1239. Rev. Rul. 72-172, 1972-1 CB 265.

The "more than 80 percent in value" test of Section 1239 not determined solely by the outstanding shares. An individual owning 80 percent of the outstanding stock of a corporation sold property to it at a gain. The remaining shares were issued subject to restrictions. The restrictions as a matter of law decreased the value of the stock. The "more than 80 percent in value" test of Section 1239 is not based solely on the number of shares outstanding. Rev. Rul. 69-339, 1969-1 CB 203.

RENTS

(*See also* Business Expenses; Dividends and Distributions)

In General 502
Deductibility Of 504

In General

Section 482 properly invoked to reallocate rental income between controlled corporation and partnership. Taxpayer, a corporation controlled by four families, organized a partnership to lease and operate its assets. The lease called for an annual rent of $48,000 and resulted in the corporation's incurring net operating losses, which were carried back to prior years as claims for refunds. The IRS disallowed the claims, invoking Section 482, and contended that a reasonable rent would be $78,000 per annum. The Tax Court sustained the IRS. *Held:* Affirmed. The two elements required to invoke Section 482, common control and the necessity to reflect proper income, were present. Although the partnership was not a sham because it reallocated income as between family members, the function of Section 482 would have been frustrated if distortion of income had been permitted. Taxpayer's argument that the lease terms were reasonable was not valid, since the facts indicated that the rent was insufficient to cover fixed expenses. The IRS' determination was based on actual rents in the area, and taxpayer did not sustain its burden of proving the calculation erroneous. South Tex. Rice Warehouse Co., 366 F2d 890, 66-2 USTC ¶ 9619, 18 AFTR2d 5517 (5th Cir. 1966), cert. denied, 386 US 1016 (1967).

Losses on rents to taxpayer's corporations not deductible. Taxpayer, an officer and the controlling stockholder of three plumbing supply corporations, leased personally owned buildings to the corporations. The rent was fixed at an amount equal to the carrying charges. Taxpayer reported a net loss from the rents after deducting depreciation. The IRS disallowed the depreciation. The Tax Court held that taxpayer was not entitled to depreciation. *Held:* Affirmed. Taxpayer entered into

RENTS: *In General*

the transaction knowing that he would suffer losses. Since the business of each lessee was not taxpayer's business, taxpayer did not incur these losses in connection with a trade or business. Yanow, 358 F2d 743, 66-1 USTC ¶ 9365, 17 AFTR2d 806 (3d Cir. 1966).

Full net profits paid as rent to related lessees were unreasonable; excess was dividend. Several individuals formed a partnership to acquire a racetrack lease. After the acquisition, they formed taxpayer corporation and subleased the track to the corporation at 100 percent of the net profits, a much higher rent. The partners urged that the rent provided by the sublease was reasonable because the partnership was subject to the basic lease obligations, made substantial capital improvements, furnished all of the financial backing for the corporation, and operated and maintained the track. As a further argument to support a payout of all of the corporate profit, they argued that the corporation stood merely as agent for the partnership. *Held:* For the IRS. The court rejected both arguments. On the basis of the close relationship between the corporate stockholders and the partnership, and considering lease arrangements of other tracks, it found the rent excessive and unreasonable. It also found that the corporation was the true operator of the track and was not a mere agent in carrying on its operations. The portion of the rent found to be excessive and not deductible as rent was considered as a dividend distribution to the partner-stockholders; as such they were taxable as ordinary income only to the extent of available earnings and profits. In determining earnings and profits available for dividends, the court held that interest on contested deficiencies determined against the corporation were properly accruable at the end of each year. It also ruled that the contract entered into between the partnership and the corporation, although couched in terms generally applicable to a sale, was in fact a sublease and not an assignment of the partners' entire interest in the lease. The income therefrom was properly taxable as rental income. Fairmount Park Raceway, Inc., 327 F2d 780, 64-1 USTC ¶ 9183 (1964).

Prepaid rent was income to controlled sublessee where stockholders were identical. A New York corporation made an agreement to lease property. It incorporated taxpayer to execute the lease. The lease was for ten years with a prepayment of the last twenty months of the term. Immediately after execution of the lease, taxpayer subleased to its affiliate in New York for the same time and terms. The New York corporation gave taxpayer its check for the initial prepayment that was immediately endorsed to the primary lessor. Taxpayer kept no books or records other than a checkbook. Taxpayer contended that no papers existed that indicated a loan from the sublessee to the lessee, and testimony of corporate officers indicated that no repayment was expected. The IRS found the payment to be a prepayment of rent includible in taxpayer's gross income. *Held:* For the IRS. The payment was received with the understanding that it was to be used for its immediately beneficial interest. Further, since the lease was coupled with an option to purchase and an application of the "rent" on the purchase price, taxpayer could not deduct the payment over to the lessor as a current operating expense. Kohler-Campbell Corp., 298 F2d 911, 62-1 USTC ¶ 9237, 9 AFTR2d 587 (4th Cir. 1962).

Additional rental payments to related entities justified. Taxpayer corporation paid rent to a corporation and a trust. Both rent recipients had been created by the president of taxpayer corporation for the benefit of his four children. Subsequent addenda were made in the leases to the above two real estate entities. The IRS disallowed the additional rental payments made under the addenda on the theory that such payments were not "required" to be made as a condition to the continued use of the respective properties. *Held:* For taxpayer. The facts indicated that there were valid business reasons for the additional payments. These included the right to use additional property. The payments were therefore deemed reasonable. Riggs Tractor Co., 73-2 USTC ¶ 9704 (ED Ark. 1973).

Rental of home owned by his corporation was additional compensation to president stock-

Rents: *Deductibility Of*

holder. A residence owned by taxpayer corporation was leased to its president and a principal stockholder for $150 a month. The IRS contended that the fair rental value was $300 a month, and that the difference was dividend income to taxpayer. *Held:* For taxpayer, in part. The district court held that the excess of a fair rent over the rent actually paid was additional compensation to the president, not a dividend. The court gave no reasoning for this conclusion. R.A. Heintz Constr. Co., 65-2 USTC ¶ 9455, 16 AFTR2d 5001 (D. Ore. 1965).

Loss on rental of residence to stockholder denied. Taxpayer maintained a residence that it rented to its president, a 50 percent stockholder. It claimed a loss representing the difference between the rental income from the officer and the expenses of maintaining the residence. *Held:* For the IRS. The loss was denied. Taxpayer offered no evidence on this issue, and failed to meet its burden of proof. Wilson Agency, Inc., 24 TCM 579, ¶ 65,109 P-H Memo. TC (1965).

Fixed amounts received as rents and paid for the right to use property qualify under Section 543(a)(2). Taxpayer entered into an agreement to receive amounts designated as rents, computed on the basis of one dollar per acre and payable semiannually for the right to use natural gas and oil property. The gross payment was subject to diminution of a stated number of acres upon the bringing in of either a producing or nonproducing oil or gas well. Such amounts qualify as rents under Section 543(a)(2), as they are fixed sums payable in advance at specified dates for the use of land. Rev. Rul. 70-153, 1970-1 CB 139.

Income from operation of farms not rent. Rents are included in personal holding company income unless they constitute 50 percent or more of corporate gross income. A corporation that owned farms contracted with farmers to work the property. They paid a stated percentage of crops as compensation. The corporation kept detailed records of the operations and exercised active management and supervision through an agent. *Held:* For taxpayer. The Tax Court held that the income derived from the farm operations was not rent; it was income from farm operations. Nonacquiescence published in CB 1956-2 was withdrawn. Webster Corp., 25 TC 55 (1955), acq. 1956-2 CB 11.

Deductibility Of

Company that negotiated arm's-length rent from unrelated parties could deduct same amount for rent from stockholders. Taxpayer, a company that conducted horse-drawn-carriage tours, rented most of the carriages and licenses from its stockholders and a few from nonstockholders. Taxpayer paid each of its stockholders about $1,500 a year. Nonstockholders received $1,600. The Tax Court upheld the IRS' disallowance of everything over $600 paid to stockholders on the ground the rent was not set at arm's length. *Held:* Reversed. The payments to stockholders were fully deductible. The proper standard was not whether taxpayer negotiated at arm's length with its stockholders but whether the payment exceeded what taxpayer would have been required to pay had it dealt at arm's length with a stranger. Mackinac Island Carriage Tours, Inc., 455 F2d 98, 72-1 USTC ¶ 9242, 29 AFTR2d 72-554 (6th Cir. 1972).

Constructive receipt of income by stockholder was basis for allowing related corporations contra deduction. The IRS disallowed taxpayer corporations' deduction for rent accrued as due to a controlling stockholder, since controlling stockholder did not report such rent as income until a later period. The district court held against the IRS. *Held:* Affirmed. The controlling stockholder constructively received the rental income, since he had authority to draw checks on the corporations' bank accounts once the rents became due and was therefore subject to his unqualified demand. Therefore, taxpayer corporations were not barred under Section 267(a)(2) from claiming rental deductions. Fetzer Refrigerator Co., 437 F2d 577, 71-1 USTC ¶ 9202, 27 AFTR2d 71-613 (6th Cir. 1971).

Issue of deductibility of rents paid by corporation to stockholders remanded. Certain individuals owned licenses to operate horse-

RENTS: Deductibility Of

drawn-carriage tours on a resort island. Later, the licensing authority required the tours to be operated by a corporation, which was accordingly organized (taxpayer). The individuals became taxpayer's stockholders and rented their licenses annually to taxpayer. Taxpayer also rented licenses from a few nonstockholders. For 1961 through 1963, taxpayer paid (and deducted as rent) its stockholder lessors $1,200, $1,550, $1,500, respectively, and its nonstockholders $1,600. The IRS argued that the rents were paid solely for the licenses and disallowed the claimed deductions in excess of $600 per lessor. Taxpayer argued that the rents were paid for carriages as well as licenses. The Tax Court upheld the IRS on taxpayer's failure of proof. *Held:* Remanded for additional evidence. The Tax Court holding was unclear because (1) it ignored evidence that the carriages were still in use although fully depreciated; (2) it did not decide the allowable rent for licenses owned by nonstockholders; and (3) it used one basis of computation for 1961 and 1963 and another for 1962 without explanation. Mackinac Island Carriage Tours, Inc., 419 F2d 1103, 70-1 USTC ¶ 9158 (6th Cir. 1970).

Payment under sale-leaseback arrangements not made at arm's length not deductible to the extent that they exceed the fair rental value of the leased assets. In order to avoid contractual prohibitions against the sale of stock of two corporations, sale-leaseback arrangements were made with respect to the assets of those corporations. The IRS contended, and the Tax Court found, that the sale-leaseback arrangements were not made in arm's-length negotiations. Therefore, rental payments in excess of what was found to be the fair rental value of the assets were disallowed. *Held:* Affirmed. The Tax Court's findings were not clearly erroneous. However, the Tax Court was reversed on its disallowance of multiple surtax exemptions, since the uncontradicted testimony of the owner and of the taxpayer that separate corporations were formed in separate localities for economic, not the tax reasons, should have been controlling. Southeastern Canteen Co., 410 F2d 615, 69-1 USTC ¶ 9396, 23 AFTR2d 69-1362 (6th Cir. 1969), cert. denied, 396 US 833 (1969).

Excessive rental payment to stockholder lessor not deductible. A corporation leased a building from its president and stockholder at a rent of 2 percent of annual net sales. The Tax Court found that the lease was not entered into in an arms-length transaction and disallowed rent on the property in excess of $12,000 per year; it considered the excess a dividend. *Held:* Affirmed on the basis of the findings of fact and opinion of the Tax Court. Kirk Inc., 289 F2d 935, 61-1 USTC ¶ 9451, 7 AFTR2d 1412 (6th Cir. 1961).

Excessive rental payments to related interests disallowed. Rent paid by taxpayer corporation to a principal stockholder in excess of $10,000, plus a percentage of profits, plus payments for insurance, taxes, and repairs was found on the facts to be excessive and unreasonable and therefore not deductible. *Held:* For the IRS. The rent represented at least a 15 percent return on cost of the property. Rents paid by prior unrelated tenants did not exceed $5,000. Potter Elec. Signal & Mfg. Co., 286 F2d 200, 61-1 USTC ¶ 9206, 7 AFTR2d 511 (8th Cir. 1961).

Repayment of rent disallowed by the IRS was not deductible. Taxpayers rented property to a related corporation. The IRS argued that the rent deduction to the corporation was unreasonable. Taxpayers thereupon entered into an agreement with the corporation to refund the amount of rent that the IRS ultimately determined to be unreasonable. The district court allowed the deduction in the year repayment was made. *Held:* Reversed. There was no legal or moral obligation to make the refund. It was prompted solely by tax-saving considerations. Simon, 281 F2d 520, 60-2 USTC ¶ 9631, 6 AFTR2d 5274 (6th Cir. 1960).

Absence of arm's-length dealing between corporation and stockholders defeats rental deduction. Taxpayer corporation, which was owned by members of a single family, was engaged in the business of renting steel scaffolding in Georgia and other states. In order to satisfy the corporation's need for larger storage facilities, the stockholders individually purchased unimproved property to be used

Rents: *Deductibility Of*

exclusively in the business and leased it to the corporation. By the terms of a ten-year net lease executed in 1948, the corporation was to pay a monthly rent of $200, and it was permitted to make improvements. Shortly after executing the lease, the corporation erected a building at a cost of $128,025. At the expiration of the ten-year lease term, the parties entered into a new lease whereby the corporation paid the stockholders an annual rent of $21,600. The IRS, noting that the rent was based on the value of the property improved by the addition of the building, disallowed the deduction to the extent that it was for the use of the improvements. *Held*: For the IRS. The court found that the second lease was not entered into by parties dealing at arm's length. The corporation received no economic benefit from the remaining useful life of the building because it reverted to the stockholders without compensation. In ordinary commercial leases, a tenant who constructs a building on another's land generally has renewal options to protect its position. The absence of such a safeguard was treated by the court as evidence of a lack of arm's-length dealing. Safway Steel Scaffolds Co., 76-2 USTC ¶ 9800, 39 AFTR2d 77-396 (ND Ga. 1976).

Rental payments to related stockholders held to be dividends. Taxpayer, which was wholly owned by *W*, was sold to *W*'s daughter by an installment purchase and sale. To effect the transfer, *W* transferred 200 of the 300 outstanding shares of taxpayer's stock to his daughter and exchanged the remaining 100 shares for taxpayer's real estate. *W* then executed a 10-year leaseback to taxpayer for a rent of $150 per month plus 40 percent of taxpayer's pretax profits. Later, *W* built new facilities and executed a 20-year lease whereby taxpayer paid *W* $500 a month plus 40 percent of taxpayer's pretax profit. The IRS determined that the percentage sums paid as rentals were dividends and not deductible business expenses by taxpayer. *Held:* For the IRS. Because the lease was based on net profits before taxes and the amounts obtained through the percentage provision exceeded fair rents and the lessor retained an equity interest in the corporation, the percentage amounts claimed for rent were not ordinary and necessary business expenses and hence not deductible by taxpayer. The sharing of the profits was a dividend. Sunnyside Beverages, Inc., 71-2 USTC ¶ 9752, 28 AFTR2d 71-6096 (ND Ind. 1971).

Taxpayer corporation's rental payment to related stockholder deemed reasonable. The owner of a corporation in the funeral business charged his corporation $1,000 per month for the rent of premises occupied by lessor and his family during his lifetime and, after his death, by his wife. The IRS determined a reasonable rent to be $700, accordingly, the corporation was assessed to have a tax deficiency on the difference in the amounts. The owner transferred certain assets, equipment, and fixtures to taxpayer in exchange for a promissory note and chattel mortgage. The IRS determined the notes and mortgage to be equity and not a loan and the basis of the transferred assets to be less than taxpayer claimed. *Held:* For taxpayer, in part. Because evidence was supplied showing the rent to be reasonable, the corresponding deduction by taxpayer was permitted. Because the characteristics of a note secured by a mortgage indicated a long-term investment rather than a debt, the property was a contribution to capital. The IRS' determination of lowered basis more accurately reflected the true value of the assets transferred. Parsons Funeral Home, Inc., 70-2 USTC ¶ 9699, 26 AFTR2d 70-5790 (NDNY 1970).

Percentage lease with related parties resulted in unreasonable rents. The principal stockholder of taxpayer, as guardian for his minor children, acquired a factory building that was rented to taxpayer. The building was acquired at a cost of $18,000. A lease was entered into providing for a nominal fixed rent plus a percentage rent based on taxpayer's sales. *Held:* For the IRS. The lease resulted in unreasonable rents. At the time the lease was made, it could have been anticipated that taxpayer's sales would increase. In fact, the lease resulted in rents of up to $50,000 a year. The court found that only $6,000 was reasonable rent. Tube Processing Corp., 65-1 USTC ¶ 9216 (SD Ind. 1964).

Rents to related partnership were reasonable. Because of a shortage of capital, taxpayer corporation rented heavy-duty construction equipment rather than purchasing it. The equipment was rented from a partnership composed of some, but not all, of the stockholders. Evidence of a reasonable rental rate included rates shown in a trade association manual. *Held:* For taxpayer. From this and other evidence, the court concluded that the rent charged was reasonable and allowed the deduction. Arkhola Sand & Gravel Co., 190 F. Supp. 29, 61-1 USTC ¶ 9161, 7 AFTR2d 310 (WD Ark. 1960).

Amount paid as rent found reasonable by jury. Taxpayer corporation leased its building from a related corporation. The lease provided for the payment of a percentage rent with a minimum. Taxpayer deducted $38,712.17 as a rental expense. The IRS contended that the amount in excess of $18,000 for 1955 was excessive and represented a distribution of earnings and profits. *Held:* For taxpayer. The jury found that a reasonable amount for the use and occupancy of the building during the year 1955 was the sum paid by the taxpayer. Natrona County Tribune, 60-2 USTC ¶ 9620 (D. Wyo. 1960).

Rent deduction partially disallowed in leaseback sale to charity. Taxpayers sold their stock in a dairy to a charitable foundation under the accepted bootstrap method: taxpayers owned 48 percent of the newly formed operating company, which leased the assets of the liquidated dairy from the foundation for 80 percent of net profits with the foundation in turn paying taxpayers (in payment for the stock) 90 percent of the rent received. The IRS disallowed part of the 80 percent-of-profits "rent" paid to the foundation. *Held:* For the IRS. In negotiating the sale, taxpayers did not inquire whether the 80 percent figure was reasonable; therefore, there was no arm's-length bargaining as to this aspect of the transaction. The court determined, on the basis of all the factors, that 50 percent of the profits was proper. Royal Farms Dairy Co., 40 TC 172 (1963).

Full amount of rental payments made by corporation to lessor-stockholder allowed. A corporation was unable to obtain a lease without its stockholders assuming personal liability. Stockholders possessing 70 percent of the stock agreed to lease the property and then sublet it to the corporation at a higher price than what they paid under the lease. The differential was to be compensation for the personal assumption of liabilities. The IRS claimed that the payments were not negotiated at arm's length; therefore, the payments were not completely deductible. *Held:* For taxpayer. While transactions between related parties must be scrutinized, rents paid to the stockholders were reasonable. Roman Sys., Ltd., 42 TCM 7, ¶ 81,273 P-H Memo. TC (1981).

Corporation allowed to deduct rent paid to stockholder consisting of base amount and percentage of gross sale. Taxpayer corporation was in the business of distributing groceries and related nonfood items to institutional customers such as schools, hospitals, and restaurants. Taxpayer's stockholders purchased land on which a facility for distributing such products could be constituted. The stockholders agreed, as a condition of the loan used to purchase the land and begin improvements thereon, that such premises would be leased to taxpayer for at least 20 years at a rent of $60,000 per year. The lease was enacted with payment of a base rent and 1 percent of taxpayer's gross sales above $4 million. The rental base was increased by the addition of a cold storage space. Other increases to the base rent were made through improvements to the building. In 1972, the gross sales exceeded $4 million, although no percentage was paid to the stockholders as rent. Taxpayer deducted the amounts paid as rent in 1974, 1975, and 1976. The IRS disallowed portions of the deductions in that the amounts paid were unreasonable. *Held:* For taxpayer. Section 162 permits a deduction for ordinary and necessary business expenses incurred during a year for carrying on a trade

Rents: *Deductibility Of*

or business. Such expenses include rents required to be paid for the continued use of property in the trade or business to which taxpayer will not take title or has no equity therein. The allowance of a Section 162 deduction for rent is not limited by a standard of reasonableness. The lease was fair and its rental provisions reasonable in light of industry standards. Thus, such rental payments were not a device to funnel corporate distributions to stockholders. Taxpayer's stockholders engaged in the lease arrangement only because the taxpayer was unable to borrow sufficient funds with which to construct a facility. William E. Davis & Sons, 41 TCM 1263, ¶ 81,178 P-H Memo. TC (1981).

Reasonable rent from corporation to sole stockholder determined. Taxpayer leased property from its sole stockholder for an annual rent of $24,000. The IRS argued that a reasonable rent was $12,000 and reduced taxpayer's deduction. *Held:* The court, after hearing expert witnesses, held the proper rent at $18,000. S&S Meats, Inc., 38 TCM 706, ¶ 79,163 P-H Memo. TC (1979).

Fair rental value of property rented to corporation by sole stockholder determined. Taxpayer corporation rented a manufacturing facility from its sole stockholder for $19,572. The IRS disallowed $12,823 of rental deduction. *Held:* For taxpayer, in part. Based on expert testimony as to comparable property, the fair rental value of the property was determined to have been $14,000 for fiscal years 1964 and 1965, and $15,000 for 1966, which was the deductible amount. Capital Refrigeration, Inc., 31 TCM 1021, ¶ 72,107 P-H Memo. TC (1972).

Amounts in excess of reasonable rental were not deductible and constituted constructive dividends. One taxpayer corporation leased land and machinery from its sister corporations, all owned by the same individuals, and claimed rental deductions, a portion of which the IRS disallowed. *Held:* For the IRS. The leasing corporation was denied deductions for rentals paid to the extent that such amounts exceeded a reasonable rental for the property. But while the excessive rental amounts were deemed constructive dividends to the individuals, the salaries paid to them for personal services were reasonable. Sparks Nugget, Inc., 29 TCM 318, ¶ 70,074 P-H Memo. TC (1970).

Fair rent between related corporations determined by Tax Court. Prior to October 1955, a very successful furniture business that also owned various real property was conducted as an individual proprietorship. In 1955, the business retained a CPA management consultant who suggested that two corporations be formed, one to operate the furniture business (taxpayer here), and the other to own and lease the real property, primarily to taxpayer. The reasons advanced for this move were limited liability and the fact that the corporate tax rate was limited to 30 percent on taxable income up to $25,000. The advice was acted upon, and all assets were transferred to two newly formed corporations in exchange for their stock. Ownership and management of the new corporations were retained by the same persons who had operated the sole proprietorship. A percentage lease was executed for the several properties obligating the taxpayer to make rental payments to the realty corporation. These payments remained fairly constant over the next four years ($25,000 to $28,000 per annum) despite the fact that several new properties were made available to taxpayer, one of the parcels was considerably improved, and two of the properties were disposed of. The IRS fixed the allowable rent deductions at $8,000 to $10,000 per year. *Held:* For the IRS, in part. The court found that if taxpayer had been dealing at arm's length with a stranger, it would not have "held still" on the rents provided for in the lease. Based on the evidence, it determined that the fair rent of the properties in an arm's-length lease between strangers ranged from $14,000 to $15,000. Roark Furniture, Inc., 22 TCM 193, ¶ 63,051 P-H Memo. TC (1963).

REORGANIZATIONS: In General

Rent to related lessor unreasonable. A payment of $18,000 by a corporation for the rent of printing presses from a company owned by the wives of the lessee's stockholders was considered unreasonably high by the IRS even after considering the limited availability of such presses. *Held:* For the IRS. The court redetermined the deductible rent at $8,000. International Color Gravure, Inc., 20 TCM 61, ¶ 61,015 P-H Memo. TC (1961).

Rents paid by corporation to its stockholders were unreasonable. Individual taxpayers were members of a family that used a corporation to carry on the family business. Payments were made by the corporation to various family members as rent for the use of machinery, automobiles, and real property owned by the members in their individual capacities. *Held:* For the IRS. The court found the rent excessive and sustained the IRS' determination that disallowed all amounts deducted as auto expenses (separate from the rent deduction), since the family members maintained and operated their own autos at their own expense. It also sustained the IRS' use of a 10-year life for depreciation of machinery owned by the individuals (rather than the two- to four-year life claimed) and its allowance of only 50 percent of the depreciation claimed by the individuals on the autos rented to the corporation. Ideal Tool & Die Co., 19 TCM 502, ¶ 60,096 P-H Memo. TC (1960).

REORGANIZATIONS

(*See also* Liquidations—Reincorporations; Transfers to Controlled Corporations)

In General	509
Acquisition of Assets (C Reorganizations)	514
Acquisition of Stock (B Reorganizations)	518
Boot	526
Business Purpose	529
Carry-Over of Net Operating Losses and Other Tax Attributes	532
Changes in Identity or Form (F Reorganizations)	543
Continuity of Business	544
Continuity of Interest	546
Dividend Equivalence	549
Expenses	550
Mergers (A Reorganizations)	551
Recapitalizations (E Reorganizations)	557
Reverse Acquisitions	559
Spin-Offs and Other Divisive Reorganizations (D Reorganizations)—Generally	559
Spin-Offs and Other Divisive Reorganizations—Active Business Requirement	568
Step-Transaction Doctrine	573

In General

Deferred receipt of stock in reorganization includes Section 483 interest. Taxpayer transferred stock of his closely held corporation to X Corporation in a B reorganization. Some of the X stock he received in return was withheld for three years as security for warranties. When the deferred stock was delivered to taxpayer, the IRS asserted that part of it was imputed interest taxable under Section 483. The Tax Court upheld the IRS. *Held:* Affirmed. The Section 483 regulations properly apply the provision to reorganizations. Kingsley, 662 F2d 539, 81-2 USTC ¶ 9785, 49 AFTR2d 82-306 (9th Cir. 1981).

Imputed interest applicable to reorganizations involving contingent stock. Taxpayers were parties to a reorganization in 1968. The reorganization agreement provided that additional shares would be issued if the value of the shares received in 1968 had not increased 20 percent within three years. In 1971, since such value increase had not occurred, the additional shares were issued. The IRS held that the contingent stock received in 1971 was subject to the imputed interest provisions of Section 483. The Tax Court found for the IRS. *Held:* Affirmed. The broad language of Section 483 was found to apply to reorganizations involving a deferred payment. The exceptions of Section 483(f) were not applicable. Katkin, 570 F2d 139, 41 AFTR2d 78-614 (6th Cir. 1978).

Acquisition of savings and loan association was purchase and reorganization. Taxpayer, a savings and loan association, purchased the guaranteed stock of two other savings and loan associations. A short time later, taxpayer acquired the withdrawal shares and investment certificates of the two entities in exchange for its own shares and proceeded to operate the business of the acquired entities. The IRS argued that taxpayer's acquisition of the two entities was a purchase followed by a liquidation, while taxpayer argued that the acquisition of the withdrawal shares and investment certificates made the transaction a reorganization. The lower court held for taxpayer. *Held:* Reversed. The withdrawal shares and investment certificates were found to be debt, not equity. They were found to compare with an ordinary savings account. Home Sav. & Loan Ass'n, 514 F2d 1199, 75-1 USTC ¶ 9423, 35 AFTR2d 75-1391 (9th Cir. 1975).

Transfer of assets through sole stockholder was a reorganization, not liquidation. Taxpayer, a U.S. corporation, was liquidated under Section 337 and claimed nonrecognition of gains realized on the sale of securities. The proceeds of the sale and other assets were distributed to the sole stockholder. During the period of the liquidation, the stockholder transferred cash and securities, some of which had been received from the liquidated U.S. corporation, to a wholly owned Panamanian corporation in exchange for stock. He also transferred to the Panamanian corporation shares representing his 50 percent ownership in another U.S. corporation actively engaged in manufacturing in the United States. After it changed its name, the Panamanian corporation qualified to do business in New York, and shortly thereafter the sole stockholder transferred to it additional securities but not in exchange for stock or securities. Taxpayer argued that the corporation was completely liquidated and was not reorganized. The IRS contended that the transfer of assets of taxpayer in liquidation constituted a reorganization and that the gain realized on the sale of assets was therefore to be recognized. The Tax Court found for the IRS. *Held:* Affirmed. Although taxpayer was liquidated according to the formalities of Section 337(a), the transferee was in effect a continuation of that business, since the liquidation could not be considered an isolated transaction but had to be viewed together with the related transfer from the sole stockholder to the transferee. Under Section 368(a)(1)(D), reorganization includes a transfer by a corporation of all or part of its assets to another corporation controlled by the same stockholders. In addition, the transferee received all of the stocks and properties and an amount of cash equal to that held by taxpayer in exchange for stock, which was distributed to the stockholder according to a plan, which did not have to be in writing. The gain in the reorganization was taxable since a ruling under Section 367 was not obtained. The transferee also contended that it was not liable for the deficiency as a transferee because the stockholder was willing and able to pay the taxpayer's deficiency. However, the IRS had a choice of proceeding against the assets in the hands of the transferee corporation or the stock in the hands of the stockholder, or both. Abegg, 429 F2d 1209, 70-2 USTC ¶ 9513, 26 AFTR2d 70-5154 (2d Cir. 1970), cert. denied, 400 US 1008 (1971).

Transaction did not qualify under Section 354 or Section 346. Taxpayers were stockholders in Pacific. In 1961, pursuant to a plan, Pacific transferred part of its business to a new corporation, Northwest, in exchange for all the latter's stock and a $200 million note. In the same year, Pacific issued to its stockholders rights to acquire 57 percent of its Northwest stock (the remaining 43 percent was offered in 1963). Taxpayers exercised their rights under which six rights plus $16 could be exchanged for a share of Northwest stock. The IRS argued that the difference between the amount paid by taxpayers and the value of the stock received was a dividend. Taxpayers argued that the receipt of Northwest stock was tax free under Section 355 or 354, or was entitled to capital gain treatment under Section 346. The Tax Court held for taxpayers under Section 355 but was reversed by the Ninth Circuit. Ultimately, the U.S. Supreme Court affirmed the Ninth Circuit but remanded for a consideration of Sections 354 and 346. On remand, the Tax Court found neither statute applicable and held for the IRS. *Held:* Affirmed. First, the stock rights were not stock or securities under Section 354(a)(1). The rights represented no voting, dividend, or liquidating rights in Pacific and thus were not stock. Even if they were securities, their distribution would have resulted, under Sections 301 and 317(a), in the same tax now disputed. Also, there was no reorganization as required by Section 354. If a D reorganization occurred, Section 354(b) was not satisfied since Pacific did not transfer "substantially all" its assets to Northwest and Pacific did not distribute 43 percent of the Northwest stock or the $200 million note. That the transaction may also have been an F reorganization did not change the result. All divisive reorganizations were intended to satisfy Section 354(b) or 355. Second, there was no redemption as required by Section 346(a)(2) and Pacific did not distribute all the proceeds or assets of the discontinued business as required by the provisions of Section 346(b). Baan, 450 F2d 198, 29 AFTR2d 72-331 (9th Cir. 1971).

Corporate reorganization not effected; gain recognized to individual stockholders on dissolution. Taxpayers were the sole stockholders of *O* Corporation and the principal stockholders of *W* Corporation. Early in 1958, both corporations adopted resolutions agreeing to a merger. On June 26, 1958, *O* Corporation was dissolved and it distributed its net assets to taxpayers in liquidation. Taxpayers contended that at the time O was dissolved they were not stockholders of *O*, having exchanged their stock on June 19, 1958 for stock in *W* Corporation. Hence, they claimed no gain on dissolution. *Held:* For the IRS. The Tax Court was affirmed in its finding that taxpayers did not exchange their stock on June 19, but remained the sole stockholders of *O* Corporation on the date of its liquidation. They were thus required to recognize any gain on the liquidation. There had not been a tax-free reorganization since there had been no actual merger, no exchange of stock, and no transfer of "substantially all the assets" to *W* corporation. Andersen, 341 F2d 584, 65-1 USTC ¶ 9258 (9th Cir. 1965).

Triangular transaction did not qualify as either B or F reorganization. Taxpayer parent, *P*, owned approximately 61 percent of the stock of operating company, *T*. *P* subsequently created subsidiary *S* by issuing its stock for all the stock of *S*. *S* then exchanged its stock in *P* for the stock of *T* and then canceled the *T* stock. *S* then proceeded to assume the management, business, and name of *T*. The IRS disallowed NOL carry-backs from the 1964 and 1965 years of *S* to the 1963 year of *T*. Taxpayer argued that the transaction fell within either the purview of a B or F reorganization so that the carry-back could be allowed. *Held:* For the IRS. This was not a B reorganization because the proprietary interests were substantially changed. *P* owned 61 percent of *T* but became the sole stockholder of *S*. Aetna Casualty & Surety Co., 403 F. Supp. 498, 75-2 USTC ¶ 9803, 36 AFTR2d 75-6287 (D. Conn. 1975).

Continuation of same business with same stockholders constituted a reorganization, not a liquidation. Taxpayers conducted their business through *A* Corporation until the IRS assessed a tax against *A* by virtue of a disallowance of certain salaries and expenses. At the time of the disallowance, the stockholders of *A* formed *B* Corporation, which either purchased or leased *A*'s assets necessary to conduct the business. *A* was left with sufficient assets to pay the tax assessments if the IRS prevailed. The IRS lost its case, and *A* sold its remaining assets for notes to *B* and distributed the notes to its stockholders. The IRS assessed the *A* stockholders on the value of the *B* notes that they received on the liquidation and that they retained on the ground that there was a D reorganization and a dividend to the *A* stockholders. Taxpayers contended that there was no intention to avoid taxes and that there was no reorganization. *Held:* For the IRS. Since the same stockholders operated the same business through a new corporation, it was a reorganization and not a

REORGANIZATIONS: *In General*

liquidation. Yeaman, 69-2 USTC ¶ 9585, 24 AFTR2d 69-5455 (ED Wash. 1969).

Reorganization principles control stock sale that was part of a liquidation. In a reorganization qualifying for tax-free treatment under Sections 361 and 368(a)(1)(C), taxpayer's predecessor, F, transferred substantially all of its assets to W in exchange for W's common stock and W's assumption of certain of taxpayer's liabilities. Taxpayer also adopted a plan for a 12-month liquidation under Section 337. As part of the plan, taxpayer sold for cash its shares of W at a gain, which it maintained was nonrecognizable by operation of Section 337. *Held:* For the IRS. The exchange of assets for stock was, as intended, a reorganization in purpose and effect. Therefore, taxpayer had to recognize the gain it realized from the sale of the acquired stock. The reorganization provisions were separate from, and prevailed over, the liquidation provisions. FEC Liquidating Corp., 548 F2d 924, 77-1 USTC ¶ 9160, 39 AFTR2d 77-709 (Ct. Cl. 1977).

Reorganization a sham. Taxpayer corporation owned an interest in a piece of land. Its sole stockholder owned an interest in an adjoining piece. When a publicly held corporation became interested in the land, both interests were transferred to a new corporation in exchange for stock. The stock of the new corporation was exchanged for stock of the publicly held corporation. After that, the new corporation was dissolved. Taxpayer claimed that the exchange was a nontaxable exchange of stock for stock. *Held:* For the IRS. The exchange was taxable. Although the transaction literally fit the definition of Section 368(a)(1)(B), the transaction was not a bona fide reorganization. The only function of the new corporation was to act as a conduit for the transfer of land. If taxpayer had exchanged the land directly for stock of the publicly held corporation, the transaction would have been taxable. Since the new corporation had no business purpose, the court ignored its existence. West Coast Mktg. Corp., 46 TC 32 (1965).

Regulated investment company failed to qualify under reorganization rules. X Corporation, which was engaged in manufacturing, sold all of its assets to unrelated Z Corporation for cash. This sale was made in anticipation of X's acquisition by Y Corporation, an open-end diversified investment company that qualified as a regulated investment company. Pursuant to an agreement between X and Y, X transferred all of its assets (cash and short-term treasury notes that X had purchased with the proceeds from the sale of its assets) to Y in return for 1,000 shares of Y. As provided in the agreement, X dissolved after the transfer and distributed the stock of Y to its stockholders, individuals A and B, in exchange for their X stock. In denying tax-free treatment, the IRS noted that a transfer of cash or short-term treasury notes for stock does not qualify as a reorganization under Section 368(a)(1) because in substance it represents a purchase by X of the shares of Y prior to X's liquidation. The fair market value of the Y stock distributed by X to its stockholders in complete liquidation had to be treated as in full payment in exchange for their X stock under Section 331. Rev. Rul. 79-434, 1979-2 CB 155.

Exchange of warrants subject to Section 1001 recognition. X Corporation acquired all the stock of Y pursuant to a plan of reorganization. Y also had warrants outstanding on its own stock for which X issued its own warrants. The reorganization qualified for nonrecognition, but the exchange of warrants was a separable transaction under Rev. Rul. 69-142, 1969-1 CB 107, and was therefore subject to Section 1001. Rev. Rul. 78-408, 1978-2 CB 203.

IRS ruled on reorganization of a domestic corporation's foreign subsidiaries. A domestic parent corporation, P, had two foreign subsidiaries, $S1$ and $S2$. $S2$ held the stock of three sub-subsidiaries, X, Y, and Z. In a reorganization transaction, P initially transferred all of $S1$'s stock to $S2$ in exchange for $S2$ stock. Then, the assets of $S1$, X, Y, and Z were transferred to N, a new subsidiary of $S2$, in exchange for N stock. Finally $S1$, X, Y, and Z were liquidated, with $S2$ receiving the

N stock from the liquidated companies. The initial transfer by *P* was not a Section 351 exchange. Instead, it was viewed as an acquisition by *N* of the assets of *S1* that qualified as a C reorganization. The transfer of assets by *X, Y,* and *Z* to *N* qualified as D reorganizations. Rev. Rul. 78-130, 1978-1 CB 114.

Reorganization held valid although acquired corporation did not transfer previously held stock of acquiring corporation. *Y* Corporation owned five shares of *X* Corporation plus a parcel of land. In order that *X* could acquire *Y*'s land, *X* and *Y* agreed to a reorganization in which *X* acquired *Y*'s assets in return for seven shares of *X* stock plus assumption of *Y*'s liabilities. However, to avoid a state transfer tax, *X* transferred only two of its shares to *Y,* which, combined with the five shares *Y* already held, formed the seven shares agreed to. Therefore, *Y* did not formally transfer the five shares to *X,* but the IRS ruled that the reorganization met the requirement under Section 368(a)(1)(C) that all of *Y*'s assets be transferred to *X.* Rev. Rul. 78-47, 1978-1 CB 113.

Return of escrowed stock received in reorganization did not result in realized gain or loss. The sole stockholder of an acquired corporation in a Section 368(a)(1)(B) reorganization returned the escrowed stock of the acquiring corporation because of the failure of the acquired corporation to attain specified earning levels. Such return did not result in the realization of gain or loss by the stockholder. Rev. Rul. 76-42, 1976-1 CB 102.

Reasonable redemption premium qualifies when market conditions would have disqualified it. Two corporations went through an A reorganization. The IRS treated as a reasonable redemption premium a redemption premium on the preferred stock of the acquiring corporation that was issued to the stockholders of the acquired corporation. That corporation had failed to meet the 10 percent limitation of Regulation § 1.305-5(b)(2) solely because of external market conditions that affected the fair market value of the acquired corporation's stock after determination of a qualifying exchange ratio but before the exchange. Rev. Rul. 75-468, 1975-2 CB 115.

Acceleration of a contingent stock agreement of a B or C reorganization prior to a subsequent reorganization involving the new parent qualified for nonrecognition. Where *P* Corporation acquired *S* Corporation in a B reorganization, and *P* Corporation provided both for the payment of additional *P* stock to the former *S* stockholders, depending on *S*'s future earnings, and for the acceleration of the payment if *P* were subsequently to be acquired in a reorganization, the former *S* stockholders recognized no gain or loss on the accelerated exchange under Section 354(a)(1). The same results would have occurred if *P* acquired *S*'s assets and liabilities in a C reorganization and used a contingent stock provision but no acceleration clause, and if *P* and *S* had agreed to a final settlement of the contingency prior to a subsequent reorganization involving *P.* Rev. Rul. 75-237, 1975-1 CB 116.

Gain recognized on A/D reorganization. In a reorganization that is both an A and D transaction, in which an individual's corporation acquires his 90 percent owned corporation's assets for stock in a statutory merger, and assumes all its liabilities which exceed the adjusted basis of the assets, gain must be recognized under Section 357(c)(1)(B) because Section 361 applies to a D reorganization. Rev. Rul. 75-161, 1975-1 CB 114.

Convertible shares received at premium need not be reported as premium. Stockholders of an acquired corporation in a statutory merger who receive for each share of their common stock an equal value share of the acquiring corporation's new convertible preferred stock need not include the premium in their gross income if the premium is reasonable. Even an 83 percent premium can be reasonable if the effect is a penalty for premature redemption. Rev. Rul. 75-179, 1975-1 CB 103.

Parent's shares used in acquisition by subsidiary. When a parent transfers shares of its voting stock to its subsidiary and the subsidiary, through a transitory subsidiary and statutory merger using the parent's stock, acquires all of the stock of an unrelated corporation, the transaction can qualify as a reorganization under Section 368(a)(1)(B). Rev. Rul. 74-565, 1974-2 CB 125.

Corporation that changes its name or issues preferred stock for its common stock is a party to a reorganization. The IRS ruled that a corporation that changes its name and issues new certificates bearing the new name of the corporation, and a corporation that issues previously authorized preferred stock in exchange for outstanding common stock are both parties to a reorganization. Rev. Rul. 72-206, 1972-1 CB 104.

Conversion of bonds into stock of another corporation is not excepted from the recognition of gain or loss. The conversion of bonds of one corporation into common stock of another corporation in accordance with the terms of the bond issue is not one of the transactions excepted from gain or loss recognition. (IT 3056 superseded.) Rev. Rul. 69-135, 1969-1 CB 198.

Nonstock federal savings and loan acquisition of assets and liabilities of stock savings and loan does not qualify as either an A or C reorganization. The acquisition, by a federally chartered nonstock savings and loan association, of all the assets and liabilities of a state-chartered savings and loan association having outstanding capital stock does not constitute a reorganization under either Section 368(a)(1)(A) or Section 368(a)(1)(B). Rev. Rul. 69-6, 1969-1 CB 104.

Dollar values need not be fixed on stock options in a corporate reorganization. Section 425(h) provides in part that if the terms of an option to purchase stock are modified, a new option is deemed granted. A modification is defined under Section 425(h)(3) as additional benefits to the employee. Where an employee in a corporate reorganization issues or assumes a stock option, no new option is deemed issued if the spread between the fair market value of the option shares immediately after the substitution or assumption over the aggregate option price of the shares is no more than the excess of the aggregate fair market value of all shares subject to the option immediately before such substitution or assumption over the aggregate option price of its shares. Regulation § 1.425-1(a)(7) permits any reasonable method to be used to determine the fair market value of the shares. The IRS ruled that the spread limitation of Section 425(a)(1) is satisfied in the following situation: X Corporation acquires all of Y Corporation's assets in exchange for X voting stock. The number and value of the substantiated shares to be received on exercise of the options is not determinable at the time of the substitution or assumption because such determination is fixed by a formula established at the time of the reorganization. The formula gives the optionees the right to acquire exactly the same number and kind of shares of X that they would have been entitled to receive in Y had they exercised their option immediately prior to the reorganization. Rev. Rul. 66-366, 1966-2 CB 194.

Acquisition of Assets (C Reorganizations)

Transfer of bank's assets deemed a C reorganization. The district court held against the IRS and found that the transfer by taxpayer, a state-chartered building and loan association, of its assets and liabilities to a federal savings and loan association constituted a C reorganization. Therefore, taxpayer was not required to restore the balance in its bad debt reserve to gross income for the final taxable year. *Held:* Affirmed. The court found that the fully paid shares and savings shares of the federal savings and loan association constituted voting stock within the meaning of Sections 368(a)(1)(C) and 368(a)(2)(B), and also that the transaction met the "continuity of interest" test for a C type reorganization. Everett, 448 F2d 357, 71-2 USTC ¶ 9629, 28 AFTR2d 71-5591 (10th Cir. 1971).

Transfer of assets of corporation to another corporation owned in substantially the same proportions was a reorganization. Taxpayers owned all of the stock of A Corporation. The parties formed B Corporation and held stock interests in B in substantially the same pro-

Reorganizations: *Acquisition of Assets (C Reorganizations)*

portions as were held in *A*. Taxpayers sold their *A* stock, and then *B* purchased all of the assets of *A*. The amount paid to taxpayers and other individuals was based on their stock interest in *A* and *B* on the amount paid by *B* to *A* for its assets. The net result of the transaction was that taxpayers owned substantially the same stock interest in *B* as they owned in *A,* and *B* continued to conduct the business formerly conducted by *A*. The IRS contended that the transaction was a reorganization, and proceeds of the sale were a dividend to taxpayers. *Held:* For the IRS. Substance governed over form, and since the same stockholders were conducting the same business both before and after the sale, the transaction was either a D or F reorganization, and the cash received by taxpayers was a dividend. Nutil, 69-1 USTC ¶ 9229, 23 AFTR2d 69-486 (CD Cal. 1968).

C reorganization lost when court telescoped transactions. Grede Foundries, Inc. owned 70 percent of the outstanding shares of Liberty Foundry Corporation. The other 30 percent of Liberty's shares were held by Grede's stockholders. Pursuant to a plan of reorganization, Grede issued 5,000 of its Class A voting common to Liberty in exchange for Liberty's assets. Upon receipt of the shares, Liberty distributed them to its stockholders in exchange for outstanding Liberty stock. The result was that Grede received 3,500 of its own shares back. The IRS determined that the transaction was not a tax-free C reorganization because taxpayer did not acquire the assets of Liberty *solely* for its own stock. *Held:* For the IRS. The court held that the gain must be recognized. The Supreme Court ruled that the exchange of voting stock *plus anything else* voids a C reorganization. Helvering v. Southwest Consol. Corp., 315 US 194 (1942). Taxpayer gave its shares of Liberty as well as its own shares, in effect, when it acted on a plan that would culminate in that result. Since there were two steps to the plan, the distribution of Grede shares followed by the exchange of some of the distributed shares for other (Liberty) shares, they must be viewed together. Grede Foundries, Inc., 202 F. Supp. 263, 62-1 USTC ¶ 9357 (D. Wis. 1962.)

Transaction did not qualify as D reorganization. Ten stockholders of *S,* holding 20 percent of *S*'s common stock, created taxpayer corporation *P*. The stockholders' *S* common stock holdings ranged from about one percent to about 4 percent, and each held 10 percent of *P. S* transferred substantially all of its assets to *P* for $21,000. *P* assumed *S*'s obligations and work in progress and issued additional shares to the 10 stockholders in proportion to their holdings in *P,* not to their holdings in *S*. The taxpayer contended that the transaction qualified as a D reorganization, but the IRS determined the transaction did not qualify. *Held:* For the IRS. There was no transfer of stock from the taxpayer to the transferor or a distribution of this stock by the transferor to its stockholders. Therefore, the statute's formal requirements for a D reorganization were not met. Furthermore, since taxpayer's and transferor's stock ownerships were not identical, actual distribution was required. Warsaw Photographic Assocs., 84 TC 21 (1985).

Transfer in liquidation to related corporation treated as reorganization. Taxpayer owned two corporations, Agency and Associates. Agency operated a general insurance business, and Associates sold large group insurance contracts. A large portion of the assets of Associates consisted of investments in stocks. Apart from receivables, the chief business assets of Associates were commission agreements with a large insurance company. Associates sold its commission agreements to Agency and liquidated by distributing its remaining assets to taxpayer. Taxpayer reported the gain as capital. The IRS contended that the transaction was a reorganization and treated the distributions as dividends. *Held:* For the IRS. The transaction was a reorganization as defined in Section 368(a)(1)(D) of the type previously adjudicated in Armour, 43 TC 295 (1964). The Court found that substantially all assets were transferred to Agency because the primary business assets (the commission agreements) were transferred. Wilson, 46 TC 334 (1966).

Attempted C reorganization fails. *P* Corporation owned 100 percent of the stock of *S-1,* and S-2. P wanted S-1 to obtain substantially all of the assets of X, an unrelated corporation. Pursuant to a plan, S-2 purchased some of X's stock, which was designed to eliminate possible adverse minority interests in X. X transferred its asset and liabilities to S-1 in exchange for P voting stock. The liabilities exceeded 20 percent of the fair market value of X's assets. After the exchange, X was dissolved, and the P stock was distributed to X's stockholders in exchange for the surrender and cancellation of all X stock. The IRS ruled that the transaction did not qualify under Section 368(a)(1)(C). When S-2 purchased some of the stock of X for cash, there was an indirect transfer of nonqualifying consideration by the acquiring corporation, S-2. Therefore, in computing whether S-1 obtained 80 percent of the fair market value of all the property of X, the liabilities assumed by S-2 were treated as money under Section 368(a)(2)(B). Because the liabilities exceeded 20 percent of the fair market value of X's assets, the transaction did not qualify as a C reorganization. Rev. Rul. 85-138, 1985-36 IRB 5.

Return of stock placed in escrow after C reorganization taxable to acquired corporation's sole stockholder. X Corporation acquired the assets of Y Corporation in a C reorganization. Some of the X stock issued to Y's sole stockholder, A, was placed in escrow pending the resolution of a contingent liability of Y. Later, part of the escrowed shares were returned to X to indemnify X for the liability. During the escrow period, the stock appreciated in value. The return of the shares to X produced taxable gain to A, since he benefited from the appreciation of the escrowed stock in determining the number of shares that had to be returned. The basis of the remaining X stock was increased by the amount of the liability satisfied. Rev. Rul. 78-376, 1978-2 CB 149.

Reorganization of foreign subsidiary to avoid nationalization was tax-free. X, a subsidiary of a domestic corporation in foreign country A, conducted business in both A and another country, B. When A began a nationalization program against foreign businesses, X organized a subsidiary, Y in country B. X then transferred all of its assets, except those that were in A and could not be moved, to Y in exchange for stock, and then transferred the Y stock to its domestic parent. The transfer from X to Y was a valid D reorganization, and the distribution to the parent was tax-free under Section 355. Rev. Rul. 78-383, 1978-2 CB 142.

Acquiring company's stock paid into escrow as part of a C reorganization may, in settlement of claims, be partially seized and combined with cash before actual transfer to target stockholders. The IRS held that when an acquiring corporation's stock was placed in escrow as part of the exchange of stock in a C reorganization, the return of half of such stock as part of a settlement of the acquiring corporation's claims against the target's stockholders, together with cash, did not violate the "solely for voting stock" requirement of Section 368(a)(1)(C). The stockholders would be required to treat the transaction as a redemption of one half of the returned shares and a forfeiture of the other half, resulting in an adjustment to their basis in the remaining shares acquired in the reorganization. Rev. Rul. 76-334, 1976-2 CB 108.

Dividends paid immediately before a C reorganization. The regular quarterly cash dividend is not taken into account in determining whether "substantially all of the properties" were acquired when the dividend was paid immediately prior to a C reorganization. Rev. Rul. 74-457, 1974-2 CB 122.

C reorganization exists where corporation continues. The IRS ruled that a transaction in which a corporation transfers substantially all its assets to a second corporation for part of the voting stock is a C reorganization, even though the transferor corporation remains in existence and in a new business. Rev. Rul. 73-552, 1973-2 CB 116.

Formation of subsidiary to acquire assets of another corporation with stock of parent with subsidiary subsequently liquidating qualifies as a C reorganization. Parent corporation organized subsidiary S solely for the purpose of participating in the proposed transaction. S then acquired all the assets of an unrelated corporation, subject to liabilities, in a statutory merger. All the acquired stock was exchanged for parent stock. S was then liquidated into the parent. The entire transaction will be considered as the acquisition of assets pursuant to Section 368(a)(1)(C). Rev. Rul. 72-405, 1972-2 CB 217.

"Solely for voting stock" requirements not met where stock of the acquired corporation was previously purchased for cash. The acquisition of substantially all of the properties of a corporation is not considered to be an exchange "solely for voting stock" where stock of the acquired corporation was previously purchased for cash pursuant to an overall plan of reorganization. Rev. Rul. 69-48, 1969-1 CB 106.

"Solely for voting stock" requirement of C reorganization not violated where acquiring corporation substitutes its stock for warrants and options of acquired corporation. The "solely for voting stock" requirement of Section 368(a)(1)(C) is not violated where, pursuant to a plan of reorganization, an acquiring corporation substitutes its stock for the outstanding unexercised warrants and employee stock options of the acquired corporation. In determining whether an exchange is solely for stock, Section 368(a)(1)(C) provides that the assumption by the acquiring corporation of a liability of the other, or the fact that property is acquired subject to a liability, shall be disregarded. The issuance of warrants and options constitutes a contractual liability within the purview of Section 368(a)(1)(C). Rev. Rul. 68-637, 1968-2 CB 158.

Requirements of a C reorganization are met when all the assets of the corporations involved are transferred to a corporation that owned no stock in either corporation. The "solely for voting stock" requirement of Section 368(a)(1)(C) may be satisfied where two corporations, one of which owns stock of the other, transfer all their assets to a corporation that owned stock in neither of the two transferors prior to the reorganization. Such an approach circumvents the decision in Bausch & Lomb Optical Co., 267 F2d 75 (2d Cir. 1959), where it was held that the "solely for voting stock" requirement was not satisfied because the effect of the transaction was the acquisition by the acquiring corporation of the assets of the acquired corporation in exchange for voting stock of the acquiring corporation plus the surrender of the stock of the acquired corporation held by the acquiring corporation. Rev. Rul. 68-526, 1968-2 CB 156.

C reorganization qualified even though transferor remained in existence solely to hold stock of acquiring corporation. For valid business reasons, a C reorganization was entered into between preexisting unrelated corporations. As a result of the reorganization, the transferring corporation received approximately 43 percent of the transferee corporation. The transferor corporation was not immediately dissolved, but did not conduct any business. The stockholders of the transferor corporation desired to keep the corporation in existence solely to hold the stock of the transferee corporation. The transaction still qualified as a C reorganization. Rev. Rul. 68-358, 1968-2 CB 156.

Section 351 applied to exchange of property by three corporations and an individual pursuant to an overall plan of reorganization. In order to consolidate the operations of five businesses, all the assets, subject to liabilities, were transferred to an existing corporation solely for voting stock. The transaction qualified as a reorganization under Section 368(a)(1)(C). The stock received by the transferor corporations was distributed to the stockholders. The fact that the corporate transferor distributed part or all of the stock that it received in the exchange to its stockholders was not taken into account in determining whether Section 351 applied. Accordingly, no gain or loss was recognized by the transferors of their assets to the remaining corporation nor was gain or loss recognized to the stockholders of the transferor corporations on the exchange of their stock of these corporations for voting stock of the remaining corporation. Rev. Rul. 68-357, 1968-2 CB 144.

REORGANIZATIONS: *Acquisition of Stock (B Reorganizations)*

Acquisition of all assets of a corporation by a parent corporation and its "grandson" corporation did not prevent a C reorganization. The IRS ruled that if a parent corporation and a subsidiary wholly owned by the parent's wholly owned subsidiary acquire all assets of an unrelated corporation solely in exchange for the parent corporation's voting stock, the transaction constitutes a C reorganization under Section 368. Rev. Rul. 64-73, 1964-1 CB 142.

Successor corporation in reorganization not required to carry on its old business. M Corporation was engaged in the manufacture of toys and N Corporation in the distribution of steel. At some time in the past, M sold most of its operating assets to a third party for cash. It more recently sold all but a small part of its remaining assets for cash, also to a third party. Subsequently, for valid business reasons, it acquired all of the assets of N solely in exchange for its voting stock. N then distributed the M stock to its stockholders and dissolved. M continued and expanded the steel business that had formerly been conducted by N. The IRS ruled that the transaction qualified as a tax-free reorganization under Section 368(a)(1)(C) and that the continuity of interest requirement had been met even though the toy business was discontinued. An earlier ruling, Rev. Rul. 56-330, 1956-2 CB 204, which held that the continuity of interest requirement was not met where the successor corporation engaged in a business different from that of its predecessor was revoked. Rev. Rul. 63-29, 1963-1 CB 77.

Acquisition of Stock (B Reorganizations)

Prior purchase disqualifies an exchange for tax-free treatment as B reorganization. Taxpayers held stock in H, a corporation that ITT wanted to acquire. ITT purchased 8 percent of H's stock for cash and then tried to merge H into its wholly owned subsidiary. The IRS issued a private letter ruling to ITT advising that the proposed merger would qualify as a tax-free reorganization under Section 368(a)(1)(B), providing that ITT disposed of its H stock before the merger. Thereafter, ITT sold its 8 percent holding in H stock to M. Four years after a reorganization plan had been approved and carried out, the IRS determined that ITT had committed fraud in its sale of H stock to M, and revoked its ruling retroactively. The IRS concluded that the merger did not qualify as a B reorganization because of the 8 percent purchase of H stock and disallowed the tax deferral of the realized gain by taxpayers. The Tax Court and district court both held that the transaction did qualify as a B reorganization because ITT controlled H after acquiring H's stock. *Held:* Reversed. A B reorganization not only requires control by the acquiring corporation after the exchange, but the exchange also has to involve no consideration other than the voting stock. The 8 percent purchase of H stock for cash was boot that disqualified the exchange from tax-free treatment. Heverly, 621 F2d 1227, 45 AFTR2d 80-1122 (3d Cir. 1980), rev'g and remanding Reeves, 472 F. Supp. 957 (D. Del. 1979), Pierson, 71 TC 727 (1979).

For a valid B reorganization, none of acquired corporations' stock may be acquired in the reorganization transaction for consideration other than voting stock in the acquiring corporation. Taxpayer, pursuant to an offering, exchanged his Hartford Fire Insurance Co. stock for voting stock in ITT and, claiming that such offering was a B reorganization, reported no gain on the exchange. The IRS contended that the exchange was not a B reorganization because, prior to the offering, ITT bought 8 percent of Hartford's stock for cash. In 1968, ITT acquired for cash 8 percent of Hartford's stock as part of a plan to acquire Hartford. ITT received a ruling from the IRS indicating that an exchange of ITT stock for Hartford stock would qualify as a B reorganization, provided that ITT, prior to the exchange, would unconditionally sell the 8 percent interest in Hartford. ITT made this sale to an unrelated third party. Although a merger was initially planned, later problems caused ITT to instead make the exchange offer in which taxpayer and 95 percent of the Hartford stockholders participated. The IRS retroactively revoked its ruling and assessed the Hartford stockholders. Taxpayer moved for a summary judgment (conceding for purposes of this motion that the cash purchase of Hartford stock and exchange offer were related and that the IRS had valid grounds to revoke its ruling). The Tax Court granted taxpayer's motion on the ground that having acquired more than 80 percent of Hartford's stock for its voting stock, ITT did not violate the "solely for voting stock" requirement of a B reorganization. *Held:* Reversed. The B reorganization's "solely for voting stock" requirement means that 100 percent of the stock acquired in the reorganization transaction must be acquired for voting stock. Chapman, 618 F2d 856, 45 AFTR2d 80-1290 (1st Cir. 1980).

Interest income imputed on additional stock received in merger. Pursuant to a B reorganization, taxpayers were to receive additional shares in the future, dependent on certain contingencies. No provision was made for the payment of interest on these shares. The IRS determined that interest should be imputed upon receipt of the additional shares. *Held:* For the IRS. Although the contractual rights to the additional shares were not payments under Section 483, they were in the nature of evidences of indebtedness, and payments under the terms of such indebtedness come within the ambit of Section 483. Therefore, the delivery of the additional shares constituted a "payment" within the meaning of the statute. The nonrecognition provisions of the reorganization provisions did not prohibit the recognition of other types of income. Catterall, 68 TC 413 (1977), aff'd, Vorbleski, 589 F2d 123, 78-2 USTC ¶ 9839, 42 AFTR2d 78-6330 (3d Cir. 1978).

Settlement of acquired corporation's contingent liability by acquiring corporation increased acquiring corporation's basis in acquired corporation's stock. D&R, Inc., a family owned corporation engaged in shipping, owned all of the stock of States, which owned all of the stock of Pacific Transport. New States was owned by Dent, who also owned 19 percent of D&R Inc. New States purchased the stock of States and, after operating it as a subsidiary, liquidated it pursuant to Section 334(b)(2). New States settled a claim against States arising from a cargo loss prior to acquisition. Although all parties were aware of the claim, the price of States was not discounted to reflect it. After the purchase, an unexpected court decision significantly enlarged States' potential liability under the claim. New States deducted the settlement payment. The IRS asserted that the payment should be considered part of the cost of States' stock. *Held:* For the IRS. Pacific Transp. Co., 483 F2d 209, 73-2 USTC ¶ 9615, 32 AFTR2d 73-5663 (9th Cir. 1973).

Acquired corporation in B reorganization was a "party to the reorganization" even though it did not actively participate in the reorganization. Taxpayer corporation exchanged its voting stock for all the voting stock held by the stockholders of another corporation. The acquired corporation was operated by taxpayer as a subsidiary and was then dissolved. Taxpayer claimed a loss on the dissolution based on its cost of the subsidiary's stock. The IRS argued that the transaction was a reorganization. *Held:* Affirmed. The loss was limited to taxpayer's basis in such stock, which was the same as the basis of the transferors. The exchange was a B reorganization, so taxpayer had a substituted basis under Section 362(b). Taxpayer's contention, that the acquired subsidiary was not a "party to the reorganization" because it did not actively participate in the reorganization, was contrary to the literal meaning and congressional intent of Section 368(b)(2). The Tax Court was therefore correct in finding that the acquisition agreement was a "plan of reorganization." Hays Corp., 331 F2d 422, 64-1 USTC ¶ 9465, 13 AFTR2d 1367 (7th Cir.), cert. denied, 379 US 842 (1964).

Reorganization was a B, not an F reorganization. *X* Corporation and *Y* Corporation were involved in a corporate reorganization. Subsequent to the reorganization, *Y*, the continuing corporation, attempted to carry-back losses to the preorganization years of *X*. *Y* contended that this was on F reorganization, while the IRS held that this was a B reorganization so that a net operating loss carry-back to *X* was prohibited by virtue of Section 381(b). *Held:* For the IRS. The substance of the transaction amounted to a massive

Reorganizations: *Acquisition of Stock (B Reorganizations)*

change in corporate structure, ownership, and method of doing business. In addition, changes in the accounting method and the closing of X Corporation's tax year on the date of the reorganization strongly indicated that a B reorganization was effected. Spinoza, Inc., 375 F. Supp. 439, 74-1 USTC ¶ 9463 (SD Tex. 1974).

Exchange of voting common stock for nonvoting was tax-free. Taxpayer and her brother owned all of the outstanding common stock of a corporation. Because the brother wanted sole voting control, the capitalization of the corporation was changed. New Class A common voting stock was issued to the brother for his stock. A new series of Class B nonvoting redeemable common was issued to taxpayer for her stock. It was understood, the court found, that the Class B stock would be redeemed shortly. Taxpayer transferred the new Class B stock to a trust in which she had a life estate (remainder to her children). The IRS argued that (1) her exchange of common stock for nonvoting common stock was tantamount to the issuance of a preferred stock that had no reason or purpose germane to the conduct of the corporate business and that (2) the transfer to the trust, followed by the redemption of some of the shares from the trust, was part of a single plan or transaction looking to the exchange of stock for a trust life estate. *Held:* For taxpayer. The court held that there was a tax-free reorganization, stating that Section 1036 applied even though voting stock was exchanged for nonvoting stock or nonvoting stock was exchanged for voting stock. The reorganization had a business purpose germane to the successful continuance of the business, and it eliminated the problem of dividend ownership. According to the court, although taxpayer created the trust at the time of the reorganization and directed that a new stock be issued to the trustee, the reorganization was not incidental to any plan of liquidation, but rather had a legitimate business purpose of its own. Accordingly, the court found that the exchange was tax-free. Carnahan, 188 F. Supp. 461, 60-2 USTC ¶ 9773 (D. Mont. 1960).

Court of Claims remands to determine whether a B reorganization did in fact result. In an earlier decision, the court held that the acquisition by taxpayer corporation of another corporation was not a reorganization because taxpayer did not obtain 80 percent control within a single 12-month period. Upon reconsideration, the IRS contended that the 12-month rule was a mere guideline to determine which exchanges of stock qualified for a B reorganization and that if a series of purchases over more than 12 months were part of a continuing offer to purchase, it qualified as tax free under the reorganization provisions. The IRS also contended that the final acquisition of 52 percent of the subsidiary stock qualified as a tax-free exchange within the definition of a B reorganization. *Held:* Remanded. Because the facts of the relationship between the two offers and several exchanges and their relationship to the later liquidation revolved around unsettled questions of fact, the case was remanded for a redetermination on the issue of whether a B reorganization had occurred. American Potash & Chem. Corp., 402 F2d 1000, 68-2 USTC ¶ 9650, 22 AFTR2d 5820 (Ct. Cl. 1968).

Stock received in lieu of dividend in B reorganization was taxable. Taxpayer, sole stockholder of his corporation, agreed to exchange all of his stock for 168,000 shares of Ashland Oil. Dividends were accrued after December 15 on the shares received by taxpayer, regardless of the date of closing; however, in the event the closing did not take place until after December 15, no cash dividend would accrue and in lieu thereof taxpayer would receive additional stock. The closing occurred on December 16, because of a delay in getting a favorable ruling, and on receipt of the additional stock the IRS determined there was a taxable transaction, as to that stock. *Held:* For the IRS. There were two separate transactions here; the receipt of the additional shares was severable from the B reorganization and such shares represent a dividend. Taxpayer had the right to receive stock, rather than cash, and the fact that he ultimately received stock was of no consequence. Section 305(b)(2) was not applicable here. Fisher, 62 TC 73 (1974).

Reorganizations: Acquisition of Stock (B Reorganizations)

Subsidiary's purchase of stock causes intended B reorganization to fail. In a transaction by P to obtain control of X, P acquired 90 percent of X's stock solely in exchange for P voting stock and had its subsidiary S obtain the other 10 percent for cash. The cash paid by S was not obtained directly or indirectly from P, and S retained ownership of the X stock it purchased. The IRS ruled that the transaction did not qualify under Section 368(a)(1)(B). The acquisition by S of 10 percent of X's stock for cash was part of the overall plan between P and X for P to obtain control of X. Therefore, P failed to meet the requirements under Section 368(a)(1)(B) that P obtain all of X's stock in exchange solely for voting stock. Rev. Rul. 85-139, 1985-36 IRB 6.

Acquisition of bank by holding company qualified as B reorganization. A bank holding company, P, acquired a national bank, S, in a B reorganization. P acquired all shares from S's stockholders except for a few shares retained by S's directors to meet federal stock ownership requirements. P received options from each of S's directors to buy their shares when they ended their directorships. P assigned the option to new directors when they were appointed. The cash to buy the shares came from the new directors, not from P. The exercise of the options did not violate the "solely for voting stock" rule for B reorganizations. Rev. Rul. 79-100, 1979-1 CB 152.

Cash contribution to pay acquired corporation's debt may be acceptable in "B" reorganization. P Corporation acquired all of the stock of T Corporation in exchange for P stock, and then contributed cash to T to discharge a debt of T to an unrelated creditor. Although the cash contribution was part of the plan, it was not a condition to the stock exchange. The values of the P and T stock exchanged were equal, and the cash was intended to improve T's financial condition. Under these facts, the cash contribution did not violate the "solely for voting stock" rule of Section 368(a)(1)(B). Rev. Rul. 79-89, 1979-1 CB 152.

No B reorganization when acquiring corporation discharged corporate debt for which stockholder had personal liability. X Corporation's stock was wholly owned by A, who was guarantor of a loan made by X. Due to X's existing capitalization, A was treated for tax purposes as the true debtor when X exchanged its stock for the stock of an acquiring corporation, Y, in a purported B reorganization. Y agreed to make a capital contribution to X sufficient to repay the loan. This capital contribution discharged the liability of X and A. A was treated as receiving boot, which violated the "solely for voting stock" requirement and rendered the acquisition taxable. Rev. Rul. 79-4, 1979-1 CB 150.

Rental income imputed. P Corporation owned all of the stock of S Corporation. P exchanged all of the S stock for all of the P stock owned by an individual, A. The exchange was made for valid business reasons. The P stock was worth 85 percent of the value of the S stock for which it was exchanged, the difference being a payment of rent by P to A for premises leased to P. The exchange did not qualify for Section 355 treatment to the extent that the S stock was in excess of the value of the P stock. Rev. Rul. 77-20, 1977-1 CB 91.

Corporation's grant of voting rights to its preferred stock enabled acquiring corporation to qualify under Section 368. Y Corporation had 81 shares of voting common and 19 shares of nonvoting preferred outstanding. X desired to acquire Y's stock in a Section 368(a)(1)(B) transaction, but did not wish to acquire the preferred stock. Y's charter was amended to give the preferred the same voting rights as common. The IRS held that X's acquisition of the Y common qualified under Section 368(a)(1)(B), since following the transaction X had control within the meaning of Section 368(c). Rev. Rul. 76-223, 1976-1 CB 103.

"Solely for voting stock" not met in cash purchase. If a corporation exchanges its voting stock for 80 percent of a corporation's shares and purchases the remaining 20 percent for cash, the "solely for voting stock" require-

REORGANIZATIONS: Acquisition of Stock (B Reorganizations)

ment of Section 368(a)(1)(B) is not met. Rev. Rul. 75-123, 1975-1 CB 115.

Preferred shares satisfy "solely for voting stock" requirement. When stockholders of an acquired corporation are issued shares of voting convertible-preferred stock that provide for additional dividends under special circumstances, the issuance does not violate the "solely for voting stock" requirement of Section 368(a)(1)(B). Rev. Rul. 75-33, 1975-1 CB 115.

Section 354 applies to subsequent transfer of shares in B reorganization. Section 354 applies to additional voting stock transferred within one year of a B reorganization to former stockholders of the acquired corporation where the fair market value of the acquired corporation's shares had been erroneously computed. Rev. Rul. 75-94, 1975-1 CB 111.

Parent's stock may be used in B reorganization by subsidiary. The following transaction qualified as a reorganization under Section 368(a)(1)(B): A parent contributed shares of its voting common stock to a newly formed corporation to enable its wholly owned operating subsidiary to acquire the outstanding publicly held minority interest in the subsidiary's 98 percent owned operating company and then, through a statutory merger, the minority held shares were exchanged for the parent's stock. Rev. Rul. 74-564, 1974-2 CB 124.

Stock-for-stock exchange followed by a distribution to a parent not a C reorganization. A C reorganization did not result from a transaction in which a parent's wholly owned subsidiary, whose assets consisted principally of shares of other wholly owned subsidiaries, transferred all of its assets except for some receivables, notes, and cash to a newly formed corporation for all of that corporation's voting shares, distributed those shares to its parent in exchange for most of its own shares, and continued to exist but did not engage in the active conduct of a trade or business. Rev. Rul. 74-545, 1974-2 CB 122.

Acquisition qualifies as a B reorganization. The IRS ruled that a reorganization that includes the acquisition by a corporation of all the outstanding shares of an unrelated corporation solely in exchange for 20 percent of its voting shares qualifies as a B reorganization. Section 301 applies to a distribution by the acquired corporation of 30 percent of the value of its assets. Rev. Rul. 74-35, 1974-1 CB 85.

A B reorganization was not foiled by a contingent stock payout. The "solely for voting stock" requirement of a B reorganization was met notwithstanding the use of a contingent stock payout that was based on a formula using the acquired corporation's earnings performance during the five-year period following the exchange to determine the ratio at which the preferred stock issued by the acquiring corporation might be converted into the acquiring corporation's common stock. Rev. Rul. 73-205, 1973-1 CB 188.

The acquisition of the stock of a second-tier subsidiary from the first-tier subsidiary in exchange solely for the parent's stock qualifies as a B reorganization. A parent corporation, in exchange solely for its voting stock, acquired all the outstanding stock of a second-tier subsidiary owned by a first-tier subsidiary. The IRS ruled that such a transaction qualifies as a reorganization as defined in Section 368(a)(1)(B). Rev. Rul. 73-28, 1973-1 CB 187.

A valid B reorganization occurs when pursuant to a plan, one corporation exchanged stock with another corporation. Pursuant to one plan, and for valid business reasons, one corporation exchanged its stock to acquire all of the outstanding stock of another corporation, and immediately thereafter the first corporation's stock was acquired by a third solely in exchange for its stock. The IRS ruled that such a plan qualifies as a reorganization pursuant to Section 368(a)(1)(B). Rev. Rul. 73-16, 1973-1 CB 186.

Prearranged sale of target stock not fatal to B reorganization treatment. P and Y corporations were publicly owned. Y had outstanding various classes of preferred stock and 9 million shares of common stock of which 300,000 shares had been purchased for cash, on the open market, within a short period of time before the transactions described herein. P sought to acquire the stock of Y in a transaction that would qualify under Section 368(a)(1)(B). Because of its prior purchase of Y stock, P sought to preclude the possibility that such purchase, and the subsequent exchange of Y stock for voting stock of P, would be treated as a single transaction that would violate the "solely for voting stock" requirement. Therefore, prior to the offer of exchange, P unconditionally sold for cash all of its Y stock to X, an unrelated third party. P had no agreement or other arrangement to reacquire the stock of Y. P thereafter acquired all of the outstanding stock of Y in exchange for voting stock of P. On these facts, the IRS found a valid tax-free B reorganization. In the IRS' view, the unconditional sale of the Y shares to X was accorded independent significance for tax purposes, as it was neither transitory nor illusory and in no way dependent or conditioned on the subsequent reorganization. After the purchase from P of the Y stock, X was free to retain its shares of Y or exchange them for shares of P. Moreover, P had no agreement or other arrangement to reacquire the shares of Y if the reorganization did not take place. Rev. Rul. 72-354, 1972-2 CB 216.

Tax consequences of an exchange of warrants for all the outstanding voting stock of an acquired corporation. A corporation acquired all the outstanding voting stock of a corporation in exchange solely for the issuance of its own stock warrants. The exchange did not qualify as a reorganization within the meaning of Section 368(a)(1)(B), since stock warrants are not voting stock. The receipt of the warrants by the stockholders of the acquired corporation was a taxable exchange, resulting in the recognition of gain. No gain or loss was recognized by the acquiring corporation on the issuance of warrants. Rev. Rul. 72-198, 1972-1 CB 223.

Exchange of stock options did not violate B reorganization. Pursuant to a plan of reorganization, two corporations exchanged their stock in a transaction that would have otherwise qualified as a reorganization under Section 368(a)(1)(B). However, because the acquired corporations had outstanding stock options, the acquiring corporation substituted its own options in their place. There was no modification of the prior options as defined by Section 425(h). The transaction qualified as a B reorganization as only voting stock was utilized as consideration in the acquisition of stock. Rev. Rul. 70-269, 1970-1 CB 82.

Assignment of federal refund claim to parent prior to subsidiary acquisition in B reorganization did not violate "solely for voting stock" requirement. Immediately prior to acquisition by an unrelated corporation, a subsidiary assigned all its rights to a federal income tax claim. The acquisition of the voting stock of the subsidiary by an unrelated corporation met "solely for voting stock" requirements of Section 368(a)(1)(B) as the refund claim was not part of the consideration given by the acquiring corporation. Rev. Rul. 70-172, 1970-1 CB 77.

"Solely for voting stock" provisions not met where liabilities were assumed as part of a two-step transaction. X and Y were corporations actively engaged in business; 60 percent of the outstanding stock of Y was owned by Z Corporation. The balance was owned by unrelated individuals. X acquired all of the assets of Z including the Y stock, in exchange solely for its own voting stock, plus the assumption of the liabilities of Z. X then exchanged its own voting stock for the remaining 40 percent of the Y stock held by individuals. The stock of Y was not acquired solely in exchange for X stock under Section 368(a)(1)(B) as X assumed the liabilities of Z. The disregarding of liabilities provision only applies to C reorganizations. Rev. Rul. 70-65, 1970-1 CB 77.

Acquisition of debentures as part of an exchange of stock for stock is not considered a part of a B reorganization. A corporation entered into a transaction that qualified as a B reorganization. The corporation also ac-

Reorganizations: Acquisition of Stock (B Reorganizations)

quired the outstanding debentures of the acquired corporation in exchange for its own stock. The IRS ruled that such a transaction is not considered part of the B reorganization and any gain or loss is recognized as provided by Section 1002. Rev. Rul. 70-41, 1970-1 CB 77.

Dividend from subsidiary met control requirements. A corporation gained control of another corporation by acquiring 75 percent of the entire stock solely for its voting stock. At the same time, a subsidiary of the acquired corporations, which held the other 25 percent of stock, agreed to distribute the stock as a dividend to the acquiring corporation. Since only voting stock was used in the exchange, the transaction qualified as a B reorganization. Rev. Rul. 69-585, 1969-2 CB 56.

Payment of dividend after B reorganization did not adversely affect the "solely for voting stock" requirements. An acquired corporation declared a dividend prior to a corporate reorganization and paid the dividend subsequent to the reorganization. The dividend was in no way part of the consideration given as part of the exchange. Therefore, the "solely for voting stock" requirements of Section 368(a)(1)(B) were not adversely affected. Rev. Rul. 69-443, 1969-2 CB 54.

Liquidation of subsidiary 1, which owned 80 percent of subsidiary 2, and the exchange of the parent's stock for the remaining minority stock did not qualify as a B reorganization. A parent corporation, wishing to own directly 100 percent of a corporation's stock of which a subsidiary owned 80 percent, liquidated the subsidiary and exchanged its own stock for the remaining 20 percent minority interest. An exchange under Section 368(a)(1)(B) must be solely for voting stock of the acquiring corporation or for voting stock of a corporation in control of the acquiring corporation. In the present plan, part of the stock of subsidiary 2 (including the assets of subsidiary 1) was received by the parent in full payment in exchange not for its own stock but for the stock of subsidiary 1. It cannot be said that the parent acquired the stock of subsidiary 2 solely for its own voting stock. Rev. Rul. 69-294, 1969-1 CB 110.

IRS examines tax-free treatment where multi-tiered subsidiaries exchange assets for convertible stock. J Corporation was the wholly owned subsidiary of A Corporation, which in turn was the wholly owned subsidiary of D Corporation. Pursuant to a plan of reorganization that was intended to meet the definition of a reorganization in Section 368(a)(1)(C), A, for valid business reasons, proposed to acquire substantially all of the assets, subject to the liabilities of X, an unrelated corporation, in exchange for voting convertible preferred stock of A. The voting preferred stock of A was convertible into common stock of D at the election of the stockholders at any time after five years from the date of the reorganization. After the transaction, A was still in control of J as defined in Section 368(c). The IRS stated that these facts raise the issue of whether the right to convert the stock issued in the transaction is a right that should be considered for property other than voting stock. If the right in these circumstances is other property, then the foregoing requirement of Section 368(a)(1)(C) is not satisfied. The answer to the question depends on particular facts in addition to those stated above. For example, the agreement could provide that the stockholders of A (other than D) present their voting convertible preferred stock of A directly to D, which would issue its voting common stock directly to the stockholders in exchange for their stock of A. Because A did not, in this situation, own any stock of D, it could not issue stock convertible into stock of D, unless D had granted to A the right to do so. Pursuant to the agreement, D granted to A the right to have A stock converted into stock of D on the conversation date. A in turn distributed to the D stockholders the right granted by D to convert its stock to the stock of D. Thus, A issued to the stockholders of D its own stock plus the right that D granted to A to have such stock converted to the stock of D. The additional right obtained from D represented other property when distributed by A to the stockholders of X. Thus, the assets of X were not acquired by J soley for voting stock of its parent *A*. Accordingly, in this case, the transaction was not a reorganization within the meaning of Section 368(a)(1)(C). Rev. Rul. 69-216, 1969-1 CB 109.

Use of debentures held not fatal to stock-for-stock reorganization. *X* Corporation acquired all of the outstanding capital stock of *Y* Corporation in exchange for voting stock of *X*. *Y* was at all times a solvent corporation. Prior to the exchange, *Y* had an issue of 6 percent, 10-year debentures outstanding. Pursuant to the plan of reorganization, *X* acquired all of the outstanding debentures of *Y* in exchange for an equal amount of new 6 percent 10-year debentures of *X*. Some of the debentures of *Y* were held by its stockholders, but a substantial proportion of the *Y* debentures was held by persons who owned no stock. The IRS, determining the applicability of Section 368(a)(1)(B), held that this exchange did not constitute an indirect nonqualifying consideration and therefore, tax-free treatment would be proper under these facts. Rev. Rul. 69-142, 1969-1 CB 107.

B reorganization qualified even though majority stockholder of acquiring corporation purchased 50 percent of acquired corporation stock prior to reorganization. The requirements of Sections 368(a)(1)(B) and 354(a) were met despite the fact that the majority stockholder of the acquiring corporation (acting solely in an individual capacity) purchased 50 percent of the acquired corporation prior to reorganization. Since the principal stockholder purchased the stock solely for his own account and in his own behalf, the acquiring corporation was considered not the purchaser of the acquired corporation stock. Rev. Rul. 68-562, 1968-2 CB 157.

Reorganization existed even though escrow account established for stock purchases. A banking corporation acquired the outstanding stock of another banking corporation under a plan designed to comply with state law whereby the acquired corporation contributed cash to an escrow fund for payment to its dissenting stockholders. The IRS ruled that the acquisition of the stock of the acquired corporation in exchange for voting stock of the acquiring corporation was a B reorganization even though, in accordance with state banking law, an escrow account was established in order to pay dissenting stockholders for their stock and even though the stock of some dissenting stockholders was not redeemed until after the consummation of the exchange. Rev. Rul. 68-285, 1968-1 CB 147.

Series of steps held to be a B reorganization. Pursuant to a plan of reorganization, a parent corporation issued some of its voting shares to its new subsidiary, which immediately merged into an unrelated corporation in a transaction that qualified as a statutory merger under applicable state law. The effect of the series of steps was that the stockholders of the subsidiary received shares of the parent, and the parent received 80 percent or more of the shares of the unrelated corporations. The IRS ruled that in the transaction, the parent, solely in exchange for part of its voting stock, acquired stock of the subsidiary within the meaning of Section 368(a)(1)(B). Rev. Rul. 67-448, 1967-2 CB 144.

Cash in lieu of fractional shares did not kill "for stock only" reorganization. In Mills, 331 F2d 321 (5th Cir. 1964), the court ruled that the "solely for stock" requirement of a B reorganization was satisfied when the acquiring corporation distributed its stock plus cash in lieu of fractional shares. The IRS will follow *Mills* in similar situations involving B and C reorganizations, where the cash represents mechanical rounding off rather than a separately bargained for consideration. In the latter case, in an A, D, or C reorganization, by reason of Section 368(a)(2)(B), the cash will be considered boot. In reorganizations where the cash payment made by the acquiring corporation is not bargained for, but is in lieu of fractional share interests to which the stockholders are entitled, the payments are treated as a redemption of the fractional shares. The transaction results in capital gain or loss unless the distribution is essentially equivalent to a dividend. In the latter case the distribution will be taxed as an ordinary dividend under Section 301. If the cash payment is in lieu of fractional shares of stock that is Section 306 stock, the distribution will be taxed as an ordinary dividend, unless the IRS is satisfied that none of the plan's principal purposes was avoidance of federal income tax. (Rev. Rul. 56-220 clarified). Rev. Rul. 66-365, 1966-2 CB 116.

"Solely for voting stock" requirement not violated by right to additional stock. M Corporation was owned equally by Y Corporation and X Corporation. Y, in agreeing to acquire all the M stock held by X in exchange for Y stock, also agreed to give X additional voting shares of stock up to an agreed maximum depending on the earnings of M for the four years following the exchange. The right acquired by X was not assignable, and the contractual right could give rise to the receipt of only additional voting shares. The IRS ruled that under the facts the "solely in exchange for voting stock" requirement of Section 368(a)(1)(B) was satisfied. The IRS distinguished this holding from the position taken in Rev. Rul. 57-586, where negotiable certificates of contingent interest were received. That ruling stated that the transferrable interest contained a dividend income element and that, therefore, something more than a mere right to receive additional common stock was involved. Rev. Rul. 66-112, 1966-1 CB 68.

Boot

Transfer of assets between 100-percent-owned corporations followed by liquidation of transferor held, despite no showing of tax-avoidance motive, to be a D reorganization with a boot dividend. Taxpayer owned all of the stock of two corporations actively engaged in business. Taxpayer caused one of these corporations to transfer all of its operating assets to the other. Taxpayer then liquidated the transferee corporation receiving all of its remaining assets (cash). The transferee continued the transferor's business, which consisted mostly of drying the transferee's lumber. Taxpayer reported a capital gain on the liquidation. The IRS asserted that the transfer and liquidation constituted a D reorganization, and that the cash distribution constituted a boot dividend. *Held:* For the IRS. The four requirements of a D reorganization were satisfied: (1) taxpayer owned 100 percent of both corporations prior to and after the transfer; (2) distribution of stock was unnecessary because ownership of transferor and transferee was identical; (3) focus of transfer of "substantially all" of transferor's assets was on operating assets, and all of these were transferred; and (4) a formal written plan of reorganization is unnecessary where steps taken show evidence of a plan. Further, the fact that no tax avoidance can be shown does not prevent the characterization of the transfer and liquidation as a D reorganization. *Rose,* 640 F2d 1030, 81-1 USTC ¶ 9271, 47 AFTR2d 81-1070 (9th Cir. 1978).

In determining the existence of a boot dividend under Section 356(a)(2) in which two corporations are consolidated, the court applies Section 302 analysis with regard solely to consolidated corporation and compares percentage of stock received with percentage that would have been received in absence of boot. Taxpayer and another owned, respectively, 56 percent and 30 percent in X Corporation and 99 percent and 0 percent in Y Corporation. It was decided that X and Y would be consolidated, taxpayer and his fellow stockholder holding roughly the same proportionate interests that they held in a third corporation, namely, 72 percent and 28 percent, respectively. To effect these proportionate stockholdings, it was necessary that, upon consolidation, taxpayer receive a note from the consolidated corporation. The IRS treated this note as a boot dividend taxable as ordinary income. *Held:* For taxpayer. In determining whether the value of the note should be taxed as a dividend under Section 356(a)(2), Section 302's redemption rules were used. According to them, the "redemption" should be deemed to have occurred between the taxpayer and the consolidated corporation. In other words, taxpayer should be treated as having received the amount of the consolidated corporation's stock he would have received if no note had been issued and he had received only stock. The amount of stock he actually received should then be compared with this hypothetical percentage. Using this analysis, taxpayer had a 23.3 percent reduction, causing his stock interest to drop from a possible 85 percent to 61.7 percent. This was a "meaningful reduction" in a state in which a two-thirds stockholder vote is necessary for a corporation's "extraordinary" acts. Wright, 482 F2d 600, 73-2 USTC ¶ 9583, 32 AFTR2d 73-5490 (8th Cir. 1973).

Boot disqualified a B reorganization. Taxpayer exchanged his stock for stock of another corporation plus $3 million in cash. He argued that the code and the regulations treat the exchanges as a B reorganization, recognizing gain only to the extent of the cash received as boot. The Tax Court agreed, noting that courts have so held and that the regulations seem to have concurred even to the extent of containing an illustration of a case like this. *Held:* Reversed. From a lengthy examination of legislative history, the court concluded that a B reorganization exists only if the exchange is solely for stock. The boot provisions have no application to a B reorganization. The exchange was fully taxable. Turnbow, 286 F2d 669, 61-1 USTC ¶ 9148, 7 AFTR2d 357 (9th Cir. 1960), aff'd, 368 US 337 (1962).

Certificates of contingent interest were stock, not boot, in merger. Taxpayer owned stock in two corporations that were merged into another corporation. Under the terms of the merger, the taxpayer received stock of the surviving corporation and certificates of contingent interest for additional stock of the surviving corporation. The certificates of contingent interest were issued because at the time of the merger, one of the corporations possessed two unresolved but potentially substantial liablities. One was its possible obligation for unsettled federal income and excess profits taxes for certain past taxable years. The other was litigation pending in a federal court in the state of Washington. The surviving corporation lacked complete information concerning these matters in the controversy, and, in order to protect its own stockholders, agreed that a certain number of shares of its common stock that would otherwise have been issued to the stockholders of the merging corporations would be set aside as reserve shares pending the determinination of those liablities, and that certificates of contingent interest would be issued in respect to the reserved shares. As the liabilities became fixed and expenses in connection with them incurred, the reserved shares where to be reduced monthly by charges computed according to a formula based on quoted values of common stock of the surviving corporation. After all deductions of this kind had been made, any remaining reserve shares were to be distributed to the then-holders of the certificates of contingent interest. The IRS conceded that the merger was a statutory merger for purposes of reorganization but argued that the certificates of contingent interest were other property, to be treated as boot under Section 356(a). *Held:* For taxpayer. The court held that the certificates of contingent interest were stock that came to taxpayer under Section 354(a)(1) without recognition of gain. According to the court, the purpose of the reorganization sections, the practical and realistic aspects of the situation, the precedent of the tax treatment of the fractional share, and the substance of the transactions, justified the conclusion that the certificates of contingent interest in this reorganization were stock within the meaning of Section 354(a)(1). Thus, the taxpayer did not have recognized income on receipt of the certificates of contingent interest. Carlberg, 281 F2d 507, 60-2 USTC ¶ 9647, 6 AFTR2d 5316 (8th Cir. 1960).

Cash received by stockholder in bank consolidation was ordinary income. Taxpayer owned 450 shares of stock in a trust company that consolidated with a national bank. To avoid unreasonably small fractional shares, the bank gave one share of its stock and $36 for each eight shares of trust company stock surrendered. Payment was made out of some $450,000 set aside by the national bank before the consolidation. The Court of Claims found that the transaction was a reorganization but that the cash was taxable as ordinary income. The distribution of $2,025 received by the taxpayer was, it found, essentially equivalent to a dividend. *Held:* Affirmed. It was immaterial whether the boot was paid out of the national bank funds or trust company funds. Because the purpose of the cash payment was to give trust company stockholders precisely the appraised value of their shares, the segregated $450,000 was in reality funds of the trust company. Taxpayer's argument that the payment was not essentially equivalent to a dividend because his proportionate interest was changed in the transaction was also without merit. Such changes are inherent in any statutory consolidation. Taxpayer had the same right to receive dividends and to share in the assets upon dissolution of the consolidated bank, as he would have had if the trust company had declared a dividend. Ross, 173 F. Supp. 793, 59-2 USTC ¶ 9493, 3 AFTR2d 1569 (Ct. Cl.), cert. denied, 361 US 875 (1959).

Liquidation found to be reorganization so that cash distribution was boot. P Corporation owned all the stock of X. In October 1965, P formed wholly owned subsidiary, Y. On July 1, 1966, X sold its operating assets to Y, and on July 7, 1966, a plan of liquidation regarding X was approved. X's remaining cash asset was distributed to P. The IRS contended that the cash distribution was taxable as a boot dividend, and taxpayer contended that this was a nontaxable liquidation pursuant to Section 332. *Held:* For the IRS. The sequence of events constituted a reorganization with the effect that Y was continuing the business of X. Therefore, taxability of the cash distribution was determined under Section 356(a)(2). Central Soya Co., 80-1 USTC ¶ 9367, 46 AFTR2d 80-5025 (ND Ind. 1980).

Spin-off treated as part of merger; gain recognized on distribution. Taxpayers were stockholders of a corporation that entered into a merger with another corporation. Taxpayers' corporation, in addition to its regular business, operated a warehouse business. The merging corporation was not interested in the warehouse. It was therefore transferred to a new corporation, and the stock of this new corporation was distributed to taxpayers. The merger was then consummated. *Held:* For the IRS. The court held that the distribution, which standing by itself would constitute a tax-free spin-off under Section 355, was boot received in the merger and was thus taxable. The court further held that in computing the gain, each separate block of stock was to be treated separately; it was not proper to aggregate all of the cost bases. Curtis, 215 F. Supp. 885, 63-1 USTC ¶ 9362 (ND Ohio 1963).

Savings accounts did not constitute boot in reorganization. A bank corporation, F, was merged into taxpayer bank corporation under Section 368(a)(1)(A). F gave each savings account holder one vote for each $100 in his or her account, each borrower one vote, and each guarantee stockholder one vote. Under state law, F's stockholders had a proportionate proprietary interest in F's net assets and earnings that was subordinate to the creditors' claims, but its account holders did not. Taxpayer's accounts did not have the indicia of ownership, that is, voting rights and the right to share in corporate assets upon liquidation, as did F. On the date of merger, all the savings accounts and guarantee stock held by F's members were converted into voting, withdrawable savings accounts in taxpayer. The IRS determined that the right to withdraw characterized the relationship of a former F stockholder with taxpayer as that of a creditor with a debtor and, consequently, constituted boot. *Held:* For taxpayer. Taxpayer's accounts were closer to equity than to debt and therefore did not constitute boot in the reorganization. The factors that made the accounts seem like stock included voting rights, proprietary interests granted by state law, the right to receive dividends that cannot be set at a fixed rate under state law, and the right to share, subordinate to the claims of the association's creditors, proportionately in the association's assets upon liquidation. Capital Sav. & Loan Ass'n, 607 F2d 970, 79-2 USTC ¶ 9648, 44 AFTR2d 79-5849 (Ct. Cl. 1979).

Stock warrants received in reorganization were boot, taxable as capital gain. Taxpayer was a stockholder in a corporation that was merged with another corporation. He exchanged his shares of common stock in the old corporation for common stock and stock purchase warrants in the new corporation. The warrants, which were traded on an exchange, had a fair market value even though the price that the warrant holder had to pay for a share of stock in the new corporation exceeded the value of a share of such stock on the reorganization. Taxpayer did not report the value of the warrants as income, claiming that they were stock received in a tax-free exchange under Section 354(a)(1). The IRS assessed the value of the warrants as ordinary income under Section 356(a)(2) as having the effect of a dividend. *Held:* For taxpayer. The Tax Court held that the warrants were taxable, but as capital gains. The warrants did not constitute stock under *Southwest Consol. Corp.*, 315 US 194 (1941). However as boot, they had none of the characteristics of a dividend distribution. Nothing was distributed out of either of the corporations; the only thing obtained was the right to buy stock at a price higher than its then market value. The leading case, *Bedford's Estate*, 325 US 283 (1945), was distinguished as involving cash. *Bateman*, 40 TC 408 (1963), nonacq. 1965-2 CB 7.

Court looks to earnings of both corporations for "boot" dividend in asset sale and liquidation that it held to be a reorganization. Capital Sales, Inc. sold its operating assets to another corporation and liquidated and distributed cash and stock to its stockholders. The cash and stock were distributed to the stockholders in proportion to their ownership interest in Capital Sales. The same three stockholders, including taxpayer, owned 94 percent of Capital Sales and 98 percent of the corporation purchasing its assets. The Court of Appeals determined that the sale and liquidation constituted a Section 368 reorganization. *Held:* For the IRS. Because the distribution was pro rata to the stockholders, the distribution was a boot dividend under Section 356(a)(2). The court, in determining the amount of the dividend, looked to the earnings of both corporations because of the *Golsen* rule. *Simon*, 43 TCM 269, ¶ 82,006 P-H Memo. TC (1982).

Business Purpose

Merger of brother-sister corporation was for valid business purpose. *A* and *B* were brother-sister corporations owned entirely by individual *I*. *A* became insolvent and subsequently entered into a merger transaction with *B*. Some of *A*'s assets were immediately sold to a former employee; later, the remaining assets were sold. The IRS and the Tax Court held that the merger was not a valid reorganization because it lacked a business purpose and continuity. *Held:* Reversed. The potential bankruptcy of *A* might have reflected on both *B*'s and *I*'s business reputation. The later sale of *A*'s remaining assets was not part of the merger transaction. *Laure*, 653 F2d 253, 48 AFTR2d 81-5354 (6th Cir.), rehearing denied, 81-2 USTC ¶ 9517 (1981).

Tax-free spin-off denied where there was no bona fide business reason for the reorganization. Taxpayers operated a furniture store business as *W* Corporation. *P* was formed, and *W*'s conditional sales contracts from furniture sales were transferred to *P*. Then, $69,020 of *P's* stock was distributed to each taxpayer, and the accumulated earnings and profits at the time was $48,889. The Tax Court agreed with the taxpayers that the event was a tax-free spin-off although the court found none of the three business reasons given for the spin-off to be valid. *Held:* Reversed. Because there was no valid business purpose for the reorganization, Section 355 was inapplicable, even though there was no tax-avoidance motive. Accordingly, a gain was recognized on the distributions to the stockholders. *Wilson*, 353 F2d 184, 66-1 USTC ¶ 9103 (9th Cir. 1965).

Business division was not tax-free Section 355 transaction. *B*, a closely held family corporation, was engaged in three interrelated businesses. Two new corporate entities, *C* and *D*, were formed with the same stockholders as *B*. Each received certain assets from *B* constituting one of the three enterprises. The IRS contended that the receipt of the stock of *C* and *D* corporations constituted a taxable distribution of corporate property to the stockholders. Taxpayer argued that this was a tax-free distribution pursuant to Section 355. *Held:* For the IRS. The real estate business of *C* was found not to be a separate active business, as required by Regulation § 1.355-1(c)(2), since most of the property involved was leased to a sister corporation. The device was found to be an inefficient method of avoiding stockholder conflict and insulating corporate liability, and therefore the "valid business purpose" rule of Section 355 was not met. Gada, 460 F. Supp. 859, 78-2 USTC ¶ 9739, 42 AFTR2d 78-6148 (D. Conn. 1978).

Taxpayer's transfer of stock was a step to reorganization, distribution taxable as dividends. Taxpayer transferred his stock in an old corporation to a new corporation in a transaction in which he received the same proportion of the amount paid by the new corporation as his stock bore to the total stock of the old corporation, reporting a capital gain. The IRS determined that the transaction was an F reorganization and that ordinary income resulted to the extent of the earnings and profits of the old corporation. *Held:* For the IRS. The circumstances of the sale showed it to be void of substance since there was no business purpose in the transaction. Consequently, the distribution to taxpayer with respect to his stock was taxable as ordinary income to the extent of the old corporation's earnings and profit. Nutil, 68-2 USTC ¶ 9583 (CD Cal. 1968).

Spin-off of corporation served sound business purpose. Taxpayer and his brothers owned several stores in Cleveland and Buffalo. In order to prevent labor difficulties with its Cleveland stores from affecting its Buffalo operations, it spun off the stock of the Buffalo store to taxpayer and his brothers. *Held:* For taxpayer. The distribution was not a dividend because it served a valid business purpose. Transfer of the spun-off shares to a trust for stockholders' wives did not warrant the conclusion that the distribution was a device to distribute earnings and profits. Olson, 48 TC 855, 49 TC 84 (1967), acq. 1969-1 CB 171.

Depreciation and losses on equipment acquired from related corporation disallowed for lack of business purpose. Taxpayer corporation operated a profitable business of selling a preventive against the corrosion of steel. Taxpayer's controlling stockholder also owned all the stock of a second corporation that had contracted to apply the preventive material. Because of uncertainties in developing offshore drilling, the second corporation was left with a substantial amount of equipment and no work while taxpayer continued in business through the sale of other products. Taxpayer purchased the equipment of the second corporation, assumed its debts, and cancelled the inter-company obligations. The price paid for the equipment was in excess of its fair market value. The equipment was later sold at a loss by taxpayer. The IRS disallowed deductions for depreciation and losses on the sale of this equipment. *Held:* For the IRS. The transfer of the equipment was designed to result in tax benefits to taxpayer. Had the transfer been a bona fide transaction, the price of the equipment would have been fair market price. Bywater Sales & Serv. Co., 24 TCM 849, ¶ 65,160 P-H Memo. TC (1965).

Retaining services of key employee ruled valid business purpose under Section 355. A key employee threatened to leave taxpayer's company, Division II, if he were not offered the opportunity to acquire a controlling interest in that business. Because the employee lacked the funds to acquire the necessary additional stock, taxpayer transferred the business the employee was involved in to a new corporation in exchange for all of its stock, and distributed stock constituting a controlling interest in the new corporation to the employee in exchange for all of his stock in taxpayer's company. The IRS ruled that the distribution of stock of the new corporation was supported by a valid business purpose within the meaning of Regulation § 1.355-2(c) because it was designed to retain the services of a key employee. Rev. Rul. 85-127, 1985-33 IRB 8.

Business purpose requirement of Section 355 met if distribution effected pursuant to advice of underwriter. Taxpayer was a closely held corporation that owned and operated a profitable golf and tennis resort in one state and also owned the stock of the subsidiary that owned and operated an unprofitable ski resort in another state. Taxpayer sought to raise additional working capital by issuing debentures. On an underwriter's advice, taxpayer decided to divest itself completely of its subsidiary by distributing the subsidiary's stock to its stockholders. The IRS ruled that the distribution satisfied the business purpose requirement of Regulation § 1.335-2(c) because it was the result of a recommendation of an independent, experienced underwriter who had advised that any relationship between taxpayer and its subsidiary would have an adverse impact on the issuance of the debentures. Rev. Rul. 85-122, 1985-32 IRB 7.

Business purpose under Section 355. The IRS held that the business purpose requirement of Regulation § 1.355-2(c) was met when a Section 355 reorganization was undertaken following the advice of underwriters that a computer technology parent could not "go public" unless it divested itself of a real estate subsidiary. Rev. Rul. 82-130, 1982-2 CB 83.

Desire to make a subsidiary's stock more attractive as consideration in an asset acquisition suffices as business purpose for a Section 355 distribution. X, a public corporation actively engaged in the construction materials production business, owned all the stock of Y, which was engaged in the television broadcasting business. Y desired to acquire the television broadcasting properties of Z, an unrelated corporation. However, Z's management did not want to accept Y's stock as consideration, since Y was controlled by a company not engaged in or identified with the broadcast business. X made a Section 355 distribution of Y stock to its stockholders. The IRS ruled that this satisfied the business purpose requirement of Regulation § 1.355-2(c). Rev. Rul. 76-527, 1976-2 CB 103.

Stock distribution to reduce state and local taxes met business purpose requirement of Regulation § 1.355-2(c). P Corporation was acquired by N Corporation, a newly formed holding company. P's stockholders transferred their stock to N in exchange for N stock. Subsequent to the above transaction, P distributed all of the stock of S, its wholly owned subsidiary, to N. This transaction was necessary under state law to avoid a double payment of a subsidiary capital tax on the value of S. Because of this, the IRS held that the business purpose test of Regulation § 1.355-2(c) was met, and the distribution was not taxable to N under Section 355(a)(1). Rev. Rul. 76-187, 1976-1 CB 97.

Distribution of stock to prevent nationalization met business purpose requirements of Section 355. In order to minimize the effect of nationalization in its country of incorporation, a foreign subsidiary transferred some of its assets to a newly formed subsidiary in another foreign country in exchange for all the stock of the new subsidiary. This stock was immediately distributed to the domestic parent corporation. Both the initial transfer of assets and the subsequent distribution of stock were held to be germane to the business of the corporations because of imminent nationalization. Therefore, the initial transfer of assets constituted a reorganization under Section 368, and the distribution of stock was not taxable to the parent under Section 355. Rev. Rul. 76-13, 1976-1 CB 96.

Spin-off of a car rental business held nontaxable because supported by sufficient business purpose. A corporation holding an auto dealership franchise was 53 percent owned by a 70-year-old individual. The corporation had a subsidiary that operated an auto rental business. The majority stockholder of the corporation had several daughters, only some of whom were active in the dealership. The auto company required that either the manager of the dealership be a majority stockholder or that all stockholders be active. The aging manager could satisfy the franchise requirements in case of his death and the business purpose test of Regulation § 1.355-2(c) if the corporation distributed its subsidiary's stock to him and his inactive daughters in exchange for their stock in the dealership corporation. Rev. Rul. 75-337, 1975-2 CB 124.

IRS ruling illustrates application of "business purpose" requirements in various factual contexts. The IRS issued a ruling illustrating the application of the business purpose requirement prescribed by Regulation § 1.355-2(c) as it affects a distribution of stock of a controlled corporation that otherwise qualifies under Section 355. In one of the situations presented, the corporation had been engaged in business as a liquor wholesaler for five years. The stock of X was owned equally by A (president) and B (general manager), who were unrelated to each other. Serious disputes between A and B concerning expansion, marketing channels, and discount policy had created a situation in which the parties were so antagonistic that the normal operations of the business were seriously affected. It was therefore proposed that 50 percent of the operating assets and liabilities relating thereto be transferred to Y Corporation in exchange for all the stock of Y, followed by the distribution of the Y stock to B, solely in exchange for the surrender by B of all of his X stock. The IRS held that the non-pro rata distribution was undertaken for reasons germane to corporate business problems and was necessary for the future conduct of the business. Therefore, the business purpose requirement as set forth in Regulation § 1.355-2(c) was satisfied. Rev. Rul. 69-460, 1969-2 CB 51.

IRS discussed the extent to which it will follow the decision in *Mary Archer W. Morris Trust* case. The IRS stated that it will follow the decision in Mary Archer W. Morris Trust, 367 F2d 794 (1966), to the extent it holds that (1) the active business requirements of Section 355(b)(1)(A) were satisfied even though the distributing corporation, immediately after the spin-off, merged into another corporation, (2) the control requirement of Section 368(a)(1)(D) implies no limitation on a reorganization of the transferor corporation after the distribution of stock of the transferee corporation, and (3) there was a business purpose for the spin-off and merger. Rev. Rul. 68-603, 1968-2 CB 148.

Carry-Over of Net Operating Losses and Other Tax Attributes

Tax Court held triangular reorganization between a shell subsidiary, and active transferor qualifies as an F reorganization. In 1968, taxpayer was formed as a shell subsidiary of Beverly Enterprises. It remained a shell until 1970, when, by means of a triangular merger, it acquired the assets of another corporation. After the merger, taxpayer suffered a loss that it sought to carry back against the acquired corporation's premerger income. The Tax Court held for the IRS in denying this carry-back. *Held:* Reversed. The main issue presented was whether, under the carry-back rules, a shell transferor in a triangular merger can carry back postmerger losses against the transferor's premerger income. The policies underlying Section 381 were not violated by permitting a carry-back under the above facts. First, the mere fact that the transferee's stockholders after the merger held stock in the transferor's parent did not present a finding that an F reorganization occurred. Furthermore, the reorganization did not change the transferor's business. In fact, it was the same business that produced the loss sought to be carried back that produced the income intended to be offset by the carry-back. Bercy Indus., Inc., 640 F2d 1058, 81-1 USTC ¶ 9303, 47 AFTR2d 81-1200 (9th Cir. 1981).

Carry-back from postreorganization year allowed. The IRS sought a rehearing in order to deny the carry-back of postreorganization net operating losses against prereorganization income. *Held:* Rehearing denied. The reorganization was found to be an F reorganization and therefore Section 381(b)(3) did not bar the carry-back. Aetna Casualty & Sur. Co., 568 F2d 811, 77-1 USTC ¶ 9120, 39 AFTR2d 77-400 (2d Cir. 1977).

Lack of continuity of business enterprise resulted in denial of acquiring corporation's deduction of target corporation's net operating losses. Payment of target's debts did not result in bad debt deductions. Taxpayer acquired the target corporation from taxpayer's stockholders. At the time of the acquisition, the target had ceased business operations and was not in a strong financial position. After acquisition, taxpayer did not attempt to resurrect the target's business. It did, however, make payments on certain of the target's debts, namely, debts for which their once common stockholders were guarantors. Taxpayer claimed a net operating loss deduction for the target's net operating losses under the Code's reorganization provisions. *Held:* For the IRS. Because the target's business had ceased at

REORGANIZATIONS: Carry-Over of Net Operating Losses

the time of the acquisition and was not resurrected by taxpayer (i.e., no continuity-of-business enterprise), there was no C reorganization (nor any other tax-free reorganization). Accordingly, taxpayer could not use the Code's reorganization provisions to deduct the target's net operating losses. Furthermore, taxpayer was not under legal obligation to pay the target's creditors, and therefore the payments do not give rise to bad debt deductions. In fact, these payments were constructive dividends to its stockholders, who were relieved of their guarantor liability by reason of such payments. Wortham Mach. Co., 521 F2d 160, 75-2 USTC ¶ 9665, 36 AFTR2d 75-5607 (10th Cir. 1975).

Section 382(b)'s continuity-of-interest provision did not automatically bar the transferee's use of transferor's losses after a nonliquidating C reorganization. Taxpayer acquired, in a transaction qualifying as a C reorganization, all the operating assets of X Corporation in exchange for 23.6 percent of taxpayer's stock. X did not distribute taxpayer's stock to its stockholders and continued as a holding company to retain a significant voice in taxpayer's operations. Y Corporation had substantial losses that taxpayer used, according to Section 581, to offset its income. The IRS asserted that under Section 382(b), such losses were unavailable to taxpayer because X did not distribute taxpayer's stock. The essence of the IRS' position was that Section 382(b) requires that for an acquired corporation's losses to be usable, the loss corporation's stockholders directly hold stock in the acquiring corporation. *Held:* For taxpayer. Section 382(b)'s reference to "stockholders of the loss corporation" should not be read literally, but in light of the general concept of continuity of interest. Because it is clear that there was sufficient continuity of interest to support a valid C reorganization, even though the transferor did not distribute the transferee's stock, there was no reason to require a greater degree of continuity of interest under Section 382(b). World Serv. Life Ins. Co., 471 F2d 247, 73-1 USTC ¶ 9162, 31 AFTR2d 73-594 (8th Cir. 1973).

Loss carry-back from single corporation to premerger multiple entities was allowed. The IRS disallowed the NOL carryback of taxpayer corporation to the consolidated premerger profits of its predecessor corporations; there were 123 corporations that had merged into taxpayer corporation. The IRS' contention was that such merger was not a mere change in identity, form, or place of organization. The district court held that in substance the merger was an F reorganization and, therefore, postmerger losses could be carried back to premerger years in accordance with Section 381(b). *Held:* Affirmed. Taxpayer corporation, in accordance with Libson Shops, 353 US 382 (1957), took advanatage of the carry-back to the extent that it did not obtain any more favorable tax treatment than it would have received had the loss occurred under the business's premerger form. The current corporate vehicle was merely the alter ego of the former 123 corporations. Home Constr. Corp. of Am., 439 F2d 1165, 71-1 USTC ¶ 9267, 27 AFTR2d 71-837 (5th Cir. 1971).

Premerger loss carry-overs apportioned between taxpayer and its subsidiaries. Taxpayer corporation acquired stock of a loss corporation, which was subsequently merged into taxpayer corporation. Some of the loss corporation's assets were placed in operating subsidiaries of taxpayer corporation. The IRS disallowed the net operating loss carry-over because the loss corporation's assets were divided among taxpayer corporation and its subsidiaries; therefore it was not possible for taxpayer corporation as the acquirer to continue in "substantially the same business" as required under Libson Shops, 353 US 382 (1957). The district court held for taxpayer corporation. *Held:* Affirmed. The court allocated the carry-over to taxpayer corporation and its subsidiaries in proportion to the income earned by each from continuation of the premerger business. The court based its holding on grounds that substance prevails over form. Amherst Coal Co., 71-1 USTC ¶ 9223, 27 AFTR2d 71-460 (4th Cir. 1971).

Failure to comply with statute in merger caused reduction of net operating loss carry-

REORGANIZATIONS: *Carry-Over of Net Operating Losses*

over. Members of a family owned 900 of the 1200 shares of a profit corporation and all 180 shares of a loss corporation. An employee owned the remaining 300 shares of the profit corporation, subject to a buy-sell agreement in favor of the corporation or the other stockholders. The stockholders merged the loss corporation into the profit corporation, issuing one share of the profit corporation for each share of the loss corporation. As a result of the merger, holders of shares in the loss corporation held 13 percent (180/1380) of the shares of the merged corporation. Although the employee's interest in the merged corporation fell to 21.74 percent (300/1380), under an amendment to the buy-sell agreement, the employee was to receive 25 percent of the value of the merged corporation, excluding the value of the loss corporation, on a sale. The Tax Court, strictly interpreting Section 382(b)(1), held that the merged corporation could carry over only 65 percent of the net operating loss. Only the shares that the stockholders of the loss corporation received as a result of the merger, and not the shares of the profit corporation, which they had previously owned, could qualify in the 20 percent test. Since the employee owned 25 percent of the stock of the merged corporation but had owned no interest in the loss corporation, the court concluded the two corporations were not owned "substantially by the same persons in the same proportions" as required by Section 382(b)(3). *Held:* Affirmed. Taxpayer (the merged corporation) did not show that the employee's shares differed in value from those held by the other stockholders. Commonwealth Container Corp., 393 F2d 269, 68-1 USTC ¶ 9319, 21 AFTR2d 1062 (3d Cir. 1968).

Carry-forward of premerger losses denied. Taxpayer and a sister corporation operated textile mills. Taxpayer's mill in North Carolina operated at a loss, and the mill of the sister corporation in Virginia operated at a profit. All designing, management, and recordkeeping emanated from central headquarters in New York. By 1953, taxpayer was heavily indebted to a bank and had defaulted in a working capital requirement. Negotiations with the bank resulted in a plan of reorganization providing for the merger of the sister corporation with taxpayer. Pursuant to this plan, taxpayer acquired the Virginia mill in exchange for stock. In 1954, taxpayer closed the mill in North Carolina and transferred all orders to the Virginia mill. Taxpayer deducted the net operating losses of the North Carolina mill on its 1957, 1958, and 1959 returns. The IRS denied the deductions. *Held:* For the IRS. The deductions were denied on the authority of *Libson Shops*. The two mills constituted separated businessses even though the operations were almost identical and control was centralized. The losses of one could not be applied against the gains of the other. This situation was similar to that in Garfinckel, 335 F2d 744 (1964). Rev. Rul. 63-40 was not applicable because the case did not involve the purchase of an unrelated corporation. Frank Ix & Sons Va. Corp., 45 TC 532, aff'd, 375 F2d 867, 67-1 USTC ¶ 9369 (3d Cir.), cert. denied, 389 US 900 (1967).

Carry-over of net operating loss for "revived corporation" disallowed. Taxpayer corporation was sales agent for a related corporation. Both corporations were bought in 1958 by a competitor. The competitor paid $10 for taxpayer's stock and kept taxpayer alive, although inactive. In 1960, taxpayer resumed operations as a sales agent for the related corporation and deducted prior net operating losses against its income. The IRS contended that, because of its inactivity, taxpayer was not carrying on the same trade or business and denied the carry-over deduction under Section 382. The Tax Court overruled, however, reasoning that inactivity of a corporation for a short time followed by a resumption of the same type of business meets the business continuity requirement. *Held:* Reversed. The statute requires both that the nature of the business not be changed and that operations continue despite the change of ownership. Section 382 provides that only purchasers who intended to carry on the business and use the loss deduction and who, therefore, presumably compensated the persons who suffered the loss can obtain the deduction. Here, during 1958, following the purchase, and during 1959, taxpayer did not continue to carry on the same business it was engaged in before the stock purchase. Barclay Jewelry Inc., 367 F2d 193, 66-2 USTC ¶ 9704 (1st Cir. 1966).

Loss corporation was inactive; loss not carried over by purchaser. In 1955, taxpayer acquired the stock of a corporation with a large net operating loss carry-over. The losses had been incurred in lead and zinc mining. During 1953 and 1954, the loss corporation had some income from equipment sales, but conducted no regular business. It had filed articles of dissolution before the purchase of stock, but taxpayer kept it alive as a subsidiary for several years before liquidating. The IRS contended that the loss corporation was inactive and that taxpayer did not continue the previous business, causing the disallowance of the carry-over under Section 382(a). The jury in the district court allowed the carry-over. *Held:* Reversed. The evidence was clear that the loss corporation had abandoned the mining business and had no active business at the time of the purchase of stock by taxpayer. Fenix & Scisson, Inc., 360 F2d 260, 66-1 USTC ¶ 9407, 17 AFTR2d 996 (10th Cir. 1966), cert. denied, 386 US 1036 (1967).

Brewery loss carry-over denied after merger with construction equipment company. A brewery corporation ceased operations after many years and sold all of its property except real estate that could not be sold at a suitable price. The corporation had substantial losses in its last years of brewery operations and small losses in the three years that it rented the real estate. Taxpayer was a profitable corporation selling construction equipment. Its land was about to be condemned, and through a series of intricate steps it merged with the brewery. Taxpayer deducted the loss carry-over of the brewery. The Tax Court denied the deduction, finding that there was a "substantial change" in the business conducted by the loss corporation after the change in stock ownership, so that Section 382 applied. *Held:* Affirmed. Since the real business of the loss corporation was its brewery operations, not the renting of real estate, this was not a case of continuing the old business and "adding" a new line. In any case, the rental income was only 1 percent of taxpayer's gross income, which was not "substantial." Euclid-Tennessee, Inc., 352 F2d 991, 65-2 USTC ¶ 9763, 16 AFTR2d 6003 (6th Cir. 1965), cert. denied, 384 US 940 (1966).

Section 269 used to bar postacquisition loss carry-over; sale of loss corporation's notes disguised dividend. Arlington corporation suffered substantial net operating losses in 1955 and 1957 in its machine shop business and was virtually insolvent. Its sole owner was interested in selling Arlington because he did not want to be connected with a bankruptcy. In 1956, taxpayers, stockholders in two of Arlington's creditors, *M* and *I* Corporations, bought the Arlington stock and all the outstanding notes held by creditors and continued to operate Arlington unsuccessfully for about a year. After that time, Arlington, then a corporate shell, acquired the assets of *M* and *I* in exchange for shares of its own stock, changed its name and place of business, and thereafter carried on only steel distribution, the business theretofore carried by *M* and *I*. Arlington, now called Interstate, claimed a net operating loss carry-over deduction in 1958 for its 1955 and 1957 losses. The Tax Court denied both the premerger and the postmerger carry-over losses under Section 269. In addition, it held that the proceeds from the taxpayer's sale of the Arlington notes constituted ordinary income, not capital gain. The acquisition of the notes was in reality an equity investment. Neither the sale of the notes nor the payments of any of the amounts due thereon would have been possible except for the merger whereby the assets of *M* and *I* were made subject to the payment thereof. Thus, the purported sale of the notes by taxpayer was in reality a distribution of earnings of *M* and *I* in the nature of a dividend. *Held:* Affirmed. The Tax Court's findings were not clearly erroneous. Its application of Section 269 to postacquisition losses was supported by legislative history. Taxpayers realized in advance of the purchase that they would have to continue to operate Arlington in order to avoid the change of stock ownership provision of Section 382 and thus benefit by the loss carry-over. Furthermore, the acquisition of the outstanding notes also was a necessary incident of the scheme. Denial of capital gains treatment on the sale of the notes was proper; and as the purchase of the notes was in reality part of taxpayer's investment in Arlington, disallowance of the purchase price in computing the gain also was proper. Finally, as Section 269 provides for a mandatory disallowance of a tax benefit, the IRS' failure to assert it in its notice of deficiency was not fatal. Luke, 351 F2d 568, 65-2 USTC ¶ 9686, 16 AFTR2d 5738 (7th Cir. 1965).

Premerger losses not available as carry-overs to surviving corporation's other business units. Taxpayer operated a department store at a loss, and late in 1953 merged with another department store corporation. In 1956, two more corporations were merged into taxpayer. On its 1955 return, taxpayer claimed net operating loss carry-overs from 1951 and 1952; in its 1957 return taxpayer claimed carry-overs from 1952, 1954, and 1956. The Tax Court applied *Libson Shops* and disallowed the premerger losses for 1952 and 1954. *Held:* Affirmed. The Second Circuit found that only the carry-over from 1956 was allowable. All the other carry-overs were governed by the 1939 Code and the reasoning of *Libson Shops*. Since the losses, including those of 1954, were sustained prior to the merger, such premerger losses were only available against income from the same business that incurred the losses. They could not be used to offset postmerger income of other units in the surviving corporation. Allied Cent. Stores, Inc., 339 F2d 503, 65-1 USTC ¶ 9493, 14 AFTR2d 6112 (2d Cir.), cert. denied, 381 US 903 (1965).

Net operating loss carry-over disallowed where stock owned by new group. Taxpayer corporation, which operated a cement tile roofing business on the East Coast, showed net operating losses in 1950, 1951, and 1952. In 1953, taxpayer merged with another corporation in the same line of business, with taxpayer emerging as the surviving corporation. All the old stockholders of taxpayer sold their interests to a new group of stockholders, and substantially all of taxpayer's assets were transferred to the new group. The new corporation operated in the Midwest. *Held:* For the IRS. The Tax Court's holding that taxpayer could not offset the prior net operating loss against income of 1953 through 1956 was affirmed. The new corporation did not operate substantially the same business as its predecessor. An entirely new group owned the stock of the new corporation, and that new corporation operated in a different part of the country. Hence, the requisite continuity of business enterprise was lacking. The appellate court also disallowed a loss on the sale of assets to the old stockholders; the sale was arranged before the sale of their stock, so they were then effectively in control. Federal Cement Tile Co., 338 F2d 691, 64-2 USTC ¶ 9803, 14 AFTR2d 5803 (7th Cir. 1964).

Merged corporation could offset postmerger losses against prior income. Taxpayer corporation and its subsidiary merged in a transaction that qualified as both a merger and a liquidation of a subsidiary. Taxpayer carried back postmerger losses to offset the subsidiary's premerger income. The IRS disallowed the carry-back. *Held:* For taxpayer. The merger was an F reorganization because it involved a mere change of form and identity. Therefore, the tax attributes carried over and the surviving corporation's postmerger losses could be offset against the subsidiary's premerger income. The fact that the merger also met Section 332 parent-subsidiary liquidation standards did not preclude relief to the resulting corporation. Thus, the net operating loss carry-back was allowed. Charles C. Chapman Bldg. Co., 74-2 USTC ¶ 9813, 34 AFTR2d 74-6193 (CD Cal. 1974).

Net operating loss was fully deductible by successor corporation. Pursuant to a C reorganization, taxpayer acquired the assets of X Corporation in exchange for 24 percent of the fair market value of taxpayer's shares. Instead of a direct distribution to the X stockholders, the stockholders chose to have a successor corporation to X hold the shares received from taxpayer. The IRS contended that taxpayer could not deduct X's net operating loss carry-over. *Held:* For taxpayer. The former stockholders of X owned more than 20 percent of taxpayer. Despite Regulation § 1.382(b)-1(a)(2), it was not necessary for the

REORGANIZATIONS: Carry-Over of Net Operating Losses

shares of taxpayer to be distributed by X directly to its stockholders on an individual basis. World Service Life Ins. Co., 471 F2d 247, 73-1 USTC ¶ 9162, 31 AFTR2d 73-594 (8th Cir. 1973).

Taxpayer that acquired property in a Section 381 transfer not entitled to a carry-back of a net operating loss against premerger income of the acquired corporation. BC, Inc. had modest profits for taxable years ending in 1957, 1958, and 1959, but a loss in its taxable year ending in 1960. During the year, taxpayer purchased all its stock and subsequently acquired all its assets in exchange and cancellation therefor. During the following year, taxpayer was evicted from the premises and sustained a substantial loss and sought to carry back against the premerger profits of the acquired corporation the losses of both the acquisition year and its own year following acquisition. The IRS disallowed the carryback. *Held:* For the IRS. Taxpayer was a corporation acquiring property in a transfer or distribution to which Section 381 generally applies. Section 381(b)(3) expressly forbade the carry-back of taxpayer's loss in the year following acquisition, and the loss for the year of acquisition fared no better. Ebbets Lanes, Inc., 68-2 USTC ¶ 9498 (EDNY 1968).

Acquisition of stock of dissatisfied stockholders was good business purpose; net operating loss carry-over allowed. Three principal groups of stockholders owned the stock of taxpayer corporation. After losses of $503,000 in two years of operation, two of the groups became dissatisfied with the operations of the company, and under pressure of these groups, taxpayer acquired their stock. *Held:* For taxpayer. Taxpayer was entitled to carry over its operating losses. The limitations under Section 382 were not applicable, since taxpayer carried on the same business after the acquisition. Nor was Section 269 applicable, since there was a good business purpose for the acquisition and the purpose was not tax evasion or avoidance. Residential Developers, Inc., 63-2 USTC ¶ 9700 (ED La. 1963).

Net operating loss disallowed where merged loss corporation was a mere shell. Prior to its merger with two other corporations, taxpayer was a mere corporate shell that had nothing other than a net operating loss accumulation. *Held:* For the IRS. The court found that the inclusion of taxpayer in the merger was a sham since it had been de facto dissolved prior to the merger. The utilization of its net operating loss, rather than any valid business purpose, was the sole reason for its inclusion. Continental Sales & Enters., Inc., 63-2 USTC ¶ 9506 (ND Ill. 1963).

Obligation assumed fully deductible despite partial reimbursement from owners of the transferor corporation. Taxpayer corporation acquired X and Y corporations in a tax-free merger. Taxpayer subsequently deducted $234,297 in connection with the settlement of a contract claim of a former officer of X. However, the IRS stated that X was not entitled to such deduction to the extent of $171,512, such amount having been reimbursed to taxpayer by previous owners of X and Y under an indemnification agreement executed prior to the effective date of the merger. Section 381(c)(16) bars an otherwise allowable deduction where a corporation is reimbursed for such amount, and the reimbursement obligation is reflected in the consideration transferred. *Held:* For taxpayer. The regulations indicate that a deduction that is barred by Section 381(c)(16) because consideration has been received for it would be allowable under Section 381(c)(4), which deals with continuation of a transferor's method of accounting. Therefore, the entire $234,297 was deductible. VCA Corp., 77-2 USTC ¶ 9736, 40 AFTR2d 77-6047 (Ct. Cl. 1977).

Merger with subsidiary qualified as F reorganization. Color was a wholly owned subsidiary of taxpayer. Color was merged into taxpayer in order to simplify bookkeeping and administration. After the merger, there was continuity of interest on the part of taxpayer's stockholders, and there were no changes in the operation of either business. During the taxable year 1969, taxpayer incurred a net operating loss of approximately $3.8 million,

REORGANIZATIONS: *Carry-Over of Net Operating Losses*

of which $3.3 million was incurred with respect to the conduct of the business acquired from Color. Taxpayer, as successor to Color, claimed a refund of the 1966 income tax of $954,849, paid by Color, by a carry-back to Color's 1966 taxable year of the postmerger $3.3 million net operating loss. Taxpayer contended that the merger with its 100 percent-owned subsidiary qualified as an F reorganization, thereby entitling taxpayer to carry back a postmerger net operating loss to premerger taxable years of its subsidiary. The IRS determined that the merger of the two operating companies could not be an F reorganization and disallowed the carry-backs. *Held:* For taxpayer. Because the merger met the F reorganization definition, it was immaterial that the merger also came within the Section 332 parent-subsidiary liquidation definition. Because the merger met the F reorganization definition, the carry-back of postmerger losses was proper. Movielab, Inc., 494 F2d 693, 74-1 USTC ¶ 9309, 33 AFTR2d 74-905 (Ct. Cl. 1974).

Deficit in earnings and profits did not survive recapitalization under bankruptcy proceeding. Taxpayer received distributions from a corporation that had previously undergone a bankruptcy reorganization and had a large deficit. As a result of the reorganization, the interests of the old stockholders were eliminated, and the bondholders were given an equity interest. The corporation had sufficient accumulated earnings and profits from the date of reorganization to pay a taxable dividend. Taxpayer contended that the prior deficit survived the reorganization and that, therefore, the distributions were a return of capital. *Held:* For the IRS. The dividend was taxable. The elimination of the old stockholders' interests and the cancellation of the old indebtedness worked fundamental changes in the corporation, including the elimination of the deficit. The effective date for the recapitalization was at the time the reorganization plan was approved, not the date when the proceedings began. McCullough, 344 F2d 383, 65-1 USTC ¶ 9359, 15 AFTR2d 726 (Ct. Cl.), cert. denied, 382 US 901 (1965).

Suspension of business for over four years killed continuity; net operating loss denied. Taxpayer, a slaughterhouse and meat packing corporation, ceased operation on account of large operating losses. It did not resume the slaughterhouse business until nearly five years later, when it was bought by the present owner in 1957. During this period, taxpayer's sole activities consisted of leasing its buildings. The present owner bought 10 percent of taxpayer's outstanding stock under a sales agreement, which provided that the remaining shares would be subject to an escrow agreement. Under the escrow agreement, the remaining 90 percent of the stock was placed in a state of suspended animation and would eventually become treasury stock. Taxpayer carried over net operating losses from years prior to the suspension to 1957. The IRS disallowed the carry-over on the grounds that there was no continuity of business. *Held:* For the IRS. Taxpayer was barred by Section 382(a) from carrying over net operating losses to 1957. The present owner owned no stock at the beginning of 1957 or 1956 and owned all of the outstanding stock at the end of 1957. It seemed that a temporary break would not destroy the continuity required by the statute. But the hiatus here was between four and five years. Thus, operations under the present owner could not be considered a continuation of the business that had been discontinued for the above period. It was the inauguration of a new business of the same kind. Glover Packing Co. of Tex., 328 F2d 342, 64-1 USTC ¶ 9249 (Ct. Cl. 1964).

No amortizable discount generated where exchange of debentures for stock constituted a recapitalization. Taxpayer exchanged 12 percent debentures due in 1994 for about 11 percent of its outstanding capital stock. The excess of the principal amount of the debentures over the market value of the acquired stock amounted to $540,573, the discount amount. Following the exchange, taxpayer claimed deductions for the amortization of the discount amount for the remainder of 1974 and for subsequent years. The IRS determined that the debentures were issued as part of a reorganization in the form of recapitalization and that their issue price equalled

REORGANIZATIONS: Carry-Over of Net Operating Losses

their redemption price. *Held:* For the IRS. The exchange of debentures for common stock was a recapitalization, since the exchange of debentures for 11 percent of the outstanding stock constituted a significant enough shift of funds within the corporate structure to qualify as a recapitalization. Since the exchange constituted a reorganization, it did not produce the original issue discount. Golden Nugget, Inc., 83 TC 28 (1984).

Postreorganization operating loss could not be carried back to prereorganizational tax year. On December 26, 1974, *S*, taxpayer's subsidiary, merged with and into taxpayer in a qualified F reorganization. Taxpayer and its affiliates sustained a consolidated net operating loss for the tax year ended December 28, 1974, none of which was attributable to the business formerly operated by the subsidiary. Taxpayer claimed a refund based on the carry-back of the postreorganizational loss to a prereorganization (separate tax return) year of the subsidiary. The IRS disallowed the carry-back. *Held:* For the IRS. The availability of a carry-back of a postreorganization net operating loss to a prereorganization year of the transferor corporation is limited to those instances where the loss in question is generated by a separate business activity formerly operated by the transferor corporation. Since no part of the 1974 net operating loss of the consolidated group was attributable to the business formerly operated by the transferor, the IRS properly disallowed the claimed carry-back. A loss-tracing requirement as a condition to a loss carry-back in connection with an F reorganization is proper. National Tea Co. & Consol. Subsidiaries, 83 TC 8 (1984).

Net operating loss could be carried over following statutory merger. Goldstein owned all of the stock of taxpayer corporation and substantially all of the stock of Cleveland when Cleveland sold its assets to Webster. Taxpayer was engaged in the jobbing business of producing bronze castings. Cleveland was engaged in the same jobbing business but also manufactured and sold its own product line of valves. Following the sale, Webster did not conduct a jobbing business, and Cleveland retained some of its jobbing business equipment and continued its jobbing business at taxpayer's plant until a merger of Cleveland and taxpayer occurred. Following the merger, taxpayer deducted the operating loss carry-overs of Cleveland. The IRS contended that the loss carry-over could not be deducted because no reorganization had occurred due to the lack of a valid business purpose. *Held:* For taxpayer. The regulations under Section 368 require a continuity of interest, continuity of business enterprise, and a business purpose for a reorganization to be recognized. All of these conditions were met here, and therefore the reorganization qualified under Section 368(a)(1)(A). The operating losses could be carried over and deducted on the surviving corporation's return. American Bronze Corp., 64 TC 1111 (1975).

Merger qualified as F reorganization, allowing carry-backs of investment tax credit and net operating losses. After obtaining a ruling that a transaction qualified under Section 332, an 80 percent subsidiary was merged into its parent holding company. Taxpayer filed a consolidated return but followed it with an amended return deducting investment tax credits and net operating losses on the premise that the merger was in fact an F reorganization and that accordingly both items were deductible. The IRS determined that Section 381(b)(3) applied and disallowed the carry-backs of the investment tax credit and net operating losses. *Held:* For taxpayer. Because the parent corporation was merely a holding company, the merger by its 80 percent subsidiary into such a holding company qualified as an F reorganization. Accordingly, the carry-backs of both the investment tax credit and net operating losses were allowed. Eastern Color Printing Co., 63 TC 27 (1974).

Losses not recognized in nontaxable reorganization. Taxpayer's farming cooperative was merged into another cooperative. After the merger, taxpayer exchanged participation certificates in the old cooperative for preferred stock in the merged cooperatives. A loss deduction based on the difference in value of the certificates and the preferred stock was disallowed. *Held:* For the IRS. The participation certificates constituted an equi-

Reorganizations: Carry-Over of Net Operating Losses

ty interest, not a debt, so a claim of partial worthlessness of a debt was not valid. Further, the exchange was made pursuant to a recapitalization (nontaxable E reorganization) and the loss was not recognized by reason of Section 354(a)(1). Atwood Grain & Supply Co., 60 TC 412 (1973).

Preacquisition loss carry-over allowed. Taxpayer, a manufacturer of crimped yarn, purchased the stock of a loss corporation that had been in the business of manufacturing hosiery. Following the acquisition, taxpayer converted the acquired production facilities to the manufacture of crimped yarn fabrics. The corporations were merged, and taxpayer sought to carry over the preacquisition operating losses over the IRS' objections. *Held:* For taxpayer. The use of the loss carry-overs was not barred by Section 382(a)(1) because both before and after the acquisition, the loss corporation engaged in substantially the same business. Nor was the loss barred under Section 269(a)(1) because the principal purpose of the acquisition was not tax avoidance but rather to acquire needed productive capacity for flat fabric. Glen Raven Mills, Inc., 59 TC 1 (1972).

Subsequent liquidation did not strip recapitalization of its tax-free character. Taxpayer, along with his wife and children, owned a corporation. Taxpayer and his wife's ownership was represented by preferred stock that was entitled to liquidating distributions plus all unpaid cumulative dividends before common stockholders. The corporation, in turn, was a very substantial stockholder in a publicly traded company. In April 1964, the corporation adopted a plan of recapitalization whereby the outstanding preferred stock was exchanged for common stock, and dividend arrearages were cancelled. The corporation was liquidated in November 1965. The IRS contended that the exchange was not a tax-free reorganization within the meaning of Section 368(a)(1)(E). *Held:* For taxpayer. On the stipulated facts, taxpayer showed a valid business purpose: elimination of the dividend arrearages. In order for the IRS to cast this aside, it was incumbent upon the IRS to show that although this was in form a recapitalization, it nevertheless occurred in such a setting as to strip it of its otherwise tax-free nature. The IRS failed to do this, basing its case on inferences that were not reasonably justified. Kaufman, 55 TC 1046 (1971), acq. 1971-2 CB 3.

Debtor-creditor relationship between corporations did not invalidate merger. S owned approximately 99 percent of taxpayer, C, and R, both engaged in the sale and service of automobiles. Pursuant to an agreement approved by the secretary of state, C and R were merged into taxpayer. At the time of the merger, C and R had considerable net operating losses that had not been carried back, and both were indebted to taxpayer. Taxpayer claimed deductions related to the loss carry-overs from C and R. The IRS disallowed the deductions, contending that C and R were insolvent as of the date of transfer, resulting in worthless stock, and therefore the stockholders of C and R did not receive a proprietary interest in taxpayer. Conversely, the merger was contended to satisfy indebtedness because of C's and R's debts to taxpayer. *Held:* For taxpayer. Because the corporations met the requirements of Section 368(a)(1)(A), the merger was not invalidated by the worthlessness of transferors' stock or the debtor-creditor relationship of the transferors and transferee. Hence, the deductions claimed for net operating loss carry-overs from the prior operations of the sister corporations were allowed. Norman Scott, Inc. 48 TC 598 (1967).

Net operating loss carry-over allowed to purchasers of stock who merely expanded old business. Taxpayer corporation was engaged in the wholesaling of glassware, dishes, alumininum wares, and other hard goods in about five states. In 1956, taxpayer's stock was purchased by a successful dry goods corporation. Subsequent to the purchase, taxpayer continued to sell hard goods, but also sold dry goods and eventually commenced retailing activities. Taxpayer also changed the location of its wholesale outlet, although the location was still within the same area of its pre-1956 activities. Taxpayer claimed that it was entitled to use pre-1956 net operating losses to offset its income for the years 1956,

1957, and 1958. The IRS denied the net operating loss carry-over (1) under Section 382(a), which eliminates such loss carry-overs if there are certain changes in the ownership (which was here conceded) and there is also a change in taxpayer's business; and (2) under Section 269, which disallows such carry-overs if the principal purpose of the stock acquisition is tax avoidance. *Held:* For taxpayer. The court, with two judges dissenting, allowed the carry-over finding that although taxpayer added dry goods to its inventory and expanded into a retail outlet, taxpayer continued to carry on, after the change in stock ownership, substantially the same business it had conducted before the change. The court also found that the stock was not acquired for tax avoidance purposes within Section 269. Goodwyn Crockery Co., 37 TC 355 (1961).

Losses incurred subsequent to acquisition were deductible by the acquiring corporation. Taxpayer corporation acquired more than 80 percent of a second corporation which then incurred losses on the sale of poultry farm assets and inventory. When taxpayer deducted the losses on a consolidated return, the IRS disallowed the losses and the filing of such return. *Held:* For taxpayer. The notice of deficiency was not framed to raise the issue of deductibility of the losses, and since the IRS conceded that a consolidated return was appropriate, the losses were properly deducted. The court added that even if the losses were in issue, taxpayer would have been entitled to the deduction. The losses, incurred on the sale of the properties, were attributable to the decision of taxpayer's management to rid itself of the poultry business, were made after the acquisition of the second corporation, and therefore, were not attributable to events preceding the acquisition date. Mississippi Steel Corp., 30 TCM 83, ¶ 71,018 P-H Memo. TC (1971).

Net operating loss carry-overs allowed where no tax-avoidance motive was shown. Taxpayer corporation, the result of a merger between three corporations, claimed a net operating loss that the IRS disallowed. *Held:* For taxpayer, in part. The merger occurred because one corporation wanted the rights to a casting process owned and licensed by the other two corporations, and since the loss deductions were not a bargaining consideration, the court determined that the merger was not principally for tax avoidance, but for legitimate business purposes and the net operating loss deductions were proper. Furthermore, the disallowance of the prime cost method of valuing inventory was proper since such method did not clearly reflect income. Arwood Corp., 30 TCM 6, ¶ 71,002 P-H Memo. TC (1971).

Acquiring corporation may succeed to entire net operating loss. The IRS ruled that X Corporation could acquire the total net operating loss carry-over of Y Corporation through a merger under Section 368(a)(1)(A), where the stockholders of the loss corporation acquire at least 20 percent of the fair market value of the outstanding stock of the acquiring corporation in exchange for their stock in the loss corporation. Section 382(b)(1) does not operate to reduce the net operating loss carry-over to the acquiring corporation even where the acquiring corporation had issued a nontaxable preferred stock dividend in a recapitalization designed to reduce the fair market value of the outstanding common stock to meet the 20 percent test upon merger with Y. The preferred stock would be Section 306 stock and would be excluded from the definition of outstanding stock for Section 382 purposes. Rev. Rul. 77-227, 1977-2 CB 120.

Net operating losses allowed after stock purchase. Creditors of a corporation acquired 85 percent of the voting stock of the corporation in a bankruptcy reorganization. The IRS ruled that the corporation could use its net operating losses, since this acquisition was not a purchase within the meaning of Section 382(a)(4). Rev. Rul. 77-81, 1977-1 CB 97.

Newly created subsidiary acquiring assets of partially owned subsidiary in C reorganization could carry back later losses to prior years of transferor. P Corporation owned 99 percent of the outstanding stock of S Corporation, an operating subsidiary. For good business reasons, P created a new subsidiary corporation, N, which acquired substantially all of the assets of S solely in exchange for shares of the voting stock of P and the assumption by N of the liabilities of S. S distributed the stock of P to its stockholders in exchange for all of its outstanding stock and then dissolved. The transaction qualified as a reorganization, since substantially all of the assets of S were acquired by N solely in exchange for part of the voting stock of P, which was in control of both S and N, and all of the P stock received was exchanged for all of the stock of S. Upon these facts, the IRS held that Section 361 was not applicable because P did not qualify as a party to a reorganization within the definition of Section 368(b) applicable to reorganizations described in Section 368(a)(1)(F). Because Section 361 was not applicable to the transfer of the property of S to N for purposes of Section 368(a)(1)(F), the transaction was not a reorganization under Section 368(a)(1)(F). Rev. Rul. 69-413, 1969-2 CB 55.

Acquisition of stock followed by liquidation a C reorganization; limitations on net operating loss carry-overs applied. Under a plan of reorganization, Y Corporation acquired all the outstanding stock of X Corporation from stockholders in exchange for Y stock. X was liquidated, the business being continued by Y. Former X stockholders held 16 percent of the fair market value of Y stock. The IRS ruled that, in substance, Y acquired the assets of X, and that came under Section 368(a)(1)(C). Since Section 381(a)(2) applied, Section 382(b) relating to limitations on net operating loss carry-overs where a change of ownership occurs as a result of a reorganization was also applicable. Rev. Rul. 67-274, 1967-2 CB 141.

Premerger losses allowed in statutory merger. Three individuals each owned one third of the stock of two loss corporations. After a statutory merger under Section 368(a)(1)(A), the surviving corporation discontinued the business it had previously run and carried over its premerger operating losses against the income from the business formerly conducted by the other corporation. The IRS ruled that the carry-over was proper. The limitations in Section 362(b) did not apply, since the transferor corporation and the acquiring corporation were owned by substantially the same persons in the same proportions. The *Libson Shops* doctrine was also not applicable, since Rev. Rul. 58-603, states that this decision would not be relied on to disallow a net operating loss carry-over in a statutory merger. Section 269(a)(1) applied only to the acquisition of a corporation and not to the acquisition of assets in a statutory merger. Finally, Section 269(a)(2) did not apply, since it excludes intercorporate property acquisitions where 50 percent or more of the stock of the corporations is commonly controlled. Rev. Rul. 66-214, 1966-2 CB 98.

Carry-over of expropriation loss available to acquiring corporation in Section 332 liquidation. Y Corporation sustained a foreign expropriation loss as defined in Section 172(k). Subsequently, Y distributed all of its assets to X Corporation in a Section 332(a) liquidation. The IRS ruled that X was entitled to make the election for the ten-year carry-over of the foreign expropriation loss provided for in Section 172(b)(1)(D). Rev. Rul. 66-169, 1966-1 CB 54.

Carry-over rules apply even where reorganization involves foreign corporations. The fact that foreign corporations engage in a C reorganization so that no immediate tax consequences result does not make inapplicable the rules that the earnings, profits, and the basis of the assets of the transferor corporation are carried over to the acquiring corporation. However, a pre-September 15, 1960 transfer of assets between foreign corporations do not qualify as a tax-free liquidation or reorganization unless a U.S. taxpayer establishes that it qualified as such or unless gain on the transaction was not recognized to a U.S. taxpayer under Section 332 or 361. Where tax treatment of stockholders of controlled foreign corporations under Section 957 is dependent upon the amount of earnings and profits carried over in a prior foreign corporation reorganization, a reasonable approximation will be acceptable where it is costly and difficult to obtain the data. Rev. Rul. 64-158, as amended by TIR No. 596 (1964). 1964-1 CB 140.

Reorganizations: Changes in Identity or Form (F Reorganizations)

After split-up, successor corporations cannot use net operating loss of transferor. After divisive reorganization, a "split-up" under Section 355(a) of the 1954 Code, an unused net operating loss carry-over of the transferor corporation may not be taken into account by any of the successor corporations. Both the Code and the Senate Finance Committee Report make it clear that loss carry-overs are not permitted through a divisive reorganization. Rev. Rul. 56-373, 1956-2 CB 217.

Changes in Identity or Form (F Reorganizations)

An F reorganization found to exist, even though transferor's minority stockholders received interest in acquiring corporation's parent. The parent corporation formed taxpayer solely to acquire the assets and business of a subsidiary in which the parent held a 62 percent interest. Taxpayer's only asset was stock in its parent. The subsidiary was merged into taxpayer, and its stockholders received stock in the parent corporation in exchange for the subsidiary's assets. Taxpayer carried back postmerger losses against the subsidiary's premerger income. The district court, agreeing with the IRS, held that the merger did not constitute on F reorganization because of the change in the ownership interest in the minority stockholders' interest. Accordingly, no carry-back was allowed. *Held:* Reversed. The appellate court held that the merger was an F reorganization, irrespective of the conversion of the minority stockholders' interest. The Aetna Cas. & Sur. Co., 568 F2d 811, 77-1 USTC ¶ 9120, 39 AFTR2d 77-400 (2d Cir. 1977), reh'g denied, 77-1 USTC ¶ 9266.

Merger of two active corporations is an F reorganization where the proprietary interest of the transferor and transferee is identical and there is continuity of business enterprise. In a reorganization determined by the Tax Court to be a statutory merger, taxpayer acquired another corporation and gave the new joint corporation a new name. All corporations were owned by the same individual, and each had the same, although separately functioning board of directors. The IRS challenged taxpayer's carry-back of net operating loss against premerger income on the ground that the above transaction was not an F reorganization because both corporations were active prior to the merger. The Tax Court held for the IRS. *Held:* Reversed. An F reorganization can involve more than one active corporation if the proprietary interest in the transferor and the transferee are identical and business continuity is not interrupted. The postmerger loss of transferee (taxpayer) may be carried back against the transferor's premerger profits. Associated Mach., 403 F2d 622, 68-2 USTC ¶ 9635, 22 AFTR2d 5780 (9th Cir. 1968).

Merger of three corporations into fourth corporation could qualify as an F reorganization. Taxpayer was the sole owner of three corporations, each engaged in the same business but in different locales. Each had the same officers and directors. Taxpayer decided to relocate operations, and so he formed a New Mexico corporation into which all three active corporations would merge. The merger resulted in no change in ownership, operations, or locale. After the merger, the New Mexico corporation (survivor of the four corporations), incurred tax losses, and pursuant to Section 381, carried them back against the taxable income of the three corporations that existed prior to the merger. The IRS disallowed the carry-back on the ground that the merger did not constitute an F reorganization. *Held:* Reversed for taxpayer. Despite the IRS' assertion to the contrary, an F reorganization may involve more than one corporation. The key is whether the surviving corporation received the transferor corporation's operating assets, whether it functioned as the transferor's alter ego, whether the identity of proprietary interest remained intact and whether the transferors' businesses continue unimpaired. However, postmerger losses from operations should be carried back to offset income from those operations that were conducted in corporate form. Estate of Stauffer, 403 F2d 611, 68-2 USTC ¶ 9634, 22 AFTR2d 5771 (9th Cir. 1968).

Bulk sale to new corporation pursuant to common law settlement with creditors was F reorganization. Taxpayer entered into a common

REORGANIZATIONS: *Continuity of Business*

law settlement with its creditors in 1962. Under the settlement, taxpayer made a bulk sale of its assets to a newly organized corporation that continued to operate the same business. The creditors received 22.50 percent of their claims in cash and the promise of the new corporation for an additional 17.50 percent in installments over 18 months. The creditors could claim the balance only if the new corporation failed to pay the installments. Taxpayer's sole stockholder owned all the stock of the new corporation. The trustee in bankruptcy of the new corporation sought to carry back its net operating losses against taxpayer's profits. He contended that the common law settlement resulted in an F reorganization. *Held:* For taxpayer. There was a change of corporate vehicle, not a change of substance. The same stockholder owned both the old and the new companies, the corporate assets were the same, and so were the liabilities, although scaled down somewhat. Holliman, Trustee, 275 F. Supp. 927, 67-2 USTC ¶ 9737 (SD Ala. 1967).

IRS loosens restrictions on use of loss carrybacks in F reorganization situations. Citing nine cases decided contrary to its long-held position on the use of loss carry-backs following F reorganizations, the IRS capitulated and announced a policy consistent with the overwhelming weight of judicial authority. Accordingly, the IRS now holds that the combination of two or more corporations may qualify as a reorganization within the meaning of Section 368(a)(1)(F) provided three requirements are satisfied: (1) There must be complete identity of stockholders and their proprietary interests in the transferor corporations and acquiring corporations. In the case of wholly owned subsidiary-into-parent merger, this requirement will be deemed to be satisfied when the stockholders and their proprietary interests in the parent do not change as a result of the merger; (2) The transferor corporations and the acquiring corporation must be engaged in the same business activities or integrated activities before the combination; and (3) The business enterprise of the transferor corporations and the acquiring corporation must continue unchanged after the combination. Rev. Rul. 75-561, 1975-2 CB 129.

Cash received in lieu of fractional shares. In an F reorganization, the cash received in lieu of fractional shares is treated as a distribution in redemption of fractional share interests if it is not, in fact, separately bargained for consideration. Rev. Rul. 74-36, 1974-1 CB 85.

IRS did not follow the decision in the *Estate of Stauffer*. The IRS stated that it will not follow the decisions of the Ninth Circuit in Estate of Stauffer, 403 F2d 611 (1968), and Associated Mach., 403 F2d 622 (1968), nor a portion of the decision of the Fifth Circuit in Davant, 366 F2d 874 (1966). The decisions held that a combination of two or more commonly owned operating corporations may qualify as an F reorganization. Rev. Rul. 69-185, 1969-1 CB 108.

Trust acquisition of assets and liabilities of corporation qualifies as reorganization. A domestic corporation, desiring to operate as a trust, forms a domestic trust that is taxable as a corporation under Section 7701(a)(3). The trust acquires the corporate assets and liabilities in exchange for transferable certificates of beneficial interest. The corporation will then distribute the certificates in exchange for its stock and dissolve. The IRS ruled that the transaction qualifies as a reorganization under Section 368(a)(1)(F). Rev. Rul. 67-376, 1967-2 CB 142.

Continuity of Business

Surviving corporation need not continue same business after merger to qualify for tax-free treatment. Two months after taxpayer corporation was organized, it merged with a loss corporation. At that time, taxpayer had no earnings. Taxpayer deducted the losses of the old corporation. The district court allowed the deduction when a jury found taxpayer's primary purpose in effecting the merger was not tax avoidance. The court's charge to the jury emphasized that the principal purpose for acquisition means that purpose that outranks or exceeds in importance any other single purpose. Relying on Libson Shops, 353

US 382 (1957), the IRS on appeal contended that the merger was not a tax-free reorganization because it did not satisfy the continuity of interest test. The owner of 99 percent of the stock of the loss corporation, who was also one of the corporation's principal creditors, received approximately one-sixth of the stock of taxpayer. Taxpayer, however, had the right of first refusal to purchase the stock as well as the stock of all other stockholders at the par value of $1 per share. The IRS contended that the existence of this right in taxpayer negated all of the attributes of its stock ownership. *Held:* Affirmed. Contrary to the IRS' argument, the stock that the principal stockholder of the old corporation received on the merger did satisfy the continuity of interest test. Except for the restriction on sale, which was the same with respect to all stockholders and which probably was not binding on a stockholder's estate, the stockholder had all of the stockholder's usual rights. The evidence did not justify a finding that the old corporation was insolvent before the merger and that, therefore, the stockholder received these rights other than as a stockholder. With respect to the IRS' argument that there was no continuity of business enterprise, the court found that the Libson Shops decision did not apply under the 1954 Code. Rev. Rul. 63-29 makes it clear that, although the surviving corporation in a merger must engage in a business enterprise, the enterprise need not be the same one that was conducted by its predecessor. The temporary suspension of taxpayer's business did not constitute a break in the continuity of the business enterprise. Adkins-Phelps, Inc., 400 F2d 737, 68-2 USTC ¶ 9609, 22 AFTR2d 5637 (8th Cir. 1968).

Reorganization tax free even though same business not continued. Three corporations, which had been engaged in land development, were consolidated to form an insurance company. The assets of the land development corporations were transferred to a newly created insurance company in exchange for its stock, and the stock was distributed in liquidation of the development corporations. *Held:* For taxpayer. The court held this was a tax-free reorganization. There was continuity of business even though the transferee was in a different type of business. There is no requirement that the same business be carried on before and after reorganization. Bentsen, 199 F. Supp. 363, 62-1 USTC ¶ 9257, 9 AFTR2d 685 (SD Tex. 1961).

IRS illustrates application of continuity rules. In a transaction meant to qualify as a tax-free reorganization under Sections 368(a)(1)(A) and (a)(2)(C), X Corporation, a holding company, acquired under the applicable state merger laws, a significant portion of the historic business assts of Y Corporation, a manufacturing business. Immediately thereafter, X transferred all assets received from Y to Z Corporation, its wholly owned subsidiary engaged in a manufacturing business. Z then used the assets in its manufacturing business. On these facts, the IRS held that the application of the continuity-of-business-enterprise rules of Regulation § 1.368-1(d) would not prevent the transactions between X and Y from qualifying as tax-free reorganizations under Sections 368(a)(1)(A) and (a)(2)(C). Rev. Rul. 81-247, 1981-2 CB 87.

Reorganization taxable where no continuity-of-business enterprise. X, a manufacturing corporation, sold all of its assets to Z, an unrelated corporation. Pursuant to a plan of reorganization, Y, a corporation that manufactured different items than X, acquired all of X's stock in exchange for voting in Y. X then engaged in a business unrelated to its previous manufacturing activities. The reorganization was not tax free under Section 368(a)(1)(B). There was no continuity of business enterprise under Regulation § 1.368-1(d) because Y neither continued X's manufacturing business nor used a significant portion of X's historic assets in a business conducted through a subsidiary. Rev. Rul. 81-92, 1981-1 CB 133.

Continuity of transferee's business not required. The continuity of business requirement of Regulation § 1.368-1(b) does not apply to the business or business assets of the transferee-corporation prior to a reorganization under Section 368(a)(1) as reflected in

REORGANIZATIONS: *Continuity of Interest*

the recent amendment of Regulation § 1.368-1(d). Rev. Rul. 81-25, 1981-1 CB 132.

Continuity of Interest

Exchange of guarantee stock for savings accounts did not qualify as tax-free exchange. Pursuant to a merger plan, taxpayers exchanged guarantee stock in a state chartered savings and loan association for savings accounts in a federally chartered mutual (nonstock) savings and loan association. The savings accounts carried certain proprietary rights, including the right to vote, the right to pro rata distributions of earnings, and the right to share in the distribution of assets upon liquidation. Taxpayers treated the exchange as an A reorganization that resulted in no recognized gain or loss pursuant to Section 354(a). The IRS determined that taxpayers were required to recognize gain realized on the exchange on grounds that there was no "continuity of interest." *Held:* For the IRS. The Supreme Court held that taxpayers were not entitled to tax-free treatment. The Court stated that the debt characteristics of the savings accounts outweighed their equity characteristics. The accounts were cash equivalents. They were not subordinated to creditors' claims, were not considered permanent contributions to capital, and the account holders had a right to withdraw the face amount of their deposits in cash. Thus, the Court held, taxpayers had failed to meet the continuity of interest requirement of Section 368. Paulsen, 105 S. Ct. 627 (1985).

Merger allowed because of continuity of interest. The IRS attacked a statutory merger of an Ohio state-chartered savings and loan association that had a limited amount of par value capital stock outstanding in addition to savings accounts, into taxpayer, a mutually owned federal savings and loan association, whose capital consisted solely of savings accounts. The IRS contended that the requirement for a continuity of proprietary interest was not met. The district court held for taxpayer and concluded that a tax-free reorganization was effected. *Held:* Affirmed. There was a continuity of interest between holders of the merged association and those of taxpayer, the surviving association, because each stockholder of the merged entity acquired an interest that was definite and material and represented a substantial part of the stock that was given up. West Side Fed. Sav. & Loan Ass'n, 494 F2d 404, 74-1 USTC ¶ 9315, 33 AFTR2d 74-960 (6th Cir. 1974).

Savings deposit accounts represented continuity of interest in merger transaction. Taxpayer X, a non-stock federal savings and loan association, entered into a merger agreement with Y, a state chartered stock savings and loan association. Pursuant to such agreement, X acquired the common stock and savings deposits of Y while the holders of Y common stocks were given savings deposit accounts of X in return for their Y stock. X contended that this transaction was a tax free A or C reorganization pursuant to Section 368. *Held:* For taxpayer. The savings accounts received by the former stockholders of Y represented an adequate continuity of proprietary interest in the successor corporation. First Fed. Sav. & Loan Ass'n, 452 F. Supp. 32, 78-1 USTC ¶ 9398 (ND Ohio 1978).

Continuity-of-interest doctrine applied to deny reorganization status to merger. Taxpayer was the exclusive franchise dealer within its state for buses made by a certain manufacturer. An unrelated corporation held the exclusive franchise for the same manufacturer's recreational vehicles. Following a decline in sales of motor homes and recreational vehicles, the unrelated corporation could no longer perform its franchise obligations. After negotiations with the taxpayer, taxpayer's stockholders acquired all the other corporation's outstanding stock, dissolved it, and merged it into the taxpayer. Following the transactions, taxpayer owned all assets and liabilities of the acquired corporation and on its return for the acquisition year, sought to use the net operating loss incurred by the acquired corporation for its last taxable period. The IRS determined that the transactions did not qualify as a tax-free reorganization and denied the use of the net operating loss. *Held:* For the IRS. Applying the step-transaction doctrine, the continuity-of-interest requirement had not been satisfied because the historic stockholders did not retain an interest in the surviving corporation; thus, the merger was not a tax-free reorganization. Absent a qualifying Section 368 reorganization, the surviving corporation may not use the net operating loss of the acquired corporation. Superior Coach of Fla., Inc., 80 TC 895 (1983).

Integration of stock purchase and merger fails continuity-of-interest test, even though stockholder's interest in merged corporation was retained through purchasing corporation. Taxpayer was a minority (less than 1 percent) stockholder in ACRA. Other minority stockholders in ACRA developed the following plan to gain control over it: (1) formation of a new corporation controlled by this group of minority stockholders, (2) purchase at least 80 percent of ACRA by the new corporation, and (3) merger or liquidation of ACRA into the new corporation. The plan was carried out, and the new corporation acquired 84 percent of ACRA. Taxpayer did not participate in the new corporation's purchase offer. As a consequence, taxpayer received stock in the new corporation upon the merger-liquidation of ACRA. Taxpayer reported no gain or loss on the exchange of ACRA stock for stock in the new corporation, treating the transaction as a tax-free reorganization. *Held:* For the IRS. The purchase of ACRA stock and the merger were part of the same integrated transaction. Accordingly, the merger did not qualify as a tax-free reorganization for failing to maintain "continuity of interest" in ACRA. Although some of ACRA's stockholders (i.e., the minority group) held a significant posttransaction interest in ACRA through the new corporation, continuity of interest was measured by comparing the prepurchase offer stockholders of ACRA with the postpurchase offer (but premerger) stockholders of ACRA (without regard to indirect interests held through the new corporation). Kass, 60 TC 218 (1973).

Chapter X bankruptcy exchange of second mortgage bonds for preferred stock meets continuity of interest test. Taxpayer, organized to effectuate a reorganization under Chapter X of the Bankruptcy Act, claiming that it had received its assets in a tax-free reorganization and therefore was entitled to use its transferor's basis for the assets received. In the reorganization, the first mortgage bondholders of the insolvent corporation received similar bonds of the taxpayer, the second mortgage bondholders received $435,000 of preferred stock of taxpayer, and $100,000 of taxpayer's new common stock was issued for cash. The IRS claimed that there was no continuity of interest, which is necessary to constitute a tax-free reorganization. *Held:* For taxpayer. The court disagreed, finding: (1) that the second mortgage bondholders would be considered "former owners," notwithstanding that the upset price (a sale was never consummated) was less than the amount owed to the first mortgage bondholders, since the bankruptcy court determined that the second mortgage bondholders did have an equity of $435,000, and (2) that while both first and second mortgage bondholders could be considered "former owners," only the second mortgage bondholders would be so considered, since the first mortgage bondholders received bonds and not stock. On this basis, the second mortgage bondholders obtained 80 percent of the stock of taxpayer, and the continuity of interest requirement was met. Atlas Oil & Refining Corp., 36 TC 675 (1961).

Exchange held to be sale rather than merger because of lack of continuity of interest. Taxpayers, who held less than one third of the outstanding shares of a company, exchanged their stock for bonds and notes of a second corporation pursuant to a plan whereby their old company was merged into the other. IRS contended that the merger was a statutory reorganization and that the notes received were property that was not received tax-free and that had the effect of a dividend. Consequently, it determined that the notes were a distribution of earnings and profits taxable as a dividend. *Held:* For taxpayer. The court found the exchange was a sale rather than a reorganization; it was not a statutory merger because the stockholders of the selling corporation did not continue their proprietary interests in the purchasing corporation. Accordingly, the entire gain realized by them was taxable as long-term capital gain.

REORGANIZATIONS: *Continuity of Interest*

Truschel, 29 TC 433 (1958), acq. 1960-2 CB 7.

IRS rules on recapitalization involving swap of new debentures for stock and old debentures. In a ruling setting forth detailed facts, the IRS held that a corporation's issuance of new debentures in exchange for either its outstanding debentures or its preferred stock qualifies under Section 368(a)(1)(E), even though the continuity of proprietary interest is not maintained. The transaction does not give rise to original issue discount on the new debentures under Section 1232. The exchange of new debentures for the stock is treated as a distribution in redemption of the stockholders' stock under Section 302, and the exchange of new debentures for the old debentures results in the nonrecognition of gain or loss under Section 354. Rev. Rul. 77-415, 1977-2 CB 311.

Section 355 distribution of stock in controlled corporations to former partners of a dissolved partnership, which held stock in the distributing corporation satisfied continuity of interest. P Corporation, engaged in one line of business, owned all the stock of S, which was engaged in a separate line of business. P stock was owned 10 percent each by A, B, C, and D and 60 percent by the $ABCD$ partnership, in which A, B, C, and D were equal partners. As part of a plan to divide control of the businesses, $ABCD$ was dissolved, so that the partners held the P stock directly (25 percent each). P then formed N, to which it transferred its business assets in return for N stock. P then dissolved, distributing N stock to A, B, and S stock to C and D. The IRS stated that this transaction satisfied the continuity-of-interest requirements of Regulation § 1.355-2(c). Following the dissolution of $ABCD$, the partners stood in its shoes as qualified persons to receive and continue stock interests in N and S. Rev. Rul. 76-528, 1976-2 CB 103.

Continuity-of-interest requirement not violated in spin-off. A corporation's spin-off of its wholly owned subsidiary, followed by a vote of the then spun-off corporation's stockholders to enter into a statutory merger with a totally unrelated corporation neither violated the continuity-of-interest requirement of Regulations §§ 1.355-2(c) and 1.368-1(b) nor constituted a device to distribute earnings and profits prohibited by Section 355(a). Rev. Rul. 75-406, 1975-2 CB 125.

Continuity of interest preserved through voting trust. Two 50 percent stockholders who transferred all their shares to a voting trust in exchange for an equal amount of voting trust certificates were considered the owners of the shares for the continuity-of-interest test. Rev. Rul. 75-95, 1975-1 CB 114.

Disposal of stock under court order did not affect continuity-of-interest requirement. Section 368(a)(1)(A) requires a continuity of interest by the owners of the enterprises involved in a statutory merger or consolidation. The IRS was asked if the continuity-of-interest requirement was met under the following circumstances: The oustanding stock of Y Corporation was owned 40 percent by the public and 60 percent by X Corporation. Because of this control, X and Y were sued by the United States for violation of the antitrust laws. In a subsequent consent decree, Y agreed to merge with an unrelated corporation (Z Co). A further provision of the decree required X to dispose of the Z stock that it received for its shares of Y stock. X agreed to dispose of the Z stock over a seven-year period, although at the time of the merger no preconceived plan or arrangement had been made for the disposition. The IRS ruled that the continuity-of-interest requirement was satisfied where the stockholder of the transferor corporation received stock of the transferee without any preconceived plan or arrangement for disposing of any of the stock and the ownership was definite and for a substantial period, generally exceeding five years, despite the fact that a court decree required disposition of the stock by the end of that period. This ruling would not be changed even if X actually sold some of Z's stock within a five-year period, since no preconceived plan existed. Rev. Rul. 66-23, 1966-1 CB 67.

REORGANIZATIONS: *Dividend Equivalence*

Dividend Equivalence

Distribution treated as dividend, not Section 331 liquidation, pursuant to D reorganization. Pursuant to an informal agreement, the assets of *A* Corporation were transferred to *B* Corporation, a related corporation, with a cash distribution being made to taxpayers, stockholders of *A*. Taxpayers reported the distribution as a capital gain on liquidation of *A*. The IRS contended the distribution was taxable as a dividend pursuant to a D reorganization. The Tax Court held for the IRS. *Held:* Affirmed. It was immaterial that taxpayers did not transfer a license under a personally owned patent that had been granted to *A* but not to *B*. The owner of a patent may grant a license by conduct as well as by contract. In essence, substantially all the assets of *A* were transferred where taxpayers controlled *B* and acquiesced in manufacture of patented product for their own benefit. DeGroff, 444 F2d 1385, 71-1 USTC ¶ 9483, 27 AFTR2d 71-1573 (10th Cir. 1971).

Transfer of assets between two controlled corporations was a reorganization with dividend resulting. Taxpayer, owner of all the stock of *X* Corporation and *Y* Corporation, desired to transfer the assets of *X* to *Y* and to liquidate *X*. He arranged for a third party to buy the stock of *X*, sell the operating assets to *Y*, and liquidate *X*. Taxpayer, contending that a bona fide sale of *X* was made to the third party, reported his profit as a long-term capital gain. The IRS contended that a corporate reorganization had taken place, resulting in dividend income to the extent of earnings and profits of both corporations. The Tax Court held that a D reorganization had taken place, resulting in a dividend to the extent of *X*'s earnings and profits. *Held:* Affirmed. All of the steps taken here were for the sole purpose of converting dividend income into capital gain. There was never a bona fide sale of *X*'s stock, since the purchaser was merely a conduit for the passage of funds from *Y* to *X* and then to taxpayers; the transaction was devoid of substance. Taxpayer's contention that a Section 331 liquidation and a sale of assets under Section 337 took place was not valid, since no function was served other than to bail out corporate earnings at capital gain rates. The only business purpose served by the events—the elimination of corporate shells and combination of businesses—could have been accomplished under the reorganization provisions by the transfer of *X*'s assets, earnings, and profits to *Y* without the necessity of funds being distributed to taxpayer. A complete liquidation did not take place under Section 331, since taxpayers did not intend to give up the corporate form of business. The IRS' contention that a D or E reorganization took place had to be upheld. What took place was a mere change in form because the enterprise continued uninterrupted, except for the distribution of some liquid assets. The IRS' position could also be upheld under Sections 354 and 356, since cash or liquid assets received as part of a reorganization are treated as a dividend, or under Section 482, to prevent evasion of taxes by reallocations between controlled corporations. Davant, 366 F2d 874, 66-2 USTC ¶ 9618, 18 AFTR2d 5523 (5th Cir. 1966), cert. denied, 386 US 1022 (1967).

Tax Court aggregates subsidiary's operating asset sale and liquidation and finds a D reorganization with a boot dividend. *X* Corporation (taxpayer) owned all of the stock of *Y*, a U.S. corporation, and all of the stock of *Z*, a foreign corporation. *Y* sold its operating assets (less than 20 percent of its total assets) to *Z* for cash, leaving *Y* with cash and receivables that it distributed to *X* in liquidation. *X* treated this distribution as tax free under Section 332. The IRS treated this transaction as a D reorganization with either a boot dividend under Section 356(a)(2) or a separate dividend under Section 301 in an amount equal to the liquidating distribution. *Held:* For the IRS. The sale and liquidation were integral parts of a D reorganization, and *X*'s gain upon liquidation of *Y* was, to the extent of *Y*'s earnings and profits, taxable as a dividend under Section 356(a)(2). The sale and liquidation qualified as a D reorganization, even though less than 20 percent of *Y*'s assets were sold, because that 20 percent constituted 100 percent of its operating assets. Furthermore, because the distribution to *X* was made as an intregrated part of this reorganization, Section 356(a)(2) (not Section 301)

REORGANIZATIONS: *Expenses*

applied in determining dividend treatment of the distribution. The amount of the dividend was determined only by the earnings and profits of *Y*, not the combined earnings and profits of *Y* and *Z*. American Mfg. Co., 55 TC 204 (1970).

Expenses

Expenses of tax-free merger on disposition of acquired businesses deductible. The IRS determined that in two separate transactions involving taxpayer and its predecessor, two corporations had been merged tax free under Section 368(a)(1)(A). On taxpayer's tax return, the IRS allowed only $40,000 out of $146,000 in expenses for the merger as a current deduction and required the rest to be capitalized. Upon disposition of the acquired businesses six years later, taxpayer deducted the capitalized expenses. The district court agreed with the IRS' determination that taxpayer's expenses were merger expenses and therefore not deductible as a current expense. *Held:* Reversed and remanded. The deduction may be allowed to the acquiring corporation for expenses of tax-free stock for stock exchange on disposition of acquired businesses. Expenses incurred in the acquisition were treated as costs in the purchase of assets, with costs related to the purchasing aspects deductible on the sale of the acquired businesses. McCrory Corp., 651 F2d 828, 81-2 USTC ¶ 9499, 48 AFTR2d 81-5319 (2d Cir. 1981).

Attorney fees incurred in the division of a corporation into two active corporations nondeductible capital expenditures. Because of dissension between taxpayer's two 50 percent stockholders, taxpayer's business was divided into two seperate businesses. This division was effected through the redemption of one of the stockholder's stock interest in taxpayer. Taxpayer deducted the attorney fees incurred because of the divisions. The IRS contended that the fees were nondeductible capital expenditures incurred in the course of a tax-deferred reorganization. The Tax Court held for taxpayer, reasoning that taxpayer received no particular economic benefit or enhancement by incurring these expenses. *Held:* Reversed. Value was added to taxpayer. Before division, taxpayer was incapable of operating because of stockholder dissension. The division resulted in two viable corporations, and thus value was added to both corporations. The divisions were a reorganization, and attorney fees were nondeductible capital expenditures. Bilar Tool & Die Corp., 530 F2d 708, 76-1 USTC ¶ 9243, 37 AFTR2d 76-850 (6th Cir. 1976).

Organization expenses did not become deductible on merger. Taxpayer corporation's predecessor corporations incurred organization expenses that, although conceded to be nondeductible when incurred, were deducted on predecessors' merger into taxpayer corporation. The IRS and district court denied the deduction. *Held:* Affirmed. The benefits to which the organization expenses pertained were not lost, but continued in taxpayer corporation, the survivor. Vulcan Materials Co., 446 F2d 690, 71-1 USTC ¶ 9449, 27 AFTR2d 71-1488 (5th Cir. 1971).

Costs of registering stock were a cost of the acquiring corporation and not "other property" to stockholders in a reorganization. Pursuant to a plan of reorganization under Section 368(a)(1), an acquiring corporation paid costs necessary to register with the SEC the stock issued to stockholders in the reorganization. The IRS held that the costs of registering its own stock were properly attributable to the acquiring corporation and were not other property received in the reorganization by the stockholders of the acquired corporation. Rev. Rul. 67-275, 1967-2 CB 142.

IRS rules on proper treatment of expense items incurred in connection with tax-free reorganization. Pursuant to a plan of reorganization, *X*, a new wholly owned subsidiary formed by *L*, acquired all of the assets of *M* in a transaction qualifying as a reorganization under Section 368(a)(1)(C) in exchange for voting stock of *L*. Pursuant to the plan of reorganization, the stock received by *M* in the exchange was in turn distributed in liquidation to its stockholders. Rather than have *M* pay the brokerage fee and the legal, acounting, and related expenses that it incurred in connection with the plan of reorganization, the stockholders of *M* voted to be assessed pro rata, according to the number of their respective shares, to cover such expenses. None of the expenses related to tax advice to the individual stockholders of *M;* the expenses were all incurred by *M* in connection with the plan of reorganization, which included the liquidation of *M*. The IRS held that these facts established that the brokerage, legal, accounting and related expenses were expenses of *M* that were incurred in connection with the plan of reorganization that included the liquidation of *M*. Accordingly, the reorganization expenses of *M* paid by its stockholders were capital expenditures and were not deductible by the stockholders under Section 212. However, each stockholder may increase his basis in *L* stock, which he acquired according to the reorganization, by the amount of the reorganization expenses paid by him. Rev. Rul. 67-411, 1967-2 CB 124.

Mergers (A Reorganizations)

Boot received upon merger was dividend. Taxpayer argued that a pro rata cash distribution, received in the merger of a small corporation into a larger one, should be taxed as a long-term capital gain. The IRS held that the cash distribution was a dividend pursuant to Section 356(a)(2), taxable as ordinary income. The district court found for taxpayer, ruling that he experienced a meaningful reduction of interest in changing from majority stockholder of a small corporation to a minor stockholder of the big one. *Held:* Reversed. The "meaningful reduction" test is used to determine the treatment of stock redemptions; it does not fully apply to reorganizations. Taxpayer continued his proprietary interests in the enterprise in modified corporate form. A pro rata distribution from a continuing corporation is a boot dividend under Section 356(a)(2). Shimberg, Jr., 577 F2d 283, 78-2 USTC ¶ 9607, 42 AFTR2d 78-5575 (5th Cir. 1978), cert. denied, 439 US 1115 (1979).

Exchange of stock for the target's debt instruments disqualifies merger for tax-free reorganization treatment. Taxpayer, as part of a plan of acquisition, purchased 20,000 shares of guaranteed stock of a fellow savings and loan association by means of cash payments to the stockholders. The 20,000 shares represented all of the outstanding guaranteed stock of the target, which also had outstanding a total of 650,252 withdrawable shares, consisting of 31,130 fully paid and 619,122 cumulative shares. The withdrawable shares were eligible for surrender and reissue of similarly withdrawable stock of taxpayer. From May through July 1956, the same procedure was used to effect a merger with yet another savings and loan. On its financial books, taxpayer treated the mergers as an acquisition of assets and an assumption of liabilities. Thus, the $8 million paid to the guaranteed stockholders in the January transaction was apportioned among the acquired assets. Taxpayer thereafter sought to amend its tax treatment of the transactions by claiming that there had been a statutory merger under the Section 368(a)(1)(A) reorganization rules. The IRS objected to taxpayer's new characterization of these acquisitions, contending that they more nearly resembled the purchase of stock followed by a liquidation. As a result, the IRS disallowed a refund claim based on a sizable bad debt reserve deduction arising from the two mergers. The net effect of this determination was to restore $6.3 million to income. *Held:* For the IRS. The Ninth Circuit, reversing the district court, agreed with the IRS that the mergers were purchase liquidations and not statutory A reorganizations. Consequently, taxpayer was required to allocate the purchase price among the target assets and could not claim the bad debt reserve amounts as a surviving tax deduction. The court reached its conclusion primarily on the basis that the withdrawable shares more nearly resembled debt than equity and that therefore there had been no exchange of stock for stock as required under Section 368(a)(1)(A). Home Sav. & Loan Ass'n, 514 F2d 1199, 67-2 USTC ¶ 9702, 35 AFTR2d 75-1391, 75-1 USTC ¶ 9423 (9th Cir.), cert. denied, 423 US 1015 (1975).

Parent-subsidiary merger qualifies as F reorganization. A subsidiary corporation merged into a parent corporation and contended that the merger constituted a reorganization under Section 368(a)(1)(F), and so the subse-

REORGANIZATIONS: *Mergers (A Reorganizations)*

quent losses of the parent attributable to the business of its former subsidiary could be carried back to a seperate taxable period of the subisdiary. The IRS determined the reorganization did not qualify as an F reorganization. Upon receiving the evidence, the district court held that the merger made no substantive change in the business enterprise and that the merger qualified as an F reorganization, and therefore taxpayer was entitled to carry back its net operating loss as permitted by Section 381(b). It also determined that the result was not precluded by the fact that the F merger also fell within the definition of a liquidation under Section 332. *Held:* Affirmed. Because a wholly owned subsidiary was merged into a parent corporation and there was no change in proprietary interests or business after the merger, the merger qualified as an F reorganization. Therefore, the parent's net operating loss could be carried back and off set against the subsidiary's income. Performance Sys. Inc., 501 F2d 1338, 74-2 USTC ¶ 9613, 34 AFTR2d 74-5582 (6th Cir. 1974).

Merger of savings banks is A reorganization. Taxpayer savings bank argued that the merger of another savings bank into it was an A reorganization; therefore, taxpayer did not have to take the other bank's bad debt reserve into income. *Held:* For taxpayer. The savings accounts that taxpayer transferred to the acquired bank's depositors constituted voting stock because the depositors had voting rights. Rocky Mountain Fed. Sav. & Loan Ass'n. 473 F. Supp. 779, 79-2 USTC ¶ 9560, 44 AFTR2d 79-5542 (D. Wyo. 1979).

Loss carry-back disallowed where acquisition purchased. *A* Corporation acquired the stock of *B* Corporation. Four days later, *B* was merged into *A*. The IRS held that *A* could not carry-back post-merger losses attributable to *B* against the premerger income of *B*. *Held:* For the IRS. The transaction was found to be a purchase, not a merger, involving a mere change in identity, form, or place of organization. In re NBH Land Co., 78-1 USTC ¶ 9358, 42 AFTR2d 78-5068 (D. Colo. 1978).

Merger of subsidiary into parent was F reorganization. *S*, a wholly owned subsidiary of taxpayer parent, was merged into taxpayer. Taxpayer argued that a portion of its post-reorganization losses, attributable to activities that it conducted as successor to *S* could be carried back to the seperate premerger years of *S*. *Held:* For taxpayer. The merger was found to qualify as an F reorganization. The requirements of Rev. Rul. 75-561 were met. TFI Cos., 77-2 USTC ¶ 9710, 40 AFTR2d 77-5688 (CD Cal. 1977).

Merger not an F reorganization. In 1968, four active corporations, *A,B,C,* and *D,* merged into taxpayer corporation, a fifth active corporation. The premerger companies engaged in disparate and nonintegrated business activities that were continued in the postmerger corporation. Prior to the merger, *R,* an individual, owned 17.4 percent of the stock of *A,* 63.58 percent of the stock of *B,* 71.56 percent of the stock of *C,* and 53.08 percent of the stock of *D.* After the merger, *R* held 61.36 percent of taxpayer's postmerger corporation's stock. The postmerger corporation sustained a net operating loss and sought to carry back the loss to offset the premerger income of *A*. The IRS determined that the reorganization did not qualify as an F reorganization; accordingly, the loss could not be carried back against the premerger income of *A*. *Held:* For the IRS. The merger did not constitute an F reorganization because there was no identity of proprietary interest before and after the merger, and the different corporations were engaged in disparate business activities. Romy Hammes, Inc., 68 TC 900 (1977).

Reorganization did not qualify under Section 368(a)(1)(F). In a statutory merger, four active corporations that were controlled by related individuals were merged into a new corporation. The surviving corporation reported a taxable loss and carried back the loss to the years prior to the merger. The IRS determined that the merger did not qualify as an F reorganization; accordingly the loss was not subject to carry-back. *Held:* For the IRS. If two or more operating corporations are merged, whether one into the other or both into a third corporation organized for that purpose, the result is more than a mere change in identity, form, or place of organization as required by Section 368(a)(1)(F). This was particularly true in the present case, since there was a substantial change in the percentage or ownership in the corporation acquired by the stockholders of the merged corporations. Berger Mach. Prods., Inc., 68 TC 358 (1977).

Consolidation of a wholly owned bank subsidiary with an existing banking association qualified as a reverse triangular merger. B was a national banking association. P was a bank holding company formed by certain stockholders of B. P formed S, a wholly owned bank subsidiary. S was then consolidated under B's charter pursuant to the National Banking Act. Under the consolidation agreement, B acquired all of the assets and assumed all of S's liabilities. The IRS ruled that under the National Banking Act the consolidation of S with B qualified as a reverse triangular merger under Sections 368(a)(1)(A) and 368(a)(2)(E). Rev. Rul. 84-104, 1984-2 CB 94.

Acquiring corporation allowed deduction for payment of merged corporation's liability. X Corporation merged with Z Corporation whereby X obtained all the assets and assumed all the liabilities of Z. As a condition of the merger, A and B, the stockholder's of Z, agreed with X to reimburse X for any after-tax expenses that X might incur as a result of a specific contingent claim that C, an employee of Z, had against Z. X transferred stock to Z equal to the fair market value of Z's assets less Z's fixed liabilities. After X settled C's claim, A and B reimbursed X in an amount equal to X's after-tax cost of the settlement with C. X, the acquiring corporation, was allowed under Sections 162 and 381(c)(4) to deduct the amount expended to settle C's claim against Z and did have not to report as income the reimbursement that it received from A and B. In addition, under Sections 354(a) and 358(a)(1), A and B were to increase their bases in stock X in an amount equal to the reimbursement paid to X and not to deduct the reimbursement. Under the principle of relation back, the indemnity payments were treated as contributions to the capital of Z made by A and B before the merger. Rev. Rul. 83-73, 1983-1 CB 84, clarifying Rev. Rul. 58-374, 1958-2 CB 396.

Two separate reorganizations found. For valid business reasons, taxpayer transferred all of its assets to two newly formed controlled subsidiaries. It then merged an unrelated corporation into a subsidiary in return for the parent's stock and reincorporated by merger into a newly formed corporation in another state. The arrangement involved separate A and F reorganizations. Rev. Rul. 79-250, 1979-2 CB 156.

IRS terms merger a sale rather than a reorganization. The stockholders in a statutory merger exchanged their stock in the merged corporation for cash received indirectly from the acquiring corporation and stock in a subsidiary of the acquired corporation. The transaction was a taxable sale of part of their stock to the acquiring corporation and a redemption of the remainder. Gain had to be recognized. The reorganization was disregarded for tax purposes. Rev. Rul. 79-273, 1979-2 CB 125.

Merger of service and lessor corporations was F reorganization. A service business and a corporation whose sole activity was leasing a building to it were owned equally by the same two stockholders. They were merged into a new corporation that continued the business and took title to the building. The IRS ruled that the merger qualified as an F reorganization, although the leasing business was terminated by the transaction. Rev. Rul. 79-71, 1979-1 CB 151.

Merger of banks qualified as F reorganization. X, a national bank, was 98.4 percent owned by a bank holding company, 0.9 percent owned by the general public, and .7 percent owned by X's directors, who were required to own stock under federal banking laws. X merged with Y, another bank owned 99.3 percent by the same holding company and .7 percent by Y's directors. The change of less than one percent in stock ownership in the merger did not prevent it from qualifiying as an F reorganization. The stock owned by the directors was disregarded in computing the change of stock ownership. Rev. Rul. 78-441, 1978-2 CB 152.

Circular cash flow to meet capitalization requirements has no effect. Cash transferred from a parent to a subsidiary to effect a reorganization merger has no tax effect when, as part of the plan of reorganization, it is returned to the original holder. Rev. Rul. 78-397, 1978-2 CB 150.

IRS illustrates exception to gain recognition rule under Section 357(c). P Corporation owned all the stock of S-1 and S-2 corporations. For valid business reasons, the decision was made to combine S-1 and S-2 pursuant to a plan of reorganization under which S-1 transferred all its assets and liabilities to S-2 in a statutory merger pursuant to state law. As a preliminary step, P gratuitously cancelled the principal amount of a debt owed by S-1 to P so that the basis of S-1's assets would exceed the total amount of its liabilities prior to the reorganization. The debt had been incurred for valid business reasons and had been outstanding for a number of years prior to the reorganization. The IRS held that P's cancellation of the principal amount of the debt owed by S-1 to P would be given substance as a contribution by P to the capital of S-1. Section 357(c) does not apply to the subsequent merger transaction, as the liabilities of S-1 assumed by S-2 did not exceed the adjusted basis of the S-1 assets transferred to S-2. Accordingly, no gain was required to be recognized. Rev. Rul. 78-330, 1978-2 CB 147.

Merger that eliminates minority stockholders deemed a redemption. The controlling stockholder of X Corporation created new Y Corporation and, thereafter, merged Y into X. In the merger, the majority stockholder received X stock while the minority stockholders received cash. The IRS ruled that the separate existence of Y would be disregarded, and the transaction would be treated as a redemption by X of the minority stockholders' stock, with its tax treatment determined under Section 302. Rev. Rul. 78-150, 1978-1 CB 214.

Cash contributed to subsidiary to avoid issuance of fractional shares not taken into account in determining whether the "substantially all" requirement was met. Contributions of cash by a parent to a subsidiary to avoid the issuance of fractional shares after an A reorganization were not taken into account in determining whether the surviving corporation held substantially all of the properties of both parties to the merger. The IRS ruled that the transaction qualified under Sections 368(a)(1)(A) and 368(a)(2)(E). Rev. Rul. 77-307, 1977-2 CB 117.

IRS adamant on *World Service Life* position. Despite judicial authority to the contrary, the IRS held that in a tax-free reorganization under Section 368(a)(1)(A) involving the merger of an individual's wholly owned corporation into its wholly owned subsidiary, the surviving corporation's use of its net operating loss carry-overs from earlier taxable years is limited by Section 382(b)(2), and application of the limitation is not prevented by Section 382(b)(3). The IRS noted that the constructive ownership of stock rules of Section 318(a) have no application to the provisions of Section 382(b). Accordingly, the IRS will not follow the decision in World Serv. Life Ins. Co., 471 F2d 247 (8th Cir. 1973). Rev. Rul. 76-36, 1976-1 CB 105.

IRS rules on merger of domestic corporation into foreign corporation's domestic subsidiary. S Corporation, a wholly owned subsidiary of P Corporation, desired to acquire all of the assets of X, an unrelated corporation. P was incorporated under the laws of a foreign country. S and X were domestic corporations. It was proposed that the acquisition be accomplished by merging X into S with the X stockholders exchanging their X stock for P stock. No stock of S could be used in the transaction. In the merger, S received all of the assets of X and assumed all of X's liabilities. The IRS held the that proposed transaction met the requirements of a reorganization under Section 368(a)(1)(A) such as business purpose, continuity of business enterprise,

REORGANIZATIONS: Mergers (A Reorganizations)

and continuity of interest. In addition, the transaction satisified the special requirements of Section 368(a)(2)(D). Therefore, it qualified as a reorganization under Section 368(a)(1)(A) by reason of the application of Section 368(a)(2)(D). Rev. Rul. 74-297, 1974-1 CB 84.

Statutory merger wherein a subsidiary distributed acquired assets and liabilities to its own subsidiary qualified as tax-free. A wholly owned subsidiary, in exchange for its parent's stock, acquired an unrelated corporation's assets and liabilities pursuant to a statutory merger. The subsidiary then distributed the acquired assets and liabilities to its wholly owned subsidiary. The transaction qualified as a statutory merger pursuant to Section 368(a)(1)(A). Rev. Rul. 72-576, 1972-2 CB 217.

Treatment of sale of stock to related corporation that merged with an unrelated corporation. An individual owned the stock of two corporations. One of the corporations merged with an unrelated corporation pursuant to Section 368(a)(1)(A). The individual retained about 85 percent of the stock after the merger. The stock of the other corporation was then sold to the new corporation for a price that was deemed to be its fair market value. The IRS ruled that the transaction was controlled by Sections 304 and 302; accordingly, the purchase of the stock was considered a distribution taxable as a dividend under Section 302(d). Rev. Rul. 72-569, 1972-2 CB 203.

Treatment of interest in a statutory merger that provided for contingent stock. Two domestic corporations agreed to merge in a transaction that would qualify as a reorganization under Section 368(a)(1)(A). As part of the plan of reorganization, provision was made for the issuance of additional shares of stock based on earnings in excess of stated amounts. The agreement provided for simple interest on the contingent shares. No part of the interest would accrue as a deduction until there was a fixed liability to pay such additional shares. Rev. Rul. 72-32, 1972-1 CB 48.

Merger of parent into subsidiary qualified as an A reorganization. Parent purchased all the stock of its subsidiary within a 12-month period. Within two years of the last stock purchase, parent was merged into subsidiary for valid business reasons. Since the parent could accomplish its desired objective of combining the two businesses by either liquidation of the subsidiary or merger, it could choose whichever form it desired. Accordingly, the merger of the parent into the subsidiary qualified as a reorganization within the meaning of Section 368(a)(1)(A). Rev. Rul. 70-223, 1970-1 CB 79.

No gain or loss recognized on the distribution of stock after merger of two corporations that owned the distributed stock. Two corporations owned all of the stock in a third corporation. Each corporation was engaged in the active conduct of a trade or business for at least five years. The stock of the first two corporations was owned by one individual. To comply with state law and for valid business reasons, the two corporations merged and distributed the stock of the third corporation to the sole stockholder. All the requirements of Section 355 were met; accordingly, no gain or loss was recognized to the sole stockholder. Rev. Rul. 70-18, 1970-1 CB 74.

Merger of corporation with one created in another state qualified as F reorganization, even though part of overall C reorganization. As part of an overall plan involving a C reorganization, a corporation giving up its assets for valid business purposes reincorporated in another state pursuant to a transaction qualifying as an F reorganization. The F reorganization qualified even though it was part of an overall plan qualifying as a C reorganization. The stockholders of the corporation giving up its assets at all times maintained their continuity of interest. Rev. Rul. 69-516, 1969-2 CB 56.

Merger of two buildings and loan associations whereby passbook and equity shares were exchanged qualified as an A reorganization. Stockholders of a building and loan association exchanged their passbook accounts and equity interests for equal passbook accounts

REORGANIZATIONS: *Mergers (A Reorganizations)*

and guarantee shares of another building and loan association. Such an exchange qualified as an A reorganization under Section 368(a)(1)(A). Rev. Rul. 69-646, 1969-2 CB 54.

Merger of two mutual savings and loans associations qualified as a reorganization where passbooks of identical amounts were exchanged. The IRS ruled that the merger of two mutual savings and loan associations qualified as a reorganization under Section 368(a)(1)(A) where passbooks of identical cash deposits were issued by the acquiring association to the share account holders of the acquired association. The savings and loan associations were both federally chartered nonstock membership banks that were owned entirely by their respective share account holders. The share accounts were evidenced by passbooks. Rev. Rul. 69-3, 1969-1 CB 103.

Options given to redeem noncallable preferred stock in a statutory merger were "other property." The IRS ruled that in a statutory merger, an option to redeem preferred stock at a fixed price from the acquired to the surviving corporation was "other property" subject to the provisions of Section 356(a). An option to redeem noncallable preferred stock at a fixed price in the future was in effect a call and something other than stock. Rev. Rul. 69-264, 1969-1 CB 102.

Assets may be transferred to more than one corporation in merger. X Corporation, which operated through six divisions, merged into Y Corporation. Immediately after the merger, the assets of the six divisions were transferred to six wholly owned subsidiaries. The IRS ruled that the transaction was a reorganization within the meaning of Sections 368(a)(1)(A) and 368(a)(2)(C) even though the assets were transferred to more than one corporation controlled by the acquiring corporation. Regulation § 1.368-2(h) provides that as used in Section 368, if the context so requires, the singular "corporation" includes the plural. Rev. Rul. 68-261, 1968-1 CB 147.

No taxable "disposition" of taxpayer's installment obligations from two corporations upon their subsequent merger. Taxpayer was a substantial stockholder in X and Y corporations. In 1955, he sold an asset to X, and in 1958, he sold one to Y. Both agreements of sale provided for installments by the respective corporations, and taxpayer elected the installment method of accounting under Section 453. In 1959, X and Y entered into a tax-free statutory merger under Section 368. The outstanding installment obligations of each corporation were not changed in amounts and maturities. The IRS ruled that there was no satisfaction or disposition of the installment obligations of either corporation resulting in gain or loss to taxpayer under Section 453(d). There was no substitution of a new or different obligor or obligation. Rev. Rul. 61-215, 1961-2 CB 110.

Distributions of cash for fractional shares on merger of common trust funds is taxable gain. When two common trust funds merge, cash is usually distributed to the holders of the shares of the funds to eliminate any fractional units of participation. The exchange of shares on such a merger does not usually result in the realization of gain or loss by the stockholders; but the IRS stated that when cash is distributed to eliminate fractional units, the receipt of that cash is deemed a partial withdrawal of the stockholder's interest in the fund, and that withdrawal is treated as a sale or exchange. Gain or loss on that withdrawal is determined by measuring the difference between the amount received by the stockholder and his adjusted basis in the interest withdrawn. Rev. Rul. 60-240, 1960-2 CB 192.

Merger was tax free despite subsequent redemption of 26 percent of shares. M Corporation, a regulated investment company, transferred all of its assets to N Corporation in exchange for stock plus a small amount of cash, which was received in lieu of fractional shares. Subsequent to the merger and not pursuant to a preconceived plan, N redeemed approximately 26 percent of the shares for cash. The transfer of the assets to N and the subsequent redemption of its stock were held to constitute two separate and distinct transactions. Accordingly, the merger qualified as a reorganization under Sections 368(a)(1)(B)

REORGANIZATIONS: *Recapitalizations (E Reorganizations)*

and 368(a)(2)(C). Rev. Rul. 56-345, 1956-2 CB 206.

Recapitalizations (E Reorganizations)

No gain or dividend on transfer to corporation pursuant to recapitalization. Taxpayers each owned an undivided interest in an office building that was operated as a partnership. The adjusted basis of the building was $140,000 and the capital of the partnership was $92,000. Taxpayers also owned all of the common stock and most of the preferred stock of a corporation. During a two-day period, taxpayers (1) contributed their preferred stock to the corporation that subsequently cancelled same, (2) surrendered their 20 shares of common (total par value $2,000) in exchange for 2,000 shares of common (total par value also $2,000) and, (3) conveyed all the partnership assets and liabilities to the corporation at book value ($92,000), payable $30,000 in cash and the balance as a capital contribution. The $30,000 cash was actually paid to a bank to discharge a loan that taxpayers had taken out when they purchased the corporation's preferred stock. The IRS determined that the $30,000 was a dividend or was taxable as boot under Section 351. *Held:* For taxpayers. No gain was realized by taxpayers under Section 351 because the amount paid by the corporation for the building did not exceed the taxpayers' adjusted bases in the realty. Since the $30,000 was paid with respect to the purchase of the realty, and not with respect to taxpayers' stock, no dividend resulted. There were good business reasons for each of the transactions. Cobbs, 64-2 USTC ¶ 9628 (ND Ala. 1964).

Cash received in an integrated transaction pursuant to recapitalization plan not a dividend. *X* Corp. adopted a recapitalization plan that permitted a stockholder to exchange voting common stock for either nonvoting preferred stock or cash. Pursuant to this plan, *A* exchanged half of his voting common stock in *X* for cash, then exchanged the other half of his voting common stock for nonvoting preferred stock. For purposes of Sections 368(a)(1)(E) and 356(a)(2), *A*'s exchanges constituted two steps in a single integrated transaction. When *A* exchanged his voting common stock in an integrated transaction for cash and nonvoting preferred stock pursuant to a recapitalization plan, his receipt of cash did not have the effect of the distribution of a dividend within the meaning of Section 356(a)(2). Rev. Rul. 84-114, 1984-2 CB 90.

Continuity of business enterprise not required in a recapitalization. Advice was sought concerning whether a recapitalization required a continuity-of-business enterprise. The IRS ruled that a continuity-of-business enterprise was not required for a recapitalization to qualify as a reorganization under Section 368(a)(1)(E). A continuity-of-business enterprise was concerned with determining whether a transaction was a tax-free reorganization or a taxable event. Because a recapitalization involves only one corporation, the transfer of assets from one corporation to another was not considered and therefore was not a requirement under Section 368(a)(1)(E). Rev. Rul. 82-34, 1982-1 CB 59.

Revenue Ruling 72-57, relating to E reorganization, was modified. Rev. Rul. 69-34, 1969-1 CB 105, concluded that cash paid for fractional shares in a recapitalization was treated under Section 302 because the payment represented a mere rounding off of fractional interests. In Rev. Rul. 72-57, 1972-1 CB 103, the same principles were applied when the primary purpose was to eliminate minority interests. The IRS modified Rev. Rul. 72-57 to say that payments for majority stockholder would be treated under Section 356(a). Rev. Rul. 78-351, 1978-2 CB 148.

Recapitalization tax free, although new stock sold to public. A recapitalization in which a corporation's common and preferred stock were converted into one class of common stock was tax free, even though 80 percent of the new stock was then sold to the public. The continuity of interest requirement need not be met in an E reorganization. Rev. Rul. 77-479, 1977-2 CB 119.

No income in E reorganization. No amount is includable in the income of debenture hold-

REORGANIZATIONS: *Recapitalizations (E Reorganizations)*

ers as a result of the exchange of their debentures for common or preferred shares in a recapitalization qualifying as an E reorganization. Rev. Rul. 75-39, 1975-1 CB 272.

No distribution resulted from recapitalization. A recapitalization in which shares of one class of common stock were exchanged for shares of a second class with a higher par value and increasing the exchanging stockholder's proportionate interests in the assets or earnings of the corporation was an isolated transaction, not part of a plan to increase their interest periodically, and it did not result in a distribution to which Sections 301 and 305(b)(2) applied. Rev. Rul. 75-93, 1975-1 CB 101.

IRS rules on a recapitalization involving the swap of preferred for common stock. Applying the statutory rules governing tax-free reorganizations, the IRS ruled that when, in accordance with a corporation's plan of recapitalization, newly issued preferred stock is exchanged for all the common stock held by its majority stockholder, the transaction constitutes a reorganization within the meaning of Section 368(a)(1)(E), and so no gain will be recognized, provided that the fair market value of the preferred stock equals that of the common. However, if the fair market value of either stock exceeds the other, the difference must be treated as having been used for the purpose otherwise indicated by the facts. Rev. Rul. 74-269, 1974-1 CB 87.

Reclassification of a subsidiary's common stock and redemption of minority stock was an E reorganization. A parent corporation owned 99 percent of the stock of its subsidiary. In an attempt to eliminate the minority stock, holdings of the subsidiary were recapitalized. Cash was paid in lieu of fractional shares. The transaction was classified as a reorganization under Section 368(a)(1)(E), not an exchange of stock under Section 1036(a). Rev. Rul. 72-57, 1972-1 CB 103.

Exchange of securities for stock and cash treated as gain from the exchange of property under Section 356. Pursuant to a transaction that qualified as a recapitalization under Section 368(a)(1)(E), a corporation issued stock and cash in exchange for outstanding debentures. The IRS ruled that any gain realized by the security holders would be treated as a gain from the exchange of property under Section 356. Rev. Rul. 71-427, 1971-2 CB 183.

Tax effect of recapitalization. Stockholders of a corporation agreed to a recapitalization in which all stockholders agreed to surrender 50 percent of their outstanding capital stock. The cost or other basis of the surrendered stock would be added to the basis of the stock retained by each stockholder. No gain or loss would be recognized to the stockholder. (IT 1168 and SM 4447 superseded.) Rev. Rul. 70-291, 1970-1 CB 168.

Exchange of revolving fund credits for share interests in a farmers' co-op was an E reorganization. A farmers' cooperative rearranged its capital structure by exchanging revolving fund certificates for share interests. Such a transaction qualified as a reorganization under Section 368(a)(1)(E). Rev. Rul. 70-298, 1970-1 CB 82.

Section 355 distribution after a recapitalization in order to meet 80 percent test qualified. A corporation recapitalized, giving minority stockholders new stock in the corporation. All rights remained the same, except that voting power was diluted, giving the majority parent stockholder 80 percent of the voting stock. The stock of the subsidiary was then distributed to the stockholders of the parent. No gain or loss was recognized to the stockholders of the parent corporation because all the requirements of Sections 355(a) and (b) were met. Rev. Rul. 69-407, 1969-2 CB 50.

Exchange of co-op stock for revolving fund credits was a recapitalization. A cooperative organization issued a new series of revolving fund certificates in amounts equal to the par value of its capital stock, solely in exchange for all of its outstanding capital stock. The exchange represented merely a change in the form of proprietary interest in the company and qualified as a recapitalization under Section 368(a)(1)(E). Rev. Rul. 69-216, 1969-1 CB 109.

Cash payment in lieu of fractional shares treated as redemption in a recapitalization. Cash payments received as part of a recapitalization in lieu of fractional shares will be treated as redemption distributions not equivalent to a dividend. The payments must represent the mere mechanical rounding off of fractions resulting from the exchange rather than separately bargained for consideration. Rev. Rul. 69-34, 1969-1 CB 105.

Reverse Acquisitions

Reverse acquisition rules of Regulation § 1.1502-75(d)(3) apply even though one of the corporations not a member of an affiliated group. The IRS held that in a reverse acquisition situation wherein an unaffiliated corporation acquires 99 percent of the stock of a parent corporation in a reverse acquisition, Regulation § 1.1502-75(d)(3) would be applied to determine the surviving corporation and short taxable years. Rev. Rul. 72-322, 1972-1 CB 287.

Reverse acquisition rules applied. In a series of transactions, the common parent of one affiliated group acquired over 80 percent of the outstanding stock of the common parent of another affiliated group. The reverse acquisition rules of Regulation § 1.1502-75(d)(3) were applied to the specific facts noted. Rev. Rul. 72-30, 1972-1 CB 286.

Spin-Offs and Other Divisive Reorganizations (D Reorganizations)— Generally

Distribution of stock warrants held taxable in spin-off. Taxpayer held stock in W, a public utility, which owned all the stock of S. In a capital restructure, taxpayers received a number of warrants and subscription privileges. Taxpayer contended that both the warrants and the later exercise of the warrants were tax free under Section 355. The Tax Court agreed with taxpayers that the transaction met the requirements of a tax-free spin-off, and therefore the distributions were tax-free. *Held:* Reversed. To qualify under Section 355, a distribution must consist solely of stock or securities and not stock warrants. The warrants had independent significance and were not a necessary step in achieving distribution. Therefore, taxpayers received a taxable distribution. Redding, 630 F2d 1169, 80-2 USTC ¶ 9637, 46 AFTR2d 80-5654 (7th Cir. 1980), cert. denied, 450 US 913 (1981).

Sister corporation's sale of assets to brother corporation and liquidation constituted a D reorganization in which there was complete identity of stock ownership, and brother corporation continued a significant portion of sister's business. Taxpayer and another corporation were wholly owned by the same individual. In 1970, the other corporation sold all of its assets to taxpayer and liquidated, distributing the sales proceeds to its stockholders. No stock in the taxpayer was received by its sister corporation or distributed to the common stockholders. Taxpayer, with only a short interruption, continued the business acquired from its sister corporation as a hedge against the interruption of supplies. The IRS argued that this sale and liquidation constituted a D reorganization. Therefore, taxpayer inherited its sister's earnings, and the distribution to the stockholder was a boot dividend under Section 356(a)(2). The Tax Court held for the IRS. *Held:* Affirmed. This sale and liquidation constituted a D reorganization, even though the liquidation formalities were followed. Futhermore, because there was complete identity of ownership between the two corporations, the formality of receiving and distributing stock in the acquiring corporation was not necessary for a D reorganization. Finally, even though there was no tax-avoidance purpose, the transaction was a D reorganization because of the continuity-of-business enterprise. Atlas Tool Co., 614 F2d 860, 80-1 USTC ¶ 9177, 45 AFTR2d 80-645 (3d Cir. 1980).

Spin-off did not qualify under Section 354 or 346. Taxpayers were minority stockholders in Pacific. In 1961, pursuant to a plan, Pacific transferred part of its business to a new corporation, Northwest, in exchange for all the latter's stock and a $200 million note. In the same year, Pacific issued to its stockholders rights to acquire 57 percent of its Northwest stock. The remaining 43 percent was offered in 1963. Taxpayers exercised their rights under which six rights plus $16 could be exchanged for a share of Northwest stock. The IRS argued that the difference between the amount paid by taxpayers and the value of the stock received was a dividend. Taxpayers argued that the receipt of the Northwest stock was tax-free under Section 355 or 354 or was entitled to capital gain treatment under Section 346. The Tax Court held for the taxpayers under Section 355 and was affirmed by the Second Circuit. The Supreme Court reversed, however, and remanded for a consideration of Sections 354 and 346. On remand, the Tax Court found neither statute applicable and held for the IRS. *Held:* Affirmed. (1) The stock rights were not "stock or securities" under Section 354(a)(1). The right represented no voting, dividend, or liquidating rights in Pacific and were thus not "stock." Even if they were "securities," their distribution would have resulted, under Sections 301 and 317(a), in the same tax now disputed. Also, there was no reorganization as required by Section 354. If a D reorganization occurred, Section 354(b) was not satisfied because Pacific did not transfer "substantially all" its assets to Northwest, and Pacific did not distribute 43 percent of the Northwest stock or the $200 million note. That the transaction may also have been an F reorganization did not change the result. All divisive reorganizations were intended to satisfy Section 354(b) or 355. (2) Section 346 was applicable. There was no redemption as required by Section 346(a)(2), and Pacific did not distribute *all* the proceeds or assets of a discontinued business as required by the provisions of Section 346(b). Gordon, 424 F2d 378, 70-1 USTC ¶ 9279, 25 AFTR2d 70-820 (2d Cir. 1970).

Value of stock rights in excess of fair market value not a dividend. Taxpayers owned stock in *P*, an 80 percent controlled subsidiary of AT&T. Under a reorganization plan, *P* spun off a portion of its assets to a newly organized corporation, *N*, in exchange for its stock. It then gave taxpayers transferable rights to subscribe to *N*'s stock at a price below its fair market value. In order to raise capital, the purchase rights required taxpayers to pay $16 per share plus six stock rights. The IRS contended that the excess of the fair market value of the stock over the subscription price was a taxable dividend to taxpayers. The Tax Court held that the transaction qualified as a tax-free spin-off under Section 355; therefore, taxpayers did not receive a taxable dividend. However, upon a later sale of the stock rights at a profit, the Tax Court held the gain to be a dividend taxable as ordinary income. *Held:* Affirmed, in part. Because the division was for valid business reasons and adhered to the technical requirements of Section 355, and the transaction did not have tax avoidance as a purpose, the transaction was tax free. The receipt of the stock rights did not result in a dividend. Taxpayers' later sale at a profit was taxable as capital gain, not ordinary income, because of its original classification under Section 355. Gordon, 382 F2d 499, 67-2 USTC ¶ 9592, 20 AFTR2d 5255 (2d Cir. 1967).

Reorganization was D; distribution was a dividend. A state bank, of which taxpayer was a principal stockholder, was reorganized as a national bank. The operating assets of the state bank were transferred to the national bank, subject to liabilities. The real estate was transferred to the stockholders and leased back to the national bank. The IRS contended that the assets distributed to the stockholders were a dividend. The district court agreed, holding that the transaction was a D reorganization because taxpayer had control of the acquiring corporation. *Held:* Affirmed. Taxpayer continued his interest in the going concern. The distributed assets were boot and taxable as a dividend. Babcock, 372 F2d 240, 67-1 USTC ¶ 9236 (10th Cir.), cert. denied, 387 US 918 (1967).

Transfer of assets treated as reorganization rather than as liquidation. Taxpayer, an investment house dealing in stocks and bonds, acquired 50 percent of a utilities corporation that supplied electric, gas, telephone, and water services. Prompted in part by its fear that the water service assets would be lost through condemnation, taxpayer wanted to separate the water service assets from the other assets. The corporation was liquidated pursuant to a plan under which a trustee acting for the stockholders transferred electric, gas, and telephone service assets to a newly formed corporation. The water service assets were similarly transferred to another newly formed corporation. The trustee turned over the stock of the transferee corporations to the former stockholders of the utilities corporation. The IRS contended that the split of one corporation into two was a reorganization and not a liquidation under Section 331. *Held:* For the IRS. Based on the circumstances, there was a reorganization. The split of one corporation into two was admittedly a change in business form and identity. However, there was no substantial change in ownership or operation. The same stockholders who controlled the liquidated corporation also owned the transferee corporations, and the proportion of ownership was substantially the same. The transferee corporations conducted the same business that had been conducted by the liquidated corporation. Stephens, Inc., 321 F. Supp. 1159, 70-2 USTC ¶ 9677 (ED Ark. 1970).

Portion of regulations that denies tax-free spin-off to single business again held invalid. To satisfy objections of its principal customer, taxpayer, which operated three plants, organized a new corporation to which it transferred one of its plants. The stock of the new corporation was then distributed to taxpayer's stockholders in the same proportion as their ownership in taxpayer. The IRS asserted that under Regulation § 1.355-1(a), the transaction did not qualify for tax-free spin-off treatment. *Held:* For taxpayer. The court found that Regulation § 1.355-1(a) was invalid to the extent that it denies the benefits of Section 355 to a division involving a single business. Marett, 63-2 USTC ¶ 9567 (ND Ga. 1962).

Capital contribution and split-off were in substance a taxable exchange of business interests. Taxpayer and another corporation each owned 50 percent of the stock of a third corporation, and each had a 50 percent interest in the assets of a joint venture. Differences of opinion arose regarding the operations of the businesses. As a consequence, taxpayer and the other corporation agreed to a complete separation. It was the intention of the parties that a division would be effected whereby taxpayer would own 100 percent of the third corporation and the joint venture would be owned by the other corporation. Accordingly, the joint venture interests were contributed to the third corporation, and it split off the joint venture, leaving taxpayer in complete control of the third corporation. Taxpayer reported no gain on the transactions. *Held:* For the IRS. The various steps were merely a circuitous route taken in the hope of transmuting the fundamental nature of the entire transaction along the way. The events were in substance one transaction in which taxpayer exchanged its interest in the joint venture for the complete control of the third corporation. Accordingly, the exchange resulted in taxable gain, and the amount realized by taxpayer was the measure of the value, as determined, of the third corporation's stock that it received. Portland Mfg. Co., 56 TC 58 (1971).

Separation of selling function deemed natural and proper; "spun-off" partnership was separate entity. Taxpayer, with the assistance of Kann, his brother-in-law, set up a corporation to import ceramic products from Japan. On behalf of the corporation, taxpayer traveled to Japan and participated in the design of the products that the firm imported. Kann became dissatisfied with the results of the operations and attributed the venture's lack of success to taxpayer's preoccupation with design at the expense of selling. To remedy the situation, Kann suggested that a separate selling business be established in which he could play a larger role. In response, taxpayer formed a family partnership to handle the merchandising and selling functions of the business and gave part of his proprietary interest to two trusts for the benefit of his minor children. Kann, a trustee of the children's trusts, did most of the work of the partnership. Attacking the partnership, the IRS alleged that the partnership had no separate existence from the corporation and that the trusts were not valid partners. *Held:* For taxpayer. The Tax Court held the partnership to be a separate entity and ruled that the trusts were valid partners. Although the selling function could have been performed by a separate division of the corporation, good business considerations motivated the separation of functions. The trusts were valid partners because the trustees were not subservient to taxpayer, and the trusts were not used to discharge the obligation of taxpayer to support his children. Hartman, 43 TC 105 (1964), acq. 1965-2 CB 5.

Spin-off feature in consolidation nontaxable. American, a state bank, and Security, a national bank, agreed to consolidate under the charter of the national bank. American had operated an insurance department for 50 years. Since a federal bank is prohibited by law from conducting an insurance business, the consolidation agreement provided that American divest itself of this business. American accomplished this by setting up a new corporation, transferring the insurance business to the new corporation, and distributing to its stockholders the stock it received in the exchange. The IRS contended that the distribution was a dividend. *Held:* A valid spin-off was effected. After the distribution, the stockholders had the same economic interest as before. Federal law provided a good business purpose. The control requirement was satisfied, as the distribution was from American rather than from the combined group. American was regarded as being in the active conduct of a business after the distribution and loss of identity in the consolidation. A section of the National Banking Act provides for a separate corporate existence of banks consolidating under federal law. The court considered this law as dispositive of the issue. Morris Trust, 367 F2d 794, 66-2 USTC ¶ 9718, 18 AFTR2d 5843 (4th Cir. 1966).

Non-pro rata split-off not "stock swap," hence nontaxable under Section 355; no constructive boot. Taxpayer and Tuttle, who each owned 50 percent of the stock of A and B, decided, as a result of management differences, to divide the two businesses equally. Pursuant to an agreement, they transferred their B stock to A as a contribution to A's capital. A new corporation, C, was then formed, to which A transferred the operating assets of its Portsmouth division, cash, and all of the B stock, in exchange for all the stock of C. (Thus A became sole stockholder of C, which became sole stockholder of B.) All of the C stock was then transferred by A to taxpayer in exchange for all of his A stock. The result of these transactions was that taxpayer became sole stockholder of C, which in turn owned all the B stock, and Tuttle became sole stockholder of A. After these transfers, all three corporations continued their active businesses, C continuing the Portsmouth operation. The IRS contended that (1) the transaction did not qualify as a split-off since it resulted in a prohibited stock swap and (2) even if it qualified, taxpayer was chargeable with the constructive receipt of boot, since it was originally intended that he receive boot (cash and B stock) but the plan was altered for tax-avoidance purposes. *Held:* For taxpayer. The court found no merit in either contention, and held that all the conditions of Section 355 had been satisfied, and the transaction was therefore nontaxable. Badanes, 39 TC 410 (1962).

Sale and liquidation deemed a reorganization and dividend distribution. Taxpayers, W and P, each owned 50 percent of two corporations, A and B. A was engaged in manufacturing, and B leased its principal asset, a parcel of improved real estate, to A. In 1973, B transferred the real estate to A. B received cash and a mortgage as payment. B then distributed all its assets to W and P in exchange for their stock in B. Taxpayers contended that the foregoing transactions amounted to a sale of assets followed by a liquidation of B, giving rise to capital gains treatment on the amounts received. The IRS argued that the transactions were merely steps in a corporate reorganization under Sections 368(a)(1)(D) and 354 coupled with a distribution of a dividend. *Held:* For the IRS. The corporations were related, controlled by the same stock holders, and the transactions were pursuant to a general plan approved by all interested parties. Altenpohl, 36 TCM 1377, ¶ 77,342 P-H Memo. TC (1977).

REORGANIZATIONS: Spin-Offs and Other Divisive Reorganizations

Corporate exchanges not a reorganization or a spin-off. Two families, K and S, each owned 50 percent of the stock of A and B corporations. Dissension arose between the two families, and it was decided to divide the businesses between them. Accordingly, S family assigned to B their 50 percent interest in A, and K family assigned to A their 50 percent interest in B. Then A and B exchanged the stock each received in the other corporation. The IRS contended that the exchanges qualified neither as a tax-free reorganization under Section 368 nor as a tax-free spin-off under Section 355. *Held:* For the IRS. Each corporation acquired its own stock in the exchange, and neither distributed to its stockholders any stock or securities of the corporation to which the assets were transferred. Although the transaction might have been cast in a form that would qualify for nonrecognition of gain, it was not, and the decision must be made upon the basis of what was actually done rather than upon what might have been done. Penn-Warrington Hosiery Mills, Inc., 20 TCM 1050, ¶ 61,211 P-H Memo. TC (1961).

Bausch & Lomb rationale not applied to nondivisive D reorganization. P Corporation owned 50 percent of the outstanding stock of T Corporation and 80 percent of the outstanding stock of S. S owned 50 percent of T, and both P and S acquired their stock in T for cash over 20 years earlier. The parties did not file consolidated returns. The parties entered into a nondivisive D reorganization whereby T transferred its assets to S for S voting stock, and S assumed T's liabilities. S's 50 percent stock interest in T was canceled; the S stock received by T was distributed to P in exchange for T stock; T dissolved. The IRS ruled that although the Bausch & Lomb rationale restricted the use of C reorganizations, in which the acquiring corporation already owns part of the stock of the corporation whose assets are to be acquired, it did not apply in determining whether the acquisition of T's assets by S met the requirements of Section 368(a)(1)(D), because the definition in the section contains no "solely for voting stock" requirement. Rev. Rul. 54-396, 1954-2 CB 147, was distinguishable on the same basis. Accordingly, the reorganization qualified under Section 368(a)(1)(D) even though S owned stock in T before acquiring T. Rev. Rul. 85-107, 1985-30 IRB 15.

Spin-off is tax-free, although gain reorganized under Section 357(c). Corporation X transferred one of its two active businesses to Corporation Y and then distributed the Y stock to X's stockholders. Y assumed liabilities of X that exceeded the basis of the property transferred to Y, so X had to recognize gain under Section 357(c). However, this gain recognition did not violate the Section 355(b)(2)(C) rule that neither active business be acquired in a transaction in which gain was recognized. The gain also did not cause the Y stock to be considered boot to the stockholder under Section 355(a)(3). The transaction qualified as a tax-free spin-off. Rev. Rul. 78-422, 1978-2 CB 143.

Distribution of cash to dissenting stockholders did not cause spin-off preceding merger to be treated as a Section 355 device. X Corporation sought to acquire P Corporation but did not want to acquire S Corporation, a subsidiary of P. Accordingly, P distributed its S stock to its stockholders pro rata, and then X acquired P stock in a B reorganization from all the stockholders of P except those who dissented to the acquisition. The dissenters, who owned 5 percent of P's stock, received cash from P for their shares. The distribution of cash to the dissenters would not cause the spin-off on S stock to be deemed a device to distribute earnings and profits under Section 355(a)(1)(B). Rev. Rul. 78-150, 1978-1 CB 214.

Qualifying Section 303 redemption did not disqualify split-off. X, a holding company, held the stock of Y and Z companies. The stock of X was held 80 percent by the estate of A and 20 percent by B, an individual. Pursuant to a split-off, the stock of Y and Z was distributed to X's stockholders. Due to liquidity problems, part of the stock of Y and Z was redeemed under Section 303. Because the redemption would have qualified under Section 303 prior to the split-off, the IRS ruled that the distribution was not used as a device for the distribution of earnings and profits, and the transaction qualified under Section 355. Rev. Rul. 77-377, 1977-2 CB 111.

Entire net operating loss available to transferor corporation following a split-off. M Corporation formed and split off S Corporation. M transferred 50 percent of its assets and liabilities to S in transactions that qualified as a D reorganization and satisfied the requirements of Section 355. The IRS distinguished this from a corporate split-up because the split-off did not involve the liquidation of M. The IRS held that Section 381(a)(2) was inapplicable, since M did not transfer substantially all of its assets. Therefore, M's entire net operating loss was available to M following the split-off. Rev. Rul. 77-133, 1977-1 CB 96.

Distribution in redemption of shares followed by a reincorporation of the assets constitutes a reorganization. For business reasons, pursuant to an integrated plan, X Corporation distributed the assets of one of its active businesses to its stockholders in redemption of part of their X stock. The stockholders in turn transferred all of these assets to Y, a newly organized corporation. The IRS ruled that there was a D reorganization rather than a partial liquidation. Rev. Rul. 77-191, 1977-1 CB 94.

IRS ruled on spin-off involving asset division. In a factually complex ruling, the IRS was asked to advise on the tax consequences of a situation in which two corporations, whose stock was owned equally by two unrelated stockholders, formed a third corporation by transferring one half of the assets of each to the new corporation in exchange for a proportionate share of its stock and then transferred the stock of the new corporation to one of the stockholders in exchange for all the stock held by that stockholder in the two original corporations. Rev. Rul. 77-11, 1977-1 CB 93.

Conversion ratio increase concerning a nontaxable spin-off to common stockholders not a deemed dividend. An increased conversion ratio for preferred shares was used to compensate for dilution in the value of common shares arising from a Section 355 spin-off. The IRS considered this adjustment as having been made pursuant to a bona fide adjustment formula. Therefore, the conversion would not be treated as a deemed distribution of stock to which Section 301 would apply. Rev. Rul. 77-37, 1977-1 CB 85.

Foreign government requirements, in respect of merger terms, disqualifies D reorganization attempt. X Corporation, a domestic entity, owned 85 percent of Y Corporation and 100 percent of Z Corporation, both of which were incorporated under the laws of a foreign country. The foreign country enacted a law that required foreign stockholders that engaged in certain basic industries to enter into agreements providing for the gradual complete takeover by the government of such corporations as Y and X. In anticipation of the involuntary sale and for other valid reasons, X decided to merge Y into Z. After formulation of a merger plan but before it had been effected, X was formally notified by the foreign government that in order to get approval, X would be required to sell 51 percent of its stock interest in Z to the government. Because X still wished to merge the corporations, it entered into an agreement with the foreign government to sell it 51 percent of the stock of Z simultaneously with the completion of the merger of Y into Z. Subsequently, Y transferred all of its assets to Z, and Z assumed all the liabilities of Y. Y dissolved and X received additional shares of Z for its Y stock. Immediately thereafter, X delivered 51 percent of the stock of Z to the foreign government in exchange for local currency. In disqualifying the reorganization from tax-free treatment, the IRS noted that at the time of the transaction, X was under a binding obligation to transfer control of Z to the foreign government immediately after the merger. Moreover, X wished to merge Y into Z to put its corporation structure in the most advantageous position pending its gradual complete takeover by the foreign government. Therefore, although the subsequent sale of stock to the government was compulsory in that it was necessary in order to get approval of the merger and was made under threat of eventual expropriation, it was an integral part of the plan of reorganization. Accordingly, the sale by X of 51 percent of the Z stock to the foreign government prevented the merger of Y into Z from qualifying as a reorganization. Rev. Rul. 76-108, 1976-1 CB 103.

IRS clarified why a pro rata spin-off discussed in a prior ruling qualified for nonrecognition of gain or loss under Section 355. Rev. Rul. 73-44, 1973-1 CB 182, concerning nonrecognition of gain or loss in a pro rata spin-off, was clarified as follows: Y, the wholly owned subsidiary of X, qualified as a corporation engaged in the active conduct of a trade or business under Section 355(b)(2) only because of its conduct of the glass container business. The newspaper business, operated by Y, was acquired by X within the five-year period preceding the date of distribution in a transaction in which gain was recognized and then transferred to Y in exchange for Y stock in a transaction in which gain or loss was not recognized. The newspaper business did not meet the requirements of Section 355(b). Rev. Rul. 76-54, 1976-1 CB 96.

Treatment of a stockholder in a Section 355 split-off. A cash distribution does not have the effect of a dividend under Section 356(a)(2), and the recognized gain on the exchange is treated as gain on the exchange of property where a stockholder exchanged his shares in the distributing corporation for cash and stock of a subsidiary in a split-off as described in Section 355. Rev. Rul. 74-516, 1974-2 CB 121.

Split-off qualifies where control acquired as part of the split-off. A distribution of stock pursuant to a split-off may qualify for nonrecognition of gain under Section 355 where control is acquired as part of the split-off. Rev. Rul. 71-593, 1971-2 CB 181.

Spin-off qualified where both parent and subsidiary did not have current or accumulated earnings and profits. A parent corporation distributed to its stockholders all the stocks of a wholly owned subsidiary. Neither the parent nor the subsidiary had current or accumulated earnings and profits. Such a transaction qualified under Section 355 as the distribution and could not be used as a device for the distribution of earnings and profits. Rev. Rul. 71-384, 1971-2 CB 181.

No gain or loss recognized in non-pro rata distribution of subsidiary's stock to certain stockholders of parent. A corporation, pursuant to a reorganization qualifying under Section 368(a)(1)(B), acquired all of the outstanding stock of the subsidiary in point. Later, and for valid business reasons, the parent decided to divest itself of the subsidiary. It did so by distributing the stock of the subsidiary to its original stockholders in exchange for 85 percent of the stock of parent that was issued as part of the original B reorganization. Immediately prior to the exchange, a substantial capital contribution was made by the parent to the subsidiary in order to reduce the disparity in the market values of the respective stocks. No gain or loss was recognized, as the transaction qualified as a distribution pursuant to the provisions of Section 355. Rev. Rul. 71-383, 1971-2 CB 180.

Spin-off followed by a stock-for-stock exchange qualified as a B reorganization. A company engaged in two distinct businesses for over five years. One of these businesses was spun off to the stockholders of the corporation. The distributing corporation then exchanged its stock for the stock of an unrelated corporation. The distributing corporation was to remain a subsidiary of the acquiring corporation. Such a transaction qualified as a reorganization under Section 368(a)(1)(B). Rev. Rul. 70-434, 1970-2 CB 83.

Distribution of stock of wholesale drug division nontaxable under Section 355. A corporation operated both a wholesale and retail division in the drug business. The majority of the sales of the wholesale division were to the retail division, although the balance of the sales produced substantial income. A new corporation that received all the assets and liabilities of the wholesale division was formed, and the stock of the new corporation was distributed pro rata to the stockholders. The original corporation operated both divisions

REORGANIZATIONS: *Spin-Offs and Other Divisive Reorganizations*

for more than five years; the new corporation remained in business after the distribution. The IRS ruled that the transaction was a reorganization under Section 368(a)(1)(D). Further, no gain or loss was recognized to the stockholders on the distribution of the stock of the new corporation. Rev. Rul. 68-407, 1968-2 CB 147.

Vacant land could not be spun off tax-free. A manufacturing company that also operated rooming houses boarded them up in 1956, demolished them in 1957, and leased the vacant land to an unrelated party. The corporation merely collected the rents and paid the real estate taxes on the land. The corporation proposed to transfer the vacant land to a new corporation in a D reorganization and then distribute the stock. The IRS ruled that the proposed distribution of stock did not qualify as a nontaxable distribution under Section 355 and was not a reorganization under Section 368(a)(1)(D) because the passive receipt of rental income was not a trade or business. There was no gain to the corporation on the transfer of the property to a new corporation solely in exchange for stock, but the distribution of this stock was treated as a taxable distribution to the stockholders. Rev. Rul. 68-284, 1968-1 CB 143.

Reorganization did not change spin-off rules. Section 355 permits a corporation to spin off a subsidiary's stock without tax consequences under certain conditions. One of these conditions is that the stock not be acquired in a taxable transaction within five years of the distribution. The IRS ruled that a corporation that owned 90 percent of the stock of a subsidiary for more than the required five years and later acquired the remaining 10 percent in a taxable exchange may exchange this stock for new subsidiary stock in a recapitalization under Section 368(a)(1)(E) and then distribute this new stock under Section 355 without the *entire* stock distribution being deemed "other property" under Section 355(a)(3). The acquisition date for the five-year period related back to the original acquisition date. Only the 10 percent of the stock that was held for less than five years was considered "other property." Rev. Rul. 65-286, 1965-2 CB 92.

"Illusory" control does not qualify spin-off. The IRS ruled that in a tax-free spin-off, the distributing corporation must have 80 percent control of the corporation whose stock it distributes "immediately before the distribution." A owned all of the stock of X and 30 shares of Y stock. X owned the other 70 shares of Y stock. A contributed 10 shares of Y stock to X (giving the latter 80 shares, or 80 percent control), and X immediately thereafter distributed the 80 shares of Y stock to A. Such a transaction did not qualify as a nontaxable transaction under Section 355, since X did not have "control" of Y within the meaning of Section 368(c) except in a transitory and illusory sense. Section 355 cannot be made to apply to a transaction in which an immediately preceeding contribution to capital is made solely in an attempt to qualify the distribution. Rev. Rul. 63-260, 1963-2 CB 147.

Spin-off of hotel business did not qualify where hotel earnings financed retained business during five-year period. A corporation engaged in the hotel and real estate business for over five years could not spin off tax-free the hotel business for stock in a new corporation pursuant to Section 355, where within the five-year period prior to the distribution, it acquired substantial new rental properties earnings. Rev. Rul. 59-400, 1959-2 CB 114.

"Split-off" reorganization involving sale of stock to key employee tax-free. All of the stock of a corporation engaged in two independent businesses (manufacturing and brokerage) for over five years was owned by a husband, his wife, and their son. For business reasons, they decided to split off the brokerage business and give a key employee a minority interest in it. This was accomplished by having the employee buy from the wife for cash some of the stock of the old corporation that she held. Immediately thereafter, a new corporation was organized to carry on the brokerage business. The old corporation turned over the assets pertaining to the brokerage business to the new corporation in return for all of its preferred and common stock. At the same time, the husband and the employee (but not the wife or the son) surrendered all of their stock in the old corporation for the preferred and common of the new. The employee's interest in the entire stock equity of the new corporation was 18 percent, and the husband owned the balance of the stock. The IRS ruled that the prior sale to the employee did not affect the tax-free nature of the split-off, since the transaction did not constitute a device to distribute earnings and profits and did not violate the continuity-of-interest requirement. It also ruled that the preferred stock was Section 306 stock in the hands of the stockholder receiving it. Rev. Rul. 59-197, 1959-1 CB 77.

Distributing operation not separate business; spin-off taxable. A soft drink bottling company distributed its beverages through facilities in different localities. It transferred its distributing operations at three of the locations to three new corporations in return for their capital stock. It then distributed the stock to its stockholders on a pro rata basis. The distribution of the stock in the three corporations was held to constitute a dividend. It did not qualify as a tax-free divisive reorganization under Section 355 because the operations at the three locations were not considered separate businesses, but part of one integrated enterprise. Rev. Rul. 58-54, 1958-1 CB 181.

Publisher of four magazines could spin off one tax free. Taxpayer published four trade magazines, one for the metal working field, the others for the electrical industry. It transferred all the assets pertaining to the metal magazine business to a new corporation in return for all the latter's common stock, which was then distributed pro rata to the stockholders of the old corporation. The transaction was held to constitute a nontaxable spin-off reorganization. The metal magazine had separate editorial staff and salesmen, and it was a business separate from the electrical magazines. Rev. Rul. 56-451, 1956-2 CB 208.

Spin-off of branch operations to new location tax free. A corporation that engaged in turkey raising, processing, and marketing transferred its net assets used in its western and southern activities to a new corporation in exchange for common stock of the latter. Under the plan, the stock was distributed to stockholders who favored the branch business in exchange for their stock. The IRS ruled that this was a tax-free spin-off transaction under Section 368(a)(1)(B). The branch business was a separate one; consequently, the transfer was of an already existing five-year business to a new location, not the formation of a new business. The distribution of the stock to some of the stockholders of the old in return for all or a portion of their old stock resulted in no gain or loss. Rev. Rul. 56-344, 1956-2 CB 195.

Real estate not separate business; could not be spun off. A corporation was engaged in the operation of a chain of grocery stores and in the manufacture and distribution of bakery and creamery products. It owned the real estate on which some of the stores were situated. The corporation could organize separate corporations for the bakery and creamery products and spin off the stock of these corporations tax free to its stockholders. However, the operation of the real estate did not constitute a separate trade or business, and the real estate could not be similarly spun off tax-free under the provisions of Section 355. Rev. Rul. 56-266, 1956-1 CB 184.

Distribution of subsidiary's stock to a group of parent's stockholders was a tax-free split-up. A corporation engaged in the hardware business owned all of the common and 12 percent of the preferred stock of a subsidiary appliance corporation. Both corporations had been engaged in the active conduct of their respective businesses for more than five years. In order to effect a separation, the following plan was adopted: First, the subsidiary issued additional shares of its common in exchange for its preferred that were owned by stockholders other than the parent corporation. After this exchange, the parent owned 93 percent of the preferred. Then, the parent distributed the stock of the subsidiary to a dissident group of its stockholders in exchange for their stock in the parent. The latter exchange was held tax-free as a divisive reorganization under Section 355. While the parent acquired control (80 percent of the voting and nonvoting stock) within five years of the split-up, the acquisition of over 80 percent of the preferred was in a tax-free exchange. Such acquisitions do not come within a five-year ban. Rev. Rul. 56-117, 1956-1 CB 180.

Spin-Offs and Other Divisive Reorganizations—Active Business Requirement

Active trade or business requirement for nonrecognition in split-off. A corporation had been engaged in the real estate business. One of its properties was destroyed by fire. Disagreement arose among the stockholders regarding rehabilitation; as a result, the property was transferred to a new corporation whose stock was distributed to taxpayer and another in exchange for their stock in the old corporation. Thereafter, activities directed toward returning the property to income-producing status were engaged in on behalf of the new corporation. Taxpayer excluded his gain on the exchange under Section 355. The Tax Court held against taxpayer. *Held:* Affirmed. A trade or business consists of a specific existing group of activities being carried on for the purpose of earning income or profit. The property that was transferred, together with the activities in connection therewith, was not sufficient to constitute the "active conduct of a trade or business." The gain on the exchange was therefore taxable. Spheeris, 461 F2d 271, 72-1 USTC ¶ 9395 (7th Cir. 1972).

Split-off taxable where five-year active business requirements not met. As a result of a disagreement among stockholders, a wholly owned subsidiary was liquidated, and certain of its operating assets were transferred to a new corporation at the end of 1955. Taxpayer then exchanged his minority holdings in the parent corporation for all the stock of the new corporation and treated the transaction as a tax-free Section 355 split-off. The Tax Court held that the transaction did not qualify, since control of the subsidiary had been acquired in a taxable transaction within the prescribed five-year period. *Held:* Affirmed. While negotiations for the acquisition of the subsidiary had started in 1950, the court concluded that no control was acquired before April 17, 1951, and no ownership was assumed before March 26, 1951. Since the new stock was distributed on December 31, 1955 (or at the latest February 9, 1956), the five-year requirement was not complied with. The court further found that (1) no tax-free reorganization (merger or consolidation) took place, since under state law the transaction resulted in a liquidation and dissolution, and taxpayer's exchange of his stock was a subsequent transaction and (2) no Section 368(a)(1)(D) reorganization resulted, since the requirements of that section were not met. Russell, 345 F2d 534, 65-2 USTC ¶ 9448 (5th Cir. 1965).

Corporation's rent of half its building not separate business under Section 355. Taxpayers were stockholders of a corporation engaged in the business of real estate and insurance brokerage. Since 1947, the corporation had owned and managed a building, 50 percent of which it occupied and the remainder of which it leased to others. In 1955, the corporation transferred the building to a newly formed corporation, distributing the stock of the new corporation to taxpayers. The new corporation then leased back the building to the old corporation for 10 years. Taxpayers contended that their receipt of stock was tax-free under Section 355, which allows a tax-free spin-off if certain conditions are met, including the requirement that the old corporation have conducted two or more separate businesses for a five-year period. The Tax Court held that this requirement was not met, since the old corporation never conducted a business engaged in the active rental of real estate. *Held:* Affirmed. The corporation occupied 50 percent of the floor space of the building and its own rent constituted 70 percent of the total rent received. Appleby, 296 F2d 925, 62-1 USTC ¶ 9178, 9 AFTR2d 372 (3d Cir. 1962).

REORGANIZATIONS: *Spin-Offs and Other Divisive Reorganizations*

Section 355 split-up of single business upheld. Taxpayer and another were each 50 percent stockholders in a corporation actively engaged in a construction business for more than five years. Because of differences, the stockholders agreed to divide the business. The old corporation transferred half of its assets (cash, equipment, and one construction contract) to a newly formed corporation in return for all of its stock. The old corporation then distributed to taxpayer the new corporation's stock in exchange for his stock. The IRS determined that gain was recognized on the exchange. Taxpayer argued that no gain should be recognized under Section 355, which provides for nonrecognition of gain to stockholders upon the distribution of stock of a corporation controlled by the distributing corporation if, immediately after the distribution, both corporations are actively engaged in a trade or business that had been actively conducted for five years. *Held:* For taxpayer. The regulations interpret Section 355 as applicable only to the separation of two or more businesses, formerly operated by a single corporation. The court found this regulation unreasonable and inconsistent with the Code and declared it invalid. It concluded that Congress intended to permit the tax-free division of a corporation operating a single business. The purpose of the active business rule was merely to prevent a tax-free split into active and inactive entities. Coady, 289 F2d 490, 61-1 USTC ¶ 9415, 7 AFTR2d 1322 (6th Cir. 1961).

Reorganization did not qualify as a tax-free division. Taxpayer and *H* each owned 50 percent of the stock of *H-A* Corporation. Pursuant to a plan to divide the corporation, *A-E* Corporation was formed. In return for all *A-E*'s stock, *H-A* transferred to it various properties that had been transferred to *H-A* only a few days before the reorganization. Subsequently, taxpayers changed all their stock in *H-A* for all of the shares of *A-E*. *H-A* retained the operating assets it used in its business. The IRS determined that the transaction did not qualify under Section 355. *Held:* For the IRS. *H-A* represented a mere conduit through which payment was made by *H* for the value of taxpayer's interest in the operating assets of *H-A*. *H-A* did not transfer a trade or business to *A-E* that *H-A* had actively conducted through a five-year period. Atlee, 67 TC 395 (1976), acq. 1977-1 CB 1.

Tax Court determined, for purposes of Section 355, that two hospitals owned by the same corporation were separate businesses. Taxpayer owned stock in Oak Park Community Hospital, Inc., a corporation formed in 1956 to operate a Stockton, California hospital. In 1961, Oak Park purchased an additional hospital located in Los Angeles. Each hospital was essentially run as a separate business. Disputes between the stockholders resulted in a plan by which Oak Park would separately incorporate each hospital and distribute, in liquidations, the stock of one newly formed subsidiary to one group of stockholders and the stock of the second new subsidiary to the other group of stockholders. This plan was carried out in 1964. Both corporations were actively engaged in business after the split-up. The taxpayer reported a capital gain on the exchange of his Oak Park stock for stock in one of the new subsidiaries. The IRS claimed that under Section 355, taxpayer was not entitled to capital gains treatment on the ground that the Los Angeles hospital was a separate business of Oak Park operating for less than five years. Taxpayer argued that Oak Park operated a single hospital business (of which the Los Angeles hospital was but a part) and that the five-year active business requirement of Section 355 was met. *Held:* For the IRS. The Los Angeles hospital was a separate business from the Stockton hospital. Because there was no integration of each hospital's income-producing activities (aside from sharing the same top management), the Los Angeles hospital business was not a part or extension of the Stockton hospital business, that is, each had its own assets and employees and thus was self-sufficient. Accordingly, the Los Angeles hospital, purchased only three years before the split-up, was not an active business in Oak Park's hands for the five years required under Section 355. Nielsen, 67 TC 311 (1973).

Rental business failed to meet active conduct requirement of Section 355. Taxpayers wholly owned *A* Corporation, a distributor and processor of steel, and *C* Corporation, a steel products warehouse. *A* formed *B,* a wholly owned subsidiary, to which it transferred real property in exchange for *B*'s stock. *B* leased the property back to *A* and later acquired additional real property, on which it constructed a plant that it leased to *C.* From 1961 through 1965, *B*'s income was derived strictly from its rentals to *A* and *C.* In 1965, all of *B*'s issued and outstanding stock was distributed to taxpayers and treated as a nontaxable transaction under Section 355. The IRS determined that the distribution was (1) used principally as a device to distribute earnings and profits; (2) *B* had not met the five-year active conduct requirement before the distribution; and (3) the distribution constituted a taxable dividend. *Held:* For the IRS. Because *A* Corporation's activities consisted of lease-back arrangements with related corporations, it did not meet the five-year active conduct requirement of Section 355 for a spin-off. The corporation had no employees and claimed no deductions for its officers' compensation or services rendered. Hence, the distribution of *B*'s stock to taxpayers was a taxable dividend. Rafferty, 55 TC 490 (1970).

Distribution of stock of a subsidiary 2.5 years after the business was acquired not a tax-free distribution under Section 355. Taxpayer owned stock in a corporation that operated a hospital and that acquired a second hospital. In the course of operating the two hospitals, disputes arose among the stockholders. Splitting up the corporation was the only acceptable solution. This was accomplished by the formation of two new corporations to which the old corporation transferred the respective hospital properties in exchange for its stock. The stock of the new corporations was then distributed pro rata to the stockholders. Taxpayer and other dissident stockholders received stock in the corporation to which the recently acquired hospital had been transferred. Taxpayer maintained that the distribution was tax free under Section 355. *Held:* For the IRS. The trade or business conducted by the new corporation after the old corporation's distribution of its stock was the same business that the distributing corporation had acquired 2.5 years earlier. Although the case did not present a purposeful attempt to bail out corporate earnings by the acquisition of a business for later distribution, and the record established a valid business purpose for the split-up, the transaction clearly did not meet the five-year active business requirements. Boettger, 51 TC 324 (1968).

Spin-off of branch store successful. A corporation located in Pueblo, Colorado had been a distributor of radio parts for many years. In 1954, spurred by a new demand for television parts, the corporation opened a branch store in Grand Junction. A local businessman was induced to manage the new store. Under his guidance, the store prospered, and when he evinced a desire to invest in the business, the stockholders were agreeable. In 1957, the assets of the branch were transferred to a new corporation in exchange for stock of the new corporation. The stock of the new subsidiary was then distributed to the stockholders of the parent company. Land was contributed to the new corporation by the manager, who received stock in exchange. The business was thereafter operated on this land. The IRS admitted that the distribution was not a device to distribute profits, but claimed that the five-year active business requirement of Section 355 was not met, as the opening of the branch constituted a new business. *Held:* For taxpayer. The distribution was tax-free. The branch was an expansion of a pre-existing activity and was not a new business. Burke, 42 TC 1021 (1964).

Split-off qualified even where active business was continued by entity other than the distributing or controlled corporation. Taxpayer and his brother were the principal stockholders of a corporation that had been actively engaged in three lines of business for over five years. After differences arose between the brothers, they decided to separate by transferring the assets of two of the businesses to an inactive subsidiary and then having taxpayer exchange his stock in the parent for all the stock in the subsidiary. Because of the strained relationship, the parties did not wait for the mechanics to be worked out. Instead, taxpayer took over the assets of the two businesses and operated them for 14 months as a sole proprietorship. At the end of that period, the actual split-off took place, and taxpayer transferred his sole proprietorship business to the subsidiary. The IRS argued that the transaction was not tax free under Section 355 because that section requires that the business be conducted by either the distributing corporation or the controlled corporation during the five-year period preceding the distribution. In effect, it contended that the 14 months of a sole proprietorship operation was a fatal hiatus. *Held:* For taxpayer. The Tax Court held that Section 355 was applicable. There is nothing in the Code or the Committee Reports to suggest that the five-year active business requirement can be met *only* by the distributing corporation and the controlled corporation. The transaction satisfied the language and purpose of Section 355, and the 14-month period during which the proprietorship conducted the business did not interrupt the necessary five years. W.E. Gabriel Fabrication Co., 42 TC 545 (1964), acq. 1965-2 CB 5.

Spin-off was tax free even though only one business was carried on; Coady approved. Taxpayer was a stockholder in General Auto, which operated as a warehouse distributor and jobber. General Auto formed a new corporation, Automotive Warehouse, to which it transferred all of its warehouse distribution property in exchange for stock. General Auto then distributed the stock to its stockholders pro rata. The IRS contended that the spin-off provisions of Section 355 did not apply because (1) taxpayer conducted a single integrated business, (2) the actual business requirements had not been met, and (3) the transaction was a device for the distribution of earnings. *Held:* For taxpayer. The Tax Court held that because all the conditions of Section 355 had been met, the transaction was tax free. Taxpayer had conducted two separate businesses; the fact that only one business was carried on did not render the section inapplicable. Coady, 289 F2d 490 (1961). The transfer of cash to Automotive Warehouse for working capital did not disqualify the transaction. Finally, the transaction was motivated by sound business reasons. Lester, Jr., 40 TC 947 (1963), acq. 1964-2 CB 6.

Spin-off failed to qualify under five-year active conduct test. A corporation engaged in manufacturing and selling potato sorting machinery organized a Maine subsidiary in 1954 to promote business in that state. In 1956, the corporation distributed the subsidiary's stock to taxpayer, its stockholder. Taxpayer contended that the distribution qualified under Section 355 as a tax-free spin-off. *Held:* For the IRS. In the absence of evidence that the Maine business was actively conducted by the subsidiary and its parent prior to its organization for the requisite five-year period, the distribution did not qualify under Section 355. The Maine business was actively conducted only from 1953, at which time the parent started to solicit business throughout Maine. Since the parent had adequate earnings, the distribution constituted a taxable dividend. Estate of Lockwood, 23 TCM 1233, ¶ 64,205 P-H Memo. TC (1964).

Spin-off of real estate operation not conducted five years prior to distribution treated as dividend in year of transfer. From 1946 through 1956, a corporation that was owned by taxpayer engaged in the wholesale distribution of linoleum and carpets leased a small portion of its premises to its largest supplier as an accommodation. For a period of five and a half years prior to 1954, the corporation also rented to a poultry business a small building on the property adjoining its premises. It decided to raze the building on the adjoining property to erect a new building. To secure the necessary construction funds, it was required by the lending bank to form a new corporation, which acquired the property from the old corporation and immediately leased it back to the latter. The loan was made to the new corporation, which assigned to the bank the rent to be paid by the old corporation. Although the property was transferred to the new corporation in 1956 in return for its $100 par value stock, no stock certificates were actually issued until 1957. At this time, the certificate of incorporation was amended to reduce the par value of the authorized stock to $1 so that the par value of the stock to be issued did not exceed the value of the property transferred. Although the stock certificates were not actually issued until 1957, the IRS determined that taxpayers were the stockholders of the new corporation in 1956, when the property of the old corporation was transferred. *Held:* For the IRS. The court noted that stock ownership in a corporation does not necessarily have to be evidenced by a certificate. The fact that property paid in for stock is less than the par value of the stock issued therefor does not, under Section 69 of the N.Y. Stock Corporation Law, invalidate the shares, but only makes them voidable under certain circumstances. The court also ruled that the distribution to taxpayer of stock of the new corporation by the old corporation was a taxable dividend in 1956, not a tax-free spin-off under Section 355. Taxpayers failed to show that the old corporation was actively engaged with real estate rental business (which the new corporation was conducting) during the five years prior to the distribution to taxpayer of the new corporation's stock. Bonsall, 21 TCM 820, ¶ 62,151 P-H Memo. TC (1962).

Clarification of applicablity of Section 355 to a plant temporarily shut down. For more than five years, taxpayer corporation owned all the stock of a manufacturing subsidiary, which had only one customer. In the fifth year, the customer went bankrupt. The plant was inactive during that year and had no income. At the end of that year, taxpayer distributed the subsidiary's stock to its stockholders in a transaction that would have qualified as a Section 355 tax-free spin-off, except that Section 355(b) requires that the subsidiary be engaged in "the active conduct of a trade or business" throughout the five-year period ending with the spin-off. The IRS ruled that active conduct of business ordinarily must include the collection of income, but that this case was a permitted exception. During the fifth year, the subsidiary incurred expenses for maintaining the plant and redesigning its product. Thus, it was engaged in the same trade or business it had conducted in prior years, and the distribution was tax free. Rev. Rul. 82-219, 1982-2 CB 82.

Despite having no employees of its own, a corporation qualifies under active business test. A controlled corporation that had no paid employees of its own was engaged in acquiring, renovating, refurbishing, maintaining, servicing, and leasing real estate. It used the employees of a sister corporation and the common officers of a controlled group under a reimbursement arrangement for over five years prior to the holding company parent's distribution of all of the controlled corporation's stock to stockholder in exchange for all the stockholder's stock of the parent. By continuation of its real estate activities after the distribution through direct employment of most of the same individuals, the controlled corporation satisfied the active business requirement of Section 355(b). Rev. Rul. 79-394, 1979-2 CB 141.

Securities ownership and management not a business under Section 355. Section 355 provides for the distribution, without recognition of gain or loss to stockholders, of stock of a corporation controlled by the distributing corporation where both corporations are engaged in the *active* conduct of a trade or business. Distribution of stock of a subsidiary that owned and managed an investment portfolio of considerable size and that required the full-time services of 20 employees did not meet the "active conduct of a trade or business" test provided by Section 355(b). Trading in stock or securities held for one's own account is an investment function and is not the active conduct of a trade or business. Rev. Rul. 66-204, 1966-2 CB 113.

Successive distributions after spin-off qualified for nonrecognition. A bank's 100-percent-owned subsidiary realty corporation was actively engaged in a rental operation for over five years. Among the subsidiary's holdings were two apartment houses that regulatory authorities advised the bank to dispose of because they were unrelated to the business of banking. The bank had acquired the stock of the subsidiary over five years before and had engaged in its own banking business for over five years. Since a sale of the buildings was deemed unwise, a plan was adopted whereby the subsidiary transferred the two "tainted" buildings to a newly formed subsidiary corporation in exchange for all of the latter's stock. Such stock was then distributed by the realty corporation to the parent bank, which in turn distributed the stock to its own stockholders. The IRS ruled that this plan met the requirements of Section 351 and that no gain was recognized to the subsidiary on the transfer of the buildings to the newly formed corporation. In addition, the plan met the requirements of Section 355, and no gain was recognized to either the bank or its stockholders on receipt of the stock of the newly formed corporation. The successive distributions were each within the purview of Section 355. In each case, the active businesss requirement and valid business purpose were satisfied. In addition, the transaction, when viewed as a whole, satisfied the continuity-of-interest requirements of that section. The same stockholders and aggregate interests were involved. The basis of each stockholder in the bank stock had to be allocated to the bank stock and the stock of the newly formed corporation in proportion to the fair market value of each at the time of distribution. Rev. Rul. 62-138, 1962-2 CB 95.

Distribution of competitive subsidiary to minority tax free. A printing corporation owned 80 percent of a typesetting corporation. For valid business reasons, it intended to divorce itself from the ownership of the typesetting subsidiary by distributing the stock to a minority of its stockholders in exchange for all the stock they held in it. Both corporations would continue to engage in the conduct of their respective businesses after the exchange, and no sales of stock were contemplated. The IRS ruled that the split-off was nontaxable under Section 355. The typesetting subsidiary was a controlled corporation; both corporations were engaged in the active conduct of their businesses and had been for five years. Rev. Rul. 56-450, 1956-2 CB 201.

Step-Transaction Doctrine

A stock-for-stock reorganization followed by the planned sale of stock by acquired company's stockholders was held to be taxable by reason of the step transaction doctrine even though stockholders were not under a binding commitment to sell such stock. McDonald's wanted to acquire the assets of several corporations, all owned by the same group of stockholders, for stock. The stockholder group would agree only to a sale for cash. Negotiations resulted in an agreement to transfer the stock of these corporations for unregistered stock in McDonald's, which shortly thereafter would "piggyback" a registration of McDonald's stock to be sold to the public. The stockholder group would not be compelled to sell its McDonald's stock but could force registration and offering of the stock; without registration, the stock received would not be transferable. The transaction occurred as negotiated, and although the registration was postponed, the stock given to the stockholder group was registered and sold within six months of the exchange. Treating this acquisition as a cash purchase for tax purposes, McDonald's liquidated the acquired corporations, claimed a stepped-up basis in their assets, and contributed the assets to several subsidiaries. The IRS challenged the subsidiaries' depreciation and amorization deductions based on the stepped-up basis. Claiming that the acquisition constituted an A reorganization, the IRS position was that the McDonald's subsidiaries held the acquired assets with the same basis as did the corporations from which the assets were acquired, that is, a carry-over basis. The Tax Court agreed with the IRS. It held that under the step transaction doctrine, the stock acquisition and the sale of McDonald's stock by the group of stockholders was not part of the same transaction. Accordingly, the assets were acquired in an A reorganization, and the McDonald's subsidiaries thus acquired them with a carry-over basis. *Held*: Reversed. Under any of the tests alternatively applied by the courts under the step transaction doctrine (i.e., the "end result" test, the "interdependence" test, and the "binding commitment" test), the stockholder group's sale of McDonald's stock for cash was part of the merger transaction. Although the Tax Court determined otherwise under an analysis consistent with the "binding commitment" test, this determination was erroneous. The mere fact that the stockholder group was not legally obliged to sell their Mc-

Donald's stock was not material under the facts. Furthermore, before continuity of interest, necessary to a nontaxable merger, can exist, it must be shown that the transfer plan was not predicated upon the transferor stockholders' prompt disposal of the stock received in the exchange. McDonald's Restaurants of Ill., 688 F2d 520, 82-2 USTC ¶ 9581, 50 AFTR2d 82-5750 (7th Cir. 1982).

Stepped-up basis lost because acquisition structured in wrong way. Two individuals engaged through various corporations in the cigarette vending business bought all the stock of a competitor corporation. Their CPA suggested that if they could not buy the corporation's assets (cigarette vending machine locations) directly, they should buy all the corporation's stock and then liquidate the corporation. The individuals did not liquidate the acquired corporation until the end of the year of purchase. Following the liquidation, the individuals transferred the cigarette vending machine locations to the new corporation's taxpayer. The individuals then substituted the stock of taxpayer as collateral to secure payment of the purchase price. The contract for the sale of stock contained a provision that required "that the corporate existence of the Company be maintained at all times in good standing." The Tax Court, finding that the contract provision evidenced a clear expression of a purpose *not* to liquidate the acquired corporation, held the *Kimbell-Diamond* rule inapplicable. The court, concluding that taxpayer acquired the assets of the old corporation in a tax-free reorganization, denied taxpayer a stepped-up basis for the cigarette vending machine locations. *Held*: Affirmed. The Tax Court did not err in finding that the stock purchase and liquidation was not a single, integrated transaction. It also correctly held that the liquidation of the old corporation and transfer of assets to taxpayer qualified as a D and F reorganization. Even if *Kimbell-Diamond* were applicable, however, the cigarette vending machine locations would not be properly subject to amortization. The reason was that there was no way to accurately determine the useful life of the locations. Griswold, 400 F2d 427, 68-2 USTC ¶ 9559, 22 AFTR2d 5481 (5th Cir. 1968).

Step transaction doctrine used to characterize transaction as reorganization. Taxpayers were stockholders and officers of a corporation engaged in engineering consultation. The corporation had a substantial surplus, and taxpayers had personally suffered large capital losses. Pursuant to an accountant's plan, a new corporation was formed with taxpayers as principal stockholders. The stock was paid for by loans from the old corporation. The old corporation's employees and operating assets were then shifted to a new corporation. The old corporation remained in existence only to complete certain nonassignable contracts and to make collections. Fourteen months later, the old corporation distributed its remaining assets to taxpayers, who reported capital gains thereon. Taxpayers then partially invested the proceeds in the new corporation. The Tax Court upheld the IRS' determination that distributions were boot incident to a corporate reorganization under Section 368(a)(1)(D) and were taxable as ordinary income. *Held*: Affirmed. The Tax Court was correct in its conclusion that the steps taken were part of an integrated plan of reorganization. Although the percentage of assets transferred was less than 65 percent, substantially all the assets were considered transferred, since the successor had the use and benefit of all the assets neccessary to the conduct of the business. Only the nonoperating assets were retained by the old corporation. Moffatt, 363 F2d 262, 66-2 USTC ¶ 9498, 17 AFTR2d 1290 (9th Cir. 1966), cert. denied, 386 US 1016 (1967).

Sale of stock for stock and boot was governed by Section 356 where it was a step in a reorganization. Taxpayer was a stockholder of Tenco. In 1959 through 1960, Minute Maid merged with Tenco under Section 368(a)(1)(A) as follows: Taxpayer and the other Tenco stockholders sold their Tenco stock to Minute Maid for Minute Maid stock (constituting over 50 percent of the consideration), cash, and notes. Minute Maid then liquidated Tenco and some other subsidiaries. Taxpayer argued that its sale of Tenco stock was a step in a reorganization and was thus governed by Section 356. The IRS argued that the sale was taxable as an independent transaction. *Held:* For taxpayer. First, the sale was a step in a reorganization. Second, taxpayer's gain to be recognized under Section 356 was a dividend under Section 356(a)(2) to the extent of taxpayer's share of Tenco's earnings and profits. The boot was distributed pro rata and effected no change in equity interests. Third, the above dividend was subject to the 85 percent dividends received deduction of Section 243(a)(1). King Enters., Inc., 418 F2d 511, 69-2 USTC ¶ 9720, 24 AFTR2d 69-5866 (Ct. Cl. 1969).

Merger did not result in complete liquidation. Taxpayer's controlling stockholder agreed to sell his stock to another corporation. The acquiring corporation created a subsidiary to purchase the stock. Following that sale, the subsidiary created its own subsidiary, which purchased the stock owned by taxpayer's minority stockholders. After the latter sale, both subsidiary corporations were merged into taxpayer. Taxpayer increased its basis in its assets to the price paid for its stock by the acquiring corporation. The IRS determined that the assets were required to be valued at their historical cost, since this was not a liquidation with a step-up under Section 334(b)(2) and the integrated transaction doctrine did not apply. *Held:* For the IRS. The requirement that a complete liquidation take place in order to claim stepped-up basis was not met by the merger of the two subsidiaries into taxpayer, since taxpayer remained active throughout. Nor did the intergrated transaction doctrine allow disregard of the transaction's intermediate steps, since the sales and mergers as structured were not equivalent to a purchase of the corporation's assets in exchange for the purchase price of its stock, and the purchaser did not intend to liquidate taxpayer after acquiring its assets through the stock purchase. New York Fruit Auction Corp., 79 TC 564 (1982).

Step-transaction doctrine not applicable in reorganization. Taxpayer purchased a small amount of Missouri Pacific Class B common stock while a lawsuit was in progress by Class B stockholders against the company and the majority stockholder of the Class A shares. The suit was settled and taxpayer received shares of a new class of common stock plus cash. He then sold a substantial portion of his new common stock to the former Class A majority stockholder. Taxpayer combined the cash received and treated the aggregate as capital gains. The IRS determined that, although the exchange of stock for stock was nontaxable, the cash distributed was a dividend. *Held:* For the IRS. Although there was a recapitalization and the exchange of stock for stock was tax free, the recapitalization and the tender offer by the former Class A majority stockholder were not interdependent parts of the settlement agreement, so the step-transaction doctrine did not apply. Taxpayer was not an obliged to tender his stock, and the basic objective in the settlement agreement was accomplished without regard to taxpayer's participation. Johnson, 78 TC 564 (1982).

Step transaction did not invalidate reorganization where business purpose for new corporation was shown. In July 1965, taxpayer transferred his mineral interest by lease to a revocable trust of which he and his wife were beneficiaries. Thereafter, a corporation that acquired the lease in exchange for its stock was formed. In September 1965, the corporate stock held by the trust was exchanged for stock in a public corporation. The IRS contended that all the events were steps by which taxpayer made a lease of his mineral interests and received an advance royalty. *Held:* For taxpayer. The exchange of stock was a tax-free reorganization because it had been shown that there was a business purpose for the organization of the corporation. Taxpayer did not know of the possibility of doing business with the public corporation until he formed his corporation to develop the mineral rights. Moreover, the corporation served to resolve certain of taxpayer's title problems. Consequently, there was a valid tax-free reorganization. It was further held that payments received for the location of wells, flowlines, and roads on the property were in the nature of rent and were taxable as ordinary income. In addition, payments received for water

REORGANIZATIONS: *Step-Transaction Doctrine*

rights were properly reportable as capital gains since taxpayer did not retain an economic interest in the water in place. Vest, 57 TC 128 (1971).

Sale of assets to related corporation converted Section 337 liquidation into taxable reorganization. Taxpayers, stockholders of construction company (Armour), formed a new corporation, (Excavating) to limit their liability under certain hazardous construction jobs. Excavating performed the actual work, using machinery rented from Armour and others. Eventually, Excavating began to specialize in a safer type of construction work and also began to buy its own equipment due to the imposition of a state sales tax on rentals. It accumulated sizable earnings and profits. When it became apparent that two separate corporations were no longer needed, taxpayers decided to liquidate Armour pursuant to Section 337. As part of the liquidation, Armour sold its equipment, furniture and fixtures, and automobiles to Excavating and distributed all its assets to taxpayers. The IRS treated the transaction as a D reorganization and determined that taxpayers had received a dividend of $1.11 million under Section 356(a)(2), rather than a capital gain in that amount. *Held:* For the IRS, in part. The transaction resulted in a reorganization. The step-transaction doctrine indicated that there was a transfer of substantially all the assets of a corporation to another corporation controlled by the same persons. The fact that no securities were exchanged was unimportant because no further issuance was necessary to retain the same proprietary interests. The basis of the assests in the hands of Excavating was found to be equivalent to the cash price. However, taxpayers'dividend on the surrender of their Excavating/stock was limited to the amount of Excavating's earnings and profits, $670,000. the IRS' arguments that the *total* gain should be recognized part of it constituted an informal dividend from Armour paid through Excavating as a conduit was without merit. Further, the gain was not reduced by the additional taxes found to be due by taxpayers as transferees in later years. James Armour, Inc., 43 TC 295 (1964).

Step-transaction doctrine applied; redemption held to be reorganization plus dividend distribution. Taxpayer was a stockholder of a corporation that operated an automobile dealership. The corporation had substantial accumulated profits but had never declared a dividend. The corporation transferred all its assets and liabilities to a new corporation for cash. The corporation then redeemed all its stock except for that held by one stockholder other than taxpayer. The stockholders also received voting stock of the new corporation. All these transactions occurred within two weeks. Taxpayer contended that the amount he received on the redemption was capital gain under Section 302. *Held:* For the IRS. The Tax Court held that there was a reorganization, part of which was taxable as ordinary income that had the effect of a dividend. There was a continuity of business and of ownership. The net effect of the series of steps was a reorganization under Section 368(a)(1)(D), and the distribution of the old corporation's surplus in the process had the effect of a distribution of a dividend under Section 356(a)(2). Grubbs, 39 TC 42 (1962).

RESEARCH EXPENDITURES

(*See* Business Expenses—In General)

RESERVES

(*See* Bad Debts—Reserves For; Liquidations—Unused Bad Debt Reserve)

RETAINED EARNINGS

(*See* Earnings and Profits)

RIGHTS, STOCK

(*See* Dividends and Distributions—Stock Dividends and Rights)

ROYALTIES

Royalties-under-license agreements distributed in liquidation were ordinary income; they had fair market value when distributed. Taxpayer organized a corporation for the manufacture of a patented float valve. He invested $1,300 for a one-third interest. The corporation later granted to another company the exclusive right to manufacture, use, and sell the valve in the United States and Canada. Shortly thereafter, the corporation was liquidated under a one-month liquidation provision. Taxpayer received for his share $500 in cash and a one-third interest in the license agreement, which he valued on his return at $417. The loss on liquidation of $383 ($1,300 minus $917) was treated as a nonrecognized loss. Royalties received under the license agreement subsequent to the liquidation (over $16,000) were treated as long-term capital gains under the theory that by virtue of the one-month liquidation, taxpayer had stepped into the tax shoes of his corporation. Taxpayer further contended that the license agreement had no ascertainable value at the time of its distribution. The Tax Court held for the IRS. *Held:* Affirmed. Taxpayer's loss was recognized because the one-month liquidation provisions only apply to nonrecognition of *gains* . As to the valuation of the license agreement, testimony indicated that such agreements were capable of valuation, and taxpayer's own valuation of $417 was accepted in absence of proof of a greater value. The transaction was thus closed, and any royalty payments received in excess of basis were ordinary income. Slater, 356 F2d 668, 66-1 USTC ¶ 9235, 17 AFTR2d 337 (10th Cir. 1966).

Royalty of 3 percent of sales of baking products paid to sole stockholders of baking corporation found reasonable. Taxpayer and another individual operated a bakery as partners. They incorporated in 1960 and transferred the partnership business to the corporation except for the formulas for certain bakery products. These formulas were licensed to the corporation for a royalty of 5 percent of sales. The IRS contended that the royalty was a dividend. *Held:* For the IRS, in part. Only a royalty of 3 percent of sales was proper and deductible. The 2 percent excess was taxable to the stockholders as a dividend. Neuberger, 69-1 USTC ¶ 9264, 23 AFTR2d 69-557 (D. Ore. 1968).

Royalty payments to related corporation for the use of patented machinery were excessive. Taxpayer deducted as rents and royalties $55,000 paid to a corporation wholly owned by its stockholders. The amount was paid for the use of machinery on which the stockholders held patents that were licensed to the lessor corporation. The agreement provided that the lessor make available to taxpayer and maintain over the life of the agreement all machines required for taxpayer's business at a consideration based on the number of units produced. The amounts paid and deducted during each year were approximately three times the cost of all the machines used, and maintenance costs required of the lessor were nominal. The IRS allowed $15,000 as an ordinary and necessary business expense, disallowing the remainder as unreasonable. Taxpayer contended that the machine was patented (a secret process was involved) and that the cost per unit was comparable to other royalty payments. *Held:* For the IRS. Even the monopoly premium that a patent may command did not justify a payment in excess of what "the traffic will bear." Evidence also showed that a comparable machine could be purchased for an amount below the annual rent of one of the lessor's machines. Taxpayer failed to introduce evidence to justify the unit cost in comparison to royalty payments for other patented machinery. Taken in its entirety, the corporations did not bargain at arm's length, as would unrelated parties. The costs were unwarranted and unreasonable. E-Z Sew Enters., Inc., 260 F. Supp. 100, 66-2 USTC ¶ 9599, 18 AFTR2d 5607 (ED Mich. 1966).

Royalty payments between related companies deductible. Taxpayer, a manufacturer and distributor of food products, entered into a license arrangement with a British affiliate wherein taxpayer received a patented process for converting raw potatoes into granular form, was licensed to sell the product in the United States, and was to pay the British company a royalty of 3 percent of its net sales of mashed potatoes, in return for which the British company was to use its know-how to assist in this venture. Subsequently, the agreement was modified, deleting reference to the patents and requiring taxpayer to pay a royalty of 2 percent of its net sales. The IRS allocated to the taxpayer, as income, the royalties it paid to the British company after this modification, contending that the taxpayer received no real benefits from the royalties in that it had developed a research capacity of its own, and the process for which it had entered into the licensing agreement was widely understood and of no monetary value. *Held:* For taxpayer. The agreements were such as might have been made by unrelated parties dealing at arm's length. The modification was required because of a patent infringement suit, and reference to the patents would have been deleted even if the agreement had been between unrelated parties. R.T. French Co., 60 TC 836 (1973).

Reasonableness of royalty based on percentage of sales determined. Taxpayer entered into an agreement with his controlled corporation whereby the corporation was to pay him a royalty for use of a system he had developed in the amount of 30 percent of net sales. This percentage was subsequently reduced in ensuing years to 16 percent and 8 percent. Each year, the corporation determined the royalty due to taxpayer and issued him its notes bearing 5 percent interest. The corporation then paid the notes as funds became available. The IRS determined that the royalty paid in excess of 6 percent of net sales constituted a dividend. *Held:* For the IRS. The court determined that based on testimony, the amount allowable as a reasonable royalty was 6 percent of net sales. The excess over that amount was a dividend as the corporation was not financially able to pay on demand the amounts accrued as owing to the taxpayer. Omholt, 60 TC 541 (1973).

Unreasonable royalties were dividends. Clyborne acquired various leases on coal properties and assigned them to taxpayer corporation, Paragon, of which Clyborne was sole stockholder, in return for overriding royalties of 30 cents per ton of coal extracted. Clyborne paid part of this royalty to the landowners and others, retaining about 10 to 15 cents for himself. Paragon deducted the full 30 cents as royalty expense, while Clyborne treated his net royalty as capital gains under Section 631. The IRS disallowed most of the deduction to Paragon and treated the net royalty as a dividend on the grounds that Clyborne had no assignable interest in the leases and that the transaction was designed to obtain a tax advantage by payment of unreasonable royalties. *Held:* For the IRS, in part. The Tax Court found an assignable interest, but concluded from the evidence that a reasonable royalty was 25 cents. Accordingly, 5 cents was a dividend, 25 cents was deductible by Paragon, and the excess of 25 cents over the amounts paid to others was capital gain to Clyborne. Merritt, 39 TC 257 (1962).

Part of royalty payments to controlling stockholder unreasonable. Taxpayer corporation purchased patents from its controlling stockholder in consideration for payment of 80 percent of the net profits to be derived from the patents. The IRS determined that the sale was not the result of arm's-length negotiation and disallowed a part of the royalties as unreasonable. *Held:* For the IRS. All the indicia of arm's-length dealing were missing. Taxpayer made no effort to check shop rights, ease of avoidance, or validity of the patents. No counter offer was made. Further, the patents were not even recorded. This left the seller free to resell them. The agreements constituted attempts to escalate the drain of additional corporate profits into the hands of the stockholder's family at capital gains rates. The court concluded, after considering all facts and circumstances, that 50 percent of the net profits were fair and reasonable royalties. Differential Steel Car Co., 25 TCM 344, ¶ 66,065 P-H Memo. TC (1966).

Royalty payments by corporation to its stockholders for use of patent were reasonable. The principal stockholders of a corporation formed a partnership to acquire certain patents from an unrelated party and then offered the corporation an exclusive license for their use. The idea of purchasing the patents was previously turned down by the corporation for business reasons, although its business success depended upon its right to manufacture the articles covered by the patents. The IRS denied the corporation a deduction for the royalty payments made to the partnership, holding that the distributions were disguised dividends. *Held:* For taxpayer. The patents were purchased by the partnership in form as well as in substance. The royalty payments made thereto by the corporation were reasonable in amount and thereby fully deductible as royalty payments. Chase, 24 TCM 1054, ¶ 65,202 P-H Memo. TC (1965).

SALARIES

(*See* Compensation for Personal Services; Dividends and Distributions—Excessive Salaries)

SECTION 306 STOCK

Section 306 not applicable to redemption of preferred stock that was previously issued in exchange for stock originally purchased. In 1954, taxpayer's corporation issued 600 shares of preferred stock to him. Taxpayer reported as capital gains the proceeds received from the redemption of 451 shares of preferred stock in 1959. The IRS contended that the proceeds were ordinary income under Section 306. *Held:* For taxpayer, in part. Section 306 was not applicable to 65 of the redeemed shares because they were received in 1954 in exchange for taxpayer's original holding of preferred stock for which he paid consideration in 1948. It was immaterial that when taxpayer exchanged 65 shares of old preferred for 65 shares of new preferred in 1954, he also received an additional 535 shares of preferred, and both blocks of stock were evidenced by one certificate. The use of one certificate did not merge both blocks of stock into one distribution under Section 306(a)(1)(A), where the 65 shares were received pursuant to a recapitalization under Section 368(a)(1)(E). Nor did 128 (24 percent of 535 (600 minus 65)) of the redeemed shares constitute Section 306 stock, since taxpayer sold 24 percent of his common stock in 1958. Taxpayer need not have disposed of all his common stock before any disposition of his Section 306 stock in order to qualify for the exception under Section 306(b)(4)(B). The proceeds from 258 of the redeemed shares were ordinary income. Fireoved, 318 F. Supp. 133, 71-1 USTC ¶ 9182, 27 AFTR2d 71-717 (ED Pa. 1970).

Lack of common stock does not bar Section 306 classification. All the holders of a corporation's only class of common stock exchanged their shares for newly created stock that was preferred as to dividends and liquidation distributions. As part of the same transaction, taxpayer later purchased stock in another newly created class of stock that provided an unrestricted interest in the corporation's future equity growth. The first class of stock was preferred stock even if there was no common stock outstanding at that time. Under the circumstances, it was Section 306 stock. Taxpayer was considered to have exchanged old common shares for an equal number of new preferred shares, and the balance of the old common shares plus cash for the new common shares. Rev. Rul. 82-191, 1982-2 CB 78.

Preferred stock received in an A reorganization in exchange for "substantially the same" stock not Section 306 stock. In a reorganization pursuant to Sections 368(a)(1)(A) and 368(a)(2)(D), a corporation merged with its second-tier subsidiary. The stockholder exchanged all his preferred stock (not Section 306 stock) in the former parent for all the preferred stock in the former first-tier subsidiary. The IRS ruled that the "cash in lieu of" test of Regulation § 1.306-3(d) does not apply where the new preferred stock received was substantially the same as the old preferred stock exchanged therefor. Thus, the new preferred stock, which represented the same assets as the old stock, was not Section 306 stock. Rev. Rul. 82-118, 1982-1 CB 56.

Section 306 Stock

Part of Section 306 stock redemption price allocated to capital account. In a Section 303 redemption of preferred stock (Section 306 stock), the reduction of the corporation's earnings and profits did not include the amount of the distribution properly chargeable to a capital account. Where the preferred stock was issued as a stock dividend instead of paid-in capital, the corporation's capital account was to be allocated between the common stock and preferred stock in proportion to their respective fair market values on the distribution date. Rev. Rul. 74-266, 1974-1 CB 73, is modified. Rev. Rul. 82-72, 1982-1 CB 57.

Preferred stock received in recapitalization exchange not Section 306 stock. The sole stockholder of a corporation received preferred stock for 97 percent of his common stock and gave the remaining 3 percent to those whom he wished to control and continue the business. The transactions were part of an integrated plan; cash received in lieu of the preferred stock would not have been treated as a dividend because of the complete termination of interest. Thus, the preferred stock was not considered Section 306 stock. Rev. Rul. 81-186, 1981-2 CB 85.

IRS found equality of voting rights spares stock issue from Section 306 taint. The subject corporation issued shares of two new classes of stock in exchange for each share of its single class of common stock outstanding in a recapitalization. One class (Class B) was preferred to the extent of an annual cumulative 6 percent par value dividend and repayment of par value upon liquidation, but both classes had equal voting rights and otherwise shared equally in dividends and liquidation proceeds. The IRS, holding that the preferred stock was not Section 306 stock, noted that the Class B stock enjoyed voting rights on an equal basis with the Class A stock, the only other class of stock outstanding. After satisfaction of its preference regarding dividends and assets in the event of liquidation, the Class B stock would share equally with the Class A stock. These rights in the Class B stock to participate in corporate growth were deemed to be significant. Thus, a sale of the Class B stock could not occur without a loss of voting control and interest in the unrestricted growth of the corporation. Rev. Rul. 81-91, 1981-1 CB 123.

Cash in lieu of fractional Section 306 shares treated as Section 302(a) redemption. In a recapitalization under Section 368(a)(1)(E), a corporation distributed cash to certain minority stockholders in lieu of fractional shares of preferred Section 306 stock. Since the deemed redemption of the fractional shares was an isolated disposition, and the stockholders lacked sufficient control to direct a bailout distribution, Section 306(b)(4)(A) applied, and the distribution was treated as a Section 302(a) redemption. Rev. Rul. 81-81, 1981-1 CB 122, amplifying Rev. Rul. 66-365, 1966-2 CB 116.

Contribution of Section 306 stock. Section 306 stock was issued to a controlling stockholder in a reorganization to prevent dilution of the earnings per share of the common stock. The amount of a charitable contribution was reduced by the amount that would have been ordinary income if it had been sold under Section 170(c)(1)(A) because taxpayer failed to prove that a principal purpose of issuing the preferred stock was not tax avoidance. Also, Section 306(b)(4)(A) would not be available to except a sale of the Section 306 stock from the ordinary income characterization of Section 306(a)(1). Rev. Rul. 80-33, 1980-1 CB 69.

Tax-free exchange yields Section 306 stock. The owners of a corporation transferred all of the common stock to a second corporation that they organized for all of its voting preferred stock and voting common stock. The IRS ruled that the voting preferred stock was Section 306 stock. Although the requirements of Section 351 were met for a nontaxable exchange, there was also a B reorganization. Section 306 applies to preferred stock received in a reoganization. Rev. Rul. 79-274, 1979-2 CB 131.

Preferred stock received in F reorganization not 306 stock. Preferred stock received in an F reorganization (involving a change of place), is not Section 306 stock if received for the same number of shares with the same terms and was not previously tainted by the exchanging stockholder. Rev. Rul. 79-287, 1979-2 CB 130.

Stock with limited rights is Section 306 stock and not common stock. The holders of one type of stock that was received in an E reorganization were entitled to receive only the par value of the stock upon liquidation of the corporation. Holders of a second type were limited to dividends of 6 percent of par value in any taxable year. The IRS ruled that for purposes of Section 306(c), such stock, with restrictions as to dividends or limited rights to assets upon liquidation, would not be considered common stock. Rev. Rul. 79-163, 1979-1 CB 131.

Preferred stock received in a qualifying Section 355 distribution was Section 306 stock. A parent and its subsidiary were engaged in separate active businesses for more than five years. The parent had earnings and profits in excess of the value of the subsidiary stock, but the subsidiary had no earnings and profits. The subsidiary stock was part common and part preferred stock. The parent distributed its subsidiary's stock pro rata in a distribution qualifying under Section 355. The IRS ruled that the preferred stock was Section 306 stock. On a disposition other than by redemption, the gain is computed as though the preferred stock were issued by the parent. In a redemption, the amount taxable as a dividend is based on the subsidiary's earnings and profits at the time of the redemption. Rev. Rul. 77-335, 1977-2 CB 95.

Section 306 stock retains taint after Section 351 exchange. Stockholders transferred all of their preferred stock to a corporation that was owned by them in exchange for that company's preferred stock. The stock held by the corporation and the corporation's preferred stock held by the stockholders were treated as Section 306 stock. It was immaterial that the corporation had no earnings and profits. Rev. Rul. 77-108, 1977-1 CB 86.

No possibility of a bailout results in no taint for newly issued common stock in recapitalization. Pursuant to a plan of recapitalization, the subject corporation issued shares of new voting common stock and new nonvoting common stocks pro rata to its stockholders in exchange for shares of its outstanding common stock. The exchange was not taxable pursuant to Section 354. The corporation's certificate of incorporation granted it a 90-day right of first refusal to purchase shares of the newly issued voting common stock at their net book value whenever a stockholder desired to sell or otherwise dispose of any of such stock. The 90-day period was to start when the corporation received written notice of a stockholder's decision. However, if the stockholder failed to give the required notice, the option was to start on the date the new voting common stock certificates were to be presented for transfer on the corporation's books. The IRS noted that the new voting common stock, which was common stock in all other respects, was not redeemable but merely subject to the corporation's right of first refusal. That right applied only with respect to individual stockholders. Thus, if a stockholder desired to dispose of some or all of the new voting common stock, thereby giving rise to the corporation's right of first refusal, the stockholder would necessarily part with some or all of the interest in the growth of the corporation. Therefore, the new voting common stock could not be used to achieve a prohibited bailout. Accordingly, the new voting common stock, although issued subject to the corporation's right of first refusal, constituted common stock for purposes of Section 306(c)(1)(B). Rev. Rul. 76-386, 1976-2 CB 95.

Cash received by noncontrolling stockholders in reorganization not considered exchanged for Section 306 stock. The IRS ruled that when stockholders who exercised no control over a corporation exchanged common stock for new common stock and cash and exchanged Section 306 nonvoting stock for Section 306 voting stock in a recapitalization, the old Section 306 stock was not considered as exchanged for money. The corporation's stock was widely held and traded, and the transactions were at arm's length. Rev. Rul. 76-15, 1976-1 CB 98.

In reorganization involving the controlling stockholder, cash first considered as received in exchange for any Section 306 stock. In an effort to avoid the application of Section 356(e), a corporation's controlling stockholder exchanged voting common stock for cash and Section 306 stock for nonvoting common stock (not Section 306 stock) in a recapitalization. However, because taxpayer had control of the corporation, the identification of stock in the exchange was not given substantive effect. Instead, the cash received was first considered as received in exchange for the Section 306 stock and was treated as a distribution of property to taxpayer to which Section 301 applied. Rev. Rul. 76-14, 1976-1 CB 97.

Recapitalization resulted in Section 306 stock. Where a corporation issued two new classes of stock for its one outstanding stock issue, no gain or loss resulted to the stockholders under Section 354(a)(1), but the voting stock that was limited and preferred regarding dividends, had limited rights upon liquidation, and did not participate in corporate growth was Section 306 stock. Rev. Rul. 75-236, 1975-1 CB 106.

Section 306 stock not a result in E reorganization. In an E reorganization, when old common stock was exchanged for two new classes of stock, neither of which was redeemable at a specified price and which differed from the old stock only in cash dividend and conversion rights, the new stocks were not "stock other than common stock" within the meaning of Section 306(c). Rev. Rul. 75-222, 1975-1 CB 105.

Recapitalization converted common stock into Section 306 stock. A corporation had outstanding $100 par value common stock. Under a Section 368(a)(1)(E) reorganization, the stock was reclassified as Class A stock. Stockholders could either retain the new Class A stock or receive a package consisting of one share of new preferred stock and one share of new Class B stock. Cumulative dividends of $7 per share were payable first to the preferred stock, then to Class A stock; then the Class A and B stock shared dividends equally. On asset distribution, the preferred would take first, then Class A to the extent of one and a half times par value, thereafter Class A and B would stock share equally. Only Class A and B stock could vote. Some stockholders exchanged all Class A, others only part, and still others exchanged none of the new Class A. The IRS ruled that: (1) for stockholders who exchanged all Class A for preferred and Class B, the preferred stock was Section 306 stock, since it was similar to a receipt of a stock dividend in preferred shares; (2) for stockholders who exchanged only a portion of Class A for preferred and Class B, the retained Class A as well as the preferred stock was Section 306 stock, since Class A stock was also preferred as to dividends over Class B stock; (3) to the Class A stockholders who retained all the Class A stock, none of the stock was Section 306 stock. To them it was the same as exchanging old common for participating Class A preferred stock. Rev. Rul. 66-332, 1966-2 CB 108.

New preferred stock in nontaxable merger and recapitalization free from Section 306 taint. New preferred stock received pursuant to a nontaxable merger and recapitalization by holders of the old preferred of the surviving corporation was held not to constitute Section 306 stock under the following facts: (1) All shares of the surviving corporation, before and after the merger, were widely held by the public; (2) the largest individual holder of the old preferred owned only 1.5 percent of the outstanding issue and held no common stock; and (3) only persons who owned 17.6 percent of the common after the merger would also own preferred, and all of these would own only about 24 percent of the preferred. Rev. Rul 60-1, 1960-1 CB 143.

Some stockholders have Section 306 stock after recapitalization. In a recapitalization, a corporation issued new common and preferred stock for all of its old common. All shares had the same fair market value at the time of the exchange. Some stockholders received new common or new preferred only, while others received shares of both issues. The IRS ruled that preferred stock received by a stockholder would not be Section 306 stock if he owned no common after the exchange. However, stockholders who receved preferred and also had the same or a greater percentage interest in the common stock equity, received, in effect, a dividend on common, and the preferred stock was Section 306 stock. Rev. Rul. 59-84, 1959-1 CB 71.

Nonvoting common was Section 306 stock. Under a plan of recapitalization, a corporation issued new voting common and new nonvoting common in exchange for its outstanding common stock. The only other difference between the voting and the nonvoting was that the nonvoting was redeemable at the discretion of the corporation. Because of the redemption feature, the nonvoting stock was held to be Section 306 stock. Rev. Rul. 57-132, 1957-1 CB 115.

No taint on Section 306 stock in absence of tax-avoidance plan. In a nontaxable reorganization, a publicly held corporation acuired for bona fide business reasons all the assets of a closely held corporation that had only common stock in return for 5 percent of its outstanding voting preferred and common. The IRS held that the preferred constituted Section 306 stock. The Code specifically provides that the disposition of Section 306 stock is the sale of a capital asset if it is established that the distribution and disposition are not in avoidance of tax. In this case, gain or loss on the sale or other disposition of the preferred stock was not treated as ordinary income, since the issuance was not part of a tax-avoidance plan. Rev. Rul. 57-103, 1957-1 CB 113.

Preferred stock received in tax-free merger was Section 306 stock, but gain on disposition was possibly capital. Under a plan of merger of two publicly held corporations, the surviving corporation issued preferred and common stock to the common stockholders of the merged corporations. The exchange was held tax-free, and the preferred stock received in connection with the merger was Section 306 stock because it was preferred received in a tax-free exchange. However, the provisions of Section 306(a)(1) that treat the gain on disposition of such stock as ordinary income were held not applicable; there was good business reason for the issuance. The earnings of the merged company were stable but low. The preferred stock was used to limit the participation of its stockholders in the combined earnings. For this reason, the acquisition of the preferred was not in pursuance of a plan of tax avoidance. To avoid ordinary income on sale, the sale, if it occurs, must not be in anticipation of redemptions. Rev. Rul. 56-116, 1956-1 CB 164.

Capital gain realized on sale of Section 306 stock to employees' trust. M Corporation, pursuant to a plan of recapitalization, issued new preferred and common for the old capital stock, about 80 percent of which was owned by employees. The recapitalization was tax-free, but the preferred was Section 306 stock. The qualified profit-sharing fund created by the corporation had previously agreed to purchase the stock of M owned by certain retiring employees. The agreement had been made when only a single class of capital stock was outstanding but did provide for the substitution of the new shares if and when issued. The IRS ruled that the gain or loss realized by each retiring employee upon the sale of his new shares of preferred and common to the trust would be capital and would not be subject to the limitations of Section 306 because this disposition did not have as a principal purpose the avoidance of tax. Rev. Rul. 56-223, 1956-1 CB 162.

SECTION 1244 STOCK

Section 1244 treatment of loss denied where the corporation issuing stock could not show that it was "largely an operating company" under Regulation § 1.1244(c)-1(g)(2). To re-enter the machine tool business, taxpayer and his family formed Bates Investment Corp. (BIC) in 1969. The stock was offered in a Section 1244 plan. BIC acquired, for almost all its cash, a majority stock interest in another

Section 1244 Stock

corporation. BIC never had gross receipts, and the only asset BIC ever owned was this stock. The acquired corporation declared bankruptcy, BIC was liquidated, and taxpayer claimed, under Secion 1244, an ordinary loss on BIC liquidation. The IRS asserted that taxpayer was not entitled to Section 1244 treatment because BIC was not an operating company as required by its regulations. The district court held for the IRS on the ground that although the "operating company" requirement of its regulations does not appear in the statute, the IRS' regulations are, under Section 1244, legislative regulations. Furthermore, the legislative history of Section 1244 supports this requirement by indicating that Section 1244 is not to be available to investment or holding companies. The facts show that BIC merely held stock and engaged in no other activities. *Held:* Affirmed for the IRS. Bates, 581 F2d 575, 78-2 USTC ¶ 9592, 42 AFTR2d 78-5480 (6th Cir. 1978).

Tax Court required that valid Section 1244 stock plan expressly limit the offering of such stock to a two-year period. Taxpayer, under a stock purchase plan set up by his employer, acquired stock to Ranchers, Inc. In 1963, Ranchers was liquidated at a loss to its stockholders. Taxpayer claimed this loss as ordinary by reason of Section 1244. The IRS challenged, on the basis of Regulation § 1.1244(c)-1(c), the deduction of an ordinary loss because no document executed in the formation of Ranchers or the issuance of its stock limited the offering of its stock to two years as required by Section 1244. Taxpayer offered evidence showing that the failure to expressly limit the offering to a two-year period was an oversight and that, in any event, all of Ranchers' stock would have been acquired within two years under the stock purchase plan. The Tax Court held for the IRS. *Held:* Affirmed. The offering of stock qualifying under Section 1244 must be expressly limited to not more than two years after the Section 1244 plan is adopted. Warner, 401 F2d 162, 68-2 USTC ¶ 9589, 22 AFTR2d 5621 (9th Cir. 1968).

Stock received in merger did not qualify as Section 1244 stock. In 1967, taxpayer acquired stock of *K* Corporation that qualified as Section 1244 stock. There followed a series of reorganizations. In 1973, an ancestor of the original company was adjudicated bankrupt, and taxpayers claimed an ordinary loss from the Section 1244 stock. The IRS determined that the stock did not qualify. *Held:* For the IRS. The company's stock did not qualify for carry-over of the *K* Corporation stock's Section 1244 status, since there was a merger which was neither an E or F reorganization. Accordingly, the loss was a capital loss. Role, 70 TC 341 (1978).

Preincorporation discussions with attorney constituted a Section 1244 plan allowing taxpayer to deduct Section 1244 loss. To obtain a GM dealership, taxpayer was required to capitalize his dealership corporation with $84,000. In forming this corporation, taxpayer fully discussed with his attorney the tax aspects of issuing the stock pursuant to Section 1244 and indicated his intent to have the corporation's stock be Section 1244 stock. The corporation's stock was issued and the GM franchise acquired; subsequently, a written Section 1244 plan was adopted. The corporation's business failed in 1970, and taxpayer claimed an ordinary loss for the worthlessness of his stock. The IRS challenged the deduction, asserting that the corporation's stock had been issued before a formal Section 1244 plan was adopted and thus that Section 1244 did not apply. *Held:* For taxpayer. A formal written Section 1244 plan need not be adopted before the Section 1244 stock is issued to gain the benefits of Section 1244. It is sufficient that an informal plan exist before the stock is issued. This informal plan existed as a result of taxpayer's preincorporation discussions with his attorney. Reddy, 66 TC 335 (1976).

Shares received from corporation in cancellation of indebtedness did not qualify as Section 1244 stock. Taxpayer was issued shares in a corporation in 1964, and at the same time 10-year options to purchase stock were issued to other parties. In 1967, these options were cancelled, and taxpayer received additional shares in cancellation of an indebtedness from the corporation to her for loans made from 1964 through 1967. On a subsequent liquidation, taxpayer claimed an ordinary loss pursuant to Section 1244. The IRS disallowed the claim, contending that the stock did not qualify as Section 1244 stock. *Held:* For the IRS. There was no plan to issue the shares within a 2-year period as required by the statute, and the minutes of the 1964 meeting included 10-year options and indicated no qualifying plan. Nor did the shares issued in exchange for loans qualify, since the stock must have been issued for money or property, and the loans here were in the nature of capital contributions. Kaplan, 59 TC 178 (1972).

Corporate payment was for stock, not for waiver of indebtedness, then reducing loss of Section 1244 stock. Taxpayers waived an indebtedness owed to them by their bankrupt corporation, later reaffirmed it, and claimed that a $30,000 distribution was for the indebtedness so that they would have a $40,000 loss for the total cost basis of their stock. The IRS determined that the payment was for the stock, and that taxpayers had only a $10,000 stock loss. *Held:* For the IRS. Taxpayers' waiver of the indebtedness caused it to lose the characterization and become a contribution to capital. The later reaffirmation of the debt did not validate it for tax purpose so as to minimize taxes. The Section 1244 stock's basis was reduced by the distribution so that taxpayer was only entitled to a $10,000 ordinary loss. Eger, 28 TCM 850, ¶ 69,171 P-H Memo. TC (1969).

SECURITIES

(*See* Bonds and Debentures; Capital Gains and Losses; Reorganizations; Tax-Free Incorporations)

SHAM TRANSACTIONS

(*See also* Allocations Among Related Taxpayers—Sham Transactions; Tax Avoidance)

Sale to estate beneficiary recognized. Taxpayer was sole beneficiary and sole executor of his father's estate. In an attempt to split the taxable income between himself and the estate, he arranged a sale of certain oil leases to himself, reserving on oil payment for the estate. The probate court approved the sale, but the district court held that it was a sham, since, as beneficiary, he had possession of the entire interest in the leases. *Held:* Reversed. The estate and taxpayer-beneficiary were separate taxable entities. The amount received by the estate was the fair value that it would have received if the transaction had been at arm's length. The tax-saving motive was immaterial. Davis, 282 F2d 623, 60-2 USTC ¶ 9715 (10th Cir. 1960).

Shift from abandonment loss to affiliate denied. Taxpayer was organized and incorporated to operate drive-in theaters. In 1952, taxpayer's stockholders organized a sister corporation. Prior to August 1954, the business of the sister corporation had so declined that it discontinued operations. In August 1954, taxpayer purchased the sister corporation's theater at book value. The theater was subsequently damaged by Hurricane Hazel and completely abandoned. Taxpayer claimed an abandonment loss on its 1955 return. The IRS took the position that the purchase was a sham, undertaken only to shift the abandonment loss from the sister corporation which could not use it, to taxpayer. The IRS made a reallocation under Section 482 and denied the loss. The district court agreed with the IRS, disallowing the deduction of the abandonment loss. *Held:* Affirmed. Taxpayer failed to show that the IRS acted arbitrarily or capriciously in allocating to the sister corporation the stated deductions claimed by taxpayer in arriving at its net operating loss carry-back. The theater, which was the subject of the sale contract, had not operated for about two months prior to the purchase, during the peak of the drive-in theater season. The additional fact that the sister corporation had already suffered sufficient losses to recover all the taxes that it had ever paid was significant in leading the IRS to the rather convincing conclusions that the sale was not in furtherance of any real or valid business purpose, and that the sole objective of the transfer was to attribute the deductions and corresponding loss to taxpayer, which could utilize the loss and reap a tax benefit. Aiken Drive-in Theatre Corp., 281 F2d 7, 60-2 USTC ¶ 9616, 6 AFTR2d 5233 (4th Cir. 1960).

Purchase and immediate sale of stock held a sham. Taxpayer corporation entered a tax-avoidance scheme whereby it purchased stock in a corporation, "dividend on," and then sold the same stock a day later, ex dividend. In this manner, taxpayer received a dividend and became entitled to a deduction in the amount of 85 percent of the dividend received. Upon the sale of the stock at a price reduced by the dividends distributed, taxpayer realized a short-term capital loss that it could apply against capital gains. The IRS determined the purchase and sale to be part of a sham and disallowed the 85 percent deduction and the short-term loss. *Held:* For the IRS. Because there was no bona fide purchase of stock, taxpayer did not receive dividends; therefore, it was not entitled to an 85 percent deduction. Good faith did not change the nature of what was otherwise a sham transaction. Malden Knitting Mills, 42 TC 769 (1964).

Tax Court denied net operating loss deduction to sole stockholders of small corporation in which the stockholders' claimed investments in corporation were sham. Taxpayers, a husband and wife, were the sole stockholders of a small corporation. Individually, the husband transferred six parcels of real property to the corporation, and jointly the couple transferred one parcel. After these transfers, the husband treated two of the parcels as his own individual property. No impediments prevented taxpayers from similarly treating the other five parcels. Taxpayers claimed losses incurred by the corporation on their joint federal income tax returns for three taxable years. The IRS disallowed the deductions on the ground that taxpayers' holdings of stock had a zero basis during the years in question. *Held:* For the IRS. The Tax Court rejected taxpayers' claim that the property transfers represented additional investment in the corporation. The alleged contributions were sham transactions unrelated to the business of the corporation and were made for the sole purpose of obtaining for taxpayers the net operating losses of the corporation as losses. Hodge, 29 TCM 1313, ¶ 70,280 P-H Memo. TC (1970).

Timber acquired by partner stockholders with corporate funds held owned by partnership, not corporation. Timber was purchased in the name of two individual partner stockholders, paid for with corporate funds, and then sold to the corporation under timber-cutting contracts. The timber was sold to the corporation at stumpage market prices as the corporation needed it, the stumpage credited against the advances made by the corporation for the original purchase of the timber. The IRS determined that purchase by the partnership was a sham, and that the timber was in fact acquired and owned by the corporation. *Held:* For taxpayer. The books and records of both corporation and partnership clearly and carefully recognized and recorded the transactions, and the tax returns of all parties reflected the ownership of the timber by the partnership. The court found that the facts clearly showed that no sham arrangement existed. Lowes Lumber Co., 19 TCM 727, ¶ 60,141 P-H Memo. TC (1960).

SPIN-OFFS, SPLIT-OFFS, AND SPLIT-UPS

(*See* Reorganizations—Spin-Offs and Other Divisive Reorganizations)

SPLITTING OF INCOME

(*See* Affiliated Corporations; Allocations Among Related Taxpayers)

STATUTORY MERGERS

(*See* Reorganizations-Mergers)

STEP-TRANSACTION DOCTRINE

(*See* Reorganizations—Step-Transaction Doctrine; Transfers to Controlled Corporations—Step-Transaction Doctrine)

STOCK REDEMPTIONS

(*See* Redemptions)

STOCK RETIREMENT

(*See* Liquidations; Redemptions; Reorganizations)

STOCK RIGHTS

(*See* Dividends and Distributions—Stock Dividends and Rights)

STOCK, SALES OF

Holding company permitted *Corn Products* loss on sale of securities purchased to protect its goodwill and reputation. Taxpayer, a holding and service company, derived nearly all of its income from service fees paid and dividends declared by its subsidiaries. Taxpayer executed a purchase contract to acquire a controlling interest in an unrelated corporation. While awaiting government approval of the acquisition, the financial condition of the prospect significanty deteriorated. Taxpayer's attorney advised taxpayer that because of this deterioration, it was no longer required to acquire the prospect's stock under the purchase agreement. Taxpayer, however, went through with the stock purchase to protect its reputation and goodwill. After a year of looking for a purchaser, taxpayer was finally able to sell its stock in this corporation. Taxpayer claimed that it realized an ordinary loss on the sale of this stock. The district court held for taxpayer. Because when taxpayer acquired its stock interest its intent was no longer motivated by investment (i.e., to acquire a subsidiary), but to preserve its reputation, the *Corn Products* doctrine supported an ordinary loss treatment on the sale of such stock. *Held:* Affirmed. A holding company may hold stock with sufficient purpose to avail itself of the *Corn Products* doctrine. The IRS' claim that the doctrine was applicable solely to "hedging" transactions was invalid. Campbell Taggart, Inc., 744 F2d 442, 54 AFTR2d 84-6135 (5th Cir. 1984).

Corporation realized gain when foundation sold stock transferred to it by corporation. Taxpayer, engaged in the investment and rental business, was one of many corporations controlled by *C*. Foundation, one of *C*'s corporations, was a nonprofit, tax-exempt corporation that indirectly owned 87 percent of taxpayer's stock. Taxpayer donated stock of another corporation, *W*, to Foundation, but kept the stock pledged to a bank as security for a loan. The stock remained pledged to the bank until the loan was paid. Thereafter, the stock was released from taxpayer's account and transferred to the liability account of *W* as collateral on its note, which the bank had just purchased. Three years later, the stock was released to *W* when its note was paid in full. While Foundation held the stock, monies it received went to pay off taxpayer's indebtedness. The IRS advised Foundation that it was losing its tax-exempt status. Later, the IRS determined that taxpayer had realized a long-term capital gain on the disposition of *W*'s stock to Foundation. *Held:* For the IRS. The substance of the transaction was a sale where the transferee received property subject to an encumbrance. The amount of the loans assumed were part of its sales price. Taxpayer did not have a right to contribute more that its equity in the stock, since the stock was pledged to a bank to secure taxpayer's note. First Nat'l Indus., Inc., 404 F2d 1182, 69-1 USTC ¶ 9145, 23 AFTR2d 69-332 (6th Cir.), cert. denied, 394 US 1014 (1969).

Ordinary income on proceeds of sale of stock allocable to dividends. Taxpayers owned prior preference stock in a parent company that was undergoing a bankruptcy reorganization. Its subsidiary was to transfer new common stock plus a cash dividend thereon to the parent in exchange for the old common held by the parent. Then the parent was to distribute the new subsidiary common plus the cash to its securityholders for their securities. Upon consummation of the plan, the parent was to be completely dissolved. Had taxpayers participated in the plan, they would have received a cash dividend of $103,000. Instead, they sold their stock to a third party and realized a gain of $468,000, which they reported as long-term capital gains. The district court upheld the IRS' contention that $103,000 of the gain must be reported as ordinary income. *Held:* Affirmed. Taxpayers were held to have received the dividend constructively. After the date set for distribution, the parent ceased to exist as an operating company, and its stock represented merely a right to other property. Consideration received from the sale of a right to ordinary income was taxable as ordinary income. The one dissenter noted, however, that the majority's theory would result in the dividend being taxed to each of numerous holders who may have traded the stock before the distribution. Brundage, 275 F2d 424, 60-1 USTC ¶ 9261 (7th Cir.), cert. denied, 364 US 831 (1960).

Sale of stock by corporation's directors voided and viewed as corporation's sales within Section 1032. Taxpayer's directors contracted with taxpayer to acquire some of its unissued authorized stock. The directors sold these contracts to others. According to a legal opinion received by these directors and taxpayer, the directors turned over to taxpayer the entire net proceeds of these sales. The attorney's opinion was that the directors, as fiduciaries of taxpayer, could not, under state law, retain the profits on these contracts; thus, viewing them as taxpayer's agents, their contracts with taxpayer should be ignored. Taxpayer did not recognize income on receipt of these funds. The IRS assessed a deficiency against taxpayer, arguing that Section 1032 did not apply because the funds received by taxpayer in excess of the subscription price in the contracts with its directors was not received in exchange for its stock. *Held:* For taxpayer. Because of their fiduciary relationship to taxpayer under state law, the directors never validly owned their shares but held them as agents of taxpayer. Thus, their sales should be viewed as sales by taxpayer, in which event Section 1032 applies. The court distinguished its opinion in General Am. Ins. Co., 19 TC 581 (1952), aff'd, 211 F2d 522 (2d Cir. 1954), aff'd, 345 US 434 (1955), where the profits from the sale of a corporation's stock were turned back to the corporation under federal, and not state, securities laws. The Cardinal Corp., 52 TC 119 (1969).

Sale of stock, incident to corporate contraction, not a dividend. Taxpayer was the controlling stockholder of a corporation that decided to discontinue one of its two lines of business. A prospective purchaser agreed to first buy out several of the minority stockholders. The corporation was then to redeem the stock so acquired by turning over one of the businesses. Because the shares held by the selling minority stockholders did not total to the agreed-upon price for the business, taxpayer sold about 2000 shares to his son, who in turn sold them to the purchaser of the assets. Actually, his son paid taxpayer out of the proceeds of the second sale. The IRS treated taxpayer's sale as a redemption equivalent to a dividend. *Held:* For taxpayer. The court found that there was a bona fide sale by taxpayer, not a dividend. Even if there were a redemption, the court would refuse to find it equivalent to a dividend. The facts show that it was not. Standard Linen Serv., Inc., 33 TC 1, acq. 1960-2 CB 7.

Regulated investment company; bidding period for short sales. The IRS ruled that if a regulated investment company sold short shares that it held for four months and closed the sale one month later, the shares would be considered as having been held for not less than three months. However, if the sale were closed by delivering identical stock that was purchased after the short sale, the closing would be considered as delivering stock held less than three months, and the initial stock holding period would have begun on the closing date of the short sale. Rev. Rul. 74-434, 1974-2 CB 195.

Treatment of common, preferred, and dual stockholders in an exchange. Taxpayers engaged in a transaction in which common shares were exchanged for common, and preferred shares were exchanged for cash. The IRS ruled that no gain was recognized on the exchange of the common shares, and the cash received by stockholders owning both classes of shares was a distribution not having the effect of a dividend on which gain, but not loss, was recognized. The exchange by stockholders owning only preferred stock was treated as a redemption. Rev. Rul. 74-515, 1974-2 CB 118.

STOCK VS. DEBT

(*See* Bonds and Debentures; Contributions to Capital; Debt vs. Equity)

STRAW CORPORATIONS

(*See* Associations Taxable as Corporations; Corporations as Taxable Entity)

SUBSIDIARIES

(*See* Affiliated Corporations; Consolidated Returns)

SUBSTANTIATION

(*See* Business Expenses—Substantiation)

SUBSTITUTED BASIS

(*See* Basis of Property)

SUCCESSOR CORPORATIONS

(*See* Affiliated Corporations; Net Operating Loss; Reorganization—Carry-Over of Losses and Tax Attributes)

SURPLUS

(*See* Earnings and Profits)

TAXABLE INCOME OF CORPORATIONS

(*See also* Capital Gains and Losses)

Advertising income paid to small related corporation includable in larger corporation's income. K and B owned all the stock of N and were the majority and controlling stockholders of taxpayer. The Tax Court held that sums totaling approximately $142,000 paid by taxpayer to N under the guise of "advertising participation program payments" were taxpayer's income and were taxable to it. Additionally, the court found that such payments could not be deducted by taxpayer as a business expense, and that the payments were taxable to K and B as constructive dividends. *Held:* Affirmed. Where the transactions were not genuine and had no business purpose, a large newspaper corporation could not omit advertising income paid over to a small related corporation under advertising income participation agreements. There was no substantial contribution by N to taxpayer's production of income, and the payments were not deductible as business expenses. Payments were constructive dividends because the exercise of power to procure payment from one corporation to the other was enjoyment and realization of income. Equitable Publishing Co., 356 F2d 514, 66-1 USTC ¶ 9298, 17 AFTR2d 514 (3d Cir. 1966).

Membership fees held not to be received in exchange for stock. Taxpayer ran three department stores that were open only to members and their guests. Members paid a small fee that primarily bought the privilege of shopping in taxpayer's stores. The district court held that the membership certificates represented stock for the purpose of Section 1032 and that the members were stockholders. Hence there was no recognition of gain by taxpayer for membership fees received. *Held:* Reversed. Membership fees were taxable and not received in exchange for stock. The rights that members received were minor and more theoretical than real. Federal Employees Distrib. Co., 322 F2d 891, 63-2 USTC ¶ 9712 (9th Cir. 1963), cert. denied, 376 US 951 (1964).

Distribution of water to stockholders without charge did not result in taxable income to mutual water company. Taxpayer was a nonprofit mutual water company. It distributed water to its stockholders without charge. Miscellaneous sources of income and stockholder assessments provided it with funds to operate and to make necessary capital improvements. The IRS contended that taxpayer realized taxable income in an amount equal to the fair market value of the water distributed. Alternatively, the IRS contended that taxpayer could not deduct the costs of gathering, impounding, and distributing the water. Finally, the IRS argued that taxpayer had to include stockholder assessments in income. *Held:* For taxpayer on the first two issues and in part on the third. Since taxpayer had no right to receive anything from its stockholders in exchange for distributing water to them, it could claim no taxable income as a result of making the distributions. The Ninth Circuit decision in Anaheim Water Co., 321 F2d 253 (1963), foreclosed denying taxpayer a deduction for its costs related to gathering, impounding, and distributing water to its stockholders. The fact that taxpayer received its stockholder assessments without restriction as to their use supported the IRS' contention that the assessments were income to taxpayer. However, the fact that the assessments were levied without regard to the amount of water a stockholder used and that taxpayer made the assessments in part to provide funds for capital supported a different construction. So did the fact that in other cases, the IRS had successfully argued that stockholders could not deduct similar assessments on the grounds that the assessments were contributions to capital. These conflicting factors required an allocation, one that would allow taxpayer to exclude from income that portion of the assessments that equaled the ratio of taxpayer's capital expenditures to the total of its assessments, and to exclude as well its miscellaneous income from its nonstockholder sources. Bear Valley Mut. Water Co., 427 F2d 713, 70-2 USTC ¶ 9551, 25 AFTR2d 70-1434 (9th Cir. 1970).

IRS disallowed tax-option election by stockholders. Three siblings owned extensive oilbearing acreage. They formed taxpayer corporation, to which they transferred title to their property without warranty or consideration, reserving for the former partners beneficial title to the property and all rights to the proceeds of existing leases for mineral rights and rights of way. The corporation was set up to continue the business in the event of the death of a party. The corporate charter limited the corporate activities; by agreement, the corporation's expenses were to be charged against the three individuals in equal amounts by means of deductions from proceeds of operations distributed periodically to the former partners. From 1960 through 1963, individual taxpayers filed separate federal tax returns reporting the income and expenses allocated to them by the corporation. The IRS determined that the corporation, not the individuals, were responsible for the taxes. *Held:* For the IRS. Profits from oil leases were taxable to the corporation that held title to the property and not to its stockholders, who had retained beneficial ownership for themselves by means of an alleged agency agreement. The corporate entity could not be ignored because it was set up for the acceptable business purposes of providing efficient management in the event that a partner died and of decreasing the need for signatures of all three owners in routine operations. Harrison Property Management Co., 475 F2d 623, 73-1 USTC ¶ 9292, 31 AFTR2d 73-946 (Ct. Cl.), cert. denied, 414 US 1130 (1973).

Incentive payment to relocate business was income. Taxpayer corporation operated an authorized Ford dealership in an undesirable section of a city. In 1965, Ford, which held none of taxpayer's stock, paid taxpayer to induce taxpayer to move its dealership to a better neighborhood in an improved facility. Taxpayer subsequently moved and spent the funds on leasehold improvements at the new location and charged the amount to a leasehold improvement account. Relying on Sections 118 and 362(c)(2), taxpayer, on its 1965 income tax return, reduced the cost of the leasehold improvements by the amount received from Ford. The IRS determined that the amount received from Ford was income to taxpayer, and taxpayer was entitled to a deduction stemming from the amortization of the leasehold improvements. *Held:* For the IRS. An incentive payment designed to finance improvement was an accession to taxpayer's wealth; accordingly, it was includable in income under Section 61(a). Arguments excluding the amounts as contributions to capital were invalid where taxpayer made improvements on his own property and not as a lessee on leased property. Also, Ford's payments clearly had a reasonable nexus with taxpayer's services, and Ford only anticipated benefits it relied upon when establishing the dealership. White, 55 TC 729 (1971).

Bank that acquired homesites and financed home construction was taxable on gains. During 1956 through 1958, taxpayer bank acquired various homesites that it carried on its books as loans receivable from Security Building Co., a corporation controlled by the wife of taxpayer's president. Security was later taken over by State Guaranty. Construction of homes was done by Johnnies (owned by the sister-in-law of taxpayer's president) for a fee of 10 percent of the actual construction costs. Taxpayer financed the construction, and State Guaranty provided assistance to Johnnies without the benefit of any written agreement. State Guaranty also guaranteed all notes received on the sale of homes, and taxpayer provided the mortgage funds. In its 1956 and 1957 returns, taxpayer included in its income the full profit on the sale of homes. In its 1958 return, it included only one half, paying State Guaranty the other half for its services. Taxpayer contended that no income should have been reported for 1956 and 1957, since half of the income belonged to State Guaranty and the other half constituted unearned discount on the notes. Taxpayer also contended that it took title to the homesites for security purposes only and that State Guaranty in reality built and sold the homes. Taxpayer argued that it had merely purchased the notes from State Guaranty at a discount (a cost equalling the amount paid for the land and the construction costs, including the 10 percent paid to Johnnies). Taxpayer further claimed that it retained half the 1956–1957 profit to secure State Guaranty's endorsement of the notes received upon the sale of homes. *Held:* For the IRS. The court, after evaluating the evidence, rejected all these contentions and held that the gains were taxable to taxpayer as reported in its returns. As to the fair market value of the notes, taxpayer failed to show that these values were less than the face value of the notes. First Sav. & Loan Ass'n, 40 TC 474 (1963).

Property transferred to controlling stockholder followed by a leaseback revested rights to income in corporation. Taxpayer transferred contracts for real estate purchases to his closely held corporation. The corporation made purchases with funds loaned by taxpayer including land it later leased to M. To secure borrowings for another investment, taxpayer had the corporation transfer the property leased by M to taxpayer in a leaseback arrangement in exchange for a credit against money the corporation had owed him. The corporation reported the rental income on its tax return. The IRS determined that the rents were taxable to taxpayer and not the corporation. *Held:* For taxpayer. By the contemporaneous leaseback, taxpayer revested in the corporation the right to the rents under the M lease; accordingly, the rental income was taxable to the corporation and not taxpayer. Roy, 27 TCM 475, ¶ 68,099 P-H Memo. TC (1968).

TAXABLE INCOME OF STOCKHOLDERS

(*See also* Dividends and Distributions; Capital Gains and Losses)

Stockholder beneficiary received corporate insurance tax free. A corporation took out life insurance on its president, who, with his wife, owned 40 percent of its stock. The corporation itself was beneficiary, reserving the right to change the beneficiary at will. Similar policies were taken out on the lives of the other two stockholder officers. The plan was to change the beneficiary so that the corporation would receive nothing when the insured officer died, and the stockholders would share in the proceeds of the policy in proportion to their stockholdings. This was done.

Tax Avoidance

The Tax Court held that the policy was purchased as part of a plan to distribute corporate profits to stockholders, and the stockholder beneficiaries were not entitled to exclude the proceeds from their income as amounts received under a life insurance contract paid by reason of the death of the insured. *Held:* Reversed. The policy was valid under applicable Ohio law. Since the corporation did not in fact receive the proceeds, the court refused to treat the transaction as if it had, and then distributed the proceeds to the taxpayer stockholder. Ducros, 272 F2d 49, 59-2 USTC ¶ 9785 (6th Cir. 1959).

Stockholder officer taxed on stock issued for accrued salary. A corporation in which taxpayer was an officer and principal stockholder issued to him shares of common stock to wipe out its liability to him for accrued salary and unreimbursed travel expenses. This was done to enable the corporation to present a better statement for obtaining a Reconstruction Finance Corporation loan. Taxpayer contended that the stock distributed to him constituted a nontaxable stock dividend. *Held:* For the IRS. The court held that taxpayer's contention was without merit, since taxpayer's proportionate interest in the corporation increased as a result of the stock distribution. Accordingly, the fair market value of the shares, as determined by the court, was included in his taxable income. Morison, 19 TCM 1364, ¶ 60,243 P-H Memo. TC (1960).

TAX AVOIDANCE

(*See also* Acquisitions to Avoid Tax; Allocation Among Related Taxpayers; Reorganizations; Sham Transactions)

Section 269 did not override Section 334(b)(2). Taxpayer corporation liquidated its subsidiary under the provisions of Section 334(b)(2). Thus, as to an installment obligation received in the liquidation, taxpayer used as its basis an allocable portion of the cost of the subsidiary's stock. The IRS contended that the basis for the note was the basis to the subsidiary, because using Section 334(b)(2) in this situation to give a stepped-up basis was considered tax avoidance within the purview of Section 269. The district court upheld the IRS. *Held:* Reversed. There was no tax avoidance where a taxpayer determined its tax liability in accordance with the rules specified by Congress (here, Section 334(b)(2)) and paid the tax that Congress intended it to pay. Supreme Inv. Corp., 468 F2d 370, 72-2 USTC ¶ 9689, 30 AFTR2d 72-5614 (5th Cir. 1972).

Tax avoidance finding disallowed net operating loss carry-forwards. The IRS held that the principal purpose behind a merger was tax avoidance; therefore, taxpayer-survivor's use of net operating carry-forwards of the acquired corporations was disallowed. The district court found for the IRS. *Held:* Affirmed. Taxpayer corporation had not come forth with sufficient evidence to overcome the IRS' findings. Vulcan Materials Co., 446 F2d 690, 71-1 USTC ¶ 9449, 27 AFTR2d 71-1488 (5th Cir. 1971).

Tax avoidance had to exist immediately before transfer. In 1953, taxpayer refinanced separate mortgages on four parcels of real property used by him in a parking lot business. In 1957, he transferred the parcels to controlled corporations, each of which assumed a share of the indebtedness. In the same year, after extensive tax consultation, taxpayer mortgaged a fifth property, which he then conveyed to a fifth corporation. The various corporations leased the properties back to taxpayer after their separate incorporations. The IRS contended that taxpayer's primary purpose in transferring the properties to the corporations was tax avoidance and that, therefore, under Section 357, he should be required to recognize his gains to the extent of the assumed indebtedness. The Tax Court agreed. Taxpayer's correspondence showed that he was very tax-conscious and was aware of the tax savings inherent in the transfers. Under Section 1239, the gain on the parking lot properties was held taxable as ordinary income. Further evidence of a tax motive was that part of the proceeds from the mortgage loans was used to purchase tax-exempt securities. A bank account in the name of taxpayer's wife was used to conceal the transaction. A portion of the interest paid on the loan was disallowed. *Held:* Reversed as to the transfer of the parcels mortgaged in 1953; affirmed as to other issues. Section 357 provides that the assumption of a mortgage on a transfer to a controlled corporation is taxable as boot if the principal purpose of the taxpayer *with respect to the assumption* was to avoid income tax *on the exchange*. In the instant case, there was no evidence that, whatever taxpayer's purpose in borrowing funds in 1953, it was to avoid taxes *on the exchange* made four years later. In this regard, the Tax Court's conclusion that taxpayer had no business purpose for incorporating his properties was clearly erroneous. The purpose was to put his real estate investments in more manageable condition for estate planning and generally to obtain the advantages attendant upon operating in the corporate form. With respect to the fifth property, however, taxpayer did not prove that his purpose in incorporating the property was not tax avoidance. On the contrary, taxpayer's using the borrowed funds to buy exempt obligations through what was nominally his wife's bank account, as well as expressions of his intention shortly before the incorporation, indicated that the opposite was true. Drybrough, 376 F2d 350, 67-1 USTC ¶ 9340, 19 AFTR2d 1076 (6th Cir. 1967).

Court ignored corporate entities in taxing income to stockholders. Taxpayers, brothers, were equal partners in a citrus grove. For tax purposes, they reported on a calendar-year basis. In 1958, taxpayers established three corporations to which they transferred undivided interests in the partnership assets. The corporation reported on a fiscal-year basis. Beginning in 1959, taxpayers made gifts of minority stock interests in the three corporations to members of their family. Two of the corporations first elected Subchapter S treatment for their fiscal year ending in 1959; the third corporation first made the election for its fiscal year ending in 1963. The IRS, ignoring the existence of the three corporations, taxed all their income to taxpayers. At the trial, the IRS conceded that the income attributable to the minority stock interests was taxable to the minority stockholders. *Held:* For the IRS. For a corporation to be considered a separate entity for tax purposes, it must engage in some business activity beside avoiding taxation. Here, the corporations engaged in no activities until they were used to effect a transfer of portions of taxpayers' assets. Their income, until they were so used, was includable in the income of taxpayers. Britt, 292 F. Supp. 6, 68-2 USTC ¶ 9557 (MD Fla. 1968).

Organization of separate corporations not for primary purpose of avoiding tax. Fourteen taxpayers were subsidiaries of the same parent corporation that managed all their affairs. Each taxpayer owned a special type of vessel that it leased to others to service submersible oil drilling barges. After acquiring the stock of the first three taxpayers in a tax-free reorganization, the parent organized the remaining taxpayers as it negotiated new leasing ventures. Taxpayers executed formal lease agreements with the prospective lessees on incorporation, and then, with financing arranged for by the parent, taxpayers purchased the necessary vessels. The vessels of all the taxpayers secured the individual loans to each. The IRS denied taxpayers multiple surtax exemptions, relying alternatively on Sections 269 and 1551 and claiming that the principal purpose of their formation was to avoid tax or that a major purpose of the parent's transferring its various business opportunities to them was to claim the multiple surtax exemption. *Held:* For taxpayers. The fact that the stockholders of taxpayer's parent were sophisticated business people who undoubtedly were aware of the tax benefits of separate corporations did not establish that tax avoidance was the principal purpose for their actions. The facts established that the principal purpose of their actions was to insulate the liability of each corporation and that claiming multiple surtax exemptions was not even one of their major purposes. Moreover, legislative history indicates that Section 1551 does not apply to the expansion of an existing business, and that a business opportunity is not property for purposes of that provision. Tidewater Hulls, Inc., 68-1 USTC ¶ 9405 (ED La. 1968).

Distribution of installment obligations to successor corporations not taxable, although tax avoidance was a major consideration. Three predecessor corporations built and sold tract homes on the installment basis. While they still had unreported installment income, the stockholders sold their stock to three successor corporations, which thereupon liquidated their predecessors under Section 332. The successors applied a stepped-up basis to the installment obligations under Section 334(b)(2). The IRS assessed deficiencies against the predecessor corporations on the full amount of the installment obligations not previously taxed. In the alternative, the IRS sought to hold the successors and the stockholders as transferees on the theory that they did not acquire a stepped-up basis on liquidation. Taxpayers contended that no gain should be recognized to the successors under Section 332, and that, therefore, Section 453(d)(4)(A) precluded recognition of gain to the predecessors on disposition of the installment obligations. The IRS countered that the transactions were a sham, and that Section 269 should be invoked, since the only result was to bail out corporate earnings at capital gains rates. *Held:* For taxpayers. The predecessor corporations did not, in fact, dispose of their installment obligations by refinancing, as the IRS contended. The evidence clearly showed that they desired to avoid a costly accelerated tax and desired to retain the obligations to maturity. The stockholders made a bona fide sale of their stock to the successor corporations, which in turn brought about a bona fide liquidation of the predecessors. Although tax avoidance was a major consideration, as long as the actions were not mere shams, the tax consequences were to be determined by the substantive acts of the parties. Applying Sections 332 and 453 to these facts, it was apparent that there was no gain recognized on the liquidation or on the distribution of the installment obligations. Use of a stepped-up basis was inescapable when Section 334(b)(2) was applied as originally enacted. In addition, Section 269 was inapplicable, since the evidence disclosed that the principal purpose of the entire series of transactions was to enable the successors to engage in regular business activities; the avoidance complained of was not the obtaining of a deduction, credit, or other allowance. Cherry, 264 F. Supp. 969, 67-1 USTC ¶ 9282, 19 AFTR2d 899 (CD Cal. 1967).

Stockholders taxed on income from property contributed to their loss corporation. Taxpayers, a father, his sons, and their wives, had invested about $80,000 in X Corporation, whose attempt to market an insecticide spray failed. After the sprayer business had ceased, taxpayers tranferred their income-producing farming property to the corporation. The IRS taxed the income of each piece of property to the stockholder who had contributed it to the corporation. *Held:* For the IRS. There was no business purpose in operating through the corporation; the plan was merely an attempt to use the losses of the corporation to avoid tax on the income-producing property. In fact, there was no corporate management of the farms. The receipts and disbursements for each parcel were kept in separate bank accounts and paid over to the contributor of the property, and, in general, the previous owners continued to manage the land parcels in the same way that they had prior to the transfer of title. Haberman Farms, 182 F. Supp. 829, 60-1 USTC ¶ 9397 (D. Neb. 1960).

Assumption of liabilities not made for tax-avoidance reasons. In a series of transactions, taxpayer transferred the assets of two businesses to a newly formed controlled corporation. To provide the corporation with more working capital, taxpayer also transferred to it income-producing securties subject to liabilities, which the corporation assumed. The liabilities were slightly less than taxpayer's basis for the securities. The IRS contended that taxpayer had recognized gain on the transaction under the authority of Section 357(b), which provides that gain is recognized to the extent of liabilities assumed if tax avoidance is the principal purpose of the exchange, or if the principal purpose is not a bona fide business purpose. *Held:* For taxpayer. The Tax Court held that while tax considerations did have an important role in dictating the form of the transaction, the principal purpose was not tax avoidance, and the transaction did have a bona fide business purpose. Therefore, the exchange was tax free. Simpson, 43 TC 900, acq. 1965-2 CB 6.

Newly formed corporation could not be disregarded as a sham so as to attribute dividends it received at formation directly to its stockholders. Taxpayer, a successful motion picture director, was until July 26, 1962 the sole stockholder of *S*, a corporation that lent taxpayer's services to various motion picture producers, collected the fees for such services, and made payments to taxpayer in smaller amounts on a deferred basis. On that date, taxpayer transferred all of his stock in *S* to a newly organized corporation, *P*, in exchange for all of *P*'s stock. On the same date, *S* declared a dividend of $137,000, which it paid to *P* on July 30. *S*'s fiscal year ended July 31. On October 15, *S* declared and paid another dividend of $4,000 to *P*. The IRS determined that these two dividends, although paid to *P*, were constructively received by taxpayer and, therefore, includable in his income. *Held:* For taxpayer. Although the IRS accepted *S* as a viable entity, it sought to show that since *S* was on the verge of becoming a personal holding company as its income from taxpayer's personal services approached the statutory 80 percent limit, the dividend to *P* was intended merely to avoid the personal holding company penalty surtax. The remedy that the IRS sought in effect ignored *P*'s corporate entity by treating the dividend, which in fact was paid to *P*, as belonging to taxpayer. This could not be done because *P* could not be disregarded as a sham entity. *P*, in fact, did carry on bona fide business activities that were separate and distinct from *S*, and taxpayer was fully justified in placing such business in a separate corporation. A second issue, a painting in which taxpayer donated a remainder interest to a university, was found to have a fair market value of $60,000 as determined by the IRS, and not $85,000 as alleged by taxpayer. Cukor, 27 TCM 89, ¶ 68,017 P-H Memo. TC (1968).

TAX-BENEFIT RULE

Tax-benefit rule did not apply where taxes paid by bank on behalf of stockholders and deducted under Section 164(e) were refunded to stockholders. Taxpayer, an incorporated bank, customarily paid the Illinois property tax imposed on its stockholders' stock. Under Section 164(e), taxpayer was permitted a deduction for the amount of the tax, but the stockholders were not. Illinois amended its constitution in 1970 to prohibit the tax, and in 1972, following challenges by the state court, the amendment's constitutionality was upheld by the Supreme Court. Taxpayer had paid the taxes for its stockholders in 1972, taking the Section 164(e) deduction, and the state authorities had placed the receipts in escrow. In 1973, the amounts in escrow together with accrued interest were refunded to taxpayer's stockholders. On its 1973 return, taxpayer recognized no income from this series of events. The IRS claimed that the returned amounts should have been included in taxpayer's income, and so assessed a deficiency. On redetermination, the Tax Court held that the returned taxes, but not the payment of accrued interest, could be included in taxpayer's income. The Seventh Circuit affirmed on appeal. *Held:* For taxpayer. The court prefaced its analysis by observing that the tax-benefit rule would "cancel out" an earlier deduction only where there was a later event that was fundamentally inconsistent with the premise on which the deduction was initially based. In determining whether specific nonrecognition provisions prevailed over the principle of the tax-benefit rule, careful examination of the particular provisions was mandated. The court found that taxpayer was not required to recognize income under the tax-benefit rule. The court noted that taxpayer had paid a constructive dividend in satisfying a liability of its stockholders. Section 164(e) entitled taxpayer to an otherwise unavailable deduction for the dividend, and the refund to stockholders did not alter this privilege. The purpose of Section 164(e) was to provide relief for corporations making payments for their stockholders of this kind. The court stated that because taxpayer's payments had not been negated by a refund to taxpayer, the change in the character of the funds in the hands of the state did not require taxpayer to recognize income. Hillsboro Nat'l Bank, 460 US 370, 83-1 USTC ¶ 9229, 51 AFTR2d 83-874 (1983).

Tax-benefit rule requires that income be recognized where expensed item is assigned a stepped-up basis in a Section 334(b)(2) liquidation. Taxpayer purchased all of the stock of another corporation that it temporarily operated as a subsidiary before it was liquidated. Among the assets received by taxpayer in the liquidation were items whose cost was properly deducted in the year of purchase. Taxpaer claimed a stepped-up basis in these items and deducted them on such basis as a business expense. The IRS asserted and the Tax Court held that the value of such items was income to taxpayer in the year of liquidation. *Held:* Affirmed. As in the case of Section 337 liquidations, the tax-benefit rule overrode the nonrecognition treatment provided under Section 336. Furthermore, it was not necessary for an actual recovery of the deducted item to occur before the tax-benefit rule could be applied. Even if a recovery were required, the deduction of the expensed item here was made under the assumption that it would be "consumed." There was a "fictional" recovery when the acquired corporation was liquidated and its value was attributed to the expensed item. Tennessee-Carolina Transp., Inc., 582 F2d 378, 78-2 USTC ¶ 9671, 42 AFTR2d 78-5716 (6th Cir. 1978), cert. denied, 440 US 909 (1979).

Tax-benefit rule overrode nonrecognition provisions of Section 337. The IRS held that proceeds from the sale of previously expensed corporate property did not qualify for nonrecognition in a liquidating sale under Section 337. *Held:* For the IRS. The proceeds were includable in ordinary income under the tax-benefit rule. Krajeck, 75-1 USTC ¶ 9492, 36 AFTR2d 75-5634 (D. ND 1975).

Tax-benefit rules applicable in a 12-month liquidation. As taxpayer corporations had deducted the excess of the costs of buying hens over their farm-price inventory value in prior years, the IRS held that the excess of selling price paid for them over inventory value, which was less than the prior deductions, was not eligible for nonrecognition in a 12-month liquidation, even though there was a bulk sale. *Held:* For the IRS. The provisions of Section 337, dealing with a 12-month liquidation, do not alter the application of the tax-benefit rules derived from other sections of the Code. Thus, under the tax-benefit rule, the excess was ordinary income. Bishop, 324 F. Supp. 1105, 71-1 USTC ¶ 9165 (MD Ga. 1971).

Tax-benefit rule applied in Section 337 liquidations. S.E. Evans, Inc. was a corporation that was organized and did business in Arkansas. In 1965, the corporation was liquidated in accordance with Section 337. This section generally provides for the nonrecognition of gain on sales of property made under the liquidation plan. Accordingly, taxpayer treated the sale of previously expensed parts and supplies as having no recognized gain. The IRS assessed a deficiency, claiming that the tax-benefit rule applied and overrode Section 337's nonrecognition treatment. *Held:* For the IRS. The court cited both Anders, 414 F2d 1283 (10th Cir. 1969), and Spitalny, 430 F2d 195 (9th Cir. 1970), as supporting the IRS' claim. In enacting Section 337, Congress never intended to eliminate the tax-benefit rule. When expensed property is sold in a liquidation plan, the tax-benefit rule applies and requires the recognition of gain. "The [property] involved is treated as representing the income which was offset by a deduction and the [gain] is but a recovery of that income." Even though the nonrecognition rule appears to apply, the tax-benefit rule says it does not. S.E. Evans, Inc., 317 F. Supp. 423, 70-2 USTC ¶ 9612, 26 AFTR2d 70-5532 (WD Ark. 1970).

Previously expensed items were reconverted to property sale. The IRS held that upon liquidation, taxpayer, a corporation that had been engaged in the business of renting various laundered items, had to recognize income on the sale of such items under the tax benefit doctrine. *Held:* For the IRS. The tax-benefit rule applied because the rental items had been previously expensed. The court then stated that the gain in this situation was not realized from the sale of these items but from reconverting these previously expensed items into property. Anders, 462 F2d 1147, 72-2 USTC ¶ 9561, 30 AFTR2d 72-5138 (Ct. Cl. 1972), cert. denied, 409 US 1064 (1969).

Recovery of amounts previously deducted notwithstanding Section 337 sale-liquidation were taxable. Section 337 provides that if within one year of a corporation's adoption of a plan of complete liquidation all of its assets are distributed in complete liquidation no gain or loss shall be recognized from its sale or exchange of property in that year. Taxpayer corporation availed itself of Section 337 and sold its entire assets to a single purchaser. Included in this sale were items that had been fully deducted in taxable years prior to the year of sale. The IRS ruled that part of the sales proceeds represented a recovery of previous deductions and accordingly was not to be treated as gain from the sale under Section 337 but as ordinary taxable income under Section 61. The recovery of an amount previously deducted constitutes ordinary income to the extent of a prior tax benefit. Rev. Rul. 61-214, 1961-2 CB 60.

TAX-EXEMPT ORGANIZATIONS

Membership organization's deductions were limited to its income. Taxpayer was an organization whose membership was limited to salaried and retired employees of Armour, a manufacturer of consumer products. Taxpayer provided entertainment and recreational activities for its members, and operated a retail store where it sold some of Armour's reject products. Taxpayer deducted the expenses for membership activities. The IRS limited such deductions to the income derived from its dues on the ground that taxpayer was a social club subject to the limitations of Section 277. *Held:* For the IRS. The taxpayer was a nonexempt social club operated primarily to furnish services and goods to its members. Its activities focused on sponsoring several social functions whose cost far exceeded membership income. The club members directly benefited by taxpayer's activities, and the sale of Armour's reject products constituted a minor activity. Accordingly, taxpayer's deductions for membership activities were limited to the amount of its income from initiation fees and dues. Armour-Dial Men's Club, Inc., 708 F2d 1287, 83-1 USTC ¶ 9388, 52 AFTR2d 83-5140 (7th Cir. 1983).

A nonprofit corporation's membership fees, which principally offer to members shopping privileges were not payments in exchange for stock. Taxpayer, a nonprofit membership organization, operated department stores for the exclusive use of its members and their guests. Regular members paid an initiation fee and received, along with shopping privileges, the right to vote for directors and the right to share in taxpayer's assets upon liquidation. Regular members had no right to share in taxpayer's profits. The IRS determined that the membership fees should be treated as income to taxpayer, derived from the granting of discount shopping privileges. The Tax Court agreed with the IRS. *Held:* Affirmed. Under the circumstances, the members received no interest of substance in taxpayer other than the privilege to buy goods at a discount. Accordingly, the initiation fees paid by members were not exempt from tax as amounts paid in exchange for stock under Section 1032. Affiliated Gov't Employees Distrib. Co., 322 F2d 872, 63-2 USTC ¶ 9707, 12 AFTR2d 5606 (9th Cir. 1963).

Loss disallowed on sale of stock by corporation to related exempt foundation. The IRS disallowed a loss claimed by taxpayer, an insurance holding company, on the sale of stock to an exempt organization founded by taxpayer. *Held:* For the IRS. The evidence indicated that taxpayer controlled the foundation within the meaning of Section 267(b)(9). The foundation's six trustees also were members of taxpayer's 12-man board. The six men knew that taxpayer was selling the stock for less than it was worth. As a practical matter, those responsible for selling the stock were those responsible for buying it. This was the first case to interpret the meaning of control in the context of Section 267(g)(9). Nationwide Corp., 72-1 USTC ¶ 9430 (SD Ohio 1972).

Offering goods in return for contributions was unrelated business. The IRS determined that a veterans' group's practice of offering books, maps, and wrist calendars to contributors produced unrelated business taxable income. The IRS also argued that the sale of its waiting list produced such income. *Held:* For taxpayer, in part. The solicitations in which the contributions were near the retail value of the items given out constituted an unrelated business; but in cases where the contributions greatly exceeded the items' value, no such business existed. The sale of its waiting list was an unrelated business for lack of a relation to its exempt purpose. Disabled Am. Veterans, 650 F2d 1178, 81-1 USTC ¶ 9443, 48 AFTR2d 81-5047 (Ct. Cl. 1981).

Qualification as exempt cooperative phone company denied. A company owned and operated a two-way radio system for its member taxicab drivers. It claimed exempt status and that the initiation fees, dues, and payments for radio rights received from its members were excludable from its income. *Held:* For the IRS. The company failed to meet Section 501(c)(12)'s requirement that at least 85 percent of a qualifying organization's gross income be collected to cover expenses and losses because it built up a net worth far in excess of its reasonably anticipated needs. The amounts members paid to the company were paid to insure direct and current receipt of its services and were taxable. Dialcab Taxi Owners Guild Ass'n, 42 TCM 590, ¶ 81-410 P-H Memo. TC (1981), aff'd, 697 F2d 289 (2d Cir. 1982).

Organization designed to advance personal rather than the public interest was not tax exempt. Taxpayer formed an organization that provided a forum to attack government proceedings against his corporations. The IRS denied taxpayer's claim for tax-exempt status. *Held:* For the IRS. The organization did not further the public interest. Save the Free Enter. Sys., Inc., 42 TCM 515, ¶ 81,388 P-H Memo. TC (1981).

Organization failed to susbstantiate claim for exempt status. Taxpayer was an unincorporated association that conducted ecumenical evangelical services. It maintained no documentation of the use of its funds and its organizational documents contained no statement of purpose. The IRS denied its ruling request for exempt status under Section 501(c)(3) *Held:* For the IRS. Taxpayer failed to show that it was organized and operated exclusively for an exempt purpose. Truth Tabernacle, 41 TCM 1405, ¶ 81,214 P-H Memo. TC (1981).

Unrelated income to exempt organizations not taxed if from royalties. Taxpayer was an exempt organization whose purpose was to improve the economic conditions of its members, professional athletes. Taxpayer licensed its trademarks, trade names, and the like to promote products. The money received was not unrelated income because it was derived from royatlies. The organization also arranged product endorsements through its members' personal appearances. The activities were unrelated and generated personal service income rather than royalty income. Rev. Rul. 81-178, 1981-2 CB 135.

Organization with gross income normally in excess of $5,000 not exempt from filing. Taxpayer was organized and operated exclusively for charitable purposes. Taxpayer, a nonprofit foundation, had gross receipts for its first taxable year of less than $7,500; however, its aggregate gross receipts for its first two years exceeded $12,000. Taxpayer applied for tax-exempt status more than 90 days following the end of its second taxable year. *Held:* Taxpayer was not exempt under Section 501(c)(3) during the first two years because it failed to satisfy the notification requirement of Section 508(a) by filing within 90 days following the end of its second taxable year. It was not within the income exception of Section 508(c)(1)(B) because its aggregate gross receipts averaged over $5,000 per year during the first two years. Taxpayer was exempt under Section 501(c)(3) for its third year. Rev. Rul. 81-177, 1981-2 CB 132.

Private foundation's interest in business acquired by re-executed will is not excess business holding. A Section 509(a) private foundation was the residuary beneficiary under a will executed prior to May 26, 1969. A second will executed later expressly revoked the first, but did not change the residuary beneficiary. Although the interest in the business acquired under the will exceeded the percentage of permitted holdings under Section 4943(c)(2), it came within the transitional rules of Sections 4943(c)(4) and 4943(c)(5). It was not an excess holding. Rev. Rul. 81-119, 1981-1 CB 512.

Certification of export documents not unrelated trade or business. A chamber of commerce, exempt under Section 501(c)(6), certified export documents for members and nonmembers for the same fee. Since the documents' certification stimulated the community's business conditions by facilitating international commerce, it was not an unrelated trade or business under Section 513. Rev. Rul. 81-27, 1981-1 CB 357.

Organization operated for benefit of fraternal societies not exempt. An organization that did not operate under the lodge system or conduct fraternal activities held property for the benefit of societies that were exempt under Section 501(c)(10). The organization did not qualify under Section 501(c)(10). Regulation § 1.501(c)(10)-1 does not incorporate Section 501(c)(8) organizations, which are operated for the benefit of fraternities operating under the lodge system in its definition of Section 501(c)(10) organizations. Rev. Rul. 81-117, 1981-1 CB 346.

TAX-FREE EXCHANGES

(*See* Involuntary Conversions; Like-Kind Exchanges; Reorganizations; Transfers to Controlled Corporations)

TAX-FREE INCORPORATIONS

(*See* Reorganizations: Transfers to Controlled Corporations)

TAX-FREE REORGANIZATIONS

(*See* Reorganizations)

TAX SHELTERS

(*See* Tax Avoidance)

THIN CAPITALIZATION

(*See* Debt vs. Equity—Thin Capitalization)

TRADE OR BUSINESS, DEFINITION OF

(*See* Business Expenses—Profit Motive Requirement; Reorganizations—Spin-Offs and Other Divisive Reorganizations—Active Business Requirement)

TRANSFEREE LIABILITY

(*See* Assessment and Collection—Transferee Liability)

TRANSFERS TO CONTROLLED CORPORATIONS

(*See also* Reorganizations)

In General	600
Basis of Property Transferred	603
Control Defined	605
Step-Transaction Doctrine	607
Taxable Transfers	608
Tax-Free Transfers	614

Transfers to Controlled Corporations: *In General*

In General

General rule of assignment of income subordinated to broad congressional interest expressed in Section 351(a). A four-member partnership in the construction business complexed a tax-free incorporation pursuant to Section 351(a). The partnership transferred its business and most of its assets to taxpayer corporation solely in exchange for all of taxpayer's stock. The partnership had employed the cash method of accounting in computing its income for federal income tax purposes. Thus, it neither took uncollected receivables into income nor used inventories in the calculation of its taxable income. Taxpayer also employed the cash method of accounting. As accounts receivable were collected, taxpayer included the amounts in income when computing taxable income. The IRS determined that the cash method of accounting had not been appropriate for the taxpayer and adjusted taxpayer's income for two fiscal years using the accrual method. Taxpayer's beginning inventory was fixed at zero, resulting in a significant increase in taxpayer's taxable income for the years at issue. The IRS assessed deficiencies, and the district court held for the IRS. *Held*: Affirmed. The court rejected taxpayer's contention that the doctrine of assignment of income as developed by the Supreme Court required that the partnership, as transferor, bear the tax liability for accounts receivable, as they were collected by taxpayer. The court stated that the broad congressional interest in facilitating the incorporation of ongoing businesses, as expressed in the nonrecognition of gain or loss provision of Section 351(a), overrides the mandate of the assignment of income rule. Hempt Bros., 490 F2d 1172, 74-1 USTC ¶ 9188, 33 AFTR2d 74-570 (3d Cir.), cert. denied, 419 US 826 (1974).

Section 351 protects taxpayer from dividend treatment of boot under Sections 304 and 302. Taxpayer transferred stock in two corporations he controlled to a third corporation he controlled in exchange for cash and stock in the third corporation. All corporations were active at the time of the transfer. Evidence clearly showed that the transfer was motivated principally by business reasons relating to effecient operation of all three companies. Taxpayer reported gain realized from the receipt of cash as long-term capital gain. The IRS assessed deficiencies on the ground that under Sections 304 and 302, the cash received was a dividend. *Held*: For taxpayer. Although payment to taxpayer was clearly "essentially equivalent to a dividend" within the meaning of Section 302, Section 351 overrode application of Section 304. Accordingly, because taxpayer held over 80 percent of the transferee's stock after the transfer, Section 351 applied. Thus, capital gain treatment of the cash received was appropriate. Stickney, 399 F2d 828, 68-2 USTC ¶ 9551, 22 AFTR2d 5502 (6th Cir. 1968).

Shares subscribed for but not issued considered outstanding stock. Under Section 1239, an individual realizes ordinary income on the sale of depreciable property to a corporation in which he owns more than 80 percent of the outstanding stock. Taxpayer transferred such property to a corporation in which he originally subscribed for and received 80 percent of the shares, and another person subscribed for 20 percent. The other person did not pay the full purchase price, and stock certificates were issued only for the shares that were fully paid. If the unpaid stock that were considered outstanding, taxpayer did not own more than 80 percent of the outstanding shares. *Held*: For taxpayer. The shares allotted to the other person were considered to be outstanding, and Section 1239 did not apply. Under applicable Louisiana law, the subscription gave the other person rights as a stockholder to all shares for which he subscribed. Parker, 242 F. Supp. 117, 65-2 USTC ¶ 9491 (WD La. 1965).

Reserve must be restored to income on transfers to controlled corporations. Taxpayer transferred all the assets of a sole proprietorship to a controlled corporation pursuant to Section 351. As of the date of transfer, there was a balance in the reserve for bad debts, part of which was added during the current period. The IRS contended that the addition to the reserve was improper and that the reserve balance should be restored to income. *Held*: For the IRS. Regulation § 1.166-4 specifies that additions to the reserves are to be made only at the end of the taxable year. The deduction was not permitted for additions made during the year. The unabsorbed reserve balance was taxable income in the year of transfer to taxpayer, who had previously received tax benefit. Hutton, 53 TC 37 (1969).

Sale by proprietor of his business to a controlled corporation did not result in receipt of any dividend income. Taxpayer sold his sole proprietorship, a beverage company, to a corporation in which he owned all the common stock. The preferred stock was owned by his sisters. Of the total purchase price of $23,800, the agreement of sale allocated $6,500 to the net tangible assets and $17,300 to goodwill. The IRS determined that the $17,300 allegedly paid for goodwill actually represented a dividend from the purchasing corporation and was taxable as ordinary income, not capital gain. *Held:* For taxpayer. Transaction did not result in the receipt of a taxable dividend. The sale of the property to the corporation was at arm's length and was prompted solely by an effort to resolve a conflict-of-interest charge raised by the preferred stockholders, and the sales price was agreed to by independent interests protecting the latter. Lamble, 26 TCM 912, ¶ 67,185 P-H Memo. TC (1967).

Sale to controlled corporation a nullity. Taxpayers, who were officers and sole stockholders of a fuel company, allegedly acquired mineral leases in their own names and later transferred them at a gain to the corporation. They reported the gain as a capital gain. The IRS contended that the leases had originally been acquired for the corporation, so the sale was a nullity, and the payments were merely disguised dividends. *Held:* For the IRS. Taxpayers were acting for their corporation when they purchased the leases. Therefore, the payments received were dividends. However, one of the payments was a repayment of a loan and was not taxable. Stern, 24 TCM 1239, ¶ 65,242 P-H Memo. TC (1965).

Transfer of indebtedness and cash to controlled corporation for debentures tax free; **value of debentures determined.** Taxpayer owned all the stock of a corporation. He exchanged cash, accounts, and notes payable of the corporation for its 20-year 6 percent subordinated debentures. *Held:* The court found that the indebtedness and cash transferred constituted "property;" the transfer was solely in exchange for stock or securities of the corporation, and the transferor was in control of the corporaton immediately after the exchange. Accordingly, no gain or loss was recognized. Taxpayer had donated some of the debentures to charity and had claimed the full face value as his deduction, whereas the IRS asserted that the bonds had no value. The court disagreed with both and determined a fair market value at less than par. Dillard, 20 TCM 137, ¶ 61,030 P-H Memo. TC (1961).

Successive transfers to subsidiaries viewed separately. Taxpayer corporation transferred assets to its 80 percent owned subsidiary in exchange for stock. The subsidiary transferred those assets to its second-tier 80 percent owned subsidiary in exchange for stock. Such transfers are viewed as separate transactions. As each transfer satisfied the Section 351 requirements, no gain or loss was recognized. Rev. Rul. 83-34, 1983-1 CB 79.

Each transfer in a plan viewed separately to determine whether tax free. *P* transferred certain assets to its solely owned subsidiary, *S-1*, which set up an out-of-state branch operation in state *B*. In order to secure financing at favorable rates, *S-1* formed Newco Corporation in state *B*. Newco contributed borrowed funds to the partnership, and *S-1* contributed the assets it received from *P*. The partnership conducted the business of the state *B* branch operation under the sole management of *S-1*. The IRS ruled that no gain was recognized by the transferors because the transfer from *P* to *S-1* and Newco to the partnership satisfied Section 721. Each transfer was to be viewed separately as a transaction. Rev. Rul. 83-156, 1983-2 CB 66, amplifying Rev. Rul. 77-449, 1977-2 CB 110.

In a transaction to which both Sections 351 and 368(a)(1)(C) apply, Sections 357(c) and

Transfers to Controlled Corporations: *In General*

381(a) also apply. *P* Corporation transferred all of its assets to newly formed *S* Corporation in exchange for all the *S* stock and the assumption by *S* of *P*'s liabilities, which exceeded the basis of the assets exchanged by *P*. *P* remained in existence and did not distribute or intend to distribute the *S* stock. The IRS ruled that this transaction qualified both as a Section 368(a)(1)(C) reorganization and a Section 351 exchange. Further, Section 357(c), requiring the recognition of gain in a Section 351 transaction to the extent that liabilities assumed exceed to the transferor's basis, was found applicable to this transaction, although it also qualified as a C reorganization. Finally, Section 381(a) applied, so that *S* would succeed to and take into account various attributes of *P* as specified in Section 381(c). The IRS based its opinion on the lack of any statutory exception in Sections 381 and 357(c) that would prevent their simultaneous application. Rev. Rul. 76-188, 1976-1 CB 99.

The IRS will not follow the decision in *Estate of Haserot*. The IRS announced that it would not follow the decision in Estate of Haserot, 399 F2d 828 (6th Cir. 1968), which held that when Section 351 applies to a transaction also described in Section 304(a)(1), the transaction will be governed by Section 351. Rev. Rul. 73-2, 1973-1 CB 171.

Section 1036 applied to exchange of common stock where one class had voting and preemptive rights. Two individuals, both stockholders in the same corporation, exchanged their stock. One stockholder exchanged one class of stock that had voting and preemptive rights; the other class had no voting rights and no preemptive rights or certain other benefits available to the other class of stock. The exchange qualified under Section 1036(a), which provides that no gain or loss will be recognized if common stock is exchanged for common stock of the same corporation. The class of stock that had voting and preemptive rights was not reclassified as preferred stock. Rev. Rul. 72-199, 1972-1 CB 228.

Interest on notes and mortgages acquired in a Section 351 transaction does not qualify as "adjusted income from rents." Individuals sold rental property that received notes and mortgages. The notes and mortgages were transferred to a newly created corporation along with other rental property pursuant to Section 351. As the notes and mortgages did not relate to property that could meet the "activity" requirements of Section 543(b)(3), the interest related thereto did not qualify as "adjusted income from rents" as described in Section 543(a)(2). Rev. Rul. 72-318, 1972-1 CB 172.

Stock transfers to employees treated as nondeductible, taxable event. Pursuant to a plan formulated by the majority stockholder of a corporation, taxpayer transferred to it some of his stock of the corporation. In accordance with this plan, the corporation then transferred the stock to certain of its employees, the number of shares dependent on the number of years of the employee's service to the corporation. The corporation had no obligation to pay additional compensation to the employees. Based on these facts, the IRS ruled that the transfer of the stock by the corporation to its employees had to be treated for federal income tax purposes as if the transfer had been made directly by the majority stockholder to the employees of the corporation. Accordingly, the value of the stock transferred by the corporation to the employees was not deductible by the corporation under Section 162. The fair market value of such shares, however, was includable in the gross income of the employees under the provisions of Section 61. Rev. Rul. 69-369, 1969-2 CB 27.

Gain or loss for each asset transferred under Section 351 computed separately. The IRS ruled that in order to determine the amount of gain recognized under Section 351(b) when several assets are transferred, each asset must be considered as transferred separately in exchange for a portion of each category of consideration received, and the fair market value of each category of consideration received must be separately allocated to the transferred assets in proportion to the relative fair market values of the transferred assets. If a loss is realized with respect to any asset as a result of such allocation, it is not recognized. Rev. Rul. 68-55, 1968-1 CB 140.

Tax-free exchanges by investment companies discussed. Section 351(d), as amended by Section 203 of Public Law 89-809, deals with restrictions on the exchange of property for stock and securities to be issued by an investment company under a registration statement to be filed with the SEC. One of the provisions requires the transferred property to be deposited before May 1, 1967. In connection with the deposit cutoff date, the IRS held that it would consider a stock split or stock dividend on stock deposited before May 1, 1967 to have been deposited before May 1, 1967 if the investment company required the split stock or dividend stock to be deposited and its value was taken into account in the exchange and, further, that the stock split or dividend took place before June 30, 1967. With respect to the Section 351(d) requirement dealing with the filing of the registration statement by the investment company with the SEC before January 1, 1967, the IRS ruled that where such registration statement was amended after January 1, 1967, the tax treatment of the exchange would not be affected if the amendent did not result in the offering of a new or a different security. Rev. Rul. 67-122, 1967-1 CB 78.

Liabilities in excess of basis determined on an individual basis. The IRS ruled that in a Section 351 exchange, the provisions of Section 357(c) apply separately to each transferor so that the gain to each transferor is the excess of the sum of his liabilities assumed over the adjusted basis of all property transferred by him to the corporation, without regard to the adjusted basis and liabilities of any other transferor. Rev. Rul. 66-142, 1966-1 CB 66.

IRS announces policy on transfers of "know-how" in respect of Section 351. In response to inquiries concerning the transfer of "know-how" by U.S. manufacturers to newly formed foreign corporations, the IRS noted that the domestic transferor typically grants to the transferee rights to use manufacturing processes in which the transferor has exclusive rights by virtue of process patents or the protection otherwise extended by law to the owner of a process. The transferor also often agrees to furnish technical assistance in the construction and operation of the plant and to provide on a continuing basis technical information as to new developments in the field. The IRS observed that on exchange, the transferee typically issues to the transferor all or part of its stock. In such situations, the stock received in consideration of services rendered is taxable to the extent of the fair market value of the stock without regard to Section 351. Where and to the extent that "property" is the consideration issued in "exchange" for the stock, the transaction is nontaxable provided that the other requirements of Section 351 are met. Rev. Rul. 64-56, 1964-1 CB 133.

Basis of Property Transferred

Sale to controlled corporation not a contribution to capital. To obtain a stepped-up basis for equipment at the cost of a capital gain tax, taxpayers sold the equipment belonging to their partnership to a corporation that they had organized several months before. The corporation, which had only nominal capital, borrowed $240,000 to purchase the equipment. The loans were guaranteed by taxpayers. In denying the corporation the stepped-up basis, the district court held that the purported sale was really a contribution to capital. *Held:* Reversed. The fact that taxpayers were personally responsible for the bank loan did not mean that the loan was made to them and not to the corporation. Since the loan was to the corporation, the organization of the corporation and the sale of the equipment to it could not be collapsed into one transaction. Murphy Logging Co., 378 F2d 222, 67-1 USTC ¶ 9461, 19 AFTR2d 1623 (9th Cir. 1967).

Transfer to controlled corporation in exchange for 10-year note was tax free; failure to make election to capitalize interest resulted in disallowance. Taxpayer purchased a parcel of land from its stockholders and gave them its 10-year note in consideration. Interest on the note was accrued by taxpayer, but instead of deducting the interest, taxpayer added it to the balance-sheet land inventory, which was reflected at cost. *Held:* For the IRS. The district court held that the exchange between taxpayer and its stockholders was a Section 351 transaction; hence, taxpayer's basis for the land was the same as its stockholders. It also disallowed the capitalization of the interest on the note because taxpayer had failed to make the election on its return. Parkland Place Co., 354 F2d 916, 66-1 USTC ¶ 9164, 17 AFTR2d 097 (5th Cir. 1966).

Stepped-up basis denied for transfer to controlled corporation. The IRS contended that the transfer of land to a newly formed corporation was not a sale but a contribution to capital, and taxpayer should not be permitted a step-up in basis. *Held:* For the IRS. The evidence indicated that taxpayer was thinly capitalized, the stockholders had made pro rata loans to taxpayer, which were subordinated to other corporate debts. Florida-Georgia Corp., 331 F. Supp. 30, 71-2 USTC ¶ 9580, 28 AFTR2d 71-5445 (D. Ga. 1971).

Property transfer to controlled corporation was a contribution to capital, not a sale. On incorporation in 1952, taxpayer's capitalization was $10,000. Mowry and his family owned all its outstanding stock. Through 1958, taxpayer remained inactive. In 1959, Mowry transferred three apartment buildings to it for $3.2 million; Mowry's basis was $800,000. Taxpayer "paid" the purchase price with $30,000 down, and the balance (after assuming a first mortgage) of $2.3 million in promissory notes was payable in $30,000 semiannual installments. The contract was the only evidence of the down payment; all taxpayer's cash was on deposit in Mowry's personal account. The parties initially did not record the deeds or affix revenue stamps to them. It was not until 1961, when the IRS began auditing the parties' books, that they took steps to publicize the transfers of property and properly account for them. Even then, Mowry did not enforce the terms of the promissory notes on taxpayer's default. The IRS contended that the sale to taxpayer was in substance a contribution to capital. It thus denied taxpayer a step-up in basis from Mowry's $800,000 as well as the benefit of the nonrecognition provision under Section 1033 with respect to certain unimproved property that taxpayer had held before condemnation. On the latter issue, the IRS also contended that the acquired property was not similar in service or use to the condemned property. *Held:* For the IRS. Substance, not form, controls. The transaction here was little more than a tax gimmick. Under the traditional tests developed by the authorities to determine whether a stockholder's transfer to his corporation is a sale or a capital contribution, including the debt-equity ratio and the objective intent of the parties, this transaction fell within the latter category. As taxpayer did not reinvest its condemnation proceeds (and, alternatively, since it did not reinvest the proceeds in similar property), it was not entitled to defer recognition of its gain. Gyro Eng'g Corp., 276 F. Supp. 454, 67-2 USTC ¶ 9704 (CD Cal. 1967).

Partnership property incorporated regains its community property status; no stepped-up basis. In 1954, a partnership was formed with community property. Under local law, such property loses its character as community property. In 1962, the partnership property was transferred to taxpayer in exchange for stock that was issued to the partners under their individual names. Taxpayer contended that since the stock was issued to individual stockholders, their wives owned half of the stock; therefore, the transfer did not meet the 80 percent test of Section 351 and was taxable. As a consequence, taxpayer argued that it was entitled to a stepped-up basis for the assets. *Held:* For the IRS. Under local law, a wife acquires a specific interest in her husband's share of the partnership in exchange for loss of community property status. When the assets leave the partnership, the community property status returns. Thus, the wives were included in the group that transferred property to taxpayer, and the 80 percent test was met. Therefore, Section 351 applied and taxpayer was required to use the partnership's basis. Miller Bros. Elec., Inc., 49 TC 446 (1968).

Transfers to Controlled Corporations: Control Defined

Incorporation tax free: stepped-up basis denied. When the owner of a typesetting business contemplated retiring, several of his employees organized a corporation to continue the business. The corporation got an option to purchase the assets and was about to exercise it when the owner sought tax counsel. Counsel advised that the owner would avoid a substantial long-term capital gain tax if both he and the corporation transferred their assets to a new corporation (taxpayer) in exchange for preferred stock for himself and common stock for the employees' corporation. This plan was adopted, and taxpayer claimed that the basis for the assets so acquired by it was at fair market value, the price called for in the original option, which was also the same as the value of the preferred stock received by the owner. The IRS held that the transaction qualified under Section 351 and that taxpayer had a substituted basis under Section 362. *Held:* For the IRS. Even if, as claimed, the owner practiced fraud on the employees' corporation, that had no relevance to the tax consequences. The form-versus-substance rule of the *Gregory* case was inapplicable: taxpayer was not a paper corporation, but a real functioning entity, even though it was originally created as a standard tax-saving device. Finally, although the deal could have been made as originally planned with different tax consequences, it was not, and what was done must control. Gus Russell, Inc., 36 TC 965 (1962).

Stepped-up basis denied on transfer to controlled corporation where transferor failed to prove he owned less than 80 percent of stock. An individual transferred assets to taxpayer corporation in return for 60,000 of its 60,002 shares. Taxpayer claimed a stepped-up basis for the assets, but the IRS disallowed the portion of depreciation related to the additional basis. *Held:* For the IRS. The property basis, determined under Section 362(a)(1), was the same as that in the hands of the transferor under a Section 351 transaction. The transferor owned over 80 percent of the taxpayer's stock at the time of the transfer. A subsequent reduction of ownership did not control. Alaska Redi-Mix, Inc., 28 TCM 1165, ¶ 69,218 P-H Memo. TC (1969).

Transfer to a controlled corporation was equity, not a loan; therefore, interest deduction was not allowed. Three partners transferred property to taxpayer corporation for a $60,000 note in 1955. By 1963, taxpayer deducted $34,000 as a net operating carry-forward loss and interest and used a cost basis for the property. The IRS denied the deductions and gave the property a carry-over basis. *Held:* For the IRS. Taxpayer failed to overcome the presumption that there was no sale, but in fact an investment. Therefore, no interest or loss deductions were allowable. The property was limited to a carry-over and not a cost basis. Cal-Glen Dev. Corp., 28 TCM 240, ¶ 69,042 P-H Memo. TC (1969).

IRS sets forth proper method for determining basis for Section 351 transfer of receivables. Taxpayer transferred property used in a sole proprietorship, including accounts receivable, to a newly formed corporation solely in exchange for all of the stock of the corporation in a transaction pursuant to Section 351(a). Taxpayer had accounts receivable with a face amount of $100x$ and a reserve for bad debts of $5x$. Prior to the transfer, taxpayer used the accrual method of accounting under Section 446(c) in the business and had previously deducted additions to a reserve for bad debts with respect to such accounts pursuant to Section 166(c). All additions to the reserve for bad debts in prior years resulted in tax benefits. The value of the stock received for the accounts receivable was $95x$. On these facts, the IRS held that, for purposes of applying Sections 358(a)(1) and 362(a), the basis of the transferor in the transferred accounts receivable was $95x$, their net value. Rev. Rul. 78-280, 1978-2 CB 139.

Control Defined

Transfer fails to qualify under Section 351. Four individual taxpayers owned 76 percent of the stock of X. Two of them, as trustees for the wife of another, held in excess of 13 percent. Taxpayers individually owned all the stock of Y. For bona fide business reasons, X decided to acquire a certain amount of Y stock in exchange for its stock. After the exchange, taxpayers held 77.3 percent of X, and the trust's interest was reduced to just under 13 percent. Taxpayers maintained that the transaction was a tax-free exchange under Section 351 because the combined holdings of taxpayers and the trust exceeded 80 percent. The IRS disagreed, after determining that the "control" group was limited to taxpayers as former owners of *Y* stock. The Tax Court agreed with the IRS, which had relied in part on Regulation § 1.351-1(a)(1)(ii). *Held:* Affirmed. The First Circuit found that other than the fact that the trust's participation was incorporated into the acquisition agreement, there was no relation between the exchange of *Y* shares and what was considered a minor purchase by the trust. Therefore, under Regulation § 1.351-1(a)(1)(ii), only the individual taxpayers were considered in the control group. Kamborian, 468 F2d 219, 72-2 USTC ¶ 9747, 30 AFTR2d 72-5744 (1st Cir. 1972).

Beneficial ownership of trust not counted for determining control under Section 1239. Taxpayers, husband and wife, and their adult son each owned one third of a building. They had the same ownership in a corporation, but the son transferred his shares to trusts for himself and his minor sister. Taxpayers then sold the real estate to the corporation. The IRS determined that taxpayers realized ordinary income on the transfer under Section 1239. The district court held for taxpayer. *Held:* Affirmed. Section 1239 did not apply to the transaction. For the purpose of Section 1239, ownership does not include the beneficial ownership of trusts. The comprehensive attribution rules of other Code sections were not applicable here. Thus, taxpayers did not have 80 percent ownership in the corporation. Rothenberg, 350 F2d 319, 65-2 USTC ¶ 9663, 16 AFTR2d 5591 (10th Cir. 1965).

Trust beneficiaries counted as owners of trust's stock to disallow capital gain on sales to corporation. In 1948, taxpayer contributed stock of his corporation to three irrevocable trusts for his three minor children. In 1954, taxpayer claimed capital gains on depreciable property sold to this corporation. At this time, taxpayer, his wife, and his minor children owned more than 80 percent of the value of the outstanding stock of the corporation *if* the stock held by the trust for his minor children could be considered as owned by the minor children under Section 1239. That section disallows capital gains treatment to an individual who sells depreciable property to a corporation, 80 percent or more of which is owned by him, his wife, or his minor children, based on the value of the outstanding stock. The IRS disallowed capital gains treatment, relying on Regulation § 1.1239-1, which treats stock as owned if it is "beneficially" owned. Taxpayer argued that: (1) no such rule is in Section 1239; and (2) the legislative history of Section 1239 indicates that the "beneficient" attribution rules were originally included in the House of Representatives' version of Section 1239, but were eliminated by the Senate on the ground that too many bona fide transactions would be covered by the House version. *Held:* For the IRS. The court held that the regulation must be upheld, since it is not clearly unreasonable, while admitting that, absent the regulations, they would draw their own inferences from the congressional history. The court also rejected taxpayer's argument that the children were not beneficial owners, since, if they died before age 21, they would receive nothing. The court found that even if the children had no vested present interest, the value of their expectancy interest, coupled with taxpayer's and his wife's interest, was clearly over 80 percent of the value of the outstanding stock. Mitchell, 35 TC 550 (1961).

Section 351 only available for shifts in ownership among transferors. *Z* Corporation and a group of investors transferred property to a new corporation in exchange for 80 percent and 20 percent of its stock, respectively. Under a contract, the corporation sold some of the stock to the investors and reduced its ownership to 49 percent. The transaction qualified for Section 351 nonrecognition because the transferors had control immediately after the exchange. Where the investors received only 1 percent of the new corporation's stock, the exchange did not qualify under Section 351. The stock issued directly to them was of relatively little value in comparison to all the stock received by them in the transaction. Viewing the transaction as a whole, the transferor corporation did not have the requisite 80 percent control. Rev. Rul. 79-194, 1979-1 CB 145.

State merger law indicates control under Section 351. Stockholders of a widely held corporation exchanged their shares for those of a newly formed corporation in a merger that was subject to state law, which provides that the acquiring corporation becomes owner of all shares except those of dissenting stockholders. Those must be paid in cash. Those stockholders who exchanged shares are in control for Section 351 purposes. Rev. Rul. 74-502, 1974-2 CB 116.

Section 351 did not apply and no Section 367 ruling was required when a domestic and foreign corporation exchanged stock in subsidiaries. Two unrelated corporations, one domestic and one foreign, each formed a subsidiary in their own country. The two corporations then exchanged 49 percent of their stock interest in their subsidiary. The transaction did not qualify as a tax-free exchange as the "control" requirements of Section 351 could not be met. In addition, a Section 367 ruling would not be required. Rev. Rul. 70-522, 1970-2 CB 81.

Step-Transaction Doctrine

Step-transaction doctrine used to defeat tax-free exchange. Taxpayer purchased part of his one-third interest in a corporation from the other two stockholders and still owed them $54,000 on the transaction. Unable to agree on certain corporate policies, taxpayer decided to buy out the other two stockholders. His tax adviser feared that if the corporation redeemed the stock of the other two stockholders and paid off the $54,000 note, there would be a dividend to taxpayer as the remaining stockholder. Therefore, a plan was devised whereby taxpayer transferred his shares (as well as the $54,000 liability) to a newly formed corporation for most of its common stock while the other two stockholders sold their stock to the new corporation. To raise part of the cash to pay off the retiring stockholders, the new corporation sold its preferred stock to the old corporation's profit-sharing trust. On the same day, the old corporation was merged into the new, and the resulting entity paid off the balance from the two retiring stockholders as well as the taxpayer's $54,000 liability. The new entity continued the same business as the old and even changed its name to one similar to that of the old corporation. The Tax Court used the step transaction to "telescope" the entire transaction back into a simple redemption by the old corporation, coupling it with a payment of taxpayer's personal obligation, which resulted in a dividend. It held that the new corporation was merely a temporary repository of the stock and that there was in reality no transfer within the contemplation of Section 351. *Held:* Affirmed. Taxpayer did not sustain the burden of proving that the Tax Court's finding was clearly erroneous. Wolf, Jr., 357 F2d 483, 66-1 USTC ¶ 9316, 17 AFTR2d 601 (9th Cir. 1966).

In absence of binding commitment to transfer property to a corporation, court refused to apply step-transaction doctrine and upheld incorporation as tax free. A partnership of individuals *X* and *Y* owned a certain parcel of land. *Z* offered to purchase *Y*'s partnership interest. It was suggested by the partnership's counsel that *Y*'s interest should be sold to a corporation that would own the land. Nevertheless, *Y* sold his partnership interest directly to *Z*, and *X* and *Z* operated as a partnership until taxpayer was formed five months later. *X* and *Z* transferred their interests to taxpayer in exchange for all its stock. The IRS asserted that the transfer to taxpayer was governed by Section 351, and thus taxpayer acquired a carry-over basis in the partnership's land. Taxpayer asserted that *Y*'s sale of his partnership interest and its incorporation were parts of a single integrated transaction. Accordingly, *Y* (and not *Z*) should have been viewed as a transferor of property to taxpayer. Because *Y* received no stock, Section 351 did not apply because the transferors (*X* and *Y*) to taxpayer did not receive at least 80 percent of the taxpayer's stock as required for tax-free treatment under that section. In such instances, taxpayer's acquisition of the property is a purchase that provides a cost (i.e., fair market value) basis. *Held:* For the IRS. The sale of the partnership interest and incorporation should not be so integrated "in absence of a binding commitment on the part of *X* and *Z* to form taxpayer and transfer the property to it." Edlund Co., 288 F2d 17, 61-1 USTC ¶ 9305, 7 AFTR2d 970 (2d Cir. 1961).

Step-transaction doctrine inapplicable to attempted Section 351 transfer. Taxpayer owned all the stock of *P* Corporation, which in turn owned all the stock of *S* Corporation. *S* made loans to taxpayer in 1970 and 1971, and during those years, taxpayer transferred several properties to *S* in exchange for cash, releases of indebtedness between taxpayer and *S*, and assumption of liabilities. *S* transferred the 1970 properties to *P* in exchange for consideration equal to *S*'s book value in the properties. The IRS determined that the property transfers to *S* were not tax free under Section 351. *Held:* For the IRS. Although the transfers were not for stock or securities of *S*, taxpayer contended that the step transaction doctrine applied because after the transactions were completed, the corporations had the properties, and taxpayer had the *P* stock. However, *S* was not obligated to transfer the properties to *P*, and *S* did not act as *P*'s agent in accepting the properties. The court further held that Section 1239 did not apply to transform the gain into ordinary income, since the sales were not made directly to *P*, which was a separate entity from *S*. Yamamoto, 73 TC 946 (1980), aff'd (9th Cir. 1982).

Transfer of sole proprietorship to corporation and acquisition of corporation by another did not qualify under Section 351. An individual transferred the assets of his sole proprietorship to his controlled corporation for additional stock in the corporation. Pursuant to an integrated plan, an unrelated corporation acquired all of the controlled corporation's stock in exchange for its own stock. The transfer of the assets of the sole proprietorship to the controlled corporation did not qualify under Section 351, as the sole proprietor did not maintain control, taking all the transactions as one. Rev. Rul. 70-140, 1970-1 CB 73.

Taxable Transfers

Transfer of receivables resulted in consideration that offset payables in Section 357(c) calculation. The Tax Court held that a cash-basis partnership realized income in a Section 351 transfer to a controlled corporation to the extent that assumed partnership liabilities exceeded the basis of the assets transferred. Although a basis was assigned to accounts payable, a zero basis was assigned to accounts receivable for purposes of the calculation under Section 357(c). *Held:* Reversed. In transferring the receivables, the partnership in effect sold such receivables to the corporation and received as consideration the extinguishment of the partnership's payables. This resulted in a set-off of the payables against the receivables and avoided gain under Section 357(c). Thatcher, 533 F2d 1114, 76-1 USTC ¶ 9324, 37 AFTR2d 76-1068 (9th Cir. 1976).

Section 351 transfer disregarded and Section 482 allocation upheld. Taxpayer operated several pharmacies and created a corporation to run the largest one, which had for some years been a loss operation. He decided to sell the assets of one of the pharmacies and of the corporation. To avoid taxes on the increased value of the pharmacy's inventory, taxpayer contributed the pharmacy's assets to his corporation for no consideration. Thereafter, he liquidated the corporation under Section 337 and sold the assets. The IRS determined that the contribution of the assets for no consideration was to evade taxes and that the tax returns did not reflect the realized income. The district court agreed with the IRS and held that the transfer was to be disregarded and the income reallocated. *Held:* Affirmed. The Fifth Circuit noted that because taxpayer contributed assets to a corporation for no consideration and followed the transfer by a liquidation and a sale of the assets, the purpose of the transaction was strictly to evade taxes on the increased value in assets. Accordingly, the transfer was disregarded and the income reallocated. West, 72-2 USTC ¶ 9666, 30 AFTR2d 72-5398 (5th Cir. 1972).

Notes constituted other property and therefore caused recognized gain under Section

TRANSFERS TO CONTROLLED CORPORATIONS: *Taxable Transfers*

351. Taxpayer corporation transferred cash and equipment to a newly formed controlled corporation in exchange for stock of the second corporation; such a transaction was deemed tax-free under the provisions of Section 351. However, the IRS determined that the constructive receipts of notes in connection with the above transfer to two stockholders was recognized gain under Section 351(b)(1)(B). Although originally contending that such gain was ordinary income, the IRS subsequently argued that such gain was taxable as capital gain; the Tax Court upheld the determination. *Held:* Affirmed. The appellate court found that there was recognized gain because the constructive receipt of the notes constituted "other property" under Section 351. Lovell & Hart, Inc., 456 F2d 145, 72-1 USTC ¶ 9273, 29 AFTR2d 72-640 (6th Cir. 1972).

Excess of liabilities assumed by newly formed corporation over basis of assets transferred by taxpayer was held taxable gain. Taxpayer formed a corporation and transferred to it the assets of an advertising agency that he had previously conducted as a sole proprietor. The corporation assumed his liabilities, which exceeded the assets. Immediately after the transfer and assumption, taxpayer was in control. The corporation did not prosper as taxpayer had expected. It deteriorated, and three years after its formation, taxpayer filed a voluntary petition in bankruptcy. For the year of the transfer, however, the IRS determined that taxpayer had realized income under Section 357(c) as a result of the assumption of liabilities by the corporation in excess of assets transferred. The Tax Court held for the IRS. Taxpayer possessed a small net worth after the transfer of assets to, and the assumption of liabilities by, the corporation, but it asserted that Section 357(c) did not apply because he was insolvent both before and after the transfer. *Held:* Affirmed. Section 351 provides for nonrecognition of gain or loss on the transfer of property to a controlled corporation solely in exchange for stock. Section 357(a) provides that assumption of liabilities does not prevent such nonrecognition unless, by reason of Section 357(c), the liabilities assumed exceed the assets transferred. The latter subsection applied. Taxpayer's assertion that his interest in a family residence should be eliminated from the financial statement prepared after the transfer neglected to consider that the residence was subject to a mortgage that was the principal liability set forth in the statement. De Felice, 386 F2d 704, 67-2 USTC ¶ 9748, 20 AFTR2d 5917 (10th Cir. 1967).

Where geologist received joint venture interest in return for his services, subsequent incorporation not tax free. Taxpayer, a geologist, had an interest as joint venturer in certain oil leases. He had controlled the entire operation, having authority to commit the venture for most expenditures. He drew a salary from a drawing account monthly, and after the full cost had been recovered by the other venturers, he had a participating interest in the lease. When the venture was incorporated, he received stock. The district court held that the incorporation was tax free to taxpayer. The Fifth Circuit reversed, holding that the stock was received as compensation for services, not property, except to the extent of the value of the maps that taxpayer contributed as property. The fact that he had a joint venture interest did not in itself constitute a contribution of property. Taxpayer petitioned for a rehearing, citing Section 721, which deals with transfers of an interest in partnership capital. *Held:* Rehearing denied. The court ruled that Section 721 did not apply to the instant case. Frazell, 335 F2d 487, 64-2 USTC ¶ 9684, reh'g denied, 339 F2d 885, 65-1 USTC ¶ 9125 (5th Cir.), cert. denied, 380 US 961 (1964).

Hotel building not similar to condemned office building; gain recognized. Taxpayer owned an office building in Cincinnati that it sold at a gain under the threat of condemnation. The proceeds were entirely invested in 80 percent of the stock of a corporation that owned a hotel in New York City. The IRS contended that taxpayer would have to recognize gain on the sale. *Held:* For the IRS. Although stating that it was immaterial that the new building was in a different city from the old and that the proceeds were used to buy stock, not the building itself, the Tax Court held that the nonrecognition provisions of Section 1033 did not apply. The new property was not "similar or related in service or use" to the old property. One was an office building, the other a hotel. The fact that both were held for the same purpose, rental income, was not sufficient. Clifton Inv. Co., 312 F2d 719, 63-1 USTC ¶ 9246 (6th Cir.), cert. denied, 373 US 921 (1963).

Transfer of mortgaged property to controlled corporation was sale; gain was taxable. Taxpayer was a 50 percent stockholder of a corporation that owned all of the stock of a financially distressed insurance company. He also owned mortgaged real estate worth about three times its basis. He obtained a new mortgage in excess of the basis of the property, paid off the old mortgages, and personally retained about $40,000. He then transferred the property subject to the new mortgage to his corporation for a consideration of $100 never paid. The corporation in turn transferred the property to the insurance company, which was also subject to the mortgage. Taxpayer contended that he merely made a capital contribution that did not result in gain or loss. It appeared that the other stockholder also transferred property to the insurance company. Both sold out within the next year. The Tax Court found that the substance of the transaction was a sale of the property to the corporation at a price equal to the outstanding mortgage, resulting in a gain equal to the difference between his basis and the amount of the mortgage. *Held:* Affirmed. The fact that the value of the property at the time of the transfer exceeded the mortgage and that one of taxpayer's motives was to render financial assistance to the insurance company did not alter the result. If taxpayer really intended a mere capital contribution, he would have transferred the property before refinancing. Simon, 285 F2d 422, 61-1 USTC ¶ 9136, AFTR2d 6077 (3d Cir. 1960).

Stock received as compensation; not Section 351 transfer. The IRS contended that stock received by taxpayer was for services rendered rather than for the transfer of property. *Held:* For the IRS. The facts indicated that taxpayer received the stock for services rendered. Reasonable value was $8.50 per share on the date of the stock presented to the taxpayer, not $15, the subscription price and the price at which the stock was sold to the public four months later. Boles, 72-2 USTC ¶ 9493, 29 AFTR2d 72-1468 (SD Ohio 1972).

Even though taxpayer remains liable on liabilities transferred to corporation, the excess of these liabilities over the basis of the assets transferred in a Section 351 exchange is taxable gain. Taxpayer transferred all the assets and liabilities of his sole proprietorship to a newly formed corporation in exchange for 100 percent of its stock. Taxpayer, however, remained liable for the transferred liabilities. At the time of the transfer, the assumed liabilities exceeded the basis of the transferred assets. Taxpayer reported neither gain nor loss on the transfer. *Held:* For the IRS. Even though taxpayer remained liable for the liabilities transferred, Section 357(c) applied. Accordingly, taxpayer realized a gain on the transfer of assets and liabilities to the corporation to the extent that such liabilities exceeded the adjusted basis of those assets at the time of the transfer. Rosen, 62 TC 11 (1974).

Transfer of property to controlled corporation was sale to unrelated corporation that acquired controlled corporation in tax-free exchange. Taxpayer, an independent oil operator, owned producing and nonproducing leaseholds. He also owned 100 percent of the stock of one corporation and 80 percent of the stock of another corporation, each of which owned producing leaseholds and other assets. According to a prearranged plan, taxpayer transferred his properties to the 100 percent owned corporation for additional shares. Taxpayer and the other stockholders then exchanged all of their stock in the corporations for stock of an unrelated publicly held corporation in a tax-free exchange. Taxpayer treated the transfer of his properties as nontaxable under Section 351 except to the extent of liabilities assumed in excess of his basis. The IRS contended that the transfer of properties should be treated as a taxable sale to the public corporation and that the consideration should be measured by the fair market value of the properties exchanged. *Held:* For the IRS, in part. Taxpayer conceded that the properties transferred should be considered a taxable sale pursuant to Rev. Rul. 70-140, 1970-1 CB 73. Accordingly, it was so held. However, the amount realized on the sale had to be measured by the value of the consideration received, not the value of the properties transferred, notwithstanding the difficulty of such a determination. The amount of the consideration received was determined based on the facts. It further held that taxpayer did not have dividend income from the purchase of stock from his controlled corporation, as there was no bargain purchase. Rodman, 57 TC 113 (1971).

Transfer of promissory note to controlled corporation did not prevent gain where liabilities exceeded basis of assets transferred. Taxpayers conducted a lumber trucking business as a sole proprietorship. Upon deciding to incorporate, they transferred assets, which consisted solely of depreciable trucks and trailers, and liabilities incurred on open account and those secured by the assets. Since the liabilities exceeded the adjusted basis of the transferred assets, taxpayers issued their promissory note payable to the corporation to make up such excess. The IRS contended that taxpayers recognized gain on the transfer. *Held:* For the IRS. Section 357(c) requires that gain be recognized where liabilities exceed the adjusted basis of assets transferred to a corporation pursuant to Section 351. The basis of the note was zero in the hands of the corporation, since taxpayers incurred no cost in making it. Gain was therefore recognized on the transfer. Based on Section 1239, the gain was taxable as ordinary income, since depreciable assets were transferred between individuals and their controlled corporations. Alderman, 55 TC 662 (1971).

Stock received as compensation was not for property. Taxpayer received 50 percent of the stock of a new corporation as a result of his promoting planning, and constructing a rental apartment project. Other individuals received the other 50 percent of the stock in return for the transfer of appreciated land. Taxpayer contended that, as a result of the work he performed, he acquired certain contract rights that constituted property; therefore, the exchange of property for stock in the corporation was a tax-free exchange. *Held:* For the IRS. Based on the evidence, taxpayer received his shares of stock in return for services performed by him, because no property was transferred by him within the meaning of Section 351. The fair market value of the stock was, therefore, taxable as ordinary income. It was further held that inasmuch as taxpayer received his stock for services, the transferors of property were not in control of the corporation immediately after the transfer; therefore, the transferors were taxable on the gain realized. James, 53 TC 63 (1969).

Income incurred on transfer of business to corporation to extent liabilities exceed basis. A cash-basis taxpayer transferred all the assets of his contracting business to a new corporation. In addition to capital stock, he took a demand note from the corporation. The principal assets transferred were zero-basis accounts receivable. Because of this zero basis, the liabilities assumed exceeded the adjusted basis of the assets transferred. The IRS contended that taxpayer incurred income under Section 357(c). The IRS also contended that Section 351 did not apply to the demand note in that a demand note is not a "security" required by that section. *Held:* For the IRS. Taxpayer incurred income in two ways. Liabilities assumed did exceed the adjusted basis of assets transferred. The court rejected an argument that the receivables had a cost. Because the note was payable on demand and was paid quickly, the court found that the note was not a security, but was "other property," taxable under Section 351(b)(1)(B). Raich, 46 TC 604 (1966).

For tax-free exchange treatment, savings accounts in a federally chartered savings and loan not stock. Taxpayer exchanged guaranteed stock in a state-chartered savings and loan for a savings account in a federally chartered mutual savings and loan association. The Tax Court held the exchange to be a tax-free exchange under Section 354(a). In reaching its decision, it relied on Paulsen, 78

Transfers to Controlled Corporations: *Taxable Transfers*

TC 291 (1982). After *Paulsen* was reversed by the Ninth Circuit, 716 F2d 563 (9th Cir. 1983), the IRS moved under Tax Court Rule 161 for reconsideration of the decision. Thereafter, the Supreme Court affirmed the Ninth Circuit Court holding that a savings account in a federally chartered savings and loan was not stock for purposes of the reorganization provisions. *Held:* For the IRS. Taxpayer recognized gain when she exchanged guarantee stock in a state-chartered savings and loan for savings accounts in a federally chartered mutual savings and loan. The predominant characteristic of the exchange was equity (stock) for debt or cash (savings account). Owens, 49 TCM 1101, ¶ 85,156 P-H Memo. TC (1985).

Nonrecognition of gains treatment disallowed. Taxpayers' closely held corporation sold real estate and claimed nonrecognition of gain treatment under Section 337. The IRS disallowed the nonrecognition of the gain. *Held:* For the IRS. The corporation did not distribute $67,000 in the form of an account and a note receivable and rent within the 12-month period following the adoption of the plan of liquidation. Furthermore, the negligence penalty was upheld where taxpayers could not show that they furnished adequate and correct information to their agents. Stevenson, 34 TCM 1103, ¶ 75,257 P-H Memo. TC (1975).

Sale of property by promoters to newly formed corporation not tax free under Section 351 where control after transfer was lacking. Taxpayer, together with two other promoters, purchased a ranch and sold it at a profit to a new corporation that they organized for cash, stock, and assumption of liabilities. Each promoter received three shares of stock for promotional and other services, and the corporation obtained the necessary funds to acquire the ranch by selling its stock to various persons. Taxpayer reported the transaction as coming within the nonrecognition of gain provisions of Section 351. *Held:* For the IRS. Section 351 was inapplicable because the three seller-promoters emerged with considerably less than 80 percent control. The subscribers to the stock could not be included with the promoters as one unit in determining control. Even assuming that the transaction was otherwise within Section 351, the court held that since the value of money and other property received was in excess of the admitted gain, all of the gain was recognizable. Winterburn, 27 TCM 910, ¶ 68,187 P-H Memo. TC (1968).

Stock found to have been issued for services rather than property, could not come under tax-free exchange provisions of Section 351. Taxpayer was president and manager of a factoring corporation all of whose stock was owned by another individual. The stockholder, who was not active in the business, wanted to sell, and through a representative, orally agreed to give taxpayer a 60-day option in which to sell the factoring business on the basis of an amount of at least $125,000 in excess of book value. Other terms and conditions of the sale were to be worked out to the satisfaction of the stockholder. A third party formed a new corporation to acquire the business and agreed with taxpayer that he would, in consideration for making the option available and for continuing to remain manager of the business, be granted 10 percent of the stock in the new purchasing corporation. Taxpayer received the stock interest and contended that since it was issued to him for property transferred (i.e., an option to purchase the factoring business), the receipt of the stock was pursuant to a nontaxable exchange under Section 351. *Held:* For the IRS. Taxpayer did not have an option to purchase, but was merely authorized to act as agent for the stockholder in effecting a sale. Thus, the stock in the new corporation was not issued to him for property transferred, but for services rendered or to be rendered by taxpayer to the new corporation; it was therefore taxable to him as compensation. The fair market value of the stock was to be determined primarily from the net asset value of the company. Washburne, 27 TCM 577, ¶ 68,122 P-H Memo. TC (1968).

Transfer to corporation for equity interest nontaxable under Section 351. In 1954, taxpayer transferred to a newly formed corporation real estate having a fair market value not in excess of $42,000 in return for a purchase-money mortgage and bond in the face amount of $75,000. All of the voting stock was issued to taxpayer's husband and brother-in-law in exchange for a prepaid fire insurance policy and some cash. Taxpayer held one nonvoting share to remain a director. In 1956, taxpayer transferred the mortgage and bond to a trust for her childrens' benefit. The IRS contended that the transfer of real estate to the corporation was not a sale but a transfer of assets for stock or securities, and that since taxpayer did not own at least 80 percent of the stock after the transfer, the nonrecognition-of-gain provisions of Section 351 were inapplicable. *Held:* For taxpayer. The purchase-money mortgage and bond received by taxpayer represented an equity interest in the corporation. Since taxpayer made the transfer in conjunction with her husband and the third party, and immediately thereafter the three transferors controlled the corporation, Section 351 applied. Interest deductions claimed by the corporation in the purchase-money mortgage were disallowed. Premiums paid by the corporation on life insurance policies owned by taxpayer, denominated by the corporation as advances, were held to be dividends, since taxpayer never intended repayment. Marsan Realty Corp., 22 TCM 1513, ¶ 63,297 P-H Memo. TC (1963).

Incorporation not tax free when stock is sold under prearranged plan. Taxpayers transferred property to a new corporation, N, for its stock. Under a prior binding agreement, taxpayer sold 40 percent of its N stock to Y, who also bought securities from N for cash. The IRS ruled that taxpayer's transfer to N was not tax free because the prearranged sale resulted in taxpayer acquiring 60 percent control, less than the 80 percent required under Section 351. Y was not a transferor whose stock could be counted with taxpayer's stock for purposes of the 80 percent test. Rev. Rul. 79-70, 1979-1 CB 144.

Exchange of stock for stock and issuance of additional stock as consideration for employment contract found to consist of two separate transactions. The sole stockholder of a corporation exchanged all his voting stock for voting stock of another corporation. Pursuant to a provision in the exchange agreement, the sole stockholder received additional shares of voting stock of the other corporation as consideration for entering into an employment contract. For tax purposes, the transaction constituted two separate transactions, a stock-for-stock exchange, which qualified as a nonrecognition transaction, and an issuance of additional shares, which was used as consideration for employment, the fair market value of which was includable in taxpayer's income. Rev. Rul. 77-271, 1977-2 CB 116.

IRS recasts Section 351 transaction where incorporators received stock interests disproportionate to their contributions. A, an individual, owned all of X Corporation. A organized Y, contributing $50x$ cash for all Y's common stock, and caused X to purchase all of Y's nonvoting preferred stock for $255x$. Upon liquidation, holders of common and preferred would each get 50 percent of net Y assets. Since A received more Y stock than he would have had it been issued in proportion to the cash contributions, the IRS ruled that Regulation § 1.351-(b)(1) could be applied to recast the transaction for tax purposes. X was treated as receiving all the preferred and enough of the common that the total value of stock received equaled X's cash contribution. X was then considered to have distributed the Y common to A as a dividend. Rev. Rul. 76-454, 1976-2 CB 102.

Section 1036 does not apply to an exchange between individual stockholders of common stock for preferred stock of the same corporation. The nonrecognition provisions of Section 1036 were not applied to an exchange between individual stockholders of common stock for preferred stock of the same corporation. Gain or loss was recognized to each stockholder on the exchange measured by the difference between the cost or other basis of the stock surrendered and the fair market value of the stock received. (OD 1008 superseded.) Rev. Rul. 69-20, 1969-1 CB 202.

IRS illustrates nonapplicability of tax-free incorporation rules in transfer of patent rights to foreign subsidiary. X, a domestic corporation,

Transfers to Controlled Corporations: *Tax-Free Transfers*

planned to grant certain patent rights in a chemical compound to *Y*, its foreign subsidiary, in exchange for *Y's* stock. The patent rights in question included the exclusive rights to import, make, use, sell, and sublicence other parties under patents owned and registered by *X* in the country in which *Y* was organized and operated, covering the manufacturer of the chemical compound. However, *Y* was prepared to agree not to assert these rights to prevent *X* and its subsidiaries from importing, using, and selling the chemical compound in *Y's* country of operation. The rights to import, use, and sell the chemical compound in *Y's* country of operation were substantial rights. Based on these facts, the IRS held that the overall effect of the transaction was that *X* would retain for itself and its subsidiaries the substantial rights to import, use, and sell the chemical compound in the country in which *Y* operated. Accordingly, since *Y* would not have all substantial rights in the patent, the grant of the patent rights would not constitute a transfer of property within the meaning of Section 351, and the receipt of stock of *Y* by *X* would therefore result in ordinary income to *X*. Rev. Rul. 69-156, 1969-1 CB 101.

Transfer of assets to a corporation by an individual causes loss of nontaxable advantages of Section 351 where another corporation also transfers assets to qualify individual's transfer. Section 351 did not apply where an individual who owned appreciated property that another corporation desired to acquire for use in its business transferred the appreciated property to a newly formed corporation, and the corporation that sought the appreciated assets transferred all of its assets subject to its liabilities to the newly formed corporation. The newly formed corporation was formed for the purpose of enabling the individual owning the appreciated property to transfer it without recognition of gain. Rev. Rul. 68-349, 1968-2 CB 143.

Partly tax-free transfer produces ordinary income where property is depreciable and parties are related. Section 1239 of the Code was intended to block a sale of depreciable property to a related interest so that stepped-up depreciation basis is acquired at the cost of only a capital gain tax. The section makes such gains ordinary, not capital. The IRS ruled on the application of that section where the transfer is partly tax free, partly taxable. The first situation was the creation of a controlled corporation through a transfer of depreciable property for stock and a short-term note. The note, not meeting the definition of security, was boot and thus taxable. Because of Section 1239, the IRS ruled that the recognized gain was ordinary. The second situation was a transfer to a controlled corporation of property encumbered by a mortgage in excess of basis. The assumption of the debt was income to the transferor under Section 357; because of Section 1239, it was ordinary income. The IRS based its position on the language of Section 1239, which refers to "any gain recognized . . . from the sale or exchange" of the depreciable property. Rev. Rul. 60-302, 1960-2 CB 223.

Tax-Free Transfers

Retention of intracorporate accounts receivable was not receipt of other property. The IRS held that when taxpayer corporation incorporated one of its divisions as a wholly owned subsidiary, taxpayer realized gain because it retained an intracorporate account receivable that was owed by the incorporated division. Such receivable was found to constitute "other property" pursuant to Sections 351(b) and 361(b). Furthermore, such gain was held to be ordinary income under Section 1245 to the extent that the recomputed basis of the former division's Section 1245 property exceeded the adjusted basis of such property. *Held:* For taxpayer. The account receivable in question was found not to be "other property" but a mere loan for which taxpayer received only a return of capital. Wham Constr. Co., 600 F2d 1052, 79-2 USTC ¶ 9471, 44 AFTR2d 79-5260 (4th Cir. 1979).

Sale of land to corporation formed eight years earlier was a Section 351 transaction. Land was sold to taxpayer corporation for $247,000, and a four-year promissory note was secured by a mortgage on the property. At the time of the sale, taxpayer had assets of

$100. It had issued its stock to its stockholder (not the seller of the land) four years earlier. Taxpayer had been organized eight years earlier with an initial capital of $4,500. Subsequently, taxpayer sold portions of the land at a gain. The IRS argued that (1) the sale was a Section 351 exchange, so that taxpayer's basis in the land was determined under Section 362; and (2) the gain on the land sales was ordinary income. The district court upheld the IRS. *Held:* Affirmed. (1) The acquisition of the land was not a sale in substance but rather the capitalization that gave life to taxpayer. Prior to this, taxpayer could not engage in business. Notwithstanding the eight-year lapse, taxpayer's organization and land acquisition were treated as one transaction under Section 351. (2) Taxpayer held the land for sale to customers. One week after acquiring the land, it contracted to have it subdivided, developed, and sold. Stanley, Inc., 421 F2d 1360, 70-1 USTC ¶ 9276, 25 AFTR2d 70-955 (6th Cir.), cert. denied, 400 US 822 (1970).

Transfer by taxpayer to his own corporation in return for a one-year note was a tax-free exchange. Taxpayer formed a corporation to consolidate all of his business and investment assets and was advised that there would be no income tax liability in the exchange of his assets for the stock of the corporation. Accordingly, he transferred the assets, and the corporation assumed all of his liabilities. Taxpayer, in exchange, received all of the outstanding stock and a promissory note due one year thereafter with interest. Since the fair market value of the transferred assets exceeded their basis to taxpayer, the IRS determined that taxpayer had recognized a gain to the extent of the conceded fair market value of the note. Although the IRS contended at the trial in the district court that a short-term note on its face is generally not held to be a security, the jury found for taxpayer, who testified that he used the short-term note to receive interest, that it was his custom to renew the note every year, and that it was not his intention that the principal be repaid. *Held:* Affirmed. All of the questions were for the jury, and its verdict was amply supported by the evidence. The promissory note was found by the jury to be a security, and the appellate court not was constrained to disturb the findings. The term "security" is not defined in the Code or Regulations, and the determination must be made on a case-by-case basis on its particular facts. Mills, Jr., 399 F2d 944, 68-2 USTC ¶ 9503, 22 AFTR2d 5302 (5th Cir. 1968).

Transfer to corporation owned by wives and brothers not a sale. Taxpayers acquired a tract of land for $100,000 and thereafter transferred it to a corporation owned by their wives and brothers, who had transferred $4,500 to the corporation. The land at the time of transfer was worth $165,000. Taxpayers received $330,000 in promissory notes, and the corporation assumed a mortgage of $30,000. Taxpayers reported capital gains on the transaction in 1959, when the corporation paid the promissory notes. The IRS determined that taxpayers had realized dividend income and increased the corporation's taxable income for 1958 through 1960 by reducing the basis of the land that was sold in those years to $100,000. *Held:* For taxpayers. Taxpayers made a tax-free transfer to a controlled corporation within the meaning of Section 351(a). The notes given to them by the corporation for the purchase price were therefore preferred stock, and the payments to the extent of the corporation's earnings were dividends and profits. Burr Oaks Corp., 365 F2d 24, 66-2 USTC ¶ 9506, 18 AFTR2d 5018 (7th Cir. 1966), cert. denied, 385 US 1007 (1967).

No gain or income realized on transferring bad debt reserve to corporation under Section 351. Taxpayer operated a sole proprietorship from 1935 through 1959. This business, on the accrual method of accounting, used the reserve method to account for bad debts pursuant to IRS permission. In 1959, taxpayer transferred his business to a new corporation in exchange for its stock (par value $45,000) and an agreement to assume all liabilities of the business. Accounts receivable ($915,000) were transferred, subject to a reserve of $27,000, and thus the net value of the receivables was reduced by the reserve. The IRS assessed taxpayer, asserting that transfer of the

Transfers to Controlled Corporations: *Tax-Free Transfers*

reserve to the corporation resulted in income to him in the amount of the reserve but no loss because of Section 351. *Held:* For taxpayer. The value of the accounts receivable was their net amount (as reduced by the reserve). Accordingly, taxpayer had neither gain nor loss on the transfer of accounts receivable. Estate of Schmidt, 355 F2d 111, 66-1 USTC ¶ 9202, 17 AFTR2d 242 (9th Cir. 1966).

Transfer was not a sale but a capital contribution. Taxpayers were members of a joint venture that transferred its only asset, a real estate purchase contract, to a corporation in exchange for stock and notes. Taxpayer treated the transaction as a sale. The IRS determined that it was a capital contribution. *Held:* For the IRS. The members of the joint venture and corporation were found to be identical in person and interest and were in control of the corporation. The notes were non-interest bearing and unsecured. Therefore, the transaction was a nontaxable transfer pursuant to Section 351. In re Drage, 78-2 USTC ¶ 9632, 42 AFTR2d 78-5869 (MD Fla. 1978).

Part of assets transferred to corporation was for stock, part considered a loan. In incorporating his proprietorship business, taxpayer transferred about $15,000 worth of equipment for capital stock of that amount. An additional $13,000 worth of assets was later transferred for a credit on the corporation's books. The IRS contended that the entire transfer was for capital stock and that the later repayment of the "loan" was really a dividend. *Held:* For taxpayer. On instructions of the court that the intent of the parties governs the tax treatment, the jury found that a loan was intended. Martin, 246 F. Supp. 147, 65-2 USTC ¶ 9717 (ND Tex. 1965).

Where business purpose present, transfer to a controlled corporation was tax free despite assumption of transferor's liabilities. Taxpayers transferred their 3 percent interest in a partnership and a corporation to a newly formed corporation in exchange for all of the latter's stock. The new corporation also assumed certain indebtedness of taxpayers in consideration of the transfer. *Held:* For taxpayer. The exchange was a tax-free transfer to a controlled corporation under Section 351. The motive for incorporating was not tax avoidance; there was a good business purpose on both sides. From taxpayers' point of view, the incorporation was part of their overall estate planning. From the new corporation's point of view, the principal purpose was to gain a valuable business property. Wheeler, 63-2 USTC ¶ 9805 (ND Tex. 1963).

Transfer of nonexclusive patent license to foreign-controlled corporation in exchange for stock given Section 351 nonrecognition treatment. Taxpayer sought a ruling that a proposed transfer of a nonexclusive patent license to a controlled foreign corporation would result in nonrecognition under Section 351. The IRS determined that such a transaction would not receive nonrecognition status under Section 351 because taxpayer did not give up all rights in the patent. Taxpayer organized the corporation and contributed the patent thereto despite the adverse ruling. The IRS claimed a setoff of the amount of the stock received in exchange for the patent license. *Held:* For taxpayer. Section 351 does not include sale or exchange requirements in its language. The nonexclusive patent license constituted property within Section 351, thus requiring nonrecognition treatment. E.I. DuPont de Nemours & Co., 471 F2d 1211, 73-1 USTC ¶ 9183 (Ct. Cl. 1973).

Transfer to controlled corporation was tax free notwithstanding disproportionate distribution. Taxpayer and his family owned various corporations. A decision was made to form a holding company; the accountant determined the number of new shares to be received by each stockholder based on the book value of his respective stock on a certain date. Taxpayer received a larger amount based on the book value of his contribution. The parties treated the transaction as a tax-free incorporation under Section 351. The IRS determined that taxpayer realized taxable income in the amount that he received as an excess credit for his contribution to the new company. *Held:* For taxpayer. Taxpayer did not receive stock in the holding company greater in value than his contribution because the value of the stock he contributed was sufficiently greater than its book value. There is no disproportionate distribution apparent from the face of the plan of incorporation. Taxpayer did not receive more than his proportionate share in the exchange, since the book value of the stock he surrendered did not accurately reflect those corporations' fair market value. Weisbart, 79 TC 521 (1982).

Purported purchase held Section 351 exchange. Taxpayer was organized, its initial capital supplied by D and his wife, but five sixths of its stock was issued to D's children and one sixth to D's wife. Within ten days, D transferred his business assets to taxpayer in exchange for $15,000, the assumption of a liability of D, and a $96,000 obligation of the taxpayer payable to D on demand. The IRS determined that the transaction fell within Section 351; accordingly, taxpayer's basis for depreciation in the assets acquired was limited to D's basis. *Held:* For the IRS. The stock exchange and asset acquisition were, in substance, parts of a single integrated transaction. The demand notes were securities, and the issuance of stock to D's wife and children did not deprive D of control immediately after the exchange. Accordingly, Section 351 applied. D'Angelo Assocs., Inc., 70 TC 121 (1978), acq. 1979-1 CB 1.

Stock transferred for stock and cash not a distribution with respect to stock. Taxpayer corporation transferred stock of its subsidiary to a principal stockholder in exchange for its own stock and a cash payment. This was done to equitably divide the businesses of taxpayer and its subsidiary among its two principal stockholders. On the transaction, taxpayer sustained a loss that it claimed as a deduction on its tax return. *Held:* For taxpayer. The transaction could not be fragmented into two separate transactions, namely, a distribution with respect to its stock and a sale for cash. It must be treated as a single exchange of stock for stock and cash in a distribution under Section 311. The loss, therefore, was deductible. Owens Mach. Co., 54 TC 877 (1970).

Asset transfer and stock purchase part of single transaction under Section 351(a). Taxpayer and T were partners in an air-conditioning contracting business. To expand their operations, they organized a corporation to which they initially caused the partnership to transfer $4,000 in exchange for 40 shares of $100 par value common stock. A day after the initial transfer, taxpayer and T executed an agreement whereby the corporation purchased the partnership's assets, including cash and accounts receivable, for $3,290 in cash plus a promissory note for $73,889. The IRS determined the transfer of cash and assets to be capital contributions under Section 351 and the note to be evidence of an equity interest whereby payments on the note were dividend income to taxpayer and T, and not deductible interest payments to the corporation. In addition, the IRS imposed a carryover basis for the assets under Section 362. *Held:* For the IRS, in part. Because there were no valid business reasons for dividing the transaction, the asset transfer was inseparable from the $4,000 transfer, and so Section 351 applied. Taking into account such factors as potential earnings capacity and capitalization, the note represented a valid debt. Accordingly, only the payments of principal in excess of the basis were taxable as long-term capital gains under Section 1232(a)(1); interest payments were deductible by the corporation; and the assets acquired by the corporation from the partnership took a carry-over basis. NYE, 50 TC 203 (1968).

Exchange held tax free. Taxpayer, owner of a corporation, formed another corporation and transferred some of its property to the new corporation. The IRS asserted that the exchange was taxable, since the new corporation had not issued stock certificates for several years. *Held:* For taxpayer. The stock certificates themselves were not relevant to the control test of Sections 351 and 368(c). Bielec, 35 TCM 1691, ¶ 76,373 P-H Memo. TC (1976).

Gain not recognized on Section 351 transfer. Taxpayers transferred their farm business to a newly formed corporation, received stock, and reported no gain under Section 351. The

IRS claimed a debt to taxpayers was created and that they therefore recognized income. *Held:* For taxpayers. No evidence of an intent to create a debt was found; in fact, no debt was created. Taxpayers received no corporate obligation in addition to their stock and recognized no gain. Shisler Farms, Inc., 33 TCM 635, ¶ 74,141 P-H Memo. TC (1974).

Loan from partners to corporation at time of incorporation of partnership not considered "other property" under Section 351. The partners of a business transferred all of the inventory, furniture, fixtures, and the prepaid assets of the partnership to a corporation. They also transferred enough of the accounts receivable (minus all of the partnership liabilities assumed by the corporation) to produce a net value of $850,000, the agreed-upon capitalization of the corporation. It was decided that all of the accounts receivable of the partnership would be transferred to the corporation until it could be determined how much of them would be required to bring the net value of the assets transferred up to $850,000, with the understanding that any amount of the accounts receivable collected by the corporation in excess of the required amount would be returned to the partnership. At the same time, the partnership loaned the corporation $100,000, for which it received a 5 percent demand note. Taxpayer-partners reported the incorporation as a tax-free exchange under Section 351(a). The IRS contended that the $100,000 cash and the excess of accounts receivable collected by the corporation for the partnership were part of the partnership property transferred to the corporation in the exchange, and that the note and receivable from the corporation to the partnership constituted "other property" under Section 351(b), so that gain was to be recognized on the exchange to the extent of such boot. *Held:* For taxpayer. The transfer of the cash and the excess accounts receivable were independent of the Section 351 exchange. Such transfer could not be considered steps in a single transaction, whereby partnership assets were transferred to the corporation in exchange for stock and "other property." Also, the loan to the corporation by the partnership and the note received as evidence of the loan were not "other property" within the meaning of Section 351(b). Makover, 26 TCM 288, ¶ 67,053 P-H Memo. TC (1967).

Note issued for receivables subsequent to incorporation of proprietorship was not "other property" within meaning of Section 351. Prior to 1960, taxpayer owned a sole proprietorship. On January 19, 1960, she signed and executed the necessary documents to accomplish the incorporation of the proprietorship and transferred the tangible assets of the business, other than the accounts receivable, for 2,998 shares of the corporation's stock. On February 8, 1960, the corporation executed a $100,000 note to taxpayer upon transfer to it of $100,000 in receivables. The IRS contended that taxpayer received in the Section 351 transfer, in addition to stock, "other property" in the form of the $100,000 note and other credits that resulted in a tax on the transfer. The IRS' contention was based on the corporate book entries showing all transfers to have occurred on January 1, 1960. *Held:* For taxpayer. Book entries were indisputably wrong as to date and completely ignored instruments of transfer and other underlying documents. The accounts receivable were not transferred as parts of the Section 351 exchange but for the later $100,000 note transaction. Thus, the note was not "other property" on the exchange. Hartley, 26 TCM 186, ¶ 67,038 P-H Memo. TC (1967).

Partnership's loss on sale to controlled corporation disallowed. A partnership owned by two brothers sold its logs at a loss to a corporation. The brothers owned two thirds of the corporation. The sale was made in the ordinary course of the partnership's business. The IRS disallowed the loss under Section 267, which provides for nonrecognition of losses on transactions between related parties. *Held:* For the IRS. The loss was not recognized. There was no merit in taxpayer's contention that Section 267 was not meant to apply to sales made in the ordinary course of business. It applies to all sales between related parties even if the sales are made in good faith. McGrew, 24 TCM 1391, ¶ 65,256 P-H Memo. TC (1965).

Transfers to Controlled Corporations: *Tax-Free Transfers*

Contract was property qualifying for tax-free incorporation. Taxpayer's nominee assigned a valuable real estate contract to a corporation in return for over 80 percent of corporate stock and bonds. *Held:* For taxpayer. Contrary to the IRS' determination, the court found that taxpayer did not receive the securities for services, but for his interest in the contract in a transfer that fell under Section 351. Taxpayer therefore realized no income on the transfer. Ungar, 22 TCM 766, ¶ 63,159 P-H Memo. TC (1963).

Transfer to corporation that was fully controlled immediately after transfer resulted in nonrecognition. Taxpayer wanted to have real property rezoned to business use and retained lawyers to handle the legal proceedings. The attorneys agreed to form a corporation to hold and develop the property. After the property was transferred to the corporation, they would perform services for the corporation in the development of the property in return for 25 percent of the corporate stock. Upon formation of the company, taxpayer subscribed to 75 percent of the stock and the attorneys to 25 percent. Immediately thereafter, the attorneys assigned to taxpayer their right to subscribe to the stock, thus leaving taxpayer as the sole subsidiary stockholder. No stock was ever issued. The property was rezoned and transferred to the corporation, but the attorneys never performed any services in developing the property. They eventually received $4,000 upon executing releases to taxpayer and the company. Taxpayer contended that the transfer of property to the corporation resulted in no recognition of gain, since he had 100 percent control of the corporation immediately after the transfer. *Held:* For taxpayer. The court noted that the intent was that the attorneys would not acquire the 25 percent interest until they performed services for the corporation, an event that never occurred. Kaczmarek, 21 TCM 691, ¶ 62,131 P-H Memo. TC (1962).

Transfer of land to 80 percent-controlled corporation was tax free. Two tenants in common, each of whom held an undivided one-half interest in land, transferred their interests to a corporation in exchange for shares of the corporate stock. Immediately after the exchange, the transferors together owned 80 percent of the issued stock and total voting power of the corporation. Taxpayer reported a capital gain but here claimed that the transaction was tax free. *Held:* For taxpayer. The court held that the IRS' characterization of the transaction as a "sale" upon which ordinary income was realized was not supported by the facts. In precisely such a situation, Section 351(a) directs that "no gain or loss shall be recognized." Cotter, 20 TCM 1027, ¶ 61,202 P-H Memo. TC (1961).

Section 351 treatment available to transfers within an acquisitive reorganization that failed to qualify for tax-free treatment. A owned 14 percent of T's stock. P, an unrelated entity, wanted all of T's stock. For A to avoid recognition of gain, P and A formed S, to which P transferred cash and other property solely in exchange for S's common stock. A transferred T stock to S solely in exchange for all of S's preferred stock. S created D Corporation and transferred to it all the cash it had received from P in exchange for all of D's common stock. These transfers were intended to be tax free under Section 351. D was merged into T, and so each share of T stock, except those held by S, was surrendered for cash equal to the stocks' fair market value, and each share of D stock was converted into T stock. Rev. Rul. 80-284, 1980-2 CB 117, concluded that because the purported Section 351 exchange was part of a larger pattern of an acquisitive reorganization that failed because of the lack of continuity of interest, the transaction resembled a sale and did not qualify under Section 351. Similarly, in Rev. Rul. 80-285, 1980-2 CB 119, purported Section 351 transfers of assets were disqualified because they were part of a larger acquisitive transaction that failed. The IRS ruled that the failure of a larger acquisitive transaction to meet the requirements for tax-free treatment under the reorganization provisions did not preclude transfers within the transaction from receiving tax-free treatment under Section 351. Rev. Rul. 84-71, 1984-1 CB 106, revoking Rev. Rul. 80-284, 1980-2 CB 117 and Rev. Rul. 80-285, 1980-2 CB 119.

Transfers to Controlled Corporations: *Tax-Free Transfers*

IRS rules on status of intracompany debt where operating division incorporated under Section 351. The subject corporation, X, operated its business in two entirely separate divisions, keeping a separate bank account and a separate set of books for both divisions. Each division also maintained an intracompany account in its respective books, and transactions between the two divisions were recorded therein. For valid business reasons, X organized a new corporation, Y. All the assets of one division were transferred by X to Y at net book value in exchange for all of the stock of Y. At the time of the transfer, the intracompany account payable due from that division to the other was $100x$. On its opening balance sheet, Y listed an account payable to X of $100x$, and X, conversely, listed an account receivable from Y of $100x$. Within one year after the transfer the account payable of Y was paid in full to X. Applying Section 351, the IRS held that the account receivable to X from Y was a note or other evidence of indebtedness received by X in a Section 351 transaction and constituted "other property" for purposes of Section 351(b). This holding was based on the fact that the preincorporation intracompany accounts could not have given rise to a debtor-creditor relationship between X and Y because X could not, prior to incorporation of Y, have been liable for a debt to itself. The intracompany accounts were mere bookkeeping entries by X, a single corporation, to show the activities of separate divisions for internal accounting purposes. Rev. Rul. 80-228, 1980-2 CB 115.

Transfer qualified under Section 351. The transfer of all operating assets, including accounts receivable, in exchange for all of the stock of a new corporation plus the assumption by the corporation of all of the liabilities of the sole proprietorship qualified taxpayer for nonrecognition of gain under Section 351. There was a valid business reason for the transfer. Rev. Rul. 80-198, 1980-2 CB 113.

Transfer of name to foreign corporation may be Section 351 transfer. The IRS ruled that the transfer by a domestic corporation to a foreign one of a corporate name and associated goodwill was a Section 351 transfer. A Section 367(a)(1) ruling request must be filed to obtain nonrecognition treatment. However, where the corporation had no rights, the name was not property until incorporation (except for goodwill). Rev. Rul. 79-288, 1979-2 CB 139.

No gain on stock-for-stock exchange. Taxpayer corporation transferred all the stock it owned in another corporation in exchange for cash and all of its own stock that the other corporation owned. Under Section 311(a)(2), no gain was recognized by either corporation for the exchange of stock for stock. The exchange for stock for cash would result in recognized gain. Rev. Rul. 79-314, 1979-2 CB 132.

Public offering of part of stock may not prevent qualifying under Section 351. A newly incorporated business offered half of its stock to the public through an underwriter, U. The public offering could be made in a "best efforts" underwriting, where U would only promise to try to sell the stock, or a "firm commitment" underwriting, where U would actually purchase the stock. In either case, the transaction would qualify under Section 351 if the public offering were completed within a short time (two weeks of the ruling). If the offering took longer, however, the "best efforts" underwriting might not meet the requirement of 80 percent control by the transferor group immediately after the exchange. Rev. Rul. 78-294, 1978-2 CB 141.

Successive transfers of assets for stock in controlled corporations qualify for tax-free treatment. P Corporation, the parent corporation, transferred certain machinery to its subsidiary, $S1$, solely in exchange for $S1$'s stock. $S1$ then transferred this same machinery to its subsidiary, $S2$, solely in exchange for $S2$'s stock. The IRS ruled that the transactions were to be viewed separately and that each transaction qualified for tax-free treatment under Section 351. Rev. Rul. 77-449, 1977-2 CB 110.

**Transfer of stock from two wholly owned corporations to a newly formed corporation fol-

Transfers to Controlled Corporations: *Tax-Free Transfers*

lowed by liquidation of one of the transferor corporations qualified under Sections 351 and 368(a)(1)(C). *A* owned all of *X* Corporation, and *B* owned all of *Y* Corporation. *A* and *B* transferred all of their stock to *Z*, a newly organized corporation. *A* received 60 percent of the *Z* stock, and *B* received 40 percent plus cash. *X* then liquidated into *Z*, and *Y* remained as a wholly owned subsidiary of *Z*. The transfer of *A*'s *X* stock to *Z* and the liquidation of *X* by *Z* were interdependent steps in a plan treated as a reorganization under Section 368(a)(1)(C), followed by a distribution by *X* of the *Z* stock to *A* in exchange for all of *A*'s *X* stock. Accordingly, no gain or loss was recognized by *X* under Section 361(a), or by *A* under Section 354(a). In addition, the transfer by *X* of its property to *Z* in liquidation and the transfer by *B* of *B*'s *Y* stock to *Z* qualified under Section 351(a). Accordingly, *B* recognized no loss and no gain in excess of the cash *B* received in the exchange. Rev. Rul. 76-123, 1976-1 CB 94.

Corporation required to divest itself of 95 percent of its stock in a subsidiary bank distributed the stock without recognizing gain or loss. A corporation that owned several subsidiaries, including all the stock of a bank, was required either to qualify as a bank holding company (which it could not readily do without divesting itself of its other subsidiaries) or to divest itself of the bank. The corporation chose to distribute 95 percent of its bank stock to its stockholders (some of whom would hold as much bank stock as the corporation), while retaining 5 percent to use as collateral for short-term financing transactions. The distribution qualified under Section 355(a), the corporation recognized no gain or loss, and the stockholder received no income as a result of the transaction. Rev. Rul. 75-321, 1975-2 CB 123.

Corporation's assumption of expenses not boot to individual. An individual who transferred his property to a corporation in exchange for all of its shares was not considered to have received boot because the corporation assumed the individual appraisal and legal fees, and shipping and packaging expenses. Rev. Rul. 74-477, 1974-2 CB 116.

Unqualified transfer of secret process qualifies under Section 351. The IRS ruled that the unqualified transfer of the exclusive right to use a trade secret until it becomes public knowledge and no longer protectable under the laws of the country where the transferee operates is a transfer of property under Section 351. Rev. Rul. 71-564, 1971-2 CB 179.

Section 357(c) applied where promissory note issued for excess liabilities over adjusted basis of assets in a Section 351 transaction. Gain was recognized under Section 357(c) where a promissory note was issued by an individual for the excess of liabilities over the adjusted basis of assets transferred by a sole proprietorship to a controlled corporation. Section 1012 provides that the basis of property is its cost, except as otherwise provided. Since taxpayer incurred no cost in making the note, its basis to him was zero. Therefore, the transfer of the note to the corporation did not increase the basis of the assets transferred. Rev. Rul. 68-629, 1968-2 CB 154.

No tax to corporation in Section 351 transaction where part of stock received distributed to stockholder. A corporation formed a subsidiary and transferred property to the new corporation solely in exchange for its stock. Immediately after the receipt of the stock, the parent distributed 25 percent of it to a stockholder, in complete redemption of his stock in the parent. The fact that the distributee was no longer a stockholder in the parent after the distribution to him of the stock of the subsidiary did not alter the fact that the distribution was made under a corporate stockholder relationship. The special rule of Section 351(c) applied to the corporation so that no gain or loss was recognized to the parent. Gain or loss was recognized to the distributee on the exchange. Rev. Rul. 68-298, 1968-1 CB 139.

Conversion of stock from separate property to community property was nontaxable exchange. In accordance with the law of their state, a husband and wife converted their separate stock ownership into community property ownership. The IRS ruled that the conversion of the stock was a nontaxable exchange within the meaning of Section 1036(a). Rev. Rul. 66-248, 1966-2 CB 303.

Tax on exchange of mortgaged farms. Taxpayers exchanged their respective farm properties consisting of farmlands, buildings, personal residences, and unharvested crops. Each of the properties was encumbered by a substantial mortgage, which was assumed by the taxpayer receiving it. The IRS ruled that: (1) the exchange of *unencumbered* farm lands, buildings, and unharvested crops was a nontaxable exchange of "like property"; (2) if the mortgages reciprocally assumed did not cancel each other, any gain resulting from such assumption was taxable as boot under Section 1031, and loss was not recognized under that section; and (3) the exchange of the personal residences (with mortgages thereon) was to be treated as a separate transaction; it could qualify for nonrecognition of gain on sale and replacement of a residence. Rev. Rul. 59-229, 1959-2 CB 180.

TRAVEL AND ENTERTAINMENT EXPENSES

(*See* Business Expenses—Travel and Entertainment Expenses)

TWELVE-MONTH LIQUIDATIONS

(*See* Liquidations—Twelve-Month Liquidations)

UNDISTRIBUTED INCOME

(*See* Accumulated Earnings Tax; Personal Holding Companies)

UNREASONABLE ACCUMULATIONS OF SURPLUS

(*See* Accumulated Earnings Tax)

UNRELATED BUSINESS INCOME

(*See* Tax-Exempt Organizations)

USEFUL LIVES

(*See* Depreciation and Amortization)

VALUATION OF PROPERTY

Dividend of gold coins taxed at fair market value. The IRS and lower court held that gold coins received as a corporate dividend were property, not cash, and were taxable at their full fair market value. *Held:* Affirmed. Although the gold coins were legal tender and hence "money" for some purposes, they were also "property" to be taxed at fair market value because they had been withdrawn from circulation and had numismatic value. Cordner, 671 F2d 367, 82-1 USTC ¶ 9275, 49 AFTR2d 82-1353 (9th Cir. 1982).

Tax Court's valuation of leasehold received in Section 334(b)(2) liquidation. Taxpayer purchased the stock of a TV station, liquidated it, and claimed a cost basis for its assets under Section 334(b)(2). The IRS challenged taxpayer's basis in both a leasehold interest in the studio facilities and TV rights to major league baseball games. Taxpayer complained that the Tax Court's valuation was too low. *Held:* Affirmed and reversed, in part. The Tax Court's valuation of the lease was not supported, and so the case was remanded for new findings. The valuation of the baseball TV rights was upheld. Miami Valley Broadcasting Corp., 594 F2d 556, 81-2 USTC ¶ 9747, 43 AFTR2d 79-769 (6th Cir. 1979).

Valuation of intangibles upheld. The Tax Court, in considering a liquidation pursuant to Section 334(b)(2), found that taxpayer failed to assign basis to goodwill and certain other nondepreciable intangible assets. *Held:* Affirmed. The use of the residual value method in valuing such intangible assets was proper. Also, the basis of a note did not have to be adjusted for unstated interest, since the interest rate of such note was 4 percent. R.M. Smith, Inc., 591 F2d 248, 79-1 USTC ¶ 9179, 43 AFTR2d 79-526 (3d Cir.), cert. denied, 444 US 828 (1979).

Value of unrelated business assets determined. Taxpayer was a publicly held corporation engaged in mining that the Tax Court held was subject to the accumulated earnings tax for 1966. In determining taxpayer's earnings and profits for 1966, the court took into account the current market value of taxpayer's liquid unrelated business assets. In a motion for reconsideration, taxpayer contended that the Tax Court erred both in taking into account the unrealized increment in the market value of taxpayer's securities and in failing to consider the effects of the capital gains tax, selling expenses, and the principle of blockage in determining that the value of taxpayer's securities in 1966 exceeded its reasonable business needs. *Held:* For the IRS. Because the market value was a more meaningful and realistic estimate than the historical cost, the court properly valued taxpayer's securities by using its current market value to compute earnings and profits. Because taxpayer both purchased and sold stock on a daily basis and could manipulate sales to minimize its capital gains tax, it was impossible to include any calculation with respect to computing earnings. Because it was highly speculative to say that the taxpayer's securities would be sold by a block sale or would incur certain costs, the court properly excluded these items from consideration in its computation of earnings and profits for the accumulated earning tax. Golanda Mining Corp., 507 F2d 594, 74-2 USTC ¶ 9845, 35 AFTR2d 75-336 (9th Cir. 1974).

Securities valued at fair market value less conversion costs in determining whether earnings were unreasonably accumulated. Taxpayer invested in certain securities whose value appreciated significantly over the years. At a later date, the IRS determined that taxpayer had unreasonably accumulated earnings. In its determination, the IRS valued the securities at their fair market value less the expense of conversion into cash. The district court held for taxpayer, concluding that liquid assets should be measured at their original cost. *Held:* Reversed. In determining whether a corporation had unreasonably accumulated earnings, the proper valuation of securities purchased by the corporation was the fair market value of the securities less the expenses of their conversion into cash. Ivan Allen Co., 493 F2d 426 (5th Cir. 1974).

Book value used to determine basis of stock of liquidated corporation. Taxpayer purchased some shares of a corporation for $12,000. These shares were exchanged for other shares that had no market value at that time. Pursuant to a plan of liquidation, taxpayer received a liquidating distribution of $12,200 and shares in a related corporation. The IRS, using book value to determine the value of all of the shares in these transactions, determined that taxpayer had a gain of $4,400. *Held:* For the IRS. Under the circumstances, the use of book value was correct. On another issue, negligence penalties were sustained against taxpayer. He failed to prove that he had made a complete disclosure of his income to his tax consultant. Fabacher, 454 F2d 722, 72-1 USTC ¶ 9204 (5th Cir. 1972).

District court examines methods of valuing depreciable property for purposes of allocating purchase price to acquired corporation's assets. Taxpayer corporation acquired an existing company by purchasing all of its stock. Taxpayer claimed operating losses as the result of this and a similar acquisition, and it carried these losses back to previous years. The IRS, on audit, reduced the claimed loss and issued deficiency notices primarily on the grounds that taxpayer used overvalued figures for allocating the purchase price to leasehold improvements, depreciable machinery, and equipment. At trial, three varying estimates were presented as evidence: one by the president of taxpayer, another by an IRS employee, and a third by an expert appraiser retained by taxpayer. *Held:* For taxpayer. The district court examined the testimony of the three parties and concluded that the method used by the expert appraiser provided the best evidence of fair market value. The expert looked at the potential earnings from use of the machinery in addition to its replacement cost, and he presented a cost-benefit ratio that took a variety of relevant factors into account. Concrete Pipe & Prods. Co., 37 AFTR2d 76-399, 76-1 USTC ¶ 9115 (ED Va. 1975).

Court determined fair market value of a bargain purchase. The IRS determined that taxpayers made a bargain purchase from their corporation when they purchased property at $0.92 per square foot; the IRS determined the fair market value to be $1.40 per square foot and asserted deficiencies against taxpayers on the difference. *Held:* For the IRS, in part. Based on evidence submitted, the fair market value was found to be $1.05 per square foot. Richardson, 330 F. Supp. 102, 71-2 USTC ¶ 9562, 28 AFTR2d 71-5375 (SD Tex. 1971).

Value of geological maps contributed to joint venture determined to be amount that it would have cost venture to construct maps. Taxpayer, a geologist, entered into a contract with two oil producers whereby, in return for his recommendation of certain properties, he was to receive a salary plus expenses and a specified interest in the acquired property after the producers recovered their expenses. At a later date, the properties were transferred to a corporation in which taxpayer received 13 percent of the stock. He did not include in income the fair market value of the stock on the grounds that it was received in a tax-free exchange under Section 351(a). The IRS determined a deficiency, and, although the district court held for taxpayer, the Court of Appeals reversed, ruling that under state law, the incorporation agreement constituted a joint venture, not a corporation, and the transfer did not constitute an exchange under Section 351. This case arose on remand from that court to resolve the two questions of (1) whether taxpayer contributed certain valuable geological maps to the joint venture or kept them as his own property and (2) if he contributed them, what their value was at the time of contribution. The IRS conceded the former question to taxpayer but valued the maps at no more than $2,000, while taxpayer contended that their value was approximately $367,000. *Held:* The maps were worth not less than $25,000. Taxpayer's method of valuation was based on statistical averages but was rejected because of its highly speculative nature. The basis for this type of valuation should be the value to the venture, and this would take into account what it would have cost to reconstruct the maps. Frazell, 269 F. Supp. 885, 67-2 USTC ¶ 9530 (WD La. 1967).

Jury determined fair market value of land and timber distributed on corporate liquidation. Land and timber were distributed to taxpayer on the liquidation of a corporation with respect to the capital stock thereof. Taxpayer claimed that the value of the land was not more than $5 per acre and the timber not more than $66. The IRS claimed that the value of the land was not less than $9 per acre and the timber not less than $76 per acre. *Held:* The jury found that the value of the land was $5 per acre and the timber $65 per acre. Harrigan, 66-2 USTC ¶ 9650, 18 AFTR2d 5693 (SD Ala. 1966).

Value of patent not ascertainable at time of corporate liquidation. The principal asset received by taxpayers of a corporation was a patent for the manufacture of titanium. A German corporation had an exclusive license to use the patent, and the Alien Property Custodian took control of the patent during World War II. At time of the liquidation, the corporation had a suit in the Court of Claims to determine royalties due from the United States during the period of its custodianship. *Held:* For taxpayer. Under the circumstances, the court found that the patent could not be valued. The liquidation was open, and payments received would be capital gain. Schulein, 62-2 USTC ¶ 9679 (D. Ore. 1962).

Allocation of cost of subdivided realty. A corporate taxpayer paid $75,000 for land, which it subdivided and on which it built houses. The IRS determined the cost of the lots on the assumption that the tracts had identical value. However, some land was higher in altitude than other land, and some was developed and some was not. *Held:* The jury found that approximately 55 percent of the cost should be allocated to approximately 38 percent of the land sold during the period. Point City Dev. Co., 60-2 USTC ¶ 9801, 7 AFTR2d 401 (ED Va. 1960).

Alternate valuation determined. Following the death of Charles Smith on August 13, 1967, his estate elected the alternate valuation date for valuing his assets. The decedent owned shares of Consolidated Cigar, which was merged into Gulf & Western in January 1968. The estate reported no taxable gain on this transaction, and the IRS determined that the estate realized gain as a result of the merger. *Held:* For taxpayer. Regulation § 1.1014-3 provides that if alternate valuation is elected and property is exchanged within one year of the decedent's death by the person who acquired it from the decedent, the value applicable in determining the basis is the value at the date of the exchange. Therefore, the estate's basis in the Consolidated stock was to be determined as of January 11, 1968, and since the transaction was at arm's length, the value of the stock received equals the value of the stock surrendered. Estate of Smith, 63 TC 722 (1975).

IRS improperly valued stock of closely held corporation. In 1961, taxpayers sold shares of stock that represented a minority interest in a closely held corporation to their son, and donated other stock. The stock was valued at $10 per share because taxpayers had sold shares at arm's length for that price in the months prior to the transfer. Four months later, the corporate stock was offered to the public at more than $30 per share. Accordingly, the IRS determined the value of the shares to be this public offering price, less a discount for lack of marketability on the valuation dates. The IRS deemed the sale of the stock to be a partial gift to the extent that the proposed value exceeded $10 per share. *Held:* For taxpayer. There was no partial gift of stock where the stock valuation had been determined by prior sales at arms' length. The IRS' proposed method, which was based on subsequent public sales less a discount of marketability on the valuation dates, was not the best method for evaluating the worth of the stock. Messing, 48 TC 502 (1967).

Rights to insurance renewal commissions valued. Taxpayer had been a stockholder in an insurance agency corporation that was liquidated in 1950. He had received part of the rights to renewal commissions on some 5,000 policies. At issue here was the treatment of the collection of such commissions in 1953 and 1954. *Held:* For taxpayer. The Tax Court found that, although at the time of liquidation it might not have been possible to determine whether any particular policy would be renewed, the insurance industry had techniques for valuing these rights, which are frequently used as collateral in commercial loans. Lacking evidence on which to find value in that way, the court applied the *Cohan* rule and valued the rights. Renewal commissions received in the years at issue, to the extent they exceeded the value at liquidation, were ordinary income. Goldstein Estate, 33 TC 1032 (1960), acq. 1960-2 CB 5.

Date on which final contingencies removed held to constitute proper valuation date for stock involved in taxable exchange. Taxpayers were partners in an equipment business in California. As part of a prearranged plan, the partnership was incorporated. In January 1969, the stockholders in the newly formed corporation entered into an executory contract to exchange their stock for stock in an existing corporation. However, the stock-for-stock exchange was contingent on approval by the stockholders of the acquiring corporation. On the date of the actual exchange, April 1, 1969, the newly formed corporate stock had a value of $18 per share. At the time of ratification by the acquiring corporation's stockholders in October 1969, the stock was valued at only $14.75 per share. Taxpayers, in reporting gain from the exchange, valued their transferred shares on the basis of the lower, October 1969 per-share price. They contended that the transaction was not completed until the acquiring stockholders' consent had been obtained. *Held:* For taxpayers. The issue of when, for tax purposes, a sale takes place is a question of fact to be decided by weighing all of the facts surrounding the transaction. As a general rule, a sale takes place when the benefits and burdens of ownership pass from seller to buyer. Since the ap-

Valuation of Property

proval of the acquiring stockholders was "an important condition precedent to the [a]greement," taxpayers were not entitled to acquire the new stock until the ratification was obtained. Accordingly, the proper valuation date was October 1969. Perry, 35 TCM 1718, ¶ 76,381 P-H Memo. TC (1976).

Court determined fair market value of stock in closely held corporation. The IRS determined that the fair market value of taxpayer's stock was based on net asset value. Taxpayer had used a higher value in determining his loss on the liquidation of his corporation. *Held:* For the IRS. The IRS' valuation was upheld, since any errors made were in taxpayer's favor. Andrews, 35 TCM 459, ¶ 76,106 P-H Memo. TC (1976).

Value of transferred property determined for loss purposes. Taxpayer corporation exchanged its property and cash for property of another party. It claimed a $208,186 loss on the difference between its property and the cash and the purported value of the property received. The IRS disallowed the loss. *Held:* For the IRS. Taxpayer did not present sufficient evidence to prove the value of the property received. Therefore, the IRS' presumption of an equal exchange value of property and cash for property was held, and no loss deduction was allowed. Valley Title Co., 34 TCM 312, ¶ 75,048 P-H Memo. TC (1975).

Property basis of liquidated property determined. A corporation purchased stock of a second corporation that was merged with a subsidiary and valued the assets at $8.76 million. The IRS determined a $21.27 million fair market value. *Held:* For taxpayer. Since the sale was negotiated at arm's length, the $8.76 million value was the proper fair market value. Moss Am., Inc., 33 TCM 1121, ¶ 74,252 P-H Memo. TC (1974).

Liquidation proceeds valued. Taxpayer, a one-third stockholder, and the other stockholder liquidated their corporation. Taxpayer claimed to have received about $19,000 less than one third of the value of the assets under a stockholder's agreement. The IRS used a higher valuation for the assets received. *Held:* For the IRS. Taxpayer failed to document his claim for the lower valuation in the agreement. Therefore, he received a full one third ($193,333) of the assets valued at $580,000. Dwight, 33 TCM 832, ¶ 74,193 P-H Memo. TC (1974).

Fair market value of liquidated property determined. Taxpayer received a building pursuant to a corporate liquidation and computed his gain based on an $85,000 fair market value for the building. The IRS used a $150,000 fair market value. *Held:* For taxpayer, in major part. The taxpayer's expert witness' capitalization-of-earnings method of computing fair market value was adjusted to result in a $100,000 fair market value. The IRS' reference to the comparable sales method was not as appropriate, since the sales of other apartment buildings were not comparable, new construction was minimal, and the land in that area was not in demand. Gottlieb, 33 TCM 765, ¶ 74,178 P-H Memo. TC (1974).

Determination of fair market value for gains purposes. Taxpayer corporation produced lumber and elected to treat the cutting of timber as a capital transaction. Gain was reported to the extent of the difference between the fair market value and the adjusted basis. The IRS determined a lesser fair market value and asserted deficiencies. *Held:* For taxpayer, in major part. The fair market value of the timber was higher than claimed by the IRS. The quality of the timber, comparable prices, distance to the sawmill, size of tracts, and existing market conditions were all considered. Thus, the deficiency was reduced substantially. Martin Timber Co., 31 TCM 1266, ¶ 72,255 P-H Memo. TC (1972).

Fair market value of real estate determined. Taxpayer, through several corporations, purchased real estate for $38,130. He had one corporation transfer it to another for the same price, and had the second corporation liquidated into a trust created for the benefit of his family. The IRS determined that taxpayer received a constructive dividend ($71,500), a return of capital ($107,000), and a capital gain ($81,000), and that the sole stockholder trust received a net liquidating dividend ($256,000) in excess of liabilities. *Held:* For taxpayer, in part. The fair market value of the property had increased to $61,000 by the time it was sold to the second corporation, and since taxpayer enjoyed the benefit of such increase, he was deemed to have realized a $22,870 constructive dividend. However, the assets received by the trust had no net value at the time of liquidation as there was a $358,000 claim against the corporation by a construction company, and therefore the trust was not in receipt of a dividend. Spitz Trust, 30 TCM 43, ¶ 71,008 P-H Memo. TC (1971).

Value of building received as a liquidating distribution determined. Taxpayer received an uncompleted public garage building constructed on leased premises in liquidation of a corporation in which he was the sole stockholder. After the liquidation, taxpayer requested, and received, an appraisal of the property, which was valued at $1.2 million by the local real estate board. The IRS contested the appraisal, which was based on a projected income approach, contending that the value should be $1.587 million. *Held:* After considering the method of proposed operation, the expected rental values, and estimated real estate taxes and replacement costs, the court found the proper value at time of liquidation to be $1.338 million. In determining the cost basis of taxpayer's stock, the court included payments that taxpayer had made to the corporation as capital contributions on or after the date that the corporation adopted its plan of liquidation. Taxpayer had guaranteed performance of all the obligations of the corporation and had to supply the funds for the corporation to pay these obligations. The court also ruled that taxpayer could claim depreciation on the portions of the building that were uncompleted on the date of distribution only from the date such portions became completed for use in taxpayer's business. Livingston, 25 TCM 277, ¶ 66,049 P-H Memo. TC (1966).

Value of collapsible corporation's assets determined. Upon liquidation of a corporation engaged in real estate development, taxpayer received certain partially improved subdivision lots, an option to purchase additional acreage, and certain reserved funds. The parties stipulated that the corporation was collapsible and that the assets involved were Section 341 assets. The only issue was that of valuation (i.e., whether, based on the determined value of the assets distributed, the gain realized on the Section 341 assets was more than 70 percent of the total gain as required by Section 341(d)(2)). *Held:* After considering a mass of evidence involving local real property valuation, the court determined the fair market values of the Section 341 assets, which it submitted to the parties for the necessary computations. Barry, 22 TCM 1129, ¶ 63,225 P-H Memo. TC (1963).

Court determined fair market value of speculative stock with restriction on disposition received in taxable exchange. Taxpayer corporation transferred assets in a taxable exchange for newly issued stock of another corporation. One of the conditions of the exchange was that taxpayer could not dispose of the acquired stock for three years without the consent of the NYSE, on which the stock was listed. Taxpayer contended that the amount of gain or loss realized on the sale could not be ascertained because the stock had no ascertainable fair market value. It based its conclusion on the fact that the security was speculative and could not be disposed of for three years. *Held:* For the IRS. The court found that the nature of the stock was not too highly speculative to preclude a valuation. It was not a new company; there was no indication that its management was inexperienced; there was no high degree of uncertainty as to its future; and its sales and earnings were continually increasing. As to the restriction imposed on the disposition, the court noted that the restriction was not absolute and was not such as to make sale of the stock by taxpayer either impossible or so improbable that it should be considered impossible for practical purposes. The court therefore determined the fair market value of the stock on the basis of all the evidence. North Am. Philips Co., 21 TCM 1497, ¶ 62,284 P-H Memo. TC (1962).

Valuation of Property

Value of real estate received on liquidation determined. Taxpayer was the sole stockholder of a corporation that, upon liquidation, distributed two parcels of real estate to him. Taxpayer and the IRS disagreed on the date of valuation and the value of the properties. *Held:* For the IRS, in part. Because the evidence indicated that there were no material differences between the two dates that could be used for valuation purposes, the court did not have to choose the one more favorable to the IRS. The values of the properties as determined by the evidence were between the figures offered by the parties. Capaldi, 21 TCM 1441, ¶ 62,271 P-H Memo. TC (1962).

Property dividend valued at subsequent sale price. Taxpayer sold all his stock in a trucking corporation. However, prior to the sale, land and a building had been distributed to him as a dividend. Taxpayer learned that the city was interested in the site for off-street parking and offered the property to the city for $32,500. The city, however, lacked sufficient funds at that time. Taxpayer sold the property to a third party for $32,500, with the understanding that the city would buy the property from the third party at that price, which it in fact did. Taxpayer contended that the fair market value of the property for dividend purposes at the time of the corporate distribution was $12,000, based on opinion evidence. The IRS asserted that the value was the sale price. *Held:* For the IRS. The court found the sale at $32,500 that occurred almost concurrently with the distribution of the property to taxpayer, supplied a more satisfactory criterion of fair market value than the type of opinion evidence submitted. Wolf, 20 TCM 1408, ¶ 61,269 P-H Memo. TC (1961).

Insurance agency's goodwill at liquidation valued at zero. A corporation that operated an insurance agency in a town with a population of 1,900 liquidated and transferred its assets to the stockholders who continued to carry on the insurance business as partners. The court held that the corporate goodwill had a value of zero at the time of liquidation, even though the corporate bonds had shown goodwill of $19,400. It found that a purchaser would not have paid for the business anything more than fair price for tangible assets. Any goodwill at the time of liquidation was due to the personal liability, business acquaintances, and other individual qualities of its stockholders. Shareholders' gain or loss on liquidation was computed by comparing the value of tangible assets received with basis for the stock. Bryden, 18 TCM 810, ¶ 59,184 P-H Memo. TC (1959).

WITHHOLDING OF TAX

(*See* Assessment and Collection–Withholding Tax)

WORTHLESS SECURITIES

(*See* Bad Debts; Capital Gains and Losses; Contributions to Capital; Debt vs. Equity; Losses)

YEAR DEDUCTIBLE

(*See* Accounting Methods; Bad Debts; Inventories)

YEAR INCLUDIBLE IN INCOME

(*See* Accounting Methods)

Table of IRC Sections

IRC §	
11	413, 440
11(d)	54, 57
26(h)	274
38	341, 347
46(b)	469
48(g)	341
61	68, 74, 80, 253, 254, 597, 602
61(a)	591
61(a)(12)	284
69	572
79	299
101(b)	142
103(b)(6)(A)	107
105(b)	136
109	308
111(c)(2)	437
118	590
118(a)	223
162	66, 125, 128, 129, 133–135, 138, 140, 141, 143, 171, 181, 183, 349, 351, 368, 425, 501, 507, 508, 553, 602
162(a)	130, 134, 145, 173, 178, 368
162(a)(1)	128, 183, 188
162(a)(3)	138
162(c)(2)	128
162(e)(2)(B)	126
163	111, 134, 241, 425
164(d)	65
164(e)	595
165	59, 103, 143, 284, 376
165(a)	242
165(c)	408
165(c)(2)	153
165(g)	227
165(g)(1)	407
165(g)(3)	103, 150, 232, 407
165(g)(3)(B)	151
166	208, 244
166(a)	407
166(c)	605
166(d)(1)	408

IRC §	
166(f)	143
167	501
170	126, 156, 157
170(a)(2)	156
170(c)(1)(A)	580
170(c)(2)	156
172(b)(1)(D)	542
172(b)(1)(F)	221
172(k)	542
174	124
203	603
212	138, 365, 551
212(1)	364, 365
222(f)	381
243	59, 336, 455, 492
243(a)	54, 297
243(a)(1)	575
243(a)(3)	336
246(c)	337
263	130
264(a)(1)	299
265	364
267	127, 141, 207, 244, 378, 415, 495–500, 618
267(a)(2)	1, 113, 127, 143, 504
267(b)(2)	498
267(b)(9)	597
267(c)	498
267(g)(9)	598
268	369
269	6, 41–52, 58, 60–62, 68, 72, 80, 81, 220, 254, 412–415, 535–537, 541, 592–594
269(a)	6, 42, 47
269(a)(1)	53, 540, 542
269(a)(2)	46, 53, 542
269(c)	43
270	81
274	125
275	217
277	597
301(a)	319

T-1

Table of IRC Sections

IRC §
301(c) 152, 284, 293, 299, 308,
    318–320, 331, 340, 382, 384, 428,
    449, 456, 458, 460, 462, 469, 471,
    482, 511, 522, 525, 549, 558,
    560, 564, 582
301(c)(1) 462, 474
301(c)(2) 332
301(d)(1) 340
302 .... 14, 287, 294, 341, 383, 442,
    443, 445, 447, 449, 450–453, 455,
    461, 465–467, 469, 472, 473, 477,
    484, 492, 526, 548, 554, 555,
    557, 576, 600
302(a) 93, 339, 340, 362, 381,
    450, 459, 460, 462, 464, 466,
    469, 474, 476, 486, 493, 580
302(a)(2)(B) 491
302(b) 381, 447, 460, 469, 480, 483
302(b)(1) ... 240, 447, 450, 452, 454,
    462, 464–466, 468, 469, 472, 473,
    475, 477, 484, 485
302(b)(2) 444, 447, 462, 463, 468,
    472, 485, 486
302(b)(2)(C) 487
302(b)(2)(D) 486
302(b)(3) 446, 447 450, 451, 462,
    468, 487–493
302(b)(4) 381, 439
302(c) 488
302(c)(2) 448
302(c)(2)(A) 446–448, 450
302(c)(2)(A)(i) 448, 450, 491
302(c)(2)(A)(ii) 450, 492
302(c)(2)(A)(iii) 447, 450, 451,
    488, 490–492
302(c)(2)(B) 449
302(c)(2)(B)(i) 450
302(c)(2)(B)(ii) 450
302(d) 382, 469, 474, 483, 555
302(e) 439
302(e)(1) 381
303 ...... 14, 32, 449, 451, 474, 477–479,
    563, 580
303(a) 478, 479
303(b)(1)(A) 478
303(b)(2)(A) 478
304 ...... 287, 294, 324, 352, 426, 445,
    453, 455, 458, 470–473, 483,
    555, 600
304(a) 454
304(a)(1) 351, 352, 362, 482, 602

IRC §
304(a)(2) 313
304(b)(2)(B) 291, 294
305 .... 318–320, 462
305(a) 277, 317–319
305(b) 318
305(b)(1) 319
305(b)(1)(A) 319
305(b)(2) 319, 340, 462, 520, 558
305(b)(4) 318
305(c) 318, 340
305(d)(1) 319
306 ...... 477, 525, 541, 567, 579–583
306(a)(1) 580, 583
306(a)(1)(A) 579
306(b)(4)(A) 580
306(b)(4)(B) 579
306(c) 581, 582
306(c)(1)(B) 581
311 .... 110, 617
311(a) 284, 443, 492
311(a)(2) 492, 620
311(c) 463
311(d) 463, 469
311(d)(1) 469, 492
311(d)(2)(A) 492
312 106
312(a) 284
312(c) 339
312(d)(1)(B) 340
312(e) 340
312(f)(1) 340
312(i) 339
312(k) 272
316 .... 276, 295, 340, 421, 456
316(a) 293, 336, 454
316(a)(1) 275
316(b) 421
316(b)(2) 420, 421
316(b)(2)(A) 421
316(b)(2)(B) 428
317 352
317(a) 319, 511, 560
318 ...... 93, 105, 361, 446–448, 451,
    462, 468, 471, 481, 488
318(a) 361, 447, 449, 471, 554
318(a)(1) 446
318(a)(1)(A) 362
318(a)(2)(B)(i) 451
318(a)(3) 446
318(a)(3)(B) 450
318(a)(3)(C) 226

T-2

TABLE OF IRC SECTIONS

IRC §	
318(a)(4)	93
331	88, 347, 355, 357, 372–374, 381, 385, 424, 439, 512, 549, 561
331(a)	353
331(a)(1)	385
331(a)(2)	381, 383, 388
332	52, 54, 55, 65, 83, 354–356, 360–362, 373–375, 382, 389, 395, 399, 411, 414, 416, 439, 528, 536, 538, 539, 542, 549, 552, 594
332(a)	406, 542
332(b)(1)	357
332(b)(2)	356
332(b)(3)	356
332(c)	382
333	83, 165, 170, 339, 341, 375–379, 390, 391, 396, 439
333(c)	376
333(c)(1)	378
333(c)(2)	392
333(d)	376
333(e)	377, 378
333(e)(2)	378
333(f)	378
333(f)(1)	392
334	361, 374
334(b)	362
334(b)(1)	360–362, 414
334(b)(2)	65, 105, 272, 346, 354, 355, 360–363, 373–375, 406, 519, 575, 592, 594, 596, 622
334(b)(2)(B)	54, 362
334(b)(3)	105, 362
334(b)(3)(A)	362
334(c)	376
336	356, 359, 368, 375, 378, 380, 406, 596
337	21, 131, 134, 135, 146, 149, 157, 160, 163–166, 233, 337, 340, 343, 346, 347, 354, 356–359, 363–371, 374, 377, 385–387, 389, 392–406, 428, 439, 475, 510, 512, 549, 576, 596, 597, 612
337(a)	388, 397, 401, 510
337(a)(2)	403
337(b)	403
337(b)(1)	405
337(b)(1)(B)	369, 405
337(b)(2)	403–405

IRC §	
337(c)(2)	83, 399
337(c)(2)(A)	375
337(c)(2)(B)	374
341	157–160, 163, 165, 168–170, 627
341(a)	163, 165, 170
341(b)	160, 163, 164, 168, 169, 403
341(b)(1)	169
341(c)	165
341(d)	169, 170
341(d)(2)	169, 627
341(d)(3)	163, 165, 166, 169
346	14, 342, 382, 383, 389, 457, 465, 469, 510, 511, 559, 560
346(a)	384, 439
346(a)(1)	388, 469
346(a)(2)	380–384, 469, 470, 511, 560
346(b)	379, 382, 457, 469, 470, 511, 560
346(b)(1)	357, 470
351	2, 71, 104, 107, 133, 146, 225, 241, 269, 272, 329, 346–351, 360, 361, 411, 415, 455, 471, 473, 513, 517, 557, 573, 580, 581, 600–621, 624
351(a)	320, 352, 471, 600, 605, 615, 617–619, 621, 624
351(b)	350, 602, 614, 618, 620
351(b)(1)(B)	609, 611
351(c)	621
351(d)	603
354	392, 394, 510, 511, 522, 548, 549, 559, 560, 562, 581
354(a)	525, 546, 553, 611, 621
354(a)(1)	163, 511, 513, 527, 529, 540, 560, 582
354(b)	511, 560
355	292, 317, 339, 383, 458, 510, 511, 516, 521, 528–531, 555, 558–573, 581
355(a)	543, 548, 558, 621
355(a)(1)	320, 531
355(a)(1)(B)	563
355(a)(3)	563, 566
355(b)	292, 357, 558, 565, 572
355(b)(1)(A)	532
355(b)(2)	565
355(b)(2)(C)	563
355(b)(2)(D)	292
356	388, 391, 549, 558, 574, 575

T-3

Table of IRC Sections

IRC §

356(a) 149, 527, 556, 557
356(a)(1) 495
356(a)(2) 485, 495, 526, 528, 529,
    549, 551, 557, 559, 565, 575, 576
356(c) 149
356(e) 582
357 .... 348, 350, 592, 593, 614
357(a) 351, 352, 609
357(b) 351, 352, 594
357(c) 349–352, 554, 563, 601–603,
    608–611, 621
357(c)(1) 350
357(c)(1)(B) 513
358(a)(1) 553, 605
361 .... 512, 513, 542
361(a) 621
361(b) 614
362 .... 605, 615, 617
362(a) 362, 605
362(a)(1) 346, 605
362(b) 519, 542
362(c)(2) 590
367 .... 375, 510, 607
367(a)(1) 620
367(d) 226
368 .... 394, 401, 411, 518, 521, 529,
    531, 539, 546, 547, 556, 563
368(a)(1) 512, 545, 550
368(a)(1)(A) 292, 336, 514, 528,
    539, 540–542, 545, 548, 550, 551,
    553–556, 574
368(a)(1)(B) 512–514, 518,
    521–526, 545, 565, 567
368(a)(1)(C) 49, 149, 352, 388,
    512–514, 516–518, 524, 525, 542,
    550, 556, 601, 602, 621
368(a)(1)(D) 339, 388, 394, 495,
    510, 515, 532, 562, 563, 566, 568,
    574, 576
368(a)(1)(E) 176, 485, 540, 548,
    557, 558, 566, 579, 580, 582
368(a)(1)(F) 542, 544, 551–553
368(a)(2)(B) 514, 516, 525, 557
368(a)(2)(C) 545
368(a)(2)(D) 555, 579
368(a)(2)(E) 336, 553, 554
368(b) 542
368(b)(2) 519
368(c) 471, 521, 524, 566, 617
381 .... 46, 105, 360, 382, 413, 416,
    439, 532, 537, 543, 602

IRC §

381(a) 2, 105, 414, 601, 602
381(a)(2) 542, 564
381(b) 519, 533, 552
381(b)(3) 532, 537, 539
381(c) 416, 602
381(c)(1) 360
381(c)(4) 350, 537, 553
381(c)(16) 537
381(c)(22) 360
382 .... 43, 45–48, 411, 412, 414,
    534, 535, 537, 541
382(a) 45, 49, 51, 220, 411, 412,
    416, 535, 538, 541
382(a)(1) 540
382(a)(1)(C) 411, 415
382(a)(4) 415, 541
382(b) 411, 416, 533, 542, 554
382(b)(1) 534, 541
382(b)(2) 554
382(b)(3) 534, 554
392 366
392(b) 366
395 338
404 .... 141, 425
404(a) 142
425(a)(1) 514
425(h) 514, 523
425(h)(3) 514
442(a)(1) 381
442(c)(1) 381
443(b) 210
443(b)(1) 209
446 .... 1, 359
446(b) 65
446(c) 605
453 .... 2, 369, 404, 405, 556, 594
453(b)(2)(A)(ii) 147
453(d) 556
453(d)(1) 146
453(d)(4)(A) 594
461 115
461(c) 65
461(f) 431, 437
481 .... 1, 2, 217
482 .... 60, 62–82, 90, 94, 131, 139,
    227, 241, 246, 253, 254, 433, 485,
    502, 549, 608
483 .... 345, 509, 519
483(f) 510
501(a) 87
501(c)(3) 277, 598, 599

T-4

Table of IRC Sections

IRC §	
501(c)(6)	599
501(c)(8)	599
501(c)(10)	599
501(c)(12)	598
508(a)	598
508(c)(1)(B)	598
509(a)	599
511	227
513	599
531	3–8, 10, 14–18, 20–22, 25–28, 30, 32–34, 36, 38, 40, 64
532	38
532(a)	23
533(b)	6, 10, 18
534	5, 7, 8, 11, 16, 25, 33
534(a)	10
534(b)	9
534(c)	8–10, 34
535	14
535(c)(2)	6
537	19, 23
537(b)(2)	32
542	134, 425, 428
542(a)	435
542(b)(2)	435
542(c)(2)	424, 426
542(c)(6)	424–427
542(c)(6)(C)	423, 424
542(c)(6)(D)	426
542(d)(1)	424
542(d)(1)(A)(iv)	426
542(d)(2)(A)	425
543	434, 436
543(a)	432, 434, 435
543(a)(2)	433, 504, 602
543(a)(6)	419, 431, 435
543(a)(7)	419, 427, 429, 430, 433
543(a)(8)(B)	432, 435
543(b)(2)	436
543(b)(3)	437, 602
544(a)(1)	419
545	434
545(b)	418, 437
545(b)(5)	435
547	420–422
547(c)	420, 421
551(b)	418
562	21, 422
563	21
563(b)	423
581	420, 424, 533

IRC §	
585	104, 221
586	221
593	221
595	208
631	578
631(a)	361
671	93
671(c)	401
677	93
690(c)(1)	390
721	601, 609
736(a)(2)	133
856	292
902	342
931	213, 214, 272
957	542
963	215
964	215
992(a)(1)(A)	337
993(a)(1)	337
995(c)(2)	337
1001	352, 390, 474, 492, 512
1002	352, 524
1012	621
1016	338
1031	165, 352, 378, 622
1031(a)	352
1032	588, 589, 597
1033	348, 604, 610
1036	520, 602, 613
1036(a)	558, 602, 622
1071	348
1201	413
1201(a)	84
1211	228
1212	228
1221	151, 403
1223(1)	361
1223(2)	151, 378
1231	347, 368, 369
1232	154, 548
1232(a)	120
1232(a)(1)	617
1232(a)(3)(A)	108
1232(b)(2)(B)	108
1234	320
1239	463, 497, 500–502, 592, 600, 606, 608, 611, 614
1239(a)	2
1239(b)	501
1244	583–585

T-5

Table of IRC Sections

IRC §	
1245	226, 272, 367, 395, 411, 614
1245(b)	272
1250	226
1250(a)	463
1348	189
1361	353, 371
1374(c)(2)(A)	417
1374(c)(2)(B)	106, 417
1501	56, 210, 213, 215
1502	212, 213
1504	56, 212
1504(a)	55, 211, 212
1504(b)(4)	214
1504(d)	210
1551	60, 62, 593
1552(a)(2)	221
1561(a)	58
1562	336
1563	54, 55, 57, 58, 60, 212
1563(a)(1)	58
1563(a)(2)	54–57, 438
1563(a)(2)(A)	54
1563(c)(2)(B)	56
1563(c)(2)(B)(ii)	54
1563(e)(6)	58
2035	478
3505	82

IRC §	
4943(c)(2)	599
4943(c)(4)	599
4943(c)(5)	599
6081(b)	441
6152	82, 440, 441
6154	440
6155	5
6164	82
6203	82
6411(b)	411
6601	5
6601(a)	4
6601(f)(3)	4
6601(f)(4)	5
6653(a)	5, 295
6655(a)	440
6655(c)	5, 440
6655(d)(1)	440
6655(d)(2)	440
6672	82, 84–87, 439, 441
6901	84
6901(c)(1)	332
7503	396
7701	90
7701(a)(3)	92, 544
7805	412

Table of Treasury Regulations

Treas. Reg. §	
1.61-5	442
1.61-3(a)	130
1.61-12(c)(1)	110
1.119-1(b)	321
1.162-7(a)	200
1.162-7(b)(2)	195
1.162-12	369
1.163-3(c)(1)	111
1.165-1(b)	59
1.166-4	600
1.243-4(c)	336
1.302-2(c)	477, 492
1.303-2(f)	478
1.304-2(a)	362
1.305-5(b)(2)	513
1.306-3(d)	579
1.312-1(d)	340
1.312-10(a)	339
1.312-10(b)	339
1.331-1(c)	388
1.334-1(c)	375
1.334-1(c)(4)(v)(b)(1)	375
1.335-2(c)	531
1.337-2	233
1.341-4(a)	163
1.341-4(c)(2)	170
1.346-1(a)	383
1.346-1(a)(2)	383
1.351-1(a)(1)(ii)	606
1.355-1(a)	561
1.355-1(c)(2)	529
1.355-2(c)	277, 292, 530–532, 548
1.368-1(b)	545, 548
1.368-1(d)	545, 546
1.368-2(h)	556
1.382-1(h)(7)	411
1.382(a)-1(h)(4)	412, 416
1.382(a)-1(h)(6)	48, 50, 411, 416
1.382(b)-1(a)(2)	536
1.425-1(a)(7)	514
1.461-1(a)(2)	115
1.471-6(g)	347
1.482-2(e)(2)(i)	78

Treas. Reg. §	
1.501(c)(10)-1	599
1.535-3(b)(1)(ii)	6
1.537-2(b)(4)	36
1.537(b)(1)	36
1.537(b)(2)	36
1.545-2(a)(1)(i)	437
1.562-1	420
1.562-1(a)	420, 422
1.963-1(a)(4)	215
1.964-1(c)(3)	215
1.1014-3	625
1.1239-1	606
1.1244(c)-1(c)	584
1.1244(c)-1(g)(2)	583
1.1501-13(d)	59
1.1501-13(e)	59
1.1501-13(f)	59
1.1502	209
1.1502-5	211
1.1502-5(a)(1)	210
1.1502-11(a)	211
1.1502-11A	214
1.1502-11A(a)	213
1.1502-13	216
1.1502-14(a)	209
1.1502-14(d)	94, 208
1.1502-14(d)(1)	104
1.1502-15(a)(1)	216
1.1502-15(a)(4)(i)(b)	216
1.1502-18(a)	213
1.1502-21(c)	218
1.1502-21(d)	55
1.1502-31(a)(4)	221
1.1502-31(b)(1)	477
1.1502-31A(d)	219
1.1502-32	106
1.1502-32(b)(2)(iii)(b)	59
1.1502-32(f)(2)	210
1.1502-32A	1
1.1502-33(d)(3)	214
1.1502-38(c)	216
1.1502-75(b)	215
1.1502-75(b)(2)	215

T-7

Table of Treasury Regulations

Treas. Reg. §		Treas. Reg. §	
1.1502-75(d)(2)(ii)	55	1.1563-1(a)(3)	56, 57, 438
1.1502-75(d)(3)	559	1.1564-1(b)	214
1.1502-75(d)(3)(i)	212	1.5521-1(a)(2)	210
1.1502-75(h)(2)	215	1.6012-2(a)(2)	89
1.1502-77(a)	215	1.12323A	108
1.1502-79	221	301.7701	88
1.1502-79(a)(1)(i)	220	301.7701-4(c)	92
1.1502-79(a)(2)	219	301.7701-4(d)	353

Table of Revenue Rulings

Rev. Rul.		Rev. Rul.	
215	441	59-197	567
54-34	430	59-229	622
54-396	563	59-233	451
55-702	420	59-240	384, 470
56-50	166	59-258	477
56-103	452	59-296	95
56-116	583	59-308	402
56-117	568	59-326	216
56-137	170	59-400	566
56-220	526	59-412	363
56-223	583	60-1	582
56-266	567	60-34	343
56-286	379	60-37	111
56-330	518	60-50	389
56-344	567	60-68	170
56-345	557	60-194	430
56-347	348	60-232	384
56-360	211	60-240	556
56-372	368	60-245	217
56-373	543	60-262	363
56-387	402, 403	60-302	614
56-450	573	60-322	384, 470
56-451	567	60-331	422
56-485	477	60-344	420
56-513	470	61-96	284
56-556	452	61-156	402
56-584	452	61-214	597
57-103	583	61-215	556
57-132	583	61-224	222
57-140	403	62-12	169
57-586	526	62-45	65
57-602	211	62-128	104
58-54	567	62-131	277
58-68	292	62-138	573
58-325	93	62-155	93
58-374	553	62-204	214
58-603	542	63-29	518, 545
59-60	470	63-40	414, 534
59-84	583	63-63	341
59-108	368	63-73	126
59-119	493	63-103	420
59-120	402	63-104	211
59-172	431	63-107	88

T-9

Table of Revenue Rulings

Rev. Rul.		Rev. Rul.	
63-114	170	67-298	157
63-215	396	67-299	383
63-225	320	67-334	211
63-228	93	67-376	544
63-245	399	67-411	551
63-260	566	67-423	437
64-56	603	67-425	479
64-73	518	67-448	525
64-93	218, 222	68-9	440
64-100	368	68-21	445
64-146	342	68-23	149
64-158	542	68-55	603
64-239	347	68-114	127
64-251	213	68-258	440
64-257	379	68-261	556
65-96	417	68-284	566
65-184	169	68-285	525
65-258	105	68-296	157
65-259	419, 435	68-298	621
65-286	566	68-348	391, 392
65-289	479	68-349	614
65-293	214	68-357	517
66-23	548	68-358	517
66-35	342	69-359	416
66-37	477	68-388	451
66-91	221	68-407	566
66-112	526	68-409	14
66-142	603	68-472	163
66-169	542	68-484	156
66-186	375	68-526	517
66-204	572	68-527	2
66-214	542	68-547	477
66-237	5	68-562	525
66-248	622	68-602	416
66-290	375	68-603	532
66-332	582	68-623	212
66-336	342	68-629	621
66-353	341	68-637	517
66-365	526, 580	68-641	215
66-366	514	69-3	556
66-374	221	69-6	514
67-16	384, 437	69-15	320
67-122	603	69-20	613
67-125	130	69-34	557, 559
67-146	215	69-48	517
67-186	416	69-80	156
67-189	211	69-117	347
67-202	53	69-126	212
67-273	398	69-135	514
67-274	542	69-142	512, 525
67-275	550	69-156	614

Table of Revenue Rulings

Rev. Rul.		Rev. Rul.	
69-163	215	70-291	558
69-182	210	70-298	558
69-185	544	70-301	6
69-216	525, 559	70-378	210
69-243	111	70-379	210
69-261	291	70-409	392
69-264	556	70-432	277
69-293	277	70-434	565
69-294	524	70-470	58
69-299	419	70-489	95
69-339	502	70-496	474
69-369	602	70-497	7
69-378	163	70-522	607
69-407	558	70-531	341
69-413	542	70-551	419
69-426	362	70-609	341
69-440	295	70-612	426
69-442	352	70-638	53
69-460	532	70-639	493
69-515	416	70-642	14
69-516	555	71-79	277
69-534	357	71-83	212
69-543	347	71-129	441
69-559	126	71-165	341
69-562	93	71-211	451
69-585	524	71-250	383
69-588	437	71-261	451
69-590	215	71-262	451
69-591	56	71-326	375
69-594	479	71-336	474
69-613	154	71-372	430
69-620	437	71-383	565
69-622	210	71-384	565
69-623	221	71-426	493
69-630	79	71-427	558
69-646	556	71-440	215
70-6	151	71-473	357
70-18	555	71-531	437
70-41	524	71-562	492
70-65	523	71-563	474
70-93	170	71-564	621
70-101	90	71-569	272
70-106	357	71-593	565
70-140	608, 611	71-596	436
70-153	504	72-30	559
70-172	523	72-32	555
70-223	555	72-48	169
70-240	495	72-57	557, 558
70-252	56	72-75	90
70-269	523	72-137	373
70-271	352	72-148	436

T-11

Table of Revenue Rulings

REV. RUL.
72-172	502
72-198	523
72-199	602
72-206	514
72-251	422
72-258	215
72-274	54
72-278	436
72-306	419
72-317	173
72-318	602
72-321	218
72-322	559
72-324	5
72-354	523
72-380	450, 492
72-405	517
72-464	111
72-530	292
72-569	555
72-576	555
72-603	214
73-2	602
73-16	522
73-28	522
73-44	565
73-179	426
73-204	478
73-205	522
73-233	226
73-234	292
73-236	292
73-237	292
73-246	320
73-264	402
73-332	436
73-378	163
73-432	147
73-460	92
73-500	169
73-551	402
73-552	516
74-5	292
74-29	398
74-35	522
74-36	544
74-54	148
74-79	357
74-87	445
74-127	115
74-211	362

REV. RUL.
74-266	341, 580
74-269	558
74-296	383
74-297	555
74-326	210
74-337	2
74-339	340
74-378	210
74-382	292
74-396	375
74-407	126
74-423	221
74-431	346
74-432	430
74-434	588
74-441	54
74-454	522
74-457	516
74-463	445
74-465	383
74-476	379
74-477	621
74-501	320
74-502	607
74-515	589
74-516	565
74-544	375
74-564	522
74-565	514
74-569	478
74-573	474
74-585	210
74-589	217
74-598	55
75-2	451
75-3	383
75-13	149
75-33	522
75-39	558
75-54	209
75-80	210
75-93	558
75-94	522
75-95	548
75-117	108
75-123	522
75-161	513
75-179	513
75-183	277
75-186	151
75-202	436

Table of Revenue Rulings

Rev. Rul.		Rev. Rul.	
75-212	210	76-338	337
75-222	582	76-386	581
75-223	382, 383	76-393	214
75-236	582	76-398	147
75-237	513	76-403	343
75-248	415	76-429	389
75-320	462	76-430	104
75-321	621	76-454	613
75-330	5	76-496	450
75-335	156	76-514	347
75-337	531	76-527	531
75-379	353	76-528	548
75-406	548	76-563	440
75-447	487	77-11	564
75-450	352	77-20	521
75-468	513	77-31	90
75-502	450	77-37	564
75-512	450	77-67	65
75-514	463	77-81	541
75-515	340	77-93	492
75-521	357	77-108	581
75-561	544, 552	77-109	401
76-13	531	77-127	436
76-14	582	77-133	564
76-15	582	77-149	319
76-39	343	77-150	398
76-42	513	77-166	470
76-54	565	77-190	403
76-90	375	77-191	564
76-107	319	77-218	445
76-108	565	77-226	492
76-123	621	77-227	541
76-145	415	77-238	445
76-151	226	77-245	470
76-164	212	77-256	492
76-175	378	77-271	613
76-186	340	77-293	464
76-187	531	77-306	163
76-188	602	77-307	554
76-223	521	77-321	378
76-239	340	77-335	581
76-240	226	77-336	436
76-243	79	77-337	378
76-258	319	77-360	483
76-289	382	77-368	6
76-302	214	77-375	382
76-316	147	77-376	382
76-317	356	77-377	564
76-331	156	77-415	548
76-334	516	77-426	477
76-337	495	77-427	362

T-13

Table of Revenue Rulings

Rev. Rul.
77-449	601, 620
77-456	362
77-467	450
77-468	382
77-479	557
78-47	513
78-55	461
78-60	462
78-115	462
78-123	340
78-130	513
78-150	554, 563
78-197	444
78-269	348
78-278	406
78-279	406
78-280	605
78-294	620
78-330	554
78-350	378
78-351	557
78-369	411
78-375	319
78-376	516
78-383	516
78-397	554
78-401	469
78-402	470
78-408	512
78-422	563
78-441	554
78-442	352
79-3	398
79-4	521
79-8	173
79-10	373
79-20	272
79-21	212
79-42	319
79-50	299
79-59	419
79-60	436
79-70	613
79-71	553
79-82	378
79-89	521
79-100	521
79-104	337
79-156	426
79-163	581
79-184	382

Rev. Rul.
79-194	607
79-226	166
79-235	165
79-250	553
79-257	382
79-258	352
79-273	553
79-274	580
79-275	381
79-279	209
79-287	581
79-288	620
79-289	352
79-314	492, 620
79-334	450
79-376	340
79-394	572
79-434	512
80-26	93
80-33	580
80-46	53
80-79	411
80-101	492
80-150	353
80-154	319
80-189	291
80-198	620
80-228	620
80-238	337
80-239	291
80-240	351
80-283	463
80-284	619
80-285	619
80-292	319
81-3	381
81-25	546
81-27	599
81-37	426
81-41	487
81-81	59, 580
81-88	410
81-91	580
81-92	545
81-117	599
81-119	599
81-177	599
81-178	598
81-186	580
81-190	444
81-233	450

Table of Revenue Rulings

Rev. Rul.
81-238	92
81-247	545
81-289	469
80-358	362
82-11	336
82-34	557
82-48	82
82-65	440
82-72	580
82-118	579
82-129	450
82-130	531
82-152	55
82-158	318
82-187	381
82-191	579
82-204	151
82-212	90
82-219	572
83-14	216
83-34	601
83-42	318
83-61	378
83-65	347
83-73	553
83-114	292
83-119	318
83-155	133
83-156	601
84-2	356
84-33	55
84-68	133
84-71	619

Rev. Rul.
84-76	478
84-79	212
84-83	87
84-101	6
84-114	557
84-135	491
84-136	221
84-137	435
84-141	318
85-14	487
85-19	491
85-48	391
85-106	469
85-107	563
85-122	531
85-127	530
85-138	516
85-139	521

REVENUE PROCEDURES

Rev. Proc.
59-1	419
63-1	419
64-31	270
65-10	341
65-17	64, 79
67-12	341
67-29	270
84-75	439

T-15

Table of Cases

A

A&A Distribs.	438
Abatti	63
Abott, Jr., B.	223
Abegg (2d Cir.)	510
Abegg (TC)	388
Abraham	90
Abramson	85
Achiro	68
Acro Mfg. Co.	355
Adams (8th Cir.)	455
Adams (TC)	400
Adelson	266
Adkins-Phelps, Inc.	545
Aero Indus. Co.	58
Aetna Casualty & Sur. Co. (2d Cir.)	532, 543
Aetna Casualty & Sur. Co. (D. Conn.)	511
Affiliated Gov't Employees Distrib. Co.	597
Affiliated Research, Inc.	242
A.F. Gallun & Sons Corp.	22
Agway, Inc. (Fed. Cir.)	443, 484
Agway, Inc. (Ct. Cl.)	484
Aiken Drive-in Theatre Corp.	586
Ainsworth	501
Air-Vent Aluminum Awning Mfg. Co.	113
Akten Realty Corp.	204
Alabama Coca-Cola Bottling Co.	20
Alabama-Georgia Syrup Co.	124
Alaska Redi-Mix, Inc.	605
Albert Van Luit Co.	190
Alderman	611
Aldon Homes, Inc.	243
Alexander	390
Alex Brown, Inc.	427
Alicia Ruth, Inc.	295
Alioto	86
Allen (7th Cir.)	224
Allen (TCM)	301
Allen Indus., Inc.	136
Allen Oil Co.	54
Allied Cent. Stores, Inc.	536
Allied Indus. Cartage Co.	431
Allied Util. Corp.	55
Allison Corp.	206
Alma Piston Co. (6th Cir.)	23
Alma Piston Co. (TCM)	37
Alper, Louis, Estate of	162
Aphaco, Inc.	134
Alphatype Corp.	4
Altec Corp.	370
Altenpohl	562
Alterman Foods	324
Altorfer	391
Ambassador Apartments, Inc. (2d Cir.)	231
Ambassador Apartments, Inc. (TC)	262
American Bronze Corp.	539
American Int'l Coal Co.	171
American-La France-Foamite Corp.	238
American Lawn Mower Co.	30
American Mfg. Co.	550
American Metal Prods. Corp.	16
American Natural Gas Co.	348
American Potash & Chem. Corp.	520
American Processing & Sales Co.	97
American Terrazzo Strip Co.	78
American Trading & Prod. Corp.	27
AMF, Inc.	109
Amherst Coal Co.	533
Amis, Jr.	305
Anaheim Union Water Co.	74, 590
Anbaco-Emig	414
Anchorage Nursing Home, Inc.	370
Anders (10th Cir.)	596
Anders (Ct. Cl.)	597
Andersen	511
Anderson	337
Anderson & Son, Inc.	44
Andrews	626
Andrews Distrib. Co.	139
Annabelle Candy Co.	321
Antrim, Jr., Estate of	454
Apollo Indus., Inc.	9

T-17

Table of Cases

Appleby	568
Appleton Elec. Co.	192
Apschinkat	313
Aqualane	116
Arcade Realty Co.	134
Archbold	487, 488
Aristar Inc.	77
Arkansas La. Gas Co.	136
Arkhola Sand & Gravel Co.	507
A.R. Lantz Co.	230
Armour	515
Armour-Dial Men's Club, Inc.	597
Aronov Constr. Co.	112
Art Sawyer, Inc.	28
Arwood Corp.	541
A.S. Barber, Inc.	321
Associated Mach.	543, 544
Associated Tel. & Tel. Co.	105
Astleford	228
Atkinson	244
Atlanta Biltmore Hotel Corp.	123, 179
Atlantic Commerce & Shipping Co.	15
Atlantic Properties, Inc.	40
Atlas Oil & Ref. Corp.	547
Atlas Tool Co.	559
Atlee	569
Atwood Grain & Supply Co.	540
Audrey Realty, Inc.	425
Austin State Bank	424
Austin Village, Inc.	229
Avery, Estate of	98
Aylsworth	298

B

Baan	511
Babcock	560
Bachman	376
Badanes	562
Badias & Seijas	401
Bagley	310
Bahan Textile Mach. Co.	15
Bains	458
Baird	302
Baker	502
Baker Commodities, Inc.	105
Baldwin Bros.	67
Baldwin-Lima Hamilton Corp.	67
Ballenger	453, 475
Ballou Constr. Co.	373
Baltimore Aircoil Co.	131
Baltimore Steam Packet Co.	110
B&M Investors Corp.	57
Banister	294
Bank of Kimball	74, 77
Bank of Winnfield & Trust Co.	64
Barclay Co.	51
Barclay Jewelry Inc.	535
Bardahl	19, 32, 34, 35, 428
Bardahl (TCM)	281
Bardahl Int'l Corp.	37
Bardahl Mfg. Corp. (9th Cir.)	4
Bardahl Mfg. Corp. (TCM 1965)	36
Bardahl Mfg. Corp. (TCM 1960)	194
Bardes	308
Barlow	391
Barrett Hamilton, Inc.	31
Barrow Mfg. Co.	16
Barry	627
Bartel	390
Barton-Gillet Co.	196
Barton Naptha Co.	58
Barton Theatre Co.	268, 442
Basic Inc.	275
Basila	175
Bateman	529
Bates	584
Bauer	257
Bausch & Lomb Optical Co.	517
Baynham, Estate of	316
Bayou Verret Land Co. (5th Cir.)	432
Bayou Verret Land Co., Inc. (TC)	435
Bay Sound Transp. Co.	43
Bear	404
Bear Valley Mut. Water Co.	590
Beauchamp & Brown Groves Co.	369
Beaver	351
Bedford's Estate	529
Beggs	147
Bellamy	184
Bell, Estate of	391
Bell Oldsmobile	146
Bell Realty Trust	434
Bell III	69
Benedek	158
Benedict Oil Co.	135
Benjamin	455
Bennett (Ct. Cl.)	339
Bennett (ED Wash.)	496
Bennett (TC)	443
Bentsen	545
Bercy Indus. Inc.	532
Berenbaum	465

Berenson	151	Borge	81
Berger (TC)	173	Boshwit Bros.	10
Berger (TCM)	315	Bourque	330
Berger Mach. Prods., Inc.	553	Boyle Fuel Co.	180
Berghash	386	Bradbury	288, 475, 481
Berkley Mach. Works	286	Braddock Land Co.	147
Berkowitz	230	Brake & Elec. Corp.	237
Berkshire Hathaway, Inc.	440	Brams	471
Berlin	309	Brandtjen-Kluge Inc.	199, 345
Berner	137	Braswell	84
Bernstein	284	Braswell Motor Freight Lines	59
Berthold	333	Braude	161
Best Realty Co.	367	Braun Co.	71
Best Universal Lock Co.	124	Braunstein (2d Cir.)	160
Betson, Jr.	252	Braunstein (TC)	161
Betts	103	Breech, Jr.	385
Bev Andersen Chevrolet, Inc.	203	Bremerton Sun Publishing Co.	40
Bibb	333	Brick Milling Co.	52
Biblin	99	Brighton Recreations, Inc.	114
Bielec	617	Britt	593
Bihlmire	305	Brittingham (5th Cir.)	80
Bijou Park Properties, Inc.	361	Brittingham (TC)	78
Bilar Tool & Die Corp.	550	Broadview Lumber Co.	313
Biltmore Homes, Inc.	141	Broadway Drive-In Theatre, Inc.	241
Binda	304	Brock	299
Bird Management, Inc.	396	Brook	150
Bishop	596	Brookfield Wire Co.	14
Blackmon, Jr.	288	Brown (6th Cir.)	464
Black Motor Co.	94	Brown (WDNC)	500
Blair Holding Co.	435	Brown, Clay	151
Blais	85	Brown Corp. of Ionia	330
Blaise, Inc.	120	Browning Turkey Farms, Inc.	259
Blanco	466	Bruce	224
Blaschka	457	Bruce-Flournoy Motor Corp.	271
Bleily & Collishaw, Inc.	490	Bruce Oil Co.	295
Blinsinger	334	Brumley-Donaldson Co.	43
Bliss Dairy	373	Brundage	588
Bloch	484	Bryan	167
Bloomington Hotel Co.	404	Bryden	628
Blount	483	Buder, Jr.	422
Blue Creek Coal, Inc.	293	Buffalo Batt & Felt Corp.	18
Bluefeld Caterer, Inc.	69	Bulkley Dunton & Co.	265
Bodzy	99, 407	Bunton Inv. Co.	184
Boettger	570	Bunton, Sr.	482
Bohac Agency, Inc.	10	Burke	570
Boise Cascade Corp. (9th Cir.)	354	Burke Concrete Accessories, Inc.	214
Boise Cascade Corp. (TCM)	352	Burke Golf Equip. Corp.	113
Boles	610	Burman Co.	140
Bongiovanni	349	Burr Oaks Corp.	116, 262, 615
Bonsall	572	Busby	102
Book Prod. Indus., Inc.	221, 401	Busch	323
Booth, Earnest, M.D., P.C.	13	Busch, Jr.	323

T-19

Table of Cases

Bush Bros. & Co. 293
Bush Hog Mfg. Co. 62
Byerlite Corp. 96
Byrne 105
Bywater Sales & Serv. Co. 530

C

Cabax Mills 361, 373
Cadillac Textiles Inc. 79
Calderazzo 149
Caletta Blueberry Co. 97
Cal-Glen Dev. Corp. 605
Callan 421
Callan Court Co. 474
Calley & Clark Co. 399
Callner 300
Cambridge Hotels, Inc. 139
Campagna 355
Campbell 143
Campbell County State Bank (8th Cir.) 76
Campbell County State Bank (TC) .. 494
Campbell Taggart, Inc. 587
Canal-Randolph Corp. 140
Canaveral Int'l Corp. 47
C&E Canners 175
Capaldi 628
Capital Refrigeration, Inc. 508
Capital Sav. & Loan Ass'n 528
Capitol Fin. Co. 201
Capitol Market, Ltd. 186
Cappuccilli 94
Capri Inc. 220
Cardinal Corp. 588
Carey 484
Carlberg 527
Carlen Realty Co. 39
Carnahan 520
Carole Accessories, Inc. 178
Carolina Rubber Hose Co. 41
Carr 85
Carrington 464
Carter (TCM 1977) 298
Carter (TCM 1960) 335
Cary 490
Casali 316
Casa Loma, Inc. 396
Casco Bank & Trust Co. 228
Casco Prods. Corp. 444
Case, Jr. 328

Cash & Lincoln Fence 308
Cashion, Inc. 290
Casner 284
Caspers 294
Castle Heights, Inc. 241
Cates 157
Catterall 519
C.A. White Trucking Co. 171
C. Blake McDowell, Inc. 420
C.E. Estes, Inc. 20
Central Credit 27
Central Foundry Co. 124
Central Freight Lines, Inc. 190
Central Motor Co. 11
Central Oil Co. 279
Central Soya Co. 528
Central Tablet Mfg. Co. 367
Challenge Mfg. Co. 132, 144
Champaign Realty Co. 119
Chaney & Hope, Inc. 12
Chapman (1st Cir.) 519
Chapman (TCM) 276
Chappell & Co. 30
Charles Baloian Co. 57
Charles C. Chapman Bldg. Co. 536
Charles Town, Inc. 74
Charter Wire, Inc. 236
Chartier Real Estate Co. 413
Chartrand 86
Chase 579
Chee 149
Chemplast, Inc. 153
Cherry 594
Chertkof 446
Chesapeake Mfg. Co. 325
Cheyenne Newspapers, Inc. 15
Childers & Venters Motors, Inc. ... 186
Chism Ice Cream Co. 203
Chock Full O'Nuts 109
Christensen 283
Christie Coal & Coke Co. 97
Christopher, Jr. 351
Chrome Plate, In re 360
Ciba-Geigy Corp. 68
Cities Serv. Co. 108
Citizens Acceptance Corp. 406
Citizens Bank & Trust Co. (Ct. Cl. 1978) 307
Citizens Bank & Trust Co. (Ct. Cl. 1977) 471
City Bank of Washington 400
Claggett 429

Clare Co.	415
Clarksdale Rubber Co.	414
Clark, W.G.	27
Clayton	395
Clements	314
Clifton Inv. Co.	610
Clymer, Jr.	176
Coady	569, 571
Coastal Casting Serv., Inc.	17
Coast Coil Co.	404
Coast Quality Constr. Corp.	411
Coast Sash & Door Co.	258
Coates	159
Coates Trust (9th Cir.)	455
Coates Trust (TC)	455, 473
Cobbs	557
Coca-Cola Co.	123
Cockey	84
Coddington	391
Coe Laboratories, Inc.	125
Cohan	77
Cohen (EDNY)	475
Cohen (TC)	160
Cohen (TCM)	334
Cohron	456
Cole, Estate of	478
Coleman Good, Inc.	234
Colley, Estate of	314
Collins	453
Collins Elec. Co.	77
Columbia Iron & Metal Co.	156
Colvin	476
Combs II	157
Comess	475
Commercial Bank at Daytona Beach	240
Commercial Fin. Co.	429
Commonwealth Container Corp.	534
Complete Fin. Corp.	56
Computer Sciences Corp.	160
Comtel Corp.	393
Concrete Pipe & Prods. Co.	624
Condit	408
Connery	369
Continental Bank	107
Continental Mach. & Tool Corp.	52
Continental Sales & Enters., Inc.	537
Coors	21
Copley	247
Cordner	622
Cordy Tire Co	188
Corn Belt Hatcheries of Ark.	214
Corn Products	151–153, 587
Cornwall	485
Cotter	619
Court Holding Co.	494
Covered Wagon, Inc.	365
Covey Inv. Co.	116
Covil Insulation Co.	209
Cox	314
Coyle	472
Cozart Packing Co. (4th Cir.)	171
Cozart Packing Co. (TCM)	201
Craigie, Inc.	219
Craigs Drug Store, Inc.	179
Crane	350
Crawford	448
Crescent Oil, Inc.	374
Creston Corp.	243
Creswell	204
Cropland Chem. Corp.	198
Crosby	321
Crosby Valve & Gage Co.	155, 156
Crow	152
Crowe	160
Crown	476
Cruser	335
Cruvant	447
Cuckler	274
Cukor	595
Culberson's, Inc.	300
Culligan Water Conditioning, Inc.	272
Cummins Diesel Sales Corp.	456
Cummins Diesel Sales of Colo. Co.	359
Cummins Diesel Sales of Ore., Inc.	39
Curry (4th Cir.)	339
Curry (5th Cir.)	233
Curry (TC)	269
Curtis	528
Cuyuna Realty Co. & Misabe Realty Co.	241

D

Dahlem Constr. Co.	30, 197
Dahlem Found., Inc.	25
Dallas Ceramic Co.	79
Daly	322
D'Angelo Assocs., Inc.	617
Danskin, Inc.	143
Darco Realty Corp.	136
Daro Corp.	270
Daron Indus. Inc.	220

Table of Cases

Datamation Servs. Inc. 150
Davant 544, 549
Dave Inv. Co. 155
Davidson Bldg. Co. 122
Davies 439
Davis (US) 452, 464, 466, 468,
                                469, 473
Davis (6th Cir.) 150
Davis (10th Cir.) 585
Davis (DNM) 100
Day 168
Daytona Beach Kennel Club, Inc. 46
Daytona Mach. Supply Co. 113
Dayton Hydraulic Co. 87
Dean 275
Decker 459
De Felice 609
DeGroff 549
Delhar, Inc. 71
Delk Inv. Co. 433
Dellinger 280
Delta Metalforming Co. 58
Demian, Ltd. 200
Demmon 339
Denison Poultry & Egg Co. 183
Deviney Constr. Co. 331
Dewmar Constr. Co. 58
Dialcab Taxi Owners Guild Ass'n ... 598
Diamond Bros. Co. 236
DiAndrea, Inc. 377
Dickman Lumber Co. 25
Diecks, Estate of 160
Dielectric Materials Co. 32
Dietrich Mfg. Co. 184
Dietzsch 317
Differential Steel Car Co. 578
Dillard 601
Dillin 324
Disabled Am. Veterans 598
Divine 338
Dixie, Inc. 8
Dixo Co. 202
Dockery 206
Dr. Pepper Bottling Co. 206
Dodd 237
Dolese 324
Donisi 232
Donruss Co. 38
Doornbosch Bros. 137, 269
Dorba Homes 254
Dorsey 475
Dothan Coca-Cola Bottling Co. 426

Doug-Long, Inc. 7
Drage, In re 616
Drew (Ct. Cl.) 83
Drew (TCM) 125
Drexel Park Pharmacy, Inc. 200
Dritz 332
Drive Indus. Park 227
Drybrough (6th Cir.) 593
Drybrough (TC) 361
Ducros 592
Dudley Co. 413
Duell 154
Duffey 310
DuGrenier 130
Du Gro Frozen Foods, Inc. 239
Dunavant 377
Dunn (2d Cir.) 487
Dunn (WD Okla.) 274
Dwight (2d Cir.) 366
Dwight (TCM) 626
Dwyer 87

E

Earl, Lucas v. 74
Eastern Color Printing Co. 539
East Tenn. Motor Co. 196
Ebbets Lanes, Inc. 537
Eberle Tanning Co. 28
Economy Cash & Carry, Inc. 190
Edler, Jr. 312, 454
Edlund Co. 608
Edminster 459
Edmiston 86
Eduardo Catalano Inc. 189
Edwards (TC 1976) 77
Edwards (TC 1968) 120
Edwards Motor Transit Co. 304
Edwin's, Inc. 183
Eger 585
Ehrlich 191
E.I. DuPont de Nemours & Co. 616
800 S. Fourth St., Inc. 60
84 Woodbine St. Realty Corp. 368
Electric Regulation Corp. 33
Electronic Modules Corp. 96
Electronic Sensing Prods., Inc. 220
Eli Lilly & Co. Subsidiaries 72
Eliott H. Raffety Farms, Inc. 228
Eller 433
Elliots, Inc. (9th Cir.) 199

T-22

Table of Cases

Elliots, Inc. (TCM)	199
Elliott	101
Ellis Corp.	435
Elward	106
Emmerson	279
Empire Land Corp.	22
Engineering Corp. of Am.	17
Engineering Sales Inc.	75
Epstein	136
Equipment Rental Co.	410
Equitable Publishing Co.	589
Erickson (9th Cir.)	63
Erickson (SD Ill.)	481
Erlich	104
Ernest, Holdeman & Collett, Inc.	183
Erwin Properties Inc.	209
Esrenco Truck Co.	62, 122
Estelle Wyler, Inc.	290
Estill	353
Ettle Co.	202
Euclid-Tennessee, Inc.	535
Everett	514
Evwalt Dev. Corp.	226
Exel Corp.	412
E-Z Sew Enters., Inc.	6, 577

F

Fabacher	623
Faber Cement Block Co.	19
Fackler	501
Factories Inv. Corp.	12
Fairfax Auto Parts of N. Va., Inc. (5th Cir.)	54
Fairfax Auto Parts of N. Va., Inc. (TC)	57
Fairfield Communities Land Co.	49
Fairmount Park Raceway, Inc.	503
Faist	302
Falkoff	274
Fall River Gas Co.	132
Family Record Plan, Inc.	359
Fanning	71
Farber	161
Farkas	244
Faucher	154
Fausek, Jr.	279
Fawn Fashions, Inc.	48
F.D. Bissett & Son, Inc.	113
F.D. Rich Co.	219
FEC Liquidating Corp.	392, 512
Federal Cement Tile Co.	536
Federal Employees Distrib. Co.	589
Federal Lithograph Co.	188
Federal Ornamental Iron & Bronze Co.	40
Federbush	293, 408
Fegan	66
Fehrs	447
Fehrs Fin. Co.	483
Feilen Meat Co.	33
Felix	162
Fellinger	117
Fellows Sales Co.	180
Fenco, Inc.	26
Fenix & Scisson, Inc.	535
Fenn, Jr.	330
Ferguson	500
Fetzer Refrigerator Co.	504
Fibel	400
Fidelity Commercial Co.	427
Fine Realty, Inc.	61
Fin Hay Realty Co.	232
Finley & Co.	330
Fireoved	579
Firstco Co.	23
First Fed. Sav. & Loan Ass'n	546
First Nat'l Bank of Omaha	145
First Nat'l Indus., Inc.	587
First Sav. & Loan Ass'n	591
First Sec. Bank	494
First Sec. Bank of Utah	73
Fischer	239
Fischer Bros. Aviation	263
Fischer Lime & Cement Co.	31
Fisher	520
Fishing Tackle Prods. Co.	138
Fitzgerald Motor Co.	67
Five Lakes Club	142
Fleming	249
Fletcher	420, 421
Flomaton Wholesale Co.	118
Florida-Georgia Corp.	604
Focht	350
Foglesong	80
Foos	200
Foresun, Inc.	223
Fors Farm, Inc.	259
Foster (US)	339
Foster (TCM)	60, 367
Fotocrafters, Inc.	194
Fowler Hosiery Co.	342
Frank	264

T-23

Table of Cases

Franke Exploration Corp. 144
Frank Ix & Sons Va. Corp. 534
Frank Spenger Co. 289
Frazell (5th Cir.) 609
Frazell (WD La.) 624
Frazier 246
Freedom Newspapers, Inc. 21
Freeman 85
Freeman, Estate of 482
Freer 246
Freidus 298
Freitas 170
Friend 465
Fugate 331
Fulman 420, 422
Fumigators, Inc. 139
Furr 468

G

Gada 530
Gahm 463
Gallagher 388
Gallina 367
Gamble Constr. Co. 418
Garbini Elec., Inc. 80
Gardens of Faith, Inc. 325
Gardner 312
Garfinckel 534
Garrison 390
Garriss Inv. Corp. 253
Garrow 376
Garvey 59
Gay Gibson, Inc. 198
General Aggregates Corp. 325
General Alloy Casting Co. 117
General Am. Ins. Co. 588
General Bancshares Corp. 124
General Geophysical Co. 106
General Housewares Corp. 392
General Mfg. Corp. 209
General Roofing & Insulation Co. .. 177
Generes 101
Genito 326
Gentry, Jr. 64
Georgia Crown Distrib. Co. 176
Georgia Pac. Corp. 216
Georgia R.R. & Banking Co. 335
Gettler 73
Gibbs 306

Gilbert, B. 328
Gilboy 263
Gilday 106
Giles Indus., Inc. (Cl. Ct. 1981) .. 175
Giles Indus., Inc. (Ct. Cl. 1974) .. 175
Gilman Paper Co. 197
Gilmore 104
Ginsburg 371
Gladstone-Arcuni, Inc. 194
Glasgow Village Dev. Corp. ... 181, 289
Glass, Jr., Estate of 360
Glenn-Minnich Clothing Co. 291
Glen Raven Mills, Inc. 540
Globe Prod. Corp. 217
Gloninger 453
Gloucester Ice & Cold Storage Co. .. 112
Glover Packing Co. of Tex. 538
Godfrey, Jr. 84
Gokey Properties, Inc. 112
Golanda Mining Corp. 623
Golden Nugget, Inc. 539
Gold-Pak Meat Co. 208
Goldstein 278
Goldstein Estate 625
Golsen 529
Good Chevrolet 177
Gooding 379, 469
Gooding Amusement Co. 239
Goodling 380
Goodstein 282
Goodwyn Crockery Co. 541
Gordon (2d Cir. 1970) 560
Gordon (2d Cir. 1967) 560
Gordon Turnbull, Inc. 13
Gorton 356
Goss 461
Gottesman & Co. 12
Gottlieb (ED La.) 306
Gottlieb (TCM) 626
Gould 141
GPD, Inc. 38
Grabowski Trust 449
Graham 190
Grant (D. Vt.) 86
Grant (TCM) 485
Gravois Planning Mill Co. 364
Gray (9th Cir.) 463
Gray (TC 1979) 418
Gray (TC 1971) 289, 458
Great Lakes Pipe-Line Co. 271
Grede Foundries, Inc. 515

T-24

Table of Cases

Green	463
Green Bay Structural Steel, Inc.	114
Greenberg	389
Greenthal	311
Greer	409
Gregory	605
Griffin & Co.	180, 252
Griswold	574
Griswold Rubber Co.	193
GROB, Inc.	26
Grubbs	576
Gsell & Co.	8
Gulf Inland Corp.	423
Gunlock Corp.	220
Gurtman	325
Gus Russell, Inc.	605
Guyer	329
Gyro Eng'g Corp.	604

H

Haag	152
Haberman Farms	594
Haensli	385
Hagist Ranch, Inc.	251
Haley	267
Half Trust	93
Hall	137
Hall Paving Co.	42
Hamabe Realty Corp.	35
Hambergers York Road, Inc.	72
Hamer	328
Hamilton Erection, Inc.	123
Hammond Lead Prods. Inc.	191
Hammond Sheet Metal Co.	205
Hampton Corp.	197
Hampton Pontiac, Inc.	271
Hanco Distrib. Co.	421
Hankenson	144
Hanna, Estate of	498
Hansen	271
Hanson	292
Harbor Medical Corp.	136
Hardin	24, 309
Hardin's Bakeries, Inc.	30
Hardy	330
Harlan	266
Harrigan	624
Harris	499
Harrison Bolt & Nut Co.	40
Harrison Property Management Co.	590
Harry A. Koch Co.	18
Harry Fox, Inc.	206
Hartley	618
Hartman (2d Cir.)	166
Hartman (ED Wis.)	475
Hartman (TC)	562
Hart Metal Prods. Corp. (7th Cir.)	43
Hart Metal Prods. Corp. (Ct. Cl.)	418
Hartwell	286
Hasbrook	471
Haserot	468
Haserot, Estate of	602
Haskel Eng'g & Supply Co.	109
Havens & Martin, Inc.	30
Haynes	133
Hays	468
Hays Corp.	519
Hayutin	223
Hearn & Curran, Inc.	267
Hedrick	331
Heft	166
Heim	423
Helgesen Properties, Inc.	280
Hempt Bros.	600
Henderson (5th Cir.)	234
Henderson (WD Wash.)	370
Henry C. Beck Builders, Inc.	217, 473
Herculite Protective Fabrics Corp.	43
Herculoc Corp.	240
Hersloff (Ct. Cl.)	89
Hersloff (TC)	89
Herzog	476
Heverly	518
H.F. Ramsey Co.	48
H.G. Cockrell Warehouse Corp.	18
Higgins	101
Hilldun Corp.	130
Hillsboro Nat'l Bank	368, 369, 596
Hilton Hotel Corp.	129
Himmel	465
Hines, Jr.	70
Hinrichsen, Estate of	485
Hipp	460
Hippodrome Bldg. Co.	121
Hirs	260
Hirshfield	429
Hitke	348
HMW Indus.	360
Hodge	586

T-25

Table of Cases

Hoffman 303
Hogg's Oyster Co. 3
Holland, Jr. 227
Holliman, Trustee 544
Home Constr. Corp. of Am. 533
Home Improvement Co. 172
Home Interiors & Gifts, Inc. 188
Home Sav. & Loan Ass'n 510, 551
Honaker Drilling, Inc. 163
Honigman 279
Hooper, Inc. 32
Hoover 311
Hoover Motor Express Co. 139
Horner 408
Horst 359
Houston Oil Field Material Co. 222
Howell 396
Huckins Tool & Die, Inc. 197
Huddle, Inc. 52
Hudlow 126
Hudspeth 359
Humphrey 473
Hurst-Rosche, Inc. 27
Husky Oil Co. 110
Hutchins Standard Serv. 245
Hutton (6th Cir.) 256
Hutton (TC) 601
Hvidsten 252
H. Wetter Mfg. Co. 420
Hydrometals, Inc. 415
Hyneman Gin, Inc. 205
Hynes, Jr. 92
Hyplains Dressed Beef, Inc. 143

I

Ideal Tool & Die Co. 509
Imperial Car Distribs. Inc. 255
Independent Laundry & Linen Serv.,
  Inc. 18
Inductotherm Indus., Inc. 414
Industrial Life Ins. Co. 38
Industrial Suppliers, Inc. 48
Ingalls 498
Inland Asphalt 140, 312
Inland Terminals, Inc. 12
Inness 407
Intercounty Dev. Corp. 398
Inter County Title Co. 27
Interior Sec. Corp. 81

Intermed, Inc. 351
Intermountain Furniture & Mfg.
  Co. 259
International Canadian Corp. 75
International Color Gravure, Inc. .. 509
International Trading Co. 145
Investors Ins. Agency 431
Irbco Corp. 98
Irby Constr. Co. 198
Iron County Lumber Co. 268
Iron Range Plastics, Inc. 313
Irving Berlin Music Corp. 433
Irving Levitt Co. 192
Isaac Engel Realty Co. 204
ISC Indus., Inc. 351
Ivan Allen Co. 623
Ivers Dep't Store, Inc. 205
Ivey (2d Cir.) 376
Ivey (5th Cir.) 160

J

Jack Ammann Photogrammetric
  Eng'rs 146
Jack Daniel Distillery, Inc. 261
Jackson Oldsmobile, Inc. 412
Jacobs (6th Cir. 1983) 323, 479
Jacobs (6th Cir. 1968) 358
Jacobson 158
Jaeger Auto Fin. Co. 256
Jaeger Motor Car Co. 306
Jaffe 460
James 611
James Armour, Inc. 576
James M. Pierce Corp. 19
James W. Salley, Inc. 428
Jarvis, William D.P. 337, 340
Jaybee Mfg. Corp. 172
Jeanese, Inc. 404
J.E. Craig Fin. Co. 187
Jeffers 345
Jefferson Memorial Gardens, Inc. .. 233
J.E. Hawes Corp. 407
Jerome 499
Jewell Ridge Coal Corp. 236
Jim Burch & Assocs. 219
J.J. Dix, Inc. 293
JJJ Corp. 32
Joe Esco S.W. Tire Co. 55
John B. Lambert & Assocs. 32

T-26

TABLE OF CASES

John C. Nordt Co.	142
Johnson (3d Cir.)	227
Johnson (6th Cir.)	299
Johnson (8th Cir.)	452
Johnson (TC 1982)	575
Johnson (TC 1980)	298
Johnson (TCM 1977)	268
Johnson Bronze Co.	254
Johnson, Estate of	498
Johnson Inv. & Rental Co.	434
Johnston	467
John Town, Inc.	233
Jones (5th Cir.)	287
Jones (6th Cir.)	358
Jones (10th Cir.)	465
Jones (DNJ)	466
Jones (TC)	410
Jones (TCM)	381
Jones, Jr.	235
Jones Livestock Feeding Co.	495
Jones, Robert Trent	315
Jordano's, Inc.	311
Jos. K., Inc.	425
Joseph L. O'Brien Co.	336
Joseph Lupowitz Sons, Inc.	435
Joseph P. Kropf, Inc.	174
Journal Box Servicing Corp.	187
Jove	103
J.S. Biritz Constr. Co.	257
J.T. Slocomb Co.	44
Julio	434
Jump v. Manchester Life & Casualty Management Corp.	218
Jupiter Corp.	46

K

Kaczmarek	619
Kamborian	606
Kamis Eng'g Co.	399
Kansas Sand & Concrete, Inc.	354
Kaplan (TC 1972)	585
Kaplan (TC 1965)	329, 340
Karon Corp.	425
Kass	547
Katkin	510
Kaufman	540
K-C Land Co.	255
KDI Navcor, Inc.	84
Keller, Daniel	70

Kelley	168
Kellner	165
Kelson	103
Ken Miller Supply, Inc.	190
Kennedy	308
Kennedy, Jr. (6th Cir.)	195
Kennedy, Jr. (TC)	198
Kent Mfg. Corp.	366
Kenton Meadows Co.	379, 469
Kentucky Utils. Co.	274
Kern's Bakery of Virginia, Inc.	416
Kerr	472
Kershaw	502
Kershaw Mfg. Co.	51
Kewavnee Eng'g Corp.	177
Key Buick Co.	50
Killhour Sons, Inc.	114
Kimball Farms Inc.	225
Kimbell-Diamond	354, 360, 362, 374, 574
Kind	387
King (5th Cir.)	169
King (TC)	317
King Enters., Inc.	575
King Flour Mills Co.	14
King, Quirk & Co.	179
Kingsbury Invs., Inc.	20
Kingsley	509
Kinney	366
Kinsel	224
Kinsey	358
Kipnis	283
Kirk Inc.	505
Kittitas Ranch Inc.	107
Klausner	290
Kluge	278
Knapp Brothers Shoe Mfg. Corp.	156
Knapp King-Size Corp.	346
Knifflen	350
Knodel-Tygrett Co.	195
Knowlton	377
Kobacker	314
Kohler-Campbell Corp.	503
Kopp's Co.	141
Koscot Interplanetary, Inc., In re	266
Kountz	334
Krajeck	596
Krapf	321
Kraus	82
Krauskopf	381
Krueger Co. & Merri Mac Corp.	433

TABLE OF CASES

Kruse Grain Co. 238
Kuckenberg 359, 403
Kuper 493
Kurt Frings Agency, Inc. 427

L

Lacy 278
Lacy Contracting Co. 1
La Fera Contracting Co. 476
Lake Gerar Dev. Co. 434
Lake Iola Groves, Inc. 396
Lake Textile Co. 6
Lakewood Mfg. Co. 182
Lamark Shipping Agency 34
LaMastro 172
Lambert 376
Lamble 601
Lammerts, Estate of 477
Lancaster 248
Landy Towel & Linen Serv., Inc. ... 213
Lane 226
Lang 389
Langley Park Apartments, Sec. C., Inc. 197
Lanrao, Inc. 354, 363
Lansall Co. 258
Larrabee 286
LaSalle Trucking Co. 21
Las Cruces Oil Co. 346
Latchis Theatres of Keene, Inc. 26
Latimer 86
Laure 529
L.C. Bohart Plumbing & Heating Co. 423
Lear, Estate of 299
Leck Co. 421
Ledford 190
Leedy-Glover Realty & Ins. Co. 31
Lefkowitz 200
Leisure Time Enters., Inc. 164
Lemoge 102
Lennard, Estate of 448
Lester, Jr. 571
Lettman 491
Levenson Klein, Inc. 188
Levin 447
Levitt 138
Levy 449
Lewis (TC 1966) 490
Lewis (TC 1960) 449

Lewis (TCM) 290
Lewis & Taylor, Inc. 204
Lewis Food Co. (SD Cal. 1964) .. 18, 186
Lewis Food Co. (SD Cal. 1961) ... 198
Liberty Loan Corp. 77
Liberty Nat'l Bank & Trust Co. (10th Cir.) 395, 405
Liberty Nat'l Bank & Trust Co. (WD Ky.) 185
Libson Shops 45, 411–414, 533, 534, 544
Linczer 253
Linsker 305
Lion Assoc. 213
Lisle 491
Liston Zander Credit Co. 336
Litchfield Sec. Corp. 418, 433
Little 120
Livernois Trust 324, 332
Livingston 627
Lizak 332
Loans & Serv., Inc. 251
Lockwood (TCM 1962) 154
Lockwood, Estate of (TCM 1964) .. 571
Lodge & Shipley Co. 439
Loewen 347
Loftin & Woodward, Inc. 305
Logan, Burnet v. 339
Lohoefer, Inc. 185
Lombardo 201
Long Corp. 408
Loper 3
Lots, Inc. 263
Louisquisset Golf Club, Inc. 122
Louisville Chair Co. 282
Louisville Store of Liberty, Ky., Inc. .. 61
Lovell & Hart, Inc. 609
Lowes Lumber Co. 335, 586
L.R. Schmaus Co. 174
Lubbock United Gen. Agency, Inc. .. 145
Lucar-Naylor Egg Ranches 272
Lucas 87
Lucas, Estate of 3, 287
Lucas v. Earl 74
Luckman 338
Luden's Inc. 113
Ludwig Baumann & Co. 96
Luff Co. 404
Luke 536
Lumb 133
Luna Indus. Inc. 220
Lundeen 294

TABLE OF CASES

Lundgren	100
Lundy Packing Co.	189
Lupowitz Sons, Inc.	432
LX Cattle Co.	431
Lynch (5th Cir.)	280
Lynch (CD Cal. 1974)	7
Lynch (ND Ga. 1971)	240
Lynch (TC)	489

M

MacArthur	471
MacDonald	370
Mackinac Island Carriage Tours, Inc. (6th Cir. 1972)	504
Mackinac Island Carriage Tours, Inc. (6th Cir. 1970)	505
Madison Square Garden Corp.	355
Magic Mart, Inc.	19
Magill	144
Magnon	307
Mahaska Bottling Co.	207
Maher (8th Cir.)	482
Maher (TC)	458
Mains, Donald L.	379
Makover	618
Malden Knitting Mills	586
Male	397
Malone & Hyde, Inc. of Mo.	262
Maloney	455
Manassas Airport Indus. Park, Inc.	166
Manchester Life & Casualty Management Corp., Jump v.	218
M&K Farms, Inc.	172
M&M Corp.	266
Mangrum	248
Mangurian	290
Manilow	83
Manson W. Corp.	9
Marc's Big Boy-Prospect, Inc.	78
Marcus	75
Marett	561
Margulies, In re	152
Marie's Shoppe, Inc.	35
Marin Canalways & Dev. Co.	249
Markham & Brown, Inc.	129
Marks	287
Mar Monte Corp.	441
Marsack Estate	372
Marsan Realty Corp.	613
Marsden	301

Marshall Inv. Co.	419
Martell Builders, Inc.	140
Martin (D. Md. 1966)	306
Martin (ND Tex. 1965)	616
Martin Timber Co.	626
Marwais Steel Co.	146
Mason-Dixon Sand & Gravel Co.	265
Massell, Jr.	355
Master Eagle Assocs.	443
Mathis, Estate of	459
Maxine Dev. Co.	397
May Dep't Stores	223
Maynard Hosp., Inc.	83
Maytag	101
McClung Hosp., Inc.	204
McCullough	538
McCurdy	99
McDonald	467, 473
McDonald's Restaurants of Ill.	574
McDowell, Inc.	422
McGah	265
McGee	90
McGinty	480
McGlothlin	151
McGregor	372
McGrew	618
McGuire	80
McHenry	245
McKeown	314
McKinley Corp. of Ohio	322
McLemore (6th Cir.)	297
McLemore (TCM)	331
McMinn, Jr.	37, 334
McNair Realty	380
McNutt-Boyce Co.	134, 425
McPherson	165
McShain	486
McSorley's, Inc.	118
McWane Cast Iron Pipe Co.	172
McWhorter, Estate of	328
Mead, Estate of	365
Mead's Bakery, Inc.	22
Medical & Professional Servs., Inc.	291
Medical Collection Corp.	128
Medical Tower, Inc.	119
Medina	189
Melinda L. Gee Trust	426
Melvin Asphalt Prods. Corp.	61
Mennuto	261
Merchants' Nat'l Bank of Mobile	82
Meridian Inc.	133
Merlite Indus.	103

Muskogee Radiological Group,
   Inc. 125
M.W. Wood Enters. 107
Myron's Enters. 24

N

Naeter Bros. Publishing Co. 48
Nakatani 389
Nalco Chem. Co. 131
Nassau Lens Co. 110
Nasser 327
Nat Harrison Assocs. 75
National Acceptance Co. 85
National Farmers Union Serv.
   Corp. 496
National Sav. & Trust Co. 92
National Tea Co. & Consol.
   Subsidiaries 539
National Underwriters, Inc. 201
Nationwide Corp. 598
Natrona County Tribune 187, 507
NBH Land Co., In re 552
Neff 457
Neils 176
Nelson (5th Cir.) 99
Nelson (10th Cir.) 278
Nemours Corp. 33
Neuberger 577
Newark Morning Ledger Co. 129
New England Wooden Ware 29
Newman 255
New York Fruit Auction Corp. 575
Niagara Falls 200
Nibur Building Corp. 218
Nicholls, North, Buse Co. 286
Nickerson Lumber Co. 310
Niedermeyer 471
Nielsen 569
Nix 204
Noble 285
Nodell Motors Inc. 10
Noll's Food Co. 147
Noonan 252
Nor-Cal Adjusters 282
Norden-Ketay Corp. 413
Norfolk Indus. Loan Ass'n 424
Norman Scott, Inc. 540
North Am. Philips Co. 627
Northeastern Consol. Co. 232
Northern Pac. Ry. Co. 60

TABLE OF CASES

Northlich, Stolley Inc. 282
North Valley Metabolic Laboratories .. 35
Northwestern Nat'l Bank of Minn. ... 63
Northwestern Steel & Supply Co. 57
Novelart Mfg. 38
Num Specialty, Inc. 185
Nutil 515, 530
NYE 617
Nystrom, Jr. 246

O

Oak Hill Fin. Co. 243, 425
Oak Motors, Inc. 257
Oak Woods Cemetery Ass'n 336
Obermeyer 240
O.B.M. Inc. 392
O'Dowd 371
Of Course, Inc. 363
Office Communications Co. 202
Offutt 288
Ogden Co. 329
Ogier 333
Ogiony 250
Oil Base, Inc. 76
O'Keefe 281
Oklahoma Press Publishing Co.
   (10th Cir. 1975) 24
Oklahoma Press Publishing Co.
   (10th Cir. 1971) 15
Oklahoma Transp. Co. 76
Old Colony Ins. Serv., Inc. 189
Old Dominion Plywood Corp. 126
Old Town Corp. 138
Olmsted 356
Olson 530
Olton Feed Yard, Inc. 296
Olympic Foundry Co. 409
Omaha Aircraft Leasing Co. 423
Oman Constr. Co. 41
Omealia Research & Dev., Inc. 47
Omholt 578
124 Front St., Inc. 352
O'Neill 251
1661 Corp. 111
ON-RI-GA Medical Professional
   Ass'n 145
Oregon Pulp & Paper Co. 345
Orgill Bros. & Co. 213
Orner 137
Osborne Motors, Inc. 178

T-31

TABLE OF CASES

Otmar Real Estate Corp. 10
Overhead Door Co. of Albuquerque
.... 212
Owens 612
Owens Mach. Co. 617
Owings 393
Oxenhandler 327

P

Pacella 68
Pacific Dev., Inc. 251
Pacific Grains, Inc. (9th Cir.) 196
Pacific Grains, Inc. (TCM) 179
Pacific Northwest Food Club, Inc. ... 81
Pacific Sec. Cos. 424
Pacific Transp. Co. 519
Page, George 363
Palmer (1st Cir.) 498
Palmer (TC) 156
Palo Alto Town & Country Village,
  Inc. 285
Paparo 467
Parfrey 301
Parker (WD La.) 600
Parker (TCM) 486
Parkland Place Co. 604
Parkside Inc. 432
Parsons 351
Parsons Funeral Home, Inc. 506
Pastene 399
Patten Seed Co. 186
Patterson 464
Patton 195
Paula Constr. Co. 287
Paul E. Kummer Realty Co. 179
Paulsen (S. Ct.) 546
Paulsen (9th Cir.) 612
Paulsen (TC) 611
Pearce 488
Peavey Paper Mills, Inc. 439
Peck 70
Peco Co. 247
Peerless Inv. Co. 343
Pelton Steel Casting 16
Penley Realty Corp. 207
Pennsylvania Containers, Inc. 194
Penn-Warrington Hosiery Mills,
  Inc. 563
PEPI, Inc. 42

Pepsi-Cola Bottling Co. of Salina ... 174
Perfection Foods, Inc. 11
Performance Sys. Inc. 552
Perlmutter 199
Perrotto 322
Perry 626
Peters 41
Petersen (TCM 1971) 410
Petersen (TCM 1965) 257
Peterson (8th Cir.) 149, 357
Peterson (TCM) 461
Petro-Chem Mktg. Corp. 175
Petroleum Heat & Power Co. 1
Petrozello Co. 34
P.F. Scheidelman & Sons, Inc. ... 145, 265
PGG Indus., Inc. 69
Phelon 316
Philbrick 344
Philipp Bros. Chems. 73
Phillips Co. 138
Phillips, Jr. 131
Piedmont Corp. 116
Pierce 301
Pierson 518
Pigeon-Hole Parking, Inc. 134
Pitts 372
P.J. Anderson & Sons 283
Plantation Patterns, Inc. 229
Plastic Toys Inc. 121
Plimpton Tool Co. 191
Pliner 454
P.M. Fin, Corp. 118
Point City Dev. Co. 625
Pomponio 158
Poro 84, 153
Portland Mfg. Co. 561
Posey 376
Post Corp. 241
Potozky 87
Potter Elec. Signal & Mfg. Co. 505
Powder Mill Realty Trust 36
Powell's Pontiac-Cadillac, Inc. 394
Powers 66
PPG Indus. 78
Pre-Mixed Concrete, Inc. 63
Prescott (8th Cir.) 354
Prescott (TC) 371
P.R. Farms, Inc. 311
Pridemark, Inc. 363, 386
Princeton Aviation Corp. 50
Pritchett 441
Producers Realty Corp. 430

T-32

Table of Cases

Protzmann 94
Pumi-Blok Co. 95
Purdy 303
Putnam 143, 153

Q

Quarrier Diner Inc. 296
Quinn 183

R

Radnitz 472
Rafferty 570
R.A. Heintz Constr. Co. 504
Raich 352, 611
Railroad Dynamics, Inc. 176
Ram Corp. 112
Rapid Elec. Co. 307
Rapoport 329
Ravano 264
Rawlins Bucking House Lodge 187
Ray 22
Ray Eng'g Co. 56
Raymond 228
Raymond I. Smith, Inc. 26
R.C. Owen Co. (6th Cir.) 438
R.C. Owen Co. (Ct. Cl.) 120
R.C. Owen Co. (TCM) 121
R.C. Tway Co. 29
Reade Mfg. Co. 349
Ready Paving & Constr. Co. 7
Realty Settlement Corp. 88
Rebelle, III 85
Redding 559
Reddy 584
Reeves 518
Regal, Inc. 213
Reitz 284
REM Enter., Inc. 253
Reppel Steel & Supply Co. 181
Republic Nat'l Bank of Dallas 399
Republic Petroleum Corp. 2
Residential Developers, Inc. 537
Resorts Int'l Inc. 411
Rhombar Co. 4
Rialto Realty Co. 119
Richards Chrysler Plymouth Corp.,
  In re 208
Richardson 94, 624

Richardson Carbon & Gasoline Co. .. 155
Richmond, Fredericksburg &
  Potomac R.R. Co. 108
Rich Plan of N. New England, Inc. .. 189
Rickey, Jr. 446, 447
Riggs, Inc. 395
Riggs Tractor Co. 503
Riley 162, 495
Ringwalt 387
Rink 131
Rinker 316
Ripson, Estate of 245
Riss & Co. 309
Riss, Sr. 64
Ritsos 246
R.J. Nicoll Co. 206
R.M. Smith, Inc. 623
Road Materials, Inc. 231
Roark Furniture, Inc. 508
Robbins 293
Robbins Door & Sash Co. 214
Robert Louis Stevenson Apartments,
  Inc. 182
Robert R. Walker, Inc. 321
Roberts & Porter Inc. 110
Robin Haft Trust 448
Robinson 466
Robishaw 501
Rocco, Inc. 46
Rocky Mountain Fed. Sav. &
  Loan Ass'n 552
Rodebaugh 65
Rodman 611
Roebling 467
Rohman 91
Role 584
Rollins 99
Rolwing-Moxley Co. 227
Roman Sys., Ltd. 507
Rommer 394
Romy Hammes, Inc. 552
Ronholt 86
Rooney 77
Roschuni (5th Cir.) 326
Roschuni (TCM) 304
Rose 526
Rosen 610
Rosenbaum 308
Rosenberg (Cl. Ct.) 317
Rosenberg (CD Cal.) 267
Ross 528
Roth 490

T-33

Table of Cases

Rothenberg	606	Sansberry	240
Roth Properties Co.	14	Santa Anita Consol., Inc.	243
Rouse	247	Santulli	456
Roussel	103	Sarkisian	253
Roux Laboratories, Inc.	183	Savage	332
Roy	591	Save the Free Enter. Sys., Inc.	598
Royal Crown Bottling Co. of Winchester	173	Savko Bros.	182
		Sayles Finishing Plants, Inc.	120
Royal Farms Dairy Co.	507	Schafer	258
Royal Oak Apartments, Inc.	132	Schanchrist Foods, Inc.	178
Royalty Serv. Corp.	269	Schine Chain Theatres, Inc.	236
Royle Co.	62	Schleppy	222
Roy Miller	500	Schlosberg	251
R.T. French Co.	578	Schlude	1
Rubin (2d Cir.)	74	Schlumberger Tech. Corp.	152
Rubin (TC 1971)	75	Schmidt, Estate of	616
Rubin (TC 1968)	74	Schneider	370
Ruck, Inc.	202	Schneider & Co.	195
Ruddick Corp.	72	Schner-Block Co.	310
Runnels, Estate of	485	Schott, Estate of	444
Ruprecht	365	Schuerholz, F.	253
Rushing	108	Schulein	624
Rushton	364	Schumann	381
Russell (5th Cir.)	568	Schwartz (TC)	297
Russell (TCM)	370	Schwartz (TCM)	309
Russos	144	Scofield	104
Ruth	181	Scotland Mills, Inc.	95
Rutter	9	Scott Krauss News Agency, Inc.	193
R.W. Mitscher Co.	39	Scriptomatic, Inc.	115
R-W Specialties, Inc.	268	Scroll	42
Ryanco Sales Co.	204	Sears Oil Co.	25
		Security Fin. & Loan Co.	260
		Security Homes, Inc.	61
S		Seda	489
		S.E. Evans, Inc.	596
Sack	409	Segura	83
Sackett	281	Sekulow	245
Safety Eng'g & Supply Co.	182	Seven Canal Place Corp. (2d Cir.)	171
Safway Steel Scaffolds Co.	506	Seven Canal Place Corp. (TCM)	193
Saia Elec., Inc.	201	Sexton	347
Saigh	276	SFH Inc.	412
Saint Paul Bottling Co.	438	Shaker Apartments Inc.	80
Salem Packing Co.	198	Shantz, Estate of	199
Saltzman	165	Sharp	387
Salvadore	270	Shaw-Walker Co. (TC)	5
Salvatori	454	Shaw-Walker Co. (TCM)	10
Sammons	278	Shea (ND Ala.)	300
Sanders	178	Shea (TC)	154
Sandersville R.R. Co.	27	Shea Co.	153
S&S Meats, Inc.	508	Shereff	390
Sandy Estate Co.	23	Sherry Park, Inc.	268
Sankary	227	Sherwood Memorial Gardens, Inc.	235

Table of Cases

Shilowitz	159
Shimberg, Jr.	551
Shisler Farms, Inc.	618
Shore	372
Shore, Dean R.	2
Short	162
Shotmeyer	189
Sich	427
Siegel	72
Siff	297
Sika Chem. Corp.	95
Silco, Inc.	322
Silverman & Sons Realty Trust	431
Silverman, Estate of	276
Simmons	301
Simon (3d Cir.)	610
Simon (6th Cir.)	505
Simon (TCM 1982)	529
Simon (TCM 1961)	477
Simpson (ED Va.)	299
Simpson (TC)	595
Sinclair Oil Corp.	54
Singleton, Jr.	216
688 E. Ave.	159
Six Seam Co.	411
Skaggs Cos.	130
Skyland Oldsmobile, Inc.	191
Skyline Memorial Gardens, Inc.	460
Slater	577
Smith (5th Cir.)	349
Smith (6th Cir.)	234
Smith (TCM 1980)	331
Smith (TCM 1965)	192
Smithback	136
Smithco Eng'g, Inc.	244
Smith, Estate of	625
Smith, Jr.	481
Smith Leasing Co.	346, 405
Smothers	385
Snyder (TCM 1983)	415
Snyder (TCM 1981)	396
Snyder Bros.	117
Snyder Sons Co. (7th Cir.)	44
Snyder Sons Co. (TC)	49
Soden	300
Solomon, Sidney R.	345
Sooner Fed. Sav. & Loan Ass'n	208
Sorem	472
Southeastern Canteen Co.	505
Southern Bank Corp.	64
Southern Gas & Water Co.	124
Southern Silk Mill	217
South Lakes Farms, Inc.	65
Southland Corp.	44
South Tex. Rice Warehouse Co.	502
Southwest Consol. Corp., Helvering v.	515, 529
Southwestern Rubber & Packing Co.	178
Southwest Properties, Inc.	164
Spain	263
Spangler	167
Sparks Nugget, Inc.	508
Spheeris (7th Cir. 1972)	568
Spheeris (7th Cir. 1960)	326
Spicer Theatre, Inc.	81
Spinoza, Inc.	520
Spitalny	369, 596
Spitz Trust	627
S.P. Realty Co.	264
Sproul Realty Co.	161
Squier, Estate of	449
Stahl (DC Cir.)	407
Stahl (TCM)	162
Stahl, Estate of	149
Stamler	401
Standard Asbestos Mfg. & Insulating Co.	310
Standard Corrugated Case Corp.	20
Standard Linen Serv., Inc.	132, 459, 470, 588
Standard Lumber Co.	211
Stange Co.	50
Stanley, Inc.	615
Starks Bldg. Co.	36
Starman Inv., Inc.	6
State Office Supply, Inc.	34
State Pipe & Nipple Corp.	132
Stauffer, Estate of	543, 544
Steadman Credit Co.	297
Steel Constructors, Inc.	177
Steel Improvement & Forge Co.	494
Steelmasters, Inc.	13
Steffen	143
Steiner	245
Stephens	479
Stephens, Inc. (8th Cir.)	385
Stephens, Inc. (ED Ark.)	561
Sterling Distribs., Inc.	15
Stern	601
Sterno, Inc. (2d Cir.)	496
Sterno, Inc. (TCM)	193
Stetson Co.	52
Steuben Sec. Corp.	93

T-35

Table of Cases

Stevenson (2d Cir.)	4
Stevenson (TCM)	612
Stevens Pass, Inc.	361
Steves, III	168
Stewart	73
Stickney	600
Stierwalt	88
Stinnett's Pontiac Serv., Inc.	226, 296
Stirling	302
Stokes	405
Stone Mountain Grit Co.	119
Storz	357
Stout	283
Strasburger	254
Strickland Paper Co.	184
Strong	250
Stroupe	390
Stubbs	155
Stuchell	281
Sullivan	480
Summit Farms, Inc.	20
Sundstrom Trust	423
Sunny Isles Ocean Beach Co.	249
Sunnyland Ref. Co.	28
Sunnyside Beverages, Inc.	506
Sun Properties	116
Superior Beverage Co. of Marysville, Inc.	54
Superior Coach of Fla., Inc.	547
Superior Garment Co.	51
Superior Motors Inc.	191
Supreme Inv. Corp.	592
Suwannee Lumber Mfg. Co.	35
Swan	325
Swanson	387
Swiss Colony, Inc.	414
Switches, Inc.	441

T

Tabery	480
Tampa & Gulf Coast R.R. Co.	115
Tarrson	333
Taschler, Estate of	324
Taylor	250
Taylor, Estate of	84
T.C. Heyward & Co.	39
Teakle	101
Ted Bates & Co.	37
Tele-ception of Winchester, Inc.	203
Telephone Answering Serv. Co.	395
Television Indus.	456
Temple Square Mfg. Co.	49
Templeton Coal Co.	28
10-42 Corp.	2
Tennessee-Carolina Transp., Inc.	596
Tennessee Sec., Inc.	98
Terris	280
Terwilliger	476
Testor	350
Texas Farm Bureau	227
Textron, Inc.	407
TFI Cos.	552
Thaler	246
Thatcher	608
Theilen, Jr.	159
Thistlethwaite	303
Thomas (TCM)	65
Thomas P. Byrnes, Inc.	433
Thomas Worcester, Inc.	333
Thompson	349
320 E. 47th St. Corp.	419
Tidewater Hulls, Inc.	593
Tillotson	67
Times Publishing Co.	31
Title Ins. & Trust Co.	446
Tobias	168
Tollefsen	328
Tomlinson Fleet Corp.	499
Touchett	151
Tovrea Land & Cattle Co.	364
Towanda Textiles, Inc.	367
Towne Square, Inc.	245
Tracy	443
Trade Winds Inv., Inc.	45
Transamerica Corp.	135
Transamerica Ins. Co.	96
Trans-Atlantic Co.	115
Transport Mfg. & Equip. Co.	497
Transport Mfg. & Equip. Co. of Del.	70
Tribune Publishing Co.	56
Trinity Quarries, Inc.	127
Trotz	500
Trucks, Inc.	181
Truck Terminals, Inc.	225
Trunk	150
Truschel	548
Truth Tabernacle	598
Tube Processing Corp.	506
Tuboscope Co.	93
Tulia Feedlot, Inc. (5th Cir.)	296
Tulia Feedlot, Inc. (Ct. Cl.)	296

T-36

TABLE OF CASES

Turnbow 527
Turner, In re 439
Turner 267
Turner Advertising of Ky., Inc. 374
Turner Tire Co. 256
Twentieth Century-Fox Film Corp. ... 498
Tyler 230

U

Ullman 46
Uneco, Inc., In re 228
Ungar 619
Union Mut. Ins. Co. of Providence .. 256
Union Offset 14
Union Plumbing & Heating, Inc. 82
Unistruck Corp. 8
United Contractors, Inc. 271
United Mercantile Agencies 88
United States Holding Co. 374
United States Steel Corp. 66
Universal Castings Corp. 237
Uris, Estate of 293
Utah Bit & Steel, Inc. 50

V

Vahlsing Christina Corp. 460
Valley Camp Coal Co. 494
Valley Paperback Mfrs., Inc. 410
Valley Title Co. 626
Van Heusden 164
Van Hummell, Inc. 25
Van Keppel 488
Van's Chevrolet, Inc. 192
Vantress 121
VCA Corp. 350, 537
Velvet O'Donnell Corp. 94
Vernon C. Neal, Inc. 217
Vern Realty, Inc. 392
Vest 576
V.H. Monette & Co. 128, 189
Victor Constr. Inc. 106
Victorson 480
Viereck 387
Vinnell 459
Virginia Materials Corp. 294
Vogel Fertilizer Co. 56, 57, 212, 438

Von Hessert 309
Vulcan Materials Co. 550, 592
Vuono-Lione, Inc. 11

W

Wachovia Bank & Trust Co. 102
Wagner Elec. Corp. 260, 269
W.A. Krueger Co. 225
Wales 377
Walker 92
Wall 456
Wallace 142
Walsh 189
Walsh Food Serv. 127
Walthan Netoco Theatres, Inc. 149
Walton Mill, Inc. 36
Ward 457
Ward Trucking Corp. 193
Warner 584
Warsaw Photographic Assocs. 515
Washburne 612
Washington Trust Bank 364
Waste Disposal, Inc. 263
Waterman S.S. Corp. (5th Cir.) 148
Waterman S.S. Corp. (TC) 276
Way Eng'g Co. 181
W.C. Leonard & Co. 141
W.D. Gale, Inc. 305
Weaver Airline Personnel School,
    Inc. 186
Weaver Popcorn Co. 114
Webb (5th Cir.) 427
Webb (TC) 340
Webber, Sr., Estate of 488
Webster Corp. 504
W.E. Gabriel Fabrication Co. 571
Wegman's Properties, Inc. 219
Weil 286
Weisbart 617
Weise-Winckler Bindery Inc. 207
Weiskopf, Estate of 448
Weiss 428
Wekesser 482
Wellman Operating Corp. 33
Wells 128
Wendell 366
Wentworth 303
West 608
West Coast Ice Co. 418
West Coast Mktg. Corp. 512

T-37

Table of Cases

Western Credit Co.	428
Western Hills, Inc.	224
West Seattle Nat'l Bank	406
West Side Fed. Sav. & Loan Ass'n	546
West St.-Erie Boulevard Corp.	393
West Va. Northern R.R. Co.	137
West Va. Steel Corp.	104
Weylin Corp.	119
Wham Constr. Co.	614
Wheeler (WD Tex. 1974)	327
Wheeler (ND Tex. 1963)	616
Whipple	100
Whitaker	331
White	591
White-Delafield-Morris Corp.	497
White Tool & Mach. Co.	66
Whiting	318
Whitson	394
Wilbur Sec. Co.	238
Wilcox	293
Wilcox Mfg. Co.	35
Wilkinson	317
Wilkof	323
William E. Davis & Sons	508
Williams (TCM 1984)	125
Williams (TCM 1976)	331, 460
Williams Contracting Co.	247
Williams Oil Co.	34
Williamson	372
Willie Teeter Farming, Inc.	496
Willmark Serv. Sys., Inc.	142
Wilson (9th Cir.)	529
Wilson (TC)	515
Wilson (TCM)	272
Wilson Agency, Inc.	504
Wimp	405
Winer Enters., Inc.	346
Winn	168
Winnefield Heights, Inc.	264
Winnek	461
Winterburn	612
Wisconsin Big Boy Corp.	73
Wise	417
Wiseman	288
W.O. Covey, Inc.	114
Woesner Abstract & Title Co.	199
Wofac Corp.	45
Wojciechowski	281
Wolf	628
Wolf, Jr.	607
Wolter Constr. Co.	218
Wood Harmon	250
Wood Preserving Corp. of Baltimore, Inc.	235
Woods Inv. Co.	106
Woodson-Tenent Laboratories, Inc.	133
Woodward	129
Woolley Equip. Co.	501
Workman	401
World Serv. Life Ins. Co.	533, 537, 554
Worster, Estate of	299
Wortham Mach. Co.	533
Wrenn, Jr., In re	326
Wright (7th Cir.)	408
Wright (8th Cir.)	527
W.R. Vermillion Co.	174

Y

Yaffe Iron & Metal Corp. (8th Cir.)	60
Yaffe Iron & Metal Corp. (WD Ark.)	438
Yamamoto	608
Yanow	503
Yeaman	512
Yeckes	397
Yellow Cab Co.	410
Young (9th Cir.)	130
Young (ND Tex.)	85
Young & Rubicam	131
Young Door Co.	497
Young Motor Co.	16
Youngs Rubber Co.	7

Z

Zeigenhorn	102
Zenz	487
Zephyr Mills, Inc.	238
Ziegler Steel Serv. Corp.	194
Zilkha & Sons, Inc.	261
Zimmerman, Estate of	468
Zivnuska	244
Zongker	168
Zorn	169